Evidence Law and Practice

Evidence Law and Practice

EIGHTH EDITION

Steven I. Friedland
PROFESSOR OF LAW AND SENIOR SCHOLAR
ELON UNIVERSITY SCHOOL OF LAW

Paul Bergman
PROFESSOR OF LAW EMERITUS
UNIVERSITY OF CALIFORNIA AT LOS ANGELES SCHOOL OF LAW

Dustin B. Benham
PROFESSOR OF LAW
TEXAS TECH UNIVERSITY SCHOOL OF LAW

CAROLINA ACADEMIC PRESS
Durham, North Carolina

ISBN: 978-1-5310-2255-6
eISBN: 978-1-5310-2256-3
LCCN: 2023939080

Carolina Academic Press, LLC
700 Kent Street
Durham, NC 27701
(919) 489-7486
www.cap-press.com

Printed in the United States of America

Contents

Table of Cases

Preface

From its inception, *Evidence Law and Practice* has reflected its authors' interests in practical learning and classroom teaching. Explanations, examples (including many in the form of mini-transcripts) and Practice Tips help students understand the meaning of evidence rules and how to apply them in the context of trial testimony. The problems and role play exercises that follow the explanations vary from testing students' understanding of rules' basic applications to providing opportunities to develop arguments about rules in situations when their application is uncertain.

This 8th Edition of the book is based on the latest version of the Federal Rules of Evidence (Appendix 1). As of the date of publication, proposals for additional rule amendments are pending and are likely to be enacted into law. Appendix 2 compiles these amendments. Appendix 3 sets forth many of the important differences between the Federal Rules and the California Evidence Code, the first modern codification of Evidence law that was enacted about a dozen years before the Federal Rules.

Evidence Law and Practice is a study aid as well as a textbook for class. Chapters 19 and 20 allow students to review evidence rules in three different contexts:

- A hypothetical criminal prosecution that can serve as the basis of a mock trial.

- Multiple Choice questions taken from recent law school examinations.

- Transcripts of trial testimony. Some of these transcripts are based on trials that in their day stirred people across the country and in some instances the world, such as the O.J. Simpson murder trial and the trial of Ethel and Julius Rosenberg, the so-called "Atomic Spies." Other transcripts are based on trials featured in courtroom movies.

We have done our best to produce a book that not only focuses on practical evidentiary issues but also incorporates discussions of courtroom strategies and courtroom history. Knowledge of evidence rules is important for all lawyers, not just litigators. Trials are the most public aspect of U.S. justice and their influence is often as great as substantive laws. We authors will grant you the right to make up any substantive law you like, so long as you grant us the right to create the evidence rules that affect their application.

We hope that instructors and students alike find the book stimulating and an effective teaching and learning tool.

Steve Friedland
Paul Bergman
Dustin Benham

Evidence Law and Practice

Chapter 1

Introduction to Evidence

§ 1.01 Chapter Checklist

1. How do the rules of evidence affect the conduct of a lawsuit?

2. What role does evidence law play at trial?

3. What are several well-established meanings of the term "evidence"?

§ 1.02 Relevant Federal Rules of Evidence

Rule 101. Scope; Definitions

(a) Scope. These rules apply to proceedings in United States courts. The specific courts and proceedings to which the rules apply, along with exceptions, are set out in Rule 1101.

(b) Definitions. In these rules:

(1) "civil case" means a civil action or proceeding;

(2) "criminal case" includes a criminal proceeding;

(3) "public office" includes a public agency;

(4) "record" includes a memorandum, report, or data compilation;

(5) a "rule prescribed by the Supreme Court" means a rule adopted by the Supreme Court under statutory authority; and

(6) a reference to any kind of written material or any other medium includes electronically stored information.

Rule 102. Purpose

These rules should be construed so as to administer every proceeding fairly, eliminate unjustifiable expense and delay, and promote the development of evidence law, to the end of ascertaining the truth and securing a just determination.

Rule 106. Remainder of or Related Writings or Recorded Statements

If a party introduces all or part of a writing or recorded statement, an adverse party may require the introduction, at that time, of any other part — or any other writing or recorded statement — that in fairness ought to be considered at the same time.

§ 1.03 Lawsuits and Rules of Evidence

The rules of evidence are best understood in context, operating as part of a larger process, a lawsuit. Despite notorious claims of "justice denied" (such as wrongful convictions or the converse, wrongful acquittals), lawsuits play an important role in the United States. Institutionally, lawsuits serve as a nonviolent method of dispute resolution and offer an accepted method of fact-finding. The evidentiary rules are critical to the smooth and predictable operation of lawsuits.

The Federal Rules of Evidence, the focus of this book, govern court proceedings in the federal court system. Many states have adopted evidence codes to govern proceedings in state courts. The state rules often track the Federal Rules of Evidence.

The Federal Rules superseded common-law evidence rules upon their adoption in 1975. The Federal Rules of Evidence were designed with lofty goals in mind, reminiscent of a document imbued with equally broad ambitions in 1776. The evidence rules were intended to "secure fairness . . . to the end that the truth may be ascertained . . . ." Rule 102. From a practical perspective, the evidentiary rules were created to promote an "even playing field" and to provide advance notice of the rules of the adversarial process. In this respect, the evidentiary rules help the trial to proceed in a routine and predictable manner, acting as a stabilizing backbone of the trial.

The rules of evidence apply in both civil and criminal cases. While the application of the rules is generally uniform, at times they are specifically tailored to assist the differing functions of the criminal and civil justice systems. (For example, a criminal defendant is given several special dispensations because of the great burden of a conviction. *See, e.g.*, Rules 404(a), 609.)

In addition to supplying rules at trial, the rules of evidence reach some pre-and post-trial matters, such as formal interviews under oath of persons with relevant information, called "depositions," the discovery of relevant information, some pre-trial motions, and post-trial proceedings.[1] However, the rules primarily apply to the trial stage of a lawsuit.

The rules can be sorted according to function. There are traffic rules concerning the smooth operation of the trial, such as Rule 611, on the order and development of the testimony. There are "accuracy" rules promoting truthful verdicts, such as Rule 403, which excludes unfairly prejudicial evidence. There are "policy" rules advancing external policies larger than the individual lawsuit, such as Rule 501 on privileges.

Each rule can be viewed as advancing one or more of the traffic, accuracy, and policy functions. For example, Federal Rule of Evidence 106, known as the rule of completeness, offers an illustration of an accuracy rule. It provides an opposing

---

1. *See, e.g., United States v. Davis*, 170 F.3d 617, 622 (6th Cir. 1999), in which the court held that hearsay is admissible in a sentencing hearing.

party with the opportunity to introduce the remainder of a writing or recording in the interest of fairness. Accuracy is further preserved by the interpretation of the rule, which limits proffered remainders to that which is relevant to the case. The goal in allowing filtered remainders as evidence is to minimize the prejudicial impact on the jury.

A major purpose of the Federal Rules of Evidence is to provide a coherent and fair structure for the resolution of legal disputes. The biggest challenge for many law students is to synthesize the rules into a usable and unified framework. All too often, the Rules seem to spin in their own individual orbits, rather than in concert with each other.

While both state and federal courts currently rely on codified evidentiary rules, vestiges of the earlier common-law system still remain. The Federal Rules of Evidence still rely on the earlier common law in certain instances, such as in the domain of privileges.[2]

The creation of the Federal Rules of Evidence was an interesting exercise in statutory construction. A decade in the making, the Rules were originally composed in 1965 by an "Advisory Committee" appointed by then Chief Justice Earl Warren. The Advisory Committee's proposal was revised prior to being finally approved by the Supreme Court. The Court then forwarded the rules to Congress for review and revision. Congress disagreed with several provisions, and enacted the rules with modifications. The Federal Rules of Evidence went into effect on July 1, 1975.

Since that time, the Rules have been periodically revised on an individual basis. Revisions have been proposed for different reasons. Some rules needed more clarity. Other Rules needed upgrades in functionality. In 2011, for example, the Rules were restyled en masse specifically for the purpose of updating the clarity of the language, without changing their substantive effect. On April 27, 2017, two amendments were adopted, going into effect on December 1, 2017. The amendments involve a hearsay rule and an authentication rule but were both directed at the changing landscape of a digital world. The amendments are reproduced below (the deleted material is in brackets; the added material is in italics):

Rule 803. Exceptions to the Rule Against Hearsay — Regardless of Whether the Declarant Is Available as a Witness

The following are not excluded by the rule against hearsay, regardless of whether the declarant is available as a witness:

* * * *

(16) *Statements in Ancient Documents.* A statement in a document [that is at least 20 years old] *that was prepared before January 1, 1998,* and whose authenticity is established.

---

2. Rule 501 refers to the pertinent federal common law to determine what privileges apply in federal courts.

Rule 902. Evidence That Is Self–Authenticating

The following items of evidence are self-authenticating; they require no extrinsic evidence of authenticity in order to be admitted:

* * * *

(13) *Certified Records Generated by an Electronic Process or System. A record generated by an electronic process or system that produces an accurate result, as shown by a certification of a qualified person that complies with the certification requirements of Rule 902(11) or (12). The proponent must also meet the notice requirements of Rule 902(11).*

(14) *Certified Data Copied from an Electronic Device, Storage Medium, or File. Data copied from an electronic device, storage medium, or file, if authenticated by a process of digital identification, as shown by a certification of a qualified person that complies with the certification requirements of Rule 902(11) or (12). The proponent also must meet the notice requirements of Rule 902(11).*

In 2020, Rule 404(b) was amended to impose additional notice requirements on the prosecution if it intends to use "other act" evidence under the rule. The new rule, under 404(b)(3), requires the following:

Rule 404. Character Evidence; Other Crimes, Wrongs, or Acts

* * * *

(b) Other Crimes, Wrongs, or Acts.

(1) *Prohibited Uses.* Evidence of any other crime, wrong, or act is not admissible to prove a per-son's character in order to show that on a particular occasion the person acted in accordance with the character.

(2) *Permitted Uses.* This evidence may be admissible for another purpose, such as proving motive, opportunity, intent, preparation, plan, knowledge, identity, absence of mistake, or lack of accident.

(3) *Notice in a Criminal Case.* In a criminal case, the prosecutor must:

(A) provide reasonable notice of any such evidence that the prosecutor intends to offer at trial, so that the defendant has a fair opportunity to meet it;

(B) articulate in the notice the permitted purpose for which the prosecutor intends to offer the evi-dence and the reasoning that supports the purpose; and

(C) do so in writing before trial—or in any form during trial if the court, for good cause, excuses lack of pretrial notice.

§1.04 The Different Meanings of "Evidence"

One of the initial points of confusion in an Evidence course is the different uses of the term "evidence." There are at least three commonly used definitions of "evidence," especially at trial. The definitions include: (1) *proof* of a cause of action, claim, or defense; (2) the *rules* governing the admissibility and exclusion of proof at trial; and (3) what is *in evidence*, that is, the *things* that jurors can take back with them to the jury room for the process of deliberations.

(1) *Proof* refers to the entirety of the "stuff" offered by the parties at trial to meet the legal requirements for showing the elements of a claim, cause of action, or defense. Despite the rush to judgment that often occurs in celebrated trials, the American system revolves around the proof admitted in the case and not the innuendo, rumors, and inadmissible allegations that might be swirling around the lawsuit. Lawsuits are generally won or lost through the admissible proof offered by the parties.

Proof takes a variety of forms, from the testimony of witnesses, to tangible material marked as "exhibits," to intangible information or data. Because proof is so important to the effective functioning of the legal system, certain prerequisites or foundations must be met prior to offering it at trial.

(2) *The rules* governing the admissibility of proof not only provide the focus of a law school course but also guide how a judge conducts a trial. These rules can be found in the Federal Rules of Evidence or state codifications, as well as in the common law. Significantly, the rules contain numerous evidentiary "foundations" — elements that are prerequisites to the admissibility of evidence at trial. Thus, much like a tort or a crime that has elements that must be proven to win, evidence law has elements that must be shown before evidence can be admitted and considered by the trier of fact. Lawyers and law students alike struggle to understand and apply these foundations, which are crucial to the introduction of evidence. Those who can best negotiate these foundations maximize their chances for success at trial. (One pointed example to the contrary can be found in the film, *The Verdict*, starring Paul Newman as a plaintiff's attorney. In the film, the court excluded crucial evidence provided by a nurse about the medical negligence of several defendant physicians. Despite the exclusion, the jury obviously considered the evidence in a stunning finding for the plaintiff.)

(3) The third common use of the term "evidence" refers to the items of proof that were admitted *into evidence*. Such evidence has met the requirements of the rules and may be taken back to the jury room by the jury and considered during deliberations. This type of evidence, which includes a large portion of tangible proof under meaning (1) above, is distinguished from mere demonstrative evidence, which is used only to illustrate a point, usually during testimony. Demonstrative evidence is generally not subject to the same rigorous admissions requirements as other evidence and is not permitted to be taken by the jury back to the jury room. Once proposed exhibits are admitted "in evidence," they no longer are controlled by the

parties, but become a part of the official case file and are under the control of the court.

Example

Dr. Amy Millsap is sued by her patient, Lenny Alberto, for medical malpractice. Surgeon Millsap allegedly performed an important operating procedure with the incorrect scalpel. At trial, the plaintiff introduced the scalpel that Dr. Millsap is believed to have used during the operation. *Does the scalpel constitute evidence?*

Answer: The scalpel used by Dr. Millsap touches on all three uses of the term "evidence." The scalpel may be relevant to proving malpractice and thus might be admitted as the "stuff" offered by a party at trial. The scalpel also must satisfy the rules governing admissibility, including being properly authenticated and shown to be relevant to the case.[3] If the scalpel is admitted "in evidence" as an exhibit, and not merely as a demonstrative aid to assist the testimony of a witness, the scalpel is considered "in evidence" and may be brought to the jury room for the jury's deliberations.

Problem 1-1: Prove It

Mr. Rick Turkish, owner and President of Turkish Advertising, Inc., created an advertising campaign for Bill's Furniture Store. Rick had negotiated the advertising deal for Bill's with one of Bill's employees, Sarina, who agreed to a fee of $40,000 for Rick's services. Sarina told Rick to send her an invoice for the work. After completing the work, Rick dropped off at Bill's an invoice for $40,000, the only written confirmation of the job. Eleven months later, Rick still had not been paid by Bill's Furniture, so Rick filed suit to collect his fee.

What are the legal grounds for recovery? What should Rick allege in his complaint? Why? Write a brief complaint.

Suppose Rick testified at trial on his own behalf.

Excerpt of Rick's Direct Examination

PLAINTIFF'S ATTORNEY: Rick, would you please state your name for the record and spell it for the court reporter.

A: Rick Turkish, that's R-i-c-k. T-u-r-k-i-s-h.

PLAINTIFF'S ATTORNEY: What do you do for a living, Mr. Turkish?

A: I own a small advertising firm.

PLAINTIFF'S ATTORNEY: What is your family status?

A: I have been married for 17 years and have three children.

---

3. If it was not *the* scalpel in question, but rather a different scalpel, it may not be admitted.

PLAINTIFF'S ATTORNEY: Please describe what happened on the afternoon of October 1st.

A: I spoke to Sarina Johnson, of Bill's Furniture Store, about doing an advertising campaign for the store. I agreed during the conversation to design and set up several advertisements in the local newspapers for Bill's Fall Sale.

PLAINTIFF'S ATTORNEY: What happened after you agreed to do the work?

A: I created and designed the advertising campaign and gave the ad campaign to the store — all of the materials, master copies and the like. I dropped them off at Bill's with one of his employees, Jimmy, along with an invoice for the work.

PLAINTIFF'S ATTORNEY: Who's Jimmy?

A: He used to work at Bill's. I gave the ad campaign to him because Sarina and Bill were not in the office that day.

PLAINTIFF'S ATTORNEY: What happened after that?

A: Nothing. I didn't hear from Bill's. And I would like to get paid for the work I did for them.

What additional questions would you want to ask Rick, keeping in mind that proof is required in this contract action and all other actions at trial? What are your goals in asking these questions?

If you represented Bill's, how would you cross-examine Rick? What would be your objectives?

Problem 1-2: Inspector Clousseau

Inspector Clousseau investigates the scene of a gruesome murder. He finds, among other things:

1. A blueprint of the building in which the murder occurred.
2. One of the victim's earrings lying on the ground near the victim's body.
3. A paint brush spattered with blood.
4. A photograph of the scene without the body in it.
5. A "Saturday Night Special" handgun, lying under a nearby bed.

The Inspector then interviews three people who are standing in the area. One of the three, a neighbor, knew the murder victim. The neighbor, Bill, tells Clousseau that the victim was Jane Duplane and that she was having a torrid affair with Bill's best friend. During the interview, Clousseau observes the maid furtively placing an object in her pocket, and a young man running away with what appeared to be an earring in his hand.

Which of Clousseau's findings or interviews constitutes proof of the crime? What rules of evidence might apply to that proof? What proof might the jury be allowed to take back with them to the jury room? Why?

§ 1.05 Real, Representative, and Testimonial Evidence

Another useful way to classify evidence is to categorize it as: (a) real, (b) representative, or (c) testimonial. "Real" evidence is physical, tangible evidence, the thing itself. It is the gun used in an armed robbery, the fender from a car in an auto accident or the original contract in a breach of contract action. Representative evidence is evidence that represents another thing—a diagram, chart, photograph, x-ray, etc. Testimonial evidence comes from witnesses "viva voce," meaning by voice. An example is the eyewitness testifying to what she observed at the pertinent time. These three forms of evidence have differing requirements for admissibility, particularly in the area of authentication, which is covered in Chapter 18.

Problem 1-3: Clousseau Revisited

In Problem 1-2, above, which of the evidence would qualify as real evidence? Representative evidence? Testimonial evidence? Explain.

§ 1.06 Another Helpful Distinction — Direct or Circumstantial Evidence

Evidence also can be categorized as either direct or circumstantial in nature. Circumstantial evidence requires an inference to be drawn for the evidence to be relevant. To illustrate, a reasonable inference from observing people walking in the streets all bundled up in hats, scarves, and heavy jackets is that it is cold outside. Thus, circumstantial evidence is used indirectly through inferences to show helpful facts. Direct evidence does not require an inference to be drawn from it to be relevant. Instead, it proves a fact — generally a material fact — without requiring any deductions. For example, an eyewitness to a murder who testifies "I saw the defendant fire the gun, killing the victim," provides direct evidence of the killer's identity. A bloody knife found at the scene of the crime, on the other hand, provides indirect or circumstantial evidence of the murder, as does the fact that a suspect fled the scene after the killing. The bloody knife and running suspect both require inferences to prove the material fact, in this case that the suspect committed a murder.

Example

Julie Janson, a schoolteacher of modest means, is charged with the larceny of her neighbor's priceless Picasso painting. She was arrested three weeks after the theft, following her purchase of a $2 million yacht. *Is the purchase of the yacht direct or circumstantial evidence of the larceny?*

Answer: The newly purchased yacht would be circumstantial evidence of the larceny. It can be inferred from Julie's recent purchase of the yacht that she suddenly obtained a significant amount of money and that the windfall was consistent with the theft and sale of a priceless Picasso painting. Direct evidence of the larceny would be an eyewitness who actually observed Julie take the painting.

Problem 1-4: Drawing Inferences in the Sand

Which of the following are examples of circumstantial evidence? Which are examples of direct evidence? Explain.

1. To show that a letter was received, evidence is offered that the letter was properly postmarked, addressed, and mailed.

2. On the issue of whether it was raining on March 14th, Ellie testified, "I looked out my window and saw rain falling."

3. On the issue of whether it was raining on March 14th, Paul testified, "When people came into the office on that day, they were wearing raincoats and shaking water from their umbrellas."

4. On the issue of whether the elephant that escaped from the circus had crossed Alexandra's backyard, Alexandra testified, "I looked into my backyard and saw huge elephant footprints."

5. On the issue of whether Betty robbed the bank, a police department employee testified that the handgun the perpetrator had dropped at the bank was registered in Betty's name.

6. On the issue of whether Larry robbed Sandra, a bystander testified, "I saw Larry rob Sandra."

7. On the issue of whether Barney attended the hockey game, Sheila's statement, "Ed told me he saw Barney walking towards the arena where the hockey game was played."

Problem 1-5: Taken Out of Context

Vanessa, the CEO of a large online marketing company, fired Ethel, a 64 year-old employee. Ethel claimed age and gender discrimination and filed suit. Vanessa offered two paragraphs of a letter Ethel wrote to Vanessa a year before her firing.

A. Ethel seeks to offer the rest of the letter, to correct a misimpression of what the two paragraphs reflect, under Rule 106. Vanessa objects to the addition based on hearsay. Does Rule 106 allow for additional part of the letter or does it depend on whether it is hearsay?

B. Ethel also desires to offer an unrecorded oral conversation between her and Vanessa discussing the letter after it was received. Does Rule 106 include unrecorded oral conversations? How would you argue this question?

[Note that the Advisory Committee in 2022 proposed an amendment to Rule 106 to deal with the issues posed by this problem.]

§ 1.07 Evidence in the Trial Courts

While appellate courts rule on a wide variety of evidentiary issues, the primary locus of evidentiary rulings lies in the trial courts. Evidentiary issues arise throughout a trial and the numerous evidentiary rulings by trial courts are seldom appealed, let alone reversed on appeal. For example, an improper leading question will rarely be considered by a court on appeal or constitute a ground for reversal because the question likely does not impact the outcome of the case. Thus, competent trial lawyers must know how to negotiate the evidence rules to successfully advance their cases.

Transactional lawyers who may never set foot in a courtroom (as per their desire) still must have great familiarity with evidence rules. While transactional attorneys generally provide advice to businesses on how to avoid legal problems, the attorneys must prepare clients for the possibility of a lawsuit. Transactional attorneys must know how to maintain records, analyze the evidentiary significance of documents and other business-related materials, and otherwise protect clients under the rules of evidence if litigation should arise.

To better understand how the rules work in practice, it is useful to situate the rules within the broader context of a lawsuit. The lawsuit includes far more than the evidentiary rules, extending to: (1) the pleadings that initiate the case and propel it forward, either to trial or an alternative disposition, such as a plea or settlement; (2) lawyering strategies and arguments; and (3) jury selection and deliberation.

United States v. Wayne Gillis

The following excerpt from a narcotics prosecution is based on a real case that occurred in Washington, D.C. Many similar cases are brought on a daily basis throughout the United States. The inclusion of this case is intended to provide useful background information; it offers an opportunity to observe how evidence exists within the context of a lawsuit.

A. The Facts of the Case

The basic facts of the case are in dispute. The facts according to the prosecutor and defense follow.

1. The Facts According to the Prosecutor

On August 24th, at approximately 2:15 p.m., W-1 (Officer Friday), a Park Police officer, was traveling north on Rock Creek Parkway in Washington, D.C.

As he passed by Parking Lot # 6, he observed a 1990 Green Volvo without a front tag. The officer drove up to the car, approached the driver's window, and motioned for the driver to open it. The driver, later identified as the defendant, rolled down the window several inches.

1 · INTRODUCTION TO EVIDENCE

W-1 smelled marijuana. He then asked the defendant to get out of the car. The defendant showed W-1 his license and registration for the car. Defendant's license and registration were from the State of Alabama. The defendant was asked whether there was any marijuana inside the car. Defendant went back into the car, pulled out the front ashtray, and brought it outside to W-1.

W-1 then asked the co-defendant, a male who was sitting in the front passenger seat, to get out of the car. W-1 discovered rolling papers and a package of white powder under the right front mat. W-1 then conducted a complete search of the car. When W-1 removed the thick seat mats off the front seat, he observed a .22 caliber Smith & Wesson pistol wedged in the crack separating the back of the driver's seat and the driver's seat itself. Nothing was discovered on the defendant. A large quantity of green weed in a plastic bag was found on the passenger.

W-1 seized all of the evidence and field-tested the powder and weed. The green weed discovered on the co-defendant tested positive for marijuana. The package of white powder tested positive for cocaine.

Defendant did not appear to be under the influence of narcotics, but the co-defendant did. Both were extremely cooperative.

The defendant and co-defendant were read their rights. During the reading, the defendant spontaneously said, "That stuff you found was not mine! But I'm not going to say anything more without a lawyer."

2. The Facts According to the Defense

The defendant, Wayne Gillis, is 34 years old. He is not married, but resides part of the time with his girlfriend, with whom he has two children, Samantha (age three) and Chase (age five). He is employed as a long-distance trucker by Amalgamated Trucking, Inc., and is consequently out-of-town for long periods of time.

On August 24th, Gillis had driven to Rock Creek Park to relax after a five-day trip to Nebraska for Amalgamated. He was accompanied by his good friend, Bob, who was sitting in the passenger's seat. Wayne routinely lets friends borrow the car while he is out-of-town and had let his friend Jim use it during this past trip.

At the park, Wayne and Bob were chatting in the car, minding their own business, when a police officer approached Wayne and tapped loudly on the window. The officer rudely asked Wayne what he was doing and then ordered him out of the car. The officer searched them and the car without permission. When the officer confronted Wayne, claiming to have found a gun and drugs in the car, Wayne told the officer that he (Wayne) knew nothing about it. Later, Wayne informed me (his attorney) that the stuff was either planted by the police or left there by his friend, Jim.

Wayne did not have Jim's address or last name; Jim was a friend from the neighborhood. Wayne said that there were others in the neighborhood who could verify that Jim lived and hung out there, although Jim had not been seen lately.

Wayne states that he had been convicted of the possession of marijuana eight years ago and disorderly conduct seven years ago. Five years ago, he was charged with conspiracy to distribute cocaine and weapons possession, but all of the charges were dropped. Wayne also thought he should mention that 15 years ago, when he was in middle school, he had been caught taking a teacher's car for a joyride with a classmate. As a result, the boys were sent to a juvenile home for a few months.

B. The Criminal Case File

Excerpts from a case file constructed by the prosecutor follow. *When reviewing these excerpts: (1) identify the possible evidence in the case; and (2) arrange the evidence in a persuasive manner, first for the prosecution and then for the defense.*

1. The Information

[The following is the prosecutor's charging document, called the "Information."]

United States v. Wayne Gillis

Misdemeanor # 468459-98Washington, D.C.

Criminal Division

The United States Attorney for the District of Columbia informs the Court that within the District of Columbia:

DEFENDANT'S NAME   Wayne (FIRST)   Gillis (LAST)   (PDID)

DEFENDANT'S ADDRESS
1204 P Street N.W.
Washington, D.C.

Defendant did on or about <u>August 24, 1998</u> commit the crime or crimes indicated

herein and identified by an X-mark or X-marks.

POSSESSION OF A CONTROLLED SUBSTANCE — in that he unlawfully, knowingly, and intentionally had in his possession a controlled substance consisting of <u>Cocaine</u> in violation of 33 District of Columbia Code, Section 541(c).

POSSESSION OF A CONTROLLED SUBSTANCE — in that he unlawfully, knowingly, and intentionally had in his possession a controlled substance consisting of <u>Cannabis</u>, in violation of 33 District of Columbia Code, Section 541(c).

DISTRIBUTION OF A SCHEDULE V CONTROLLED SUBSTANCE — in that he unlawfully, knowingly, and intentionally did distribute a quantity of <u>Cannabis</u>, a Schedule V controlled substance, in violation of 33 District of Columbia Code, Section 541(a)(1).

POSSESSION WITH INTENT TO DISTRIBUTE A SCHEDULE V CONTROLLED SUBSTANCE — in that he unlawfully, knowingly, and intentionally did possess with intent to distribute a quantity of <u>Cannabis</u>, a Schedule V controlled substance, in violation of 33 District of Columbia Code, Section 541(a)(1).

CARRYING PISTOL WITHOUT A LICENSE — in that he carried openly and concealed on and about his person, a <u>Pistol</u> without a license therefor issued as provided by Section 22-3206, District of Columbia Code, in violation of Section 22-3204, District of Columbia.

UNITED STATES ATTORNEY FOR THE DISTRICT OF COLUMBIA BY ASSISTANT UNITED STATES ATTORNEY FOR THE DISTRICT OF COLUMBIA

BY: Janet Parker DATE: 9/3/98 OFFICER: Friday DISTRICT: Rock Creek Park, Washington, D.C.

2. The Prosecutor's Notes

Summary of Case

8/24/98-2:15 p.m.

6th Parking Lot, Rock Creek Park, N.W.

Charges: Possession of Cocaine, Possession of Marijuana, Carrying a Pistol Without a License

Witnesses

Witness #1	Arresting Officer/Chain of custody
Witness #2	Assisting Officer
Witness #3	Crime Scene Search Officer — Took fingerprints
Witness #4	Transporting Officer

Evidence	Who and Where Found
1 .22 Caliber Pistol	Witness # 1: wedged in the front seat.
1 Bag of Marijuana	Witness # 1: in possession of passenger.
3 Marijuana Cigarettes	Witness # 1: front ashtray.
2 Packets of Cocaine	Witness # 1: under front passenger's mat.
1 Package of Rolling Paper	Witness # 1: under front passenger's mat.
1 Hemostat	Witness # 1: under front driver's mat.

3. Deposition Transcript of Eyewitness, Ronald Samoa

[taken on September 14, 1998, in the office of the defense counsel]

DEFENSE COUNSEL: Would you please state your name for the record?

A: Ronald T. Samoa

DEFENSE COUNSEL: Where do you live, Mr. Samoa?

A: I live at 1405 Cleveland Park Circle, N.W., Washington, D.C.

DEFENSE COUNSEL: Where were you on August 24, 1998, at approximately 2:15 p.m.?

A: I was in Rock Creek Park, taking a walk.

DEFENSE COUNSEL: What did you see at that time, if anything?

A: I saw a police officer go over to a parked car and animatedly say something through a rolled up window. The driver rolled down the window a crack and I saw what looked like smoke come out of it.

DEFENSE COUNSEL: Then what happened?

A: The driver then got out of the car, put his hands up in front of him, and seemed to tell the officer to take it easy. The passenger got out at the same time. Then the officer practically dove into the car and emerged with some stuff in his hands.

DEFENSE COUNSEL: Where did the stuff in his hands come from?

A: I could not see.

DEFENSE COUNSEL: When the officer went into the car, can you describe what he was doing with his hands?

A: The officer's right hand was balled up, like a fist, but I couldn't see if he was holding anything in it; I just am not sure.

DEFENSE COUNSEL: Thank you.

How would you approach the case as the prosecutor? As the defense counsel? Explain your strategy for each side.

What would you include in an opening statement to the jury in this case? Note that the opening statements by counsel are not evidence. Instead, they can be thought of as the "road maps" of what the evidence will show. They offer a peek at all of the pieces in the puzzle, presented whole before the evidentiary component of the trial begins, much like the table of contents for a book. Note that when evidence is finally presented at trial, the organization and clarity of the opening statement is often torn apart by necessity. Sometimes a single witness can testify only about pieces of several events; likewise, several witnesses often are required to explain a part of the overall narrative. The opening statement is not an opening argument about the other side's evidence. While attorneys construct their openings subject to personal preference, common features include: (1) a one-line theme for the case, much like the title of a book or film; (2) a story about what happened (that is, what the evidence will show); and (3) a request for a favorable verdict based on the evidence.

§ 1.08   A Jury of Her Peers

Problem 1-6: A Jury of Her Peers

Susan Glaspell's classic short story, A Jury of Her Peers, *is included below. In reading the story, identify what types of evidence the women rely upon: Character? Opinion (lay or expert)? Eyewitness? Circumstantial or direct? Physical evidence? Hearsay? How probative (or persuasive) is each item of evidence? Do the men and the women assign different probative values to the same kinds of evidence? Do they discover and focus attention upon different kinds of evidence? Do they interpret the evidence differently? What do the answers to these questions suggest to you about whom you would want on a criminal jury trying the wife if you were defense counsel? If you were the prosecution? What sorts of opening and closing arguments should each side make? What story will each side want to tell? Which story is more persuasive and why?*

A JURY OF HER PEERS — 1917

Susan Glaspell

When Martha Hale opened the storm-door and got the north wind, she ran back for her big woolen scarf. As she hurriedly wound that round her head her eye made a scandalized sweep of her kitchen. It was no ordinary thing that called her away — it was probably farther from ordinary than anything that had ever happened in Dickson County. But her kitchen was in no shape for leaving: bread ready for mixing, half the flour sifted and half unsifted.

She hated to see things half done; but she had been at that when they stopped to get Mr. Hale, and the sheriff came in to say his wife wished Mrs. Hale would come too — adding, with a grin, that he guessed she was getting scared and wanted another woman along. So she had dropped everything right where it was.

"Martha!" now came her husband's impatient voice. "Don't keep folks waiting out here in the cold."

She joined the three men and the one woman waiting for her in the sheriff's car.

After she had the robes tucked in she took another look at the woman beside her. She had met Mrs. Peters the year before, at the county fair, and the thing she remembered about her was that she didn't seem like a sheriff's wife. She was small and thin and didn't have a strong voice. Mrs. Gorman, the sheriff's wife before Gorman went out and Peters came in, had a voice that seemed to be backing up the law with every word. But if Mrs. Peters didn't look like a sheriff's wife, Peters made it up in looking like a sheriff — a heavy man with a big voice who was particularly genial with the law-abiding, as if to make it plain that he knew the difference between criminals and non-criminals. And right there it came into Mrs. Hale's mind that this man who was so lively with all of them was going to the Wrights' now as a sheriff.

"The country's not very pleasant this time of year," Mrs. Peters at last ventured.

Mrs. Hale scarcely finished her reply, for they had gone up a little hill and could see the Wright place, and seeing it did not make her feel like talking. It looked very lonely this cold March morning. It had always been a lonesome-looking place. It was down in a hollow, and the poplar trees around it were lonely-looking trees. The men were looking at it and talking about what had happened. The county attorney was bending to one side, scrutinizing the place as they drew up to it.

"I'm glad you came with me," Mrs. Peters said nervously, as the two women were about to follow the men in through the kitchen door.

Even after she had her foot on the doorstep, Martha Hale had a moment of feeling she could not cross this threshold. And the reason it seemed she couldn't cross it now was because she hadn't crossed it before. Time and time again it had been in her mind, "I ought to go over and see Minnie Foster" — she still thought of her as Minnie Foster, though for twenty years she had been Mrs. Wright. And then there was always something to do and Minnie Foster would go from her mind. But now she could come.

The men went over to the stove. The women stood close together by the door. Young Henderson, the county attorney, turned around and said, "Come up to the fire, ladies."

Mrs. Peters took a step forward, then stopped. "I'm not cold," she said. And so the two women stood by the door, at first not even so much as looking around the kitchen.

The men talked about what a good thing it was the sheriff had sent his deputy out that morning to make a fire for them, and then Sheriff Peters stepped back from the stove, unbuttoned his outer coat, and leaned his hands on the kitchen table in a way that seemed to mark the beginning of official business. "Now, Mr. Hale," he said in a sort of semi-official voice, "before we move things about, you tell Mr. Henderson just what it was you saw when you came here yesterday morning."

The county attorney was looking around the kitchen.

"By the way," he asked, "has anything been moved?" He turned to the sheriff. "Are things just as you left them yesterday?"

Peters looked from cupboard to sink; to a small worn rocker a little to one side of the kitchen table.

"It's just the same."

"Well, Mr. Hale," said the county attorney, "tell just what happened when you came here yesterday morning."

Mrs. Hale, still leaning against the door, had that sinking feeling of the mother whose child is about to speak a piece. Lewis often wandered along and got things mixed up in a story. She hoped he would tell this straight and plain, and not say unnecessary things that would make it harder for Minnie Foster. He didn't begin at once, and she noticed that he looked queer, as if thinking of what he had seen here yesterday.

"Yes, Mr. Hale?" the county attorney reminded.

"Harry and I had started to town with a load of wood," Mrs. Hale's husband began.

Harry was Mrs. Hale's oldest boy. He wasn't with them now, for the wood never got to town yesterday and he was taking it this morning, so he hadn't been home when the sheriff stopped to say he wanted Mr. Hale to come over to the Wright place and tell the county attorney his story there, where he could point it all out. With all Mrs. Hale's other emotions came the fear Harry wasn't dressed warm enough — they hadn't any of them realized how that north wind did bite.

"We come along this road," Hale was going on, "and as we got in sight of the house I says to Harry, 'I'm goin' to see if I can't get John Wright to take a telephone.' You see," he explained to Henderson, "unless I can get somebody to go in with me they won't come out this branch road except for a price I can't pay. I'd spoke to Wright about it before; but he put me off, saying folks talked too much anyway, and all he asked was peace and quiet — guess you know about how much he talked himself. But I thought maybe if I went to the house and talked about it before his wife, and said all the women-folks liked the telephones, and — that in this lonesome stretch of road it would be a good thing — well, I said to Harry that that was what I was going to say — though I said at the same time that I didn't know as what his wife wanted made much difference to John — "

Now, there he was! — saying things he didn't need to say. Mrs. Hale tried to catch her husband's eye, but fortunately the county attorney interrupted with:

"Let's talk about that a little later, Mr. Hale. I do want to talk about that, but I'm anxious now to know just what happened when you got here."

When he began this time, it was deliberately, as if he knew it were important.

"I didn't see or hear anything. I knocked at the door. And still it was all quiet inside. I knew they must be up — it was past eight o'clock. So I knocked again, louder, and I thought I heard somebody say, 'Come in.' I wasn't sure — I'm not sure yet. But I opened the door — this door," jerking a hand toward the door by which the two women stood, "and there, in that rocker" — pointing to it — "sat Mrs. Wright."

Everyone in the kitchen looked at the rocker. It came into Mrs. Hale's mind that this chair didn't look in the least like Minnie Foster — the Minnie Foster of twenty years before. It was a dingy red, with wooden rungs up the back, and the middle rung gone; the chair sagged to one side.

"How did she — look?" the county attorney was inquiring.

"Well," said Hale, "she looked — queer."

"How do you mean — queer?"

He took out note-book and pencil. Mrs. Hale did not like the sight of that pencil. She kept her eye on her husband, as if to keep him from saying unnecessary things that would go into the book and make trouble. Hale spoke guardedly: "Well, as if she didn't know what she was going to do next. And kind of — done up." "How did she seem to feel about your coming?" "Why, I don't think she minded — one way or other. She didn't pay much attention. I said, 'Ho' do, Mrs. Wright. It's cold, ain't it?' And she said, 'Is it?' — and went on pleatin' of her apron." "Well, I was surprised. She didn't ask me to come up to the stove, but just set there, not even lookin' at me. And so I said, 'I want to see John.' And then she-laughed. I guess you would call it a laugh." "I thought of Harry and the team outside, so I said, a little sharp, 'Can I see John?' 'No,' says she — kind of dull like. 'Ain't he home?' says I. Then she looked at me. 'Yes,' says she, 'he's home.' 'Then why can't I see him?' I asked her out of patience with her now. ''Cause he's dead.' Says she just as quiet and dull and fell to pleatin' her apron. 'Dead?' says I, like you do when you can't take in what you've heard." "She just nodded her head, not getting a bit excited, but rockin' back and forth."

"'Why — where is he?' says I, not knowing *what* to say."

"She just pointed upstairs — like this — pointing to the room above."

"I got up, with the idea of going up there myself. By this time I — didn't know what to do. I walked from there to here, then I says, 'Why, what did he die of?'"

"'He died of a rope around his neck.' Says she; and just went on pleatin' at her apron."

Hale stopped speaking, staring at the rocker. Nobody spoke; it was as if all were seeing the woman who had sat there the morning before.

"And what did you do then?" the attorney asked.

"I went out and called Harry. I thought I might — need help. I got Harry in, and we went upstairs." His voice fell almost to a whisper. "There he was — lying over the — "

"I think I'd rather have you go into that upstairs," the county attorney interrupted, "where you can point it all out. Just go on now with the rest of the story."

"Well, my first thought was to get that rope off. It looked — "

He stopped; he did not say how it looked.

"But Harry, he went up to him and he said, 'No, he's dead all right, and we'd better not touch anything. So we went downstairs."

"She was still sitting that same way. 'Has anybody been notified?' I asked. 'No' says she, unconcerned."

"'Who did this, Mrs. Wright?' said Harry. He said it business-like, she stopped pleatin' at her apron. 'I don't know,' she says. 'You don't *know*?' says Harry. 'Weren't you sleepin' in the bed with him?' 'Yes,' says she, 'but I was on the inside.' 'Somebody slipped a rope around his neck and strangled him, and you didn't wake up?' says Harry. 'I didn't wake up,' she said after him."

"We may have looked as if we didn't see how that could be, for after a minute she said, 'I sleep sound.'"

"Harry was going to ask her more questions, but I said maybe that weren't our business; maybe we ought to let her tell her story first to the coroner or the sheriff. So Harry went fast as he could over to High Road — the Rivers' place, where there's a telephone."

"And what did she do when she knew you had gone for the coroner?"

"She moved from that chair to this one over here, and just sat there with her hands held together and looking down. I got a feeling that I ought to make some conversation, so I said I had come in to see if John wanted to put in a telephone; and at that she started to laugh, and then she stopped and looked at me — scared."

At sound of a moving pencil the man who was telling the story looked up.

"I dunno — maybe it wasn't scared; I wouldn't like to say it was. Soon Harry got back, and then Dr. Lloyd came, and you, Mr. Peters, and so I guess that's all I know that you don't."

He said this with relief, moved as if relaxing. The county attorney walked to the stair door.

"I guess we'll go upstairs first — then out to the barn and around there."

He paused and looked around the kitchen.

"You're convinced there was nothing important here?" he asked the sheriff. "Nothing that would — point to any motive?"

The sheriff too looked all around. "Nothing here but kitchen things," he said, with the insignificance of kitchen things.

The county attorney was looking at the cupboard. He opened the upper part and looked in. After a moment he drew his hand away sticky.

"Here's a nice mess," he said resentfully.

The two women had drawn nearer, and now the sheriff's wife spoke.

"Oh — her fruit," She said, looking to Mrs. Hale for understanding. "She worried about that when it turned so cold last night. She said the fire would go out and her jars might burst."

Mrs. Peters' husband broke into a laugh.

"Well, can you beat the women! Held for murder, and worrying about her preserves!"

The young attorney set his lips.

"I guess before we're through with her she may have something more serious than preserves to worry about."

"Oh, well," said Mrs. Hale's husband, with good-natured superiority, "women are used to worrying over trifles."

The two women moved closer together. Neither of them spoke. The county attorney seemed to remember his manners — and think of his future.

"And yet," said he, with the gallantry of a young politician, "for all their worries, what would we do without the ladies?"

The women did not speak. He went to the sink to wash his hands, turned to wipe them on the roller towel, pulled it for a cleaner place.

"Dirty towels! Not much of a house-keeper, would you say, ladies?" He kicked his foot against some dirty pans under the sink.

"There's a great deal of work to be done on a farm," said Mrs. Hale stiffly.

"To be sure. And yet" — with a little bow to her — "I know there are some Dickson County farm-houses that do not have such roller towels."

"Those towels get dirty awful quick. Men's hands aren't always as clean as they might be."

"Ah, loyal to your sex, I see," he laughed. He gave her a keen look. "But you and Mrs. Wright were neighbors. I suppose you were friends too."

Martha Hale shook her head.

"I've seen little enough of her of late years. I've not been in this house — it's more than a year."

"And why was that? You didn't like her?"

"I liked her well enough," she replied with spirit. "Farmers' wives have their hands full, Mr. Henderson. And then — " She looked around the kitchen.

"Yes?" he encouraged.

"It never seemed a very cheerful place," said she, more to herself than to him.

"No," he agreed; "I don't think anyone would call it cheerful. I shouldn't say she had the home-making instinct."

"Well, I don't know as Wright had either," she muttered.

"You mean they didn't get on very well?"

"I suppose anything Mrs. Peters does 'll be all right?" the sheriff inquired. "She was to take in some clothes for her, you know — and a few little things. We left in such a hurry yesterday."

The county attorney looked at the two women they were leaving alone among the kitchen things.

"Yes — Mrs. Peters," he said, his glance resting on the woman who was not Mrs. Peters, the big farmer woman who stood behind the sheriff's wife. "Of course Mrs. Peters is one of us," he added in a manner of entrusting responsibility. "And keep your eye out, Mrs. Peters, for anything that might be of use. No telling; you women might come upon a clue to the motive — and that's the thing we need."

Mr. Hale rubbed his face in the fashion of a slow man getting ready for a pleasantry. "But would the women know a clue if they did come upon it?" he said. Having delivered himself of this, he followed the others through the stair door.

The women stood motionless, listening to the footsteps, first upon the stairs, then in the room above them.

Then, as if releasing herself from something too strange, Mrs. Hale began to arrange the dirty pans under the sink, which the county attorney's disdainful push of the foot had upset.

"I'd hate to have men coming into my kitchen, snoopin' round and criticizing."

"Of course it's no more than their duty," said the sheriff's wife, in her timid manner.

"Duty's all right, but I guess that deputy sheriff that come out to make the fire might have got a little of this on." She gave the roller towel a pull. "Wish I'd thought of that sooner! Seems mean to talk about her for not having things slicked up, when she had to come away in such a hurry."

She looked around the kitchen. Certainly it was not "slicked up." Her eye was held by a bucket of sugar on a low shelf. The cover was off the wooden bucket, and beside it was a paper bag — half full.

Mrs. Hale moved towards it.

"She was putting this in there," she said to herself — slowly.

She thought of the flour in her kitchen at home — half sifted, half not sifted. She had been interrupted, and had left things half done. What had interrupted Minnie Foster? Why had that work been left half done? She made a move as if to finish it — unfinished things always bothered her, and then she saw that Mrs. Peters was watching her, and she didn't want Mrs. Peters to get that feeling she had of work begun and then — for some reason — not finished.

"It's a shame about her fruit," she said, going to the cupboard. "I wonder if it's all gone."

"Here's one that's all right." she said at last. She held it towards the light. "This is cherries, too." She looked again. "I declare I believe that's the only one."

"She'll feel bad, after all her hard work in the hot weather. I remember the afternoon I put up my cherries last summer."

She put the bottle on the table, and was about to sit down in the rocker. But something kept her from sitting in that chair. She stood looking at it, seeing the woman who had sat there "pleatin' at her apron."

The thin voice of the sheriff's wife broke in upon her: "I must be getting those things from the front room closet." She opened the door into the other room, started in, stepped back. "You coming with me, Mrs. Hale?" She asked nervously. "You — you could help me get them."

They were soon back. "My!" said Mrs. Peters, dropping the things on the table and hurrying to the stove.

Mrs. Hale stood examining the clothes the woman who was being detained in town had said she wanted.

"Wright was close!" she exclaimed, holding up a shabby black skirt that bore the marks of much making over. "I think maybe that's why she kept so much to herself. I s'pose she felt she couldn't do her part; and then, you don't enjoy things when you feel shabby. She used to wear pretty clothes and be lively — when she was Minnie Foster, one of the town girls, singing in the choir. But that — oh, that was twenty years ago."

With a carefulness in which there was something tender, she folded the shabby clothes and piled them at one corner of the table. She looked up at Mrs. Peters, and there was something in the other woman's look that irritated her.

"She don't care," she said to herself. "Much difference it makes to her whether Minnie Foster had pretty clothes when she was a girl."

Then she looked again, and she wasn't so sure; in fact she hadn't at any time been sure about Mrs. Peters. She had that shrinking manner, and yet her eyes looked as if they could see a long way into things.

"This all you was to take in?" asked Mrs. Hale.

"No," said the sheriff's wife; "she said she wanted an apron. Funny thing to want," she ventured in her nervous way, "for there's not much to get you dirty in jail, goodness knows. But I suppose just to make her feel more natural. She said they were in the bottom drawer of this cupboard. Yes — here they are. And then her little shawl that always hung on the stair door."

She took the small grey shawl from behind the door leading upstairs.

Suddenly Mrs. Hale took a quick step towards the other woman.

"Mrs. Peters!"

"Yes, Mrs. Hale?"

"Do you think she — did it?" Mrs. Peters looked frightened, "Oh I don't know," she said, in a voice that seemed to shrink from the subject.

"Well, I don't think she did," affirmed Mrs. Hale. "Asking for an apron, and her little shawl. Worryin' about her fruit."

"Mr. Peters says — " Footsteps were heard in the room above; she stopped, looked up, then went on in a lowered voice: "Mr. Peters says — it looks bad for her. Mr. Henderson is awful sarcastic in a speech, and he's going to make fun of her saying she didn't wake up."

For a moment Mrs. Hale had no answer. Then, "Well, I guess John Wright didn't wake up — when they was slippin' that rope under his neck," she muttered.

"No, it's *strange*," breathed Mrs. Peters. "They think it was such a — funny way to kill a man."

"That's just what Mr. Hale said," said Mrs. Hale, in a resolutely natural voice. "There was a gun in the house. He says that's what he can't understand."

"Mr. Henderson said, coming out, that what was needed for the case was a motive. Something to show anger — or sudden feeling."

"Well, I don't see any signs of anger around here," said Mrs. Hale. "I don't — " She stopped. Her eye was caught by a dish-towel in the middle of the kitchen table. Slowly she moved towards the table. One half of it was wiped clean, the other half untidy. Her eyes made a slow, almost unwilling turn to the bucket of sugar and the half-empty bag besides it. Things began — and not finished. She stepped back. "Wonder how they're finding things upstairs? I hope she had it in better shape up there. Seems kind of *sneaky* locking her up in town and coming out here to get her own house to turn against her!"

"But, Mrs. Hale," said the sheriff's wife, "the law is the law."

"I s'pose it is," answered Mrs. Hale shortly.

She turned to the stove, saying something about that fire not being much to brag of. "The law is the law — and a bad stove is a bad stove. How'd you like to work on this?" with the poker pointing to the broken lining. She opened the oven door. The thought of Minnie Foster trying to back in that oven — and the thought of her never going over to see Minnie Foster — . She was startled by hearing Mrs. Peters say, "A person gets discouraged — and loses heart." The sheriff's wife had looked from the stove to the sink — the pail of water which had been carried in from outside. The two women stood there silent, above them the footsteps of the men who were looking for evidence against the woman who had worked in that kitchen. That look of seeing into things, of seeing through a thing to something else, was in the eyes of the sheriff's wife now. When Mrs. Hale next spoke to her, it was gently.

"Better loosen up your things, Mrs. Peters. We'll not feel them when we go out."

Mrs. Peters went to the back of the room to hang up the fur tippet she was wearing. "Why, she was piecing a quilt," she exclaimed, and held up a large sewing basket piled high with quilt pieces.

Mrs. Hale spread some of the blocks on the table.

"It's log-cabin pattern," she said, putting several of them together. "Pretty, isn't it?"

They were so engaged with the quilt that they did not hear the footsteps on the stairs. As the stair door opened Mrs. Hale was saying, "do you suppose she was going to quilt it, or just knot it?"

The sheriff threw up his hands.

"They wonder whether she was going to quilt it, or just knot it!"

There was a laugh for the ways of women; a warming of hands over the stove, and then the county attorney said briskly, "Well, let's go right out to the barn and get that cleared up."

"I don't see as there's anything so strange," Mrs. Hale said resentfully, after the outside door had closed on the three men — "our taking up our time with little things while we're waiting for them to get the evidence. I don't see as it's anything to laugh about."

"Of course they've got awful important things on their minds," said the sheriff's wife apologetically.

They returned to an inspection of the blocks for the quilt. Mrs. Hale was looking at the fine, even sewing, preoccupied with thoughts of the woman who had done that sewing, when she heard the sheriff's wife say, in a startled tone, "Why, look at this one."

"The sewing," said Mrs. Peters, in a troubled way. "All the rest of them have been so nice and even — but — this one. Why, it looks as if she didn't know what she was about!"

Their eyes met — something flashed to life, passed between them; then, as if with an effort, they seemed to pull away from each other. A moment Mrs. Hale sat there, her fingers upon those stitches so unlike the rest of the sewing. Then she had pulled a knot and drawn the threads.

"Oh, what are you doing Mrs. Hale?" asked the sheriff's wife.

"Just pulling out a stitch or two that's not sewed very good," said Mrs. Hale mildly.

"I don't think we ought to touch things." Mrs. Peters said.

"I'll finish up this end," answered Mrs. Hale.

She threaded the needle and started to replace bad sewing with good. Then in that thin, timid voice, she heard: "Mrs. Hale!"

"Yes, Mrs. Peters?"

"What do you suppose she was so — nervous about?"

"Oh, I don't know," said Mrs. Hale, as if dismissing a thing not important enough to spend much time on. "I don't know as she was — nervous. I sew awful queer sometimes when I'm just tired."

"Well, I must get these clothes wrapped. They may be through sooner than we think. I wonder where I could find a piece of paper — and string."

"In that cupboard, maybe," suggested Mrs. Hale.

One piece of the crazy sewing remained unripped. Mrs. Peter's back turned, Martha Hale scrutinized that piece, compared it with the dainty, accurate stitches of the other blocks. The difference was startling. Holding this block it was hard to remain quiet, as if the distracted thoughts of the woman who had perhaps turned to it to try and quiet herself were communicating themselves to her.

"Here's a bird cage," Mrs. Peters said. "Did she have a bird, Mrs. Hale?"

"Why, I don't know whether she did or not." She turned to look at the cage Mrs. Peters was holding up. "I've not been here in so long." She signed. "There was a man round last year selling canaries cheap — but I don't know as she took one. Maybe she did. She used to sing real pretty herself."

"Seems kind of funny to think of a bird here. But she must have had one — or why would she have a cage? I wonder what happened to it."

"I suppose maybe the cat got it," suggested Mrs. Hale, resuming her sewing.

"No; she didn't have a cat. She's got that feeling some people have about cats — being afraid of them. When they brought her to our house yesterday, my cat got in the room, and she was real upset and asked me to take it out."

"My sister Bessie was like that," laughed Mrs. Hale.

The sheriff's wife did not reply. The silence made Mrs. Hale turn. Mrs. Peters was examining the bird cage.

"Look at this door," she said slowly. "It's broke. One hinge has been pulled apart."

Mrs. Hale came nearer.

"Looks as if someone must have been — rough with it."

Again their eyes met — startled, questioning, apprehensive. For a moment neither spoke nor stirred. Then Mrs. Hale, turning away, said brusquely, "If they're going to find any evidence, I wish they'd be about it. I don't like this place."

"But I'm awful glad you came with me, Mrs. Hale." Mrs. Peters put the birdcage on the table and sat down. "It would be lonesome for me — sitting here alone."

"Yes, it would, wouldn't it?" agreed Mrs. Hale. She had picked up the sewing, but now it dropped to her lap, and she murmured: "But I tell you what I *do* wish, Mrs. Peters. I wish I had come over sometimes when she was here. I wish — I had."

"But of course you were awful busy, Mrs. Hale. Your house — and your children."

"I could've come. I stayed away because it wasn't cheerful — and that's why I ought to have come. I" — she looked around — "I've never liked this place. Maybe because it's down in a hollow and you don't see the road. I don't know what it is, but it's a lonesome place, and always was. I wish I had come over to see Minnie Foster sometimes. I can see now."

"Well, you mustn't reproach yourself. Somehow we just don't see how it is with other folks till — something comes up."

"Not having children makes less work," mussed Mrs. Hale, "but it makes a quiet house. And Wright out to work all day — and no company when he did come in. Did you know John Wright, Mrs. Peters?"

"Not to know him. I've seen him in town. They say he was a good man."

"Yes — good," conceded John Wright's neighbor grimly. "He didn't drink, and kept his word as well as most, I guess, and paid his debts. But he was a hard man, Mrs. Peters. Just to pass the time of day with him — " She shivered. "Like a raw wind that gets to the bone." Her eye fell upon the cage on the table before her, and she added, "I should think she would've wanted a bird!"

Suddenly she leaned forward, looking intently at the cage. "But what do you s'pose went wrong with it?"

"I don't know," returned Mrs. Peters; "unless it got sick and died."

But after she said this she reached over and swung the broken door. Both women watched it.

"You don't know — her?" Mrs. Hale asked.

"Not till they brought her yesterday," said the sheriff's wife.

"She — come to think of it, she was kind of like a bird herself. Real sweet and pretty, but kind of timid and — fluttery. How — she — did — change."

Finally, as if struck with a happy thought and relieved to get back to everyday things: "Tell you what, Mrs. Peters, why don't you take the quilt in with you? It might take up your mind."

"Why, I think that's a real nice idea, Mrs. Hale. There couldn't possibly be any objection to that, could there? Now, just what will I take? I wonder if her patches are in here?" They turned to the sewing basket.

"Here's some red," said Mrs. Hale, bringing out a roll of cloth. Underneath this was a box. "Here, maybe her scissors are in here — and her things." She held it up. "What a pretty box! I'll warrant that was something she had a long time ago — when she was a girl."

She held it in her hand a moment; then, with a little sigh, opened it.

Instantly her hand went to her nose. "Why!"

Mrs. Peters drew nearer — then turned away.

"There's something wrapped up in this piece of silk," faltered Mrs. Hale.

"This isn't her scissors," said Mrs. Peters, in a shrinking voice.

Mrs. Hale raised the piece of silk. "Oh, Mrs. Peters!" she cried. "It's — "

Mrs. Peters bent closer.

"It's the bird," she whispered.

"But, Mrs. Peters!" cried Mrs. Hale, "*Look* at it! Its *neck* — look at its neck! It's all — other side *too*."

The sheriff's wife again bent closer.

"Somebody wrung its neck," said she, in a voice that was slow and deep. The eyes of the two women met — this time clung together in a look of dawning comprehension, of growing horror. Mrs. Peters looked from the dead bird to the broken door of the cage. Again their eyes met. And just then there was a sound at the outside door.

Mrs. Hale slipped the box under the quilt pieces in the basket. The county attorney and sheriff came in.

"Well, ladies," said the attorney, as one turning from serious things to little pleasantries, "have you decided whether she was going to quilt it or knot it?"

"We think," said the sheriff's wife hastily, "that she was going to knot it."

"Well, that's very interesting, I'm sure." He caught sight of the cage. "Has the bird flown?"

"We think the cat got it," said Mrs. Hale in a prosaic voice.

He was walking up and down, as if thinking something out.

"Is there a cat?" he asked absently.

Mrs. Hale shot a look up at the sheriff's wife.

"Well, not *now*," said Mrs. Peters. "They're superstitious, you know; they leave."

The county attorney did not heed her. "No sign at all of anyone having coming in from the outside," he said to Peters, continuing an interrupted conversation. "Their own rope. Now let's go upstairs again and go over it, piece by piece. It would have to have been someone who knew just the — "

The stair door closed behind them and their voices were lost.

The two women sat motionless, not looking at each other, but as if peering into something and at the same time holding back. When they spoke now it was as if they were afraid of what they were saying, but could not help saying it.

"She liked the bird," said Martha Hale. "She was going to bury it in that pretty box."

"When I was a girl," said Mrs. Peters, under her breath, "my kitten — there was a boy took a hatchet, and before my eyes — before I could get there — " She covered her face an instant. "If they hadn't held me back I would have" — she caught herself, and finished weakly — "hurt him." Then they sat without speaking or moving. "I wonder how it would seem," Mrs. Hale began, as if feeling her way over strange ground — "never to have had any children around." Her eyes made a sweep of the kitchen. "No, Wright wouldn't like the bird — a thing that sang. She used to sing. He killed that too."

Mrs. Peters moved. "Of course we don't know who killed the bird."

"I knew John Wright," was the answer.

"It was an awful thing was done in this house that night, Mrs. Hale," said the sheriff's wife. "Killing a man while he slept — slipping a thing round his neck that choked the life out of him."

Mrs. Hale's hand went to the bird-cage. "His neck. Choked the life out of him."

"We don't *know* who killed him," whispered Mrs. Peters wildly. "We don't *know*."

Mrs. Hale had not moved. "If there had been years and years of nothing, then a bird to sing to you, it would be awful — still, after the bird was still."

"I know what stillness is," whispered Mrs. Peters. "When we homesteaded in Dakota, and my first baby died — after he was two years old — and me with no other then — "

Mrs. Hale stirred. "How soon do you suppose they'll be through looking for the evidence?"

"I know what stillness is," repeated Mrs. Peters. Then she too pulled back. "The law has got to punish crime, Mrs. Hale."

"I wish you'd seen Minnie Foster when she wore a white dress with blue ribbons, and stood up there in the choir and sang."

The picture of that girl, the thought that she had lived neighbor to her for twenty years, and had let her die for lack of life, was suddenly more than the woman could bear.

"Oh, I *wish* I'd come over here once in a while!" she cried. "That was a crime! That was a crime! Who's going to punish *that*?"

"We mustn't — take on," said Mrs. Peters, with a frightened look towards the stairs.

"I might 'a *known* she needed help! I tell you, it's *queer*, Mrs. Peters. We live close together, and we live far apart. We all go through the same things — it's all just a different kind of the same thing! If it weren't — why do you and I *know* — what we know this minute?"

Seeing the jar of fruit on the table, she reached for it. "If I was you I wouldn't *tell* her her fruit was gone! Tell her it *ain't*. Tell her it's all right — all of it. Here — take this in to prove to her! She — she may never know whether it was broke or not."

Mrs. Peters took the bottle of fruit as if glad to take it — as if touching a familiar thing, having something to do, could keep her from something else. She looked about for something to wrap the fruit in, took a petticoat from the pile of clothes she had brought from the front room, nervously started wading that round the bottle.

"My!" she began, in a high voice, "it's a good thing that men couldn't hear us! Getting all stirred up over a little thing like a — dead canary. As if that could have anything to do with — with — My, wouldn't they *laugh*?"

There were footsteps on the stairs.

"Maybe they would," muttered Mrs. Hale — "maybe they wouldn't." "No, Peters," said the county attorney, "it's all perfectly clear, except the reason for doing it. But you know juries when it comes to women. If there was some definite thing — something to *show*. Something to make a story about. A thing that would connect up with this clumsy way of doing it."

Mrs. Hale looked at Mrs. Peters. Mrs. Peters was looking at her. Quickly they looked away from one another. The outer door opened and Mr. Hale came in.

"I've nailed back that board we ripped off," he said.

"Much obliged, Mr. Hale," said the sheriff. "We'll be getting along now."

"I'm going to stay here awhile by myself," the county attorney suddenly announced. "You can send Frank out for me, can't you?" he asked the sheriff. "I want to go over everything. I'm not satisfied we can't do better."

Again, for one brief moment the women's eyes met.

The sheriff came up to the table.

"Did you want to see what Mrs. Peters was going to take in?"

The county attorney picked up the apron. He laughed.

"Oh, I guess they're not very dangerous things the ladies have picked out."

Mrs. Hale's hand was on the sewing basket in which the box was concealed. She felt that she ought to take her hand off the basket. She did not seem able to. She picked up one of the quilt blocks she had piled on to cover the box. She had a fear that if he took up the basket she would snatch it from him.

But he did not take it. With another laugh he turned away, saying, "No, Mrs. Peters doesn't need supervising. For that matter, a sheriff's wife is married to the law. Ever think of it that way, Mrs. Peters?"

Mrs. Peters had turned her face away. "Not — just that way," she said.

"Married to the law!" chuckled Mrs. Peters' husband. He moved towards the door into the front room, and said to the county attorney, "I just want you to come here a minute, George. We ought to take a look at these windows."

"Oh — windows!" scoffed the county attorney.

"We'll be leaving in a second, Mr. Hale," Mr. Peters told the farmer, as he followed the county attorney into the other room.

"Can't be leavin' too soon to suit me," muttered Hale, and went out.

Again, for one final moment, the two women were alone in the kitchen.

Martha Hale sprang up, her hands tight together, looking at the other woman, with whom it rested. At first she could not see her eyes, for the sheriff's wife had not turned back since she turned away at that suggestion of being married to the law. Slowly, unwillingly, Mrs. Peters turned her head until her eyes met the eyes of the other woman. There was a moment when they held each other in a steady, burning look in which there was no evasion nor flinching. Then Martha Hale's eyes pointed the way to the basket in which was hidden the thing that would convict the third woman — that woman who was not there, and yet who had been there with them through that hour.

For a moment, Mrs. Peters did not move. And then she did it. Threw back the quilt pieces, got the box, tried to put it in her hand-bag. It was too big. Desperately she opened it, started to take the bird out. But there she broke — she could not touch the bird. She stood there helpless, foolish.

There was a sound at the door. Martha Hale snatched the box from the sheriff's wife and got it in the pocket of her big coat just as the sheriff and the county attorney came back into the kitchen.

"Well, Henry," said the county attorney, facetiously, "at least we found out that she was not going to quilt it. She was going to — what is it you call it, ladies?'

Mrs. Hale's hand was against the pocket of her coat.

"We call it — knot it," was her answer.

§ 1.09 Chapter Review Problems

Review Problem 1-A

A famous movie star is arrested for shoplifting three expensive dresses from the Durn's Department Store. The star asserts her innocence and claims, "It was all a huge misunderstanding. I just wanted to show my personal assistant the cute buttons on the front of the dresses and she happened to be standing outside the store." At trial, the star offers the fact that she already was the owner of similar dresses, which she often wore to fancy dinner parties. The star testified, "Why would I need additional similar dresses? My own dresses are fabulous."

Which of the following is the most accurate statement about the star's own dresses?

1. The fact that the star owned similar dresses is relevant because it is direct evidence of her attendance at numerous dinner parties.

2. The similar dresses constitute representative evidence of the dresses allegedly shoplifted by the star.

3. The similar dresses require no evidentiary foundation from the star's attorney because they "speak for themselves."

4. The similar dresses constitute relevant circumstantial evidence in the case.

Review Problem 1-B

Arturo Montejo is charged with the murder of Sandy Mitrani. At trial, the prosecutor, Ms. Parnell, offers Sandy's statement as she lay dying from a bullet wound to the abdomen. The defense counsel, Ms. Sarno, objected and the Judge called both attorneys to the bench to discuss the question of admissibility.

JUDGE: Ms. Parnell, please proffer what the statement Sandy allegedly made was?

MS. PARNELL: The statement Sandy made that we would like to introduce is: "I can't believe this! I left myself open for being shot, and by that $%@#%@#^ Montejo!" The statement is a dying declaration, Your Honor.

MS. SARNO: Your Honor, a dying declaration requires the maker of the statement to be unavailable to testify, that the statement be about the circumstances of the maker's death, that the person believe death was imminent at the time of the statement, and that the statement be made in a homicide or civil case. The pertinent rule is Federal Rule of Evidence 804(b)(2) and pursuant to that rule, Sandy's statement was not a dying declaration.

Which of the following propositions is most accurate regarding the admissibility of Sandy's statement?

1. The statement is direct evidence of Sandy's death.

2. The prosecutor, Ms. Parnell, has an affirmative obligation to offer some evidence that Sandy knew death was imminent prior to the judge admitting it into evidence.

3. Since the jury must decide whether Sandy believed her death was imminent, the prosecutor, Ms. Parnell, need not lay any foundation concerning that point.

4. The prosecutor, Ms. Parnell, must show that Sandy died from the gunshot wound or was otherwise unavailable to testify beyond a reasonable doubt.

Chapter 2

The Roles of Judges, Juries, and Attorneys at Trial

§ 2.01 Chapter Checklist

1. How is the judge the "gatekeeper" of the evidence admitted at trial?

2. How can attorneys satisfy their dual roles of representing their clients zealously and serving as officers of the court?

3. How can attorneys represent their clients zealously at trial and preserve the record for a potential appeal at the same time?

4. Why is the jury described as the "judge of the facts"?

5. Is it important for jurors to evaluate the credibility of evidence?

§ 2.02 Relevant Federal Rules of Evidence

Rule 103. Rulings on Evidence

(a) Preserving a Claim of Error. A party may claim error in a ruling to admit or exclude evidence only if the error affects a substantial right of the party and:

(1) if the ruling admits evidence, a party, on the record:

(A) timely objects or moves to strike; and

(B) states the specific ground, unless it was apparent from the context; or

(2) if the ruling excludes evidence, a party informs the court of its substance by an offer of proof, unless the substance was apparent from the context.

(b) Not Needing to Renew an Objection or Offer of Proof. Once the court rules definitively on the record — either before or at trial — a party need not renew an objection or offer of proof to preserve a claim of error for appeal.

(c) Court's Statement About the Ruling; Directing an Offer of Proof. The court may make any statement about the character or form of the evidence, the objection made, and the ruling. The court may direct that an offer of proof be made in question-and-answer form.

(d) Preventing the Jury from Hearing Inadmissible Evidence. To the extent practicable, the court must conduct a jury trial so that inadmissible evidence is not suggested to the jury by any means.

(e) Taking Notice of Plain Error. A court may take notice of a plain error affecting a substantial right, even if the claim of error was not properly preserved.

Rule 104. Preliminary Questions

(a) In General. The court must decide any preliminary question about whether a witness is qualified, a privilege exists, or evidence is admissible. In so deciding, the court is not bound by evidence rules, except those on privilege.

(b) Relevance That Depends on a Fact. When the relevance of evidence depends on whether a fact exists, proof must be introduced sufficient to support a finding that the fact does exist. The court may admit the proposed evidence on the condition that the proof be introduced later.

(c) Conducting a Hearing So That the Jury Cannot Hear It. The court must conduct any hearing on a preliminary question so that the jury cannot hear it if:

> (1) the hearing involves the admissibility of a confession;
>
> (2) a defendant in a criminal case is a witness and so requests; or
>
> (3) justice so requires.

(d) Cross-Examining a Defendant in a Criminal Case. By testifying on a preliminary question, a defendant in a criminal case does not become subject to cross-examination on other issues in the case.

(e) Evidence Relevant to Weight and Credibility. This rule does not limit a party's right to introduce before the jury evidence that is relevant to the weight or credibility of other evidence.

§ 2.03 Introduction

Judges, juries, and attorneys have different responsibilities at trial. The responsibilities encompass the gathering, offering, objecting to, and admission of evidence. While evidence rules play a significant role in the division of these duties, general rules of trial procedure and standards of professional conduct have a large impact as well.

§ 2.04 The Trial Judge's Role

Judges are responsible for the overall management of trials. As the trial's "chief operating officer," the judge is at once an umpire of disputes and an air traffic controller. The judge must ensure that the case progresses in an orderly and predictable fashion (*see* Rule 611). As part of this general responsibility, it is the judge's job to rule on evidentiary objections and on the admissibility of evidence. The Federal Rules of Evidence give judges discretion in making evidentiary rulings and constrain judges' power. For example, while judges can call witnesses (*see* Rule 614) and may even comment on the evidence, they must exclude both irrelevant evidence (*see* Rule 402) and improper lay opinion testimony (*see* Rule 701). Further, a federal judge's ability to comment on the evidence is limited to the extent that it must not interfere with the jury's fact-finding function.

A judge makes admissibility determinations about whether evidence is hearsay, whether a witness is properly qualified to testify, whether a sufficient foundation has been laid for an exhibit, and whether a privilege applies to certain evidence. In making these and other admissibility determinations, a judge has wide latitude to consider many types of evidence. In the interest of accurate rulings, the judge is even permitted to consider inadmissible evidence, including hearsay. Nevertheless, the rules prohibit judges from considering privileged information when making admissibility determinations (*see* Rule 104(a)). Privileged information is consequently unique; judges cannot consider it when deciding whether evidence is admissible and a trier of fact cannot consider it when determining the facts of the case.

Example

At 2:00 a.m. on January 6th, two cars collided on Interstate 95. One of the cars was going the wrong way. After the crash, the cars were turned and entangled in such a manner that it was difficult to determine which driver was at fault.

At a civil trial between the drivers of the two cars, both of whom survived with serious injuries, the plaintiff offered in evidence a piece of metal located approximately 40 feet away from the crash, claiming that it was part of the defendant's car. The plaintiff offered the piece of metal because its location supported the plaintiff's theory that the defendant's car was the one traveling in the wrong direction.

At an earlier part of the trial, an expert from the Ford Motor Company had testified that this piece of metal "looked like" the kind that came from a 1994 Ford Galaxy, the defendant's car. An eyewitness had testified that he had seen the accident and that the impact had spewed pieces of metal everywhere, even as much as 60 feet away.

From the judge's perspective, the eyewitness was not very credible, and evidence suggested that the expert witness had made several mistakes in the past. Further, an affidavit from a passenger of another car, who attempted to describe the accident, was filled with statements made by other bystanders. The affidavit generally supported the plaintiff's claim about the piece of metal, however. Despite all of these deficiencies, the judge admitted the piece of metal on the basis that a reasonable juror could decide that the piece of metal was indeed a part of the defendant's car.

The judge also believed the jury could reasonably discredit the evidence of the eyewitness and the expert, and find that the metal was not part of the defendant's car. However, that possibility was not a reason under the rules to exclude the metal. The basic fact-finding function belongs to the jury and not the judge. It was simply the judge's job to screen out "bad" evidence, meaning evidence whose relevance was not supported by evidence sufficient to support a finding of fact pursuant to Rule 104(b).

A. Questions of Admissibility

Perhaps the best-known job of the judge is the duty to rule on questions of admissibility. Judges must decide whether to sustain (uphold) or overrule (deny) a party's objections to evidence. If the attorneys fail to object to evidence or make a proffer, judges generally bite their tongues and remain silent, as it is the prerogative of the attorneys to try their own cases.

When a judge is asked to rule on a question of relevancy, the judge bases the ruling on reason and experience and the supporting evidence presented. (*See, e.g.,* Advisory Committee Note to Rule 401.) When a judge is asked to rule on other evidentiary areas, the judge may need to apply additional legal rules and principles. In areas like hearsay and privilege, the judge must determine whether evidentiary prerequisites have been met. Since admissibility rulings often involve the particular facts of a case, each ruling may pose new and challenging considerations that permit a judge to use her discretion. (*See* Rules 104(a), 104(b).) (Some admissibility questions, like those involving judicial notice, are not intended to promote diverse results from case to case or judge to judge. *See* Rule 201, which is discussed in Chapter 16.)

Rule foundation admissibility questions, meaning whether the requirements of the Rules are met, are governed by Rule 104(a). These questions depend on fact as well as law, such as whether a proposed "excited utterance" hearsay statement was made under the stress of excitement or whether an expert is relying on data or information of the type reasonably relied on in the expert's field. Thus, the judge alone decides if an out-of-court statement meets the criteria for an excited utterance or whether an expert is basing her testimony on information "reasonably relied on in the field", but it is the jury that decides whether to give that excited utterance or expert any credit or weight.

The burden of supplying supporting facts and laying a foundation for the admissibility of evidence is generally placed on the party offering the evidence and requires a preponderance of proof. The Advisory Committee observes that, for fact determinations, "the judge will of necessity receive evidence pro and con on the issue." Advisory Committee Note 104(a). Significantly, the supporting evidence is not limited by the Rules, meaning a judge can even consider inadmissible evidence in making the admissibility decision, except a judge is not permitted to consider evidence that qualifies as privileged in making the admissibility determination. (*See* Rule 104(a).)

The preponderance of proof includes witness credibility questions. This means that a judge must resolve credibility questions should they arise. For example, if two witnesses contradict each other on the existence of a foundational fact, the judge must decide which witness to believe. Of course, the judge's *preliminary* determination of fact is not dispositive; the jury may disregard the evidence if it chooses.

Conditional relevance admissibility determinations are governed by Rule 104(b) and have a different standard of admissibility. These questions, as discussed further in the section on conditional relevance in the Relevance chapter, involve the facts surrounding the claimed event. Conditional relevance, also called relevance conditioned on fact, asks whether there is enough evidence to support a party's claims about what the facts are. For example, what actually happened at a meeting, an auto accident, or homicide may all depend on a supporting fact or facts. Under the minimal threshold of Rule 104(b), the judge simply must ask whether sufficient evidence has been introduced for a reasonable jury to find that the fact exists. If the judge concludes a reasonable jury *could* find — not necessarily *would* find — that the fact exists, the judge will admit the evidence for the jury's consideration.

Unlike preliminary competency determinations pursuant to Rule 104(a), the judge does not resolve credibility questions in finding conditionally relevant foundational facts. That is, the judge generally assumes the truthfulness of the proponent's foundational witnesses. These standards of proof are not recited in either Rule 104(a)'s or 104(b)'s text, but result from a "judicial gloss" on the rules. This is not the only area where holes in the rules are filled by "judicial gloss," but it is one of the more important ones. *See Huddleston v. United States*, 485 U.S. 681 (1988) (104(b) conditional relevancy standard); *and Bourjaily v. United States*, 483 U.S. 171 (1987) (104(a) competency standard).

Example

In a breach of contract action brought by a fencing manufacturer against its primary supplier, the plaintiff manufacturer offers the testimony of a witness to the agreement. The testimony includes the following:

DEFENDANT'S ATTORNEY: Objection, Your Honor, the witness' answer will be riddled with inadmissible hearsay. May we approach the bench?

JUDGE: Certainly. (at sidebar) Plaintiff's counsel, please proffer what Sheila will say if she is allowed to answer the question.

PLAINTIFF'S ATTORNEY: Of course, Your Honor. She will testify she heard the defendant's brother say to the defendant, "You realize the agreement does not allow us to supply the manufacturer with materials from our usual supplier in Maine and that it's going to cost us a heap more to get supplies elsewhere?" and that the defendant just stared back at his brother prior to signing the agreement.

JUDGE: Why is this objectionable, counsel?

DEFENDANT'S ATTORNEY: It is inadmissible hearsay, Your Honor.

JUDGE: I rule that the evidence is admissible, constituting an adoptive statement by a party opponent by silence. The defendant acquiesced in the statement and it is offered against him, as Rule 801(d)(2) provides. I am satisfied, based on the entire record in this case, that the evidence is relevant to the breach of contract issue and is not hearsay because it qualifies as a statement by a party opponent.

Problem 2-1: Alimony Al

Al sues his ex-wife, Anne, for increased alimony payments. Anne seeks to introduce at trial a journal that Al regularly kept of his expenses. Al objects, claiming that the book is a fake. Al submits a letter from a person who claims to have written the journal in exchange for a $4000 payment from Anne.

1. Can the judge consider the letter from the purported author of the journal in determining whether to admit the book? Why?

2. Anne calls Al's new wife, Kristine, to the witness stand. Al objects, relying on the marital communications privilege. What standard of admissibility applies in determining whether the privilege exists? How does the standard compare to general relevancy determinations?

Exercise: The Judge's Role

A judge often rules on evidence objections in seconds. The speed at which a judge must react is like the speed cars travel on the interstate — fast, to say the least. Thus, judges must become adept at saying "overruled" (the question or evidence will be permitted), or "sustained" (the question or evidence will be excluded), after objections are lodged by counsel. In addition, judges often ask for a response by opposing counsel prior to ruling.

The exercise below is intended to provide students with the opportunity to experience the judge's role at trial. If possible, students should stay in role during the entire exercise.

* * *

Exercise

For a statement to be admitted under the hearsay exception commonly referred to as "dying declarations," Rule 804(b)(2), the attorney must lay a foundation showing that the statement was made "by a [currently unavailable] declarant while believing that the declarant's death was imminent, concerning the cause or circumstances of what the declarant believed to be impending death." Thus, the attorney has several evidentiary foundations to meet prior to a judge finding the statement admissible. The attorney must show the unavailable declarant not only made a statement about his death, but he believed he was about to die at the time of the statement. (Note that the rule does not require the declarant to die, just for the declarant to believe she was about to die.)

Assume that a trial has commenced concerning the following fact pattern: Joan Jacobs was shot in an aborted robbery attempt outside a shopping mall in broad daylight on a very hot July day. As she slumped against her sports utility vehicle in the parking lot, she started rambling to the security guard, Sharon Stanley, who had come to help her, and the crowd of bystanders that had gathered. Jacobs muttered, "Get me a priest . . . and a last glass of water . . . I am bleeding everywhere. I am in big trouble. Does anyone else have the chills? It is cold here. If I ever see that guy who shot me again, I would recognize him anywhere! He looks just like Tom Cruise, only taller, about six feet tall. And oh yeah, he had a beard and a scar across his right cheek. I better not talk now, I am really hurting and may not make it. Tell my husband I love him . . . oh, I really want to hug my dog. Get Dr. Smaltz over here to help me; he's the best."

Joan subsequently dies. You are the prosecutor in the murder trial. James Jackson is accused of the murder. At trial, you first called Sharon Stanley to the witness stand to lay the appropriate foundations for the dying declaration.

After Sharon Stanley has testified, you call another witness who was a bystander in the crowd surrounding the deceased. The bystander, Bobby Barnwell, will testify that as he was leaving the shopping mall, he was attracted by a small crowd around a woman, who he later learned was named Joan Jacobs. Barnwell will state:

"I saw a man walking quickly in the other direction look back over his shoulder several times — as if he was hiding something. I think, but can't be sure, it was the defendant here. The guy slyly dropped something into a garbage can, but I couldn't see what it was." (The garbage can was later searched and discovered to contain a handgun with one of the defendant's fingerprints on it.)

Barnwell is currently unemployed and has been arrested four times for disorderly conduct.

Place Mr. Barnwell on the witness stand and ask him questions on direct examination to elicit information about the man he saw walking in the other direction. In addition, be prepared to ask the questions listed below.

Because you are just starting your journey of learning the rules of evidence, for the purposes of this exercise, the opposing counsel should object to those questions believed to be impermissible with the following phrase, "Objection, Your Honor; that was improper." (In actual trials, lawyers must identify the precise bases of their objections. "C'mon, Your Honor, she can't ask that" may be good enough for TV lawyers, but not for real ones.) The judge can ask the prosecution for a brief response, stating why the form or substance of the question is appropriate (pointing out, for example, that the response will help to prove the case or that the response is not unfairly prejudicial). The judge must then rule, either overruling the objection or sustaining the objection.

Some of the questions in the list below are clearly admissible or inadmissible. Many of the questions, however, are borderline acceptable, depending on the judge and the factual context of the questioning for their propriety. A student playing the examining attorney should ask the questions, and a student playing a witness should answer the questions. Also, a student playing opposing counsel should object to those questions believed to be improper and, after brief advocacy from each counsel, one or more students playing judges should rule.

The questions that counsel should ask the witness ought to include the following:

1. How did Ms. Jacobs appear when you first saw her?
2. What was the man doing when he walked in the other direction?
3. What did you have for breakfast that morning, Mr. Barnwell?
4. Why were you at the shopping mall?
5. Were you arrested for disorderly conduct recently?
6. Explain.
7. Did you think Ms. Jacobs was dying?
8. How long have you been unemployed?
9. Where do you live?
10. Describe the parking lot in the area where Ms. Jacobs was lying.
11. What did you hear Ms. Jacobs say about Tom Cruise?

B. Appellate Judges: The Standard of Review on Appeal

An appellate judge usually does not retry a case on appeal. This means that the judge must take the record made below "as is," including the facts. The standard of review, meaning the test the appellate judges apply in considering the issues on appeal, can vary, depending on the nature of the issue. Variables include the type of error alleged, (e.g., Did the error involve a constitutional right? Was the error made by the jury, prosecutor, judge, or other person?), and whether the error occurred in a criminal or civil case.

Standards of review include: abuse of discretion, *de novo*, and plain error. *Abuse of discretion* means a rule afforded discretion to a trial judge and the judge's evidentiary ruling exceeded the boundaries of that discretion. *De novo* review occurs when the issue is a question of law and the appellate court starts with a clean slate for its review. *Plain error* is an evidentiary error that concerns important evidence and is so apparent from the record that an appellate court is likely to consider it, even though a party failed to object to the evidence. The appellate court is saying, in effect, "I know it when I see it." Reversible error generally cannot be found in an evidentiary ruling unless the error caused harm that rendered the trial proceedings unfair. The pertinent Federal Rule of Evidence requires that an error affect a "substantial right" of the parties to amount to reversible error. (*See* Rule 103(d).)

Problem 2-2: *"Justice Was Done, So Appeal Immediately"*

Rebecca is tried on charges of robbing a grocery store. In her defense, Rebecca offers to testify that she exchanged blows with the grocery store's manager more than one year prior to the alleged robbery and had not been in the store since that time. The prosecution objects, claiming the evidence is irrelevant. The trial judge improperly sustains the objection, ruling that no mention of the altercation would be allowed. Rebecca is convicted. She appeals the conviction, claiming the exclusion of the evidence was in error. *What is the appropriate standard of review by the appellate court?*

§ 2.05 The Jury's Role

The jury is commonly called the "judge of the facts." As fact-finder, the jury weighs the admissible evidence according to the applicable standard of proof (e.g., preponderance of the evidence or beyond a reasonable doubt). On a different level, the jury's role transcends the individual case. In a jury-based legal system, the jury arguably becomes an integral part of democratic governance, particularly in criminal cases, where an accused is entitled to a jury selected from a cross-section of society. (*See* the United States Constitution, Sixth Amendment.)

Especially in criminal cases, the jury becomes the conscience of the community. As the community's moral conscience, a jury has considerable power, including the power to nullify the law and return a verdict of "not guilty," no matter how rationally compelling the prosecutor's evidence. This law-shaping power is not expressly communicated to the jury at a trial, but to a certain extent is accepted as implied. *See, e.g.,* M. Harrington, *The Law-Finding Function of the American Jury*, 1999 WIS. L. REV. 377 (1999) ("Most [judges] recognized that juries might ignore their instructions, and bring in a verdict contrary to the law stated in the charge."). The law-finding function makes sense if one views the jury as having important constitutional and democratic dimensions, drawn from the community at large and acting on its behalf.

The jury's role differs from that of the judge. While the judge oversees the trial process and can make preliminary factual determinations, the jury comprises the basic trial machinery, acting as the final arbiter of the facts as they relate to guilt, liability, and other weighty matters.

The determination of the facts is perhaps the jury's most important responsibility. The jury's job is to weigh the evidence, decide how events took place, and apply the law to the facts. For example, a jury must decide in a breach of contract action whether there was a contract and then whether it was breached. Of course, the jury's role is interdependent with the attorneys, who must offer admissible evidence for the jury's consideration.

Fact determination is complex. This is attributable in large part to the nature of human behavior. Studies have shown that even though a juror's "common sense" may indeed be common, it does not always make sense. These studies indicate that people tend to forget information much more rapidly immediately after an event than later on (a phenomenon called "the forgetting curve"), and that the confidence of eyewitnesses in their identifications often does not correlate with the accuracy of their identifications. While jurors are supposed to use common sense when evaluating witness' credibility, their common sense may not include awareness of these studies.

The rules of evidence intrude on the jury's fact-finding role when there are special kinds of proof problems. On rare occasions in civil cases, for example, when facts are beyond dispute, the court will instruct juries to accept certain facts as true. (*See* Rule 201.) This judicial declaration of fact is called judicial notice. On some occasions an opposite problem may exist, a lack of proof that threatens to deny justice. In this situation, the rules of evidence permit the creation of a presumption, which shifts at least some of the burden of proving the case to the opposing party in order to flush out evidence and promote fairness. (*See* Rule 301.) (Judicial notice and presumptions are discussed in Chapter 16.)

The judge and jury actually share some fact-finding responsibilities under the rules, with the judge making preliminary fact-finding decisions in several contexts. In one context, judges often must make preliminary determinations of fact in ruling on the competency of evidence, determining whether the evidence meets the admissibility standards set forth in the Federal Rules of Evidence. In another context, judges determine questions of *conditional relevance*, meaning whether facts exist to sufficiently connect evidence to the case.

§ 2.06 The Attorney's Role

An attorney must juggle two different roles at trial. Counsel must keep one eye on strategy in an attempt to win the case at hand and the other eye on creating a record for a potential appeal. Further, an attorney is both an officer of the court with a responsibility to the judicial system and a zealous representative of the client. These sometimes conflicting responsibilities increase the difficulty of the attorney's role.

A successful case depends not only on what evidence is offered by counsel but also on how the evidence is marshaled in support of counsel's theory of the case. An unsuccessful case generally permits an appeal, but only if the attorney creates an adequate record. The duty to create an appellate record translates into several requirements for the competent attorney. These include objecting to the admission of evidence and making a proffer or "offer of proof" for the record when the court has excluded an attorney's evidence or an answer to a question. More specifically:

1. *Objection.* If an adversary offers improper evidence, a lawyer must object, setting forth the specific basis for the objection *See* Rule 103(a)(1). A general objection of "irrelevant, incompetent and immaterial" is rarely sufficient.

2. *Proffer.* If a judge excludes evidence and it is not apparent from the record what the excluded evidence consisted of, the offering lawyer must make an

offer of proof, called a proffer, identifying the substance of the excluded evidence. *See* Rule 103(a)(2).

3. *Plain Error.* If the attorney fails to object or make a proffer, the point is generally foreclosed on appeal. However, one major exception to the proffer requirement exists. An appellate court can consider plain error, even though there was no objection or proffer (*see* Rule 103(d)). Attorneys should not rely on the plain error rule to save them from objection omissions, but rather should use it only as a last resort.

Practice Tip — Ask it twice:

If an objection to a question is overruled, a new trial attorney often follows up by instructing the witness to answer the question. Instead, counsel should ask the question again, just in case the jury missed it during the objection interplay. Even if the witness starts to answer before the question can be reasserted, control the witness with a quick hand "stop sign" motion, so that you can re-ask the question prior to eliciting the answer.

Trial attorneys must juggle another duality in roles. Attorneys are considered officers of the court and, as such, have a duty to act ethically and maintain the integrity of the judicial system. Lawyers also serve as representatives of their clients. In this capacity, attorneys must act competently and zealously on their clients' behalf. Sometimes these roles yield underlying tensions and even outright conflict, such as when a client informs counsel she intends to testify falsely (or has already done so).

The dual roles of the trial attorney seem to unite in one of the attorney's most important tasks — laying foundations for the admissibility of evidence. Laying foundations for evidence cannot be underestimated as a lawyering responsibility. This task means being able to demonstrate the prerequisites to admissibility as required by the rules of evidence. These evidentiary prerequisites are better thought of as affirmative admissibility ingredients, rather than as negative prohibitions. If the right foundational ingredients are shown, the evidence is admitted. With the notable exception of irrelevant evidence, most evidence can be offered for some purpose, either to prove an element of the case or to impeach a witness.

Attorneys' arguments to the judge about evidence issues typically focus on the sufficiency of foundations, not on "what the rules ought to be." Foundations can be viewed as the organizational center of evidence law; they serve as the primary intersection of evidence law in a classroom and evidence law in the courtroom. That is why this textbook emphasizes the laying of foundations.

Exercise: The Attorney's Role in Laying Evidentiary Foundations

Remember that for a hearsay statement to be admitted under the hearsay exception commonly referred to as "dying declarations," Rule 804(b)(2), the attorney must lay a foundation showing the statement was made "by a declarant while believing that the declarant's death was imminent, concerning the cause or circumstances of what the declarant believed to be impending death."

Assume the same facts as "The Dying Declaration" problem in the Judge's Role section, above. [In brief, Joan Jacobs had been shot in an aborted robbery attempt outside a shopping mall in broad daylight on a very hot July day. As she slumped against her sports utility vehicle in the parking lot, she started rambling to the security guard, Sharon Stanley, who had come to help her, and the crowd of bystanders that had gathered. Jacobs muttered, "Get me a priest . . . and a last glass of water . . . I am bleeding everywhere. I am in big trouble. Does anyone else have the chills? It is cold here. If I ever see that guy who shot me again, I would recognize him anywhere! He looks just like Tom Cruise, only taller, about six feet tall. And oh yeah, he had a beard and a scar across his right cheek. I better not talk now, I am really hurting and may not make it. Tell my husband I love him . . . oh, I really want to hug my dog. Get Dr. Smaltz over here to help me; he's the best." Joan subsequently dies.]

You are the prosecutor in the subsequent murder trial of James Jackson. At trial, you call the security guard, Sharon Stanley, to the witness stand to lay the appropriate foundation for the dying declaration.

You want to ask Stanley six questions in order to lay the foundation about Joan's belief of impending death. Your questions are to be asked after the following testimony. (Please write out the six questions.)

PROSECUTOR: Good morning, Ms. Stanley.

STANLEY: Good morning.

PROSECUTOR: Please state your name for the court reporter and spell your last name if you would.

STANLEY: Sure. Sharon Stanley. S-t-a-n-l-e-y.

PROSECUTOR: Ms. Stanley, why are you testifying in court today?

STANLEY: I was one of the first people to respond to the parking lot, aisle 21, of the Town and Country Mall on January 14th, where Joan Jacobs lay dying.

PROSECUTOR: [*begin your questions*]

Practice Tip:

Listening to your witness is an important trial skill. You may certainly refer to notes during a trial, but you need to pay complete attention to witnesses while they answer your questions. Resist the temptation to look down and review your notes while a witness is testifying. If you do that, the jury may be left with the wrong impression — that everything has been scripted or you do not care what a witness says. You also might miss something significant in the witness' answer.

Problem 2-3: My Cousin, the Lawyer, Vinnie

Vinnie, a new member of the bar, was conducting his first trial, a murder defense of his cousin in a small, conservative Southern town. In its case-in-chief (initial presentation of evidence), the prosecution offered evidence that the defendant had committed adultery on several occasions and had made contributions to animal rights groups. Vinnie objects to the evidence, saying "No way those things are admissible, Judge! The evidence is incompetent, immaterial, and irrelevant, and I object." The defendant was convicted and he appealed. *Should the appellate court consider these objections? Explain.*

Practice Tip—Never let the others in the courtroom see you perspire: You may need a bit of seasoning before you feel comfortable speaking in public as a trial attorney. One way to deal with those inevitable moments of "brain freeze," when you start perspiring even though the courtroom is ice cold, is to ask the judge for a brief chance to consult your notes or co-counsel, if there is one. Say in a cool, calm, and collected voice, "May I— —have a moment, Your Honor?" While you may feel lost, you do not appear so to the court or the jury.

§ 2.07 Summary and Review

1. Can the judge, *sua sponte* (i.e., on his or her own motion), offer strategic or tactical ideas to a party?

2. What are the two different types of admissibility determinations made by judges?

3. How do those admissibility determinations differ?

4. What are the ethical limitations on attorneys at trial?

5. Why should attorneys state the specific grounds of an objection?

6. Who decides how much weight to give evidence?

7. What does the term "evidentiary foundations" mean?

8. What is an offer of proof?

§ 2.08 Chapter Review Problems

Review Problem 2-A

In a case involving the murder of a convenience store clerk late at night in a store located right off the interstate highway, the prosecution offers the confession of the defendant, a 19-year-old youth. Over objection, the judge admitted the confession into evidence, ruling that it was voluntarily made in conformity with the Due Process Clause of the Constitution. At trial, the defendant offers evidence of coercion, noting the proximity of the officers asking the questions from the defendant, the length of the interrogation, the location of the confrontation and other such factors. The prosecutor objects to these questions. *How should the judge rule on the objection?*

1. Overrule the objection, since the defense in a criminal case can revisit the legal issue of whether a confession was voluntarily made.

2. Overrule the objection, if the questions go to the weight and credibility of the confession.

3. Sustain the objection, because once the evidence is admitted, the facts relating to the ruling are off-limits.

4. Sustain the objection, because Constitutional questions are within the province of the court and the court alone.

Review Problem 2-B

In a breach of contract action between the plaintiff, Ralph's Remodeling Company (Company), and Marsha Johnson, the defendant, the Company alleges non-payment after remodeling Marsha's kitchen. In her defense, Marsha claims that the job was not completed and that the work done was entirely inadequate.

At trial, the Company calls one of its project supervisors, Alberto Martin, who testifies about the work performed. The judge, Martha Pelos, had a gut feeling that Martin was misstating the facts and was somewhat unbelievable, although she recognized that reasonable people might find Martin reliable. *What should the judge do after Martin testifies?*

1. Inform the jury that Martin's testimony is being struck from the record because the judge found it to be questionable.

2. Strike the testimony from the record if the judge believes the jury would discredit it.

3. Allow the testimony if the judge concludes that the jurors could rationally believe Martin's testimony.

4. Allow the testimony if Martin's testimony is important to the defense.

Review Problem 2-C

In a diversity action alleging strict products liability arising from the rollover of a sports utility vehicle, the plaintiff's expert explained how the vehicle's defects contributed to the rollover. The cross-examination eroded the witness' credibility, undermining her opinion that the defect caused the rollover. The jury, however, found for the plaintiff and awarded considerable damages. *Upon the return of the verdict, what action should the judge take?*

1. The judge should accept the verdict because the jury's verdict is final no matter what the jury considered in reaching its determination, even if it drew straws.

2. The judge should accept the verdict because it is within the province of the jury to weigh the evidence, including the credibility of experts, even if the judge disagrees with the jury's assessment.

3. The judge should order a new trial if the jury's consideration of the expert's testimony gave the expert somewhat excessive credibility.

4. The judge should order a new trial if the jury's consideration of the expert's testimony would not be in accord with a preponderance of jurors.

Chapter 3

Relevance

§ 3.01 Chapter Checklist

1. Why is it important to ask, "To what is the evidence relevant?" and not just, "Is the evidence relevant?"

2. What do inferences have to do with relevance?

3. What do relationships have to do with relevance?

4. What does *probative* mean in the definition of relevance?

5. What does *fact of consequence* mean in the definition of relevance?

6. How does the *probative* prong of the relevance test relate to the *fact of consequence* prong?

7. How difficult is it for evidence to meet the threshold test of relevance?

8. Why is some evidence *conditionally relevant?*

9. At what point in time during a party's case can proof of a conditionally relevant fact be offered during the trial?

10. How does *Knapp* v. *State*, 79 N.E. 1076 (1907) (*see* the case library at the end of this chapter), shed light on the concept of relevance?

§ 3.02 Relevant Federal Rules of Evidence

Rule 401. Test for Relevant Evidence

Evidence is relevant if:

(a) it has any tendency to make a fact more or less probable than it would be without the evidence; and

(b) the fact is of consequence in determining the action.

Rule 402. Generally Admissibility of Evidence

Relevant evidence is admissible unless any of the following provides otherwise:

- the United States Constitution;
- a federal statute;
- these rules;

- or other rules prescribed by the Supreme Court.

Irrelevant evidence is not admissible.

Rule 104. Preliminary Questions

(a) In General. The court must decide any preliminary question about whether a witness is qualified, a privilege exists, or evidence is admissible. In so deciding, the court is not bound by evidence rules, except those on privilege.

(b) Relevance That Depends on a Fact. When the relevance of evidence depends on whether a fact exists, proof must be introduced sufficient to support a finding that the fact does exist. The court may admit the proposed evidence on the condition that the proof be introduced later.

(c) Conducting a Hearing So That the Jury Cannot Hear It. The court must conduct any hearing on a preliminary question so that the jury cannot hear it if:

(1) the hearing involves the admissibility of a confession;

(2) a defendant in a criminal case is a witness and so requests; or

(3) justice so requires.

(d) Cross-Examining a Defendant in a Criminal Case. By testifying on a preliminary question, a defendant in a criminal case does not become subject to cross-examination on other issues in the case.

(e) Evidence Relevant to Weight and Credibility. This rule does not limit a party's right to introduce before the jury evidence that is relevant to the weight or credibility of other evidence.

§ 3.03 The Importance of Relevance

Why is relevance an important concept? The answer lies partly in its primacy; relevance is the first hurdle to admissibility. Just as the judge is the gatekeeper of admissibility determinations, relevance is a threshold through which evidence must pass. Significantly, all evidence must be relevant to be admissible. *See* Rule 402. Serving as the first in a long line of evidentiary requirements is significant enough, but relevance also plays a recurring role on the "evidence highway." It is a factor in assessing the admissibility of hearsay, impeachment, and other forms of evidence as well.

Relevance determinations also help with sorting evidence. For example, relevance dictates whether evidence applies to proving the elements of the case, impeaching a witness, or both. While relevance decisions depend on several factors, including everyday human experience, science, and the facts of the case, the relevance rules offer at least one bright line: irrelevant evidence is inadmissible. *See* Rule 402. Irrelevant evidence is distracting, unhelpful, and counterproductive to judicial economy.

Of course, the fact that evidence is relevant does not mean that it will be admitted. (If that were the case, a course in Evidence Law might be extraordinarily short.) Not all relevant evidence is admissible. Relevant evidence still must overcome other exclusionary obstacles to qualify for admission, such as those concerning character, hearsay, privilege, and improper impeachment, among others. Thus, rather than acting as the sole hurdle to admissibility, relevancy only serves as one of many prerequisites.

§ 3.04 Defining Relevance

The definition of relevance is often divided into two distinct parts. Evidence is relevant pursuant to Rule 401 if it is (1) probative of (2) a fact of consequence in determining the action.

The term "probative" essentially means making something else more or less likely. Evidence is probative of a fact at issue in the case if it makes such a fact more or less likely. This also means that there is a relationship between the evidence and the fact, such that a "chain of inferences" can be constructed connecting the evidence to the case. The fact that the evidence also yields inference chains that do not relate to the case is of no significance; all that is needed is one inference chain that bears on the case at hand. Further, evidence satisfies this standard even if it only makes the pertinent fact a tiny bit more or less likely. As the Advisory Committee observed, "[a]ny more stringent requirement is unworkable and unreasonable." Advisory Committee Note, Rule 401.

Example 1

The accused, Joey, was charged with the robbery of a clothing store, The Glow. At trial, the prosecutor, Jenna, offers evidence that Joey was in the store the day before the robbery, and that he walked around the aisles without purchasing anything before he left. *Is this evidence probative of whether Joey robbed the store?*

Answer: On the one hand, inferences may be drawn from Joey's presence in the store that are not probative of whether he committed the crime, such as: (1) Joey likes that Glow store; (2) Joey likes to shop for clothes; (3) Joey does not buy clothes often; or (4) Joey knows what kind of merchandise is sold at Glow stores. On the other hand, the fact that Joey was in the store the day before the robbery is probative in two different ways. If Joey was in the store the day before and was just looking around, it makes it more likely he was the robber because it appears that he was "casing the store" in preparation for the robbery. From the defense perspective, if Joey was in the store the day before the robbery, it makes it less likely that he was the robber, because a person would be afraid of being recognized if he were going to rob the store the very next day.

A "fact of consequence in determining the action" is a fact helpful to resolving the suit, also sometimes described as a fact "properly provable" in the case. Facts of consequence include: (1) an element of the cause of action, claim, or defense; (2) the credibility of the witnesses; and (3) background facts (e.g., helpful facts filling in gaps in the evidence). The term "material fact," commonly used prior to the Federal Rules of Evidence, was abandoned by the Advisory Committee in favor of "fact of consequence." As the Advisory Committee noted in its Comment on Rule 401, the word "material" was "loosely used and ambiguous." Advisory Committee Note, Rule 401.

It is worth noting that the relevance definition does not exclude evidence simply because the evidence concerns a fact of consequence not in dispute. To the contrary, many parties offer evidence about facts of consequence that are not in dispute; the parties want to bolster their cases on relevant matters. If objections are lodged to this evidence the judge can still exclude it, but only because the evidence was unfairly prejudicial (perhaps as a waste of time or cumulative) not because it concerned an undisputed fact of consequence.

Example 2

Balou sued Rodriguez for breach of contract regarding a deck that Rodriguez had agreed to build in Balou's backyard. Balou claimed that the deck was incomplete; Rodriguez had left woodwork unfinished and excess garbage everywhere. Rodriguez responded by claiming the deck was finished and the contract completed. At trial, Balou testified that a similar agreement between the same parties for a different deck on the side of Balou's house included the purchase and application of a wood sealer and the removal of garbage. Rodriguez objected to this evidence, claiming it was irrelevant. Later, on cross-examination of Balou, Balou was asked whether he had been convicted of grand theft auto, a felony, five years earlier. Balou objected to this evidence as well. *How should the judge rule on these objections?*

Answer: Both objections should be overruled. The prior agreement clarifies a fact of consequence in the case, namely the intent of the parties as it relates to their current agreement, and makes it more likely that Balou's claim will succeed. The impeachment of Balou with a felony conviction also makes a fact of consequence, Balou's believability, less likely, and therefore makes it less likely that Balou's claim will succeed. While the facts of consequence differ, both the intent of the parties and the believability of the witnesses are important to resolving the suit.

––––––––––

The key to understanding relevance is that it describes how one thing *relates to* another thing, if at all. (*See* Advisory Committee Note, Rule 401.) A relationship indicates that there is some connection between the evidence and something else. Relevance indicates that the evidence is connected through a process of inferences to the case at hand. A single piece of evidence can give rise to a wide variety of inferences, all based on logic, science, and experience.

Because there is usually some uncertainty about what may be inferred from particular evidence, relevance is oriented around probabilities. That is to say, if we want to know whether it was raining at the time of an accident, evidence that pedestrians were wearing raincoats makes it more probable that it was raining than it was before the evidence was introduced. For that matter, the reconstruction of prior events, what fact-finding really constitutes at trial, is hardly ever based on certainty. Instead, most facts are really probabilities, no matter how sure we are of their existence. Even scientific evidence, which some say is "certain," is subject to differing opinions, exceptions, revisions, and new discoveries. (Consider, for example, the debates about the origins of the universe, "nature versus nurture," and other continuing scientific disagreements.)

The drawing of inferences in the relevance enterprise differs from general forms of logic. One judge has noted that relevance analysis is unlike the process of deduction, where major and minor premises are supplied. Instead, "[i]nferential processes . . . generally proceed from one proven premise to a conclusion. The one drawing the inference supplies the missing premise, typically from a reservoir of experience." *United States v. Hannigan,* 27 F.3d 890, 898 n.3 (3d Cir. 1994) (Becker, J., concurring). Thus, relevance determinations are rooted in a combination of science and experience. *See* Advisory Committee Note, Rule 401.

Judge Becker offered an illustration of relevance in *Hannigan,* stating that an eyewitness who hears gunfire can only assume that the gunshot hit the victim who was standing nearby. If a bullet in fact was fired from the gun and struck a victim, it was traveling much too fast for the witness to actually see it go by. Yet, logic and experience dictate that if one observes a person aim a gun at another person and pull the trigger (with the gun making a loud retort), and the person in the line of fire falls down covered with blood, then a bullet must have been fired from the gun and must have struck the victim. This kind of probabilistic reasoning occurs routinely and, generally, unconsciously. With relevance, however, a more conscious approach is favored. *See United States v. Hannigan,* 27 F.3d 890, 898 n.3 (3d Cir. 1994) (Becker, J., concurring).

In relevance analysis, numerous helpful inferences may be drawn from a single fact. To illustrate, in a case involving the attempted robbery of a person in a shopping mall parking lot, eyeglasses found on the ground at the scene of the crime could relate to several pertinent conclusions. For example, the found glasses could indicate the alleged victim struggled to prevent the robbery (if it is shown the glasses belonged to the alleged victim), or that the alleged victim wore glasses and needed them to perceive the alleged perpetrator (which relates to the witness' credibility), or that the alleged perpetrator wore glasses (which relates to identification). On the other hand, the pair of eyeglasses found at the scene may relate to a variety of irrelevant facts as well. The glasses might belong to a person not involved in the incident. Even if they did belong to a participant, the glasses could still indicate irrelevancies, such as which brand of eyeglasses the wearer prefers, whether the glasses are designed for athletic usage, or whether the glasses are made with special shock-resistant glass.

This "eyeglasses" example illustrates how a single piece of evidence can relate to a wide variety of facts. The example also demonstrates that relevancy is not an inherent characteristic of a piece of evidence, but depends on the facts of the case. *See, e.g.,* Advisory Committee Note, Rule 401. For example, if a banana peel is found on the floorboard beneath the passenger seat of an automobile, it may be probative of many facts, including: the driver eats in the car; the driver is messy; the driver carries groceries in the car; the driver has a pet monkey; there was a passenger in the car; the passenger eats in the car; the passenger is messy; and so on. Thus, the relevance of the banana peel depends on the specific issues in the case.

With such a wide variety of inferences that can be drawn from a single piece of evidence, the task for the attorney is to find a connection between the evidence and the substantive issues at trial, the credibility of witnesses, the background facts, or a combination of these things. Whether the evidence can be linked to the case requires an answer to the question: "Relevant to what?" Stated differently, the operative question to answer in resolving relevance issues becomes, "What is the evidence being offered to prove?"

Example 3

One evening, Bruce was killed in a one-car accident. The only issue in a subsequent lawsuit was whether Bruce's death was an accident or a suicide.

Bruce's close friend, Natasha, said that on the day of the crash, Bruce appeared to be "very sad." *Is this evidence relevant?*

Answer: The evidence that Bruce appeared to be very sad prior to the accident is relevant to something, but to what? This fact may be relevant to the case if Bruce's sadness is probative of (makes more likely) a fact in issue (the reason Bruce died). The sadness is probative of suicide because sadness tends to make it more likely that Bruce was depressed, which in turn could provide a motive for suicide. While there may be many other explanations for Bruce's sadness, the alternative inference chains probably would be irrelevant to the case. As long as one inference chain can be connected to the case, making it even a little bit more (or less) likely that Bruce died as a result of a suicide, the evidence will be considered relevant.

———————

Appellate courts typically review trial courts' relevance determinations under an "abuse of discretion" standard. This standard reflects the factual and contextual nature of relevance rulings and that, particularly with such a low threshold for relevancy requirements, appellate courts should avoid second-guessing trial judges' relevance determinations.

The following problems provide the opportunity for you to apply the relevance rules by constructing inference chains that link various types of evidence to the case. In drawing these inference chains, it becomes clear that the application of the doctrine of relevance can be quite complex.

Problem 3-1: Judge Judy

Judge Judy was asked to decide a most difficult question: which of two women claiming to be the mother of an infant child was indeed the biological mother? Each woman claimed that the child was hers. Judge Judy told the women that there was an easy solution — she was going to cut the child in half. At this pronouncement, one of the women began to cry. She shouted, "No! I can't stand it; don't do it!" The other woman was ashen-faced, but silent.

1. Are the women's reactions to Judge Judy's decision relevant? To what issue is their reaction relevant?

2. What assistance do the Advisory Committee Notes provide in resolving the relevancy issues in this problem?

3. If the parable instead involved two men who both claimed to be the father of the child, would their reactions be similarly relevant or irrelevant? Compare the relevancy of the reactions of the alleged mothers to the reactions of the alleged fathers.

Problem 3-2: Bermuda Love Triangle

Freddy Krueger is accused of killing his friend, Jason, with a single blow to the head. At trial, the prosecution wishes to introduce love letters written by Freddy to Jason's wife only months before Jason's death. The defense objects to the introduction of the letters.

If Freddy did write the letters, are the letters relevant? To what are they relevant? Write out the chain of inferences that makes the letters relevant.

Problem 3-3: Missing

Joan accidentally left her purse on the snack bar after purchasing popcorn at the local movie theater. Joan remembers seeing other patrons in the area, but cannot describe any of the people, even in the most general of terms because she was in a hurry to catch the beginning of the feature film. In her purse were four new $50 bills. The purse was recovered after the movie. All of the money was missing from the purse.

Which of the following evidence is relevant in determining who took the money? Explain your answers by describing the inferences you drew from the evidence.

1. Bob, another patron, paid for popcorn right before the movie started with a new $50 bill.

2. Patrons Susan and Jamie left the movie theater halfway through the film.

3. Harvey, another patron, was convicted of the possession of marijuana in 1990.

4. The purse was found in the restroom. (Does it matter whether the purse was recovered in the women's room or the men's room? Why? If the purse was recovered in the women's room, what impact, if any, is there on the relevance of the evidence in parts 1, 2, and 3, above?)

Problem 3-4: Eddie From Boston

Eddie from Boston was accused of robbing the First City Bank of Massachusetts. Eddie is alleged to have used a "Saturday Night Special" revolver during the robbery.

Which of the following items of evidence would be relevant to the prosecution's case? Explain, using inference chains.

1. Eddie withdrew money at the same bank the day prior to the robbery after having a friendly 10-minute conversation with the teller (no one else was in line).

2. Eddie had an eight-year-old bank robbery conviction in a different state, Maryland.

3. Eddie was fired from his previous job as a clerk in a convenience store as a result of an unproven allegation that he stole money from the cash register.

4. Eddie had participated in two barroom brawls the week before the bank robbery.

5. Eddie was divorced and delinquent in his payments of $400 per month in child support.

6. Eddie was virtually broke. His only asset was a $49 savings account at a different bank.

7. Eddie owned a rifle.

8. Eddie has two children, ages two and seven.

9. Eddie has been convicted of marijuana possession on two separate occasions in the past four years.

10. Eddie prefers "rock" to Bach and gin without tonic.

Problem 3-5: The Reel Thing

Wanda brought suit against three insurance companies, all of which had insured the life of her husband, Harry. She claimed that the body recently found in Pond Apple Creek was Harry's and that, as the beneficiary, she should be paid the million dollars from the insurance policies on Harry's life. Wanda offers in evidence an authenticated letter from Harry's fishing buddy, Al. Al wrote to Harry saying, "I look forward to fishing with you at the Pond Apple Creek at the end of September." Harry has been missing since September 30th.

Is this letter relevant? If yes, relevant to what? Write out the inference chain that justifies your conclusion.

Problem 3-6: "Beam Me Up . . ."

Scotty was a driver for the Letrek Company. While driving a Letrek truck, Scotty collided with a car driven by Kirk. Kirk sued the Letrek Company for damages in tort based on the theory of *respondeat superior*. The parties reached a written stipulation on most of the facts. The only issue at trial was whether Scotty was acting within the scope of his employment at the time of the accident or whether he was on a "fun and frolic" detour outside of his job. Plaintiff Kirk offers evidence that "at the time of the accident, Scotty was not looking where he was going. In fact, he was falling asleep."

Is this evidence relevant? If so, relevant to what?

Problem 3-7: Fire! (a.k.a. Burning Down the House)

Hal was driving in his car when he turned on the radio and heard that his own house had burst into flames. Hal was subsequently charged with burning down his house to obtain insurance proceeds. At trial, the prosecutor intended to offer evidence that Hal took out additional fire insurance seven months before the fire. The following exchange occurred at trial:

PROSECUTOR: Wanda, as the insurance agent for the defendant, Hal, could you please describe the insurance that Hal had on the house, especially within the past year of its destruction?

DEFENSE COUNSEL: Objection, your honor. Irrelevant.

JUDGE: Counsel, please approach the bench.

How would you argue this objection if you were the prosecutor? How would you argue the objection if you were the defense counsel? What ruling would you make if you were the judge?

Problem 3-8: I Wuz Robbed!

John and Johanna are being prosecuted for robbing a bank on June 4th at 9:00 a.m. Their defense is mistaken identity. At trial, Tommy, the bank teller who was robbed, testified about the robbery.

PROSECUTOR: Tommy, directing your attention to 8:55 a.m. on June 4th, where were you?

DEFENSE ATTORNEY: Objection! Where the teller was at that particular time is irrelevant.

1. Is the question necessarily irrelevant? What answer would make the question relevant?

PROSECUTOR: How did you feel, Tommy, as the robbers handed you the note that read "your money or your life"?

A: I felt —

DEFENSE ATTORNEY: Objection! Irrelevant. How the teller felt is irrelevant to whether a robbery occurred.

1. You are the prosecutor; how would you respond?

2. How should the judge rule and why?

Problem 3-9: Benny and Jets

The defendant, Benny, is charged with the *distribution* of cocaine. The prosecution calls Benny's friend, Jets, to the witness stand to testify that he, Jets, had *used* cocaine with the defendant three months prior to the defendant's arrest.

PROSECUTOR: Jets, please tell the ladies and gentlemen of the jury where you were on March 6th, at approximately 3:00 p.m.?

A: I was at the Giants football game with my friend, Benny.

PROSECUTOR: Describe what happened between you and Benny at the game.

DEFENSE COUNSEL: Objection. Irrelevant.

Is this evidence relevant to the charge of distribution? Explain.

Problem 3-10: Ahnald

The defendant, Franz, is prosecuted for assault and battery on Ahnald. Franz claims self-defense. Franz testified that immediately before the altercation with Ahnald, Franz was told by a third party that Ahnald, a weight lifter, was out to get him.

1. Is this testimony relevant? Relevant to what?

2. Does it matter whether Ahnald was in fact "out to get" Franz?

3. If Franz cannot recall who told him that Ahnald was out to get him, is the evidence still relevant?

Problem 3-11: Ahnald's Younger Brother

Ahnald's younger brother, Sly, was stopped by the police late one Saturday night while driving on the interstate. He was glassy-eyed and appeared to be intoxicated. When he refused to cooperate with the detaining officer, the officer called for backup. Before the backup arrived, the officer mistakenly thought that Sly was reaching for a gun, and shot him dead. In a civil rights action brought by the survivors of Sly, the officer testified as follows:

OFFICER TOOJAY: I saw Mr. Sly move his hand toward the pocket of his jacket, like he was reaching for a gun. I thought he was going to shoot at me, so I took the safety off of my weapon and shot him.

The plaintiff wishes to offer in evidence that in a search of the victim after the shooting, no weapon was found. *Is this evidence admissible? Explain.*

Problem 3-12: Sexual Battery

Joe is charged with sexual battery. To prove the victim's age, which is relevant to the elements of the offense, the government offers evidence that Joe generally dates women between the ages of 15 and 18.

If you were the judge, would you find that this evidence is relevant to this case? Why? See Francis v. State, 512 So. 2d 280 (Fla. 2d Dist. Ct. App. 1987).

Problem 3-13: The Commuter

Sean was approached by four youths while riding on a nearly empty commuter train one weekend morning. The youths stood on both sides of Sean, two to a side. One of them said, "Give me five dollars." Sean, fearing an attack that would result in serious bodily harm, took out a revolver and shot the four youths, injuring each of them seriously. *In a subsequent prosecution for attempted murder, which of the following facts is relevant?*

1. Sean (or any of the four youths) is female, male, trans, or non-binary.

2. Sean (or any of the four youths) is of color or white.

3. Sean (or any of the four youths) is younger or older than 21.

4. Sean (or any of the four youths) is of high, average, or low socioeconomic status.

5. Sean (or any of the four youths) is gay, lesbian, bisexual, transgender, questioning or straight.

6. Any of the four youths has a prior criminal record.

7. The train is in a subway or above ground.

8. The train is located in a rural area, the suburbs of a city, or an inner city.

9. The incident occurred at night or during the day. Or during the summer or the winter.

10. Sean had been mugged once before, but not on a train. *Explain* your conclusions.

"The Commuter" is based on the so-called "subway vigilante" case, *People v. Goetz*, 73 N.Y.2d 751, 532 N.E.2d 1273 (1988). The defendant, Bernhard Goetz, was found not guilty by a jury on charges of attempted murder. Goetz shot and injured four youths on December 22, 1984, in a New York City subway train after the youths flanked him and one of the youths asked Goetz to give him five dollars. Goetz successfully claimed that he acted in self-defense. The following is an excerpt from the jury instructions given by Justice Stephen Crane of the Supreme Court of New York (the trial court) in *People v. Goetz.*

Justice Crane's jury instruction stated:

> Please note that before he can be justified in using deadly physical force in defense of the person, the defendant must have reasonably believed that he was being threatened with deadly physical force.

> What then is a reasonable belief? A determination of reasonableness must be based upon the circumstances facing the defendant or his situation in terms encompassing more than the physical movements of the potential assailant or assailants. These terms include any relevant knowledge the defendant had about that person or persons; they also necessarily bring in the physical attributes of a person's involvement, including the defendant.

Furthermore, the defendant's circumstances encompass any prior experiences he had, which would provide a reasonable basis for belief that another person's intentions were to injure him or that the use of deadly force was necessary under the circumstances.

A person may be said to reasonably believe that deadly physical force is about to be used against him, if a reasonable person in his shoes, that is, in the same circumstances and situation that he faced, would so believe. In other words, in this case you must scrutinize the reasonableness of any belief the defendant claims to have had by reference to a hypothetical reasonable person who was transported into the subway car on December 22, 1984, and who faced the exact situation which confronted the defendant.[1]

1. How is the *Goetz* jury asked to deal with the particular circumstances of the shooting?

2. How does the jury instruction define the scope of relevant evidence in the case?

3. In light of the jury instructions, how broad is the permissible scope of relevant evidence?

4. How is the scope of relevant evidence affected by whether the self-defense instruction is "objective" or "subjective"?

Problem 3-14: A Bottle of Red

Billy was observed purchasing a bottle of red wine at a liquor store at 2:00 p.m. on Tuesday. At 7:00 p.m. on the same day, he was arrested for driving while intoxicated on the local highway. The prosecution offers evidence about Billy's wine purchase in Billy's subsequent trial for driving while intoxicated. The defense objects.

1. Should the judge admit the evidence? Why?

2. Would it be relevant if Billy was seen carrying an empty, rather than a full, bottle of wine at 2:00 p.m.?

3. Would it be relevant if Billy was seem carrying a half-empty wine bottle at 2:00 p.m.?

4. Would the 2:00 p.m. purchase of wine be relevant, if, at the time Billy was arrested, he smelled of beer? Explain.

Problem 3-15: "Name Your Price"

The defendant offers the testimony a witness, Price, in a workers' compensation action. Price states, "The plaintiff tried to bribe me to testify in his favor."

Is this testimony relevant? If so, relevant to what? Explain.

---

1. Charge to Jury, Justice Stephen Crane, Supreme Court of the State of New York, County of New York, Criminal Term: Part 81. *The People of the State of New* York v. *Bernhard H. Goetz.*

Problem 3-16: Too Rough Justice

Centuries ago, in the days of yore, Judge Martin presided over the judicial system. The primary test used at that time to determine guilt or innocence in criminal cases was the "jump" test. An accused was told to jump off of a 50-foot cliff into the trees and jagged rocks below. It was widely believed that an innocent person would survive the fall without serious injury.

Haynes is charged with battery after biting his former friend, Jockey. Judge Martin tells Haynes, "Jump thou, Sirrah!" Haynes refuses, saying, "Hearest thou me well, thou dost not appreciate my situation if thou thinkest I would go over yon cliff."

1. Is Haynes's refusal to jump relevant? To what?

2. Is it relevant if Haynes, prior to being told to jump, attempted to escape while in custody? Why?

Problem 3-17: "Lions and Tigers and . . ."

The defendant, Bear, is charged with extortion. Bear allegedly threatened to shoot the local butcher if the butcher did not pay for "protection." At trial, the government offers evidence that the defendant kept several guns in his bedroom.

Is this evidence relevant? Explain. See United States v. Gilley, 836 F.2d 1206 (9th Cir. 1988).

Problem 3-18: Evidence, Politics, and Race

Mike Espy was indicted for taking gifts while serving as Secretary of Agriculture. Espy, an African-American, claimed that some of the charges were outright lies and that others were misinterpreted. Espy did not deny that he took some of the things that might be described as gifts, but argued that he did not have wrongful intent in doing so. He further stated that some of his failures to comply with the law were mistakes or oversights, given the extreme pressures he faced in his job.

Richard Douglas, a deputy agriculture secretary under Espy, was called to testify by the prosecution. On cross-examination by the defense, Douglas admitted that Espy made major changes at the Department by promoting women and minorities. Douglas further testified that some of the people who worked in the Department could not fathom that a Black person could hold such a position of decision-making power. The prosecutor objected to Douglas' testimony. *Should the objection be sustained?*

Problem 3-19: Exploding Tire

The plaintiff, Petra, was injured by an exploding tire at the Fox's Used Tire Superstore. At trial, one of the defendants, Uniyear Treads, called several experts to testify that the RH5 design of the tire was entirely safe. On cross-examination,

Petra wished to ask the defendant's experts about other accidents involving the RH5 design to test the witnesses' credibility.

Can she ask the witnesses about the other tire accidents? See, e.g., Cooper v. Firestone Tire and Rubber Co., 945 F.2d 1103 (9th Cir. 1991).

Problem 3-20: Parnell v. Asbestos, Inc.

The plaintiff, Parnell, sued the defendant, Asbestos, Inc., for injuries relating to alleged long-term exposure to asbestos. The plaintiff offered several premises showing causation. The first premise was that all forms of asbestos cause cancer. The second premise was that Parnell had been exposed to the asbestos products of several different manufacturers, including the defendant's asbestos. Therefore, according to the plaintiff, the defendant's products had at least in part caused the asbestosis. In rebuttal, the defendant wishes to call an expert witness to testify that one form of asbestos, chrysolite asbestos, does not cause cancer at all.

What is this evidence offered to show? Is it relevant? To what? Should it be admitted?

Problem 3-21: Blowing Smoke

Morris Philip is charged with the murder of Chester Fields. Philip offers evidence of an alibi. To strengthen his defense, Philip seeks to offer evidence that Marley Burroughs, Fields's former partner in an insurance business, had a motive to kill Fields. The motive evidence consists of testimony that after finding out that Fields had embezzled more than $100,000 from the business and caused it to go bankrupt, Burroughs swore, "I'll get back at Fields for this outrage if it's the last thing I do." *Is the motive evidence relevant?*

§ 3.05 Conditional Relevance

When the relevance of evidence depends on the existence of a fact, the evidence is considered to be "conditionally relevant." Rule 104(b) of the Federal Rules of Evidence codifies conditional relevance. Rule 104(b) gives judges the discretion to conditionally admit evidence so long as the missing link in that evidence will be connected up by proof of the missing fact. For example, if a gun is offered in a murder case, its admissibility depends on a fact of whether it was the gun used in the murder or has some other connection to the crime. Likewise, when a person claims another person was present at a meeting, that claim is predicated on a meeting occurring.

Judges can admit this evidence upon a subsequent showing that the gun was used in the crime and that a meeting took place, respectively. Conditionally relevant evidence will be admitted by the judge if a reasonable jury *could* find by a preponderance of the evidence that the fact exists. The judge does not actually determine whether the fact really exists; the judge's role is simply to exclude the evidence if no reasonable jury *could* find that the fact exists. Thus, a judge acts to screen facts when making these relevance determinations.

Given the way conditional relevance distinguishes between the judge's prefatory fact-finding role and the jury's primary fact-finding responsibility, it can be viewed as more about the division of fact-finding responsibilities at trial than about relevance. The procedural orientation of Rule 104(b) is further illuminated by the fact that a judge can admit this type of evidence "subject to" the later introduction of the missing fact. Thus, the Rule also can be viewed as a timing mechanism.

Conditional relevance also can be considered an example of foundational evidence, since it serves as a prerequisite to admissibility. There are many other types of foundations, from authenticating exhibits to meeting the requirements of hearsay exceptions to establishing a claim of privilege. In another sense, conditional relevance poses a type of competency requirement, because it demands that evidence have a minimum level of connection to the facts in the case. Without a sufficient showing of a connection, the evidence is incompetent and ineligible for consideration by a jury.

From another perspective, conditionally relevant evidence is like a chain with one or more of its links missing. The missing link signifies the omitted but necessary separate fact. When evidence is conditionally admitted, this means that counsel promises to supply the missing fact or facts at a later time. If the missing link is not provided, the evidence will be subject to exclusion.

Conditional relevance situations arise for a variety of reasons. A single witness may not be able to lay the entire foundation required for a piece of evidence, in which case the party must use additional evidence or witnesses. Further, even if a party is able to offer its evidence chronologically, so as to avoid gaps, the party may choose to rearrange its order of presentation for strategic purposes. Thus, a party may rely on several witnesses to lay the foundation for a single piece of evidence, such as a gun or a computer printout, even though a fragmented approach is not necessary.

The admissibility of conditionally relevant evidence provides needed flexibility to attorneys in presenting their case. It allows the attorneys to control what evidence to present and in what order. While a counsel's ordering of witnesses may be confusing to the jury, the opening statement and closing arguments can offer clarity and guidance.

Example

Jorge was charged with the shooting death of his girlfriend, Lourdes. A gun was found outside of the house where Lourdes was killed. *Is the gun relevant evidence?*

Answer: The gun may be conditionally relevant to the shooting death of Lourdes if additional evidence shows that it was the particular gun used in the shooting (and not a gun unconnected to the incident). The gun may be admitted in evidence pending a later showing, through ballistics tests or otherwise, that this was the gun in question.

Problem 3-22: On a Cloudy Day

With wispy white clouds drifting lazily overhead one hot and sunny June day, Gilligan was severely injured while cutting the hedges. He claimed that he was injured when the rotary hedge cutter he was using suddenly exploded. At trial, Gilligan offers a piece of steel blade found 10 yards away from the accident site.

1. The defendant objects to this evidence. What is the basis for this objection?
2. How is this evidence conditionally relevant?
3. Does adding visual language to the problem, such as "[w]ith wispy white clouds drifting lazily overhead one hot and sunny June day," affect the way this problem is considered? How would this visual language be received by a jury?

Problem 3-23: Stone Crabs

Alice is accused of breaking into Jim's Stone Crab Restaurant through a rear window and stealing 80 stone crab claws and two tins of mustard sauce. No fingerprints were discovered. At trial, the prosecution offers in evidence a pair of thin black kitchen gloves found near the perpetrator's point of entry. The defendant objects to this evidence.

Are these gloves conditionally relevant? Why?

What must be shown for the gloves to be admitted?

Problem 3-24: Defective Paint

Assume that a painting contractor buys five large drums of white paint from the Power Paint Company. Four months later, the contractor buys five drums of yellow paint from the same company. After buying the yellow paint, the contractor starts using the white paint and realizes that it is defective. The contractor then refuses to pay for the yellow paint, and sends it back unopened. The contractor is sued.

The judge rules, "It is irrelevant that the white paint was defective. There's no connection between white paint and yellow paint manufactured four months later."

What foundational evidence might you *offer to show a connection between the two sets of paint drums?*

Problem 3-25: An Accident?

Vanessa De La Beckworth and Daniel Jimenez lived together for 13 months as girlfriend and boyfriend. One night, they had a fight in the kitchen over who was to feed their dog, a pit bull. Vanessa called 911 and stated, "Help! I've been cut by my boyfriend, Daniel! I need a doctor. Fast!" Police and an ambulance arrived shortly after the call, and found that she had been cut and bruised.

Three weeks later, Daniel was charged with two counts of aggravated domestic violence. The prosecutor requested an interview with Vanessa, and during the interview she stated that the bruise and cut had been of her own doing. She explained that she blamed it on Daniel because she was angry with him. She also told the prosecutor that, while she knew Daniel had faults, she loved Daniel and would not testify against him or do anything to hurt him.

The prosecution intends to go forward with the case. The prosecutor subpoenas Vanessa to testify, knowing that she will deny that her injuries are Daniel's fault and that the prosecution will have to rely on what she said to the 911 operator. The prosecution wishes to call Eric Mendleson, PhD, to testify about Battered Woman's Syndrome. The prosecutor proffers the following will be Mendleson's testimony if it is permitted:

PROSECUTOR: Dr. Mendleson, tell us what happens to battered women when they are confronted about their injuries at the hands of their significant other.

A: At first, in their agitated and injured state, they often blurt out the truth about what caused their injuries. Only later do they often recant. In fact, one study showed that 80 percent of women will recant after an assault. Further, many women assaulted by their boyfriends exhibit the Stockholm Syndrome — which is where some hostages view their attackers as essentially a good person who is just misunderstood.

If the defense attorney objects based on relevance, what should defense counsel argue in support of the objection? Why?

How is this evidence only conditionally relevant?

The trial court admitted the testimony subject to a limiting instruction by the judge pursuant to Federal Rule of Evidence 105.

If you were the judge, how would you craft the limiting instruction?

On appeal, what would you argue was improper about giving a limiting instruction? Why? See People v. Gomez, 72 Cal. App. 4th 405, 85 Cal. Rptr. 2d 101 (1999).

Exercise: Relevance Foundations

Johnny Blutone is prosecuted for battery on Patrick Houston after a fight in a local bar; the defense is self-defense. Johnny and Patrick knew of each other from living in the same town, but had never met until the bar fight. At trial, Johnny wished to testify that Johnny heard that Patrick had started a previous bar fight with another person, brutalizing that person and sending him to the hospital with severe injuries. The prosecutor objected to the evidence and the judge ruled at the bench the evidence was inadmissible unless the defense offers additional information making the prior bar fight conditionally relevant. Specifically, the judge stated that in order to be admissible, the defendant must show he, Johnny, knew about the prior fight before the one in question had occurred. Johnny thereupon offered a new witness, Fariq Abdul, a friend, to testify that Abdul told Johnny about the attack about a week prior to the bar fight in question, while they were sitting at lunch at the Quarterdeck restaurant.

1. You represent the defendant, Johnny. Lay the foundation for the prior bar fight evidence as the judge instructed. In other words, question Fariq Abdul about what he told Johnny. Include: (1) Fariq's name and brief background (personalize him), (2) the setting (describe where they were), and (3) the action (what was said in the conversation).

2. A student should play Fariq and testify, staying in role while on the witness stand. Another student or students can role-play opposing counsel. At the end of the examination, a person acting as judge should rule whether a foundation has been created to make the prior bar fight relevant pursuant to Rule 104(b).

Problem 3-26: Joe C. Boss

Joe Celebrity Boss admitted various improper romantic office affairs with employees in a lawsuit brought by one of the women involved. In the subsequent lawsuit brought by another former female employee alleging a similar affair with Boss, the plaintiff wished to use the prior statement by Joe that he "had various improper affairs with women employed by me at the same company."

(a) Is Joe's statement in the prior suit a binding judicial admission?

(b) Is Joe's statement in the prior suit relevant in the later suit?

§ 3.06 Comparing Rules

Compare Federal Rule of Evidence 401 with a different approach, formerly used in Texas:

Test of Relevancy

(a) "Materiality" inquires whether there is any rational relationship or pertinence of the offered evidence to any provable or controlling fact issue in dispute.

(b) "Relevancy" inquires whether the offered evidence has probative value tending to establish the presence or absence, truth or falsity, of a fact.

(c) Test: Is it material? If not, exclude. If yes, and only in that event, is it relevant? If not, exclude. If yes, admit.

Which is the clearer rule, the Texas rule or the Federal Rule of Evidence? Why?

§ 3.07 Summary and Review

1. Why is the application of the relevance rules dependent on the particular case?

2. What is the definition of relevance under the Federal Rules of Evidence?

3. Compare the concept of "probativeness" with the concept of "fact of consequence."

4. Define conditional relevance.

5. Specify whether each of the following statements is True or False:

    a. Only certain select forms of irrelevant evidence are admissible at trial.

    b. If evidence is relevant, it will be admitted at trial.

    c. Evidence requiring more than 15 links to connect it with the issues in the case will be excluded.

    d. Circumstantial evidence is more likely to be relevant than direct evidence.

    e. Conditionally admitted evidence is admitted for a limited purpose.

    f. Relevance objections are almost always sustained.

§ 3.08 Chapter Review Problems

Review Problem 3-A: The Swallower

The defendant, Alan Onano, is charged with knowingly possessing heroin with the intent to distribute it in violation of 21 U.S.C. § 841(a). On March 14th, Onano was a passenger on Nigerian Airlines Flight 859, traveling from Nigeria to Kennedy Airport in New York. He was arrested at the airport after acting suspiciously. Several days later, following a bowel movement, he was found to have swallowed 83 condoms containing heroin. At trial, the defendant did not deny swallowing the condoms, but claimed that he believed he was swallowing diamonds, not drugs. The defendant offered an expert witness, Dr. Elliot Berns, a gemologist and a professor at the Fashion Institute of Technology. Dr. Berns was expected to testify on two points: the feasibility of smuggling diamonds by ingesting condoms, and the value of the smuggling venture if diamonds had been placed in the 83 condoms.

1. Is Dr. Berns' testimony relevant? Explain.

2. If Dr. Berns is allowed to testify, is his testimony conditionally relevant? Why?

3. How would you question Dr. Berns on direct examination? How would you question him on cross-examination? Prepare both examinations.

Review Problem 3-B

JK Lassiter is accused of forgery, allegedly writing several false checks in his employer's name and then cashing them. When the prosecutor asks the defendant to submit handwriting exemplars to further identify the forged handwriting, he refuses. The prosecutor wishes to offer evidence of the refusal at the subsequent trial, and the defense objects. *Which of the following is the most accurate statement about the defendant's refusal?*

1. The evidence is irrelevant because the defendant's pretrial refusal to do something is not related to a fact of consequence in the case.

2. The evidence is irrelevant because the defendant's pretrial refusal is not probative of his frame of mind at a previous time.

3. The evidence might be excluded, but not because of its lack of relationship to the case.

4. The evidence should be excluded because it violates the false hearsay document rule, unless its substantive value outweighs its probative nature.

Review Problem 3-C

Which of the following examples will most likely be excluded as irrelevant?

1. In a prosecution for the destruction of property, when the defendant was arrested, he used a false name. The prosecutor wants to offer the fact that the defendant offered a false name as evidence of guilt.

2. In a prosecution for defacing government property, a protester allegedly had thrown ashes and mud at the Pentagon walls. In his defense, the protester wants to introduce evidence about the vagaries of United States policy toward nuclear weapons control.

3. In a tort action for strict products liability after a tire exploded, the defendant used a substantially similar tire to test whether the same type of tire was defective.

4. In a prosecution for securities fraud, the fact that just before the defendant was arrested, the defendant deleted many of the files on his computer.

Review Problem 3-D: On the Tube: The Practice

Paul Stuart is on trial for the murder of Melissa, with whom he had been having an extramarital affair. Melissa's next-door neighbor Betty White testifies that she saw Stuart running out of Melissa's house at 10:30 PM on the night of the murder. White had previously provided an alibi for Stuart when she told police officers that she never saw Stuart in Melissa's house on the night of the murder. White testifies that she had lied to the police because Stuart's mother Wendy had paid her $500,000 to do so. *Is evidence of Wendy's payment to White admissible to prove that Stuart killed Melissa?*

During closing argument, Stuart's lawyer argues to the jurors that other people had a motive to kill Melissa. The defense lawyer points to Stuart's mother Wendy, a priest with whom Melissa had been having an affair, and Melissa's ex-spouse, who had to make large alimony payments to Melissa as people who had a motive to kill Melissa. *Is the defense lawyer's argument proper?*

§ 3.09 Case Library

Knapp v. State

Supreme Court of Indiana
168 Ind. 153, 79 N.E. 1076 (1907)

Chapter 4

Relevant but Inadmissible — Unfairly Prejudicial Evidence

§ 4.01 Chapter Checklist

1. Compare prejudicial evidence to unfairly prejudicial evidence. Why doesn't Rule 403 exclude all prejudicial evidence?

2. What is the test to determine if unfair prejudice exists?

3. How many steps are there in analyzing whether unfairly prejudicial evidence exists?

4. What are the two main types of unfairly prejudicial evidence that are excluded by Rule 403?

5. What do certain types of probability evidence in criminal cases, excessively violent evidence, similar acts or occurrences, and scientific tests have in common?

6. What is the significance of a limiting instruction?

§ 4.02 Relevant Federal Rules of Evidence

Rule 402. General Admissibility of Relevant Evidence

Relevant evidence is admissible unless any of the following provides otherwise: the United States Constitution; a federal statute; these rules; or other rules prescribed by the Supreme Court. Irrelevant evidence is not admissible.

Rule 403. Excluding Relevant Evidence for Prejudice, Confusion, Waste of Time, or Other Reasons

The court may exclude relevant evidence if its probative value is substantially outweighed by a danger of one or more of the following: unfair prejudice, confusing the issues, misleading the jury, undue delay, wasting time, or needlessly presenting cumulative evidence.

———————

The Advisory Committee Note to Rule 403 states in part, "These circumstances [in which relevant evidence is excluded] entail risks which range all the way from inducing decision on a purely emotional basis, at one extreme, to nothing more harmful than merely wasting time, at the other extreme."

§ 4.03 Introduction

Not all relevant evidence is admissible. As Rule 402 provides, relevant evidence may be made inadmissible by the "Constitution of the United States, by Act of Congress, by these rules, or by other rules prescribed by the Supreme Court pursuant to statutory authority." The reasons for excluding relevant evidence may vary, from violation of a criminal defendant's constitutional rights to violation of the hearsay rule.

Pursuant to Rule 403, trial courts have the authority to exclude relevant evidence if it poses a significant risk of unfair prejudice, misleads the fact finder, confuses the issues, or simply wastes time. In effect, there are two types of unfairly prejudicial evidence — one that misleads the jury and one that wastes its time. "Dangerous unfair prejudice" does not simply mean that the evidence strongly influences the jury. Evidence is usually offered by a party for the very purpose of persuading jurors to decide in that party's favor. That is, evidence is offered by parties to "prejudice" the jury in a party's favor. Most evidence in fact will cause jurors to form immediate initial impressions or judgments — effectively triggering some prejudging — based on the jurors' own experiences and natures. According to the Advisory Committee, evidence creates "unfair prejudice" when it has "an undue tendency to suggest a decision on an improper basis, commonly, though not necessarily, an emotional one." *See* Advisory Committee Note to Rule 403. Thus, the risk of "unfair prejudice" is the risk that the jury may not be able to assess or evaluate the evidence properly. This risk arises when admission of the evidence would be perceived as unfair or when the evidence would adversely affect the fairness of the trial process.

Not all evidence posing a danger of unfair prejudice is excluded under Rule 403. Instead, the court must administer a weighted balancing test and decide whether the probative value of the evidence is *substantially* outweighed by one or more of these prejudice factors.

Some evidence that is highly prejudicial is also highly probative of a fact in issue. Prior acts of a party offered to show a party's propensity to act in a certain manner, for example, can be both highly probative and highly prejudicial at the same time. Thus, in a robbery case, the fact that the defendant stole a car the day before the event to use in the robbery makes it more likely that the defendant was indeed the robber — but also carries the inference that the defendant has a propensity toward criminal behavior (i.e., that he is a one-man crime gang). Under the Federal Rules of Evidence, the need for relevant evidence often is considered greater than the potential harm that could result from the admission of at least some prejudicial evidence. Thus, evidence that poses a danger of unfair prejudice is excluded only if the danger of unfair prejudice "substantially outweighs" the probative value of the evidence. This weighted balancing test favors admissibility by exhibiting a preference for relevant evidence, even if the relevant evidence presents a risk of prejudice. However, the application of the balancing test is firmly committed to the judge's sound discretion, and rulings under Rule 403 are rarely reversed on appeal.

As the Advisory Committee Note to Federal Rule of Evidence 403 points out, excluding evidence because it is unfairly prejudicial should be a last resort. Exclusion should occur only after the judge has determined that a limiting instruction to the jury will not be sufficient to offset any prejudice. A limiting instruction is a directive by the judge to the jury to use the evidence only for a legitimate purpose. For example, if a judge in the robbery case admits evidence at trial showing that the defendant stole a car on the day preceding the robbery, the judge may instruct the jury to use the evidence only as it pertains to the robber's common scheme or plan and not as it relates to the defendant's propensity to violate the law.

One case that traces the intricacies of the unfair prejudice balancing test is *Old Chief v. United States*, 519 U.S. 172 (1997). (*See* Case Library.) In *Old Chief*, the accused was charged with possessing a firearm as a previously convicted felon. The accused offered to stipulate to the fact that he was a prior felon, but the prosecution refused to accept the stipulation. Instead, the prosecution wished to offer evidence at trial of the prior crime, which was one of violence. The district court and the court of appeals both sided with the prosecution, allowing the government to prove its own case. The Supreme Court reversed.

While the Court found that the type of conviction was relevant to the current charge and observed that the prosecution usually has the option of proving its own case as it sees fit (even on matters that are not in dispute), the Court found that the evidence still should have been excluded as unfairly prejudicial. In defining "unfair prejudice," the Court turned to the Advisory Committee Note to Rule 403, which defined "unfair prejudice" as "an undue tendency to suggest decision on an improper basis, commonly, though not necessarily, an emotional one." Justice Souter concluded that unfair prejudice of this sort had occurred in the case of Johnny Lynn Old Chief. Said Justice Souter's majority opinion:[1]

> Such improper grounds certainly include the one that Old Chief points to here: generalizing a defendant's earlier bad act into bad character and taking that as raising the odds that he did the later bad act now charged (or, worse, as calling for preventive conviction even if he should happen to be innocent momentarily).

Justice Souter went on to discuss the analytical method that courts should employ in balancing probative value against the risk of unfair prejudice under Rule 403. He observed that a court's decision on admissibility might require a review of evidentiary alternatives as well as the evidence in question: "what counts as the Rule 403 'probative value' of an item of evidence, as distinct from its Rule 401 'relevance,'

---

1. 519 U.S. at 181–182.

may be calculated by comparing evidentiary alternatives." These alternatives might include revealing only the general nature of the offense to the jury or some other method of minimizing prejudice.

Example

Susan alleges that she was raped by an acquaintance, John. At the criminal trial, John introduces a photograph of Susan dancing with him one year prior to the alleged rape. The photograph shows Susan wearing a strapless gown. Does the photograph present a risk of unfair prejudice?

Answer. The photograph may have some probative value, such as showing that Susan and John were acquainted with each other prior to the incident in question. However, the danger of unfair prejudice would be substantial.

If Susan's manner of dress on an earlier occasion would lead some jurors to consider punishing her through a verdict, the jury would be influenced to decide the issue based on emotion and not on the requirements of the law. The photograph consequently would obfuscate the relevant facts and hinder the jury in fulfilling its duty to find the truth. If Susan claimed she did not know John, and the photograph is the only evidence that the two were acquainted, then the photograph would have stronger probative value, yielding a much greater chance of admissibility.

Problem 4-1: "One Drink Too Many"

On a dark, moonless night in late November, a truck and passenger car collided on a remote section of the interstate. The driver of the car, Albert, was killed. Albert's estate filed a negligence suit against the driver of the truck, Tina, and her company, Studio 53, Inc. At trial, the defendants called Dr. Robert Orsky, a hematologist at the Regional Crime Laboratory, to discuss blood tests performed on Albert after the accident that showed the presence of intoxicants in his blood, indicating that he was drunk. The plaintiff objected and called for a sidebar, at which time the following discussion occurred.

JUDGE: What is the basis for your objection, counsel?

PLAINTIFF'S ATTORNEY: The blood test done by Dr. Orsky is not reliable, Your Honor, and should be excluded on grounds of unfair prejudice. We proffer the testimony of Nurse Wilma Jones, who, only minutes before the horrible accident, had assisted in taking the stitches out of Albert's hand at the nearby medical office. Nurse Jones will testify that she came within 18 inches of Albert's face and that Albert in no way, shape, or form smelled of alcohol.

JUDGE: Defense Counsel, any reply?

How should the defense counsel reply to the plaintiff's assertions?

JUDGE: In this case, because I find the nurse's testimony believable and the blood test of questionable value, I find that admitting the results of the blood test would unfairly prejudice the plaintiff's case. The blood test evidence will be excluded.

Did the judge rule correctly? Explain. See Ballou v. Henri Studios, Inc., 656 F.2d 1147 (5th Cir. 1981).

Problem 4-2: A Day in the Life of Susan White

Susan White, a crane operator at a major road construction site, was severely injured in a crane accident. Susan brought suit against the crane manufacturer based on a theory of strict products liability. To show damages, Susan offered a film depicting an average day in her life subsequent to the accident, including how she eats, gets out of bed, bathes, and travels on the city streets with other pedestrians.

Is such a "day in the life" film unfairly prejudicial?

Problem 4-3: In a New York State of Mind

[The following problem is based on an actual incident that occurred in New York City in the fall of 1992. The facts apply not only to the groups mentioned, but to all stereotypes that can enter into jurors' interpretive assumptions relating to an event. Professor Claude Steele, who later became the Provost of Columbia University, describes the phenomenon of "stereotype threat." This occurs when individuals live up — or down — to stereotypes of themselves by others. In essence, a person is sometimes treated by others based on their "social identity," which includes group membership in categories such as age, gender, race, and ethnicity. Everyone is subject to such threats, not simply minorities. *See, e.g.*, C. Steele, A Threat in the Air: How Stereotypes Shape the Intellectual Identities and Performance of Women and African-Americans, 52 Am. Psychologist 613 (1997)].

Dora and Bart, a white female and white male, respectively, were transit police officers in New York City. One day, while on an anti-crime detail, they came upon two young black males in the subway who they believed to be robbing a woman subway rider. The black males were holding handguns. Dora and Bart quickly opened fire, wounding one of the apparent assailants. It turned out that the apparent assailants, Johnny Patton and George Diamond, were undercover police officers from a different district who were in the process of arresting a suspect. Officer Patton was injured.

Assume for the purposes of this problem that Dora and Bart are charged with aggravated assault for the injuries caused to Officer Patton. Dora and Bart wish to argue that their conduct was not culpable.

1. What is the relevance, if any, of perceptions, stereotypes, and statistical data about race?

2. What is the relevance of the fact that the apparent assailants were male and relatively youthful in appearance?

3. Are generalizations about a group always an improper use of stereotypes and, therefore, unfairly prejudicial?

A plethora of evidence may be labeled "unfairly prejudicial," but certain kinds of evidence are particularly susceptible to exclusion on this basis. Consequently, the rest of this chapter will focus on recurring types of evidence often believed to present a special danger of unfair prejudice: (1) probability evidence about identity in criminal cases (specifically, the likelihood of another person with the same characteristics committing the crime charged), (2) evidence depicting violence in a manner that is physically revolting, (3) novel scientific evidence, and (4) similar events, happenings or occurrences.

§ 4.04 Probability Evidence of Identity in a Criminal Case

Statistical evidence is routinely admitted at trial to assist the trier of fact. One type of statistical evidence, however, is particularly misleading and is generally excluded. This type of evidence, denoted here as "probability evidence of identity," is specifically offered to show the unlikelihood of another person with the same characteristics as the defendant committing the crime charged. Such evidence suffers from a variety of defects, not the least of which is its power to exert extreme influence over a jury. A problem will illustrate this concept.

Problem 4-4: Chances Are . . .

The defendant, Lester, is charged with first-degree murder in Walhalla, South Carolina, a rural town of 4,000 people. At trial, the prosecution introduced evidence showing that the defendant had the same general physical description, the same type of accent, and the same brand of sneakers (Nike) as the person linked to the crime by various witnesses. The defendant claims mistaken identity. In rebuttal, the prosecution offers a professor of statistics, Dr. Egbert Einstein. Dr. Einstein intends to testify there is an extreme improbability, one in 12 million, of these characteristics belonging to a second person in Walhalla.

(a) What flaws, if any, can you find in Professor Einstein's evidence? (b) Should his testimony be admitted? (c) Why? See, e.g., People v. Collins, 68 Cal. 2d 319, 66 Cal. Rptr. 497, 438 P. 2d 33 (1968), which is reprinted in the Case Library at the end of this chapter.

§ 4.05 Evidence of Excessive Violence

Evidence showing the results of violence is a routine part of many trials, particularly in criminal homicide cases. Homicide requires proof of an unlawful killing of another human being. In a murder case, for example, the prosecutor must prove that a person died. The death may have been horrific. While evidence of the death is permitted in order to prove the case, Rule 403 imposes some limitations.

Specifically, it is improper to offer evidence that so blinds a jury to the facts of the case that the jury makes an emotional determination. A shorthand description of this limit is that the evidence cannot be so violent in appearance that a reasonable jury will "lose its lunch" as a result of viewing it.

Problem 4-5: Lose Your Lunch

Ernest and Samantha, the leaders of a radical political party, were found shot to death in their living room. The scene was gruesome, and the stench of death was everywhere. Franklyn, a known contract killer, was charged with the murders. At trial, the government offers testimony of a crime scene search officer, Jan, who testified that she visited the scene immediately following the murders and took color photographs of the bodies. The prosecutor then attempted to introduce in evidence the glossy 8 × 10 photographs taken by Jan. Franklyn's attorney objected.

1. How should a judge rule on the objection?
2. Should the prosecutor agree to stipulate to the fact that Ernest and Samantha were killed by gunshots?
3. Should the judge approve the stipulation if both parties agree to it?

Problem 4-6: Legs

Ned Carlyle lost both of his legs to amputation after an automobile accident. After being fitted with prosthetics, he learned to walk again. Ned sued the driver of the other car for damages. At trial, Ned testified about the accident.

PLAINTIFF'S ATTORNEY: Ned, please describe the injuries you received from the accident.

A: My legs were crushed from the knees down. The "jaws of life" were used to extract me from the car. Here's what happened—

DEFENDANT'S ATTORNEY: Objection. This evidence is unnecessary and unfairly prejudicial.

JUDGE: *What ruling and why?*

PLAINTIFF'S ATTORNEY: Can you show the ladies and gentlemen of the jury what your legs look like today?

A: Certainly. (Ned begins to remove his prosthetics to show the jury his stumps, intending to point to where his legs once were.)

DEFENDANT'S ATTORNEY: Objection. Your Honor, the witness' actions are unfairly prejudicial.

JUDGE: *What ruling and why?*

If the judge rules in favor of the defendant, but the plaintiff already has engaged in the forbidden behavior, does the defense counsel have any recourse?

What can the defense counsel do?

§ 4.06 Scientific Evidence

Scientific experiments that seek to replicate or simulate the events on which a lawsuit is based have the potential to be both highly probative and highly misleading. Consequently, experimental scientific evidence likely will be excluded as unfairly prejudicial, unless it is found to be "substantially similar" to what it intends to recreate.

While any form of novel scientific evidence, whether based on experiment, observation, or other formulation, also may be unfairly prejudicial, courts have placed the analysis of most scientific evidence questions squarely within the expert testimony rules, Rule 702 et seq. *See* Chapter 9 for extensive discussion of the admissibility of scientific evidence through expert testimony.

Example

Al Wiley is prosecuted for white-collar fraud after allegedly bilking several large health care companies of millions of dollars. At trial, the prosecutors offer the testimony of Dr. Ziggy Topstein, an expert in polygraphy. Dr. Topstein intends to testify that he has administered "lie detector" tests for 20 years and has an advanced degree specializing in interpreting the physiological data from such tests. He administered a "lie detector" test to the defendant, Wiley, immediately after the allegations against him. The test was conducted at Wiley's request, but the results indicated that Wiley was evasive and likely untruthful about the events in question. The defendant objected to the testimony. *How should the judge rule?*

Answer: Despite claims about the accuracy of polygraph tests, the judge should exclude the evidence as both unfairly prejudicial and insufficiently reliable to meet the standards for reliable scientific evidence under Rule 702. Jurors may tend to overvalue such evidence, and may forsake their own independent review of the defendant's credibility. Moreover, the testimony does not yet have a sufficiently reliable scientific basis. Many experts find that the human interpretation of polygraph tests is subjective, to the extent that the results are subjective and solely within the "eye of the beholder." Further, there may be disputes about replicating such tests in a laboratory setting.

A brief preview of how courts have approached novel scientific evidence follows. (This area will receive in-depth coverage in Chapter 9.)

Frye vs. Daubert

Courts have been struggling with the admissibility of novel scientific evidence for decades. From 1923 until fairly recently, the federal courts mostly applied the singular test of whether the evidence was "sufficiently established to have gained general acceptance in the particular field in which it belongs." *Frye v. United States*, 293 F. 1013, 1014 (D.C. Cir. 1923). In 1993, however, the Supreme Court held that the

Frye test had been superseded by the adoption of the Federal Rules of Evidence. Under the Federal Rules, the appropriate test allows trial courts to consider multiple factors. These factors include the following: (1) whether the subject matter was "scientific knowledge," (2) whether the theory or technique can be or has been tested, (3) whether the theory or technique has been subjected to peer review and publication, (4) whether the technique has a known or potential rate of error, (5) whether standards controlling the technique's operation exist and are maintained, and (6) finally, but not exclusively, the *Frye* test of general acceptance in the particular field. *See Daubert v. Merrell Dow Pharmaceuticals, Inc.*, 509 U.S. 579, 593–594 (1993). Justice Blackmun stated:

> Faced with a proffer of expert scientific testimony, then, the trial judge must determine at the outset, pursuant to Rule 104(a), whether the expert is proposing to testify to (1) scientific knowledge that (2) will assist the trier of fact to understand or determine a fact in issue. This entails a preliminary assessment of whether the reasoning or methodology underlying the testimony is scientifically valid and of whether that reasoning or methodology properly can be applied to the facts in issue.[2]

The meaning of the multiple-factor test of *Daubert* is still unfolding. Courts are being asked to admit novel scientific evidence in a wide variety of cases, many dealing with illness and injury allegedly caused by faulty products or pharmaceuticals. The Supreme Court has decided subsequent cases in an effort to clarify the meaning of *Daubert*.

In *Kumho Tire Co., Ltd. v. Carmichael*, 526 U.S. 137 (1999), for example, a suit resulting from an automobile accident allegedly caused by a defective tire, the Supreme Court attempted to further delineate the scope of the *Daubert* test. The Court considered whether the *Daubert* reliability test should be used for a non-scientific expert, in this case an expert in tire failure analysis. The Court held that the *Daubert* test also must be applied to testimony by "technical" or other non-scientific experts, such as engineers, but emphasized that the *Daubert* reliability test was a flexible one. The Court referred to its prior decision in *General Electric Co. v. Joiner*, 522 U.S. 136 (1997), where it held that courts of appeals must use an "abuse of discretion" standard when reviewing reliability findings by the district courts. *Id.* at 143. (In *Joiner*, the Supreme Court reviewed the exclusion of an expert witness' opinion on whether a type of chemical, PCBs (polychlorinated biphenyls), caused the plaintiff's cancer.) The chapter on expert testimony delves into these cases and the rules governing experts in great detail. The problem that follows illustrates the role Rule 403 still plays with some scientific evidence.

---

2. 509 U.S. at 592–593.

Problem 4-7: Videotape Replay

A tractor-trailer truck collided with a Buick Riatta automobile. The driver of the Buick brought suit against the tractor-trailer driver and his insurance company. At the time of the accident, 1:00 p.m., the pavement was dry and the weather was clear.

At trial, the plaintiff offered in evidence the results of an experiment between a tractor-trailer truck similar to the one involved in the accident and an identical Buick automobile to show that the defendant must have been driving the tractor-trailer at an excessive speed at the time of the accident. The plaintiff could not obtain the actual truck that collided with the car because it had been too badly damaged in the crash. The only differences between the experiment and the actual crash were that the experimental truck was approximately 115 pounds heavier than the truck involved in the accident and the experiment occurred on a slight incline, not on flat land like the actual accident.

1. Are the results of the experiment unfairly prejudicial? Why?

2. Would it be reversible error if the experiment results were improperly admitted? Why?

Problem 4-8: To Tell the Truth

After a series of rapes committed by a masked rapist, the police apprehended a suspect. There was no positive eyewitness identification of the defendant as the perpetrator of the crime. Instead, the prosecution relied on:

(a) DNA testing, which revealed that the semen found on the clothes of two of the victims was that of the defendant; and (b) a witness who claimed after hypnosis that she remembered observing the defendant at the scene of a rape immediately prior to their occurrences.

1. Is either the DNA or hypnosis evidence relevant? Why?

2. Is either the DNA or hypnosis evidence unfairly prejudicial? Why?

3. What is the relevance of *Daubert v. Dow Pharmaceuticals, Inc., Kumho Tire Co., Ltd. v. Carmichael*, or *Frye v. United States*?

4. Which of the following types of evidence would most likely be excluded:

(a) polygraph evidence, (b) handwriting analysis (graphology) evidence, (c) voice spectrography identification evidence, or (d) blood alcohol testing? Why? Discuss.

§ 4.07 Similar Occurrences, Happenings, and Events

Evidence of similar occurrences, happenings, and events is generally offered to corroborate or bolster a party's theory of the case. Often, there is an insufficient quantity of direct evidence about an incident or event to explain it adequately. For example, there may be inadequate information about the cause of a person's slip and fall on a dimly lit sidewalk or why a person became ill an hour after eating at a restaurant. When there is a lack of information, comparisons to other events or occurrences are especially useful. In a broad sense, the history of an event may be instructive as to its cause, its significance, or its meaning.

This type of evidence has great potential for unfair prejudice, however, leading to the general rule, "*res inter alios acta*," meaning things between others are inadmissible. Prior events, happenings, or occurrences often occur under widely disparate circumstances. Dissimilarities in the circumstances between the other events and the event in question diminish the net worth of the evidence. In addition, jurors may be misled or distracted by other events, to the extent that they are led to focusing on the nuances of other events instead of the event at issue. Further, no matter how similar or helpful to the jury the other occurrences are, the prior events are nevertheless collateral to the specific facts to be decided. For all of these reasons, evidence of similar occurrences, happenings, and events is often excluded at trial.

Exceptions to the general exclusion of similar occurrences exist. Sometimes, the evidence overcomes the specter of unfair prejudice, in part because of substantial similarities. Similar events evidence has been admitted in the following contexts: (1) to show causation (such as that of an illness or injury); (2) to show a dangerous condition existed (such as a bump or hole in the road); (3) to show the mental state of a party when it is at issue (such as in a suit claiming discrimination); (4) to rebut a party's claim of impossibility (such as subsequent similar events the defendant claimed could not occur); (5) to show the sales of other real property (to prove value); (6) to show the meaning of a contract, contract provision, or document (by offering prior dealings between the parties); and (7) to show the meaning of a contract, contract provision, or document (by the custom or usage in the industry). These exceptions are limited, however, and do not swallow up the general rule of exclusion.

A lack of similar occurrences, sometimes offered to show a lack of culpability, fault, or responsibility, is even more prejudicial than the existence of similar events and is generally excluded. The fact that an injury occurred for the very first time at the hands of an experienced taxi driver, surgeon, waiter, or store manager does not accurately portray whether negligence, fault, or responsibility on the part of the defendant existed. This evidence misleads a jury because a first-time accident could very well be the result of negligence or fault, there may have been reporting problems about prior similar events, and the prior experience may not have been under similar circumstances (e.g., the surgeon removed gall bladders for years and this was her first removal of an appendix).

Example

Josephine's house was condemned by the state after a new highway was designated to run through her kitchen. The only issue at trial was what constituted just compensation for her house. Josephine introduced the sale price of other homes in her neighborhood. *Are the prices of these other sales admissible?*

Answer. The other sale prices are relevant and not unfairly prejudicial, provided that the other houses being used for comparison are comparable to Josephine's. If the other houses are not sufficiently similar, and can be distinguished based on differences in size, features, location, etc., the admission of the sale prices of other homes probably would be unfairly prejudicial.

Problem 4-9: Slipped Up

Wally Witness testifies for the plaintiff in a "slip and fall" personal injury case. The plaintiff contends that the defendant negligently permitted puddles of water to accumulate on the defendant's walkway where the plaintiff fell.

Can Wally testify that he had observed puddles regularly form on the walkway during the three weeks prior to the plaintiff's fall? Can Wally testify that he had seen three people other than the plaintiff fall on the same walkway that week? Why?

Problem 4-10: Spoiled Shrimp

Memphis Frozen Foods, Inc., shipped three tons of frozen shrimp with Benner Shipping. The shrimp spoiled en route, and Memphis Frozen Foods brought suit against Benner Shipping for damages. The key issue was how to interpret the requirements of the contract. Benner Shipping attempted to introduce in evidence prior contracts between the parties concerning the sale of scallops and clams. Memphis Frozen Foods objected, claiming that the prior contracts were irrelevant because they did not deal with shrimp.

How should a judge rule on this objection? Why?

Problem 4-11: Double Decker

Suzanne was injured when she was thrown from a ride at the State Fair called the "Double Decker." Suzanne sued the ride's owner and its manufacturer. At trial, the defendants attempted to introduce evidence that no one had been injured in 5,000 previous rides on the Double Decker.

How is this problem different from other offers of similar acts, occurrences, or happenings evidence? Is this evidence unfairly prejudicial?

Problem 4-12: Sugar or Sweetener?

Polly, an employee in an artificial sweetener factory, was severely injured when a "No-Sweet" machine exploded. Polly sued the manufacturer of the machine. At trial, Polly attempted to introduce evidence concerning other "No-Sweet" machine explosions.

Should such evidence be considered unfairly prejudicial? Why? See generally Ponder v. Warren Tool Corp., 834 F.2d 1553 (10th Cir. 1987).

Problem 4-13: Harassment

The plaintiff, Janet Fife, brought suit in 1995 against her boss and former employer (Ace Barnes and Ace Hardware, Inc., respectively), claiming sexual harassment and unlawful retaliation. The plaintiff testified at trial.

PLAINTIFF'S ATTORNEY: Do you know if you are the only person to make allegations of this kind against the defendant?

DEFENDANT'S ATTORNEY: Objection. This question calls for an irrelevant and unfairly prejudicial answer.

JUDGE: *How should the judge rule on this objection? [Assume the objection was overruled.]*

A: Actually there were three other complaints — one by Barnes's former secretary in 1988, one by his store clerk in 1997, and one by his truck driver in 1999.

PLAINTIFF'S ATTORNEY: What were the outcomes of those other complaints?

DEFENDANT'S ATTORNEY: Objection, Your Honor. This question calls for an irrelevant and unfairly prejudicial response.

JUDGE: Counsel, please approach the bench.

How should the judge rule on this objection if the answer to the question were as follows:

A: One of the complaints, the one by the truck driver, was dismissed. The other two complaints were found to have merit by the administrative body that reviewed the complaints, and damages were awarded.

Problem 4-14: Unfair Prejudice

The accused in a bank fraud prosecution, Serena Ortuno, had worked for the bank for seven years and allegedly defrauded the bank for five of those seven years. You are the defendant's attorney. In the course of the direct examination of Serena, you attempt to elicit the following information: (1) the various jobs held by the defendant in the bank; (2) the number and names of the defendant's siblings; (3) that the bank recovered its entire corpus of funds; (4) that the defendant sometimes suffered from impaired judgment; (5) that the defendant took and passed a lie detector test given by her attorney in front of three neutral observers (not associated with the prosecution); (6) that the bank changed its procedures for accounting for $50 bills, the ones allegedly stolen, after the defendant's arrest; (7) that the defendant would offer a computerized reenactment of how the defendant usually walked through the vault; and (8) that the defendant received a Girl Scouts award for honesty, years before.

With a student role-playing Serena, ask her about the eight items above. Other students can be given the role of opposing counsel and asked to object, based on either irrelevance or unfair prejudice. A different student can role-play a judge and rule on the admissibility of these items.

Problem 4-15: People v. Penny

Jimmy Penny was prosecuted for molesting a six-year-old girl. At trial, the prosecution offered the following evidence. Which evidence is unfairly prejudicial?

(a) Pornographic magazines of young children that police officers found in Penny's home when executing a valid search warrant.

(b) Pornographic magazines depicting only adults that the police found in Penny's home when executing the same search warrant.

(c) Non-pornographic pre-teen and teen magazines depicting children in stylish clothing that the police found in Penny's home when executing the same search warrant.

§ 4.08 Summary and Review

1. Should a judge exclude evidence that is more prejudicial than probative upon a proper objection?

2. What is the difference between unfairly prejudicial evidence and prejudicial evidence?

3. Why do the Rules use a weighted balancing test for excluding unfairly prejudicial evidence?

4. Why is most statistical evidence allowed even though courts usually exclude probability evidence about the likelihood of a person other than the accused committing the alleged crime?

5. What are the dangers of other similar acts evidence?

6. Why admit gruesome evidence of a murder scene?

7. Should scientific test or experiment evidence always be admitted when performed by a qualified scientist?

8. Does the Supreme Court's approach to the admissibility of scientific evidence make sense? Why or why not?

§ 4.09 Chapter Review Problems

Review Problem 4-A

Arlen Spanos was prosecuted for securities fraud after skimming from several mutual funds he managed. At trial, the defendant offered a psychiatrist who testified that Spanos had "impaired judgment" during the relevant time period. When the prosecutor confronted the psychiatrist on cross-examination, she admitted that the condition did not rise to the level of insanity. The prosecution then objected to the testimony and requested that it be struck from the record. *How should the judge rule?*

1. The testimony should be excluded because it was an irrelevant opinion about the defendant's state of mind.

2. The testimony should be excluded because while it was relevant to the defendant's state of mind, it would mislead jurors into thinking the defendant was insane during the relevant period.

3. The testimony should be allowed, because it was relevant to a crucial aspect of fraud, the defendant's state of mind.

4. The testimony should be allowed, unless the jury would be influenced by the psychiatrist's status as an expert in the field of "impaired judgment."

Review Problem 4-B

Alou was charged with conspiracy to distribute cocaine. At trial, the judge overruled an objection by the defense to evidence that Alou participated previously in a similar operation involving the distribution of cocaine. The court ruled the evidence was not unfairly prejudicial. *If Alou was convicted and appealed the trial court's ruling, how should the appellate court rule?*

1. Uphold the trial judge's decision, unless other trial courts have excluded similar evidence under identical circumstances.

2. Uphold the trial judge's decision, because of the great deference by appellate courts to trial judges, in large part because the appellate court must decide based only on a "cold" record.

3. Reverse the trial judge's decision if it fails the litmus test of being a reliable decision more likely than not.

4. Reverse the trial judge's decision if the ruling affected a substantial right of the defendant.

Review Problem 4-C

Ali Staton, the manager of a successful coffee shop, was charged with embezzling funds from the business. At trial, the prosecutor offered evidence that Staton earned an annual salary of $45,000 from the coffee shop, with yearly bonuses of up to $10,000. The prosecutor then offered a new witness to testify that in the months leading up to the arrest, Staton was seen leasing a Porsche Boxster and traveling to Hawaii in the first-class section of the airplane. *If the defense objects to this evidence, how should the judge rule?*

1. Admit the evidence, providing the defense has an opportunity to rebut it under the "rule of completeness," permitting opposing parties to submit remainders.

2. Admit the evidence, but only if its prejudicial impact is not very high.

3. Exclude the evidence, but not if the probative value and danger of unfair prejudice of the evidence are both considerable.

4. Exclude the evidence because it is not relevant to whether the defendant embezzled as charged.

Review Problem 4-D

Rasheed went to the Lotus Room one Friday night for a dinner of Chinese food. Later that evening, he became very ill and attributed it to food poisoning. After being out of work for several weeks and still feeling unable to work at a competent level, he sued the restaurant for damages. At trial, Rasheed wished to offer the fact that in the month before Rasheed's dinner there, eight other people, all in separate parties, had become ill after eating at the Lotus Room for dinner. *If the defendant objects to this evidence, how should the judge rule?*

1. The judge should admit the evidence, because it is relevant to how Rasheed became ill.

2. The judge should admit the evidence, because everyone else became ill after eating dinner, just like the plaintiff.

3. The judge should exclude the evidence, because it is hearsay and irrelevant.

4. The judge should exclude the evidence, unless additional evidence is offered showing a much greater similarity between the other events and the dinner in question.

Review Problem 4-E: Law Firm Philadelphia

Andrew Beckett sues the law firm in which he had been employed as an associate for wrongful termination. Beckett claims that he was illegally fired because he had AIDS, which a law firm partner recognized from seeing a lesion on his face. The law firm's defense is that the partners were unaware that Beckett had AIDS and that they fired him for poor work performance.

During cross-examination of Beckett, defense lawyer Belinda Conine holds up a mirror to his face and asks him if he can see any lesions on his face. Beckett examines his face in the mirror and responds that no lesions are visible. *Is Conine's mirror demonstration proper?*

Following the cross-examination, Beckett's lawyer Joe Miller asks Beckett whether he has lesions anywhere on his body that resemble the lesion he had on his face when he was fired. Beckett replies that he has AIDS lesions on his torso. Miller then asks Beckett to remove his shirt and hold the mirror in front of his chest. In the mirror are a chest full of red lesions. *Is Miller's use of the mirror proper rebuttal to Conine's demonstration?*

§ 4.10 Case Library

People v. Collins

Supreme Court of California
68 Cal. 2d 319, 66 Cal. Rptr. 497, 438 P.2d 33 (1968)

Sullivan, Justice:

We deal here with the novel question whether evidence of mathematical probability has been properly introduced and used by the prosecution in a criminal case. While we discern no inherent incompatibility between the disciplines of law and mathematics and intend no general disapproval or disparagement of the latter as an auxiliary of the fact-finding processes of the former, we cannot uphold the technique employed in the instant case. As we explain in detail, *infra*, the testimony as to mathematical probability infected the case with fatal error and distorted the jury's traditional role of determining guilt or innocence according to long-settled rules. Mathematics, a veritable sorcerer in our computerized society, while assisting the trier of fact in the search for truth, must not cast a spell over him. We conclude that on the record before us defendant should not have had his guilt determined by the odds and that he is entitled to a new trial. We reverse the judgment.

. . . .

On June 18th, 1964, at about 11:30 a.m., Mrs. Juanita Brooks, who had been shopping, was walking home along an alley in the San Pedro area of the City of Los Angeles . . . . As she stooped down to pick up an empty carton, she was suddenly pushed to the ground by a person whom she neither saw nor heard approach . . . . She managed to look up and saw a young woman running from the scene. According to Mrs. Brooks the latter appeared to weigh about 145 pounds, was wearing "something dark," and had hair "between a dark blond and a light blond," but lighter than the color of the defendant Janet Collins' hair as it appeared at trial. Immediately after the incident, Mrs. Brooks discovered that her purse, containing between $35 and $40, was missing.

About the same time as the robbery, John Bass, who lived on the street at the end of the alley, was in front of his house watering his lawn . . . . [H]e saw a woman run out of the alley and enter a yellow automobile parked across the street from him . . . . The latter then saw that it was being driven by a male Negro, wearing a mustache and beard. At the trial Bass identified defendant as the driver of the yellow automobile . . . .

. . . .

At the seven-day trial the prosecution experienced difficulty in establishing the identities of the perpetrator of the crime. The victim could not identify Janet and had never seen the defendant. The identification by the witness Bass, who observed the girl run out of the alley and get into the automobile, was incomplete as to Janet and may have been weakened as to the defendant . . . .

In an apparent attempt to bolster the identifications, the prosecutor called an instructor of mathematics at a state college. Through this witness he sought to establish that, assuming the robbery was committed by a Caucasian woman with a blond ponytail who left the scene accompanied by a Negro with a beard and mustache, there was an overwhelming probability that the crime was committed by any couple answering such distinctive characteristics. The witness testified, in substance, to the "product rule," which states that the probability of the joint occurrence of a number of mutually independent events is equal to the product of the individual probabilities that each of the events will occur. Without presenting any statistical evidence whatsoever in support of the probabilities for the factors selected, the prosecutor then proceeded to have the witness assume probability factors for the various characteristics which he deemed to be shared by the guilty couple and all other couples answering to such distinctive characteristics.[3]

Applying the product rule to his own factors the prosecutor arrived at a probability that there was but one chance in 12 million that any couple possessed the distinctive characteristics of the defendants. Accordingly, under this theory, it was to be inferred that there could be but one chance in 12 million that defendants were innocent and that another equally distinctive couple actually committed the robbery. Expanding on what he had thus purported to suggest as a hypothesis, the prosecutor offered the completely unfounded and improper testimonial assertion that, in his opinion, the factors he had assigned were "conservative estimates" and that, in reality "the chances of anyone else besides these defendants being there, . . . having every similarity, . . . is somewhat like one in a billion."

Objections were timely made to the mathematician's testimony on the grounds that it was immaterial, that it invaded the province of the jury, and that it was based on unfounded assumptions. The objections were "temporarily overruled" and the

---

3. (Court's original footnote 10.) Although the prosecutor insisted that the factors he used were only for illustrative purposes — to demonstrate how the probability of the occurrence of mutually independent factors affected the probability that they would occur together — he nevertheless attempted to use factors which he personally related to the distinctive characteristics of the defendants. In his argument to the jury he invited the jurors to apply their own factors, and asked defense counsel to suggest what the latter would deem reasonable. The prosecutor himself proposed the individual probabilities set out in the table below. Although the transcript of the examination of the mathematics instructor and the information volunteered by the prosecutor at that time create some uncertainty as to precisely which of the characteristics the prosecutor assigned to the individual probabilities, he restated in his argument to the jury that they should be as follows:

Characteristic	Individual Probability
A. Partly yellow automobile	1/10
B. Man with moustache	1/4
C. Girl with ponytail	1/10
D. Girl with blond hair	1/3
E. Negro man with beard	1/10
F. Interracial couple in car	1/1000

In his brief on appeal the defendant agrees that the foregoing appeared on a table presented in the trial court.

evidence admitted subject to a motion to strike. When that motion was made at the conclusion of the direct examination, the court denied it, stating that the testimony had been received only for the "purpose of illustrating the mathematical probabilities of various matters, the possibilities for them occurring or re-occurring."

. . . .

As we shall explain, the prosecution's introduction and use of mathematical probability statistics injected two fundamental prejudicial errors into the case:

(1) The testimony itself lacked an adequate foundation both in evidence and in statistical theory; and (2) the testimony and the manner in which the prosecution used it distracted the jury from its proper and requisite function of weighing the evidence on the issue of guilt, encouraged the jurors to rely upon an engaging but logically irrelevant expert demonstration, foreclosed the possibility of an effective defense by an attorney apparently unschooled in mathematical refinements, and placed the jurors and defense counsel at a disadvantage in sifting relevant fact from inapplicable theory.

We initially consider the defects in the testimony itself. As we have indicated, the specific technique presented through the mathematician's testimony and advanced by the prosecutor to measure the probabilities in question suffered from two basic and pervasive defects — an inadequate evidentiary foundation and an inadequate proof of statistical independence. First, as to the foundation requirement, we find the record devoid of any evidence relating to any of the six individual probability factors used by the prosecutor and ascribed by him to the six characteristics as we have set them out in footnote 10, *ante*. To put it another way, the prosecution produced no evidence whatsoever showing, or from which it could be in any way inferred, that only one out of every ten cars which might have been at the scene of the robbery was partly yellow, that only one out of every four men who might have been there wore a mustache, that only one out of every ten girls who might have been there wore a ponytail, or that any of the other individual probability factors listed were even roughly accurate . . . .

We can hardly conceive of a more fatal gap in the prosecution's scheme of proof. A foundation for the admissibility of the witness' testimony was never even attempted to be laid, let alone established. His testimony was neither made to rest on his own testimonial knowledge nor presented by proper hypothetical questions based upon valid data in the record . . . .

But, as we have indicated, there was another glaring defect in the prosecution's technique, namely an inadequate proof of the statistical independence of the six factors. No proof was presented that the characteristics selected were mutually independent, even though the witness himself acknowledged that such condition was essential to the proper application of the "product rule" or "multiplication rule." . . . To the extent that the traits or characteristics were not mutually independent (e.g., Negroes with beards and men with mustaches obviously represent overlapping categories . . .), the "product rule" would inevitably yield a wholly erroneous and exaggerated result even if all of the individual components had been determined with precision . . . .

In the instant case, therefore, because of the aforementioned two defects — the inadequate evidentiary foundations and the inadequate proof of statistical independence — the technique employed by the prosecutor could only lead to wild conjecture without demonstrated relevancy to the issues presented. It acquired no redeeming quality from the prosecutor's statement that it was being used only "for illustrative purposes" since, as we shall point out, the prosecutor's subsequent utilization of the mathematical testimony was not confined within such limits.

We now turn to the second fundamental error caused by the probability testimony. Quite apart from our foregoing objections to the specific technique employed by the prosecution to estimate the probability in question, we think that the entire enterprise upon which the prosecution embarked, and which was directed to the objective of measuring the likelihood of a random couple possessing the characteristics allegedly distinguishing the robbers, was gravely misguided. At best, it might yield an estimate as to how infrequently bearded Negroes drive yellow cars in the company of blonde females with ponytails.

The prosecution's approach, however, could furnish the jury with absolutely no guidance on the crucial issue: *Of the admittedly few such couples, which one, if any, was guilty of committing this robbery?* Probability theory necessarily remains silent on that question, since no mathematical equation can prove beyond a reasonable doubt (1) that the guilty couple *in fact* possessed the characteristics described by the People's witnesses, or even (2) that only *one* couple possessing those distinctive characteristics could be found in the entire Los Angeles area.

As to the first inherent failing we observe that the prosecution's theory of probability rested on the assumption that the witnesses called by the People had conclusively established that the guilty couple possessed the precise characteristics relied upon by the prosecution. But no mathematical formula could ever establish beyond a reasonable doubt that the prosecution's witnesses correctly observed and accurately described the distinctive features which were employed to link defendants to the crime . . . . Conceivably, for example, the guilty couple might have included a light-skinned [African-American] with bleached hair rather than a Caucasian blonde; or the driver of the car might have been wearing a false beard as a disguise; or the prosecution's witnesses might simply have been unreliable. (Footnote omitted.)

The foregoing risks of error permeate the prosecution's circumstantial case. Traditionally, the jury weighs such risks in evaluating the credibility and probative value of trial testimony, but the likelihood of human error or of falsification obviously cannot be quantified; that likelihood must therefore be excluded from any effort to assign a *number* to the probability of guilt or innocence. Confronted with an equation which purports to yield a numerical index of probable guilt, few juries could resist the temptation to accord disproportionate weight to that index; only an exceptional juror, and indeed only a defense attorney schooled in mathematics, could successfully keep in mind the fact that the probability computed by the prosecution can represent, *at best*, the likelihood that a random couple would share the characteristics testified to by the People's witnesses — *not necessarily the characteristics of the actually guilty couple.*

As to the second inherent failing in the prosecution's approach, even assuming that the first failing could be discounted, the most a mathematical computation could *ever* yield would be a measure of the probability that a random couple would possess the distinctive features in question. In the present case, for example, the prosecution attempted to compute the probability that a random couple would include a bearded Negro, a blonde girl with a ponytail, and a partly yellow car; the prosecution urged that this probability was no more than one in 12 million. Even accepting this conclusion as arithmetically accurate, however, one still could not conclude that the Collinses were probably *the* guilty couple. On the contrary, as we explain in the Appendix, the prosecution's figures actually imply a likelihood of over 40 percent that the Collinses could be "duplicated" by at least *one other couple who might equally have committed the San Pedro robbery.* Urging that the Collinses be convicted on the basis of evidence which logically establishes no more than this seems as indefensible as arguing for the conviction of X on the ground that a witness saw either X or X's twin commit the crime.

Again, few defense attorneys, and certainly few jurors, could be expected to comprehend this basic flaw in the prosecution's analysis. Conceivably even the prosecutor erroneously believed that his equation established a high probability that *no* other bearded Negro in the Los Angeles area drove a yellow car accompanied by a ponytailed blonde. In any event, although his technique could demonstrate no such thing, he solemnly told the jury that he had supplied mathematical proof of guilt.

Sensing the novelty of that notion, the prosecutor told the jurors that the traditional idea of proof beyond a reasonable doubt represented "the most hackneyed, stereotyped, trite, misunderstood concept in criminal law." He sought to reconcile the jury to the risk that, under his "new math" approach to criminal jurisprudence, "on some rare occasion . . . an innocent person may be convicted." "Without taking that risk," the prosecution continued, "life would be intolerable . . . because . . . there would be immunity for the Collinses, for people who chose not to be employed to go down and push old ladies down and take their money and be immune because how could we ever be sure they are the ones who did it?"

In essence this argument of the prosecutor was calculated to persuade the jury to convict defendants whether or not they were convinced of their guilt to a moral certainty and beyond a reasonable doubt . . . . Undoubtedly the jurors were unduly impressed by the mystique of the mathematical demonstration but were unable to assess its relevancy or value. Although we make no appraisal of the proper applications of mathematical techniques in the proof of facts, . . . we have strong feelings that such applications, particularly in a criminal case, must be critically examined in view of the substantial unfairness to a defendant which may result from ill conceived techniques with which the trier of fact is not technically equipped to cope . . . . We feel that the technique employed in the case before us falls into the latter category.

We conclude that the court erred in admitting over defendant's objection the evidence pertaining to the mathematical theory of probability and in denying defendant's motion to strike such evidence . . . . The judgment against defendant must therefore be reversed.

. . . .

Appendix

. . . .

Hence, even if we should accept the prosecution's figures without question, we would derive a probability of over 40 percent that the couple observed by the witnesses could be "duplicated" by at least one other equally distinctive interracial couple in the area, including a Negro with a beard and mustache, driving a partly yellow car in the company of a blonde with a ponytail. Thus the prosecution's computations, far from establishing beyond a reasonable doubt that the Collinses were the couple described by the prosecution's witnesses, imply a very substantial likelihood that the area contained *more than one* such couple, and that a couple *other* than the Collinses was the one observed at the scene of the robbery . . . .

Old Chief v. United States

United States Supreme Court
519 U.S. 172, 117 S. Ct. 644, 136 L. Ed. 2d 574 (1997)

SOUTER, J., delivered the opinion of the Court, in which STEVENS, KENNEDY, GINSBURG, AND BREYER, JJ., joined. O'CONNOR, J. filed a dissenting opinion, in which REHNQUIST, C.J., and SCALIA and THOMAS, JJ., joined.

Subject to certain limitations, 18 U.S.C. Section 922(g)(1) prohibits possession of a firearm by anyone with a prior felony conviction, which the Government can prove by introducing a record of judgment or similar evidence identifying the previous offense. Fearing prejudice if the jury learns the nature of the earlier crime, defendants sometimes seek to avoid such an informative disclosure by offering to concede the fact of the prior conviction. The issue here is whether a district court abuses its discretion if it spurns such an offer and admits the full record of a prior judgment, when the name or nature of the prior offense raises the risk of a verdict tainted by improper considerations, and when the purpose of the evidence is solely to prove the element of prior conviction. We hold that it does.

In 1993, petitioner, Old Chief, was arrested after a fracas involving at least one gunshot. The ensuing federal charges included [possession of a firearm by a convicted felon.] . . . . The earlier crime charged in the indictment against Old Chief was assault causing serious bodily injury. Before trial, he moved for an order requiring the Government "to refrain from mentioning . . . the prior criminal convictions of the Defendant, except to state that the Defendant has been convicted of a crime punishable by imprisonment exceeding one (1) year." The Assistant United States Attorney refused to join in a stipulation, insisting on his right to prove his case his own way, and the District Court agreed . . . .

We granted Old Chief's petition for writ of certiorari . . . because the Courts of Appeals have divided sharply . . . . As a threshold matter, [the nature of the prior conviction is relevant.] A documentary record of the conviction for that named offense was thus relevant evidence in making Old Chief's Section 922(g)(1) status more probable than it would have been without the evidence.

. . . .

The principal issue is the scope of a trial judge's discretion under Rule 403, ... The term "unfair prejudice," as to a criminal defendant, speaks to . . . "an undue tendency to suggest decisions on an improper basis . . . . Advisory Committee's Notes on Fed. Rule Evid. 403.

Such improper grounds certainly include the one that Old Chief points to here: generalizing a defendant's earlier bad act into bad character and taking that as raising the odds that he did the later bad act now charged . . . . There is, accordingly, no question that propensity would be an "improper basis" for conviction . . . . [W]hen a court considers "whether to exclude on grounds of unfair prejudice," the "availability of other means of proof may . . . be an appropriate factor." Advisory Committee's Notes on Fed. Rule Evid. 403 . . . .

. . . Where a prior conviction was for a gun crime or one similar to other charges in a pending case, the risk of unfair prejudice would be especially obvious, and Old Chief sensibly worried that the prejudicial effect of his prior assault conviction, significant enough with respect to the current gun charges alone, would take on added weight from the related assault charge against him.

. . . In arguing that the stipulation or admission would not have carried equivalent value, the Government invokes the familiar, standard rule that the prosecution is entitled to prove its case by evidence of its own choice, or, more exactly, that a criminal defendant may not stipulate or admit his way out of the full evidentiary force of the case as the government chooses to present it . . . .

This is unquestionably true as a general matter. The "fair and legitimate weight" of conventional evidence showing individual thoughts and acts amounting to a crime reflect the fact that making a case with testimony and tangible things not only satisfies the formal definition of an offense, but tells a colorful story with descriptive richness . . . .

This recognition that the prosecution with its burden of persuasion needs evidentiary depth to tell a continuous story has, however, virtually no application when the point at issue is a defendant's legal status, dependent on some judgment rendered wholly independently of the concrete events of later criminal behavior charged against him . . . .

. . . In this case, . . . the only reasonable conclusion was that the risk of unfair prejudice did substantially outweigh the discounted probative value of the record of conviction, and it was an abuse of discretion to admit the record when an admission was available.

. . . .

The judgment is reversed, and the case is remanded to the Ninth Circuit for further proceedings consistent with this opinion.

Chapter 5

Character and Habit Evidence

§ 5.01 Chapter Checklist

1. Is the evidence being offered "character" evidence or "other acts" evidence that establishes character circumstantially?

2. If yes, what is the purpose for which evidence of a person's character is being offered?

    a. Is the person's character itself a material fact, that is, an essential element of a crime, claim, or defense?

    b. Is the person's character offered to prove that a person acted on a particular occasion in accordance with his or her propensity?

    c. Is the person's character offered to prove or disprove the person's character for truthfulness as a witness?

3. If the evidence is being offered to prove propensity, do any of the exceptions to the general bar on propensity evidence for criminal defendants or victims apply?

4. Is this a homicide or sexual assault case, to which special character evidence rules apply?

5. If the evidence is being offered via a defendant or victim exception, what is the form of the character evidence being offered?

    a. The person's reputation?

    b. An opinion about the person's character?

    c. Specific acts in which the person has previously engaged?

6. Is evidence that looks like character-propensity evidence but is not—such as non-propensity uses of prior bad acts—being offered and, if so, for what purposes?

7. Is other-act evidence being offered to establish habit, rather than character-propensity?

§ 5.02 Relevant Federal Rules of Evidence

Rule 404. Character Evidence; Crimes or Other Acts

  (a) **Character Evidence.**

(1) Prohibited Uses. Evidence of a person's character or character trait is not admissible to prove that on a particular occasion the person acted in accordance with the character or trait.

(2) Exceptions for a Defendant or Victim in a Criminal Case. The following exceptions apply in a criminal case:

(A) a defendant may offer evidence of the defendant's pertinent trait, and if the evidence is admitted, the prosecutor may offer evidence to rebut it;

(B) subject to the limitations in Rule 412, a defendant may offer evidence of an alleged victim's pertinent trait, and if the evidence is admitted, the prosecutor may:

(i) offer evidence to rebut it; and

(ii) offer evidence of the defendant's same trait; and

(C) in a homicide case, the prosecutor may offer evidence of the alleged victim's trait of peacefulness to rebut evidence that the victim was the first aggressor.

(3) Exceptions for a Witness. Evidence of a witness's character may be admitted under Rules 607, 608, and 609.

(b) **Other Crimes, Wrongs, or Acts.**

(1) Prohibited Uses. Evidence of any other crime, wrong, or act is not admissible to prove a person's character in order to show that on a particular occasion the person acted in accordance with the character.

(2) Permitted Uses. This evidence may be admissible for another purpose, such as proving motive, opportunity, intent, preparation, plan, knowledge, identity, absence of mistake, or lack of accident.

(3) Notice in a Criminal Case. In a criminal case, the prosecutor must:

(A) provide reasonable notice of any such evidence that the prosecutor intends to offer at trial, so that the defendant has a fair opportunity to meet it;

(B) articulate in the notice the permitted purpose for which the prosecutor intends to offer the evidence and the reasoning that supports the purpose; and

(C) do so in writing before trial — or in any form during trial if the court, for good cause, excuses lack of pretrial notice.

Rule 405. Methods of Proving Character

(a) **By Reputation or Opinion.** When evidence of a person's character or character trait is admissible, it may be proved by testimony about the person's reputation or by testimony in the form of an opinion. On cross-examination of the character witness, the court may allow an inquiry into relevant specific instances of the person's conduct.

(b) **By Specific Instances of Conduct.** When a person's character or character trait is an essential element of a charge, claim, or defense, the character or trait may also be proved by relevant specific instances of the person's conduct.

Rule 406. Habit; Routine Practice

Evidence of a person's habit or an organization's routine practice may be admitted to prove that on a particular occasion the person or organization acted in accordance with the habit or routine practice. The court may admit this evidence regardless of whether it is corroborated or whether there was an eyewitness.

Rule 412. Sex-Offense Cases: The Victim's Sexual Behavior or Predisposition

(a) **Prohibited Uses.** The following evidence is not admissible in a civil or criminal proceeding involving alleged sexual misconduct:

(1) evidence offered to prove that a victim engaged in other sexual behavior; or

(2) evidence offered to prove a victim's sexual predisposition.

(b) **Exceptions.**

(1) *Criminal Cases.* The court may admit the following evidence in a criminal case:

(A) evidence of specific instances of a victim's sexual behavior, if offered to prove that someone other than the defendant was the source of semen, injury, or other physical evidence;

(B) evidence of specific instances of a victim's sexual behavior with respect to the person accused of the sexual misconduct, if offered by the defendant to prove consent or if offered by the prosecutor; and

(C) evidence whose exclusion would violate the defendant's constitutional rights.

(2) *Civil Cases.* In a civil case, the court may admit evidence offered to prove a victim's sexual behavior or sexual predisposition if its probative value substantially outweighs the danger of harm to any victim and of unfair prejudice to any party. The court may admit evidence of a victim's reputation only if the victim has placed it in controversy.

(c) **Procedure to Determine Admissibility.**

(1) *Motion.* If a party intends to offer evidence under Rule 412(b), the party must:

(A) file a motion that specifically describes the evidence and states the purpose for which it is to be offered;

     (B) do so at least 14 days before trial unless the court, for good cause, sets a different time;

     (C) serve the motion on all parties; and

     (D) notify the victim or, when appropriate, the victim's guardian or representative.

   (2) Hearing. Before admitting evidence under this rule, the court must conduct an in camera hearing and give the victim and parties a right to attend and be heard. Unless the court orders otherwise, the motion, related materials, and the record of the hearing must be and remain sealed.

(d) Definition of "Victim." In this rule, "victim" includes an alleged victim.

Rule 413. Similar Crimes in Sexual-Assault Cases

(a) Permitted Uses. In a criminal case in which a defendant is accused of a sexual assault, the court may admit evidence that the defendant committed any other sexual assault. The evidence may be considered on any matter to which it is relevant.

(b) Disclosure to the Defendant. If the prosecutor intends to offer this evidence, the prosecutor must disclose it to the defendant, including witnesses' statements or a summary of the expected testimony. The prosecutor must do so at least 15 days before trial or at a later time that the court allows for good cause.

(c) Effect on Other Rules. This rule does not limit the admission or consideration of evidence under any other rule.

(d) Definition of "Sexual Assault." In this rule and Rule 415, "sexual assault" means a crime under federal law or under state law (as "state" is defined in 18 U.S.C. § 513) involving:

   (1) any conduct prohibited by 18 U.S.C. chapter 109A;

   (2) contact, without consent, between any part of the defendant's body — or an object — and another person's genitals or anus;

   (3) contact, without consent, between the defendant's genitals or anus and any part of another person's body;

   (4) deriving sexual pleasure or gratification from inflicting death, bodily injury, or physical pain on another person; or

   (5) an attempt or conspiracy to engage in conduct described in subparagraphs (1)–(4).

Rule 414. Similar Crimes in Child-Molestation Cases

(a) Permitted Uses. In a criminal case in which a defendant is accused of child molestation, the court may admit evidence that the defendant committed any other child molestation. The evidence may be considered on any matter to which it is relevant.

(b) **Disclosure to the Defendant.** If the prosecutor intends to offer this evidence, the prosecutor must disclose it to the defendant, including witnesses' statements or a summary of the expected testimony. The prosecutor must do so at least 15 days before trial or at a later time that the court allows for good cause.

(c) **Effect on Other Rules.** This rule does not limit the admission or consideration of evidence under any other rule.

(d) **Definition of "Child" and "Child Molestation."** In this rule and Rule 415:

   (1) "child" means a person below the age of 14; and

   (2) "child molestation" means a crime under federal law or under state law (as "state" is defined in 18 U.S.C. § 513) involving:

      (A) any conduct prohibited by 18 U.S.C. chapter 109A and committed with a child;

      (B) any conduct prohibited by 18 U.S.C. chapter 110;

      (C) contact between any part of the defendant's body — or an object — and a child's genitals or anus;

      (D) contact between the defendant's genitals or anus and any part of a child's body;

      (E) deriving sexual pleasure or gratification from inflicting death, bodily injury, or physical pain on a child; or

      (F) an attempt or conspiracy to engage in conduct described in subparagraphs (A)–(E).

Rule 415. Similar Acts in Civil Cases Involving Sexual Assault or Child Molestation

(a) **Permitted Uses.** In a civil case involving a claim for relief based on a party's alleged sexual assault or child molestation, the court may admit evidence that the party committed any other sexual assault or child molestation. The evidence may be considered as provided in Rules 413 and 414.

(b) **Disclosure to the Opponent.** If a party intends to offer this evidence, the party must disclose it to the party against whom it will be offered, including witnesses' statements or a summary of the expected testimony. The party must do so at least 15 days before trial or at a later time that the court allows for good cause.

(c) **Effect on Other Rules.** This rule does not limit the admission or consideration of evidence under any other rule.

Rule 608. A Witness's Character for Truthfulness or Untruthfulness

(a) **Reputation or Opinion Evidence.** A witness's credibility may be attacked or supported by testimony about the witness's reputation for having a character for truthfulness or untruthfulness, or by testimony in the form of an opinion about that character. But evidence of truthful character is admissible only after the witness's character for truthfulness has been attacked.

(b) **Specific Instances of Conduct.** Except for a criminal conviction under Rule 609, extrinsic evidence is not admissible to prove specific instances of a witness's conduct in order to attack or support the witness's character for truthfulness. But the court may, on cross-examination, allow them to be inquired into if they are probative of the character for truthfulness or untruthfulness of:

(1) the witness; or

(2) another witness whose character the witness being cross-examined has testified about.

By testifying on another matter, a witness does not waive any privilege against self-incrimination for testimony that relates only to the witness's character for truthfulness.

Rule 609. Impeachment by Evidence of a Criminal Conviction

(a) **In General.** The following rules apply to attacking a witness's character for truthfulness by evidence of a criminal conviction:

(1) for a crime that, in the convicting jurisdiction, was punishable by death or by imprisonment for more than one year, the evidence:

(A) must be admitted, subject to Rule 403, in a civil case or in a criminal case in which the witness is not a defendant; and

(B) must be admitted in a criminal case in which the witness is a defendant, if the probative value of the evidence outweighs its prejudicial effect to that defendant; and

(2) for any crime regardless of the punishment, the evidence must be admitted if the court can readily determine that establishing the elements of the crime required proving—or the witness's admitting—a dishonest act or false statement.

(b) **Limit on Using the Evidence After 10 Years.** This subdivision (b) applies if more than 10 years have passed since the witness's conviction or release from confinement for it, whichever is later. Evidence of the conviction is admissible only if:

(1) its probative value, supported by specific facts and circumstances, substantially outweighs its prejudicial effect; and

(2) the proponent gives an adverse party reasonable written notice of the intent to use it so that the party has a fair opportunity to contest its use.

(c) **Effect of a Pardon, Annulment, or Certificate of Rehabilitation.** Evidence of a conviction is not admissible if:

(1) the conviction has been the subject of a pardon, annulment, certificate of rehabilitation, or other equivalent procedure based on a finding that the

person has been rehabilitated, and the person has not been convicted of a later crime punishable by death or by imprisonment for more than one year; or

(2) the conviction has been the subject of a pardon, annulment, or other equivalent procedure based on a finding of innocence.

(d) Juvenile Adjudications. Evidence of a juvenile adjudication is admissible under this rule only if:

(1) it is offered in a criminal case;

(2) the adjudication was of a witness other than the defendant;

(3) an adult's conviction for that offense would be admissible to attack the adult's credibility; and

(4) admitting the evidence is necessary to fairly determine guilt or innocence.

(e) Pendency of an Appeal. A conviction that satisfies this rule is admissible even if an appeal is pending. Evidence of the pendency is also admissible.

§ 5.03 Character Evidence Basics

A. Defining "Character Evidence" and "Propensity"

Rule 404(a)(1), the general rule concerning character evidence, reads as follows:

> Evidence of a person's character or character trait is not admissible to prove that on a particular occasion the person acted in accordance with the character or trait.

This rule excludes a particular type of evidence ("character") offered for a particular forbidden purpose (to prove that "on a particular occasion the person acted in accordance with the character or trait"). Much of the character-evidence analysis turns on whether proof that tends to prove character is being offered for the forbidden purpose — also known as "propensity" — or for some other permitted purpose. If offered for any other purpose, character evidence is admissible subject to Rule 403 and the other rules of evidence. Thus, it is helpful when analyzing character evidence to begin with the question, "What is this being offered to prove?"

But before examining the inferential chain connecting character evidence to the elements of the case, it might be helpful to explore what evidence of "character" includes.

"Character," in common understanding, refers to the "kind of person" someone is: kind or cruel, peaceful or violent, careful or sloppy. "Character" is often used broadly to describe much of a person's nature. For example, to say "Charles is an honest man" is to describe him as an overall good person, who would neither steal nor lie nor mislead another. The term "character trait" is used more narrowly to refer to a particular aspect of our character, perhaps as punctual, quick-tempered, or fastidious. Most people judge others quite readily based on their confident assessments of others' characters. We believe that honest people won't lie, punctual people won't be late, and fastidious people won't leave dirty dishes.

Sometimes, parties offer evidence of character directly, by calling a witness to testify that "Johnny is a thug" or that "Denise is dishonest." Often, however, character is implicated less directly, by introducing evidence of seemingly extraneous events — "Johnny beat up a guy in a bar several years ago" or "Denise lied on her job application during high school" — to prove character or a character trait. To connect the event to the case, the offering party contends that the other act, like assaulting or lying, proves (at least circumstantially) that a person involved in the current case is a thug or a liar.

As mentioned above, this type of character proof runs afoul of Rule 404(a)(1) when its relevance in the case depends on the forbidden propensity inference (i.e., the character evidence is offered to prove that a person acted in accordance with it on a particular occasion).

Imagine, for example, that Johnny has been charged with assaulting Vinnie. Johnny claims self-defense. The prosecutor seeks to offer a previous, unrelated incident where Johnny beat up a guy in a bar. The relevance of the previous incident might be described this way:

1. Johnny previously beat up a guy in a bar.

2. Thus, Johnny is violent.

3. Therefore, Johnny was more likely the aggressor in the fight with Vinnie and not simply defending himself.

4. Accordingly, Johnny is guilty of assault.

It is the third of the four steps (or inferences) that runs afoul of the propensity ban. In other words, you cannot offer the previous fistfight to establish that Johnny acted in "accordance with his [violent] character" at the particular time in question — his alleged assault of Vinnie.

Some might ask, "why not? Someone who has beaten people up on previous occasions is unlikely to be a wallflower during the incident with Vinnie. Shouldn't the jury hear about who the defendant *is* to best determine what happened at the time in question? Isn't more proof better when it comes to finding the truth?"

Courts and the rule drafters have long answered "no" in the context of character-propensity evidence. In a sense, Rule 404 is Congress' judgment that the risks of character evidence offered for propensity are so great that they substantially outweigh the probative force of the proof as a matter of law. Instead of allowing case-by-case balancing under Rule 403, Rule 404 commands courts to exclude character-propensity evidence, unless an exception applies.

At trial, character-propensity evidence carries several risks:

Jurors may overvalue character proof.

Most people are willing to make quick, confident judgments about another person's character based on very little evidence. For example, we might label someone a liar whom we once catch in a significant lie when that untruth may have been an aberration. Indeed, character is not very predictive of how people will react in particular situations. Character describes average behavior only. A "nasty-tempered person" may be grumpy more often than most other people. Nevertheless, he or she may still often, perhaps even usually, be friendly and kind. (Remember Vito Corleone in *The Godfather*, gently playing with his grandchildren one minute, then ordering killings of "business" associates the next!) The more broadly defined and "cross-situational" the character trait, the less its predictive power. Thus, we might expect a person we label as "tardy" to be late for all or most appointments. In fact, such persons may often be tardy for social events but punctual at their job.

Character can change over time, often in subtle but important ways that jurors might ignore in light of dramatic evidence of earlier positive or negative character traits. Even violent persons can have a religious experience that leads them to peace. Age can temper youthful aggression. Someone who steals as an impoverished youth may never do so in a more affluent adulthood.

Jurors may punish a person for reprehensible conduct even when that conduct is not at issue in the current case.

Character evidence has moral overtones. Jurors may dislike someone they perceive as dishonest. Jurors may, therefore, feel that defendants "deserve" punishment, convicting them more for who they are than for what the evidence has shown that they have done.

This risk can become even more acute when jurors learn of a previous incident for which a person has not yet been punished. For instance, imagine in the example above if jurors learn that Johnny severely injured a person in the previous bar fight but that he was never charged or convicted of a crime. The jury may very well choose to punish Johnny for the previous assault, regardless of whether the evidence proves Johnny committed the assault for which he is currently on trial. This violates the fundamental principle that people should be put on trial for specific, charged conduct and not extraneous events or as a generalized character inquiry.

Character proof consumes time and risks confusing jurors about the issues on trial.

Proof of extraneous events can quickly devolve into a sideshow. Court time is a limited resource and courts often face backlogs, with the costs running to taxpayers and the prejudice from delay running to litigants. Putting someone on trial for a lifetime of conduct would significantly extend the process.

At the same time, jurors are given a difficult task — determining what occurred during a months- or years-old incident. Layering in additional, potentially older, incidents solely to establish a person's character runs the risk of distracting or even confusing jurors.

The Advisory Committee aptly highlighted some of the concerns this way:[1]

"Character evidence is of slight probative value and may be very prejudicial. It tends to distract the trier of fact from the main question of what actually happened on the particular occasion. It subtly permits the trier of fact to reward the good man and to punish the bad man because of their respective characters despite what the evidence in the case shows actually happened."

Example

Ronald Meldman is charged with armed robbery. Meldman is a 28-year-old postal clerk caught by police officers running near the scene of the crime and arguably fitting the offender's description. Meldman, in handcuffs and surrounded by four police officers, is brought before the victim and told, "We found this guy running from the scene, and he seems to fit the description." The victim responded, "Well, he does sort of look like the guy." There were no other eyewitnesses. Meldman told the police he was running to catch the bus to work when they grabbed him.

At trial, the prosecution offers evidence in its case-in-chief that Meldman was convicted nine years earlier of robbery. If this evidence is admitted, there is a grave danger that the jury will simply assume, "He robbed before, so, of course, he did it again. Those people never change." The jury might ignore the nine years in which Meldman earned an honest living, suggesting he has indeed changed. Or the jury might ignore the unique circumstance that he committed the armed robbery when he was homeless and starving, a situation that has now changed. Most important, the jury might ignore the weak evidence that Meldman committed the current crime — the tenuous identification, the lack of corroborating evidence, and any plausible explanation for his alleged "flight." If the prior conviction caused the jurors to ignore all these things, they would be convicting him simply because they think he is a bad man. For reasons like these, evidence of Meldman's prior crime will in fact be inadmissible to prove that he committed the current one, pursuant to Rule 404(a)(1).

Practice Tip: What's the Story?

Understanding each party's litigation story can help you identify whether proffered evidence constitutes character evidence. Thus:

1. Evidence that is itself part of the story of a dispute cannot be character evidence.

2. Evidence that is relevant to a story but not part of the dispute is often character evidence.

3. One way to overcome an "improper character evidence" objection is to convince a judge that proffered evidence is in fact part of the story of a dispute, in other words part of the transaction or occurrence at issue.

---

1. FED. R. EVID. 404, advisory committee's note to subdivision (a) (quoting California Law Revision Committee).

For example, assume that D is charged with a murder of victim V that took place on July 30.

1. The prosecutor offers evidence that D stole the gun that was used to shoot V. Evidence of the theft cannot be character evidence as it is part of the story of the killing of V.

2. The prosecutor offers evidence of an uncharged and unrelated crime: D's killing of X on June 30. Evidence of the killing of X is character evidence.

3. The prosecutor offers evidence that D's motive for killing V was to prevent V from telling the police that V had seen D kill X on June 30. Evidence of D's killing of X is now part of the story of the charged crime of killing V, and so is now not character evidence.

Problem 5-1: At the Movies: Insane Anatomy of a Murder

In the film *Anatomy of a Murder*, Lt. Manion is charged with murdering Barney Quill. Manion admits that he killed Quill, but claims that he did so as a result of "irresistible impulse," a form of temporary insanity resulting from finding out that Quill had raped and beaten Manion's wife, Laura. The prosecution theory is that Quill and Laura were lovers, and that Manion killed Quill after learning of the affair. Cross-examining Manion, the prosecutor asks Manion how many enemy soldiers he has killed in combat. The prosecutor argues that Manion's wartime experience may have conditioned him to killing. The defense objects, claiming that evidence of wartime combat killing is irrelevant and an improper attempt to show that Manion has a propensity to be violent. *How should the judge rule on the objection?*

Problem 5-2: Arsenal

Late one evening, four men were repairing a car on a Brooklyn street. A young lady walked along the opposite side of the street. One of the group of men insulted her as she walked past. Her husband, following behind her after buying a newspaper, learned about the exchange and cussed out the men before returning home.

When husband and wife made it back to their apartment, the wife revealed details about the insult (one of the men propositioned her and offered her $2 in exchange).

Enraged, the husband returned to the scene and a fight ensued. The husband killed one of the four men ("Coppola") with a pistol he brought to the scene in his pocket.

At trial, the defendant-husband admits killing Coppola, but he claims it was not done with premeditation. Instead, defendant claims that he acted out of sudden rage stemming from the incident.

The prosecution seeks to admit evidence collected from the defendant's apartment when police arrested him. The evidence includes three pistols and a tear gas gun. The defendant did not bring any of these items to the scene and, indeed, each of the pistols is a different caliber than the weapon that killed Coppola. No one alleges that the defendant employed tear gas in the incident. Except where otherwise stated, answer questions 1 to 5 below by consulting only Rules 401, 402, and 403.

1. Would evidence of the arsenal in defendant's apartment concern his "character" — as defined in everyday usage — or something else? Why?

2. If the evidence does concern "character," what character trait or traits is the prosecutor likely trying to prove, or is the defendant's "general character" at issue?

3. For what purpose or purposes might the prosecutor want to offer the evidence of defendant's weapons in the state's case-in-chief at trial? Why?

4. What is the likely impact of the evidence on the jury, and is that impact "unfair"? Might the defense argue for exclusion of any or all of these sorts or forms of evidence under Rule 403? How?

5. As a matter of basic relevance, should any of this evidence be admissible if the defendant were on trial for defrauding his employer instead of murder? Would any of the evidence be relevant in such a trial? Why?

How and why might that additional information alter your answers to the above questions?

6. Would the evidence in Questions 1, 3, and 5 be admissible if we now consider the character rules?

See People v. Zackowitz, 254 N.Y. 192 (1930).

B. Rule 404(b) — Specific Acts Relevant to Character but Offered for Non-Propensity Purposes

1. General Principles and Problems

Remember from the previous discussion that character evidence is inadmissible under Rule 404(a)(1) *only* if its relevance depends on propensity — that a person acted in accordance with a character trait on particular occasion. But evidence that tends to cast negative or positive light on a person's character may very well be relevant for a non-propensity purpose. When this is so, admitting the evidence does not violate Rule 404(a)(1).

Rule 404(b)(1) reads:

(b) Other Crimes, Wrongs, or Acts.

(1) Prohibited Uses. Evidence of any other crime, wrong, or act is not admissible to prove a person's character in order to show that on a particular occasion the person acted in accordance with the character.

Rule 404(b)(1) makes plain what is implicit in 404(a)(1) — a person's "other" acts are not admissible when their relevance depends on a propensity theory. This aspect of Rule 404(b) is largely duplicative of Rule 404(a)(1). Indeed, evidence that "Johnny beat up a guy in a bar" (a "crime, wrong, or act" tending to prove character) raises concerns just like evidence that "Johnny is violent" (character evidence) would.

Rule 404(b)(2) reads:

> (2) **Permitted Uses.** This evidence may be admissible for another purpose, such as proving motive, opportunity, intent, preparation, plan, knowledge, identity, absence of mistake, or lack of accident.

Consider these principles as you complete the next problem.

Problem 5-3: Arsenal 2

Assume the same facts from Problem 5-2: Arsenal, but this time imagine that the defendant contests that he killed Coppola. Suppose that defendant claims he was in New Jersey at the time of the shooting. In this version, the police find four pistols near the body. Only one of the guns was used in the killing, and the police are able to tie it to the shooting because the caliber of the weapon matches a shell casing and is consistent with the mortal wound. Upon arresting the defendant, police discover purchase receipts for each of the four weapons in the defendant's apartment. The prosecutor offers all the weapons at defendant's murder trial.

1. Are the guns relevant? If so, why? Are any of the guns relevant for a non-propensity purpose? Is the murder weapon relevant for different reasons than the other guns? If so, precisely how?

2. Does any of the evidence have a tendency to shed light on defendant's character? Could one purpose (permissible or not) of the evidence rely on propensity? If so, describe the inferences.

3. Assume that the defendant's attorney objects that introducing the guns violates Rule 404(a)(1). How should the court rule?

[a] Purposes Other Than Character

Rule 404(b)(2) sheds light on three key character evidence concepts.

Other-acts evidence may be admissible for non-propensity purposes.

The rule correctly recognizes that other-acts evidence may be relevant for multiple reasons, meaning that a party might offer it for a propensity (forbidden) or other purpose (permitted).

Problem 5-4: Master Key

Samantha pled guilty to burglarizing an apartment in a complex near her home. She did so by using a master key stolen from a maintenance closet at the complex and took items out of the apartment to pawn for drugs. A few months after the original burglary, but before Samantha was arrested for that crime, a person was murdered in a botched burglary at the same complex. There were no signs of forced entry, but property was stolen. Samantha claims that she did not commit the murder, and the prosecutor seeks to introduce details of Samantha's previous stolen-key burglary during the state's case-in-chief. The defense objects that the previous burglary incident is inadmissible per Rule 404. *How should the court rule (assume Samantha does not testify)?*

The list of permissible purposes for other-acts evidence in Rule 404(b)(2) is illustrative but not exhaustive or exclusive.

You may have noticed that Rule 404(b)(2) highlights "opportunity" as one among several permissible uses of other-acts evidence, along with motive, intent, preparation, plan, knowledge, identity, absence of mistake, or lack of accident.

This list illustrates several common, permissible non-propensity purposes for other-acts evidence. But other possibilities exist, and a few of them are covered below. The list is not exhaustive or exclusive.

Likewise, just because someone nominally offers other-acts evidence for one of the purposes in Rule 404(b)(2), the evidence does not automatically avoid Rule 404's propensity ban.

Example

David was convicted of killing Vaughn by shooting him in the head at point-blank range, execution style. He served his time and was released. A few months later, Walter was killed at David's house. David admits shooting Walter, but he claims it was an unintentional accident. During its case-in-chief, the prosecution seeks to admit evidence of David shooting Vaughn to establish that David indeed intended to kill Walter. The prosecutor cites Rule 404(b)(2) to the court and argues, "this goes to his intent Your Honor, the defendant clearly intended the first killing and likely intended this one, too."

Although the prosecution phrased the offer in terms of "intent," the evidence's relevance on this theory clearly turns on propensity.

The prosecution is contending that because David killed with intent before, he is the type of person who kills with intent, and therefore he likely intended to shoot Walter. If the prosecutor offered the proof to establish "lack of accident," the proof would fare no better. To prove lack of accident, the prosecutor is still contending that David is less likely to have accidentally shot Walter because he is the kind of person who intentionally kills others and did so in the case at hand. Both theories rely on propensity reasoning and violate Rule 404(a)(1), (b).

Contrast this example with Problem 5-4, Master Key, above. In that case, the evidence was relevant to show that Samantha was one of a few people who could have committed the crime because she had a key that allowed her to commit it, not that she is the type of person who commits such crimes and acted in accordance.

The important point, then, is not to view the examples (e.g., intent, plan, opportunity) of non-propensity purposes in Rule 404(b)(2) as outright exceptions to the propensity ban. They are merely illustrative scenarios that encompass some common non-propensity purposes for other-acts evidence. Merely saying the magic words, "this goes to intent" or "this goes to opportunity" is not enough to get around Rule 404's propensity ban. Instead, the offering party must demonstrate that the relevance of the evidence does not depend on the propensity inference.

Even when other-acts evidence is relevant for a non-propensity purpose, courts "may" exclude it pursuant to Rule 403.

While other-acts evidence may be admissible for a non-propensity purpose per Rule 404(a)(1), (b), Rule 403 may still provide grounds for exclusion. Think of the Rule 404(b) analysis as two distinct questions:

1. Is the evidence relevant for a non-propensity purpose?

2. Is the probative value of the non-propensity purpose substantially outweighed by the Rule 403 risks (unfair prejudice, wasted time, misleading the jury)?

Often, other-acts evidence that is relevant for a non-propensity purpose simultaneously connects to the case through a propensity inference. This creates a potentially unfairly prejudicial scenario. Consider why as you tackle the next problem.

Problem 5-5: Master Key 2

Consider the facts of Problem 5-4, Master Key, above. Further imagine that, consistent with those facts, the prosecutor offers the evidence of the details of Samantha's previous burglary to "establish that she had an opportunity to enter the crime scene Your Honor, she had a key." The court responds, "I do believe you are on to something. It seems that this does show opportunity."

1. Should the court admit the evidence without further analysis? If you were the defense attorney, would your raise further objection? On what basis?

2. Identify the permissible probative value of the state's offer.

3. Identify any 403 risks arising from the state's offer.

4. Considering your answers to the previous questions, if you were the judge, would you admit or exclude the proof?

5. If you decided to admit the proof, would you provide any special instruction to the jury? If so, craft an instruction. If not, identify and articulate why an instruction is unnecessary.

[b] Proof of Specific Acts

The most common use of Rule 404(b)(2) is as justification for introducing a criminal defendant's prior misconduct to prove matters such as intent, knowledge, or identity. However, Rule 404(b)(2) authorizes the use of specific-acts evidence in both civil and criminal cases. In fact, *any* specific act can be offered under Rule 404(b)(2) for a purpose other than showing propensity.

While we often, for shorthand, speak of *"prior"* specific acts, acts occurring *after* the events at issue (e.g., after the charged offense) can also sometimes be relevant. In addition, while we generally speak of prior "misconduct," good acts may sometimes be offered under Rule 404(b)(2) to show lack of guilt or responsibility for the current behavior on trial.

Under Rule 404(b)(2), the specific act must be shown by evidence sufficient to enable a reasonable jury to conclude by a preponderance of the evidence that the prior acts occurred and that the defendant or other relevant actor committed them. *See Huddleston v. United States*, 485 U.S. 681, 689, 108 S. Ct. 1496, 99 L. Ed. 2d 771 (1988). For example, the mere fact of arrest is not sufficient to meet this burden; there must be evidence that the defendant actually committed the prior crime. *See, e.g., United States v. Robinson*, 978 F.2d 1554, 1559 (10th Cir. 1992). Convictions constitute sufficient proof of specific acts of misconduct, but Rule 404(b) also applies to "uncharged misconduct" — misconduct that has not resulted in an arrest or formal charge. Indeed, misconduct can include criminal charges that resulted *in an acquittal*, provided that the occurrence of the earlier crime is shown by the appropriate standard of proof required for that jurisdiction. This conclusion follows from the differing standards of proof for conviction of a crime and for admission of Rule 404(b)(2) evidence. An acquittal establishes only that the state could not prove guilt beyond a reasonable doubt; it does not prove the accused innocent. Thus, a prosecutor could offer sufficient evidence to enable a reasonable jury to find guilt by a preponderance of the evidence under Rule 404(b)(2) even though another jury has entered an acquittal.

Dowling v. United States, 493 U.S. 342, 110 S. Ct. 668, 107 L. Ed. 2d 708 (1990), supports this conclusion. Dowling had been charged with a bank robbery in which the perpetrator wore a ski mask and carried a handgun. At trial, a prosecution witness testified, over defense objection, that she had been assaulted in her home two weeks after the robbery by two men who entered without her permission, one of whom wore a ski mask and carried a handgun. She was able to identify that man as Dowling, because she pulled off his ski mask while struggling with him. She also identified a man named Christian as the other assailant. Dowling was charged with burglarizing and robbing her but was acquitted. At Dowling's trial for the bank robbery, the prosecutor nevertheless offered this woman's testimony to strengthen its identification of Dowling and to link him to Christian, who drove the getaway car in the charged bank robbery. The Third Circuit held that this was error, albeit harmless, because Rule 404(b) did not sanction admission of other crimes evidence that resulted in acquittal. On further appeal to the Supreme Court, the other-crimes evidence was challenged under the collateral estoppel component of the Double Jeopardy Clause (not under Rule 404(b)). The Court rejected this challenge, partly because of the different standards of proof concerning criminal guilt and Rule 404(b) evidence: "Because a jury might reasonably conclude by a preponderance of the evidence that Dowling was the masked man who entered Henry's home, even if it did not believe beyond a reasonable doubt that Dowling committed the crimes charged at the first trial, the collateral estoppel component of the Double Jeopardy Clause is inapposite."

While the Rule 404(b) question was not before the Court, the *Dowling* rationale suggests that bad acts may be admissible under Rule 404(b)(2) even though the defendant has been acquitted of those acts. We say "may," however, because a defendant remains free to argue in a particular case that the act has minimal probative value in light of the acquittal. As the Supreme Court has said elsewhere, "the strength of the evidence establishing the similar act is one of the factors the court may consider when conducting the Rule 403 balancing."

[c] Notice Required

Finally, Rule 404(b)(3) contains a notice requirement. Rule 404(b)(3) provides:

> **(3) Notice in a Criminal Case.** In a criminal case, the prosecutor must:
>
> **(A)** provide reasonable notice of any such evidence that the prosecutor intends to offer at trial, so that the defendant has a fair opportunity to meet it;
>
> **(B)** articulate in the notice the permitted purpose for which the prosecutor intends to offer the evidence and the reasoning that supports the purpose; and
>
> **(C)** do so in writing before trial — or in any form during trial if the court, for good cause, excuses lack of pretrial notice.

Rule 404(b) was amended in 2020 to strengthen and clarify an existing notice requirement in criminal cases. The rule now makes clear that a prosecutor must provide "[n]otice [of 404(b) evidence] . . . before trial in such time as to allow the defendant a fair opportunity to meet the evidence, unless the court excuses that requirement upon a showing of good cause." (Advisory Committee Note). The prosecutor is obligated to provide notice whether or not the defendant requests it.

The notice must specify the non-propensity purpose for which the prosecutor intends to offer the evidence, rather than just identifying the evidence. This notice must be in writing before trial, though written notice includes electronic formats. (Advisory Committee Note).

Courts may, in certain circumstances, excuse a late or incomplete notice:

> The good cause exception [to the notice requirement] applies not only to the timing of the notice as a whole but also to the timing of the obligations to articulate a non-propensity purpose and the reasoning supporting that purpose. A good cause exception for the timing of the articulation requirements is necessary because in some cases an additional permissible purpose for the evidence may not become clear until just before, or even during, trial. (Advisory Committee Note).

Trial courts may, however, exclude 404(b) evidence for failure to provide proper pretrial notice, where the prosecutor does not establish good cause for the failure.

2. Motive

Rule 404(b)(2) states that evidence of specific other acts may be admissible to prove motive. There is sometimes a fine line between "motive" and character-propensity evidence, a distinction that is not clarified by the rules or their drafting history. Motive may speak to whether someone acted at all, whether they acted with the requisite mental state, or both. Mueller and Kirkpatrick note that motive is:

> [a]ptly described as an inducement or state of feeling that impels and tempts the mind to indulge in a criminal act, motive is perhaps best viewed as a circumstantial fact that usually need not be shown to prove guilt but is often relevant as a basis to infer both intent and act.

> CHRISTOPHER B. MUELLER & LAIRD C. KIRKPATRICK, 1 FEDERAL EVIDENCE § 4:32 (4th ed. 2017) (internal quotations omitted).

Example 1

Imagine, for example, that Jane is accused of a murder-robbery but denies that she is the killer. Further assume that Jane was desperate for money to pay off debts arising from her involvement in organized crime. Jane's need for money makes it at least somewhat more likely that she was involved in the crime because she was *motivated* to commit it.

This theory of relevance does not depend on the forbidden propensity inference (i.e., Jane is the type of person, in general, who is involved with crime and thus is more likely to have acted in accordance with this propensity at the time the victim was killed). Instead, the evidence is relevant to show that Jane had a specific reason to rob — to obtain money to pay off her debts.

You will also note that although the evidence's relevance does not depend upon the propensity inference, it does carry the risks associated with character-propensity evidence. There is a substantial chance a jury, confronted with evidence that Jane participated in organized crime, would engage in propensity reasoning instead of its proper purpose (to establish motive). Moreover, the jury might convict Jane notwithstanding the evidence on the murder-robbery charge to punish her for past criminal transgressions or preemptively incapacitate her as a participant in future organized crime.

Example 2

Harry Osterling, a 30-something accountant, shows up at a Jewish daycare center, shoots three five-year-old children, and flees. Assuming that he is sane, it is clear from the nature of his acts that he meant to cause serious bodily injury or death to these children. But *why* would such a man want to hurt innocent children? Investigation reveals that he is a neo-Nazi who was personally insulted by the daycare center's rabbi, who called Osterling a "hateful, powerless barbarian" the day before the shooting.

Would evidence of the exchange between Osterling and the rabbi be admissible over Osterling's objection that admitting the evidence would violate Rule 404? Moreover, would the prosecutor be able to prove Osterling's status as a neo-Nazi by evidence of instances of his wearing swastikas and giving racist speeches?

Assume we know that *someone* shot the children at the Jewish daycare center, but we do not yet know who. Investigation reveals circumstantial evidence that Osterling was in the vicinity of the daycare center shortly before the shooting and that he is a skilled marksman. To bolster its murder charge against Osterling, the prosecution offers evidence of his neo-Nazi affiliations. This "motive" evidence is offered to prove that Osterling, and not someone else, committed the act of shooting the Jewish children. The evidence is relevant to show Osterling was motivated against the victims in this case. This theory of relevance avoids the forbidden inference — that Osterling has a murderer's character and acted upon his murderous propensities the day in question. The distinction between motive and propensity is a fine one, and there is substantial risk the jury might consider the neo-Nazi proof to establish his character and propensity to murder. Thus, the neo-Nazi proof would be admissible, but a judge would also apply Rule 403 to account for the risks in admitting the proof.

The disagreement between Osterling and the daycare center's rabbi is also likely admissible to show that Osterling was motivated against the victims. Because of the previous disagreement with the rabbi, Osterling had reason to retaliate against the rabbi. Attacking the rabbi's students would be one way to get back at him. Thus, proof of the disagreement would be relevant to establish that Osterling had a reason to attack the children and, accordingly, was more likely to have committed the crime than someone without a motive.

Problem 5-6: Infidelity

Montana Redwood is on trial for homicide. In cross-examining prosecution witnesses, defense counsel revealed the defense theory, that Redwood killed Molly Ringwater because Ringwater was attacking Redwood's wife. The prosecutor offered evidence that Redwood had been unfaithful on numerous occasions during the year before the killing. *Admissible? Why or why not? Should the ruling change if the prosecution also offers evidence that Ringwater had told Redwood's wife of Redwood's infidelity in a conversation that took place shortly before Ringwater's demise?*

Problem 5-7: Gangs

David is a member of a street gang, the Bloods. One night, Vinnie, a member of a rival gang, the Crips, is killed in a drive-by shooting. The Bloods and Crips have been in a long war with each other over turf, control of a lucrative drug market, and revenge for previous killings. After investigation, the police arrest David and charge him with first degree murder. David disputes that he was involved in the crime. During its case-in-chief, the state attempts to prove that David was a member of the Bloods and that Vinnie was a Crip. David objects to the proof of his gang membership under Rules 404 and 403. *How should the court rule?*

Problem 5-8: Demerol

Brady was a nurse at Memorial Hospital. As part of a DEA investigation of stolen drugs at Memorial, Brady was charged with stealing Demerol (a pain drug). Based on an eyewitness and hospital records, the government alleged that Brady had withdrawn a small amount of the drug from many syringes over a three-month period. Brady denied that he stole the drug. The prosecution seeks to admit proof that Brady was a Demerol addict, and Brady has moved to exclude any proof or reference to his addiction. *How should the court rule? See United States v. Cunningham*, 103 F.3d 553 (7th Cir. 1996).

3. Opportunity

Rule 404(b)(2) states that evidence of specific acts may be admissible to prove opportunity. "Opportunity," as used in Rule 404(b)(2), means access to or presence at the scene of a crime, or having distinctive or unusual skills or abilities employed in the commission of the crime charged. Remember that "opportunity" is not an element of the crime. Rather, opportunity is one link in the inferential chain that tends to prove identity — the defendant is more likely to have committed the crime because he or she had a specific opportunity to do so. For one example of how opportunity proof works in disputed identity cases, see Problem 5-4, Master Key.

Example

Robin Macduff is accused of burglarizing a local mansion. While items were missing, there were no signs of forced entry, and all windows were protected by bars and all the doors were locked. The prosecutor offers evidence, however, that Macduff is a locksmith, and that she had picked thousands of locks in the past 10 years as part of her job. This special ability demonstrates the kind of "unusual skill" that might offer her the opportunity to commit a crime that others could not.

Problem 5-9: High-Tech Terrorism

Lteef Ulima was arrested for the bombing of a federal office building after police viewed a videotape that showed Ulima hurriedly leaving the building moments before the explosion. Forensic analysis revealed that the explosion was caused by an experimental explosive device, one that was part of a government research project contracted to a private entity. The State offers evidence that, three weeks before the explosion, Ulima burglarized a warehouse of Regotech Corporation, the private contractor working on the experimental explosive device. *Admissible or not? Why?*

Problem 5-10: Medium

Purported medium Jane Johnson is charged with fraudulently accepting money for putting clients "in touch" with their dead relatives. Johnson would hold séances during which the "dead" would talk to the living. The prosecution proffers evidence of Johnson's involvement in three scams in which she would mimic other persons' voices and appearance to gain access to that person's bank accounts, stock trading accounts, and pension funds. The defense objects to the proffer. *How should the court rule and why?*

4. Modus Operandi

Rule 404(b)(2) states that evidence of specific acts may be admissible to prove identity. "Identity" is the ultimate purpose for which much of Rule 404(b) evidence is offered. *See, e.g.,* motive discussion in [2], above. One method of proving identity is through *"modus operandi"* proof. *"Modus operandi"* means the criminal's method of operating. It proves identity by relying on the argument that the pattern and characteristics of the crimes are so unusual and distinctive as to be like a signature.

A *modus operandi* argument does not arise simply because crimes are of the same general type. It is improper to argue, for example, that merely because the accused burgled homes three times before, the jury should believe that he burgled again. That sort of inference is the classic character propensity inference. Instead, the two crimes must involve some sufficiently unusual pattern or tool to have high probative value in suggesting that the same person committed both crimes. Some courts even speak of the "uniqueness" of the method or pattern, though it is doubtful that uniqueness (being one of a kind) is literally required. But the signature trait concept is nevertheless often stringently applied.

The essential *modus operandi* inference is not "the defendant burgled before, therefore he is the type of person who burgles and likely burgled again" (classic forbidden propensity reasoning). Instead, the inference is that the method of committing the prior act and current crimes is so idiosyncratic, and the acts involved so similar, that only the defendant could have committed it.

Example

Five men are found murdered in Beverly Hills at different times and places over the course of a year. In each of the five killings, the deadly deed was done by stabbing the victim in the heart with a three-sided knife — one that promotes rapid bleeding and prevents healing. Moreover, in each case, such a knife was used to carve a different zodiac sign on the victim's body. Ronny Wood has been linked to the first four killings because his fingerprints were found at the crime scenes. But no physical evidence linked him to the fifth killing. At Wood's trial on the fifth killing, the prosecutor will likely succeed, over defense objection, in admitting evidence of the occurrence and manner of the first four killings, and of Wood's connection to them, as "signatures" showing that Wood, by using the distinctive knife and by his zodiacal signing, effectively identified himself as the perpetrator of the fifth killing.

Problem 5-11: Count Dracula

On October 31st (Halloween), at midnight, a man wearing a ski mask and a "Count Dracula-like cape" held up a taxicab driver at gunpoint. No one saw the offender's face, but Richard Harrington has been charged with the crime. The prosecution's case consisted entirely of witnesses who linked Harrington to each of four prior cabbie robberies. Each of these robberies took place one year apart, each happening at midnight on Halloween for each of the four years preceding the current robbery. In the first three robberies, eyewitnesses saw Harrington's face when he removed his mask and fled. Harrington was tried but acquitted of all three offenses. In the next case, eyewitnesses saw a caped, ski mask-wearing man flee into Harrington's apartment building. Subsequent police searches with warrants uncovered a cape but no mask. The offender fled and was thus never arrested. *Should evidence of the previous three, acquitted, mask robberies be admitted? The uncharged case in which the offender fled? Why or why not?*

Problem 5-12: Gambling for Drugs

On March 31 of last year, two local detectives saw Dan Davidson accepting money from passersby, then immediately handing each of them a brown paper bag that he plucked from the wheel well of a pick-up truck. After each transaction, Davidson crossed the street and handed something to Dr. Moriss Dolittle, who stood in front of his store, Dolittle's Video. As it turned out, Dolittle owned the pickup truck. On that date, one of the detectives purchased what appeared to be cocaine and marijuana from Davidson via this procedure. When the detectives later legally searched the pickup truck and Dolittle's Video, they found illegal lottery betting slips in both locations. However, Dolittle was not then charged with illegal bookmaking.

Five months later, officers executed a search warrant at 555 Co-op City Avenue, based on an informant's report of drug dealing at that address. They found crack cocaine, a triple-beam scale, a digital scale, small bags of the kind used to package cocaine, and $12,000 cash in a suitcase, as well as illegal lottery numbers and lists of bets written on them.

At Dolittle's trial for possessing the cocaine found at 555 Co-op City Avenue, the prosecution seeks to offer evidence of (1) the Davidson investigation of last year and the betting slips uncovered during that investigation, (2) Dolittle's conviction five years ago for running an illegal lottery, and (3) the lists of bets found during the Co-op City Avenue search. The prosecution argued that these items are admissible to prove Dolittle's identity as the owner of the Co-op City apartment. *How should the trial judge rule and why?*

Problem 5-13: Drug Courier Profile

Jason Mellwood is on trial for possession of cocaine with intent to distribute it. The prosecution called a police expert on drug courier profiles to testify that Mellwood fit most of the elements of the following drug courier profile:

Flight arrival from or departure to an identified source city, such as Miami.

Arrival carrying little or no baggage, or large quantities of empty suitcases.

Unusual itinerary, such as rapid turnaround time for a lengthy airplane trip.

Use of an alias.

Carrying unusually large amounts of currency (many thousands of dollars), usually on the person, in briefcases, or in bags.

Purchasing airline tickets with a large amount of currency in small denominations.

Unusual nervousness, beyond that ordinarily exhibited by airplane passengers.

The almost exclusive use of public transportation, particularly taxicabs in departing from the airport.

Making a telephone call immediately after deplaning.

Leaving a false or fictitious call-back telephone number with the airline.

Excessively frequent travel to source or destination cities.

Mellwood was observed engaging in the same profile-like behavior on five separate occasions over the course of the three months preceding his arrest. Only on the fifth occasion did officers arrest him as he picked up a bag from the luggage carousel, a bag they later found to have cocaine stored in hidden pockets. The state's proffer includes these officers' testimony.

Mellwood's defense is that he simply picked up the wrong baggage at the luggage pickup area, since the bag containing the cocaine had no tags identifying its owner. Defense counsel objects to the profile testimony as relying on a prohibited propensity evidence. The prosecutor responds that the evidence is offered to prove both *modus operandi* and that Mellwood did not merely possess the cocaine for his own use. Rather, he was a "drug courier," i.e., a person who acted with the intention of aiding in the distribution and sale of cocaine to ultimate buyers. *What ruling and why?*

5. Intent or Knowledge

Rule 404(b)(2) states that evidence of specific acts may be admissible to prove intent or knowledge. In other words, evidence of other similar acts may help to establish that a defendant did not act mistakenly, accidentally, or unknowingly, but rather with intent or knowledge required.

Example

David is charged with murdering Vincent. According to the state, David shot Vincent when the two were alone in the woods. David's defense is that he and Vincent were hunting and that he accidentally shot Vincent when Vincent came between David and a covey of quail. The prosecutor seeks to admit evidence that David killed another hunting buddy, Alan, four years ago. David claimed that in that instance, he accidentally shot Alan while attempting to shoot a pheasant. The prosecutor claims that the evidence is relevant to show intent and lack of accident.

The state has articulated a valid non-propensity relevance theory for the evidence of Alan's death. Note that the inferential chain is not that David killed Alan on purpose and therefore is more likely to have killed Vincent on purpose. Instead, the proper non-propensity theory would be that having accidentally killed Alan a few years ago, David would have been much more careful when hunting to avoid accidentally shooting someone again. Thus, the proof reduces the chances that David shooting Vincent was an accident and makes it more likely that it was intentional conduct.

The reasoning does have some force — after the horror of shooting and killing one friend in an accident, most people would be extremely careful in the future (if they hunted again at all). Still, the risks of the proof are quite high as well. The jury might misuse the proof, reasoning that the first killing was intentional and that this one must have been as well. Depending on the circumstances surrounding the uncharged incident, courts would be within their discretion to admit or exclude the proof via Rule 403.

Huddleston v. United States, 485 U.S. 681, 108 S. Ct. 1496, 99 L. Ed. 2d 771 (1988), further illustrates using other acts to prove intent via knowledge. There, Huddleston allegedly sold 5,000 stolen blank videocassette tapes. He was charged with selling stolen goods in interstate commerce and possessing stolen property in interstate commerce. The only issue at trial was whether Huddleston knew that the tapes were stolen. To prove such knowledge, the government successfully used similar-acts testimony from two witnesses: first, the owner of a record store testified that, about three months before the current incident, Huddleston offered to sell him thousands of new television sets for only $28 each. And, second, an undercover FBI agent testified that Huddleston, posing as a buyer for an appliance store, offered to sell the agent many refrigerators and icemakers. Huddleston himself testified that he got the tapes, televisions, and appliances from a third party, who assured him that the items were legitimate. The trial court instructed the jury that the similar-acts evidence was to be considered only in determining Huddleston's knowledge that the items he sold were stolen, and could not be considered to prove his character. The jury convicted Huddleston on the stolen property charge.

The Sixth Circuit initially reversed, because the state had not proven by "clear and convincing" evidence that the televisions were indeed stolen (one of the two "similar acts"). After a rehearing, however, the court affirmed the convictions, concluding that proof by a preponderance of the evidence was sufficient and that the evidence concerning the televisions was admitted for a proper purpose not outweighed by its potential prejudicial effect.

The Supreme Court accepted *certiorari*. "The threshold inquiry," said the Court, "before admitting similar acts evidence under Rule 404(b) is whether that evidence is probative of a material issue other than character." (485 U.S. at 686.) Rule 404's text itself "contains no intimation that any preliminary showing is necessary before such evidence may be introduced for a proper purpose." Accordingly, "the evidence is subject only to general strictures limiting admissibility such as Rules 402 and 403." (485 U.S. at 687–688.) Indeed, the Advisory Committee Note expressly rejected any "mechanical solution" to the admission of evidence under Rule 404(b). Rather, said the Advisory Committee, a trial court must decide "whether the danger of undue prejudice outweighs the probative value of the evidence in view of the availability of other means of proof and other factors appropriate for making decisions of this kind under Rule 403."

The relevance of the similar-acts evidence turned on whether the acts occurred and whether Huddleston committed them. When the relevance of an item of evidence turns on proof of preliminary facts, the problem is one of "conditional relevance," which is controlled by Rule 104(b). The Court noted that Rule 401 defines relevance as whether evidence has any tendency to make a fact of consequence more or less probable. In light of this low threshold, the Court concluded that the appropriate standard for proving conditional relevance is this: whether a reasonable jury could find the preliminary foundational facts (here, the occurrence of the similar acts and defendant's involvement in them) by a preponderance of the evidence. The trial court need not itself be convinced that these acts occurred. On the introduction of sufficient evidence, the issue is to be resolved by the jury (or court in a bench trial). The similar acts in question — and they were similar — would be probative of a material issue other than character, namely, whether Huddleston had the necessary state of mind. The evidence was important in this case, because the only means available in the case for proving mental state were inferences drawn from conduct.

As to Huddleston's argument that the low standard for conditional relevancy would allow the admission of other-acts evidence that might be unduly prejudicial, the Court explained:

> We share petitioner's concern that unduly prejudicial evidence might be introduced under Rule 404(b). We think, however, that the protection against such unfair prejudice emanates not from a requirement of a preliminary finding by the trial court, but rather from four other sources: first, from the requirement of Rule 404(b) that the evidence be offered for a proper purpose; second, from the relevancy requirement of Rule 402 as enforced through Rule 104(b); third, from the assessment the trial court must make under Rule 403 to determine whether the probative value of the similar acts evidence is substantially outweighed by the potential for unfair prejudice, . . . :

and fourth, from Federal Rule of Evidence 105, which provides that the trial court shall, upon request, instruct the jury that the similar acts evidence is to be considered only for the proper purpose for which it was admitted.

Problem 5-14: Unlucky Wives

Consider the following facts from *United States v. Henthorn*, 864 F.3d 1241 (10th Cir. 2017):

In September 2012, Harold Henthorn's second wife, Toni, died after falling more than 100 feet from a cliff in Rocky Mountain National Park. She fell in a remote location with poor cellular service and no nearby aid stations. Henthorn first called 911 around 6:00 pm, but — due to the remoteness of the location — by the time the first ranger arrived on the scene, it was after 8:00 pm and Toni was dead. After an investigation, Henthorn was charged with and tried for first-degree murder on the government's theory that he, with premeditation and malice aforethought, pushed Toni over the cliff to her death.

. . .

[Henthorn claimed Toni fell off the cliff by accident]. An investigation of the incident raised a number of questions about Henthorn's version of events.

. . .

[T]he investigation [also] revealed Henthorn had taken out several large life insurance policies on Toni's life prior to her death and recently made himself the beneficiary of a life insurance annuity originally naming their seven-year-old daughter as the beneficiary.

During the course of the investigation, prosecutors learned of two prior incidents involving Henthorn and his wives. *First*, they became aware of the mysterious circumstances surrounding the death of Henthorn's first wife, Lynn, in May 1995. Lynn died while she and Henthorn were changing a tire on the side of the road; she was crushed under the car and died from internal injuries consistent with traumatic asphyxiation. Prior to that incident, Henthorn had also taken out a large life insurance policy on Lynn, but no legal action came as a result. *Second*, they discovered an incident in May 2011 when Henthorn threw a heavy beam off a deck he was repairing at the couple's vacation cabin near Grand Lake, Colorado. The beam struck Toni in the back of the neck and upper back, injuring her neck. The prosecution seeks to admit evidence of both incidents.

Over defense objection, how should the court rule?

Problem 5-15: The Mysterious Crib Death

Lolly Faludi's three-month-old baby recently died, in what she claimed was an instance of crib death. Crib death is a sudden and unexpected cessation of breathing or an inability to take in sufficient oxygen. In effect, babies "drown" in a sea of air. This is Faludi's third child to die of apparent crib death, and she has been charged with homicide. *Will the prosecution succeed in admitting evidence of the two prior crib deaths at Faludi's homicide trial? Why or why not? What additional information, if any, will help you decide?*

Problem 5-16: The Malicious Prisoner

Quentin Kress is charged with malicious assault of a fellow prisoner. "Malicious assault" in this jurisdiction is defined as assault done with "malice," which is "a purpose to cause intense physical pain or psychological humiliation." The prosecutor seeks to offer evidence of Kress' subsequent acts of cruelty toward the same victim. *Will the prosecutor succeed in admitting this evidence? Why or why not? What additional information, if any, will help you in making this decision?*

Problem 5-17: The Confused Bookkeeper

Dalton Rumbo admits that he made a serious error in bookkeeping but told his employer that this was an unknowing mistake. An auditor uncovers 10 similar such mistakes by Rumbo during the past year. *Should evidence of these 10 earlier mistakes be admitted at Rumbo's embezzlement trial based on his most recent bookkeeping error? Why or why not?*

Problem 5-18: Brass Knuckles

Bluto Olive claims self-defense at his trial for aggravated assault. Over defense objection, the trial court admits evidence that, shortly before the assault, Olive purchased brass knuckles and put them into his pants pocket. Possession of brass knuckles constitutes the crime of "possessing an instrument of crime." *Did the trial judge rule correctly? Why or why not?*

6. Common Plan, Scheme, or Design

One common non-propensity use of other-acts evidence under Rule 404(b)(2) is:[2]

> To prove the existence of a larger plan, scheme, or conspiracy, of which the crime on trial is a part.... [E]ach crime should be an integral part of an over-arching plan explicitly conceived and executed by the defendant or his confederates. This will be relevant as showing motive, and hence the doing of the criminal act, the identity of the actor, or his intention.

Example

Daria Daniels is on trial for possession of a controlled substance (cocaine) with intent to distribute. She was observed from afar passing a suitcase from one vehicle to another. The vehicle that received the suitcase was stopped a few blocks away, and the suitcase was recovered. It contained several kilos of cocaine. Daniels' defense is that she isn't the person who passed the suitcase and that the agent observing the transaction misidentified her. The

---

2. 1 KENNETH S. BROUN, MCCORMICK ON EVIDENCE § 190, at 754–55 (Kenneth S. Broun ed., 6th ed. 2006).

prosecutor seeks to admit proof that Daniels is part of a gang that specializes in drug distribution. The proof is relevant to establish that Daniels was motivated by her membership in the gang to engage in the transaction and thus it was more likely Daniels who passed the suitcase.

Note that acts committed pursuant to a common scheme can also become admissible if the charging instrument includes them in the charged offenses, e.g., by charging a conspiracy. In many jurisdictions, each co-conspirator is liable for all acts done by other co-conspirators during the course of, and in furtherance of, the conspiracy. Even in jurisdictions where there is no joint liability for co-conspirators, a similar rule generally governs accomplice liability. Moreover, especially in a conspiracy case, the defendant may be tried on all charges stemming from the criminal agreement in a single trial. Thus, numerous criminal acts may be provable at the same trial to prove the elements of the crimes charged, even though the acts might otherwise be admissible under Rule 404(b)(2) to show a "common plan, scheme, or design."

Problem 5-19: Bank Robbery Spree

Darryl Dees is accused of robbing a local bank (First National), along with another person. The robbers wore masks, slid a note to the teller demanding money "or else," and one of them put a pistol in her face. They escaped out a side door with more than $2,000 in cash. Twenty minutes later, Darryl was stopped for a traffic violation in a car about one-half mile from the bank. He was alone and the police did not recover money from the vehicle.

At trial, Darryl denies that he robbed the bank. The prosecutor seeks to admit two other bank robberies allegedly involving Darryl. Both took place in the same city as the First National robbery. The first occurred seven months ago. In it, Darryl walked into a bank alone (different from the first but in the same town) and allegedly demanded money. About that time, a plainclothes police officer nearby tackled Darryl and arrested him before any money changed hands. Darryl was unarmed. A federal grand jury indicted him, but the case is still pending for trial and Darryl was released on bond. In another incident, about two months ago, a man clearly resembling Darryl (as viewed from a security video) walked into yet another bank and demanded money, though he did not display a weapon. The teller complied and the robber made off with $1,000. Darryl has not been indicted in the incident.

Darryl's attorney objects to admitting the other two incidents at the trial of the First National bank robbery. The prosecution responds that the incidents are part of a "plan" as contemplated by Rule 404(b). *How should the court rule?*

Problem 5-20: Inheriting by Murder

Eight persons are found murdered over the course of one year. All are murdered in very different and bizarre ways: (1) stabbed with a three-sided knife, (2) thrown out a window, (3) run over by a car, (4) poisoned, (5) killed by an exploding car bomb, (6) died because heart medication had been stolen, (7) bludgeoned with a hammer, and (8) shot in the heart. There is circumstantial evidence linking Fenton Armstrong to the first seven killings but not to the eighth. He is charged with the eighth killing and goes to trial. At the trial, the prosecutor seeks to offer evidence of Armstrong's involvement in the first seven killings as a way to prove that he committed the eighth. The prosecutor also has evidence that each of the murder victims was in line to inherit a fortune from Armstrong's uncle, Michael O'Malley. With all eight victims dead, however, Armstrong will inherit the money. The defense objects to all the proffered evidence. *Should the defense objections be sustained or overruled? Why or why not? Would any additional information aid your inquiry? What information?*

Problem 5-21: Government Kickbacks

George Felberg is in charge of hiring construction firms on various government projects. He is charged with hiring overly expensive firms that do shoddy work because they paid him kickbacks. At his trial for taking one such kickback, the prosecutor offers evidence of 10 other kickbacks he received from similarly incompetent but expensive construction companies over the past year. *Should this evidence be admissible?*

§ 5.04 Exceptions to the Rule 404(a)(1) Propensity Ban

A. Admissible Instances of Propensity Evidence

Even though "propensity" evidence is generally prohibited under Rule 404, there are several exceptions to that prohibition. Distinct from Rule 404(b) evidence, Rule 404(a)(2) and (3) offer true exceptions to the character-evidence ban — parties are allowed to offer character evidence to establish a person's conformance with a propensity to act so long as the exception applies.

Exceptions pertaining to defendants and victims in criminal cases (Rules 404(a)(2)) are addressed below, with sexual assault and child molestation cases (Rules 413, 414) and impeachment (Rule 404(a)(3)) addressed later in this chapter.

Another distinction between Rule 404(b) evidence and Rule 404(a)(2) character-evidence-exception proof is that Rule 404(a)(2) proof must be offered in specific forms detailed in Rule 405 (reputation, opinion, or specific instance). This chapter takes up that topic after considering the applicability of the criminal defendant and victim exceptions.

B. Character of the Accused: Rule 404(a)(2)(A)

Rule 404(a)(2)(A) creates, among other things, one particularly important exception to the propensity bar — a criminal defendant may offer proof of his or her own pertinent character trait.

Rule 404. Character Evidence; Crimes or Other Act

    (a) Character Evidence.

        (2) Exceptions for a Defendant or Victim in a Criminal Case. The following exceptions apply in a criminal case:

            (A) a defendant may offer evidence of the defendant's pertinent trait, and if the evidence is admitted, the prosecutor may offer evidence to rebut it.

Example

Chunah Rubenstein is charged with assault. After the prosecution rests (its sole testimony being from the alleged assault victim), the defense calls a rabbi and a priest to the stand, both of whom testify that, in their opinion, Rubenstein is a peaceful man. In rebuttal, the prosecution calls Rubenstein's ex-wife, who opines that Rubenstein is a violent man. All this testimony is propensity evidence; the rabbi and priest suggest that such a peaceful man is unlikely to commit a violent crime, and the ex-wife suggests the opposite. Yet none of the testimony is barred, because all of it fits within the Rule 404(a)(2)(A) exception. "Peacefulness" and "violence" are character traits "pertinent" to an assault charge; thus, evidence of the former may be offered by the accused, and evidence of the latter may be offered in rebuttal by the prosecutor.

The requirement that the character trait be "pertinent" has been explained this way:[3]

Not all aspects of the accused's character are open to scrutiny under this exception. The prevailing view is that only pertinent traits — those involved in the offense charged — are provable. One charged with theft might offer evidence of honesty, while someone accused of murder might show that he is peaceable, but not vice versa.

Other sources, however, have defined "pertinent" as synonymous with "relevant," as it is defined in Rule 401: evidence having *any* tendency to make the existence of any fact that is of consequence to the determination of the action more probable or less probable than it would be without the evidence. Arguably, an honest person is at least marginally less likely than a dishonest one to commit any crime, thus less likely to commit murder (rephrased in a way that will help you as you study character for truthfulness in the later sections on impeachment, "honesty" might be more precisely characterized as "law-abidingness"). Under this very broad view, therefore, the trait of being law abiding is "pertinent" to both a theft case and a murder trial. Even under such a reading of "pertinent," however, an argument for exclusion might be made under Rule 403 that the minimal probative value of law-abiding-character

---

3. 1 KENNETH S. BROUN, MCCORMICK ON EVIDENCE § 191, at 769 (Kenneth S. Broun ed., 6th ed. 2006).

evidence in a murder trial is substantially outweighed by the risk of unfair prejudice. In practice, therefore, the differing approaches might rarely (though perhaps
sometimes) lead to different results. Thus, a person's general character for being law
abiding has some probative force, and many courts would allow criminal defendants to admit at least some proof of the trait. But as the evidence becomes cumulative or time-consuming, courts retain discretion to exclude it as the waste of time
substantially outweighs its probative force.

The justification for the rule is murky. But there are several rationales available:
Most notably, the rule recognizes that the defendant is typically vastly outmatched
by the resources of the prosecution. Thus, the defendant is given the advantage of
character evidence to prove that he or she is not the kind of person to have committed the crime. The feature of the rule that gives only the defendant the option
to inject character into the case may reflect the idea that good character evidence
is less worrisome than bad in a system that presumes innocence. Alternatively, the
rule may simply be an act of mercy toward a defendant who has generally led a good
life. In any event, the rule is a well-established one with deep roots in evidentiary
history.

An accused taking advantage of the rule must be cautious, however. Introducing character evidence on one's own behalf opens the door to prosecution rebuttal.
Thus, if a defense character witness opines that the defendant is kind, the prosecution might call a witness to testify that, to the contrary, the defendant is cruel. The
prosecutor would not have been permitted to offer that evidence if there had been
no defense character witness.

A Civil Versus Criminal Case Caution: It is important to emphasize that the
"mercy rule" exception applies only in a criminal case, not a civil one. Thus, if a
defendant in a civil case seeks to offer evidence of his good character to show that
he had a propensity not to perform certain bad acts, therefore making it less likely
that he did the bad acts alleged in the current suit, that evidence will still be inadmissible. It is excluded by Rule 404(a)(1)'s broad general bar on admitting propensity evidence. The Advisory Committee Note to the 2006 amendments to Rule 404
explained the rationale for excluding such evidence in civil cases but admitting it,
when offered by the accused as to a pertinent trait, in criminal cases:

> The circumstantial use of character evidence is generally discouraged
> because it carries serious risks of prejudice, confusion and delay.... In
> criminal cases, the so-called "mercy rule" permits a criminal defendant to
> introduce evidence of pertinent character traits of the defendant and the
> victim. But that is because the accused, whose liberty is at stake, may need "a
> counterweight against the strong investigative and prosecutorial resources
> of the government." C. Mueller & L. Kirkpatrick, *Evidence: Practice Under
> the Rules*, pp. 264–5 (2d ed. 1999). *See also* H. Richard Uviller, *Evidence of
> Character to Prove Conduct: Illusion, Illogic, and Injustice in the Courtroom*,
> 130 U. Pa. L. Rev. 845, 855 (1982) (the rule prohibiting circumstantial use
> of character evidence "was relaxed to allow the criminal defendant with so

much at stake and so little available in the way of conventional proof to have special dispensation to tell the fact-finder just what sort of person he really is"). Those concerns do not apply to parties in civil cases.

C. Forms of Proof When Character Evidence Is Offered via Rule 404(a)(2)

Even though Rule 404(a)(2) allows character evidence if offered by the criminal defendant, among other circumstances discussed below, another rule — Rule 405(a) — restricts the form of character testimony.

Character evidence typically comes in these three forms:

1. *Reputation:* what people in a relevant community say about a particular person's character.

2. *Opinion:* what an individual who knows another person well thinks of that other person's character (as opposed to what the individual has heard other people say about that character).

3. *Specific acts:* specific instances of a person's behavior that reveal something about his or her character.

In general, whenever character evidence is admissible to prove propensity via a Rule 404(a)(2) exception, character may be proven by reputation or opinion but not by specific acts, as the first sentence of Rule 405(a) explains:

Rule 405. Methods of Proving Character

(a) **By Reputation or Opinion.** When evidence of a person's character or character trait is admissible, it may be proved by testimony about the person's reputation or by testimony in the form of an opinion. On cross-examination of the character witness, the court may allow an inquiry into relevant specific instances of the person's conduct.

Although specific acts are arguably more probative of character than either reputation or opinion evidence, the latter forms of character evidence are less time-consuming and less likely to lead to confusing collateral issues. For these reasons, therefore, the Federal Rules of Evidence generally prefer these latter two forms of proof.

The form of proof allowed when offered through Rule 404(a)(2)'s propensity exceptions varies based on whether it is elicited on direct or cross-examination.

Direct Examination — Opinion and Reputation

The party entitled to introduce character proof via a Rule 404(a)(2) exception is limited to opinion ("What is your opinion of the defendant's character for peacefulness?") or reputation ("In your community, what is the defendant's reputation for peacefulness?").

Rule 405(a) limits character witnesses' testimony to these forms because, e.g., evidence law developed (both at common law and in the rule-drafting process) to constrain character proof. Rule 405's form limitations are aimed at preventing the trial of a specific criminal offense from devolving into sideshow mini-trials of other alleged misconduct. The most a witness can testify to is her character opinion or knowledge of the defendant's reputation and not the specific occurrences that may underlie that testimony. This limitation constrains the amount of time that character proof takes to present, and it also blunts the force of even permitted propensity proof—the jury gets a general impression, not a laundry list of specific incidents.

Example 1

In a criminal perjury trial, the defense calls a witness to testify to specific instances in which most people would lie (for example, because an honest answer would have cost defendant his job) but the defendant nevertheless told the truth. This evidence is offered by the accused to prove the "pertinent" trait of truthfulness to show that he was unlikely to lie on the stand, that is, to commit perjury. Under Rule 404(a)(2)(A), he may offer some form of character evidence. But under Rule 405(a), he is prohibited from proving character by the specific instances of conduct he proffers.

Example 2

Same case as Example 1, but instead of proffering specific instances of truthful conduct, the defendant offers a witness to testify to the defendant's reputation in his community as a truthful person. Objection overruled. If this witness is properly qualified, this form of character evidence (reputation) is specifically sanctioned by Rule 405(a).

Example 3

Same case as Example 1, but the witness testifies that he has been the defendant's best friend for 25 years and, in his opinion, the defendant is a truthful person. Objection overruled. Opinion evidence on direct examination is specifically allowed by Rule 405(a)

Cross-examination of character witnesses, however, is a different exercise.

Cross-Examination—Specific Instances

When cross-examining a "character witness," the cross-examiner may inquire into specific instances that would be relevant to the jury's assessment of the character testimony ("Were you aware that the defendant was in four bar fights in the past two years?").

The theory of admissibility of this proof is that the character witness, after having offered her opinion or knowledge of another person's reputation, ought to be subject to adversarial testing. Thus, if a character witness has testified that he has known the defendant for 20 years and that the defendant is a peaceful person, it is fair game for the prosecution to test the basis of that opinion.

The method that Rule 405 prescribes is by cross of relevant specific instances of the person's conduct. Building on the examples above, if the character witness has offered "opinion" testimony that the defendant is "peaceful," the prosecutor might ask on cross whether the witness knew that the defendant was convicted of aggravated assault. The valid purpose of this proof is not to establish that the defendant did commit the previous assault, rather it is to establish that the witness' opinion may be ill-founded (a fine and controversial inferential line).

Example 4

Benjamin Rodegard is charged with murder. The defense calls Benjamin's next-door neighbor, Rabbi Joseph Gold, to testify that Benjamin has a reputation in his community as a peaceful person. On cross-examination, the prosecution may ask the rabbi whether he had heard that Rodegard earlier that year had stabbed two other neighbors in a bar brawl that he started. If the rabbi says "no," that suggests he really does not know much about critical relevant aspects of Rodegard's reputation. If he says "yes," the rabbi's judgment is suspect: How can someone with a reputation as a stabbing bar brawler be described as a person known to be "peaceful"?

Good Faith Basis for the Question and Rule 403

The cross-examiner must have a good faith basis to ask a specific-instance question. This is because specific-instance questions are often very damaging, whatever the witness' answer. If for example, you ask a character witness, "Are you aware that the defendant shot a man?" and the witness answers "No," the question and answer have not technically undermined the witness' opinion testimony. But in reality, the jury has heard the question and is left to surmise — did the defendant really shoot a man? Did the witness just not know about it? Thus, a minimal safeguard built into the specific instance rule is that counsel must have a good faith basis to believe that the defendant did indeed shoot a man and that the character witness could have heard about it.

And recall that the point of specific-instance proof is not to establish whether the instance happened or not, rather it is admissible to test the character witness' opinion. Often specific instances run the significant risk of being misused by a jury, e.g., as evidence that the incidents occurred, establishing general dangerousness or to punish the person for an unpunished specific bad act.

As a result, Rule 403 is an additional safeguard against admitting specific instances that would inject substantial unfairness into the process. But beware — a Rule 403 objection following an unfair, damaging question (e.g., "Are you aware that Dana Daniels physically abused her children five years ago?") will hardly unring the bell the jury heard in the question. Even if the objection is sustained, the jury is left to speculate about whether the conduct occurred. Thus, a pretrial motion in limine for specific instances is a must, particularly when a defendant plans to put character witnesses on via Rule 404(a)(2).

Extrinsic Proof Disallowed

Even when Rule 405(a) permits proof of relevant specific instances on cross, courts do not allow extrinsic proof. The common way trial lawyers convey this rule is that the cross-examiner must "take the answer" of the character witness on cross. Even if the witness denies the specific instance, the extrinsic-proof bar prevents the cross-examiner from introducing evidence — through exhibit or testimony from another witness — to contradict the denial. Nor can the cross-examining attorney impeach the witness with evidence contrary to the witness' denial of a specific instance.

Example 5

Same facts as previous example, but this time the rabbi did not testify to Rodegard's reputation as peaceful but rather to the rabbi's personal opinion that Rodegard is a peaceful person. Inquiry into specific acts is still permissible on cross-examination of the character witness (the rabbi). In cross-examining an opinion witness, the question would probably be phrased, "Didn't you know that Rodegard stabbed two neighbors in a bar brawl?" rather than "Hadn't you heard that Rodegard stabbed two neighbors in a bar brawl?" This is because opinion turns on the witness' personal knowledge of the person's behavior rather than on what the witness heard others say about the person's behavior. However, while traditional character evidence rules were often meticulous about the "Have you heard" versus "Do you know" distinction, the drafters of the Federal Rules of Evidence viewed the words as formulaic mantras. The Rules permit cross-examining character witnesses about specific instances of conduct regardless of the precise form of the words used.

The cross-examiner must, as mentioned above, have a good-faith basis to believe that the specific acts happened. Those acts must also be relevant and must survive weighing under Rule 403. Furthermore, and related to these points, the acts must be of a type likely to be known by the witness or the community. Arguably private acts, such as Rodegard's secret violence against his children, would not fit the bill. Also, as mentioned above, the cross-examiner must take the witness' answer. In other words, if during cross-examination the witness denies knowledge of the specific acts, the questioner may not offer extrinsic evidence (evidence from another witness, document, or other evidence rather than from the cross-examined witness's own mouth while on the stand) that those acts in fact took place. Even if the witness concedes knowledge of the acts, however, the jury should be instructed *not to use the answers as proof that the acts happened*. Instead, the answers may be used only to test the witness' standard for forming an opinion about, or for evaluating the reputation of, the person about whose character the witness testifies.

Problem 5-22: The Criminal Assailant

Charlton Hestown is on trial for assault. In this jurisdiction, the elements of criminal assault are attempting to cause or purposely, knowingly, or recklessly causing bodily injury to another person.

1. Hestown calls his priest to the stand, who testifies that Hestown has a reputation as a "good, kind man." Admissible? Why or why not?

2. Assume instead that the priest testifies that Hestown's reputation is that of a "law-abiding man." Does this change the result?

3. What if, instead, the priest opines that Hestown is a "peaceful person"? What result, and why?

4. What if the priest also says that Hestown is an "honest man"?

5. What if the priest testifies that he knew "Hestown broke up a fight between neighbors" and did not become violent "when someone spit in his face during an altercation at a church softball game"?

6. The prosecution now calls Hestown's former best friend to testify that Hestown in fact has a reputation as a violent thug. Assume that the priest testified that Hestown is a "peaceful person."

7. The prosecution now calls Hestown's former best friend to testify that Hestown in fact has a reputation as a drug dealer.

8. Do your answers to any of the questions change if Hestown is sued civilly, instead of prosecuted criminally? Why?

Problem 5-23: Bar Fight

Denise Donaldson is on trial for assaulting Vaughn Vincent during a bar fight. Denise claims she was not at the fight and was instead at work. During its case-in-chief, the state calls a character witness to testify that Denise had a reputation as a violent thug. The defense objects. *How should the court rule?*

Problem 5-24: Treason

Don Davidson, a U.S. citizen, is charged with treason following an allegation that he assisted a foreign power in tampering with an election in the United States. A defense witness testifies that Davidson is a "great guy." *Is the witness' testimony admissible under the so-called "mercy rule" Rule 404? Would your answer change if the suit was a civil one for damages for revealing state secrets rather than a criminal one for treason?*

Problem 5-25: The Warden Cross-Examined

John Quinn, a prison inmate, is charged with assaulting another inmate. The prison warden, Warden Jamison, was permitted to testify on the defendant's behalf that, in his opinion, Quinn is a peaceful person, and Quinn has a reputation in the prison community as a peaceful person. *Should the prosecution be permitted, despite defense objections, to ask the following questions on cross-examination?*

1. Wasn't Quinn written up twice for starting fights in the mess hall?

2. Didn't Quinn severely beat his cellmate when first admitted to the prison five years ago?

3. Doesn't Quinn have a reputation as a vicious man whom other inmates feared?

4. Doesn't Quinn have a reputation for involvement in failed prison escapes, though there was never enough evidence to prosecute him?

Problem 5-26: Group Therapy

The psychiatrist who has been treating a prison inmate, Johnny Berro, who is now charged with assault, is called to the stand by the defense to testify that Berro is peaceful. *Can the prosecution properly ask the psychiatrist on cross, "Didn't Mr. Berro assault another patient in a group therapy session under your care?"*

D. Foundation for Character Proof

Once we have determined that a particular form of character evidence is admissible, we must be able to lay the required foundation for the evidence at issue. These foundational requirements are dictated more by general rules of logical and pragmatic relevancy (respectively, Rules 401 and 403) than by any specific language in the character evidence rules.

Reputation

A reputation witness must be shown to be familiar with the subject's reputation in the relevant community. The courts split on what "communities" are "relevant." Some common-law cases limit the term to the neighborhood in which the subject lives. Other cases also include the subject's workplace, and still others include any group of persons likely to be familiar with the pertinent character trait involved. The broadest view seems to make the most sense, because in the modern world a person may have closer acquaintances among workmates or church members than neighbors. The Federal Rules seem to take a broad view, by creating a hearsay exception for reputation of a person's character "among associates" or "in the community" (Rule 803(21)).

Opinion

With opinion evidence, the question is whether the witness personally knew, from his or her own observations and not merely from the views of others, data sufficient to allow the witness to make a judgment about the subject's character. Testimony about how the character witness knows the subject, how long the relationship has existed, and how recent the character witness' contact with the subject has been is all pertinent to whether the witness has a sufficient basis for a character opinion.

E. Character of the Victim in Cases Other than Homicide and Sexual Misconduct: Rule 404(a)(2)(B)

Rule 404(a)(2)(B) and (C) create additional exceptions to the propensity bar. Rule 404(a)(2)(B) provides:

> subject to the limitations imposed in Rule 412, a defendant may offer evidence of an alleged victim's pertinent trait, and if the evidence is admitted, the prosecutor may:
>
> (i) offer evidence to rebut it; and
>
> (ii) offer evidence of the defendant's same trait.

The word "pertinent" here apparently has the same meaning as under Rule 404(a)(2)(A) (*see* [B], above). And just like evidence offered under Rule 404(a)(2)(A) (defendant's character), evidence offered under Rule 404(a)(2)(B) must comply with the form requirements of Rule 405(a).

Example

Patricia Fun is charged with assaulting Renee Schlager. Fun, in the defense's case-in-chief, calls Marci Wilt, a neighbor of Schlager's, to the stand to testify that Schlager has a reputation in the community as a violent person. Fun claims self-defense, arguing that Schlager was the first aggressor. The prosecution's objection will be overruled, as this testimony fits within the exception to the propensity rule created by Rule 404(a)(2)(B). The victim's violent nature is "pertinent" to the defendant's claim of self-defense. However, the prosecution would then be entitled to call a character witness to the stand who will testify, in rebuttal, that Schlager's true reputation in the community is as a very gentle and kind individual.

Note the difference between this example and the Chunah Rubenstein example in [B], above. Chunah, the defendant, was permitted under the mercy rule to offer evidence of his own good character under Rule 404(a)(1)(A). But, in this current example, Fun offers evidence not of her own character concerning violence but rather of her alleged victim's character for violence under Rule 404(a)(2)(B). Likewise, the prosecution's rebuttal evidence concerns the victim's character, not the defendant's.

Rule 404(a)(2)(B)(ii) would also permit the prosecutor, if she so chose, to offer evidence of the defendant's character on the same trait on which the defendant attacked the victim's character (here: character for violence), as we will see in more detail below.

Problem 5-27: Urban War Syndrome

Harry Howdeen claims self-defense at his assault trial. The defense makes the following offer of proof: Leonard Jesperson, a psychiatrist who has examined the victim, Margie O'Laris, will testify in the defense case-in-chief that O'Laris suffered from Urban War Syndrome. This behavioral syndrome results in unpredictably violent behavior among its sufferers, those who have lived in the inner-city and have been surrounded by violence. *Should the prosecution objection be sustained? What sort of foundation, if any, would improve the chances of admitting Jesperson's testimony? If the objection is overruled, will the prosecution succeed in rebuttal in admitting evidence that Margie O'Laris had been cured?*

Problem 5-28: Frauds and Fraudsters

During the defense case-in-chief, defendant Daniel Jones calls to the stand at his fraud and embezzlement trial Wanda Webster, a neighbor of the alleged victim, Vareen Alpaz. Jones, an accountant, is on trial for embezzling funds out of a local small business. Jones's defense is that Alpaz (the business owner) actually drained the business of money himself because he was seeking to shield assets from the IRS. Webster begins to recount her opinion that Alpaz is a "dishonest crook," but the prosecution objects. *Should the trial court sustain or overrule the objection? Why? If the objection is overruled, will the prosecution succeed in admitting evidence that:*

1. Alpaz has a reputation among other business owners as being a "boy scout"?

2. Alpaz has a reputation in the community as being "peaceful"?

Problem 5-29: False Pretenses

Marty Cunningham's defense at his trial for the crime of false pretenses is that his alleged victim, Hollis Holloway, is well-known as a skeptical, distrustful man. The trial judge sustains the prosecution's objection and instructs the jury to disregard the witness' testimony to this effect. False pretenses requires proof of (1) a false representation of a material present or past fact, (2) which causes the victim (3) to pass title to his property (4) to the wrongdoer, (5) who (a) knows his representation to be false and (b) intends thereby to defraud the victim. *Do you agree with the trial judge's ruling? Why or why not?*

Problem 5-30: The Violent Victim

A defendant is charged with attempted homicide on a victim named Margie O'Laris. The defendant claims self-defense, arguing that O'Laris was the first aggressor. To support this claim, the defense offered evidence that the victim was a violent person. *Can the prosecution offer evidence that the victim, Margie O'Laris:*

1. Had a reputation among students in her nighttime GED program as a peaceful woman?

2. Was, in the opinion of her co-workers at McDonald's, a peaceful woman?

3. Despite being punched three times in the face by a neighbor, had never defended herself or retaliated with violence?

F. Prosecutor Attack on the Criminal Defendant's Same Character Trait Permitted Once the Defense Has Attacked the Victim on That Trait

Remember that under Rule 404(a)(2)(B), the defendant in a criminal case can offer evidence of a pertinent trait of character of the alleged victim. Rule 404(a)(2)(B)(i), however, permits the prosecutor to respond by defending the victim's character on that same trait. But Rule 404(a)(2)(B)(ii) also permits the prosecutor then to attack the defendant's character on that same trait. Restated, once the defense attacks a pertinent trait of the victim's character in a criminal case, the prosecutor can not only defend the victim's character on that trait but can also attack the defendant's character on that same trait. A defendant choosing to attack a victim's character thus opens the door to an attack on the defendant's own character by the prosecution that would otherwise be barred. That can be a risky gamble.

Example

In an earlier example, Patricia Fun, a criminal defendant in an assault case, offered evidence of the violent character of her alleged victim to show that the victim was the first aggressor. Under the original law, the prosecution could under Rule 404(a)(2) respond only with evidence of the victim's peaceful nature. Old Rule 404(a)(1) barred any attack on the *accused's* character because she did not first offer evidence of her own good character. Under the current, amended law, however, the result is different. Now when the defense offers evidence about the victim's violent character, the prosecution becomes free also to present evidence of *defendant Fun's* violent nature to prove that she, not the victim, was indeed the first aggressor.

The Advisory Committee Note, relied upon by the Judicial Conference, explained that, without this provision, unfairness and distortion would result when the defendant offers evidence, for example, of the victim's violent character:

If the government has evidence that the defendant has a violent character, but is not allowed to offer this evidence as part of its rebuttal, the jury has only part of the information it needs for an informed assessment of the probabilities as to who was the initial aggressor. This may be the case even if evidence of the accused's prior violent acts is admitted under Rule 404(b), because such evidence can be admitted only for limited purposes and not to show action in conformity with the accused's character on a specific occasion. Thus, the amendment is designed to permit a more balanced presentation of character evidence when an accused chooses to attack the character of the alleged victim.

Problem 5-31: More Fraudster

Imagine that the facts are the same as above in 5-28, Frauds and Fraudsters. During its rebuttal case, the prosecution attempts to elicit proof that Jones has a well-known reputation in the community for being a fraudster. The defense objects. *How should the court rule?*

Problem 5-32: More Urban War Syndrome

Return to the facts of Problem 5-27. Still assume that the prosecutor's objection to testimony that the assault victim suffered from Urban War Syndrome was overruled. In rebuttal, the prosecutor offers evidence that defendant Harry Howdeen has a reputation as an extremely violent man. *Would this testimony be admissible under the old Rule 404(a)(2)? Under the amended Rule 404(a)(1)? Why? Would your answers change if this were a civil rather than a criminal case?*

Caution:

We will see later in this chapter that special rules govern the use of evidence of the victim's character in a proceeding involving alleged sexual misconduct. *See* Rule 412. Indeed, that is why the Rule 404(a)(2) exception declares that it is "subject to the limitations imposed by Rule 412." Similarly, as the immediately following section of this chapter will explain, special rules govern evidence of a homicide victim's character. *See* Rule 404(a)(2)(C).

Civil Versus Criminal Case Caution: Again, as with Rule 404(a)(2)(A), this Rule 404(a)(2)(B) exception applies only in criminal cases. In civil cases, no Rule 404(a)(2)(B) exception will apply, and the same evidence admissible in a criminal case will now be inadmissible in a civil one.

G. Character of the Victim in Homicide Cases: Rule 404(a)(2)(C)

Rule 404(a)(2)(C) creates another exception to the character-propensity ban. This exception is limited, however, to criminal homicide cases and authorizes the admission of propensity evidence in such cases only under the following circumstances:

> (C) In a homicide case, the prosecutor may offer evidence of the alleged victim's trait of peacefulness to rebut evidence that the victim was the first aggressor.

Civil Versus Criminal Versus Criminal Homicide Caution: This exception, it must be remembered, applies only in criminal cases, and, even then, only in one kind of criminal case: homicide. The exception does not, therefore, even apply to attempted homicide. Rather, it applies only to the completed, successful crime of homicide, meaning that the victim must die. The exception does not apply to civil cases, thus rendering inadmissible evidence of the alleged victim's peaceful character to rebut evidence that the victim was the first aggressor in a civil assault or civil wrongful death suit.

Exception Available to Rebut Even Non-Character Evidence of Victim Aggression: Rule 404(a)(2)(C) allows prosecution proof of the peaceable character of the victim *even if* the defendant has offered *no* character evidence about the victim, so long as the defendant first introduces evidence that the victim was the first aggressor *in a homicide case.*

For instance, the defense might offer eyewitness proof that the alleged victim first raised a gun at the defendant during a killing. This proof is not character evidence, yet it still triggers Rule 404(a)(2)(C) and allows the prosecutor to rebut it with character proof that establishes the victim was peaceful and therefore unlikely to be aggressive at the event in question.

One feature, and rationale, underlying this exception, is that the homicide has deprived the prosecution of the alleged victim's version of events (he or she is dead). Thus, the rule at least makes the decedent's peaceful character available as circumstantial proof that he or she would not have acted aggressively to rebut defense proof to the contrary.

Example

After a heavy night of drinking, Diana Davey stabbed Victoria Vaughn in the chest with a butcher knife. Victoria died as a result of the wound. At her criminal murder trial, Diana's defense is that Victoria came at her first with another knife, also recovered from the scene and thus Diana acted in self-defense. Diana calls an eyewitness from the night of the killing to testify to her version of events, and the witness does indeed testify that Victoria came at Diana first. In its rebuttal case, and over defense objection, the prosecution calls two of Victoria's sisters who testify that in their opinion, Victoria was peaceful and "wouldn't hurt a fly." The court should overrule the objection because Rule 404(a)(2)(C) allows the prosecutor to establish the victim's pertinent character trait to rebut defense claims that the victim was the first aggressor.

Problem 5-33: Street Fight

Darryl is on trial for murder for killing Victor in a street fight. During the defense opening, Darryl's lawyers admit that Darryl killed Victor but claim Darryl acted in self-defense. Darryl himself takes the stand during the defense case-in-chief and testifies as follows:

Defense Counsel: What happened when you first saw Victor in the street?

Prosecutor: Objection Your Honor. This is getting into Victor's character. [How should the court rule? Why?]

Judge: Overruled.

Darryl: He ran straight at me with a pipe over his head, swinging it at me, and screaming that he was going to kill me.

Defense Counsel: And, at that time, what did you know about Victor's previous conduct?

Prosecutor: Objection. Now we are getting into Victor's character your honor. [How should the court rule? Why?]

Judge: Overruled.

Darryl: He'd shot two men dead at a gas station two years before.

Defense Counsel: Why was that information important to you?

Darryl: It made me terrified that he was serious and was going to kill me with the pipe.

Based on this testimony, what is the defense theory of admissibility for the gas-station shooting?

Problem 5-34: Street Fight II

In the same case as Problem 5-33, the prosecutor cross-examines Darryl as follows:

Prosecutor: Are you the same Darryl who beat a man unconscious at a local bar the month before you killed Victor?

Defense Counsel: Objection. Improper character evidence.

How should the court rule? Why?

Further, assume the prosecutor calls Victor's longtime best friend who testifies that, in the best friend's opinion, Victor was harmless and peaceful. The defense objects to improper character evidence. *How should the court rule? Why?*

H. Specific Instances Admissible Where Character Is an Essential Element

In cases in which a person's character is directly in issue as an essential element of a charge, claim, or defense, the parties may introduce specific instances of conduct as proof of character. Thus, specific acts are admissible when character evidence is offered as direct evidence of an element of a charge, crime, claim, or defense, instead of as circumstantial proof of propensity. This rule is set forth in Rule 405(b):

Rule 405.

(b) **By Specific Instances of Conduct.** When a person's character or character trait is an essential element of a charge, claim, or defense, the character or trait may also be proved by relevant specific instances of the person's conduct.

Rule 405(b) is not a true exception to Rule 404(a)(1)'s propensity ban. That is because proof admitted via Rule 405(b) does not rely on propensity reasoning for its relevance and is thus not prohibited by Rule 404(a)(1) in the first place. Instead, Rule 405(b) addresses situations where character itself is an "essential element" of a criminal charge or civil claim.

Note the use of the word "also" in Rule 405(b). Rule 405(a), which permits reputation and opinion as forms of character testimony, applies not only to propensity evidence but to all cases ("when[ever]") in which evidence of a person's character or character trait is admissible. Thus, reputation and opinion evidence are appropriate forms of proof when character evidence is being used directly, to prove elements, not merely for circumstantial propensity uses. But Rule 405(b) makes clear that, when direct proof of elements is involved, proof may "also" be in the form of specific acts, a form of proof that is prohibited with propensity evidence.

It is important not to over spot Rule 405(b) issues — the rule applies rarely and only when character is an actual element of a claim being tried; it does not apply when character is used to establish some other element circumstantially.

Take, for example, a self-defense murder case. The defendant relies on a defense that he reasonably feared for his own life and as a result killed the alleged victim. In such a case, specific evidence of the alleged victim's previous violent episodes (unknown to the defendant at the time of the incident being tried) are relevant. They tend to establish that the victim was aggressive in the past, therefore had an aggressive character, and thus was more likely the aggressor in the incident in question. And the defendant is entitled to introduce victim-character evidence per Rule 404(a)(2)(B). But such specific-instance evidence surely violates Rule 405(a)'s requirement that Rule 404(a)(2) evidence be in the form of opinion or reputation.

The alleged victim's character as violent is not an element of the defense. Thus, it is not admissible per Rule 405(b). Rather, his or her character is an intermediate link in the chain ultimately proving an element — the defendant's reasonable fear of the victim.

There are few instances in criminal or civil law where the character of a person is an actual element. A few examples:

- The defendant's predisposition to commit a particular crime to rebut the defendant's entrapment defense.[4] When a criminal defendant claims that the government "entrapped" her into committing a crime, the government may offer evidence of specific past criminality to establish that defendant's character as a criminal trumped any government encouragement.

- Specific bad acts committed by a defamation plaintiff to establish the truth of allegedly defamatory statements. Imagine that Mayor Susan Smith sues the KANSAS CITY TELEGRAM for calling her a "crook" in an editorial. At trial, the TELEGRAM may put on specific-instance evidence to prove Mayor Smith was indeed a crook (she embezzled money from a company, assaulted a subordinate, etc.), subject of course to Rule 403.[5]

- A few other examples:

---

4. *See* MICHAEL H. GRAHAM, 3 HANDBOOK OF FED. EVID. § 405:2 (8th ed. 2017).
5. *Cf. id.*

- Truthfulness in a perjury prosecution.

- Good character as a parent in assessing the best interest of a child in a custody proceeding.

- Character as a careless driver in a negligent entrustment case.[6]

As a reminder — Rule 405(b) is not the only rule that allows proof of character by specific instances. Rule 404(b) allows specific-instance "other acts" proof when it does not depend on propensity reasoning, Rule 404(a) allows specific instances on cross of a character witness, and (as we will soon discuss) Rule 608 allows specific instances in certain impeachment scenarios and the sexual character rules allow proof of specific instances in certain circumstances.

Problem 5-35: United States v. Lorean

The defendant, Lorean, is charged with possession with intent to distribute cocaine after a government "sting" operation. Lorean admits to possessing the cocaine, but claims that he was entrapped by an undercover police officer. The jurisdiction uses a subjective test of entrapment, which asks (1) whether the police induced or created the crime and (2) whether the defendant was predisposed to committing the crime charged.

Which, if any, of the following evidence offered by Lorean is admissible?

1. Testimony by Lorean's father stating that his son would never violate any criminal laws whatsoever. To the father's knowledge, his son had violated the law only once, when he stole a ball at the local five-and-dime store. Admissible?

2. Lorean's brother testifies that, in his opinion, Lorean is an extremely honest person. Admissible?

3. Can the prosecution offer evidence that Lorean was arrested for the possession of marijuana 15 years prior to trial?

§ 5.05 Sexual Offenses and Sexual Misconduct: Criminal and Civil

A. The Rape Shield Law: Rule 412

1. The General Rule: Rule 412(a)

We have now finished reviewing the major exceptions to the prohibition against propensity evidence. Here we consider an exception to one of those exceptions, that is, a reinstitution of the bar on propensity evidence for one class of persons: victims of rape and similar offenses. The federal "rape shield" statute accomplishes this

---

6. *Cf. id.*

reinstitution, and we address it here because you should now be ready to understand its complexities and assess its policy wisdom.

The exception embodied in Rule 404(a)(2) that permits propensity attacks on pertinent traits of a victim's character, discussed in [B], above, is politically charged. Whether a trait is "pertinent" very much depends on the lawmakers' worldview. For many years, under common-law analogues to Rule 404(a)(2)(B), and for several years under Rule 404(a)(2)(B) itself, evidence of a rape victim's promiscuous character was considered "pertinent" to whether she consented to sexual intercourse. Moreover, judges were rarely willing to exclude such evidence as unfairly prejudicial under a 403-like analysis. Testimony that a victim had a reputation as a "slut," that "everyone knew she slept around," and of the specific nitty-gritty alleged incidents of the victim's sex life became standard fare at criminal and civil trials.

The federal rape shield law, Rule 412, seeks to reduce dramatically, without completely eliminating, the use of such victim character evidence at criminal and civil trials involving allegations of sexual misconduct. Rule 412, in its original form, became law several years after the Federal Rules of Evidence were adopted. The current version of Rule 412, substantially amended from the original version, was adopted in 1994 and amended for stylistic reasons in 2011.

Subsection (a) states a general ban on victim character evidence:

Rule 412. Sex-Offense Cases: The Victim's Sexual Behavior or Predisposition.

(a) **Prohibited Uses.** The following evidence is not admissible in a civil or criminal proceeding involving alleged sexual misconduct:

(1) evidence offered to prove that a victim engaged in other sexual behavior; or

(2) evidence offered to prove a victim's sexual predisposition.

Rule 412, subsection (a), thus carves out a general exception to the exception from the propensity ban established by Rule 404(a)(2)(B). Rephrased, Rule 412, subsection (a), reinstates the propensity bar for one category of crime victims (as well as reaffirming the bar in similar civil cases): victims of alleged sexual misconduct, such as rape.

The Advisory Committee did not justify this general prohibition on victim propensity evidence on grounds of its irrelevance. Rather, the Committee viewed the new rule as creating incentives to identify accurately and prosecute such misconduct while protecting victim privacy:

> The rule aims to safeguard the alleged victim against the invasion of privacy, potential embarrassment and sexual stereotyping that is associated with public disclosure of intimate sexual details and the infusion of sexual innuendo into the fact-finding process. By affording victims protection in most instances, the rule also encourages victims of sexual misconduct to institute and to participate in legal proceedings against alleged offenders.

While the Committee did not consider victim character irrelevant in a Rule 401 sense, the Note makes clear that Rule 403-like concerns about unfair prejudice also underlay the new rule. The rule also reaches beyond substantive propensity uses to bar impeachment uses, except in certain designated circumstances discussed under the topic of Rule 412(a) exceptions below.

Example 1

An alleged rape victim has finished her direct testimony at trial. The defense concedes sexual intercourse but argues consent. The defense offers evidence of the victim's sexual trysts with numerous third parties on other occasions. The defense argues that this evidence is offered to impeach, because promiscuous women are usually liars. This sort of inference, and thus the proffered evidence, is barred by Rule 412(a).

Rule 412 does not bar evidence that the victim made numerous allegedly false prior claims of others' sexual misconduct, however. Such evidence can be viewed as character-based impeachment evidence; Rules 404(a)(3) and 608 govern instead.

Rule 412's broad general prohibition against any evidence of "sexual predisposition" extends beyond reputation or opinion evidence of a victim's promiscuous nature and specific instances of sexual conduct. The word "behavior" is here meant to include "activities of the mind, such as fantasies or dreams," as well as any activity that implies sexual contact, such as using contraceptives or having a venereal disease. Furthermore, concludes the Advisory Committee, the prohibition is "designed to exclude evidence that does not directly refer to sexual activities or thoughts but that the proponent believes may have a sexual connotation for the fact finder." Illustrations might include evidence relating to the victim's mode of dress, speech, or lifestyle.

Example 2

The defendant in a rape case offers evidence that the victim wore a short, tight dress, with a deep "V" neck, to prove that she consented to sexual intercourse with the defendant. This evidence will ordinarily be barred by Rule 412(a).

Rule 412(a) thus excludes a broad range of victim sexual behavior (and even thought) evidence. And the Rule's express language seems to prohibit *any* use of such evidence, whether offered to prove propensity or something else, and whether offered to prove a substantive element of a crime, claim, or defense or to impeach.

Civil Versus Criminal Cases: The rule extends to all criminal and civil cases because the social policies involved may matter in any case where sexual misconduct is alleged, not just rape prosecutions. For example, the rule would apply in a kidnapping charge where evidence of the defendant's sexually assaulting the victim is offered to prove motive or as background for the kidnapping. As we will soon see, however, different exceptions apply to the rule in criminal versus civil cases. Do not worry about these exceptions yet in doing the problems immediately below.

Problem 5-36: At the Movies: Pre-Shield

In the film *Town Without Pity*, four U.S. soldiers stationed in Germany are charged with raping a young German woman. Their defense is that she consented to sexual intercourse. To prove that the sexual conduct was consensual, defense attorney Maj. Garrett aggressively cross-examines the young woman and elicits evidence that she often exercised naked in front of her window, with the blinds pulled up. Moreover, she often allowed her boyfriend to see her naked. *Imagine that you are practicing in a jurisdiction without a Rape Shield law. Would this evidence be admissible in light of the remaining character evidence rules? Would this evidence be admissible under Rule 412?*

Problem 5-37: On the Tube: Liar

In the made-for-TV film *Defense of Edward Brannigan*, successful lawyer Brannigan is charged with raping his law clerk. Brannigan's defense is that his clerk consented to engage in sexual intercourse. To attack the law clerk's credibility on the witness stand, the defense seeks to offer evidence that some years earlier, the clerk had had a child out of wedlock and falsified the father's identity on the hospital birth record. The prosecutor objects that the evidence is inadmissible under the Rape Shield law, because it would reveal the law clerk's prior sexual behavior. *Should the judge sustain the prosecutor's objection?*

Problem 5-38: At the Movies: At the Bar

In the film *The Accused*, the defendant is charged with raping Sarah Tobias. The defendant claims that Sarah consented to sexual intercourse. The defendant seeks to testify that he met Sarah for the first time on the night of the rape, in a bar. Sarah was inebriated, and dressed in a low-cut mini-dress. Prior to their having sex, Sarah had danced provocatively with the defendant, with other men in the bar, and alone in the middle of the dance floor. They left the bar together and had sex in his truck; he then dropped her off at home. *What part, if any, of this testimony would be admissible under Rule 412?*

Problem 5-39: At the Movies: Quick Re-Marriage

In the film *Anatomy of a Murder*, Lt. Manion is charged with murdering Barney Quill. Manion admits that he killed Quill, but claims that he did so as a result of "irresistible impulse," a form of temporary insanity resulting from finding out that Quill had raped and beaten Manion's wife, Laura. The prosecution's theory is that Quill and Laura were lovers, and that Manion killed Quill after learning of the affair. Cross-examining Laura, the prosecutor elicits testimony that she had married Manion only three days after divorcing her first husband. *Does the evidence of the quick re-marriage constitute evidence of "other sexual behavior" within the meaning of Rule 412? If so, does Rule 412 render the evidence inadmissible?*

Problem 5-40: Rhonda's Outrage

In a criminal rape case, the victim, Rhonda Sun, angrily responds as follows to cross-examination by the defense suggesting that she consented to sexual intercourse: "Sir, I am devoutly religious and unmarried. My religion prohibits premarital sexual intercourse. I have not had, and until I am married will not have, consensual premarital sex with any man, much less that beast." In response, the defense seeks to offer evidence that Rhonda had consensual sexual intercourse with at least three men during her lifetime. The prosecution objects, citing Rule 412(a). *Ruling? Cf. State v. Williams*, 477 N.E. 2d 221 (Ohio Ct. App. 1984), *aff'd*, 487 N.E. 2d 560 (Ohio 1986).

Problem 5-41: Stained Reputations

Now the defense in Problem 5-40 offers evidence that Rhonda filed false rape charges against three other men in other cities — all of whom were acquitted — under very similar circumstances to the charges made here. The prosecutor objects. *What ruling? What additional information, if any, would help to guide your decision? Does it matter that Rhonda stands ready to testify that the other charges were true and that the prosecutor has evidence that both the assaults and the acquittals were motivated by prejudice against practitioners of Rhonda's religion?*

Problem 5-42: Romantic Dreams

In a civil sexual harassment case filed by Betty Nomad against her employer, Kirk McCoy, McCoy plans to argue that Betty both invited and welcomed his caresses of her breasts and buttocks. To support this claim, he calls to the stand one of Betty's co-workers, who begins to recount a conversation that she had with Betty in which Betty said that on many nights she had had dreams of intimate sexual contact with Mr. McCoy. Betty's counsel objects. *Ruling?*

To further support his argument, McCoy offers evidence, over Betty's counsel's objection, that Betty routinely wore low-cut dresses to the office covered by a shawl. But she removed the shawl whenever Mr. McCoy entered the room and did so near the time of the alleged harassing conduct. *Did the trial judge rule correctly?*

2. Exceptions in Criminal Cases: Rule 412(b)(1)

Rule 412(b)(1) creates exceptions, however, to this reinstated propensity bar as to victims of alleged sexual misconduct in criminal cases:

(b) **Exceptions.**

    (1) *Criminal Cases.* The court may admit the following evidence in a criminal case:

        (A) evidence of specific instances of a victim's sexual behavior, if offered to prove that someone other than the defendant was the source of semen, injury, or other physical evidence;

(B) evidence of specific instances of a victim's sexual behavior with respect to the person accused of the sexual misconduct, if offered by the defendant to prove consent or if offered by the prosecutor; and

(C) evidence whose exclusion would violate the defendant's constitutional rights.

The effect of these exceptions is to retain a flat bar on reputation or opinion evidence of a victim's sexual behavior in criminal cases but to permit evidence of specific instances of a victim's sexual conduct in two very narrowly defined circumstances and in the rare situation in which the Constitution demands admissibility. In theory, of course, there may be circumstances under which the constitution would also mandate admissibility of reputation or opinion evidence. This text focuses largely on the Federal Rules of Evidence, so we will focus only tangentially on the constitutional issues in the examples below.

Example 1

Hope Elkhoond alleges that she was raped by Monty Mountebank. Monty, however, claims that Hope's mother found evidence that Hope was having sexual intercourse with her father. To divert evidence from her dad, Hope claimed that she had been raped by Monty, against whom she already had a variety of grudges anyway. Hope's mom rushed her to the hospital, where tests were run and semen found. Because of a laboratory problem, no DNA profile was extracted from the sample before it was destroyed. At his rape trial, Monty seeks to introduce evidence of specific instances, near the time of the hospital visit, when Hope had sexual intercourse with her father to prove that the abusive father, not Monty, was the source of the semen. This testimony will likely be admissible under Rule 412(b)(1)(A).

Example 2

Same case as Example 1, but this time Monty concedes that the semen was his but argues that Hope consented. To prove his point, he offers evidence that he and Hope had consensual sexual intercourse on five prior occasions during the month before the alleged rape. The prosecutor's Rule 412 objections would be appropriately overruled by the trial judge because the proof establishes the victim's previous sexual behavior with respect to the accused, per Rule 412(b)(1)(B).

The Rule 412(b)(1)(B) exception, as the Advisory Committee has noted, extends beyond prior instances of sexual activities between the alleged victim and the accused to include "statements in which the alleged victim expressed an intent to engage in sexual intercourse with the accused, or voiced sexual fantasies involving the specific accused."

Although Rule 403 is not expressly mentioned in Rule 412, it may be relied on as a ground for excluding evidence that would otherwise be admissible under Rule 412(b)(1).

Problem 5-43: Satanic Rites

Rape defendant Harry Harlan, in support of his consent defense, offers evidence that the victim, Cheryl Browner, had engaged in group consensual sexual activity with Harlan and a series of other men on three prior occasions, one five years ago, one a year ago, and one the month before this incident. All three incidents were part of Satanic prayer rites, Ms. Browner being a Satanist. *Should the prosecution's objection be sustained? Cf. People v. Keith, 118 Cal. App. 3d 973, 173 Cal. Rptr. 704 (1981);* Eyes Wide Shut *(Stanley Kubrick 1999).*

Would your ruling change if Harlan tried to prove that the rape occurred during such a group Satanic rite, and that Ms. Browner made clear that she no longer wanted to participate? What if Harlan says that he backed off, but others in the group would not do so, despite his efforts to stop them? In the hubbub, he argues, Browner mistook him for one of the rapists.

Problem 5-44: Fantasies

In the same prosecution as in Problem 5-43, Harlan offers evidence that Ms. Browner often told co-workers that she frequently fantasized about Harlan making love to her. *Should this evidence be admissible? How, if at all, does this problem differ from the fantasies of Betty Nomad in Problem 5-42? Ignore hearsay issues for now.*

Harlan also offers evidence that Ms. Browner has a reputation of being "loose" with other members of her coven, of which Harlan was one. *Is this evidence admissible under Rule 412? Would your view change if the coven's Master Warlock offered his opinion that Ms. Browner was promiscuous with her coven "brethren"?*

Problem 5-45: Kobe Bryant

NBA superstar Kobe Bryant is accused of raping a woman in a hotel room. Kobe admits sexual intercourse but claims consent. A rape kit taken at a hospital after the alleged assault returns with DNA from semen that is not Kobe's. The rape exam showed vaginal injuries consistent with sex by force. Kobe's defense team seeks to admit evidence that the alleged victim had sex with other men and suffered the vaginal injury in the days before the incident. The defense also seeks to introduce the DNA evidence from the rape kit, establishing that at some point prior to the rape exam, the victim had intercourse with another man. *If the prosecutor objects to this evidence, how should the court rule?*

Problem 5-46: Homage to "To Kill a Mockingbird"

Tom Robinson, an African American, is on trial for raping Mayella Ewell, a white woman; his defense is consent. They both reside in a small Southern town that maintains many of the cultural vestiges of the Old South, including the social unacceptability of sexual relationships between blacks and whites. Robinson offers evidence that on previous occasions Mayella had been intimate with three other African Americans. *Admissible?*

3. Exception in Civil Cases: Rule 412(b)(2)

In civil cases, Rule 412(b)(2) creates a very different set of exceptions than Rule 412(b)(1) recognizes in criminal cases:

> **(2) Civil Cases.** In a civil case, the court may admit evidence offered to prove a victim's sexual behavior or sexual predisposition if its probative value substantially outweighs the danger of harm to any victim and of unfair prejudice to any party. The court may admit evidence of a victim's reputation only if the victim has placed it in controversy.

Subdivision (b)(2), governing only civil cases, employs a balancing test rather than listing specific exceptions like those recognized in criminal cases under subdivision (b)(1). According to the Rule 412 Advisory Committee Note, the rule adopted this approach "in recognition of the difficulty of foreseeing future developments in the law." "Greater flexibility is needed to accommodate resolving causes of action such as claims for sexual harassment." Moreover,

> [T]his test for admitting evidence offered to prove sexual behavior or sexual propensity in civil cases differs in three respects from the general rule governing admissibility set forth in Rule 403. First, it reverses the usual procedure spelled out in Rule 403 by shifting the burden to the proponent to demonstrate admissibility rather than making the opponent justify exclusion of the evidence. Second, the standard expressed in subdivision (b)(2) is more stringent than the original rule; it raises the threshold for admission by requiring that the probative value of the evidence substantially outweigh the specified dangers. Finally, the Rule 412 test puts "harm to the victim" on the scale in addition to prejudice to the parties.

Evidence of an alleged victim's reputation may be received in a civil case, but only if the alleged victim has "put his or her reputation into controversy."

Example 1

Renee Wilt has brought a Title VII sexual harassment suit against her employer, the local fire department, for creating a "hostile environment" by permitting the posting of pornography throughout the fire station. The fire department seeks to offer evidence of Renee's reputation as a longtime consumer of pornography to show that there was nothing personally intimidating to her in the fire station environment. Her objection under Rule 412(b)(2) will likely be sustained, as it is hard to argue that her allegations of improper conduct by the department put her reputation at issue.

Example 2

Same case as Example 1, but instead of offering reputation evidence, the fire department offers evidence of specific recent instances in which Renee both collected pornography for her own use and jokingly posted it in the fire station. A trial judge would likely be well within her discretion to overrule any objection, by finding that the probative value of the specific-instance evidence substantially outweighs the danger of harm to Renee, the alleged victim, and of any unfair prejudice to any party.

Example 3

Same case as Example 1, but Renee testifies at trial that the men in the fire station put a photo of Renee's face on the head of a nude woman in each of the pornographic photos and spread rumors throughout the department and the neighborhood that Renee was a "well-known slut." She seeks damages for the harm to her reputation. Now the department offers evidence that Renee had a reputation as a slut long before her co-workers spread any rumors to that effect. This evidence arguably would be admissible, because Renee placed her reputation "in controversy," and the probative value of the evidence may under the circumstances be deemed high relative to unfair prejudice.

Problem 5-47: Sexual Harassment

Lilah Falew has filed a civil sexual harassment suit against her employer, a well-known insurance company, Mandebell Insurance. Falew was a very successful insurance agent. She claims that her fellow agents, all male, subjected her to repeated sexually tinged verbal abuse. For example, one agent might smile when Falew wore a short skirt to work, saying, "Now I know why you get so many clients." In another example, an agent told Lilah, "Oh, baby, you can insure me any time!" Falew also alleged that male agents openly commented on the attractiveness of various parts of her body. All the comments were severe and pervasive in creating a hostile working environment, and they continued despite her objections. Falew testified about each of these incidents at the civil trial. *Answer the following questions.*

1. May Mandebell's lawyer call rebuttal witnesses to say that, "Lilah had quite a reputation for sleeping with her clients. You know, she slept her way to the top"? What if they instead testified that she generally had a "promiscuous reputation"? Would your answer to either question change if Lilah blurted out on direct examination, "I was so upset by these comments. I'm single, and a very religious woman, and I pride myself on my reputation — I don't sleep around. They were killing my reputation"?

2. May Mandebell's lawyer call Lilah's former best friend, a female co-worker in the claims department, to say, "In my opinion, Lilah loved these comments. She loved the attention, and she loved men. She wore those short skirts because she wanted to elicit their comments. And if she liked one of the guys, she might just take his comment as a clue to, shall we say, try to get more intimate"?

3. Now Mandebell's lawyer calls witnesses to testify to specific and repeated instances in which Lilah herself made sexual comments, smilingly, about the anatomy of various male agents. Furthermore, they recite instances in which the men indeed made sexually suggestive comments, and Lilah responded

with her own, often cruder suggestions. Moreover, these comments continued over a course of years. Lilah did not file this lawsuit until shortly after her boss told her that her sales were slipping and that she would have to shape up or ship out. Should any or all of this testimony be admissible?

4. Finally, Mandebell calls a secretary who said that she overheard Lilah telling a friend during a phone conversation, "I just love when the men make dirty comments. It turns me on." Admissible or not? Why or why not?

4. Procedure to Determine Admissibility: Rule 412(c)

Under any of the Rule 412 exceptions, the following procedures must be followed:

(c) Procedure to Determine Admissibility.

(1) Motion. If a party intends to offer evidence under Rule 412(b), the party must:

(A) file a motion that specifically describes the evidence and states the purpose for which it is to be offered;

(B) do so at least 14 days before trial unless the court, for good cause, sets a different time;

(C) serve the motion on all parties; and

(D) notify the victim or, when appropriate, the victim's guardian or representative.

(2) Hearing. Before admitting evidence under this rule, the court must conduct an *in camera* hearing and give the victim and parties a right to attend and be heard. Unless the court orders otherwise, the motion, related materials, and the record of the hearing must be and remain sealed.

Example

In the Renee Wilt sexual harassment case (*see* [3], above), the department files in court, and serves on Renee, 13 days before trial, a motion stating its intention "to offer various evidence of plaintiff's sexual obsessions to disprove her claims of perceived intimidation and her damages." The motion should be summarily denied, both because it is untimely without stating good cause for the delay and it is so vague that it fails "specifically" to describe the evidence and state the purpose for which it is offered.

Problem 5-48: Mandebell's Notice

In Problem 5-47, assume that Mandebell did not file written notice of its intention to use any of the evidence until five days before trial. Mandebell maintains that no witnesses were willing to come forward before that time, despite Mandebell's best efforts. The notice finally filed included only the following substance (along with a caption, signature block, and other procedural formalities): "Mandebell will call witnesses to establish that the plaintiff invited and enjoyed the sorts of comments about which she now complains and now says merit awarding her damages. These witnesses will testify to specific acts by the plaintiff, as well as to her reputation, showing how she sought out, participated in, and often initiated what she now says were lewd comments." *Should the trial judge excuse the late filing of this notice, and is the notice adequate?*

B. Character of the Defendant in a Criminal or Civil Sexual Assault or Child Molestation Case: Rules 413, 414, and 415

Rule 404 generally bars use of propensity evidence subject to the few exceptions noted in that rule. However, Rules 413, 414, and 415 create additional exceptions for criminal or civil cases involving, or predicated on, offenses of sexual assault or child molestation. Rules 413, 414, and 415 are identical in all but one respect. Rule 413 governs criminal sexual assault cases only, Rule 414 governs criminal child molestation cases only, and Rule 415 governs civil sexual assault or child molestation cases. Jointly read, therefore, these three rules apply roughly the same standards to criminal and civil sexual assault or child molestation cases.

Rule 413(a) is thus representative of all three rules and states the core standard:

Rule 413. Similar Crimes in Sexual Assault Cases

(a) **Permitted Uses.** In a criminal case in which a defendant is accused of a sexual assault, the court may admit evidence that the defendant committed any other sexual assault. The evidence may be considered on any matter to which it is relevant.

Notice that Rule 413 limits the prior offense evidence to offenses of the same type as the one charged. Thus, in a current case charging rape, which is an offense of sexual assault, the rule permits evidence of other rapes or other sorts of sexual assaults, but not of child molestation. That being said, certain child molestation conduct (i.e., nonconsensual sex with a minor) could be within the scope of the broad definition of sexual assault (discussed below) in Rule 413(d). Rule 414 requires that current child molestation cases permit use of prior offenses of child molestation but not of adult rape because adult rape does not involve a "child" within the terms of Rule 414(d). While Rule 415 is less clear, it is probably best read similarly as permitting in civil cases based on sexual assault, for example, the use of character evidence only of a prior sexual assault.

Rule 413(d) defines "sexual assault" broadly, including: "contact, without consent, between any part of the defendant's body — or an object — and another person's genitals or anus," "contact, without consent, between the defendant's genitals or anus and any part of another person's body," "deriving sexual pleasure or gratification from inflicting death, bodily injury, or physical pain on another person," and any attempt or conspiracy to engage in any of this conduct. This definition obviously includes rape, some indecent assaults, and other common sexual offenses. Importantly, there is case law holding that the Rule's reference to an offense of "sexual assault" requires only proof that the specified conduct happened but not that it resulted in an arrest, charge, or conviction.

Rule 414 defines "offense of child molestation" in a fashion similar to Rule 413's definition of "offense of sexual assault," but with a child, whose consent is irrelevant.

Because the exceptions in Rules 413–415 permit use of prior offenses for any relevant purpose, they create another set of exceptions to the rule against propensity evidence. The exceptions are apparently justified by the difficulty of proof in sexual assault cases, especially consent defense cases, where there rarely is a third-party witness or corroborating physical evidence of force. Other justifications can also be articulated, rooted in jurors' biased preconceptions about sexuality that may cloud their ability fairly to consider a rape victim's tale. *See* ANDREW E. TASLITZ, RAPE AND THE CULTURE OF THE COURTROOM (1999); *see also* Steven I. Friedland, *Date Rape and the Culture of Acceptance*, 43 Fla. L. Rev. 487 (1991). Nevertheless, the exceptions are controversial ones, arguably representing a sea change in our thinking about character evidence. To the critics of Rules 413–415, the same character dangers apply in sexual assault cases as in robbery cases. Accordingly, they see no justification for carving out a special exception for one class of cases but not the other.

One other troubling aspect of original Rule 413 was whether it was limited by Rule 403. Original Rule 413 flatly said that evidence of other sexual assault offenses "is admissible," rather than "may be" admissible, making no reference to Rule 403 whatsoever (original Rules 414 and 415 contained similar language). Yet Rule 403 presumptively applies to all evidence questions, unless another rule expressly states otherwise (as, for example, portions of Rule 609 do). Moreover, the original rule said that the evidence "may" be considered for its bearing on any relevant matter, not that it "must" be considered, in apparent contradiction to the rule's earlier "is admissible" language and opening the door to a Rule 403 analysis. The Floor Statement of the principal House Sponsor, Representative Susan Molinari, also says:

> In other respects, the general standards of the rules of evidence will continue to apply, including the restrictions on hearsay evidence and the Court's authority under Evidence Rule 403 to exclude evidence whose probative value is substantially outweighed by its prejudicial effect.

Molinari's view had generally been adopted by the courts, resulting in substantially different outcomes compared to a contrary interpretation that ignores Rule 403.

The 2011 restyling of the Federal Rules of Evidence eliminated any ambiguity on this point, replacing the "is" admissible language with "may" be admissible language, a phrasing much more consistent with Rule 403, balancing still being available as a ground for exclusion of evidence otherwise admissible under Rule 413.

Some factors that courts might consider when admitting proof admitted via Rules 413–415 include, e.g., similarity to the charged offense, wrongfulness of the prior act and likely emotional impact on the jury, proximity in time, degree of certainty that the prior offense occurred, and possibility of minimizing unfair prejudice in admitting the proof.[7]

Example 1

Wealthy socialite Wilhelm Cannady Smythe is charged with raping Cathy Bator while on a date. Smythe concedes that he engaged in sexual intercourse with Bator but maintains that it was consensual, though this theory has so far become clear only on cross-examination of the state's witnesses, as its case-in-chief is still proceeding. Near the end of that case, the state calls three women to the stand to testify that each of them were raped by Smythe while on dates with him during the past year under circumstances similar to those described by Bator. None of them originally reported the crimes because of their fear of mistreatment by the judicial system. Their testimony will likely be admissible under Rule 413 for "any matter to which it is relevant." Thus, it may, based on a propensity inference, tend to show that Smythe acted "forcibly" (an element of the rape statute in this jurisdiction), as well as that Bator did not consent and that Smythe knew. Admissibility is, as mentioned above, subject to Rule 403.

Example 2

Same facts as in example 1, but Smythe denies ever engaging in sexual intercourse with Bator. The evidence of Smythe's prior sexual assaults is now offered to prove that he committed the current act of intercourse. The evidence will still likely be admissible under Rule 413, subject to Rule 403.

Example 3

Assume instead that the three women who testify against Smythe all recount events that occurred 20 years earlier, while he was a teenager. At that time, he had squeezed their buttocks and fondled their hips through their clothing without their permission but stopped immediately when each slapped him and said, "No!" These are circumstances very different from those testified to by Bator. Rule 403 applies, and a trial judge might exclude this evidence as stale and of low probative value in proving rape, given the less serious and distinct nature of the earlier offenses and the very different circumstances under which they took place.

Rule 413(b) also imposes a notice requirement when the prosecution expects to use Rule 413(a) evidence at trial. The attorney for the government "must" disclose the evidence to the defendant at least 15 days before the scheduled trial or at such later time as the court may for good cause allow. That disclosure must include statements of witnesses or a summary of the substance of any testimony that is expected to be offered. Rules 414(b) and 415(b) contain similar notice requirements.

---

7. Christopher B. Mueller & Laird C. Kirkpatrick, 2 Federal Evidence § 4:84 (4th ed. 2017).

Problem 5-49: Pinched Buttocks

At Thornell Hamhurst's trial on charges of rape, the prosecution calls several female witnesses to testify that Hamhurst pinched each of their buttocks, while making lascivious comments about their bodies, at a variety of fraternity parties during the past two years. The defense objects. *Ruling? Would your ruling change if Hamhurst had instead sought to grab each of these women's breasts? To grab each of the women between their legs?*

Problem 5-50: S & M

Refer to the previous problem, but assume instead that Thornell Hamhurst is charged with indecent assault, which is defined in this jurisdiction as a non-consensual touching of the defendant's genitals to any part of another person's body but not involving sexual intercourse. Hamhurst's defense is mistaken identity: someone near Hamhurst on a crowded subway had apparently pressed his crotch against a female passenger, and the passenger mistook Hamhurst for the culprit. The prosecutor offers evidence in its case-in-chief that Hamhurst was convicted of aggravated assault for whipping a prostitute severely as part of a sadomasochistic ritual. No notice of the prosecutor's intention to offer this evidence had been given because, said the prosecutor, he had never imagined that Hamhurst would have the gall to raise a mistaken identity defense when there were so many eyewitnesses in the brightly lit train. The defense objects. *Ruling? Would your ruling change if the prosecutor instead offers evidence that the earlier aggravated assault took place when Hamburst had been tried for, but acquitted of, that offense? Why or why not?*

§ 5.06 Impeachment: Rules 404(a)(3), 607, 608, and 609

A. Distinction between Impeachment and Substantive Evidence

Rule 404(a)(3) excepts from the propensity bar, "[e]vidence of a witness's character," which "may be admitted under Rules 607, 608, and 609." Thus, the special standards recited in Rules 607, 608, and 609 apply when character evidence is used to impeach a witness with character evidence.

What does it mean to "impeach" a witness? Put simply, impeachment is discrediting a witness, on the theory that they are lying, mistaken, or both.[8] This places impeachment in a special category of evidence because it is relevant to the propositions in the case indirectly: to show that witness testimony establishing material fact X should not be believed and therefore fact X is less likely to be true. Compare this

---

8. *Impeachment*, Black's Law Dictionary (10th ed. 2014) (defining impeachment as "[t]he act of discrediting a witness . . . [t]he act of challenging the accuracy or authenticity of evidence.").

type of impeachment proof with what we might refer to as "substantive" evidence. Substantive evidence speaks directly or circumstantially to the issues in the case: e.g., an eyewitness account of the robbery at issue.

Rephrased, substantive evidence is relevant to establish facts in issue while impeachment evidence affects the weight to be given substantive evidence, weight that may, for example, be diminished if the witness is lying, confused, or mistaken. If the party with the relevant burden fails to offer a witness to testify to evidence supporting the existence of an element of a crime, claim, or defense, that party has not met its burden. Accordingly, judgment will be entered in his opponent's favor. On the other hand, if evidence *is* offered by the party with the relevant burden as to every element on which he has that burden, then the case will generally get to the jury. But whether the jury in fact finds for a party will turn in part on whose witnesses they believe.

Either party may offer impeachment evidence to suggest that another party's witness is just wrong—either lying or mistaken. Indeed, impeachment evidence is offered to persuade the jury to find in favor of a party on the theory that a witness cannot be believed. There are many forms of impeachment evidence, character being but one form, but it is that form that is the focus of most of this chapter. An understanding of the difference between character-based and non-character impeachment is critical and discussed in more detail below in Section [B].

Example

The defendant in a homicide case calls witness X to the stand. X testifies that defendant could not have been at the scene of the crime because defendant was with witness X at another location. This is substantive evidence that, if believed, helps to disprove identity by providing an alibi.

The prosecutor might then respond with evidence that witness X has been convicted twice for perjury. This evidence is impeachment offered to suggest that because X has lied under oath in the past, X has a liar's character and thus X is more likely to be lying now on the stand. If the jurors in fact conclude that X is now lying, they will discount X's testimony. They will thus rely more heavily on other evidence in deciding whether the state has met its burden of persuading the jury beyond a reasonable doubt that the defendant committed the crime.

Impeachment can generally be accomplished either by cross-examining the witness in an effort to get him to admit to the impeaching facts or by offering other witnesses and exhibits to impeach on rebuttal. (This ability to offer extrinsic evidence of impeachment, however, has limitations as we will see under Rule 608.)

B. Character-Based Impeachment versus Non-Character Impeachment

It is important to keep in mind, however, that much of what we call "impeachment" does not implicate the character-propensity ban at all and is thus not subject to the character evidence rules. The key distinction between character-based and non-character impeachment lies in the chain of inferences between the impeachment proof and the ultimate impeachment proposition (i.e. that the witness is not telling the truth).

Here are the typical character-based impeachment inferences:

1. The witness has a character for untruthfulness (as indicated by reputation, opinion, or specific instances of untruthful conduct).

2. The witness is acting in accordance with the propensity for untruthfulness.

3. Thus, the witness is less likely to be telling the truth on the witness stand today.

Inference No. 2 is forbidden. This type of character-based impeachment implicates the character-evidence rules. Indeed, where the relevance of impeachment evidence depends upon propensity, the evidence would run afoul of Rule 404(a)(1)'s character-propensity bar but for Rule 404(a)(3), which allows witness-character evidence via Rules 607, 608, and 609.

But not all impeachment depends on the character-propensity chain of inferences. Non-character impeachment evidence includes proof indicating that the witness is *lying* in this specific case for some reason, not that the witness is lying because he or she is a *liar*. Likewise, non-character impeachment may establish that the witness is mistaken in his or her testimony, because of perception or memory. Non-character impeachment ordinarily does not implicate the character-evidence rules.

Non-character impeachment generally falls into one of four categories:[9]

1. Bias

Evidence of a witness' bias is relevant to show that the witness is motivated to lie in this specific case (not that the witness is a liar in general and therefore lying).[10]

Example 1

In a civil negligence case stemming from an intersection collision, the brother of the plaintiff testifies that the plaintiff "definitely had a green light, and the defendant ran her light and was speeding." On cross-examination, the defendant's lawyer interrogates the witness as follows:

Q: "Your brother wants to win this lawsuit?"

A: "Yes."

Q: "And you want the best for your brother?"

---

9. Mark S. Brodin et al., 4–608 Weinstein's Federal Evidence § 608.02 (2018).

10. *See* Fed. R. Evid. 601, advisory committee's note (noting that "[i]nterest in the outcome of litigation . . . [is] highly relevant to credibility and require[s] no special treatment" without reference to character); *see also* Christopher B. Mueller & Laird C. Kirkpatrick, 1 Federal Evidence § 4:26 (4th ed. 2017); *see also, e.g.*, United States v. Abel, 469 U.S. 45 (1984).

A: "Yes, I do."

Q: "Testifying that your brother had a green light helps him win?"

A: "I guess it does."

Q: "And by testifying today, you want to do what you can to help your brother?"

A: "Yes, but I'm telling the truth!"

Q: "The truth is that you love your brother, correct?"

A: "Of course I do, but I'm telling the truth!"

This line of inquiry is appropriate to establish the witness' bias — that he loves his brother and is therefore motivated to lie or shade the truth to help him win. Note that the lawyer is not establishing that the witness is a liar and is therefore lying. Rather, the testimony establishes that the witness has a specific reason to lie in this one case and therefore should not be believed. Because the relevance of the evidence does not depend on the character and propensity of the witness, the character evidence rules do not bar its admission and the evidence is relevant, subject to 403.

2. Prior Inconsistent Statement

A witness' prior inconsistent statement is admissible to show the witness said different things at different times about the same matter. The reasoning goes that someone who changes their story over time is less likely to be telling the truth than someone with a consistent story. Thus, impeachment by prior inconsistent statement is non-character impeachment because the relevance of the evidence does not depend on an inference that the person is a liar and therefore is lying. Instead, the prior inconsistent statement is used to demonstrate that the witness is lying or mistaken on a particular matter in this one case. The character-evidence rules simply do not apply.

Authorities have recognized that impeachment by multiple prior inconsistent statements may become so pervasive that it rises to a character attack. Likewise, the inconsistent statement could be misused to imply that the witness is a liar in general. Both of these situations might give rise to character evidence objections. The circumstances will indicate whether the impeachment has crossed the line into a character attack.[11]

In addition, Federal Rule of Evidence 613 governs the method and form of proof of impeachment by prior inconsistent statement. That rule is beyond the purview of this chapter and will be discussed in more depth in Chapter 7, dealing with witnesses.

---

11. FED. R. EVID. 608, advisory committee's note to subdivision (a) ("Whether evidence in the form of contradiction is an attack upon the character of the witness must depend upon the circumstances.").

Example 2

A prosecution witness in a criminal assault trial testifies that the defendant, Dana Davis, was the first aggressor. On cross-examination, the defense confronts the witness with grand jury testimony in which the witness stated, "I really can't blame Dana — it is hard not to react when you are punched in the mouth." The defense attorney asks the witness, "Did I read your sworn grand jury testimony correctly?" and the witness answers, "Yes."

This evidence would be admissible, subject to Rule 403, without reference to the character evidence rules. The defense is simply pointing out that the witness said different things at different times about the same topic, not that the witness is a liar in general.

Note that the contradiction is not crystal clear. When did Dana get punched in the mouth? At the beginning of the altercation or later? Who punched her? There are plausible readings of the grand jury testimony in isolation that are still consistent with the prosecution's theory that Dana was the first aggressor. Most courts hold that the contradiction need not be perfect or even compelling. Instead, a statement is "inconsistent if under any rational theory it might lead to any relevant conclusion different from any other relevant conclusion resulting from anything the witness said."[12]

3. Impeachment by Contradictory Evidence

Evidence in a trial generally comes from more sources than a single witness. And often the evidence on a single point may be in conflict. A witness account of an event or fact may be challenged by this contradictory evidence in an attempt to persuade the jury to give the witness account less weight. A witness may testify that a criminal defendant was six feet tall. That witness can be confronted with evidence showing that the defendant is actually five feet, four inches tall. This is non-character impeachment, in most circumstances.[13]

4. Impeachment by Attack on Memory or Perception

Another form of non-character impeachment involves attacking the witness' memory or perceptive capacities. For example, a witness may claim to have had a great view of an event. The opposing party might attack the testimony by pointing out that the witness has bad eyesight and was not wearing glasses or contacts that day. Likewise, the attorney may point out that the scene was dark or that the view

---

12. Mark S. Brodin et al., 4–613 Weinstein's Federal Evidence § 613.04 (2018).

13. Like prior-inconsistent-statement impeachment, impeachment by contradictory evidence can be so pervasive, or employed in such a manner, as to raise inferences about the witness' character for truth-telling generally. In such circumstances, Rules 404, 608, and 609 are implicated. *See* Fed. R. Evid. 608, advisory committee's note.

was actually obstructed. Any of these routes do not involve a character-propensity inference. Instead of saying that the witness has a liar's character and is therefore lying, the impeaching party asserting that the witness could not have seen (or perhaps did not see so clearly), as a matter of physical reality, what the witness claims to have seen. In this way, the impeaching party seeks to persuade the jury to give the evidence less weight. Likewise, an attorney may point out through questioning that the passage of time or other circumstances have undermined the witness' memory of the event.

5. The Importance of the Character-Based versus Non-Character Impeachment Distinction

Very often, what lawyers think of as impeachment does not implicate the character evidence rules. Being able to recognize non-character impeachment is critical because a character-based objection (based on Rule 404, 608, or 609) should be overruled.

On the other hand, the character evidence rules do impose substantial limitations on character-based witness impeachment. That topic is what the balance of this chapter is about. We will see that the form of proof of character-based impeachment is limited, in much the same way admissible character-propensity proof about the criminal defendant or victim is limited by Rule 405. Likewise, extrinsic proof of specific instances tending to establish a character for untruthfulness is generally not admissible (though special rules apply for impeachment by criminal conviction).

Knowing when an impeachment is character-based, and thus knowing when these limitations apply, is critical in responding to impeachment objections at trial. When impeachment is character-based, Rule 608 is often an early stop in the analysis.

C. Rule 608 — Witness Character for Truthfulness or Untruthfulness

Rule 608 creates different rules based on the form and timing of the character impeachment evidence — one rule, in paragraph (a), for proof of character by opinion and reputation; another rule, in paragraph (b), for proof of character by specific acts:

Rule 608. A Witness's Character for Truthfulness or Untruthfulness

(a) **Reputation or Opinion Evidence.** A witness's credibility may be attacked or supported by testimony about the witness's reputation for having a character for truthfulness or untruthfulness, or by testimony in the form of an opinion about that character. But evidence of truthful character is admissible only after the witness's character for truthfulness has been attacked.

(b) **Specific Instances of Conduct.** Except for a criminal conviction under Rule 609, extrinsic evidence is not admissible to prove specific instances of a witness's conduct in order to attack or support the witness's character for truthfulness.

But the court may, on cross-examination, allow them to be inquired into if they are probative of the character for truthfulness or untruthfulness of:

(1) the witness; or

(2) another witness whose character the witness being cross-examined has testified about.

By testifying on another matter, a witness does not waive any privilege against self-incrimination for testimony that relates only to the witness's character for truthfulness.

1. Opinion and Reputation: Rule 608(a)

Rule 608(a) declares that the "a witness's credibility may be attacked or supported by testimony about the witness's reputation . . . or by testimony in the form of an opinion . . ." However, under Rule 608(a), a credibility attack must involve evidence that refers *only* to "character for . . . untruthfulness." Other types of character traits may not, therefore, be used as the basis for impeachment.

Example

Jolly Jamison is an alibi witness for his friend, Bart Timpson, at Timpson's robbery trial. During rebuttal, the prosecutor seeks to call two witnesses to the stand to impeach Jamison: first, Jamison's next-door neighbor, who will testify that Jamison has a reputation in his neighborhood as an untruthful man; second, Jamison's ex-wife, who will testify to her opinion that Jamison is a thief and a violently abusive man. The next-door neighbor's testimony attacks witness Jamison's character for untruthfulness and therefore should be admitted via Rule 608(a). But the ex-wife's testimony concerns character traits (thievery and violence) that have nothing to do with truthfulness or its opposite and should thus be beyond the scope of what is authorized by this Rule.

Wilson v. City of Chicago
United States Court of Appeals for the Seventh Circuit
June 1, 1993, Argued; October 4, 1993, Decided

Judges: Before POSNER, Chief Judge, and COFFEY and EASTERBROOK, Circuit Judges.

POSNER, *Chief Judge.* In 1982 Andrew Wilson shot and killed two Chicago policemen. He was convicted of first-degree murder and sentenced to death. The Supreme Court of Illinois reversed his conviction on the ground that his confession, which had been part of the evidence against him at trial, had been coerced. . . . Wilson had "testified that he was punched, kicked, smothered with a plastic bag, electrically shocked, and forced against a hot radiator throughout the day on February 14 [the day of his arrest], until he gave his confession," . . . and his testimony had been corroborated by extensive contemporaneous medical and photographic evidence.

Wilson was retried, again convicted, and this time sentenced to life in prison without possibility of parole; his appeal from the second conviction is pending. Meanwhile he had brought this suit for damages under *42 U.S.C. §1983*, claiming that the torture inflicted upon him to make him confess denied his right to due process of law. Named as defendants were the City of Chicago and several police officers, including a lieutenant, Jon Burge, who were alleged to have participated in the torture of Wilson. A first trial, which lasted eight weeks, ended in a hung jury. A second trial of the same length resulted in a special verdict that, while finding that Wilson's constitutional rights had been violated, exonerated all the officers. Although the jury found that the City of Chicago had had a de facto policy authorizing its police officers physically to abuse persons suspected of having killed or injured a police officer, the jury also found that the policy had not been a direct and proximate cause of the physical abuse visited on Wilson. So judgment was entered in favor of all defendants, though meanwhile the Police Board of Chicago, in disciplinary proceedings against the officers, had found three of them guilty of misconduct, suspended two of them, and fired the third — Burge. The decision of the Police Board is under appeal to a state court. The Fraternal Order of Police was unsuccessful in its effort to enter a float in the most recent St. Patrick's day parade honoring Burge and the other officers who were disciplined.

Wilson challenges a number of the district judge's rulings at the second trial . . .

Since there must be a new trial at which other issues presented by this appeal may recur, we shall indicate our view of them for the guidance of the district court.

. . .

The judge excluded the testimony of a British journalist, Gregory Miskiw, that one of the defense witnesses, William Coleman, was a liar. Coleman had shared a cell with Wilson in 1987, before Wilson's second criminal trial, and he testified that Wilson had told him that at his trial he was going to fabricate a tale of having been coerced to confess, in order to beat a murder rap. An odd suggestion; at the time of the alleged conversation the Supreme Court of Illinois had already suppressed the confession as coerced. In any event the plaintiff wanted to impeach Coleman's credibility with testimony by Miskiw that Coleman had once fed him two pieces of juicy gossip, one concerning a cousin of the Queen of England, that had turned out to be false.

The rules of evidence permit (with various limitations) impeaching a witness by evidence that he has a reputation for untruthfulness or even — a novelty — by *opinion* evidence that he is untruthful. *Fed. R. Evid. 608(a)*; Note to *Rule 608(a)* of Advisory Comm. on 1972 Proposed Rules. The fact that Coleman had lied to Miskiw about Queen Elizabeth's cousin would not fit the older or newer version of the rule. The telling of a lie not only cannot be equated to the possession of a *reputation* for untruthfulness, but does not by itself establish a *character* for untruthfulness, as the rule explicitly requires whether the form of the impeaching evidence is evidence of reputation or opinion evidence. Trials would be endless if a witness could be impeached by evidence that he had once told a lie or two. Which of us has never lied? Cf. David Nyberg, *The Varnished Truth: Truth Telling and Deceiving in Ordinary Life* (1993). But there is more here. Miskiw wanted to testify that Coleman had a reputation for untruthfulness among people who had worked with Coleman and members of his family, who regarded him as "the blackest of the black sheep of the family." Was this a "community" within the meaning of the rule? We suppose so. Coleman is a peripatetic felon. He is not a member of any stable community, but that is true of a lot of law-abiding people in our mobile society, and a community doesn't have to be stable in order to qualify under the rule. Cf. *McCormick on Evidence* § 43 at p. 159 (4th ed. 1992). It was Miskiw's job as a reporter to determine Coleman's reputation for trustworthiness in order to decide whether to place any credence in his gossip about the royal cousin. His interviews with members of Coleman's "community" enabled him to testify to Coleman's reputation in that community on the basis of personal knowledge.

Miskiw had also spent a fair amount of time with Coleman himself, in an effort to determine whether the gossip was accurate. On the basis of his personal contacts with Coleman he formed the apparently well-substantiated opinion that Coleman was "a consummate liar." This opinion was admissible wholly apart from evidence about Coleman's reputation in his own community.

. . .

Affirmed in Part, Reversed in Part, and Remanded.

Problem 5-51: Maintenance Man

Ginger Paulson sues her landlord, John Damon, for negligence and punitive damages after she fell from a balcony at her apartment complex that had a loose railing. The central witness for the plaintiff's case, Wally Williams, testified that John had instructed him not to fix the railings because they were "good enough" and were "too expensive" to fix. During the defense case, John calls Wally's ex-best-friend, Isaac, who testifies that he has known Wally for 10 years and was his best friend until a few weeks before trial (they had a falling out over a debt). Over plaintiff Paulson's objection, Isaac goes on to testify that Wally is a "total liar." Again over objection, Isaac goes on to recount three of Wally's most egregious lies. *How should the court have ruled on each objection?*

Problem 5-52: Criminal Defendant

Dana Dial is on trial for murder. Dana invokes the Fifth Amendment and her sole witness at trial is Harvey, who testifies that on the night of the murder, Dana was with him in another town. During the prosecution's rebuttal case, prosecutors call a character witness, over defense objection. The witness, a local who has run in the same circle as Dana and Harvey for years, testifies that Harvey has a well-founded reputation in the community as a liar and that Dana is a "liar too." *How should the court have ruled on the defense objection?*

2. Specific Acts: Rule 608(b)

Rule 608(b) declares that, "[e]xcept for a criminal conviction under Rule 609, extrinsic evidence is not admissible to prove specific instances of a witness's conduct in order to attack or support the witness's character for truthfulness." The rule continues:

> But the court may, on cross-examination, allow them to be inquired into if they are probative of the character for truthfulness or untruthfulness of
>
> (1)   the witness; or
>
> (2)   another witness whose character the witness being cross-examined has testified about. . . .

Remember that the general rules governing the use of character-propensity evidence on traits other than witness truthfulness, Rules 404(a)(2) and 405, permit proof on direct examination of a character witness only by reputation or opinion evidence but not by evidence of specific acts. Like Rule 405, Rule 608(b) allows specific acts may be used to impeach character on cross-examination of the witness whose character is at issue or a witness testifying to the character of another witness.

But such proof is only allowed if those specific acts are elicited "intrinsically," meaning from the mouth of the witness who is being cross-examined.

If the witness being cross-examined denies committing or knowing about the alleged wrongful acts, the cross-examiner is thus not permitted to call another witness (one whose testimony is "extrinsic" to the witness being cross-examined) or introduce an exhibit to prove the contrary *unless* that testimony has some relevance additional to that of proving the witness' untruthful character. The cross-examiner is stuck with the challenged witness' denial, false or not.

Example 1

Robert Deck is a witness who testifies for the defense in a "date" rape trial. Deck testifies that he was at the fraternity party where the rape allegedly happened and saw the victim being the sexual aggressor. The prosecutor asks Deck whether he once committed perjury by lying about the size of his assets when testifying at his recent divorce trial. Deck denies that he lied at that earlier trial. Deck has never been convicted of perjury, or even charged with it. The prosecutor seeks to call witnesses to establish: (1) the amount of money Deck testified to having in the bank in his divorce case, and (2) the much greater amount of money Deck in fact had in the bank at that time. A defense objection to these witnesses' testimony should be sustained if the sole purpose of this testimony is to prove Deck's character for untruthfulness. Their testimony would be extrinsic evidence of

Deck's act of lying under oath at his divorce trial, an act that Deck has just denied in his testimony at the rape trial.

Important reminder: Note that Rule 608(b) refers to "specific instances of a witness's conduct," *not* "specific instances of conviction." If a witness is being cross-examined about prior *convictions* of crime to impeach his character for truthfulness, then Rule 609 (discussed below) controls.

But if the evidence concerns only the fact that the relevant act happened, even if the defendant was never even tried much less convicted of that act — indeed, even if the act is not itself a crime but does go to character for truthfulness or untruthfulness — then Rule 608(b) applies. That is why Deck could be asked whether he *committed* perjury, there being no evidence that he was *convicted* of such a crime.

The original rule prohibited using extrinsic proof of specific acts to attack or support a witness' "credibility." The rule was amended to replace the word "credibility" with the phrase "character for truthfulness." The point of this change was to "clarify that the absolute prohibition on extrinsic evidence applies only when the *sole reason* for proffering that evidence is to attack or support the witness' character for truthfulness." *See* Advisory Committee Note, amended Rule 608(b):

The "Rule 608(b) extrinsic evidence prohibition does not apply when it is offered for a purpose other than proving the witness' character for veracity." *Id.* Thus, if extrinsic evidence is offered to impeach on grounds other than character — such as by contradiction or a showing of bias — Rules 402 and 403 control.

At its root, the amendment was meant to clarify that non-character impeachment is not subject to the limitations of Rule 608(b) and thus extrinsic evidence is permissible. So, for instance, if Deck had previously testified at a grand jury proceeding that the victim was *not* the sexual aggressor, the prosecutor could introduce the transcript to impeach Deck, subject to Rule 613.

Likewise, the prosecutor could call a witness in rebuttal to testify that Deck and the defendant were fraternity brothers and lifelong friends. Such evidence would establish that Deck was biased in favor of the defendant and motivated to protect him. The impeachment evidence is extrinsic, but this is fine because the prosecutor is not trying to establish that Deck is a liar by nature and is thus lying today; rather, the prosecutor seeks to establish that Deck has a specific motivation to lie in this specific case.

The primary rationale for barring extrinsic proof of acts going to truthful or untruthful character is that it wastes time. The trial court becomes bogged down in a series of mini-trials over whether events relatively peripheral to the current case ever happened. Perhaps the intended effect of the amended Rule is to prohibit initial use of extrinsic proof of character in the hope that the witness will admit his lies (given the risk of perjury prosecution), thus avoiding a mini-trial.

Note, moreover, that even efforts to prove a witness' specific acts "intrinsically" may be made only if the acts are probative of the witness' character for truthfulness or untruthfulness. Like proof of opinion or reputation under Rule 608(a), questions about specific instances of conduct under Rule 608(b) may not address other character traits (ones unconnected to truthfulness or its opposite) or attack the witness' credibility on some basis other than character. Furthermore, the court has discretion whether to permit intrinsic proof at all, making a case-specific judgment that balances the act's probative value against other concerns. That is why the Rule declares that the relevant acts "may," ... be inquired into on cross-examination if probative of character for truthfulness or untruthfulness.

Example 2

Now assume that witness Deck's alleged perjury at his divorce trial took place 10 years ago (Deck is an older student, returning to college). A trial judge might consider the event so remote as to have little probative value regarding Deck's current character for truthfulness. The judge might, therefore, exercise discretion to bar the prosecutor from questioning Deck about the perjury.

Example 3

Now the prosecutor asks Deck whether he assaulted his roommate two days ago. The defense objection will be sustained, as the answer would not concern Deck's character for truthfulness or untruthfulness.

On a different point, the Advisory Committee further declares: "It should be noted that the extrinsic evidence prohibition of Rule 608(b) bars any reference to the consequences that a witness might have suffered as a result of an alleged bad act." The Advisory Committee explained the point thus:

> For example, Rule 608(b) prohibits counsel from mentioning that a witness was suspended or disciplined for the conduct that is the subject of impeachment, when that conduct is offered only to prove the character of the witness. *See United States v. Davis*, 183 F. 3d 231, 257 n.12 (3d Cir. 1999) (emphasizing that in attacking the defendant's character for truthfulness "the government cannot make reference to Davis's forty-four day suspension or that Internal Affairs found that he lied about" an incident because "[s]uch evidence would not only be hearsay to the extent that it contains assertion of fact, it would be inadmissible extrinsic evidence under Rule (608(b)"). *See also* Stephen A. Saltzburg, *Impeaching the Witness: Prior Bad Acts and Extrinsic Evidence*, 7 Crim. Just. 28, 31 (Winter 1993) ("counsel should not be permitted to circumvent the no-extrinsic-evidence provision by tucking a third person's opinion about prior acts into a question asked of the witness who has denied the act.").

So far, we've discussed the application of Rule 608(b) when challenging the credibility of the testifying witness. It also applies to "another witness whose character the witness being cross-examined has testified about." In other words, on cross-examining a witness who has testified about the character of another witness, the witness being cross-examined may be questioned about acts relating to that other witness' character for truthfulness or untruthfulness.

Example 4

Now assume that Deck and the defendant both testified at the rape trial. The defendant claimed that the alleged victim consented. In rebuttal, the prosecution called Norman, a well-qualified witness who testified that the defendant has a reputation in his neighborhood as a liar. Deck testified in response for the defendant that, in his opinion, the defendant has the character of a very truthful man. The prosecutor cross-examines Deck as follows: "Weren't you present when the defendant purchased liquor from The Brewery Pub using a false identification card, incorrectly representing his age as 21 at a time when he was in fact only 16 and thus well below the legal age for drinking?"

This question fits within the scope of Rule 608(b). Deck has just testified that another witness (the defendant) has a truthful character. It is therefore within the trial judge's discretion to permit a question to challenge Deck's claim about the other witness by suggesting (via specific acts) that the other witness in fact has an untruthful nature.

Note an important difference between this rule and the last sentence of Rule 405(a). First, the person about whose character the character witness vouches need not have been a witness for the last sentence of Rule 405(a) to apply. By contrast, Rule 608(b) allows specific-instance cross about "witnesses." Additionally, Rule 608(b) is limited to authorizing questioning about *only one relevant character trait:* a character for truthfulness or untruthfulness. Rule 405(a) applies when character evidence about "pertinent" traits is being introduced. What is pertinent depends on the case (e.g., in an assault, violent propensities are relevant). But both rules are similar in one important way: they both permit proof of prior acts only by *intrinsic,* not extrinsic, evidence.

Example 5

Now assume that Deck has testified at the rape trial but the defendant has not. Assume further that Deck's testimony on direct was that the defendant had a reputation for peacefulness, and the trial court admits this testimony as relevant to proving that a peaceful man was less likely than most men to commit rape, an act of violence. On cross-examination, the prosecutor asks, "Had you heard that just one week before this rape, the defendant beat his next-door neighbor, Johnny Crenshaw, to a pulp, hospitalizing Crenshaw?" This question is not objectionable under the character evidence rules because it fits within the terms of Rule 405(a), last sentence: "On cross-examination, inquiry is allowable into relevant specific instances of conduct." Here, unlike Example 4, Rule 608(b) does not govern for two reasons: first, character witness Deck has testified about a character trait other than truthfulness or untruthfulness (and Rule 608 applies only to those truth-related character traits); second, the defendant (for whose character Deck vouches) has not been a witness at the trial. Like Rule 608(b), however, Rule 405(a) prohibits *extrinsic impeachment* because inquiry is allowable *only* on cross-examination. Thus, if Deck denies hearing about the defendant's beating of Crenshaw, no other witness may be called to contradict Deck's testimony.

Problem 5-53: Corporate Misfeasance

Jane Voight has been charged with criminal fraud and embezzlement stemming from her time as CEO of BigCorp, Inc. BigCorp is a publicly traded, Fortune 500 company. Jane is alleged to have used her position to divert money from the company to her private use, including plane and yacht travel, without authorization. She is also alleged to have directed company officers and employees to hide losses from the public by making misrepresentations in SEC reports. *How should the judge rule on objections to each of the following pieces of evidence? If the court admits the evidence, how might it instruct the jury?*

1. During its case-in-chief, the prosecution puts on a reputation witness to testify that Jane has a terrible reputation for truthfulness.

2. Assume that the prosecution does not call the reputation witness described in No. 1. During the defense case-in-chief, Jane does not testify but does call a witness to testify to her well-founded opinion that Jane is an honest person.

3. Same facts as No. 2, above. Jane calls an additional witness to testify that Jane was scrupulously honest as a company employee and reported fraud among her colleagues on at least three different occasions.

4. Same facts as No. 2, above. Jane testifies during the defense case-in-chief before the opinion-character witness.

5. Same facts as No 2., above (including the fact that Jane does not testify). During rebuttal, the prosecution calls a reputation witness to testify that Jane has a terrible reputation for honesty and truthfulness.

6. Jane does not call any character witnesses in her case-in-chief, but she does testify. During rebuttal, the prosecution calls a reputation witness to testify that Jane has a terrible reputation for honesty and truthfulness.

7. Same facts as No. 6, above. Imagine that the judge overrules the defense objection to the prosecution's character witness. During cross of the prosecution's character witness, Jane's attorney asks, "Have you heard that Jane turned in three different colleagues for fraud during her time at the company?"

8. Same facts as No. 6, above. The witness answers, "No, I have not." Jane's attorney attempts to introduce the three incident reports to demonstrate that Jane did turn the other employees in for fraud.

3. Rehabilitating Character: Rule 608(a)

Rule 608(a) and (b) provide methods to impeach a witness with character evidence establishing that the witness has an untruthful character. But Rule 608(a) also allows parties to offer positive character evidence to establish that a witness has a truthful character. The second sentence of the Rule provides:

> But evidence of truthful character is admissible only after the witness's character for truthfulness has been attacked.

Fed. R. Evid. 608(a).

Thus, a witness cannot be proven truthful by character evidence via Rule 608(a) until *after* a party has attacked the same witness' truthful character.

Example 1

Recall the Timpson example, in the Rule 608(a) section, above. Defendant Timpson is charged with robbery and his primary alibi witness was impeached with evidence of an untruthful character. On sur-rebuttal, the defense calls witness Jamison's pastor to testify. The pastor testifies to his own opinion that, based on a relationship that began 10 years earlier and continues to this day, Jamison has an honest character. This testimony should be allowed pursuant to Rule 608(a) to rehabilitate Jamison's character for truthfulness after the prosecution attacked it.

But under Rule 608(a), evidence of truthful character may not be admitted unless that particular character trait has first been attacked. The current restyled version of the rule does not expressly state the form of evidence to be used to constitute an attack on character for truthfulness. Courts have held, however, that the right to rehabilitate character for truthfulness with positive character evidence is triggered by character-based attacks on the same trait, e.g., impeachment by opinion or reputation for dishonest character, impeachment by conviction, and impeachment by specific dishonest acts per Rule 608(b). As discussed above, non-character impeachment — e.g., impeachment by bias, inconsistent statement, contradictory evidence — generally does not implicate Rule 608. Thus, it does not constitute an attack on "character for truthfulness" that would trigger the opportunity to rehabilitate the witness' character.

In certain cases, whether an impeachment technique not overtly involving character for truthfulness in fact constitutes an attack is a case-specific question guided by the circumstances. It may turn, for example, on the egregiousness and nature of the inconsistency. Was it so extreme or made under such circumstances that it would not be expected to be uttered from the lips of someone whose general character — their nature or on-average behavior relative to most other people — is other than that of a liar, the kind of person who lies? Whether such a showing has been made will often be the subject of heated debate at trial and is subject to no simple or easy litmus test.

Example 2

Morris Manor is accused of committing a robbery that occurred two months ago. Manor offers an alibi defense, taking the stand and testifying that he was at home with his mother watching TV on the date of the robbery and that he even remembers what they were watching: the hit television show *24*. If the defense next calls Manor's mother to the stand to testify that she was indeed home with him at the time of the crime, but she admits on cross that they were watching the opera, not *24*, that inconsistency with her son's testimony may easily be explained as his memory simply failing him on a relatively minor matter, particularly if he was not arrested until many weeks later so that nothing unusual happened to give him any reason accurately to remember what was on TV.

Accordingly, his mother's cross-examination testimony would not likely constitute an attack on his "character" for truthfulness, so he could not offer evidence of his truthful character in response.

On the other hand, if he did not call his mom to the stand but rather the prosecution did, and if she testified that he was not home with her that night because it was his birthday, and he always goes out with his friend, George, on his birthday for a big celebration at a special restaurant, and if George next testifies that for the first time in 10 years he and the defendant did not see each other on the defendant's birthday, that might arguably constitute an attack on Manor's "character for truthfulness." Manor would debatably be highly likely to remember where he was on his birthday, especially because he makes such a big deal out of it and it was only two months ago, and he follows a regular birthday celebration routine. Moreover, his inconsistency is one so easily caught — the prosecution could simply call his mother to the stand, as they did.

Under these circumstances, a trial judge might easily conclude that this inconsistency was so likely a lie under such outrageous circumstances as to suggest to the jury that the defendant is a liar, that is, that he has a *character* for untruthfulness. Accordingly, the trial judge might permit the defendant to respond with evidence that he in fact has a truthful, not an untruthful, character.

Problem 5-54: Married Robbers

Derrick Lowell testifies at his trial on a robbery charge involving a crime that took place in New York City. Lowell swears that he was in San Francisco visiting a friend on the date of the crime. The prosecutor calls Lowell's ex-wife to the stand, who tearfully recounts that Lowell was indeed in New York City on the relevant date, a date she cannot forget because it is the date that she and Lowell married. In rebuttal, Lowell calls a priest to testify that Lowell is a kind, truthful man. The prosecutor objects. *Should the objection be sustained or overruled? Why?*

Problem 5-55: Married Robbers Revisited

At the same trial of Derrick Lowell summarized in Problem 5-54, which of the following would trigger Lowell's right to call a witness to testify to Lowell's truthful character:

1. Lowell admits that he absconded with $3,000 he obtained from the parents of a terminal 8-year-old cancer patient. Lowell had falsely told them that the money would fund a novel but effective cancer treatment that Lowell had invented. No such treatment existed. Lowell was never convicted.

2. The prosecution calls Lowell's best man to the stand to testify that he saw Lowell at Lowell's wedding on the date of the alleged crime.

3. The prosecutor calls Lowell's former roommate to the stand. Lowell and the roommate lived together before Lowell married and at the time of the crime. Lowell had testified that he never owned or wore a red running suit, which was what the robber wore. The roommate testifies, however, that Lowell indeed owned such a suit at the time of the crime, and the roommate saw Lowell wear the suit on many occasions.

4. The prosecution calls the same roommate to testify that Lowell had said, on several occasions before the crime, that he knew and despised the robbery victim because Lowell believed that the soon-to-be victim was having an affair with Lowell's fiancée.

D. Rule 609 — Impeachment by Prior Convictions

Rule 609 divides recent criminal convictions that can be used to impeach a witness into two categories:[14] (a) crimes involving dishonesty or false statement, regardless of whether they are felonies, misdemeanors, or summary offenses; and (b) felonies (crimes "punishable by death or imprisonment for more than one year"), regardless of whether they did or did not involve a false statement. The latter sort of convictions are addressed below first. Although a record of conviction is a form of hearsay, it falls under an exception to the hearsay rule found in Rule 803(22), though the hearsay exception has several additional requirements for conviction records.

1. Felony Convictions: Rule 609(a)(1)

Rule 609(a)(1) reads as follows:

(a) In General. The following rules apply to attacking a witness's character for truthfulness by evidence of a criminal conviction:

    (1) for a crime that, in the convicting jurisdiction, was punishable by death or by imprisonment for more than one year, the evidence:

---

14. Fᴇᴅ. R. Evɪᴅ. 609(b) addresses standards for admitting older convictions.

    (A) must be admitted, subject to Rule 403, in a civil case or in a criminal case in which the witness is not a defendant; and

    (B) must be admitted in a criminal case in which the witness is a defendant, if the probative value of the evidence outweighs its prejudicial effect to that defendant.

We use the term "felony" as a shorthand for crimes "punishable by death or by imprisonment for more than one year," though a particular criminal code might not necessarily classify such a crime as a felony. Some jurists long considered any such crimes as probative of credibility. The theory was that anyone who would maim, kill, or steal large amounts will worry little about lying under oath. Other jurists considered only crimes involving falsehood to be probative of credibility. Rule 609(a)(1) takes a compromise position: some felonies are significantly probative of falsehood, some are not.[15] The admissibility determination is a case-specific judgment requiring the trial judge to balance unfair prejudice against probative value.

Rule 609(a)(1) sets up two different balancing tests, depending on the nature of the witness being impeached: one test for a witness who is a criminal defendant, another test for all other witnesses. For witnesses other than criminal defendants, Rule 609(a)(1)(A) applies the usual Rule 403 balancing test.

For a witness who is also a criminal accused, the court may admit the evidence under Rule 609(a)(1)(B) only if it determines that the "probative value of the evidence outweighs its prejudicial effect to that defendant." This latter test places the burden of admitting the evidence on the proponent, requires the probative value exceed undue effects, and is thus more protective of the accused than the test of Rule 403. In other words, Rule 403 favors admissibility while the special Rule 609(a)(1)(B) test for criminal defendants favors exclusion.

Neither Rule 609 nor its commentary explains what should guide a court's discretion in applying the special balancing test for a criminal accused. However, the following factors have been identified by commentators as helpful in gauging the degree of prejudice in such cases:[16]

1. The degree to which the crime reflects on credibility. For example, a violent crime may not reflect on credibility as much as a theft conviction.

2. The nearness or remoteness of the prior conviction. A person who has led a blameless life for years after a conviction is entitled to more consideration as honest than one who was recently convicted . . . .

3. The similarity of the prior offense to the offense charged. This is a factor that weighs against admissibility when the only theory of admission is

---

15. *Cf.* Christopher B. Mueller & Laird C. Kirkpatrick, 3 Federal Evidence § 4:42 (4th ed. 2017).

16. *See, e.g.*, Roger C. Park et al., Evidence Law: A Student's Guide to the Law of Evidence as Applied in American Trials § 9.09, at 455 (1998).

impeachment of the accused as a witness. The reason is that the jury may use the evidence not for its bearing upon the credibility of the witness, but for the inference that "because she did it before she probably did it again" — or, even worse, decide to re-punish the accused for the prior crime whether or not the current one was committed. Thus, a stronger case can be made for receiving a prior auto theft conviction as impeachment in a bank robbery case than in an auto theft case.

4. The extent to which defendant's testimony is needed for fair adjudication of the trial. If defendant's testimony is crucial for his defense, this fact weighs against the admissibility of the prior convictions, because if the evidence will be admissible, it is less likely that the defendant will testify.

5. Whether the defendant's credibility is central to the case. Some courts will consider whether the witness' credibility can be explored adequately without using evidence of the witness' prior conviction. If the witness can be impeached convincingly using other means (e.g., bias, prior inconsistent statement) the existence of such alternative impeachment methods is a factor weighing against allowing use of the prior conviction.

Example 1

Tony Leduca is charged with simple assault. Leduca takes the stand and claims self-defense. The prosecutor seeks to impeach Leduca with evidence that he was convicted nine years ago of felony assault, a crime punishable by up to 20 years in prison, for an incident that occurred on his eighteenth birthday. That offense involved Leduca smashing his girlfriend's suspected lover on the head with a metal pipe, an act of jealous revenge. The current simple assault charge arises out of Leduca's punching a co-worker who insulted Leduca based on Leduca's ethnicity. There were no eyewitnesses to the current simple assault case: it is Leduca's word against his co-worker's. However, Leduca's brother is a reluctant witness to whom, says the prosecution, Leduca admitted starting the fight in the current case with very little provocation for doing so. A trial court would be well within its discretion to exclude the prior conviction because assault, a crime entirely of violence, reflects little on credibility; the conviction is stale; the two offenses are quite similar; the defendant's testimony is essential to his defense given the lack of eyewitnesses; the defendant's credibility is central to the case; and there are other adequate means for challenging that credibility, namely the testimony of Leduca's brother.

Note Concerning Grounds for Appeal: In *Luce v. United States*, the United States Supreme Court held that a trial court's *in limine* (generally meaning before trial) ruling to permit impeachment of the accused with a prior felony conviction under what is now Rule 609(a)(1)(B) is preserved for review only if the accused testifies at his trial. If he chooses not to testify for fear of being cross-examined about his prior felony conviction, he thus loses his right to object to the Rule 609(a)(1)(B) admissibility ruling on appeal. The Court reasoned that an appellate court would otherwise have to speculate whether the impeachment in fact would have happened since *in limine* rulings are subject to change during trial and the prosecution might have tactical reasons for ultimately foregoing that type of impeachment. Additionally, it is speculative to assume that the sole reason a defendant did not testify was because of an adverse Rule 609(a)(1)(B) ruling. Furthermore, the details of the defendant's testimony are necessary for a reviewing court to judge the weighing of prejudice against probative value that Rule 609(a)(1)(B) requires. *See also Ohler v. United States*, 529 U.S. 753 (2000) (reaffirming the Court's willingness to follow and extend *Luce*).

Example 2

Assume in Example 1 above that the trial court ruled *in limine* that Leduca's assault conviction would be admissible to impeach him if he testified at trial. Leduca is convicted in the current case and, on appeal, seeks to claim that he chose not to testify because of this incorrect Rule 609(a)(1)(B) ruling. As *Example 1* explained, Leduca had a good argument for excluding this impeachment evidence. Nevertheless, because he chose not to testify at trial, he has waived his right to complain on appeal about the Rule 609(a)(1)(B) decision, as the *Luce* rule requires.

2. Crimen Falsi Convictions: Rule 609(a)(2)

Rule 609(a)(2) reads as follows:

(a) **In General.** The following rules apply to attacking a witness's character for truthfulness by evidence of a criminal conviction:

. . .

(2) for any crime regardless of the punishment, the evidence must be admitted if the court can readily determine that establishing the elements of the crime required proving — or the witness's admitting — a dishonest act or false statement.

Under Rule 609(a)(2), evidence that a witness has been convicted of a crime requiring proof of a dishonest act or false statement "must be admitted." The trial judge has no discretion to weigh prejudice against probative value. Rule 609(a)(2) convictions, unlike virtually all other evidence, are not subject to Rule 403.

Nevertheless, exclusion is still possible if one of the limitations stated in Rule 609(b) (old convictions), (c) (effect of pardon), or (d) (juvenile adjudications) applies. These limitations are addressed below.

Crimes of dishonesty or false statement (i.e., "*crimen falsi*") are admissible under Rule 609(a)(2) whether they are felonies or misdemeanors. (*Caution:* A misdemeanor — here meaning a crime punishable by one year or less imprisonment.) Non-*crimen-falsi* misdemeanors are not admissible via Rule 609 because they are neither Rule 609(a)(1) felonies nor Rule 609(a)(2) crimes requiring proof of "dishonest act[s] or false statement."

The difficult question in applying Rule 609(a)(2) is determining what constitutes a crime of dishonesty or false statement. The Advisory Committee Note to the 1990 amendments to Rule 609 listed some offenses clearly meeting the test:

> Congress extensively debated the rule, and the Report of the House and Senate Conference Committee states that "[b]y the phrase dishonesty and false statement, the Conference means crimes such as perjury, false statement, criminal fraud, embezzlement, or false pretense, or any other offense in the nature of *crimen falsi*, commission of which involves some element of deceit, untruthfulness, or falsification bearing on the accused's propensity to testify truthfully."

The 1990 Advisory Committee went on, however, to disapprove of "some decisions that take an unduly broad view of 'dishonesty,' admitting convictions such as bank robbery or bank larceny." The comment suggests an intention to exclude stealing as a crime of dishonesty.

Example

A plaintiff had earlier been convicted of the misdemeanor offense of tampering with electric meters, a kind of theft of electricity. Tampering with an electric meter means modifying or interfering with it in a way that makes it report less electricity consumed than was actually used. Courts have held that this type of theft requires proof of a dishonest act because tampering with an electric meter always involves deception — the thief deceives the meter reader into believing a false number on the electric meter. Depending on the elements of the crime, potential statements of admitted facts that comprise part of the guilty plea process, or the indictment in the case (more discussion on sources courts use to evaluate whether crimes require proof of false statement or dishonest act below), tampering with an electric meter often requires proof of deception.

This example, though, illustrates the difficulty courts have had in deciding whether a crime is *crimen falsi*, especially when the crime's elements might not on their face suggest that the crime is always of that nature but, in the particular case, acts of dishonesty or false statement may have been involved in the course of committing the crime.

In part to clarify this confusion, Rule 609(a)(2) was amended in 2006 to declare that "evidence that any witness has been convicted of a crime shall be admitted regardless of the punishment," but only "if it *readily can be determined* that establishing the elements of the crime *required* proof or admission of an act of dishonesty or false statement by the witness." (emphasis added). Note the presence of the word "required" to emphasize that the acts of dishonesty had to be *necessary* to proving the crime's elements, even if the statutory elements on their face did not expressly refer to deceit. Here is how the Advisory Committee explained this necessity requirement:

> The amendment provides that Rule 609(a)(2) mandates the admission of evidence of a conviction only when the conviction required proof of (or

in the case of a guilty plea, the admission of) an act of dishonesty or false statement. Evidence of all other convictions is inadmissible under this section, irrespective of whether the witness exhibited dishonesty or made a false statement in the process of the commission of the crime of conviction. Thus, evidence that a witness was convicted of a crime of violence, such as murder, is not admissible under Rule 609(a)(2), even if the witness acted deceitfully in the course of committing the crime.

The Advisory Committee went on in its note concerning the 2006 amendment to emphasize how truly narrow its definition of "dishonesty or false statement" was:

> This amendment is meant to give effect to the legislative intent to limit the convictions that are to be automatically admitted under subsection (a)(2). The Conference Committee provided that by "dishonesty or false statement" it meant "crimes such as perjury, subornation of perjury, false statement, criminal fraud, embezzlement, or false pretense, or any other offense in the nature of *crimen falsi*, the commission of which involves some element of deceit, untruthfulness, or falsification bearing on the [witness's] propensity to testify truthfully." Historically, offenses classified as *crimen falsi* have included *only those crimes in which the ultimate criminal act was itself an act of deceit* (emphasis added).

In another sense, however, this definition of crimes of "dishonesty or false statement" is not as narrow as it could have been because, as noted above, it still can include some crimes not expressly mentioning deceit in the defining statute. "For example, evidence that a witness was convicted of making a false claim to a federal agent is admissible under this subsection regardless of whether the crime was charged under a section that expressly references deceit (e.g., 18 U.S.C. sec. 1001, Material Misrepresentation to the Federal Government) or a section that does not (e.g., 18 U.S.C. sec. 1503, Obstruction of Justice)." *See* FED. R. EVID. 609, advisory committee's note to 2006 amendment.

In arguing that a crime is *crimen falsi*, a party may thus go beyond the text of the statute, inquiring into its logic as to what proof it necessarily requires, and may go even further by arguing that, *in this specific case*, the ultimate criminal act was one of deceit. However, this does not entitle the proponent to a wide-ranging evidentiary issue on this question. It is important to note that only a narrow range of evidence may be consulted by the trial court in answering the *crimen falsi* question, for Rule 609(a)(2)'s current version now expressly declares that convictions fall within its terms only if "the court can readily determine that establishing the elements of the crime required proving — or the witness's admitting — a dishonest act or false statement." What does it mean to say that these things can "readily be determine[d]"? The Advisory Committee Note to the 2006 amendment answered this question thus:

> The amendment requires that the proponent have ready proof that the conviction required the factfinder to find, or the defendant to admit, an

act of dishonesty or false statement. Ordinarily, the statutory elements of the crime will indicate whether it is one of dishonesty or false statement. Where the deceitful nature of the statute is not apparent from the statute and the face of the judgment — as, for example, where the conviction simply records a finding of guilt for a statutory offense that does not reference deceit expressly — a proponent may offer information such as an indictment, a statement of admitted facts, or jury instructions to show that the factfinder had to find, or the defendant had to admit, an act of dishonesty or false statement in order for the witness to have been convicted . . . . But the amendment does not contemplate a "mini-trial" in which the court plumbs the record of the previous proceeding to determine whether the crime was in the nature of *crimen falsi.*

3. Old Convictions Subject to Rule 609(b)

Rule 609(b) reads as follows:

> **(b) Limit on Using the Evidence After 10 Years.** This subdivision (b) applies if more than 10 years have passed since the witness's conviction or release from confinement for it, whichever is later. Evidence of the conviction is admissible only if:
>
> > (1) its probative value, supported by specific facts and circumstances, substantially outweighs its prejudicial effect; and
> >
> > (2) the proponent gives an adverse party reasonable written notice of the intent to use it so that the party has a fair opportunity to contest its use.

Under Rule 609(b), evidence of a conviction that is more than 10 years old (as measured from the date of conviction or date of release from confinement) is presumed inadmissible.[17] Indeed, an old conviction is only admissible per Rule 609(b) if the court determines, in the interests of justice, that "its probative value, supported by specific facts and circumstances, substantially outweighs its prejudicial effect." This is effectively a reverse-403 balancing test that is set up to presumptively exclude old convictions.

In addition to satisfying Rule 609(b)'s reverse-403 balancing test, the proponent must give the adverse party sufficient advance written notice of the intent to use such evidence to provide a fair opportunity to contest admissibility. Whether notice is reasonable is case specific, and courts have significant discretion to exclude Rule 609(b) convictions where notice is given close to trial.

Note that Rule 609(b) applies to both old felonies and old *crimen falsi* convictions. Even though a conviction under Rule 609(a)(2) would be mandatorily admissible if

---

17. FED. R. EVID. 609(c), (d).

it were fresh, once it is subject to Rule 609(b), it is presumed *inadmissible* and is subject to Rule 609(b)'s reverse-403 balancing test.

4. Special Qualifications to Rule 609

Crimes that have been pardoned and juvenile adjudications are also usually inadmissible. However, impeachment by a pardoned conviction will be permitted if the pardon was not based on a finding of innocence and the offender was convicted of a subsequent felony. Additionally, juvenile adjudications may be used to impeach witnesses other than the accused if the trial court finds impeachment necessary for a fair determination of guilt or innocence.

The pendency of an appeal does not render evidence of a conviction inadmissible, but evidence of the pendency of the appeal is admissible.

Example

Paulo Victor has testified at his embezzlement trial, denying any wrongdoing. The prosecutor seeks to impeach Paulo with a conviction for felony robbery, which is punishable by up to 20 years in prison. Paulo was convicted 12 years ago and served five years in prison, being released upon a pardon based on a finding that he had been rehabilitated. Unfortunately, Paulo was arrested one year later for committing a felony assault, of which he was also convicted but for which he served only two years. The prosecutor also seeks to impeach Paulo with a juvenile rape adjudication received 20 years ago, for which Paulo served two years in confinement at a juvenile home. The special qualifications in Rule 609(b), (c), and (d) will not bar impeaching Paulo with the adult robbery conviction. Because he was released from prison seven years ago, the conviction is not more than 10 years old in the terms of Rule 609(b), although the date of conviction was 12 years ago. While he was ultimately pardoned of that crime, that pardon was not based on a finding of innocence. And the fact that he was convicted of a subsequent crime punishable by more than one year in prison means that Rule 609(c) does not bar the impeachment. However, Rule 609(d) prevents the prosecutor from impeaching Paulo with the juvenile adjudication, because he is the criminal accused. Even were this not true, the prosecution would have a heavy burden to show great probative value under Rule 609(b), because the adjudication was well over 10 years old.

5. Extrinsic Evidence

Rule 608(b) bars the use of extrinsic evidence to impeach a witness by proof of specific acts concerning the witness' character for truthfulness or untruthfulness that did not result in a conviction (*see* [B] [2], above). Under Rule 609, on the other hand, impeachment by a prior conviction may be done by intrinsic or extrinsic evidence. Thus, the cross-examiner need not accept a witness' denial that he or she was previously convicted of the impeaching crime. The conviction may be proven by, e.g., a public record.

6. Eliciting Details of Prior Convictions

How much detail about a prior conviction may be elicited before the jury? There is no single approach followed by all courts. Under one view, the impeacher may ask only about the existence and name of the crime and when the conviction occurred. Under another view, the impeacher may also inquire about the length of the punishment imposed. It is also commonly held that details of the crime itself may be elicited if the witness impeached tried to explain the conviction away, for example, by claiming that he pled guilty to protect a loved one or that he was drunk at the time of the crime.

Example

At Harding's trial for felony cocaine distribution, the prosecutor seeks to impeach Harding's testimony with evidence of Harding's felony conviction for possession of marijuana with intent to sell. Although the trial court permits impeachment by noting the name, existence, and date of the marijuana conviction, and even by further noting the punishment imposed, it excludes further details. Specifically, the prosecutor had sought to show that the earlier crime involved 80 pounds of marijuana found in the defendant's home and that the marijuana was actually in the defendant's home at the time of his arrest on the cocaine charge. The trial court thought that these details unduly stressed the similarity between the two crimes, with the risk that the marijuana offense would become evidence of substantive guilt rather than of a lack of credibility.

Problem 5-56: The Matasow Corporation

Ronald Matasow's corporation, in which he is the sole shareholder, has been civilly sued for sexual harassment. The basis for the suit by his ex-secretary, Mary Beckett, is her allegation that Matasow inappropriately touched Ms. Beckett against her will, despite her protests. She finally quit. Matasow testifies at the trial that he never touched Ms. Beckett and that she resigned because she knew that she would otherwise soon be fired for incompetence. Matasow is cross-examined by Beckett's counsel. *In connection with that cross-examination, consider the following:*

1. Matasow is asked whether he was convicted nine years ago of a felony rape of his then-secretary, Mary Baldwin. Should defense counsel's objection be sustained? Why or why not? Would deleting any details — and, if so, which — from the question improve the chances of the objection's being overruled? Why or why not?

2. If the objection in Question 1 is overruled but Matasow denies the conviction, what options, if any, does Beckett's counsel have for proving that

Matasow was in fact convicted? What documents, if any, would be required, and what witnesses, if any, should be called to the stand and when? What questions would you ask the witness or witnesses? What details should you elicit?

3. Would your answer to Question 1 change if the rape conviction happened 11 years ago and resulted in a time-served sentence? If it happened 11 years ago, resulting in a prison sentence of five years? If Matasow only served three years when he was pardoned based upon a finding of his innocence of the crime? If the rape conviction is still tied up in the courts, going through a ponderous process of appeals?

4. Would your answer to Question 1 change if, instead of a civil harassment trial, the trial were a criminal misdemeanor sexual assault trial naming Matasow as the defendant? A criminal rape trial against Matasow?

5. Suppose at the civil harassment trial Matasow is now asked, "Weren't you recently convicted of a bank robbery that occurred two years ago?" Should the defense objection be sustained? Why or why not? Would your answer change if this question is asked of Matasow at his criminal misdemeanor sexual assault trial? His criminal felony rape trial? Why or why not? Could you elicit any of the following details, whether at one of the criminal trials or at the civil harassment trial:

   a. Matasow wore a convincing disguise at the time of the bank robbery, gaining entrance to the bank after banking hours by presenting a phony identification card naming him as the newly hired manager of the bank to replace the acting manager?

   b. Matasow was sentenced to 10 years' imprisonment for the bank robbery?

6. Would your answers to Question 5 change if the bank robbery conviction involved a 15-year-old juvenile adjudication?

Problem 5-57: Johnny Winter's Lament

Johnny Winter has been charged with burglary. He testifies at the trial that he broke into the victim's home because he was cold and homeless, not because he planned to commit any crime inside. His story, if believed, will reduce his crime from burglary to criminal trespass. The prosecutor, over defense objection, elicits on cross-examination an admission by Winter that he had been convicted of a burglary five years earlier. Unasked, Winter adds, "But I didn't do it. I pled guilty to save my mother the agony of attending my trial, rest her soul. She died recently." The prosecutor now seeks to ask questions about the details of the earlier burglary, designed to show that: (1) Winter was the mastermind, supervising a gang of thieves in pulling off a massive theft of goods from a furniture warehouse; and (2) Winter's mother was in fact a member of the gang. *Should these details be admitted into evidence? Why or why not?*

Problem 5-58: At the Movies: Snitch Attack

In the film *Anatomy of a Murder*, Lt. Manion is charged with murdering Barney Quill. Manion admits that he killed Quill, but claims that he did so as a result of "irresistible impulse," a form of temporary insanity resulting from finding out that Quill had raped and beaten Manion's wife, Laura. Miller, incarcerated in the same cell as Manion, testifies on the prosecution's behalf that Manion told him during the trial that "I'm pulling the wool over the eyes of my lawyer and the jury, and will take care of Laura after I get out of here." On cross-examination, defense lawyer Paul Biegler elicits testimony that Miller had previously been convicted of three felonies: arson, assault with a deadly weapon, and larceny. Moreover, Miller had been arrested for indecent exposure, perjury, and disorderly conduct. *What, if any, of this evidence would be admissible under Rules 608 and 609? Would it matter if the convictions were for misdemeanors rather than for felonies?*

Problem 5-59: Forging a Defense

George Parker is charged with homicide. Parker testifies that he acted in self-defense. The prosecutor seeks to impeach Parker by eliciting on cross-examination Parker's misdemeanor forgery conviction five years ago, for which he received probation. *Should the defense objection be sustained? Why or why not?*

E. Habit

A proper understanding of character-propensity evidence requires distinguishing it from habit evidence. "Habit," unlike character-propensity evidence, is routinely admissible:

Rule 406. Habit; Routine Practice

Evidence of a person's habit or an organization's routine practice may be admitted to prove that on a particular occasion the person or organization acted in accordance with the habit or routine practice. The court may admit this evidence regardless of whether it is corroborated or whether there was an eyewitness.

The starting place for gauging the distinction between character and habit is the Rule 406 Advisory Committee Note:

Character is a generalized description of one's disposition, or of one's disposition in respect to a general trait, such as honesty, temperance, or peacefulness. Habit in modern usage, both lay and psychological, is more specific. It describes one's regular response to a repeated specific situation. If we speak of character for care, we think of the person's tendency to act prudently in all the varying situations of life, in business, in family life, in handling automobiles, and in walking across the street. A habit, on the other hand, is the person's regular practice of meeting a particular kind of situation with a specific type of conduct, such as the habit of going down a particular stairway two stairs at a time, or of giving the hand-signal for a left turn, or of alighting from railway cars while they are moving. The doing of the habitual acts may become semi-automatic.

Equivalent behavior on the part of a group is designated "routine practice of an organization" in the rule.

There is general agreement that habit evidence is highly persuasive as proof of conduct on a particular occasion. Again quoting McCormick § 152, p. 341:

Character may be thought of as the sum of one's habits though doubtless it is more than this. But unquestionably the uniformity of one's response to habit is far greater than the consistency with which one's conduct conforms to character or disposition. Even though character comes in only exceptionally as evidence of an act, surely any sensible man in investigating whether X did a particular act would be greatly helped in this inquiry by evidence as to whether he was in the habit of doing it.

Note that "habit" evidence, as opposed to "character" evidence, is admissible to prove that the person conformed with their propensity to engage in the habit on a particular occasion.

Why is habit evidence admissible for a purpose forbidden for character evidence? One reason is that the probative value of habit evidence to prove conformity is high.

The excerpted portion of the Advisory Committee Note sets forth what Professor Thomas Mengler has called the "probability theory" of habit.[18] Under this theory, the probability of someone reacting in a specific, predictable way to a narrow, specific situation is quite substantial. The person always or nearly always reacts as expected.

Example 1

Joanie Mirez showers immediately upon awakening each morning. She will not eat, play with her kids, or read the newspaper until she showers. Her husband of 20 years remembers only one exception to this rule: the day he thought he was having a heart attack, and she had to rush him to the hospital. This likely qualifies as Rule 406 habit evidence, and is admissible to prove Joanie showered on a particular occasion.

Example 2

Andrew Paslitz watches the television science fiction show *Sliders* every Thursday night at 8:00 p.m., even when it is in reruns. He turns down professional and social invitations rather than miss this show. This behavior is regular and specific, like habit, but may lack some of the non-volitional hallmarks that tend to accompany habit evidence. Andrew likely is fully conscious of the behavior (as opposed to brushing his teeth or buckling his

---

18. *See* Thomas M. Mengler, *The Theory of Discretion in the Federal Rules of Evidence*, 74 Iowa L. Rev. 413, 417 (1989).

seatbelt). Arguments exist either way and courts would be within their discretion to deem this television-watching behavior habit or not.

However, the meaning of "habit" is not limited to a definition based on the "probability theory." An alternative definition has been based on the "psychological theory."[19] According to this theory, habits are "unconsciously mechanical — Pavlovian."[20] The Advisory Committee Note discussed the non-volitional nature of habits:

> In *Levin v. United States*, 338 F.2d 265, 119 U.S. App. D.C. 156 (1964), testimony as to the religious "habits" of the accused, offered as tending to prove that he was at home observing the Sabbath rather than out obtaining money through larceny by trick, was properly excluded:

> It seems apparent to us that an individual's religious practices would not be the type of activities which would lend themselves to the characterization of "invariable regularity." [1 Wigmore 5201]. Certainly the very volitional basis of the activity raises serious questions as to its invariable nature, and hence its probative value.

One modern court has similarly defined "habit," as have many lower courts, as "semi-automatic, almost involuntary and invariably specific responses to fairly specific stimuli."[21] The idea is that if the behavior is barely, if at all, under your conscious control, you are highly unlikely to vary it, both because you are not really aware of it and because changing it may even be beyond your control.

Example 3

Reginald usually arrives at faculty meetings precisely on time. He is certainly far more punctual than his colleagues, most of whom have developed the custom of arriving "fashionably late." There is rarely a quorum until at least 15 minutes after the official meeting time. For these reasons, Reginald's colleagues often joke that he is "compulsive about time." In fact, however, Reginald is a good 10 minutes late about three times per year, and is the last to arrive once each year. A hot sports game on the radio, a publication offer from a prestigious law journal, or an occasional fit of pique will slow Reginald down. But most faculty members, who arrive even later than he, don't notice his 10-minute tardiness and view his one exceptional lateness each year as aberrational. However, as there are only 10 faculty meetings each year, "Punctual Reggie" is actually late 40 percent of the time!

Reggie's 40 percent tardy rate makes it hard to predict with a high degree of confidence that Reggie will be on time for any particular faculty meeting. But Reggie has never, since his fourth birthday, failed to brush his teeth upon

---

19. *Id.*
20. *Id.*
21. *Wash. State Physicians Ins. v. Fisons Corp.*, 122 Wash. 2d 299, 325, 858 P.2d 1054, 1068 (1993).

wakening. We can be almost 100 percent confident on any given randomly selected morning that Reggie will brush his teeth. The "habit" of Reggie's "brushing-teeth-upon-wakening" therefore has a much higher probative value than Reggie's intermittent behavior of being "punctual at work."

Example 4

Doug Lars is a chain smoker. When he finishes one cigarette, he lights another. Even if he promises a host at a party not to smoke, shortly thereafter he is lighting up. When the hostess complains, Doug responds with genuine surprise, "I'm so sorry! I didn't even realize that I was doing that." Evidence of Doug's smoking habit would be admissible to prove that he was smoking on a particular occasion. The behavior is specific, regular, and non-volitional.

The Advisory Committee Note states both the probability and psychological theories of habit but does not choose between them. Yet choice is necessary. Thus, in the earlier example in which Paslitz watches the *Sliders* television show every Thursday night, the behavior is specific, oft-repeated, and regular, but probably not semi-automatic. The behavior would be more likely habit under the probability theory but not under the psychological theory.

Mengler argues that the Advisory Committee intended for the courts to resolve the dispute. Indeed, given the rules' general preference for trial court discretion and distrust of appellate review, Mengler concludes that trial courts were meant to resolve the question on a case-by-case basis. This would permit different definitions of habit to prevail in different cases, as the needs of the case dictated.

One important use of habit in modern trials is its manifestation as the "routine practice of an organization." In busy, often large, corporate or government entities, overworked staff may often forget the details of specific transactions. But businesses set up procedures that they rely on to maintain profit, efficiency, and effectiveness that function much like habits.

Example 5

The chair of a large law firm's litigation department is being deposed. He cannot remember whether he attended a particular department meeting on January 3, 2004, which was a Monday. However, further questioning reveals that the written firm policy manual mandates a litigation department meeting every Monday to be attended by all department members and presided over by the department chair. The Manual further requires written notice from any attorney who cannot attend any meeting, and requires the notice to be kept in the attorney's personnel file. No such note from this department chair is in his personnel file. Furthermore, the chair concedes that the firm has always rigidly enforced the terms of its policy manual. This evidence of the routine practice of the law firm strongly suggests that the chair was indeed present at the January 3 meeting and would likely be admissible per Rule 406.

Problem 5-60: Stolen Sneakers

The defendant was accused of stealing sneakers from My Left Foot, a sporting goods store. The defendant claimed at trial that he purchased the goods but was not given a sales receipt. The prosecution then attempted to introduce evidence showing that it was the custom of the store to give sales receipts with every purchase.

Is the evidence admissible? Why?

Must specific examples of the store's practice regarding receipts be provided prior to the admission of evidence showing the habit of a person or a routine business practice?

Problem 5-61: "The Hurrieder I Go, The Behinder I Get"

A fiery crash occurred between cars driven by plaintiff and defendant. Plaintiff claimed that defendant negligently caused the accident.

At trial, plaintiff attempted to introduce evidence that defendant "is always in a rush." *Admissible? Why?*

Plaintiff testifies that she "regularly uses turn signals" to prove that she used one at the time of the crash. *Is this permissible habit evidence? Why?*

Problem 5-62: Chivas

The defendant, Rob, is prosecuted for driving while intoxicated at 1:00 p.m. on a Tuesday. The state introduced evidence at trial that the defendant always drank a shot of Chivas Regal liquor promptly at noon every day.

Is the evidence admissible? Why?

Would it be admissible habit evidence if the state offered to show that Rob was in a habit of getting drunk every day around noon?

Problem 5-63: Don't Do Me Like That

The plaintiff claims he was fired from the police force because he exercised his First Amendment right to freedom of speech. The plaintiff offers evidence at trial that the police department routinely fired individuals who exercised their First Amendment rights, evidence that the department fired several different people for speaking out. *Is this evidence admissible? Why? See McWhorter v. City of Birmingham, 906 F.2d 674 (11th Cir. 1990).*

§ 5.07 Character Evidence Review Problems

In doing the problems below, first determine whether character evidence is admissible at all, then, if it is, in what form.

Problem 5-64: O.J. Mimpson Defamed

O.J. Mimpson, a well-known actor and former football star, has civilly sued Fred Moldman for defamation that occurred earlier this year. Moldman has said in newspaper interviews that "Mimpson is a wife-beater, and he finally killed his ex-wife and my son too, because he got in the way." The story concerned the stabbing-murder of Mimpson's ex-wife, Mikel Mimpson, and her friend, Bob Moldman, by a thus far unidentified assailant just four months ago. Mimpson is also being criminally prosecuted for murdering Mikel Mimpson and Bob Moldman.

1. Mimpson, in his civil case-in-chief, calls a well-qualified witness, Roland Butler, to testify that Mimpson has a reputation as a kind, peaceful man. Should Moldman's objection to this testimony be sustained? Would your answer differ if this were a criminal trial in which defendant Mimpson called this same witness in his case-in-chief?

2. If Butler were permitted to testify in the civil case, could Moldman's counsel on cross ask Butler:

   a. Did you know that 12 years ago defendant Mimpson was observed by police standing shirtless in his driveway, his then-wife Mikel in bra and panties crying nearby, while Mimpson held a baseball bat that he had just used to smash his car's windshield?

   b. Have you heard that seven years ago Mimpson hit Mikel on her forehead, then repeatedly slapped her, bruising her face and resulting in his no-contest plea to assault?

   c. Didn't Mr. Mimpson three years ago kick in his now ex-wife Mikel's double French doors, breaking the glass and threatening to kill Mikel?

3. Assume instead that Mimpson never called Butler to the stand. However, Mimpson himself offers this brief testimony: "I did not stab or kill my wife." Can Moldman's counsel successfully make any of the inquiries of Mimpson that were made of Butler in question 2a-c above?

4. Assume now that Mimpson's objections in Question 3 above were sustained. Can Moldman succeed in admitting evidence from any of the following witnesses:

   a. Harry Hamlin, to testify in the civil case that Mimpson has a reputation as a wife-beater? That Mimpson has a reputation as a violent man? Does your answer change if Hamlin were called by the prosecution in its case-in-chief in the criminal case?

   b. Rosy O'Gear, to testify in the civil case that he has been Mimpson's friend for 30 years, and, unfortunately, it is his opinion that Mimpson is a wife-beater? A violent man? Does your answer change if O'Gear were called by the prosecution in its case-in-chief in the criminal case?

   c. Various witnesses in the civil case, to testify from their personal knowledge to the incidents recounted in Questions 2a-c above? Does your answer change if the witnesses were called by the prosecution in its case-in-chief in the criminal case?

Problem 5-65: Wherefore Art Thou, Romeo?

Ronald Speiser shot Victor Romeo, paralyzing him from the waist down. Speiser's defense was that he was trying to protect his brother, Randy, from attack by Romeo and two other angry men. Randy testified in part as follows:

DEFENSE COUNSEL: Randy, were you present in this courthouse yesterday, the first day of this trial?

A: I was.

DEFENSE COUNSEL: Where precisely were you in the courthouse at about 2:00 p.m.?

A: I was in the hallway outside this courtroom, waiting for the lunch break to end.

DEFENSE COUNSEL: What, if anything, happened at that time?

A: Victor Romeo . . .

PROSECUTOR: Objection, Your Honor! Irrelevant. I'd ask for an offer of proof.

JUDGE: Counselor?

DEFENSE COUNSEL: *(at side bar)* Your Honor, this witness will testify that Romeo slammed the witness against the wall, smacked him in the face, and said, "This time your brother won't be able to protect you."

PROSECUTOR: I renew my irrelevance objection, and object as well on character evidence and hearsay grounds.

What ruling on the character evidence and relevance objections? Why? Would your ruling change if Randy instead just testified, "Everyone knows Victor Romeo, and he is a nasty, violent guy you want to stay clear of."

Problem 5-66: The Drunken Suspect

Gonzo Ravel is facing trial for burglarizing a supermarket; he stole meat, beer, and money by cutting a hole in the roof. Ravel's counsel calls Leonard Rundy to the stand to testify to Ravel's reputation as an honest, law-abiding citizen. The following exchange took place:

DEFENSE COUNSEL: Mr. Rundy, do you know others in your community who know Mr. Ravel?

A: Yes, practically everybody in the building. I am the janitor of 24 units and practically everybody in the units knows him because he does favors for them occasionally.

DEFENSE COUNSEL: Have you heard others in your community discuss . . . . ?

PROSECUTOR: Your Honor, may we approach the bench?

PROSECUTOR: *(at the bench)* Fair warning, Mr. [Counsel]. He has 20 public drunkenness arrests, two of which resulted in convictions. Once you put his character in evidence, I can ask this man about each and every one of them.

DEFENSE COUNSEL: Whose character, the defendant or the witness?

PROSECUTOR: You are starting to put the defendant's character in evidence, aren't you?

DEFENSE COUNSEL: What does Your Honor have to comment about this argument?

JUDGE: I am afraid it is correct.

DEFENSE COUNSEL: Well, I disagree and so note it for the record, but I will withdraw the question.

JUDGE: All right.

Should the trial court's ruling be reversed on appeal? Why or why not?

Problem 5-67: Officer's Character

Denny is on trial for dealing drugs. The sole witness to the alleged drug deal is a police officer, Officer Smith. Smith testifies that Denny sold him three grams of crack. The prosecutor then puts on another witness, Willie, who testifies that in Willie's experience with Officer Smith as a friend, spanning 12 years, Officer Smith is a truthful person. *Is Willie's testimony admissible?*

1. No, because the testimony's probative value does not substantially outweigh its unfairly prejudicial effect.

2. No, because evidence of the witness' character for truth telling is inadmissible.

3. Yes, so long as the testimony satisfies Rule 403.

4. Yes, so long as the testimony satisfies Rule 403, but if Officer Smith did not testify, Willie's testimony would be inadmissible.

Problem 5-68: Wife's Character

Denise is on trial for murdering her husband, Van. During her case-in-chief, which revolves primarily around self-defense, Denise calls a character witness, Wayne, to testify that he's lived in the same neighborhood as Denise for 14 years and that everyone in the neighborhood believes that Denise is a peaceful person because she broke up three different domestic disputes between her neighbors in recent years. *Is Wayne's testimony admissible?*

1. Yes, because Wayne may give opinion testimony about Denise's character.

2. Yes, because the testimony comprising other people's statements about Denise's character is not hearsay.

3. No, because the testimony is inadmissible character evidence.

4. No, because Wayne's testimony does not conform to an appropriate method of proving character.

Problem 5-69: Fruits and Vegetables

In 2012, Dantry is on trial for conspiracy to commit murder and testifies that she did not participate in the conspiracy because she was out of state at the time the murder was planned. In 2008, she was convicted of theft by deception for tampering with a scale in a small convenience store that she owned. She rigged the scale to add extra weight to customer's vegetable and fruit purchases, increasing the price. A state statute provided that a person commits theft by deception when they "obtain or exert unauthorized control of another person's property by deception or trick." The prosecutor seeks to admit a record of the 2008 conviction. *Permissible?*

1. Yes, because admitting the conviction is mandatory.

2. No, because the conviction is not probative of a pertinent character trait in the murder trial.

3. Yes, so long as the conviction's probative value outweighs its unfairly prejudicial effect.

4. No, because extrinsic evidence of Dantry's scale tampering is inadmissible pursuant to Rule 405.

Problem 5-70: Job Application

Dennis died in 2011. In a civil case tried in 2012 against Dennis' estate, Paul sued Dennis for fraud. Paul alleged that Dennis misrepresented the value of a business Paul purchased from Dennis by making false statements in a 2010 filing with the Securities and Exchange Commission. In 2005, Dennis filled out a job application at an unrelated business (Burger Emperor) and, under education, listed a master's degree from Texas Tech University that he never earned. During his case-in-chief, Paul seeks to introduce Dennis' statements in the job application at the 2012 fraud trial. *Is the job application admissible to establish Dennis' statements?*

1. No, because the job application contains inadmissible character evidence.

2. No, because the job application contains inadmissible hearsay.

3. Yes, so long as the court gives a proper limiting instruction.

4. Yes, because the job application establishes that Dennis had a character for untruthfulness.

Problem 5-71: Orwellian Defamation

Maxwell has civilly sued George Orwell for defamation. Maxwell's first Witness, Blue True, at trial testified that he overheard Orwell tell a local newspaper, *The Daily Globe:* "John Maxwell is a well-known liar; he raped my daughter, Rosetta, and now he's trying to lie his way out of it; just like he always does." *The Globe* printed this quote in a story about Rosetta's rape. When Maxwell calls his second witness, Father

O'Reilly (Maxwell's next-door neighbor and parish priest for the past 23 years), to testify that Maxwell has a reputation for truthfulness in the community in which they both live, Orwell objects. *Orwell's objection should be:*

1. Overruled because O'Reilly's testimony is admissible under both Rule 405(b) and Rule 608(a).

2. Overruled because O'Reilly's testimony is admissible under Rule 405(b) only.

3. Sustained because O'Reilly's testimony is a propensity use of character evidence.

4. Sustained because the mercy rule does not apply.

Problem 5-72: Perjuring Clergy

On cross-examining Father O'Reilly, Orwell's counsel asks the following question: "Isn't it true that you perjured yourself 11 years ago, lying to a grand juror about whether your brother ran an illegal gambling operation?" Assume that O'Reilly was never convicted of perjury, but that he did lie to the grand juror. *Maxwell's objection to this question should be:*

1. Sustained under Rule 609 because the perjury occurred more than 10 years ago.

2. Overruled under Rule 609 if Orwell gave sufficient written notice to Maxwell of the intent to ask the question, offered a fair opportunity to contest its admissibility, and provided specific facts and circumstances demonstrating that the evidence's probative value substantially outweighs it prejudicial effect.

3. Admissible under Rule 608(b) subject to Rule 403 and in the discretion of the court.

4. Inadmissible under Rule 608.

Problem 5-73: Perjuring Clergy Revisited

Assume that the trial judge permits the question in multiple-choice Problem 5-72 above to be asked, and in response, Father O'Reilly denies the perjury. Orwell's counsel later seeks in the defense case to call O'Reilly's brother to testify that he, the brother, had indeed been an illegal gambler, and had told O'Reilly about the gambling, and heard O'Reilly admit to lying about that knowledge to a grand jury. *Maxwell's objection to this testimony should be:*

1. Sustained because it is extrinsic evidence offered solely to prove character for truthfulness or untruthfulness.

2. Overruled because prior crimes used to impeach a witness may be proved by extrinsic evidence.

3. Overruled because, although it is extrinsic evidence that may prove character for truthfulness or untruthfulness, it is also relevant as proper impeachment by specific contradiction, provided it survives Rule 403 balancing.

4. Sustained because it is hearsay not fitting within a recognized exception.

Problem 5-74: False Cries

Same facts as Problem 5-71. But now assume that, instead of being at a civil defamation trial, Maxwell is the defendant in a criminal trial on charges that he raped Rosetta, and Rosetta has testified in the prosecution's case. The defense seeks to cross-examine Rosetta as a means of offering evidence that she falsely cried rape on three earlier occasions involving three men (one man per occasion) other than Maxwell. *This evidence should be:*

1. Inadmissible under Rule 412.

2. Admissible under Rule 412.

3. Admissible under Rule 413.

4. Admissible under Rule 608(b).

Problem 5-75: Reasonable Belief?

Now assume that Maxwell's defense at his rape trial is that he reasonably believed that Rosetta had consented. The prosecution proffers evidence that on three prior occasions Maxwell had sexual intercourse with three other women who charged Maxwell with rape, though each dropped the charges before the trial because they feared that the wealthy Maxwell would besmirch their names in the press. *The proffered evidence is:*

1. Inadmissible character-propensity evidence.

2. Admissible character-propensity evidence.

3. Admissible, if the trial court concludes that a reasonable jury could by the preponderance of the evidence believe that the three earlier incidents happened and involved the defendant as the three women described.

4. Admissible, if the trial court concludes that she is personally convinced by a preponderance of the evidence that the three earlier incidents happened and involved the defendant as the women described.

Problem 5-76: Simply Assaulting

Assume Maxwell takes the stand at his criminal rape trial and raises an alibi defense. On cross-examination, the prosecutor asks Maxwell to admit that he was convicted of misdemeanor simple assault one year ago. *Defense counsel's objection should be:*

1. Sustained because simple assault is not relevant to the issues in the case.

2. Overruled because simple assault is *crimen falsi*.

3. Sustained under both Rule 609 and Rule 404(a).

4. Sustained only under Rule 403.

Problem 5-77: Tax Fraud

Defendant Ozzie Harriet takes the stand as part of his defense. On cross-examination, the prosecutor asks Harriet whether he was convicted two years ago for tax fraud. *The question is:*

1. Proper to show Harriet is inclined to lie.

2. Proper to show that Harriet is inclined to steal.

3. Improper because the conviction has insufficient similarity to the crime charged.

4. Improper because the probative value of the evidence is outweighed by the danger of unfair prejudice.

Chapter 6

Other Exclusions of Relevant Evidence: The Quasi-Privileges

§ 6.01 Chapter Checklist

1a. Is evidence of "subsequent remedial measures" being offered, that is, of measures taken after an injury or harm occurs that make its reoccurrence less likely? *See* Rule 407.

1b. If yes, is the evidence offered to prove negligence, culpable conduct, a defect in a product's design, or a need for a warning or instruction, in which case it is not admissible, or is it instead offered for some other purpose, such as proving ownership, control, or feasibility of precautionary measures, in which case it may be admissible? *See* Rule 407.

2a. Is evidence being offered of (1) furnishing or offering or promising to furnish, or (2) accepting or offering, or promising to accept a valuable consideration to compromise or attempt to compromise a claim that is disputed as to either validity or amount, or of (3) conduct or statements made in compromise negotiations? *See* Rule 408.

2b. If yes, is the evidence offered to prove liability for or invalidity of a claim or its amount, in which case it is — with one exception — inadmissible, or is it instead offered for some other purpose, such as proving bias or prejudice of a witness, negating a contention of undue delay, or proving an effort to obstruct a criminal investigation, in which case it may be admissible? *See* Rule 408.

2c. Even if the evidence is offered to prove liability for or invalidity of a claim or its amount, which would ordinarily make it inadmissible, does the evidence consist of conduct or statements made in compromise negotiations in a criminal case in which the negotiations related to the claim of a public office or agency in the exercise of regulatory, investigative, or enforcement authority? If yes, contrary to the usual rule, the evidence is admissible.

3a. Is evidence being offered of furnishing or offering or promising to pay medical, hospital, or similar expenses occasioned by an injury? *See* Rule 409.

3b. If yes, is it offered to prove liability for injury, in which case it is inadmissible? *See* Rule 409.

4a. Is evidence being offered in any civil or criminal proceeding of (*see* Rule 410):

    (1) a plea of guilty later withdrawn?

    (2) a plea of *nolo contendere* (that is, "no contest," meaning that the defendant neither admits nor denies the crime but nevertheless agrees to be sentenced for it)?

    (3) any statement made in the course of any proceedings under Rule 11 of the Federal Rules of Criminal Procedure or comparable state procedure regarding either of the foregoing pleas?

    (4) any statement made in the course of plea discussions with an attorney for the prosecuting authority which does not result in a plea of guilty or which results in a plea of guilty later withdrawn?

4b. If yes, is the statement offered in any proceeding wherein another statement made in the course of the same plea or plea discussions has been introduced and the statement ought in fairness to be considered contemporaneously with it, or in a criminal proceeding for perjury or false statement if the statement was made by the defendant under oath, on the record, and in the presence of counsel? *See* Rule 410.

4c. If yes to 4b, the evidence may be admissible, but, if no, is the evidence offered against the defendant who made the plea or was a participant in the plea discussions, in which case it is inadmissible? *See* Rule 410.

5a. Is evidence offered that a person was or was not insured against liability? *See* Rule 411.

5b. If yes, is it offered on the issue whether the person acted negligently or otherwise wrongfully, in which case it is not admissible, or is it instead offered for another purpose, such as proof of agency, ownership, or control, or bias or prejudice of a witness in which case it may be admissible?

See Rule 411.

§ 6.02 Relevant Federal Rules of Evidence

Rule 407. Subsequent Remedial Measures

When measures are taken that would have made an earlier injury or harm less likely to occur, evidence of the subsequent measures is not admissible to prove:

- negligence;
- culpable conduct;
- a defect in a product or its design; or
- a need for a warning or instruction.

But the court may admit this evidence for another purpose, such as impeachment or — if disputed — proving ownership, control, or the feasibility of precautionary measures.

Rule 408. Compromise Offers and Negotiations

(a) PROHIBITED USES. Evidence of the following is not admissible — on behalf of any party — either to prove or disprove the validity or amount of a disputed claim or to impeach by a prior inconsistent statement or a contradiction:

(1) furnishing, promising, or offering — or accepting, promising to accept, or offering to accept — a valuable consideration in compromising or attempting to compromise the claim; and (2) conduct or a statement made during compromise negotiations about the claim — except when offered in a criminal case and when the negotiations related to a claim by a public office in the exercise of its regulatory, investigative, or enforcement authority.

(b) EXCEPTIONS. The court may admit this evidence for another purpose, such as proving a witness's bias or prejudice, negating a contention of undue delay, or proving an effort to obstruct a criminal investigation or prosecution.

Rule 409. Offers to Pay Medical and Similar Expenses

Evidence of furnishing, promising to pay, or offering to pay medical, hospital, or similar expenses resulting from an injury is not admissible to prove liability for the injury.

Rule 410. Pleas, Plea Discussions, and Related Statements

(a) PROHIBITED USES. In a civil or criminal case, evidence of the following is not admissible against the defendant who made the plea or participated in the plea discussions:

(1) a guilty plea that was later withdrawn;

(2) a nolo contendere plea;

(3) a statement made during a proceeding on either of those pleas under Federal Rule of Criminal Procedure 11 or a comparable state procedure; or

(4) a statement made during plea discussions with an attorney for the prosecuting authority if the discussions did not result in a guilty plea or they resulted in a later-withdrawn guilty plea.

(b) EXCEPTIONS. The court may admit a statement described in Rule 410(a)(3) or (4):

(1) in any proceeding in which another statement made during the same plea or plea discussions has been introduced, if in fairness the statements ought to be considered together; or

(2) in a criminal proceeding for perjury or false statement, if the defendant made the statement under oath, on the record, and with counsel present.

Rule 411. Liability Insurance

Evidence that a person was or was not insured against liability is not admissible to prove whether the person acted negligently or otherwise wrongfully. But the court may admit this evidence for another purpose, such as proving a witness's bias or prejudice or proving agency, ownership, or control.

§ 6.03   Overview

Exclusionary evidence rules are most often justified in one of two ways:

1. The evidence, if admitted, will mislead the jury or otherwise impede an accurate and efficient search for the truth.

2. Exclusion of the evidence will promote some public policy that has little to do with the "truth" in a specific case. For example, excluding illegally seized but highly probative evidence (a matter beyond the scope of this course) is often thought to encourage police to respect individuals' Fourth Amendment right to be free from unreasonable searches and seizures.

Evidence rules seen as primarily serving the second of these two goals are often called "privileges." There is no common term for rules that primarily serve the first goal, but that category would include most evidence rules other than privileges. Thus, the hearsay rule, the exclusion of most forms of character evidence, and the court's power to exclude unfairly prejudicial evidence with low probative value are often justified as aiding the search for the truth at trial. "Quasi-privileges" are rules justified as serving *both* the determination of truth and external public policies. Recent scholarship suggests, however, that *all* evidence rules at least partly serve goals unconnected with "truth" and that "truth" itself may be a notion imbued with value judgments. But we avoid entering that debate here. *See, e.g.,* Robert P. Burns, A Theory of the Trial (1999); Andrew E. Taslitz, *What Feminism Has to Offer Evidence Law*, 28 Sw. U. L. Rev. 171 (1999). Moreover, while some scholars prefer alternative phraseology, we find the term "quasi-privileges" a useful shorthand.

The major quasi-privileges are: (1) Rule 407's exclusion of much evidence of subsequent remedial measures; (2) Rules 408 and 410, which exclude much evidence of compromise negotiations; (3) Rule 409's bar on admitting evidence of offers to furnish, or payment of, a person's medical expenses to prove the offeror's liability for the injury; and (4) Rule 411's bar on admitting much evidence that a person was insured against liability.

§ 6.04   Subsequent Remedial Measures: Rule 407

After an incident that causes an injury, persons or organizations that are potentially responsible for the harm may take measures to prevent its recurrence. But if those persons or entities are later sued by the injured parties, those parties might offer evidence that the defendants took such "subsequent remedial measures." There are many reasons that evidence of subsequent remedial measures might be offered. Among the most problematic of such reasons is proving that the remediator was at fault for not fixing the problem sooner.

Example 1

John Smith drove a Volvo truck whose rear end was at the height of the heads of the drivers of most ordinary cars. One day, Smith suddenly changed lanes without signaling and was hit from behind. He was hit by a GM car driven by Ronald Patterson, who was instantly decapitated. Volvo immediately recalled all its trucks of the model involved in the accident to install "safety bars" that effectively lowered the rear of the trucks in a way that should avoid future decapitations in accidents like Patterson's. Patterson's estate sued Volvo, both for negligence in designing its truck and for defectively designing the truck, a theory of strict products liability. The estate sought at trial to offer evidence of the trucks' recall and of the installation of the safety bars (1) to prove Volvo's negligence in not earlier installing such bars on all trucks of this model, and (2) to show that the model's design was defective. This evidence seemed to be relevant under Rule 401 to show both Volvo's negligence and the defective design of the truck. However, were the evidence to be admitted at trial, Volvo might be reluctant to take corrective measures after future accidents revealing other defects, because Volvo would fear that evidence of such measures would be used against it at trial.

Partly to encourage such remedial measures, Rule 407 requires the exclusion of evidence like that immediately above against Volvo:

Rule 407. Subsequent Remedial Measures

When measures are taken that would have made an earlier injury or harm less likely to occur, evidence of the subsequent measures is not admissible to prove:

- negligence;
- culpable conduct;
- a defect in a product or its design; or
- a need for a warning or instruction.

But the court may admit this evidence for another purpose, such as impeachment or — if disputed — proving ownership, control, or the feasibility of precautionary measures.

The Advisory Committee considered the "social policy of encouraging people to take, or at least not discouraging them from taking, steps in furtherance of added safety" to be the "more impressive ground" for exclusion. Advisory Committee Note, Rule 407. The Committee noted that courts had applied this principle to exclude evidence of "subsequent repairs, installation of safety devices, changes in company rules, and discharge of employees" and that "the language of the present rule is broad enough to encompass all of them." While conceding that subsequent remedial measures might in a particular case have *some* relevance (*some* probative value) for each of the prohibited purposes, the Committee saw the probative value as minimal, thus further justifying the rule:

> The conduct is not in fact an admission, since the conduct is equally consistent with injury by mere accident or through contributory negligence. Or, as Baron Bramwell put it, the rule rejects the notion that "because the world gets wiser as it gets older therefore it was foolish before."

Some commentators describe Rule 407 as an "inclusionary rule," because the last sentence makes clear that subsequent remedial measures are admissible under Rule 407 (though they may be excluded by other rules) for any other purpose than the prohibited ones listed in the Rule's first sentence. The specific admissible purposes noted in the last sentence are, therefore, really just *non-exhaustive* examples of admissible purposes. Nevertheless, to avoid speculative claims that evidence is offered for an admissible purpose, given the dangers that jurors will use it for an inadmissible one, the last sentence requires that there be a real controversy about one of the listed issues to justify admissibility.

Example 2

Jana Fallahy, attending a party, slips on highly polished kitchen tile and severely injures her back. Reginald Melbourne, who gave the party, later replaces the tile with slip-resistant carpet. Jana sues Reginald for negligence in inviting partygoers into a home with slippery tile and offers evidence that the defendant replaced the tile with carpet. The defendant objects.

If the evidence is offered to prove Reginald's negligence in not earlier installing the carpet, the defense objection should be sustained. Suppose Jana's counsel argues that the evidence is really offered simply to show that Reginald owned the home in which the accident took place, which would render him responsible for its condition. For the evidence to be admissible for that purpose, the issue of ownership must be "controverted." If Reginald admitted ownership in his answer to the complaint, ownership is conceded, and the objection should be sustained. If, on the other hand, Reginald's answer denied ownership (perhaps claiming that he was just house-sitting and is at least not solely responsible for the injuries), then ownership is in dispute, and the objection should probably be overruled.

A careful lawyer must also be sensitive to this timing issue: to what event must the remedial measure be "subsequent"? Again, the 1997 Advisory Committee Note answers this question:

> [Under] the [1997] amendment to Rule 407 . . . , the words "an injury or harm allegedly caused by" were added to clarify that the rule applies only to changes made after the occurrence that produced the damages giving

rise to the action. Evidence of measures taken by the defendant prior to the "event" do not fall within the exclusionary scope of Rule 407 even if they occurred after the manufacture or design of the product.

Example 3

Assume that in the first example in this chapter, Volvo realized that its trucks created a decapitation danger because numerous Volvo trucks had been involved in similar accidents before Ronald Patterson's accident. All but one of the trucks — the one that killed Patterson — had the new "safety bars" added by the time Patterson was killed. Patterson offered, over defense objection, evidence of the recall and safety bar installation concerning all the other trucks to prove Volvo's negligence in the Patterson case. The objection should be overruled because the remedial measures, while "subsequent" to the "manufacture or design of the product," were not "subsequent" to the "occurrence that produced the damages giving rise to the action."

Problem 6-1: The Ruptured Bulldozer

John Faro was injured while operating a Ford F4 bulldozer. The injury occurred when a hydraulic hose ruptured; it sprayed him and the engine with a flammable liquid, which ignited on contact. Forty-eight percent of Faro's body was burned. Faro, who had been injured in New York State, sued Ford, a Michigan corporation, in federal court, on theories of negligent design and strict products liability. Specifically, Faro argued that a protective shield should have enclosed the driver, protecting him from being sprayed if any hose ruptured. Faro sought to call a witness who would testify that Ford in fact installed such shields on its F5 earth-moving scraper, three weeks after Faro's injury. But, upon Ford's objection, the trial court excluded this evidence.

At the motion *in limine* on whether to exclude this evidence, Faro's expert had testified that the F5 moving scraper's design was not different from the F4 bulldozer's design in any significant way that would prevent installing such deflection shields on the bulldozer too. Prior to this motion *in limine*, however, Faro had succeeded in admitting all of the following evidence to support the proposition that deflecting shields could have been installed on the F4 bulldozer: an instructional aid on mechanical engineering, an engineering code of ethics, an alleged shielding standard published by the International Standards Organization, internal Ford memoranda, magazine articles, and service letters regarding the effects of possible ruptures in the F4 hoses.

1. Did the trial judge rule correctly? Would any additional information help you to answer this question? Should the trial judge's ruling be reversed on appeal?

2. Would your answer to Question 1 change if Ford had offered an expert at the motion *in limine* who testified that F5 wheeled-earth moving scrapers, which scrape rocky roads flat, are of a radically different design from, and serve different functions than, the F4 bulldozer, which moves large amounts of earth

and dirt? What if he further testified that installing a shield on the F4 bull-dozer would have raised its cost by $10,000? That it was not yet scientifically feasible to install an effective deflecting shield on bulldozers?

3. Assume that, after excluding the evidence about the F5, and after plaintiff Faro rested, defendant Ford called an expert to the stand. Would your answer to Question 1 above change if the expert testified:

   a. That it is not scientifically feasible yet to install deflecting shields on bulldozers?

   b. That it is feasible but is prohibitively expensive?

   c. That it is not feasible on any construction equipment?

   d. That it is prohibitively expensive on any construction equipment?

Problem 6-2: The Painful Beach Party

John Patrick rented a beach house from Maurice Applebaum. One day, when Patrick threw a beach party at the house, a guest slipped in the outdoor shower and sustained serious back and neck injuries. Applebaum, hearing about the incident, came by one day and installed non-slip rubber mats on the shower floor. The guest sued both Patrick and Applebaum for the injuries suffered as a result of the slip in the shower. At trial, the plaintiff seeks to offer evidence of Applebaum's installing the non-slip mats. *Will this evidence be admissible against one or both of the defendants?*

Problem 6-3: Rotund University

A Rotund University School of Law student was recently raped while studying late at night in one of the study carrels in the stacks. The University hired an outside consulting firm to prepare a report on what steps, if any, the school could take to avoid future such incidents. The consultant recommended that the library be locked during night hours; that only students, faculty, and staff have keys; that locks be changed each semester; and that video cameras and emergency alarm buttons be installed on every floor. However, none of these changes has yet been implemented. The rape victim sues the University for damages and seeks to offer the report into evidence. *Ignoring hearsay issues, should the University's objection be sustained or overruled?*

§ 6.05 Offers to Compromise: Rules 408 and 410

A. Importance of Compromise in Civil and Criminal Cases

High percentages of both civil and criminal cases are resolved by compromise, generally by settlement agreements (civil cases) or plea bargains (criminal cases). Our legal system generally seeks to encourage compromises as fair and efficient ways to settle disputes, thus reducing the otherwise unmanageable burden on trial courts. At the same time, some claims are settled to avoid the costs and risk of a trial, rather than as an admission of responsibility or guilt, thus suggesting that compromises are of limited probative value in proving fault or guilt at trial. The Rules, in recognizing these policy concerns, often exclude evidence of compromises reached or statements made during compromise negotiations, though negotiations arising in the civil versus the criminal context are treated somewhat differently.

B. Evidence of Civil Settlement Agreements and Negotiations: Rule 408

Rule 408 addresses use of evidence of civil settlement agreements and negotiations in trials arising in the same or other cases than the one in which the negotiations took place:

Rule 408. Compromise Offers and Negotiations

(a) PROHIBITED USES. Evidence of the following is not admissible — on behalf of any party — either to prove or disprove the validity or amount of a disputed claim or to impeach by a prior inconsistent statement or a contradiction:

(1) furnishing, promising, or offering — or accepting, promising to accept, or offering to accept — a valuable consideration in compromising or attempting to compromise the claim; and (2) conduct or a statement made during compromise negotiations about the claim — except when offered in a criminal case and when the negotiations related to a claim by a public office in the exercise of its regulatory, investigative, or enforcement authority.

(b) EXCEPTIONS. The court may admit this evidence for another purpose, such as proving a witness's bias or prejudice, negating a contention of undue delay, or proving an effort to obstruct a criminal investigation or prosecution.

The Advisory Committee explained that it based Rule 408 (compromises and offers to compromise) on essentially the same two grounds as support Rule 407 (subsequent remedial measures):[1]

As with evidence of subsequent remedial measures, dealt with in Rule 407, exclusion [under Rule 408] may be based on two grounds: (1) The evidence is irrelevant, since the offer may be motivated by a desire for peace rather than from any concession of weakness of position. The validity of this position will vary as the amount of the offer varies in relation to the size of the claims and may also be influenced by other circumstances. (2) A more

---

1. Advisory Committee Note, Rule 408.

consistently impressive ground is promotion of the public policy favoring the compromise and settlement of disputes.

The Advisory Committee worried, however, that these purposes were not well served by the traditional approach, which excluded only the compromise itself, but admitted evidence of both negotiations leading up to a compromise and offers to compromise:[2]

> The practical value of the common law rule has been greatly diminished by its inapplicability to admissions of fact, even though made in the course of compromise negotiations, unless hypothetical, stated to be "without" prejudice, or so connected with the offer as to be inseparable from it. McCormick § 251, pp. 540–541. An inevitable effect is to inhibit freedom of communication with respect to compromise, even among lawyers. Another effect is the generation of controversy over whether a given statement falls within or without the protected area. These considerations account for the expansion of the rule herewith to include evidence of conduct or statements made in compromise negotiations, as well as the offer or completed compromise itself.

Example 1

Matt Wrightley is dying from lung cancer, allegedly caused by his 50 years of chain-smoking Winston-Salem cigarettes. He sues Winston-Salem, the manufacturer of the cigarettes, for failing to warn consumers adequately of the dangers of smoking, as these dangers were known to the cigarette manufacturers long before they were known to the federal government. During the course of settlement negotiations, the attorney for Winston-Salem concedes that a single study conducted by the company itself 40 years ago concluded that cigarettes could cause lung cancer but denies that this lone study constituted "knowledge" of a cancer danger. Winston-Salem did not at any point in the litigation produce such a report during discovery despite the plaintiff's requests. The company's attorney offered $1,000,000 to settle the suit. The plaintiff, declaring the offer obscenely low, walked out of the settlement negotiations, and the case proceeded to trial. Rule 408 prohibits introduction of either the $1,000,000 offer or the Winston-Salem lawyer's admission about the company's report concerning cancer danger if offered to prove either: (1) that Winston-Salem is liable for failing to convey early adequate warnings of cancer dangers to its customers, or (2) that Winston-Salem caused the plaintiff to suffer at least $1,000,000 in damages.

Example 2

Same example as above, but the case was indeed settled for $1,000,000. A new plaintiff sues Winston-Salem on the same theory as did Matt Wrightley,

---

2. *Id.*

seeking at trial to offer evidence of the Wrightley settlement as an admission of liability generally for negligently failing to make early and adequate warnings of the cancer dangers of its product. Winston-Salem's objection to this evidence will be sustained.

Rule 408 bars admitting evidence of accepting a compromise to settle a claim disputed as to validity or amount *at any future civil or criminal trial* to prove liability for the claim. An earlier version of the Rule declared that the Rule "does not require the exclusion of any evidence otherwise discoverable merely because it is presented in the course of compromise negotiations." This language was deleted by a 2006 amendment but, according to the Advisory Committee, this deletion was not done to effect any change in meaning but because the language was "superfluous." Although the "intent of the sentence was to prevent a party from immunizing admissible information, such as a pre-existing document, through the pretense of disclosing it during compromise negotiations," explained the Advisory Committee, "even without the sentence, the Rule cannot be read to protect pre-existing information simply because it was presented to the adversary in compromise negotiations."

Example 3

In the first Winston-Salem hypothetical above, assume that Winston-Salem does indeed admit in response to interrogatories that it has copies of its damaging internal cancer report in its possession. It refuses to produce the report, however, and later moves *in limine* to bar its introduction at trial, because the report was discussed during the failed settlement negotiations. While the *mention* of the report during settlement negotiations is inadmissible to prove liability or damages at trial, Rule 408 does not bar admission of the *report itself* for the same purposes. The Rule was never intended as a shield for otherwise discoverable documents.

Furthermore, because the report is likely admissible at trial, under rules consistent with the Federal Rules of Civil Procedure, Winston-Salem cannot withhold the report during discovery on the ground that the report is either inadmissible or unlikely to lead to admissible evidence.

Importantly, the Rule applies only to compromise offers concerning a claim that is "disputed as to either validity or amount." Rule 408. The Advisory Committee explains: "The policy considerations which underlie the rule do not come into play when the effort is to induce a creditor to settle an admittedly due amount for a lesser sum."

Example 4

The Classic Books Club sends one of its customers, Martha Evans, a letter threatening to sue her for $5,000 she owes them for books ordered and received at her request. She calls Classic Books, admits that she owes them the full $5,000, but says that it will cost her little to contest that fact and represent herself in any lawsuit. She therefore offers to pay $3,000, but not one penny more, arguing that it is in the company's interest to accept the settlement rather than face the litigation costs of suit. The company rejects her offer, files a complaint, and seeks to use her $3,000 settlement offer and admission of $5,000 liability against her at trial. Her objection under Rule 408 will be overruled because the negotiation statements concerned a matter not seriously disputed as to either "validity or amount."

Like Rule 407, Rule 408 is arguably an inclusionary rule because civil settlements, offers, and statements during compromise negotiations are not excluded by Rule 408 if offered for *any* purpose *other than* proving the validity or liability of the claim then in dispute. In particular, the Rule expressly declares that the use of compromise evidence for "proving bias or prejudice of a witness, negating a contention of undue delay, or proving an effort to obstruct a criminal investigation or prosecution" does "not require exclusion." To say that Rule 408 does not require exclusion does not mean, however, that some other rule might nevertheless exclude the evidence if a proper objection under another rule is made.

Example 5

Carter, Guttman, Inc., has been civilly sued for wrongful termination by its former employee, Harold Carswell. Carswell is also the star witness against Carter, Guttman, Inc., executives in a criminal bribery prosecution. The Chief Executive Officer of Carter, Guttman, Inc., offers to pay Carswell $2,000,000 to settle his civil suit for wrongful termination ($1,000,000 more than he asked for in that suit) if Carswell will leave the country before he can be subpoenaed in the criminal case and not return until the criminal case is resolved. Carswell refuses and reports the Carter, Guttman, Inc., proposal to the local prosecutor. The company's CEO is indicted for attempted obstruction of justice. In the criminal prosecution, the CEO objects under Rule 408 to evidence of his offer to settle the civil wrongful termination suit and of his related statements during settlement negotiations. This objection will be overruled. The evidence is not offered to prove that the company is liable for the civil claim but rather to prove the CEO's effort, in an unrelated case, "to obstruct a criminal investigation or prosecution."

Example 6

The Federal Railroad Administration ("FRA") has assessed a substantial civil fine against the Kay-Cee Railroad Company for violation of federal railroad safety regulations. Kay-Cee disputes both whether it has engaged in any violations in the first place and the size of the fines. The attorney for the FRA enters into negotiations over this matter with Kay-Cee. During those negotiations, Kay-Cee's President admits to knowing that certain safety violations had caused a railroad engineer's death yet ordered that the violations not be corrected because it would be cheaper just to pay the fine. As a result, as the company President further admits, a second engineer died, so the President finally ordered those violations corrected. The company and the FRA do ultimately agree to settle their fine dispute for approximately half the amount that FRA originally sought.

Subsequently, the U.S. Attorney files negligent homicide charges against Kay-Cee. At trial, the government seeks to offer testimony about the above statements made by Kay-Cee's President during the civil dispute. Kay-Cee objects under Rule 408 on the grounds that these were statements made during compromise negotiations. Although ordinarily such statements would be barred by the rule, the objection should be overruled because the statements fit within the exception for statements made during compromise negotiations relating to a civil claim "*by a public office or agency in the exercise of regulatory, investigative, or enforcement authority.*" Note that this exception applies only to the statements made during the civil negotiations, *not* to the furnishing or offering or accepting of consideration. As the Advisory Committee Note to the 2006 amendment that created this exception explains:

> The amendment distinguishes statements and conduct (such as a direct admission of fault) made in compromise negotiations of a civil claim by a government agency from an offer or acceptance of a compromise of such a claim. An offer or acceptance of a compromise of any civil claim is excluded under the Rule if offered against the defendant as an admission of fault. In that case, the predicate for the evidence would be that the defendant, by compromising with the government agency, has admitted the validity and amount of the civil claim, and that this admission has sufficient probative value to be considered as evidence of [criminal] guilt. But unlike a direct statement of fault, an offer or acceptance of a compromise is not very probative of the defendant's guilt. Moreover, admitting such an offer or acceptance could deter a defendant from settling a civil regulatory action, for fear of evidentiary use in a subsequent criminal action.

Remember too that the exception is only to Rule 408, not to other rules. Thus the statements by Kay-Cee's President still might be excluded under Rule 403 under appropriate circumstances. As the Advisory Committee Note again explains:

> Statements made in compromise negotiations of a claim by a government agency may be excluded in criminal cases where the circumstances so warrant under Rule 403. For example, if an individual was unrepresented at the time the statement was made in a civil enforcement proceeding, its probative value in a subsequent criminal case

may be minimal. But there is no absolute exclusion imposed by Rule 408.

Example 7

Assume instead that the family of the second engineer killed as a result of the Kay-Cee Railroad Company's safety violations mentioned in Example 6 has brought a civil suit for wrongful death against the railroad. The FRA has not yet assessed civil penalties or begun any negotiations with the company. However, during negotiations between the company and the engineer's family in the wrongful death suit, Kay-Cee's President admits that he knew that these violations had already caused one other death, that he did not order them corrected because of the expense of doing so, and that his failure contributed to this second engineer's death. No settlement agreement can be reached, however, so the case is scheduled for trial. Meanwhile, the local prosecutor's office brings criminal charges against Kay-Cee for negligent homicide. At the criminal trial, Kay-Cee objects under Rule 408 when the engineer's family member present at the civil negotiations is called to testify to the President's statements made during those negotiations. This objection will be sustained. Rule 408 generally bars admission of offers to settle, settlements, or statements made during civil settlement negotiations to prove fault or guilt respectively at *any* later civil or criminal trial *other than where the later criminal trial involves offering statements made during civil negotiations with a government regulatory, investigative, or enforcement agency.*

Why does the Rule prohibit offering civil compromise negotiation statements made in negotiations *between private parties* to prove guilt at a criminal trial but *not* prohibit them if the civil negotiations were with a government regulatory, investigative, or enforcement agency? Here is the Advisory Committee's justification for the general prohibition on using civil settlement negotiation statements at later criminal trials to prove guilt:

> [S]tatements made during compromise negotiations of other disputed claims [that is, *other than* those claims involving the government] are not admissible in subsequent criminal litigation, when offered to prove liability for, invalidity of, or amount of those claims. When private parties enter into compromise negotiations they cannot protect against the subsequent use of statements in criminal cases by way of private ordering. The inability to guarantee protection against subsequent use could lead to parties refusing to admit fault, even if by doing so they could favorably settle the private matter. Such a chill on settlement negotiations would be contrary to the policy of Rule 408.

By contrast, the Advisory Committee believed that it was fair to admit such statements where negotiations were with the government rather than with private parties. There were two reasons for this conclusion: first, the parties should expect that statements made to one governmental entity might be reported to another one; and, second, governmental negotiators may be able to gain concessions from, or at times bind, other governmental actors (specifically prosecutors) where that is necessary to obtaining a civil settlement. In other words, the civil parties can by contract negotiate prohibitions against use of civil compromise negotiations in a later criminal trial — prohibitions not created by Rule 408. The underlying theory seems to be that the default position should be admissibility because that empowers governmental negotiators. However, those negotiators can move away from that default where it is in the public interest to do so. It will be in the public interest to do so where the state sees it as worthwhile to forego using the civil settlement negotiation statements as evidence in a criminal case where that is the only way to get the other side to agree to settle the civil matter. The other side, correspondingly, sees it as not worth settling the civil case if it risks criminal conviction in a serious matter. In the Advisory Committee's words:

> [T]he [2006] amendment provides that Rule 408 does not prohibit the introduction in a criminal case of statements or conduct during compromise negotiations regarding a civil dispute by a government regulatory, investigative, or enforcement agency. *See, e.g., United States v. Prewitt,* 34 F.3d 436, 439 (7th Cir. 1994) (admissions of fault made in compromise of a civil securities enforcement action were admissible against the accused in a subsequent criminal action for mail fraud). Where an individual makes a statement in the presence of government agents, its subsequent admission in a criminal case should not be unexpected. The individual can seek to protect against subsequent disclosure through negotiation and agreement with the civil regulator or an attorney for the government.

Example 8

Jason Dunkin is involved in a car crash in which he hits another car at high speed, seriously injuring the other car's driver. That driver has sued Jason for damages caused by Jason's negligent driving. The whole suit turns on whether Jason ran a red light. During settlement negotiations, Jason admits that he ran the red light, but no settlement is reached because the two parties cannot agree on damages. The case goes to trial, and Jason takes the stand, this time testifying that the light facing him was green, not red, when he entered the intersection. Plaintiff's counsel seeks to cross-examine Jason with reference to his admission during settlement negotiations that the light facing him was in fact red, not green, at the time of the accident. Plaintiff's counsel's theory for admission is that the statement is simply being offered to impeach by a prior inconsistent statement, not to prove validity or invalidity of the claim or amount. Jason's lawyer objects. His objection should be sustained, for Rule 408, as amended in 2006, expressly states that when the requirements set forth in parts (1) or (2) of the rule are otherwise met, the rule bars using settlement offers or statements made during them to impeach if the impeachment method is by contradiction or use of a prior inconsistent statement. Here is the 2006 Advisory Committee Note's justification for this position:

> The amendment prohibits the use of statements made during settlement negotiations when offered to impeach by prior inconsistent statement or through contradiction. Such broad impeachment would tend to swallow the exclusionary rule and would impair the public policy of promoting settlements. *See* McCormick on Evidence at 186 (5th ed. 1999) ("Use of statements made in compromise negotiations to impeach the testimony of a party, which is not specifically treated in [original] Rule 408, is fraught with danger of misuse of the statements to prove liability, threatens frank interchange of information during negotiations, and generally should not be permitted."). *See also EEOC v. Gear Petroleum, Inc.*, 948 F.2d 1542 (10th Cir. 1991) (letter sent as part of settlement negotiation cannot be used to impeach defense witness by way of contradiction or prior inconsistent statement; such broad impeachment would undermine the policy of encouraging uninhibited settlement negotiations).

Example 9

Assume that during the negotiations in the immediately preceding example, Jason Dunkin had also said, "I never went one mile per hour past the speed limit" and that the plaintiff alleged that Jason was negligent both in running a red light and in speeding. No settlement is reached, and the case goes to trial. At trial, Jason seeks to offer his own statement made during the negotiations denying speeding as substantive evidence that he in fact was not speeding at the time. The plaintiff objects. The objection will be sustained. According to the Advisory Committee, again in its 2006 Note:

> The amendment makes clear that Rule 408 excludes compromise evidence even when a party seeks to admit its own settlement offer or statements made in settlement negotiations. If a party were to reveal its own statement or offer, this could reveal the fact that the adversary entered into settlement negotiations. The protections of Rule 408 cannot be waived unilaterally because the Rule, by definition, protects both parties from having the fact of negotiation disclosed to the jury. Moreover, proof of statements and offers made in settlement would often have to be made through the testimony of attorneys, leading to the risks and costs of disqualification. *See generally Pierce v. Tripler & Co.*, 955 F.2d 820, 828 (2nd Cir. 1992) (settlement offers are excluded under Rule 408 even if it is the offeror who seeks to admit

them; noting that the "widespread admissibility of the substance of settlement offers could bring with it a rash of motions for disqualification of a party's chosen counsel who would likely become a witness at trial.").

Problem 6-4: The Car Crash

Two cars collide. One driver, Harry Marsden, said to the other driver, Julian Cort, "Look, let's not hassle this; will you take $1,000, and let's forget the whole thing?" Cort subsequently files a civil complaint against Marsden, seeking damages caused by Marsden's negligence. *Will any or all of Marsden's statements be admissible at the subsequent trial on this complaint? Why or why not?*

What if, instead, Marsden said, "I screwed up; I wasn't paying attention. How about taking $1,000 to forget the whole thing?" *Will any or all of these statements be admissible? Why or why not?*

Problem 6-5: The Non-Settling Defendant

Plaintiff Robert Belton filed a diversity action against Pittsburgh Corning and 15 other defendants, alleging that exposure to their asbestos-containing products caused him to develop various diseases. Immediately before trial, the 15 defendants other than Corning settled with plaintiff Belton. Corning, in its opening statement to the jury, stated that it would prove that plaintiff had been exposed to asbestos-containing products manufactured by 15 other companies, identifying them by name. Those companies were the settling defendants, though the jury did not yet know this. Thus, Corning argued, plaintiff could not prove that any of his injuries were caused by Corning's products. Over Corning's objection, however, plaintiff presented evidence in the liability phase of the trial that each of the 15 other defendants had settled immediately before trial, though the amounts of the settlements were not revealed. The jury entered a verdict in favor of the plaintiff, and the case proceeded to the damages phase.

At the damages phase, again over defense objection, the plaintiff presented evidence of the precise amount of the settlement agreements. The jury returned a massive verdict against Corning. *Were either or both of the trial judge's rulings in error? Why?*

Problem 6-6: The Recalcitrant Health Insurer

Dallas Park's health insurer was Aetna Life Insurance Company. Park obtained "immuno-augmentative" anti-cancer treatment at the Immunology Center (IC) in Freeport, Bahamas, when more traditional treatments had failed. Aetna refused to reimburse Park for the cost of these treatments on the ground that the treatments were not broadly accepted in the medical profession and were not necessary to treat her cancer.

1. At trial, Park offers evidence that another Aetna insured who had been treated with the same sort of anti-cancer therapy at the IC was reimbursed in full by Aetna without any dispute. Aetna objects. If you were the trial judge, how would you rule and why?

2. Assume the same facts, but with one variation: Aetna had, by letter, expressed a concern to the earlier insured about the efficacy and necessity of these treatments. That insured asked to have an Aetna representative meet with the insured and her physician. Mid-way during that meeting, the Aetna representative said, "Well, you've convinced me. These really are effective treatments in cases like yours, and we will be happy to cover them." Again, if you were the trial judge in *Park v. Aetna*, how would you rule, and why?

3. Now assume that, in the present case of *Park v. Aetna*, the parties met to try to negotiate a settlement. This time, the Aetna representative says, during the negotiations, "This really is an effective, promising treatment in many cases, but the amount you are requesting to settle the claim is ridiculously large." At trial, another Aetna representative, much higher in the company hierarchy, testified, "We long ago concluded that these treatments are worthless in fighting Mr. Park's sort of cancer, and all our representatives are trained to understand this conclusion." Plaintiffs counsel asks this latter Aetna representative, "Didn't Mr. McAuliffe [the first Aetna representative] meet with my client and admit that this treatment is effective? Didn't he contest only the amount of the claim?" Aetna objects. How should the trial judge rule?

4. Returning to the facts of Problem 6-5, assume that plaintiff Belton calls each of the settling co-defendants to the stand to testify during the liability phase that each of them manufactured a type of asbestos different from the unique type made only by Corning. They so testify to lay the groundwork for plaintiff's experts to testify that the asbestos particles found in plaintiff's lungs were of the unique type made by Corning. Assume further in this variation that the trial judge has not told the jury of Belton's settlements with the 15 co-defendants and has no intention of doing so. Corning's counsel on cross-examination asks each co-defendant, "Isn't it true that you were originally named as a co-defendant in this lawsuit and that you settled with the plaintiff immediately before this trial? And isn't it further true that a condition of this settlement was that you would testify as you now have at his trial?" Objections to both questions were sustained as to each witness. Did the trial judge rule correctly?

5. What if, in part 2 above, Aetna offered to settle the claim for $50,000? At trial, an Aetna representative testifies that the medical treatment is worthless in fighting cancer. Can plaintiff's counsel impeach the representative with the $50,000 settlement offer, arguing that it shows that Aetna did, contrary to the representative's testimony, recognize that the treatment indeed had value?

6. Assume the facts of part 2 above. At trial, Park seeks to have his physician testify about the same medical research presented during the part 3 settlement negotiations that enabled Park to get Aetna tentatively to concede the value of the treatment. Aetna objects on the ground that the jury would be exposed to "evidence of conduct or statements made in compromise negotiations." How should the trial judge rule?

Problem 6-7: Megatech

Marc Wayne is the CEO of Megatech, Inc, a corporation involved in agribusiness. Megatech has allegedly failed to obey Environmental Protection Agency ("EPA") regulations governing the disposal of animal waste on its farms. Small family-run corn farmers on adjacent land maintain that the run-off of animal waste from Megatech farms is killing nearby corn crops. The small farmers jointly bring a class action suit against Megatech for damages for negligence and for an injunction in abatement of a nuisance. The farmers also report the matter to the EPA, which begins an investigation. As a result of that investigation, the EPA concludes that there have been serious violations of its regulations, and they seek civil penalties as well as strict future compliance with the law, threatening to sue Megatech if their demands are not promptly met. Megatech meets with the farmers to discuss settlement of their suit. During that meeting, CEO Wayne says, "I've known for years that our run-off was draining into your farms, but I had no idea that animal waste run-off could be dangerous to corn crops, I don't see how I could have known, and we just aren't responsible for any damages." After much haggling, the suit is settled for $1,000,000. The EPA thereafter meets with Megatech, insisting that the settlement is a paltry sum and does not prevent future harms. The EPA still seeks civil penalties and wants an agreement to changes in farming practices that will minimize future run-off. During this negotiation with EPA, CEO Wayne says, "Look, my employees have been telling me for at least two years that animal waste run-off could harm the adjacent corn crops, but they never showed me any scientific evidence to support it, and I wasn't going to kill our profits by putting big bucks into alleviating the problem if it didn't really hurt anyone." EPA refuses to settle and files a civil action against Megatech. Simultaneously, the United States Attorney files federal criminal charges against Megatech for violating federal criminal environmental law statutes.

1. At the criminal trial, the prosecution seeks to offer into evidence CEO Wayne's statement from Megatech's negotiation with the small farmers, "I've known for years that our run-off was draining into your farms." Megatech objects. Sustained or overruled?

2. Suppose that the objection in Question 1 is sustained. Now Megatech, in its case-in-chief, seeks to offer into evidence the statement of its CEO made during settlement negotiations with the small farmers that he "had no idea that animal waste run-off could be dangerous to corn crops, I don't see how I could have known, and we just aren't responsible for any damages." The CEO has not taken the stand, but other Megatech employees present at the negotiation

are available to testify to CEO Wayne's statements. The prosecution objects. How should the judge rule?

3. Assume now that CEO Wayne takes the stand at Megatech's criminal trial and denies ever having been aware, until the farmers complained to him, that any Megatech animal waste was running onto adjacent farmers' land. On cross-examination, the prosecution seeks to have Wayne admit to his statement during his civil negotiation with the small farmers that he had "known for years that our run-off was draining onto your farms." Megatech objects to the question. Sustained or overruled?

4. The prosecution seeks to offer into evidence the fact that Megatech settled with the farmers for $1,000,000, arguing that that settlement constituted an admission of guilt. Megatech objects. How should the trial judge rule?

5. The prosecution next seeks to offer in its case-in-chief at the criminal trial the statement that CEO Wayne made to the EPA: "Look, my employees have been telling me for at least two years that animal waste run-off could harm adjacent corn crops." Megatech objects. How should the trial judge rule?

6. Assume that the objection in Question 5 is sustained. CEO Wayne later takes the stand in Megatech's case-in-chief, testifying that no one had ever warned him before he met with the farmers that animal waste run-off could kill corn crops. The prosecution seeks on cross to have Wayne admit to his statement to the EPA that "my employees have been telling me for at least two years that animal waste run-off could harm adjacent corn crops." Megatech objects. Sustained or overruled?

7. Wayne is still on the stand. Prosecutors seek on cross to have him admit to his statement to the EPA that he "wasn't going to kill our profits by putting big bucks into alleviating the problem [of run-off harming corn crops]." Megatech objects. Sustained or overruled? Does your answer depend upon whether the objection to Question 6 was sustained or overruled?

8. Megatech seeks in its case-in-chief to offer evidence of Wayne's statement during Megatech's negotiations with the small farmers that he had "no idea that animal waste run-off could be dangerous to corn crops" and he "didn't see how [he] could have known," and Megatech just is not "responsible for any damages." The prosecution objects. How should the trial judge rule?

9. Could Megatech's attorney have reduced the risk of evidence of Wayne's statements made during civil negotiations with the EPA being admitted in evidence against Megatech at a potential later criminal trial? How?

10. Would your answers to any of the above questions change if CEO Wayne himself, and not Megatech, was being criminally tried?

11. Would your answers to any of the above questions change if, instead of CEO Wayne making the statements noted above, Megatech's lawyer had made the statements, that is, for example, the lawyer admitted that Wayne knew

about the run-off for years? (Assume that Wayne was not even present at the negotiations.)

12. Would your answers to any of the above questions change if the evidence noted were sought to be offered at the trial of the civil suit brought by the EPA rather than at a criminal trial?

C. Plea Bargains and Related Statements in Criminal Cases: Rule 410

Rule 410 addresses the use of evidence in any proceeding, civil or criminal, of guilty plea negotiations arising from a criminal case. Rule 410's general prohibition on using such evidence reads as follows:

Rule 410. Pleas, Plea Discussions, and Related Statements

(a) **PROHIBITED USES.** In a civil or criminal case, evidence of the following is not admissible against the defendant who made the plea or participated in the plea discussions:

(1) a guilty plea that was later withdrawn;

(2) a nolo contendere plea;

(3) a statement made during a proceeding on either of those pleas under Federal Rule of Criminal Procedure 11 or a comparable state procedure; or

(4) a statement made during plea discussions with an attorney for the prosecuting authority if the discussions did not result in a guilty plea or they resulted in a later-withdrawn guilty plea.

(b) **EXCEPTIONS.** The court may admit a statement described in Rule 410(a)(3) or (4):

(1) in any proceeding in which another statement made during the same plea or plea discussions has been introduced, if in fairness the statements ought to be considered together; or

(2) in a criminal proceeding for perjury or false statement, if the defendant made the statement under oath, on the record, and with counsel present.

The purpose of this rule is to encourage plea negotiations between the prosecution and the defense, by assuring defendants that, if the negotiations fail, the defendants' statements will not be used against them at trial. If the prosecution and defense reach a plea agreement, that agreement must be approved by the trial judge. The trial judge conducts a "colloquy" in open court in which the defendant is questioned under oath to ensure that his or her decision to plead guilty was knowingly, intelligently, and voluntarily made. The defendants will thus be informed of the content and implications of the rights being waived by entering the guilty plea (such as the right to a jury trial); of the potential penalties that may result from pleading guilty; and of the limited grounds for appealing or withdrawing a guilty plea. Additionally, the prosecutor usually reads a summary of the facts to which the defendant admits.

Once a plea is entered, it may be withdrawn only for a very few, narrow reasons such as that the plea was involuntary or that defense counsel was ineffective in advising the defendant to plead guilty. Even then, proving these grounds can be hard, since the plea would not have been accepted until after a detailed colloquy in which the defendant, for example, denied that he or she was pressured in any way to enter into the plea. Nevertheless, if the court does permit the plea to be withdrawn and the case proceeds to trial, subsection (1) prohibits using the fact of the plea against the defendant at that trial or in any other civil or criminal proceeding. Subsection (2) extends similar protection to statements made during the colloquy, which is the procedure described in subsection (3) as a "proceeding on either of those please under Federal Rule of Criminal Procedure 11 or comparable state procedure . . . ." The prohibition against using colloquy statements applies in any future civil or criminal proceeding, even if the resulting guilty plea is not withdrawn.

A "*nolo contendere*" or "no contest" plea is, in common sense terms, a statement by the defendant that, "I will neither admit nor deny that I am guilty, but I will not contest the charge, and I therefore agree to allow the state to sentence me as if I were guilty." A defendant entering a no contest plea faces the same criminal penalties as one entering a guilty plea. However, there is one huge advantage in entering a *nolo* plea: the plea may not usually (though there are some exceptions beyond the scope of this course) be used against a defendant as an admission of guilt in a subsequent civil case. A colloquy is also required, though a defendant may be asked only to concede that the state can prove an agreed-upon summary of facts rather than admitting (as he would with a guilty plea) that those facts actually happened.

Subsections (2) and (3) of Rule 410 extend the same evidentiary protections to a no contest plea as they extend to a guilty plea later withdrawn, including protection of statements made during the colloquy. Subsection (4) further extends protection to any statements made between the defendant or defense counsel and the prosecutor while attempting to negotiate a guilty plea, even if no plea ever results or a plea does result but is later withdrawn. In this respect, Rule 410 differs from the analogous Rule 408 for civil settlement negotiations. Under Rule 408, statements made during negotiations with any person involved in the case are protected (for example, with an insurance company agent trying to settle a civil claim before suit is brought). Under Rule 410, however, negotiations are protected only if they are made *with the prosecutor*. Statements to the police are outside Rule 410's scope. Thus, statements made during purported negotiations between a defendant and interrogating police officers are not barred by this rule (unless, of course, the officers are acting as agents for the prosecutor for these purposes — in which case the statements made to the police would be protected by Rule 410 because they would in effect really be statements to the prosecutor). Although statements made to police officers during purported settlement negotiations where the officers are not acting on behalf of the prosecutors are not protected by Rule 410, they may under certain circumstances be barred by other rules, such as the constitutional prohibition against involuntary confessions.

Rule 410 provides broader protection than Rule 408 in at least one respect, however: evidence of a guilty plea later withdrawn or a *nolo* plea may not be admitted to show bias or for any other purpose unconnected to criminal liability for the offense charged. Unlike Rule 408, under which civil settlement offers or agreements are excluded from trial only if offered for the purpose of proving liability for or invalidity of the claim or its amount, Rule 410 excludes withdrawn pleas or offers to plead for *any purpose whatsoever*, other than two narrow exceptions discussed below. The same is true for statements made in the course of plea discussions with the prosecuting authority. These discussions must, however, involve an attempted *quid pro quo*, thus involving a "plea" and not simply an admission. *Compare United States v. Leon Guerrero*, 847 F. 2d 1363, 1367 (9th Cir. 1988) (making this determination by inquiring whether the offender had an actual and reasonable expectation that he was negotiating a plea), *with State v. Fox*, 760 P. 2d 670, 674–675 (Haw. 1988) (Rule's language requires only a subjective inquiry into the offender's state of mind).

Importantly, however, Rule 410 does not extend protection against using a guilty plea against the declarant in another civil or criminal case if the plea is never withdrawn and becomes the basis for a conviction. A guilty plea in a criminal case is therefore often admissible as a party admission in a civil case. *See* Chapter 13.

> Rule 410 continues with the following provisions creating exceptions to the general rules outlined above:
>
> **EXCEPTIONS.** The court may admit a statement described in Rule 410(a) (3) or (4):
>
> (1) in any proceeding in which another statement made during the same plea or plea discussions has been introduced, if in fairness the statements ought to be considered together; or
>
> (2) in a criminal proceeding for perjury or false statement, if the defendant made the statement under oath, on the record, and with counsel present.

The rationale for the first exception (concerning statements that ought in fairness be considered together) has been explained by the Rules of Criminal Procedure Advisory Committee Note to Rule 11(e)(6) of the Federal Rules of Criminal Procedure, which Rule corresponds to Rule 410, thus:

> This change is necessary so that, when evidence of statements made in the course of or as a consequence of a certain plea or plea discussion are introduced under circumstances not prohibited by this rule (e.g., not "against" the person who made the plea), other statements relating to the same plea

or plea discussions may also be admitted when relevant to the matter at issue. For example, if a defendant upon a motion to dismiss a prosecution on some ground were able to admit certain statements made in aborted plea discussions in his favor, then other relevant statements made in the same plea discussions should be admissible against the defendant in the interest of determining the truth of the matter at issue.

The second exception permits, for example, a perjury prosecution based on the defendant's lies under oath in a guilty plea colloquy. The colloquy statements may be used against the defendant at a perjury trial.

The United States Supreme Court has read a third exception into the Rule as implied by its nature and the nature of the adversary system: a defendant may waive the right to the rule's protection if the prosecutor insists on such a waiver as a precondition to the plea negotiations.

The Court recognized this waiver rule in *United States v. Mezzanatto* (513 U.S. 196, 115 S. Ct. 797, 130 L. Ed. 2d 697 (1995). There, a defendant charged with possessing methamphetamine with intent to distribute it sought to negotiate a plea with the prosecutor. The prosecutor agreed to do so only if the defendant first agreed — which he did — that any statements made during the negotiation could be used to impeach him should the case go to trial. During the negotiations, however, the defendant sought to shift primary responsibility to another individual, a Mr. Shuster. The prosecutor thus cut short the negotiations, believing that the defendant had lied. At trial, the prosecutor, over defense objection, impeached the defendant with prior inconsistent statements that he had made during the plea bargaining. The jury convicted him, and he appealed, arguing that he had been impeached in violation of Rule 410 of the Federal Rules of Evidence. The Ninth Circuit reversed the defendant's conviction, holding that, because neither Rule 410 nor its two narrowly drafted exceptions said anything about waiver, Congress must have meant to preclude it.

The United Stated Supreme Court, however, reversed the Ninth Circuit, reinstating the conviction. First, the Court was unconvinced that the Rule's silence about waiver mattered, given the routine trial practice of granting waivers for tactical purposes. Second, the Court believed that the waiver agreements before it would enhance truth-seeking by discouraging lies. Third, said the Court, the Rule's reference to making certain statements inadmissible "against" the defendant, and its exception where a defendant has first offered such statements in his favor, contemplates the tactical freedom of a defendant to agree to the use of such statements where he believes that the result may work in his favor. Fourth, and most importantly, the Court rejected the argument that permitting waivers would defeat the Rule's purpose of encouraging plea bargains:[3]

> To use the Ninth Circuit's metaphor, if the prosecutor is interested in "buying" the reliability assurance that accompanies a waiver agreement, then

---

3. 513 U.S. at 208.

precluding waiver can only stifle the market for plea bargains. A defendant can "maximize" what he has to "sell" only if he is permitted to offer what the prosecutor is most interested in buying. And while it is certainly true that prosecutors often need help from the small fish in a conspiracy in order to catch the big ones, that is no reason to preclude waiver altogether. If prosecutors decide that certain crucial information will be gained only by preserving the inadmissibility of plea statements, they will agree to leave intact the exclusionary provisions of the plea-statement rules.

Justice Souter dissented on a number of grounds, most importantly rejecting the conclusion that Congress meant to leave waiver to the mercy of market forces. Souter believed that waivers would diminish the "zone of unrestrained candor" because a defendant must pause to think whether the guilty plea negotiations are worth the risk, thus undermining the Rule's pro-plea-negotiation purpose.[4]

Problem 6-8: Rodney Ransom

Rodney Ransom is the driver of a car that was involved in an accident with a car driven by Myron Cohen. A police officer who arrived on the scene gave Ransom a ticket for reckless driving. Cohen civilly sues Ransom on a negligence theory. When Ransom meets with his newly retained defense lawyer, Lola Brandon, Ransom says, "I'll just go down to traffic court and plead guilty, so at least that will be over with, and we can concentrate on the silly civil suit. OK?" *What advice should Ransom's lawyer give him in response to this question? Why?*

Problem 6-9: Turning on Mr. Big

Morris Mumford is arrested on a charge of distributing cocaine. Detective Jacob Marlee tells Mumford, "Look, I know you're just a little guy. If you turn in Mr. Big, the prosecutor has promised me you'll get probation." Mumford then recounted the complete details of his involvement in the cocaine distribution scheme, and this confession was admitted against him at trial, over Mumford's objection. *Did the trial judge rule correctly? Does it matter, in reaching this decision, whether Marlee told Mumford the truth?*

Problem 6-10: Waiving Rule 410

Assume that in Problem 6-9 above, the prosecutor joins Marlee's discussions with Mumford, but the prosecutor agrees to discuss a plea with Mumford only if he first waives his right to exclude his statements from trial under Rule 410. At first, Mumford refuses, saying he does not understand what Rule 410 is and does not want to give up something without knowing its importance. The prosecutor leaves the room to make a phone call. While he is gone, Marlee tells Mumford, "Trust me, if you don't agree to this waiver thing, you're going away for at least 20 years." When the

---

4. *Id.* at 214–215.

prosecutor returns, Mumford agrees to the waiver and confesses everything. The prosecutor believes that Mumford is lying about some details and refuses to agree to a plea. At Mumford's trial, the prosecutor calls Marlee to the stand to recount Mumford's confession. The defense objects. *How should the trial judge rule? Are there any additional facts that would help you in answering this question? What facts?*

1. What if, on this same set of facts, Mumford and the prosecutor do reach an agreement. Mumford recounts the details of the crime during the plea colloquy, and a plea is entered. Subsequently, the prosecutor obtains evidence that some of what Mumford said during the colloquy was false. May the colloquy statements be admitted against Mumford at his later perjury trial?

2. Suppose in a civil case against Mumford for the wrongful death of a teenager who died from an overdose of drugs sold to him by Mumford, Mumford takes the stand and denies any involvement in a drug distribution scheme.

   a. Under the original set of facts here, in which no plea agreement is reached, may Mumford's statements made during plea negotiations be used to impeach him at his civil trial?

   b. Under variation 1, may the fact of his plea be used to impeach him at the civil trial?

   c. Under variation 1, assume that Mumford successfully withdraws his guilty plea. Before that criminal case proceeds to trial, he testifies in the civil case, denying involvement in the drug scheme. May his colloquy statements be used to impeach him at the civil trial?

§ 6.06 Payment of Medical and Similar Expenses

Rule 409 reads as follows:

Rule 409. Offers to Pay Medical and Similar Expenses

> Evidence of furnishing, promising to pay, or offering to pay medical, hospital, or similar expenses resulting from an injury is not admissible to prove liability for the injury.

Example 1

Layla DePaul rear-ends a car driven by Lindsey Lee. Lindsey exits the car, able to speak but complaining of back pain. Layla says, "Don't worry. We'll get you immediate medical care, and if your insurance company won't pay for it, I will." Layla's statement will be excluded from evidence, upon Layla's objection, at any trial in which Lindsey or someone acting on her behalf seeks to recover damages from Layla.

The Advisory Committee Note explains the rationale for the rule:[5]

> [G]enerally, evidence of payment of medical, hospital, or similar expenses of an injured party by the opposing party, is not admissible, the reason often given being that such payment or offer is usually made from humane impulses and not from an admission of liability, and that to hold otherwise would tend to discourage assistance to the injured person.

Rule 409 differs from Rules 408 and 410 in that Rule 409 does not extend to "conduct or statements not a part of the act of furnishing or offering or promising to pay." Advisory Committee Note. The Advisory Committee explains that this difference arises "from a fundamental difference in nature. Communication is essential if compromises are to be effected, and consequently broad protection of statements is needed. This is not so in cases of payments or offers or promises to pay medical expenses, where factual statements may be expected to be incidental in nature."

Example 2

In Layla's accident with Lindsey above, assume that Layla really said, "Don't worry. I'm so sorry. It's all my fault. I shouldn't have tailgated you. We'll get you immediate medical attention, and if your insurance company won't pay for it, I will." In a subsequent suit by Lindsey against Layla, Rule 409 will result in the exclusion of the offer to pay medical expenses. But Rule 409 will not apply to exclude the statements clearly admitting fault, such as, "It's all my fault. I shouldn't have tailgated you." It also would not exclude the apology ("I'm so sorry"), which could be viewed as an admission of fault on the theory that people do not apologize unless they have done some wrong calling for an apology. Of course, a judge has discretion to exclude an apology like "I'm sorry" under Rule 403.

No dispute is necessary for Rule 409 to apply. Moreover, the offer need not have been made directly to the injured party; it can be made to anyone who can accept payment. Importantly, the Rule's prohibition is only against using the evidence to "prove liability for the injury." But furnishing, offering, or promising to pay medical expenses can be used for any other purpose, such as showing control or identity.

Example 3

In Layla's accident with Lindsey above, assume that Layla and Linda were in the car that hit Lindsey. Layla said to Lindsey, "We'll get you to a hospital. Don't worry about the money. If your insurance company won't pay the cost, I will." Lindsey did not, however, see who drove the car that hit

---

5. Advisory Committee Note, quoting Annot. 20 A.L.R.2d 291, 293.

her, and there were no eyewitnesses outside the cars. Moreover, Linda died before her deposition could be taken. Lindsey offers into evidence Layla's offer to pay Lindsey's medical expenses. This offer is made not to prove Layla's fault but merely to show that Layla had control over the car, that is, that Layla was the driver.

The argument would be that the driver is the one most likely to feel responsible enough (in the sense of having some active involvement in the events, even if not "at fault") to offer to pay medical expenses. Of course, other inferences are possible (maybe Layla was the passenger but just a nice person), but Layla's being the driver is at least a relevant plausible inference. Rule 409 would not bar this evidence. However, a trial court might nevertheless fear that a jury would make the prohibited fault inference and that a limiting instruction would not cure the problem. Accordingly, the trial judge still might exclude the evidence under Rule 403.

Problem 6-11: Med X

After a frustrating business meeting, Jan hurried away, lost in thought. Jan crashed her car into Arsenio, knocking him over. As Arsenio writhed in pain on the ground, Jan stated, "I'm really sorry; I was preoccupied, and this mess was all my fault. If you don't bring suit, I'll be more than happy to pay for all of your medical expenses. Hey, I'll even pay for your ripped pants and for any embarrassment this incident may have caused you. What do you say?" Arsenio said, "No," and filed suit. *Are any of Jan's statements admissible at trial?*

Problem 6-12: Kommander Condominium Club

One crisp fall day at the Kommander Condominium Club, Rob Arbuckle was late for his 10:30 a.m. tennis appointment. He left the elevator while looking at his watch and bowled over 86-year-old Alfred Macumber. A distraught Rob exclaimed, "Oh Mac! I hope you're okay. Why don't you go to the Mellon Hospital, and I'll pay for the check-up?" Later that night, Mac's attorney called Rob and told him that Mac was thinking of bringing suit because of his fairly severe injuries. Rob responded, "Look, I don't want any trouble. I admit I was not looking when I ran into Mac; I was in a hurry. If I gave Mac $1,000, would this whole thing go away?" The attorney refused Rob's proposal. Prior to the civil trial, Rob was prosecuted for battery on Mr. Macumber. He sought a plea bargain in which he would admit guilt if he received a suspended sentence. The prosecutor rejected Rob's offer. *Which, if any, of Rob's statements are admissible against him in the civil trial?*

§ 6.07 Liability Insurance: Rule 411

Rule 411 reads as follows:

Rule 411. Liability Insurance

Evidence that a person was or was not insured against liability is not admissible to prove whether the person acted negligently or otherwise wrongfully. But the court may admit this evidence for another purpose, such as proving a witness's bias or prejudice or proving agency, ownership, or control.

Example 1

Assume the facts, set forth in § 6.06, about Lindsey's suit against Layla, which arises out of an automobile accident. At trial, Lindsey offers evidence that Layla was insured to prove Layla's own awareness of her poor driving skills and thus her effort, by obtaining insurance, to protect herself against the consequences of her own carelessness. Layla's objection will be sustained.

The Advisory Committee Note sets forth two justifications for the rule: (1) "(at best the inference of fault from the fact of insurance coverage is a tenuous one, as is its converse)"; and (2) "the feeling that knowledge of the presence or absence of liability insurance would induce juries to decide cases on improper grounds." Commentators have also described the rule as encouraging people (and companies) to obtain insurance by limiting the risk that the insurance contract will create an inference of their carelessness.

The rule is not limited to evidence that the *defendant* was insured against liability; it was broadly drafted "so as to include contributory negligence or other fault of a plaintiff as well as fault of a defendant."

Note that the Rule does not prohibit using the evidence for purposes other than proving negligence or wrongful conduct.

Example 2

Layla, in varying our continuing example above, had been driving a truck with the phrase, "Acme Trucking Company," emblazoned on its side. Part of Lindsey's claim is that the truck's owner was negligent for not maintaining its brakes in tip-top shape. Lindsey's suit is only against Layla. Layla, in her answer to the complaint, denies owning the truck. She denies being responsible for its maintenance, and alleges that the maintenance responsibility belongs to the Acme Trucking Company. Lindsey introduces evidence at trial that the truck was insured in Layla's name, to prove that Layla was the truck's true owner and therefore was obligated to keep it well-maintained. Layla's objection under Rule 411 will probably be overruled, because the evidence is offered to prove ownership, not to prove Layla's negligence or otherwise wrongful conduct. However, the evidence may be excluded if the trial judge is not convinced that jurors will comply with a limiting instruction directing them to use the evidence of insurance only for the permitted purpose.

Problem 6-13: "I Forgot"

Defendant is sued for injuries resulting from an automobile accident. The defendant did not have automobile liability insurance; he "forgot to buy some." At trial, the defendant testified on direct examination.

DEFENDANT'S ATTORNEY: How careful a driver are you?

PLAINTIFF'S ATTORNEY: Objection. This evidence is irrelevant and unfairly prejudicial.

JUDGE: *(How should the judge rule? Why?)*

DEFENDANT'S ATTORNEY: What is your motive to be careful while driving?

PLAINTIFF'S ATTORNEY: Objection.

DEFENDANT'S ATTORNEY: (at the bench) I will proffer, Your Honor, that the defendant will say that "I'm a careful driver in large part because I forgot to take out car insurance; I knew that I could be held personally liable if I was in an automobile accident."

PLAINTIFF'S ATTORNEY: Objection.

JUDGE: *(How should the judge rule? Why?)*

Is this evidence admissible if it is offered to rebut the implicit assumption that, because many people have automobile insurance, the defendant likely has automobile insurance as well?

Problem 6-14: Go Ahead and Jump

Plaintiff, Laurie, brought suit against a bungee-jumping facility in Michigan. Plaintiff jumped and was injured when the rope broke. Plaintiff offered evidence at trial that the defendant was insured, to corroborate her claim that the defendant operated the business with a lackadaisical attitude. The facility's unofficial motto was: "Why worry? Be happy." *Is this evidence admissible?*

Problem 6-15: Columbo

Defense witness, Samantha, testified about the position of two cars involved in an automobile accident at a busy intersection. On cross-examination, she was asked by an apparently bumbling attorney named Columbo whether she was employed by the defendant's insurer. The defendant objected to the question and the court sustained the objection. *Should the lower court's ruling be affirmed on appeal?*

Problem 6-16: Statutory Interpretation Exercise

Read *United States v. Mezzanatto* (513 U.S. 196 (1995)), and answer the following questions:

1. *Text and Silence:* What role did text play in the majority's analysis? The dissent's? How much weight did each opinion give to text? What audience was assumed to assign the text meaning? What was the relative weight given to text versus silence, that is, what the text failed to say? Why?

2. *Truth:* What respective weight did the majority and dissenting opinions give to truth-finding as a value? Why did each opinion give truth its respective weight?

3. *The Free Market:* What significance did each opinion give to the importance of a free versus a regulated market in plea bargains? Why? What was the source of each opinion's view of the relevance meaning, an importance of this market? What narrative did each opinion craft, and what was the role of the free market in that narrative?

4. *Congressional Intent Versus Congressional Purpose and Its Alternatives:* Did any of the opinions relay on "actual" congressional intent on "actual" congressional purpose? What intent or purpose would Congress have had, had it thought specifically about the matter before the Court? What sources did each opinion rely on for these real or imagined designations of legislative intent? What was the relative role of the Advisory Committee and the Supreme Court in determining legislative intent or purpose, real or imagined? What weight did intent or purpose receive relative to other data sources on which each opinion relied?

5. *Candor:* Is there a difference between what each opinion claims to be doing in its approach to statutory interpretation and what it is in fact doing?

§ 6.08 Review Problems: Synthesizing the Quasi-Privileges

Problem 6-17: Let's Make a Deal

Barbara owed Alice $500. When Barbara saw Alice hanging out in front of the local convenience store, Barbara asked Alice, "If I give you $350 and a ticket to the Harry Connick Jr. concert, would that be an adequate settlement? I don't have the full $500 I owe you, and I just won't have it by the agreed date. I'm very short on cash at the moment." *If Alice does not accept Barbara's offer, can Alice introduce Barbara's statements in a later trial for payment of the $500?*

Problem 6-18: Engulf and Devour

Johann is sued by a business partner, Domino. Domino claimed that Johann understated profits by $1 million over a period of five years and clandestinely siphoned off partnership money for personal use. During negotiations with Domino, Johann admitted to taking some money because he needed to pay off gambling losses. Johann claimed, however, that he did not owe Domino anything because Domino had swindled him at the time they had formed the partnership, and, therefore, the money he took was rightfully his.

Can Domino offer Johann's statements at trial?

If Johann, hoping to get a more favorable settlement by showing his meager current assets, had produced during the negotiations all of the tax forms relating to the years in question and the betting slips verifying his losses, could these documents still be offered at trial?

If Johann had agreed that he owed Domino the $1 million as Domino claimed, but offered during negotiations to pay "500 grand" to have the lawsuit dropped, are any factual admissions made in conjunction with Johann's offer to pay admissible?

If subsequent criminal proceedings are initiated against Johann for his failure to pay income taxes on the monies in question, would the statements he made during the previous settlement negotiations be admissible in the subsequent criminal case?

Problem 6-19: Battery

Jessel is sued by Cohan for damages resulting from an alleged battery outside of a local nightclub, Crickett Place. Cohan and Jessel engaged in a series of discussions about settling the suit before trial. During one discussion, Cohan stated, "The only reason I hit you from behind was because you were doing a song and dance with my girlfriend inside the club." Negotiations were unsuccessful. At trial, Cohan takes the stand and states, "I was in the club until after Jessel left; I didn't learn about him getting hurt until I heard the sirens and ran outside to see what had happened."

Jessel seeks to impeach Cohan with the admissions he made during settlement negotiations. Is this permissible?

Problem 6-20: Gorkey Park

McGillicuddy is charged with two counts of breaking and entering the kitchen of a local restaurant, Sim's Place. A day after the charges were filed, McGillicuddy visited a local police officer, Officer Gorkey. McGillicuddy and Gorkey were social acquaintances. McGillicuddy proposed to Gorkey that "if you ditch these charges against me, I can help you catch some big-time crooks. I admit I broke into Sim's, but I was hungry and wanted some food; you can understand that, right?"

At McGillicuddy's trial for breaking and entering, can the prosecution offer McGillicuddy's statements to Officer Gorkey?

Assume that McGillicuddy's friend, Bobby, also is charged with breaking and entering as an aider and abettor. But the real mastermind of the operation, says Bobby, was McGillicuddy, who planned everything. Bobby agrees to testify against McGillicuddy, provided that the prosecution drops the charges against Bobby. *Can statements made by Bobby while entering a plea of guilty be used by McGillicuddy to impeach Bobby on cross-examination (e.g., a statement in which Bobby describes his own planning activity in a way suggesting that he, not McGillicuddy, was the mastermind, so McGillicuddy could show that he was just Bobby's innocent dupe)?*

McGillicuddy unsuccessfully attempted to negotiate a plea directly with the prosecutor. At trial, McGillicuddy introduces some of his own statements made during plea discussions with the prosecutor. These are statements suggesting that McGillicuddy thought he had permission to enter the kitchen. *What can the prosecutor do in response to McGillicuddy's evidence, if anything?*

After reading Rule 410 of the Federal Rules of Evidence, McGillicuddy concluded that the Rule is designed to protect the accused during plea bargaining. Consequently, McGillicuddy offered the statements made by the prosecutor during their unsuccessful plea negotiations. *Are the prosecutor's statements admissible?*

Problem 6-21: Did I Say That?

Leslie is sued by her neighbor, Murray, for breaking a very expensive mirror in Murray's house. During settlement negotiations, Leslie admitted she had been smoking marijuana at Murray's at the time the mirror broke. She denied, however, actually breaking the heirloom. The following month, Leslie is prosecuted for the possession of marijuana at her neighbor's house.

Can the prosecution offer the admission about marijuana use that Leslie made during the earlier settlement negotiations?

If Leslie had pled guilty to using marijuana at her neighbor's house, and then was sued in a civil action by her neighbor for breaking the mirror, could the guilty plea be used against her in the later civil trial?

Problem 6-22: The Singing Sparrow

The defendant, Sparrow, is charged with murdering Goodot. During a plea negotiation with the prosecutor, the defendant blurts out, "You guys don't know who you're up against! You think I killed Goodot, but you really should ask me about the unsolved murder of Blaine in the next county. I have personal knowledge about that one, and you coppers are way off base in your investigation!"

Sparrow is subsequently charged with Blaine's murder. *At that trial, can the prosecutor offer Sparrow's inculpatory statements made during the Goodot plea negotiations?*

Problem 6-23: Rosetta's Orwellian Plight

Rosetta sues Maxwell civilly for injuries growing out of Maxwell's alleged sexual assault. Rosetta seeks to testify to the following: "I called an ambulance right after the rape and was rushed to the Center City Hospital Emergency Room. Maxwell was waiting there and said to me: 'I'm sorry that I hurt you. I just couldn't control myself. I promise to pay all your medical expenses if you promise not to tell the cops what happened, even if they ask you, and not to sue me.'" *This testimony, in the face of a proper objection, should be:*

(a) Admissible if there is a limiting instruction prohibiting the jurors from using the words, "I promise to pay all your medical expenses" as showing Maxwell's consciousness of guilt for in fact raping Rosetta.

(b) Inadmissible under Rule 408.

(c) Inadmissible under Rule 409.

(d) Inadmissible under both Rules 408 and 409.

Problem 6-24: Maxwell's Comeuppance

Just before the criminal trial arising from the situation mentioned in the immediately preceding multiple-choice question, defense counsel approaches the prosecutor to begin plea discussions. The prosecutor refuses to negotiate unless the defendant responds personally to the prosecutor's question during the negotiation and further waives his right to raise any Rule 410 objections at any future trial. Additionally, the prosecutor promises to seek the highest possible sentence if the defendant is convicted of the rape charge if the defendant does not immediately agree to the Rule 410 waiver. Reluctantly, the defendant and his counsel agree to the prosecutor's terms. During the negotiation, defendant Maxwell admits that he raped Rosetta, and the prosecutor immediately cuts off negotiations and proceeds to trial. Defendant Maxwell testifies at his rape trial that he did not rape Rosetta but, rather, that she consented. The prosecutor seeks to cross-examine Maxwell with this statement made during the plea negotiations and later files perjury charges against Maxwell for lying under oath at his rape trial. *Select the best answer:*

(a) Maxwell's statement made during the plea negotiations is admissible at both the rape trial and the perjury trial.

(b) Maxwell's statement made during the plea negotiations is inadmissible at the rape trial but admissible at the perjury trial, so long as the trial court concludes by a preponderance of the evidence that the waiver was not voluntary.

(c) Maxwell's statement made during the plea negotiations is not admissible at either the rape trial or the perjury trial.

(d) Maxwell's statement made during the plea negotiations is admissible at the rape trial but not the perjury trial.

Chapter 7

The Examination and Impeachment of Witnesses

§ 7.01 Chapter Checklist

1. Is a witness testifying at a hearing, proceeding, or trial?

2. Is the witness under oath and subject to cross-examination?

3. Is the witness offering evidence about the background of the case, an element of a claim, defense, or cause of action, or the impeachment of another witness?

4. Is the witness on direct, cross, redirect, or recross-examination?

5. If this is the proponent's witness, what objections to the witness' testimony can be anticipated?

6. If the witness is being impeached, is the impeachment intrinsic (from the witness' mouth) or extrinsic (through other evidence or another witness)?

7. If the impeachment is intrinsic, is it in a permissible form?

8. If the impeachment is extrinsic, does it satisfy the collateral issue rule?

§ 7.02 Relevant Federal Rules of Evidence

Rule 601. General Rule of Competency

Every person is competent to be a witness unless these rules provide otherwise. But in a civil case, state law governs the witness's competency regarding a claim or defense for which state law supplies the rule of decision.

Rule 602. Lack of Personal Knowledge

A witness may testify to a matter only if evidence is introduced sufficient to support a finding that the witness has personal knowledge of the matter. Evidence to prove personal knowledge may consist of the witness's own testimony. This rule does not apply to a witness's expert testimony under Rule 703 .

Rule 603. Oath or Affirmation

Before testifying, a witness must give an oath or affirmation to testify truthfully. It must be in a form designed to impress that duty on the witness's conscience.

Rule 604. Interpreters

An interpreter must be qualified and must give an oath or affirmation to make a true translation.

Rule 605. Competency of Judge as Witness

The presiding judge may not testify as a witness at the trial. A party need not object to preserve the issue.

Rule 606. Competency of Juror as Witness

(a) **At the Trial.** A juror may not testify as a witness before the other jurors at the trial. If a juror is called to testify, the court must give a party an opportunity to object outside the jury's presence.

(b) **During an Inquiry into the Validity of a Verdict or Indictment.**

(1) *Prohibited Testimony or Other Evidence.* During an inquiry into the validity of a verdict or indictment, a juror may not testify about any statement made or incident that occurred during the jury's deliberations; the effect of anything on that juror's or another juror's vote; or any juror's mental processes concerning the verdict or indictment. The court may not receive a juror's affidavit or evidence of a juror's statement on these matters.

(2) *Exceptions.* A juror may testify about whether:

(A) extraneous prejudicial information was improperly brought to the jury's attention;

(B) an outside influence was improperly brought to bear on any juror; or

(C) a mistake was made in entering the verdict on the verdict form.

Rule 607. Who May Impeach

Any party, including the party that called the witness, may attack the witness's credibility.

Rule 608. Evidence of Character and Conduct of Witness

(a) **Reputation or Opinion Evidence.** A witness's credibility may be attacked or supported by testimony about the witness's reputation for having a character for truthfulness or untruthfulness, or by testimony in the form of an opinion about that character. But evidence of truthful character is admissible only after the witness's character for truthfulness has been attacked.

(b) **Specific Instances of Conduct.** Except for a criminal conviction under Rule 609, extrinsic evidence is not admissible to prove specific instances of a witness's conduct in order to attack or support the witness's character for truthfulness. But the court may, on cross-examination, allow them to be inquired into if they are probative of the character for truthfulness or untruthfulness of:

(1) the witness; or

(2) another witness whose character the witness being cross-examined has testified about.

By testifying on another matter, a witness does not waive any privilege against self-incrimination for testimony that relates only to the witness's character for truthfulness.

Rule 609. Impeachment by Evidence of Conviction of Crime

(a) **In General.** The following rules apply to attacking a witness's character for truthfulness by evidence of a criminal conviction:

(1) for a crime that, in the convicting jurisdiction, was punishable by death or by imprisonment for more than one year, the evidence:

(A) must be admitted, subject to Rule 403 , in a civil case or in a criminal case in which the witness is not a defendant; and

(B) must be admitted in a criminal case in which the witness is a defendant, if the probative value of the evidence outweighs its prejudicial effect to that defendant; and

(2) for any crime regardless of the punishment, the evidence must be admitted if the court can readily determine that establishing the elements of the crime required proving — or the witness's admitting — a dishonest act or false statement.

(b) **Limit on Using the Evidence After 10 Years.** This subdivision (b) applies if more than 10 years have passed since the witness's conviction or release from confinement for it, whichever is later. Evidence of the conviction is admissible only if:

(1) its probative value, supported by specific facts and circumstances, substantially outweighs its prejudicial effect; and

(2) the proponent gives an adverse party reasonable written notice of the intent to use it so that the party has a fair opportunity to contest its use.

(c) **Effect of a Pardon, Annulment, or Certificate of Rehabilitation.** Evidence of a conviction is not admissible if:

(1) the conviction has been the subject of a pardon, annulment, certificate of rehabilitation, or other equivalent procedure based on a finding that the person has been rehabilitated, and the person has not been convicted of a later crime punishable by death or by imprisonment for more than one year; or

(2) the conviction has been the subject of a pardon, annulment, or other equivalent procedure based on a finding of innocence.

(d) **Juvenile Adjudications.** Evidence of a juvenile adjudication is admissible under this rule only if:

(1) it is offered in a criminal case;

(2) the adjudication was of a witness other than the defendant;

(3) an adult's conviction for that offense would be admissible to attack the adult's credibility; and

(4) admitting the evidence is necessary to fairly determine guilt or innocence.

(e) **Pendency of an Appeal.** A conviction that satisfies this rule is admissible even if an appeal is pending. Evidence of the pendency is also admissible.

Rule 610. Religious Beliefs or Opinions

Evidence of a witness's religious beliefs or opinions is not admissible to attack or support the witness's credibility.

Rule 611. Mode and Order of Interrogation and Presentation

(a) **Control by the Court; Purposes.** The court should exercise reasonable control over the mode and order of examining witnesses and presenting evidence so as to:

(1) make those procedures effective for determining the truth;

(2) avoid wasting time; and

(3) protect witnesses from harassment or undue embarrassment.

(b) **Scope of Cross-Examination.** Cross-examination should not go beyond the subject matter of the direct examination and matters affecting the witness's credibility. The court may allow inquiry into additional matters as if on direct examination.

(c) **Leading Questions.** Leading questions should not be used on direct examination except as necessary to develop the witness's testimony. Ordinarily, the court should allow leading questions:

(1) on cross-examination; and

(2) when a party calls a hostile witness, an adverse party, or a witness identified with an adverse party.

Rule 612. Writing Used to Refresh Memory

(a) **Scope.** This rule gives an adverse party certain options when a witness uses a writing to refresh memory:

(1) while testifying; or

(2) before testifying, if the court decides that justice requires the party to have those options.

(b) **Adverse Party's Options; Deleting Unrelated Matter.** Unless 18 U.S.C. § 3500 provides otherwise in a criminal case, an adverse party is entitled to have the writing produced at the hearing, to inspect it, to cross-examine the witness about it, and to introduce in evidence any portion that relates to the witness's testimony. If the producing party claims that the writing includes unrelated matter, the court must examine the writing in camera, delete any unrelated portion, and order that the rest be delivered to the adverse party. Any portion deleted overobjection must be preserved for the record.

(c) **Failure to Produce or Deliver the Writing.** If a writing is not produced or is not delivered as ordered, the court may issue any appropriate order. But if the prosecution does not comply in a criminal case, the court must strike the witness's testimony or — if justice so requires — declare a mistrial.

Rule 613. Prior Statements of Witnesses

(a) **Showing or Disclosing the Statement During Examination.** When examining a witness about the witness's prior statement, a party need not show it or disclose its contents to the witness. But the party must, on request, show it or disclose its contents to an adverse party's attorney.

(b) **Extrinsic Evidence of a Prior Inconsistent Statement.** Extrinsic evidence of a witness's prior inconsistent statement is admissible only if the witness is given an opportunity to explain or deny the statement and an adverse party is given an opportunity to examine the witness about it, or if justice so requires. This subdivision (b) does not apply to an opposing party's statement under Rule 801(d)(2).

Rule 614. Calling and Interrogation of Witnesses by Court

(a) **Calling.** The court may call a witness on its own or at a party's request. Each party is entitled to cross-examine the witness.

(b) **Examining.** The court may examine a witness regardless of who calls the witness.

(c) **Objections.** A party may object to the court's calling or examining a witness either at that time or at the next opportunity when the jury is not present.

Rule 615. Exclusion of Witnesses.

At a party's request, the court must order witnesses excluded so that they cannot hear other witnesses' testimony. Or the court may do so on its own. But this rule does not authorize excluding:

(a) a party who is a natural person;

(b) an officer or employee of a party that is not a natural person, after being designated as the party's representative by its attorney;

(c) a person whose presence a party shows to be essential to presenting the party's claim or defense; or

(d) a person authorized by statute to be present.

§ 7.03 The Examination of Witnesses

A. Overview

Witness testimony, sometimes referred to as *viva voce*, or "by voice," is one of the most common and compelling types of evidence at trial. Witnesses produce potentially powerful evidence, and witness examination sometimes becomes a "trial within a trial," much like the individual battles within a war. Because of the significance of witness testimony, special rules have been adopted to govern it. Many trials are won or lost on the nature and impact of witness testimony and how the attorneys negotiate the rules governing the admissibility of that testimony.

The Rules place the examination of witnesses squarely within the control of the judge. Under Rule 611, the judge has the discretion to decide whether to allow witness testimony and if so, in what form and at what time. For example, the judge has the authority to govern the use of leading questions on direct examination, to determine the length of time for cross-examination, and to limit the scope of cross-examination. *See* Rule 611. Of course, the Federal Rules of Evidence provide the judge with guidance and impose a variety of prohibitions, including those related to the subject matter of the questions. For example, questions must concern a relevant matter under Rules 401 and 402 and not elicit privileged information under Rule 501.

The Federal Rules of Evidence impose several different types of limits on witness testimony. These limits range from who may testify (i.e., witness competency), to the substance of the testimony, to the form of the questions asked. Competency restrictions, such as those imposed on judge and jurors as provided in Rules 605 and 606, help to maintain the fundamental fairness of the trial process. Substantive limits are utilized to deter suspect evidence, such as hearsay, propensity character evidence, and settlement offers. Form limits also are intended to foster fairness and efficiency in the stylized "dance" that constitutes a trial.

B. Competency: Who May Testify

The competency of witnesses to testify in federal court is generally determined by Federal Rule of Evidence 601. While it may seem obvious that federal law should govern in federal courts, there exists one glaring exception in the area of witness competency. Rule 601 directs that state laws govern the competency of witnesses in a federal civil action or proceeding when the state law provides the rule of decision. In this manner, Rule 601 becomes a choice-of-law rule. The use of state law in federal court is not restricted solely to competency matters. State law sometimes may be used in federal court when determining whether evidence is privileged. *See* Rule 501. Privileges are discussed in Chapter 17. *See also* Presumptions, Rule 302.

Under the Federal Rules of Evidence, all witnesses are presumptively competent to testify under Rule 601. Rule 601 reverses the common law practice, which for many years excluded from the witness stand various categories of persons, such as those convicted of certain crimes, persons having an interest in the action (such as a party or a party's spouse), and persons without religious beliefs. These grounds of incompetency have largely disappeared from both federal and state courts, with the one remaining vestige in some state courts, often called "Dead Man's Statutes." These statutes essentially prohibit interested parties from testifying about an oral transaction or communication against a deceased or incompetent person essentially because such a person would not be able to rebut that testimony. Under the federal rules, at least, all of the aforementioned persons are permitted to testify, although some prior conduct, such as convictions of crime, may be the subject of impeachment. An example of a "Dead Man's Statute" follows.

Idaho Code § 9-202. Who may not testify [Dead Man's Statute]

The following persons cannot be witnesses:

3. Parties or assignors of parties to an action or proceeding, or persons in whose behalf an action or proceeding is prosecuted against an executor or administrator, upon a claim or demand against the estate of a deceased person, as to any communication or agreement, not in writing, occurring before the death of such deceased person.

The presumption of competency under Rule 601 is not a free pass to testify. The presumptive witness must meet the foundational requirement of understanding what it means to tell the truth, must possess some relevant information, and must bypass several carefully delineated prohibitions involving testimony by the judge and jurors.

The primary foundational requirement for witness competency is that the witness must be able to understand what it means to tell the truth. This prerequisite has no bright-line litmus test, perhaps because imposing a bright-line standard would be difficult, if not impossible. As the Advisory Committee Note to Rule 601 aptly stated, "No mental or moral qualifications for testifying as a witness are specified. Standards of mental capacity have proved elusive in actual application." Consequently, it is assumed in the Rules that the overwhelming majority of witnesses understand their obligation to testify truthfully. This assumption extends even to convicted perjurers (who will be given an opportunity to incur yet another perjury conviction). There is one category of witness for which the "meaning of truthfulness" requirement is regularly tested, however, and that is the child witness. An attorney must carefully lay a foundation with child witnesses to establish their understanding of the difference between truth and falsehood.

Example

ATTORNEY: Hi, Rebecca. How are you?

C: Fine.

ATTORNEY: Good. I am going to ask you a few questions, Okay?

C: Okay.

ATTORNEY: May I call you Becca?

C: My Mommy and Daddy do.

ATTORNEY: Becca, how old are you?

C: Four. Last week!

ATTORNEY: Did you have a party on your birthday?

C: Yes. With cake.

ATTORNEY: With whom do you live, Becca?

C: My Mommy and Daddy and Emma.

ATTORNEY: Who is Emma?

C: My sister.

ATTORNEY: Becca, do you know what it means to tell the truth?

C: Yes.

ATTORNEY: What happens when you don't tell the truth?

C: Mommy sends me to time-out.

ATTORNEY: What is that?

C: It is when I am in trouble.

ATTORNEY: What happens during time-out?

C: I stand in a corner. I'm not allowed to talk.

ATTORNEY: Is it fun?

C: Noooo.

ATTORNEY: What happens if you tell the truth?

C: Nothing.

ATTORNEY: No time-out?

C: No.

ATTORNEY: Are you going to tell the truth here today?

C: Yes. (nodding her head up and down)

ATTORNEY: If I told you that I was wearing a green tie, would that be the truth or a lie?

C: That's silly. That would be a lie.

ATTORNEY: And if I told you that Santa Claus and the Easter Bunny were phony merchandising creations of a capitalist economy . . . please don't cry Becca, I withdraw the question.

ATTORNEY: Now, remember when there was a fire at your house?

C: Yes.

ATTORNEY: Who was home at the time?

Problem 7-1: The Habitual Drug Addict

Paul observed an armed robbery in Pacific Heights one foggy Sunday morning. When Paul was called to testify for the prosecution, the defense objected. In an earlier deposition, Paul admitted that he was a heroin addict, and had been one for more than a decade. *Should Paul's testimony be permitted?* Explain.

Problem 7-2: Say What?

Archie Oakley, age 102, was on his front porch when he observed a purse snatching approximately 20 yards away. While Archie could not positively identify the assailant, he was called to testify by the prosecution to provide other relevant information. Archie concedes that he is deaf in one ear, needs a hearing aid in the other, and has very poor vision. The defendant objects to Archie's testimony, claiming it is extremely unreliable. *Is Archie competent to testify?* Explain.

Problem 7-3: Dead Again and Again

Josie agreed in writing to sell Bernard her boat, pending an inspection. The inspection occurred and it was a complete success. Before the completion of the sale, however, Josie died. Bernard then brought suit against Josie's estate based on diversity of citizenship. Bernard sought specific performance of the contract. At trial, Bernard took the witness stand to testify about the terms of the contract. *Will Bernard be allowed to testify about the agreement if a "Dead Man's Statute" applies?* Explain.

Problem 7-4: Hypnotized

Lil, the victim of an armed robbery at gunpoint, could not remember what happened during the robbery, no matter how hard she tried to recall the events, with the exception of the general time and place. After she made numerous unsuccessful attempts to recall the crime, a certified police neuropsychologist hypnotized her. After the hypnosis, Lil was able to recall what had occurred during the robbery and even remembered the identity of the perpetrator. *Will Lil be allowed to testify at trial?* Explain.

C. Requirement of Personal Knowledge

Federal Rule of Evidence 602 generally requires lay witnesses to possess personal knowledge in order to testify. Without personal knowledge, a layperson likely violates the Rules in at least two ways: (1) the testimony is probably based on hearsay, in which case the hearsay declarants would be the preferable witnesses; and (2) the testimony is probably speculation, which would distract the jury from drawing its own inferences from the admitted evidence.

Rule 602 permits some witnesses to testify without personal knowledge. The most significant example of testimony without personal knowledge involves expert witnesses, who routinely testify based on facts supplied to them either before or during their testimony. *See* Rule 703. Similarly, out-of-court admissions of party opponents (generally offered through the testimony of in-court witnesses) are admissible in evidence, even if they were not based on the party's personal knowledge. *See* Rule 801(d)(2). These exceptions are discussed at length in Chapters 9 and 13, respectively.

Rule 602 can be viewed in conjunction with Rule 701, which describes when laypersons may offer opinions. As Rule 701 explains, a lay witness may offer opinions or inferences if the opinions are:

(a) rationally based on the witness's perception;

(b) helpful to clearly understanding the witness's testimony or to determining a fact in issue; and

(c) not based on scientific, technical, or other specialized knowledge within the scope of Rule 702.

Thus, the personal knowledge requirement leaves some room for lay witnesses to offer opinions and inferences, but only within narrow guidelines.

Example

Peter brings suit against his neighbor, Stanley, for civil assault, trespass, and conversion. At trial, Peter calls another neighbor, Howard, to testify. The following exchange occurs on direct examination:

PLAINTIFF'S ATTORNEY: Now, Howard, what happened at 6:45 p.m. on January 4th?

A: Stanley walked across the path between his and Peter's house. He was carrying a disgusting dead animal and—

DEFENDANT'S ATTORNEY: Objection. Lack of personal knowledge, Your Honor.

JUDGE: Please approach the bench, counsel.

PLAINTIFF'S ATTORNEY: Your Honor, Howard had seen Peter walk across that path innumerable times on prior occasions, if not this one, and was told by Elma, who is always a reliable source of information for what happens in that part of the neighborhood, that Peter walked across the path on this occasion with the dead animal.

JUDGE: I am going to sustain the objection. Even if Howard had observed Peter traverse the path many times before, he cannot opine that Peter did so on this occasion. If anyone should testify about Peter's alleged trip with the dead animal, it ought to be Elma. Instead, Howard's testimony is hearsay when he offers Elma's statement as his own. There is a preference for putting Elma on the witness stand to hear about her observations directly. Please continue with the examination. Again, the objection is sustained.

Problem 7-5: Robbin the Hood

Robbin the Hood is prosecuted for bank robbery. At trial, Robbin's wife, Gayle, testifies for the defense. She states that before Robbin robbed the bank to give to the poor, he was despondent about the state of affairs in this country. The prosecution objects to this testimony, claiming that Gayle lacks personal knowledge about Robbin's state of mind. *What ruling and why?*

D. Competency of Judges and Attorneys as Witnesses (Rule 605)

Rule 605 sensibly disqualifies judges from testifying in trials over which they preside. Serious doubts about objectivity would arise if a judge were called to testify at the behest of a party. In practice, a situation in which a party seeks to have a judge testify to case-related information is unlikely to arise. If judges have personal knowledge about events giving rise to litigation they are supposed to preserve both the reality and the appearance of impartiality by recusing themselves, regardless of whether they are likely to be called as witnesses.[1] In the unlikely event a party does call a presiding judge to testify, Rule 605 provides that the adversary need not object to preserve the impropriety for appeal. The automatic objection protects a party from having to directly challenge a judge's competency in open court.

The Federal Rules of Evidence do not have a rule barring attorneys from testifying in cases in which they appear as counsel. Again, the situation rarely arises because ethical rules generally bar lawyers from appearing as counsel in trial if they are likely to be called as witnesses.[2] However, the lack of a rule flatly rendering attorneys incompetent as witnesses means that judges sometimes do allow attorneys to testify to uncontested and formalistic matters. For example, a judge may allow an attorney of record to testify to efforts to locate an unavailable witness for the purposes of establishing a hearsay declarant's unavailability under Rule 804(a).

Problem 7-6: Anyone but You

Judge Liz Wilber lived in a suburban neighborhood outside of Chicago. One cold Saturday morning, while she was walking her dog, Pudge, the Judge witnessed two of her neighbors engaged in a fistfight. The fight ended when one neighbor took out

---

1. For an analysis of whether judges must disqualify themselves from presiding over cases in which they have personal knowledge of case-related matters regardless of whether any party intends to call the judge as a witness, *see* Glen Weissenberger and James Duane, Federal Rules of Evidence: Rules, Legislative History, Commentary and Authority 253–256 (LexisNexis 2005).

2. *See, e.g.*, Rule 3.7(a) of the Model Rules of Professional Conduct. If the need for an attorney's testimony arises only after the attorney-client relationship is underway, the attorney should withdraw as counsel unless doing so would cause "substantial hardship." *Id.*

a knife and stabbed the other, causing a serious wound. Judge Wilber coincidentally drew the case and presided over the trial.

The defense calls Judge Wilber as a "necessary" witness.

1. Can she testify if she states from the bench that testifying will not impede her impartiality?

2. If no objection is lodged by the opposing counsel, can Judge Wilber then testify?

3. Can the bailiff, who also lives in the neighborhood, testify?

4. Can the court reporter, who is a friend of the defendant, testify as a character witness?

5. Can the defendant's best friend, who was convicted of murder twice and perjury once, testify for the defendant on a minor question of fact?

6. Suppose Judge Wilber had recessed the case for the day and was heading to her car. As she did so, she overheard a witness who had just testified say, "My testimony today really pulled the wool over their eyes; I can't believe they bought that garbage!" What should the judge do?

7. Suppose that instead of Judge Wilber overhearing the witness, it was the opposing counsel. What should the opposing counsel do?

Problem 7-7: The Deal

Enos, Nasty, and Usta are members of a radical environmental group that allegedly fire-bombed the office of the Sierra Club, killing two people. Only Nasty and Usta are charged with the bombing. Enos is called to testify for the prosecution. The defense counsel believes that Enos has been offered a deal by the prosecution in exchange for his testimony, but that he would refuse to acknowledge such a deal at trial. The defense counsel wants to call in rebuttal the assistant prosecutor who negotiated with Enos. *Can the assistant prosecutor be asked to testify? See United States v. Newman, 476 F.2d 733 (3d Cir. 1973).*

Practice Tip: Competency to testify — why attorneys use investigators:

Often, lawyers interview the adverse witnesses in a case prior to trial, either formally, in depositions, or informally. When lawyers cross-examine the opposing witnesses after such interviews, the witnesses are "locked in" to their stories based on the interviews.

Sometimes, witnesses at trial deny having made the prior statements, especially those made during informal interviews. This situation could create a significant dilemma. Counsel does not want to testify to impeach the witness, but similarly does not want to let the witness' credibility remain untested. The answer lies in the use of investigators. If an investigator had been employed, the investigator could be called to testify about what was said, consequently impeaching the witness and letting the attorney play the sole role at trial for which she prepared — lawyer, not witness.

E. Competency of Jurors as Witnesses (Rule 606)

Rule 606(a) closely resembles Rule 605, in that it bans jurors from testifying in cases where they are sitting as jurors. The primary difference, should the unlikely scenario of a juror being called as a witness occur, is that an adversary has to object to preserve the point for appeal. The rule allows the adverse party to object out of the jury's presence, reducing the risk that the objection will prejudice the remaining jurors. A mistrial likely would result should a party seek to call a juror to testify. Removing the juror from the jury and continuing with the trial in front of the remaining jurors (perhaps with the addition of an alternate) is unlikely to be a satisfactory solution, since the ability of the remaining jurors to evaluate the credibility of their ex-colleague's impartiality would be in question.

It might be unimaginable that judges and jurors would testify in actions in which they are professionally involved. However, Rules 605 and 606(a) sit at the polar extreme from trial procedures as they initially evolved in England. Hundreds of years ago, judges and jurors had firsthand knowledge of the parties and their disputes. Rather than listening to evidence, they reviewed what they knew and rendered judgments accordingly. Implicit in Rules 605 and 606(a), by contrast, is the policy that judges and jurors should not be personally acquainted with parties or their disputes.

Unlike Rules 605 and 606(a), Rule 606(b) applies to scenarios that arise often. After a verdict is rendered and a jury is discharged, the losing party may talk to jurors and uncover deliberative improprieties that the party thinks justify setting aside the verdict. There are numerous possible improprieties. A party may find out that, despite an out-of-court statement being admitted only for a limited, non-hearsay purpose, the jurors in fact violated the hearsay rule by using it for its truth. Similarly, jurors might have used evidence admitted for a non-character use as evidence that a defendant was a bad person and therefore deserved to be convicted despite doubts over whether the defendant committed the charged crime. Perhaps the jurors speculated about inadmissible evidence or agreed they had no idea what the phrase "malice aforethought" meant, but were too embarrassed to ask the judge for clarification. In addition, some jurors might have changed their votes because they wanted to conclude the deliberations quickly.

Rule 606(b)'s response to such problems is consistent with the aphorism widely attributed to Otto Von Bismarck, "If you like laws and sausages, you should never watch either one being made." That is, while such happenings hardly symbolize the jury system's finest moments, the rule keeps the deliberations largely hidden from view by forbidding jurors from testifying about them: "Upon an inquiry into the validity of a verdict . . . a juror may not testify as to any matter or statement occurring during the course of the jury's deliberations or the effect of anything upon that or any other juror's mind or emotions as influencing the juror to assent to or dissent from the verdict . . . or concerning the juror's mental processes in connection therewith . . . ." Rule 606(b) rests in part on a judgment that perfection in the trial process is impossible to achieve and the need for finality means that improprieties in the jury process generally must be tolerated. In addition, underlying Rule 606(b) is a fear that a general policy admitting evidence about jury deliberations would chill jurors' abilities to speak openly and would encourage losing parties to hound jurors who suffered from "buyer's remorse" into describing improprieties that might not have occurred.

Example 1

Tanner was convicted of mail fraud. Following his conviction, in an effort to obtain a new trial, Tanner submitted affidavits from two of the jurors describing events that had taken place during the trial and the deliberations. The affidavits claimed that a number of the jurors smoked marijuana regularly during the trial, and others had snorted cocaine. In addition, one juror sold marijuana to another during the trial, and a number of jurors fell asleep. Further, jurors consumed beer and wine during lunch breaks and at recesses. Despite these apparent events, the United States Supreme Court still upheld the verdict, concluding that Rule 606(b) barred the use of the affidavits. *See Tanner v. United States*, 483 U.S. 107 (1987).

Rule 606(b) does not turn a completely blind eye to jury improprieties. The rule's exceptions permit jurors to "testify on the question whether extraneous prejudicial information was improperly brought to the jury's attention or whether any outside influence was improperly brought to bear upon any juror." Even if a judge considers such evidence, jurors are nevertheless not allowed to testify to the impact of the improper influence on their reasoning processes. Rather, a judge decides what the impact would have been on a "reasonable juror," and either upholds a verdict or sets it aside accordingly.

Example 2

Assume that a juror in *Tanner* had submitted an affidavit stating that while the bailiff was escorting the jurors to lunch, the bailiff had told the juror, "This wasn't allowed in evidence, but you all should know that Tanner is a really bad guy. He has a string of convictions for mail fraud a mile long." The juror's affidavit also states, "I never would have voted to convict Tanner if the bailiff hadn't said that." The judge can consider the juror's affidavit when deciding whether the bailiff's statement was sufficiently prejudicial to justify setting aside the guilty verdict. However, the juror's assertion as to the effect of the impropriety on the juror's vote is inadmissible.

Rule 606(b) governs inquiries "into the validity of a verdict." Often, serious problems in the jury process become evident prior to the time a jury arrives at a verdict. Rule 606(b) does not bar jurors from testifying to improprieties that arise prior to the time of verdict.

Problem 7-8: At the Movies

In the film *12 Angry Men*,[3] jurors debate whether a young Puerto Rican defendant is guilty of stabbing his father to death with a knife. During the deliberations, the following incidents take place:

1. The prosecution claims that the knife found lying next to the victim and owned by the defendant was an extremely unusual one. During the deliberations, Juror #8 counters the prosecutor's claim by producing an almost exact replica of the knife. Juror #8 tells the other jurors that he bought it the night before in a shop while walking in the defendant's neighborhood.

2. An elderly prosecution witness who walks with a limp testified that he lives directly underneath the victim's apartment. On the night of the victim's death, the witness heard a violent argument coming from the victim's apartment and heard the door slam and someone run out of the apartment. The witness walked from his bedroom to his front door in time to see the defendant run past. In the jury room in front of all the jurors, Juror #8 conducts an experiment in which he walks with a limp over the distance from the witness' apartment to his front door. The experiment suggests that the witness could not have gotten to his front door in time to see the defendant run past.

3. Juror #10 argues that the defendant is guilty because "We all know that these kind of people are violent and that human life doesn't mean the same to them as it does to us," the jurors.

Following the verdict, which, if any, of these incidents would jurors be competent to testify about under Rule 606(b)?

Problem 7-9: Stop the Reading!

1. Maryann Twonnette is on trial for murder. While the jury is deliberating, a group of jurors seeks to inform the judge that one of the jurors refuses to deliberate. Instead, the juror continuously sits in a corner and reads a book, and tells the other jurors, "Tell me when you're done deliberating, then I'll vote not guilty and we can get out of here."

Can the judge consider this information? If so, how, if at all, might the judge be able to respond?

2. The jury convicts Maryann Twonnette of first-degree murder. One of the jurors later informs Twonnette's attorney that during the deliberations, another juror had violated the judge's order to ignore media reports about the case by bringing into the jury room a newspaper article detailing Twonnette's lengthy prior criminal history. Some, but not all, of the information in the article had been introduced into evidence at trial. The juror also tells the defense attorney that a few of the jurors changed their votes from "not guilty"

---

3. United Artists (1957).

to "guilty" after reading the article. The defense attorney submits a motion for a new trial, attaching as exhibits the newspaper article and an affidavit from the juror swearing to the above information.

What, if any, information can the judge consider in ruling on the motion for a new trial?

F. The Sequential Order of Witness Testimony and Form Objections

Witness examination usually unfolds in a ritualistic order. The party that calls a witness to testify is generally called the witness's proponent. The proponent then examines the witness on direct examination. After direct examination, the opposing party has the opportunity to conduct cross-examination. Rule 611(b) provides that cross-examination "should be limited to the subject matter of the direct examination and matters affecting the credibility of the witness." Following the cross-examination, the proponent may conduct a redirect examination. As its name implies, a "redirect" examination is a variant of direct examination and is governed by rules similar to the initial direct examination, particularly with respect to the rule prohibiting leading questions. Redirect examination allows a rebuttal or exploration of points raised on cross-examination.

Order of Testimony

1. Direct Examination

2. Cross-Examination

3. Redirect Examination

4. Recross-Examination

A wide variety of objections can be raised concerning a witness' testimony, particularly objections to the form of the examiners' questions. Some of the more common objections, and their definitions, are offered below:

1. Leading questions: questions that suggest an answer. Questions calling for a yes or no response are often leading. Primary examples of leading questions are questions beginning with words such as Was, Were, Did, Does, Have, or Had.

2. Asked and answered questions: questions that have already been asked of the witness and answered.

3. Compound questions: questions that actually incorporate two or more questions in a single sentence.

4. Questions assuming facts not in evidence: questions that assume the existence of facts not yet testified to by a witness or otherwise introduced into evidence.

5. Argumentative questions: questions that are phrased in such a way that they don't seek information but rather they merely engage the witness in improper argument.

6. Questions calling for speculation: questions asking for information beyond the witness' personal knowledge or questions asking the witness to provide an inadmissible opinion. *See* Rule 701 and Chapter 8. In such cases, the witness has either no knowledge or insufficient information about the subject matter of the testimony.

7. Non-responsive answers: answers by witnesses that do not respond to the examiner's question.

8. Narrative answers: answers by witnesses that exceed the scope of the questions put to them. A party may object to a vague or overbroad question that would likely result in an objectionable answer; in that case, the objection would be phrased as "Calls for a Narrative Answer."

G. Witness Strategy

1. General Principles

An attorney may follow various strategies with witness testimony, particularly when it is recognized that effective testimony "paints a picture," or "tells a story," and that there are many ways to paint a single picture or tell a story. Trial practice strategies include the tone of voice attorneys adopt with witnesses, where attorneys stand when examining witnesses, in which direction attorneys face, or how they frame particular questions. Much of what a jury receives from testimony lies in its nonverbal subtext and not in the words themselves. Some attorneys hire jury consultants, who assist with jury selection or suggest how to approach the witnesses at trial in the most persuasive manner.

One strategy commonly followed by trial lawyers is embodied in Rule 615. This rule permits attorneys (or the judge, *sua sponte*) to request that prospective witnesses be excluded from the courtroom when other witnesses are testifying. This rule is commonly known among trial attorneys as "The Rule on Witnesses." Attorneys sometimes use verbal shorthand, asking the judge "to invoke the rule." Despite invocation of the rule, certain witnesses must be permitted to remain in the courtroom: the parties; certain experts; and persons whose presence might be authorized by statute, such as the victims of crimes.

2. Direct Examination

The function of direct examination is to elicit information that is relevant to the cause of action, claim, or defense. The testimony of a witness on direct examination can be viewed as consisting of three parts: background, scene, and action.

The "background" component establishes the witness as a three-dimensional person and not merely as a blank conduit of information. Juries and judges can identify more with a whole person than with an empty name with nothing behind it. The background also helps lay a foundation of authenticity (a showing that this witness is who she says she is) and of credibility (that this witness is believable). Common background questions address the witness' age, employment, education, and family status.

The "scene" component of testimony is usually the locus or place in which the action occurs. If the case is a prosecution for bank robbery, the scene is the bank. If the case is a domestic family dispute, the scene is the family house. The scene component, while very important, often is given short shrift. Many attorneys jump right into the action part of the testimony instead.

The "action" component is usually the focal point of the testimony and is readily identifiable. In a bank robbery, the action is the robbery itself. In a family dispute, the action is the actual dispute.

The prohibition against leading questions on direct examination has several rationales. One reason for the rule is to allow the jury to hear the testimony directly from the witness and not from the attorney. If leading questions were permitted, an attorney could present the entire factual story through leading questions, with the witness serving as nothing more than a stage prop. A second reason is that witnesses are considered to be aligned with the party who called them to the witness stand, and, consequently, there is no need for the attorney to lead the witness through the testimony.

The assumption about witness alignment, however, is not always accurate. Sometimes a party must call a hostile witness, i.e., a person who is biased in favor of the opposing side or is otherwise aligned with an opposing party. For example, an eyewitness with important information may be a family member or neighbor of the opposing party. If the witness is considered to be hostile to the examiner, the examiner may seek the judge's permission to ask leading questions on direct examination, or simply, "to lead the witness."

The rule prohibiting the use of leading questions on direct examination is subject to several exceptions in addition to the one for hostile witnesses. The usual non-leading questions may be inappropriate with a witness who is aged, infirm, or a child. Thus, Rule 611(c) provides that leading questions are allowed on direct examination if the court decides they are necessary to develop the witness' testimony.

Example

PROSECUTOR: (on direct examination) Wally, where do you live?

DEFENSE COUNSEL: Objection! Leading.

JUDGE: Objection overruled.

[The judge most likely ruled in this manner because the question was not leading. Like most "where," "why," "when," or "how" questions, this question does not suggest an answer. Further, the question properly elicits background information.]

A: I live on the corner of 4th and Overland Street.

PROSECUTOR: What happened on July 10th, at 7:00 p.m.?

A: I saw Johnny B. Badd shoot and kill Louie Ratatooie.

PROSECUTOR: Did Johnny shoot Louie with a revolver?

DEFENSE COUNSEL: Objection. Leading.

JUDGE: Objection sustained.

[The judge concluded that the question suggests an answer — that Johnny shot Louie with a revolver. There is no reason to lead the witness during this portion of the direct examination pursuant to Federal Rules of Evidence 611.]

PROSECUTOR: So Johnny shot Louie dead? And after the shooting, in which direction did Johnny drive away and where did he hide the gun?

DEFENSE COUNSEL: Objection on three grounds, Your Honor —, asked and answered, compound question, and assuming facts not in evidence.

[If the judge permits an explanation, probably at a sidebar, the defense counsel might elaborate as follows. "First, the question of whether Johnny shot Louie dead has been asked and answered. Second, the question asked by the prosecutor about the events after the shooting is objectionable because it is really two separate questions posed in compound form. The witness was asked where did Johnny drive and where did Johnny hide the gun. Finally, the question is objectionable because it assumes facts not in evidence — that Johnny drove away (he may have walked, taken a boat, or even remained at the scene) and that he hid the gun (he may not have hidden it at all)."]

Problem 7-10: Returning to Form Objections

Plaintiff sues Defendant for breach of contract. Plaintiff is questioned at trial on direct examination.

PLAINTIFF'S ATTORNEY: Would you state your name for the record?

A: Alfreida Cohen.

PLAINTIFF'S ATTORNEY: You live in San Francisco, right?

DEFENDANT'S ATTORNEY: Objection! (*On what grounds?*)

JUDGE: (*How should the judge rule? Why?*)

PLAINTIFF'S ATTORNEY: Do you live in San Francisco, or somewhere else?

DEFENDANT'S ATTORNEY: Objection! (*On what grounds?*)

JUDGE: (*How should the judge rule? Why?*)

PLAINTIFF'S ATTORNEY: Where were you on the night of June 1st, at 9:00 p.m.?

DEFENDANT'S ATTORNEY: Objection! (*On what grounds?*)

JUDGE: (*How should the judge rule? Why?*)

A: I was at the Burger King, having a candlelight dinner.

PLAINTIFF'S ATTORNEY: What did you see and hear at that time?

DEFENDANT'S ATTORNEY: Objection! (*On what grounds?*)

JUDGE: (*How should the judge rule? Why?*)

A: I saw the defendant selling goods to my competitor.

PLAINTIFF'S ATTORNEY: So you saw the defendant selling goods to someone else?

DEFENDANT'S ATTORNEY: Objection! (*On what grounds?*)

JUDGE: (*How should the judge rule? Why?*)

PLAINTIFF'S ATTORNEY: After you saw the defendant with your competitor, what happened next?

A: They left and I went to my office. Later that week I saw the defendant's sister. Now she's in business with the defendant and —

DEFENDANT'S ATTORNEY: Objection! (*On what grounds?*)

JUDGE: (*How should the judge rule? Why?*)

Problem 7-11: More Form

At a trial in a civil conversion case, the plaintiff testifies on direct examination as follows:

PLAINTIFF'S ATTORNEY: When you saw the defendant walk by your house at 3:30 p.m., on July 5th, what did you do?

DEFENDANT'S ATTORNEY: Objection! (*On what grounds?*)

JUDGE: (*How should the judge rule? Why?*)

PLAINTIFF'S ATTORNEY: What happened at 3:30 p.m. on July 5th?

DEFENDANT'S ATTORNEY: Objection! (*On what grounds?*)

JUDGE: (*How should the judge rule? Why?*)

PLAINTIFF'S ATTORNEY: Did the defendant have anything in his hands when, as you say, he walked by your house at 3:30 p.m.?

DEFENDANT'S ATTORNEY: Objection! (*On what grounds?*)

JUDGE: (*How should the judge rule? Why?*)

A: Yes, he held what appeared to be a glass statue.

PLAINTIFF'S ATTORNEY: Do you think the defendant looked suspicious or shifty?

DEFENDANT'S ATTORNEY: Objection! (*On what grounds?*)

JUDGE: (*How should the judge rule? Why?*)

A: (if objection overruled) Yes, definitely.

PLAINTIFF'S ATTORNEY: So where were you when you saw the defendant?

A: At first, I was still in front of my house. Then I went inside to telephone the police. I was steaming! By 4:00 p.m., the police came and I had calmed down some. It took until 5:00 p.m. before I was fully relaxed. I did drink a beer at 4:50 p.m., but then I was itching to —

DEFENDANT'S ATTORNEY: Objection! (*On what grounds?*)

JUDGE: (*How should the judge rule? Why?*)

3. Cross-Examination

On cross-examination, it is generally a good practice to ask short, clear questions, the answers to which are known by the questioner.

Cross-examination is the part of the trial approached by some attorneys with unrestrained exuberance. Novices in particular often labor under the mistaken belief that a good cross-examination always crushes a witness into tiny pieces. Nothing could be further from the truth. Cross-examination of a witness should depend on what can be achieved in the context of the case. The witness might have helpful information as well as hurtful evidence, and even the hurtful information may not hurt that much. Belligerent cross-examination of an unimportant witness, especially one who happens to be sympathetic in the jury's eyes, can be much more harmful to the case than not cross-examining the witness at all.

Leading questions are permitted on cross-examination, and many effective cross-examinations, particularly those in which impeachment of the witness is the primary objective, consist almost entirely of leading questions. In fact, leading questions are the preferred type. When a cross-examiner uses a series of well-framed leading questions, it almost seems as if the attorney is testifying, and not the witness.

It is an oft-stated maxim that examiners should not ask a question to which they do not know the answer. A nonleading question, such as, "Why did you do that?", invites a new and possibly harmful response by the witness, one that could surprise the examiner and greatly damage the case. For example, the question, "So if you did not observe the defendant stab the victim, how can you testify he did it?" could result in the extremely unfortunate answer, "I saw the videotape of the knifing" or "I saw everything up to the point of impact." In addition, a non-leading question permits the witness to explain, bolster, or augment the testimony previously given on direct examination.

Arguing with witnesses about major points of the witness' testimony is usually a vain attempt to get the witness to recant what the witness stated on direct examination. Instead, it is more useful to make smaller points, especially those about which the attorney already knows the answer. The attorney can argue the salient central questions (such as guilt or liability), using inferences and logic in the closing argument to the jury. It is the rare case, indeed, where a witness collapses on the stand with bowed head, saying, "Yes, you're right. I will finally, after all of these years, admit I did it. I am the culprit who committed the evil deed!"

Example

An eyewitness to an automobile accident, Lucy Lubner, has testified on direct examination about how the accident occurred. She is now on cross-examination. This cross-examination suggests inferences that can be argued and aggregated for the jury during closing argument.

DEFENDANT'S ATTORNEY: Now, Lucy, you say the accident occurred at approximately 5:00 p.m.?

A: Yes, about that time.

DEFENDANT'S ATTORNEY: You were on your way home after working a six-hour shift in the town mill?

A: Yes, I work from 10:00 a.m. to 5:00 p.m. on Fridays.

DEFENDANT'S ATTORNEY: Is it fair to say that your work requires you to stand over a moving machine for most of the day?

A: Yes, that's right.

DEFENDANT'S ATTORNEY: While you are standing over that machine, you are also operating it, right?

A: Yes.

DEFENDANT'S ATTORNEY: Now this accident occurred on December 18th, true?

A: Yes.

DEFENDANT'S ATTORNEY: The sun was setting at that time, right?

A: Yes.

DEFENDANT'S ATTORNEY: Some of the cars around you had their headlights on.

A: Yes.

Problem 7-12: Scope

Bam was employed as a truck-driver for a mouthwash company. After detouring from his usual delivery route to visit his friend, Barney, Bam was involved in an accident with a pedestrian, Fred. Fred sued Bam and Bam's employer. The only issue at trial was whether Bam was acting outside of the scope of his employment at the time of the accident. At trial, Bam was called to testify by the plaintiff, Fred. Bam was asked only four questions that elicited whether he was working at the time of the accident. On cross-examination, Bam was asked several additional questions:

DEFENDANT'S ATTORNEY: Bam, were you distracted at the time of the crash by your friend, Pebbles, yelling at you from the sidewalk?

PLAINTIFF'S ATTORNEY: Objection! (*On what grounds?*)

JUDGE: (*How should the judge rule? Why?*)

DEFENDANT'S ATTORNEY: Had you been drinking any alcoholic beverages immediately prior to the crash?

PLAINTIFF'S ATTORNEY: Objection! (*On what grounds?*)

JUDGE: (*How should the judge rule? Why?*)

DEFENDANT'S ATTORNEY: Describe what you saw immediately after the crash occurred.

PLAINTIFF'S ATTORNEY: Objection! (*On what grounds?*)

JUDGE: (*How should the judge rule? Why?*)

Problem 7-13: Succa Mucca Rucca . . .

Arsenic, a prominent local banker, sues Lacy, the mayor of the town, for slander. Lacy called Arsenic a "succa mucca rucca cheat whose business deals are all criminal in nature." At trial, plaintiff Arsenic calls his business partner, Sharon, to testify.

A. Before Sharon can take the witness stand, defendant Lacy asks to approach the bench and states, "I believe that while the proposed witness, Sharon, was excluded from the courtroom during prior testimony, she was exposed to at least some prior testimony when she had dinner with Arsenic last night. Rule 615 prohibits witnesses from the courtroom so they "cannot hear other witnesses' testimony" but the prohibition, Your Honor, was intended to extend to prohibit witnesses from having access to other trial testimony in any place outside of the courtroom as well." How should the judge interpret Rule 615? Note that there is a 2022 proposed Amendment to Rule 615 to settle this issue.

B. Assume that Sharon is allowed to testify. Sharon states that Arsenic is an honest businessman whose truthfulness, in her opinion, is beyond reproach. Sharon is asked the following questions on cross-examination:

DEFENDANT'S ATTORNEY: Sharon, didn't Arsenic take 20 legal pads owned by the bank for his own personal use two years ago?

PLAINTIFF'S ATTORNEY: Objection! The question is irrelevant.

JUDGE: (*How should the judge rule? Why?*)

DEFENDANT'S ATTORNEY: Sharon, is it true that you cheated on your civil service examination last year?

PLAINTIFF'S ATTORNEY: Objection! The question is beyond the scope of the direct examination, your honor.

JUDGE: (*How should the judge rule? Why?*)

§ 7.04 Impeachment of Witnesses

> **Key Words: Attack — Witness — Truth (or Accuracy)**

A. Introduction

"To impeach a witness" means to attack the witness' believability, often called credibility. A witness' credibility may be undermined by showing that their testimony is either untrue or inaccurate. Even a well-intentioned witness may have low credibility, if only because the person needs eyeglasses or has a poor memory. Thus, impeachment is not simply about whether a witness is lying or deceitful. An examiner generally impeaches a witness to undermine the weight that will be accorded the witness' testimony by the trier of fact. It bears emphasizing that the impeachment of a witness can be viewed almost as a trial within a trial, since it is distinct from the admissibility of the witness' initial evidence.

Under the common-law "voucher rule," parties were presumed to vouch for the credibility of their own witnesses. Consequently, parties were forbidden to impeach their own witnesses unless the witnesses were shown to be hostile or adverse. The Federal Rules of Evidence and the evidence codes of many states have abandoned the voucher limitation. *See* Rule 607. The modern rules recognize that parties often do not have a real choice in selecting their own witnesses. Consequently, parties should be able to impeach those witnesses when appropriate. Further, parties may seek to impeach their own witness for strategic purposes. The proponent of the witness may wish to "lessen the sting" or "soften the blow" of harmful impeachment evidence by offering the evidence on direct examination. The disclosure makes it appear that the party has not attempted to hide damaging testimony.

Two of the primary considerations in understanding the impeachment rules are the type of impeachment, e.g., proof of bias or prior convictions, and whether the impeaching evidence is considered *intrinsic* or *extrinsic*. The intrinsic-extrinsic distinction is the first important analytic step in determining the admissibility of evidence offered to impeach a witness. Essentially, intrinsic and extrinsic impeachment methods are governed by different parameters.

B. Comparing Intrinsic and Extrinsic Impeachment

Whether impeachment will be permitted will often depend on whether it is intrinsic or extrinsic in nature. The most common form of impeachment is intrinsic.

Definition of Intrinsic Impeachment

Intrinsic impeachment means that an attack on a witness' truthfulness essentially rests on the answers given by the witness being impeached. It is impeachment from the witness' "own mouth." Intrinsic impeachment questions include, "Didn't you cheat on your driver's license exam?", "Didn't you tell a different story last month compared to what you are saying today on the witness stand?", and "Don't you owe the defendant, on behalf of whom you are now testifying, $20,000?"

Extrinsic evidence impeachment, on the other hand, depends on either a new witness, a witness other than the one to be impeached, or the introduction of new evidence, such as a document. Thus, confronting a witness during cross-examination with inconsistent testimony that the witness had previously given in a deposition is a form of intrinsic evidence impeachment, whereas introducing the inconsistent portion of the deposition itself into evidence constitutes a form of extrinsic evidence impeachment.

Most types of impeachment — notably (1) *contradiction,* (2) *bias,* (3) *convictions of certain crimes,* (4) *prior acts relating to a witness' truthfulness,* (5) *testimonial capacities,* and (6) *prior inconsistent statements* — are permissible forms of intrinsic evidence impeachment. Extrinsic evidence impeachment, on the other hand, is more restricted because it has greater potential for wasting time and distracting the jury.

The rule governing when a witness may be impeached through extrinsic evidence is popularly called the "collateral issue" rule. This rule prohibits the use of extrinsic evidence to impeach a witness on a collateral matter. Correspondingly, it permits extrinsic evidence impeachment only for non-collateral (i.e., important) matters. The non-collateral or important matters that are properly the subject of extrinsic impeachment are: (1) *bias,* (2) *impeachment relating to a fact at issue,* (3) *the witness' testimonial capacities,* (4) *convictions of a crime,* and (5) *reputation or opinion evidence about the truthfulness or veracity of another witness.*

Under the collateral issue rule, therefore, extrinsic evidence may not be used to impeach a witness when: (1) contradicting the witness on a collateral (unimportant) fact, (2) showing a witness' prior inconsistent statement on a collateral fact, or (3) offering a prior act by the witness relating to the witness' truthfulness. To ensure that judges do not admit extrinsic evidence of prior untruthful act impeachment, Rule 608(b) includes an express prohibition of such evidence.

C. Common Types of Impeachment

1. Overview

Most types of impeachment are implicitly accepted by tradition and case law, rather than expressly described in the Federal Rules of Evidence. Types of impeachment commonly employed at trial include the following:

- Contradiction (*see* [2], *below*).
- Bias (*see* [3], *below*).
- Criminal convictions (*see* [4], *below*).
- Prior untruthful acts (*see* [5], *below*).
- Testimonial capacities (*see* [6], *below*).
- Prior inconsistent statements (*see* [7], *below*).
- Poor character for truthfulness (*see* [8], *below*).

Example

The witness, Amy Sue, testified on direct examination that she observed the defendant rob the Charley's Chicken restaurant on 9th Street and escape through the side door. The following occurred on cross-examination of Amy Sue.

This is an example of impeachment by contradiction:

DEFENSE COUNSEL: Now, Amy Sue, the Charley's Chicken restaurant that was robbed is actually located at 3200 S.W. 9th Street, not 3400 S.W. 9th Street, as you just testified, right?

A: Actually, you're correct, come to think of it.

This is an example of impeachment by showing bias:

DEFENSE COUNSEL: Amy Sue, you hate people who are charged with violent crime, isn't that right?

A: Well, that's true, but this defendant is the person who I saw rob Charley's.

This is an example of impeachment by prior, untruthful acts:

DEFENSE COUNSEL: Please just answer the question asked. Last March, you committed mail fraud against the United States Postal Service, did you not?

A: So? What about it?

This is an example of impeachment by prior felony conviction:

DEFENSE COUNSEL: You were convicted nine years ago of attempted murder, right?

A: Yes, but that so-called conviction was a colossal mistake. I was framed!

This is an example of impeachment by showing defects in the witness' testimonial capacities:

DEFENSE COUNSEL: You were not wearing your prescription eyeglasses at the time you say you observed the alleged robber, were you?

A: No, I was not wearing my glasses.

This is an example of impeachment by prior inconsistent statement:

DEFENSE COUNSEL: So it is your testimony here in court that the robber was about 5 feet, 10 inches tall and had brown hair?

A: Yes.

DEFENSE COUNSEL: Didn't you say to your mother after the incident that "the robber was about 6 foot 2 and had blonde hair"?

A: Yes, I did say that to my mother.

[Note: Most attorneys probably would not be able to squeeze in all six forms of intrinsic impeachment with a single witness unless the witness is Attila the Hun or otherwise thoroughly discreditable.]

Problem 7-14: Cross My Heart: An Overview

Jim Stone is sued by his neighbor for the conversion of his neighbor's very expensive Cannondale bicycle, which disappeared at around 11:45 a.m. At trial, Jim testifies on his own behalf, claiming misidentification. Jim offered an alibi. He asserted that he was at work several miles away from 9:00 a.m. to noon, including the time when the alleged theft occurred. On direct examination, Jim stated, "If someone took that fancy bicycle of yours, I'm really sorry. But I can tell you this, I was at work several miles away from 9:00 a.m. until noon on that day." On cross-examination, Jim is questioned as follows:

PLAINTIFF'S ATTORNEY: Isn't it true that on the day in question, you worked in the morning from 8:00 a.m. to 11:25 a.m., and not to 11:45 a.m. as you just testified?

DEFENDANT'S ATTORNEY: Objection! Irrelevant!

JUDGE: (*How should the judge rule? Why?*)

PLAINTIFF'S ATTORNEY: Are you going to lose your job if you are found liable in this case?

DEFENDANT'S ATTORNEY: Objection! (*On what grounds? What type of impeachment is occurring? Explain.*)

JUDGE: (*How should the judge rule? Why?*)

PLAINTIFF'S ATTORNEY: Weren't you convicted of a felony, the distribution of marijuana, three years ago?

DEFENDANT'S ATTORNEY: Objection! *(On what grounds? What type of impeachment is occurring? Explain.)*

JUDGE: *(How should the judge rule? Why?)*

PLAINTIFF'S ATTORNEY: You cheated on your Law School Admission Test last year, didn't you?

DEFENDANT'S ATTORNEY: Objection! *(On what grounds? What type of impeachment is occurring? Explain.)*

JUDGE: *(How should the judge rule? Why?)*

PLAINTIFF'S ATTORNEY: You have intermittent amnesia, Mr. Stone, don't you?

DEFENDANT'S ATTORNEY: Objection! *(On what grounds? What type of impeachment is occurring? Explain.)*

JUDGE: *(How should the judge rule? Why?)*

PLAINTIFF'S ATTORNEY: Didn't you say in your deposition on June 5th that you drove to work via the Parkway, not U.S. 1, as you just testified?

DEFENDANT'S ATTORNEY: Objection! *(On what grounds? What type of impeachment is occurring? Explain.)*

JUDGE: *(How should the judge rule? Why?)*

2. Contradiction

Contradiction occurs when the examining attorney disputes the witness' testimony about a fact (e.g., "Ms. Witness, you said on direct examination that the house at Greentree Place has no garage, when in fact it has a two-car garage, isn't that right?"). On cross-examination, a witness may be impeached by contradiction concerning facts that need not be dispositive or even important to the outcome of the case. The theory of impeachment by contradiction is that if a witness is inaccurate about one fact, she is more likely to be inaccurate about other facts as well.

a. Extrinsic Contradiction Impeachment: Permitted Only if Important to the Case

If the witness denies the asserted contradicting facts, however, the cross-examiner will not be allowed to prove them by extrinsic evidence, unless the subject fact is important to the case. For example, the color of the traffic light as the defendant's car proceeded through the light's intersection in a negligence action would be a fact important to the case and a proper basis for extrinsic impeachment.

Problem 7-15: Cross.com

Carolyn testified in a commercial litigation action. *Which of the following questions are permissible during the cross-examination of Carolyn? Explain.*

1. "You used your personal computer to make notes of the meeting with the opposing party only two days after the meeting occurred, not immediately thereafter as you testified on direct examination, isn't that right?"

2. "You have a Macintosh computer, not a Dell as you just testified on direct, isn't that correct?"

3. "You left your office last Wednesday at 5:30 p.m., not 7:30 p.m. as you testified on direct examination, right?"

4. "Your boss, Ms. Sanders, was wrong when she testified that she deposited the March proceeds on March 4th, wasn't she?"

5. "Isn't it true that you are one huge liar?"

3. Bias

Bias is a form of impeachment in which a witness is shown to be influenced, prejudiced, or predisposed toward or against a party. Bias may exist because the witness is hostile, interested in the outcome, or otherwise non-neutral (e.g., "Mr. Witness, is it true that you owe the plaintiff money, that you hate the plaintiff because he's now married to your ex-wife, and that you were promised a job by the plaintiff's brother if the plaintiff wins this case?"). The attack usually occurs on cross-examination, but also can be advanced sometimes through extrinsic evidence.

a. Extrinsic Bias Impeachment: Permitted

Extrinsic impeachment of bias is routinely permitted because bias is considered non-collateral to the case. Extrinsic bias impeachment generally follows failed intrinsic bias impeachment, where the witness has denied the allegation of bias. Watch for extrinsic evidence of specific acts used to show bias. This extrinsic evidence is generally permitted, despite being confused with prior untruthful acts, which cannot be used extrinsically.

Problem 7-16: The Right Direct-Ion

Shawn is prosecuted for allegedly battering Bobbi on a Colorado ski slope. The only eyewitness is Shawn's sister, Tya. The prosecutor calls Tya as a witness. On direct examination, the prosecutor questions Tya.

PROSECUTOR: Tya, you are the sister of the defendant, Shawn, correct?

DEFENSE COUNSEL: Objection. The question is leading and therefore improper.

JUDGE: (*How should the judge rule? Why?*) *If this is proper impeachment, can it occur on direct examination? Why?*

PROSECUTOR: Tya, are you currently facing a criminal charge of attempted murder?

DEFENSE COUNSEL: Objection. This question is improper impeachment on several grounds. (*What are the grounds for this objection?*)

JUDGE: (*How should the judge rule? Why?*)

PROSECUTOR: Have any deals been made in return for your testimony?

DEFENSE COUNSEL: Objection! (*What are the grounds for this objection?*)

JUDGE: (*How should the judge rule? Why?*)

Problem 7-17: Just Friends

The defendant, Alexander, is charged with the unlawful possession of a firearm by a felon. At trial, the defendant's friend, Preston, testifies for the defense. Preston states that the gun in question, found on the ground near Alexander, was really Preston's. On cross-examination, the prosecutor asks Preston whether he and Alexander are both members of the same gang, "Red 'N Blue Violins."

Is this evidence permissible impeachment? Explain.

Problem 7-18: Losing Religion

Shawana is prosecuted for the distribution of cocaine. Father O'Malley testifies for the prosecution as an eyewitness to the crime. On cross-examination he is asked by defense counsel, "Father, isn't it true that Shawana was at one time a member of the church where you are the priest, but she quit the church after having an argument with you?"

Is this question permissible? Explain.

4. Convictions of Crime

The underlying theory of impeachment by conviction is that a witness who has been convicted of certain types of crime is less believable. According to Federal Rule of Evidence 609, two types of crimes affect a witness' credibility and can be used to impeach the witness: (1) crimes of dishonesty or false statement, that involve deception or fraud, regardless of the potential length of incarceration; and (2) felonies, that are punishable by more than one year in prison. Other crimes, such as misdemeanor crimes of violence or drug possession, cannot be used to impeach witnesses, although state rules often vary from jurisdiction to jurisdiction. Likewise, Rule 609 generally excludes juvenile adjudications and "stale" convictions, which are less probative of truthfulness. Convictions are stale if more than 10 years have elapsed since the date of the conviction or of the witness' release from incarceration, whichever is later. Under Rule 609, for example, a witness could not be impeached with an 11-year-old felony conviction for which the sentence was probation and a fine.

a. Crimes of Dishonesty or False Statement

What qualifies as a crime of "dishonesty or false statement" is not always clear from the face of the crime. In *United States v. Brackeen*, 969 F.2d 827 (9th Cir. 1992) (*per curiam*), for example, the defendant was indicted on one count of aiding and abetting an armed bank robbery and two counts of unarmed robbery. The defendant pled guilty to both counts of unarmed robbery and was tried and convicted of aiding and abetting the armed bank robbery. At the trial of the aiding and abetting charge, the court permitted the defendant to be impeached with the robbery convictions under Federal Rule of Evidence 609(a)(2) as crimes of dishonesty or false statement. On appeal, the Ninth Circuit, *en banc*, reversed. The Court held that the unarmed robberies were not crimes of dishonesty or false statement for purposes of Rule 609. The phrase "dishonesty or false statement" could have been intended to refer either to crimes broadly evidencing a lack of integrity or those more narrowly indicating a breach of trust, such as deceit or fraud. The Court chose the narrower construction, stating that Congress, in enacting the rules, intended the narrower view. The phrase is limited to crimes that are "crimen falsi," i.e., crimes that are bad in and of themselves and have some relationship to deceit and lying. It does not include "those crimes which, bad though they are, do not carry with them a tinge of falsification." *Id.* at 830–31. The Court proceeded to cite with approval similar constructions from other circuits.

If a crime does not require proof of fraud or deception on its face, such as obstruction of justice, it still can qualify as a crime of dishonesty or false statement under some circumstances. As an amendment to the original text of Rule 609 helped to clarify, if the prosecutor had to prove dishonesty or false statement to obtain a conviction, the crime qualifies as a permissible conviction under Rule 609.

b. Unfair Prejudice

Crimes of dishonesty or false statement are directly probative of the truthfulness of a witness and generally are not subject to the Rule 403 balancing test. Appellate courts also view the use of limiting instructions given by the trial court to the jury as an extra safeguard against the risk of unfair prejudice.

c. Felony Convictions

Prior felony convictions are not automatically permitted for the purpose of impeaching a witness. Under Rule 609, the use of felony convictions first must satisfy the unfair prejudice test of Rule 403 for all witnesses, with the exception of a testifying criminal defendant, a situation that warrants a special balancing test. The exclusion of some felonies reflects the belief that a felony conviction is less likely to bear on a witness' truthfulness than a crime of dishonesty or false statement. (For the situation that preceded the rule change, *see Green v. Bock Laundry Machine Co.*, 490 U.S. 504 (1989)). Rule 609 provides greater protection to criminal defendants who choose to testify on their own behalf. The rationale for this special treatment is to prevent felony convictions offered to impeach the accused from being used by the trier of fact as substantive evidence of guilt. Under a special balancing test, felony convictions will be permitted to impeach the testifying accused only if their probative value outweighs the prejudicial effect to the accused. This balancing test reverses Rule 403's built-in presumption in favor of admissibility and favors the accused.

Courts may consider a variety of factors in determining whether a defendant's felony conviction will be unfairly prejudicial when offered as impeachment evidence. One important factor is the similarity between the impeachment felony and the crime charged. The greater the similarity, the greater the likelihood that the impeachment will be misused by the jurors as evidence that "if the defendant did it before, it is more likely the defendant did it again" (e.g., "Once a criminal, always a criminal"). Other factors that might be considered include the importance of the defendant's credibility to the case, the nature and date of the impeachment crime, and the significance of the defendant's testimony to the case overall. *See, e.g., United States v. Sloman*, 909 F.2d 176, 180–81 (6th Cir. 1990).

The admissibility of a crime offered to impeach a testifying accused is not tied to the use of that crime in other ways, such as its use as an "other act" under Rule 404(b). A conviction may be used to impeach even if the underlying crime has been offered—and rejected by the trial court—as an "other act" pursuant to Rule 404. In essence, the fact that evidence is impermissible for one purpose does not mean it is impermissible for another purpose. *See, e.g., United States v. Haslip*, 160 F.3d 649, 653–54 (10th Cir. 1998). Of course, with evidence admitted for one purpose and not another, a limiting instruction accompanying the evidence may be appropriate. *Id.* at 655.

What constitutes a "conviction" for impeachment purposes can be perplexing, especially to a layperson. A conviction can result from a jury or court verdict, or a guilty plea. Having been indicted, arrested, or otherwise charged with a crime is insufficient to qualify as a conviction under the rules. Further, contrary to a popular misconception, a conviction is fodder for impeachment regardless of whether the accused received a sentence of incarceration, probation, or no penalty at all. A person who has been given probation and has never stepped foot in a jail cell can still have multiple felony convictions. Like other types of impeachment (*see* Rule 607), a witness' criminal convictions may be offered on either direct or cross-examination. Parties may offer evidence during direct examination of a favorable witness that the witness has been convicted of a crime to "soften the blow" of the ensuing cross-examination and demonstrate to the jury that counsel is not hiding anything.

i. Extrinsic Conviction Impeachment: Permitted

If a witness denies a conviction on cross-examination, it may be proved by extrinsic evidence. The form of the extrinsic evidence is limited, though, usually to a certified copy of the conviction. Thus, the judge or the members of the jury that convicted a witness cannot be called to testify to the conviction.

Problem 7-19: Forgery, Fake, Fraud

Sylvia is prosecuted for forging signatures on applications for food stamps. The prosecution, in its case-in-chief, offers a witness, Wally, who will testify that Sylvia (1) has been convicted of forgery on three prior occasions, and (2) was charged with embezzlement on a fourth prior occasion.

Are these convictions and the criminal charge admissible? Why?

If it had been Wally, and not Sylvia, who was convicted of forgery and charged with embezzlement, would the convictions and charge be admissible?

Problem 7-20: Medical Mal

Mal brought suit against Dr. Sloan for failing to diagnose Mal's prostate cancer. At trial, the plaintiff's expert, Dr. Inos, testified. On cross-examination, the defendant wished to question the doctor about his misdemeanor conviction for willfully failing to file a federal income tax return.

Is this impeachment permissible? See Cree v. Hatcher, 969 F.2d 34 (3d Cir. 1992).

May Dr. Inos be asked about a pending suspension of his medical license by the State of Iowa if he is testifying in an Arkansas federal court? Explain.

Problem 7-21: One Bad Apple

Johnny Apple was prosecuted for attempted murder. Johnny testified at trial and denied committing the crime charged. On cross-examination, the prosecution attempted to impeach Johnny with the following crimes. *Can any of the crimes be used to impeach Johnny? In addition, what test applies in determining whether impermissible prejudice would result?*

1. A 15-year-old conviction for attempted murder.

2. A seven-year-old conviction for assault, punishable by six months in jail and a fine of $1,000.

3. A 19-year-old juvenile adjudication for murder.

4. A 10-year-old conviction for aggravated battery, punishable by a maximum of three years in prison, for which the defendant was sentenced to two months incarceration, sentence suspended.

5. A six-year-old conviction for grand theft, for which the defendant was sentenced to six months' incarceration.

5. Prior Untruthful Acts

Impeachment by prior acts under Rule 608(b) is limited to specific prior acts of the witness that reflect on the witness' capacity for truthfulness or veracity. These acts are the functional equivalent of the acts underlying the dishonesty or false statement convictions under Rule 609. Prior untruthful acts impeachment, as it is sometimes called, is still distinguishable from impeachment by conviction, because no conviction is required for bad acts impeachment. In fact, the act may not have been the subject of a criminal charge at all or might even have been the subject of a criminal charge resulting in an acquittal.

Describing this conduct as "bad acts" is a misnomer of sorts because there is a limit on the type and nature of the prior acts that fall in this category. The acts that may be used for impeachment are limited to those involving truthfulness or veracity, such as fraud, obtaining property under false pretenses, or perjury. Acts of violence, such as disorderly conduct, battery, or even murder, do not constitute "bad" acts relating to truthfulness and generally cannot be used to impeach. Acts such as drug use, driving at excessive speed, failing to return a library book on time, and filing for bankruptcy also fail to be sufficiently related to witness truthfulness to be admissible untruthful act impeachment.

Sometimes, a judge will probe beneath the surface of a crime that does not on its face appear to involve dishonesty to determine if the manner in which the crime was committed was deceitful. For example, if a larceny was directly intertwined with deceit, it might meet the requirements of Rule 608(b) impeachment. *See, e.g., United States v. Payton*, 159 F.3d 49 (2d Cir. 1998).

If impeachment by a prior act is proper, the witness may be asked only about the underlying act itself and not about an arrest, charge, indictment, suspension, or expulsion relating to the act. The witness' truthfulness does not hinge on the arrest, indictment, etc., but rather on commission of the act itself. Thus, it is permissible to ask, "You defrauded your insurance company, didn't you?" but not, "You were indicted for defrauding your insurance company, weren't you?"

The original language of Rule 608(b) was clarified by an amendment that deleted the bracketed words and added the italicized words:

> (b) Specific instances of the conduct of a witness, for the purpose of attacking or supporting the witness' [credibility] *character for truthfulness*, other than conviction of crime as provided in Rule 609, may not be proved by extrinsic evidence. They may, however, in the discretion of the court, if probative of truthfulness or untruthfulness, be inquired into on cross-examination of the witness (1) concerning the witness' character for truthfulness or untruthfulness, or (2) concerning the character for truthfulness or untruthfulness of another witness as to which character the witness being cross-examined has testified.

The giving of testimony, whether by an accused or by any other witness, does not operate as a waiver of the accused's or the witness' privilege against self-incrimination when examined with respect to matters [which] *that* relate only to [credibility] *character for truthfulness.*

The rationale behind substituting the phrase, "character for truthfulness," for the word, "credibility," is not immediately apparent. The answer lies in the fact that the term "credibility" can have broader connotations than the phrase "character for truthfulness." As the Committee Note explaining the change observes, "The rule has been amended to clarify that the absolute prohibition on extrinsic evidence applies only when the sole reason for proffering that evidence is to attack or support the witness' character for truthfulness." Advisory Committee Note to Rule 608(b). What the amendment emphasizes is that the prohibition of extrinsic evidence is limited to prior acts impeachment under Rule 608(b); other forms of impeachment are governed separately. As the Committee Note elaborates, "By limiting the application of the Rule to proof of a witness' character for truthfulness, the amendment leaves the admissibility of extrinsic evidence offered for other grounds of impeachment (such as contradiction, prior inconsistent statement, bias and mental capacity) to Rules 402 and 403." (citations omitted).

a. Extrinsic Untruthful Act Impeachment: Disallowed

Permissible prior untruthful act impeachment cannot be proven by extrinsic evidence. If the witness denies the act, the questioner generally must take the witness' answer without any further follow-up. *See* Rule 608(b). Otherwise, a mini-trial would result, and the jury would be distracted.

Problem 7-22: Liar, Liar

Janet is prosecuted for committing perjury during her testimony before the grand jury. At trial, she testifies on her own behalf and is asked the following questions on cross-examination:

PROSECUTOR: You were arrested for lying on your income tax statement last year, weren't you?

DEFENSE COUNSEL: Objection. Improper impeachment.

JUDGE: (*How should the judge rule? Why?*)

PROSECUTOR: You deceived your boss three weeks ago, didn't you, when you claimed you missed an important meeting because your train was late?

DEFENSE COUNSEL: Objection. Improper impeachment.

JUDGE: (*How should the judge rule? Why?*)

6. Testimonial Capacities

The term "testimonial capacities" refers to aspects of a witness' testimony that are important for accuracy: (1) perception — what the witness saw, heard, smelled, or touched at the time in question; (2) memory — the ability of the witness to recall the prior occurrence, happening, or event; (3) narration — the ability of the witness to communicate this perception and memory to others; and sometimes (4) sincerity (which is often viewed as a combination of the other three capacities) — a measurement indicating a lack of prevarication. Sincerity is distinct from accuracy, because a witness can be sincere but still inaccurate.

Attacking a witness' testimonial capacities is accomplished by presenting intrinsic or extrinsic evidence revealing defects in any one or more of these capacities. By revealing these defects, the jury is shown the limits of a witness' ability to provide an accurate recounting of prior events. For example, many witnesses have limited and inaccurate memories, particularly with the passage of time. Additionally, the opponent is allowed to present extrinsic evidence (*see* [C], *below*) of a witness' reputation for untruthfulness, or offer a qualified witness' opinion of another witness' untruthfulness under Rule 608(a).

Defects in testimonial capacities often extend beyond common deficiencies to encompass physiological defects that result in problems of perception, memory, or narration. These problems are more severe than those reflected by statements such as "I forgot" or "I could not hear something so far away," which happen to everyone, and instead concern some physical or psychological condition, such as bad eyesight, amnesia, hearing loss, or schizophrenia. Physiological defects are particularly injurious to a witness' ability to be accurate.

a. Extrinsic Testimonial Capacities Impeachment: Permitted

Testimonial capacities impeachment is considered important in a case and is routinely permitted. It generally follows a failed attempt on cross-examination to impeach a witness' testimonial capacities intrinsically.

Problem 7-23: Psychotic Chips

In a tort action for false imprisonment, Don Geo is about to testify as an eyewitness for the defense. As he takes the witness stand, he yells to the jury, "Would you like some of my fantastic psychotic chips?" referring to a bag of potato chips he is carrying. Don adds, "They're mind-altering."

1. On cross-examination, the plaintiff's attorney questions Don about two previous hospital stays for undifferentiated schizophrenia. *Are such questions permissible? Why?*

2. Don also is questioned on cross-examination about whether his psychotic chips contain any mind-altering substances. *Admissible?*

3. May Don be asked on cross-examination whether he was under the influence of alcohol or other drugs at the time he observed the alleged false imprisonment?

4. May he be asked whether he is currently under the influence of a mind-altering substance at the time of trial? Why?

7. *Prior Inconsistent Statements*

Impeachment by a prior inconsistent statement pursuant to Rule 613 is actually a specialized form of impeachment by contradiction, namely self-contradiction. Two statements by the witness are necessary for this type of impeachment. One of the statements usually occurs during the witness' testimony at trial, and the second statement generally occurs prior to the testimony. The two statements must, on the whole, be inconsistent. The statements can be in the form of oral, written, or assertive conduct and need not be sworn.

If the witness at trial forgets facts while testifying and says "I don't remember" in response to a question, or fails to make a certain statement at trial, there is no trial statement. If there is then only the one statement prior to trial, impeachment with that prior statement is generally forbidden. If the witness is acting in bad faith by intentionally "forgetting" the facts at trial, however, an exception is made to this requirement of two statements, and the prior statement may be used to impeach.

Federal Rule of Evidence 613 drops the common-law requirement of *The Queen's Case*, 2 Br. & B. 284, 129 Eng. Rep. 976 (1820). That case created a "fairness" rule by requiring the examining counsel to give a witness the opportunity to deny or explain the witness' own prior written statement before being impeached on it. However, Rule 613 imports its own version of fairness by requiring the contents of a prior statement to be shown or disclosed to opposing counsel on request.

a. Extrinsic Prior Inconsistent Statement Impeachment: Permitted Only if the Subject Matter Is Important to the Case

Many parties who attempt to impeach a witness through a prior inconsistent statement will have to take the witness' answer if it involves a question unimportant to the issues in the case. The relative importance to the issues of the case raises a relevance inquiry for the judge, who will make the admissibility decision. For this category, the analysis is similar to that of contradiction impeachment—no extrinsic evidence of a prior inconsistent statement is allowed, unless the subject matter is non-collateral. The judge must exercise some discretion in determining what is non-collateral.

Example

Jean sues Ted for allegedly breaching a commercial lease extension for Ted's Tender Chicken, a fast food restaurant located in Jean's shopping center. Ted's defense is that no extension occurred. An important issue at trial concerned a meeting at Ted's restaurant on June 24th. An eyewitness to the meeting, Sophia, testified that on the day in question at the restaurant, both Jean and Ted met, discussed the lease, appeared to agree on an extension, and signed several documents. On cross-examination, Sophia was impeached by a prior inconsistent statement.

DEFENDANT'S ATTORNEY: Now, Sophia, you have just testified on direct examination that Jean and Ted signed several documents during the meeting on the day in question?

A: That is correct.

DEFENDANT'S ATTORNEY: You discussed what happened at this meeting with me before, didn't you?

A: Yes, I believe so.

DEFENDANT'S ATTORNEY: It was during your deposition, way back in May, right?

A: Yes, I think it was in May.

DEFENDANT'S ATTORNEY: The meeting occurred only five months or so prior to the deposition, true?

A: Yes.

DEFENDANT'S ATTORNEY: At the deposition, you were under oath?

A: True.

DEFENDANT'S ATTORNEY: You swore to tell the truth?

A: Definitely. Yes.

DEFENDANT'S ATTORNEY: The whole truth and nothing but the truth?

A: Sure.

DEFENDANT'S ATTORNEY: Referring opposing counsel to the witness' deposition, page eight, line nine, I asked you during the deposition: "How many documents did Jean and Ted sign?" You answered: "They signed only one document." Isn't that correct?

A: Yes, that is what you asked and I answered.

8. Poor Character for Truthfulness — Extrinsic Impeachment Only

Poor character for truthfulness is a type of extrinsic impeachment expressly permitted under Rule 608(a). Thus, when assessing the relative importance of this type of impeachment, it is fair to say it is non-collateral and allowed. Under Rule 608(a), a witness can have his or her truthfulness attacked by another witness in the form of reputation or opinion testimony only. Extrinsic evidence of specific acts of that prior witness is not permitted. *See* Rule 608(b). When opinion or reputation evidence is offered, counsel must lay a foundation showing that the character witness has an adequate basis for forming an opinion about the impeached witness' character or for having heard about the impeached witness' reputation.

A critical intersection that often arises is between character evidence offered to impeach and character evidence offered to prove an issue in the case. Reputation or opinion-type testimony offered to impeach a witness is only about the witness and the witness' truthfulness. Reputation or opinion-type testimony offered as character evidence is about a party or victim and is generally circumstantial character evidence about a party's guilt, fault, or liability.

Problem 7-24: Truth-o-Meter

The prosecutor called Paula as a witness in a DUI manslaughter case. When Paula testified, she stated that she saw the defendant's car swerve in front of her car and that the driver of her car, Sadie, yelled, "That driver is going at least 90 mph!" Because Sadie had already testified for the prosecution and been impeached by Defendant, Paula was asked, "Do you have an opinion as to Sadie's truthfulness?" Paula responded, "If Sadie said the guy was doing 90, I, for one, would certainly believe her."

If Defendant objected to Paula's statement about Sadie's truthfulness, what ruling and why?

Problem 7-25: Cavalier and Convicted

Joe Cavalier was convicted of receiving stolen property nine and a half years prior to his trial for mail fraud and conspiracy to commit mail fraud. Cavalier testified in his own defense, and the prosecution offered evidence of the prior conviction in order to impeach him. The defense objected. *What ruling and why?*

D. Two-Way Admissibility of Some Prior Inconsistent Statements

Significantly, some prior inconsistent statements are admissible for two purposes — for their truth as well as to impeach a witness. To determine when this "two-way" admissibility situation exists, the context of the prior inconsistent statement matters. As discussed further in Chapter 12, on Rule 801, if a prior inconsistent statement of a witness has certain qualifying features (e.g., it was made under oath and in a prior proceeding, like statements in a deposition), it will be admitted not only for its impeachment value, but also for the truth of the matter asserted. This means that in the example above, if the deposition statement by the witness, Sophia, qualifies under Rule 801, it can be considered by the jury not only for the effect of the apparent inconsistency on Sophia's believability, but also for the truth of the matter asserted — what was actually signed at the meeting and by whom.

Special significance also accrues to prior statements of testifying parties offered against them. These statements may qualify as admissions of a party opponent under Rule 801(d)(2) and would be admitted for their truth as well as for impeachment purposes.

Sometimes, a witness confronted with a prior inconsistent statement denies making the statement, even if the statement was taken down by a court reporter as part of a deposition. If this occurs, the witness may be impeached by extrinsic evidence of the statement (such as a writing or a witness) but only if the inconsistency is about a matter at issue in the case. If extrinsic impeachment is permitted, a foundation must be laid for the extrinsic evidence. To promote efficiency, it is worth attempting to use the witness to be impeached to help lay the foundation. If a new witness is required, and the witness to be impeached may be needed at a later time, it is important not to excuse the witness, but rather to explain to the court the intended additional use of the witness.

Problem 7-26: Yeah, Right

Ted, the primary witness for the defense in a tort action, states on direct examination that he was not aware that a lawsuit had been filed until four days prior to trial. On cross-examination, Ted is asked whether he told a good friend eight months earlier, right after the suit had been brought, "I heard that good old Plaintiff filed suit this week." *Is this question permissible impeachment?*

E. More Impeachment Problems

Problem 7-27: "You Took the Tag Off of Your Mattress?!"

Cheryl is prosecuted for shoplifting from the "We R Toys" store. The store clerk, Laurie, testifies for the prosecution. On cross-examination, the clerk is asked the following questions:

DEFENSE COUNSEL: Isn't it true that the "We R Toys" store has only four parking spaces out front and not five, as you testified?

PROSECUTOR: Objection. (*On what grounds?*)

JUDGE: (*How should the judge rule? Why?*)

DEFENSE COUNSEL: You've been arrested for child abuse, haven't you?

PROSECUTOR: Objection. (*On what grounds?*)

JUDGE: (*How should the judge rule? Why?*)

DEFENSE COUNSEL: Laurie, you faked a workers' compensation injury last year to collect benefits, didn't you?

PROSECUTOR: Objection. (*On what grounds?*)

JUDGE: (*How should the judge rule? Why?*)

DEFENSE COUNSEL: You were told by your boss that you'd get an extra vacation day if you testified today, isn't that correct?

PROSECUTOR: Objection. (*On what grounds?*)

JUDGE: (*How should the judge rule? Why?*)

DEFENSE COUNSEL: Laurie, you were convicted last year of shoplifting at a "Toys R Not U" store, isn't that right?

PROSECUTOR: Objection. (*On what grounds?*)

JUDGE: (*How should the judge rule? Why?*)

DEFENSE COUNSEL: You took the tag that says "Do Not Remove" off of your mattress, didn't you?

PROSECUTOR: Objection. (*On what grounds?*)

JUDGE: (*How should the judge rule? Why?*)

Problem 7-28: Defamation Redux

Sue is called an "inept, tabloid-loving, dimwit surgeon" in the local newspaper. She sues for libel. At trial, her brother, Bob, also a surgeon, testifies on her behalf as a character witness about Sue's professional competence. Bob is cross-examined by counsel for the defendant newspaper.

DEFENDANT'S ATTORNEY: So, Bob, isn't it true that you punched the defendant newspaper editor in the nose outside of Rosie O'Sady's restaurant last week?

PLAINTIFF'S ATTORNEY: Objection. Improper impeachment.

JUDGE: (*How should the judge rule? Why?*)

DEFENDANT'S ATTORNEY: Bob, you are aware that there were two incidents in which your sister was cited by the hospital for cutting into the wrong location, correct?

PLAINTIFF'S ATTORNEY: Objection! Improper impeachment.

JUDGE: (*How should the judge rule? Why?*)

DEFENDANT'S ATTORNEY: You said on direct examination that your sister has participated in at least 800 operations. Yet, in your deposition on October 5th, at page three, line four, you were asked, "In how many operations did your sister participate?" and you answered, "Oh, I don't know, maybe 400."

PLAINTIFF'S ATTORNEY: Objection! Improper impeachment.

JUDGE: (*How should the judge rule? Why?*)

DEFENDANT'S ATTORNEY: Bob, didn't you misrepresent your college class rank on your medical school application?

PLAINTIFF'S ATTORNEY: Objection. Improper impeachment.

JUDGE: (*How should the judge rule? Why?*)

Problem 7-29: The Young Freud

The young Dr. Von Freud testified about the cause of death in a prosecution for homicide.

1. Dr. Von Freud is asked on cross-examination whether his opinion is consistent with *Gray's Anatomy*, which is considered to be an authoritative medical treatise in the field. *Admissible? Why?*

2. He also is asked on cross-examination whether he has been convicted of child abuse. *Permitted?*

3. Dr. Von Freud is questioned on cross-examination about whether he had been fired from his previous employment because he had forged medical records. *Admissible? Why?*

Extrinsic Impeachment Example

Harold testified for the plaintiff, Maude, in a breach-of-contract action. On cross-examination, Harold was asked if: (1) he was dating Maude, (2) Maude had agreed to enter into the contract without qualification, (3) Harold had been convicted of mayhem 10 years earlier, and (4) Harold had lied on his bar application four years earlier. Harold answered "no" to all four questions. On rebuttal, can the defendant offer a new witness to testify: (1) Harold was dating Maude, and (2) Maude had agreed to the contract offer without qualification? Can the defense also offer: (3) a certified copy of Harold's prior conviction for mayhem, and (4) a copy of his bar application with the allegedly untruthful statement?

Answer: The collateral issue rule permits the defendant to impeach Harold extrinsically in three of the four instances because in those instances the impeachment is considered important or non-collateral. The new witness may testify about: (1) whether Harold and Maude were dating, because it shows bias, which is never collateral; and (2) the dispute about Maude's responses to the contract offer, because it involves a fact in issue. The certified copy of Harold's conviction for mayhem is admissible, because convictions of crime are considered to be non-collateral matters as well. However, the prior bad act — the alleged lie on the bar application — cannot be the subject of extrinsic impeachment because prior bad acts are considered collateral. Even if Harold is lying anew with respect to the bar application, the questioner must take the witness' answer.

Problem 7-30: Extrinsically Yours

Xavier testifies for the defense in an action involving the sale of real property. Xavier was an eyewitness to the alleged contract to sell the property.

1. During cross-examination by the plaintiff, Xavier is asked whether he had been convicted of attempted robbery 10 years earlier. *Is this question permissible?*

2. Xavier denied having been convicted of attempted robbery. ("Preposterous!" he exclaimed). *Can the opposing counsel now offer in evidence a certified copy of the attempted robbery conviction? Why?*

3. On cross-examination, Xavier is asked whether he was wearing his hearing aid at the time of the alleged sale. Xavier responded by saying that he was indeed using his hearing aid. *Can the opposing counsel now call a different witness, Alec, to testify that Xavier was not wearing a hearing aid at the time of the alleged sale?*

4. On cross-examination, Xavier is asked whether he had worn white sneakers on the day in question, not red ones as he had testified on direct. Xavier answered the question by denying that he had worn white sneakers. *Can the opposing counsel now call a different witness in rebuttal to testify that Xavier was wearing white sneakers at the meeting about the sale?*

5. Xavier also is asked whether he had said in a deposition two months before trial, "I was the first one there for the meeting about the sale," when on direct he testified that he "was only the third or fourth person there." *If Xavier claims he made no such prior statement, can a rebuttal witness who was present at the deposition testify that Xavier made the statement?*

6. *If Xavier is asked on cross-examination whether he owes the defendant a large sum of money and he denies it, may the plaintiff call a different witness in rebuttal to confirm this fact?*

Problem 7-31: More Perjury

Clark is being prosecuted for perjury. He calls his best friend, Lenny, with whom he went to grade school, to testify on his behalf.

DEFENSE COUNSEL: What is Clark's reputation for truthfulness?

A: Clark's reputation in the community is one of complete honesty; he would never lie.

PROSECUTOR: (on cross-examination) Have you heard, Lenny, that Clark was expelled from night school for cheating on an examination two years ago?

(Does this question relate to impeachment, to character evidence, or to both?)

DEFENSE COUNSEL: Objection. *(On what grounds?)*

JUDGE: *(How should the judge rule? Why?)*

Lenny finishes testifying, and the prosecutor calls Sheila, a rebuttal witness, who testifies as follows:

A: In my opinion, Lenny is a liar. Furthermore, everyone in this community says that Clark is about as truthful as that television character, Bart Simpson; basically, Clark has a reputation for having no veracity at all.

DEFENSE COUNSEL: Objection. *(On what grounds?)*

JUDGE: *(How should the judge rule? Why?)*

Sheila finishes testifying, and the defense calls Sheila's estranged husband, George, to testify on behalf of Clark. On direct examination, after being asked about Sheila's and Lenny's reputations, George declares:

A: In my opinion, Sheila is a liar. In any event, Lenny's reputation in the community is one of unimpeachable honesty.

PROSECUTOR: Objection. *(On what grounds?)*

JUDGE: *(How should the judge rule? Why?)*

Problem 7-32: Bigfoot

Bernie is charged with conspiracy to import heroin. At the time of his arrest, which occurred one week after the alleged conspiracy concluded, Bernie was apprehended with alleged heroin in his shoe. At trial, Bernie testified in his own defense and denied being a part of a conspiracy.

1. On cross-examination, the prosecution asked Bernie if he had heroin in his shoe at the time he was apprehended. Is the question permissible?

2. If the question is permitted, and Bernie denies having had heroin in his shoe, may the prosecutor then call the arresting officer to the witness stand to testify to that fact?

Problem 7-33: Buddies Revisited

Alexander is prosecuted for a felony. At trial, Alexander's fellow gang member, Preston, testifies on the defendant's behalf. On cross-examination, Preston is asked whether he belongs to the same gang as the defendant. Preston says no. On rebuttal, the prosecution calls a police officer specializing in gangs to testify that both Preston and Alexander belong to the gang, "R U Blud." The officer further testifies that the gang is known for lying to protect fellow members. Alexander is convicted, and he appeals, claiming that both the cross-examination of Preston and the police officer's extrinsic testimony should have been excluded.

What ruling and why? See United States v. Martinez, 962 F.2d 1161 (5th Cir. 1992).

Problem 7-34: Edna to Rachel to Frank

In a civil assault-and-battery action, the defense calls an eyewitness, Edna. She testifies that the defendant was not the first aggressor, but was merely defending himself.

1. In rebuttal, the plaintiff calls Rachel, who testifies that, in her opinion, Edna is not a very truthful person. *Should this testimony be allowed?*

2. In surrebuttal (the reply to the rebuttal), the defendant calls a new witness, Frank, who testifies that Edna has a stellar reputation for truthfulness in the community. *Should a judge permit this testimony?*

Problem 7-35: Mortgage

The defendant, Adin, was charged with the unlawful possession of a firearm.

1. The central prosecution witness, Tylie, testified in the prosecution's case-in-chief. On cross-examination, she was asked whether she had made a false statement on her recent mortgage application. *Is the question permissible?*

2. After Tylie denied making any false statements, the judge permitted the prosecutor to offer the mortgage application in evidence. *Was this error?*

Problem 7-36: Interregnum

In a slip-and-fall negligence action, the defendant, Belinda, testified about the fall. Belinda stated that she observed boxes flying all around the plaintiff, Irving, as he fell. On cross-examination, plaintiff's counsel asked Belinda about her deposition, which was taken one month prior to trial.

1. The plaintiff's counsel questioned Belinda about her failure to mention flying boxes when she was asked during the deposition to describe the incident. *Is this question permissible impeachment?*

2. Plaintiff's counsel also asked Belinda whether Irving had ever fired her from a job. Belinda responded, "No!" *Can plaintiff offer Belinda's former co-worker to testify that Belinda had been fired by Irving? Why?*

F. Rehabilitation of Witnesses

Steps: (1) Impeachment; then (2) Rehabilitation

A witness' character for truthfulness can be rehabilitated only after his or her veracity has been directly attacked. A direct attack on a witness' character includes prior convictions, prior untruthful bad acts, and reputation or opinion evidence of untruthfulness. As noted earlier, preemptive rehabilitation, which occurs in anticipation of impeachment, is not permitted. Rehabilitation can occur either through questions on redirect examination or through a separate reputation or opinion witness testifying about the impeached witness' good character for truthfulness or veracity.

Note that rehabilitation generally occurs on redirect examination. This new direct examination permits the witness to explain his or her answers on cross-examination, if appropriate. The explanations, however, are still limited by Rule 403 and unfair prejudice.

A significant form of rehabilitation occurs under Rule 608(a). After a witness' character for truthfulness has been directly attacked, the proponent of the witness can then offer opinion or reputation evidence bolstering the witness' veracity. This form of rehabilitation involves calling a new witness whose primary purpose is to rebut the attacks on the other witness' character.

Problem 7-37: Rehab

Maryanne was the star defense witness in a forfeiture action. The government claimed that a considerable amount of marijuana was found in the back seat of the defendant's car, justifying the car's forfeiture. Anticipating a ferocious cross-examination of Maryanne, the defense first called Maryanne's partner, Marcy, to testify that, in her opinion, Maryanne has an unimpeachable character for truthfulness and veracity.

The prosecution objects to Marcy's testimony. *What ruling and why?*

After Maryanne testified on direct examination, the prosecution zealously cross-examined her, suggesting that Maryanne recently fabricated her testimony to assist the defendant's case. On redirect examination, the following occurred:

DEFENSE COUNSEL: When did you first learn of this incident?

A: Almost immediately after the forfeiture occurred.

DEFENSE COUNSEL: What did you do upon hearing about it?

A: I immediately told my friend Julian the same exact thing that I just testified to on direct, that the hitchhiker had unloaded and then repacked his bag in the back seat before leaving the car.

PROSECUTOR: Objection! (*What is the basis for the prosecutor's objection?*)

JUDGE: (*How should the judge rule? Why?*)

G. Refreshing the Witness's Memory

Stuck somewhat incongruously in the middle of the impeachment rules, Rule 612 pertains to refreshing a witness's memory. The Rule appears misplaced in several ways. Refreshing a witness's memory most often occurs during the direct examination of the proponent's own witness and is generally performed to bolster the witness's credibility by facilitating an accurate memory of events or occurrences. Thus, it effectively accredits the witness, instead of impeaching the witness's credibility. A witness who has forgotten events that happened long ago often appears more believable than one who remembers prior events with crystal clarity.

Another incongruity is that impeachment is a form of evidence to be considered by the jury, while refreshing a witness's recollection is not. Because the items used to refresh memory are not being offered into evidence, but rather are being used as memory aids, whatever an attorney may employ to refresh a witness's memory is not subject to the rules of authentication or put to the usual test of admissibility. This means that inadmissible hearsay, or even inadmissible real evidence, may be used to refresh a witness's memory. While this may sound like a "free ride," a way to sneak in evidence under the guise of refreshing memory, it is not; the items must be disclosed to the opposing counsel and may be used to impeach the witness as well.

The process of refreshing memory comes closest to impeachment when it is being employed during cross-examination, when a witness's forgetfulness may be highlighted by an examiner to show duplicity or inaccuracy, particularly if a prior written statement made by the witness exists. (The hearsay exemption for certain kinds of witnesses' prior inconsistent statements is addressed in Chapter 13.)

Judges retain discretion to refuse to permit some writings to be used for refreshing the recollection of witnesses. If a writing is to be used as the actual basis for testimony and not merely to refresh a witness's memory, for example, it may be excluded by the court.

Problem 7-38: "Sammy Says"

Sammy testifies for the plaintiff in a complex commercial litigation action. He is asked on direct examination about a particular business meeting the previous year and he answers, "Hmmmm, I really don't remember it." Counsel then shows Sammy the notes Sammy took during the meeting.

1. May plaintiff's counsel give Sammy his own meeting notes to refresh his memory? What is the proper procedure by which to refresh recollection? May Sammy read the notes to the jury?

2. Do the notes have to be authenticated?

3. Does it matter if the notes were not taken by Sammy, but instead were taken by someone else at the meeting? May Sammy still rely on the notes to refresh his memory about the meeting? May Sammy read the notes to the jury?

4. If Sammy reviews his notes during the direct examination, may he be questioned about the notes on cross-examination?

5. If Sammy carefully took the notes immediately after the meeting when the events were fresh in his mind, but he has no current recollection about the meeting, may the notes be admitted in evidence at trial? *See* Rule 803(5).

H. Impeachment Statutes

Compare the current form of Federal Rule of Evidence 609(a) with various preliminary draft proposals.

House Subcommittee Draft (1973)

> For the purpose of attacking credibility of a witness, evidence that he has been convicted of a crime is admissible if, but only if (1) the crime involved dishonesty or false statement, or (2) the crime was punishable by death or imprisonment in excess of one year under the law under which he was convicted, unless the judge determines that the danger of unfair prejudice outweighs the probative value of the evidence of conviction.

House Bill H.R. 5463 (February 1974)

> For the purpose of attacking the credibility of a witness, evidence that he has been convicted of a crime is admissible only if the crime involved dishonesty or false statement.

Senate Judiciary Committee Draft (October 1974)

> For the purpose of attacking the credibility of a witness, evidence that he has been convicted of a crime may be elicited from him or established by public record during cross-examination but only if the crime (1) involved dishonesty or false statement or (2) in the case of witnesses other than the accused, was punishable by death or imprisonment in excess of one year under the law under which he was convicted, but only if the court

determines that the probative value of admitting this evidence outweighs its prejudicial effect.

Current Version

For the purpose of attacking the credibility of a witness, (1) evidence that a witness other than an accused has been convicted of a crime shall be admitted subject to Rule 403, if the crime was punishable by death or imprisonment in excess of one year under the law under which the witness was convicted, and evidence that an accused has been convicted of such a crime shall be admitted if the court determines that the probative value of admitting this evidence outweighs its prejudicial effect to the accused; and (2) evidence that any witness has been convicted of a crime shall be admitted if it involved dishonesty or false statement, regardless of the punishment.

Compare the current Federal Evidence Rule 609(a) with the following state rules:

Alaska 609(a)

(a) General rule. For the purpose of attacking the credibility of a witness, evidence that he has been convicted of a crime is only admissible if the crime involved dishonesty or false statement.

Montana 609

For the purpose of attacking the credibility of a witness, evidence that the witness has been convicted of a crime is not admissible.

Compare the Federal Rules of Evidence with the following state laws on impeachment:

N.Y. CPLR § 4514

In addition to impeachment in the manner permitted by common law, any party may introduce proof that any witness has made a prior statement inconsistent with his testimony if the statement was made in a writing subscribed by him or was made under oath.

Indiana Code Chapter 34-1-15-1

When a witness, whether a party to the record or not, is cross examined to lay the foundation for his impeachment by proof of an act or statement inconsistent with his testimony, and is asked if he did not do the act or make the statement, and he answers that he does not recollect having done the act or made the statement, the party thus laying the foundation for impeachment shall have the right to introduce evidence of the act or statement in the same manner as if the witness had answered that he had not done the act or made the statement.

Hawaii Chapter 626, Rule 609.1

(a) General rule. The credibility of a witness may be attacked by evidence of bias, interest, or motive.

(b) Extrinsic evidence of bias, interest, or motive. Extrinsic evidence of a witness' bias, interest, or motive is not admissible unless, on cross-examination, the matter is brought to the attention of the witness and the witness is afforded an opportunity to explain or deny the matter.

§ 7.05 Summary and Review

1. Compare impeachment evidence and character evidence. What are the major differences? What are the major similarities?

2. How are prior inconsistent statements a form of contradiction?

3. Why is extrinsic impeachment more restrictive than intrinsic impeachment?

4. Define "bias."

5. What types of crimes may be used to impeach a witness?

6. Why are the permissible forms of impeachment by conviction limited to felonies and crimes of dishonesty or false statement?

7. Why did the Federal Rules of Evidence adopt a special "prejudice" balancing test for the use of felony convictions to impeach a criminal defendant?

8. What types of acts are permissible in "prior bad acts" impeachment? Why?

9. What is impeachment by omission?

10. What are the permissible ways to refresh a witness' memory?

§ 7.06 Chapter Review Problems

Review Problem 7-A

Accountant Zakkiah Jones was arrested for driving under the influence of alcohol one dark night on the main road of her Pennsylvania town. Jones testified in a subsequent trial, stating she made a left turn onto Main Street from 3rd Avenue prior to being stopped. The prosecutor did not ask her any questions on cross-examination about how she ended up on Main Street, but called Officer Lemke in rebuttal. Lemke testified, "After she was stopped, Ms. Jones told me she turned onto Main Street from 4th Avenue." *Which of the following statements about the Officer's testimony is the most accurate?*

1. It is admissible as prior inconsistent statement impeachment, so long as the two statements were inconsistent.

2. It is admissible as prior inconsistent statement impeachment if the prior statement had been made under oath.

3. It is not admissible as prior inconsistent statement impeachment because the statement's probative value is substantially outweighed by its danger of unfair prejudice.

4. It is not admissible as prior inconsistent statement impeachment because it is offered by Officer Lemke.

Review Problem 7-B

In a negligence action arising from an automobile accident, the plaintiff called an eyewitness, Sheila Scranton, to testify about what she observed on the pertinent morning at approximately 8:00 a.m. The witness testified that after leaving the International House of Pancakes, where she had breakfast, she almost immediately observed the accident. On cross-examination, Sheila is asked, "Isn't it true that you were eating that morning at the Original Pancake House and not at the International House of Pancakes?" *If there is an objection to this question, how should the judge rule?*

1. Allow the question because it is permissible impeachment by prior inconsistent statement.

2. Allow the question because it contradicts Sheila's testimony.

3. Disallow the question because it is collateral to the issues in the case.

4. Disallow the question because it is confusing and unfairly prejudicial.

Review Problem 7-C

Allan Jackson is charged with larceny. At trial, he takes the witness stand to deny committing the crime. On cross-examination, the prosecutor wishes to ask him about a nine-year-old conviction for robbery, for which the defendant received probation. *Can the prosecutor use the conviction to impeach Jackson?*

1. Yes, since the conviction is less than 10 years old.

2. Yes, if the prejudicial impact does not substantially outweigh the conviction's probative value.

3. No, because the defendant did not serve any jail time on the conviction.

4. No, unless the judge determines that the probative value of the conviction outweighs its prejudicial impact on the defendant.

Review Problem 7-D

In a murder trial, a critical witness for the defense is the cashier at the convenience store where the killing took place. The cashier will testify that the police never asked him whether the defendant looked like the perpetrator and ignored his protests about arresting the defendant. In the prosecution's case-in-chief, a police officer is called to testify that he had previously arrested the cashier and at the time the cashier kept saying, "I hate cops; I hate cops." This testimony is:

1. Admissible to impeach the cashier based on bias.

2. Admissible to impeach the cashier based on prior bad untruthful acts.

3. Inadmissible to impeach the cashier because it occurred in the prosecution's case-in-chief.

4. Inadmissible to impeach the cashier because the impeachment is extrinsic, not intrinsic.

Chapter 8

Lay Opinion Evidence

§ 8.01 Chapter Checklist

1. Is the exhibit or testimony an opinion?

2. Is the opinion "lay" or "expert"?

3. If the testimony involves "lay opinion," is the opinion:

   a. "rationally based" on the perception of the witness, and

   b. helpful to a clear understanding of the witness's testimony or the determination of a fact in issue?

§ 8.02 Relevant Federal Rules of Evidence

Rule 701. Opinion Testimony by Lay Witnesses

If a witness is not testifying as an expert, testimony in the form of an opinion is limited to one that is:

(a) rationally based on the witness's perception;

(b) helpful to clearly understanding the witness's testimony or to determining a fact in issue; and

(c) not based on scientific, technical, or other specialized knowledge within the scope of Rule 702.

§ 8.03 Distinguishing between Lay and Expert Opinion Testimony

A. Facts versus Opinions

Opinion testimony is testimony that relies on the reasoning and analytical abilities of the witness, not simply his or her raw perceptions. Everyday examples are myriad. Some examples: temperature ("it was hot"), distance ("it was nearby"), height ("she was tall"). Laypersons (basically meaning ordinary people) are permitted to offer opinion testimony that doesn't require scientific or technical knowledge. Expert witnesses, by contrast, are allowed to render technical or scientific opinions.

For example, an expert physician might testify thus: "In my opinion, the plaintiff will never walk again."

At common law, laypersons were generally prohibited from testifying to opinions, but under the current rules, laypersons may do so as long as the opinion satisfies Rule 701.

"Fact" and "opinion" are not always clearly divisible; sometimes the distinction is a matter of degree. Ordinary folks speak all the time with less than absolute certainty, but neither in everyday life nor in the courtroom does that hesitation render their testimony opinion. For a witness to say, "I think the car was red," is to testify from personal knowledge rather than to offer an opinion.

Example

The following is a section of testimony in an assault case:

PROSECUTOR: What did you observe that night?

A: I saw George looking at Joey with rage.

DEFENSE COUNSEL: Objection, improper lay opinion. The witness can know and recount only what he saw, heard, etc. He can't read minds, and he shouldn't be allowed to speculate on what my client was thinking or feeling that night.

JUDGE: I think the foundation is a little thin, but I'll overrule.

The witness, let us say a neighbor, may have seen George furrow his brow, squint his eyes, and turn the corners of his mouth downward. Such observations might support the inference that George felt anger. Recounting the observations (the state of the brow, eyes, and mouth) was seen, at least at common law, as the witness' role; drawing the inferences from those observations (George looked at Joey with rage) was the jury's role.

But the example makes clear that the jury will have a difficult time drawing the proper inference without the assistance of the witness. What does "rage" look like? Surely the witness describing raw perceptions — how the face literally looked — will have difficulty conveying the composite meaning of the observations; that, taken together, the expression conveyed anger. Thus, the judge appropriately overruled the objection (though she also properly noted that the witness needed to give more foundation (i.e., underlying facts) to support the opinion).

B. When Laypersons Can Offer Opinions

1. Rationally Based on Perceptions of Witness

Rule 701 declares that a witness "not testifying as an expert" may testify in the form of opinions or inferences if, and only if, they are limited to those opinions or inferences that are "rationally based on the witness's perception."

The advisory committee notes to Rule 701 indicate that this standard "is the familiar requirement of first-hand knowledge or observation." In other words, lay witnesses must have personal knowledge of enough facts to rationally render an opinion on the matter. The word "rational" requires the judge to decide whether the witness's firsthand knowledge is adequate to support the opinion.

Example 1

Imagine the following exchange in a civil negligence action:

DEFENSE ATTORNEY: What did you see that night?

A: It was so foggy, I couldn't see my hand in front of my face.

[Intervening Questions]

DEFENSE ATTORNEY: Do you have an opinion about how far ahead of you the plaintiff's vehicle was?

A: Far away.

PLAINTIFF'S ATTORNEY: Objection, Your Honor. Under Rules 602 and 701, the witness did not have the ability to perceive distance that night. [The witness's vision was obscured by fog.]

JUDGE: Sustained.

Despite the slightly delayed objection, this is likely the appropriate ruling under Rule 701(a). The defense attorney, of course, may attempt to lay more foundation. Perhaps the fog cleared? Or there was another circumstance that explains how the witness could rationally perceive the distance of the car? The defense attorney can attempt to lay more foundation to establish the witness' firsthand knowledge, but if unable to do so, the objection should be sustained again.

Example 2

A witness has testified that he was 200 feet away from the scene of an auto accident, facing in the opposite direction. He heard squealing brakes and a loud crash. From these observations alone, he testifies that the defendant's car was traveling at 65 mph on a residential street when it entered the intersection. Absent any special training (or perhaps even with training), the witness cannot so precisely determine the defendant car's speed merely from the sound of the crash, especially when the witness was 200 feet away.

2. Helpful to the Jury

According to Rule 701, a lay opinion must be "helpful" to the jury in "understanding the witness's testimony or to determining a fact in issue." The advisory committee made clear that "helpful" does not mean that the opinion is absolutely necessary. Indeed, the rule envisions that the adversary system will largely govern itself in determining which opinions help the jury—advocates are incentivized to put on specific, concrete opinion testimony that moves the case forward on one or more important issues. To do otherwise would risk losing the jury to inattention or another advocate's more powerful case. Likewise, generalized opinions that are not well supported will face the crucible of cross-examination.

While undoubtedly broad, the requirement that lay opinions be "helpful" mandates that those opinions do not "amount to little more than choosing up sides" by "introduce[ing] meaningless assertions." This is a low bar, but it prevents witnesses from taking the stand to merely proclaim that "he's guilty" or "I think she ought to pay."

Lay opinions are most helpful, however, when testimony about raw perceptions cannot adequately convey meaning. In other words, situations in which "you had to be there" (e.g., cases in which this witness' recounting of details alone cannot fully capture the reality of what happened).

Opinions may also be helpful because they aid clear expression. Thus a witness' opinion that the defendant was "smiling" more clearly conveys what the witness saw than does the statement, "The left corner of his mouth upturned one-eighth of an inch."

Also known as "collective facts," this type of opinion testimony is really a shorthand rendition of what the witness perceived. The event observed may involve so many details that what registers in the witness' mind is an overall impression more than specifics.

Example

PROSECUTOR: What, if anything, did you observe about the defendant's demeanor that night?

A: He was very drunk.

Many, probably most, judges would permit this answer as a lay opinion, assuming an adequate foundation establishing that the opinion was "rationally based on the perception of the witness" (as described above).

3. Not Based on Scientific, Technical, or Other Specialized Knowledge

The distinction between the realms of lay and expert opinion can be fuzzy. But Rule 701(c) is clear that lay opinions are appropriate only where the opinion is not "based on scientific, technical, or other specialized knowledge." This means that expert opinions are not admissible via Rule 701 and must pass the more demanding requirements of Rule 702.

Note that the rule does not treat witnesses as just "lay" or "expert." A given witness might testify to lay opinions (subject to the Rule 701 analysis) and expert opinions (subject to Rule 702).

Knowing which opinions are based on expert knowledge and which opinions are based on lay knowledge is critical—the analyses for admissibility under the two pertinent rules are very different. In many instances, the expert versus lay opinion analysis is quite straightforward: a medical opinion about cause of death is based on expert medical knowledge (scientific, technical, and specialized); an engineering opinion about the inherent dangers of a defective product is based on expert engineering knowledge (same); an opinion about the quality of plumbing in a building is based on expert plumbing knowledge (technical and specialized).

On the other end of the spectrum, Rule 701 lay opinions include, among other things, "prototypical examples . . . relating to the appearance of persons or things, identity, the manner of conduct, competency of a person, degrees of light or darkness, sound, size, weight, distance, and an endless number of items that cannot be described factually in words apart from inferences."[1]

In other instances, the distinction is more muddled — occasionally courts treat what looks like expert opinion as lay opinion. The advisory committee notes single out two of these anomalies and place them under the heading of "particularized knowledge." The first is opinion testimony of narcotics users identifying a substance as a narcotic. Thus, someone who has used cocaine regularly may identify it by taste or inhalation, and the resulting taste or high. The second area of lay opinion that looks a lot like expert opinion is business valuation by business owners. Many courts allow a business owner to testify to the value of his or her own business. This is true even when an expert accounting opinion would be necessary if the testimony were coming from someone other than the owner. Beyond these two seeming anomalies, some courts have also permitted lay opinion on the value of one's own home or other property.

Practice Tip

Litigants often end up fighting about whether opinions are based on expert or lay knowledge when litigating the timeliness of pretrial expert designations. Some propositions in cases *require* expert testimony. A lay opinion won't suffice, and if a party with the burden on the matter does not have an expert opinion, the court might grant summary judgment or judgment as a matter of law at trial.

But experts and their opinions must be disclosed months before trial in many instances. Sometimes a party simply overlooks the expert designation deadlines. Other times, the expert is deemed unqualified, or the opinion unreliable. In other cases, lawyers may designate an expert and disclose some opinions, while forgetting or omitting opinions on a single critical issue that could end the case.

In these situations, when the court won't grant a continuance to allow for additional expert disclosures, lawyers will sometimes try to contend that the issue is the proper province of lay opinion. And they will have a witness at hand to deliver the lay opinion. In this way, lawyers and litigants

---

1. FED. R. EVID. 701 advisory committee's note. Internal quotes omitted.

sometimes seek to work around the pretrial scheduling order by using lay opinion as a loophole.

When you practice, be sure to have expert testimony on every important issue. And resist the other side's attempts to "supplement" their expert disclosure through undisclosed lay testimony.

4. Opinions on Ultimate Issues

Rule 704 provides:

> **(a) In General** — Not Automatically Objectionable. An opinion is not objectionable just because it embraces an ultimate issue.
>
> **(b) Exception.** In a criminal case, an expert witness must not state an opinion about whether the defendant did or did not have a mental state or condition that constitutes an element of the crime charged or of a defense. Those matters are for the trier of fact alone.

The common law flatly banned opinions on "ultimate issues," such as whether the crane operator was negligent or whether the killer acted in the heat of passion. Rule 704(a) abolishes this prohibition for both lay and expert testimony, except for a subcategory of expert opinion to be discussed in Chapter 9. But ultimate issue opinions may still be excluded if unhelpful under Rule 701 (lay opinions) or of no assistance to the factfinder under Rule 702 (expert opinions), or if prejudice and related concerns substantially outweigh their probative value under Rule 403. For example, one upshot of Rule 704(a) is that an opinion such as, "The driver was going too fast to make the turn safely" may well be acceptable, while an opinion that, "The driver was negligent" may not be helpful.

§ 8.04 Problems

Problem 8-1: High on Marijuana

Two automobiles collided at the corner of Third and Elm Streets, seriously injuring one of the drivers, Ronald Patterson. Patterson has sued the other driver, Gerald Rabinowitz, alleging that he caused the accident by negligently running a red light. Patterson's passenger, Jose Ramirez, testifies at trial that, immediately after the accident, Ramirez and Rabinowitz both left their cars and chatted. You are Patterson's attorney and want to call Ramirez to the stand to testify that Rabinowitz was obviously very high on marijuana at the time of the accident. You know from pretrial discovery that Rabinowitz's defense will be that the light facing him was in fact green, and it was Patterson who ran the red light.

1. What is your theory of the relevance of Ramirez's testimony?

2. Is any portion of Ramirez's testimony opinion, or does it all involve personal observation?

3. If any portion is opinion:

   a. Is it lay or expert?

   b. What questions would you ask to establish the foundation for admissibility of the opinion? Why?

   c. What cross-examination questions (on voir dire or in the regular course of cross) do you anticipate from opposing counsel? Why?

Problem 8-2: My Cousin Vinnie and Tire Marks

Vinnie Barbarino is a recent law school graduate. His cousin, Johnny Barbarino, allegedly shot and killed the cashier at a 7-Eleven during the course of a robbery. An eyewitness has testified that he saw Johnny and his cohort, Merv Griffin, fleeing from the robbery in a 1967 green Camaro. Johnny was in fact stopped while driving a car matching that description 10 minutes after the killing. At that time, he admitted to the police that he had purchased something at the 7-Eleven 10 to 15 minutes before being stopped. The police examination at the 7-Eleven shows tire tracks leaving the scene. The prosecution expert has testified that these tracks were consistent with those that would be left by the sort of tires that can be used on 1967 Camaros. Vinnie, representing Johnny at trial, calls to the stand his girlfriend, Fran Chabowski, to offer the opinion that the tire impressions in the police photographs at the 7-Eleven could not have been made by a 1967 Camaro, both because the impressions left were more like those of a heavier car and because the tire marks had unusual curlicues found only on tires used exclusively on 1967 Buick LeSabres. Vinnie seeks to qualify Ms. Chabowski to offer this opinion:

DEFENSE COUNSEL (Vinnie): Ms. Chabowski, what do you do for a living?

A: I am a hairdresser.

DEFENSE COUNSEL: And what do your father and brother do for a living?

PROSECUTOR: Objection, Your Honor. Irrelevant.

DEFENSE COUNSEL: Your Honor, the relevance will soon be clear.

JUDGE: It had better be, Mr. Barbarino. Proceed.

DEFENSE COUNSEL: So what do your father and brother do for a living?

A: They run their own car repair business.

DEFENSE COUNSEL: Have you ever been involved in that business?

A: Yes, I worked there for 12 years.

DEFENSE COUNSEL: I am handing you a photograph marked P-1. Could those tire marks in the photo have been made by a 1967 Camaro?

PROSECUTOR: Objection, inadequate foundation.

JUDGE: Objection sustained.

1. Was the opinion that Vinnie sought to elicit "lay" or "expert"? Would your answer change if Ms. Chabowski had never worked for an auto repair shop but instead was simply a car buff, who read extensively on auto design and repair and spent all her free time for the past decade repairing and restoring classic cars, including 1967 Camaros and LeSabres?

2. Was the prosecution's objection precise enough? How could you have more precisely and convincingly stated that objection?

3. What questions should Vinnie have asked to improve the chances that the foundation laid would be found adequate to justify admitting the opinion? Why?

4. If, instead of sustaining the objection, the trial judge first permitted cross-examination by the prosecutor on voir dire, what questions should the prosecution ask? Why?

5. Should the Questions in 3 and 4 above be asked within, or outside of, the jury's hearing? Why?

Problem 8-3: The Stolen Ring

Drew Gavel is charged with felony theft of a diamond ring from a jeweler. For the offense to be a felony, rather than a mere misdemeanor, the fair market value of the ring must be more than $5,000. Officer John Kelly is called to the stand by the prosecution to testify that the ring stolen by Gavel has a fair market value of at least $7,000. The bases for Officer Kelly's opinion are that: (1) he had recently comparison-shopped at more than 20 jewelry stores for an engagement ring for his fiancé; and (2) he had also for the last three months read extensively on the quality and pricing of diamond rings, relying largely on Internet searches for information. The defense objects that Officer Kelly has not been properly qualified as an expert in jewelry appraisal. The judge sustains the objection. The prosecutor responds by saying that Officer Kelly is offering a "lay opinion." The defense objects, "improper lay opinion."

1. What ruling and why?

2. Would another sort of witness have been a better choice? Who? Why?

3. What if the fair market value of a single-family home, owned by the testifying witness, was the subject of the opinion testimony?

Problem 8-4: The Wound

Dr. Richard Speck has been sued for negligently treating Arnold Paslitz's ankle wound, by prescribing only an antiseptic and a Band-Aid. The wound turned out to be the bite of a poisonous brown recluse spider. It developed an infection common in such bites but left so long untreated that permanent physical damage was done to the ankle. Paslitz maintains that he delayed seeking treatment solely because of Speck's advice that there was nothing to worry about that a Band-Aid and a little Bactine couldn't cure. Paslitz calls his wife, Patricia, to testify about her observations of the wound that ultimately led her to urge her husband to go to the emergency room. She is a securities lawyer with no medical training. The following exchange took place at trial as she was being questioned by Paslitz's counsel:

PLAINTIFF'S ATTORNEY: Please describe the wound, as you observed it on that day.

A: Its appearance was very unusual. There was a round two-inch hole on Arnold's ankle. Green pus oozed out of the hole. A half-inch ring of what looked like charred black flesh surrounded the hole. A bright red, swollen, tender-looking circle, about two inches in thickness and elevated, like a little volcano, surrounded the charred-looking area. Every part of the wound was sensitive to touch, causing great pain. The wound was hot to the touch, as was Arnold's whole ankle and foot. The foot was itself a bright red, hugely swollen, and sensitive to touch.

DEFENDANT'S ATTORNEY: Objection, improper opinion. Move to strike.

[In a real trial, the objection likely would have preceded the answer, at which point Paslitz's counsel may have made an offer of proof outside the jury's hearing (perhaps at sidebar), to aid the trial judge in her ruling.]

1. What ruling? Why?

2. Are some parts of the answer more objectionable than others? Which portions of the answer should be deleted to increase the likelihood of the testimony's being admitted without sacrificing too much tactical gain for Paslitz? How should the witness be prepared to articulate her answer most effectively given the requirements of the rules of evidence? To deal with objections that are sustained?

3. What if the witness' answer had simply been, "The wound was the grossest I've ever seen — sore, swollen, oozing pus, green, and ugly. Arnold was in pain and scared." *Does any or all of this answer in any way alter your analysis? What portions, if any, of this answer are opinion? Could the witness be prepared to answer in a way that seems more like a recitation of fact than opinion?*

Problem 8-5: The Insanity Defense

Wolin Yerguson boarded a Long Island Railroad rush hour train and pulled out a gun, screaming, "You evil haters must die and save us all!" He then indiscriminately shot 20 passengers, one by one, killing five of them and seriously wounding the rest. He mumbled throughout this episode; the other passengers were able to make out only a word or phrase here and there. His bloodshot eyes kept whirling in circles, never making contact with his victim's eyes. As he fired his last bullet, he screamed, "This will appease the dragon."

1. One of the passengers was asked by Yerguson's lawyer on cross-examination at trial, "Did he appear sane during this incident?" The prosecution objects. What ruling? Why?

2. Would your answer change if Yerguson's brother, with whom Yerguson is quite close, were asked that same question about his observations of Yerguson at the police station one-half hour after the crime? The two brothers had spent an hour together at the police station before Yerguson was questioned by the police. Why?

Problem 8-6: The Plane Crash

A small plane crashed onto a busy highway, injuring the passengers of the plane and the occupants of two cars. Anna was an eyewitness. At trial, Anna testified on direct examination.

PLAINTIFF'S ATTORNEY: Anna, in your opinion, how fast was the car traveling when it was hit by the plane?

DEFENDANT'S ATTORNEY: Objection.

JUDGE: (*How should the judge rule? Why?*)

The examination continues:

PLAINTIFF'S ATTORNEY: Anna, how fast was the plane traveling just before it collided with the car?

DEFENDANT'S ATTORNEY: Objection.

JUDGE: (*How should the judge rule? Why?*)

The examination switches gears:

PLAINTIFF'S ATTORNEY: After the plane touched down, you testified that the pilot wobbled out of the craft. Can you describe the pilot?

A: (1) First, I saw him stumble.

A: (2) It smelled like he had been drinking some sort of alcohol.

A: (3) I'd estimate he was about six feet, two inches tall, and 195 pounds.

A: (4) He looked like he'd been without sleep for a while; he appeared disoriented.

A: (5) By the way he carried himself, it also appeared as if he had a very large ego; I can usually tell these things right off the bat.

Which of the above five statements, if any, are proper lay opinions? Explain your conclusions.

Problem 8-7: The Wink

Detective Kim Gorel was testifying in a homicide trial about her interview with the defendant, Ken. The defense had claimed mistaken identity in its opening statement.

PROSECUTOR: What happened when you were talking with the defendant?

A: The defendant said, "It's a shame that a person was killed," and then he winked at me.

DEFENSE COUNSEL: Objection! Improper opinion.

JUDGE: (*How should the judge rule? Why?*)

The questioning continues:

PROSECUTOR: What do you mean by, "he winked"?

A: He raised his left eyebrow and then quickly closed and opened that same eye.

PROSECUTOR: What did you take that to mean?

DEFENSE COUNSEL: Objection. Calls for speculation.

JUDGE: (*How should the judge rule? Why?*)

The prosecution calls a second witness, Al, to testify. It had already been established that a bottle of Kouros cologne was found in the knapsack the defendant was carrying at the time he was arrested.

PROSECUTOR: What did you observe at 9:40 p.m. in the alley adjacent to John's street?

A: I saw a man raise up a knife and stab another person. Then he ran quickly by me.

PROSECUTOR: What did you observe when he ran by you?

A: Actually, I was so startled and the shadows were so thick, I did not see his face. But I can tell you this, the guy was wearing Kouros cologne.

DEFENSE COUNSEL: Objection! Improper opinion.

How would you rule on this objection if you were the judge and why? How could the prosecutor have done a better job?

Problem 8-8: Hammered

Joey is on trial for DWI. When he was pulled over, Joey refused field sobriety tests and also refused the Breathalyzer. To establish that he was drunk while driving, the prosecutor offers a video of Joey from a convenience store, taken immediately before Joey was pulled over, showing him stumbling to the counter to purchase cigarettes. The prosecutor also seeks to offer the testimony of the convenience store clerk that Joey looked "hammered." *How should the court rule on a defense objection that this constitutes "impermissible lay opinion"?*

Problem 8-9: Human Lie Detector

Officer Jones testifies in the prosecution's rebuttal case in a murder trial that, in his opinion, defendant Donnie lied in his testimony about not being involved. He bases his opinion on 20 years of police experience and his personal experience with gangs. Based on his work with gangs, Jones testifies that he can read the demeanor of gang members for "tells" that help him know when a gang member is lying. *Is Jones's testimony admissible?*

1. Yes, so long as the testimony satisfies Rule 403.

2. No, because the testimony is an inadmissible credibility opinion.

3. No, because Officer Jones is not qualified to give opinions about gang activity — he doesn't have a Ph.D. in a relevant field.

4. Yes, so long as Donnie takes the stand in his own defense.

Problem 8-10: Cocaine Werewolf

Joanna is on trial for distribution of cocaine acquired from an international drug organization. The government's primary evidence against Joanna is the testimony of her former roommate, Carl, who will testify that he found a large bag of a white substance in Joanna's purse, snorted it, and determined that the substance was cocaine. Carl based this testimony on his extensive experience using cocaine. On voir dire, Carl testifies that, at the time he identified the cocaine in Joanna's purse, he had used cocaine approximately 300 times, that he often used it for several days at a time, and that his nickname, at one point, was The Cocaine Werewolf. Joanna disputes that she possessed any white substance, much less cocaine.

Should the court admit Carl's cocaine-identification testimony? Why or why not?

Problem 8-11: Accident Reconstruction

George is on trial for intoxicated manslaughter. He was allegedly drunk when he ran into a pedestrian, killing the pedestrian. The prosecutor calls Will, a city parks employee who is responsible for cleaning the gutter of the street in question, to testify to his opinion about the skid marks at the scene. Will did not see the accident but testifies that, as he observed the day following the crash, the skid marks were about "sixty feet long," and Will goes on to testify that, based on the marks, he estimates that "the car was going real fast, probably eighty miles an hour." Is Will's testimony admissible?

1. No, because Will did not observe the accident firsthand.

2. No, because Will is not qualified as an expert.

3. Yes, because the opinion is the proper subject of lay testimony.

4. Yes, because Will is qualified as an expert.

Problem 8-12: Home Valuation

In a divorce case, Daniella, a Ph.D. physicist, is prepared to testify that the value of the home she owns with her husband is $432,000. They have lived in the home for ten years (before their very recent separation). Among other issues, the size of the marital estate is in dispute in the case. Daniella's husband objects to Daniella's testimony. Should the court exclude the testimony?

1. Yes, because Daniella is not an expert in home valuation.

2. Yes, because, although qualified as a home valuation expert, Daniella's testimony is not helpful to lay jurors who would be able to assess home values for themselves.

3. No, because the testimony is relevant, helpful, and within the province of lay opinion.

4. No, because Daniella, as a Ph.D. physicist, is qualified as an expert.

Problem 8-13: Suspicious Shopper

At a shoplifting trial, Officer Johnson testifies for the prosecution that the defendant, Don, was acting "suspiciously" as he left the store, prompting Officer Johnson to scrutinize a security video of Don at the self-checkout line. The prosecution never specifically qualified Officer Johnson as an expert. In the video, Officer Johnson observed Don dropping items into his bag without scanning them. Don defends the case by claiming he absent-mindedly put the items in the bag and did not intend to steal them. Is Officer Johnson's testimony about Don's suspicious demeanor admissible?

1. Yes, because it is helpful to the jury and within the province of a lay witness.

2. Yes, because police officers are automatically qualified to testify about criminal behavior.

3. No, because the testimony is irrelevant.

4. No, because, although helpful, the testimony is admissible only through a properly qualified expert.

Chapter 9

Expert Opinion Evidence

§ 9.01 Chapter Checklist

1. What are the major and minor premises of the "expert syllogism"?

2. To what relevant issues does any proffered expert testimony relate?

3. Is a proposed expert "qualified" by knowledge, skill, experience, training, or education to testify in the form of an opinion or otherwise?

4. If the expert is so qualified, does the expert's testimony involve: (a) scientific knowledge; (b) technical knowledge; or (c) other specialized knowledge? Does this matter?

5. Is the expert basing an opinion on:

   a. a hypothetical question?

   b. observations personally made by the expert in the courtroom?

   c. observations personally made by the expert outside of the courtroom?

   d. information provided to the expert prior to trial?

6. Does the expert offer his or her opinion to a "reasonable degree of professional certainty"? Does this matter?

7. Has the expert testified to an "ultimate issue" by stating an opinion or inference as to whether a criminal defendant did or did not have a mental state or condition constituting an element of a charged crime or defense?

8. Have the principles and methods (techniques) used by the expert been shown to be both relevant and "reliable," with reliability shown by weighing a wide range of pertinent factors, including:

   a. Whether the principles and techniques are testable and have been tested (that is, has a hypothesis been generated, and have adequate efforts been made to falsify that hypothesis, with no such falsification yet having been achieved)?

   b. Have the theory and technique been subjected to:

      (1) peer review?

      (2) publication?

   c. What is the technique's known or potential error rate?

   d. Has the principle or technique attained "widespread acceptance"?

   e. Are there standards controlling the technique's operation?

9. Has the witness reliably applied the general principles and methods to the facts of the specific case?

10. If the expert has based any portion of an opinion on otherwise inadmissible facts or data, are those facts or data of the type "reasonably relied upon" by other experts in the field?

11. Has cross-examination of the expert inquired into such matters as:

   a. The nonexistence of any particular basis on which the expert relied that might, if shown, alter the opinion?

   b. The existence of contrary or additional bases that would alter the expert's opinion or arguably undermine the accuracy of the opinion?

   c. The materials the expert reviewed or failed to review?

   d. The tests or other investigations the expert conducted or failed to conduct?

   e. Any financial compensation the witness received for giving advice and testimony?

   f. The contradiction between his assertions and those by others in the "learned treatises" exception to the hearsay rule?

§ 9.02 Relevant Federal Rules of Evidence

Rule 702. Testimony by Expert Witnesses

A witness who is qualified as an expert by knowledge, skill, experience, training, or education may testify in the form of an opinion or otherwise if the proponent has demonstrated by a preponderance of the evidence that:

(a) The expert's scientific, technical, or other specialized knowledge will help the trier of fact to understand the evidence or to determine a fact in issue;

(b) The testimony is based on sufficient facts or data;

(c) The testimony is the product of reliable principles and methods; and

(d) The expert's opinion reflects a reliable application of the principles and methods to the facts of the case.

Rule 703. Bases of an Expert's Opinion Testimony

An expert may base an opinion on facts or data in the case that the expert has been made aware of or personally observed. If experts in the particular field would reasonably rely on those kinds of facts or data in forming an opinion on the subject, they need not be admissible for the opinion to be admitted. But if the facts or data would otherwise be inadmissible, the proponent of the opinion may disclose them to the jury only if their probative value in helping the jury evaluate the opinion substantially outweighs their prejudicial effect.

Rule 704. Opinion on an Ultimate Issue

(a) **In General** — Not Automatically Objectionable. An opinion is not objectionable just because it embraces an ultimate issue.

(b) **Exception.** In a criminal case, an expert witness must not state an opinion about whether the defendant did or did not have a mental state or condition that constitutes an element of the crime charged or of a defense. Those matters are for the trier of fact alone.

Rule 705. Disclosing the Facts or Data Underlying an Expert's Opinion

Unless the court orders otherwise, an expert may state an opinion — and give the reasons for it — without first testifying to the underlying facts or data. But the expert may be required to disclose those facts or data on cross-examination.

Rule 706. Court-Appointed Expert Witnesses

(a) **Appointment Process.** On a party's motion or on its own, the court may order the parties to show cause why expert witnesses should not be appointed and may ask the parties to submit nominations. The court may appoint any expert that the parties agree on and any of its own choosing. But the court may only appoint someone who consents to act.

(b) **Expert's Role.** The court must inform the expert of the expert's duties. The court may do so in writing and have a copy filed with the clerk or may do so orally at a conference in which the parties have an opportunity to participate. The expert:

(1) must advise the parties of any findings the expert makes;

(2) may be deposed by any party;

(3) may be called to testify by the court or any party; and

(4) may be cross-examined by any party, including the party that called the expert.

(c) **Compensation.** The expert is entitled to a reasonable compensation, as set by the court. The compensation is payable as follows:

(1) in a criminal case or in a civil case involving just compensation under the Fifth Amendment, from any funds that are provided by law; and

(2) in any other civil case, by the parties in the proportion and at the time that the court directs — and the compensation is then charged like other costs.

(d) **Disclosing the Appointment to the Jury.** The court may authorize disclosure to the jury that the court appointed the expert.

(e) **Parties' Choice of Their Own Experts.** This rule does not limit a party in calling its own experts.

§ 9.03 Nature of Expert Testimony

A. Why Experts Are Needed

Experts play an increasingly important role in both civil and criminal trials. In recent years, experts have played key roles in defective airbag cases, in proceedings overturning faulty convictions, and in property damage cases following catastrophic weather events. Other examples confirm the centrality of experts in contemporary litigation. In a medical malpractice case, for example, a professor specializing in heart surgery might testify that a defendant doctor botched a surgical procedure. In a civil antitrust case, an expert might opine that Microsoft has attained overwhelming domination of the market for computer operating systems. In a criminal case, an expert might discuss her view that George Floyd died as a result of a police officer suffocating him (as opposed to intoxication). In each instance, a party maintains that a full, fair, and informed jury decision requires expert guidance. Without such guidance, the proponents of the expert testimony argue, the jury cannot understand why the surgeon fell short, Microsoft rules, and Floyd's death was murder.

Inferences necessary to courtroom arguments are based on generalizations. For example, a prosecutor argues in a homicide trial that a married woman's male lover killed the woman's husband in a jealous rage. This argument is based on the generalizations that: (1) men in love with married women are jealous of the women's husbands, and (2) jealous men are more likely than other men to kill the person who inspires the jealousy. Generalizations like these are within factfinders' common experience, so no supporting expert testimony is needed. But some generalizations are not common in everyday experience. Thus, the generalization that "Women suffering from battered women's syndrome may see danger in their husband's or lover's behavior that is not apparent to most other observers" is not one that can be fully appreciated or understood based on average people's everyday experiences. The expert provides the knowledge and experience that the lay factfinders lack.

We have, however, up until now spoken in each case of *an* expert but, in fact, many experts are sometimes needed to make fairly specific points, as will shortly become clear. Furthermore, in addition to offering opinions, an expert may testify, in some instances, to the expert's own observations that underlie the opinions. For example, a psychiatrist might testify that the defendant emitted a wolf-like howl, or a physical therapist might testify about seeing the injured plaintiff's pained grimace. Similarly, experts might recount observations that they made in court, such as a linguist noting aspects of a defendant's speech while the defendant was testifying at trial, then matching that speech to a threatening phone caller's recorded voice.

B. The Syllogistic Nature of Expert Reasoning

To understand who may qualify as an expert, how they may testify, and what they might say, it is helpful to examine the syllogistic nature of expert testimony. *See* Edward J. Imwinkelried, *The Educational Significance of the Syllogistic Structure of*

Expert Testimony, 87 Nw. U. L. Rev. 1148 (1993). A syllogism is a form of argument consisting of a major premise (a general statement), a minor premise (a more specific statement), and a conclusion that must necessarily be true if the premises are true. For example:

Major Premise: All dogs have teeth.

Minor Premise: Lassie is a dog.

Conclusion: Therefore, Lassie has teeth.

The major premise in this example involves a broad generalization: that all dogs have teeth. The minor premise involves an observation about one particular creature, Lassie, namely, that Lassie is a dog. If both premises are true, that is, if all dogs do indeed have teeth and if Lassie is a dog, then Lassie necessarily must have teeth. But we might easily disprove the major premise, perhaps by observing at least one dog who has no teeth — an observation easy to make in a kennel of geriatric canines. If all we can then say is that some dogs have teeth, then it does not necessarily follow that Lassie, a dog, has teeth (though it may nevertheless turn out that she does). Similarly, even if it were correct that all dogs have teeth, the minor premise might be proven false: Lassie might be a wolf instead of a dog. That assertion may itself require a separate expert opinion distinguishing between dogs and wolves. Expert testimony can be analyzed in a similar fashion.

Example

In the infamous criminal trial of O.J. Simpson for murdering his ex-wife, Nicole Brown Simpson, and her friend, Ronald Goldman, the prosecution argued that blood found at the crime scene was O.J.'s blood, thus making it highly likely that he was the killer. DNA testing revealed a match between O.J.'s blood and the blood of someone other than the two victims found at the crime scene. This evidence was used to support the claim that O.J.'s blood was at the scene. The implicit syllogism was as follows:

Major Premise 1:   Each human has unique DNA.

Major Premise 2:   DNA tests can accurately identify a match between a known person's DNA and that of an unknown offender at a crime scene.

Minor Premise: O.J.'s DNA matches that found in blood at the crime scene.

Conclusion: Therefore, O.J. was the killer.

Note that this example uses two major premises, that is, two general statements. For the practical purposes of trial, there is no need to explore the technicalities of formal logic further. You should simply be aware that real arguments may have several general statements and several more specific ones. It is less important that you be able to label premises accurately as "major" or "minor" than that you understand that the argument must proceed from the most general statement to increasingly more specific ones. [1]

The syllogistic model of the form illustrated above greatly oversimplifies the true nature of the arguments involved. A DNA expert does not in fact testify that O.J.'s blood and crime scene blood are the same. Rather, the expert testifies that there is a certain "probability" of a match, which is a much more cautious statement than the flat assertion that there is indeed a match. Nevertheless, juries may use expert testimony in syllogistic fashion. Perhaps more importantly, the syllogistic model, while not 100 percent accurate, helpfully focuses our attention and trial planning on what a proponent must prove to prevail. Thus the probative value of DNA evidence requires the prosecution to prove something close to the general statements in major premises 1 and 2 above: that each human has unique DNA and that it is identifiable by testing. These are assertions that apply to any DNA. In addition, the prosecution must prove something close to the minor premise statement specific to *this case* before *this jury*: that O.J.'s unique DNA matches that in blood found at the crime scene. Moreover, the simplistic syllogism offered here can be expanded, or syllogisms can be placed within syllogisms, or other sorts of reasoning processes combined with the overall syllogism to improve its usefulness. For example, two other premises might be:

Major Premise: Any DNA testing must involve steps A through D done in a specified manner, to produce a high degree of confidence in the claimed existence of a match.

Minor Premise: The DNA testing of O.J. indeed involved steps A through D, done in the properly specified manner.

---

1. The use of more than one major or minor premise might arguably violate certain principles of formal logic. *See* Ruggero J. Aldisert, Logic for Lawyers: A Guide to Clear Legal Thinking 146 (3d ed. 1997). That problem can be avoided by breaking up what is presented here in the form of a single syllogism into multiple shorter syllogisms involving only one major and one minor premise each. *Id.* Nevertheless, this quicker and more informal way of proceeding, using multiple major and minor premises in a single "syllogism," is useful for the practical purposes of trial preparation; more closely mimics the implicit reasoning processes of practicing lawyers; and has proven itself to be a valuable educational tool. *See, e.g.* T.R. van Geel, Understanding Supreme Court Opinions 44 (5th ed. 2007) (effectively using a similar method as a way to teach students to analyze United States Supreme Court opinions on constitutional law). Furthermore, some leading evidence scholars, without using the "syllogism" terminology, have used essentially the same method: a series of premises, moving from the most general to the most specific, that must be true to support an expert's conclusion. *See* David L. Faigman et al., Modern Scientific Evidence: The Law and Science of Expert Testimony §1-3.3.1, at 24–25 (1997). The "syllogism" terminology is used here for ease of reference and to emphasize the importance of identifying premises *and identifying proof* that each premise is true, since these concepts are well-illustrated in the language of syllogisms. It is the practical value of this approach as a teaching and trial preparation tool that matters more for the purpose at hand than do the complexities of formal logic, for this approach is unlikely to lead a student or practitioner into logical error. Furthermore, while there are ways to conceptualize the expert rules other than in terms of a syllogism, the syllogism offers clarity (without distortion) to what often seems, especially to students, like chaos. *See* Edward J. Imwinkelried, *Educational Significance of the Syllogistic Structure of Expert Testimony*, 87 Nw. U. L. Rev. 1148 (1993).

| Conclusion: | Therefore, we can have a high degree of confidence in the claimed match between the crime scene blood and O.J.'s blood. |

In the real case, the defense, of course, argued in part that the DNA testing concerning the blood in this case was flawed: steps were missing or were done in an improper manner, so there could be little confidence in the claimed match.

Problem 9-1: Radioactive Taggants

A federal office building was bombed in downtown Chicago, killing many, injuring many more, and reducing the building to rubble. The bomb used was apparently a homemade one, combining some fertilizer ingredients with fuel oil. But the detonating device contained commercially produced materials, including a fuse. The fuse contained a radioactive taggant. A "taggant" is a radioactive molecule placed into the fuse as a tracking device. Its presence is designed to enable law enforcement to track the precise lot of fuses involved and thus to locate the store where this particular fuse was sold. That store's customer list then enables the FBI to link the fuse to a purchaser, who becomes a criminal suspect. Somewhat different taggants are used in each lot so that each lot of fuses has its own distinctive taggant "signature." However, sometimes one lot's taggants touch and thus "contaminate" another lot. This problem can arise at the retail level, where one lot sitting on a shelf may leave a residue that then affects another lot stored in the same location. Lab-testing errors also occasionally result in the misidentification of a particular taggant and thus of a particular lot. Moreover, undue exposure to direct sunlight sometimes causes a chemical reaction that skews lab results. Furthermore, although they are rare, the same radioactive isotopes used in these taggants sometimes appear in other natural or man-made substances in everyday use.

1. Richard McDear is on trial for planning the explosion. Write out the expert syllogism (or syllogisms) that must be proven if the prosecution seeks to introduce expert testimony linking McDear to the explosion as a purchaser of a fuse from a lot marked with a taggant found in fuse remnants at the bomb site.

2. What witnesses should the prosecution call to prove each of the major and minor premises? What sorts of questions should be asked of each witness?

3. What sorts of questions will the defense ask of each of these witnesses to challenge admissibility? What information might the defense seek in discovery and from whom?

C. Why Special Expert Admissibility Rules Are Needed

Courts and legislators have long feared jurors' reactions to expert testimony. Juries are thought to be so "overawed" by experts that they will defer to the expert's opinions and abandon their obligation as jurors independently to judge the strength and credibility of the evidence for themselves. Alternatively, courts and scholars have feared the "battle of the experts" in which two experts (often paid by the parties), one representing each side in a dispute, offer diametrically opposite opinions. In such cases, argue critics, unsophisticated jurors will simply accept the word of the clearer, flashier, more likable expert rather than the one with the soundest bases for the opinion. The concern is that these aspects of trial theater, rather than reason, will lead jurors to follow a misleading or baseless opinion. Accordingly, the rules of evidence have long required expert opinions to pass special admissibility tests — tests raising higher hurdles than those facing lay witnesses.

While the Federal Rules of Evidence supposedly liberalized — that is, relaxed — some of these tests, the tests for experts were always, and still are, more stringent than those facing lay witnesses. Moreover, media stories of enormous civil verdicts based on "junk science" (alleged science with few adequate bases) have led to court interpretations of existing expert evidence rules, or legislative modification of those rules, in the direction of greater stringency.

Problem 9-2: Taggants Revisited

Review the facts of Problem 9-1. *Is expert testimony in that problem likely to raise any of the policy concerns that justify more stringent admissibility rules for admitting expert testimony as compared to lay testimony? Are there ways to address these concerns other than excluding the testimony?*

§ 9.04 Presentation of Expert Testimony

A. Rule 702 — Helpfulness of Expert Opinion and Qualifications of Expert

Expert testimony is addressed specifically by Federal Rules of Evidence 702, 703, 704, 705, and 706. The first of these rules that we will explore is Rule 702, which currently reads:

Rule 702. Testimony by Expert Witnesses

A witness who is qualified as an expert by knowledge, skill, experience, training, or education may testify in the form of an opinion or otherwise if:

(a) the expert's scientific, technical, or other specialized knowledge will help the trier of fact to understand the evidence or to determine a fact in issue;

(b) the testimony is based on sufficient facts or data;

(c) the testimony is the product of reliable principles and methods; and

(d) the expert has reliably applied the principles and methods to the facts of the case.

Pending Amendments

The evidence rulemaking committees have recently proposed amendments, that could take effect in December 2023 (additions in <u>underline</u>; deletions in ~~strikethrough~~):

Rule 702. Testimony by Expert Witnesses

A witness who is qualified as an expert by knowledge, skill, experience, training, or education may testify in the form of an opinion or otherwise if <u>the proponent demonstrates to the court that it is more likely than not that</u>:

    (a) the expert's scientific, technical, or other specialized knowledge will help the trier of fact to understand the evidence or to determine a fact in issue;

    (b) the testimony is based on sufficient facts or data;

    (c) the testimony is the product of reliable principles and methods; and

    (d) the ~~expert has reliably applied~~ <u>expert's opinion reflects a reliable application of</u> the principles and methods to the facts of the case.

As discussed in more detail below, these amendments would clarify that the proponent has the burden to establish the sub-parts of Rule 702 by a preponderance. The amendment to sub-part (d) would emphasize that courts are to scrutinize expert application of principles and methods in reaching conclusions.

Rule 702 codifies the syllogistic approach to expert evidence. Provision (c)'s reference to reliability concerns the major premises, for example, that each human being has unique fingerprints and that a method exists for accurately identifying those unique fingerprints. Provision (d) concerns the minor premises, e.g., that fingerprints were properly taken from a specific suspect and crime scene and that the method for accurately matching that suspect's prints to those at the scene was properly applied in the case before the court. Provision (b) is ambiguous; it may apply to both the major and minor premises or instead only to the latter, a matter we will address shortly.

Having established that special admissibility rules are needed for expert testimony, we now examine in greater detail what those rules are and what they mean. This section looks at when it is appropriate to admit expert testimony, when an expert is qualified to offer expert evidence, and the proper manner for presenting expert testimony. These subjects lay the groundwork for the rest of the chapter, which examines how solid general principles applied to the case at hand properly support expert opinions.

We earlier discussed the distinction between "lay" and "expert" testimony. We must return to that distinction here because an expert must be qualified to offer an opinion on the particular subject of the expert's opinion. A person who is an expert on some things may be a mere layperson on others. Expert opinion should be limited to those matters about which the witness has adequate *expert* qualifications.

Example 1

Dr. Joseph Lewis, a skilled heart surgeon, is called to testify in a medical malpractice trial that another heart surgeon, Dr. Jesse Smith, improperly performed an angioplasty (insertion of a small tube to open up a blocked artery feeding the heart). Dr. Lewis would arguably be qualified to offer such an expert opinion. Suppose, however, that, instead of testifying about heart surgery, Dr. Lewis were called to testify in a dental malpractice trial that Dr. Bright, a dentist, had offered inadequate dental care. In that case, Dr. Lewis' opinion, as a heart surgeon, would be little more informed about dental care than a layperson's; it would be inadmissible.

What if Dr. Shine, a renowned dentist, were called to the stand at Dr. Bright's trial for dental malpractice, to opine that Bright's patient, Harvey Bateson, was in great pain for many days after being treated by Dr. Bright? Is Shine any more qualified than Bateson himself, or perhaps Bateson's wife or employer, to offer the opinion that Bateson was in pain?

The answer to this last question shows a close link between what *qualifications* are required for a person to be eligible to testify as an expert and what *topics of inquiry* are appropriate for an expert opinion. Some common-law cases have said that the only proper topics of inquiry of an expert are those "beyond the ken of laypersons." However, this means that experts must have *qualifications* enabling them to offer opinions on matters that laypersons (including jurors drawing their own inferences) could not. Of course, on the question of dental patient pain, it might be argued that no opinion is necessary at all, lay or expert. Any witness-observer might describe Bateson's grimaces, tears, and screams, from which jurors could infer that Bateson was in pain. Moreover, if some opinion is needed, it should be "within the ken" of laypersons to offer and understand it.

If, however, Dr. Shine wanted to testify that he could tell the difference between faked and real pain, based on training unavailable to laypersons, that would indeed be a subject "beyond the ken" of laypersons. But Shine would have a hard time showing that he was specially qualified by "knowledge, skill, experience, training, or education" to offer such an opinion. Dentists, unlike polygraphers (lie detector technicians), do not get any special training on how to spot their patients' lies. (Of course, close examination of the underlying empirical research would be necessary to determine whether polygraphers' special training actually makes them any better than dentists at lie identification.) The Federal Rules of Evidence relax the common law "beyond the ken" requirement. All that is necessary is that the testimony will be helpful, that is, "will help the trier of fact to understand the evidence or to determine a fact in issue."

Under this standard, experts may testify about topics that concern matters within the general knowledge of jurors, if they have special qualifications such that their opinion will nevertheless aid the jury. The Advisory Committee Note explained the topics-of-inquiry (helpfulness) link to expert qualifications this way:[2]

> There is no more certain test for determining when experts may be used than the common sense inquiry whether the untrained layman would be qualified to determine intelligently and to the best possible degree the particular issue without enlightenment from those having a specialized understanding of the subject involved in the dispute.

Note that the Advisory Committee Note expressly links "when experts may be used" (What are the proper *topics* of expert testimony?) with whether the expert is one of "those having a specialized understanding of the subject involved in the dispute" (Is the expert "qualified"?). Furthermore, the Note stresses that qualifications and topic-appropriateness must be measured as to "the particular issue" about which the expert will testify. The expert need not, however, refer only to matters "beyond the layman's ken" but rather may address any topic that enables the jury to determine an issue to "the best possible degree" by hearing from the expert. Perhaps the existence of dental pain is within lay experience. But an expert's opinion that a particular patient was in more pain than the vast majority of other patients whom the expert dentist treated in his long career might nevertheless allow the jury to make a more accurate and informed judgment.

Example 2

Jolene offers the testimony of an expert on battered women's syndrome, who will testify that: (a) some battered women display a fear of great harm from their abusers in situations where danger may not be apparent to non-battered third parties; (b) these women see no safe way to escape when others might; and (c) Jolene suffered from BWS, and was fearful that her husband would kill her.

A common-law court might hold that fear of assault and inter-spousal disagreements are within the "ken" of ordinary laypersons. Under the Federal Rules of Evidence, by contrast, a court might concede that fact but nevertheless admit the evidence after concluding that it would be helpful for jurors to learn of an expert's opinions based on research into the experiences and behaviors of battered women. With that information, they could more effectively judge Jolene's credibility and, if finding her truthful, better see the world through her eyes.

The syllogistic nature of expert testimony is important in judging an expert's qualifications, as in the following example.

---

2. FED. R. EVID. 702 advisory committee's note (quoting Mason Ladd, *Expert Testimony*, 5 VAND. L. REV. 414, 418 (1952)).

Example 3

John O'Barr, the president of a major university, is being charged with making threatening phone calls. One of his victims has recorded all his phone calls. Pursuant to a court order, O'Barr has recorded himself reciting a specified script. The prosecution wants to offer a voiceprint analysis to prove that the voice on the recording of the threatening phone call matches O'Barr's voice. The term "voiceprint" is commonly used to refer to a spectrogram, which is a visual representation of a human voice's qualities.

The prosecution calls Ronald Nelson, a police officer spectrogram technician, to the stand as the prosecution's sole expert witness. Nelson has a high school degree and has attended five training sessions on how to administer spectrograms. He has administered more than 50 voice spectrograms over the course of 10 years; in each case he testified as a voice spectrogram expert at a criminal trial. O'Barr's counsel objects on the ground that Nelson is not adequately qualified to establish the foundation necessary for his expert opinion.

The trial court should sustain the objection. The implicit syllogism is as follows:

Major Premise 1:   Each human has a unique voice.

Major Premise 2:   The voice spectrogram analyzer is a device that accurately records each person's voice's features and correctly represents those features in a written diagram.

Major Premise 3:   Voice spectrogram analyzer accuracy depends on the technician's following certain specified procedures.

Minor Premise: Those procedures were accurately followed in matching O'Barr's voice recording to the threatening phone caller's voice recording.

Conclusion: O'Barr made the threatening phone calls.

Police Officer Nelson is definitely qualified to testify concerning the minor premise, that is, to describe what procedures he followed in doing spectrographic analysis. He is probably qualified to testify as to Major Premise 3, that is, to explain what are the proper procedures. But he is not qualified to testify concerning the first two major premises. Only a scientist, preferably an academic who has done research in, or is at least familiar with, voice spectrographic analysis or voice identification more generally would be qualified to testify that each human voice is unique and that the principles and methods involved in the voice spectrograph make it a reliable way of identifying otherwise unknown speakers. Thus, the prosecution can cure Nelson's qualification problem by limiting his testimony to Major Premise 3 and the Minor Premise and calling a well-credentialed scientist to the stand to testify concerning the first two major premises.

A lawyer seeking to establish, or to challenge, an expert's qualifications must explore issues such as the following: (1) the expert's formal education and degrees received, (2) the expert's specialized training in his or her field of expertise, (3) the time the expert has spent practicing in that field, (4) the expert's professional licenses, teaching experience, publications, and membership in professional organizations, and (5) previous testimony given by the expert. Pretrial discovery may well arm an advocate with knowledge about these aspects of the expert's qualifications, especially in civil cases, where depositions are more likely to be available.

Example 4

A portion of a sample voir dire qualifying an expert witness follows. This voir dire (as used here, the term means the questioning done to establish the foundation for admitting expert testimony as qualified) arises at a hearing to determine the competency of a criminal defendant to stand trial. The prosecution calls Dr. Susan Trautman Borg to the stand as an expert in the psychiatric diagnosis and treatment of mental illness.

PROSECUTOR: Good morning, Dr. Borg. Please state your full name for the record and spell it for the court reporter.

A: Susan Trautman Borg, M.D.

PROSECUTOR: What is your educational background?

A: I received my B.A. and M.D. degrees from Case Western Reserve University. After graduating, I did my internship and residency at Jackson Memorial Hospital in Miami. I had a post-doctoral fellowship in psychiatry at the National Institute of Mental Health in Washington, DC.

PROSECUTOR: Are you employed?

A: Yes, at the South Allenton State Psychiatric Facility.

PROSECUTOR: What is your job at South Allenton State?

A: I am the Director of Psychiatric Services.

PROSECUTOR: How long have you worked there?

A: I have been the Director for seven years. I began at South Allenton as the head resident, spent two years in that position, and then served as Associate Director for three years.

PROSECUTOR: How many patients have you treated for psychiatric illness in those seven years?

A: Based on the Diagnostic and Statistical Manual III-R, which is generally used by psychiatrists and psychologists, I'd say quite a few. Probably several hundred.

PROSECUTOR: What are your job responsibilities?

A: I currently handle a reduced caseload of approximately 10 to 15 patients along with my administrative duties. These duties involve overseeing a department of 20 psychologists, 10 social workers, and 75 other staff members.

PROSECUTOR: What does Board-certified in psychiatry mean?

A: Board certification exists in various medical specialties. In psychiatry, it means that the psychiatrist has passed an examination designed to ensure an advanced degree of knowledge in the field of psychiatry and has been approved by the American Board of Medical Specialties. To become Board-certified, a person must first become Board-eligible, which requires successfully completing several prerequisites, including an examination. Only a small percentage of psychiatrists are Board-certified.

PROSECUTOR: What is your board status, Doctor?

A: I am Board-certified.

PROSECUTOR: Doctor, to which, if any, professional organizations do you belong?

A: I belong to the American Psychiatric Association, where I am the immediate past president.

PROSECUTOR: Have you published any writings in your field?

A: I published the paper "Psychotropic Drugs: the Good, the Bad, and the Ugly," in the journal Nature in 1991, and have co-authored approximately 50 other pieces in a wide variety of journals. Co-authoring is the general practice of scholars in my medical specialty.

PROSECUTOR: Have you ever testified as an expert in psychiatry?

A: About 150 times, mostly for the prosecution, but sometimes for the defense.

PROSECUTOR: Have you continued your education in psychiatry?

A: Yes. I take three continuing education courses in psychiatry each year, as required, and teach at Allenton University as an adjunct. I also participate in as many educational colloquia as time permits.

PROSECUTOR: Your Honor, I now offer Dr. Borg as an expert in the diagnosis and treatment of mental illness.

To recap: (1) There is a close connection between what topics of inquiry are appropriate for expert advice and what qualifications must be demanded of the expert. Accordingly, a good lawyer first carefully specifies the precise opinions the expert will offer, why those opinions will help the jury, and why the expert has the qualifications to offer the specific opinion requested.

(2) A good lawyer also understands the syllogistic nature of expert testimony. With this understanding, the lawyer is able to determine all the premises involved in proposed expert testimony and which experts are qualified to testify about the various premises in the syllogism — specifically, in the roles of theorist (educator), technician, and interpreter.

Problem 9-3: Bomb-Blast Terrorism

Assume the facts stated in Problem 9-1:

1. *Who would you, as the prosecutor, call to the stand as an expert in the McDear case? Would you need more than one expert?*

2. What questions would you ask the expert (or experts) to qualify him (her, or them)? Be ready to conduct the qualifying examination in class.

Problem 9-4: The Inaccurate Eyewitness

Dr. John La Rue is an academic psychologist specializing in the areas of the accuracy of human perception and memory. Jonathan Brill was robbed at gunpoint at an ATM machine at 10:00 p.m. during the month of October. Mr. Brill gave a description of his assailant to the police that night. Approximately 72 hours later, Brill picked the defendant, Horace Weatherwax, out of a lineup, saying, "I'm certain that's the man. I'd never forget that face." The defense calls Dr. La Rue to the stand at Weatherwax's trial to discuss the factors that affect the accuracy of eyewitness identifications generally, what factors were present in this particular case and their significance, and to opine that Brill's identification of Weatherwax was not trustworthy.

Which of the following are relevant to qualifying (or disqualifying) Dr. La Rue as an expert witness and why or why not:

1. He has published 17 articles on the impact of various traumas (war wounds, child abuse, and spousal abuse) on human perception and memory.

2. His Ph.D. was in clinical psychology rather than experimental psychology.

3. He has never specifically done research on the accuracy of eyewitness identification.

4. He teaches, and has for the past 10 years taught, an undergraduate course on the accuracy of eyewitness identification.

5. He has extensively read the literature on eyewitness identification accuracy.

6. He published an article in *Psychology Today* on the accuracy of bystander eyewitness testimony, as distinguished from testimony by the victim.

7. He has testified concerning eyewitness accuracy in 50 cases, each time testifying for the defense.

8. He has provided psychotherapeutic counseling to Mick Jagger, Tom Cruise, and other well-known musicians and actors.

9. He received his degree from a little-known, small-town night school.

10. He is president of the American Society of Forensic Psychologists.

11. He is a member of the American Psychological Association.

Problem 9-5: Dr. Borg

Review the illustrative voir dire of Dr. Borg in Example 4, above. *Even after this voir dire, are there plausible grounds for objection to her qualifications to offer an opinion regarding whether the criminal defendant (asserting an insanity defense) suffered from a particular mental disease or defect at the time of the crime and to explain the significance of that disease or defect? What sorts of additional questions on the voir dire by the prosecution could have reduced the chances of such objections?*

B. Direct Examination of Experts

1. The Four Data Sources and the Traditional Hypothetical Question

There are four potential sources of data on which an expert may base an opinion:

1. Firsthand observations made by the expert out of court. For example, a dermatologist testifies about the color, shape, feel, and smell of a rash that she observed on a patient's arm.

2. Facts or data made known to the expert out of court, such as a forensic internist opining about the reasons for a diagnosis, which include X-ray reports and lab tests done by other doctors and technicians that the expert examined prior to trial. This information may also include depositions.

3. Information provided to an expert in the courtroom that the expert is asked to assume is accurate.

4. An expert's observation of in-court testimony by one or several witnesses.

Example 1

The issue in a negligent driving case in which the driver's passenger was seriously injured is whether the driver exceeded the 55-mph speed limit. A police officer who arrived on the scene shortly after the accident describes his observation of the length of skid marks and the extent and nature of the damage to the defendant's car. The emergency room physician describes the plaintiff's injuries. A physicist who has listened to the officer's and the physician's testimony is later asked whether, assuming the truth of that testimony, the physicist has an opinion about what speed the defendant's car was traveling at the time of the accident.

Secondhand Information

Before the current rules, courts often required experts to base their opinions on facts or data that were already admitted into evidence, or at least facts that were admissible. Thus, data source category 2 (facts or data presented to the expert out of court) could not, in the strictest versions of the traditional rule, be the basis for expert opinion unless those facts or data were separately admitted into evidence. Usually (but courts differed on this point), they would have to be admitted *before* the experts could recite their opinions for the jury. For example, the x-ray report and results would first have to be admitted into evidence before the emergency room physician in the last example above could offer the patient's diagnosis. In less restrictive versions of the traditional rule, the x-ray and lab results would, if not already admitted, have at least to be admissible.

These traditional rules were not especially troublesome for firsthand observations made by the expert either in or outside of court because such observations are usually admissible (unless unduly prejudicial under Rule 403). In addition, observations can often be easily and concisely stated by the expert, who in this capacity serves more as an eyewitness (e.g., "He moaned in pain, had bruises across much of his calf, etc.," as recounted by an emergency-room physician treating an automobile accident victim). But data source 2, we will soon see, more often requires the expert to rely on evidence whose admissibility is questionable. Trial courts needed to police expert opinions based on such evidence. To ensure that an expert revealed the actual bases of an opinion before offering it, courts traditionally required that the opinions be elicited by a hypothetical question. Hypothetical questions in this context asked the expert to assume certain listed facts to be true and to offer an opinion based upon that assumption. Courts sometimes failed to distinguish among the four data sources, and required hypothetical questions involving any of the four sources.

The most common sort of hypothetical question expressly stated, often in list-like form, every fact that the expert was asked to assume to be true:

Example 2

Dr. Johnson, a well-known physician, is called as a knee-injury expert in a case in which the plaintiff/accident-victim's knee was treated in an emergency room. Dr. Johnson did not himself observe the plaintiff's injuries, nor has he ever treated the plaintiff. The direct examination includes this hypothetical question:

PLAINTIFF'S ATTORNEY: Dr. Johnson, please assume the following facts are true: One, Johnny Bender [the plaintiff] groaned when trying to bend his right knee. Two, he bent that knee slowly, never achieving more than a 20-degree angle. Three, the knee was swollen, red, and puffy. Four, the knee was bleeding profusely. Doctor, given these assumptions, do you have an opinion, to a reasonable degree of medical certainty, as to the nature of Mr. Bender's knee injury?

For Dr. Johnson to be allowed to offer this opinion, another witness would have had to testify (or plaintiff would have had to promise to produce such a witness) that he or she observed the plaintiff's bloody, swollen, stiff knee as well as groans in the emergency room. The emergency-room physician or, if present, the plaintiff's spouse, might be able to offer such testimony. Of course, the emergency-room physician, rather than the high-priced Dr. Johnson, could also be queried about his diagnosis of the plaintiff. Many judges traditionally would have encouraged such queries also to be done in the form of a hypothetical question. Nevertheless, the plaintiff may still want to call the better-credentialed Dr. Johnson to the stand to buttress the emergency-room physician's opinion about the extent of the plaintiff's injuries.

An alternative form of the hypothetical question, rather than reciting every fact to be assumed by the expert, simply asks the expert to assume the truth of the previous testimony of a witness or witnesses that the expert has heard testify in court:

PLAINTIFF'S ATTORNEY: Dr. Johnson, assuming the truth of the observations testified to today by Mr. Bender's spouse and the emergency room physician, do you have an opinion regarding when, if ever, Mr. Johnson will recover full use of his knee?

Such an approach may be misleading or confusing, however, if the testimony is conflicting or complex. In such a case, a court might require use of the more detailed, specific version of the hypothetical question.

2. Liberalization of Expert Opinion Bases Under the Federal Rules of Evidence

a. Rule 703

The hypothetical question was often strategically advantageous to counsel. Attorneys were able to use a hypothetical question as a mini-summation during the trial. Furthermore, credibility might be lent to an advocate's case by asking a well-respected expert to assume the truth of the advocate's witnesses.

But the hypothetical question had downsides as well. Some such questions had to be quite lengthy, which made them boring and lengthened the trial. Hypothetical questions could construct a misleading, one-sided hypothesis. And much courtroom time was consumed by attorneys arguing for and against the inclusion of various details in hypotheticals.

Moreover, they opened the door to reversals on appeal if an appellate court later concluded that some of the assumed facts were not supported by other evidence in the trial. Additionally, reciting the bases for an opinion before hearing the opinion itself may have left the jury confused, uncertain of why the data presented in the hypothetical was important.

For reasons like these, the Federal Rules of Evidence rejected the requirements that: (1) expert opinions must be based only on admitted, or at least admissible, evidence; (2) the data underlying the opinion must be revealed before presenting the opinion itself; and (3) the hypothetical question is the preferred mode of inquiry.

Lawyers remain free, however, to adhere to traditional approaches where they believe it is strategically wise to do so.

The first of these three changes to traditional rules is contained in the beginning two sentences of Rule 703 as originally drafted:

The facts or data upon which an expert bases an opinion or inference may be those received by, or made known to, an expert at or before the hearing. If of a type reasonably relied upon by experts in the particular field in forming opinions or inferences upon the subject, the facts or data need not be admissible in evidence in order for the opinion or inference to be admitted.

The provision that inadmissible evidence may be the basis for an opinion only if "reasonably relied upon" by experts in the particular field retains a hint of the traditional rules. First, some opinions still may not be based on inadmissible evidence, if the evidence is not "reasonably relied upon." Second, if an advocate is concerned about this limitation, it may be avoided by seeking opinions based only on admissible evidence. Thus, counsel may in close cases have an incentive to adhere to more traditional rules.

Why retain these shades of the traditional rules? The implicit answer: because these remnants help prevent misleading end runs around the purpose of the rules of evidence, which is "to secure fairness in administration . . . to the end that truth may be ascertained and proceedings justly determined." FED. R. EVID. 102. While not expressly relying on Rule 102, the Advisory Committee Note to Rule 703 gives this example of how Rule 703's limitations promote truth-seeking: "The language [of reasonable reliance] would not warrant admitting in evidence the opinion of an 'accidentologist' as to the point of impact in an automobile collision based on statements of bystanders, because this requirement is not satisfied." If the bystanders do not testify and cannot, therefore, be cross-examined, and if no exception to the hearsay rules justifies admitting their statements as reliable ones, then the expert's opinion is based on data whose adequacy will never be challenged before the jury and that lacks other guarantees of trustworthiness. Presumably, evidence relied upon by an expert that is independently admissible has survived the gauntlet of the other evidence rules, thus creating some minimal guarantee of trustworthiness. But nothing in an "accidentologist's" training increases the accuracy of bystander statements otherwise barred by the hearsay rules. Before we can have confidence in the expert's opinion being based on worthy data, we therefore at least require that the data either be admissible or be "reasonably relied upon" by experts in the field.

When may an expert "reasonably rely" on data or other information in forming an opinion? No consensus has emerged, but the courts have suggested some approaches. The liberal school equates "reasonable" reliance with "regular" or "customary" reliance. The judge's task is to determine whether it is the customary practice of other experts in the relevant specialty to use a particular data source in their reasoning. A more restrictive school considers "reasonable" reliance to be a matter for independent determination by the trial judge, who must conduct a searching inquiry to determine the wisdom of an expert's relying on a particular data source. The trial judge need not defer to customary practice, although that may be a relevant factor. A middle approach regards customary reliance on a data source by experts in a field as strong evidence of reasonableness, perhaps even creating a rebuttable presumption of reasonableness.

There is also a dispute over what information the "reasonable reliance" standard must apply. Rule 703 refers to facts or data being *"of a type"* reasonably relied upon by experts in the field. Some courts conclude, therefore, that the trial judge's narrow inquiry should be whether the expert properly relied on the particular "type" or category of information, rather than whether it was reasonable to rely on the *specific* facts or data of that type in this case. A contrary view reads Rule 703 as empowering the trial judge to question the expert's wisdom in relying on *particular* facts or data, not simply determining whether those relied upon were of the general sort to which experts would reasonably look.

Even if an expert "reasonably relies upon" inadmissible data, does that mean that the expert may reveal that data to the jury? If the answer is yes, again an end run might be possible around other rules of evidence. Thus an advocate might intentionally ask the expert to interview persons who will not be at trial to enable the advocate indirectly to reveal (via the expert) those persons' otherwise inadmissible hearsay statements. Yet some commentators have concluded that a new hearsay exception should be established for the data underlying an expert opinion that complies with Rule 703's reasonable reliance requirement. *See, e.g.*, Paul R. Rice, *Inadmissible Evidence as a Basis for Expert Opinion Testimony: A Response to Professor Carlson*, 40 VAND. L. REV. 583 (1987). Other courts and commentators permit revelation of the reasonably relied upon but otherwise inadmissible bases of expert testimony only on a non-hearsay rationale. The jury is instructed that it may not consider these bases for the truth of what they assert. Rather, the jury is told that the bases are offered only so that the jurors know on what the expert relies, thus enabling jurors to judge the credibility of the expert's opinion. If the jury sees no reason to believe that such bases in fact exist, or concludes that there were other ignored bases that the expert should have considered, the jury may choose not to credit the expert's opinion. Juries will often, however, use the recited bases precisely for the prohibited purpose — to prove the truth of what they assert — despite a court's instructions to the contrary.

Example

A physician testifies, based partly upon lab test results, that a patient suffered from a certain type of infection. Assume that the lab report is inadmissible, perhaps because the records were not kept in the way expected in the ordinary course of business (which would violate hearsay rules to be studied later). May the physician nevertheless reveal the content of the lab report to the jury, so long as the lab report contains a "type" of fact or datum reasonably relied upon by experts in the field? The proponent of such disclosure will argue that jurors cannot evaluate the worth of the physician's opinion without knowing the contents of the lab report on which he relied. The jury can simply be instructed that it may not use the statements in the lab report for the truth of what they assert, only to assess the credibility of the expert's opinion. For example, was there thorough investigation by the expert? Does evidence other than the statements themselves suggest that they were right? The opponent of such revelation will argue that the jury will improperly use the lab report for the truth of what it asserts, and that such use would both violate hearsay rules and unfairly prejudice the opponent under Rule 403.

To reduce the incentive for attorneys to use experts as conduits for inadmissible hearsay, Rule 703 provides:

Federal Rule of Evidence 703

An expert may base an opinion on facts or data in the case that the expert has been made aware of or personally observed. If experts in the particular field would reasonably rely on those kinds of facts or data in forming an opinion on the subject, they need not be admissible for the opinion to be admitted. But if the facts or data would otherwise be inadmissible, the proponent of the opinion may disclose them to the jury only if their probative value in helping the jury evaluate the opinion substantially outweighs their prejudicial effect.

Rule 703 specifies circumstances when the bases of an expert *opinion* render it admissible. It does not render the otherwise inadmissible bases for that expert opinion freely admissible as substantive evidence. Thus, Rule 703 does *not* create an exception to the hearsay rule. *See* Fed. R. Evid. 703, advisory committee's note to 2000 amendment. Underlying bases may be revealed under the specified conditions, but "the trial judge must give a limiting instruction upon request, informing the jury that the underlying information must not be used for substantive purposes." *Id.* That is, the information is admitted only so that the jury can know the opinion's basis and thus better assess its credibility. But the rule provides a "presumption against disclosure to the jury." *Id.* A significant burden is thus placed on the proponent to overcome that presumption. This balancing test should be contrasted with the test under Rule 403, which favors admissibility of relevant evidence by excluding it only if its probative value is substantially outweighed by unfair prejudice and related concerns. Rule 703 takes quite the opposite approach; it presumes that the inadmissible bases for expert opinion are unfairly prejudicial, but will admit those bases if their probative value in assisting the jury to evaluate the expert's opinion substantially outweighs their prejudicial effect. In engaging in this balancing process, the trial judge must consider the probable effectiveness or lack thereof of a limiting instruction. *Id.*

Rule 703 applies only to evidence of the underlying bases when offered by the *proponent* of the expert. It does not restrict "the presentation of underlying expert facts or data when offered by an adverse party." *Id.* Thus, it does not prevent the presentation of underlying facts or data on cross-examination of the expert by an adverse party. Importantly, an adversary's attack on an expert's basis on cross might open the door to an opponent's rebuttal with information that was reasonably relied upon by the expert but not initially disclosable under the balancing test. *Id.* However, in a multi-party case, even if only one party proffers the evidence, each party for whom evidence is beneficial is considered a "proponent." *Id.* Finally, Rule 702, not Rule 703, governs an opinion's reliability, regardless of whether the opinion is based on admissible or inadmissible evidence, a point that will be made clearer when we return to it later.

Rule 703 is closely related to Rule 705, so we will examine the latter before analyzing problems involving both rules.

b. Rule 705

Rule 705 embodies two changes from the traditional rules. It permits an opinion to be stated before its bases are revealed (or not to reveal the bases on direct examination at all). The rule also provides that hypothetical questions are no longer required:

Rule 705. Disclosing the Facts or Data Underlying an Expert's Opinion

Unless the court orders otherwise, an expert may state an opinion—and give the reasons for it—without first testifying to the underlying facts or data. But the expert may be required to disclose those facts or data on cross-examination.

The Advisory Committee Note makes clear that eliminating the frequent requirement of presentation by a hypothetical question was one major goal of Rule 705. Although it is no longer required, the direct examiner might choose, for strategic reasons, nevertheless to proceed via hypothetical. *See also* Fed. R. Evid. 702, advisory committee's note ("The language 'facts or data' is broad enough to allow an expert to rely on hypothetical facts that are supported by the evidence."). If the hypothetical is short, clear, and punchy, it offers the proponent the traditional advantage of a mini-summing-up midtrial. Regardless of whether a hypothetical question is used, Rule 705 gives the advocate the flexibility to determine *when*, if at all, to reveal the bases for an expert opinion at trial. Many advocates find it effective to elicit the opinion first, then its bases, enabling jurors to understand why the bases matter, to give them a road map:

Example

Dr. Reginald Gobert, a renowned psychiatrist, takes the stand at defendant Johannes Brahms' criminal trial in support of his insanity defense. Defense counsel, after eliciting Dr. Gobert's credentials, proceeds on direct examination as follows.

DEFENSE COUNSEL: Did you personally examine Mr. Brahms to assess his mental capacities at the time of the crime?

A: Yes, I examined him on at least four occasions, for a total of 10 hours of observation.

DEFENSE COUNSEL: Of what did your examination consist?

A: I interviewed him extensively about his background and his current thoughts and feelings; I observed his demeanor, the clarity and responsiveness of his speech, whether he made eye contact; and I administered a variety of written tests. [Gobert then explains what these tests and other observations involved and why they mattered].

DEFENSE COUNSEL: Did you engage in any other investigations besides meeting with the defendant to form an opinion about Mr. Brahms' mental state at the time of the alleged crime?

A: Yes. I read all the police reports; reviewed his school and employment records and his physician's files; and interviewed his family, friends, teachers, and current co-workers.

DEFENSE COUNSEL: Based upon these investigations, did you form an opinion to a reasonable degree of professional certainty whether Mr. Brahms suffered from a mental disease or defect at the time of the crime?

A: Yes.

DEFENSE COUNSEL: What is that opinion?

A: He did then, and still does, suffer from the mental disease of paranoid schizophrenia.

DEFENSE COUNSEL: What is paranoid schizophrenia?

A: *[Here Dr. Gobert explains the symptoms of the disease].*

DEFENSE COUNSEL: What are your reasons for reaching that conclusion?

A: He repeatedly insisted that he is really Napoleon Bonaparte reborn, making this point not just to me but to all his family and friends for at least two years before this incident. Moreover, *[here Dr. Gobert recites the bases for the opinion in detail and then explains why each is significant, that is, why it supports his conclusion].*

Defense counsel's manner of proceeding here—eliciting the opinion before asking for recitation of its bases—was traditionally unacceptable but is perfectly appropriate under Rule 705. Indeed, under Rule 705, defense counsel need not have begun, as he did in the above example, by reciting the general sorts of investigations he undertook (that is, for example, noting that he interviewed the defendant without then recounting what the defendant said). Rather, defense counsel could have simply proceeded this way:

DEFENSE COUNSEL: Do you have an opinion to a reasonable degree of professional certainty whether Mr. Brahms suffered from a mental disease or defect at the time of the crime?

A: Yes.

DEFENSE COUNSEL: What is that opinion?

A: He did then, and still does, suffer from paranoid schizophrenia.

DEFENSE COUNSEL: What is paranoid schizophrenia?

A: *[Here Dr. Gobert explains].*

DEFENSE COUNSEL: What investigations did you do to help you reach your opinion?

A: *[Here Dr. Gobert notes that he interviewed the defendant and his family and friends, etc.].*

Q: What were the results of those investigations, that is, the bases for your opinion?

A: *[Here Dr. Gobert recites what the defendant and his family and friends actually said during the interviews, what the test results were, etc.].*

The order of examination is thus generally in the advocate's control.

Some have objected to Rule 705's liberalization of traditional rules because the new Rule allows a direct examiner to choose not to elicit any bases at all. That would place the cross-examiner in the perhaps awkward position of eliciting bases for the first time, possibly thereby inadvertently injuring his own case. Such concerns are overblown.

Significant pretrial discovery of expert opinions and their bases is now standard procedure, especially in civil cases. A cross-examiner should, therefore, be well aware of the nature and bases of opinions to be expressed by the opponent's expert. Cross-examiners can thus elicit what they believe will help their client and harm the opposition. Moreover, where this is not the case (that is, in jurisdictions following Rule 705 but with limited discovery), the trial court has discretion under the rule to require disclosure of bases on direct, for example, where necessary to prevent unfair surprise. Finally, sound strategic reasons encourage proponents to reveal the bases for expert opinions on direct. Juries are simply not likely to credit raw opinions unsupported by convincing facts or data, especially if an opposing expert offers a well-supported opinion. An advocate might withhold some bases on direct in the hope that they will be more powerful if elicited by the opponent on cross. But that scenario is likely only if the opponent did inadequate investigation or if the trial is set in a jurisdiction with very limited expert discovery; otherwise, there would be no prospect of the opponent's being surprised by the witness' answers.

Problem 9-6: The Gullible Personality

Ms. B was charged with knowingly possessing nine stolen welfare checks. The prosecution's undisputed evidence showed that six checks, made out to different payees, were given to Ms. B by her boyfriend's good friend, Scott. Ms. B deposited the checks, which supposedly had been endorsed to Scott, into her account. One check was returned unpaid, and her account was charged accordingly, but Scott made good her loss. He subsequently gave her three more checks to deposit. The prosecution's theory is that Ms. B "must have known" that the checks were stolen, but Ms. B testified that she did not in fact believe that the checks were stolen; she believed Scott's story that the checks had been given to him in payment for a debt, and he needed her assistance because he had no bank account of his own.

Ms. B calls a psychologist to the stand at trial to testify that Ms. B's personality is characterized by an unusually high degree of gullibility and dependency. To reach this conclusion, the psychiatrist, Dr. P, administered various psychological tests, interviewed Ms. B, and interviewed: (1) her parents, who described numerous instances in which Ms. B, as a child, believed clear lies told her daily by her brother; (2) Ms. B's ex-husband, who admitted to cheating on Ms. B with other women, then telling ridiculous lies (all believed by Ms. B) to cover his deception; (3) Charlene, Ms. B's lifelong close friend, who said that she and Ms. B had frequently used hallucinogenic drugs for 10 years; and (4) Ms. B's childhood teachers, who described numerous violent assaults by Ms. B on other children. All those interviewed are outside the subpoena power of the court, and none of their statements fit within any hearsay exception or exclusion. Moreover, the results of some of the psychological tests administered by Dr. P, such as the Rorschach test and the Thematic Apperception Test, are inadmissible because they have been held by the state's appellate court to be unreliable. However, some of the other tests, such as the Myers-Briggs Personality Test, have been held to be reliable. Furthermore, the trial court ruled that Dr. P's opinion meets the *Daubert* test (discussed later in this chapter), requiring an expert opinion to be "relevant and reliable" as to its major premises, and the court ruled that the expert is well-qualified.

1. May Dr. P testify to her opinion that Ms. B has an unusually gullible personality?

2. If yes, should the trial judge permit Dr. P to reveal all of the bases for the opinion to the jury? Only some of those bases? Which ones and why? As a strategic matter, how many of Dr. P's bases will Ms. B want to elicit?

3. What questions would you use to elicit Dr. P's opinion in a form other than a hypothetical question and why?

4. Strategically, should Ms. B's counsel use a hypothetical question or some other sort of question to elicit Dr. P's opinion? Craft an appropriate hypothetical question.

5. What questions would you, as Ms. B's counsel, ask to elicit whatever bases you desire from Dr. P?

6. What questions should the prosecutor ask of Dr. P on cross-examination, and does Ms. B's counsel have any plausible grounds to object to those questions?

7. Are there any rules other than the expert evidence rules (Rules 702 through 706) that may be plausible grounds for objecting to any portions of Dr. P's testimony, whether on direct or cross? Why?

Problem 9-7: The Negligent Radiologist

John MacKinnon brings a wrongful death suit against Dr. Reginald Robinson for failing to diagnose Mr. MacKinnon's wife's breast cancer at an early stage. Dr. Joseph DePaul, a renowned radiologist, is called to testify as an expert regarding whether Dr. Robinson failed to exercise the expected degree of care in his field.

PLAINTIFF'S ATTORNEY: Dr. DePaul, do you have an opinion regarding when a competent radiologist would first have spotted Ms. MacKinnon's breast cancer?

A: Yes.

PLAINTIFF'S ATTORNEY: What is that opinion?

DEFENDANT'S ATTORNEY: Objection! Dr. DePaul has not provided the bases for his conclusions before offering them.

1. Is defense counsel correct? Why or why not?

PLAINTIFF'S ATTORNEY: Doctor, assuming that the mass was observable on the mammogram taken on October 1 but Ms. MacKinnon was not advised by Dr. Robinson or anyone else of that fact until the following March 1, what impact did that have on Ms. MacKinnon's survival chances?

DEFENDANT'S ATTORNEY: Objection! Calls for speculation!

2. How should plaintiff's counsel respond to this objection?

PLAINTIFF'S ATTORNEY: What do you rely on for your conclusion that Ms. MacKinnon would have had a very significantly greater chance of surviving her cancer had it been diagnosed in October?

A: Well, the lab report dated February 25 said . . .

DEFENDANT'S ATTORNEY: Objection! Hearsay.

3. How should plaintiff's counsel respond to this objection?

The trial judge now gets into the act:

JUDGE: Doctor, what is the basis of your conclusion that as of October 1 the mass had not spread beyond its borders?

4. Is the court permitted to ask such a question?

Problem 9-8: Monopolies and Economists

The United States government has filed an antitrust suit against Microsoft. As part of the government's case, it must prove that Microsoft effectively monopolized the market for computer operating systems. The government called to the stand Dr. Peter Kostick, a leading economist, who opined that Microsoft had indeed monopolized the noted market. That opinion was partly based on the report of an independent consumer rights organization, which had placed undercover "moles" in the employ of Microsoft. The report declared that "Microsoft controls 90% of the operating system market and sets unduly low prices, at a severe financial loss, where necessary to drive competitors out of business."

Can the economist testify if the report statement is inadmissible hearsay? If yes, can he reveal the content of the report to the jury?

3. "Or Otherwise"

Rule 702 includes this phrase: "may testify in the form of an opinion or otherwise." The "or otherwise" language is meant to permit expert witnesses to recount information clearly within the scope of their expertise but merely as background, without offering any opinion about any aspect of the case before the court. The jury then is free to apply that background to the facts of the specific case. The original Advisory Committee Note explains:

> Most of the literature assumes that experts testify only in the form of opinions. The assumption is logically unfounded. The rule accordingly recognizes that an expert on the stand may give a dissertation or exposition of scientific or other principles relevant to the case, leaving the trier of fact to apply them to the facts. Because much of the criticism of expert testimony has centered upon the hypothetical question, it seems wise to recognize that opinions are not indispensable and to encourage the use of expert testimony in nonopinion form when counsel believes the trier can itself draw the requisite inference. The use of opinions is not abolished by the rule, however. It will continue to be permissible for the expert to take the further step of suggesting the inference which should be drawn from applying the specialized knowledge to the facts.

The Advisory Committee Note to Rule 702 gives further guidance for assessing the value of such "generalized testimony." For such testimony, the rule requires that: "(1) the expert be qualified; (2) the testimony address a subject matter on which the factfinder can be assisted by an expert; (3) the testimony be reliable; and (4) the testimony 'fit' the facts of the case."

To recap: A witness can thus testify as an expert in at least three capacities:

1. *As an observer,* akin to an ordinary lay witness describing perceived events. E.g., "The wound was red, oozing a slimy green substance," or, using some expertise in the description, "The wound was red, oozing a slimy green pus."

2. *As an opinion-articulator* about the facts of the specific case. E.g. "This defendant suffers from paranoid schizophrenia."

3. *As an "or otherwise" testifier* (an educational expert), educating the jury about background principles helpful in understanding a particular case but not including an opinion about the specific case. E.g., "Paranoid schizophrenics are often so out of touch with reality that they often lose much of the ability

to tell right from wrong," offering no opinion about whether this defendant — who happens to be a paranoid schizophrenic — can tell right from wrong.

Problem 9-9: The Radiologist and Psychologist Meet

1. In Problem 9-7, in which capacity(ies) would the expert testify if permitted to respond to the various questions posed? Why?

2. In Problem 9-6, what sorts of questions should be asked of the psychiatrist, Dr. P, to avoid her giving an "opinion," thus limiting her instead to "or otherwise" background?

4. The Ultimate Issue Rule

Traditionally, evidence law prohibited any witness, lay or expert, from offering an opinion on the "ultimate issue" in the case.

Example

Imagine that, under traditional common law practice, a car owner brings a negligence action against a mechanic, alleging that faulty repair of the car's brakes caused an accident in which the car owner was severely injured. The plaintiff calls an expert mechanic to the stand. The following exchange occurs after the mechanic testifies that he examined the following: (1) the automobile brakes, (2) the extent of the damage to the car, (3) the police reports, and (4) the depositions of the plaintiff and the defendant.

PLAINTIFF'S ATTORNEY: Do you have an opinion to a reasonable degree of professional certainty whether defendant Joseph Roscoe negligently repaired the brakes on plaintiff John Roten's car?

A: Yes, I do.

PLAINTIFF'S ATTORNEY: What is that opinion?

DEFENDANT'S ATTORNEY: Objection, calls for an opinion on an ultimate issue.

JUDGE: Objection sustained.

The reason given for the ultimate issue bar was that opinion testimony about an ultimate issue "usurps the function" or "invades the province" of the jury. These vague phrases express the concern that jurors will too readily defer to an expert's views on the ultimate question. But the rule proved problematic for three reasons:

1. It often made it unreasonably difficult for advocates to present their cases, forcing the witnesses into verbal contortions to avoid the disfavored "magic phrasing."

2. Doubts grew about the ultimate issue rule's assumption that juries would be so gullible and irresponsible as to ignore weighing the reasons for an expert's opinion.

3. It was often difficult to distinguish "ultimate" from "non-ultimate" issues. The above example is clear. But what if the expert mechanic had instead been asked, "Did the defendant fail to exercise the same sort of care as other mechanics ordinarily do in repairing brakes?" Or instead: "What procedures do mechanics customarily follow in brake repairs of this kind?" "Why do they do so?" "Did the defendant fail in any way to follow such procedures?" "How?" "What impact did this have on the brakes' safety?" The sometimes substantial differences in the phrasing of these questions show that it can be hard to draw a line between "ultimate" and "penultimate" issues. Even this latter set of questions, which seems to be on the "right" side of the line, raise another question: "Do these questions really accomplish the task of fairly conveying the necessary information better than do the other options, combined with their own follow up questions?"

For similar reasons, a majority of jurisdictions have abandoned the ultimate issue rule. The Federal Rules of Evidence followed suit for most kinds of cases in Rule 704(a):

> In General—Not Automatically Objectionable. An opinion is not objectionable just because it embraces an ultimate issue.

The abolition of the ultimate issue rule does not mean that opinions on ultimate issues are always permitted. Rules 701 and 702 respectively require that opinions be helpful to the trier of fact. Rule 403 similarly gives the trial court discretion to exclude unfairly prejudicial or time-wasting opinions. The Advisory Committee Note to Rule 704 offers clarification:

> These provisions [Rules 403, 701, and 702] afford ample assurances against the admission of opinions which would merely tell the jury what result to reach, somewhat in the manner of the oath-helpers of an earlier day. They also stand ready to exclude opinions phrased in terms of inadequately explored legal criteria. Thus the question, "Did T have capacity to make a will?" would be excluded, while the question, "Did T have sufficient mental capacity to know the nature and extent of his property and the natural objects of his bounty and to formulate a rational scheme of distribution [the legal test for testamentary capacity]?" would be allowed.

Congress added Rule 704(b) in 1984 to reinstitute the ultimate issue rule for one class of cases. Rule 704(b), as recently further restyled in 2011, declares that:

> Exception. In a criminal case, an expert witness must not state an opinion about whether the defendant did or did not have a mental state or condition that constitutes an element of the crime charged or of a defense. Those matters are for the trier of fact alone.

The Senate Judiciary Committee Report concerning the amendment cites with approval an American Psychiatric Association statement as expressing the Rule's intentions:

Psychiatrists, of course, must be permitted to testify fully about the defendant's diagnosis, mental state and motivation (in clinical and common-sense terms) at the time of the alleged act so as to permit the jury or judge to reach the ultimate conclusion about which they and only they are expert.

Despite this guidance, Rule 704(b) reintroduces all the same uncertainties that have always accompanied the ultimate issue rule. For example, the Committee Report declares that a psychiatrist would be permitted to testify that a patient suffered from a "mental disease or defect." Yet whether a patient suffered from a mental disease or defect is an element of the insanity defense and thus presumably logically involves an "ultimate issue."

On the other hand, many commentators agree that Rule 704(b)'s ultimate issue rule would bar an opinion that a defendant could not appreciate the distinction between right and wrong, which is another element of the insanity defense. The most plausible way to distinguish these facially similar situations is to view the underlying policy concern as limiting experts to opinions on subjects that they commonly address in their fields and disallowing opinions about standards that the legal system creates. The term "mental disease or defect" is arguably close enough to the sorts of medical terminology used by psychiatrists every day (though even this point is debatable) so that the legal standard and professional terminology overlap. Consequently, no "ultimate issue" is involved. But whether a patient can appreciate the distinction between right and wrong seems farther afield from traditional psychiatric terms, and it involves moral judgments better made by a jury than an expert. This distinction is one of degree more than a dichotomy — that is, the term "mental disease or defect" may also involve moral judgments, but to a lesser degree than determining someone's ability to tell right from wrong. The distinction thus, again without providing bright lines, may nevertheless be helpful in resolving close cases.

Problem 9-10: Gullibility Revisited

Review Problem 9-6 concerning Ms. B's alleged gullibility. Would the expert's opining that Ms. B was "unusually gullible" be objectionable under Rule 704? What if the expert were instead asked: "In your opinion, did Ms. B know that the checks that she cashed were stolen?" What if she were asked, "In your opinion, was Ms. B capable of knowing that the checks were stolen?" Finally, what if she were asked to (a) describe the indicators of an unusually gullible personality and (b) opine on whether Ms. B displayed any or all of those indicators, identifying which ones she found to be present?

5. Reasonable Degree of Professional Certainty

Some jurisdictions insist that experts may testify only if they describe their opinions as "reasonably certain" or, in other jurisdictions, as "reasonably probable." The idea is that they must have formed their opinions to "a reasonable medical or scientific certainty." Other jurisdictions abandon these formalities, and require simply that an opinion be helpful to the factfinder. This latter approach is shared by the Federal Rules of Evidence. Under this approach, there is thus no categorical rule prohibiting opinions stated to be "mere possibilities." However, such opinions might be vulnerable to attack under Rule 702 as unlikely to assist the trier of fact or under Rule 403 as more prejudicial than probative.

6. The Opinion Rule and Out-of-Court Statements

We will examine hearsay in Chapters 10 through 15. But it is worth alerting you here to another problem at the intersection of the rules on hearsay and expert testimony: Assume that a hearsay document is admitted, for example, under the business records exception to the hearsay rule. If the document contains opinions, including expert ones, must the opinion be admitted only if it complies with the opinion rules, like Rules 701 through 705, that would apply were a live witness to state the opinion on the stand? Many courts say "yes," although common sense suggests that the rules should be more liberally applied in the hearsay setting.

Example 1

A report written by an infectious disease specialist, after describing the patient's symptoms, says: "Diagnosis: Patient suffers from cellulitis [fat cell infections], probably caused by a brown recluse spider bite. The infections have spread significantly, due to the late start of treatment." The report is offered into evidence by the plaintiff at a medical malpractice trial charging the plaintiff's family doctor with recommending hospitalization at a later point than sound professional judgment required.

The report is hearsay — an out-of-court statement offered for the truth of what it asserts. But the report probably fits within the business records exception to the hearsay rule. However, the report contains opinions, and many courts would read the business records exception as including opinions only if the requirements of Rules 701 through 705 are met. Because this opinion is offered by a highly qualified infectious disease specialist, it may be relatively easy for most or all of the excerpted statements to fulfill the opinion rules. But had those statements instead been made by the emergency-room technician (who knows far less about infectious diseases than does the specialist), the admissibility of some or all of the stated opinions would be in much greater doubt.

Furthermore, the opinion rule has long been held not to apply to statements admitted under the exclusion or exception to the hearsay rule for opposing party statements. The rationale for this exclusion partly involves adversarial rather than reliability concerns. In other words, parties should fairly expect to be bound by their own words when they bring or defend a lawsuit (see Chapter 13 for details). Moreover, parties are likely to have both the incentive and the resources to challenge any misleading or false statements purportedly their own. This rationale applies to opinions as much as to "facts."

Example 2

Plaintiff sued Ford Motor Company for personal injuries after his Ford Pinto exploded into flames when hit from behind at 5 m.p.h. The plaintiff seeks to admit into evidence this portion of a memorandum written by Ford's Chief Automotive Engineer within the scope of his employment: "The Pinto gas tank is poorly placed and may too easily spark fires in low impact collisions. Production should be postponed to address this problem." Is it admissible?

The quoted statement is offered by the plaintiff for the truth of what it asserts and is thus hearsay. However, the statement arguably fits within the opposing-party-statement exemption from the hearsay rule. Moreover (unlike the approach of many courts to the business records exception), the opposing-party-statement exemption overcomes both hearsay and opinion rule objections. Thus, no independent showing need be made that the opinion meets the requirements of Rules 701 through 705.

Broadening the opinion rule exception to documents other than those containing admissions is a trend apparently now underway in many jurisdictions. If the opinion rule is modernly thought of as a preference, where possible, for specific over general testimony, this makes sense. When documents contain otherwise admissible hearsay, the documents cannot be "prompted" in the way that a live witness could to rephrase an opinion in more specific terms.

C. Cross-Examination: Scope and Manner

Many of the restrictions on the direct examination of experts do not apply on cross-examination. Thus, traditional rules requiring bases to be revealed before opinions are elicited and requiring other admitted or admissible evidence being available to support those bases are of no concern.

Under Rule 705, if an expert has not revealed any or all the facts, data, and opinions underlying his in-court opinion, the opponent may elicit those matters on cross-examination. Available methods for impeaching the expert include the following:

- Exploring how the non-existence of any particular basis on which the expert relied would alter his or her opinion.

- Exploring how the existence of contrary or additional bases (presumably to be supported by evidence from the cross-examiner at a later stage) would alter the expert's opinion.

- Determining which materials the expert reviewed or failed to review in preparing to offer the opinion.

- Determining which tests or other investigations the expert conducted (or failed to conduct) and how they were done.

- Exploring the financial compensation received by the expert for advice and testimony.

- Revealing contradictions between the expert's assertions and those made by other experts in published works, provided those works comply with the learned treatise exception to the hearsay rule, Rule 803(18).

- Posing a hypothetical question based upon an alternative set of assumptions.

- Exploring what prior expert testimony the expert has given, for whom, its content, and whether it conflicts with the current testimony.

Problem 9-11: My Cousin Vinnie Cross-Examined

Assume the facts in the My Cousin Vinnie case, Problem 8-2, and draft a set of cross-examination questions for the putative expert.

Problem 9-12: Or Was It the Accurate Eyewitness?

Assume the facts in Problem 9-6 and draft a set of cross-examination questions for the expert psychologist.

D. Cross-Examination: Learned Treatises

Another impeachment technique is to cross-examine the expert with a learned treatise whose position contradicts that of the expert on the stand. At common law, cross-examination by learned treatises was permissible only to impeach the witness, e.g., by showing the witness's unfamiliarity with a respected work or by implying the weakness of the witness's opinion because it was contrary to such a well-respected piece of scholarship. But the treatise could not be used as substantive evidence, that is, as proof of the truth of what the treatise asserts. The common law feared that substantive use of learned treatises would confuse the jury with technical information and statements taken out of context or that statements from treatises would be unreliable because of the rapid change in the state of scientific knowledge.

The Federal Rules of Evidence took a somewhat different approach. Instead, they created a new hearsay exception for learned treatises under these circumstances. Under Rule 803(18), the following statements are not excluded by the hearsay rule:

(18) *Statements in Learned Treatises, Periodicals, or Pamphlets.* A statement contained in a treatise, periodical, or pamphlet if:

(A) the statement is called to the attention of an expert witness on cross-examination or relied on by the expert on direct examination; and

(B) the publication is established as a reliable authority by the expert's admission or testimony, by another expert's testimony, or by judicial notice.

If admitted, the statement may be read into evidence but not received as an exhibit.

The drafters of Rule 803(18) believed that the requirement that the expert must be questioned about the treatise would help prevent jurors from misunderstanding or misapplying statements from a treatise. On the other hand, the expert being challenged cannot simply block questioning by denying the authoritative nature of the treatise. Another expert or, in appropriate cases, judicial notice, may establish that the treatise has the necessary authority. Authors of treatises and other scholarly works (any scholarly work will do) have an incentive to produce reliable work to avoid criticism by professional peers so, without the hearsay exception, the jury might be deprived of valuable information. But a restriction is still imposed on "receiving" the treatise as an exhibit, that is, it may not be taken into the jury room because of the residual fear that the jury may there misapply the treatise without the expert's guidance.

§ 9.05 Relevance and Reliability of General Principles and Methods

A. Defining Terms

It is helpful, in understanding how courts treat the admissibility of expert testimony, to distinguish "principles" from "methods." The distinction is important because it is often made in case law, scholarly commentary, and codified evidence rules. Nevertheless, rarely do courts, advisory committees, or legislatures clearly define the terms. Moreover, different cases or code commentaries may suggest different meanings. Yet authorities are increasingly fond of saying that expert testimony must be the product of both reliable "principles" and "methods."

One by-no-means sharp, but still helpful, definition of these terms may be to say that they refer to differing levels of generality, but both are still best thought of as major premises in the expert syllogism. The "principle" is the most general statement, the "method" somewhat less general, but both are still broad assertions not yet applied to the facts of the specific case. Often "method" is seen as a means for applying a "principle" to a specific case. Using alternative terminology, a "method" is a *technique* for applying principles in specific instances.

Therefore, if either the principle or the method is flawed, even their perfect application to a particular situation cannot be said to reach a trustworthy result. For example, two "principles" may be that DNA exists and is unique for each person, and a "method" may be that DNA testing can accurately identify each person's unique DNA. The Advisory Committee Note to the amendments to Rule 702 offered this example:

> When a law enforcement agent testifies regarding the use of code words in a drug transaction, the principle used by the agent is that participants in such

transactions regularly use code words to conceal the nature of their activities. The method used by the agent is the application of extensive experience to analyze the meaning of the conversations.

If it is untrue that participants in drug transactions regularly use code words, then testimony that a particular suspect was using "common" drug-dealer code words is unhelpful. Similarly, the helpfulness of the agent's expert testimony is suspect if the principle of the use of code words is true but it has not been shown that drug agents are generally capable of identifying when code words are being used and what they mean. Even if we rephrase this last point to say that we need only show that *this agent* can reliably interpret drug-dealer code, we again must be confident that the agent can generally do so before we will allow him or her to interpret a particular suspect's conversation as containing such code.

While principles and methods can, therefore, be distinguished, they are also related. Thus, drug agents may base the principle that drug dealers regularly use code on their repeated experiences of hearing and identifying them doing so. Similarly, while the existence of DNA may be proposed as a theory, empirical support for the theory's accuracy may be derived from repeated experimental identification of DNA via DNA testing. Nevertheless, to say that the two concepts of "principles" and "methods" are related does not mean that the distinction is useless.

Example

Dr. Eugene Smart, a psychologist, testifies that there is a dramatically increased likelihood of recidivism by a violent criminal offender if certain factors are present. He further testifies that he is effective at identifying, from a clinical interview with a patient, whether those factors are present in that patient's case. The expert's ultimate goal is to testify that Joey Small, who was recently convicted of first-degree murder, displays the necessary traits and is thus likely to re-offend. His testimony is relevant to issues being considered by a jury in determining whether to recommend the death penalty.

Even if Dr. Smart is right that the presence of the specified factors leads to an increased probability of future violence, it does not necessarily follow that he can generally determine their presence in individual patients based solely upon a clinical interview. It may be the case, for example, that a combination of written psychological tests, interviews with family members and friends, and extended observation of the patient's behavior by a team of properly trained psychologists who reach consensus are necessary in order to accurately identify the presence of the relevant factors, and that a simple clinical interview is insufficient. Absent proof by the proponent of the trustworthiness of Dr. Smart's method for *applying* the general principle of violence-identifying-factors to individual suspects, Smart's testimony should, upon objection, be excluded.

One of the Advisory Committee Notes to Rule 702 also addresses the requirement that "the testimony is based on sufficient facts or data." The Note initially declares that this requirement "calls for a quantitative rather than a qualitative analysis." But the Note does not define "facts" or "data" other than to say that the "term 'data' is intended to encompass the *reliable* opinions of other experts" (emphasis added). The Note's point might be that the way in which either a "principle" or a "method" is derived must be trustworthy. For a magician to say that he had a dream that something called DNA (which he describes) exists and is unique for each human being (other than identical twins) would not be a sufficient "datum" upon which an expert can base an opinion. But reliance on careful, repeated laboratory studies on the same question by well-respected chemists and biologists using sound scientific procedures would be sufficient. This interpretation is further supported by the Note's declaration that "an analysis of the sufficiency of the expert's basis cannot be divorced from the ultimate reliability of the expert's opinion."

This example reveals the slipperiness of terminology. What we think of as the "scientific *method*" seems to be one sort of reliable set of "facts or data" within the meaning of the Advisory Committee's terminology. For example, the failure of repeated experiments to disprove the hypothesis that a certain vaccine wards off the flu may be given great weight if the experiments were well-designed, including adequate controls ruling out other factors (e.g., the content of clear drinking water was the same for all subjects, thus ruling out the influence of contaminants). When the Advisory Committee refers to a "method," however, it is apparently referring to the means for applying a principle to a specific case rather than to the soundness of the procedures for deriving the principle in the first place. Scientists and many legal commentators, as well as many laymen, may thus find the Advisory Committee's terminology confusing. Furthermore, the Committee's use of "facts or data" can alternatively be read to refer to case-specific bases — minor premises, instead of the procedures for deriving major premises — as some commentators urge. Or, still other commentators suggest, "facts" may refer to case-specific bases, and "data" to the soundness of procedures for deriving principles. Complete agreement on terminology among all interested persons is unlikely, and it is the distinctions underlying the terms — and whether those distinctions are useful (which we and the Advisory Committee believe they are) — that matters most, even if we may disagree about which word best labels which concept.

Problem 9-13: Principled Methods

In the problems listed below, identify the major and minor premises. Then, for each of the problems, identify the "principles and methods"/techniques involved in the major premises and the "facts or data" supporting the bases for all the listed premises.

1. Problem 9-1.

2. Problem 9-4.

3. Problem 9-5.

B. Scientific Evidence

1. The Frye Test

a. The Test Stated

Many courts had long carved out for special treatment one sort of expert testimony: that concerning "novel" "scientific" evidence. Cases have often not made clear the reasons for courts requiring additional admissibility tests, or more stringently applying existing admissibility tests, to scientific evidence. Clarification of that justification was thus often made in the first instance by commentators. Furthermore, the courts generally provided little guidance for distinguishing "scientific" from "non-scientific" evidence. The distinction was not one founded in the philosophy of science or the experience of scientists themselves. Rather, the courts seemed, sometimes implicitly, sometimes explicitly, to deem "scientific" any evidence for which the justifications for special admissibility hurdles applied.

Among the justifications for these special hurdles were that: (1) an "aura of infallibility" surrounded the evidence so that a jury was unlikely to evaluate independently, or to be skeptical of, its worth; (2) scientific evidence relies on such arcane information that it will be very difficult for jurors to evaluate its worth, even if they are not "overawed" by any view of science as infallible; therefore, jurors just won't try, it being easier simply to take the expert's word; (3) the evidence is so unfamiliar to the courts that judges will have difficulty guiding juries on how fairly to evaluate it; and (4) the evidence "invades the province of the jury" in a particularly powerful way, such as lie-detector test results determining for the jury who speaks "truth" and who does not.

Courts were particularly concerned about "novel" scientific evidence because it presented more of the above dangers to a greater degree than scientific evidence with a longer pedigree of testing in the courts. The classic test for the admissibility of novel scientific evidence was articulated in Frye v. United States, 293 F. 1013, 1014 (D.C. Cir. 1923), which barred the use of polygraph evidence:

> Just when a scientific principle or discovery crosses the line between the experimental and demonstrable stages is difficult to define. Somewhere in this twilight zone the evidential force of the principle must be recognized, and while courts will go a long way in admitting expert testimony deduced from a well-recognized scientific principle or discovery, the thing from which the deduction is made must be sufficiently established to have gained general acceptance in the particular field in which it belongs.

b. Validity versus Reliability

The Frye test raised numerous questions. Notably, what precisely was the "thing" that had to be generally accepted? One influential answer to this question is that both the "validity" and "reliability" of a scientific principle must be shown by sound empirical data. "Validity," as used by a scientist, asks, "Is this test accurate; does it measure what it is supposed to measure?" "Reliability" asks, "Does this test consistently yield the same results upon repeated challenge?"

Example

An expert seeks to testify that: (1) cocaine has a unique scent; and (2) a new "sniffer" machine (such a machine is indeed being tested as we write this text) can detect that unique scent.

If there is indeed a unique scent for cocaine, a sniffer's reaction (say, by ringing a bell or flashing a red light) might validly detect what it purports to detect — cocaine. However, sometimes the sniffer might fail to react when the cocaine scent is present, or might react when the scent is not present. If so, the sniffer test would not be "reliable" because it does not reach consistent results. Validity and reliability can, of course, be connected. Thus, if a sniffer is unreliable, that is, highly inconsistent when it reacts to cocaine, then it is hard to tell when its reaction is "valid," when the bells and lights indeed reflect what they purport to reflect: the presence of cocaine. On the other hand, a test can be "reliable" but invalid. If the sniffer consistently reacted when substance X, believed to be cocaine, was placed near the sniffer, it would be reliable. However, if substance X is in fact sugar, then the sniffer is invalid; it does not measure what it purports to measure, the presence of cocaine.

c. Defining the Relevant Field

Another problem with the *Frye* test was determining what was the relevant "scientific" field in which the technique must be accepted.

Example

An expert is called by the prosecution in a murder case to testify about his use of a "dog-scent lineup" to identify the defendant as the killer. In a dog-scent lineup, a dog sniffs an item taken from the offender, such as a hat dropped by a killer while fleeing. The dog sniffs the hat and then sniffs each of the six to eight persons placed in a line. If the pooch barks at number 7, that is the equivalent of the dog's saying, "Number 7's scent matches the scent on the hat." Such testimony would support the inference that number 7 is the killer.

Though not often recognized by the courts, several premises contribute to the value of this testimony. Its validity turns on proving that: (1) each human has a unique scent; (2) that scent remains on items of clothing for a significant period of time after they are worn; and (3) properly trained dogs can reliably match the unique scent on an item of clothing to its human source. Does the "relevant field" that must "generally accept" each of these propositions consist of biologists specializing in scenting, canine anatomy specialists, experimental dog psychologists, policemen trained in the use of dog-scent identification techniques, the scientist who invented the dog-scent lineup technique, or some combination of any or all these fields? This question highlights the difficulties in determining the relevant field. It also raises a qualifications question. Some courts would prohibit persons who made their living from inventing or applying a technique from testifying about its value or that of its underlying principles, on the theory that such persons are hopelessly biased.

Courts applying *Frye* also often reached inconsistent and seemingly random results as to what techniques were "novel" or not, "scientific" or not.

2. The Daubert *Test*

a. Holding and Rationale: Interpreting the Federal Rules of Evidence

In *Daubert v. Merrell Dow Pharmaceuticals, Inc.*, 509 U.S. 579, 113 S. Ct. 2786, 125 L. Ed. 2d 469 (1993), the Court squarely considered whether the 1923 *Frye* test survived adoption of the Federal Rules of Evidence. The plaintiff, Joyce Daubert, gave birth to a deformed child after taking Bendectin, an anti-nausea drug, during her pregnancy. She sued Merrell Dow Pharmaceuticals, Inc., the manufacturer of Bendectin. The trial court granted the defendant's motion for summary judgment on the ground that the Dauberts could not prove that Bendectin caused the birth defect. In doing so, the trial court gave no weight to affidavits of the plaintiffs' experts that addressed the issue of causation, concluding that those experts' opinions were not based on generally accepted scientific theories. The Court of Appeals for the Ninth Circuit affirmed on similar grounds, squarely questioning whether *Frye* survived the Federal Rules. The Supreme Court held that *Frye* did not survive adoption of the Federal Rules, and that in its stead the Rules established a "relevancy and reliability" test. *Daubert* vacated the lower court's decision and remanded the case for determination of the admissibility of the plaintiffs' experts' opinions under the newly announced test.[3]

The Court's analysis was straightforward and largely textual. Rule 702 governed, and nowhere did it mention "general acceptance." Moreover, there was no legislative history suggesting that Congress intended to incorporate the general acceptance tests into the rules. To the contrary, the drafting history made no mention of *Frye*. The "austere" *Frye* standard, which made it difficult to admit scientific evidence, would be contrary to the "liberal thrust" of the Rules, which took the "general approach of relaxing the traditional barriers," like *Frye*, "to 'opinion' testimony."

What replaced *Frye*, said the Court, was a new "relevancy and reliability" standard. That new test, said the Court, is rooted in Rule 702, which in relevant part says that a qualified expert may offer an opinion "[i]f *scientific*, technical, or other specialized knowledge will assist the trier of fact to understand the evidence or to determine a fact in issue" (emphasis added). The Court sought to give meat to that test by accepting the parties' assumption that the evidence before the Court was "scientific," rather than "technical, or other specialized knowledge," and that that

---

3. On remand, the Ninth Circuit Court of Appeals concluded that plaintiffs' experts' opinions were not reliable and dismissed the case. *Daubert v. Merrell Dow Pharmaceuticals, Inc.*, 43 F.3d 1311 (9th Cir. 1995).

assumption had evidentiary significance. The purported "scientific" evidence consisted of proffered expert testimony (summarized in affidavits) claimed to support the proposition that Bendectin had caused Joyce Daubert to give birth to a deformed child.

Rule 702's "clear contemplation" of regulation of expert testimony was thus obvious, said the Court, from the Rules' reference to "scientific knowledge." "The adjective 'scientific' implies a grounding in the methods and procedures of science. Similarly, the word 'knowledge' connotes more than subjective belief or unsupported speculation." The something "more" that defined knowledge was, according to Webster's, "any body of known facts or . . . any body of ideas inferred from such facts or accepted as truths on good grounds." "Scientists, however, viewed themselves as dealing with the 'scientific method,'" which is a process, not a guarantee of certainty. "Scientific knowledge" was therefore derived from the scientific method and based on "good grounds." Significantly, concluded the Court, the requirement of "good grounds" was a clear standard of "evidentiary reliability."

But the then-Rule 702 requirement that the evidence offered would "assist the trier of fact to understand the evidence or to determine a fact in issue" (today the word "assist" is replaced by the word "help") also mattered, said the Court. The Court viewed this requirement as going primarily to relevance, for evidence that is not relevant cannot be helpful to the jury. One aspect of relevance stressed by the Court is "fit," the notion that scientific validity for one purpose is not necessarily validity for other, unrelated purposes. Thus, knowledge of the phases of the moon, noted the Court, might be relevant to how dark it was on a particular night, but not to how likely it was that a particular individual behaved irrationally.

The Court also found that Rules 701, 703, and 602 embodied the relevancy and reliability requirements. Rule 701 bars lay witnesses from giving opinions unless "rationally based on the perception of the witness." This restates the "familiar requirement of first-hand knowledge or observation." Unlike lay witnesses, however, experts have wide latitude to offer opinions not based on firsthand knowledge. Under Rule 703, for example, experts may opine based on hearsay if it would be "reasonably relied upon by experts in the particular field." As the Advisory Committee Note to Rule 602 noted, the requirement of firsthand knowledge reflects a "pervasive manifestation" of the common-law insistence on the "most reliable sources of information." Thus, the Court stated, the Rules must have eliminated the firsthand knowledge requirement for experts only because it was assumed that the knowledge and experience of their disciplines provided a reliable basis for the opinion.

b. The *Daubert* Factors

i. *The Factors Stated*

Next, drawing on a wide array of sources (from philosophers of science to practicing scientists), the *Daubert* Court crafted a series of factors to guide the trial court in its decision on evidentiary reliability:

1. Are the theory (the underlying scientific principle) and the technique applying that theory (what Rule 702 refers to as "methods") testable and have they been tested? By "tested," the Court apparently meant, "Has a hypothesis been generated, and have adequate efforts been made to falsify that hypothesis, with no such falsification yet having been achieved?"

2. Have the theory and technique been subjected to peer review and publication?

3. What is the known or potential error rate of the technique?

4. Are there standards controlling the technique's operation, that is, an authoritative statement of the circumstances under which the technique's application to a particular case will be considered trustworthy?

5. Has the principle or technique attained "widespread acceptance" (something undefined but arguably less than *Frye's* general-acceptance test, though later cases seem to treat the two terms as equivalent)?

There is no need for a "yes" answer to every question for evidence to be admissible. These questions merely help to guide the trial judge's policy judgments. Moreover, these factors are not exclusive. "Many factors will bear on the inquiry," said the Court, "and we do not presume to set out a definitive checklist or test." Rather, the trial court's inquiry is to be a "flexible one." The *Daubert* factors listed are not exhaustive and not applicable to every case.

The five factors articulated by the *Daubert* Court mostly seem readily understandable, though their application to particular cases may be difficult.

ii. The Gatekeeping Function

Finally, although the Court rejected the "austere" *Frye* approach, the *Daubert* opinion makes clear that easy admission of scientific evidence is not the Court's suggested alternative. Rather, the trial court must exercise a "gatekeeping" function in reviewing the quality of scientific evidence before it reaches the jury. "We are confident," declared the Court, "that federal judges possess the capacity to undertake this review." At the same time, however, the Court recognized that its flexible test might admit some evidence that *Frye* would exclude. To this point, the Court summarily noted that rules other than Rule 702 — such as Rules 703 and 403 — might sometimes justify excluding scientific evidence. More importantly, the Court, arguably directing its comments to trial judges, urged faith in the adversarial jury system, rejecting fears that:

> abandonment of "general acceptance" as the exclusive requirement for admission will result in a "free-for-all" in which befuddled juries are confounded by absurd and irrational pseudoscientific assertions. In this regard respondent seems to us overly pessimistic about the capabilities of the jury, and of the adversary system generally. Vigorous cross-examination, presentation of contrary evidence, and careful instruction on the burden

of proof are the traditional and appropriate means of attacking shaky but admissible evidence.

Caution:

Remember that, while the *Frye* inquiry is no longer determinative, a *Frye*-like analysis may be one of the factors considered by the trial court in its flexible weighing process under *Daubert*. In addition, some state jurisdictions retain *Frye* or a similar test as a gateway for expert testimony.

Problem 9-14: Linguistic Rage

John Cheng is a graduate student in philosophy who killed the members of his doctoral thesis committee. Cheng claims that he was insane, or at least extremely emotionally disturbed, at the time of the crime.

Cheng emigrated from Hong Kong a few years ago. He came from an upper-middle-class family there, but his family severed all ties when Cheng refused to join the family business. Cheng had been an outstanding and privileged student in Hong Kong, but in the United States, he met one disappointment after another. For years, he was unable to get a teaching assistantship ("TA") or office job, finding work only as a busboy in a Chinese restaurant. When he finally did get a TA position, he got such poor teaching evaluations that his contract was not renewed. His grades were barely passing. He blamed all this on discrimination based on his accent and race, for he was confident that he otherwise had a strong command of English and a talented mind. The rejection of his dissertation was the final straw, and he reacted with violence.

His defense attorney raised a novel defense: linguistic rage. Linguistic rage is rooted in sociolinguistic studies of accent. The studies show that an accent is not physically a bar to understanding, but that it is part of a social categorization process by which outsider groups are subordinated. "People in power are perceived as speaking normal, unaccented English. Any speech that is different from that constructed norm is called an accent."

The defense plans to call a linguist to the stand who will testify that this ideology of linguistic subordination is widespread. Accent discrimination thus systematically excludes talented workers from jobs, promotions, and other kinds of recognition for achievement. Yet, after childhood, many adults are physiologically incapable of losing their accents. Moreover, accents are generally not a bar to understanding by those willing to listen. Furthermore, our ways of speaking are central to our social and individual identities, so failed efforts to lose our accents and the resulting ridicule cause great emotional pain. Additionally, accent and race discrimination are linked. While some Asian-Americans have now achieved visible success in American society, Asian accents activate the worst stereotypes about Asians. In short, "accent, when it acts in part as a marker for race, takes on special significance."

The linguist, Rosini Pfund, has published articles concerning her theories on accent discrimination in numerous prestigious professional journals, mostly ones specializing in linguistic ethnography. An ethnographic study involves careful recording and description of an individual case. For example, the speech of selected immigrants with ostensible "accents" might be recorded in their various interactions with different communities — at work, in the subject's neighborhood, at church, and at home. Information may then be gathered as well from documentation, from interviews with subjects concerning their experiences — for example, losing a job, not getting a promotion, being shunned by neighbors — and concerning others' stated perceptions (under a promise of anonymity) of the subjects. Alternatively, others' perceptions may be inferred from indirect questions; their answers to questions such as, "Did you understand what Mr. Sun just said?" or "Do you think he would make a good supervisor?" might be taken as reflecting deeper but not explicitly stated views about the connections among his accent, personality, and intelligence.

Dr. Pfund relied, for most of her testimony, on the following sources of information:

- Ethnographic studies conducted by linguists.

- Linguistic histories of various ethnic groups who have immigrated to the United States, especially Asian-Americans, and how they have fared here.

- Writings by philosophers of language on its nature and its role in human reasoning and social organization.

- Writings by political activists in the Hispanic-American and Asian-American communities.

The defense also plans to call a psychologist who will testify that, as a result of accent discrimination, Cheng suffered from a mental disease or defect. The psychologist will also testify that Cheng suffered an extreme emotional disturbance that would justify the mitigation of murder to manslaughter.

1. How would Ms. Pfund's testimony fare under each of the *Daubert* reliability factors? Why or why not?

2. Is Ms. Pfund's testimony "relevant" under *Daubert's* "relevancy and reliability" test? Why?

3. What cross-examination questions should the prosecution ask Ms. Pfund? Why?

4. Would Ms. Pfund's testimony more likely be admitted under *Daubert* or under *Frye*? Why?

Problem 9-15: The Horizontal Gaze Nystagmus Test

Patricia Kurland is on trial for drunk driving. Officer Butch Leibel testifies that he stopped her car because it was weaving slightly. To test her for drunkenness, he administered the horizontal gaze nystagmus test (HGN). HGN is based on the theory that alcohol consumption affects eye movement. Thus, an officer might, as

Officer Leibel did, ask a suspect to focus on and follow a moving pen held by the officer 12 inches from the suspect's eyes. The officer seeks to observe: (1) whether the onset of nystagmus (eye jerking) occurred when the pen was at an angle of less than 45 degrees from the center of the suspect's face; (2) whether nystagmus was moderate or distinct when the suspect's eyes have been moved as far as possible in one direction or the other; and (3) whether the suspect's eyes moved smoothly in tracking the pen.

Based on the HGN results, Officer Leibel testified that Kurland: (a) was then under the influence of alcohol and (b) that she had operated her car at a blood alcohol level of more than .10, the legal limit in this state. Officer Leibel testified that he was trained to test for horizontal gaze nystagmus at the police academy and that he has since administered hundreds of HGN tests. He testified that he had tested Kurland following the Drug Evaluation and Classification Program standards that had been developed during the 1980s and 1990s by the Los Angeles Police Department to guide its officers in the correct procedures for administering HGN. Franklin Eyeworth, a well-respected local optometrist, also took the stand. He testified that optometrists routinely look for nystagmus and generally accept the principle that it is measurably affected by alcohol consumption.

1. Should any or all of the officer's and the optometrist's testimony be excluded under *Daubert*? Why or why not?

2. Would it change your opinion to learn that the National Highway Traffic Safety Administration (NHTSA) had conducted both laboratory studies and field tests of HGN accuracy using the L.A. Police Department standards? NHTSA issued a report concluding that: (1) in laboratory studies, officers using HGN were 90 percent accurate in identifying persons who had recently consumed alcohol and 70 percent accurate in identifying who had a blood alcohol level higher than .10; and (2) in field studies (observing officers using HGN on real suspects on the street, then measuring the suspects' blood alcohol level using blood tests), the officers were 70 percent accurate in identifying who had recently consumed alcohol and 40 percent accurate in identifying who had a blood alcohol level higher than .10?

Problem 9-16: My Brand New Miata

Two brand new Miata automobiles collided at the intersection of Fourth and Vine. At trial in a personal injury action arising from the collision, the plaintiff is expected to offer a police officer as an expert in accident reconstruction. Several eyewitnesses are also expected to testify at the trial about the accident. You, as defense counsel, are about to take the deposition of the officer. *What questions should you ask him specifically to help you determine whether to file a motion in limine to exclude his testimony at trial as violative of* Daubert? *What do you think his answers are likely to be? Do you think it likely that his testimony will ultimately be admitted? Why?*

Problem 9-17: Harassment!

In a sexual harassment action, the plaintiff offered the testimony of Dr. Lucy Barnes, an expert psychologist, to describe the profile of a sexual harasser. Dr. Barnes will testify that a sexual harasser is typically married, is the victim's supervisor, and has known the victim for at least six months. Dr. Barnes bases this conclusion on surveys done of men who either voluntarily sought treatment once their alleged harassment was revealed or were ordered to do so by their employers as a condition of continued employment. *Is this testimony admissible?*

Problem 9-18: Probably Guilty

Ms. Juanita Brooks was robbed by a blonde woman wearing a ponytail who fled in a partly yellow automobile, driven by a mustached and bearded African-American man, which immediately drove away from the scene at high speed. The defendants, Robert Mollins and Sandy Travolta, were stopped by the police 10 minutes after the crime in the general vicinity of the robbery, and they fit the victim's description of the thieves, though the victim made only a tentative identification at trial of Travolta as the robber and Mollins as the lookout and getaway driver.

To bolster its case, the prosecution called an instructor of mathematics at a state college. The prosecutor asked the mathematician, Randall Numerology, the following:

PROSECUTOR: Dr., please assume the following probabilities:

Characteristic	Individual Probability
A. Partly yellow automobile	1/10
B. Man with moustache	1/4
C. Girl with ponytail	1/10
D. Girl with blond hair	1/3
E. African-American man with beard	1/10
F. Interracial couple in car	1/1000

What is the probability that the crime was committed by any single couple with such distinctive characteristics?

A: One in 12,000,000.

PROSECUTOR: How did you come up with that figure?

A: By using the product rule, which states that the probability of the joint occurrence of a number of mutually independent events is equal to the product of the individual probabilities that each of the events will occur.

PROSECUTOR: So you multiplied these probabilities?

A: Yes.

PROSECUTOR: What does it mean to say that events are "mutually independent"?

A: It means that the probability of one event's happening does not alter the probability of another event's happening. For example, the probability of rolling a "2" with one die is 1/6, as is the probability of rolling a "3." If you now roll a "2," that does not make it any more or less likely that your next die throw will be a "3." That probability was 1/6 before the "2" was rolled and is still 1/6 after.

Should defense counsel have objected under Daubert? Why or why not?

iii. Procedural Concerns

Several procedural concerns further illuminate the meaning of the *Daubert* test. First, the Court declared the reliability inquiry to be a Rule 104(a) question. The proposed December 2023 amendments to Rule 702 would emphasize this procedural point to remedy supposed court confusion on the matter. The amended rule would state that experts may testify "if the proponent has demonstrated [e.g., reliability] by a preponderance of the evidence." The advisory committee note to the amendment makes clear that the court rules on admissibility under 104(a). Accordingly, the proponent of the evidence has the burden of proving that a scientific principle or technique is reliable to the trial judge's personal satisfaction by a preponderance of the evidence. This may require a pretrial or mid-trial hearing at which the trial court will hear and resolve conflicting evidence on both sides of the reliability question. In making this judgment, the trial judge may need to resolve credibility disputes between experts. Although the court initially indicated that the focus is to "be solely on principles and methodology, not on the conclusions that they generate," subsequent cases and the December 2023 amendment would make clear the requirement that the "expert's opinion reflects a reliable application of the principles and methods to the facts of the case." FED. R. EVID. 702(d).

Thus under current Rule 702, the judge has a role to play at the level of individual application, namely ensuring that the principles and methods have been reliably applied to the individual case. *See* FED. R. EVID. 702(d) and advisory committee's note. But if there is a dispute about the underlying facts to which the principles and methods are applied, the trial court should not exclude the expert's testimony because the court believes one version of the facts and not the other. *Id.* Moreover, at any level of abstraction, two experts might each rely on competing principles or methods that are both found by the court to be reliable. *Id.*

The second procedural concern arises because, in *General Electric Co. v. Joiner*, 522 U.S. 136, 138–39, 118 S. Ct. 512, 515, 139 L. Ed. 2d 508 (1997), the Court held that a trial court's decision concerning the *Daubert* reliability requirement is subject to appellate review only for an abuse of discretion.

Later, in *Kumho Tire Co. v. Carmichael*, 526 U.S. 137, 119 S. Ct. 1167, 143 L. Ed. 2d 238 (1999), the Court held that trial judge discretion extends to two other decisions as well: (1) what factors are to be used in making the reliability judgment concerning a particular principle or technique in a particular case (in the Court's words, "whether *Daubert's* specific factors are, or are not, reasonable measures of reliability in a particular case is a matter that the law grants the trial judge broad latitude to determine"); and (2) whether it is necessary to hold a "*Daubert* hearing" in the first place, that is, whether the reliability inquiry can instead be resolved by judicial notice or by other procedures that do not require taking testimony.

This enormous discretion vested in the trial court limits the appellate courts' role in achieving consistency in the treatment of scientific evidence and implementation of *Daubert's* dictates. Indeed, even before *Kumho Tire,* many trial courts started to show increasingly close scrutiny of various forms of scientific evidence, despite the *Daubert* Court's language about the "liberal thrust" of the federal expert evidence rules. Accordingly, *Daubert* has not proven to be a more lenient standard than *Frye.* Indeed, some scholars contend that the difference in expert admissibility rates in jurisdictions retaining *Frye* or *Daubert* is negligible.

Problem 9-19: Reversal of Rage

Assume the facts of Problem 9-14 on linguistic rage:

1. Which of the original *Daubert* factors, if any, would you as trial judge apply in conducting your *Daubert* analysis? Why?

2. What additional factors, if any, would you decide are relevant to the *Daubert* inquiry if you sat as the trial judge? Why?

3. If a trial judge ruled that all the original *Daubert* factors — and no others — not only had to be considered but had to be met so that the failure of any one factor would result in exclusion in this case, would that ruling likely be reversed on appeal? Why?

Problem 9-20: Concluding Methods

Is it relevant, in assessing the reliability of principles and methods under Daubert:

1. That a psychologist concludes that a murder suspect was 100 percent incapable of committing a violent act, when all treatises in the field explain that, according to the empirical data, there are no circumstances under which psychologists can confidently make such claims?

2. That a polygrapher concludes that the subject was telling the truth when every one of the indicators on the polygraph test are the kind that standard training texts describe as indicating a lie?

3. That a handwriting examiner declares that the signature on a forged check matches the defendant's signature when scholars are split on whether handwriting examiners can make any such judgments with a high degree of confidence?

4. That a biologist testifies that an anti-nausea drug causes cancer in humans when studies on its carcinogenic effects have all involved white rats?

C. Evidence Based on Technical or Other Specialized Knowledge, Including Social Science

The *Daubert* factors, we have seen, were crafted in the context of determining when to admit "scientific" evidence. Furthermore, *Daubert* itself involved the natural, not the social, sciences. Three questions initially arose (before amendments to Rule 702 enshrined the Court's answers to some of them): (1) Does the *Daubert* test apply to non-scientific expert testimony, that is, to "technical or other specialized knowledge"? (2) If yes, how, if at all, should the *Daubert* test be modified to accommodate these other sorts of knowledge? (3) Is social science "science," and, whatever the answer to that question, how, if at all, should *Daubert* be applied differently to this sort of knowledge as compared to natural scientific knowledge?

The Court answered the first two of these questions in *Kumho Tire Co. v. Carmichael*, 526 U.S. 137, 119 S. Ct. 1167, 143 L. Ed. 2d 238 (1999). Before *Kumho Tire*, some courts admitted some evidence that would likely be excludable under a careful application of the *Daubert* factors, arguing that a more lenient standard applied because the particular principle or technique involved was not "scientific" evidence. *Kumho Tire* held otherwise, concluding that all expert testimony, including "technical and other specialized knowledge," is governed by *Daubert's* "relevancy and reliability" standard. *Kumho Tire* involved an engineer's testimony. The Court explained:[4]

> [I]t would prove difficult, if not impossible, for judges to administer evidentiary rules under which a gatekeeping obligation depended upon a distinction between "scientific" knowledge and "technical" or "other specialized" knowledge. There is no clear line that divides the one from the others. Disciplines such as engineering rest upon scientific knowledge. Pure scientific theory itself may depend for its development upon observation and properly engineered machinery. And conceptual efforts to distinguish the two are unlikely to produce clear legal lines capable of application in particular cases.

Rule 702, noted the Court, articulated a single standard for admitting expert testimony, regardless of its type. Furthermore, the reason the Federal Rules of Evidence grant experts more latitude than other witnesses, the Court concluded, is the assumption that all expert testimony has a reliable basis. All expert testimony must therefore be relevant and reliable. The opinion suggested, although this question was not specifically before the Court, that social science is governed by this same standard, whether we consider that discipline "scientific" or not.

Reliability does not necessarily have to be judged, however, by the same five factors articulated in *Daubert*:

> We can neither rule out, nor rule in, for all cases and for all time the applicability of the factors mentioned in *Daubert*, nor can we now do so

---

4. *Kumho Tire Co. v. Carmichael*, 526 U.S. 137, 119 S. Ct. 1167, 1174, 143 L. Ed. 2d 238 (1999).

for subsets of cases categorized by category or expert or by kind of evidence . . . .

Daubert itself is not to the contrary. It made clear that its list of factors was meant to be helpful, not definitive. Indeed, those factors do not all necessarily apply even in every instance in which the reliability of scientific testimony is challenged. It might not be surprising in a particular case, for example, that a claim made by a scientific witness has never been the subject of peer review, for the particular application at issue may never previously have interested any scientist. Nor, on the other hand, does the presence of *Daubert's* general acceptance factor help to show that an expert's testimony is reliable where the discipline itself lacks reliability, as, for example, do theories grounded in any so-called generally accepted principles of astrology or necromancy.

After *Kumho Tire*, trial courts will be faced with the perhaps daunting task of coming up with helpful factors to guide the admissibility decision in a wide range of very different expert disciplines. The Court has not, therefore, entirely erased the distinction between "scientific" and "non-scientific" testimony because, for example, the reliability of a physicist's opinion necessarily requires understanding what are the standards of "good physics," a natural science. But that does not correspondingly mean that, on the other hand, Freudian psychology is to be judged by the standards of "good Freudian psychology," for *Kumho Tire* requires a court to determine whether an entire discipline is reliable. Some commentators have argued that Freudian psychology, unlike some other sorts of psychology, is so subjective that there is no objective way to gauge its reliability. Thus, a Freudian psychologist might interpret a particular dream to mean that a patient was obsessively attached to his mother, while another Freudian psychologist might offer a completely different interpretation of the same dream. How would we devise a "test" to determine who is right? On the other hand, some aspects of Freudian psychology are testable but yet have not been sufficiently tested. We could thus devise tests, as some indeed have, to determine whether Freudian talking therapy alleviates depression. Some commentators would therefore insist that all Freudian psychology — indeed all social science — be judged by the same sorts of factors as were involved in *Daubert* itself, with special emphasis on "testability and testing." Where this is found wanting, the testimony should be excluded.

Much social science can and should indeed be done using procedures similar to, or at least analogous to, those in the natural sciences. But even social science that cannot, or has not, yet met such standards of pseudo-natural-scientific testing can still sometimes be useful to a jury. This can be so even if the social scientist, while drawing on general principles, uses techniques and reaches conclusions in some ways unique to the particular case. Under *Kumho Tire*, therefore, there may be certain types of expert testimony using methods significantly different than those in the natural sciences that are nevertheless arguably still reliable. *Cf.* FED. R. EVID. advisory committee's note ("In certain fields experience is the predominant, if not sole, basis for a great deal of reliable testimony."). Here are three illustrations:

Example 1: The Acute Observer

Forensic linguists study conversations that are relevant to issues at trial, to interpret to the jury meanings that might not be evident on their face. One such linguist testified for the defense in a case in which the defendant, a chemical manufacturer, was charged with conspiring to find a pill press to aid a drug dealer. The suspect's defense was that he became so uncomfortable when he finally realized what the other party had proposed, that he sought only to get out of the conversation. His audio-recorded statements did not, therefore, reveal his agreement to anything.

The linguist was able to explain why the other party's early offers were ambiguous (thus explaining why the listener would participate for so long), and to point out why the rules of social politeness would make it hard for the listener to extricate himself from the conversation. Similarly, the linguist noted that the listener-defendant brought up only 15 percent of the words used, and spoke in much shorter sentences than did the primary speaker. Furthermore, most of the listener's turns at talk were one-word utterances, largely feedback markers, "uh-huh," "yeah," "hmmm," "oh," "okay," and "man." These tactics were arguably efforts of the listener to distance himself from the conversation without alienating the primary speaker, instead of actual acceptance of the speaker's proposal.

The only direct statement of agreement by the listener was in offering to "check around," which was an indirect response to the speaker's asking where he could get a pill press. But eight days later, in a second conversation, the listener simply reports, "I haven't had any luck." This lack of specificity about where and how he looked, about his prior experiences with or contacts in locating pill presses, and his lack of enthusiasm or elaboration, are the kind of hollow offers that people often use to end uncomfortable exchanges quickly, like "Let's get together for lunch sometime."

This combination of close observation of the defendant's speech with background information on the sociodynamics of ordinary conversation arguably offered a plausible alternative to the prosecution's conspiracy theory.

Example 2: Overcoming Cognitive Blinders

A prosecution expert in a rape case involving an African-American victim testifies about empirical research showing that most people, including jurors, are likely to be more skeptical of the testimony of African-American victims than white victims. Similarly, they are more willing to believe that an African-American woman consented to the defendant's behavior than a white woman did. The defense objects that the testimony is irrelevant and only concerns generalizations, thus offering no reliable guidance concerning whether this alleged victim is telling the truth.

The prosecution responds that the testimony alerts the jurors to an unconscious racist bias that may hamper their ability to decide fairly. The testimony enhances jurors' rationality by alerting them to their own prejudices, the "cognitive blinders" that can bar them from seeing the truth. *Cf.* FED. R. EVID. advisory committee's note ("[I]t might also be important in some cases for an expert to educate the factfinder about general principles, without ever attempting to apply these principles to the specific facts of the case").

Example 3

A sociologist testifies at a sexual harassment trial in support of a hostile environment claim. A state sexual harassment statute extends gender-based harassment to include non-sexual but systematic forms of gender disparagement, exclusion, and hostility. The sociologist recounts her ethnographic study of legal practice, which revealed a discriminatory emotional division of labor. Thus, male lawyers turned social events into competitions over who could drink the most beer, routinely mistook female associates for secretaries, and considered those associates shrill if they behaved aggressively but thought them weak if they took a more relational approach. Yet male associates were praised for their "hardball" tactics. Males also laughed at women lawyers who told tales of their aggressive behavior, which put women in a one-down position. As a consequence, women lawyers generally had a lower social and professional status than male lawyers in the study. The sociologist similarly interpreted the behavior she observed in visiting the law firm involved in the current sexual harassment suit, relying on her earlier ethnographic study in evaluating the current defendant's conduct. This testimony relies on interpretive social science, which assigns meaning to human action rather than, for example, doing experiments.

Problem 9-21: Raging Against Daubert

Return again to Problem 9-14 on linguistic rage. After Kumho Tire, can you articulate arguments that Daubert's "testimony" and error rate factors should not apply (or at least not apply in the same way as with the natural sciences) to the linguistic rage inquiry? What other factors should apply?

Problem 9-22: The Best Defense

Plaintiff filed a civil rights action for damages against the Sheriff's Office, alleging that the Sheriff conducted warrantless searches of his home and office. The plaintiff called famous attorney Matlock Mason to the stand to testify as an expert. Matlock states that the officers' conduct qualifies as a "search" and that plaintiff had not legally "consented" to the search. Is Matlock's opinion admissible?

§ 9.06 Expert Evidence Review Problems

Problem 9-23: Trial Transcript Exercise:
Federal Military Institute

The Federal Military Institute ("FMI") is an all-male, government-funded school for training "citizen-soldiers." This school uses the "adversative method" of training. In this method, upperclassmen bully, abuse, taunt, physically challenge, and otherwise harass freshmen "grunts," who are expected not to resist. The method is thought to build physical and emotional strength, discipline, teamwork, subordination of individual ego to the greater good, obedience, acceptance of hierarchy, and adaptability.

Several women have brought a civil lawsuit challenging the male-only admissions policy of FMI. FMI's response was to create a small all-female school, the Federal Women's Military Institute ("FWMI") as an alternative. That school does not use the adversative method, on the theory that women better learn leadership in a more nurturing environment. FMI calls feminist historian Barbara Randall to the stand. Excerpts from her direct examination follow:

DEFENDANT'S ATTORNEY: Dr. Randall, what is your educational background?

A: I received my Ph.D. in history from Yale University in 1979, specializing in twentieth-century women's history. I did post-graduate work at Princeton's Women's Studies Programs.

DEFENDANT'S ATTORNEY: And where are you now employed?

A: I am a Full Professor holding the Elizabeth Shelbourne Chair in Women's History in the History Department of Harvard University, a post I have held since completing my post-graduate work. I also simultaneously hold a post as a tenured professor in Harvard's Women's Studies Program.

DEFENDANT'S ATTORNEY: What is your area of research specialization?

A: I study gender differences in the ways that women and men learn in many settings. Twentieth-century history is replete with examples of both mythological and real such differences.

DEFENDANT'S ATTORNEY: Do you rely entirely on historical research in your work?

A: I read widely in many disciplines — social science, philosophy, politics, literary criticism, feminist studies, all of which inform my work.

DEFENDANT'S ATTORNEY: Dr. Randall, are you familiar with FMI and FWMI?

A: Yes. I have extensively studied both institutions. I have interviewed all current students, faculty, and administrators at both schools, and have sat in classes and reviewed their curricula.

DEFENDANT'S ATTORNEY: Have you formed any opinion about whether FMI would be an institutionally effective institute for training women as citizen-soldiers?

A: Yes.

DEFENDANT'S ATTORNEY: What is that opinion?

A: FMI would be a terrible place to educate women to be any sort of soldier or leader. Few women, if any, could thrive there, and even those who might succeed would very likely do better elsewhere.

DEFENDANT'S ATTORNEY: Why is that?

A: Because women do not learn well in an adversative model.

DEFENDANT'S ATTORNEY: And do you have an opinion about whether FWMI would be more effective than FMI at training citizen-soldiers?

A: Yes.

DEFENDANT'S ATTORNEY: What is that opinion?

A: FWMI is very effective in an absolute sense, and far more effective certainly than FMI, in training women as citizen-soldiers.

DEFENDANT'S ATTORNEY: Why is that?

A: The overwhelming scholarly evidence from history and in all fields of gender studies is that, by college, young women have far less confidence in themselves than do young men. They need a chance to see females succeeding in leadership roles and to take those roles themselves to restore self-confidence. Moreover, women learn and develop best in close relationships with other women. A caring, nurturing environment — support from fellow students, from teachers, from teammates — gives them the strength and skill to be tough with opponents and to learn more effectively. FWMI provides exactly this sort of environment for young women.

DEFENDANT'S ATTORNEY: What is your opinion, if any, on whether FMI discriminates against women by FMI's males-only admissions policy?

A: FMI does not so discriminate. It does treat men and women differently, but not all differences in treatment are discriminatory. These differences are in fact necessary to equality. FMI sends the applications of all women whom FMI rejects to FWMI so that women learn to be peer soldiers with the male graduates of FMI. And, correspondingly, it is only at FMI that men learn to be the best soldiers they can be. These separate institutions are the only way to have male-female equality in the military.

DEFENDANT'S ATTORNEY: On what do you base the opinions that you have shared with us today, Dr. Randall?

A: On my observations at both institutions and my knowledge of history from my own research and on my wide multidisciplinary reading in feminist studies.

DEFENDANT'S ATTORNEY: No more questions, Thank you.

If this testimony were presented before the jury, should objections have been made at any point by the plaintiffs' counsel to any of the questions? Why? What would be the basis for such objections? How likely would the objections be to succeed? If this testimony were instead an offer of proof before the trial judge, would you permit this expert to testify before the jury? Why or why not? Consider all the bases for objections in this chapter.

Problem 9-24: The Crime Scene Investigator

A well-known former professional football player is charged with stabbing his ex-wife to death. According to police DNA forensic scientists, blood found at the crime scene matched the defendant's blood. But the defense argues that the crime scene investigation was so poorly done as to risk contamination and tampering. The defense calls Michael Straub, an experienced murder forensic investigator, to opine that the investigation did indeed raise these risks. His analysis relied on his interviews with the lead detectives on the case, the lab representatives at the crime scene, and the lab technicians who did the testing. Straub testifies that each of the officers and technicians he interviewed recounted myriad details contrary to what is required by the National Guidelines for Death Investigations. However, according to the prosecutor, each of the officers and technicians denies telling Straub what he claims they said. Straub is unquestionably well-qualified. The police officers' and technicians' out-of-court statements to Straub as he recounts them are all inadmissible hearsay.

1. Should Straub be permitted to recount his opinion to the jury? Why or why not?

2. If yes, should he be allowed to relate the bases for his opinion to the jury? Why or why not?

Problem 9-25: Psychologist's Hearsay

In the linguistic rage problem, Problem 9-14, the psychologist bases his testimony that linguistic rage rendered Cheng incapable of telling right from wrong on: (1) his interviews of Cheng, Cheng's parents, friends, and employers, all of which statements are inadmissible hearsay; and (2) the opinion of the linguist that Cheng's history and behavior fit the prototypical description of linguistic rage, again a hearsay statement not fitting within any exceptions.

1. Is the psychologist's opinion admissible? Why or why not?

2. If yes, may the bases for his testimony be revealed to the jury?

Problem 9-26: Probabilities Revisited

In Problem 9-18, assume that the prosecutor offered no proof concerning the probabilities he noted of the "independent events." Rather, he simply asked the mathematician to assume those probabilities. In his closing argument, the prosecutor told the jury that they were free to apply whatever probabilities they believed were adequate, understanding that they had to apply the product rule to whatever probabilities they chose.

1. What grounds, if any, should the defense have raised in objecting to the mathematician's testimony beyond those already discussed in Problem 9-18?

2. What additional proof could the prosecution have offered, if any, to fend off such an objection?

Problem 9-27: Bio-Mechanic 1

Joseph Elton, Ph.D., a bio-mechanic, is testifying for the plaintiff in a Texas automotive-product-defect case on the issue of causation. Dr. Elton will testify that, during a rollover accident, the plaintiff sustained a spinal cord injury as a result of the flimsy roof of an SUV being crushed. In Texas, plaintiffs must establish producing cause to recover in a product liability case. Producing cause is defined as "a cause-in-fact that is also a substantial factor" in bringing about the occurrence or injury. Dr. Elton testifies that the roof crush was a producing cause, couching his opinion within the Texas definition of producing cause. He based his opinion on a review of the evidence in the case and a series of in-depth tests that he ran with crash dummies and identical exemplar vehicles. Dr. Elton knew how to run these tests based on his extensive experience as a bio-mechanic for the Air Force and NASA. His Harvard Ph.D. is in a relevant field, and he regularly speaks and publishes on the topic of bio-mechanics. His outside tests and theories on roof crush, similar to the tests he ran in this particular case, have been published in peer-reviewed journals. Although he ran case-specific tests to render an opinion for the plaintiff, those tests echo theories he developed as part of his non-litigation scientific testing. The only difference in the non-litigation tests is that they involved dummies of different sizes and different vehicles. The dummies in the litigation tests were the same size as the plaintiff. *Are Dr. Elton's opinions admissible?*

1. No, because Dr. Elton is unqualified as an expert in bio-mechanics.

2. No, because Dr. Elton's opinion is not helpful.

3. Yes, because experts may always rely on hearsay as a basis for their opinions.

4. Yes, because Dr. Elton properly relied on the evidence in this case to form his opinion and employed a reliable methodology.

Problem 9-28: Bio-Mechanic 2

Same facts as Problem 9-27 above. To admit Dr. Elton's opinion:

1. The court must determine by a preponderance of the evidence that Dr. Elton's opinion is correct to the exclusion of other expert testimony on the subject.

2. The court must determine by a preponderance of the evidence that Dr. Elton's opinion is reliable.

3. The court must determine that a reasonable jury could find by a preponderance of the evidence that Dr. Elton's opinion is reliable.

4. The court must determine that a reasonable jury could find by a preponderance of the evidence that Dr. Elton's opinion is correct to the exclusion of other expert testimony on the subject.

Problem 9-29: Bio-Mechanic 3

Same facts as Problem 9-27 above, but Dr. Elton relies on deposition testimony from a witness, Wally, who does not testify at trial. Wally, a passenger in the subject vehicle, testified in deposition that the plaintiff's body was snugly belted in during the rollover and that he did not witness the plaintiff travel toward the roof before impacting the roof. Dr. Elton relied on this deposition testimony based on his training as a bio-mechanic to support his theory that the roof crushed down on the plaintiff to cause the injury. He testified during a hearing in front of the judge that bio-mechanics reasonably rely on eyewitness statements to support their opinions. The plaintiff never offers Wally's deposition into evidence. *Was it appropriate for Dr. Elton to rely on Wally's testimony?*

1. No, because Wally's statement was hearsay within the definition of Rule 801(a)–(c).

2. Yes, because other experts reasonably rely on eyewitness statements.

3. Yes, because Wally's testimony was not being offered for the truth of the matter asserted.

4. No, unless evidence sufficient to support a finding by a preponderance establishes that experts reasonably rely on eyewitness statements.

Problem 9-30: Physician, Heal Thyself

Robert Allen is injured in an automobile accident. He brings a civil suit against the other car's driver. At trial, plaintiff calls a physician to the stand, hired solely for purposes of this litigation, to testify that, in his opinion, the accident compressed a previously healthy nerve in plaintiff's neck, a compression likely to cause plaintiff a lifetime of pain. In reaching his opinion, the physician relied on the treating radiologist's report, the emergency-room physician's medical records, an interview with the plaintiff, and interviews with the plaintiff's family members.

1. The physician's opinion is inadmissible.

2. The physician's opinion is admissible if the proponent establishes that all its bases are of the type reasonably relied upon by other experts in the relevant field, but those bases are presumptively inadmissible.

3. Both the physician's opinion and all its bases are admissible, absent a showing of unfair prejudice to one of the parties.

4. The physician's opinion is admissible, but its bases may never be revealed to a jury on direct examination.

Problem 9-31: Coercive Indoctrination

John Dalvo is charged with murder and conspiracy to commit murder. John's defense is that "coercive indoctrination," (colloquially known as brainwashing) by John's older, more charismatic co-conspirator, rendered John temporarily insane. John calls a psychologist to the stand who will testify that in his opinion, John was indeed indoctrinated into his crime by his co-conspirator.

1. The physician's opinion's admissibility will turn on whether it is the product of reliable principles or methods reliably applicable to the facts of the case and based on sufficient facts or data.

2. *The Daubert* test does not apply to "soft" sciences like psychology.

3. The *Daubert* test does apply, but the opinion is admissible if it is generally accepted in the field of psychology.

4. The *Daubert* test applies only if the study of coercive indoctrination is based on novel principles using novel methods.

Problem 9-32: Experts Not

Which of the following statements is NOT true concerning an expert witness?

1. An expert witness may base her opinion on irrelevant information as long as it is made available to the opposing side prior to trial.

2. A person testifying as an expert witness may qualify as an expert even if she does not possess a college degree.

3. An expert witness may base her opinion on double hearsay.

4. An expert witness may not testify in a criminal case for the defendant on an ultimate mental state issue.

Problem 9-33: Reconstructionist

Tom is the defendant in a civil negligence case (car wreck). The primary issue at trial is who was at fault in the crash — plaintiff or Tom. The plaintiff calls Dr. Nora Smith to testify as an expert in accident reconstruction. Dr. Smith is well-qualified as an accident reconstructionist. To form her opinions, Dr. Smith reviewed all the depositions and exhibits in the case, the police accident report, and did a scene inspection a couple of years after the accident. She offers her opinion that Tom is at fault in the accident, based on her reconstruction. Is the opinion admissible?

1. No, because the expert did not have sufficient personal knowledge of the facts.

2. No, because the expert opinion would not be helpful to the jury.

3. Yes, so long as experts in the field would reasonably rely on the materials the expert reviewed.

4. Yes, so long as the information the expert reviewed was admissible or satisfied a reverse-403 balancing test.

Chapter 10

Protecting the Adversary System: The Hearsay Rule and the Confrontation Clause

§ 10.01 Chapter Checklist

1. What are the two types of arguments supporting the admissibility of out-of-court statements?

2. What is the Five-Step Hearsay Matrix?

3. How does the hearsay rule protect the right to cross-examination?

4. What are the four hearsay dangers?

5. How does the definition of "hearsay declarants" limit the scope of the hearsay rule?

6. What is a statement for purposes of the hearsay rule?

7. Can I avoid the hearsay rule by asking witnesses to paraphrase out-of-court statements?

8. Can witnesses' own out-of-court statements constitute hearsay?

9. What are *testimonial* hearsay assertions?

10. What is the link between *testimonial* hearsay assertions and the Confrontation Clause of the Sixth Amendment?

§ 10.02 Relevant Federal Rules of Evidence

Rule 801. Definitions That Apply to This Article; Exclusions from Hearsay (sections a–c)

(a) Statement. "Statement" means a person's oral assertion, written assertion, or nonverbal conduct, if the person intended it as an assertion.

(b) Declarant. "Declarant" means the person who made the statement.

(c) Hearsay. "Hearsay" means a statement that:

    (1) the declarant does not make while testifying at the current trial or hearing; and

(2) a party offers in evidence to prove the truth of the matter asserted in the statement.

Rule 802. The Rule Against Hearsay

Hearsay is not admissible unless any of the following provides otherwise:

- a federal statute;

- these rules; or

- other rules prescribed by the Supreme Court.

United States Constitution — Sixth Amendment.

In all criminal proceedings, the accused shall enjoy the right . . . to be confronted with the witnesses against him.

§ 10.03 Introduction

While some evidentiary rules are narrow and technical, others (such as those limiting the admissibility of character evidence) embody the U.S. conception of a fair trial. The hearsay rule, the basic principles of which are the focus of this chapter, is at the core of this conception. Reinforced in criminal cases by the U.S. Constitution's Sixth Amendment (the Confrontation Clause), the hearsay rule is virtually synonymous with the adversary system of trial because it protects a party's right to cross-examine adverse witnesses. (The hearsay rule also helps to explain the international popularity of American courtroom films and TV shows, as it promotes the *mano-a-mano* verbal confrontations between cross-examiners and witnesses that so often produce sudden plot twists.)

The hearsay rule reflects a centuries-old distrust of secondhand information. For example, early in the sixteenth century, famed Swiss alchemist Paracelsus wrote that he was not the creator of the Philosopher's Stone, and so could speak of it only from hearsay.[1] And a few years later, soon after Queen Anne Boleyn's beheading in 1536, palace governess Lady Bryan wrote a letter stating that she didn't know the current whereabouts of the Queen's daughter Elizabeth "except by hearsay."[2] The long-standing suspicious attitude toward hearsay underlies Rule 802, which sets forth the general rule that hearsay is not admissible in evidence.

Under Rule 801, a hearsay statement is one made orally, in writing, or through assertive conduct at a time or place other than on the witness stand during the trial or hearing in which the statement is offered into evidence. Judges and lawyers often reduce this definition to the shorthand term, "out-of-court statement." For example,

---

1. M. PACHTER, PARACELSUS: MAGIC INTO SCIENCE 133 (1951).
2. JOAN GLASHEEN, THE SECRET PEOPLE OF THE PALACES 40 (B.T. Batsford, 1998).

Bob would be offering Joan's out-of-court statement into evidence in the following situations:

- Bob testifies, "Soon after the accident, Joan told me that she saw the car that collided with mine run a red light."

- Bob seeks to read into the trial record Joan's deposition testimony, "I saw the car that collided with Bob's run a red light."

- Bob offers into evidence an affidavit signed under oath by Joan during pretrial discovery proceedings stating, "I saw the car that collided with Bob's run a red light."

- Bob offers into evidence a portion of the transcript from an earlier trial in which Joan testified under oath, "I saw the car that collided with Bob's run a red light."

- Bob testifies that after the accident, Joan held up a picture of a red light after he asked her, "What color was the light for the other car when it entered the intersection?"

Each excerpt of Bob's testimony refers to an out-of-court statement by Joan, because Joan made each statement other than "while testifying at the current trial or hearing" in which Bob offered Joan's statement into evidence.

Any hearsay that you picked up about the hearsay rule before enrolling in the Evidence course may be more confusing than helpful. For one thing, not all out-of-court statements constitute hearsay. Under Rule 801(c), an out-of-court statement constitutes hearsay only if a proponent offers it "to prove the truth of the matter asserted in the statement." Rule 802 does not exclude an out-of-court statement that is offered for a legitimate "non-hearsay purpose" (a purpose that does not depend on the statement's accuracy).

Second, even if a proponent does offer an out-of-court statement into evidence for the truth of what it asserts, the statement may well be admissible under one or more of the gaggle of exemptions and exceptions identified by Rules 801, 803, 804, and 807. Thus, a conclusion that an out-of-court assertion constitutes hearsay does not necessarily mean that the assertion is inadmissible in evidence at trial.

Finally, even if a hearsay statement is admissible under an exemption or exception provided by the Federal Rules of Evidence, the Confrontation Clause might bar a prosecutor from offering it into evidence against a criminal defendant.

This chapter begins hearsay analysis by focusing on Rule 801's definition of hearsay, and by explaining why the purpose for which a party offers an out-of-court statement into evidence determines its admissibility. To keep your eyes on the forest of admissibility as you go through the individual definitional trees, keep the following "Five-Step Hearsay Matrix" in mind. The questions set forth in the matrix provide a helpful approach for analyzing hearsay issues.

Five-Step Hearsay Matrix

Step One: Does evidence constitute a declarant's out-of-court statement?

Step Two: If so, for what purpose does the proponent seek to elicit an out-of-court statement?

Step Three: If the proponent offers an out-of-court statement for a non-hearsay purpose (that is, for a purpose that does not depend on the statement's accuracy), is that purpose relevant and, if so, is its probative value substantially outweighed by the risk of unfair prejudice or the other factors set forth in Rule 403?

Step Four: Can a proponent who offers an out-of-court statement for its truth satisfy the foundational requirements of an exemption or exception to the hearsay rule?

Step Five (necessary only when prosecutors offer hearsay statements into evidence against criminal defendants): Even if an out-of-court statement is admissible under the hearsay rule, does the Confrontation Clause require its exclusion? This chapter concludes with an analysis of Confrontation Clause issues.

§ 10.04 Hearsay Defined

Under Rule 801(c), an out-of-court statement is hearsay when:

- A "declarant";

- makes an out-of-court oral or written assertion; or

- engages in non-verbal conduct that is intended as an assertion; that is

- offered to prove the truth of the matter asserted in the statement.

"The truth of the matter asserted" is the definitional element that most commonly determines whether out-of-court statements are hearsay. A party offers an out-of-court statement for its truth if the statement must be accurate to be relevant. If the purpose for which a party offers a statement makes the statement relevant without regard to its accuracy, the statement is non-hearsay. Thus, *the very same statement can be either hearsay or non-hearsay, depending on the point that the offering party attempts to prove. To carry out hearsay analysis properly, you have to know what the offering party seeks to prove by offering an out-of-court assertion into evidence.*

Example

Jean is present when Melissa tells her friend Joe, "The guards in the bank where I work have blanks instead of real bullets in their guns." If Jean were asked to testify to Melissa's statement in a trial, the testimony might be hearsay. Melissa is a declarant, and she made her statement to Joe out-of-court. But whether the statement is hearsay depends on what it's offered to prove. Melissa's statement would be:

Hearsay if Joe were injured in a robbery that took place in the bank where Melissa works and sues the bank for not adequately protecting its customers, and if Joe's attorney offers Melissa's out-of-court statement as evidence that the bank's guards were armed only with blanks. Joe's attorney would then be offering Melissa's statement "for its truth," because Melissa's statement would be relevant to prove that the guards' guns were loaded with blanks only if it were accurate.

Non-hearsay if Joe is charged with robbing the bank, and the prosecution offers Melissa's statement to prove that a motive for the robbery was that Joe didn't fear being shot by the guards. Melissa's statement would now be relevant even if it were inaccurate — that is, even if the guards' guns were in fact loaded with real bullets. Hearing Melissa's statement could have led Joe to *believe* that the guards only had blanks. Joe's belief permits an inference that Joe would not be fearful of being shot during a robbery attempt, which strengthens an inference that Joe robbed the bank.

The next section explains the policies underlying the hearsay rule and describes why offering out-of-court statements for a "non-hearsay purpose" obviates the concerns giving rise to the rule.

§ 10.05 The Hearsay Rule and the Adversary System

A. Hearsay Rule Protects the Right to Cross-Examine

The primary reason that out-of-court statements are hearsay only when parties offer them for "the truth of the matter asserted" is that the adversary system of trial relies heavily on cross-examination as a method of ferreting out truth, and the hearsay rule protects a party's right to cross-examine adverse witnesses. In other words, the hearsay rule's primary purpose is to protect a party from the use of evidence from hearsay declarants the party cannot cross-examine. In the words of the great evidence scholar John Wigmore, "The hearsay rule ... signifies *a rule rejecting assertions ... which have not been in some way subjected to the test of cross-examination.*"[3] Thus, the hearsay rule is the legal equivalent of the common expression, "Tell it to the judge (or jury)." The rule reflects a belief that in an adversarial system of justice, witnesses ought to tell their stories in court, where judges and jurors can observe and evaluate them and adverse parties can cross-examine them.

If the purpose of the hearsay rule is to allow cross-examination of speakers whose out-of-court statements are offered into evidence, why aren't all out-of-court statements treated equally? Why does the bar of the hearsay rule disappear when out-of-court assertions are offered for "non-hearsay purposes"? The answer is that when an out-of-court statement is offered for a non-hearsay use, the declarant's presence on the witness stand is not necessary for meaningful cross-examination to occur.

---

3. Vol. 5, WIGMORE ON EVIDENCE — CHADBOURN REVISION § 1362 (1974) (emphasis in original).

When a statement is offered as non-hearsay, the credibility issue concerns the in-court witness who serves as the "conduit" for the out-of-court statement, not the declarant. And, of course, the adversary can cross-examine and test the credibility of the in-court witness.

By contrast, when an out-of-court statement is offered for its truth, the important credibility issues generally revolve around the *hearsay declarant*, not the "conduit" witness. That is why a hearsay declarant's presence at trial is almost always necessary for an opportunity for meaningful cross-examination to occur.

To understand why the admission of hearsay from non-testifying speakers typically precludes adversaries from testing its credibility, recognize that accepting the accuracy of hearsay gives rise to four "hearsay dangers." Depriving parties of the opportunity to cross-examine hearsay declarants prevents them from demonstrating that the presence of one or more of these dangers renders hearsay inaccurate or incomplete. The subsection below explains the four hearsay dangers and then illustrates how the opportunity for meaningful cross-examination depends on whether a statement is offered for its truth or for a non-hearsay purpose.

B. The "Hearsay Dangers"

The factors that cross-examiners are unable to probe when hearsay substitutes for in-court testimony are as follows:

Sincerity. Does a hearsay declarant's out-of-court statement actually reflect the declarant's belief? For example, was Graham intending to be accurate when he told his neighbor Beverly the day after a collision, "the Beemer ran a red light"? Beverly's testifying to Graham's out-of-court statement at trial is likely to foreclose a cross-examiner from probing Graham's sincerity and perhaps showing that Graham lied. Common motives that cross-examiners pursue at trial to probe a witness' sincerity include a witness' financial stake in a trial's outcome, close personal relationship with the adversary, or bad feelings toward the cross-examiner's client. Or, a cross-examiner might be able to show that Graham's demeanor and manner of answering questions under oath (e.g., shifty eyes, sweaty palms) demonstrate that he is insincere.

Perception. Even if a hearsay declarant was sincere, did the declarant have an adequate opportunity to observe the events to which the hearsay statement refers? For example, how well could Graham observe the Beemer that he said ran the red light? Beverly's testifying to Graham's out-of-court statement at trial is likely to foreclose a cross-examiner from probing Graham's perception and perhaps showing that Graham was too far away to observe accurately, or that the intersection was badly lit, or that Graham was preoccupied and therefore not paying close attention to the car that ran the red light.

Memory. Even if a hearsay declarant was sincere and had an adequate opportunity to observe events, how well did the declarant recall those events at the time the hearsay statement was made? For example, how well did Graham recall the color of the light and the Beemer's location at the time he said that the car ran the light? Beverly's testifying to Graham's out-of-court statement at trial is likely to foreclose a cross-examiner from probing Graham's memory and perhaps showing that Graham is unable to recall other important details, or that he has given conflicting accounts of the event.

Communication Difficulties. Even if a hearsay declarant was sincere, had an adequate opportunity to observe events, and adequately recalled those events, how accurately does a declarant's choice of words describe those events? For example, did Graham misspeak? Beverly's testifying to Graham's out-of-court statement at trial is likely to foreclose a cross-examiner from probing Graham's use of language at trial and perhaps showing that Graham meant to say that a Toyota ran the red light. In addition, admission of Graham's hearsay is likely to prevent a cross-examiner from showing that Graham uses language in an idiosyncratic way. For example, perhaps the cross-examiner could show by questioning Graham that he is especially cautious and considers any driver whose car is in an intersection when a light turns red to have "run a red light."

Practice Tip: ROTC

"ROTC" is a military mnemonic that may help you to remember the hearsay dangers. Cross-examination tests a witness' ability to <u>R</u>emember; <u>O</u>bserve; <u>T</u>ell the Truth; and <u>C</u>ommunicate.

The following samples of testimony illustrate the linkage between the hearsay rule and cross-examination. The first testimonial excerpt demonstrates how the admission of hearsay is likely to negate the opportunity for meaningful cross-examination. Assume that Melinda is a defendant in an auto accident case. Dave, the plaintiff, claims that Melinda negligently drove her Ford automobile through a red light and ran into Dave's car. To prove that Melinda was negligent, Dave is allowed to testify, "About 10 minutes after the collision, a bystander came up to me and said, 'I saw what happened. The driver of the Ford that ran into your car ran a red light.'" Because Dave has not produced the bystander (the hearsay declarant) as a witness, Melinda's attorney has to try to undermine the bystander's credibility by cross-examining Dave. A portion of the cross-examination might go as follows:

DEFENDANT'S ATTORNEY: A bystander told you that the Ford ran the red light?

A: That's correct.

DEFENDANT'S ATTORNEY: Do you know whether the bystander was acquainted with my client? (sincerity question)

A: No, I don't.

DEFENDANT'S ATTORNEY: Do you know whether the bystander had ever made negative statements about people who drive Ford automobiles? (sincerity question)

A: No, I'd never met or talked to the bystander before the collision.

DEFENDANT'S ATTORNEY: Do you know whether the bystander would be squirming uncomfortably if the bystander had to respond to my questions in court, under oath? (sincerity question)

A: Sorry, haven't a clue.

DEFENDANT'S ATTORNEY: What was the bystander's physical location at the time that the bystander claims to have seen the Ford run the red light? (perception question)

A: I don't know.

DEFENDANT'S ATTORNEY: Do you know whether the bystander was facing toward or away from the sun at the time the bystander claims to have seen the Ford run the red light? (perception question)

A: No, I don't know.

DEFENDANT'S ATTORNEY: Do you know whether the bystander was concentrating on work or family problems at the time the bystander claims to have seen the Ford run the red light? (perception question)

A: I don't know. Look, why are you asking me all these questions? All I know is what the bystander told me after the collision.

DEFENDANT'S ATTORNEY: I understand. But I suspect that this cross-examination is going to be used as an example in an Evidence textbook, so I need to show readers how use of the bystander's assertion for its truth really frustrates my opportunity to conduct meaningful cross-examination. Does the bystander now recall how fast the Ford was going when it allegedly ran the red light? (memory question)

A: I don't know.

DEFENDANT'S ATTORNEY: Well, can the bystander recall how fast your car was going when it collided with my client's car? (memory question)

A: How the heck would I know?

DEFENDANT'S ATTORNEY: Can the bystander tell us what the weather was like at the time of the collision? (memory question)

A: I have no idea.

DEFENDANT'S ATTORNEY: Has the bystander given a conflicting account of what happened to anyone else? (memory question)

A: I don't know.

DEFENDANT'S ATTORNEY: Do you know whether the bystander can accurately distinguish a Ford automobile from other makes of car? (ambiguity question)

A: I don't know.

DEFENDANT'S ATTORNEY: Do you know whether the bystander meant that the light turned red before or during the time the Ford was in the intersection? (ambiguity question)

A: I don't know.

As you can see, the admissibility of hearsay largely negates the defense attorney's opportunity for meaningful cross-examination. The bystander's out-of-court statement might be subject to any of the four dangers, but the substitution of the hearsay assertion for the bystander's in-court testimony prevents the attorney from exploring them.

If the distinction between hearsay and non-hearsay makes any sense, then an opportunity for meaningful cross-examination should be available when a party offers an out-of-court statement for a non-hearsay purpose. To test this, consider a second sample of testimony from a revised version of the previous case. As in the previous example, Melinda is a defendant in an auto accident case. And, as before, Dave, the plaintiff, claims that Melinda negligently drove her Ford automobile through a red light and ran into Dave's car. In this version, to counter Melinda's affirmative defense that Dave and not she ran the red light, Dave testifies that moments before the collision, Chuck, a passenger in Dave's car, told Dave, "Be careful at this intersection. Cops are always around and people get tickets for running red lights here all the time." Chuck's statement, Dave testifies, made him especially wary and careful not to go through a red light.

In this example, Dave offers Chuck's statement for a non-hearsay use. Even if what Chuck said about cops ticketing motorists is inaccurate, the statement is relevant because Dave claims that Chuck's remark led Dave to drive carefully as he approached the intersection where the collision occurred. Thus, if the hearsay/non-hearsay distinction makes sense, Melinda's attorney should have a reasonable chance to cross-examine Dave:

DEFENDANT'S ATTORNEY: You say that moments before the collision, Chuck told you that cops often ticket motorists for running red lights at that intersection, right?

A: That's correct.

DEFENDANT'S ATTORNEY: We only have your word for this and not Chuck's, right? (sincerity question)

A: That's true.

DEFENDANT'S ATTORNEY: Chuck moved out of the country and is not available to verify your testimony, right? (sincerity question)

A: That's correct.

DEFENDANT'S ATTORNEY: Do you recall anything else that Chuck said to you during the five minutes prior to the collision? (memory question)

A: No.

DEFENDANT'S ATTORNEY: Do you recall what if anything you and Chuck had been discussing when Chuck made this statement to you? (memory question)

A: No.

DEFENDANT'S ATTORNEY: Has Chuck previously been a passenger in your car?

A: Yes, often.

DEFENDANT'S ATTORNEY: On any prior occasion, has Chuck ever given you a warning about the presence of police officers? (memory/sincerity question)

A: Not that I can remember.

DEFENDANT'S ATTORNEY: You didn't personally see any police officers at the intersection, did you? (perception question)

A: No.

DEFENDANT'S ATTORNEY: Have you driven through that intersection previously? (memory question)

A: Sure.

DEFENDANT'S ATTORNEY: Can you estimate for us how many times in the six months prior to the events giving rise to this lawsuit that you drove through that intersection? (memory question)

A: Oh, I can't be sure. Let's say 15–20 times.

DEFENDANT'S ATTORNEY: And you'd never been stopped by a police officer for any reason connected to that intersection, isn't that true? (memory/ sincerity question)

A: I guess that's right.

DEFENDANT'S ATTORNEY: You talked to Police Officer Jones about what happened about 15–20 minutes after the accident, is that right?

A: That's about right.

DEFENDANT'S ATTORNEY: And you didn't mention to Officer Jones that Chuck had made this statement to you, did you? (sincerity/memory question)

A: No.

DEFENDANT'S ATTORNEY: Before approaching the intersection where the collision took place, you had been driving with Chuck in your car for about 15 minutes, right?

A: That's true.

DEFENDANT'S ATTORNEY: And Chuck might have made this statement earlier in the drive, isn't that right? (perception/memory question)

A: I'm pretty sure that he said it right before the accident.

DEFENDANT'S ATTORNEY: How much time elapsed between the time Chuck said this to you and the collision took place? (memory question)

A: I'm not exactly sure. A few seconds, I'd say.

DEFENDANT'S ATTORNEY: And did you ask him how he knew that cops often ticketed drivers in that area? (sincerity question)

A: No.

DEFENDANT'S ATTORNEY: Yet you say that you immediately slowed down after hearing Chuck say this?

A: Yes.

DEFENDANT'S ATTORNEY: At the time you claim that Chuck made this statement to you, you were talking on your mobile phone to your sales manager about an important customer you were going to see later in the day, isn't that right? (memory/perception question)

A: Yes.

DEFENDANT'S ATTORNEY: So you weren't paying close attention to what Chuck might have said to you, isn't that right? (sincerity/perception question)

A: I could do both things.

As may be apparent, Dave's offering Chuck's statement for a non-hearsay use allows Melinda's attorney to conduct meaningful cross-examination. What is relevant to the case is whether Chuck made the statement, whether Dave heard it, and, if so, how the statement might have affected Dave's driving. These non-hearsay uses provide Melinda's attorney with a fair opportunity to test Dave's sincerity, memory and perception.

Practice Tip: Identifying Non-Hearsay Uses

Out-of-court statements do not come neatly packaged with tags listing "possible non-hearsay uses" attached. If you become a litigator, your pretrial preparation is often likely to include developing arguments supporting non-hearsay uses for helpful out-of-court statements that you cannot offer under a hearsay exemption or exception. Anticipating potential objections, you will also commonly develop arguments that the probative value of the non-hearsay purpose outweighs the risk that jurors will improperly consider them for their truth. For more on non-hearsay uses, *see* Chapter 11.

C. Why Not Admit Hearsay "For What It's Worth"?

You might concede that the admission of hearsay is apt to frustrate cross-examination yet argue that Rule 802's general policy of excluding hearsay is unwarranted. After all, if it accomplishes nothing else, the first cross-examination above should serve as a warning to a sensible judge or juror that the accuracy of the bystander's hearsay assertion is untested. You could support your argument with the results of empirical evidence, admittedly based on simulated jury studies, suggesting that jurors are wary of untested hearsay.[4]

If this is so, why not routinely admit hearsay and rely on judges and jurors to discount its weight according to the circumstances? If we trust them to evaluate the probative worth of other evidence, shouldn't we also trust them to evaluate the probative worth of hearsay? Moreover, trial judges would retain the power under Rule 403 to exclude hearsay when particular circumstances wouldn't allow for a reasonable assessment of hearsay's probative value; in such situations, the hearsay's probative value might be substantially outweighed by the likelihood of confusion or undue consumption of time. In addition, a rule of general admissibility would be much more coherent and easier for judges and lawyers to apply in the heat of battle than a rule of exclusion accompanied by a bewildering array of non-hearsay uses and hearsay exemptions and exceptions. And the resultant time that students would save in the Evidence course could be profitably devoted to the study of oil and gas leases.

If this is your attitude, you're not alone. In fact, you can point to the support of an entire country — England's adversary system very much resembles our own, yet in the Civil Evidence Act of 1968 the English Parliament largely abolished the hearsay rule in civil cases. However, American rule-makers have thus far been unwilling to reverse the general policy of excluding hearsay. Many would probably respond to an "admit hearsay for what it's worth" argument as follows:

- In many circumstances, judges and especially jurors are unable rationally to assess hearsay's probative value. They'd be guessing, based on unarticulated and untested assumptions, and in general would probably be inclined to accord hearsay assertions more weight than they are "really" worth.

- If hearsay were generally admissible, crafty lawyers would "witness-shop," producing impressive witnesses who could repeat the hearsay assertions of percipient witnesses of questionable demeanor or background.

- The hearsay rule as presently constituted enables lawyers to predict with at least a fair amount of accuracy whether an out-of-court assertion will be admitted into evidence. This predictability helps lawyers plan trial strategies and may also foster pretrial settlements.

- The hearsay rule protects cross-examination, a fundamental trial right that is too important to be left to the uncertain whims of judges and jurors with varying degrees of judgment, experience and common sense.

- The current format of the hearsay rule is flexible enough to satisfy those who think that hearsay ought to be generally admissible. First, rule-makers can craft new exceptions as they deem warranted, and have done so.

---

4. *See, e.g.,* Margaret Kovera, Roger Park & Steven Penrod, *Jurors' Perceptions of Eyewitness and Hearsay Evidence*, 76 MINN. L. REV. 703 (1992).

Example 1: Many states have in recent years enacted a "tender years" hearsay exception for young children's out-of-court assertions of abuse.

Example 2: In response to the exclusion of prosecution evidence in the famous 1995 murder trial of O.J. Simpson, California enacted a new hearsay exception (Cal. Evid. Code Sec. 1370) for statements describing physical injuries made by victims who are unavailable to testify at trial.

Second, Rule 807's residual ("catch-all") exception allows judges to admit hearsay that they deem reliable even if it doesn't fit the foundational requirements of any of the preexisting exceptions. (see Chapter 15.) If these changes don't go as far as some would like, they perhaps relieve the pressure for a general change of hearsay policy.

D. "Hearsay Policy" Problems

Problem 10-1: The Telephone Game

True or False: The primary risk that the hearsay rule is designed to prevent is exemplified by "The Telephone Game," in which a message tends to change as it's whispered from one person to the next. That is, the hearsay rule exists because of worry that witnesses will inaccurately report out-of-court assertions.

Problem 10-2: Beyond Question?

Slip-and-Fall Case. To prove that she slipped on a wet spot in a restaurant, Lynn Oleum offers into evidence signed and sworn affidavits from three community religious leaders who happened to be dining in the restaurant that night. Each affidavit declares under oath that the affiant saw Lynn's foot slip on a wet spot on the floor. The restaurant objects that the affidavits are hearsay. Lynn argues that the affidavits are not barred by Rule 802 because like in-court testimony they were made under oath and because the stature and number of the declarants renders the hearsay dangers negligible. *Ruling?* Alternative No. 1: What if instead of affidavits relating to Lynn, the religious leaders' statements consist of testimony given in the trial of a case filed by Angel, a different patron indicating that they had seen Angel slip and fall on the same wet spot on the same night as Lynn? Alternative No. 2: What if Lynn wants to testify to the testimony she herself gave under oath in Angel's trial against the restaurant?

Problem 10-3: What's the Use?

Bart Harbour is charged with illegally poaching seals on Seal Rock in Acadia Cove. Bart's defense is that he was unaware that it was against the law to capture seals. (Assume that this is a legitimate defense to the charge.) The prosecution calls Davy Jones and elicits testimony that he is Acadia's Covemaster. The examination continues as follows:

PROSECUTOR: Are you familiar with a location known as Seal Rock?

A: I am. Seal Rock is in Acadia Cove, about 50 yards offshore. It's a large oval-shaped rock about 25 yards in length and about 10 yards across where seals breed and are commonly present.

PROSECUTOR: Are there any notices posted on Seal Rock?

A: Yes indeed. There are two signs on the rock with large, dark letters at the top saying "Illegal to Hunt or Harm Seals" and indicating that both federal and state laws forbid human contact with seals.

DEFENDANT'S ATTORNEY: Objection, hearsay, move to strike the last answer. The notices are out-of-court statements offered for their truth.

PROSECUTOR: *How will you respond to the objection?*

Problem 10-4: Hearsay Expert

You are speaking to the Hearsay Rule Sub-Committee of the Congressional Federal Rules of Evidence Oversight Committee. They have asked for your views on a proposal that the Rule 801 definition of hearsay be retained, but that Rule 802 be amended to provide, "The admissibility of hearsay is committed to the discretion of the trial judge, and trial judges' rulings shall be final except for manifestly unjust rulings that are likely to have affected a verdict. Existing hearsay exceptions shall serve only as factors that trial judges may take into account when making their rulings." *What advice will you give the Sub-Committee as to the wisdom of this proposal?*

§ 10.06 Who Are "Declarants"?

A. Definitions and Examples

Now that you've been introduced to the concept of "the truth of the matter asserted," consider next the three additional elements of Rule 801's definition of hearsay. Begin with the term "declarant," the maker of an out-of-court statement. The typical hearsay situation involves two people: the declarant (the speaker who makes the statement) and the witness (who testifies to the statement in court).

Example 1

PLAINTIFF'S ATTORNEY: What happened after the defendant's car collided with yours?

A: A bystander walked over to me and said that the car that hit mine ran the red light.

Here, the declarant is the bystander; the driver is the witness.

The hearsay definition limits declarants to "persons." Pity the animals; not only are most all of them barred from restaurants, but also they can't be declarants. Likewise, mechanical devices are not declarants.

Example 2

A driver in an auto accident case testifies as follows:

Attorney: How fast were you going at the time of the collision?

A: 35 m.p.h.

Attorney: And how do you know that was your speed?

A: Because I had just glanced at my car's digital speedometer and that was the speed it showed.

No hearsay declarant exists. The speedometer is a mechanical device and does not "assert" that the speed was 35 m.p.h.

Example 3

A landlord in an eviction case testifies as follows:

PLAINTIFF'S ATTORNEY: And how do you know the sun has just come up?

A: I hear roosters crowing in the tenant's backyard.

No hearsay declarant exists; roosters are not declarants. (The cross-examination justification for the hearsay rule suggests that this aspect of the rule makes good sense, preventing attorneys from making demands such as, "Get those roosters into this courtroom so that when the sun comes up I can cross-examine the living daylights out of them.")

B. "Declarant" Problems

Problem 10-5: Where's the Declarant?

Are there hearsay declarants in these scenarios?

1. As evidence that a statement was made by a computer store employee, the plaintiff seeks to testify that "I phoned the number that was listed for the computer store on its website."

2. To prove the magnitude of her damages in a personal injury case, professional basketball player Shirley Knott offers into evidence the "Statistics" page of the league's website showing that she was leading the league in blocked shots on the day of her injury.

3. To prove that the Fizzy Cola Co. owned and operated a truck that was involved in an accident, a bystander seeks to testify that painted on the side of the truck was a logo that read, "Fizzy Cola — The Healthy Cola."

4. Yon is called as a witness and testifies, "My name is Yon Yonsin, I come from Wisconsin."

Problem 10-6: Bloody Glove

Lerna Hand is charged with murder. To prove Lerna's identity as the murderer, the prosecution calls Police Officer Tracy, who testifies as follows:

PROSECUTOR: What led you to arrest Lerna?

A: I held the bloody glove that I found at the murder scene up to the nose of Cinders, the police bloodhound I've personally trained. Cinders sniffed the glove for a few moments and followed a scent directly to Lerna.

DEFENDANT'S ATTORNEY: Objection, hearsay. Cinders' behavior is the equivalent of the out-of-court statement, "Lerna was the murderer." I also object that the evidence of the dog's behavior is irrelevant.

PROSECUTOR: *How can you respond to these objections?*

Assume that the judge summons counsel to the bench and asks you for an "offer of proof" concerning the foundational testimony that you will elicit from Officer Tracy to support the relevance of Cinders' behavior. *What will your offer of proof consist of?*

Problem 10-7: Polly Wants a Conviction

Laurel is charged with murdering Hardy; Laurel's defense is an alibi. To prove Laurel's identity as the murderer, the prosecution calls Police Officer Tracy, who testifies as follows:

PROSECUTOR: When did you arrive at Hardy's apartment?

A: Approximately five minutes after receiving the call reporting that gunshots had been heard coming from the apartment.

PROSECUTOR: What did you see when you entered the apartment?

A: I saw Hardy lying in a pool of blood on the floor, and a parrot in a cage in the same room.

PROSECUTOR: What, if anything, did the parrot do while you were in the room?

A: The parrot repeatedly squawked, "Laurel, why'd you do it? Laurel, why'd you do it?"

DEFENDANT'S ATTORNEY: Objection, hearsay.

PROSECUTOR: No hearsay is involved, Your Honor, because the parrot is not a declarant.

JUDGE: *What is your response to the prosecutor's argument?*

A Newsworthy Parrot

A story in the Aug. 28, 2017 edition of the Detroit News reports that Glenna Duram was sentenced to life in prison after she was convicted of first degree murder for the shooting death of her husband Martin. A witness testified that after the slaying, Martin's pet parrot Bud repeated the words "don't (expletive) shoot" in Martin's voice. The article is online at: http://www.detroitnews.com/story/news/local/michigan/2017/08/28/woman-gets-life-prison-murder-witnessed-parrot/105060404/ (Thank you to UCLAW graduate David Kaye for calling this story to the authors' attention).

Problem 10-8: News to Me

Ethel is charged with murdering Fred in the apartment they shared. To prove the time of the killing, the prosecution calls next-door neighbor, Lucy, who testifies as follows:

PROSECUTOR: What time did you hear the gunshots?

A: I heard them at 3:00 p.m.

PROSECUTOR: And how do you know that?

A: Well, for one thing I looked at my watch when I heard the gunshots, my watch displayed 3:00.

PROSECUTOR: Any other reason you knew it was 3:00?

A: Yes. I had been listening to the radio, and I heard the shots right after the announcer said "Here's the 3:00 news." At the same time, I was looking out the window of my apartment, and I saw Quasimodo, the village's long-time bell-ringer, climb the church tower and by pulling the rope he rang the church bells three times.

DEFENDANT'S ATTORNEY: Objection to all this Your Honor, hearsay.

PROSECUTOR: No hearsay is involved, Your Honor. The watch, the radio and the church bells are all mechanical devices.

JUDGE: *What is your response to the prosecutor's argument?*

Problem 10-9: Photo Finish

Auto accident case. To prove the extent of the damages to his car, plaintiff Phil offers into evidence a photograph of the car, taken shortly after the accident. Defendant Dean objects that the photo is hearsay because it constitutes an assertion about the car's condition. *Is this a valid argument?*

Plaintiff's counsel: If the hearsay objection is overruled, offer the photograph into evidence after laying a proper foundation through the testimony of Phil.

Problem 10-10: Print — Out?

Auto accident case. To prove the value of her car that was totaled in the accident, plaintiff Paula's attorney makes the following request:

"Your Honor, I ask that Plaintiff's Exhibit #1 be received in evidence. Exhibit #1 is a computer printout taken from the Used Car Dealers Internet Website, indicating the fair market value for plaintiff's make and model of car."

In response to defendant Deena's hearsay objection, plaintiff states that the printout is machine-generated, so no declarant is involved. *How should the judge rule?*

Problem 10-11: My Better Side

Kay Mart is charged with armed robbery of a department store. The prosecution offers into evidence a visual recording taken by the store's security camera, showing Kay in profile pointing a gun at the store clerk and grabbing cash out of the register. In response to Kay's hearsay objection, the prosecution responds that the video camera that is the source of the recording is not a hearsay declarant. *How should the judge rule?*

Problem 10-12: Just the Ticket

Romero is on trial for speeding. Officer Ward testifies that at around 2:00 p.m. on October 12, she was assigned to traffic detail on Cyclone Ave., a residential street with a speed limit of 30 m.p.h. She was standing outside her patrol vehicle when she observed Romero's Camaro coming in her direction. Her testimony continues as follows:

PROSECUTOR: Officer Ward, what happened after you first observed Romero's Camaro?

A: I raised my radar gun and pointed it in the direction of the Camaro. I focused the radar gun on the car until a reading appeared on the screen indicating the speed of the car.

PROSECUTOR: And what was that speed?

A: 53 m.p.h.

DEFENDANT'S ATTORNEY: Objection, hearsay. The radar gun reading is an out-of-court assertion because it resulted from the officer's pointing it in the direction of the Camaro.

PROSECUTOR: *What is your response to defense counsel's argument?*

§ 10.07 Was the Statement Made "Out-of-Court"?

A. General Rule

A statement is made "out-of-court" if it is made any time other than by a witness during the trial in which the statement is offered. Even if a statement has been given under oath and in a courtroom proceeding, for purposes of the hearsay rule it is an out-of-court statement if it was not made during the trial in which it is offered.

B. "Out-of-Court" Problems

Problem 10-13: On My Word

Pola sues Dana for personal injuries growing out of an auto accident. During the trial, in an effort to prove that Dana ran a stop sign, counsel for Pola makes the following request:

> Your Honor, I ask that Pola's Exhibit #2 be received in evidence. Exhibit #2 is an excerpt from the transcript of the testimony that Stan gave when Dana's attorney took Stan's deposition. In this deposition excerpt, Stan testified that Dana's car ran a stop sign before colliding with Pola's car.

Does the deposition excerpt constitute an out-of-court statement?

Problem 10-14: On My Word Again

In Problem 10-13, counsel for Pola makes the following request:

> Your Honor, I ask that Pola's Exhibit #3 be received in evidence. Exhibit #3 is an excerpt from the transcript of the prior trial of this case, which resulted in a mistrial. In this excerpt from the prior trial, Stan testified that Dana's car ran a stop sign before colliding with Pola's car.

Does the trial excerpt constitute an out-of-court statement?

Problem 10-15: Big Mouth

In Problem 10-13, counsel for defendant Dana cross-examines plaintiff Pola as follows:

DEFENDANT'S ATTORNEY: You had just finished talking on your cellular phone when the collision occurred, correct?

A: I wouldn't say that. I'd finished talking at least three or four minutes before the collision.

DEFENDANT'S ATTORNEY: You talked about this case with a friend in the back of the courtroom during the court's morning recess, didn't you?

A: Just a little bit.

DEFENDANT'S ATTORNEY: Didn't you tell your friend during this recess that you'd finished the call just moments before the collision?

Is defense counsel's last question an attempt to offer evidence of an out-of-court statement?

Problem 10-16: Same Ol', Same Ol'

In Problem 10-13, plaintiff Pola testifies as follows:

PLAINTIFF'S ATTORNEY: What speed were you driving just before the collision occurred?

A: Exactly as I told the police officer who showed up soon after the accident, I was driving no more than 25 m.p.h.

Has the plaintiff testified to an out-of-court statement?

§ 10.08 What Is a "Statement"?

A. Definition and Examples

With this definitional underbrush behind you, consider Step One of the Five-Step Hearsay Matrix: "Does evidence constitute an out-of-court statement?" No matter what it is offered to prove, an out-of-court utterance can constitute hearsay only if it qualifies as a "statement." This term generally poses no problem under Rule 801(a), as it applies broadly to all intentional or purposeful oral or written assertions.

Example 1

PLAINTIFF'S ATTORNEY: What happened after the collision?

A: A bystander walked over to my car and said that the car that hit me had run a red light.

The bystander's post-collision remark is an assertive statement concerning a past event.

Example 2

PLAINTIFF'S ATTORNEY: What happened next?

A: Ann told me that she was going to go to Joe's office and sign the contract.

Ann's remark is an assertive statement concerning an intended future act.

Example 3

PLAINTIFF'S ATTORNEY: Police Officer Tracy, did you observe the traffic collision?

A: I did.

PLAINTIFF'S ATTORNEY: Prior to the collision, did you observe the defendant's BMW?

A: Yes.

PLAINTIFF'S ATTORNEY: And did you prepare a written accident report afterwards?

A: I did.

PLAINTIFF'S ATTORNEY: And does that accident report refer to the defendant's BMW?

A: Yes. The accident report states that the blue BMW ran the red light.

The statement in the accident report is a written assertion.

Subdivision (a) of the Advisory Committee's Note to Rule 801 states that "The effect of the definition of 'statement' is to exclude from the operation of the hearsay rule all evidence of conduct, verbal or non-verbal, not intended as an assertion." Because the definition equates the term "statement" with "intent to assert," a verbal remark constitutes hearsay only if the speaker intended to make the assertion that the statement is offered to prove.

Example 6

Testimony of plaintiff in a negligence action:

PLAINTIFF'S ATTORNEY: And what happened after you got out of your car following the collision?

A: I grabbed the back of my neck and yelled, "Ouch."

"Ouch" constitutes a non-assertive verbal reflex reaction admissible to prove that the plaintiff was in pain. Because the statement is reflexive, it is not the equivalent of the plaintiff's purposeful assertion, "My neck hurts."

Example 7

Testimony of the surviving widow who is the executor of a will in a will contest case, offered to prove that a sled is part of the decedent's estate:

ATTORNEY FOR THE WILL PROPONENT: What word did your husband Orson often utter while asleep during that period of time?

A: Almost every night during that period, my dear Orson repeatedly murmured "Rosebud" while he was sleeping.

"Rosebud" is a non-assertive remark because the circumstances do not support an inference that Orson intended to make an assertion.

B. Hidden Statements

Rule 801's formulaic definition of hearsay as a statement offered "to prove the truth of the matter asserted" would produce unjust anomalies were it to be applied mechanically to speakers' literal words. People can express the same thought in a myriad of ways. If the hearsay rule is to be fair and sensible, decisions about whether a statement is hearsay should depend on what people intend to communicate, and not merely on the happenstance of their chosen words. Similarly, people may communicate through behavior instead of or in addition to making statements, and when they do it makes sense to treat behavior as assertions.

The subsections below describe common situations in which statements are hearsay even though the words are not offered for their literal truth.

1. Sub-Assertions

A party might try to avoid the hearsay rule by offering a statement into evidence for the truth of a sub-assertion. The party might claim, "There's no hearsay problem because I'm not relying on the truth of the entire statement, but only on the accuracy of a sub-assertion. Therefore I'm not offering the statement for its literal truth." However, this argument doesn't work because a declarant's intent to assert extends to sub-assertions.

Example

Jill is charged with a murder that occurred at the top of a hill around 3:00 p.m. To prove that Jill had the opportunity to commit the murder, the prosecutor calls a witness to testify that at around 4:00 p.m. on the day of the murder, a friend told the witness, "About an hour ago, I saw Jack and Jill run up the hill to fetch a pail of water." In response to the defense attorney's hearsay objection, the prosecutor argues that "I'm offering the statement only to prove that Jill ran up the hill at around 3:00 p.m. I'm not offering the portion of the statement referring to the pail of water. Because I'm not offering the entire statement for its literal truth, it's not hearsay." The argument fails because the declarant's intent to assert extends to the sub-assertion about the time of day, and the sub-assertion's relevance depends on its accuracy.

2. Linked Assertions

You often have to go outside the boundaries of a declarant's specific remark to decide whether it constitutes an assertion and if so, what it asserts. That is, you often have to link a speaker's statement to the context in which it is made to determine whether it constitutes an assertion for hearsay purposes. For example, assume that a conversation between Al and Ed includes the following question and answer:

Al: Did Jenni run the red light?

Ed: Yes.

Here, Ed's statement has meaning only if you link it to Al's question. Ed's linked assertion is, "Jenni ran the red light."

The context that demonstrates assertiveness may consist not only of a linked remark, but also of a linked event. For example, assume that after watching a golfer sink a hole-in-one, Monica says with a sigh, "Someday maybe that will finally be me." The context suggests that Monica has asserted, "I have never had a hole-in-one."

3. Invisible Assertions

An assertion may be implied even though neither the question nor the answer refers to it explicitly. This commonly occurs when information is presented as based on a witness' own perceptions, when in reality the witness is simply a conduit for information supplied by an invisible declarant.

Example 1

PLAINTIFF'S ATTORNEY: Following the accident, did you talk to the plaintiff?

A: I did.

PLAINTIFF'S ATTORNEY: After talking to the plaintiff, what was your belief as to whether the defendant had run a red light?

A: I had the firm impression that the defendant had run a red light.

Here, neither the questions nor the answers explicitly refer to an out-of-court assertion. Yet it's obvious that the witness' "firm impression" is based on the plaintiff's out-of-court assertion that the defendant ran the red light. Since that explicit out-of-court assertion would be hearsay, so is the witness' "firm impression."

Invisible assertions are not always as apparent as in the example above. Consider this next testimonial excerpt.

Example 2

PLAINTIFF'S ATTORNEY: Did your spouse talk to the landlord?

A: Yes.

Here, the dialogue itself furnishes no clue as to whether the answer represents the witness' first-hand knowledge, or information imparted to the witness by the spouse (or by someone else). A cross-examiner who has reason to believe the latter may ask the judge for "permission to take the witness on *voir dire* for the purpose of asking foundational questions." If the judge grants permission and the foundational questioning reveals a previously invisible assertion, the cross-examiner may be able to exclude the testimony on hearsay grounds. The process might unfold as in the following example.

Example 3

PLAINTIFF'S ATTORNEY: Did your spouse talk to the landlord?

DEFENDANT'S ATTORNEY: Excuse me, Your Honor, permission to ask a few *voir dire* questions?

JUDGE: For what reason, Counsel?

DEFENDANT'S ATTORNEY: For the purpose of showing that the witness' answer is hearsay.

JUDGE: Well, I'll permit just a few questions. The jury may remain in the courtroom.[*]

---

[*] Judges have discretion to permit mid-examination interruptions for foundational questioning. Depending on the likely length of the *voir dire* questioning and the risk that the *voir dire* questioning will disclose to the jury important information that the judge might later determine is

DEFENDANT'S ATTORNEY: Were you personally present when your spouse talked to the landlord?

A: No.

DEFENDANT'S ATTORNEY: So is it fair to assume that your awareness of whether your spouse talked to the landlord is based on your spouse having told you that such a conversation took place?

A: Yes, that's right.

DEFENDANT'S ATTORNEY: Based on the witness' testimony, I object based on hearsay grounds to the witness' testifying to whether the spouse talked to the landlord.

JUDGE: I'll sustain that objection. Let's resume direct examination.

In *United States v. Brown*,[5] an income tax preparer was charged with tax fraud for overstating deductions on nearly all the tax returns he prepared. At trial, a government agent testified that she had examined the tax returns prepared by the defendant and had found that they consistently overstated deductions. The government agent never referred to out-of-court assertions during her testimony. However, the court concluded that the agent could only have known that deductions were overstated on the tax returns if the agent had talked to the taxpayers for whom the returns were prepared and been told by the taxpayers what information they had supplied to the defendant. Because the government agent's testimony "had to have been based" on out-of-court assertions, the court held that the agent's testimony was improper hearsay and reversed the conviction.

4. Vicarious Assertions

A vicarious assertion consists of a statement made by a declarant that is treated as though it had been made by a different person, who typically is a party to the lawsuit in which the assertion is offered. Rule 801(d)(2) enumerates four types of vicarious assertions, and Chapter 13 examines each of them.

Example

Butch and Sundance are charged with robbing the Last National Bank. The prosecution offers evidence that Sundance and Butch drove to the bank together, that Sundance waited in the car outside the bank with the motor running while Butch ran into the bank and held it up at gunpoint, and that Butch then ran out of the bank and jumped into the car as Sundance sped off. While inside the bank, Butch told the teller that "We've got guns and we're prepared to shoot if necessary." In Sundance's trial, under Rule 801(d)(2)(e), a judge would treat Butch's assertion as though Sundance had made

---

inadmissible, the judge also has discretion to decide whether the *voir dire* questioning should be conducted out of the jury's hearing. *See* Rule 104 (c).

5. 548 F.2d 1194 (5th Cir. 1977).

it because they conspired together to rob the bank and the statement was made in the course of the robbery.

5. Assertive Conduct

As defined in Rule 801(a), a statement includes "nonverbal conduct of a person, if it is intended by the person as an assertion." When a person uses nonverbal conduct as a substitute for verbal expression, treating the conduct as hearsay makes sense. The hearsay dangers are virtually the same, whether declarants communicate through words or conduct.

Example 1

PROSECUTOR: Police Officer Tracy, what happened after you took the defendant to the police station?

A: We conducted a lineup.

PROSECUTOR: Was Vic Timm present to observe the lineup?

A: Yes.

PROSECUTOR: And what happened?

A: I asked Vic if he recognized any of the people in the lineup as the person who held up the convenience store. Vic pointed to Number 3.

For hearsay purposes, Vic's act of pointing is a statement, the equivalent of a verbal assertion, "Number 3 is the robber." A conclusion that Number 3 robbed the store depends on Vic's sincerity as well as on the accuracy of his perception and memory. Even a form of the narrative danger remains. For example, did Vic point at the person he meant to identify?

By contrast, nonverbal conduct that does *not* reflect an intent to assert is not hearsay. "Pure conduct" (that is, conduct not intended as an assertion) is not hearsay because it is not communicative and therefore is not thought to give rise to the hearsay dangers.

Example 2

Testimony of Bystander in an auto accident case:

PLAINTIFF'S ATTORNEY: What happened before you saw the defendant's car collide with the plaintiff's car?

A: I saw the defendant's car swerving back and forth.

PLAINTIFF'S ATTORNEY: Did anything else happen before the collision?

A: Yes. A pedestrian who had started to cross the street when the light changed to green had to dive back to the corner to avoid being hit by the defendant's car.

Both the driver's swerving and the pedestrian's reactions constitute non-assertive (pure) conduct tending to prove that the defendant was driving dangerously. The defendant's driving cannot reasonably be regarded as the defendant's chosen means of communicating the idea that "I am driving dangerously." Nor are the pedestrian's reactions an intended way of asserting that "the defendant is driving dangerously" or "I'm frightened." The defendant is driving and the pedestrian is diving for cover; neither is engaged in communicative conduct.

While non-assertive conduct may not raise *hearsay* concerns, conduct may be ambiguous and, if so, its admission may raise *relevance* concerns. Assume, for example, that a party seeks to prove that a ship was seaworthy. The party's witness is an onlooker standing on a dock who testifies that an experienced ship captain looked over the ship from stem to stern, then set out to sea in it. The captain's behavior appears to be non-assertive conduct from which a judge or juror may infer that the ship was in good condition.

However, because the captain did not verbally explain what she or he was doing, the relevance of the behavior is uncertain. Perhaps the captain was not conducting a safety inspection, but instead was looking for the piece of chewing gum that had been stuck onto the side of the ship a few days earlier. Or, perhaps the captain was suicidal and sailed off despite recognizing that the ship was likely to sink. The point is that behavior unaccompanied by verbal explanations may be ambiguous. If this fact does not render the evidence of conduct irrelevant, it may reduce its probative value and hence make a judge more likely to exclude it under Rule 403.

6. Implied Assertions

The concept of "implied assertions" raises issues that Rule 801's definition of hearsay does not conclusively resolve. Implying an assertion presents no difficulty when a declarant's words do not literally express the declarant's clearly intended meaning. Again, people can express the same thought in many different ways. To prevent unfair outcomes based on insignificant and random variations in declarants' particular word choices, judges need only apply the hearsay rule as though the intended meanings had been expressed explicitly.

For example, assume that Pedro is a plaintiff in an auto accident case. If Pedro were to testify that a bystander told Pedro, "Dan's car ran the stop sign," the bystander's assertion would be hearsay if offered to prove that Dan drove negligently. But assume that Pedro testifies that the bystander had made one of these remarks:

- "I can't believe that Dan didn't notice the stop sign."
- "Dan's car was an accident waiting to happen."
- "Look at how Dan was driving and tell me that we don't need more traffic cops on our streets."
- "Teenage child of mine, I don't ever want you driving like Dan."
- "Wow — what insane driving!"
- "Didn't Dan's car go through a stop sign?"

In each instance, Pedro might argue that the hearsay rule doesn't apply because he is not trying to prove that statements are literally accurate. For example, Pedro might say, "I'm not offering the third statement to prove that more traffic cops are needed on the streets. Therefore, the remark is not hearsay." Similarly, Pedro might argue, "The last two utterances are not assertions — one is an exclamation and the other is a question."

However, a judge could reasonably conclude that in each instance the bystander simply chose different ways of intentionally expressing the same idea: that Dan was driving carelessly. If so, it's fair to apply the hearsay rule to what the bystander intended to assert. Otherwise, hearsay rulings would turn on inconsequential variations in word choices.

When the relevance of a statement depends on the accuracy of a declarant's belief, many commentators continue to argue that the statement should be treated as hearsay regardless of the declarant's intent. The famous (to Evidence aficionados, anyway) English case of *Wright v. Tatham* exemplifies their argument.

Decided by the House of Lords in 1838, the case grew out of a will contest filed by Admiral Tatham (pronounced "Tatum"), the sole surviving heir of his wealthy uncle, the decedent John Marsden. Admiral Tatham's lofty financial expectations were shattered when Uncle John left his entire estate to John's steward, Wright. Seeking what he no doubt considered his proper due, the Admiral sought to have Uncle John's will set aside on the ground that his uncle was mentally incompetent at the time he made the will. The hearsay issue involved a series of letters that Wright sought to offer into evidence to prove that Marsden was sane. Marsden had moved from England to America, and the letters at issue were written to Marsden by various acquaintances and relatives of his in England. The letters were quite ordinary. For example, one described a sea voyage that the letter writer had taken, and another asked Marsden to propose a settlement to help resolve a property dispute back in England. Wright's theory in offering the letters into evidence was that since people would not write such letters to a man who had lost his marbles, the letters constituted evidence that Marsden was competent when he signed his will. Moreover, since Wright was not offering the letters for the truth of what they asserted (for example, Wright was not trying to prove that the account of the sea voyage was accurate), the letters were not hearsay.

The majority of the House of Lords excluded the letters as improper hearsay. The reasoning was that just as the letters would have been hearsay had the letter writers directly asserted, "Marsden is sane," so should they be hearsay when a party asks for an inference of sanity to be drawn from the writers having corresponded with Marsden in a way that suggested that the writers believed him to be sane. In the words of Baron Parke, "The letters which are offered only to prove the competence of the testator, that is the truth of the implied statements therein contained, were properly rejected, as the mere statement or opinion of the writer would certainly have been inadmissible."

From the standpoint of the hearsay dangers, the outcome in *Wright v. Tatham* seems justifiable. The declarants' (letter writers') statements allow an inference that Marsden was sane only if their belief in his sanity was accurate. Thus, Admiral Tatham's lawyer could make a strong argument for needing to test the accuracy of their belief through cross-examination. The Admiral's lawyer might have wanted to probe their *sincerity:* the letter writers may have only pretended to act as though Marsden was competent in order to curry favor with him in the hopes that he would remember them in an eventual will. Similarly, the lawyer may have wanted to probe their *perception* and *memory:* had the letter writers had a sufficient opportunity to evaluate Marsden's competence in England? What did they know of his competence since he'd moved to America? And as Marsden had moved to America some time before the letters had been written, how accurate were the letter writers' memories of Marsden's competence? Subdivision (a) of the Advisory Committee Note to Rule 801 acknowledges that the credibility of assertions such as those in *Wright v. Tatham are* untested, but argues that the "Committee is of the view that these dangers are minimal in the absence of an intent to assert and do not justify the loss of the evidence on hearsay grounds." Thus, under Rule 801, the hearsay rule applies only to verbal or nonverbal language "intended as an assertion." A judge who ruled on the admissibility of the letters today would reason that they are not hearsay unless the letter writers *intended* to assert, "Marsden is sane." In the absence of such an intent, the letters constitute non-hearsay.

Nevertheless, the existence of the hearsay dangers leads many evidence scholars to support the outcome of *Wright v. Tatham.* For example, in *Federal Rules of Evidence in a Nutshell,* respected evidence scholar Michael Graham argues that the Advisory Committee's "apparent attempted rejection" of the holding in *Wright v. Tatham* is "as unfortunate as it is incorrect." For Graham, "When a statement is offered to infer the declarant's state of mind from which a given fact is inferred in the form of an opinion or otherwise, since the truth of the matter asserted [that is, the declarant's belief] must be assumed in order for the nonasserted inference to be drawn, the statement is properly classified as hearsay." At the same time, Graham recognizes that the argument is of little practical importance, as even if assertions such as those in *Wright v. Tatham* are deemed to be hearsay, they will generally be admitted under Rule 807, the residual exception that admits trustworthy hearsay.

U.S. v. Zenni (E.D. Ky. 1980) exemplifies Rule 801's approach to unintended assertions as set forth in the Advisory Committee's Note. In that case, police officers lawfully entered the defendant's residence to look for evidence of illegal bookmaking activity. While they were inside the premises, the officers answered the phone a number of times. The callers asked for bets to be placed on various sporting events, saying such things as "Put $50 on Dipsy Doodle in the fifth race at Pimlico." The prosecution offered the phone callers' statements into evidence to prove that the defendant had been engaged in bookmaking. In other words, just as Wright had offered the contents of letters as circumstantial evidence of the letter writers' belief that Marsden was sane, so the prosecutor in *Zenni* offered the contents of the phone calls as circumstantial evidence that the callers believed that they were calling a bookmaker, leading to a further inference that the defendant was a bookmaker.

The *Zenni* court held that the calls were non-hearsay. Because it was "obvious that these persons did not intend to make an assertion" that the defendant was a bookmaker, the calls were not barred by Rules 801–802.

Zenni represents the majority approach to "implied assertions." When a declarant's out-of-court assertion is used as circumstantial evidence that a fact that is not directly asserted is true, the assertion is hearsay only if the judge concludes that the declarant intended to assert the fact. However, by making the outcome turn on judges' assessments of declarants' "intent," the *Zenni* approach to whether implied assertions constitute hearsay requires subjective judicial interpretation and thereby creates uncertainty as to the application of the hearsay rule. The Advisory Committee came down on the side of admissibility of out-of-court statements when judges are undecided about whether a speaker intended to make an assertion. The Committee's Note to Rule 801(a) points out that the burden of proof is on the party claiming that an intent to assert existed.

Practice Tip: Implied Assertions and the Hearsay Dangers

The continuing debate over the application of the hearsay rule to implied assertions creates space for you to argue that a judge should consider an unintended assertion to be hearsay and therefore exclude it. The more difficult textual support for such an argument is that *Zenni* and cases like it have simply misinterpreted Rule 801(a)'s definition of what constitutes a "statement." *Zenni* reads the final phrase, "if it is intended by the person as an assertion," as applying both to "oral or written assertions" and to "non-verbal conduct." However, the placement of the comma in Rule 801(a) can give rise to a plausible argument that the phrase "if it is intended by the person as an assertion" applies only to "non-verbal conduct." Under this interpretation, the phrase "oral or written assertion" may encompass not only what a declarant intended to assert, but also the declarant's subjective beliefs that underlie the assertion, regardless of whether or not the declarant intended to assert those beliefs. You may also make a broader policy-based argument asking a judge to rule that an implied assertion is hearsay by stressing that the "hearsay dangers" exist when judges admit implied assertions into evidence as non-hearsay. For example, examine the phone callers' statements in *Zenni*. Statements such as "put $50 on Horse Hide to win the third race at Aqueduct" are relevant to prove that the recipient of the phone call is a bookie *if* the caller was sincere about wanting to place a bet and *if* the caller correctly perceived and remembered that the phone number belonged to a bookie. If your argument persuades a judge that the presence of the hearsay dangers undermines the reliability of an unintended assertion, the judge might exclude an out-of-court statement as hearsay.

C. "Statement" Problems

The following problems focus on whether offered evidence constitutes a "statement." Remember that evidence might constitute a statement yet ultimately be admissible for a non-hearsay purpose or under a hearsay exception or exemption.

Problem 10-17: Flight

Andy Amo is charged with murdering Smith. Prosecution witness Magoo is prepared to testify that Magoo heard gunshots and saw Amo running away from where the shots came from. Amo argues that as the prosecution will claim that Amo's running away shows that Amo was involved in the killing, evidence of his running constitutes testimony to an out-of-court assertion, "I'm the murderer." *Is this a valid argument?*

Problem 10-18: Knock Knock Who's There

Lucy is charged with shooting and killing Schroeder in his apartment on May 1 at around 2:00 a.m.; Lucy's defense is an alibi. Which if any of the following excerpts of testimony allow the prosecution to establish Lucy's presence at the scene of the shooting without offering evidence of an out-of-court assertion?

1. Charlie will testify that he was talking on the phone to Schroeder on May 1 at around 2:00 a.m. when he heard what sounded like a knock on a door. Shortly afterward, Charlie heard Schroeder say, "Well, well, it's Lucy."

2. Charlie will testify that he was talking on the phone to Schroeder on May 1 at around 2:00 a.m. when he heard what sounded like a knock on a door. Shortly afterward, Charlie heard Schroeder say, "Lucy, you've never looked better."

3. Charlie will testify that he was talking on the phone to Schroeder on May 1 at around 2:00 a.m. when he heard what sounded like a knock on a door. Shortly afterward, Charlie heard Schroeder say, "Lucy, please take off your shoes before coming in."

4 Charlie will testify that he was talking on the phone to Schroeder on May 1 at around 2:00 a.m. when he heard what sounded like a knock on a door. Charlie will further testify that Lucy always lets people know she's at the door by knocking in a way that imitates the theme of Beethoven's Fifth Symphony, and that's the sound of the knock that Charlie heard when he was talking to Schroeder.

5. Charlie will testify, "I visited Lucy three days after the shooting. I saw an open wall safe, looked inside and found a locked diary. I broke open the lock and looked through it, and I recognized the handwriting as Lucy's. I took it with me and gave it to the police." The prosecution offers the last entry of the diary into evidence; it reads, "May 1, 2:00 a.m. Visited Schroeder's apartment."

6. None of the above involves out-of-court assertions.

7. All of the above involve out-of-court assertions.

Problem 10-19: Hard Landing I

Flora Walker sues McBroccoli's for personal injuries after she allegedly slipped and fell on a puddle of mustard that the restaurant had failed to clean up. To prove that the floor was unsafe, Flora testifies that while lying on the restaurant's floor after having slipped, Flora heard one nearby diner say to another, "Why are restaurant personnel so careless these days?" McBroccoli's objects that the diner's remark is hearsay. Flora responds that the utterance is non-hearsay as the diner's remark does not constitute an out-of-court assertion. *Is Flora's response valid?*

Problem 10-20: Hard Landing II

Same case as previous example. To prove that the floor was unsafe, Flora proposes to testify, "I'll say again what I've said all along, that there was a huge blob of mustard on the floor." Does Flora's testimony constitute an out-of-court assertion?

Problem 10-21: Hard Landing III

Same case as previous example. To prove that the floor was unsafe, Flora proposes to testify, "Just before I slipped and fell, I noticed a McBroccoli's employee walking toward the spill holding a pail and a mop." *Is Flora testifying to the employee's out-of-court assertion?*

Problem 10-22: Help!

Caryl is charged with sexually assaulting Lorna in a car parked in a secluded spot. To counter Caryl's claim of consent, the prosecution seeks to have Lorna testify that she repeatedly honked the car's horn in an effort to summon help during the assault. *Does honking the horn constitute an out-of-court statement?*

Problem 10-23: Take Notes

Breach of contract action filed by Cain against Abel. Never having testified in court before, Cain is very nervous. Therefore, in response to direct examination questions, Cain testifies by looking at the written notes he made before trial and paraphrasing what he had written. *Is Cain testifying to out-of-court statements?*

Problem 10-24: Raise a Glass

In the breach of contract action that Cain filed against Abel, Abel's defense is that the parties never finalized the contract. To prove that the parties reached an agreement during lunch at a café on September 22, Cain calls a café server to testify, "I served lunch to Cain and Abel on September 22 and saw them toast each other with wine glasses at the conclusion of the lunch." *Is the server testifying to Cain's or Abel's out-of-court statement?*

Problem 10-25: Cell Phone

Jack Carr is charged with carjacking. Jack's defense is that he was walking down the street when a car pulled over and the driver, a stranger, asked Jack to circle the block once or twice so the stranger could pick up an order in a nearby store. When the car's owner hadn't returned after Jack circled the block once, Jack drove a few blocks away and was arrested. To prove that Jack stole the car, the prosecutor seeks to have the arresting officer testify to searching Jack incident to the arrest and finding a cell phone in his pocket. The phone rang and the officer answered it. The caller said, "The nearest chop shop is on Maple Avenue. Turn left on Maple and go about 10 blocks, then drive up the blue driveway on the right." (A "chop shop" quickly breaks down stolen cars for their parts.) *Has the caller made an out-of-court statement that is offered for its truth? Does it matter whether the defendant in the case in which the caller's statement is offered is Jack or the caller?*

Problem 10-26: Loot Lips

Jekyll is charged with bank robbery on June 4. To prove Jekyll's guilt, the prosecution calls Louie to testify as follows:

PROSECUTOR: On June 5, who was in the apartment when you arrived?

A: Hekyll and Jekyll.

PROSECUTOR: Were they both in the same room as you?

A: Yes. We were all in the living room.

PROSECUTOR: What happened after you entered the living room?

A: I saw stacks of money on a coffee table. Hekyll said that the money was the take from the bank job that he and Jekyll had pulled off the day before. Jekyll then asked me if I wanted a cup of tea. I said no, and we all left to go to the art museum to see the Impressionists exhibit.

DEFENDANT'S ATTORNEY: Objection and move to strike the last answer as irrelevant because no statement of Jekyll's pertaining to the bank robbery has been offered.

JUDGE: *What ruling?*

Problem 10-27: Slippery Slope I

The parents of Josie, a developmentally disabled 8-year-old child, sue Josie's school after Josie allegedly broke her shoulder on September 22 when using an unreasonably dangerous slide on the schoolyard without adult supervision. Josie lacks the capacity to testify. However, to prove that Josie was injured while playing on the slide, her father Wilfrid seek to testify that a few days after the accident, he walked slowly around the schoolyard with Josie and that Josie suddenly began to cry hysterically as they approached the slide. The school district's attorney objects on the ground that Josie's behavior constitutes evidence of an out-of-court statement. *As the judge, would you sustain the school district's objection?*

Problem 10-28: Slippery Slope II

In the same case, the school district seeks to offer evidence that a few days before Josie was injured, the mother of Jeff, another child with similar developmental problems, examined the slide and then allowed Jeff to play on it.

Student # 1: You are the attorney for Josie's parents. Identify the inference that the school district is likely to ask the jury to draw from the evidence of Jeff's mother's actions. Might you object to this evidence on the grounds of hearsay or lack of relevance? If so, present the argument you would make in support of your objection.

Student # 2: You are the attorney for the school district. Support the admissibility of the evidence of Jeff's mother's actions with an argument that they are relevant and do not constitute out-of-court assertions.

Problem 10-29: Slippery Slope III

During the pretrial discovery phase of the same case, the attorney for the school district takes the deposition of Josie's mother. During the deposition, Josie's mother testifies as follows:

Q: (by the school district's attorney): Do you know a father of a child in the school by the name of Max?

A: Yes, Max Dietrich.

Q: Did you ever talk to Max about Josie's injury?

A: Yes.

Q: And what did Max tell you about how Josie got hurt?

Attorney for Josie: Objection, the question calls for hearsay.

What is the effect of this objection on the deponent? Can the plaintiff's attorney instruct the client/deponent not to answer the question? Why might the plaintiff's attorney make this objection?

Problem 10-30: Slippery Slope IV

At the conclusion of pretrial discovery in the same case, the school district submits a Motion for Summary Judgment. The motion asks for the suit to be dismissed on the ground of lack of evidence that the school was responsible for Josie's injuries. Included in motion is an Affidavit of Leonard Vole. Vole's affidavit states in part that "My son attends the same school as Josie. I saw Josie in the schoolyard on September 22. When Josie left the schoolyard with her caregiver around 3:00 p.m., Josie was unhurt. On September 23, Max Dietrich, a father whose child attends the same school, told me that he was also in the schoolyard on September 22, and that he saw

Josie leave the schoolyard unhurt on that day. Max further told me that as Josie and her caregiver crossed the street, Josie stumbled and fell to the ground. According to Max, Josie immediately grabbed her shoulder and began to cry loudly.

What if any portion of this affidavit constitutes hearsay? If Josie's parents object on the ground of hearsay, should the judge sustain the objection? What are the consequences of the judge sustaining the objection?

Problem 10-31: Beersay

Tommy Ake sues The Microbrewery after he allegedly developed food poisoning as a result of drinking improperly brewed beer on the night of March 12. To prove that its beer was not the source of any symptoms that Tommy may have had, Microbrewery's manager offers to testify that the restaurant served 153 other patrons on the night of March 12 and that the manager received no other complaints about the beer. Tommy makes a hearsay objection on the ground that evidence of the lack of complaints is the equivalent of the other patrons' out-of-court assertion, "The beer was fine on March 12." *How should Tommy's lawyer respond to the objection?*

Problem 10-32: Eye Message

Jerry is charged with armed robbery. Jerry's friend Tom is present when Jerry is arrested in his apartment. The prosecution seeks to have Officer Tracy testify that after the officer told Jerry why he was under arrest and administered the "Miranda" warnings, Jerry winked at Tom and said, "Don't you remember that I was with you at the time of the robbery?"

1. The defense attorney objects to Officer Tracy's characterizing Jerry's eye movement as a wink. *How should the judge respond to this objection?*

2. The defense attorney objects to Officer Tracy's testimony that, "The defendant's wink meant that he wanted Tom to agree to a phony alibi." *How should the judge respond to this objection?*

3. The defense attorney objects to evidence of what Jerry said to Tom as hearsay. The judge should rule that:

   a. The evidence is not hearsay because Jerry is asking Tom a question, not making an assertion.

   b. The evidence is not hearsay because Jerry did not make an assertion.

   c. Under the circumstances, the judge should consider Jerry's conduct as the equivalent of the out-of-court statement, "Tom, I want you to make up an alibi for me."

   d. The evidence is not hearsay because Jerry spoke in the presence of a police officer.

Problem 10-33: A Civil Action

Environmental suit by a citizens' action group against a factory owner for allegedly polluting a stream that runs by the factory. The plant manager testifies on the factory owner's behalf as follows:

DEFENDANT'S ATTORNEY: Why did you and the plant's owner walk to the stream?

A: We were giving a tour of the factory and the grounds to a group of foreign manufacturers' representatives.

DEFENDANT'S ATTORNEY: What happened when you got to the stream?

A: The owner dipped a cup into the stream and took a drink of water.

PLAINTIFF'S ATTORNEY: Objection, hearsay. Evidence that the owner drank water from the stream is the equivalent of the owner's assertion that the stream is not polluted.

JUDGE: Defense Counsel, any response?

DEFENDANT'S ATTORNEY: Yes, Your Honor, just briefly. The owner clearly did not intend an assertion. It's not like the owner drank water from the stream during a televised news conference. Drinking the water was simply non-assertive conduct, admissible as evidence that the water is safe.

JUDGE: *Does the owner's conduct constitute the owner's out-of-court assertion?*

Problem 10-34: Need Moe Money

Sally sues Moe Torist for personal injuries resulting from a car accident.

(a) To prove that Moe was at fault, Sally offers to testify that after the collision, Sally walked over to Moe and said, "This was all your fault." Moe responded by saying "let's just exchange insurance information and get out of here." *Has Moe made a tacit out-of-court statement that he was at fault?*

(b) To prove that Moe was at fault, Sally offers into evidence a certified copy of a Judgment indicating that after a trial Moe was found guilty of misdemeanor reckless driving in the incident that resulted in the collision with Sally. *Is the Judgment of Conviction admissible in evidence? Would it matter whether trial was to a judge or a jury?*

Problem 10-35: A Ticket, Attack It

Margarita received a ticket in the mail from City for running a red light. The ticket is accompanied by two photos taken by a camera posted at the intersection that automatically takes photos of cars that run red lights. One photo depicts the car entering the intersection, the other depicts the driver. Margarita decides to fight the ticket in court. *Can she exclude the photos on the ground that they constitute out-of-court statements?*

To show that the camera was functioning properly, City offers an Operating Report that the camera equipment produces when it records a car running a red light. *Can Margarita exclude the Operating Report on the ground that it constitutes an out-of-court statement?*

Problem 10-36: Brief Case I

Hawkeye is charged with possession of illegal drugs that were found in a briefcase. To prove that the briefcase in court is the one in which the illegal drugs were found, the prosecution calls Officer Marple to testify, "I recognize the briefcase as the same one because it has the name 'Hawkeye' embossed on the side." *Is the officer testifying to the briefcase owner's out-of-court assertion? If so, what is that assertion?*

Problem 10-37: Brief Case II

Same case as Problem 10-36. To prove that the briefcase in which the illegal drugs were found belongs to Hawkeye, the prosecution calls Officer Marple to testify, "The briefcase in which I found the drugs had the name 'Hawkeye' embossed on the side." *Is the officer testifying to the briefcase owner's out-of-court assertion? If so, what is that assertion?*

Problem 10-38: Alibi-Bye

Rosie Olla is charged with murder; her defense is an alibi. To disprove Rosie's alibi, the prosecution calls Officer Gomez to testify that the officer arrested Rosie in Rosie's mother's apartment on the afternoon of the murder. When informed of the charge, Rosie immediately said that she'd been with her mother all day long. At that point, Rosie's mom fainted. *Does mom's fainting constitute an assertion? If so, what is the assertion?*

Problem 10-39: Exclamation!

Don is charged with physical abuse of his seven-year-old son, Vince. The prosecutor calls Vince's teacher Tom to testify that when arguing with a classmate during recess, Vince cried out, "At least your dad doesn't keep whipping you with a belt!" *Does Vince's exclamation constitute an assertion? If so, what is that assertion?*

Problem 10-40: At the Movies: Take Dictation

In the film *The Wrong Man*,[6] Manny goes into a loan office to seek a loan. The employees think that he is the man who robbed them about a month earlier using a note that instructed the employee to hand over the money in the cash drawer, but misspelled the last word as "draw." A loan office employee calls the police, who arrest Manny. At the police station, a police officer twice dictates the handwritten note that the robber used in the course of the robbery, each time asking Manny to

---

6. Universal Pictures (1956).

write down by hand what he dictates. The second time Manny writes down what the police officer says, Manny leaves the "er" off the final word, "drawer." Manny is charged with the robbery and the prosecution wants to offer into evidence the copies of the robbery note that Manny wrote from the police officer's dictation. *Do the copies constitute out-of-court statements by Manny?*

§ 10.09 Common Hearsay Misconceptions

In an effort to spare you some of the anguish felt by previous generations of law students, the subsections below clarify common hearsay misconceptions.

A. "It's Not Hearsay If You Paraphrase"

One common misconception is that what the hearsay rule prevents is testimony to a declarant's exact words. Paraphrasing, then, seemingly avoids the hearsay problem.

For example, a questioner seeking to introduce evidence that a bystander saw the defendant's car run a red light might try to avoid the hearsay rule by phrasing the question as follows:

Q: Without using the bystander's exact words, can you give us the gist of what the bystander said to you following the collision?

The ploy fails. No matter how loosely paraphrased a declarant's out-of-court assertion, the answer is hearsay if it's offered for the truth of its contents. In other words, the hearsay analysis of these answers would be identical:

a. "The bystander said, 'The Mercedes ran a red light.'"

b. "The bystander indicated that the light for the Mercedes was red."

c. "The bystander indicated that the Mercedes entered the intersection illegally, after the light had changed."

d. "The bystander indicated that the Mercedes driver failed to follow the driving laws."

B. "It's Not Hearsay If the Witness Is Also the Declarant"

As mentioned earlier, the typical hearsay situation involves two people: the declarant, and the in-court "conduit" witness who testifies to the declarant's out-of-court assertion. Perhaps a resulting misperception is that the hearsay rule is inapplicable when the declarant and the in-court witness are one and the same person. In reality, when a witness testifies to the witness' own out-of-court assertion, the hearsay analysis is identical. To be admissible, the out-of-court assertion must qualify either for a non-hearsay use or a hearsay exception or exemption. For example, consider this brief testimonial excerpt:

PLAINTIFF'S ATTORNEY: And on that date and time, what happened?

A: I saw two cars collide.

PLAINTIFF'S ATTORNEY: Did you speak to either of the drivers after the collision?

A: I did. I walked over and spoke to the driver of the blue car.

PLAINTIFF'S ATTORNEY: And what did you say to the driver of the blue car?

A: I told the driver that the Mercedes ran the red light.

In this example, if what the witness said to the driver of the blue car is hearsay, it is hearsay regardless of whether the driver or the witness testifies to the statement.[7]

This outcome seems to conflict with the earlier notion that hearsay protects a party's opportunity to cross-examine adverse witnesses. If the witness and the hearsay declarant are the same person, the adversary does in fact have an opportunity for cross-examination. In the example above, for example, the defense attorney can cross-examine the witness concerning what the witness said to the Mercedes driver. Therefore, you might argue, the hearsay bar should not apply when witnesses testify to their own out-of-court statements.

A technical response to this argument is that the hearsay rule provides the opportunity for *contemporaneous* cross-examination. In other words, the statement is hearsay because the cross-examiner did not have an opportunity to question the declarant *at the time the out-of-court statement was made.* This may not strike you as a compelling counter-argument, since cross-examination is never fully contemporaneous. Perhaps a better one is simply this: if the witness is in court, *the witness should testify to the event, not to the out-of-court statement.* Witnesses are supposed to provide judges and jurors with their best current recollections of past events, and they should testify to what they saw or heard, not to what they said out of court about what they saw or heard.

Thus, no hearsay problem would arise had the testimony above gone as follows:

PLAINTIFF'S ATTORNEY: And on that date and time, what happened?

A: I saw two cars collide, a blue car and a Mercedes.

PLAINTIFF'S ATTORNEY: Did you notice either of the cars prior to the collision?

A: Yes. I saw the Mercedes, and it ran the red light.

---

7. Rule 801(d)(1) does provide three categories of hearsay exceptions (though defined by the Federal Rules of Evidence as "non-hearsay") based on a declarant also testifying in court. Chapter 12 considers these "exceptions." At this point, it is enough that you realize that out-of-court statements are not routinely admissible simply because the people who made them also testify at trial.

C. "The Statement Isn't Hearsay If It's Circumstantial Evidence"

When an out-of-court statement is offered as the basis of an inference that the offering party wants the factfinder to draw, a common misperception is that the statement isn't offered for its truth because the fact asserted and the conclusion are different. In reality, *if the inference depends on the accuracy of the out-of-court statement*, the statement is hearsay.

Example

In a wrongful termination case, the plaintiff claims that she was illegally fired because of her physical disability. The plaintiff seeks to testify, "Around the time I was fired, a co-worker told me that she had seen my boss painting over the handicapped parking symbols in the office parking lot." The plaintiff offers the co-worker's testimony to prove that the boss was antagonistic to people with physical disabilities, from which the factfinder might further infer that the plaintiff's disability was the reason for the firing. The co-worker's statement is hearsay, because the plaintiff's desired inferences cannot be drawn unless the factfinder concludes that the co-worker's statement is accurate.

D. "It's Not Hearsay If the Statement Was Made in a Police Officer's Presence"

A fourth misperception (sometimes cynically called the "Philadelphia" or the "Chicago" exception to the hearsay rule) is that anything said in the presence of a police officer is admissible in evidence. As you'll see, a police officer's presence can be a relevant factor in some hearsay situations. However, no general doctrine admits out-of-court statements simply because they were made in a police officer's presence.

Practice Tip: "Who Would I Need to Cross-Examine?"

If you are uncertain as to whether something said out-of-court is a statement that is offered for its truth, you might ask yourself the question, "Who would I need to cross-examine at the time a statement is made?" If you cannot conduct meaningful cross-examination in the absence of the person whose words are offered into evidence, that is a signal that the words constitute hearsay.

§ 10.10 Hearsay Review Problems

Problem 10-41: Carded

Benny Han is charged with burglary in Denver, Colorado. Benny's defense is mistaken identity, and he testifies that he was in the state of Georgia at the time of the burglary. To substantiate this claim, Benny seeks to introduce into evidence an e-mailed receipt from Clark's Shoe Shop for the purchase of slippers. The receipt indicates an address for Clark's in Atlanta, Georgia, and is dated September 12, the day of the burglary. The last four digits of Benny's credit card number are on the receipt. *Does the receipt constitute a statement for purposes of the hearsay rule? If your answer is "yes," identify the declarant and the out-of-court assertion.*

Problem 10-42: Loretta

Loretta has been sued by homeowner Dion Tology for fraudulently inducing Dion to sign a home improvement contract. *Which if any of the items of evidence below would constitute out-of-court assertions if offered by Dion to prove that Loretta made false statements to Dion about the terms of the contract?*

1. The Better Business Bureau revoked Loretta's membership.

2. Loretta has been sued by three other customers for fraudulently inducing them to sign home improvement contracts.

3. One of Loretta's former customers said, "I'm never going to do business with a scumbag like Loretta again."

4. Loretta was fired by the home improvement company that had employed her as a salesperson.

5. Another neighbor looked out his window, saw it was Loretta ringing the bell, and refused to come to the door.

6. A citizens' action group set a pile of home improvement contracts on fire as part of a silent vigil in front of Loretta's office.

Problem 10-43: Stat!

The plaintiff in a medical malpractice case offers the following testimony of an operating room nurse to prove that the plaintiff had a life-threatening medical condition:

PLAINTIFF'S ATTORNEY: And what did the head nurse say just before the plaintiff's operation got under way?

A: The head nurse told me to order an additional three pints of blood.

DEFENDANT'S ATTORNEY: Objection, hearsay.

PLAINTIFF'S ATTORNEY: It's not hearsay because the head nurse's remark does not constitute an assertion under Rule 801. The head nurse was simply requesting additional blood, not intending an assertion about the plaintiff's medical condition.

JUDGE: *Is this a valid response to the objection?*

PLAINTIFF'S ATTORNEY: It's also not hearsay even if you rule that the nurse intended to assert that the plaintiff needed additional blood. I'd be offering that assertion only as the basis of an inference that the plaintiff had a life-threatening medical condition. Because I'd be offering the remark to prove something other than what it asserts, it's not hearsay.

JUDGE: *Is this a valid response to the objection?*

Problem 10-44: No Parking

Ruth seeks to prove that she paid a parking ticket by offering the items of evidence listed below. *Which if any of the items constitutes an out-of-court assertion that Ruth paid the ticket?*

1. Ruth's testimony that she went to the Department of Motor Vehicles two days after she received the ticket and paid it.

2. A Department of Motor Vehicles visual recording depicting Ruth handing money to a Department employee.

3. A copy of the ticket, stamped "Paid" and dated two days after the ticket was issued.

4. The absence of Ruth's name on a list compiled by a Department of Motor Vehicles employee entitled "List of Vehicle Owners With Unpaid Parking Tickets."

5. None of the above.

6. All of the above.

Problem 10-45: Instant Replay

Walt Mart is charged with stealing a jacket from a department store. The prosecution offers into evidence a visual recording made by the store security guard who observed the theft. The security guard testifies that she made the recording moments after the defendant's arrest by having a store employee play the role of the defendant and re-create the theft. Following the security guard's instructions, the recording depicts the employee walking up to the jackets, looking around, picking up a jacket and putting it on, and quickly walking out of the store. The defense makes a motion to exclude the recording, claiming that it constitutes an out-of-court assertion. *Should the judge sustain the objection?*

Problem 10-46: Bettor Beware Role-Play Exercise

In *Zenni*, the court ruled that phone callers' remarks such as "Put $50 on Ocean Wafer to win the fifth race at Pimlico" were not assertions when offered to prove that the location they were calling was used for bookmaking. The defendant to whom the phone number belonged is charged with illegal bookmaking and has pleaded not guilty.

Student # 1: You are the police officer who arrested the defendant. You answered the phone at least five times during the half-hour period you were at the bookmaking site, and in each case the caller gave an account number and placed bets of varying amounts on such events as horse racing, football, basketball, ice hockey, and tiddlywinks. You responded only with comments such as "OK" or "You're down."

(You made notes of what the phone callers said immediately after each call, and the judge has given you permission to refer to those notes during cross-examination if necessary to answer the defense counsel's questions.)

Student # 2: You are the defense attorney, and will cross-examine the arresting officer. You'll try to undermine the probative value of the phone calls as evidence that your client was engaged in bookmaking.

Remainder of Class: You are jurors whose task is to evaluate the probative value of the phone call evidence. In addition, consider whether the defense attorney had a reasonable opportunity to test the callers' sincerity, perceptions, and memories.

Problem 10-47: Reputation

Oscar the Grouch is charged with assault. To prove that he struck the alleged victim in self-defense, Oscar calls Ernie to testify that, "I have often heard the people in Oscar's neighborhood talk about him, and I can tell you that he has a reputation for peacefulness." *How should the judge rule on the prosecutor's hearsay objection? Would your answer be different if Oscar's defense were an alibi?*

Problem 10-48: Quick Hitters

Which of the offered items of evidence in the problems below constitute hearsay?

1. Testimony of an eyewitness to a bank robbery, "The suspect ran out of the bank and jumped into a Tesla," offered by the prosecutor to prove the suspect's method of escape.

2. Testimony of an eyewitness to a bank robbery, "The suspect ran out of the bank and jumped into a Tesla," offered by the prosecutor to prove that the suspect's getaway car was manufactured by Tesla Automotive Co.

3. A monthly paycheck made out to the defendant, offered by the defense to prove that the defendant did not have a motive to commit a crime.

4. A text message sent to a defendant in which the sender places an order for a quantity of illegal drugs, offered by the prosecutor to prove that the defendant is a drug dealer.

5. Testimony by a defendant's next-door neighbor that the defendant frequently hesitated when answering the neighbor's questions as to the defendant's whereabouts at the time of a murder, offered by the prosecutor to prove that the defendant's alibi testimony is phony.

6. A visual recording of a reenactment of a slip-and-fall on a sidewalk, offered by the plaintiff to prove that the sidewalk was dangerous.

7. Testimony to a statement made by the occupant of a car that rolled over and struck a tree, "It was me, and not the defendant, who was driving the car at the time of the rollover," offered by the defense in a drunk-driving prosecution to exculpate the defendant.

8. A police gang expert's testimony that two members of the 14th St. Gang told the expert that a carjacking was part of a gang initiation ritual, offered by the prosecution to support the expert's opinion that the defendant engaged in a gang activity.

§ 10.11 Hearsay and the Confrontation Clause

The "Confrontation Clause" of the Sixth Amendment states, "In all criminal proceedings, the accused shall enjoy the right ... to be confronted with the witnesses against him." While the Confrontation Clause and the hearsay rule both protect a criminal defendant's right to cross-examination, might prosecution evidence that is admissible under a hearsay exception or exemption be barred by the Confrontation Clause? The U.S. Supreme Court has confronted this issue often, and its jurisprudence has been shifting and murky. Lest you feel sorry for yourself, be glad that you are not a trial court judge having to apply this jurisprudence to a novel scenario.

In *Ohio v. Roberts*,[8] the Court ruled that hearsay was admissible under the Confrontation Clause so long as the declarant was unavailable to testify and the hearsay was admissible under a "firmly rooted" hearsay exception. If hearsay was admissible under a non-firmly rooted exception (such as Rule 807, the residual exception), hearsay could still be admissible if it had "particularized indicia of reliability."[9] Prosecutors were often able to satisfy one or the other of these pathways to admissibility, so that in practice the Confrontation Clause normally did not impose a greater obstacle to admissibility than those imposed by evidence rules.

Crawford v. Washington (U.S. Sup. Ct. 2004) literally yanked out these principles by their roots. *Crawford* re-planted the constitutional soil with a principle that admissibility for Confrontation Clause purposes turns on whether hearsay assertions are *testimonial*. Under *Crawford*, testimonial hearsay made by non-testifying and unavailable declarants is admissible against criminal defendants only if a defendant has had a previous opportunity to cross-examine the declarant. If a defendant has not had an opportunity to cross-examine a declarant, hearsay is inadmissible no matter how reliable it may appear to be and no matter how firmly rooted a hearsay exception.

In *Crawford*, the defendant was prosecuted for attempting to kill his wife Sylvia's assailant as Sylvia looked on. The defendant used a spousal privilege (*see* Chapter 17) to prevent the prosecutor from calling Sylvia as a witness. Instead, the prosecutor offered into evidence a tape recording of the statement that Sylvia had given to the police shortly after the altercation. The statement was admissible under a hearsay

---

8. 448 U.S. 56, 100 S. Ct. 2531 (1980).

9. Courts had to evaluate "indicia of reliability" by considering only the circumstances under which hearsay statements were made, and could not point to statements' consistency with other facts to conclude that the statements were reliable.

exception, Rule 804(b)(3). But *Crawford* decided that it should have been excluded because it was "testimonial." Protection against the use of testimonial assertions, said the Court, was the core of the Confrontation Clause. As the defendant in *Crawford* had not had a formal opportunity to question Sylvia (even though his own privilege claim rendered her unavailable as a witness), the statement was inadmissible under the Confrontation Clause.

Crawford did not offer a comprehensive definition of testimonial statements. Grounding the concept on the Framers' presumed understanding of what the right to confrontation encompassed in the late 1700s, the opinion opted for examples. According to the opinion, testimonial statements include affidavits, statements given to police officers in the course of custodial interrogations, depositions, courtroom testimony, and "statements that were made under circumstances which would lead an objective witness reasonably to believe that the statement would be available for use at a later trial."[10] Sylvia's statements to the police were testimonial because not only were the police gathering evidence for use at trial, but also she was herself a potential suspect at the time that she spoke with the police.

The U.S. Supreme Court cases since *Crawford* have involved one of two types of fact patterns. One fact pattern, similar to the one in *Crawford*, involves statements made by private persons *to* government agents, typically police officers. These cases are *Davis v. Washington, Michigan v. Bryant,* and *Ohio v. Clark.* The second factual scenario involves statements made *by* government agents. These cases are *Melendez-Diaz v. Massachusetts, Bullcoming v. New Mexico,* and *Williams v. Illinois.*

Statements Made TO Government Agents

The first post-*Crawford* case in the "statements to government agents" scenario was *Davis v. Washington* (U.S. Sup. Ct. 2006). In *Davis*, the Court resolved confrontation clause issues in two domestic violence prosecutions. In one case, the Court decided that Michelle McCottry's description of abuse to a 911 operator was not testimonial because it was not a result of interrogation concerning a past crime. McCottry called 911 in an effort to summon help during an ongoing emergency. McCottry was not a *witness providing information relating to a past crime* but instead was seeking police assistance to assure her safety. In the second case, the Court ruled that Amy Hammon's description of abuse to police officers was testimonial because the violence had ended by the time police officers arrived and spoke to her. Summarizing the two situations, the Court explained its reasoning as follows:

---

10. A question that *Crawford* did not address is whether courts should apply pre-*Crawford* reasoning to non-testimonial statements. In other words, if a prosecutor offers non-testimonial hearsay into evidence under a hearsay exception, must the exception be either "firmly rooted" or must the statement possess "indicia of reliability" to be admissible under the Confrontation Clause? The most likely answer is "no." The Confrontation Clause is probably not implicated when statements are non-testimonial. However, no definitive answer is possible because the Supreme Court has not yet answered the question.

Statements are non-testimonial when made in the course of police inter-rogation under circumstances objectively indicating that the primary pur-pose of the interrogation is to enable police assistance to meet an ongoing emergency. They are testimonial when the circumstances objectively indi-cate that there is no such ongoing emergency, and that the primary purpose of the interrogation is to establish or prove past events potentially relevant to later criminal prosecution.

The Court again applied Confrontation Clause analysis to a claimed "ongoing emergency" situation in *Michigan v. Bryant* (U.S. Sup. Ct. 2011). In *Bryant*, police officers interviewed Covington, a fatally wounded shooting victim. Shortly before he died, Covington provided the police with a few details about the shooting, including the shooter's identity. The Court ruled that Covington's statements were non-testimonial because the totality of the circumstances (including Covington's medical condition, the unknown whereabouts of the shooter and the informality of the interrogation) demonstrated that from an objective standpoint, the primary purpose of police questioning was to deal with an ongoing emergency rather than to gather evidence of a past crime. The decision provoked a bitter dissent from Justice Scalia, *Crawford's* author, who had gotten used to winning Confrontation Clause battles. Justice Scalia charged that the majority had created a "*faux* emergency" and demeaned the Court by leaving Confrontation Clause analysis "in a shambles."

Ohio v. Clark (U.S. Sup. Ct. 2015) is at the time of this edition the latest U.S. Supreme Court case to apply its Confrontation Clause analysis to a situation involv-ing statements made to public officials. In *Clark,* a preschool teacher asked a three-year-old boy about bruises that the teacher had noticed on the boy's body. The boy made statements indicating that the defendant was the source of the injuries. The boy did not testify at the defendant's trial for child endangerment and domestic vio-lence because the judge ruled that he was incompetent under a state law that deemed minors under 10 years of age generally incompetent to testify. In lieu of his testimony, the prosecutor called the pre-school teacher as a witness to testify to the boy's state-ments identifying the defendant as the source of the injuries. The Supreme Court held unanimously that admission of the boy's hearsay statements did not violate the Confrontation Clause. The Court ruled that the statements were not testimonial because (1) the questioner was a teacher rather than a police officer; (2) the ques-tioning occurred in the course of an ongoing emergency involving suspected child abuse; (3) the boy was not told that his answers would result in criminal charges; (4) the teacher's questioning was informal and spontaneous; and (5) statements made by very young minors were generally admissible in evidence when the Sixth Amend-ment was adopted and are unlikely to implicate the Confrontation Clause.

Statements Made BY Government Agents

Next consider the Supreme Court Confrontation Clause cases involving state-ments by government agents. In *Melendez-Diaz v. Massachusetts* (U.S. Sup. Ct. 2009), a defendant charged with drug trafficking was convicted based on an affi-davit from a police lab technician certifying that a powdery substance constituted cocaine. In *Bullcoming v. New Mexico* (U.S. Sup. Ct. 2011), the prosecutor proved a defendant's blood-alcohol level by offering into evidence a forensic laboratory report. The prosecution did call a forensic analyst to testify, but not the one who had run the test and prepared the report. In each case, a 5-4 majority ruled that admission of the laboratory reports violated the Confrontation Clause. The reports were testimonial, since they had been prepared for use at trial. The dissenters argued vehemently that the rulings misinterpreted history and angrily predicted that the rulings would hamstring the operation of already overburdened police crime labs.

Though their wisdom was bitterly contested, the majority opinions in *Melendez-Diaz* and *Bullcoming* seemed to provide relatively clear guidance to lower courts that had to rule on cases involving the admissibility of reports of test results. The clarity disappeared when the Court decided *Williams v. Illinois* (U.S. Sup. Ct. 2012). In *Williams*, prosecution DNA expert Lambatos testified to an opinion linking the defendant to a rape. The prosecutor called two other lab analysts as witnesses. One of the analysts testified to the presence of semen on vaginal swabs taken from the rape complainant. The second testifying analyst identified the defendant as the source of a DNA profile that was on the state's DNA database. Lambatos linked the DNA profile in the state's database to the DNA found on the rape complainant's vaginal swabs based on the report of a test conducted by a non-testifying analyst employed by Cellmark, a privately run out-of-state laboratory. The prosecutor did not offer the Cellmark analyst's report into evidence, nor did Lambatos testify to the contents of the Cellmark report. Instead, Lambatos testified to the very strong probability of a match between the DNA sample in the state's database and the DNA found on the vaginal swabs.

The result of *Williams* was that Lambatos' reliance on information in the Cellmark report did not violate the Confrontation Clause. Four of the justices who ruled that no violation occurred offered two bases for their opinions. One was that the Cellmark report was non-hearsay, because the information in the report was simply part of the basis of Lambatos' opinion as an expert. A second basis for the four justices' "no violation" ruling was that the Cellmark report was not testimonial because it was not inculpatory of the defendant. This portion of the four justices' opinion reads as follows:

> As a second, independent basis for our decision, we also conclude that even if the report produced by Cellmark had been admitted into evidence, there would have been no Confrontation Clause violation. The Cellmark report is very different from the sort of extrajudicial statements, such as affidavits, depositions, prior testimony, and confessions, that the Confrontation Clause was originally understood to reach. The report was produced before any suspect was identified. The report was sought not for the purpose of obtaining evidence to be used against petitioner, who was not even under suspicion at the time, but for the purpose of finding a rapist who was on the loose. And the profile that Cellmark provided was not inherently inculpatory. On the contrary, a DNA profile is evidence that tends to exculpate

all but one of the more than 7 billion people in the world today. The use of DNA evidence to exonerate persons who have been wrongfully accused or convicted is well known. If DNA profiles could not be introduced without calling the technicians who participated in the preparation of the profile, economic pressures would encourage prosecutors to forgo DNA testing and rely instead on older forms of evidence, such as eyewitness identification, that are less reliable. The Confrontation Clause does not mandate such an undesirable development. This conclusion will not prejudice any defendant who really wishes to probe the reliability of the DNA testing done in a particular case because those who participated in the testing may always be subpoenaed by the defense and questioned at trial.

Justice Thomas was the fifth justice to rule that Lambatos' testimony did not violate the Confrontation Clause. However, Justice Thomas ridiculed the arguments of the four justices who had concluded that the Cellmark report was non-hearsay and non-testimonial. Justice Thomas supplied the fifth "no violation" vote on a ground that the Cellmark report was too informal to constitute testimonial hearsay, a position that none of the other eight Justices agreed with.

The four *Williams* dissenters joined together in Justice Kagan's opinion that the information in the Cellmark report was hearsay, as Lambatos had obviously relied on its accuracy in order to arrive at an opinion that the DNA profile on the vaginal swabs matched the DNA profile of the defendant found on the state's DNA database.

In *Crawford*, Justice Scalia suggested that a great benefit of the "testimonial" concept was that outcomes of Confrontation Clause disputes would be far more uniform compared to the inconsistent outcomes that the "indicia of reliability" standard had produced. So far, however, even the Supreme Court itself is bitterly divided about the meaning and application of the Confrontation Clause. The *Bullcoming* majority argued that a testimonial statement is one whose primary purpose is to establish or prove past events. But four dissenters responded that lab reports are too reliable to exclude, possibly breathing life back into the *Ohio v. Roberts* reliability standard. Justice Thomas formed part of one majority in *Bullcoming*, and a different majority in *Williams* based on his idiosyncratic reliance on the formality of a written report.

The scope of the "ongoing emergency" concept is equally uncertain. Justice Scalia developed the concept to distinguish *Davis* from *Hammon*, then fumed when in *Bryant* Justice Sotomayor avoided the Confrontation Clause by using the same factors to create what Scalia denounced as a *faux* emergency.

Uncertainty also surrounds the "primary purpose" portion of the definition of testimonial hearsay. In *Bryant*, Justice Sotomayor suggested that judges should assess both an interrogator's purpose in asking questions (assuming that a hearsay remark isn't volunteered) and a declarant's purpose in speaking in order to evaluate primary purpose "objectively." Justice Scalia disagreed vehemently in his *Bryant* dissent: "The declarant's intent is what counts." Justice Ginsburg in *Bullcoming* tried a third tack, referring to a *statement's* primary purpose (as though a "statement" can have a "purpose").

Crawford may ultimately send mixed messages about American justice as it is reflected in the adversary system. Writing for the majority, Justice Scalia stated:

> The reliability of evidence is a *procedural* rather than a *substantive* guarantee. Whatever the reality, for purposes of the criminal justice system evidence is reliable when it is "tested in the crucible of cross-examination."

This comment seemingly drives a wedge between civil and criminal justice. The concept of "testimonial hearsay" is limited to criminal cases. As you will see, many hearsay exceptions render hearsay admissible in civil cases regardless of whether it has been "tested in the crucible of cross-examination." *Crawford* thus creates one standard of reliability for criminal cases and a different (lesser) one for civil cases. Whatever the constitutional justifications, civil litigants may justly believe that their disputes are resolved in a second-class system of justice.

Crawford emerged in 2004 looking like a legal vehicle that was seemingly designed to run forever. A couple of decades later, the decision shows a lot of wear and tear. The classic 1930s–1940s radio series *The Shadow* always ended with hero Lamont Cranston ominously warning listeners that "The weed of crime bears bitter fruit." To paraphrase Cranston, in uprooting *Ohio v. Roberts,* the weed of *Crawford* has thus far borne a lot of bitterness. With a new mix of Justices on the Court, the future direction of *Crawford* is uncertain.

Practice Tip: Prosecuting Domestic Violence Cases

More than coincidence accounts for the fact that the two rulings in *Davis* involved domestic violence. Intimidated domestic violence victims frequently refuse to cooperate with prosecutors and often absent themselves from their abusers' trials. Prior to *Crawford*, prosecutors were often able to secure convictions by offering victims' post-abuse statements to police officers into evidence. In *Davis*, the Court acknowledged that in these situations "the Confrontation Cause gives the criminal a windfall," but refused to "vitiate constitutional guarantees." At the same time, the Court pointed to a possible way out for prosecutors: the forfeiture provision of Rule 804(b)(6). If prosecutors can demonstrate that an abuser intimidated his victim into refusing to testify, the abuser "forfeits the constitutional right to confrontation." *See* Chapter 15 and the Supreme Court's interpretation of Rule 804(b)(6) in *Giles v. California*.

Practice Tip: Pretrial Depositions

Prosecutors might react to *Crawford's* interpretation of the Confrontation Clause by making witnesses who have made out-of-court statements that are admissible under the hearsay rule available for cross-examination prior to trial. Since confrontation either at or before trial satisfies *Crawford*, scheduling depositions at which defense lawyers can question witnesses might allow prosecutors to offer hearsay into evidence at trial should the witnesses later become unavailable. Of course, witnesses who make themselves unavailable for trial might try to make themselves equally unavailable for pretrial depositions. However, when formal pretrial questioning is feasible, and the importance of the case and the feared unavailability of the witness at trial combine to outweigh the time and expense, depositions are one way that prosecutors can satisfy *Crawford*.[11]

In jurisdictions in which defendants are bound over for trial based on preliminary hearings rather than grand jury proceedings, prosecutors can satisfy *Crawford* by questioning witnesses at preliminary hearings. The reason is that defendants have an opportunity to question government witnesses at preliminary hearings. However, defendants are not present at grand jury proceedings and of course have no opportunity to question witnesses who testify before grand juries. Thus, pretrial depositions may be of particular value in jurisdictions that rely on grand jury proceedings.

Problem 10-49: Facial Recognition

Ross Marshall is charged with armed robbery of a clothing store. Just after the culprit left the store, a customer ran over to the victimized clerk and said, "I got a good look at the robber. He had a big scar on his right cheek." The prosecutor calls the clerk to testify to the customer's statement to prove that Marshall, who has a facial scar, was the robber. Assume that the customer's statement would be admissible under the "excited utterance" exception to the hearsay rule (*see* Chapter 14). *The effect of the Confrontation Clause is that:*

1. The customer's statement is testimonial, and if the customer is unavailable to testify at trial the customer's statement is inadmissible unless Marshall has had a previous opportunity to cross-examine the customer.

2. Even if the customer's statement is testimonial and the customer is unavailable to testify, the statement is admissible if it has "indicia of reliability."

3. Since the customer's statement is non-testimonial, its admissibility is not affected by the Confrontation Clause.

---

11. Robert Durst, a wealthy New York real estate magnate, was charged in Los Angeles in 2015 with killing a girlfriend, Susan Berman, in December 2000. Durst's alleged motive was his fear that Berman would implicate him in the 1982 disappearance and presumed killing of his wife. With Durst's trial not scheduled to start before 2018 and many of potential witnesses older or likely to make themselves unavailable for trial, Los Angeles prosecutors questioned a number of witnesses under oath. *See, e.g.,* Maria Gerber, *Witness Distances Herself from Strong Testimony She Previously Gave against Durst in Murder Case*, L.A. TIMES, July 27, 2017 (http://www.latimes.com/local/lanow/la-me-ln-robert-durst-murder-case-20170727-story.html.) Durst and his attorneys were present and were able to cross-examine the witnesses, making the witnesses' testimony admissible if they were unavailable to testify at Durst's trial. Durst was tried and convicted of murder in 2021 and he died in prison in 2022.

4. The Confrontation Clause allows the prosecution to offer the customer's statement into evidence only if the customer testifies at Marshall's trial.

In a variation of this problem, assume that a police officer questions Customer #2 following the robbery. Customer #2 tells the officer, "Oh my God, I just remembered, the robber was missing a right earlobe." Marshall, who has two intact earlobes, calls the officer to testify to Customer #2's statement. In response to the prosecutor's hearsay and Confrontation Clause objections, the judge determines that Customer #2's statement would be admissible under the "excited utterance" exception to the hearsay rule, and that it is testimonial. *Should the judge exclude Customer #2's statement on the ground that admission would violate the Confrontation Clause?*

Problem 10-50: One and Done

Jeff Birns is charged with arson. At Birns' preliminary hearing, store clerk Lowe testified that the day before the fire that Birns is charged with setting took place, Lowe sold Birns a bag of rags, a box of matches and a gallon of gasoline. Birns' lawyer cross-examined Lowe at the preliminary hearing. At trial, though Lowe is available to testify, the prosecutor chooses not to call Lowe as a witness, and instead seeks to read the transcript of Lowe's preliminary hearing testimony into the record. *Should the trial judge grant the prosecutor's request?*

Problem 10-51: Tender Years

Wilson Narita is charged with sexually molesting his eight-year-old stepdaughter, Madison. In the course of its investigation, the prosecutor learns that two years earlier Narita had been living with another woman when he allegedly molested her four-year-old daughter, Claire. In Narita's trial for molesting Madison, the prosecutor seeks to offer "pattern witness" evidence of the defendant's molestation of Claire under the jurisdiction's rule that allows character evidence in child molestation criminal cases.

1. The judge rules without conducting a hearing that "Claire is six years old, and in my experience, children of that age are too young to testify. They can't really understand the duty to tell the truth, and the courtroom experience would be psychologically damaging. Therefore, I rule that Claire is unavailable as a witness." *Is the judge's determination proper?*

2. With Claire having been deemed unavailable to testify at Narita's trial, the prosecution calls Antonia, a police officer, to testify to a conversation that she had with Claire at the police station in the presence of Claire's mother. Officer Antonia testifies at a foundational mini-trial that Claire told her that "When my stepdaddy lived with my mom he kept putting his thing on my pee pee." Claire also told Officer Antonia that she was too scared of the defendant to say anything for a long time, but finally she told her mom, who kicked the defendant out of the house. The prosecution offers Claire's statement into evidence under the jurisdiction's "tender years" hearsay exception, which applies

to statements made by children under the age of 12 describing acts of sexual abuse or neglect. *Is Claire's statement testimonial?*

Problem 10-52: Tipping Point

Thayer is charged with illegally distributing prescription drugs. At trial, undercover government agent Nark identifies Thayer as the person who he saw engaged in the sale of a large quantity of norcodeine pills at the Third Avenue underpass. Nark testifies further that he staked out the location where the sale took place based on statements made to Nark on the street to the effect that "If you need norcodeine, Thayer is the person you want to see and his office is the Third Avenue underpass." Thayer objects to this portion of Nark's testimony under the Confrontation Clause. *Should the judge sustain the objection?*

Problem 10-53: It's Not What You Say, It's Where You Say It

Devin Michaels is charged with armed robbery. The prosecutor seeks to offer into evidence a hearsay statement made by Edna O'Toole stating that O'Toole saw the defendant with loot taken in the robbery. Assume that O'Toole's statement would be admissible as a matter of hearsay law. If O'Toole is unavailable to testify at Michaels' trial, the prosecution could offer her hearsay statement into evidence under the Confrontation Clause if:

1. O'Toole made the statement while testifying under oath to the grand jury that indicted Michaels.

2. O'Toole made the statement while testifying at Michaels's preliminary hearing. Michaels represented himself at the preliminary hearing, at which time he had a chance to cross-examine O'Toole but did not.

3. After reading a story about the armed robbery in her local newspaper, O'Toole voluntarily called the Police Department "Hot Line" and recorded a message describing what she had seen.

4. O'Toole made the statement while testifying for the prosecution in the trial of Michaels's co-conspirator, Sally Welch. Welch was tried separately prior to Michaels, and Welch's lawyer thoroughly cross-examined O'Toole in the earlier trial.

Problem 10-54: There Goes the Neighbor, Hood

1. Hope is charged with selling illegal drugs. Hope's partner in the illegal business was Benny, and the prosecution seeks to offer into evidence against Hope a conversation that Benny had with Diller. In the conversation Benny described how he and Hope did business because he believed that Diller planned to join the partnership. In fact, Diller was an undercover police officer who recorded the conversation. When Benny refuses to testify against Hope, the prosecution offers into evidence the recording of Benny's conversation

with Diller. Assume that Benny's statements would be admissible in evidence against Hope under the co-conspirator exception to the hearsay rule (*see* Chapter 13). *Are Benny's statements to Diller testimonial for purposes of the Confrontation Clause?*

2. Change the forgoing problem as follows: (a) Benny is on trial for selling illegal drugs; (b) Benny's statements to Diller that the prosecution seeks to offer into evidence were made after Diller arrested and interrogated Benny. Assume that as a matter of hearsay law, Benny's statements are admissible as opposing party statements (*see* Chapter 13). *How should the judge rule on the following argument of Benny's attorney:*

Your Honor, I object to the admission of Benny's statements to Officer Diller. Those statements are clearly testimonial. Moreover, my client intends to exercise the constitutional right to remain silent by not testifying at trial. The statements are thus inadmissible under Crawford, *because Benny's exercise of the right to remain silent means that the defense has no opportunity to question or cross-examine Benny. To admit Benny's statements into evidence would improperly punish Benny for exercising a constitutional privilege.*

Problem 10-55: Brothers in Lawlessness

The Urban Police Department (UPD) has created a special task force in an effort to cripple a violent street gang, the 17th Street Crisps, headed by the Sam brothers, Flot and Jett. The UPD has posted fill-in-the-blank electronic documents on Nextdoor Apps in neighborhoods often victimized by the Crisps' violence. Witnesses can use the Nextdoor app to send electronic reports of crimes to the police. Flot and Jett are jointly charged with murder. The prosecutor seeks to offer into evidence an electronic Nextdoor report prepared by Molly McGovern that states, "Sam brothers Flot and Jett hiding in the neighbor's bushes, loading handguns. Wearing dark clothes. Pointing guns at dark sedan. Shots fired. F. and J. jump into blue sedan, driving away south on 17th."

With McGovern unavailable as a witness, the prosecutor offers a printout of the electronic report into evidence. *Are McGovern's statements testimonial? What was the UPD's primary purpose in posting the fill-in-the-blank reports, and what is the significance of that purpose for admissibility?*

Problem 10-56: About Time

John Ramirez is charged with a murder that took place about two decades earlier. Ramirez was a fugitive from justice during this period. A search incident to Ramirez's arrest produced a knife with a distinctive cutting pattern. Based on the medical examiner's 20-year-old report describing the victim's fatal wounds, prosecution expert witness Lorena Edwards is prepared to testify to an opinion that a high probability exists that the knife found in the defendant's possession when he was arrested is the type of knife that caused the fatal wounds. Having passed away during the period when Ramirez was a fugitive from justice, the medical examiner is not available for cross-examination. *Is Edwards's testimony admissible over a Confrontation Clause objection?*

Problem 10-57: 911 Call

Tina Tyler drove away from her home in a panic after her husband yelled and fired a gun at her. While driving away, Tyler called 911 and described what happened to a 911 operator. The transcript of the call is as follows: "I'm on Fairfield. I'm driving away from the premises. He just shot at me. My husband shot — I just been shot at . . . OMG, OMG, he shot at me. . . . I got a witness, my little goddaughter is in the car. I'm in a Ford gray Mustang. I'm so scared. He's wearing a blue shirt and glasses, his girlfriend is there." Tyler also told the operator her husband's race, his date of birth, the address of the shooting, and she described the gun as a little black .22.

With Tyler unavailable to testify at her husband's trial on firearm and assault charges, the prosecution offers the transcript of the 911 call into evidence. *Are her statements to the 911 operator testimonial?*

Problem 10-58: Potpourri

Consider the admissibility of hearsay evidence under the Confrontation Clause in the following circumstances:

1. Joe is charged with driving while intoxicated under a DUI (driving under the influence) statute that makes it a felony for a minor previously convicted of drunk driving to drive while under the influence of alcohol or other drugs. To prove that Joe drove with a blood alcohol level above .08 (and thus was intoxicated), that Joe was a minor at the time of the offense and that Joe had previously been convicted of drunk driving, at trial the prosecution offers the following items into evidence:

    (a) A Court Clerk's Certificate stating that an attached document titled "Abstract of Conviction" is a genuine and accurate copy of a court record indicating that Joe was convicted of drunk driving six months prior to the date he was arrested on the current charge.

    (b) A County Clerk's Certificate stating that an attached Certificate of Birth is a genuine and accurate copy of a county record indicating that Joe was 17 years old at the time of his arrest that is the basis of the current charge.

    (c) An Analysis Report prepared and sworn to by Ronald Houston, indicating that Houston is a licensed lab analyst and that he administered a Breathalyzer test to Joe in accordance with standard lab procedures following Joe's arrest on the current charge and obtained a readout on the machine indicating that Joe's blood alcohol level was .12.

    (d) A Breathalyzer Test Record prepared and sworn to by Judy Schackelford indicating that as an employee of a Breathalyzer testing company she conducted a routine test of the Breathalyzer machine used to determine Joe's blood alcohol level two days before he was arrested and determined that the machine was in proper working order.

Assuming that the D.A. offers the documents above into evidence in lieu of live witnesses, and that Joe has not previously had a chance to cross-examine any of them, how should the judge rule on the defense attorney's Confrontation Clause objections?

2. Milt is charged with assaulting Nguyen with a deadly weapon. Officer Ahmadi finds Nguyen lying dazed and bleeding in an alley. The officer asks Nguyen, "What happened? Are you OK? Should I call an ambulance?" Nguyen then says to the officer, "Thank God! Don't know why, somebody wearing a Star Wars mask ran out of the back door of a store and slugged me with a metal pipe. My head hurts so bad." *Assume that Nguyen's statement would be admissible in evidence as a matter of hearsay law. Is the statement testimonial?*

3. Green is charged with the premeditated murder of Venutti. Supporting Green's defense of insanity is Dr. Loeb, who testifies that Green suffered from schizophrenia and that because Green had not been taking his prescribed anti-psychotic medications, Green was incapable of planning or understanding that he could harm another human being. In rebuttal, the prosecutor calls Dr. Leopold. Dr. Leopold's opinion is that Green suffers only from a mild form of schizophrenia, and that Green committed the murder to prove that he is a superior human being who can get away with crime. Dr. Leopold arrived at this opinion after extensively examining Green and interviewing Green's parents. *If Green's parents are unavailable to testify and Green has not previously had an opportunity to cross-examine them, would the Confrontation Clause prevent Dr. Leopold from testifying to their statements?*

4. Marian is called by the prosecutor to testify in a bank robbery prosecution in which the defense is mistaken identity. Marian identifies the defendant as the person who ran past her as she walked toward the bank moments after it was robbed. Marian further testifies that she paid particularly close attention to the defendant because as she approached the bank she heard an unidentified person call out from the bank's door, "The bank's been robbed! There goes the guy who did it (pointing at the running man)!" The prosecutor offers the unidentified person's shout to explain why Marian's identification is credible. *Is Marian's testimony to the statement that she says led her to pay close attention to the defendant admissible over the defense attorney's Confrontation Clause objection?*

5. Dungo is charged with murder. The prosecution contends that Dungo killed the victim Lou Pina as part of a turf war between members of rival gangs. To support this contention, the prosecutor calls police officer Luis Fuentes, who qualifies to testify as a "gang expert." Fuentes testifies to an opinion that Dungo killed Pina for the benefit of Dungo's gang. Officer Fuentes based this opinion in part on casual, unrecorded conversations that he had had with

various members of both gangs in the days preceding Pina's death. Dungo objects that the gang members' statements were testimonial and that because none of them testified, Officer Fuentes's conclusions are inadmissible under the Confrontation Clause. *How should the judge rule?*

6. Dmitri is on trial for bank robbery. A bank security guard testified that the robber rode away on a red electric bike after the robbery. The prosecutor calls Officer Martinez to testify that, "As a member of the bank robbery investigation team, the day following the robbery I talked to Hans Ohrt, who owns a bike shop two blocks away from the bank. I told Ohrt that I wanted to talk to customers who had recently purchased electric bikes. Ohrt told me that Dimitri had bought a red electric bike two days earlier." Ohrt is unavailable to testify at Dmitri's trial. *Would the Confrontation Clause prevent Officer Martinez from testifying to Ohrt's statement?*

§ 10.12 Chapter Review Problems

Review Problem 10-A

Jones is charged with DUI (driving under the influence). The police officer who arrested Jones administered a blood alcohol test at the police station. The officer seeks to testify that Jones "blew" a reading of.13 on the Breathalyzer machine, well over the legal limit of.08. Jones objects that the reading is hearsay. *The judge should:*

1. Sustain the objection because the machine's readout constitutes the arresting officer's out-of-court statement.

2. Overrule the objection because machines don't make hearsay assertions.

3. Sustain the objection because the machine's readout constitutes the Breathalyzer machine manufacturer's out-of-court statement.

4. Sustain the objection because Jones's erratic driving is the equivalent of Jones's out-of-court assertion that "I drank too much alcohol."

Review Problem 10-B

Which item(s) of evidence below would be non-hearsay if offered by the plaintiff to prove that the sun was shining brightly at the time that a traffic accident took place?

1. The plaintiff's testimony that "As my spouse and I left the store and walked to our car about five minutes before the accident occurred, I asked my spouse, 'Do you have any of that sunblock lotion that you usually carry?'"

2. The plaintiff's testimony that "As my spouse and I left the store and walked to our car about five minutes before the accident occurred, my spouse said, 'Can you believe that this morning's weather report said it was going to be cool and cloudy today?'"

3. The plaintiff's testimony that "As my spouse and I left the store and walked to our car about five minutes before the accident occurred, I saw a man walk outside the store, stop, apply lotion from a bottle labeled 'World's Best Sunblock,' then continue walking."

4. The plaintiff's testimony that "As my spouse and I left the store and walked to our car about five minutes before the accident occurred, my spouse said to me that 'I just saw a man walk outside the store, stop, apply lotion from a bottle labeled "World's Best Sunblock," then continue walking.'"

Review Problem 10-C

Which item(s) of evidence below would be non-hearsay if offered by the plaintiff to prove that a black-and-white Llasa Apso dog belonged to the defendant?

1. The plaintiff seeks to testify that "I saw the black-and-white Llasa Apso jump up on the defendant's lap and lick the defendant's face."

2. Same as #1, but the plaintiff also offers into evidence a passage from the book "Canine Behavior for Dummies" stating that "Llasa Apsos are extremely owner-loyal and will only lick the faces of their owners."

3. A receipt from the Furry Friends Pet Shop that indicates the date on which a black-and-white Llasa Apso was sold to the defendant, as well as the sale price.

4. A book entitled "How to Raise a Llasa Apso" was found on the nightstand next to the defendant's bed.

Review Problem 10-D

Which item(s) of evidence below would be non-hearsay if offered by the plaintiff to prove that a certain cell phone number belongs to Alex Graham?

1. The plaintiff seeks to testify that she called the phone number and heard a recorded message that said, "You've reached Alex Graham's message center. Please leave a message and I'll call you back if and when I feel like it."

2. A printout of the cell phone company's records indicating that the phone number is assigned to Alex Graham.

3. The plaintiff seeks to testify that "I stood near Alex Graham and dialed the phone number. When it rang, I saw a friend of Alex Graham pick the phone off a table and hand it to him.

4. The plaintiff seeks to testify that "I dialed the phone number, and a voice that I recognized as that of Alex Graham said, 'Alex Graham here.'"

§ 10.13 Case Library

Crawford v. Washington

U.S. Supreme Court

541 U.S. 36 (2004)

Davis v. Washington

U.S. Supreme Court

547 U.S. 813 (2006)

Melendez-Diaz v. Massachusetts

U.S. Supreme Court

557 U.S. 305 (2007)

Michigan v. Bryant

U.S. Supreme Court

562 U.S. 344 (2011)

Bullcoming v. New Mexico

U.S. Supreme Court

564 U.S. 647 (2011)

Williams v. Illinois

U.S. Supreme Court

567 U.S. 50 (2012)

Ohio v. Clark

U.S. Supreme Court

576 U.S. 237 (2015)

Chapter 11

Non-Hearsay Purposes for Out-of-Court Statements

§ 11.01 Chapter Checklist

1. Who determines what a statement is offered to prove?

2. What is an "assertion first" approach to case planning?

3. How is admissibility determined when a statement is offered for a non-hearsay use?

4. What are the most common non-hearsay purposes?

§ 11.02 Relevant Federal Rules of Evidence

Rule 801. Definitions That Apply to This Article; Exclusions from Hearsay (partial text)

(c) Hearsay. "Hearsay" means a statement that:

(1) the declarant does not make while testifying at the current trial or hearing; and

(2) a party offers in evidence to prove the truth of the matter asserted in the statement.

Rule 802. The Rule Against Hearsay

Hearsay is not admissible unless any of the following provides otherwise:

- A federal statute;
- These rules; or
- Other rules prescribed by the Supreme Court.

§ 11.03 Introduction

Chapter 10 reviewed various types of verbal and nonverbal behavior that constitutes "statements" within the meaning of Rule 801 and explained that the hearsay rule results in the exclusion of an out-of-court statement only if it is offered for "the truth of the matter asserted." This chapter examines a variety of circumstances in which statements can be admissible for purposes that do not rely on the statements' truth, or for what lawyers and judges commonly refer to as "non-hearsay purposes."

Chapter 10 set forth a "Five-Step Hearsay Matrix" and analyzed Steps One and Five of that Matrix. This chapter analyzes Steps Two and Three:

Step Two: What is a statement offered to prove?

Step Three: If the statement is offered for a non-hearsay purpose, is that purpose relevant, and if so, is its probative value substantially outweighed by any of the factors set forth in Rule 403?

§ 11.04 Step Two of the Hearsay Matrix: Identifying an Assertion's Non-Hearsay Purpose

In our adversarial system, when a relevance issue arises with respect to an item of evidence, the burden is generally on the offeror to establish the connection between the evidence and the fact of consequence (or credibility concern) that the offeror seeks to prove or disprove. Thus, it's up to the party who seeks to offer an out-of-court statement into evidence as non-hearsay to identify how the statement is relevant without regard to its accuracy.

A legitimate non-hearsay use for a statement may be readily apparent. Nevertheless, an adversary may object when such a statement is offered so that the judge can instruct jurors for the record that they may not consider the statement for its truth.

Example 1

Defendant Phil Abuster is charged with murdering Basil Leaf and calls Sue Asponte to support the self-defense plea. Sue's testimony proceeds in part as follows:

DEFENDANT'S ATTORNEY: What happened when you met up with Mr. Abuster, about an hour before Mr. Leaf was killed?

A: He started talking nervously about Basil Leaf.

DEFENDANT'S ATTORNEY: Do you know Basil Leaf?

A: Yes. He's someone that Phil and I used to play cards with.

DEFENDANT'S ATTORNEY: And what did Mr. Abuster say about Basil Leaf?

A: He said that Basil was a violent and vicious individual who always carried a gun and a knife.

PROSECUTOR: Your Honor, for the record I ask that admissibility of the witness' testimony concerning the defendant's statement be limited to the issue of the defendant's state of mind.

DEFENDANT'S ATTORNEY: No objection.

JUDGE: The record will reflect that the statement is admitted solely on the issue of the defendant's belief about Mr. Leaf. I instruct the jury to consider it only for that purpose and not as evidence that what Mr. Abuster said about Mr. Leaf was accurate.

In Example 1 above, the defendant's assertion about Basil Leaf is relevant without regard to its truth. The defendant's assertion that Basil always carried a gun and a knife is circumstantial evidence that the defendant was afraid of Basil. From that fear, the jurors may infer that the defendant would not have attacked Basil, an inference that supports the defendant's self-defense claim. The prosecutor therefore correctly does not object to the statement's admissibility, but also does not want the jurors to use the defendant's out-of-court assertion for its truth, that is, as evidence that Basil was violent and always carried a gun and a knife. Thus, the prosecutor asks for and obtains an instruction that the jury can use the defendant's assertion only for the non-hearsay purpose of reflecting the defendant's claimed belief about Basil. (The prosecutor might also have objected to the statement's admissibility under Rule 403, arguing that the probative value of the non-hearsay use is substantially outweighed by the danger of unfair prejudice or other Rule 403 factors.)

As this example suggests, out-of-court assertions admitted as non-hearsay resemble the shares of common stock often awarded as bonuses to corporate insiders—they are restricted. In the case of non-hearsay, lawyers and judges call the restriction a "limited purpose," meaning that a judge or juror can properly consider an assertion admitted as non-hearsay only for the limited use for which it was admitted. In jury trials, judges typically try to confine the use of non-hearsay to its limited purpose. On request or *sua sponte*, a judge may give a "limiting instruction" immediately, admonishing jurors to consider an assertion only for its non-hearsay use as soon as a witness testifies to the assertion. And during final summation, a lawyer can refer to the non-hearsay assertion only for the limited purpose for which it's been admitted. For example, the defense attorney in the example above could not say during closing argument, "We know from what Phil Abuster said that Basil Leaf was a violent and vicious individual who always carried a gun and a knife." By contrast, the defense attorney could legitimately argue that "We know from what Phil Abuster said that Abuster was afraid of Basil Leaf and therefore would not have acted aggressively towards him."

A party cannot rely on an assertion admitted for a non-hearsay purpose to prove an element of a claim or defense when proof of that element depends on the statement's accuracy. For example, change the Abuster/Leaf example so that Basil Leaf is charged with unlawfully carrying a weapon. The prosecution could not rely on Abuster's out-of-court assertion to Sue Asponte as proof of this fact.

Practice Tip: Credibility vs. Admissibility

Offering an out-of-court statement as evidence of a party's state of mind may produce an objection that the testimony is "unreliable" or "self-serving"

and therefore inadmissible under Rule 403 because the statement's probative value is outweighed by the danger of unfair prejudice. For example, the
prosecutor in the Abuster/Leaf example may object to Abuster's statement
to Sue Asponte on the ground that Abuster might have been "planting a
defense." That is, perhaps Abuster intended to kill Leaf all along, and told
Sue (and possibly others) that Leaf was always armed in order to support a
phony self-defense claim. Such objections improperly conflate credibility
with admissibility. Judges should not evaluate credibility when determining
whether evidence is admissible under Rule 403. That is a jury function. If
jurors can rationally conclude that Abuster believed that Leaf was always
armed, the judge should admit Sue's testimony and leave the ultimate determination of the testimony's credibility to the jury.

Identifying a legitimate non-hearsay use for an assertion depends on your knowing the elements of the substantive rules that you are trying to prove or disprove.
Only by tying a non-hearsay use to a particular element (or to the credibility of a
witness) can you establish an assertion's relevance. Typically, trials involve claims
and/or defenses with multiple elements, and an out-of-court assertion may constitute hearsay if you offer it to support or disprove one element but admissible non-
hearsay if you offer it to support or disprove a different element.

Example 2

Julie is injured when she slips and falls in Aisle 3 of a supermarket, and
she sues the market for failing to clean up the wet spot on the floor that
allegedly caused her fall. Under applicable substantive law, two of the elements that Julie has to prove are that (1) a wet spot made the floor unreasonably dangerous, and (2) the supermarket knew of the dangerous condition.
Julie calls Randy to testify that a few minutes before she fell, Randy had
been shopping in the market and had told the store manager, "You've got
a very slippery wet spot on the floor in Aisle 3." Randy's statement would
be inadmissible hearsay were Julie to offer it to prove Element #1. However,
Randy's statement would be admissible as non-hearsay if Julie offers it to
prove Element #2 (notice to the store). Accurate or not, Randy's statement
to the manager provided notice of the possible existence of a dangerous
condition. The judge would admit the statement for the limited purpose of
notice and admonish the jurors not to use it as evidence that the floor was
dangerously wet. Julie would have to prove that the dangerous condition
existed through some means other than Randy's out-of-court statement to
the manager.

Practice Tip: "Assertion-First" Case Planning.

In order to maximize a presentation's persuasiveness, experienced litigators may take an "assertion-first" approach to case planning. That is, a
lawyer who is anxious to offer a very helpful out-of-court assertion into

evidence may try to develop a legal theory that creates a non-hearsay use for that assertion.

Example 3

You represent a pedestrian who was injured by an allegedly drunk driver who was driving a borrowed car with the owner's permission. You have evidence that before the owner gave permission to the driver, a close friend of the driver had told the owner, "The driver is regularly stewed to the gills." This assertion would be hearsay and probably inadmissible if you offer it as evidence that the driver was drunk when your client was struck. However, the assertion is certainly one that you would want to offer into evidence on your client's behalf. You can create a non-hearsay use for the assertion if you sue not only the driver but also the owner for "negligent entrustment" of the car to a dangerous driver. The friend's assertion would probably then be admissible for the limited purpose of proving that the owner knew that the driver had a propensity to drink.

§ 11.05 Step Three of the Hearsay Matrix: Determining the Relevance of a Claimed "Non-Hearsay Use"

In the abstract, there's no magic in being able to identify a non-hearsay use for an out-of-court assertion. Virtually any statement can give rise to a myriad of non-hearsay uses. For example, assume that in a personal injury case growing out of an auto accident, Mary is prepared to testify that "Patrick told me that the blue car ran a red light." You might offer this testimony as non-hearsay to prove such matters as:

Mary is capable of hearing.

Patrick is capable of speaking.

Patrick is capable of distinguishing colors.

Patrick is aware of traffic rules.

Mary is acquainted with Patrick.

The drawback is that none of these potential non-hearsay uses is likely to have the slightest bearing on who was at fault for the accident. A claimed non-hearsay use for an out-of-court assertion can serve as a ticket to admissibility only if that use is relevant. Under the familiar relevance principle of Rule 401, this means that a non-hearsay use either must bear on a witness' credibility or must have a tendency to make a fact of consequence more or less probable than it would be without the evidence.

Thus, once the offering party has identified a non-hearsay use for an out-of-court statement, often the next step is to determine whether that use has any bearing on a fact of consequence. As is always true when relevance issues arise, that determination depends not only on abstract legal elements, but on parties' specific factual contentions.

Example

Ginger is charged with murdering Fred. Ginger claims that two days before the alleged murder, her friend Gene told her, "Fred recently told me that you're a goner the next time he sees you." Gene's statement would be relevant as non-hearsay if Ginger's claim was that she killed Fred in self-defense. Whether or not what Gene said was accurate, hearing it might make Ginger afraid of Fred. If Ginger were afraid of Fred, arguably she wouldn't attack him, which lends credence to her self-defense claim. The direct examination of Ginger eliciting Gene's statement in support of her self-defense claim might go something like this:

DEFENDANT'S ATTORNEY: Ginger, when did you next see Gene?

A: It was two days before I saw Fred.

DEFENDANT'S ATTORNEY: And at that time, did you and Gene have a conversation?

A: Yes. I was alone outside a café, having coffee. Gene walked up to me and said, "Ginger, I hate to tell you this, but Fred recently told me that you're a goner the next time he sees you."

PROSECUTOR: Objection and move to strike, Your Honor. Hearsay.

[In an actual trial, a prosecutor who anticipates Ginger's answer and thinks it improper would object after the question, before Ginger gave the answer. Delaying an objection until after an improper question is answered may lead a judge to rule that an adversary has waived the objection.]

JUDGE: Defense counsel, any response? What is this statement being offered to prove?

DEFENDANT'S ATTORNEY: The testimony is relevant as non-hearsay to show that Ginger acted in self-defense, Your Honor. Even if Gene was joking or lying or just trying to scare Ginger, what Gene said is relevant to explain why Ginger was fearful of Fred, which in turn made it highly unlikely that she would attack him, leading to the conclusion that if she killed Fred she did so in self-defense. The only issue is whether Gene made the statement to Ginger, and Ginger can be cross-examined as to that claim.

[Of course, a judge or jury might instead conclude that Ginger's fear of Fred led her to "off" Fred at her earliest opportunity. As you know, however, the possibility of conflicting inferences is quite common and does not render evidence irrelevant.]

JUDGE: I'll admit the testimony as non-hearsay.

This non-hearsay argument would not succeed, however, if Ginger's defense were an alibi. For example, assume that Ginger's defense is that she was watching an old musical at the Bijou Theater at the time Fred was killed. In this factual scenario, Ginger's fear of Fred would simply be irrelevant. If the defense attorney nevertheless did try to offer Gene's statement into evidence for this non-hearsay use, Ginger's testimony would probably go something like this:

DEFENDANT'S ATTORNEY: Ginger, when did you next see Gene?

A: It was two days before I saw Fred.

DEFENDANT'S ATTORNEY: And at that time, did you and Gene have a conversation?

A: Yes. I was alone outside a café, having coffee. Gene walked up to me and said, "Ginger, I hate to tell you this, but Fred recently told me that you're a goner the next time he sees you."

PROSECUTOR: Objection and move to strike, Your Honor. Hearsay.

[Again, in an actual trial the prosecutor would object after the question, before Ginger's answer.]

JUDGE: Defense counsel, any response? What is this statement offered to prove?

DEFENDANT'S ATTORNEY: I offer the testimony as non-hearsay to show that hearing Gene's statement made Ginger fearful of Fred.

JUDGE: Counsel, so what? There's no connection between your client's possible fear of Fred and your defense. Your client's fear might be relevant to prove how she might have reacted in the victim's presence, but because your client's claim is that she was nowhere near the victim at the time of his death, her fear is irrelevant. I'll sustain the objection, strike the response and instruct the jury to disregard it.

Again, nothing inherent in the words of an out-of-court assertion determines its relevance as non-hearsay. As with any other item of proffered evidence, you need to establish a connection between your desired non-hearsay use and a fact of consequence or the credibility of a witness.

§ 11.06 Probative Value Versus Unfair Prejudice

Even if an offering party identifies a relevant non-hearsay use, the admissibility of an out-of-court assertion can (like any other type of evidence) be derailed by other evidentiary considerations. The primary evidence rule that comes into play with non-hearsay uses is Rule 403, the flip side of the basic relevance rule set forth in Rule 401. Rule 403, as you recall, authorizes judges to exclude evidence when its probative value is substantially outweighed by such factors as the danger of unfair prejudice or undue consumption of time.[1] This section addresses Rule 403 in the context of out-of-court statements offered for non-hearsay uses.

Offering an out-of-court assertion for a non-hearsay purpose always gives rise to a potential Rule 403 argument that the risk that a jury will improperly use the assertion for the truth of its contents outweighs the probative value of the non-hearsay use. Thus, as the proponent of non-hearsay, you may have to develop an argument not only supporting the probative value of the non-hearsay use but also minimizing the risk of improper use.

Example

Return to the example of Ginger and assume that her defense to the charge that she murdered Fred is that she killed him in self-defense. Ginger seeks to offer evidence that two days before Fred was killed, Gene said to her, "Fred recently told me that you're a goner the next time he sees you." Once the defense attorney identifies the desired non-hearsay use (to show that Ginger had reason to fear Fred), the prosecutor may make a Rule 403 objection. If so, the arguments may go as follows:

PROSECUTOR: Your Honor, the government objects to the defendant's testimony concerning Gene's statement on Rule 403 grounds. The defense offers the statement as non-hearsay, to show that the defendant was fearful of Fred and therefore would be unlikely to attack him. I submit that the evidence has little probative value, because the jury would be justified in making the exact opposite inference, that if the defendant were afraid for her life, she might well attack Fred before he could harm her. And balanced against this minimal probative value is the significant risk that the jury will improperly accept Gene's statement for its truth, and infer that Fred had threatened to kill Ginger. This is exactly the reasoning that the hearsay rule is designed to prevent, so exclusion of the evidence is necessary to avoid unfairly prejudicing the government's case.

JUDGE: Defense counsel, any response?

DEFENDANT'S ATTORNEY: The government is arguing Ginger's credibility concerning her reaction to Gene's statement, and I submit that that's a matter for the jury to decide. This evidence is critical, because the jury can't possibly render a fair verdict unless it knows what was going through Ginger's mind at the time she killed Fred, and Gene's statement is the key to understanding her mental state. As for the possibility of misuse of the statement, the government has not identified any way in which the risk is greater in this case than in any other case in which

---

1. Chapter 4 examines Rule 403 in detail.

non-hearsay is offered. Your Honor should admit the statement and admonish the jurors not to use the statement for its truth.

JUDGE: I'll admit the statement and admonish the jury accordingly. Will the bailiff please ask the jurors to return to the courtroom?

With non-hearsay as with any other piece of evidence admitted for a limited purpose, there's no guarantee that jurors will obey a judge's admonishment. Evidence rules are more effective in controlling the information that reaches jurors than they are in controlling how jurors react to evidence once they've heard it. For example, assume that during deliberations in the case of *State v. Ginger,* a couple of jurors argue, "I can't believe that Gene would have told Ginger that Fred had threatened to kill her unless Fred had really made the threat. And I bet that Fred followed through and did try to kill her." These jurors would be improperly using Gene's statement for its truth.

When such misuse occurs, often the judge and the lawyers don't find out about it at all. Jurors may not talk to them after deciding a case, and even when they do, they may not talk in detail about what was said during deliberations. Moreover, if the judge and the lawyers do find out about misuse of evidence they usually do not do so until after a case has been decided. At that time, as you know, Rule 606 makes it nearly impossible to impeach a verdict on the ground that jurors misused evidence (*see* Chapter 7).

A concern that admonishing jurors not to use non-hearsay assertions for their truth may be asking jurors to perform a nearly impossible mental task is a factor that some judges will consider when deciding whether to exclude non-hearsay under Rule 403.

§ 11.07 Common Non-Hearsay Uses

A. Overview

No matter how thoroughly you pore over the Federal Rules of Evidence, you will not find a rule authorizing the use of out-of-court assertions for non-hearsay purposes. Such rules are unnecessary. The admissibility of a statement as non-hearsay depends on the existence of a logical relationship between a claimed non-hearsay use and the legal, factual, and credibility issues in a particular case, and thus is governed by general relevance principles. However, certain non-hearsay uses appear routinely in trials, and this chapter focuses on those uses. These routine non-hearsay uses include:

Assertion offered as evidence of a speaker's state of mind.

Assertion offered as evidence of a listener's state of mind.

Assertion offered as a "verbal act" or "words of independent legal significance."

Assertion offered to contradict (impeach) in-court testimony.

Assertion offered to provide context and meaning.

Practice Tip: Non-Hearsay Uses and "State of Mind"

Many substantive rules include "state of mind" elements such as "intent," "knowledge," and "willfully." As a result, one of the most common claimed non-hearsay uses for out-of-court statements involves state of mind. While having legal outcomes rest partly on state of mind elements may further important policy goals, the frequency with which they appear in substantive rules greatly expands the range of potential non-hearsay uses for out-of-court statements. If you find yourself searching for an argument for the admissibility of an out-of-court assertion, always consider "state of mind."

B. Assertion Relevant to Declarant's State of Mind

Declarants' assertions often reflect their subjective beliefs (states of mind). Whether or not the assertions are accurate, the subjective beliefs that spawned them may be relevant. Thus, an assertion may be admissible as non-hearsay when offered as circumstantial evidence of a declarant's subjective belief. A declarant's subjective belief can be relevant in two common circumstances:

The declarant's belief is itself a fact of consequence.

The declarant's belief is circumstantial evidence of the declarant's behavior.

Example: Declarant's State of Mind a Fact of Consequence

In a will contest case involving a claim that the testator was mentally incompetent to make a will, the contesting party's attorney is questioning a witness who has testified that she was a close friend of the testator:

PLAINTIFF'S ATTORNEY: How often did you speak with the testator in the weeks before he signed the will?

A: Oh, at least every other day. I'd try to visit with him as often as I could.

PLAINTIFF'S ATTORNEY: Were these conversations in any way unusual?

A: Yes. One thing was that just about every time we'd get together, the testator would say a few times, "I am the walrus."

DEFENDANT'S ATTORNEY: Objection, hearsay.

JUDGE: Response from plaintiff's attorney?

PLAINTIFF'S ATTORNEY: The statement is offered as non-hearsay to prove that the testator was delusional and therefore incompetent to make a will, a fact of consequence in this case. The making of statements claiming to be an animal is evidence of delusion.

JUDGE: Objection overruled. I'll admit the statement as circumstantial evidence of the defendant's mental state.

Example: Declarant's State of Mind as Circumstantial Evidence of Declarant's Behavior

Jill is charged with murdering her live-in boyfriend Barker; the defense is self-defense based on Battered Women's Syndrome. Jill's attorney examines Jill's close friend Madeleine:

DEFENDANT'S ATTORNEY: Do you recall a conversation with Jill that took place the day before Barker's death?

A: Yes, I do.

DEFENDANT'S ATTORNEY: How did you happen to be talking to Jill?

A: She called and asked me to come over to her apartment before Barker got there.

DEFENDANT'S ATTORNEY: How did Jill seem to be when you got to her apartment?

A: She seemed extremely nervous. She kept looking out the window. She kept repeating that Barker would be home any minute.

DEFENDANT'S ATTORNEY: Did Jill say anything else about Barker?

A: Yes. She said that Barker kept a gun hidden somewhere in the apartment, and that if she tried to leave he would find her and kill her.

PROSECUTOR: Objection, hearsay.

JUDGE: Defense attorney, any response?

DEFENDANT'S ATTORNEY: Yes. Jill's statement is non-hearsay to prove that Jill was an abused woman who feared that Barker would kill her. Apart from the accuracy of her statements, what Jill said sheds light on how she experienced her relationship with Barker. Her statements support an inference that Jill suffered from Battered Women's Syndrome and that she felt trapped in the relationship and used deadly force in the belief that her survival depended on it.

JUDGE: Objection overruled.

You might remember from Chapter 10's discussion of "implied assertions" that some evidence scholars would argue that "I am the walrus" is hearsay. The argument is that the statement's relevance is based on an implied assertion, "I believe that I am the walrus," and the belief has to be accurate for the statement to be relevant. However, the argument is of little practical importance. Even if the assertion is deemed to be hearsay, it would almost certainly be admitted under the "state of mind" exception to the hearsay rule (Rule 803(3); see Chapter 14) or as Residual Hearsay (Rule 807; see Chapter 15).

Important Limitation: A declarant's state of mind CANNOT serve as the basis of an inference about the behavior of someone *other than* the declarant.

Example: Improper Attempt to Use a Declarant's State of Mind as Circumstantial Evidence of the Behavior of a Different Person

Jill is charged with murdering her live-in boyfriend Barker; the defense is self-defense based on Battered Women's Syndrome. Jill's attorney examines Jill's close friend Madeleine:

DEFENDANT'S ATTORNEY: Do you recall a conversation with Jill that took place the day before Barker's death?

A: Yes, I do.

DEFENDANT'S ATTORNEY: How did you happen to be talking to Jill?

A: She called and asked me to come over to her apartment before Barker got there.

DEFENDANT'S ATTORNEY: How did Jill seem to be when you got to her apartment?

A: She seemed extremely nervous. She kept looking out the window. She kept repeating that Barker would be home any minute.

DEFENDANT'S ATTORNEY: Did Jill say anything else about Barker?

A: Yes. She said that Barker kept a gun hidden somewhere in the apartment, and that if she tried to leave he would find her and kill her.

PROSECUTOR: Objection, hearsay.

JUDGE: Defense attorney, any response?

DEFENDANT'S ATTORNEY: Yes. Jill's statement is non-hearsay. We can infer that Jill suffered from Battered Women's Syndrome, from which we can further infer that Barker had subjected her to past abuse.

JUDGE: Objection sustained. An assertion of the defendant's mental state cannot serve as the basis of an inference about Barker's behavior.

Problem 11-1: Up the Creek I

Jones' widow sues Life Insurance Co. to collect the proceeds of Jones's life insurance policy. To prove that the disfigured body found at the bottom of a steep cliff alongside Crooked Creek was Jones's, the widow offers into evidence a letter written by Jones stating, "In a couple of days I'm going to head west to Crooked Creek." *Can the widow offer Jones's letter for a non-hearsay use?*

Problem 11-2: Up the Creek II

Same case as Problem 11-1. To prove that the disfigured body found next to Crooked Creek was Jones's, the widow offers into evidence a second letter written by Jones stating, "Crooked Creek is like heaven on earth." *Can the widow offer Jones's letter for a non-hearsay use?*

Problem 11-3: Mother and Child

Husband and Wife each seek custody of their five-year-old son, Child. To prove that it would be in Child's best interests for Wife to have custody, Wife seeks to testify, "Last week, Child told me that Husband is mean and often hits Child." *Can Wife offer Child's statement for a non-hearsay use?*

Problem 11-4: Mine!

Prosecution of Marconi for assaulting Morse; both of whom work for the same computer company. To prove that Marconi had a motive to attack Morse, the prosecution calls Kevin to testify that a month before the alleged assault, Marconi told Kevin, "I actually wrote the program that Morse got the award for creating." *Can the prosecution offer Kevin's testimony for a non-hearsay use?*

Problem 11-5: Backache

Pedro sues D'Amato for personal injuries growing out of an auto accident. To prove that he was in pain after the accident, Pedro calls Wilton to testify, "I was with Pedro on the night of the accident, and Pedro told me that his back was really stiff and sore." *Can Pedro offer his statement to Wilton for a non-hearsay use?*

Problem 11-6: At the Movies: The Boyfriend

The film *The Good Mother*[2] involves a custody battle between divorced parents. The couple's eight-year-old daughter Molly lives with the mother and her live-in boyfriend, Leo. The father testifies that while Molly was visiting with him, she walked in on him just after he had finished showering, while he was clad only in a towel tied around his waist. The father further testifies that Molly asked him to "let me see it," and that "Leo always lets me see his penis." The mother's lawyer makes a hearsay objection to the father's testimony to Molly's statements. *Representing the father, for what, if any, non-hearsay use can you offer Molly's statements?*

Problem 11-7: At the Movies: Motive for Murder

In the film *Jagged Edge*,[3] Jack Forrester is on trial for the murder of his wealthy wife Page. The prosecution's theory is that Forrester killed Page to prevent her from obtaining a divorce that would destroy his social and economic status. Virginia Howell, a prosecution witness who was Page's good friend, testifies that shortly before Page was killed, Page told Virginia that "my husband doesn't love me, he's been seeing other women, I'm going to divorce him." *In response to the defendant's hearsay objections to these statements, for what, if any, non-hearsay use can the prosecutor offer them?*

---

2. Warner Bros./Touchstone Pictures/Silver Screen Partners (1988).
3. Columbia Pictures (1985).

C. Assertion Relevant to Listener's State of Mind

Just as statements can provide a window into a declarant's state of mind, so can hearing another's statement affect a listener's state of mind. When a listener's state of mind is *relevant*, the out-of-court statement that gave rise to that state of mind can qualify for admission as non-hearsay. As is true for a declarant's state of mind, a listener's state of mind may be relevant either because it is itself a fact of consequence, or because it constitutes circumstantial evidence of behavior.

Example: Listener's State of Mind as a Fact of Consequence

Medical malpractice case in which plaintiff Petra claims that defendant Dr. Phibes gave Petra an overdose of X-rays and severely burned her leg. The substantive law in Petra's jurisdiction allows recovery of damages for "reasonable fear of developing cancer." Petra's attorney is questioning Petra:

PLAINTIFF'S ATTORNEY: Did you seek medical advice about the condition of your leg?

A: Yes, from Dr. Frank Enstein, a dermatologist.

PLAINTIFF'S ATTORNEY: What happened when you went to see Dr. Enstein?

A: Dr. Enstein examined my leg and told me that there's a very high risk that it's going to become cancerous in the future.

DEFENSE ATTORNEY: Objection, hearsay.

PLAINTIFF'S ATTORNEY: Dr. Enstein's statement to Petra is offered as non-hearsay to prove that she reasonably feared developing cancer, a mental state which is itself a fact of consequence on the issue of damages.

JUDGE: Objection overruled.

Example: Listener's State of Mind as Circumstantial Evidence of Behavior

Jill is charged with murdering her live-in boyfriend Barker; the defense is self-defense based on Battered Women's Syndrome. Jill's attorney examines Jill's close friend Madeleine:

DEFENDANT'S ATTORNEY: Do you recall a conversation with Jill that took place the day before Barker's death?

A: Yes, I do.

DEFENDANT'S ATTORNEY: How did you happen to be talking to Jill?

A: She called and asked me to come over to her apartment before Barker got there.

DEFENDANT'S ATTORNEY: How did Jill seem to be when you got to her apartment?

A: She seemed extremely nervous. She kept looking out the window. She kept repeating that Barker would be home any minute.

DEFENDANT'S ATTORNEY: Did you say anything to Jill about Barker?

A: Yes. I told her that about a week earlier, Barker had told me that he kept a gun hidden in the apartment, and that if Jill ever tried to leave him he would find her and kill her.

PROSECUTOR: Objection, hearsay.

JUDGE: Defense attorney, any response?

DEFENDANT'S ATTORNEY: Yes. Madeleine's statement is offered as non-hearsay to support Jill's belief that Barker would kill her if she tried to end the relationship. Apart from the accuracy of what Madeleine said, her statements support an inference that Jill felt trapped in the relationship and was forced to do what she did in order to survive.

JUDGE: Objection overruled.

Problem 11-8: Bagged

Debra is charged with possession of illegal drugs. To prove that Debra knew that the substance in the baggies found in Debra's home was contraband, the prosecution calls Seller to testify, "I assured Debra that the baggies contained Grade A-1 heroin."

1. *Can the prosecution offer Seller's testimony as non-hearsay?*

2. *Is Seller's testimony admissible to prove that the baggies contained heroin?*

Problem 11-9: Medical Mal

Sue Cherr sues Hospital for negligently employing Doctor Mal, who allegedly performed an unnecessary operation on Sue. To prove Hospital's negligence, Sue offers to prove that six months before Hospital hired Dr. Mal, the monthly issue of the state's Medical Quality Assurance Board Newsletter had rated the doctor as "unqualified to practice medicine or anything else, for that matter." *Can Sue offer the Newsletter's statement as non-hearsay?*

Problem 11-10: Warning Sign

Peter sues a county fair and the operator of The Big One roller coaster ride for damages for injuries that Peter allegedly incurred because of extreme shaking while riding The Big One. The defendants seek to offer evidence that, at the time of Peter's ride, a sign posted next to The Big One's entrance read "Warning. Riders are likely to experience severe shaking on this ride." *Can the defendants offer the contents of the sign into evidence as non-hearsay?*

Problem 11-11: Ganging Up

In a prosecution for attempted murder, Police Officer Arvin testifies as an expert on street gang behavior. After qualifying Officer Arvin as an expert, the prosecutor seeks to elicit Arvin's opinion that the defendant committed the crime as part of a gang initiation rite. Arvin bases this opinion on information provided to him

418   11 · NON-HEARSAY PURPOSES FOR OUT-OF-COURT STATEMENTS

by two members of the gang. In response to the defendant's hearsay objection to Arvin's opinion, the prosecutor argues that the information is not hearsay because it is not offered for its truth but rather as the basis of the expert's opinion. *How should the judge rule on the objection?*

Problem 11-12: Hold the Dressing

Pei Pei slips and falls in the Cracked Barrel Restaurant on March 31, and sues the restaurant for negligently failing to clean up the spilled liquid that allegedly caused Pei Pei to fall. The restaurant's defense is that the floor was clean. Pei Pei calls Tal, who was eating in the restaurant on the night that Pei Pei fell, to testify to events that occurred prior to the time she fell. The defense (restaurant's) attorney and the judge should respond to the numbered portions of the transcript.

PLAINTIFF'S ATTORNEY: Do you recall where you were on the evening of March 31 last, at around 8:00 p.m.?

A: Yes, I was eating dinner with a companion in the Cracked Barrel Restaurant.

PLAINTIFF'S ATTORNEY: Do you know about an incident in which a small puddle of liquid in the restaurant caused Pei Pei to fall that night?

DEFENSE ATTORNEY: (*What objection, if any, might you make to this question?*)

JUDGE: (*Rule on any objection*)

PLAINTIFF'S ATTORNEY: Well, let me ask you this. Did you notice anything unusual about the floor near where you were dining?

DEFENSE ATTORNEY: Objection, leading question.

JUDGE: Overruled. (*Is this ruling correct?*)

A: Yes.

PLAINTIFF'S ATTORNEY: What did you notice?

A: A few feet from where I was sitting, between me and the salad bar, there was a puddle of some kind of clear liquid on the floor. I couldn't tell what it was; it looked like salad oil that had been laying there for some time.

DEFENSE ATTORNEY: Objection, improper opinion.

JUDGE: Overruled. (*Is this ruling correct?*)

PLAINTIFF'S ATTORNEY: Did you discuss this puddle with your dining companion?

A: I did. I told my companion that the spill was a dangerous one and that someone could easily slip and fall in it and get hurt.

DEFENSE ATTORNEY: Objection, hearsay.

PLAINTIFF'S ATTORNEY: Your Honor, I'm offering the statement only to corroborate the witness' testimony that a spill was on the floor, so on that basis it's not hearsay. I'll stipulate that the statement is not offered to prove that the spill was dangerous or that someone could get easily hurt.

JUDGE: (*What ruling on this response to the objection?*)

PLAINTIFF'S ATTORNEY: I also offer the statement for the non-hearsay purpose of its effect on the companion's state of mind. Hearing Tal's assertion gave the companion reason to believe that the spill was a dangerous one.

JUDGE: (*What ruling on this response to the objection?*)

PLAINTIFF'S ATTORNEY: Did you say anything else to your companion?

A: Yes, I said that I was going to notify an employee to clean it up.

DEFENSE ATTORNEY: Objection, hearsay.

PLAINTIFF'S ATTORNEY: Your Honor, I'm offering the statement to show notice to the restaurant, so it's not hearsay.

JUDGE: (*What ruling on the objection?*)

PLAINTIFF'S ATTORNEY: Did your companion respond to your comment?

A: Yes. My companion said, "You don't have to bother. I already mentioned it to the hostess."

DEFENSE ATTORNEY: Objection, hearsay.

PLAINTIFF'S ATTORNEY: Your Honor, I'm offering the statement only to prove notice to the restaurant, so it's not hearsay.

DEFENSE ATTORNEY: (*How would you respond to the plaintiff's argument?*)

JUDGE: (*Rule on the Defense Attorney's response*)

PLAINTIFF'S ATTORNEY: What happened next?

A: Just at that moment the hostess walked past the table. My companion told her, "Don't forget to take care of that spill over there near the salad bar."

DEFENSE ATTORNEY: Objection, hearsay.

PLAINTIFF'S ATTORNEY: The companion's statement is a command, not an assertion that a spill existed, and therefore is not hearsay. (*Is this a valid argument?*)

PLAINTIFF'S ATTORNEY: Also, the companion's statement is non-hearsay for the reason that it's admissible to show notice to the restaurant that a spill existed. (*Is this a valid argument?*)

D. Assertion Offered as a "Verbal Act" (also known as "Words of Independent Legal Significance" or "Legally Operative Conduct")

An assertion is non-hearsay when the assertion itself constitutes direct evidence of a fact of consequence. If this were not so, you'd have the absurdity of a substantive rule creating a legal right negated by an evidence rule preventing proof of a fact of consequence establishing the legal right. As with the other non-hearsay uses, admitting out-of-court statements as "verbal acts" protects an adversary's opportunity for meaningful cross-examination. The issue is whether words constituting direct evidence were spoken or written, and the witness who testifies that they were is in court and subject to cross-examination.

Example 1

Faye sues Ray for defamation, claiming that Ray made a false statement to a group of people that damaged Faye's reputation. Faye's attorney is questioning Faye:

PLAINTIFF'S ATTORNEY: What took place during this meeting of the California Post-Modern Club?

A: I heard Ray tell a group of club members that I like red meat and that when I order a salad I don't ask for the salad dressing on the side.

DEFENSE ATTORNEY: Objection, hearsay.

PLAINTIFF'S ATTORNEY: Ray's statement is non-hearsay because it constitutes words of independent legal significance. Faye's testimony provides direct evidence that Ray spoke the words that we claim are defamatory. That is, Ray's uttering of those words satisfies a fact of consequence that we have to prove to make out a case of defamation. We'll later offer evidence of other facts of consequence, including the falsity of Ray's statement.

JUDGE: Objection overruled.

Example 2

Arnold Schwartz sues Vic Tanney for breach of contract, alleging that Vic refused to honor a written agreement to hire Arnold as a fitness trainer in Vic's gym. Arnold's attorney offers a written exhibit into evidence:

PLAINTIFF'S ATTORNEY: Your Honor, I offer into evidence a written contract that we will show was signed by Arnold and Vic in which Vic agrees to employ Arnold as a fitness trainer in Vic's fitness club.

DEFENSE ATTORNEY: Objection, hearsay.

PLAINTIFF'S ATTORNEY: The contents of the contract constitute non-hearsay words of independent legal significance, as the contents provide direct evidence of the terms of the agreement between Arnold and Vic, and thus satisfy a fact of consequence in this breach of contract case.

JUDGE: Objection overruled.

Example 3

Kathy sues Lee for reneging on a legally enforceable gift. Kathy's attorney is examining Kathy:

PLAINTIFF'S ATTORNEY: And what happened when Lee talked to you at your thirtieth birthday party?

A: Lee handed me an ATM card and a small piece of paper with a PIN written on it, and told me that the money in the account that she had set up for me was mine as thanks for all the kindnesses I'd shown to Lee.

DEFENSE ATTORNEY: Objection, hearsay.

PLAINTIFF'S ATTORNEY: What Lee told Kathy when giving her the ATM card and the PIN constitutes non-hearsay verbal acts, as Lee's words establish that Lee made a gift to Kathy.

JUDGE: Objection overruled.

Similar considerations support the admissibility of "verbal parts of acts" as non-hearsay. When words and deeds are intertwined, and the words establish the legal character of the deed, the words are admissible as "the verbal part of the act."

Example 4

A county supervisor is charged with accepting bribes in exchange for votes. The prosecution offers evidence that the treasurer of a trash collection company handed the supervisor a cash-filled envelope and said, "This should take care of your vote on the trash collection contract." The treasurer's statements are non-hearsay because they establish the legal character of the act as a bribe rather than a loan or a donation to the supervisor's favorite charity.

Problem 11-13: Death and . . .

The Internal Revenue Service sues Dee Duction for failing to report the value of a Lexus automobile as earned income. Dee claims that the Lexus was a gift from Smith and not taxable income. To prove that the Lexus was a gift from Smith, Dee could call Wesson to testify that:

1. Smith told me, "I gave my Lexus as a gift to Dee Duction yesterday."

2. Smith told me, "I'm going to give my Lexus as a gift to Dee Duction tomorrow."

3. I was standing next to Dee and Smith when Smith said, "Dee, here are the keys to my Lexus. Accept it as my gift to you."

4. I was standing next to Dee and Smith when Dee said, "Smith, I still can't tell you how much I appreciate your giving me the Lexus yesterday."

5. All of the above.

Problem 11-14: Payback Time

George sues Gracie for failing to repay a loan of $5,000. To prove that the loan was repaid, Gracie testifies that "I handed George five $1,000 bills and told him that this was payment in full of the loan." *Is Gracie's statement to George hearsay?*

Problem 11-15: Cellar Dweller

Reggie is charged with being an "accessory after the fact" for helping Archie to evade capture after robbing a bank. The prosecutor calls Doug Head as a witness to testify that "I was visiting Reggie when Archie ran into the house and told us that he'd just robbed a bank and needed help. Reggie told Archie to hide in the cellar, that he'd be safe there. A few minutes after Archie had run into the cellar, a police officer knocked on the door and asked us if we'd seen Archie. Reggie told the officer that he had no idea of Archie's whereabouts." *What portions, if any, of this testimony constitute inadmissible hearsay?*

Problem 11-16: Protection

Nitti is charged with obtaining money from retailers through means of extortion. The prosecution calls Marcus Nieman, a small jewelry store owner, to testify that "Nitti came into my store and told me that he'd blow up my store if I didn't pay him $1,000 a month." *Does Nitti's statement constitute a verbal act?*

Problem 11-17: Mea Culpa

Whit Lasch sues May Aculpa for injuries growing out of an auto accident. Whit offers to testify that a week after the accident, May called Whit and said, "I'm really sorry. The accident was all my fault." *Does May's statement constitute a verbal act?*

Problem 11-18: Up in Arms

Bonnie is charged with armed bank robbery. To prove that Bonnie was armed at the time of the robbery, the prosecution calls Officer Ness to testify that "I arrested Clyde for robbing the bank along with Bonnie. Clyde then told me that Bonnie had used a gun during the robbery." *Does Clyde's statement to the officer constitute a verbal act?*

E. Assertion Offered to Contradict (Impeach) Testimony ("Prior Inconsistent Statement")

Evidence of a witness' out-of-court assertion that is inconsistent with the same witness' in-court testimony is admissible as non-hearsay. A judge or juror may regard a witness who "speaks with a forked tongue" to be lying or mistaken (or a reptile). Thus, regardless of the out-of-court assertion's accuracy, the mere fact that a witness has made inconsistent statements is relevant for its possible impact on the witness' credibility.

Example

Miguel sues Dustin for personal injuries growing out of an auto accident. Miguel's witness Sara testified on direct examination that Dustin's car ran a stop sign. The defense attorney's cross-examination goes as follows:

DEFENSE ATTORNEY: Sara, you saw Dustin's car run the stop sign?

A: I did, that's what I testified to.

DEFENSE ATTORNEY: Yet the day after the accident, you talked about it with Maria, your supervisor at work, correct?

A: I'm sure I did. It was pretty unnerving.

DEFENSE ATTORNEY: And didn't you tell Maria that you thought that the driver of the car that collided with Dustin's car was to blame for the accident?

PLAINTIFF'S ATTORNEY: Objection, hearsay.

DEFENSE ATTORNEY: Sara's statement to Maria is offered as non-hearsay to contradict Sara's direct-examination testimony. Sara's giving contradictory accounts of the same event may lead the jury to disbelieve Sara.

JUDGE: Objection overruled. The witness will answer the question.

Remember that even if Sara admits to making this statement to Maria, the defense attorney can't use the statement for the truth of its contents (i.e., that the plaintiff Miguel was at fault). Sara's out-of-court statement to Maria is admissible only for the limited purpose of impeachment, and the judge is likely to instruct the jurors not to use it as evidence that Miguel was at fault. (As you'll see in Chapter 12, Rule 801(d)(1)(A) makes contradictory out-of-court assertions admissible for their truth when they are made under oath, perhaps in a deposition. Some jurisdictions, such as California, go even further and admit all self-contradictory statements for their truth. *See* Cal. Evid. Code §1235.)

Practice Tip: A Bygone Common Law Practice

The late judge and law school dean Irving Younger was famous for his summer lectures for trial lawyers (among other things). Judge Younger's somewhat tongue-in-cheek teachings about impeachment with prior inconsistent statements began with the common law pre-impeachment "foundational dance" known as "time, place, and manner" questioning. Younger stressed that trials were "gentlemanly," and that a gentleman would not ask a witness about an inconsistent out-of-court statement without giving the witness a chance to think of an explanation for it. (Female litigators were few in number during the period Younger referred to.) Thus, the rules called for a pre-impeachment time, place, and manner "dance" that would warn witnesses that they were about to be impeached with their own words and give them a chance to save their honor with an explanation.

For example, let's say that Al testified for the plaintiff that an auto accident defendant ran a red light. The defense lawyer plans to impeach Al with a prior inconsistent statement—Al's statement to his neighbor Mary that he didn't see the color of the light. The pre-impeachment dance might have gone something like this:

Q: Al, you testified during direct examination that my client ran a red light?

A: Yes, that's what I said.

Q: You have a next-door neighbor named Mary, right?

A: That's correct.

Q: You've been neighbors and friends for about a decade?

A: Yes.

Q: And two months ago, in mid-July, you discussed the traffic accident with Mary, isn't that right?

A: I think so.

Q: And this conversation took place while you were each working in your front gardens, right?

A: Yes.

Q: Your memory of the accident was better two months ago then than it is now, right?

A: Possibly.

Q: In fact you even discussed the color of the light with Mary at the time of the accident, didn't you?

A: I probably did.

Q: And you told Mary at that time that you didn't see the color of the light? Didn't you say that to her?

A: Yes, but—

The time, place, and manner questions would give Al a chance to think about and offer an explanation for the inconsistency, if he had one that was consistent with the duty to tell the truth.

As the need for rules of civility suggests, litigators have for some time been unwilling to give opposing witnesses a "sporting chance" to defend their honor before impeaching them. And Federal Rule of Evidence 613(a) did away with the last vestiges of the common law "time, place, and manner" era. When questioning a witness about a prior statement the questioner need not "show it or disclose its contents to the witness."

Problem 11-19: Speed Test 1

In a personal injury case growing out of an auto accident, By Stander testifies on direct examination by the plaintiff that "The plaintiff's Mazda was traveling about 25 m.p.h. when it was struck by the defendant's Buick." Which, if any, of the following questions that the defense attorney might put to By on cross-examination constitute prior inconsistent statements?

1. "Didn't you tell the investigating officer that the plaintiff's Mazda wasn't going much faster than 20 m.p.h. just before the accident?"

2. "Didn't you tell the investigating officer that you couldn't remember how fast the plaintiff's Mazda was going just before the accident?"

3. "Isn't it true that Ahn Looker told the investigating officer that the plaintiff's Mazda was going at least 35 m.p.h. just before the accident?"

4. "Didn't you tell the investigating officer that you're not too good at judging the speed of cars?"

5. "Isn't it true that you lied about a year ago when you falsely reported to your insurance company that three laptop computers had been stolen from your car?"

6. "Didn't you tell the investigating officer that the defendant's Buick entered the intersection with the green light just before the accident?"

Problem 11-20: Speed Test 2

Same case as previous example. During the defense attorney's cross-examination of plaintiff's witness By Stander, the following testimony occurs:

DEFENSE ATTORNEY: By the way, how fast was the defendant's car going just before the accident?

A: I'm sorry, I don't remember.

DEFENSE ATTORNEY: Well, didn't you tell the investigating officer that the defendant's car was traveling no more than 30 m.p.h.?

Does the defense attorney's last question constitute proper impeachment with a prior inconsistent statement?

F. Assertions Offered to Provide Context and Meaning

In an effort to convince judges and jurors that testimony is accurate and that legal claims are valid, litigators typically strive to elicit testimony so that it portrays events in a way that makes the events appear real and memorable. Unless a witness is testifying to a performance by a mime, real-world incidents consist both of actions (e.g., "A robber entered the store carrying a gun") and words (e.g., "I heard someone say that we should run out the back door"). Thus, to help witnesses appear credible, attorneys normally elicit stories that include statements that were part and parcel of the events to which they're testifying. Such statements often qualify as non-hearsay for the simple reason that they are not offered for their truth, but to portray realistically a detailed and accurate version of events relevant to a litigated dispute. Of course, trial judges have the power under Rule 403 to exclude contextual assertions if the time necessary to recount them or their unfairly prejudicial impact outweighs their probative value.

Example

Huntz and Leo are charged with conspiring to distribute illegal drugs. The prosecutor is questioning Bobby, a former member of the conspiracy who has agreed to testify for the government concerning the conspirators' operations. Bobby is about to testify to what took place at a meeting in Leo's apartment:

PROSECUTOR: And what happened when you arrived at that location?

A: Huntz opened the door and we went into the living room. Leo was on the phone when I got there, so Huntz and I just talked about stuff for a few minutes until he was off the phone.

PROSECUTOR: Can you remember what you and Huntz talked about?

A: Nothing special. I think he told me that he hadn't been feeling well for the last few days, and that his family was really pressuring him to go back to school or get a job.

PROSECUTOR: Anything else happen before Leo got off the phone?

A: I remember telling Huntz that school wasn't such a bad idea, I was thinking along the same lines for myself. Oh, I told him I was sorry he didn't feel well, and that he looked OK to me, I think that's about it.

PROSECUTOR: Did Leo join you and Huntz at some point?

A: Yeah, he wasn't on the phone more than a few minutes. He said something about his sister having trouble with her kid, and that she hoped that Leo could talk to him.

PROSECUTOR: Then what happened?

A: Leo came over to where we were sitting and said that there was a problem with a meth delivery . . .

In this example, the alleged conspirators' comments are non-hearsay because their relevance does not depend on their accuracy. The various statements are relevant because they demonstrate that Bobby was personally present and can recall what took place at a real event. Moreover, the testimony is too brief and non-emotive to raise Rule 403 concerns.

§ 11.08 Chapter Review Problems

Problem 11-21: Summation

Darla is charged with murdering Spanky; her defense is self-defense. Darla's attorney offered evidence that a few days before Spanky's death, a friend of Darla's had told Darla that Spanky was usually armed to the teeth with weapons. The defense offered the friend's statement as non-hearsay to show that Darla had reason to fear Spanky. Based on the friend's statement, evaluate the propriety of this portion of the defense attorney's final summation:

> Ladies and gentlemen, the prosecution's argument that Darla attacked Spanky doesn't make any sense. Darla testified that she was afraid of Spanky, and we know that Darla had good reason to fear him since Spanky normally was fully armed with weapons.

Problem 11-22: My Case Is Shot

Shot Gunn is a plaintiff in a case growing out of an accident in which Shot was a passenger in a car that collided with the defendant's car. At trial, the driver of the car in which Shot was riding as a passenger testifies on direct examination as follows:

PLAINTIFF'S ATTORNEY: And what happened next?

A: Well, just moments before the collision, I heard Shot say that I had better be careful because the defendant's car was traveling way over the speed limit and was constantly changing lanes.

DEFENSE ATTORNEY: Objection, hearsay, move to strike.

PLAINTIFF'S ATTORNEY: Your Honor, the statement is offered as non-hearsay to help explain why the driver of the car in which Shot was a passenger was driving with particular care.

JUDGE: Objection overruled. I'll admit the statement for that limited purpose.

PLAINTIFF'S ATTORNEY: And what, if any, effect did Shot's remark have on your own driving?

A: I slowed down and made sure that I stayed in my lane.

Assume that at the close of Shot's case, the above testimony is Shot's only evidence as to the defendant's driving. The defendant moves for a directed verdict, asking that the judge dismiss Shot's case. *How should the judge rule on the motion?*

Problem 11-23: Policy Argument

Hy Strung's heirs file suit against Life Insurance Company after the Company refuses to pay the policy proceeds after Hy's death. The Company claims that Hy obtained the policy by lying about his health history, particularly his history of high blood pressure. The Company offers into evidence Hy's written insurance application, in which Hy wrote "none" next to the question, "Do you have any history of elevated blood pressure?" Hy's heirs object to admission of the application on the ground of hearsay. What result?

Problem 11-24: Bad Heir Day 1

This is a will contest case in which plaintiff Aggie Tator, Tess Tator's daughter and sole heir, seeks to set aside Tess's will disinheriting Aggie on the ground that the will was a product of Tess's insane delusion that Aggie was a drug addict. The beneficiary of the will, the Friends of Crabgrass Society, seeks to call three witnesses to testify that within three weeks prior to the will's execution, each of the witnesses had independently told Tess that they had seen Aggie buying and injecting heroin. *Can the Friends of Crabgrass Society offer this testimony as non-hearsay?*

Problem 11-25: Bad Heir Day 2

In this will contest case, plaintiff Darth Tator, Tess Tator's son and sole heir, seeks to set aside Tess's will disinheriting him on the ground that the will was a product of Tess's insane delusion that Darth was a drug addict. The beneficiary of the will, the Friends of Bluegrass Society, seeks to call as a witness Tess's friend Bill to testify as follows to a conversation that took place about a week before the will's execution:

DEFENSE ATTORNEY: Bill, do you have a friend by the name of Jim?

A: Yes, I do. Jim, I, and Tess Tator had all been good friends.

DEFENSE ATTORNEY: And did you speak to Jim about Tess in mid-August, about a week before Tess signed her will?

A: Yes, I did.

DEFENSE ATTORNEY: And what did Jim tell you?

A: Jim said that he'd talked to Tess the day before our conversation. He said that he'd told her that he'd recently seen her son Darth buying and injecting heroin.

PLAINTIFF'S ATTORNEY: Objection, hearsay, move to strike.

DEFENSE ATTORNEY: I offer Jim's statement to Tess as non-hearsay to show that Tess had a rational reason to disinherit Darth.

JUDGE: (*What ruling?*)

Problem 11-26: Bad Heir Day 3

In this will contest case, plaintiffs Aggie and Darth, Tess Tator's two children and sole heirs, seek to set aside Tess's will disinheriting them on the ground that the will was a product of Tess's insane delusion that they were drug addicts. The beneficiary of the will, the Friends of Greengrass Society, seeks to call Tess's friend Jim to testify as follows to a conversation that Jim had with Tess about a week before the will's execution:

DEFENSE ATTORNEY: Jim, what happened during your conversation with Tess?

A: Tess talked a little bit about Darth and Aggie, her children.

DEFENSE ATTORNEY: And what did Tess say about Darth and Aggie in this conversation?

A: Tess told me that three of Darth's and Aggie's friends had recently told her that they'd seen Darth and Aggie buying and injecting heroin.

PLAINTIFF'S ATTORNEY: Objection, hearsay, move to strike. The witness is testifying to what Tess said that some other declarants had told her.

DEFENSE ATTORNEY: The testimony is non-hearsay to show that Tess acted rationally in disinheriting her children.

JUDGE: (*What ruling?*)

Problem 11-27: Affordable Hearsay

Pavel sues Afford Motor Cars, his former employer, for wrongful termination. Afford had fired Pavel, an assistant manager, after receiving and investigating complaints from a number of female employees that Pavel had sexually harassed them. Assume that substantive law protects employers against wrongful termination suits if the employers investigate claims of employee wrongdoing and find a reasonable justification for termination. Afford commissioned an investigation, and offers into evidence the investigator's report that it allegedly considered before firing Pavel. The report recites employee accounts of Pavel's acts of sexual harassment, and concludes that Pavel committed numerous acts of sexual harassment. *You represent the employer; for what, if any, non-hearsay purpose can you offer the report into evidence?*

Problem 11-28: Honeymoon Over

Alice sues Ed for wrongful death, alleging that Ed's negligent driving caused the death of Alice's husband Ralph. In such cases, the monetary value of the husband-wife relationship is itself an element of damages. Ed calls Alice's coworker Trixie to testify, "A couple of weeks before Ralph was killed, Alice told me that Ralph had been cruel and indifferent to her throughout all the years of their marriage and had repeatedly stuck his fist in her face and threatened to send her to the moon." *Can Ed offer Trixie's testimony into evidence for a legitimate non-hearsay purpose?*

Problem 11-29: Mind the Gap

Otis sues the Sears Tower Management Co. for personal injuries as a result of Otis's tripping when he got out of an elevator car that allegedly had stopped below the level of the floor. Al Urter is prepared to testify that he was riding in the elevator car at the same time as Otis and that when the elevator door opened and before Otis started to walk out, Al said to Otis, "Watch out for the gap between the elevator and the floor."

1. Otis offers Al's statement into evidence to prove that the elevator had stopped below the level of the floor. In response to Sears Tower's hearsay objection, Otis's attorney argues that "It's non-hearsay because Al's statement does not constitute an assertion that a gap existed between the elevator and the floor." *Ruling?*

2. Sears Tower offers Al's statement into evidence to prove that Otis's own carelessness contributed to his injuries. Otis makes a hearsay objection. *Ruling?*

Problem 11-30: Garden Variety Hearsay 1

Rose sues Fern, alleging that Fern failed to make good on a promise to pay Rose $1,000 to remove all the ivy from Fern's front yard. To prove that the parties entered into a contract on March 1, Rose testifies in part as follows:

PLAINTIFF'S ATTORNEY: And what was said in this March 1 conversation with Fern?

A: Fern asked how much I would charge to clear the ivy from her front yard. I said $1,000, and Fern said that we had a deal.

DEFENSE ATTORNEY: Objection, hearsay.

JUDGE: (*What ruling?*)

Problem 11-31: Garden Variety Hearsay 2

Same case. To prove that Rose and Fern entered into a contract on March 1, Rose calls Fern's next-door neighbor Daisy, who testifies as follows:

PLAINTIFF'S ATTORNEY: And did you talk to Fern on February 28?

A: I did.

PLAINTIFF'S ATTORNEY: And what did Fern tell you?

A: Fern said that on the following day, she was going to offer Rose $1,000 to remove all the ivy from her front yard.

DEFENSE ATTORNEY: Objection, hearsay.

JUDGE: (*What ruling?*)

Problem 11-32: Garden Variety Hearsay 3

Same case. To prove that Rose and Fern entered into a contract on March 1, Rose calls Fern's next-door neighbor Daisy, who testifies as follows:

PLAINTIFF'S ATTORNEY: And did you talk to Fern on February 28?

A: I did.

PLAINTIFF'S ATTORNEY: And what did you tell Fern?

A: I told Fern that she had better clear the ivy from her front yard or she would have a terrible rat problem.

DEFENSE ATTORNEY: Objection and move to strike. Hearsay and irrelevant.

PLAINTIFF'S ATTORNEY: *Can you offer the testimony for a relevant non-hearsay use?*

Problem 11-33: Garden Variety Hearsay 4

Same case. To prove that Rose and Fern entered into a contract on March 1, Rose calls Fern's next-door neighbor Daisy, who testifies as follows:

PLAINTIFF'S ATTORNEY: Daisy, did you talk to the plaintiff, Rose, on March 3?

A: I did.

PLAINTIFF'S ATTORNEY: Where did that conversation take place?

A: In Fern's front yard, when Rose was clearing ivy from Fern's yard.

PLAINTIFF'S ATTORNEY: And what was said in this conversation?

A: I asked Rose how much she would charge to clear ivy from my yard. Rose said that Fern had agreed to pay her $1,000 to clear the ivy from Fern's yard, so she'd charge me the same if the yards were about the same size.

DEFENSE ATTORNEY: Objection and move to strike, hearsay.

PLAINTIFF'S ATTORNEY: Rose's statement to Daisy is non-hearsay because it recites the terms of the agreement.

JUDGE: (*What ruling?*)

Problem 11-34: Alternate Defenses

Ojay Simpson is charged with murdering his ex-wife, Nicole Brown. The prosecution seeks to offer evidence from Nicole's friend Sara that three days before Nicole was found stabbed to death, Nicole had told Sara, "My ex has been stalking me day and night, and yesterday he vandalized my car. I'm really scared of him." Assume either that Ojay's defense is an alibi, or that his defense is that he killed his ex-wife in self-defense after she came at him with a hammer. *Discuss the impact of these alternative defenses on the hearsay status of Nicole's statement to Sara.*

Problem 11-35: Convenience Store (Role Play)

Prosecution of Walter Denton, a teenage boy, for armed robbery of a convenience store. Denton's defense is an alibi, and the primary issue at trial is the credibility of Sharon, the security guard who was on duty the night of the robbery and who identifies Denton as the robber. A few days before the robbery, the store manager had posted an "Alert" in a section of the store's website that only employees can access. The "Alert" stated in part, "Police reports indicate that convenience stores such as ours are increasingly a target of violent robberies by teenage boys." A hearing will take place out of the jury's presence in which the prosecutor will seek a ruling that the contents of the Alert are admissible, and the defense attorney will seek to have the contents excluded from evidence.

Student # 1: You are the prosecutor, and in the hearing will argue that you should be permitted to offer the contents of the "Alert" into evidence during Sharon's direct examination. Interview Sharon outside of class and try to develop foundational evidence that Sharon can provide that allows you to offer the Alert's contents into evidence as non-hearsay. During the hearing, support your argument as to the admissibility of the Alert's contents as non-hearsay by making an "offer of proof" as to the foundational evidence that Sharon can provide, based on what you were told during the interview. With the judge's permission, you may also respond to the defense attorney's counter-argument if you think it necessary to do so.

Student # 2: You are Sharon, and will meet with the prosecutor outside of class to discuss the testimony you will give if you are permitted to testify. Like the prosecutor, try to think of what testimony you can give that will make the contents of the Alert admissible as non-hearsay, and then assume that such testimony is consistent with your duty to tell the truth.

Student # 3: You are the defense attorney who represents Walter. Try to anticipate the prosecutor's argument to support admissibility of the Alert's contents as non-hearsay and argue against admissibility. After hearing the prosecutor's argument, you may argue that the Alert is irrelevant, or that the contents are unduly prejudicial, or both.

Student # 4: As the judge, preside over the hearing and rule on the admissibility of the Alert's contents.

Problem 11-36: Zoo Suit

Annie Malle has sued a zoo for personal injuries that she sustained as a result of being bitten by an iguana. While visiting the zoo, Annie had reported to Osa, a zoo employee, that she'd seen the iguana running loose, and Osa told Annie to "please show me where you last saw it." Annie pointed out a spot on a dirt path on the far side of a sign that read "Danger; Employees Only," and told Osa that "the iguana ran into the bushes over there." Osa asked Annie to walk to where she'd last seen the iguana, saying "don't worry about that sign, it's perfectly safe." When Annie and Osa walked to the point on the path where Annie had last seen the iguana, Annie crouched down, pointed toward a bush, and was bitten. The zoo claims that Annie's own carelessness contributed to her injuries.

The zoo's attorney makes a hearsay objection to Annie's testifying to the statements that she made to Osa and that Osa made to her. *Are any of these statements admissible as non-hearsay?*

Annie's attorney makes a hearsay objection to Osa's testifying to the message on the sign. *Is this message admissible as non-hearsay?*

Problem 11-37: Last Words (Role Play)

Sunny Von is charged with murdering her husband Claus by poisoning his tea. Sunny claims that Claus was depressed and took his own life. The prosecution calls the Von family housekeeper, Alan Dersh, to testify that the day before Claus died, Claus told Alan with his last words that "I think Sunny has been poisoning me." The judge will conduct a hearing (out of the jury's presence) on the admissibility of Claus's statement to Alan. The hearing will go as follows:

Student # 1: As the prosecutor, identify a non-hearsay use for Claus's assertion and develop and present an argument in support of your proposed use. You may with the judge's permission respond to the defense attorney's argument.

Student # 2: As the defense attorney, try to anticipate the prosecutor's likely proposed non-hearsay use for Claus's assertion and develop and present an argument in opposition.

Student # 3: As the judge, preside over the hearing and rule on the assertion's admissibility.

Note: In the case of *Shepard v. United States*, 290 U.S. 96 (1933), Dr. Shepard was charged with murdering his wife. The government argued on appeal that the wife's statement, "Dr. Shepard has poisoned me," was admissible for the limited purpose of showing that the wife wanted to live and was not suicidal. Justice Cardozo dismissed the argument, for at trial the government offered the wife's statement for its truth, not for the limited purpose it belatedly put forward on appeal. However, Justice Cardozo's memorable words indicate how he would have ruled had the government offered the wife's statement for the limited purpose at trial:

> Discrimination so subtle is a feat beyond the compass of ordinary minds. The reverberating clang of those accusatory words would drown out all weaker sounds. It is for ordinary minds, and not for psychoanalysts, that our rules of evidence are framed.

Justice's Cardozo's conclusion is not, of course, binding on the judge in this problem. His opinion was dictum, and the case pre-dated the Federal Rules of Evidence by decades.

Problem 11-38: Under Cover

To prove that Dana illegally solicited an act of prostitution, Police Officer Millhone offers to testify that Dana walked up to the officer's parked car. The officer said, "I'm feeling lonely tonight." Dana replied, "I'd be glad to help you out, but if you want to have sex with me, it'll cost you $100." *Are any of the statements hearsay?*

Problem 11-39: Rite to Trial

Irv has been sued for intentional infliction of emotional distress by Dinah, whose husband Bill was struck by a car just after he left the restaurant in which he and Dinah had been eating. Irv had walked out of the restaurant just after Bill did. Irv saw a car strike Bill, and then Irv watched as a Catholic priest ran over to Bill and began administering the last rites. At that point, Irv ran back into the restaurant and told Dinah, "I'm sorry to tell you this. The fellow you were eating with was just hit by a car and is going to die at any moment." Bill survived, and Dinah has sued Irv to recover for the emotional shock allegedly caused by his statement.

1. When Dinah seeks to testify to Irv's statement to her, Irv's attorney objects on the basis of hearsay. *Is this a valid objection?*

2. When Irv seeks to testify to the priest administering the last rites, Dinah objects that his actions constitute an out-of-court statement and are hearsay. *Is this a valid objection?*

Problem 11-40: Pre-School

Mack Martin is charged with sexually abusing a four-year-old child who was a student in Mack's preschool class. Mack denies the charges.

1. At trial, the child testifies hesitantly and incompletely. The prosecutor then calls Officer Millhone to testify to the explicit details concerning the sexual act allegedly perpetrated by Mack that the child provided to the officer in a pretrial interview. *Would the officer's testimony be admissible for a non-hearsay purpose?*

2. At trial, the child testifies to the explicit details concerning the sexual act allegedly perpetrated by Mack. The defense attorney then calls Officer Millhone to testify that in a pretrial interview conducted by the officer, the child described the sexual act allegedly perpetrated by Mack hesitantly and incompletely. *Would the officer's testimony be admissible for a non-hearsay purpose?*

3. At trial, the child testifies to the explicit details concerning the sexual act allegedly perpetrated by Mack. Mack's attorney then seeks to offer into evidence a video recording of a children's services worker's pretrial interviews of the child, which depicts the child initially denying that any sexual misconduct occurred, and after repeated insistence by the children's services worker that sexual abuse had occurred, recanting the denial and agreeing with the worker. *On what non-hearsay basis might the defense attorney seek to offer the video recording into evidence?*

Related Case Note: The "Triangle Shirtwaist Fire" was a watershed event in the U.S. labor movement. The fire occurred in 1911 in a lower Manhattan garment factory, and resulted in the deaths of more than 100 mostly poor, immigrant female garment workers. The deaths were generally attributed to the factory owners' violating labor laws by keeping exit doors locked until quitting time. The owners were criminally charged with causing the death of one of the employees, who according to key prosecution witness Kate Altermann burned to death while trying to escape through a locked exit door. Defense attorney Max Steuer, representing the owners, used an unusual trial tactic when he cross-examined Altermann. Steuer asked Altermann to "describe what happened again," and her narrative response was nearly a verbatim match to the testimony she had given on direct examination. Steuer then asked Altermann to "describe what happened again," and she used the identical words when she again repeated her story. (When Steuer pointed out that she had changed one word, she quickly corrected herself.) Steuer then offered evidence of the very different language Altermann had used when she gave a statement to the prosecutor nine months prior to trial, soon after the fire. The contrast between Altermann's earlier courtroom accounts apparently undermined her credibility with the jurors, because the owners were acquitted. *What non-hearsay use did Steuer make of the out-of-court statement that Altermann gave to the prosecutor?*

Problem 11-41: Self Service

Otto Mobeel sues Van Dorr for personal injuries incurred as a result of Van's alleged physical assault on Otto after a dispute as to which of them had first arrived at an e-car charging station. Van contends that if he struck Otto at all he did so only in self-defense.

1. Otto seeks to testify that after Van got out of his car and walked toward Otto brandishing the windshield cleaning tool, Otto said two or three times, "I don't want to fight, let's stop this nonsense." *Are Otto's statements admissible for a non-hearsay purpose?*

2. Otto seeks to testify that as Van was advancing toward him with the windshield cleaning tool, another patron who was using a nearby charging station said to Otto, "It looks like that guy is going to attack you." In response to Van's hearsay objection, Otto responds, "I'm offering the statement for the non-hearsay purpose of proving that the patron believed that Van was the aggressor." *How should the judge rule on the objection?*

3. Van seeks to testify that a few minutes after Otto left the charging station, a station employee walked over to Van and said, "We'll never let that guy charge his car here again." Otto makes a hearsay objection; Van responds that the employee's statement is admissible because it is relevant to prove that Otto started the fight apart from the assertion's accuracy. *How should the judge rule?*

Problem 11-42: Parole Evidence

Carla and Trevor are charged with jointly planning and carrying out a bank robbery. Carla's defense is that she knew nothing about the robbery until Trevor forced her at gunpoint to enter the bank with him and point a gun at the bank employees while he emptied their cash drawers. The prosecution seeks to offer testimony from David that a week before the bank robbery took place, he and Carla were in their parole officer's waiting room. While they were waiting for their monthly meetings to take place, Carla said to David that "Maybe you can live like this, but this guy Trevor and me are going to score a big hit on a bank soon and get out of here."

PROSECUTOR: *Argue for the admissibility of David's testimony as non-hearsay.*

DEFENSE ATTORNEY: *Argue for the exclusion of all or a portion of David's testimony.*

JUDGE: *Preside over the arguments and rule on the admissibility of David's testimony.*

Problem 11-43: 2-B or Not 2-B

Sherm is charged with possession of illegal drugs that a police officer found stuffed under a shirt in the corner of a closet after legally entering Apt. 2-B. Sherm's defense is that he lives in Apt. 3-B and knows nothing about the drugs in Apt. 2-B. To prove that Sherm lives in Apt. 2-B, the prosecutor calls the police officer who found the drugs to testify that the officer found an envelope and a letter in a pocket of the shirt under which the drugs were stuffed. The envelope was addressed to Sherm in Apt. 2-B; inside was a letter addressed to Sherm at the same address from Knight Law School, denying Sherm's application for admission. The defense attorney objects to the envelope and letter as hearsay. *How should the judge rule?*

Problem 11-44: At the Movies: Self-Defense

In the made-for-TV movie *Final Appeal*,[4] Christine is charged with murdering her husband Ed. Christine claims that she shot Ed when he confronted her and advanced toward her, and she thought that he was going to attack her. Christine seeks to testify to an incident that took place about a week before the shooting, when Ed chased her through their house with a machete and said, "If I catch you spying on me again, you'll die." *Would Christine's testimony to Ed's statement be admissible over the prosecution's hearsay objection?*

Problem 11-45: At the Movies: Addiction

In the same film as in Problem 11-44, the prosecution calls Police Officer Ayers to testify that he investigated Christine's complaint the day after the alleged attack that her husband Ed had assaulted her with a machete. After denying that the incident had taken place, Ed told Officer Ayers that Christine was addicted to amphetamines and that she imagined many incidents that never took place. The judge strikes the testimony concerning Ed's statements as inadmissible hearsay. The judge's ruling is:

1. Improper if the prosecution's theory is that Christine killed Ed to prevent him from destroying her drug cache.

2. Improper if the prosecution's theory is that Christine killed Ed because he was about to file for a divorce that she opposed.

3. Improper if the prosecution's theory is that when Christine killed Ed she was under the influence of amphetamines.

4. Improper because Ed's statements explain why the officer failed to arrest Ed for assault with a deadly weapon.

5. Improper because Ed's statements tend to undermine Christine's claim that Ed would have confronted her and advanced on her on the day of the shooting.

Problem 11-46: Bad Call

Sue Ellen is charged with trafficking in illegal drugs. Officer Liu testifies that she and other police officers raided a warehouse filled with illegal drugs. The officers received a number of phone calls from callers who sought to make drug purchases.

---

4. Republic Television (1993).

Officer Liu testifies that two of the callers asked for "100 pounds of your finest hashish and make sure that Sue Ellen prepares the order, she always includes a little extra in a package." The prosecution offers the callers messages to prove that the warehouse was a place where drugs were being sold and that Sue Ellen was a seller. *How should the judge rule on the defense attorney's hearsay objection?*

Problem 11-47: Sold!

Auction House sues Bidder to enforce an agreement that was allegedly arrived at when its auctioneer accepted the last bid for a rare set of "Great Law Professor Trading Cards." The auctioneer seeks to testify that Bidder made the final and highest bid, after which the auctioneer said, "Sold." Bidder objects that the auctioneer's testimony is inadmissible hearsay. *How should the judge rule?*

Problem 11-48: At the Movies: The Shout

In the film *Let Him Have It*,[5] Derek Bentley and Chris Craig are charged with murdering a police officer who intervened in their attempt to burgle a warehouse. Craig fired the bullet that killed the police officer. Bentley was unarmed, but his culpability for the killing is based on the proposed testimony of a second police officer that when Craig pointed a weapon at the shooting victim, Bentley shouted, "Let him have it, Chris." *What is the relevance of Bentley's statement to the prosecution's case, and does it constitute hearsay? If Bentley does not testify at trial, should the judge sustain Craig's objection that Bentley's statement is barred by the Confrontation Clause?*

Problem 11-49: Probable Claus

Kris Kringle is charged with fraudulently posing as a department store Santa and soliciting donations by falsely telling passersby that donations will go to organizations that combat domestic violence.

(a) To prove that Kringle posed as Santa Claus, the prosecution calls Passerby A to testify, "Kringle was dressed as Santa and repeatedly said 'Ho! Ho! Ho' while standing in front of the department store."

(b) To prove that Kringle posed as Santa Claus, the prosecution calls Passerby B to testify, "Kringle asked my four-year-old, 'And what do you want for Christmas?'"

(c) To prove that he didn't fraudulently pose as Santa, Kringle seeks to testify, "The department store manager told me that the Santa they had hired had called in sick and asked me to wear their Santa suit and stand in front of the store."

What is the hearsay status of the oral remarks in these scenarios?

---

5. Luc Roeg & Robert Warr (1991).

Problem 11-50: Kidnapped

Boylen, a homeless man whose living space is a campsite in a hilly, wooded area, is charged with kidnapping Bobby, a five-year-old child. Bobby escapes after seven days in captivity. To prove that Bobby had been to the campsite, the prosecutor calls a police officer who interviewed Bobby to testify to Bobby's description of the campsite area where he was held captive. The defense attorney objects that the officer's testimony is inadmissible under the hearsay rule and the Confrontation Clause. *How should the judge rule on the objection?*

Problem 11-51: Un-Urned

Rabwin is charged with stealing an urn containing the ashes of Lee's beloved late pet Rover. *How should the judge rule on the hearsay objections in the following scenarios?*

a. To prove that Rabwin took the urn, the prosecution calls Dmitri to testify, "I saw Rabwin walking out Lee's front door carrying an urn that had a shiny plate on it that read, 'My Beloved Rover." Rabwin's attorney makes a hearsay objection to the testimony concerning the words on the shiny plate.

b. To prove that the urn contained the ashes of Lee's beloved pet Rover, the prosecution calls Dmitri to testify, "I saw Rabwin walking out Lee's front door carrying an urn that had a shiny plate on it that read, 'My Beloved Rover." Rabwin's attorney makes a hearsay objection to the testimony concerning the words on the shiny plate.

c. To prove that Rabwin took the urn, the prosecution calls Allison to testify, "Dmitri told me that he saw Rabwin walking out Lee's front door carrying an urn that had a shiny plate on it that read, 'My Beloved Rover." Rabwin's attorney makes a hearsay objection to Allison's testimony

§ 11.09 Multiple-Choice Review Problems

Review Problem 11-A

Ronald McDonald sues King Corp. for violating age discrimination laws when it terminated his employment as an accountant. McDonald seeks to offer into evidence an e-mail that he sent to his former co-workers in the accounting department stating that "King Corp. terminated my employment today as part of its effort to save money by firing older workers and bringing in new ones at much lower salaries." Assume that McDonald properly authenticates the e-mail. Which statement below is accurate?

1. The portion of the e-mail stating that King Corp. fired McDonald is non-hearsay, admissible as "words of independent legal significance" because termination of employment is a fact of consequence that McDonald has to prove.

2. The entire e-mail is non-hearsay, admissible as "words of independent legal significance" because both termination of employment and age discrimination are facts of consequence that McDonald has to prove.

3. The entire e-mail is admissible as non-hearsay because McDonald, the maker of the statement, testifies and is subject to cross-examination.

4. The entire e-mail is admissible as non-hearsay to show that McDonald's former co-workers' belief that McDonald was improperly terminated is reasonable.

5. The e-mail is inadmissible hearsay.

Review Problem 11-B

In a traffic accident case, to prove that the defendant drove negligently the plaintiff can offer evidence that:

1. Just prior to the accident, the passenger in the defendant's car said, "There's a sharp turn up ahead, you should probably slow down."

2. Shortly after the accident, the passenger in the defendant's car said, "That was a sharp turn back there, you should have slowed down."

3. Just prior to the accident, the passenger in the plaintiff's car said, "There's a sharp turn up ahead, that car coming the other way needs to slow down."

4. Shortly after the accident, the passenger in the plaintiff's car said, "That was a sharp turn back there, that car coming the other way should have slowed down."

Review Problem 11-C

Police Officer Sara O'Hara places Miggins under arrest for burglary. Miggins momentarily manages to break free and run away, but O'Hara recaptures Miggins quickly. At Miggins's trial for burglary, the prosecution seeks to offer evidence of Miggins's escape attempt. The judge should rule that the evidence of the escape attempt is:

1. Irrelevant to the issue of Miggins's guilt, as many people might try to avoid arrest regardless of whether they have committed a crime.

2. Inadmissible character evidence, tending to prove only that Miggins committed the crime of "attempted escape" and therefore has a propensity to violate the law.

3. Admissible to prove Miggins's guilt.

4. Hearsay, since Miggins's escape attempt constitutes an implied assertion, "I am guilty."

Review Problem 11-D

Miggins sues Police Officer Sara O'Hara for false arrest. At trial, Officer O'Hara seeks to offer evidence that she responded to an alarm at the home of Lemieux, who pointed in the direction of Miggins and said, "That's the guy who broke into my house." Evidence of Lemieux's statement is:

1. Admissible to show that the officer reasonably believed that Miggins had committed the burglary.

2. Admissible as non-hearsay to prove that Miggins did commit the burglary, because the statement explains why Lemieux pointed in Miggins's direction.

3. Inadmissible hearsay.

4. Admissible to prove that Lemieux believed that Miggins committed the burglary.

Review Problem 11-E

Kramden is charged with assaulting Norton; Kramden contends that Norton was the aggressor and that Kramden acted in self-defense. Kramden seeks to have Alice testify that the day before the alleged assault, Kramden told her, "That guy Norton is as mean and vicious as they come." Kramden's statement to Alice is:

1. Admissible to prove that Norton is mean and vicious and therefore was the aggressor.

2. Admissible to prove Kramden's fear of Norton, from which it can be inferred that Kramden would not have attacked Norton.

3. Inadmissible evidence of Norton's propensity for violence.

4. Inadmissible unless, pursuant to Rule 104(b), Kramden offers foundational evidence sufficient to support a finding that Norton had previously engaged in violent conduct.

Chapter 12

The Admissibility of Testifying Witnesses' Hearsay Statements

§ 12.01 Chapter Checklist

1. What are the two routes through which an out-of-court assertion may be admitted for the truth of its contents?

2. Why do the Federal Rules of Evidence distinguish between "exemptions" and "exceptions"?

3. Is the use of an out-of-court assertion affected by whether it is admitted under an exemption or an exception?

4. What rules govern hearsay foundation "mini-trials"?

5. What foundational requirements are necessary for the following types of out-of-court statements to be admissible for the truth of their contents?

    a. The statement conflicts with the same witness' courtroom testimony.

    b. The statement is consistent with a witness' courtroom testimony.

    c. The statement constitutes an identification.

§ 12.02 Relevant Federal Rules of Evidence

Rule 801. Definitions That Apply to This Article; Exclusions from Hearsay (partial text)

(d) Statements That Are Not Hearsay. A statement that meets the following conditions is not hearsay:

(1) *A Declarant-Witness's Prior Statement.* The declarant testifies and is subject to cross-examination about a prior statement, and the statement:

(A) is inconsistent with the declarant's testimony and was given under penalty of perjury at a trial, hearing, or other proceeding or in a deposition;

(B) is consistent with the declarant's testimony and is offered (i) to rebut an express or implied charge that the declarant recently fabricated it or acted from a recent improper influence or motive in so testifying; or

442 12 · THE ADMISSIBILITY OF TESTIFYING WITNESSES' HEARSAY STATEMENTS

(ii) to rehabilitate the declarant's credibility as a witness when attacked on another ground; or

(C) identifies a person as someone the declarant perceived earlier.

§ 12.03 Introduction

Chapter 11 reviewed circumstances in which hearsay statements may be admissible for non-truth purposes. In two common circumstances, however, parties seek to offer out-of-court statements for their truth:

1. A relevant non-hearsay purpose may be unavailable. That is, an out-of-court assertion may be relevant only if it is accurate.

Example 1

Auto accident case in which the driver of a silver car sues the driver of a blue car for negligence. The driver of the silver car seeks to offer evidence that Bystander saw the collision and the next day told a friend, "Yesterday I saw a blue car run a red light." In all likelihood, a relevant non-hearsay use for this statement is unavailable.

2. Even if a potential non-hearsay use is available, a party may want an out-of-court statement admitted for the truth of its contents because of its probative value.

Example 2

In the same auto accident case, Bystander testifies at trial on behalf of the blue car driver, "The blue car driver had the green light." The silver car driver could offer Bystander's inconsistent out-of-court statement to the friend into evidence to attack Bystander's credibility. However, the silver car driver would probably prefer that Bystander's statement also be admissible for its truth to prove that the blue car driver ran the red light.

The Federal Rules of Evidence establish two routes by which parties can offer hearsay statements for the truth of their contents. Rule 801 is the "exemption" or "exclusion" route. When a party offering a hearsay statement into evidence satisfies the foundational requirements for one of the subparts set forth in Rule 801(d)(1), the statement is exempt from (or excluded from) Rule 802's hearsay bar.[1]Rules 803, 804, and 807 constitute the primary "exception routes" to admissibility of hearsay. When a party proffering hearsay satisfies the foundational requirements set forth in any of these provisions, an assertion is excepted from Rule 802's hearsay bar. After providing a brief overview of exemptions and exceptions, this chapter examines

---

1. Judges and commentators sometimes refer to statements exempted from the hearsay rule as "statutory non-hearsay."

"witnesses' prior statements," one of the two major categories of exempt out-of-court statements.

Insofar as the use of statements at trial is concerned, the distinction between "exempt" or "excluded" statements and statements that are admitted into evidence under a hearsay exception is meaningless. The routes lead to the same destination: they make hearsay statements admissible for the truth of their contents. However, some commentators have cynically suggested that the array of exemptions and exceptions set forth in the rules is so great that perhaps Rule 802 ought to be phrased the other way around: "Hearsay is admissible, except on the rare occasion that an attorney can't think of an exemption or exception provided by these rules." In fact, had John Keats's interests run to Evidence law rather than romantic poetry, he might have written "Ode on a Hearsay Assertion," and begun it with the verse, "How can I admit thee? Let me count the ways . . . ."

§ 12.04 Laying Foundations for Hearsay Admissibility through "Mini-Trials"

Every exemption or exception in the Federal Rules of Evidence specifies the factors ("foundational elements") that litigants must satisfy for hearsay to be admissible. To the proponent of hearsay, the need to lay a foundation means that offering hearsay into evidence pursuant to a hearsay exemption or exception resembles painting a room. What a painter really wants to do is slap a new coat of paint on the walls. But first, the painter typically must prepare the walls by removing wallpaper, cleaning the walls, repairing cracks, and putting on a primer coat.

So too at trial, what a proponent of hearsay really wants to do is put an assertion before a judge or jury. But first, the proponent has to prepare the record by offering evidence satisfying the requisite foundational elements. In setting out different foundational elements for each exemption or exception, the Federal Rules of Evidence are more a recipe book than a collection of exclusionary rules. Just as a recipe book might tell cooks what ingredients must be assembled in order to make a chocolate cake or a Denver omelet, the Federal Rules tell lawyers and judges what foundational elements have to be satisfied for hearsay to be admissible under an exemption or an exception.

Arguments about whether hearsay is admissible under an exemption or an exception typically center on a proponent's ability to satisfy the required foundational elements (or as lawyers and judges often say, "to make the necessary foundational showing"). A proponent's effort to establish foundational elements often gives rise to a "mini-trial." Whereas in the "main" trial the issue might be whether a defendant drove carelessly or committed a crime, in a mini-trial the issue might be whether an assertion was an "excited utterance" (Rule 803(2)) or was made "in furtherance of a conspiracy" (Rule 801(d)(2)(E)).

During mini-trials, proponents may make "offers of proof" or offer testimony in support of foundational elements. In the latter situations, adversaries may cross-examine the proponents' witnesses, with questions limited to the foundational issue, and offer evidence of their own. Under Rule 104(c), in most circumstances the judge has discretion to decide whether the jury will be present during the mini-trial. (A party seeking to exclude hearsay often asks a judge to exclude jurors from the courtroom during a mini-trial, so that the jurors don't hear evidence that the judge may ultimately decide is inadmissible.) After listening to the evidence and considering the parties' arguments, under Rule 104(a) the judge decides whether the proponent of hearsay has met the burden of proving (by a preponderance of the evidence) the necessary foundational elements. (If an adversary disputes a hearsay declarant's personal knowledge, the judge resolves the dispute pursuant to the lower foundational burden established by Rule 104(b).)

Example

Pamela has sued Amanda for negligence for personal injuries resulting from an auto accident. Pamela seeks to offer into evidence a hearsay assertion made by bystander Ann Teek pursuant to the "excited utterance" exception (Rule 803(2)). Pamela is about to testify to Teek's assertion. If Amanda disputes the adequacy of the foundation, the mini-trial may unfold as follows:

PLAINTIFF'S ATTORNEY: And what happened after you got out of your car following the accident?

A: A woman named Ann Teek walked over to me and asked if she should call an ambulance.

PLAINTIFF'S ATTORNEY: Did Ms. Teek say anything to you about the events leading up to the collision?

DEFENDANT'S ATTORNEY: Objection, hearsay.

PLAINTIFF'S ATTORNEY: Your Honor, I'm offering Ms. Teek's remark as an excited utterance under Rule 803(2). I'm prepared to lay the necessary foundation.

[To lay a proper foundation, Pamela has to convince the judge that

(a) the statement related to a startling event or condition; and that

(b) Teek spoke under the stress of excitement caused by the event.]

JUDGE: Do we need to excuse the jury?

PLAINTIFF'S ATTORNEY: I don't think that will be necessary Your Honor. I think I can elicit the foundational evidence without referring to the assertion itself.

DEFENDANT'S ATTORNEY: No objection to the jury remaining.

JUDGE: Proceed with the foundation, counsel.

[At this point the "mini-trial" begins, with the issue being the adequacy of the foundation for an excited utterance.]

[If either of the attorneys or the witness will refer to the assertion during foundational questioning, the judge may decide to excuse the jury. If the judge ultimately decides that the assertion is admissible, excusing the jury may waste time. The reason is that after the jury returns the proponent is likely to repeat the foundational questioning because the information both satisfies foundational elements and supports the assertion's credibility. On the other hand, if the jury remains present during the mini-trial and the judge ultimately decides that hearsay referred to during foundational questioning is inadmissible, the less-than-satisfactory solution is for the judge to admonish the jurors to ignore what they've already heard. Rule 104(c) leaves the decision entirely up to the judge's "interests of justice" discretion in civil cases.]

PLAINTIFF'S ATTORNEY: How much time passed between the collision and the time you spoke to Ms. Teek?

A: I can't be sure of course, maybe a minute.

PLAINTIFF'S ATTORNEY: And what was her general demeanor?

A: She seemed really upset. She kept repeating "Are you OK? Are you OK?" I also remember her saying something like "My God, I can't believe you're able to walk out of your car."

[Under Rule 104(a), evidence rules (other than those relating to privileges) don't apply to foundational questioning. Thus, even if these remarks did constitute hearsay, they would not be excluded.]

PLAINTIFF'S ATTORNEY: Anything else you can remember about her demeanor or behavior?

A: She was out of breath and her face seemed flushed.

PLAINTIFF'S ATTORNEY: Nothing further on the foundation, Your Honor.

JUDGE: Defense counsel, do you wish to cross-examine?

DEFENDANT'S ATTORNEY: One or two questions, Your Honor.

[If the defense attorney thinks that the plaintiff's foundation fails to satisfy the foundational requirements by a preponderance of the evidence, the attorney may forego questioning and submit the matter on the record as it stands.]

[If the defense attorney does cross-examine, the questioning will be limited to the foundational issue. The defense attorney will have a further opportunity to cross-examine the witness on all other issues at the conclusion of the direct examination.]

[When mini-trials involve more complex foundational issues (e.g., pursuant to Rule 803(6), the reliability of a business' record-keeping procedures), the proponent may call additional witnesses, and the opposing attorney may both cross-examine and call witnesses.]

DEFENDANT'S ATTORNEY: The woman who spoke to you was calm enough to tell you that her name was Ann Teek, correct?

A: Yes, she gave me her name.

DEFENDANT'S ATTORNEY: And she also gave you a business address and phone number, right?

A: Yes.

DEFENDANT'S ATTORNEY: In fact she wrote down this information on a card and handed it to you, right?

A: Right.

DEFENDANT'S ATTORNEY: And after talking to you she walked over and spoke to Amanda, right?

A: She walked in that direction, I was really hurting and I wasn't paying that much attention to what she did.

DEFENDANT'S ATTORNEY: Nothing further. Your Honor, I renew my objection. While the collision may have been a startling event, I don't think that the record establishes that Ms. Teek spoke under the stress of excitement.

JUDGE: Plaintiff's counsel, any response?

PLAINTIFF'S ATTORNEY: The testimony amply shows that Ms. Teek spoke under the stress of excitement. She had just witnessed a head-on collision, she expressed surprise that the plaintiff was able to get out of the car, and she was flushed and out of breath.

JUDGE: I find that the foundation is adequate. The objection is overruled. Counsel, resume the direct examination.

PLAINTIFF'S ATTORNEY: Pamela, directing your attention to Ms. Teek, did she say anything to you about the events leading up to the collision?

A: Yes. She said that Amanda had run a red light.

PLAINTIFF'S ATTORNEY: Now, after speaking to Ms. Teek, what happened?

Practice Tip: "Offer of Proof" Mini-Trials

Whether you are the proponent or the opponent of hearsay, an "offer of proof" is often a speedier, alternative form of mini-trial. This form of mini-trial typically takes place with both counsel at the judge's bench. Instead of foundational testimony unfolding in question-answer format as above, the hearsay proponent summarizes the foundational evidence that supports admissibility. The adversary may respond by pointing out the weaknesses in the foundation. The judge can then rule without having to hear the actual foundational testimony. If you are the proponent of hearsay, an advantage of the "offer of proof" strategy is that you avoid having to elicit the same evidence twice, with its attendant risks that witnesses will appear less credible the second time around or will create conflicts by describing events one way during a mini-trial and a different way when the jury returns and you cover the same ground. If you are the opponent, an "offer of proof" affords you a preview of the proponent's foundational evidence, helping you decide whether to object and giving you additional time to think through cross-examination. No matter which side you find yourself on, of course, it is incumbent on you as an officer of the court to make an offer of proof that accurately summarizes the testimony you expect witnesses to give.

§ 12.05 Testifying Witnesses' Prior Statements

A. Three Categories of Exempt Statements

Rule 801(d)(1) provides that declarants' hearsay statements are "not hearsay" (i.e., are exempt or excluded from the hearsay rule) if the declarant testifies at the trial in which the statement is offered and is subject to cross-examination concerning the statement; *and* (a) the declarant's prior statement is inconsistent with the declarant's in-court testimony and was given under oath; *or* (b) the declarant's prior statement is consistent with the in-court testimony and is offered to counter an attack on the witness' credibility; *or* (c) the declarant's prior statement consists of an identification. The following sections examine each of these types of exemption.

B. Prior Inconsistent Statements (Rule 801(d)(1)(A))

Foundational Elements:

* The declarant testifies at the trial or hearing;
* The declarant is subject to cross-examination concerning the prior statement;
* The prior statement is inconsistent with the declarant's testimony;
* The prior statement was given under oath subject to the penalty of perjury at a trial, hearing or other proceeding, or in a deposition.

As you know from Chapter 11, a witness' hearsay assertion is admissible for the non-hearsay purpose of impeaching that same witness' conflicting in-court testimony. For instance, if Marcia testifies for the prosecution that "the robber was wearing a blue shirt," the defense may introduce into evidence Marcia's out-of-court statement, "the robber was wearing a green shirt," to cast doubt on Marcia's credibility. Admissibility of hearsay in this situation does not require a hearsay exemption or exception. The prior statement is admissible not for its truth (i.e., to prove that the robber was wearing a green shirt), but as non-hearsay to cast doubt on Marcia's credibility.

When the proponent of a prior inconsistent statement satisfies the foundational elements of Rule 801(d)(1)(A), by contrast, hearsay is admissible not simply to cast doubt on the declarant's credibility, but also for the truth of its contents.

Example 1

Marcia testifies for the prosecution at trial, "The robber was wearing a blue shirt." The defense cross-examination is as follows:

DEFENDANT'S ATTORNEY: You testified on direct that the robber wore a blue shirt?

A: Right.

DEFENDANT'S ATTORNEY: Your Honor, I'd like to read into the record a portion of the witness' grand jury testimony in this case, which of course was given under oath. The testimony appears on page 56, lines 12–15, of the transcript of the grand jury proceedings.

JUDGE: Prosecutor, any objection?

PROSECUTOR: None, Your Honor.

JUDGE: Proceed.

DEFENDANT'S ATTORNEY: (reading from the grand jury transcript) "Question: How was the robber dressed? Answer: The robber wore a green shirt." Marcia, were you asked that question in front of the grand jury and did you give that answer?

A: Yes.

Because Marcia's prior inconsistent statement was given under oath, Rule 801(d)(1)(A) makes it admissible for its truth — that is, as evidence that the robber wore a green shirt.

When the content of a prior inconsistent statement is not necessarily more helpful to a cross-examiner's case than in-court testimony, the proponent of the prior inconsistent statement is likely to be agnostic as to whether the statement qualifies for a hearsay exemption under Rule 801(d)(1)(A) or is admissible as non-hearsay solely for impeachment. The existence of the inconsistency is what is important, and either way the judge or jury finds out that the witness has given contradictory accounts of the same event. However, the distinction can be important if the content of the prior inconsistent statement supports the cross-examiner's legal claims. Then, Rule 801(d)(1)(A)'s hearsay exemption means that the prior statement constitutes substantive evidence for those claims. Without the exemption, the cross-examiner would be limited to arguing the prior inconsistent statement's effect on the witness' credibility.

Example 2

Marcia testifies for the prosecution at trial, "The robber had a scar on his left cheek." The defense introduces into evidence Marcia's prior inconsistent statement, "The robber had no facial markings." Assume that the defendant in fact has a scar on his left cheek.

If Marcia's prior inconsistent statement was made under oath so as to be admissible under Rule 801(d)(1)A), the defense attorney can argue that "Marcia's prior statement proves the defendant's innocence. Her previous statement, made under oath, is evidence that the robber had no facial markings. Since, as you can plainly see the defendant has a scar on his left cheek, the defendant cannot be the robber."

If Marcia's prior inconsistent statement was not made under oath and so is admissible only as non-hearsay to impeach Marcia, the defense attorney is limited to arguing that "You should not believe Marcia's testimony that the robber had a scar on his left cheek. Marcia stated previously that the robber had no facial markings, so her convenient change of testimony is not trustworthy."

Proponents of prior inconsistent statements can offer them into evidence in a variety of ways. The most common is simply to cross-examine a witness about a prior inconsistent statement.

Example 3

Q: You testified on direct examination that the robber had a scar on his left cheek?

A: That's right.

Q: However, you testified before the grand jury that you couldn't recall which of the robber's cheeks had a scar on it, isn't that right?

A: Yes.

If the witness denies giving this testimony before the grand jury, the cross-examiner can "prove up" the prior inconsistent statement by reading the inconsistent grand jury testimony into the record.

Practice Tip: Reducing the Risk of an Explanation

When you confront witnesses with prior inconsistent statements on cross-examination, you run the risk that they will immediately blurt out explanations that bolster the credibility of their in-court testimony. By way of example, assume that an adverse witness in a personal injury case growing out of an auto accident testifies that your client ran a red light. On cross-examination, you elicit the witness' testimony that shortly after the accident the witness told your client, "You had the green light, pal." The witness may add at once, "the reason I said that to your client is that he was hysterical and I was just trying to calm him down." If the judge or jury thinks this a reasonable explanation of the inconsistency, your impeachment has probably lost much of its force. (It is generally a bad idea to ask adverse witnesses to explain why they've made inconsistent statements; the likely result is an answer that is the equivalent to getting a pie in the face, as in this example. But a witness may volunteer an explanation without your asking for one. Judges often allow volunteered explanations to remain in the record so long as the volunteered information is admissible, reasoning that they are part of the give-and-take of cross-examination.)

To minimize the risk of an explanation, you may choose to forgo cross-examination about a prior inconsistent statement, and instead read the prior inconsistent statement into the record, or call a witness to testify to the prior inconsistent statement, when it is your turn to present evidence. To use this procedure, you'll obviously need either a written document that contains the statement or a witness who can testify to the prior inconsistent statement. In either situation, however, the witness whose prior statement you offer is not on the stand when you offer it, and so cannot blurt out an immediate explanation.

If you plan to use this alternative impeachment procedure, you'll need to remember the impact of couple of other rules that Chapter 7 discusses. One is the "collateral evidence rule," which limits impeachment to cross-examination if an inconsistency relates to a minor point. The second is Rule 613, which provides that "extrinsic evidence of a prior inconsistent statement" (i.e., evidence offered other than during cross-examination) is inadmissible unless the impeached witness has "an opportunity to explain or deny" the inconsistency, or unless "the interests of justice otherwise require." Rule 613 seeks to ensure that the party who called the witness whose prior inconsistent statement has been offered into evidence has an opportunity at a later point in the trial to re-call the witness and ask the witness to explain the inconsistency (if the witness has a satisfactory explanation).

Example 4

Marcia testified for the prosecution that "the robber had a scar on his left cheek." The defense attorney cross-examined Marcia on a number of points but made no reference to her inconsistent grand jury testimony. During the defense case-in-chief, the defense attorney plans to read into the record Marcia's grand jury testimony, in which she said that she didn't know which of the robber's cheeks had a scar. To comply with Rule 613, the defense attorney would conclude Marcia's cross-examination as follows:

DEFENDANT'S ATTORNEY: No further questions of the witness at this time.

JUDGE: May this witness be excused?

DEFENDANT'S ATTORNEY: No, Your Honor. I ask that she remain on call and subject to subpoena.

JUDGE: Very well. The witness may stand down but shall remain on call and subject to the previously issued subpoena.

By not excusing Marcia, the defense attorney satisfies Rule 613. The defense attorney could then read Marcia's inconsistent grand jury testimony into the record during the defense case-in-chief:

DEFENDANT'S ATTORNEY: Your Honor, I'd like to open the defendant's case by reading into the record an excerpt from Marcia's grand jury testimony. I'll be reading from page 56, lines 8–11.

JUDGE: Prosecutor, any objection? Hearing none, defense counsel may proceed.

[Defense counsel's precise reference to the transcript testimony gives the prosecutor a chance to determine whether the foundational requirements have been met, in this instance the requirement that the prior statement be "inconsistent" with Marcia's trial testimony.]

DEFENDANT'S ATTORNEY: (reading from the grand jury transcript) "Question: Did you notice whether the robber had any facial markings? Answer: Yes, the robber had a scar on his cheek. Question: Do you know which of the robber's cheeks was scarred? Answer: No, I don't." Thank you, Your Honor, I'll now proceed to call the first witness for the defense.

Practice Tip: "Close the Doors"

The "Close the Doors" technique may also help cross-examiners reduce the risk of explanations. Close the Doors consists of identifying potential explanations a witness might reasonably use to explain away an inconsistency and eliminate those explanations before offering the inconsistency into evidence. The film *My Cousin Vinny* has a wonderful illustration of this technique. Although the illustration does not arise in the context of impeachment with a prior inconsistent statement, the Close the Doors technique applies whenever a cross-examiner seeks to impeach a witness.

In the film, Vinny cross-examines a prosecution witness who testified that only five minutes elapsed between the time that the defendants entered a convenience store and the time the witness heard gunshots and saw the defendants run out of the store. The witness bases his time estimate on how long it took him to cook his breakfast grits. Vinny plans to impeach the witness' time estimate by eliciting the witness' admission that grits require 20 minutes of cooking. Before doing so, however, Vinny closes the doors on possible explanations the witness may give for why his grits were ready in five minutes. The Close the Doors portion of the cross-examination proceeds as follows:

VINNY: How do you like your grits — regular, creamy, or *al dente*?

A: Just regular, I guess.

VINNY: Do you use instant grits?

A: I use regular grits. No self-respecting Southerner uses instant grits.

These questions eliminate two potential explanations the witness might have given for his grits being ready to eat in only five minutes: he likes his grits extra-tough, and he uses instant grits. Having closed the doors to these explanations, Vinny elicits the witness' admission that grits need to be cooked for 20 minutes before they are ready to eat.

Practice Tip: Elicit an Inconsistent Statement During Direct Examination to "Take the Sting Out" of Cross-Examination

You may be the proponent of a witness who has made an inconsistent statement and you are confident that your adversary intends to elicit the inconsistent statement during cross-examination. In this situation, consider eliciting the inconsistent statement yourself, during direct examination. Doing so conveys the idea that you have nothing to hide. And if the witness has a reasonable explanation for the inconsistency, you can elicit the explanation immediately.

Problem 12-1: Try to Remember

(a) Paolo sues Deng for personal injuries suffered in an auto accident. Prior to trial, Paolo deposed Willis, who was riding in Deng's car when the accident occurred. At the deposition, Willis testified as follows:

PLAINTIFF'S ATTORNEY: Willis, was Mr. Deng talking on a cell phone when the collision took place?

A: Sorry, I don't remember.

At trial, Willis testifies on Deng's behalf that Deng was not talking on a cell phone when the collision took place.

Is Willis's deposition testimony inconsistent with his trial testimony?

(b) Assume that you represent Deng. When you meet with Willis prior to his scheduled deposition by the lawyer for plaintiff Paolo, Willis tells you that he and Deng have decided that Willis should not think about the accident at all prior to the deposition. This way, as often as possible, Willis will be able to respond to questions honestly by saying, "I don't remember." Deng and Willis have decided that this is a dandy strategy for providing as little information as possible to Paolo's attorney at the deposition. *Do you agree?*

(c) When Paolo's attorney takes Willis's deposition, Willis testifies as follows:

PLAINTIFF'S ATTORNEY: Willis, was Mr. Deng talking on a cell phone when the collision took place?

A: Yes, I think he was talking on a cell phone.

At trial, while testifying on Deng's behalf, Willis states that he cannot remember whether Deng was talking on a cell phone when the collision took place.

Can Paolo's attorney offer Willis' deposition testimony into the record as a prior inconsistent statement?

(d) When Paolo's attorney takes Willis's deposition, Willis testifies as follows:

PLAINTIFF'S ATTORNEY: Willis, was Mr. Deng talking on a cell phone when the collision took place?

A: Yes, he was on the phone having a big argument with his ex-wife about child custody arrangements.

At trial, Paolo's attorney calls Willis as a witness. Willis testifies as follows:

PLAINTIFF'S ATTORNEY: Willis, what if anything was Deng doing at the time the collision took place?

A: I'm sorry, I can't remember.

[At this point the judge allows Paolo's lawyer to try to stimulate Willis's recollection by showing Willis the portion of the deposition testimony in which Willis testified that Deng was talking on a cell phone to his ex-wife at the time of the collision. For more information about this procedure, *see* Chapter 14.]

PLAINTIFF'S ATTORNEY: Willis, now that you've had a chance to review your deposition testimony, let me ask you again what, if anything, was Mr. Deng doing at the time the collision took place?

A: I still can't remember. I really don't remember a thing about that day.

PLAINTIFF'S ATTORNEY: Do you recall being a passenger in Mr. Deng's car when a collision occurred?

A: No.

PLAINTIFF'S ATTORNEY: Since the accident, have you been under a doctor's care for any kind of medical problem relating to your mental functioning?

A: No. It's just that I don't remember anything about an accident when I was a passenger in Deng's car.

PLAINTIFF'S ATTORNEY: Are you and Mr. Deng good friends?

A: Of course. We've worked together for a few years and we hang around socially sometimes.

PLAINTIFF'S ATTORNEY: And do you know whether Mr. Deng owns a cell phone?

A: I don't remember whether he does or not.

On this record, can Paolo's attorney offer Willis's deposition testimony into the record as a prior inconsistent statement?

Problem 12-2: Blame Worthy

Alison Anderson sues Mel Atonin for personal injuries suffered in an auto accident. Mel's attorney deposes Worthy, who the police report identifies as a witness to the accident. At the deposition, Worthy testifies, "I saw Mel's car, the blue SUV, run the red light." Between the time of the deposition and the trial, however, Worthy calls both counsel and tells them that his deposition testimony was wrong, and that he didn't see the cars before hearing the crash. Worthy also tells the attorneys that if he is called as a witness at trial, he'll testify that he didn't see what happened prior to the collision. When Alison's attorney nevertheless calls Worthy as a witness at trial, the following ensues:

PLAINTIFF'S ATTORNEY: Plaintiff next calls Worthy to the stand.

DEFENDANT'S ATTORNEY: Your Honor, might the plaintiff make an offer of proof out of the jury's presence as to what information she seeks to elicit from Worthy? I believe that the plaintiff's putting Worthy on the witness stand is simply a ruse to offer hearsay.

JUDGE: Very well, counsel. I've excused the jury. Plaintiff, what evidence do you plan to elicit from this witness?

PLAINTIFF'S ATTORNEY: I'm informed by Worthy that he will testify inconsistently from his deposition that he did not see either of the cars prior to the crash. After he so testifies, I will then impeach Worthy with his deposition testimony that the defendant's blue SUV ran the red light.

DEFENDANT'S ATTORNEY: In that case, I renew the hearsay objection and ask that Your Honor not permit the plaintiff to call Worthy as a witness.

JUDGE: I'll rule based on the assumption that Worthy will testify that he didn't see what happened prior to the collision. On that basis, I'll hear argument from both counsel before ruling on the objection. You might address the impact on my ruling of Rule 607.

Student # 1: You are the defense attorney. Argue that because the plaintiff seeks to call Worthy only for the purpose of offering his deposition testimony into evidence, the judge should not permit the plaintiff to call Worthy as a witness.

Student # 2: You are the plaintiff's attorney. Argue that you can call Worthy as a witness and, if his testimony conflicts with his deposition testimony, you can offer Worthy's deposition testimony into evidence.

Student # 3: You are the judge. Preside over the arguments and rule on whether the plaintiff can call Worthy as a witness and offer Worthy's deposition testimony into evidence should Worthy testify that he did not see the cars prior to the collision.

Problem 12-3: Bar Exam 1

Donahue is on trial for assault with a deadly weapon. The prosecution claims that Donahue and Meeker exchanged heated words in a bar, and that as Meeker walked out Donahue threw a bottle at him, striking Meeker on the head and shoulder. Prosecution witness Friedman testifies on direct examination that after Donahue and Meeker got into an argument, Meeker picked up a pool cue and advanced on Donahue with it. At that point, according to Friedman, Donahue threw the bottle at Meeker. After Friedman concludes testifying, the prosecutor seeks to call Police Officer Ono to testify that on the evening of the bar fight, Friedman told Ono that "Meeker was walking away when Donahue threw the bottle at him."

Is Officer Ono's testimony admissible against Donahue under the Confrontation Clause?

Problem 12-4: Bar Exam 2

Same case as previous problem. Assume that Friedman's hearsay statement that Meeker was walking away when Donahue threw the bottle at him was not made to a police officer on the night of the bar fight, but rather under oath during a grand jury hearing. When Friedman testifies during direct examination that Donahue threw the bottle at Meeker after Meeker picked up a pool cue and advanced on Donahue with it, the prosecution seeks to read Friedman's inconsistent grand jury testimony into the record for the truth of its contents.

Is Friedman's grand jury testimony admissible against Donahue under the Confrontation Clause?

Problem 12-5: Computer Caper

In Palmer's lawsuit against his former employer for wrongful termination, Erica testifies on the employer's behalf that she was Palmer's co-worker and that she saw him steal company property. Palmer's attorney cross-examines Erica in part as follows:

PLAINTIFF'S ATTORNEY: You testified on direct examination that you saw Palmer take computer equipment that was still packed in its original cartons from a company storage closet and put it in his car, correct?

A: That's right.

PLAINTIFF'S ATTORNEY: And you testified that you saw him take monitors, printers, keyboards, and software, right?

A: Yes.

PLAINTIFF'S ATTORNEY: At your deposition, I asked you to identify what property you had seen Palmer take, right?

A: Yes, you did.

PLAINTIFF'S ATTORNEY: Yet you did not mention at that time that you had seen him take software, isn't that right?

A: No, I didn't, I must have forgotten that.

DEFENDANT'S ATTORNEY: Objection and move to strike. Counsel's question does not refer to anything that witness said at deposition that is inconsistent with the testimony she's given today at trial.

PLAINTIFF'S ATTORNEY: *What is your response to the objection?*

PLAINTIFF'S ATTORNEY: And isn't it also true that Ballam, another employee of the company, testified at her deposition that the computer equipment that Palmer took was used and marked with labels saying "To Be Trashed"?

DEFENDANT'S ATTORNEY: *What objection, if any, might you make to this question?*

Problem 12-6: *Baby Ruth*

Duncan is charged with murdering "Baby Ruth" Jackson, an elderly woman who was admired in her neighborhood for providing candy and telling stories to little children. Duncan was charged with the murder based primarily on information provided by McCarthy. McCarthy told police officers that he heard a scream coming from Baby Ruth's home and saw Duncan jump over her fence carrying a purse and a knife. McCarthy also told the officers that shortly afterwards he heard Duncan tell his mother that he'd stabbed Baby Ruth. Called as a prosecution witness at trial, however, McCarthy testifies that "I never saw Duncan on the night Baby Ruth was killed, and I didn't hear him confess to nobody." The prosecution offers McCarthy's statements to the police officers into evidence as prior inconsistent statements. McCarthy testifies that he made the statements, but that they were not true and he made them "because I was mad at Duncan for trying to steal my woman."

1. Assume that the information above constitutes the entirety of the prosecution's case linking Duncan to the murder of Baby Ruth. *Under the Federal Rules of Evidence, how should the judge rule in response to the defense attorney's Motion to Dismiss the case against Duncan?*

2. In contrast to Rule 801(d)(1)(A), California Evidence Code Section 1235 makes all prior inconsistent statements admissible for their truth, regardless of whether they were given under oath. *Under the California Evidence Code, how should the judge rule in response to the defense attorney's Motion to Dismiss the case against Duncan?*

3. Assume that McCarthy's statements implicating Duncan in the murder of Baby Ruth were made not to police officers, but under oath during federal grand jury proceedings.

Student # 1: As the prosecutor, make a brief closing argument based on the summary of evidence above in an effort to convince the jury to believe McCarthy's grand jury testimony.

Student # 2: As the defense attorney, make a brief closing argument based on the summary of evidence above in an effort to raise a reasonable doubt about Duncan's guilt.

Problem 12-7: Ask the Expert

Your local representative to the U.S. Congress seeks your advice with respect to changing Rule 801(d)(1)(A) to make all prior inconsistent statements admissible for the truth of their contents (as the California Evidence Code provides). When deciding how to respond to the Congressperson's request, consider the following questions:

(a) In adopting the rule that all prior inconsistent statements are admissible for their truth, the California Law Revision Commission stated that "the inconsistent statement is more likely to be true than the testimony of the witness at the trial because it was made nearer in time to the matter to which it relates and is less likely to be influenced by the controversy that gave rise to the litigation." Do you agree with this generalization?

(b) Do you agree with the Federal Rules drafters' position that prior statements are more likely to be truthful if they are made under oath?

(c) When judges instruct jurors to consider a prior inconsistent statement only for its effect on a witness' credibility and not for the truth of its contents, how likely are jurors to follow the admonition?

(d) In criminal cases, would the proposed change be more likely to benefit prosecutors or defense lawyers? To the extent one group is likely to benefit more than the other, is this a relevant or legitimate consideration?

(e) Would you favor an alternative amendment providing that prior inconsistent statements are admissible for their truth only if the party offering it shows that the adversary turned the witness into a "turncoat" by bribing or intimidating the witness into a changed story?

Problem 12-8: Excuse Me

David is charged with bank robbery; the defense is an alibi. Beth testifies that David was with her at the movies at the time of the robbery. After cross-examining Beth and agreeing to excuse Beth as a witness, the prosecutor learns that two months before the trial, a different prosecutor had instituted proceedings seeking to revoke Beth's probation. In the probation revocation hearing, Beth had testified that "I haven't been in David's company for over a year." The prosecutor seeks to read this portion of Beth's testimony during the probation revocation hearing into the record during David's trial. Defense counsel objects, arguing that because Beth had already been excused as a witness, granting the prosecutor's request would leave the defense with no opportunity to offer evidence to explain or deny the probation revocation testimony. *How should the judge rule on the prosecutor's request?*

Problem 12-9: The Woodshed

Paul Biegler is an Assistant U.S. Attorney who is prosecuting Laura for armed robbery. Prior to trial, Biegler meets with Fred Manion, an eyewitness who will identify Laura as the robber. When he talked to the police shortly after the robbery, Manion said that he didn't really get a good look at the robber, and that beyond thinking that the robber was female he thought he'd have a hard time identifying the person who did it. Biegler expects the defense to impeach Manion with his statements to the police. Biegler hopes that his meeting with Manion will produce a satisfactory explanation for those statements that Biegler can elicit on redirect examination of Manion. Below is a partial transcript of Biegler's pretrial meeting with Manion. *Consider whether Biegler complies with ABA Model Rule of Professional Conduct 3.4-(b), which provides that "A lawyer shall not . . . counsel or assist a witness to testify falsely."*

BIEGLER: So just to review, you're prepared to testify that Laura was the robber?

MANION: That's right. There's no doubt in my mind about that.

BIEGLER: Do you remember that when you talked to the police right after the robbery, you said you didn't get a good look at the robber, and that you thought you'd have a hard time recognizing her if you saw her again?

MANION: Yes, I do. I'm really sorry, I hope that doesn't mess you up.

BIEGLER: Well, on cross-examination you can certainly expect Laura's attorney to bring out those statements and later argue that your identification isn't worth diddly.

MANION: Is there anything we can do?

BIEGLER: Well, I can bring out what you said to the police during direct examination, and ask you to explain why you made those statements. Or, I can let the defense attorney bring the statements out during cross-examination and ask you for an explanation during my redirect. Either way, the key is giving the jury a satisfactory explanation. Can you tell me why you told the police that you didn't get a good look at the robber?

MANION: I wish I could. That whole period is kind of a blur — the robbery, seeing a gun, being questioned by the cops, it was really unnerving.

BIEGLER: Are you saying that you were frightened, maybe of retaliation by Laura or her friends, and saying that to the police was your way of not getting involved?

MANION: Yes, I'd say that's correct.

BIEGLER: That's fine. When your statements to the police are brought up, either by me or the defense, you can give that explanation. I think it's a reasonable one that the jury will accept.

Problem 12-10: Gimme Shelter

Wes Quire, Esq., is the defendant in an attorney malpractice action. The complainant alleges that Quire provided incompetent advice as to the legitimacy of a Tibetan Winery Trust as a tax shelter, causing the complainant to incur tax penalties of more than $200,000. At trial, Kirk Stark, Esq., testifies as an expert on Quire's behalf. Stark testifies that he is a tax specialist and that Quire had a reasonable basis for believing that the investment was a legitimate tax shelter. On cross-examination, Stark admits that six months earlier, he signed an affidavit under penalty of perjury stating that "Among the topics I will cover is that no competent tax professional would consider Tibetan Winery Trusts to be legitimate tax shelters." Stark submitted this affidavit to a law school when seeking an appointment to teach Tax 1 six months earlier. *Is the affidavit admissible for the truth of its contents?*

C. Prior Consistent Statements (Rule 801(d)(1)(B))

Foundational Elements:

* The declarant testifies at the trial or hearing;

* The declarant is subject to cross-examination concerning the prior statement;

* The prior statement is consistent with the declarant's testimony;

* The statement is offered to rebut an adversary's express or implied charge that the declarant's testimony is recently fabricated or the result of improper influence or motive; or to rehabilitate a declarant's credibility as a witness after it has been impeached on another ground.

A prior consistent statement consists of a witness' hearsay statement that agrees with (corroborates) the same witness' courtroom testimony. While prior *inconsistent* statements are tools for *discrediting* witnesses, prior *consistent* statements are tools for *accrediting or rehabilitating* witnesses. A prior consistent statement that satisfies the foundational elements of Rule 801(d)(1)(B)(i) or (ii) is admitted for the truth of its contents regardless of whether it was made under oath.[2]

Example

Millie is testifying against the defendant in a sexual assault case.

PROSECUTOR: Millie, what happened after the defendant offered to give you a ride home?

A: The defendant drove into a basement garage about a mile from the club.

PROSECUTOR: Did you speak to the police after escaping from the defendant's car?

A: I did. I phoned 911 as soon as I could.

PROSECUTOR: And what did you tell the 911 operator?

A: I said that the defendant had offered to drive me home from a club but instead had driven to an underground parking lot.

---

2. Consistent statements admitted under sub-section "i" are very likely to qualify for admission under the more general language of sub-section "ii." The separate sub-parts exist because they were adopted at different times.

The last answer constitutes a "prior consistent statement," as Millie offers evidence that in essence asserts, "I said the same thing before trial that I'm testifying to now."

You might reasonably expect the admissibility of prior consistent statements to be parallel to that of prior inconsistent statements. If it were, prior consistent statements would be generally admissible as non-hearsay to support a witness' credibility, and admissible for their truth under a hearsay exemption if made under oath. However, the common-law treatment of prior consistent and inconsistent statements was not parallel, and the Federal Rules of Evidence continue the non-parallel common-law tradition.

The general rule is that in the absence of an attack on credibility, prior consistent statements are not admissible as non-hearsay to bolster witnesses' credibility. A rationale for this policy is that Rule 403 factors are likely to outweigh the probative value of such statements. For one thing, undue delays would no doubt occur if hearsay rules permitted attorneys to parade in the people to whom witnesses had spoken with before trial, to testify in essence, "what do you know, the witness told me the very same thing." (And if prior consistent statements were generally admissible as non-hearsay, you can bet that lawyers would encourage important witnesses to tell their stories to as many highly credible people as possible.) Thus, the policy generally barring the use of prior consistent statements as non-hearsay to bolster witnesses' credibility is a specialized application of Rule 403.

As a result, admission of a prior consistent statement under Rule 801(d)(1)(B) normally involves a three-step process:

Step One: A witness testifies on behalf of Party A.

Step Two: Party B impeaches (or seeks to impeach) the witness' credibility.

Step Three: Party A offers evidence of the witness' prior consistent statement. (Party A may do so through the testimony of the witness who made the prior consistent statement, or through an extrinsic source, such as a witness who has personal knowledge of the consistent statement.)

Whether an impeached witness' prior consistent statement is admissible to rehabilitate the witness' credibility often depends on timing. A prior consistent statement generally is admissible to rebut impeachment only if the witness made the consistent statement *before* the basis of impeachment existed.

Example 1

Tome is charged with sexually abusing his four-year-old daughter. After the daughter testifies to acts of abuse, Tome's cross-examination suggests that the daughter lied about the abuse so that she could live with her mother instead of with Tome. To rehabilitate the daughter's credibility, the government calls social workers and medical personnel to testify to the daughter's consistent statements to them describing Tome's abuse. The daughter's prior consistent statements were not admissible, because the same motive to lie (her desire to live with her mother) existed at the time the daughter spoke to the social workers and medical personnel. *Tome v. United States* (513 U.S. 150 (1995)). (The Court remanded the case to the lower court for consideration of whether some or all of the daughter's pretrial statements were admissible under the "catch-all" hearsay exception, now Rule 807, or the hearsay exception for "statements for purposes of medical diagnosis," Rule 803(4). Please refer to Chapter 14 for further discussion of these possibilities.)

Example 2

Same case. Tome's cross-examination of his daughter suggests that the daughter lied about the abuse because she wanted to live with the new puppy her mother had adopted. Statements by the daughter describing Tome's abuse made before the mother adopted the new puppy would rebut Tome's impeachment and qualify as prior consistent statements.

Example 3

Wendy testifies for the plaintiff in a breach of contract action that Peter attended an important May 21 meeting. The defense impeaches Wendy by calling Michael to testify that on June 21, Wendy told Michael that she couldn't recall whether Peter attended the May 21 meeting. The plaintiff can rehabilitate Wendy by calling John to testify that on May 22, Wendy told John that Peter attended the May 21 meeting. Wendy's consistent statement to John was made before her inconsistent statement to Michael.

Practice Tip: "Tender Years" Hearsay

A number of states have created "tender years" hearsay exceptions that make prior consistent statements such as the ones at issue in *Tome* admissible even in the absence of an attack on credibility. For example, under California Evidence Code Section 1360, a child's hearsay statement that is consistent with the child's courtroom testimony is admissible if the following foundational elements are shown to exist:

- The statement is offered in a criminal case.
- The child was under 12 years old when the statement was made.
- The statement describes an act or acts of sexual abuse.
- The judge concludes that the statement is reliable.

Problem 12-11: The Howling

Susan Bee sues Elizabeth Cady for personal injuries resulting from an auto accident that occurred two years prior to trial. During direct examination on the issue of damages, Susan testified that, "Ever since the accident, I howl every time there's a full moon." The cross-examination of Susan included the following excerpt:

DEFENDANT'S ATTORNEY: Isn't it true that you decided to claim that you howl at the full moon only after you found out that our Supreme Court ruled last month that uncontrollable howling was an element of damages in personal injury cases?

A: That's not true.

Under Rule 801(d)(1)(B), can Susan call Harriett Beecher to testify that "Twelve months ago, Susan told me that ever since the auto accident, she howls at every full moon"?

Problem 12-12: MacMeth

In a government corruption prosecution, Mac testifies for the prosecution that on June 1, he overheard the defendant offer the mayor $100,000 in exchange for the mayor's favorable vote on a contract. The defense cross-examination of Mac includes the following testimony:

Q: Mac, you were a long-time user of methamphetamines, is that right?

A: I regret to admit that's true.

Q: In fact, you started using methamphetamines daily about a month after you claim to have overheard a conversation between my client and the mayor, correct?

A: That's correct. But I'm proud to say that I am in recovery and now have 183 days clean and sober.

Q: That's admirable. But your addiction to meth has affected your memory, has it not?

A: I wouldn't agree with that.

Q: You overdosed and went to detox twice while you were actively using methamphetamines for over a year, and your memory was unaffected?

A: I remember what your client said to the mayor.

Under Rule 801(d)(1)(B), can the prosecutor offer evidence that Mac reported the alleged conversation between the mayor and the defendant the day after it took place? What if the statement with which the prosecutor attempts to rehabilitate Mac's credibility was made to a police investigator during the time that Mac was actively using methamphetamines?

Problem 12-13: Park Place

Defendant Pancho Kramer is charged with sexual assault. Martina Budge testifies on behalf of the prosecution that while taking a walk in the park in which the attack occurred, Budge noticed a gray jacket on the ground underneath a bench near the park's tennis courts. (Assume that this testimony links the defendant to the assault.) A portion of the defense attorney's cross-examination of Budge goes as follows:

DEFENDANT'S ATTORNEY: You walk in the park regularly, correct?

A: Yes, I do.

DEFENDANT'S ATTORNEY: In fact, you've been taking evening walks in the park pretty regularly for the last four to five years, correct?

A: That's true.

DEFENDANT'S ATTORNEY: And you often see articles of clothing lying around the park when you take your walks, don't you?

A: Yes.

DEFENDANT'S ATTORNEY: So it would not be unusual for a gray jacket to be underneath a park bench?

A: No.

DEFENDANT'S ATTORNEY: You didn't stop walking to go over and take a look at the jacket, did you?

A: No.

DEFENDANT'S ATTORNEY: And you can't describe any other articles of clothing that had been left in the park that night, can you?

A: No, I suppose not.

DEFENDANT'S ATTORNEY: About five months have gone by since that evening, correct?

A: That's about right.

DEFENDANT'S ATTORNEY: Yet you claim that you remember specifically seeing a gray jacket underneath a bench near the tennis courts on the night of the alleged assault?

A: That's what I remember.

Following this questioning, under Rule 801(d)(1)(B), can the prosecution call police officer Nastase to testify that a few days after the assault, Budge voluntarily came into the police station to tell Nastase that Budge had seen a gray jacket lying underneath a bench near the park's tennis courts on the night of the attack? If not, might the police officer's testimony be admitted on any other rationale?

Problem 12-14: Just One More Thing

Dante is charged with armed sexual assault of Sean. Armed sexual assault is punishable more heavily than the crime of unarmed sexual assault. During direct examination by the prosecutor, Sean testified that, "On March 1, Dante offered me a ride home from the club, drove to a dark basement parking lot instead, and tried to pull my clothes off. I got out of the car and ran away before anything else happened." Defense counsel's cross-examination of Sean included the following excerpt:

DEFENDANT'S ATTORNEY: Isn't it true that you decided to make up this story only after Dante fired you on March 15?

A: That's not true.

To prove that Dante was armed at the time of the assault, the prosecutor seeks to call Police Officer Sakamoto to testify as follows: "On March 3, Sean came into the police station and told me that Dante had offered him a ride home but instead had driven to an underground parking lot. Sean told me that Dante pulled a knife, pointed it at him with one hand and tried to tear his clothes off with the other. Sean said that he managed to get out of the car and run away before anything else happened."

Would Officer Sakamoto's testimony be admissible as a prior consistent statement under Rule 801(d)(1)(B)?

Problem 12-15: Rescue Effort

Greig is charged with assaulting Baskin. Nilsson supports Greig's self-defense claim by testifying that Baskin initiated the altercation by attacking Greig from behind. Cross-examining Nilsson, the prosecutor impeaches Nilsson with Nilsson's felony conviction for fraud. Greig then calls Swenson to testify, "The day after Greig was arrested for attacking Baskin, Nilsson told me that Baskin had started the fight and that Greig hit Baskin to protect himself." *Is Swenson's testimony to Nilsson's consistent statement admissible to rehabilitate Nilsson? Does it matter whether the fraud conviction occurred before or after Nilsson spoke to Swenson?*

Problem 12-16: Emot ("Tome" Reversed)

The four dissenters in *Tome v. United States* argued that Rule 801(d)(1)(B) does not contain an explicit timing requirement, and that a prior consistent statement might be relevant to rebut a charge of "recent fabrication" or "improper motive" even if it was made at a time when the same motive existed as at trial. Under their view, the admissibility of a prior consistent statement would be based on general relevance principles, with a judge having the power to exclude a prior consistent statement under Rule 403 if its unfair prejudice outweighed its probative value.

Assume that the Supreme Court overrules *Tome*, or that Congress amends Rule 801(d)(1)(B) so as to adopt the dissenters' approach.

As the prosecutor faced with the facts in Tome, *what argument would you make in an effort to persuade the trial judge to admit the daughter's prior consistent statements on relevance principles?*

As the defense attorney faced with the facts in Tome, *what argument would you make in an effort to persuade the trial judge to exclude the daughter's prior consistent statements under Rule 403?*

D. Pretrial Identifications (Rule 801(d)(1)(C))

Foundational Elements:

* The declarant testifies at the trial or hearing;

* The declarant is subject to cross-examination concerning the prior statement;

* The prior statement identifies a person;

* The statement was made after the declarant perceived the person.

  This element generally refers to post-crime identifications, such as when a crime victim tells the police than the person pictured in a mug shot was the attacker.

The hearsay exemption for pretrial identifications is a powerful prosecutorial tool in criminal cases. "Identity" is often the crux of a criminal trial. Yet, weeks or even months may pass between the time that witnesses observe criminal activity and the time that trials occur. The delay can provide defendants with a strong argument that witnesses' in-court identifications are mistaken or worthless. ("Witnesses will identify whoever is seated next to the defense attorney as the perpetrator.") This hearsay exemption allows prosecutors to offer evidence of identifications that are made closer in time to actual events, and therefore perhaps of greater probative value to jurors than in-court identifications.

Witnesses whose prior identifications are admitted in evidence often repeat their identifications at trial. Thus, a hearsay statement admitted as a "prior identification" often constitutes a "prior consistent statement," but of a type that is admissible without the intermediate attack on the witness' credibility. However, this is not invariably true. In *United States v. Owens* (484 U.S. 554 (1988)), defendant Owens was a prisoner who was charged with beating a correctional counselor named John Foster with a lead pipe. Foster suffered such severe memory loss that at trial he could remember almost nothing about the attack and could not identify the attacker. However, while in the hospital, Foster told an FBI agent that Owens had attacked him, and Foster also picked out a photo of Owens as his attacker. The Court held that Foster's identification of Owens in the hospital was admissible under Rule 801(d)(1)(C). Though Owens claimed that Foster's mental condition prevented thorough cross-examination, Foster was "subject to cross-examination concerning the statement" and the rule requires nothing more. (In this pre-*Crawford* case, the Court also decided that Owens' opportunity for cross-examination, though limited, satisfied the Confrontation Clause.)

Example

In the made-for-TV movie *Criminal Justice*,[3] an assailant slashes Denise Moore's face and takes the small amount of cash that she was carrying. Moore describes her attacker to the police as follows: "Male, Black, mid-20s,

---

3. Home Box Office 1990.

6' 1," 220 pounds, dark skin, short hair." Moore then looks though mug shots, holds up a photograph of Jessie Williams, and tells the police officers: "This is him . . . this is the guy, except he had sort of a rough beard . . . I'm sure this is him." The police officers arrest Williams the next day and put him in a lineup. Viewing the lineup, Moore says that "It's Number 4 (Williams) . . . he's the one that cut me. I'm sure." Sometime later, Moore testifies during grand jury indictment proceedings that Williams is the person who slashed her face and robbed her. Each of these out-of-court statements by Moore constitutes a prior identification that is potentially admissible under Rule 801(d)(1)(C).

Practice Tip: Excluding "Prior Identifications"

When a prosecutor seeks to offer several "prior identifications" into evidence in the same case, a defense attorney may argue that the judge should exclude one or more of the out-of-court identifications under Rule 403. For example, because an identification of a mug shot suggests that a defendant has a criminal record, a judge may exclude evidence of a mug shot identification as unfairly prejudicial. Moreover, multiple prior identifications may consume an unwarranted amount of time. Thus, prior identifications may be exempt from the hearsay rule but be excluded for other reasons.

Should it matter how much time elapses between an event and an out-of-court identification? Cf. California's version of Rule 801(d)(1)(C), Cal. Evid. Code § 1238. Section 1238 includes a foundational requirement that the out-of-court identification be made "at a time when the crime or other occurrence was fresh in the witness' memory."

Practice Tip: Trading Places

In his book *Deceitful Silence,* Bruce A. Green retells a story from a 1934 biography of famed Los Angeles trial lawyer Earl Rogers, *Take the Witness* by A. Cohen & J. Chisholm. Rogers represented a defendant who was charged with stealing a horse. The horse's owner was a well-known local farmer. The owner testified that he had no doubt that Rogers' client was the horse thief. The defendant was seated next to Rogers at counsel table, "dressed in worn overalls, with a stubbly beard, nervously twirling a small green hat." On cross examination, Rogers questioned the owner on seemingly unimportant details about crops and cattle, all the while standing between the owner and the defendant. Meanwhile Rogers' assistant, who had been seated inconspicuously in the back of the courtroom and dressed similarly to the defendant (including the green hat), changed places with the defendant. Rogers then stepped to the side and asked the farmer to identify again the person who stole the horse. The farmer pointed to the assistant, seated at counsel table, and testified that he had no doubt that the person he pointed to stole the horse. The biographers conclude, "The case was literally laughed out of court." To access Green's book, visit http://www.jstor.org/stable/29760619. Added note: The 1957 pilot episode of the classic though short-lived television series *The Defenders* depicts Rogers' courtroom trickery in the context of a murder prosecution. The cast of the pilot episode includes William Shatner and Steve McQueen, two actors who went on to great fame.

Problem 12-17: Bagged

Reina, who is blind, grabs the arm of a thief who had just wrenched her purse off her arm. Reina yells for help, and holds on to the thief until a police officer arrives. Reina tells the officer that the person she is holding onto is the one who tried to steal her purse. The thief is charged with robbery. At trial, Reina describes the attempted theft of her purse but cannot identify the defendant as the robber. The police officer identifies the defendant as the person who was in Reina's grasp. The police officer also seeks to testify that when the officer handed Reina the purse that the suspect had been holding, Reina stated, "Yes, this is my purse." *Under Rule 801(d)(1)(C), can the police officer testify that (a) "Reina told me that the person whose arm she was holding onto was the person who had grabbed her purse"; and that (b) "Reina told me that the purse that I took out of the suspect's hands and placed in her hand was her purse"?*

Problem 12-18: Hitting a Brick Wall

Edna Cleary testifies for the prosecution in a case in which McCormick is charged with grand theft of bricks that were sufficient in number to build a wall. After eliciting testimony from Cleary that she watched the theft unfold from an office window, the prosecutor elicits the following testimony from Cleary:

PROSECUTOR: Do you see the individual who loaded the bricks into the bed of his truck here in the courtroom?

A: No.

PROSECUTOR: Calling your attention to the defendant McCormick, seated next to defense counsel, can you tell us whether the defendant is the person you saw loading the bricks into the truck bed?

A: He is definitely not the person who took the bricks.

Following this testimony, the prosecutor calls Chad Bourne as a witness. Bourne's testimony goes as follows:

PROSECUTOR: Mr. Bourne, do you know Edna Cleary, the witness who just testified?

A: I do. We work together.

PROSECUTOR: And calling your attention to Dec. 2, a week after the charged theft, were you and Ms. Cleary at work that day?

A: We were.

PROSECUTOR: Please tell us what took place between Ms. Cleary and you at approximately 10 AM on that date.

A: Sure. Our desks are just a few feet apart. Ms. Cleary called me over and pointed to her computer screen and said, "Look at this — there's a photo of the guy who stole the bricks last week."

PROSECUTOR: Did you look at the photo she pointed to?

A: I did.

PROSECUTOR: And do you recognize anyone here in court as the person depicted in that photo?

A: Yes, it was the defendant, seated over there (pointing to McCormick).

The defense attorney objects on the ground that Cleary's in-court denial that McCormick was the person who committed the theft means that the pretrial identification of McCormick is inadmissible. Defense counsel further objects that as Cleary's statement to Bourne is hearsay, Bourne's testimony is improper. *How should the judge rule on these objections? Would the prosecutor be better off offering Cleary's statement to Bourne into evidence as a prior inconsistent statement under Rule 801(d)(1)(A) rather than as a prior identification under Rule 801(d)(1)(C)?*

Problem 12-19: Lengthy Rivalry

Capulet is charged with attempted murder. The charges result from a savage beating that Capulet allegedly administered to Montague, a member of a rival street gang. Montague suffered severe and permanent memory loss. Asked to describe what happened at trial, Montague testifies that he remembers two men hitting him and that it was dark. He cannot recall other details of the attack nor can he identify either attacker. He recalls being in a hospital room for many days, but doesn't remember speaking to anyone while he was there. The prosecutor then makes an offer of proof that Dr. Ophelia Tybalt will testify that she provided medical care for Montague while he was in the hospital. When Montague was well enough to talk a few days after the attack, Dr. Tybalt spoke to him for a few minutes about where he was and why he was there. At one point Dr. Tybalt asked Montague how he had gotten hurt, and he answered, "It was Capulet and someone else." Dr. Tybalt asked him about the attack on a few other occasions, but Montague could say nothing more about it than he testified to in court. *Can Dr. Tybalt testify to the above information under Rule 801(d)(1)(C)? Would allowing Dr. Tybalt to testify be consistent with the principles underlying the Confrontation Clause as interpreted by* Crawford *(see Chapter 10)?*

Problem 12-20: The Lineup

Arnold Kim is charged with armed robbery of a jewelry store; the defense is an alibi. Wigmore, the store owner, later identifies the defendant in a lineup as the person who robbed her at gunpoint.

1. On the morning of trial, Wigmore calls the prosecutor and says, "I'm calling you from Bermuda. I'm not coming to court, I got an email message from

someone stating that he was a friend of Kim and that if I identify Kim as the robber in court I'm a goner. I've heard too many stories of government witnesses suddenly going missing." *Can the prosecutor offer Wigmore's lineup identification into evidence under Rule 801(d)(1)(C)?*

2. Assume that Wigmore is prepared to identify Kim at trial as the robber. Prior to trial, Kim's attorney submits a motion *in limine* asking the trial judge to rule that because the police employed improper lineup procedures, Wigmore should not be allowed to identify the defendant in court and her lineup identification of the defendant should not be admitted. The defense bases the motion on the case of *Neil v. Biggers*,[4] in which the U.S. Supreme Court ruled that a defendant can suppress both a witness' in-court and pretrial identifications if police procedures were so suggestive as to create a substantial likelihood of misidentification. The judge schedules a foundational hearing ("mini-trial") on the issue of the propriety of the lineup procedures. A partial transcript of that hearing reads as follows:

PROSECUTOR: And after viewing the lineup, Wigmore, were you able to identify the person who robbed you at gunpoint?

A: Yes, I did make an identification.

PROSECUTOR: And who did you point out as the robber?

A: That man over there (pointing to the defendant).

PROSECUTOR: And is it your testimony here today that the defendant is the person who robbed you in the jewelry store at gunpoint?

A: Yes.

PROSECUTOR: No further foundational questions, Your Honor. I ask that you rule that Wigmore can testify to the lineup identification and also that he be allowed to testify to the defendant's identity at trial if possible.

JUDGE: Defense may inquire.

DEFENDANT'S ATTORNEY: Thank you, Your Honor. Wigmore, when you viewed the six people in the lineup, you initially told the police officer that you weren't sure that you recognized any of them as the robber, is that right?

A: That's true.

DEFENDANT'S ATTORNEY: The officer then asked you to look very carefully, and told you that it was important that you identify someone if you could?

A: Yes, the officer did say that.

DEFENDANT'S ATTORNEY: And after again studying everyone in the lineup, you again told the officer that you couldn't be sure if the robber was amongst them?

---

4. 409 U.S. 188, 93 S. Ct. 375, 34 L. Ed. 2d 401 (1972).

A: That's right.

DEFENDANT'S ATTORNEY: And the police officer then asked you to look very carefully at Suspect # 3?

A: Yes.

DEFENDANT'S ATTORNEY: The officer further mentioned that Suspect #3 closely matched the description you gave of the robber just moments after the robbery?

A: The officer did say something like that.

DEFENDANT'S ATTORNEY: Do you want me to refresh your recollection as to what the officer said by playing the recording of the conversation for you?

A: No, that's what the officer said.

DEFENDANT'S ATTORNEY: And after this you said that the officer was right, that Suspect #3 was the robber?

A: Yes.

DEFENDANT'S ATTORNEY: And Suspect #3 is the defendant, the person you're prepared to identify here today as the robber?

A: Yes.

DEFENDANT'S ATTORNEY: Isn't it true that your recollection of Mr. Kim today is based entirely on having seen him at the lineup?

A: No. I recognize him from the robbery.

DEFENDANT'S ATTORNEY: Yet when you first saw Mr. Kim in the lineup, just a week after the robbery, you told the officer that you weren't sure if the robber was in the lineup?

A: That's true, I was nervous.

DEFENDANT'S ATTORNEY: Yet now you're certain that Mr. Kim was the robber?

A: Yes, quite certain.

DEFENDANT'S ATTORNEY: No further questions.

JUDGE: Prosecution, anything further?

PROSECUTOR: Thank you, Your Honor, just briefly. Wigmore, did you identify the defendant as the robber because the police officer told you to?

A: No.

PROSECUTOR: As you sit in this courtroom now, do have in your mind a clear picture of the person who robbed your store?

A: Yes.

PROSECUTOR: And do you see that person here in the courtroom?

A: Yes, it's him, seated over there (indicating the defendant).

PROSECUTOR: No further foundational questions, Your Honor.

JUDGE: If that concludes the foundational evidence, I'll hear briefly from counsel before ruling on the defense motion.

Student # 1: As the defense attorney, argue in support of the motion *in limine.* Be sure to mention which side has the burden of proof on the foundational issue, and what that burden consists of.

Student # 2: As the prosecutor, argue in support of the admissibility of the pretrial and in-court identifications.

Student # 3: As the judge, rule on the admissibility of the pretrial and in-court identifications.

Problem 12-21: At the Movies: Turncoat

In the film *Knock on Any Door,*[5] Nick Romano is charged with murdering a policeman while attempting to escape after robbing a bar. The defense is an alibi. The prosecutor calls Juan Rodriguez, Romano's friend, expecting Rodriguez to testify that he saw Romano shoot the officer. However, Rodriguez testifies that he is unable to remember anything that happened on the night of the robbery/murder. The prosecutor then reads a statement that Rodriguez admits that he gave to the police, in which Rodriguez states that he saw Romano kill the policeman. *Is Rodriguez's out-of-court statement to the police admissible as a prior inconsistent statement? As a prior identification?*

Problem 12-22: At the Movies: Better Late Than Never

In the film *Destination Murder,*[6] Laura Mansfield witnesses her father's murder. She views a lineup but tells the police that she can't identify any of the lineup participants (one of whom is Jackie Wales) as the murderer. Assume that Laura eventually testifies at Wales's trial that she saw him kill her father. *Can the defense offer the statement that Laura made to the police at the lineup into evidence under Rule 801(d)(1)(C)?*

§ 12.06 Multiple-Choice Review Problems

Review Problem 12-A

Sara Jane, who had been a fugitive from justice for 25 years, is arrested and tried for attempted murder for planting a car bomb under a police car. Three days after the bombing, Lee identified Jane as the bomber after looking through photos and

---

5. Columbia Pictures, 1949.
6. RKO Radio Pictures, 1950.

selecting the photo depicting Jane. At Jane's trial 25 years later, Lee testifies, "I'm sorry, it's been so long ago that I just can't remember whether Jane is the person who I saw plant the bomb." *Which of the following statements is accurate?*

1. The prosecution can offer evidence of Lee's photo identification to prove that Jane was the bomber.

2. The prosecution can offer evidence of Lee's photo identification as a prior inconsistent statement to prove that Jane was the bomber.

3. The prosecution can offer evidence of Lee's photo identification as a prior consistent statement to prove that Jane was the bomber.

4. The prosecution cannot offer evidence of Lee's photo identification.

Review Problem 12-B

In a slip-and-fall case filed by plaintiffs Ben and Anna Peel against a department store for damages including loss of consortium, Ben testifies that he tripped on loose carpeting in the store's sportswear department. Ben seeks to testify that "While I was being treated in the emergency room, I told a nurse that I had tripped on loose carpeting." Ben's statement to the nurse is:

1. Admissible as a prior consistent statement not for its truth, but for the non-hearsay purpose of corroborating Ben's credibility.

2. Inadmissible as a prior consistent statement because the statement to the nurse was not made under oath.

3. Admissible as a prior consistent statement after Ben admits during cross-examination that he lost his job a month after the accident and needs money to pay family bills.

4. Admissible as a prior consistent statement after the defense attorney asks Ben on cross-examination, "Isn't it true that you falsified your personal statement when you applied to law schools?" (Ben denied having done this.)

5. Admissible as a prior consistent statement after Ben admits during cross-examination that after being treated in the emergency room, he told the friend who drove him home, "I'm not really sure why I fell."

Review Problem 12-C

Josh is charged with distribution of cocaine. At trial, Jenni testifies for the government under a grant of immunity that she bought a package of what was later determined to be cocaine from Josh. On cross-examination, Josh's attorney asks Jenni, "Didn't you previously say that Jerry and not Josh was the person from whom you bought the cocaine?" Which of the following statements is accurate?

1. Jenni's prior statement is admissible to prove that Jerry was the cocaine seller if it was made under oath during grand jury proceedings.

2. Jenni's prior statement is admissible only for its truth and not to impeach her credibility as a witness if it was made under oath during grand jury proceedings.

3. Jenni's prior statement is inadmissible unless it was made under oath.

4. Jenni's prior statement is admissible as a prior inconsistent statement to prove that Jerry was the cocaine seller if it was made to the police shortly after they arrested her for possession of cocaine.

Review Problem 12-D

At trial, government witness Sarah points to the defendant Robertson as the person she saw take money at gunpoint. During cross-examination, the defense attorney seeks to elicit testimony from Sarah that when she attended a lineup that included Robertson a few days after the robbery, she told a police officer that "I don't think that any of these people are the robber." Sarah's statement to the police officer is:

1. Inadmissible because Sarah was uncertain as to whether the robber was in the lineup.

2. Admissible under Rule 801(d)(1)(C) for the purpose of proving that the person she saw commit the robbery was not in the lineup.

3. Inadmissible because Sarah was not under oath at the time she spoke to the police officer.

4. Admissible as non-hearsay for the purpose of casting doubt on Sarah's in-court identification.

§ 12.07 Case Library

Tome v. United States

U.S. Supreme Court
513 U.S. 150 (1995)

United States v. Owens

U.S. Supreme Court
484 U.S. 554 (1988)

Chapter 13

The Admissibility of Opposing Parties' Hearsay Statements

§ 13.01 Chapter Checklist

1. Must an opposing party's hearsay statement admit to wrongdoing to be admissible under Rule 801(d)(2)?

2. Can parties offer their own hearsay into evidence under Rule 801(d)(2)?

3. Can a non-party's hearsay statement be admissible under Rule 801(d)(2)?

4. Can the contents of a hearsay assertion alone support admissibility under Rule 801(d)(2)?

5. By what standard does a judge decide whether Rule 801(d)(2)'s foundational requirements have been satisfied?

§ 13.02 Relevant Federal Rules of Evidence

Rule 801. Definitions That Apply to This Article; Exclusions from Hearsay (partial text)

. . .

(d) Statements That Are Not Hearsay. A statement that meets the following conditions is not hearsay:

(1) . . .

(2) *An Opposing Party's Statement.* The statement is offered against an opposing party and:

(A) was made by the party in an individual or representative capacity;

(B) is one the party manifested that it adopted or believed to be true;

(C) was made by a person whom the party authorized to make a statement on the subject;

(D) was made by the party's agent or employee on a matter within the scope of that relationship and while it existed; or

(E) was made by the party's coconspirator during and in furtherance of the conspiracy.

The statement must be considered but does not by itself establish the declarant's authority under (C); the existence or scope of the relationship under (D); or the existence of the conspiracy or participation in it under (E).

Rule 802. The Rule Against Hearsay

Hearsay is not admissible unless any of the following provides otherwise:

- a federal statute;
- these rules; or
- other rules prescribed by the Supreme Court.

§ 13.03 Introduction

Rule 801(d)(2) exempts an "opposing party's statement" from Rule 802's hearsay bar. As a result, hearsay statements that satisfy the foundational requirements of Rule 801(d)(2) are received for the truth of their contents.

This chapter analyzes each of the five circumstances in which an "opposing party's statement" is admissible under Rule 801(d)(2). However, no matter the individual circumstances, the admissibility of opposing parties' statements under Rule 801(d)(2) is governed by the following three basic principles.

1. *Parties cannot offer their own hearsay statements into evidence under Rule 801(d) (2).* Hearsay is admissible under Rule 801(d)(2) only if an *adversary* offers an opposing party's statement into evidence.

Example 1

Plaintiff Samantha is testifying against defendant Steve in an auto accident case:

PLAINTIFF'S ATTORNEY: Samantha, did you say anything to the defendant after the police officer left the scene of the accident?

A: Yes. I walked over to him and said, "You knucklehead, this was all your fault."

DEFENDANT'S ATTORNEY: Objection, hearsay.

PLAINTIFF'S ATTORNEY: Rule 801(d)(2) Your Honor. It's Samantha's own statement, and she's a party.

JUDGE: Objection sustained. Back to Evidence class for you, counsel. You can't offer your client's own statement into evidence under that rule. (Of course, defendant Steve could offer Samantha's statement into evidence under Rule 801(d)(2), should Steve believe it in his interest to do so.)

2. *An opposing party's hearsay statement is admissible under Rule 801(d)(2) regardless of whether it confesses wrongdoing or was in any way against a party's interests at the time it was made.*

Example 2

A police officer is testifying against a defendant who is charged with robbing a jewelry store:

PROSECUTOR: And after the defendant agreed to talk to you Officer, what happened?

A: I asked the defendant where he was at 10:00 a.m., the time of the robbery.

PROSECUTOR: And how did the defendant reply?

A: He said that he didn't commit the robbery, and that he was at the movies watching *The John Dillinger Story* at that time.

The defendant's hearsay statement is an admissible opposing party statement, even though it exculpates rather than implicates the defendant. (The prosecutor might want to elicit evidence of the exculpatory statement because it is inconsistent with another exculpatory statement.)

Example 3

Plaintiff Samantha is testifying against defendant Steve in an auto accident case:

PLAINTIFF'S ATTORNEY: And what happened after you and the defendant got out of your cars after the accident?

A: We checked out the damage to the cars.

PLAINTIFF'S ATTORNEY: Did the defendant say anything to you while you were both looking at the cars?

A: Yes. He said that he'd been temporarily blinded by the sun glaring off my cell phone.

In Examples 2 and 3, the defendants' hearsay statements are admissible under Rule 801(d)(2) even though they may have been self-serving at the time they were made. Of course, in an adversary system of justice, parties do not usually offer opposing parties' statements into evidence if they support an opposing party's claims. However, a hearsay statement that seemingly promoted a declarant's interests at the time it was made can turn out to be antithetical to the speaker's interests by the time of trial. When this situation arises, Rule 801(d)(2) allows a party to offer hearsay into evidence if the declarant is the opposing party.

Example 4

Plaintiff Gale Winns sues Mommin Popp for injuries suffered when she allegedly slipped on a wet spot in Popp's convenience market. Popp's defense at trial is that the fall was due entirely to Winns' carelessness because the floor was bone-dry at the time of the fall. Gale testifies as follows:

PLAINTIFF'S ATTORNEY: And what happened when you were lying on the floor?

A: Mr. Popp walked over and said that it was my own fault that I had fallen. He said that he'd warned me to watch out for the big wet spot.

In Example 4, Popp's statement seemed self-serving (favorable to Popp) at the time Popp spoke to Winns. Nevertheless, Winns might offer Popp's statement into evidence at trial to undermine Popp's defense that the floor was bone-dry.

3. Rule 801(d)(2) can make admissible an opposing party's hearsay statement regardless of when it was made. Admissibility does not depend on a declarant being a party to a lawsuit at the time a hearsay statement is made. As a result, anything that any of us has ever said (personally or vicariously remember) is a potential ticking time bomb, just waiting for our becoming a party to the right lawsuit to light the fuse.

Example 5

When they are both in high school, Al Gebra tells Cal Culus that "No matter how long it takes, I'm going to get back at you someday for copying my geometry homework." Some years later, Al is charged with murdering Cal. Subject to judicial discretion under the general relevance provisions of Rules 401, 402, and 403, a prosecutor might successfully offer Al's high school threat as an opposing party's statement under Rule 801(d)(2) to prove that Al murdered Cal.

Practice Tip: Rule 801(d)(2) and "Party Admissions"

In earlier times, opposing party statements were called "party admissions." In some jurisdictions they still are. The FRE revisers expurgated the term "party admissions" from the text of the rules. One reason was the word "admissions" wrongly implied that statements had to admit to wrongdoing in order to be admissible. Also, even judges sometimes confused Rule 801(d)(2)'s "party admissions exemption" with Rule 804(b)(3)'s very different hearsay exception for "declarations against interest," referring to the former as "admissions against interest."[1] Recognize however that despite the change in the text of Rule 801(d)(2), judges, lawyers, state rules, and even some law professors may continue to refer to opposing party statements as "party admissions."

Practice Tip: The "Mark Twain Exemption?"

American novelist and humorist Mark Twain famously said, "It is better to keep your mouth closed and be thought a fool than to open it and remove all doubt." The FRE's exemption for opposing party statements suggests the wisdom of Twain's observation.

---

1. For a case employing this confused terminology, *see Bill v. Farm Bureau Life Insurance Co.,* 119 N.W.2d 768 (Iowa 1963).

§ 13.04 Opposing Parties' Statements and the Adversary System

Unlike the hearsay exceptions collected in Rules 803 and 804, the hearsay exemption for opposing parties' statements set forth in Rule 801(d)(2) is not based on trustworthiness. That is, the exemption does not reflect a belief that hearsay assertions made by opposing parties (or their vicarious representatives) are any more likely to be accurate or reliable than hearsay assertions made by anyone else. Rather, the exemption is rooted in an adversary system in which parties are responsible for advancing and protecting their legal rights. The considerations underlying the exemption for opposing parties' statements include the following:

- A "gotcha" attitude of "you said it, you explain it." The exemption holds people accountable for their out-of-court statements and increases the likelihood that parties' courtroom positions will be consistent with their pretrial statements.

- The "hearsay dangers" (*see* Chapter 10) are minimized: An opposing party can't readily complain about being unable to probe the party's (or vicarious agent's) own sincerity, perception, memory, or use of language. The opposing party will almost certainly be in court and available to testify and can, if warranted, explain the assertion or deny making it, consistent with the oath.

- When the exemption admits a hearsay statement made by a party's agent, the party will often have an ongoing relationship with the declarant. If so, the party can normally produce the declarant as a witness to explain or deny the statement, consistent with the oath.

The policy of allowing parties to tar adversaries with their out-of-court statements is so strong that judges typically admit opposing parties' statements into evidence even when the statements are subject to evidentiary infirmities that would result in exclusion under other rule of evidence. For example, perhaps a party spoke about an event though lacking personal knowledge of what actually happened. Or, the party's statement may consist of little more than a conclusory legal opinion. Though "defects" such as these generally result in exclusion of evidence, both statements will probably be admitted under Rule 801(d)(2). The rationale is that "if a party had a good enough basis for saying it, that's a good enough basis for admitting it into evidence." On the other hand, the exemption does not invariably run roughshod over every other rule of evidence. For example, judges can exclude opposing parties' statements if their contents are irrelevant, or if their probative value is substantially outweighed by the danger of unfair prejudice.

Example

Jon sues Barbara on a "negligent entrustment" theory for personal injuries incurred in an auto accident. Jon alleges that Barbara carelessly loaned her car to Jennifer, a driver who Barbara knew or should have known to be the town drunk. Jon calls Barbara's neighbor as a witness to testify that when the neighbor told Barbara that her car had been involved in an accident, Barbara said, "Jennifer must have been drunk." Despite the conclusory form of Barbara's statement and her lack of personal knowledge as to how the accident occurred, a judge would in all likelihood admit Barbara's statement under Rule 801(d)(2) if Jon offers it into evidence to prove both that Barbara knew of Jennifer's drinking problem and that her drinking caused the accident. However, if instead Barbara had responded to the neighbor by saying, "I hope that after the accident, the cops didn't search the car and find the mask I used in my last bank robbery," her assertion would probably be excluded as irrelevant to the issue of negligent entrustment.

§ 13.05 Declarant Is the Opposing Party (Rule 801(d)(2)(A))

Foundational Elements:

* * The declarant is a party to the lawsuit in which the hearsay is offered;

* * The declarant's adversary offers the party's statement into evidence.

Under Rule 801(d)(2)(A), a hearsay statement is admissible if offered against the party who made it, whether "in an individual or a representative capacity." The proviso prevents a party sued in one capacity from weaseling out of an assertion by claiming that "I made it in a different capacity." For example, a defendant charged with defrauding a bank cannot prevent the prosecution from offering into evidence a hearsay statement made by the defendant to a bank officer by claiming that "I was speaking to the bank officer not as an individual, but in my capacity as trustee of my parent's trust."

Problem 13-1: Multiple Choys

Mr. and Mrs. Choy sue Rhoda for personal injuries resulting from an auto accident. *Which of the following statements would be admissible as opposing party statements if the Choys offer them into evidence to prove Rhoda's liability?*

1. After the accident, Dad Choy told a bystander, "Rhoda was speeding just before she plowed into my car."

2. Rhoda testified at her deposition, "I'm guessing I was going over the speed limit just before the accident."

3. Rhoda's neighbor Katie told Mom Choy, "A couple of days after the accident, Rhoda told me that she had been speeding just before the collision."

4. After the accident, a bystander heard Rhoda mutter to herself, "Must have been the darn brakes."

5. After the accident, Rhoda told a bystander, "It was all my fault."

Problem 13-2: Who's a Party?

Maso Menos is charged with armed robbery of Des Pacio. Maso denies being the robber, and on direct examination by defense counsel Maso testifies as follows:

DEFENDANT'S ATTORNEY: And what happened next?

A: The officer placed me under arrest and drove me back to the place where the robbery had supposedly taken place.

DEFENDANT'S ATTORNEY: And then what happened?

A: The officer left me in the back seat and walked over to a man who was standing about 10 feet away, who I later learned was Des Pacio. I'd never seen Mr. Pacio before.

DEFENDANT'S ATTORNEY: OK. What happened next?

A: The officer talked to Mr. Pacio for a few minutes, then walked back over to me.

DEFENDANT'S ATTORNEY: Did you overhear any of the conversation between the officer and Mr. Pacio?

A: Yes. I heard Pacio tell the officer that he didn't get a very good look at the robber, and I heard the officer say that she was concerned about some differences between me and the description that Mr. Pacio had given of the robber.

PROSECUTOR: Objection, hearsay.

DEFENDANT'S ATTORNEY: Pacio and the police officer constitute opposing parties, so the statements are admissible under Rule 801(d)(2)(A).

JUDGE: *What ruling?*

Problem 13-3: Oh Canida

In *Mahlandt v. Wild Canid Survival and Research Center*, 588 F.2d 626 (8th Cir. 1978), the Center and its Director of Education were sued for civil damages after "Sophie," a wolf kept in the front yard of the home of the Center's Education Director, allegedly bit a 3-year-old girl in the face. Their defense was that the girl's facial injuries were a result of her having crawled into the yard under a wire fence, not a wolf bite. (The name "Wild Canid" may not have made a good impression on the jury. Perhaps organizations ought to consult with lawyers before choosing names. "*Mahlandt v. Cuddly Critter Center*" wouldn't have sounded nearly as intimidating.)

1. When informed by telephone of the child's injuries, the Education Director wrote the Center's President a note stating that "Sophie bit a child who came into my backyard." The plaintiff offers the note into evidence against the Director under Rule 801(d)(2)(A). *Is this note admissible over the Director's "lack of personal knowledge" objection?*

2. Assume that you represent the plaintiff (the child who was allegedly bitten and her parents). *How might you have used the tools of formal discovery to uncover the Director's note prior to trial? Assume that the note was either (a)*

handwritten by the Director (b) was an email message that the Director sent to the Center's President.

3. Assume that the Education Director's note to the President reads as follows: "It's been reported to me that Sophie bit a child that came into my backyard." The plaintiff offers the note into evidence against the Director under Rule 801(d)(2)(A). *Is this note admissible over the Director's "lack of personal knowledge" objection?*

4. Assume that you are the Defense Attorney representing the Education Director, and are discussing the note with the Director on the eve of trial. That discussion goes as follows:

DEFENDANT'S ATTORNEY: I may not be able to prevent the plaintiff from introducing this note into evidence. If it is admitted, of course, you'll have a chance to explain that you didn't know what had actually happened when you wrote the note. It might be helpful if you could offer the jury a good reason for writing the note anyway. Can you recall what your thinking was at the time you wrote it?

A: I was pretty shocked. I never thought Sophie capable of harming a child, and I still don't. But I'm not sure how to answer your question.

DEFENDANT'S ATTORNEY: Well, one possibility is that you wrote the note to make sure that the President would order an immediate and thorough investigation. Thinking back, might that have been in the back of your mind?

A: Well, certainly we were all concerned about what had happened. So, yes, I'd agree with that.

DEFENDANT'S ATTORNEY: OK. If we're in court and the note is admitted into evidence, I'll ask you why you wrote the note and you can say that you wanted to make sure that the President ordered an immediate and thorough investigation. That's the truth, right?

A: Yes.

Does this portion of the meeting satisfy ethical guidelines forbidding lawyers from "making up" testimony for their clients to give?

5. At trial, in lieu of offering a written note into evidence, the plaintiff calls Sara to testify that she heard the Education Director say that Sophie had bitten a child. Sara begins by testifying that at the time of the alleged biting incident, she was working as a computer technician at the Wild Canid Center. About half an hour after the incident took place, Sara heard the Education Director talking with a small group of people. When the plaintiff's attorney asks Sara to testify to the Director's hearsay statement, the trial continues as follows:

DEFENDANT'S ATTORNEY: Objection to this testimony, based on lack of foundation.

JUDGE: Counsel for plaintiff, on what basis are you offering this statement?

PLAINTIFF'S ATTORNEY: Opposing party statement, Your Honor.

DEFENDANT'S ATTORNEY: And my objection goes to foundation as an opposing party statement. Our position is that the Director did not make the statement that this witness attributes to him. I'd ask that the jury be excused for a hearing as to the adequacy of the foundation.

JUDGE: All right, the jury has been excused, counsel for plaintiff may proceed.

> [At this point a "mini-trial" begins with the plaintiff trying to lay the foundation for a straight admission, which entails offering evidence that the Director made the out-of-court assertion.]

PLAINTIFF'S ATTORNEY: Sara, what is it that you heard the Director say?

A: The Director said, "It sounds like Sophie bit a child who came into my backyard."

PLAINTIFF'S ATTORNEY: And how do you know it was the Director who said this?

A: I'd worked in the Center for over a year, I've heard the Director's voice many times and recognized it.

PLAINTIFF'S ATTORNEY: Were there any background noises that might have caused you to mishear what the Director said?

A: No, it was pretty quiet. We'd all heard about the accident and everyone was pretty subdued.

PLAINTIFF'S ATTORNEY: Nothing further.

JUDGE: Defense counsel, any questions for this witness?

DEFENDANT'S ATTORNEY: Thank you, just a couple. Your employment at Wild Canid was terminated about a month after the biting incident, correct?

A: That's right.

DEFENDANT'S ATTORNEY: And you blame the Director for your termination, don't you?

A: I didn't think the Director's evaluation of my performance was accurate, but that's all in the past.

DEFENDANT'S ATTORNEY: At this point I'd like to excuse this witness for a moment and call the defendant briefly to testify as to the foundation.

JUDGE: You may do so.

DEFENDANT'S ATTORNEY: Director, did you make the statement just attributed to you?

A: I did not.

DEFENDANT'S ATTORNEY: Did you say anything at all to indicate that you believed that Sophie bit the child?

A: No, I had no idea what had happened.

DEFENDANT'S ATTORNEY: Did anyone to your knowledge make such a statement?

A: No. I was just briefly talking to a few staffers in my office before leaving to check on the child's condition. I remember that somebody, I think it was Jean, asked if I thought that Sophie could have bitten the child. I said it didn't sound like Sophie at all, and that we shouldn't jump to any conclusions before we knew more facts. Then I left.

DEFENDANT'S ATTORNEY: Was there any other conversation at all about whether Sophie bit the child?

A: No, not that I heard, at least.

DEFENDANT'S ATTORNEY: No further questions.

JUDGE: Plaintiff, any questions of this witness?

PLAINTIFF'S ATTORNEY: Not as to the foundation, Your Honor.

JUDGE: Director, you may step down. Under Rule 104, the Director's statement is admissible once the plaintiff offers evidence sufficient to support a jury finding that the Director made the statement. Having listened to the foundational evidence, I find the evidence equally balanced on both sides but believe that the jury could reasonably conclude that the Director made the statement. Therefore, I'll admit it. Defense, you'll have a chance to have the Director testify in front of the jury that the statement was never made, and the jury can believe who it chooses. OK, recall the jury and let's get started.

Is the judge's statement of the foundational burden correct? After ruling that the plaintiff has offered sufficient evidence that the Director made the statement for it to be received in evidence, is the judge correct in saying that the Director will be able to deny making the statement in front of the jury? Based on the evidence that the attorneys elicited during the mini-trial, what ruling would you have made as to the statement's admissibility?

Problem 13-4: Wrenching an Admission

Amy sues Beth for injuries incurred when Beth allegedly struck Amy with a monkey wrench that Beth pulled out of her desk drawer:

1. During pretrial discovery, Beth responded to Amy's Request for Admission as follows:

   Amy's Request # 5: Admit that the following fact is true: You always keep a monkey wrench in your desk drawer at work. Beth's response: Admitted.

   After the judge admits Beth's response to Request #5 into evidence, can Beth testify that "I have never kept a monkey wrench in my desk drawer at work"?

2. Linda will testify when called by Amy as a witness that she works with Beth and that a week after the quarrel, Beth told Linda, "I always keep a monkey wrench in my desk drawer here at work."

After Linda testifies to Beth's statement, can Beth testify trial that "I have never kept a monkey wrench in my desk drawer at work"?

3. After she was fired for allegedly striking Amy, Beth sued her employer for wrongful termination. Beth's complaint in that lawsuit alleged in part that "Plaintiff Beth never struck Amy with the monkey wrench that she keeps in her desk drawer at work or with any other object."

Can Amy offer this allegation into evidence as an opposing party's statement made by Beth in the trial of her personal injury case?

4. Assume that Amy initially named both Beth and Jacob as defendants in her personal injury lawsuit, and that she later dismissed Jacob from the case and proceeded to trial against only Beth. Amy's initial complaint included the following allegation: "Defendant Beth or defendant Jacob, or both defendants Beth and Jacob, intentionally struck me with a monkey wrench."

Can Beth offer this allegation into evidence as an opposing party statement made by Amy (to prove that Jacob and not Beth was the cause of any injuries that Amy incurred)? When responding to this question, consider that Rule 8(e)(2) of the Federal Rules of Civil Procedure includes the following language: "A party may set forth two or more statements of a claim or defense alternatively or hypothetically . . . . All statements shall be made subject to the obligations set forth in Rule 11." (Rule 11 requires in essence a good-faith basis for claims and defenses.)

Problem 13-5: Pleading Ticket

You represent Jill, who's been sued civilly for damages by Gustavo following an auto accident in which her car collided with Gustavo's car. Gustavo's complaint alleges that the accident was caused by Jill's negligent failure to keep her car in good repair. After the accident, a police officer inspected Jill's car and wrote her a ticket for driving with bald tires. Jill tells you, "I'm planning to dispose of the traffic ticket quickly by going down to traffic court and pleading guilty. Do you think that's what I should do?" *How would you respond to Jill's question?*

Problem 13-6: Brag Art

Art is charged with armed robbery of a convenience market; the defense is an alibi. The prosecutor calls the convenience store clerk to testify that after the clerk had handed over money at gunpoint to Art, Art said "I'm having a good week. I knocked over two liquor stores the day before yesterday, and now I'm making a haul today." *As the defense attorney, what argument might you make against the admissibility of the statement?*

Problem 13-7: Nocturnal Admission?

Dion Tology is charged with armed robbery of the Belmont Bar & Grill. Vince will testify when called as a prosecution witness, "I was camping with Dion two weeks ago. One night I was awakened by Dion talking in his sleep. I shined my flashlight at him, and he looked like he was sound asleep. But he was saying all sorts of things, including that he had robbed the Belmont." *As the defense attorney, what argument might you make against the admissibility of Dion's statement?*

§ 13.06 Adoptive Statements (Rule 801(d)(2)(B))

Foundational Elements:

* A party adopted or by words or deeds manifested belief in the truth of a non-party declarant's hearsay statement;

* The party's adversary offers the hearsay statement into evidence.

Rule 801(d)(2)(B) makes a non-party declarant's hearsay statement admissible if the party against whom the statement is offered adopts the statement or by words or actions demonstrates that the party believed it to be true.

Example

Ruby Pearl is charged with robbing a jewelry store. Opal is testifying as a witness for the prosecution:

PROSECUTOR: Opal, what happened when you entered Ruby's apartment?

A: I told Ruby that I'd heard that she'd pulled off the jewelry store caper, and that she must have come away with some great stuff.

PROSECUTOR: And how did Ruby respond?

A: She just smiled at me and showed me a handful of gold rings and bracelets.

Opal's testimony lays a foundation for the prosecutor to offer her statement ("Ruby pulled off the jewelry store caper and got great stuff") into evidence against Ruby under Rule 801(d)(2)(B). Ruby's conduct adopted and manifested belief in the truth of Opal's statement.

Often, as in the example of Ruby above, a party makes a statement or engages in conduct that provides a basis for concluding that the party intended to adopt or manifested a belief in the accuracy of another person's statement. However, a party's silence can on occasion be enough for a judge to conclude that the party adopted another person's statement. If a party remains silent in circumstances when a reasonable person would have denied a statement had it not been true, an "adoption by silence" can result.

The potential scope of this exemption is extremely broad. If the foundational elements for "adoption by silence" were loosely interpreted, anything said by anyone within a party's earshot could become admissible under Rule 801(d)(2)(B). To insure that people don't have to run around shaking their heads "no" or yelling "no way" every time they overhear a statement they disagree with on pain of it being admitted as an opposing party's statement should litigation occur, judges tend to apply the foundational elements rigorously. *McCormick on Evidence* notes that a party seeking to offer a declarant's statement as an adversary's adopted statement must usually satisfy the following foundational elements:

- The circumstances must show that the party heard the statement.

- The party must have understood the statement.

- The subject matter of the statement must have been within the party's personal knowledge. (This is an exception to the general rule that personal knowledge is unnecessary for admissibility under Rule 801(d)(2).)

- Under the circumstances, a reasonable person would have denied the statement had it not been true.

Should a judge determine whether the offering party has satisfied these foundational factors pursuant to Rule 104(a) or 104(b)? Disagreement on this issue exists among courts and commentators alike. A compromise position that some favor calls for the judge to decide whether a reasonable person would have denied the statement had it not been true pursuant to Rule 104(a) and decide the other foundational factors pursuant to Rule 104(b). Under this position, the offering party has to convince the judge by a preponderance of evidence that a reasonable person would have denied the statement had it not been true but need only offer evidence sufficient to support a finding that the remaining factors are true.

Problem 13-8: On the Tube: "Barb-Accuse"

On an episode of the one-time popular television soap opera *Melrose Place*, 20-year-old Alison unexpectedly shows up at a barbecue in her parents' backyard. Many of her parents' close friends, including at least one judge, are present. Her father and mother both angrily ask her to leave, saying "you don't belong here." Alison says in a loud voice, "You going to do what you used to do to Meredith and me?" Her father says, "Alison, this is neither the time nor the place for this." Alison then shouts in a voice loud enough for everyone to hear, "Daddy, why don't you tell them all our dirty little secret, about how you used to take me and Meredith down to the basement and do things to us." Daddy stands silent for a few moments, and Alison walks away. Assume that Daddy is now charged with doing illegal things to Alison and Meredith in the basement.

Student # 1: As the Prosecutor, make a brief argument to support your position that the trial judge should admit Alison's statement as Daddy's adopted statement.

Student # 2: As the Defense Attorney, argue in response to the prosecutor's argument that the judge should not admit Alison's statement into evidence as your client's adopted statement.

Student # 3: As the Judge, preside over the argument and rule on the prosecutor's request, and state for the record the following:

1. Under Rule 104, which party has the burden of proof with respect to the foundational elements and what does the burden consist of?

2. When announcing your ruling, explain the factors that incline you to admit or exclude the statement.

Problem 13-9: Text Booked

Gresham is charged with committing a series of robberies. To prove his guilt, the prosecutor offers into evidence an exchange of text messages between a cell phone belonging to Gresham and one belonging to his mother. The thread of messages, spelled as in the original, includes the following:

Gresham: Stop telling lies!!!

Gresham: That's why Johnny left yo nasty ass. . . .

Mother: U r the 1 who needs to learn how 2 respect . . . I am ur mother and ur days r number . . .

Gresham: Why are you so hateful?

Mother: An that is why u will b locked up 4 robberies of the stores in this area.

Mother: Why do u feel hv 2 b so nasty an fowl u r sick.

(no further messaging)

Does Gresham's failure to respond to the text message regarding the robberies constitute his opposing party statement as an adoptive admission of his mother's accusation?

Problem 13-10: Silent Right

Beverly is arrested in her apartment for selling illegal drugs. The prosecutor calls the arresting officer to testify that after the officer arrested Beverly, Beverly claimed said that the drugs didn't belong to her. Beverly's partner, Danny, who was present in the apartment when the arrest occurred, then told Beverly, "Tell the truth for a change. You know that the drugs are yours." Beverly responded by hanging her head and saying nothing. *Does Beverly's silence establish a sufficient foundation for an adoption of Danny's statement?*

Problem 13-11: Car Jack

Jill sues Jack for damages resulting from an auto accident. Jill offers to testify that after the collision, both drivers got out of their cars. Jill then said, "You never even slowed down at the red light. This is all your fault."

1. Assume that Jack says nothing in response to Jill's remark. *Does his response constitute an adoption of Jill's accusation?*

2. Assume that Jack responded to Jill's remark by saying, "I'm really sorry about what happened. Let's just exchange information and let the insurance companies worry about it." *Does Jack's response amount to an adoption of Jill's accusation?*

3. Assume that Jack responded to Jill's remark by immediately jumping back into his car and driving away. *Does Jack's conduct amount to an adoption of Jill's accusation?*

4. Jill also says to Jack, "Luckily, my passenger took a picture of your car going through the red light on this cell phone." Jack then grabbed the cell phone out of Jill's hand, threw it to the ground, and stomped it to bits. *Does Jack's conduct amount to an adoption of Jill's accusation?*

Problem 13-12: I Wanna Hold Your Hand (of Cards)

Four long-time friends, John, Paul, George, and Ringo, meet regularly to play poker. In the course of dealing a hand, John says, "Paul, running through that field of strawberry bushes after grabbing that guy's valuable guitar left you with a bunch of nasty-looking scratches." Paul responds only, "Just deal the cards. I need to get even on the night." Does Paul's response constitute an adoption of John's statement that he grabbed a valuable guitar?

§ 13.07 Authorized Statements
(Rule 801(d)(2)(C))

Foundational Elements:

* A hearsay declarant was expressly or impliedly a party's authorized agent;

* The party's adversary offers the hearsay statement into evidence.

Rule 801(d)(2)(C) makes a declarant's hearsay statement admissible if the party against whom the statement is offered authorized the declarant to speak on the adversary's behalf about the statement's subject matter. Thus, a party seeking to offer an "authorized statement" must offer foundational evidence sufficient to convince a judge by the preponderance of the evidence under FRE 104(a) that the declarant had "speaking authority," and that the declarant's statement was within the scope of that authority.

A declarant may have *express* authority to speak for a party. For example, before leaving for a day at the races, Harpo might prepare a document stating that "I hereby authorize Groucho to speak on my behalf about what happened during the night at the opera." More often, a declarant's authority to speak is a by-product of agency law principles, which *imply* both authority and the scope of the authority from the declarant's relationship to a party.

Example 1

Jay and Bob are partners in a dry-cleaning business. Under agency law, partners have the power to bind each other in business dealings. Hence, an email written by Jay and sent to a bank in the course of arranging for a business loan would probably be admissible against Bob as an authorized statement in a collection action brought by the bank against Bob. However, agency law principles would not give Jay the implied authority to speak about Bob's personal marital situation. Therefore, a statement that Jay makes about Bob's plans with respect to his children would not constitute an authorized statement by Bob that his wife Oprah could offer into evidence against him in a child custody dispute.

Example 2

In the *Mahlandt* case (*see* Problem 13-3 above), assume that a member of the Board of Directors stated that "Sophie the wolf bit a young child." The statement would qualify as the organization's authorized statement, because under agency law Board members have the implied authority to speak for corporations on matters concerning corporate activities.

A foundational issue that has arisen often is the extent to which a judge can consider a declarant's claim of authority to speak when determining whether a declarant in fact had authority to speak for a party. Some courts have disregarded the agent's claim entirely and have looked only to the surrounding circumstances to determine whether authority existed. Other courts have treated a declarant's claim of authority with varying degrees of respect. Rule 801(d)(2) resolves the uncertainty in federal court cases by providing that on the foundational issue of a declarant's authority, a statement's contents must be considered but are not alone sufficient to establish a declarant's authority. Thus, a party seeking to offer an out-of-court statement as an authorized statement must offer evidence independent of the statement that authority existed.

Example 3

Anne is fired from her place of employment. A few days later, Anne's former colleague Vy Karious contacts Anne's former employer and states that "Anne is really upset by her firing and she asked me to talk to you to see if she can somehow get her job back. Anne admits that she showed up to work wasted a few times, but that was because of a personal problem that's now been resolved, and you can be sure that it will never happen again."

Anne doesn't get her job back and sues her ex-employer for wrongful termination. The employer wants to offer Vy's statement into evidence to prove that Anne had come to work wasted and relies on Vy's statement to prove that Anne had authorized Vy to speak for her. Anne however testifies during a mini-trial, "I never authorized Vy to talk about my work experiences. I just asked her to talk to the employer and make an appointment for me." Under Rule 801(d)(2), the trial judge considers Vy's statement as evidence that Anne authorized Vy to speak. However, the employer would have to offer independent evidence of Vy's authority before her statement could be admitted into evidence as Anne's authorized statement.

Problem 13-13: Lawyer Lee

Juan Lee, Esq., represents Jackson in a case involving Jackson's tripping on a toy truck on the sidewalk in front of Binder's home. After his initial interview of Jackson, Lee sends Binder a letter seeking the name of Binder's home insurance carrier. In that letter Lee outlines how Jackson's mishap occurred and describes Jackson's injuries. The letter states that "perhaps Mr. Jackson was a bit intoxicated, but that doesn't excuse your carelessness." *Can Binder offer Lee's letter into evidence against Jackson to prove that Jackson was under the influence of alcohol at the time of the mishap?*

Problem 13-14: Scoop

Eppy Demic sues Toxicity Inc. for polluting her town's drinking water. After the suit is filed, Toxicity's press secretary Bill tells a journalist that "We've never actually tested the sludge we dump into the river. How do you expect us to know whether it's safe?" *Would the press secretary's statement qualify as Toxicity's authorized statement? What if Bill is Toxicity's bookkeeper, whose job is to take care of payroll and insurance matters for the company's employees?*

Problem 13-15: Gilligan's Island

You represent Blairwood Construction, a development company that is planning to build a luxury resort complex on the island of Knott Atoll. Gilligan, who heads a local environmental group opposed to the project, claims that construction would destroy the habitat of an endangered species of bird known as the "yellow twitbill." Blairwood's President wants to send out a conciliatory press release, but doesn't want to say anything that might be used against the company should Gilligan go to court and try to stop the project. Which one of the following remarks will you recommend to the President, and why?

1. "As a good corporate citizen, Blairwood wants to minimize harm to the yellow twitbill."

2. "The yellow twitbill may be an endangered species, though the ornithological community is deeply divided over the issue."

3. "We at Blairwood are aware of and take very seriously Gilligan's claim that the yellow twitbill's habitat may be affected by the building of the resort."

4. "Blairwood has hired a local ornithologist who will suggest ways to minimize harm to the yellow twitbill."

Problem 13-16: Way Out

John L. Way, former star quarterback for the Denver Buncos, has sued the team for breach of contract for kicking Way off the team for violating the "public appearance" provision of the standard player agreement incorporated into Way's contract. The team contends that Way violated the provision by secretly demanding money for making appearances that the team arranged for and that Way was contractually obligated to attend for free. To support its claim that Way demanded payments, the team seeks to offer into evidence a statement made by players' union representative Les Strike to a newspaper reporter. Strike stated to the reporter: "I've talked to Mr. Way about the matter, and he's asked me to convey to you that he sees nothing wrong with asking for appearance money. Almost all players do the same thing." The team claims that Way authorized Strike to make this statement; Way denies that Strike had any authority to speak for him.

The team calls the reporter as a witness to testify to Strike's statement. When Way objects that the statement is inadmissible hearsay, the following mini-trial ensues:

JUDGE: Counsel for the Buncos, do you have any evidence other than the statement itself that Mr. Strike was authorized by Mr. Way to speak for him on this matter?

DEFENDANT'S ATTORNEY: I do, Your Honor.

Student # 1: You are conducting the mini-trial as the attorney for the Buncos, and seek to admit Strike's statement into evidence as Way's authorized admission. You will elicit the following foundational information from the reporter: Before speaking with Strike, the reporter saw Strike and Way conversing quietly with each other in a corner of the team's locker room for about five minutes. On a couple of occasions, Strike pointed in the reporter's direction and Way nodded his head up and down. In addition, when Strike made the statement quoted above, the reporter asked Strike for the names of other players who took money for charitable appearances. Strike excused himself, talked to Way quietly for a few moments, then returned and said that the previous statement was the only information he would provide.

Student # 2: You are conducting the mini-trial as the attorney for Way, and seek to prevent Strike's statement from being admitted as your client's admission. You may cross-examine the reporter. You may then also call Way as an opposition foundational witness. Way will testify that he did talk to Strike on the occasion in question, but that he never authorized Strike to speak to the reporter on his behalf about appearance money or anything else. According to Way, he and Strike talked generally about the issue of appearance money, but Way said that he needed time to think about the issue and wasn't ready to discuss the matter publicly. Way also claims that Strike is out to "get" Way for Way's making public statements that the standard player agreement agreed to by the union the previous year was a "sweetheart deal" that sold out the players to benefit the union executives.

Student # 3: You are the judge and will preside over the mini-trial and rule on the admissibility of Strike's statement to the reporter as an authorized statement.

§ 13.08 Employee Statements
(Rule 801(d)(2)(D))

Foundational Elements:

* A declarant is a party's agent or employee;

* The declarant's hearsay statement concerns a matter within the scope of the agency or employment.

* The declarant's hearsay statement was made during the existence of the agent/ servant relationship;

* The party's adversary offers the hearsay statement into evidence.

Example

In the *Mahlandt* case (*see* Problem 13-3 above), the Survival Center's Education Director wrote a note stating that "Sophie the wolf bit a child in my backyard." The Director's statement would be admissible both against the Director personally and against the Center (as a statement by an employee), since the Director was the Center's employee, the note talks about a matter within the scope of the Director's employment, and the Director wrote the note while a Center employee.

Rule 801(d)(2)(D) greatly liberalizes employer-friendly common law principles. This issue of employee statements often becomes important when an injured plaintiff sues an employer on a "respondent superior" theory for damages caused by an employee's alleged carelessness. In such situations, the plaintiff frequently seeks to offer into evidence against the employer a hearsay statement made by the employee following the mishap. For instance, in a civil negligence case in which the employer is a defendant, a plaintiff might seek to testify that following the collision, the employee said, "I never should have drunk those last two martinis." Prior to the adoption of the Federal Rules of Evidence, judges typically ruled that such hearsay statements of employees were not admissible against employers. The judges' reasoning tended to regard employees as little more than dog meat, paid to carry out their daily tasks but certainly not authorized to speak on behalf of their employers.

The restrictive common law approach is typified by the case of *Big Mack Trucking Co. Inc. v. Dickerson.*[2] In *Big Mack*, Leday and Dickerson were employed as truck drivers by Big Mack. They parked their loaded trucks one behind the other, Leday's truck on higher ground. As Dickerson stood between the trucks, Leday's truck rolled

---

2. 497 S.W.2d 283 (Texas 1973).

forward and crushed him between the two trucks, killing him. Dickerson's family sued Big Mack for wrongful death, alleging that the brakes on Leday's truck were defective. To prove that the brakes were defective, the plaintiffs called as witnesses a Big Mack vice-president and a police offer who had investigated the accident. Both these witnesses testified that Leday had told them that he'd been having brake trouble and that he hadn't been maintaining his brakes properly. The court decided that Leday's statements should have been excluded as inadmissible hearsay as against Leday's employer, Big Mack. In the judges' view, Leday was neither expressly nor impliedly authorized by Big Mack to explain how the accident happened. (The court also held that Leday's statements did not qualify as "spontaneous utterances," *see* Rule 803 (2), discussed in Chapter 14, because too much time had elapsed between the accident and the making of the statements.)

Rule 801(d)(2)(D) produces a dramatically different result in cases such as *Big Mack*. Leday's statements satisfies the foundational requirements of Rule 801(d)(2) (D) because:

- Leday was an employee of Big Mack.
- Leday's statements concerned a matter within the scope of his employment. His job was to drive trucks, and his statements concerned a truck driving accident.
- At the time he spoke, Leday was a Big Mack employee.

Under Rule 801(d)(2)(D), then, the plaintiffs in *Big Mack* could have offered Leday's statement into evidence against the trucking company.

As with authorized statements, Rule 801(d)(2) states that judges must consider the contents of an employee's statement when determining whether an adequate foundation has been established for its admission into evidence. For example, assume that a declarant says, "I'm in charge of explosions for my employer, Detonator Inc. I want to apologize for setting off that last explosion so close to your house. What's that? Yes, I'll speak a bit louder in the future." Under 801(d)(2), the statement itself is some evidence that the declarant was employed by Detonator Inc., and of the scope of the declarant's employment. However, the statement does not by itself by itself "establish . . . the agency or employment relationship and scope thereof." Thus, a party seeking to offer the assertion into evidence as Detonator's employee statement would need to offer evidence independent of the assertion of the declarant's employment status and job responsibilities.

Problem 13-17: Late for Class

A typical foundational dispute under Rule 801(d)(2)(D) is whether a matter about which an employee spoke is within the employee's scope of employment. Assume that one of your law school classmates slips and falls on a banana peel while rushing into a classroom so as not to be late for Evidence (quite understandably!). The injured student sues the law school for negligence, and wants to offer into evidence the statement, "That banana peel should have been picked up yesterday." This statement would qualify as an "employee statement" if it were made by (select as many declarants as you think appropriate):

1. Your Evidence instructor, who spoke after the law student hobbled into the classroom and explained what happened.

2. A law school janitor whose duties include cleaning the hallway in which the mishap occurred.

3. A law school janitor whose duties do not include the hallway in which the mishap occurred.

4. The law school's supervising janitor, whose oversees law school janitorial services but does not have clean-up duties.

5. The university's supervising janitor, who generally oversees campus janitorial services but has no direct law school responsibilities.

6. The law school's Dean.

7. The law school's Director of Admissions.

8. The University's Chancellor or President.

9. Another student enrolled in Evidence.

Problem 13-18: Pickup Line

A pedestrian is hit by a small delivery van owned by Federal Parcel Service. Lori, the van's driver, tells the pedestrian after the accident that "I didn't see you, I was checking on my next pickup." Lori's statement constitutes an employee statement by Federal Parcel:

1. If Lori made it while she was working for Federal Parcel, even if she'd been fired by the time the case came to trial.

2. If Lori made it while she was working for Federal Parcel, but only if she is still a Federal Parcel employee when the case comes to trial.

3. Only if Federal Parcel expressly or impliedly adopts Lori's statement.

4. Only if Lori has express authority to speak for Federal Parcel.

Problem 13-19: No Brakes

Rachel is injured when the car she is driving is struck by a car driven by Jeff. Rachel sues Jeff and also Sue, the car's owner, for failing to maintain the car properly. Rachel testifies that after the accident, Jeff told her that "I stepped on the brakes in plenty of time to stop before hitting you, but the car never slowed down." Rachel's attorney is conducting Jeff's direct examination, and seeks to offer Jeff's hearsay statement into evidence as Sue's statement. *Based on the foundation set forth below, how would you rule on Rachel's offer?*

PLAINTIFF'S ATTORNEY: Jeff, how did you happen to be driving Sue's car?

A: She called me from the airport, saying that she had forgotten her passport and asking me to bring it to her ASAP. She told me to use her car, since I was supposed to start it up a couple of times while she was away.

PLAINTIFF'S ATTORNEY: What happened after you received the call from Sue?

A: I went into her apartment, found the passport where she said it would be, and drove to the airport. It's when I was driving the car back to Sue's place that I collided with Rachel.

Would your answer be different if Jeff also testified that, "As she promised, Sue paid me $100 for retrieving her passport"?

Problem 13-20: Acid Remark

Seeking to rehabilitate two dilapidated inner-city apartment buildings that it owns so that they can be rented out to low- and middle-income families, City hires Get the Lead Out to remove all vestiges of lead paint from both premises. During the lead removal process, a Get the Lead Out employee spills acid on a passerby and says, "I'm sorry. I thought that was a container of juice. My bad for not sobering up before coming to work." The passerby sues City for personal injuries. *Is the Get the Lead Out employee's statement admissible against City under Rule 801(d)(2)(D)?*

Problem 13-21: Rumor Mill

In the *Mahlandt* case (*see* Problem 13-3 above), the parents of a young girl sued the Wild Canid Survival Center after Sophie, a wolf who was in the yard of the Center's Education Director, allegedly bit the girl. The parents seek to offer evidence that the day following the incident, a Wild Canid employee who cares for injured animals on the grounds of the Center itself told another employee that "I heard some talk that Sophie snapped at another kid a few weeks ago." *Is the employee's statement admissible against the Center under Rule 801(d)(2)(D)? What if the speaker were an animal caretaker who formerly worked at the Wild Canid Survival Center and who said after hearing what happened stated, "How many times do animals have to attack children before the Center takes adequate precautions?"*

§ 13.09 Co-Conspirator Statements (Rule 801(d)(2)(E))

Foundational Elements:

* The hearsay declarant is a party's co-conspirator;

   Co-conspirators are two or more people who knowingly join together to commit an illegal act.

* The statement was made in the course of the conspiracy;

* The declarant's statement was made in furtherance of the conspiracy;

* An adversary (typically a prosecutor) offers the hearsay statement into evidence.

When two or more partners engage in a common enterprise, each partner has implicit authority to speak for the enterprise so that an enterprise-related hearsay statement made by any one partner is admissible against any of the others. Rule 801(d)(2)(E) extends this general principle of agency law to illegal enterprises.

Example

Ralph is charged with selling illegal drugs. Ralph's confederate, Alice, tells the undercover police officer who pretends to be purchasing the drugs, "Ralph just got these in — our finest quality goods ever." If the Rule 801(d)(2)(E) foundational requirements are met, the government could offer Alice's statement into evidence against Ralph to prove that the drugs that Alice tried to sell to the police officer belonged to Ralph.

The hearsay exemption for co-conspirator statements is a major prosecutorial weapon. Co-conspirator statements are potentially admissible whenever two or more persons have joined together in illegal activity, even if only one of the persons is a defendant and even if a defendant isn't charged with a crime of conspiracy. For example, assume again that the government offers evidence that Alice and Ralph joined together to sell illegal drugs. Alice's statement to the undercover police officer may be admitted against Ralph under the co-conspirator exemption even if only Ralph is a defendant in the case, or Ralph is charged only with selling illegal drugs, not with the crime of conspiracy to sell illegal drugs. (As you probably recall if you've studied criminal law, "conspiracy" is itself a crime, independent of the crime that conspirators try to commit or succeed in committing.)

The United States Supreme Court clarified the foundational requirements for co-conspirator statements (and by implication for the other exemptions for vicarious opposing parties' statements) in *Bourjaily v. United States* (483 U.S. 171 (1987)). (The case name is vaguely reminiscent of a fine red wine. If so, the vintage probably left a bitter aftertaste in many defendants' mouths.) In *Bourjaily*, the defendant was charged with conspiring with Angelo Lonardo to distribute cocaine and with possession of cocaine for sale. The Court held that Lonardo's statements about the drug deal to an undercover FBI informant were admissible against the defendant as admissions of a co-conspirator. In the course of its opinion, the Court ruled that judges were to determine the admissibility of vicarious statements pursuant to Rule 104(a), meaning that the government had to convince the trial judge of the sufficiency of the foundation by a "preponderance of the evidence." And because Rule 104(a) states that courts need not adhere to evidentiary rules (except privilege) when determining whether foundations are sufficient, the trial judge could consider Lonardo's statements themselves as evidence that Lonardo and the defendant were co-conspirators.

Left open by *Bourjaily* was the question of whether a co-conspirator's hearsay statements alone could be sufficient to prove that a conspiracy existed. The

Bourjaily court did not have to decide this issue because the government in that case offered evidence independent of Lonardo's statements that Lonardo and the defendant were co-conspirators. The defendant showed up at the pre-arranged time in the parking lot, put the cocaine in his car, and at the time of his arrest had more than $20,000 in cash in his car. After *Bourjaily* was decided, Congress amended Rule 801 to ensure that a hearsay statement alone was not sufficient to establish the foundation for any type of vicarious statement. Thus, Rule 801(d)(2) currently provides that "The statement must be considered but does not by itself establish the declarant's authority under (C); the existence or scope of the relationship under (D); or the existence of the conspiracy or participation in it under (E)."

Practice Tip: Prosecutorial Discretion

The hearsay exemption for co-conspirator statements helps to explain why prosecutors often forego filing conspiracy charges even when they have evidence that two or more defendants joined together to commit a crime. Prosecutors can offer co-conspirators' statements into evidence regardless of whether a defendant is charged with conspiracy. To satisfy the foundational elements for offering co-conspirator statements into evidence, prosecutors need only convince judges by a preponderance of the evidence that a declarant and a defendant were co-conspirators. By contrast, charging a defendant with conspiracy requires prosecutors to prove beyond a reasonable doubt that a conspiracy existed. Because judges may not punish a defendant convicted of, say, "conspiracy to rob a bank" and "bank robbery" any more severely than a defendant convicted simply of "bank robbery," prosecutors often choose to lighten their burden by foregoing conspiracy charges while putting co-conspirators' statements before judges and juries under Rule 801(d)(2)(E).

When defendants are charged with conspiracy and the government seeks to offer co-conspirator statements into evidence, the foundational issue that the judge has to decide by a preponderance of the evidence ("Was there a conspiracy?") is identical to the ultimate fact that the jury has to decide beyond a reasonable doubt ("Is the defendant guilty of conspiracy?") Thus, when a judge admits a hearsay statement into evidence under Rule 801(d)(2)(E), the jury is not informed that the judge has decided that a conspiracy existed.

Problem 13-22: Double Dealer

Monohan and Edwards are on trial for illegally selling opioids. Morales is prepared to testify for the government, "I was a drug dealer before I became an undercover cop. Monohan contacted me and told me that he and Edwards were selling as many opioids as they could get hold of to high school distributors. He asked me to join them because of my great connections with pharmacies. I told him I couldn't, I had quit dealing." Are Monohan's statements to Morales admissible against Edwards under the co-conspirator exemption?

Problem 13-23: Loot Out

Tom and Dick rob a bank, and Dick is now on trial for the robbery. To prove that Dick was armed with a weapon during the robbery, the prosecutor calls Tom's friend Harry, who testifies during a mini-trial out of the jury's presence to the following events that took place on the day following the bank robbery:

PROSECUTOR: And what happened when you arrived at Tom's apartment?

A: As soon as I walked in, I saw bundles of money on the coffee table. I asked him how he'd gotten so much cash.

PROSECUTOR: Did Tom reply to this?

A: Yes. He said that he and Dick had had some luck robbing a bank, and that this was his share of the take.

PROSECUTOR: Did you respond to this remark?

A: Yes. I said, "Sorry, Tom, we've been friends for a long time, but I might have to tell the cops about this."

PROSECUTOR: And what, if anything, did Tom say in response?

A: He told me to do what I like, and then said that Dick had an itchy trigger finger. He said that Dick had used a gun in the bank and probably wouldn't hesitate to use it on me. He said that I'd been a good friend over the years, but that he and Dick had done enough time in their lives and they had decided in advance that they would do whatever it took not to go back to prison.

PROSECUTOR: That's the foundation, Your Honor. I offer Tom's statements as co-conspirator statements by Dick under Rule 801(d)(2)(E).

JUDGE: *Assume that sufficient evidence independent of this statement exists to establish as a foundational matter that Tom and Dick were co-conspirators. Should the judge admit what Tom said against Dick under the hearsay exemption for co-conspirators' statements?*

Problem 13-24: Handoff

Sol is charged with conspiring with his sister Pearl to distribute cocaine. The prosecutor offers evidence from Ben, a government informant, that on three occasions Ben bought cocaine from Pearl. According to Ben, he and Pearl would fly in a small private plane to a local airport, Pearl would go to a phone and make a call, and a short time later a cab from the Blue Cab Co. would pull up and a man would reach out and hand Pearl a package, which later turned out to contain cocaine; the cab would then drive away. When Ben asked, "Who are you calling," Pearl said, "Sol." Ben asked, "Sol isn't a government informant, is he?" Pearl said, "No, silly, Sol is my brother." After the third drug transaction, the informant arrested Pearl. Other police officers then went to Sol's house and arrested him. The government also offers records of the Blue Cab Co. showing that on two of the three dates that drug transactions took place, one of its cabs picked up a passenger on a corner two blocks away from Sol's address, took the passenger to the airport, and dropped the passenger off at the same corner. Elana, a Blue Cab Co. cabdriver, testifies at the foundational hearing that "It's possible that Sol is the person I picked up on the corner, drove to the airport, and then returned to the corner, but I can't be sure."

1. Assuming that the foundational requirements of Rule 801(d)(2)(E) are satisfied, if Pearl does not testify, is the prosecutor barred from offering Pearl's statements to Ben (a government agent) into evidence against Sol under the Confrontation Clause as interpreted by *Crawford v. Washington* (*see* Chapter 10)?

2. Foundational Argument

Student # 1: You are the prosecutor, and will argue that you've offered a sufficient foundation to admit Pearl's statements against Sol as the statements of a co-conspirator.

Student # 2: You are the defense attorney, and will argue that the foundation is insufficient for Pearl's statements to be admitted against Sol.

Student # 3: You are the judge; preside over the arguments and rule on the admissibility of Pearl's statements against Sol.

Problem 13-25: The Latecomer

Patricia is charged with armed bank robbery. The prosecutor has offered evidence that Thelma and Louise robbed a bank using weapons and then escaped in a getaway car driven by Patricia. The prosecutor also offers evidence that Thelma and Louise asked Patricia to drive the getaway car one day before the robbery took place, when they pulled out a book, *Bank Robbery in a Nutshell*, and read, "The successful robber needs a getaway car." To prove that Patricia is guilty of the more severe charge of an "armed" robbery, the government offers evidence that one week before the robbery, Thelma told Louise, "Be sure to bring your gun. We'll shoot our way out of the bank if necessary." Patricia objects to the admission of this statement as hearsay. *The court should:*

1. Sustain the objection because the passage from the *Nutshell* is inadmissible hearsay.

2. Sustain the objection because Thelma's statement was not made in the course of Patricia's membership in the conspiracy.

3. Sustain the objection because the statement was not made in Patricia's presence.

4. Overrule the objection.

Problem 13-26: At the Movies: The Two Yutes

In a variation on the classic comic courtroom film *My Cousin Vinny*,[3] two "yutes," Bill and Stan, stop at a convenience store while driving cross-country to attend

---

3. 20th Century Fox, 1992.

college at UCLA. They buy a few items and leave, but the police soon pull their car over and place them under arrest for killing the store's clerk in the course of committing a robbery. At the police station, Bill and Stan are interviewed separately. After waiving his right to talk to an attorney, Bill says in wonderment to a police officer, "Stan and I shot the clerk? Stan and I shot the clerk?" At Bill and Stan's trial on a charge of murder, the police officer repeats Bill's statements as assertions, "Stan and I shot the clerk. Stan and I shot the clerk."

True or False: Bill's statements are admissible against Stan under the co-conspirator exemption.

Problem 13-27: Unfilled Offer

Rasheed is charged with murdering Patel, a drug dealer. The prosecution claims that Rasheed and Pierre jointly planned and carried out the killing so as to take control of Patel's drug business. A police informant who had posed as a drug buyer will testify on the prosecution's behalf that when he arrested Rasheed in a quiet nighttime raid, Pierre was still at large. Pierre was apparently unaware of Rasheed's arrest because the next day, Pierre contacted the same informant and said, "I'll sell you some of the drugs that Rasheed and I took after we got rid of Patel; I'm expecting Rasheed to bring it by my place later today."

True or False: Pierre's offer to sell drugs to the informant is admissible against Rasheed under the co-conspirator exemption.

Comparative Note: *California Foundational Requirements*

California departs from the federal rules with respect to the foundational requirements for vicarious statements in two ways. First, California judges decide these issues under Evidence Code Section 403, California's equivalent of Federal Rule of Evidence 104(b). Some commentators are particularly critical of the California rule in the context of co-conspirator statements, believing that jurors are particularly likely to "bootstrap" in this context. In other words, use of the lower foundational threshold of admissibility means that co-conspirator statements are more likely to be heard by jurors in California than in federal court trials, giving California jurors the opportunity to use the statements themselves to determine the adequacy of the proof of the other foundational requirements. At the same time, as a result of a second conflict between the California and the FRE, in California the foundation for vicarious statements has to be established entirely independently of the statements' contents. Thus, the California rules take from parties against whom vicarious statements are offered with one hand and give to them with the other with respect to foundational requirements for vicarious statements.

§ 13.10 Multiple-Choice Review Questions

Review Problem 13-A

Jyoti Williamson is charged with attempting to blow up a federal building. Jyoti's first statement to the arresting officer was "Rats! All that McGregor and I needed was one more day to finish making the bomb." The government seeks to offer Jyoti's statement into evidence against McGregor. *The judge should rule that:*

1. The statement is inadmissible unless McGregor is charged with conspiring with Jyoti to blow up a federal building.

2. The statement is inadmissible unless McGregor is charged with conspiring with Jyoti to blow up a federal building and they are tried together.

3. The statement is inadmissible hearsay.

4. The statement is admissible against McGregor so long as the government also offers evidence independent of the statement that Jyoti and McGregor jointly attempted to blow up a federal building, regardless of whether McGregor is charged with conspiracy.

Review Problem 13-B

In a civil suit for personal injuries, plaintiff Jackson testifies that defendant Carter was the driver of a car that struck and injured Jackson as Jackson attempted to cross a road. Carter denies any involvement in the accident. During direct examination, Jackson seeks to testify, "When I saw Carter's photo in the newspaper about a week after the accident, I said to my spouse, 'Can you believe that the paper has a photo of the driver who hit me last week?'" *Jackson's testimony would be:*

1. Admissible under Rule 801(d)(2) to prove that Carter was the driver of the car that struck Jackson.

2. Admissible as a prior identification to prove that Carter was the driver of the car that struck Jackson.

3. Admissible as non-hearsay to support Jackson's credibility because Jackson's words don't directly assert that Carter was the driver of the car.

4. Inadmissible hearsay.

Review Problem 13-C

Poppy sues the Hi Carb Bagel Co. for damages resulting from a collision involving Poppy's car and Hi Carb delivery van # 2. Poppy seeks to offer evidence that when the driver of the van reported the accident to Arturo, Hi Carb's chief mechanic, Arturo, stated, "We should have taken care of the brakes on that van months ago." Arturo's statement is:

1. Admissible as Hi Carb's employee statement to prove that van #2 was not properly maintained.

2. Inadmissible hearsay because Arturo lacked personal knowledge of whether failure to maintain the brakes was in any way responsible for the collision.

3. Admissible as non-hearsay to show that the van's driver knew or should have known that the van was unsafe to drive.

4. Inadmissible hearsay in the absence of foundational evidence indicating that Arturo's job duties include driving delivery vans.

Review Problem 13-D

Breach of contract case brought by Pierre against de la Torre; de la Torre contends that the parties never entered into an agreement. Prior to trial, de la Torre's lawyer sends an e-mail to Pierre's attorney stating in part that "my client may have violated the contract, but it'll cost you lots of time and money to prove it, so we'll give you half of what you're asking for, take it or leave it." Pierre leaves it, and the case goes to trial. Pierre seeks to offer the above portion of the e-mail into evidence to prove that a valid contract existed. The judge should rule that:

1. The e-mail is inadmissible under Rule 408 because the statement was made in an effort to resolve the claim prior to trial.

2. The e-mail is inadmissible in the absence of foundational evidence showing that de la Torre authorized the lawyer to send the email to Pierre's lawyer.

3. The e-mail is admissible to prove that a contract existed and that de la Torre breached it.

4. Based on the e-mail, the judge should rule that as a matter of law a valid contract existed and de la Torre breached it.

Chapter 14

The Admissibility of Hearsay Statements under Rule 803

§ 14.01 Chapter Checklist

1. Does admissibility of hearsay under Rule 803 depend on a declarant's availability to testify?

2. Are the trustworthiness considerations underlying each Rule 803 hearsay exception the same?

3. How does the permitted gap between event and statement differ among the exceptions for present sense impressions, excited utterances, and past recollection recorded?

4. For an excited utterance to be admissible, does it have to have been made spontaneously?

5. If a hearsay statement satisfies any one of the Rule 803 foundational requirements, is it admissible as a matter of law?

6. Does the admissibility of an excited utterance require that an event be both objectively and subjectively startling?

7. Can a statement qualify under the medical hearsay exception if it is made to a non-physician?

8. When might a statement be admissible under the medical hearsay exception, but not under the "state of mind" exception?

9. How does the "state of mind" hearsay exception compare to non-hearsay uses of statements as circumstantial evidence of state of mind?

10. Does the "state of mind" exception make admissible an assertion of the fact giving rise to the state of mind?

11. What are three common ways of obtaining evidence from a forgetful witness? Which of these depends on the use of a document prepared or adopted by the forgetful witness?

12. Does the business records exception apply only to the records of for-profit entities?

13. What is the role of a "sponsoring witness" when a party seeks to offer a business or public record into evidence?

14. Do the business record and public record exceptions both require that a document be prepared in the regular course of operations?

15. Are police reports admissible as public records against criminal defendants?

§ 14.02 Relevant Federal Rules of Evidence

Rule 612. Writing Used to Refresh a Witness's Memory

(a) Scope. This rule gives an adverse party certain options when a witness uses a writing to refresh memory:

(1) while testifying; or

(2) before testifying, if the court decides that justice requires the party to have those options.

(b) Adverse Party's Options; Deleting Unrelated Matter. Unless 18 U.S.C. § 3500 provides otherwise in a criminal case, an adverse party is entitled to have the writing produced at the hearing, to inspect it, to cross-examine the witness about it, and to introduce in evidence any portion that relates to the witness's testimony. If the producing party claims that the writing includes unrelated matter, the court must examine the writing in camera, delete any unrelated portion, and order that the rest be delivered to the adverse party. Any portion deleted over objection must be preserved for the record.

(c) Failure to Produce or Deliver the Writing. If a writing is not produced or is not delivered as ordered, the court may issue any appropriate order. But if the prosecution does not comply in a criminal case, the court must strike the witness's testimony or — if justice so requires — declare a mistrial.

Rule 803. Exceptions to the Rule Against Hearsay — Regardless of Whether the Declarant Is Available as a Witness (partial text)

The following are not excluded by the rule against hearsay, regardless of whether the declarant is available as a witness:

(1) *Present Sense Impression.* A statement describing or explaining an event or condition, made while or immediately after the declarant perceived it.

(2) *Excited Utterance.* A statement relating to a startling event or condition, made while the declarant was under the stress of excitement that it caused.

(3) *Then-Existing Mental, Emotional, or Physical Condition.* A statement of the declarant's then-existing state of mind (such as motive, intent, or plan) or emotional, sensory, or physical condition (such as mental feeling, pain, or bodily health), but not including a statement of memory or belief to prove the fact remembered or believed unless it relates to the validity or terms of the declarant's will.

(4) *Statement Made for Medical Diagnosis or Treatment. A statement that:*

(A) is made for — and is reasonably pertinent to — medical diagnosis or treatment; and

(B) describes medical history; past or present symptoms or sensations; their inception; or their general cause.

(5) *Recorded Recollection. A record that:*

(A) is on a matter the witness once knew about but now cannot recall well enough to testify fully and accurately;

(B) was made or adopted by the witness when the matter was fresh in the witness's memory; and

(C) accurately reflects the witness's knowledge.

If admitted, the record may be read into evidence but may be received as an exhibit only if offered by an adverse party.

(6) *Records of a Regularly Conducted Activity.* A record of an act, event, condition, opinion, or diagnosis if:

(A) the record was made at or near the time by — or from information transmitted by — someone with knowledge;

(B) the record was kept in the course of a regularly conducted activity of a business, organization, occupation, or calling, whether or not for profit;

(C) making the record was a regular practice of that activity;

(D) all these conditions are shown by the testimony of the custodian or another qualified witness, or by a certification that complies with Rule 902(11) or (12) or with a statute permitting certification; and

(E) the opponent does not show that the possible source of the information or other circumstances indicate a lack of trustworthiness.

(7) *Absence of a Record of a Regularly Conducted Activity.* Evidence that a matter is not included in a record described in paragraph (6) if:

(A) the evidence is admitted to prove that the matter did not occur or exist;

(B) a record was regularly kept for a matter of that kind; and

(C) the opponent does not show that the possible source of the information or other circumstances indicate a lack of trustworthiness.

(8) *Public Records.* A record or statement of a public office if:

(A) it sets out:

(i) the office's activities;

(ii) a matter observed while under a legal duty to report, but not including, in a criminal case, a matter observed by law-enforcement personnel; or

(iii) in a civil case or against the government in a criminal case, factual findings from a legally authorized investigation; and

(B) the opponent does not show that the source of information or other circumstances indicate a lack of trustworthiness.

. . . .

(10) *Absence of a Public Record.* Testimony — or a certification under Rule 902 — that a diligent search failed to disclose a public record or statement if the testimony or certification is admitted to prove that:

(A) the record or statement does not exist; or

(B) a matter did not occur or exist, if a public office regularly kept a record or statement for a matter of that kind.

§ 14.03 Introduction

This chapter examines the major categories of hearsay statements that satisfy foundational requirements set forth in Rule 803 and thus may be admitted into evidence as exceptions to the hearsay rule. Like the Rule 801 hearsay exemptions reviewed in Chapters 12 and 13, Rule 803 exceptions make out-of-court statements admissible for the truth of their contents. However, the Rule 801 hearsay exemptions apply to situations where the maker of the out-of-court statement is present in court either as a witness or a party. By contrast, Rule 803 admits out-of-court assertions from declarants whose presence in court is immaterial. That is, under Rule 803 a party offering the hearsay statement of a declarant who is absent from the trial does not have to explain or justify the declarant's absence for the statement to be admissible.[1]

Practice Tip: Problem Witnesses

As a tactical matter, attorneys generally prefer to offer live testimony rather than hearsay because the former is more likely to impress judges and jurors. However, attorneys can take advantage of Rule 803 to get helpful evidence into the record when hearsay declarants are "problem witnesses" whose live appearance may be damaging. For example, assume that a bystander's "present sense impression" supports a plaintiff's version of how a traffic accident took place. However, the bystander is unlikely to be a convincing witness, perhaps because of poor demeanor or because the witness is likely to testify to a version of events that is less helpful to the plaintiff than the hearsay. In either event, the plaintiff's attorney may prefer to present the hearsay through the testimony of a percipient witness who heard

---

1. A hearsay declarant's absence from trial may result in exclusion of hearsay under the Confrontation Clause as interpreted by *Crawford v. Washington* (*see* Chapter 10) if a prosecutor offers the hearsay into evidence against a criminal defendant.

the bystander's remark and can provide the foundational testimony necessary for admissibility.

Rule 803 has 23 subparts, each one identifying the foundational elements of a different hearsay exception. Under Rule 104(a), the party offering a hearsay assertion into evidence pursuant to one of these exceptions generally has the burden of convincing a judge by a preponderance of the evidence that the required foundational elements exist. However, personal knowledge is a necessary though usually unidentified foundational element for virtually all of the Rule 803 hearsay exceptions. Judges decide disputes about this foundational element pursuant to the lower admissibility threshold of Rule 104(b).[2]

Rule 803's introductory phrase ("*The following are not excluded by the hearsay rule . . .*") serves as a reminder that satisfying the foundational requirements for a hearsay exception is not an automatic ticket to admissibility. Judges may exclude statements that satisfy the foundational requirements for a hearsay exception for other evidentiary failings. For example, a judge may exclude hearsay under Rule 403, ruling that because a hearsay statement is vague, conclusory, or speculative, the risk of unfair prejudice substantially outweighs its probative value. And hearsay may satisfy an exception but be barred by the Confrontation Clause.

A number of important Rule 803 hearsay exceptions tie directly to topics examined in other chapters, and are therefore covered in those other chapters rather than this one. For example, Rule 803(18) provides a hearsay exception for "learned treatises." Treatises are hearsay when parties offer them for the truth of what they assert because they embody the written statements of the author. Because this exception allows parties to introduce expert testimony in the form of statements made in treatises that have been shown to be reliable, you will find a discussion of this exception in Chapter 9. Because they address forms of character evidence, the hearsay exceptions provided for by Rule 803(21) for reputation evidence and by Rule 803(22) for certain judgments of conviction are addressed in Chapter 5. Reputation evidence involves hearsay because the declarants are the people who make the assertions from which reputations are derived (e.g., "Sara is as honest as the day is long.") With convictions, the hearsay consists of the judgments asserting that the convicted defendants committed the acts giving rise to the convictions.

§ 14.04 Trustworthiness

Trustworthiness is the common thread that ties together Rule 803 hearsay exceptions. Each exception's foundational elements define circumstances that the drafters of the Federal Rules of Evidence (who for the most part followed the lead of their common law forebears) considered likely to produce accurate assertions. The Rules

---

2. Typically, judges also resolve authenticity disputes (did the claimed declarant make the statement?) under Rule 104(b).

regard the likelihood of assertions' accuracy as an acceptable trade-off for a party's possible inability to cross-examine a hearsay declarant.

Despite the lengthy common-law pedigree of most of the Rule 803 hearsay exceptions, their soundness is debatable for a number of reasons:

- The situations defined by the exceptions grouped together in Rule 803 are wildly disparate, so that one's confidence level that an exception's foundational elements correctly identify trustworthy assertions must vary from one exception to the next. Compare, for example, the likely accuracy of an assertion by a startled declarant (Rule 803(2)) with the likely accuracy of a routinely prepared business record (Rule 803(6)).

- Even inside the fence posts of a single hearsay exception, the circumstances in which assertions are made may be very different yet still satisfy foundational requirements. For example, business records (Rule 803(6)) are likely to be admissible whether the record is that of a small, local not-for-profit organization or of a multinational corporation.

- Some of the exceptions are probably at least as much a product of folklore and tradition as empirical reality. For example, Rule 803(2) reflects the common wisdom that a startled declarant who makes a statement regarding an exciting event while under the "stress of excitement" is likely to be truthful and accurate. However, the common wisdom has not been borne out by empirical research, which often shows that startling events tend to distort observers' memory and perceptions.[3]

At the end of the day, the Rule 803 exceptions resolve these doubts in favor of admissibility, trusting to the ability of judges and jurors to recognize weaknesses and devalue even supposedly reliable hearsay to the extent warranted. Moreover, judges do have the authority to avoid the mischief that a set of pre-defined hearsay exceptions of varying degrees of reliability can create. On the one hand, though judges are not generally supposed to evaluate credibility when making admissibility determinations, at least some of the 803 exceptions incorporate trustworthiness into their foundational requirements (*see*, e.g., Rule 803 (6)). As a result, judges may have room to exclude hearsay of questionable trustworthiness. On the other, judges have the power under Rule 807 to admit a hearsay assertion even though it does not fit within any of the pre-ordained Rule 803 exceptions, so long as it has "equivalent circumstantial guarantees of trustworthiness."

---

3. The classic essay suggesting the weakness of the reasoning underlying "excited utterances" is Hutchins & Schlesinger, *Some Observations on the Law of Evidence*, 28 Colum. L. Rev. 432 (1928). *See also* Moorehead, *Compromising the Hearsay Rule: The Fallacy of Res Gestae Reliability*, 29 Loy. L.A. L. Rev. 203 (1995); Stewart, *Perception, Memory and Hearsay: A Criticism of Present Law and the Proposed Federal Rules of Evidence*, 1970 Utah L. Rev. 1.

Practice Tip: "Objection, the Statement is Self-Serving"

Though presumed trustworthiness is the common thread binding together the Rule 803 hearsay exceptions, most of them do not include an explicit foundational requirement that a hearsay statement be trustworthy. Nevertheless, and especially when parties testify to or otherwise offer into evidence their own hearsay statements, adversaries sometimes object on the ground that the evidence is "self-serving" and therefore untrustworthy. However, the "self-serving" objection does not exist and is improper. The admissibility of hearsay depends on whether it satisfies the foundational requirements of an exception, and presumably parties do not offer their own statements into evidence unless they are self-serving. A "self-serving" objection may be the equivalent of a claim that a party's own hearsay statement is motivated by self-interest and therefore is unworthy of belief. But it's up to jurors and not judges to determine the probative value of hearsay.

Problem 14-1: Redraft

The plaintiff in an auto accident case seeks to offer a bystander's statement into evidence as an "excited utterance" under Rule 803(2). The defense attorney objects and makes the following request:

> Your Honor, in support of my hearsay objection, I request that you conduct a foundational hearing out of the jury's presence so that I can make a record as to the general lack of trustworthiness of excited utterances. I am prepared to call three University researchers, who I will establish are regarded as the best experts in the field, to present the results of their independent research projects indicating that assertions made at a time when people are excited or under stress are much less likely to be accurate than statements made when people are calm and in full possession of their faculties. Based on their testimony and their research, the defense urges that the excited utterance exception is not grounded on empirical reality and that therefore you should exclude the bystander's hearsay statement.

Which, if any, of the rulings below might the judge properly make in response to the attorney's request?

1. The judge should grant the request and exclude the bystander's statement if the judge concludes that the excited utterance exception is not grounded in empirical reality.

2. The judge should deny the request and rule that because the experts' testimony would contradict Congress' findings in approving Rule 803(2), the experts' testimony is irrelevant and therefore inadmissible.

3. The judge should deny the request but allow the defense attorney to offer evidence concerning the effect of stress on accuracy for whatever weight the jury gives it.

4. The judge should deny the request and rule that expert testimony about the effect of stress on accuracy is irrelevant if the plaintiff offers evidence that establishes by a preponderance of evidence that stress tends to improve accuracy.

§ 14.05 Contemporaneous and Excited Utterances (Rules 803(1) and (2))

Foundational Elements (803(1)):

- The declarant made a statement while or immediately after perceiving an event or condition;
- The statement describes or explains the event or condition.

Foundational Elements (803(2)):

- The declarant made a statement relating to a startling event or condition;
- The declarant was under the stress of excitement caused by the event or condition at the time the declarant made the statement.

Rules 803(1) and (2) authorize the admission of hearsay statements that declarants make roughly contemporaneously with the events or conditions that the statements describe. The narrow time frame between an event and a hearsay assertion relating to that event tends to obviate memory problems and to minimize a declarant's chance to reflect and make up a lie.[4] (Back in the day, judges admitted contemporaneous and excited utterances hearsay as part of the "*res gestae*" (closely connected to relevant events). Modern evidence rules give you one less Latin term to worry about.)

Moreover, the admission of essentially contemporaneous statements usually furnishes an adversary with a reasonable opportunity to cross-examine. Either a declarant will testify to the declarant's own hearsay assertion, or a witness who personally heard the declarant make the assertion will testify to it. In the latter situation, the witness will almost certainly have witnessed the same event that the declarant did. Thus, a party will normally have an opportunity to cross-examine a percipient observer, even if not the declarant whose hearsay statement is received in evidence.

Admissibility under both of these exceptions requires that a declarant have first-hand knowledge. The personal knowledge element isn't stated explicitly in the rule, but the Advisory Committee Note to Rule 803 states that personal knowledge is an implicit requirement of these and virtually all hearsay exceptions.

---

4. Examined from a more cynical perspective, of course, the effect of the hearsay exception is to reward really fast liars.

Example 1

The plaintiff is a Chicago resident who has sued the owner of an apartment on the twentieth floor of a high-rise for damages for carelessly allowing a window air conditioner to fall out the window and injure the plaintiff, who at the time was walking under the window. The defendant denies that the air conditioner fell from his window. The plaintiff calls a passerby whose testimony is in part as follows:

PLAINTIFF'S ATTORNEY: And what happened as you walked along Wacker Drive?

A: Just after I turned the corner I heard a loud noise coming from somewhere over my head. I looked up and saw what looked like a window air conditioner falling off a window ledge.

PLAINTIFF'S ATTORNEY: Were you alone when this happened?

A: No, I was on my way to lunch with a colleague from work.

PLAINTIFF'S ATTORNEY: What, if anything, did you say to the colleague when you saw the air conditioner begin to fall.

A: As soon as I saw it, I turned to my companion and said, "Oh my God, an air conditioner just fell out of that window, the one with the 'Let's Go Cubs!' sign in the window." [The defendant's window had such a sign in it.]

Here, the declarant observes an event that most people would find startling. The statement describes the event, and the declarant made the statement while under the stress of the excitement that the event created. Thus, it is a classic excited utterance. (When trying to establish that declarants spoke under the stress of excitement, you'll find it helpful, though not absolutely necessary, if the declarants were considerate enough to preface whatever they said with "Oh my God.")

The foundational requirement that an event be startling has both objective and subjective components. The subjective aspect is that a declarant has to be personally startled. It is possible, therefore, that an assertion might be excluded for the reason that though most people would have found an event startling, the declarant in question did not. For example, a Los Angeles driver might have a hard time convincing a judge that "I was startled by the sight of three drivers completing left turns after a traffic light in their direction turned red." The objective aspect is that an event must be one that most reasonable people would find unusual and startling. Thus, an assertion such as, "Oh my God, what a terrible hangnail that man has," is unlikely to qualify as an excited utterance.

Rule 803(2) eliminates the common-law foundational requirement that a startled utterance had to be "spontaneous." A few older decisions excluded assertions that were preceded by questions such as, "What happened to you?" on the ground that they weren't made spontaneously. Rule 803(2) saves lawyers who wander past the scenes of traffic accidents from the need to rush up to ambulance attendants and bystanders and instruct them, "Don't say a thing to the injured driver. Let's see what she has to say about what happened on her own." Nevertheless, if a proffered statement was preceded by other conversation, a judge may conclude that the declarant was not under the "stress of excitement" at the time the statement was made.

Example 2

Defendant Leticia is charged with murder; her defense is an alibi. The prosecution calls a witness who can place Leticia at the murder scene around the time of the killing:

PROSECUTOR: And at that time, what were you doing?

A: I was looking out my front window, waiting for my carpool.

PROSECUTOR: And then what happened?

A: I saw Leticia walk past and go into the house next door.

PROSECUTOR: Is Leticia someone you knew?

A: Oh, yes. She used to live in the neighborhood, but she'd moved away a few months earlier.

PROSECUTOR: Did you mention to anyone that you had seen Leticia?

A: Yes. As she was walking past my window I called out to my roommate that "Leticia just walked past our house."

Here, what the witness said to the roommate constitutes a present sense impression. The statement describes an event and the witness made it while perceiving the event.

The present sense impression exception is broader in scope than the exception for excited utterances in that the former does not require that an event or condition described by a statement be startling or in any way unusual. On the other hand, the excited utterance exception is broader in that it seems to permit a greater lapse of time between the time that an event occurs and a declarant makes a statement describing the event. A present sense impression must be made during or "immediately after" an event, which the Advisory Committee Note to Rule 803(1) describes as requiring "substantial contemporaneity." By contrast, the allowable time lapse between event and statement for an excited utterance is measured not merely by the clock, but also by judges' conclusions about how startling an event was and the duration of a declarant's state of excitement. If a judge concludes that the stress of excitement caused by an event continued for hours or even longer, a statement relating to that event might qualify as an excited utterance long after it would cease to qualify as a present sense impression.

Rule 803(2) is also potentially broader than Rule 803(1) in that the latter requires that a statement *describe or explain* an act or condition, while for the former to apply a statement need only *relate to* an event or condition.

Problem 14-2: Red or Blue

Denise, a pedestrian, sues Steve and Steve's employer, Meals To Go, for injuries resulting from being struck in a hit-and-run, allegedly by Steve's red car. Steve's defense is that Denise was actually struck by a blue car that passed Steve's car shortly before the mishap. Marisa, an ambulance driver, arrived at the accident scene 10 minutes after Denise was struck. To prove that Denise was struck by a red car, her attorney calls Marisa, whose testimony is as follows:

PLAINTIFF'S ATTORNEY: Marisa, what did you see when you arrived at the scene of the accident?

A: Denise was laying on the ground, a few people were standing around her.

PLAINTIFF'S ATTORNEY: What did you notice about Denise?

A: She appeared to be in great pain. She was writhing around, yelling out, and crying.

PLAINTIFF'S ATTORNEY: Then what happened?

A: I knelt down to do a quick check on her condition. I tried to comfort her, telling her, "You'll be OK, you'll be OK." Then I asked her where she was feeling pain.

PLAINTIFF'S ATTORNEY: Did Denise respond to you?

A: Yes. Right after I started saying this she said, "I hurt so bad, especially my legs and my back. A red car hit me right after I stepped into the street."

DEFENDANT'S ATTORNEY: Objection. Hearsay.

JUDGE: From the plaintiff's description of how she was hit, I'm dubious about her claim that she had personal knowledge of the color of the car that hit her so I will exclude the word "red" on that ground. (*Is this a correct ruling?*)

PLAINTIFF'S ATTORNEY: Did you hear Denise say anything else?

A: Yes. A couple of times while she was writhing in pain, she said it was all the driver's fault.

DEFENDANT'S ATTORNEY: Objection. Hearsay.

JUDGE: (*What ruling on the objection?*)

PLAINTIFF'S ATTORNEY: What happened next?

A: My partner and I got Denise stabilized. Then we put her in the ambulance to take her to the emergency room.

PLAINTIFF'S ATTORNEY: Were there other people nearby at the time you were stabilizing Denise?

A: Yes, maybe five or six people.

PLAINTIFF'S ATTORNEY: Did you hear any conversation between any of these people?

A: Yes, I heard one person ask what happened. Another person said that a pedestrian was hit by a red car, and that the driver of the red car looked like he was texting when his car hit the pedestrian.

PLAINTIFF'S ATTORNEY: Do you know which two individuals had this conversation?

A: I don't, I was focused on helping Denise.

DEFENDANT'S ATTORNEY: I object and move to strike the unknown onlooker's remark, hearsay. I also ask that Your Honor instruct the jury to disregard that testimony.

JUDGE: (*What ruling on the objection?*)

PLAINTIFF'S ATTORNEY: One last point, Marisa. Did you see Steve, seated over there, at the scene of the accident?

A: Yes, I did. He drove up and came over to me just as we were about to take Denise to the hospital.

PLAINTIFF'S ATTORNEY: Can you describe his demeanor?

A: Yes. He was really upset, nervously looking all around, crying. He kept repeating, "I don't believe this."

PLAINTIFF'S ATTORNEY: Did he say anything else?

A: Yes. I remember that he said that his boss at Meals To Go would be furious because he still had a bunch of dinners to deliver. (*Is this statement admissible as evidence that the accident occurred in the course of Steve's employment?*)

Problem 14-3: Excited Acceptance

Assume the same factual circumstances as in Problem 14-2, except that Denise has filed a separate lawsuit against Bob for breaching a verbal agreement to buy Denise's car for $25,000. Bob denies that he agreed to buy the car. In the breach of contract suit, Denise calls Marisa, the ambulance driver, to testify that when Denise was in the ambulance still writhing in pain, Denise said, "Oh my God, I remember that Bob agreed to buy my car for $25,000." *Is Denise's statement to Marisa admissible in Denise's breach of contract suit against Bob to prove that he agreed to buy her car for $25,000?*

Problem 14-4: Stepdaddy

Max is charged with physical abuse of his five-year-old stepson, Larry. The prosecution makes an offer of proof that a police officer will testify to entering an apartment at 10:00 a.m. and finding Larry alone in the apartment and crying. The officer will also testify that Larry was standing lethargically, had numerous bruises on his face, had swollen and reddened hands, and an open cut on one of his hands. Larry did not respond to the officer's questions about what had happened. The officer took

Larry to the hospital. Larry received medical treatment and was questioned further by the doctor and the officer about what had happened but didn't answer.

The prosecutor also offers to prove that a nurse was with Larry in a hospital room when Larry's natural father, Joe, arrived at about 4:00 p.m. When Larry saw him, Larry said at once, "Oh Dad, stepdaddy keeps whipping me. You don't whip me, Dad." Finally, the parties stipulate that the doctor's examination revealed that some of Larry's injuries were new, others were a few weeks old.

Student # 1: As the Prosecutor, argue for the admissibility of Larry's statement to his father as an excited utterance, to prove that Larry's stepfather beat him.

Student # 2: As the Defense Attorney, argue that Larry's statement to his father is inadmissible hearsay.

Student # 3: As the Judge, preside over the hearing and rule on the admissibility of Larry's statement to his father.

Problem 14-5: Mach Trial 1

Julio sues Hyun for injuries resulting from a collision between their two cars that occurred on Arrow Road. Julio's witness Amanda testifies that she was a passenger in a car that was passed by Hyun's car, a two-year-old black Saab convertible, at about 3:00 p.m. on March 31, about 10 minutes prior to the collision. Please answer the italicized questions embedded in the following partial transcript of Amanda's testimony:

PLAINTIFF'S ATTORNEY: What did you notice about the defendant's car when it passed the one in which you were riding?

A: I noticed that he was going a lot faster than we were. When he passed us, I looked over at the speedometer in our car and saw that we were going at the speed limit on Arrow, 55 m.p.h. I know that was the speed limit because we had just passed a speed limit sign.

DEFENDANT'S ATTORNEY: Objection to the testimony concerning the speedometer reading and the statement on the speed limit sign, hearsay. Move to strike.

JUDGE: (*Ruling?*)

PLAINTIFF'S ATTORNEY: Since the defendant's car passed yours and yours was traveling at the speed limit, would it be fair to say that the defendant was exceeding the speed limit?

DEFENDANT'S ATTORNEY: Objection, leading question and calls for a conclusion.

JUDGE: Overruled. The witness may answer. (*Is this ruling correct?*)

A: Yes.

PLAINTIFF'S ATTORNEY: Amanda, are you a licensed driver?

518   14 · THE ADMISSIBILITY OF HEARSAY STATEMENTS UNDER RULE 803

A: Yes, for about 12 years.

PLAINTIFF'S ATTORNEY: Do you drive regularly on Arrow and similar roads?

A: Sure, I drive all the time.

PLAINTIFF'S ATTORNEY: Based on that experience, can you estimate how much faster than your car the defendant's black Saab was going when it passed you?

A: I'd say at least 10 m.p.h. faster, but I can't be sure.

DEFENDANT'S ATTORNEY: Objection, lack of foundation, speculation. Move to strike.

JUDGE: Sustained. (*Is this ruling correct?*)

PLAINTIFF'S ATTORNEY: And what happened after the defendant's car passed yours?

A: I watched him for a while, maybe half a minute, until he was out of sight.

PLAINTIFF'S ATTORNEY: Then what happened?

A: I turned to the driver and said, "I think that car is an accident waiting to happen."

DEFENDANT'S ATTORNEY: Objection, hearsay. Move to strike.

PLAINTIFF'S ATTORNEY: Present sense impression, Your Honor.

JUDGE: On the ground of hearsay, the objection is overruled. (*Is this ruling correct?*)

DEFENDANT'S ATTORNEY: I also object that the statement should be excluded because it's speculative.

JUDGE: (*How should the judge rule on this objection?*)

DEFENDANT'S ATTORNEY: I also object based on relevance. Even if Hyun was exceeding the speed limit at the point he passed Amanda, which we contest, that point was 10 minutes before the accident, and about 10 miles from the location of the accident. Thus, any evidence as to how Hyun might have been driving when Amanda observed him is irrelevant, and any relevance is substantially outweighed by the likelihood of unfair prejudice.

JUDGE: (*What ruling on the relevance objection? Would your ruling be affected by whether Arrow Road is a main highway without traffic lights or an urban street with occasional traffic lights?*)

PLAINTIFF'S ATTORNEY: Finally, Amanda, did you say anything else to the driver of the car in which you were a passenger?

A: This is a hearsay chapter, so you know I did. Just after the black Saab passed us, I said that the way the car was being driven, its driver must be drunk.

DEFENDANT'S ATTORNEY: (*What objection if any would you make to this testimony?*)

Problem 14-6: Mach Trial 2

Same case as previous problem. Assume that Amanda testifies that the car she saw pass the one in which she was riding was a black Saab convertible and that she thinks that it had a "Go Packers" sticker on the right rear bumper. (This matches the description of the defendant's car, except that the bumper sticker on the defendant's car says only "Packers.") The defense attorney then approaches the bench and asks for a mini-trial on the foundational issue of whether the car that Amanda saw was that of Hyun, the defendant. When the judge grants permission, the testimony proceeds as follows:

DEFENDANT'S ATTORNEY: You noticed that a black Saab passed you, right?

A: Yes.

DEFENDANT'S ATTORNEY: You didn't find that extremely unusual, did you?

A: No. These days you get passed all the time even though you're going the speed limit.

DEFENDANT'S ATTORNEY: So you didn't notice the license plate number of the car that passed you?

A: That's right.

DEFENDANT'S ATTORNEY: All you noticed was that the car that passed you was a black Saab?

PLAINTIFF'S ATTORNEY: (*What objection, if any, might you make to this question?*)

A: Also that it was a late-model convertible, and the bumper sticker.

DEFENDANT'S ATTORNEY: As you look at Hyun here in court, you can't testify that he personally was driving the car that passed you, right?

A: That's true.

DEFENDANT'S ATTORNEY: And did this car pass you on the left or the right?

A: On the right. That's one reason I noticed it.

DEFENDANT'S ATTORNEY: And what make and model of car were you in?

A: A blue Prius.

DEFENDANT'S ATTORNEY: Nothing further. If plaintiff has no foundational questions, I'd like to call the defendant Hyun as a foundational witness.

JUDGE: Plaintiff indicates no questions, so defense counsel you may call your client for foundational questioning only.

DEFENDANT'S ATTORNEY: Thank you, Your Honor. Hyun, I want to call your attention to approximately 3:00 p.m. on March 31. Were you driving on Arrow Road at that time?

A: Yes, I was.

DEFENDANT'S ATTORNEY: Were you exceeding the speed limit at any time prior to the accident?

A: No.

DEFENDANT'S ATTORNEY: Did you pass a blue Prius on the right?

A: No. I was in the far left lane, and, of course, I might have passed some Priuses while I was driving, but none on the right. I never pass on the right.

DEFENDANT'S ATTORNEY: Around 3:00 on that date, did you see any other black Saab convertibles on the road?

A: I did. I saw one other car, I noticed it because it was the same make and model as mine.

DEFENDANT'S ATTORNEY: Did you notice whether it had any kind of bumper sticker on it?

A: No, I didn't.

DEFENDANT'S ATTORNEY: What did you observe about how this other black Saab was being driven?

A: Very fast — it passed me, and the driver was weaving in and out of lanes.

DEFENDANT'S ATTORNEY: No further questions.

JUDGE: Plaintiff's attorney, any questions? OK, if none, I'll hear brief argument.

DEFENDANT'S ATTORNEY: Your Honor, I move to strike Amanda's testimony on the ground that if the car that passed hers was not my client's car, her testimony is irrelevant. And it's speculative as to whether it was my client's car that she saw. She didn't see him personally behind the wheel, she testified that there's nothing unusual about being passed, there was at least one other black Saab in the vicinity, and she was inaccurate about the bumper sticker.

JUDGE: Under Rule 104, it's up to the plaintiff to convince me by a preponderance of the evidence that Amanda's testimony pertains to the defendant's car. (*Is this a proper statement of the foundational burden?*)

JUDGE: I conclude that the plaintiff has satisfied the requisite foundational standard, so the motion to strike Amanda's testimony is denied. (*Is this a proper ruling?*)

PLAINTIFF'S ATTORNEY: No further questions of Amanda, Your Honor. I have one additional witness to call and make an offer of proof that this witness will testify to having seen the defendant speeding and driving erratically on the same portion of Arrow Road 10 days before the March 31 collision that gave rise to this lawsuit.

DEFENDANT'S ATTORNEY: Objection, improper character evidence.

JUDGE: (*What ruling on the defendant's objection?*)

Problem 14-7: Nine One Mum

Warren Peace is charged with murdering Diane, his former fiancée, on the evening of September 22. Peace's defense is self-defense. The police found Diane about 11:00 p.m., shot to death in her bedroom. To prove Peace's identity and intent, the prosecution calls Diane's mother to testify that Diane telephoned her around 10:30 p.m. on the evening that she died. Diane was sobbing and asking her mother for help. She told her mother, "Warren's here. He's been drinking' he's got a gun, and he's planning to use it." Diane's mother then called the police. *Please rule on the following defense objections to the mother's testimony:*

1. The defense objects to the testimony in its entirety as hearsay. The defense attorney argues that the excited utterance and present sense impression exceptions are not available because they both rest on the likelihood that the adverse party will have an opportunity to cross-examine a percipient observer, either the declarant or the witness who heard the declarant's statement. As Diane's statement was made over the phone and her mother was not at the scene of the shooting, the statement should be excluded because the defense has no opportunity to cross-examine a percipient observer.

2. The defense objects that Diane's statement is hearsay and argues that the excited utterance and present sense impression exceptions are unavailable because there is no way to ascertain whether Diane had personal knowledge.

3. The defense objects to the portion of Diane's statement, "he's planning to use it" as speculative and not based on personal knowledge.

4. Assume that Diane called 911 instead of her mother and made the same statement to the 911 operator. Assume that the 911 operator who took the call is not available to testify. However, all calls to 911 are automatically recorded, and those recordings are time- and date-stamped. Can the prosecution offer the recording of Diane's phone call into evidence?

Problem 14-8: Eek Mail

Bill is charged with threatening Jim. The prosecution calls Jim to testify that when he saw an e-mail message from an unidentified sender telling him to "prepare to die," Jim immediately told his roommate, "Oh my God, this must be another threat from Bill!" *Is Jim's statement admissible in evidence to prove that Bill sent the message?*

Problem 14-9: Mind the Gap

Jean Yuss sues The Gap, alleging that she hurt her knee when she tripped and fell in a Gap store when getting out of an elevator that stopped two inches below the level of the fourth floor. To prove that the elevator did not stop at floor level, Jean's attorney calls a Gap customer service representative as an adverse witness to testify that about 30 minutes after Jean fell, a customer told the customer service representative that "You need to check your elevators. I just saw a woman trip getting out of an elevator on the fourth floor a little while earlier because the elevator didn't stop evenly with the floor." Gap's attorney makes a hearsay objection. *How should the judge rule on the objection?*

Problem 14-10: Second Opinion

Ruth Kanal sues Dr. Oral Scrivello for dental malpractice, alleging that Dr. Scrivello improperly fitted her with a bridge. When two visits to Dr. Scrivello failed to stop the pain caused by the allegedly improperly fitted bridge, Ruth went to another dentist. To prove that Dr. Scrivello's work was substandard, Ruth seeks to testify that when the second dentist examined the bridge for the first time, the second dentist immediately said, "Oh my God, who performed this shoddy work on you?" Dr. Scrivello objects that Rhonda's testimony is inadmissible hearsay. *How should the judge rule on the objection?*

Problem 14-11: When the Bough Breaks

Phil Bert sues his neighbor Mary Birch for injuries after a limb from a eucalyptus tree on Birch's property allegedly broke off suddenly and struck Bert, who at the time was asleep in a hammock in his front yard. Bert calls Hazel to testify that while she and Kilmer were walking past Bert's and Birch's properties, Kilmer suddenly shouted, "Oh my God, did you see that, Hazel? A limb from that big tree just fell onto that man lying in the hammock in the next yard!" Kilmer is unavailable to testify, and except for Kilmer's hearsay statement, Bert has no evidence that a falling limb caused his injuries. *Is Kilmer's hearsay statement admissible to prove that Bert was struck by a limb that fell from a tree on Birch's property?*

Problem 14-12: First Words

John Jones is charged with sexually assaulting a college student, Kay Stevens. To prove that Jones assaulted Stevens, the prosecution calls Stevens's friend Todd Wilson to testify that the day after the assault, Stevens came to his dorm room around 4:00 a.m. and told him that Jones, her ex-boyfriend, had sexually assaulted her a few hours earlier. Stevens also told Wilson that he was the first person she had told. She hadn't said anything earlier because she felt shameful and guilty and was too embarrassed to go to the police or her family. Stevens finally decided to tell Wilson because she trusted him, and she wanted to protect future potential victims. *Is Wilson's testimony to Stevens' statement that Jones sexually assaulted her admissible?*

§ 14.06 Statement of Presently Existing State of Mind, Feeling, or Belief (Rule 803(3))

Foundational Elements:

- A statement identifies a declarant's concurrently existing state of mind, emotion, sensation, or physical condition;

- The offeror of the statement seeks to prove the fact that produced the state of mind only if it is relevant to issues surrounding the declarant's will.

As you may recall (*see* Chapter 11), a routine non-hearsay use for out-of-court assertions is to offer them as circumstantial evidence of either the declarant's or a listener's state of mind. When offered as circumstantial evidence of state of mind, an assertion skirts the hearsay rule. For example, a declarant's assertion that "Gene always carries a gun" would normally be admissible as non-hearsay if the declarant were charged with murdering Gene and claimed that the killing was done in self-defense. Without regard to the statement's truth, a judge or juror might infer from the declarant's having made the statement that the declarant was fearful of Gene, from that infer that the declarant would be unlikely to act aggressively toward Gene, and from that conclude that any killing would have been done in self-defense.

Rule 803(3)'s hearsay exception for statements of presently existing internal conditions or beliefs is the "other shoe," the counterpart to using out-of-court assertions as circumstantial evidence of state of mind. When declarants directly assert their beliefs, feelings, emotions, knowledge, physical conditions, and the like, non-hearsay analysis doesn't work. Rather, judges and jurors must rely on the accuracy of out-of-court statements in order to conclude that those feelings and beliefs existed. Rule 803(3) reflects a belief that assertions of "state of mind" are likely to be trustworthy. Memory problems are nonexistent because the condition or belief exists simultaneously with the statement. Perceptual problems are also largely absent, on the theory that declarants are more reliable observers and reporters of their inner selves than of the outside world.

On the other hand, admitting "state of mind" hearsay does not obviate the other two hearsay dangers. Ambiguity remains a risk. In fact, emotions, feelings, and beliefs tend to be complex, and statements about them may be, if anything, more prone to ambiguity dangers than statements about whether a person carries a gun, the color of a light, or many other aspects of the outside world. Sincerity problems also remain; mendacious declarants may conceal or misrepresent their states of mind. However, the risk of insincerity is likely to be obvious to judges and jurors, and out-of-court assertions of then-existing state of mind are likely to be at least as trustworthy as in-court testimony. Finally, the need for state of mind evidence is often great, because so many legal issues turn on the state of mind with which an act was performed. For all of these reasons, this hearsay exception is of long standing.

Rule 803(3) distinguishes assertions of fact about the world outside a declarant (e.g., "Gene always carries a gun") from assertions describing a declarant's "inner world" (e.g., "I'm afraid of Gene"), and establishes a hearsay exception only for the latter. A judge may admit evidence of an assertion of fact about the "outside world" that gives rise to an assertion about a declarant's "inner world," but only as non-hearsay and then subject to exclusion under Rule 403.

Example

Defendant Jones pleads self-defense to a charge of murdering Gene. To support the defense, Jones calls Reynoso to testify that a day before Jones shot Gene, Jones told Reynoso, "I'm really afraid of Gene. He always carries a gun and he threatened to kill me." Jones' "inner world" assertion that Jones fears Gene is admissible for its truth under Rule 803(3). Jones' "outer world" assertion that Gene always carries a gun and threatened to kill Jones is not admissible under Rule 803(3). The judge may admit these assertions as non-hearsay circumstantial evidence of Jones' state of mind of fear of Gene.

Rule 803(3) has its roots in the case of *Mutual Life Ins. Co. v. Hillmon* (145 U.S. 285 (1892)), one of the most colorful cases ever decided by the U.S. Supreme Court. The case was tried to a jury six different times over the span of nearly 25 years. In this case, Hillmon's alleged widow, Sally, sued to collect the proceeds of life insurance policies that her husband had taken out with three different life insurance companies shortly before heading west from their home in Kansas, supposedly hoping to buy a ranch. Mrs. Hillmon claimed that her husband had died and presented as proof a badly burned corpse found by the side of a campfire in Crooked Creek, Kansas. The insurance companies disagreed, claiming that the corpse was Walters, a man who disappeared around the same time as Hillmon. The companies argued that Hillmon had asked Walters to accompany him west in order to bump him off, pass the corpse off as Hillmon, and collect the insurance proceeds. (The events took place late in the nineteenth century, remember; perhaps "D" had been discovered, but "N" and "A" were still unknown.) As evidence that Walters had accompanied Hillmon, the life insurance companies offered into evidence letters written by Walters to relatives shortly before he disappeared. In a portion of one letter, written to his "sweetheart," Alvina Kasten, in 1879, Walters stated that he "will leave here to see part of the country which I never expected to see when I left home, as I am going with a man by the name of Hillmon, who intends to start a sheep ranch."

The U.S. Supreme Court's 1892 opinion reversed the jury verdict in favor of Mrs. Hillmon in Trial No. 3. The Court held that the letters were admissible to prove that Walters accompanied Hillmon to Crooked Creek. Identifying the policy now incorporated into Rule 803(3), the Court held, "Whenever the intention is of itself a distinct and material fact in a chain of circumstances, it may be proved by contemporaneous oral or written declarations of the party . . . . Wherever the bodily or mental feelings of an individual are material to be proved, the usual expressions of such feelings are original and competent evidence." Under *Hillmon* and now under Rule 803(3), an assertion of a declarant's concurrently existing intention to perform a future act is admissible to prove that the declarant followed through and did it.[5]

---

5. The *Hillmon* case became a huge political "cause célèbre," seen by many Populists of the day as pitting a poor grieving widow against rapacious business interests. The case produced a second Supreme Court decision in 1903, which reversed another verdict in favor of Mrs. Hillmon in Trial No. 6 and resulted in an order that the case be retried a seventh time. Eventually, all the insurance companies settled with Mrs. Hillmon. Neither Hillmon nor Walters were officially seen or heard from again.

Practice Tip: Pursuing the Mystery

For a detailed description of the colorful history and conflicting evidence in *Hillmon* in the form of a transcript of hypothetical closing arguments based on the evidence offered in Trial No. 6, see Bergman and Wesson, *I Am Going with a Man by the Name of Hillmon* in TRIAL STORIES (Tigar and Davis eds., 2008). The U.S. Supreme Court reversed the verdict reached by the jury in Trial No. 6. At that point the protracted dispute ended with a settlement. As a result, no judicial determination of the campfire corpse's identity exists. Decades later, Prof. Wesson exhumed the bone fragments from the grave site so that DNA analysis might provide an answer as to whether it was Hillmon or Walters who died at Crooked Creek. The chapter in TRIAL STORIES concludes with the results of Prof. Wesson's efforts.

That Rule 803(3) admits contemporaneous assertions relating only to a declarant's inner world explains the reason for its very important limitation. Rule 803(3) specifically excludes from its scope "a statement of memory or belief to prove the fact remembered or believed." This limitation is necessary because every assertion about the outside world reflects a declarant's then-existing inner belief. Without the limitation, therefore, the state of mind exception would swallow the hearsay rule. ("Good riddance," you might be thinking.)

For example, assume that Sandy, who'd been involved in a traffic accident, tells a friend a few days after the accident, "I had the green light." If Sandy's lawyer offers the statement to the friend into evidence to prove that Sandy had the green light, the assertion is garden-variety hearsay, inadmissible unless an exception applies. Now consider the Rule 803(3) argument that Sandy's lawyer might make if the exclusion of the "fact remembered or believed" did not exist:

> Your Honor, the statement, "I had the green light," was really an assertion of Sandy's then-existing state of mind. That is, what Sandy was really saying to the friend was, "My presently existing belief is that the light in my direction was green." As the assertion reflected Sandy's contemporaneous inner belief as to the light's color, it's admissible under the state of mind exception.

If Rule 803(3) did not bar the use of a "statement of memory or belief to prove the fact remembered or believed," this argument would succeed in this and perhaps every other instance in which hearsay is offered. The limitation ensures that state of mind hearsay statements are admitted only to prove a declarant's state of mind, not to prove a fact about the outside world that gave rise to that state of mind.[6]

A hearsay assertion that qualifies for admission under Rule 803(3) may be relevant because the declarant's state of mind is itself a fact of consequence.

---

6. The exception allows statement of memory or belief to prove the fact remembered or believed if they relate to the validity or terms of the declarant's will.

Example 1

Danny sues Melissa for personal injuries growing out of an auto accident. Danny calls Amy, who testifies that she spoke with Danny about six months after the accident:

PLAINTIFF'S ATTORNEY: Where were you and Danny when this conversation took place?

A: In a mall. We were shopping for a present for a colleague's baby shower.

PLAINTIFF'S ATTORNEY: And what happened?

A: Danny bent down to check on the price of a car seat. All of a sudden he winced and grabbed his back. He said that his back was killing him, and that he was in terrible pain.

Danny's statement reflects his then-existing physical condition: back pain. His back pain is itself a fact of consequence on the issue of damages in the personal injury case.

A hearsay assertion that qualifies for admission under Rule 803(3) may also be relevant because it sheds light on the declarant's conduct.

Example 2

Melissa is charged with murdering Danny; the alleged motive was Danny's failure to contribute to the cost of a car seat that Melissa and Danny gave to a colleague at a baby shower. The prosecution calls Amy to testify to a conversation that Amy had with Danny the day before he was killed:

PROSECUTOR: Where did this conversation with Danny take place?

A: In the employees' lounge. It was after work hours, and Melissa had just left the lounge. So Danny and I were alone.

PROSECUTOR: And what did Danny say to you at that time?

A: Danny said that he was going to tell Melissa that he was no longer interested in contributing to the cost of the car seat.

Danny's statement to Amy reflects his then-existing state of mind: his intention to tell Melissa that he would not contribute to the car seat's cost. Danny's intention is relevant to his conduct and Melissa's alleged motive: The trier of fact can infer from Danny's statement to Amy that he followed through and told Melissa that he would not contribute to the car seat's cost.

Most declarants are unschooled in the niceties of the state of mind exception and can therefore be forgiven for often failing to confine assertions exclusively either to facts in the outside world or to their inner world beliefs and emotions. For example, Han may say that, "I'm really angry that the stockbroker didn't tell me that a big lawsuit was about to be filed against the company she recommended that I invest in." Here, Han combines an assertion about the outside world (the stockbroker failed to provide important information) with an inner-world assertion (Han is angry).

Rule 803(3) makes the inner-world portion of the statement admissible at trial, assuming that Han's anger toward the stockbroker pertains to a fact of consequence. However, Rule 803(3) does not make Han's statement admissible to prove that the stockbroker failed to provide important information about a stock purchase. After all, had Han said only that "the stockbroker didn't tell me that a big lawsuit was about to be filed against the company she recommended that I invest in," the assertion's status as inadmissible hearsay is apparent. The inadmissibility of that portion of Han's assertion should not change merely because Han happens to utter a related remark that qualifies under the state of mind exception. However, a judge might (subject to Rule 403) admit the outer-world portion of the statement into evidence not for its truth, but for the limited purpose of providing context and meaning to the admissible inner world portion of a statement.

The seeming incongruity of having to differentiate between assertions of state of mind (admissible) and assertions about the outside world giving rise to those states of mind (inadmissible) sometimes induces judges to fudge the distinction. For example, consider the case of *United States v. Annunziato*.[7] In that case, Annunziato and other union officials were charged with unlawfully asking for and receiving kickbacks in connection with a bridge construction project. As proof that Annunziato had taken kickbacks, the government called an employee of the construction company to testify that the company's president had told the employee that, in substance, "I'm going to send some money to Annunziato because he's asked for some money on the bridge project." Judge Friendly's opinion recognized that the statement of intention to send money to Annunziato was admissible under the state of mind hearsay exception. The statement that Annunziato had previously asked for the payment was not, but in colorful language the court ruled that it was nonetheless admissible: "True also, the statement of the past event would not be admitted if it stood alone; but this would not be the only hearsay exception where the pure metal may carry some alloy along with it."

Annunziato's logic is troubling, because declarants so commonly join assertions of state of mind with assertions about the past events that produced them. Rather than twist the state of mind hearsay exception, *Annunziato* might better have regarded the company president's statement that he intended to send money to Annunziato because Annunziato had asked for a payment as a *verbal part of an act.* That is, the president's statement established the legal character of the payment: it was a bribe, not a holiday present or a loan. (*See* Chapter 11.)

Practice Tip: A Trustworthiness Foundational Element?

Does the foundation for the state of mind exception include a statement's trustworthiness? Compare Rule 803(3) with California Evidence Code Section 1252, which provides that an assertion of state of mind "is inadmissible . . . if the statement was made under circumstances such as

---

7. 293 F.2d 373 (2d Cir. 1961).

to indicate its lack of trustworthiness." While Rule 803(3) does not explicitly mention trustworthiness, some federal court judges read an element of trustworthiness into the exception. As a result, a judge might exclude an assertion that otherwise satisfies Rule 803(3) because of a declarant's apparent contemporaneous motive to fabricate. For example, assume that the day before allegedly committing a murder, the defendant tells a friend, "I'll be going out of town for a few days." A judge who believes that the statement was part of the defendant's attempt to set up a phony alibi might exclude the statement although it otherwise satisfies the foundational requirements of Rule 803(3). A judge who does so might say that the statement is "too self-serving," or that "the defendant had an obvious motive to fabricate," or that "the statement lacks probative value and I'm excluding it under Rule 403." Pronouncements such as these conflict with the text of Rule 803(3), and judges are supposed to leave credibility determinations to jurors. However, if you object to the admissibility of hearsay offered pursuant to Rule 803(3), you might ground your objection partly on the statement's lack of trustworthiness. And if you are the proponent of Rule 803(3) hearsay that a judge excludes for lack of trustworthiness, make the best record that you can that the statement satisfies the explicit foundational requirements of the rule, and hope that if the verdict is unfavorable, an appellate court will conclude that the ruling was erroneous and prejudicial.

Problem 14-13: Before and After

Spin is charged with murdering Marty. Consider the following two potential items of evidence:

1. The prosecution calls Marty's friend Darlene to testify that "I talked to Marty on the morning of the day that he was killed. During that conversation, Marty told me that Spin had visited him the day before and said that he was going to kill him." Under Rule 803 (3), the judge sustains Spin's objection that Darlene's testimony is inadmissible hearsay.

2. The prosecution calls Marty's friend Darlene to testify that "I talked to Marty on the morning of the day that he was killed. During that conversation, Marty told me that after I left he was going to pay a visit to Spin." Under Rule 803 (3), the judge overrules Spin's objection that Darlene's testimony is inadmissible hearsay.

Assume that both of these rulings are correct. Can you justify the opposite outcomes based on the statements' likely trustworthiness?

Problem 14-14: Driver's Ed

Mary sues William for personal injuries growing out of an automobile accident. Which of the following potential items of evidence should the judge receive in evidence?

1. To prove that she was driving carefully, Mary testifies that minutes before the accident she told Ed, the passenger in her car, that "I'm always afraid of getting a speeding ticket on this stretch of road."

2. To prove that she was driving carefully, Mary testifies that minutes before the accident she told Ed, the passenger in her car, that "Traffic cops like to hide in driveways along this stretch of road."

3. To prove that William was speeding, Mary testifies that minutes before the accident she told Ed, the passenger in her car, that "I'm really afraid that one of these speed demons is going to hit us."

4. To prove that the injuries caused by the accident were still bothering her one month later, Mary calls Henry to testify that when he visited Mary a month after the accident, Mary told him that "My back is really killing me. It's hurt me every day since the accident."

5. To prove that William was speeding, Mary calls Henry to testify that when he visited Mary a month after the accident, Mary told him that "My back still really hurts from when that guy William was speeding and ran into my car."

Problem 14-15: At the Movies: Last Page

Re-examine Problem 11-7 in the context of Rule 803(3). Recall that in the film *Jagged Edge*,[8] Jack Forrester is charged with murdering his wealthy wife Page. To prove that Jack's motive for killing Page was to prevent a divorce that would leave him with few assets, the prosecution calls Page's friend Virginia Howell to testify that "I spoke to Page a couple of weeks before she was killed. She told me that Jack had been seeing other women, that he didn't love her anymore, and that she wanted a divorce." *Is Ms. Howell's testimony admissible over the defendant's hearsay objection?*

Problem 14-16: Fearsay 1

Abe Yusir is charged with abusing three stepchildren. The stepchildren have been placed temporarily in the same foster home. On a day scheduled for Yusir to have a monitored visit with each stepchild, the following events take place:

A. When told that Yusir is about to visit with him, Yusir's eight-year-old stepson Hakeem immediately tells the foster mother that "I'm really afraid of my stepdad." The prosecution offer's Hakeem's statement into evidence pursuant to the state of mind exception to prove that Yusir abused Hakeem. *How should the judge rule on defense counsel's hearsay objection?*

B. When the foster mother tells Yusir's seven-year-old stepdaughter Patty that Yusir is about to visit with her, Patty screams and runs from the room. The prosecution offers Patty's reaction to prove that Yusir abused her. *How should the judge rule on defense counsel's hearsay and irrelevance objections?*

---

8. Columbia Pictures, 1985.

C. When the foster mother tells Yusir's six-year-old stepson Anthony that Yusir is about to visit him, Anthony says, "My stepdaddy was always beating me." The prosecution offers the statement as non-hearsay to prove that Anthony feared Yusir. *How should the judge rule on defense counsel's irrelevance objection?*

Problem 14-17: Fearsay 2

Attila is charged with the murder of Genghis; Attila's defense is an alibi. The prosecution calls Nero to testify that the day before Genghis's death, Genghis told Nero that "I'm afraid that one day, Attila is going to try to kill me." The court should rule that:

1. The testimony is admissible to prove that Genghis was not the aggressor.

2. The testimony is admissible under the state of mind exception to prove that Attila killed Genghis.

3. The testimony is inadmissible hearsay.

4. The testimony is non-hearsay to prove that Attila had a motive to attack Genghis.

Problem 14-18: Fearsay 3

Attila is charged with the murder of Genghis. During the defense case-in-chief, Attila testifies that, "What happened was that Genghis asked me to take out my new gun so that he could look at it. When I handed it to him, he cocked it and took his own life." The prosecution calls Nero to testify that the day before Genghis' death, Genghis told Nero that "I'm afraid that one day, Attila is going to try to kill me." *True or False: Genghis' statement to Nero is admissible to rebut Attila's testimony.*

Problem 14-19: Proof Possibles

Jerry is charged with robbery of a small convenience store. Robbery consists of "taking the property of another through means of force or fear." Which of the following out-of-court statements could the prosecution offer to prove that the robber used force or fear? (Choose as many would be admissible.)

1. Tom's testimony that "I saw the robbery and heard the clerk say, 'Please, please don't shoot me.'"

2. Tom's testimony that "As soon as the robber ran off I went to check on the clerk, who told me that 'I was really terrified that I was going to get shot.'"

3. Tom's testimony that "As soon as the robber ran off, another person and I ran over to check on the clerk. The other person said, 'Oh my God, the victim must have been terrified!'"

4. Tom's testimony that "The day after the robbery, the clerk said to me that 'I was really afraid that I was going to get shot during the robbery.'"

5. Tom's testimony that "I saw the robbery and heard the clerk call out to me, 'Stay away, he's got a gun and he's going to use it.'"

6. Sylvester's testimony that "The day after the robbery, the defendant Jerry told me that 'The clerk I stuck up yesterday was really terrified.'"

Problem 14-20: Tea Party

Earl Grey is charged with killing his wife Jasmine by poisoning her tea. Grey's defense is that Jasmine had been depressed for weeks and finally took her own life. Consider the admissibility of the following potential items of evidence.

1. To prove that Grey committed the murder, the prosecution calls Jasmine's friend Green to testify that the day before she died, Jasmine told him that "I'm afraid that my husband has been trying to poison me."

2. To rebut the defense claim that Jasmine committed suicide, the prosecution calls Jasmine's friend Green to testify that the day before she died, Jasmine told him that "I'm afraid that my husband has been trying to poison me."

3. To rebut the defense claim that Jasmine committed suicide, the prosecution calls Jasmine's friend Green to testify that the day before she died, Jasmine told him that "I want to live."

4. To prove that Jasmine was depressed, the defense calls Jasmine's friend Green to testify that two weeks before she died, Jasmine told him that "I just can't seem to stop crying these days."

5. To prove that Jasmine took her own life, the defense calls Jasmine's friend Green to testify that the day before she died, Jasmine told him that "Soon, I might just end it all."

6. To prove that Jasmine took her own life, the defense calls Jasmine's friend Green to testify that the day before she died, Jasmine's sister told Green that "I'm really sad because I just left Jasmine's house and she told me that soon she might just end it all."

7. To prove that Jasmine took her own life, the defense calls Jasmine's friend Green to testify that the day she died, Green rushed in, saw Jasmine lying on her bedroom floor and said, "Oh my God, she's taken her own life!"

Problem 14-21: Chat Room

James Naiden is on trial for using the Internet to attempt to induce a minor to have sex with him. The prosecutor offers into evidence transcripts of sexual chat room communications between Naiden and the police officer who posed as a 14-year-old girl. Naiden's defense is that he didn't believe that the person he was corresponding with was a minor. As proof of his belief, Naiden calls a friend, Louise, to testify pursuant to Rule 803(3) that during the time that Naiden was corresponding with the police officer, Naiden told Louise that he (Naiden) did not believe that the person he had recently met on the Internet was a minor. The prosecutor objects on the ground that Naiden's statement to Louise is inadmissible hearsay.

Student # 1: As the defense attorney, argue briefly that Louise's testimony is admissible under Rule 803(3).

Student # 2: As the prosecutor, argue briefly that Louise's testimony is inadmissible hearsay.

Student # 3: As the judge, preside over the arguments and rule on the objection.

§ 14.07 "I'm Off to Meet . . . (The Wizard?)"

The issue of whether an assertion describing a declarant's inner world should make admissible a closely related assertion about the outside world has arisen in a number of cases in which a declarant has announced an intention to meet another person. In these cases, the courts have often admitted the entire statement not merely to prove what the declarant did, but also to prove that the other person attended the meeting. A dramatic example is the case of *United States v. Pheaster* (544 F.2d 353, 9th Cir. 1976).

In *Pheaster,* defendant Angelo and others were charged with kidnapping Larry Adell, the teenage son of a Palm Springs multimillionaire. The prosecution offered evidence that shortly before he disappeared, Larry had told a friend that "I'm going to meet Angelo at Sambo's North at 9:30 p.m. to pick up the free pound of marijuana he promised me." The court upheld the prosecution's contention that Larry's statement was admissible to prove that Angelo had met with Larry. At the same time, in an unusual display of judicial humility, the court stated that it "recognized the force of the (defense) objection to the application of the *Hillmon* doctrine in the instant case." The court noted: "When hearsay evidence concerns the declarant's statement of his intention to do something with another person, the *Hillmon* doctrine requires that the trier of fact infer from the state of mind of the declarant the probability of a particular act not only by the declarant but also by the other person . . . . A much more significant and troubling objection is based on the inconsistency of such an inference with the state of mind exception." Moreover, the court quoted from the Notes of the House Committee on the Judiciary commenting on then-proposed Rule 803(3), which stated that "the Committee intends that the Rule be construed to limit (the *Hillmon* doctrine) so as to render statements of intent by a declarant admissible only to prove his future conduct, not the future conduct of another person." However, while the *Pheaster* court acknowledged that "the matter is certainly not free from doubt," a prior California decision helped to persuade the court that Rule 803(3) left the *Hillmon* decision "undisturbed." In *Hillmon* the Supreme Court had said that Walters's letters were admissible to prove that Walters went west "and that he went with Hillmon." Thus, under the *Hillmon* reasoning, Larry's comment was admissible to prove that he met with Angelo. The following poem may help you recall the *Pheaster* doctrine:

"A Pheaster Sonnet"

In chichi Palm Springs on one evening hot,

Larry said he was going out to a parking lot.

Angelo was the man he said he was going to see,

About some pot that could be his with no fee.

Only to find himself kidnapped and then never set free.

Resulting in Angelo's arrest before he could flee.

Now Larry's last words being heard by the jury,

Raised in defendant Angelo a terrible fury.

He knew all about the exception for state of mind,

Years ago in *Hillmon* by the Supreme Court opined.

But surely here the prosecution was in a bind,

The foundation for this hearsay the judge couldn't find.

For Larry's assertion about his own intent

Is trustworthy only as to where he went.

And not as to the whereabouts of a different gent.

How can an assertion *Hillmon* possibly cover

When a declarant refers to the conduct of another?

The court noted that the issue was not free from doubt.

But said that it would be wrong to keep it out.

To a California case the *Pheaster* court did cling,

And said it's too late to spoil a good thing.

So the state of mind exception may allow you to cheat,

When declarants refer to people they are going to meet.

The next three problems are based on the outcome of the *Pheaster* case.

Problem 14-22: Pheaster 1

Angelo is charged with drug dealing. As evidence that Angelo was selling drugs, the prosecution offers evidence that Larry told a friend, "I'm going to meet my drug dealer Angelo in the parking lot in order to stock up on my supply of illegal drugs." The friend called the cops, who came to the parking lot and arrested Angelo. Larry's statement to his friend is admissible to prove that:

1. The friend reasonably believed Angelo to be a drug dealer and therefore had probable cause to call the police.

2. Larry met Angelo in the parking lot, but it is not admissible to prove that Angelo was a dealer who was selling drugs.

3. Larry met Angelo in the parking lot and that Angelo was selling drugs.

4. Larry was in the parking lot, but it is not admissible to prove either that Angelo was in the parking lot or that he was selling drugs.

Problem 14-23: Pheaster 2

Angelo is charged with killing Larry in the parking lot of Sambo's North restaurant; Angelo's defense is an alibi. *True or False: To prove that Angelo was in the parking lot, the prosecution could offer evidence from Larry's friend Bonnie that "On the morning he died, Larry told me that Angelo was going to be in the Sambo's North parking lot later in the day."*

Problem 14-24: Pheaster 3

Angelo is charged with killing Larry in the parking lot of Sambo's North restaurant. *True or False: To prove that Larry was in the parking lot, the prosecution could offer evidence from Angelo's friend Carla that "On the morning that Angelo was arrested, Angelo told me that Larry was going to be in the Sambo's North parking lot later in the day."*

§ 14.08 Statements Made for Purposes of Medical Diagnosis or Treatment (Rule 803(4))

Foundational Elements:

- The declarant made a statement for the purpose of obtaining medical treatment or seeking a diagnosis;

- The information in the statement is reasonably pertinent to diagnosis or treatment;

- The statement concerns the declarant's medical history, past or present symptoms, pain or sensations, or the inception or general character of the cause or external source of the declarant's medical condition.

Example

Indy sues Stocker for personal injuries growing out of an auto accident. Indy is in physical therapy for many weeks following the accident. Indy's treating physician testifies to a conversation that she had with Indy about three months after the accident:

PLAINTIFF'S LAWYER: What did Indy tell you about her right arm?

A: She said that it was still very sore, and that she couldn't lift it above her shoulder.

PLAINTIFF'S LAWYER: Did she say anything else about her physical condition?

A: Yes, as I recall she mentioned that her right wrist had been sore for a long time after the accident, but that now it was feeling better.

Indy's statements to her physician are admissible under Rule 803(4) to prove the extent and duration of the injuries allegedly caused by the accident, and to support any expert opinions the doctor may give regarding Indy's prognosis. To the extent that Indy described her then-existing physical condition to the physician, the statements would also be admissible under Rule 803(3). However, Indy's statements regarding past symptoms ("my right wrist had been sore") are admissible only under Rule 803(4).

The likely trustworthiness of statements made to treating medical personnel is transparent. Declarants are likely to be careful and accurate when describing their present and past physical condition to someone who will treat them medically. ("You did what with my spleen??? I meant to say that I was interested in *gene* therapy!!!")[9]

However, statements made for purposes of diagnosis rather than treatment do not necessarily carry the same aura of trustworthiness. For example, consider a plaintiff in a personal injury case who describes his physical condition to a forensic medical expert who has been retained to testify at the plaintiff's trial to the extent of the plaintiff's injuries. The expert isn't going to treat or remove any body parts of the plaintiff, and the plaintiff certainly has a motive to exaggerate his pain and suffering. Nevertheless, Rule 803(4) extends the common law "medical hearsay" exception to include statements made for purposes of "diagnosis or treatment."

In part, the liberalization of the common law rule is based on the belief that a declarant's motive to gild the lily when speaking to a diagnosing physician is likely to be apparent to judges and jurors. In addition, even before the rule was liberalized, such statements generally were admitted anyway, when medical experts testified to the bases for their opinions. The statements were typically admitted as non-hearsay; jurors were instructed to consider them only as to the weight they gave an expert's opinions. Extending Rule 803(4) to admit statements made for purposes of diagnosis avoids the previous fiction that jurors are capable of making such fine distinctions.

To be admissible under Rule 803(4), a hearsay statement needn't necessarily be made to a doctor. Nearly any type of medical personnel will do (e.g., an ambulance attendant, a nurse, a physical therapist, perhaps even a family member), so long as the judge concludes that the statement was "reasonably pertinent to diagnosis or treatment."

A "One-Way" Exception. The medical hearsay exception applies to statements *from* patients *to* medical personnel. The exception does *not* make admissible statements *from* medical personnel *to* patients. For example, if a doctor examines Rich

---

9. Studies of patient behavior indicate that patients frequently lie and withhold information when talking to their doctors. For one such study, visit https://www.healthline.com/health-news/why-do-most-people-lie-to-their-doctor. Thus, the accuracy of the assumption underlying his hearsay exception is questionable.

and tells him, "You've got Lyme disease," Rich cannot testify to the statement as evidence that he has Lyme disease.

United States v. Tome (61 F.3d 1446 (10th Cir. 1995) suggests how judges may interpret the "reasonably pertinent" foundational requirement. The defendant in *Tome* was charged with sexual abuse of his young daughter. The Court held that the daughter's statement to a pediatrician that "my father put his thing in me" was admissible under Rule 803(4). Her statement was reasonably pertinent to treatment even though it was made during a "get acquainted" conversation, because making patients comfortable was part of the pediatrician's examination process. On the other hand, similar statements that the daughter made to a children's services caseworker were not admissible under the rule because the caseworker's role was limited to referring the daughter to other medical professionals for treatment.[10] The court's reasoning suggests that admissibility requires both a patient's subjective belief that information is pertinent to diagnosis or treatment and the objective reasonableness of that belief.

Problem 14-25: Blue Skye

Lucy is charged with the attempted murder of Skye, her former fiancée. Lucy claims that she acted in self-defense, in part as a result of months of physical abuse by Skye. Skye denies abusing Lucy. To prove that she had been abused by Skye, Lucy calls Dr. Diamond, a psychiatrist, to testify that before the incident took place, Dr. Diamond had treated Lucy for a variety of symptoms associated with "battered spouse syndrome." Dr. Diamond's testimony was in part as follows:

DEFENDANT'S ATTORNEY: Dr. Diamond, when was your first appointment with Lucy?

A: It was on the 17th of October.

DEFENDANT'S ATTORNEY: And what did she tell you on that occasion regarding her physical condition?

A: She told me that she'd been suffering from terrible headaches, was not able to sleep more than an hour or two at a time, had lost her appetite, and often started crying for no apparent reason.

DEFENDANT'S ATTORNEY: Did she tell you when these symptoms had started?

A: Yes. She said they had begun in May, after her fiancé Skye started physically abusing her when he had had too much to drink.

PROSECUTOR: Objection, hearsay. The statement is inadmissible under the medical hearsay exception because neither identifying the alleged source of

---

10. The *Tome* case had been remanded to the Court of Appeal by the U.S. Supreme Court after it had held that the daughter's statements were inadmissible as prior consistent statements under Rule 801(d)(1)(B). For a discussion of the Supreme Court's *Tome* opinion, *see* Chapter 12.

past abuse nor tying the abuse to drinking was reasonably pertinent to the doctor's treatment of Lucy.

JUDGE: *How should the judge rule on the prosecutor's objection?*

Problem 14-26: Child Abuse Expert

Ralph Waldo is charged with sexually assaulting seven-year-old Debra, the daughter of a woman he had been dating. The prosecutor retained pediatrician Dr. Joyce Weathers to examine Debra and to diagnose the cause of Debra's physical injuries. At trial, Dr. Weathers testifies that in her opinion, the physical injuries that she observed on Debra are consistent with abusive sexual contact. Pursuant to Rule 803(4), the prosecutor also seeks to have Dr. Weathers testify that while she was examining Debra, Debra told her that "My mom's friend Ralph tried to stick something down there (pointing to her vagina) and it really hurt, and he put his hand over my mouth so I couldn't scream. I couldn't breathe." *Can Dr. Weathers testify to Debra's statement, including the identity of her attacker, under the exception for medical hearsay? If Debra doesn't testify, what is the impact of* Crawford v. Washington *(see Chapter 10) on the admissibility of her statement to Dr. Weathers?*

Problem 14-27: Bitten

John sues Vicki on behalf of his three-year-old daughter Lyndon for injuries suffered by Lyndon allegedly as a result of being bitten by Vicki's dog, a breed of big dog called a "pitweiler." Vicki claims that a neighbor's small Yorkie caused the injuries. John took Lyndon to an emergency room. John calls the emergency room physician to testify that "When he brought his daughter in, John told me that she had scratches and a deep gash on her right leg, and that she seemed to be having lots of pain in the neck area. He also told me that she'd been bitten by a large dog." Vicki's attorney makes the following objections:

1. John was not the patient so his statement is inadmissible under Rule 803(4).

2. John concededly wasn't present when Lyndon was bitten. Because he lacks personal knowledge of how the injuries occurred, his statement is inadmissible under Rule 803(4).

3. Identifying the source of the injuries as a "large dog" was not reasonably pertinent to Lyndon's treatment, so that portion of his statement is inadmissible under Rule 803(4).

How should the judge rule on the objections?

Problem 14-28: At the Movies: Sister

In the film *The Verdict*,[11] the sister of a comatose patient files a medical malpractice lawsuit on her behalf against two anesthesiologists and the hospital that employed

---

11. 20th Century Fox (1982).

them. The suit alleges that the patient went to the hospital's emergency room in distress to give birth and ended up comatose because of the use of an improper anesthetic. To prove that the patient had eaten a full meal one hour before arriving at the hospital (and that therefore the defendants used an improper anesthetic), the plaintiff seeks to offer evidence that the sister, who had accompanied the patient to the hospital, told the hospital's admitting nurse that "My sister ate a full meal an hour ago."

Is the sister's statement to the admitting room nurse admissible under Rule 803(4)?

Problem 14-29: Back Talk

Jeff sues Arlene for injuries suffered in an auto accident allegedly caused by Arlene's careless driving of her sports utility vehicle ("SUV"). Arlene claims that the accident could not have caused Jeff's injuries, and that any injuries he had were the result of an earlier water skiing mishap. *Which of the following statements that Jeff might have made after the accident to his treating physician would be admissible by him under Rule 803(4)?*

1. My back really hurts.

2. My back has been hurting me ever since the accident.

3. My back has been hurting me ever since I was hit by that SUV.

4. My back has been hurting me ever since I was hit by that SUV that was going at least 30 m.p.h.

5. My back has been hurting me ever since I was hit by that SUV that was going at least 30 m.p.h., and I've never hurt my back before.

6. My back has been hurting me ever since I was hit by that SUV that was going at least 30 m.p.h. and ran the red light.

7. My back has been hurting me ever since I was hit by that SUV that a woman who must have been boozing it up was driving at least 30 m.p.h. and ran the red light.

Problem 14-30: Friendly Advice

Hedda Furst attends a dinner party and sees an old friend, Dr. Liz Ishen. Hedda has never been a patient of Dr. Ishen, an internist. However, from time to time when they have been together on social occasions, Hedda has talked to Dr. Ishen about personal medical concerns. At the dinner party, Hedda tells Dr. Ishen that "I've been getting really bad headaches for a few weeks now; they started when that auto paint shop opened up next to where I live. Do you think I should wait to see if they go away, or should I make an appointment with my doctor?" Sometime later, Hedda files suit against the auto paint shop. *Is Hedda's statement to Dr. Ishen at the dinner party admissible under the medical hearsay exception?*

Problem 14-31: Medi-Cal

Matt sues Randy for personal injuries stemming from Randy's allegedly intentionally running into Matt with the intent to injure him during an adult league ice hockey game. To prove that his injuries resulted from the collision with Randy, Matt calls Cal, the coach of his ice hockey team, as a witness to testify to what happened. Cal's testimony goes as follows:

PLAINTIFF'S ATTORNEY: And what happened after you saw Randy collide with Matt?

A: Matt skated off the ice immediately and went to the far end of the bench. When the period was over, I asked him whether he could play and he said that he couldn't, that his shoulder and his back were killing him from when Randy ran into him on purpose. He also asked me to put an ice pack on his shoulder.

DEFENDANT'S ATTORNEY: Objection, hearsay.

PLAINTIFF'S ATTORNEY: Medical hearsay exception, Rule 803(4).

JUDGE: I'll sustain the objection, subject to the plaintiff's eliciting further foundational evidence.

PLAINTIFF'S ATTORNEY: Thank you, Your Honor. Cal, does the league have any policy with respect to injuries that players suffer during league games?

A: Yes. A first-aid official is supposed to attend all games. That official's job is to check on any player who is hurt during a game. If the first-aid official thinks that an injury needs more attention than just the usual first-aid procedures, he or she is supposed to refer a player to a hospital emergency room.

PLAINTIFF'S ATTORNEY: As a coach, what is your role with respect to injured players?

A: Because coaches often have a better chance to observe how an injury occurred than players, the league encourages us to describe how an injury occurred to the first-aid official. Also, coaches are to pass along any information that players give them to the official. And of course as a coach I bring a first aid kit to every game. So if a player isn't hurt too seriously, I often provide ice packs, bandages, aspirin, and other basics.

PLAINTIFF'S ATTORNEY: Do you tell the players about your role in case of injury to a player?

A: Yes, I go over the processes in a team meeting before the start of each season.

PLAINTIFF'S ATTORNEY: Nothing further by way of foundation, Your Honor.

JUDGE: Does the defense want to make any foundational inquiries?

DEFENDANT'S ATTORNEY: Just a couple. Coach, does it happen that games are played even though a first-aid official might not be in attendance?

A: That's happened, yes. I don't like it.

DEFENDANT'S ATTORNEY: And on this occasion, did either you or Matt talk to a first-aid official after the collision with Randy?

A: I don't remember. I know Matt stayed on the bench until the end of the game.

DEFENDANT'S ATTORNEY: And so far as you remember, Matt didn't ask you to call over the first-aid official, right?

A: That's right.

DEFENDANT'S ATTORNEY: That concludes my foundational questioning.

Student # 1: As the plaintiff's attorney, argue briefly that the foundation is sufficient to admit Matt's statement to the Coach under Rule 803(4).

Student # 2: As the defense attorney, argue briefly that the foundation is insufficient to admit Matt's statement to the Coach under Rule 803(4).

Student # 3: As the judge, preside over the arguments and rule on the objection, indicating which party has the burden of establishing its position, what that burden consists of, and the reasons for your ruling.

§ 14.09 Past Recollection Recorded (Rule 803(5)); Refreshing Recollection (Rule 612)

Foundational Elements (Rule 803(5)):

- The declarant has personal knowledge of a matter;

- The declarant has insufficient recollection to testify about the matter fully and accurately;

Unlike the other Rule 803 exceptions, Rule 803(5) requires that a declarant testify if a hearsay statement is to be admitted under Rule 803(5).

- The declarant made a memorandum or record concerning the matter, or adopted a memorandum or record prepared by someone else:

- The matter was fresh in the declarant's memory at the time the memorandum or record was made or adopted;

- The declarant testifies that the memorandum or record is accurate.

- The offering party can read the contents of an admissible memorandum or record to a judge or jury; only the adverse party can offer the memorandum or record itself into evidence.

Foundational Elements (Rule 612):

- If a party uses a writing to refresh a declarant's recollection either while or (in the judge's discretion) before testifying, the adverse party may examine the writing and offer pertinent portions of it into evidence.

Despite what may be ample pretrial preparation, witnesses sometimes lose their train of thought while testifying and omit information that their questioners know that the witnesses can provide. Given this common human frailty, evidence rules give attorneys two ready ways to refresh a forgetful witness' recollection. First, questioners can use leading questions to remind witnesses of the forgotten information. While under Rule 611 leading questions are not ordinarily allowed during direct examination, an exception that most judges recognize occurs when an attorney is refreshing the memory of a witness who apparently can provide the information the attorney is seeking but has momentarily forgotten it.

Example 1

The witness is to testify to a meeting in which the purchase of new computers was discussed:

PLAINTIFF'S ATTORNEY: And who attended this meeting?

A: It was me, Hilary, Francesca, Nicholas and . . . I'm sorry, I know one other person was there, her name has slipped my mind momentarily.

PLAINTIFF'S ATTORNEY: Was it Vince?

A: Yes, thank you. Vince also was at the meeting.

The leading question is permissible in this situation because the lawyer is not putting words in the witness' mouth. It is apparent that the witness has personal knowledge that another person attended the meeting but has momentarily forgotten her name.

An attorney can also refresh the recollection of a forgetful witness under Rule 612 by showing the witness a document that refers to the forgotten information. If the document enables the witness to recall the forgotten information, the attorney re-asks the question and the examination proceeds. Under Rule 612 as at common-law, an attorney may use any document to refresh recollection. The document needn't be admissible in evidence nor authored by the testifying witness.[12]

Under Rule 612 the adversary can demand "to have the writing produced at the hearing, to inspect it, to cross-examine the witness thereon, and to introduce in evidence those portions which relate to the testimony of the witness," even if the witness used the document to refresh the witness' memory prior to testifying, perhaps during a pretrial preparation meeting. Thus, a questioner using a document to refresh a witness' recollection, either before or during trial, must be careful not to use a document that contains harmful or embarrassing information.

---

12. One colorful opinion noted that if for some reason it refreshed a witness' memory, an attorney might even refresh recollection with "the dolorous refrain of 'The Tennessee Waltz'" or "the sweet carbonation of a chocolate soda." *See Baker v. State*, 371 A.2d 699 (Md. Ct. Spec. App. 1977). Don't be too quick to bring music or a picnic basket into the courtroom, however. In practice, attorneys invariably refresh recollection with documents.

Example 2

The witness is to testify to a meeting in which the purchase of new computers was discussed:

PLAINTIFF'S ATTORNEY: And who attended this meeting?

A: It was me, Hilary, Francesca, Nicholas and . . . I'm sorry, I know one other person was there, her name has slipped my mind momentarily.

PLAINTIFF'S ATTORNEY: If I were to show you the minutes of the meeting, might they enable you to recall the name of the other person who attended it?

A: I'm sure they would.

Many judges regard this question and answer as foundational to allowing an attorney to attempt to refresh a witness' recollection.

The common protocol is for the questioner to hand a refreshing document (here, the minutes) to the witness and allow the witness time to review it. The questioner should remove the document from the witness before continuing the questioning.

PLAINTIFF'S ATTORNEY: Is your memory now refreshed as to the name of the other person who attended the meeting?

A: Yes.

PLAINTIFF'S ATTORNEY: And who was this other person?

A: It was Vince.

The memory-refreshing techniques described above do not raise hearsay issues because they do not involve offering out-of-court statements into evidence. Even when an attorney refreshes recollection with a document under Rule 612, the witness testifies from present memory, not to the contents of the document (in theory, at least). When a witness genuinely lacks present recall, however, the "refreshing" rubric is unavailable. In such situations, Rule 803(5) can make a declarant's hearsay statement admissible. If the rule's foundational requirements are satisfied, the offering party reads a document's contents into evidence. The *written memorandum or record itself is not received* in evidence unless offered by the adversary. The purpose of this restriction is to avoid giving an unfair advantage to a party whose witness lacks sufficient memory to testify from present recollection. If the memorandum or record were physically admitted into evidence, the jury could examine it during deliberations. Thus, it might have undue influence compared to other evidence in the case, most of which will be oral.

The trustworthiness rationale for Rule 803(5)'s "recorded recollection" exception is similar to that for present sense impressions (Rule 803(1)), which is the lack of time to fabricate or forget. In each case, the statement that is admitted must have been made soon after the event to which the statement refers. Rule 803(1) requires that the statement be made during the event or "immediately thereafter." Rule 803(5) has a somewhat looser standard but requires that the statement have been made "when the matter was fresh." In both situations, the short time frame perhaps obviates memory problems and reduces a declarant's chance to reflect and make up a lie.

Rule 803(5) contains an additional trustworthiness requirement: the declarant has to testify that the written statement was correct at the time the declarant made it. This makes sense, because when hearsay is admitted under Rule 803(1), the adversary generally has an opportunity to cross-examine either the declarant or a witness who personally heard the out-of-court assertion, and who therefore will usually have witnessed the same event as the declarant. Under Rule 803(5), by contrast, an opportunity for cross-examination is likely to be lacking. Typically, the only witness is the declarant, who by definition can no longer remember much about what happened.

Example 3

A witness in a bank robbery prosecution testifies that she saw the robbers leap into the getaway car. The witness wrote down the car's license plate number on the back of an envelope, but can no longer remember the number. The prosecutor lays the foundation to qualify the statement on the envelope as the witness' "recorded recollection" as follows:

PROSECUTOR: And what happened after you heard the noise and shouting coming from the bank?

A: Two men ran out of the bank, jumped into a car and drove off at high speed.

PROSECUTOR: Can you describe this car?

A: I can't remember much. It was a few years' old, dark color, sedan-type.

PROSECUTOR: Did you notice the car's license plate number?

A: Yes. I looked at it as the car drove off. I knew something was wrong, and I wanted to at least get the license plate number.

PROSECUTOR: Do you now recall the car's license plate number?

A: Not really. I remember it started with the letter "N," that's about all I really remember now.

The recorded recollection exception doesn't require that a witness be entirely devoid of memory. All that's required is that the witness have "insufficient recollection . . . to testify fully and accurately."

PROSECUTOR: After you watched the car drive off, what did you do?

A: I kept whispering the license plate number to myself. As I did that, I pulled an envelope and a pen out of my jacket pocket and wrote down the license plate number.

PROSECUTOR: How long after the car drove off did you write down the license plate number?

A: It couldn't have been more than a minute.

PROSECUTOR: So would you say that the license plate number was fresh in your mind when you wrote it down on the envelope?

> Although leading, the question is permissible under Rule 611(c), because it refers to testimony the witness has already given. Moreover, the question pertains to a foundational issue, and under Rule 104(a), when deciding foundational issues courts are not "bound by the rules of evidence except those with respect to privileges." As a result, counsel often have considerable leeway regarding the use of leading questions during foundational questioning.

A: Yes.

PROSECUTOR: Your Honor, I have here an envelope marked Government's No. 8 for Identification, which I've already shown to defense counsel. May it be shown to the witness? (The bailiff hands the envelope to the witness.) Please look at Exhibit 8 and tell us if you recognize what that is.

A: This is the envelope with the license plate number on it.

PROSECUTOR: How do you recognize it?

A: Well, it's my handwriting, and I also recognize the envelope because it has my dentist's return address on it.

PROSECUTOR: At the time, did you write down accurately the license plate number of the car you saw the two men drive off in?

A: I did.

PROSECUTOR: At this time, Your Honor, I ask permission to read into the record the license plate number as recorded on Exhibit 8.

JUDGE: Proceed.

PROSECUTOR: What's written on the envelope is NOM 1234. OK, now after you wrote down the license plate number, what happened next?

Problem 14-32: Forget It

Kris is a witness for the prosecution in an armed robbery case. Please answer the italicized questions in the transcript below.

PROSECUTOR: Kris, how many people were working behind the counter when you heard the defendant yell for them to hand over all the money in the register?

A: I know more than one, but I'm sorry, I don't remember exactly.

PROSECUTOR: Might it refresh your recollection if I show you the police report?

A: Possibly.

PROSECUTOR: Permission to show the witness the police report prepared by the investigating officer, Your Honor?

DEFENDANT'S ATTORNEY: Excuse me. Might I first ask a foundational question?

JUDGE: Go ahead.

DEFENDANT'S ATTORNEY: Did you personally speak to a police officer after the robbery?

A: No, I was too upset. I gave a police officer my name and phone number and went home.

DEFENDANT'S ATTORNEY: In that case I object to the witness being shown the police report, Your Honor. Nothing in the report is based on information from this witness.

JUDGE: That objection is overruled. The witness may be shown the report. (*Is this ruling correct?*)

PROSECUTOR: Kris, you've had a chance to look over the report. Are you now able to recall how many employees were working behind the counter when the defendant yelled for them to hand over the money?

A: According to the report, three employees were working behind the counter.

DEFENDANT'S ATTORNEY: Objection, hearsay, move to strike.

JUDGE: (*How should the judge rule on the objection?*)

PROSECUTOR: When the defendant yelled for them to hand over money, did you notice anything unusual about his manner of speaking?

A: It's possible. Again, I'm just not sure.

PROSECUTOR: Well, he slurred a number of his words, right?

DEFENDANT'S ATTORNEY: Objection, leading.

JUDGE: (*How should the judge rule on the objection?*)

A: That's right, he did.

PROSECUTOR: Did the robber have any facial marks?

A: No.

PROSECUTOR: Permission to show the police report to the witness again, Your Honor?

JUDGE: Both counsel please approach the bench. (At the bench) Why do you want to show the police report to the witness?

PROSECUTOR: To refresh the witness' recollection that the robber had a scar on his right cheek.

JUDGE: No foundation for refreshing recollection exists, so the request is denied. Both counsel may return to counsel table. (*Is the judge's ruling proper?*)

PROSECUTOR: Just one more thing I'd like to ask you about. Following the robbery, did you speak to any of the other customers who were in the store at the time of the robbery?

A: Yes, I talked to Cynthia Greene, one of the other witnesses, about a week after the robbery. She must have gotten my phone number from the police, I said it would be OK for other witnesses to call me.

PROSECUTOR: In this conversation, what, if anything, did Cynthia say about the defendant?

A: I know she said something about him, but I'm sorry, I've forgotten what she said.

PROSECUTOR: May I approach the bench, Your Honor? (At the bench, both counsel present) I'd like to show the witness the notes that Ms. Greene made following her conversation with the witness. By way of an offer of proof, I expect that the witness' memory will be refreshed that Ms. Greene, who testified earlier in the trial that she was unable to identify the defendant as the robber, told this witness that a few days after the robbery she attended a police lineup and identified Suspect #4 as the robber. Other evidence will show that Suspect #4 was the defendant.

DEFENDANT'S ATTORNEY: Object on the ground that even if the witness' memory is refreshed as to what Ms. Greene told her, the answer would constitute inadmissible hearsay.

JUDGE: Objection sustained. Counsel, the refreshing recollection technique doesn't enable you to offer evidence that is otherwise inadmissible. (*Is the judge's ruling correct?*)

Problem 14-33: Forget Me Not

Same case as Problem 32. Abbott and Costello happened to be walking past the store just after the robbery took place. The prosecutor seeks to have Abbott testify that he saw the defendant jump into a waiting car, which immediately sped down the street and around the corner. Thinking that trouble was afoot, Abbott ran after the car and chased it around the corner and down the next block, but soon lost sight of it. While chasing the car, Abbott had a chance to observe its license plate. After resting for about a minute, Abbott walked back to Costello and told him how the license plate number read. At trial, Abbott is unable to recall anything other than that the license plate started with the letter "M." The prosecutor then seeks to have Costello testify that he didn't see the car's license plate, but that he took a pen and a tissue out of his jacket pocket and accurately wrote down the information about the license plate that Abbott gave him. The tissue has written on it the words "Me Not." (*If the prosecutor were to elicit this evidence, are the words on the tissue admissible as Abbott's recollection recorded?*)

Assume that at the time Abbott told him the car's license plate number, neither pen nor tissue was available to Costello. However, Costello has an excellent memory, and is prepared to testify that Abbott told him that the license plate number of the getaway car was "Me Not." *Can Costello verbally testify to Abbott's statement regarding the license plate number of the getaway car under the exception for recollection recorded?*

Problem 14-34: Lasting Freshness

Sherrill is charged with selling illegal drugs. The primary government witness is Al, who was employed as an undercover informant. At trial, Al identifies Sherrill as a dealer from whom he bought drugs. Asked by the prosecutor to testify to the quantity of drugs he purchased from Sherrill and their price, Al replies, "I don't remember." The prosecutor then seeks to read into evidence pursuant to Rule 803(5) the following memorandum that Al wrote:

> Dealer # 4: Sherrill. Asked for a lid of cocaine. Sherrill said she could sell me a lid of nearly pure cocaine; price $500. Gave her five marked $100 bills; she went into the alley and returned with a lid of cocaine, which she gave to me.

> Evidence offered by both parties during the foundational mini-trial established the following: At the time he bought drugs from Sherrill, Al had been employed as an undercover police officer for three months. During that time, he'd been involved in about 100 purchases of illegal drugs. Al wrote the memorandum approximately one hour after the transaction with Sherrill. In the 20 minutes or so prior to the transaction with Sherrill, Al had bought drugs from three other dealers, and before writing the memorandum he purchased drugs from two more dealers. These other transactions involved from one-half to two lids of cocaine, and prices ranging from $300 to $1,200. All the drug transactions took place within a two-block radius. After completing six drug transactions, Al radioed for police backup, pointed out the individuals who were to be arrested, and then wrote out six memoranda of the type given above, in the order in which the transactions took place.

Student # 1: You are the prosecutor. Make a brief argument that the drug transaction was fresh in Al's mind at the time he wrote the memorandum and that therefore it is admissible as Al's recollection recorded.

Student # 2: You are the defense attorney. Make a brief argument that the drug transaction was not fresh in Al's mind at the time he wrote the memorandum and that therefore it is inadmissible as Al's recollection recorded.

Student # 3: You are the judge. Preside over the arguments and rule on the admissibility of the memorandum as Al's recollection recorded.

Problem 14-35: Preppie-ration

A defense attorney is about to cross-examine Sheldon Bottomhew IV, an Ivy League college student who is a government witness in a murder case. The defense attorney's first two questions to Sheldon are:

1. "Did you meet with anyone from the prosecutor's office prior to trial to go over the information that you have testified to today?"

2. After receiving an affirmative response to the prior question, the next question is, "When you met with someone from the prosecutor's office to go over that information, did you look at any documents?"

What is the potential significance of Sheldon's answer for the defense attorney's ability to gain access to documents in the prosecutor's possession?

Best Memory Ever? If there were a *Guinness Book of World Records* for evidence rulings, the case of *United States v. Senak*[13] might qualify in the category of "strangest foundation for recollection recorded." *Senak* upheld a trial court's ruling that a written statement given by a declarant to an FBI agent, describing a conversation that had occurred three years earlier, was made at a time when the event was still fresh in the declarant's memory, and so qualified as the declarant's recollection recorded.

Practice Tip: The Strategic Advantage of "Past Recollection Recorded"

Witnesses whose out-of-court statements are admitted under the hearsay exception for past recollection recorded are generally very difficult to cross-examine. They have already admitted on direct examination that they no longer remember much about the events in question, and are likely to respond to cross-examination questions with answers that consist of little more than, "Sorry, I don't remember." The lack of recollection can make it very difficult for a cross-examiner to undermine the version of events as set forth in the writing that constituted the witness' past recollection recorded. By contrast, the opportunity for meaningful cross-examination is likely to be far greater when witnesses say that a writing has refreshed their recollection. As such witnesses purport to testify from present memory, a cross-examiner can fully explore the extent and accuracy of their testimony.

§ 14.10 Business Records (Rules 803(6), (7))

Foundational Elements:

- A business entity (broadly defined) produces a memorandum, report, record, or data compilation in any form of acts, events, conditions, opinions, or diagnoses concerning the entity's business practices;

- Entity representatives with personal knowledge contributed the information contained in the memorandum, etc.;

- The representatives recorded the information at or near the time that business-related activity occurred;

---

13. 527 F.2d 129 (7th Cir. 1975).

- The entity's regular business practice is to prepare the memorandum, report, record, or data compilation;

- The acts, events, conditions, opinions, or diagnoses relate to a regularly conducted business activity.

- The elements above are shown by the testimony of a custodian or other qualified witness, or by a certification that complies with Rule 902(11) or (12).

- A custodian of records testifies to an entity's practices and procedures regarding the preparation and maintenance of records. Of course, custodians typically have no firsthand knowledge of the events described in any particular set of records. However, their testimony describing an entity's usual record-keeping procedures and the conformity of the records produced in court to those procedures, assures a judge that the records are trustworthy.

- The Rule 902 subsections create additional hearsay exceptions that enable domestic and foreign businesses to establish the elements of a business record with a short written certificate. This spares organizations whose records are often relevant to cases in which the organizations are not themselves parties (such as hospital records in personal injury cases) the time and trouble of sending a custodian to court.

- Business records are inadmissible if "the source of information or the method or circumstances of preparation indicate lack of trustworthiness." This phrasing puts the onus on a party seeking to exclude a business record from evidence to convince a judge that an otherwise qualified business record is untrustworthy.

The business records exception (Rule 803(6)) is a bedrock of modern commercial litigation. An extremely broad exception, Rule 803(6) allows organizations to prove facts by introducing their records into evidence, whether those records consist of traditional paper documents or data stored in computers.

For purposes of Rule 803(6), a covered entity includes a "business, institution, association, profession, occupation, and calling of every kind, whether or not conducted for profit." For example, a sole proprietorship, a church or synagogue, a PTA group, a labor union, and a charitable environmental organization are entities whose records would qualify for admission into evidence as business records.

As parties, entities may seek to offer their own records into evidence under Rule 803(6). Or, "outside" parties may seek to offer entities' records into evidence as business records. For example, a plaintiff in a personal injury case may offer the records of the hospital that treated the plaintiff's injuries following a mishap.

The business records exception is a product of both necessity and trustworthiness. The exception is necessary because in most modern entities, numerous employees are likely to contribute to business records. A simple wholesale transaction may begin with a salesperson "in the field" who submits an order via e-mail to another employee who transmits the order to a central order desk. From there, the order may pass through several employees, each of whom makes entries related

550 14 · THE ADMISSIBILITY OF HEARSAY STATEMENTS UNDER RULE 803

to the transaction. Eventually a record may be transmitted to the shipping department, which sends out the goods that were ordered. An evidence rule requiring foundational testimony from all employees with personal knowledge of transaction-related events would be at best tremendously burdensome and at worst (especially given employee turnover) impossible to satisfy.

Trustworthiness results from regularity of record keeping and commercial reality. Records are likely to be accurate when they are prepared according to regular business practices by employees whose continued employment rests on knowing and following those practices. Moreover, entities need to establish and follow regular and reliable procedures for reasons that have nothing to do with litigation. Entities that do not have or do not follow regular procedures often do not survive long enough to become parties to anything other than bankruptcy proceedings.

Clearly admissible under the business records exception are documents memorializing "objective" business details, such as what goods were bought, how much was paid, when they were shipped, and the like. However, the modern scope of the exception is far broader than this. As a written report made admissible by Rule 803(6) may include "opinions or diagnoses," the rule may admit a doctor's notation in a hospital record concerning a patient's prognosis. An admissible record may also consist of a "report" pertaining to "events or conditions." As a result, the report of an entity's investigation into an accident in which it was involved may also qualify as a business record.

During the common-law period of the business record exception's history, courts were likely to exclude reports resulting from companies' internal investigations, on the ground that they were likely to be "self-serving" and untrustworthy. The paradigm case was *Palmer v. Hoffman*.[14] There, a railroad was sued for the wrongful death of person struck by a train because of the engineer's alleged failure to warn of the train's approach to a crossing. The railroad offered into evidence the engineer's written statement, made two days after the accident when the railroad, as it regularly did, investigated the cause of the accident. Justice Douglas, writing for the Court, held that the statement did not qualify for admission as a business record. Justice Douglas's reasoning was that while the statement may have affected the railroad's business, it was not made "in the regular course of business" within the meaning of the hearsay exception, because "the business of the (railroad) is the railroad business," not litigating. (Actually, a count of the number of cases in which railroads appear as parties might prove Justice Douglas wrong about this.) Justice Douglas thought such statements generally untrustworthy, and he worried that businesses could bootstrap self-serving reports into evidence simply by establishing regular procedures for making them: "Any business by installing a regular system for recording and preserving its version of accidents for which it was potentially

14. 318 U.S. 109, 63 S. Ct. 477, 87 L. Ed. 645 (1943).

liable could qualify those reports" as business records. Reports like the engineer's statement lack trustworthiness because "these reports are calculated for use essentially in the court, not in the business. Their primary utility is in litigating, not in railroading."

Modern courts, however, tend to interpret Rule 803(6) so as to make organizations' internal investigative reports admissible. Judges' attitudes tend to be that almost all business records, even receipts from grocery stores, are produced partly to protect an entity should a dispute arise. Thus, so long as a judge is convinced that an entity established and followed routine procedures, and those procedures are generally trustworthy, the resulting record is very likely to be admitted into evidence. Judges trust juries to recognize that reports stemming from internal investigations may be slanted in an entity's favor and to discount their contents appropriately.

Example 1

Mike Rohard has sued Abee See Co. for damages for breach of contract, alleging that Abee See breached a written agreement to deliver 10,000 computer hard drives to Rohard by May 1. Abee See claims that the hard drives were delivered to Rohard's place of business as set forth in the agreement on April 30. To prove delivery, Abee See calls Les See, its custodian of records, to lay the foundation for records proving that delivery was made. Les' foundational testimony may proceed along these lines:

DEFENDANT'S ATTORNEY: And what are your duties as the custodian of records?

A: I'm responsible for setting up the company's record-keeping procedures, communicating them to all employees, and ensuring that they are followed. I also supervise the employees who maintain and file the records.

DEFENDANT'S ATTORNEY: Have you set up procedures for establishing that the company has shipped goods and that those goods have been received by its customers?

A: Certainly. We maintain both paper and computer records for all shipments. The shipping supervisor and the delivery driver both initial a shipping invoice as soon as goods have been moved from our warehouse to a truck. At the other end, both the driver and the customer rep sign the same invoice as soon as delivery is made. Computer records are also updated whenever an entry is made on an invoice.

DEFENDANT'S ATTORNEY: Showing you what has been previously marked as Defense Exhibit C for Identification, do you recognize what this is?

A: I do. It's an Abee See shipping invoice. It's the form I set up, we have hundreds like it in our records.

DEFENDANT'S ATTORNEY: Calling your attention to what appear to be signatures, do you recognize any of them?

A: Just the one of Baltic See, our shipping supervisor. I don't recognize the others, but this one appears to be that of our delivery driver, because it's signed twice, once when it was loaded onto the truck by us and once when it was delivered. You'll notice there's a company time stamp next to the signatures; that's also standard company practice.

DEFENDANT'S ATTORNEY: What happens to a document such as Exhibit C after the goods are delivered?

A: The driver brings it to the records office, where it's stamped as you see here in the upper left-hand corner. We then update the computer records and store the original invoice in an Invoice File. A file contains all the invoices for each year, arranged chronologically by date of delivery.

DEFENDANT'S ATTORNEY: And where did you find the invoice that is Exhibit C?

A: In this year's Invoice File.

DEFENDANT'S ATTORNEY: I ask that Exhibit C be received in evidence.

JUDGE: Exhibit C in evidence.

Here, the witness' testimony establishes that Exhibit C was prepared according to regular and timely practices. Moreover, no evidence suggests that it lacks trustworthiness. While in complex cases the foundational testimony can be far more extensive, the custodian's testimony is probably sufficient to lay the foundation for a simple shipping document.

The admissibility of a business record is not necessarily an "all or nothing" proposition. An adversary of the proponent of a business record may concede that while some portions of a record qualify for admission, other portions should be excluded. The usual arguments that attorneys make in an effort to exclude portions of a business record are that particular assertions lack trustworthiness or constitute "double hearsay" (sometimes called "hearsay upon hearsay," or in the heat of trial, "garbage").

With regard to trustworthiness, the less that a statement in a business record relates to a matter that a judge considers to be routine and objectively verifiable, the more likely a judge is to exclude it as falling outside the scope of the business records exception. Because trustworthiness partly depends on routine, judges may conclude that statements that are the product of subjective judgment lack trustworthiness. For example, consider two hospital records. One contains an orthopedist's opinion that a patient's left arm was broken. The other contains a psychiatrist's opinion that a patient suffers from "undifferentiated schizophrenia that is likely to produce grand mal seizures." A judge is more likely to admit the former statement than the latter. A judge is likely to consider diagnosing a broken arm a matter of objective routine, whereas psychiatric diagnoses are often considered subjective and non-routine.

The "double hearsay" limitation on business records originates with the case of *Johnson v. Lutz*.[15] In this wrongful death case, a motorcyclist collided with a truck, with the usual outcome. To prove that the truck had been operated carefully, the truck driver offered a police officer's accident investigation report into evidence. The court concluded that the officer's report did not qualify as a business record because the police officer did not personally observe what happened. Rather, the report was "made from the hearsay statements of third persons who happened to be present at the scene of the accident when he arrived." The business records exception "was not intended to permit the receipt in evidence of entries based on voluntary hearsay statements by third parties not engaged in the business or under any duty in relation thereto." Judges continue to exclude statements by "outsiders" (those without a business duty to be accurate) under the business records exception. Of course, if outsiders' statements qualify under a separate hearsay exception, their statements may be admissible.

Example 2

Shore Worker sues his employer for injuries suffered when a load crashed on him, allegedly because the employer neglected to maintain a winch properly. Shore is taken to an emergency room for treatment.

1. Shore offers the records of his emergency room treatment into evidence as a business record. The physician's notes indicate in part that "Patient stated that he was hurt when the winch failed to operate properly." Even if the hospital records qualify generally as a business record, Shore's statement to the physician would probably be excluded as inadmissible hearsay, because Shore is an "outsider" to the hospital entity and not under a business duty to be accurate. (Nor would a judge be likely to admit Shore's statement under the exception for "medical hearsay," because whether or not the winch was operating properly is probably not reasonably pertinent to treatment.)

2. Shore's employer offers the records of Shore's emergency room treatment into evidence as a business record. The physician's notes indicate in part that "Patient stated that he was hurt when he was unable to hold onto the rope and a beer bottle with the same hand." If the report qualifies as a business record, Shore's statement to the physician would probably also be admissible, under two different hearsay exceptions. The physician had a business duty to accurately report what Shore said about how he got hurt, and Shore's statement is an opposing party statement under Rule 801(d)(2)(A) if offered into evidence against Shore by the employer.

The Business Records Exception in the News: Former professional basketball player Chris Webber was indicted in September 2002 and charged in federal court with obstructing justice by committing perjury when he

---

15. 170 N.E. 517 (N.Y. 1930).

denied in grand jury testimony that he had received and paid back money from gambler Ed Martin while Webber was playing basketball at the University of Michigan. The government's evidence that Martin had had financial dealings with Webber and other Michigan basketball players consisted in large part of Martin's written business records consisting of the names of players to whom he had given gifts and made loans, any amounts repaid by the players, and the dates of those transactions. However, Martin died of natural causes in February 2003, before the government was able to bring the case to trial. Martin's death deprived the government of the only witness whose testimony could support the foundational elements of Rule 803(6). As a result, the government had to make a deal, and so dismissed the obstruction of justice charge in exchange for Webber's pleading guilty to a much lesser offense, criminal contempt.[16]

Problem 14-36: Floor-ida

Ida has been sued by We'll Floor You Inc. for failure to pay the $4,500 balance due the company for refinishing the wood floors in Ida's home. To prove payment, Ida offers into evidence a printout of her electronic payment register under Rule 803(6). Ida seeks to testify to her regular and routine practice to enter payment details (such as the amount, payee and the date of payment) in the register every time and as soon as she pays an invoice electronically writes a check. The printout indicates that on March 12, Ida made a payment to We'll Floor You in the amount of $4,500. *How should the judge rule on We'll Floor You's objection that the printout is inadmissible hearsay?*

To prove that Ida owes $4,500 as the balance due for floor refinishing, "We'll Floor You" offers into evidence its computer record of the work it performed in Ida's home. The record includes the contract specifying a total cost of $9,000 and a partial payment by Ida of $4,500. We'll Floor You's manager testifies to the company's method of regularly preparing such records in the usual course of business. The manager also proposes to testify that the company's bookkeeper regularly enters the words "Final Payment Received" into a record as soon as final payment is received, and that no such notation has been made on Ida's record. *Are the record and the manager's testimony admissible under Rules 803(6) and 803(7)?*

Problem 14-37: On the Tube: Dear Diary

In an episode of the television show "Murder One," Wilson is charged with murdering Kim, a prostitute. The defense seeks to show that Kim had been blackmailing a number of her clients, to show that others had a motive to kill her. As evidence that Kim had been blackmailing clients, the defense seeks to offer into evidence her diary in which she identified clients by name, and recorded the amounts of money she had demanded that the clients pay her, the dates of the demands, and any payments

---

16. *See Webber Avoids Jail, Pleading Guilty on a Contempt Charge*, N.Y. Times, July 15, 2003, at D5.

made by the clients. The prosecutor objects that the diary is inadmissible hearsay, on the grounds that (1) prostitution is illegal, (2) a prostitute is not engaged in a business activity within the meaning of Rule 803(6), and (3) the defense has failed to satisfy other foundational requirements in Rule 803(6). *How should the judge rule on these objections?*

Problem 14-38: Hotel California Alibi

Arthur A. Chester is charged with murdering Stanley Morgan in Broomall, Pennsylvania; the defense is an alibi. To prove that he was in California on the night Morgan was killed, the defendant offers into evidence a hotel registration card from the Fresno Hilton Hotel. The registration card is dated the night of the killing, and contains handwritten information consisting of the defendant's name, home and business addresses and phone numbers, and the number and expiration date of a credit card belonging to the defendant. The defendant offers evidence that the hotel regularly asks guests to fill out registration forms upon check-in and to provide the hotel clerk with a credit card and a driver's license (or other government-issued identification). *How should the judge rule on the government's objection that the registration card is inadmissible hearsay?*

Problem 14-39: Track Record 1

Oscar Ramirez, a freight train brakeman, sues his employer, the B & Uh-O Railroad, alleging that he was injured when the brakes on the train car on which he was riding malfunctioned, causing it to slam into a train car ahead of it. The Railroad claims that the cause of the accident was Ramirez's failure to set the brake properly. To prove that the brake was operating properly at the time of the accident, the Railroad offers into evidence an "inspection report" prepared by its Safety Supervisor. According to the report, the Supervisor inspected the train car on which Ramirez was riding about four hours after the accident occurred and found that the brake was working properly. The Railroad offers further foundational evidence indicating that it regularly asks for inspection reports following accidents resulting in injuries.

Student # 1: You are the attorney for Ramirez, and have objected that the inspection report is hearsay and inadmissible under Rule 803(6). Make a brief argument in support of your objection.

Student # 2: You are the attorney for the Railroad. Make a brief argument that the report is trustworthy and should be admitted to prove that the brake was operating properly.

Student # 3: As the judge, preside over the hearing and rule on the report's admissibility under Rule 803(6).

Problem 14-40: Track Record 2

Same case as Problem 39. Assume that the judge has concluded that the Safety Supervisor's inspection report is sufficiently trustworthy to qualify as a business record. *Consider which of the following statements in the report the plaintiff might be able to exclude.*

1. "A check of company maintenance records indicate that the brake had passed a complete safety inspection one month before the accident."

2. "Harry Chu, yard maintenance worker, states that Ramirez indicated to Chu that Ramirez had forgotten to pressurize the brake before moving the car."

3. "Pepper Roni, who runs a nearby diner, states that Ramirez had drunk a few beers shortly before starting work on the night of the accident."

4. "Ramirez previously worked for a trucking company. I am informed by the trucking company's personnel officer that according to that company's records, Ramirez had failed to set a brake properly on three different occasions in the six months prior to his leaving there and coming to work for our company."

5. "My conclusion is that the accident was due to Ramirez's own carelessness in neglecting to set the brake properly."

Problem 14-41: Building the Foundation

Martina sues Lewis for personal injuries arising out of an auto accident, and seeks damages for pain and suffering caused by a separated shoulder, an injury that Martina alleges was due to the accident. To support Lewis's claim that Martina's separated shoulder is unrelated to the auto accident, Lewis wants to offer into evidence the records of Martina's emergency room treatment following the accident. The records make no reference to shoulder problems. You are defendant Lewis's attorney. Under Rule 803(7), indicate who you would call as a witness and the foundational evidence you would seek to elicit to convince the trial judge to admit the records as evidence that Martina did not suffer a separated shoulder in the accident.

Problem 14-42: Truss-worthiness

Same case as previous problem. Assume that it is plaintiff Martina who wants to offer the records of her emergency treatment into evidence, and that the judge has ruled that they qualify as business records. The records include the emergency room physician's opinion that "X-rays reveal damage to three of the patient's vertebrae. Likely prognosis: patient will have permanent back pain, will have to wear a truss to support her back when standing for lengthy periods, and is at increased risk for early onset of rheumatoid arthritis."

If you represent Lewis, what objection and argument might you make under Rule 803(6) in an effort to exclude all or part of the opinion? As the judge, how would you rule on the objection?

Problem 14-43: Report In?

Same case as previous problem. To prove the extent of her injuries, plaintiff Martina offers into evidence a "Medical Report and Evaluation," prepared by

Dr. Forensic. Dr. Forensic evaluated Martina for the purpose of testifying as an expert at trial, and it is Dr. Forensic's regular practice to prepare such reports when preparing to give expert testimony. When Martina offers the report into evidence while questioning Dr. Forensic, defendant Lewis objects that the report is inadmissible hearsay under Rule 803(6). *How should the judge rule on the objection?*

Assume that when she meets with Dr. Forensic the day before Dr. Forensic is to testify, Martina tells him that "I've been doing everything the doctors said to do, but my back pain is as bad as ever." *Can Dr. Forensic testify to Martina's statement at trial?*

Problem 14-44: Nail File

Cindy Rellah sues the Silver Slipper Dance Club after a nail allegedly sticking out of the dance floor penetrated her shoe and gashed her foot. To prove that the dance floor was safe, the club offers into evidence under Rule 803(6) a written report prepared by its floor manager the day following the plaintiff's alleged injury. The report indicates that the manager made a complete visual inspection of the dance floor and did not see a nail in the dance floor or find any indication that a nail had ever been sticking out of the floor. Foundational evidence elicited by the plaintiff indicates that the manager prepared the report after getting a phone call from the owner of the club telling the manager, "I just got off the phone with one of the customers who was at the club last night. She claimed that her foot was cut open by a nail on the dance floor. She sounded like trouble. Better check it out fast and get something down on paper." *How should the judge rule on Cindy's hearsay objection to the club's offer of the floor manager's report?*

Problem 14-45: Safety Record

The parents of three-year-old Todd Lerr sue Hasbroken Toy Co. for injuries Todd suffered as the result of swallowing a button on a toy truck manufactured by Hasbroken. The lawsuit alleges design defects on one of Hasbroken's "Nuke 'Em" series of "Toy Trucks for Healthy Children." To prove that the truck's bomb release feature was safe, Hasbroken offers into evidence a computer-generated report prepared for purposes of the litigation. The report, based on company records, recites (a) all the sales of "Nuke 'Em" model trucks since Hasbroken started manufacturing them three years earlier; and (b) a statement by Hasbroken's Vice President for Safety that Hasbroken logs consumer complaints for each line of its toys, and that a check of the records revealed that Hasbroken has never received a complaint concerning the bomb release button on "Nuke 'Em" trucks. *The judge should make which of the following rulings under Rules 803(6) and 803(7)?*

1. The report is inadmissible because it was prepared specifically for use in the lawsuit in which it is offered.

2. The report is inadmissible unless Hasbroken presents foundational evidence from an expert on computers about the reliability of computers.

3. The report is inadmissible because consumers are under no business duty to report problems with the bomb release button.

4. The report is admissible if Hasbroken convinces the judge that the sales records and complaint logs upon which the computer printout was based were kept as a part of Hasbroken's regularly conducted business.

5. None of the above answers is accurate.

Problem 14-46: Testimonial Custodian

Dr. Hermione Yu, a radiologist, is charged with theft for billing a county hospital for hours that she did not actually work. To prove the hours for which Yu claimed and received compensation, the prosecutor offers into evidence under Rule 803(6) the relevant portions of the hospital's accounting records. The records are accompanied by a certificate of a hospital custodian of records certifying under Rule 902(11) that the accounting records satisfy the foundational factors set forth in Rule 803(6). The defense objects that the certificate is inadmissible under the Confrontation Clause as interpreted by *Crawford v. Washington* (*see* Chapter 10), because the certificate is testimonial and the defense has not had an opportunity to cross-examine the custodian who prepared it. *Should the judge sustain the objection?*

Problem 14-47: Lay a Foundation

Assume that a plaintiff in a personal injury case seeks to support the plaintiff's claim for damages with the record of the urgent care facility documenting the treatment and services that the plaintiff received following an alleged assault by the defendant. Two students, one the plaintiff's attorney and the other the manager of the urgent care facility, should prepare and present in class the foundational testimony that would support admission of the record into evidence as a business record pursuant to Rule 803(6). (Accuracy of the foundational testimony is not required!)

§ 14.11 Public Records (Rule 803(8))

Foundational Elements:

- Records, reports, statements, or data compilations in any form are those of a public office or agency;

- The records etc. set forth:

    (i)   the activities of the agency or office;

    (ii) matters that an agency or office has a legal duty to report (except for law enforcement reports in criminal cases); or

    (iii) in civil cases and against the government in criminal cases, factual findings resulting from an investigation carried out pursuant to legal authority.

Just as the trustworthiness of business records emanates from an entity's "business duty" to prepare and maintain accurate records, so Rule 803(8) is based on public employees' duty to accurately report and record information in the course of carrying out government duties.

Necessity is also a common basis of both exceptions. Requiring parties to bring to court the numerous public employees who typically contribute to the information stored in public records would be at best highly burdensome to parties and public agencies alike, and in many cases would be impossible.

Perhaps out of a belief that procedures vary less from one public agency to another than from one private entity to another, the foundational requirements for public records are in general less onerous than for business records. The most notable distinction is that while the business records exception requires that a record be prepared pursuant to an entity's "regular practice," and that the record pertain to a "regularly conducted business activity," Rule 803(8) omits any mention of regularity.

Rule 803(8) describes three types of public records. While the foundational requirements are different for each, many public records are admissible under at least two of the subsections. In general, Rule 803(8) broadly applies to "records, reports, statements or data compilations, in any form, of public offices or agencies." This language encompasses public agencies at all levels of government, federal, state and municipal. (For example, a public state law school's student records constitute public records for purposes of the rule.)

Rule 803(8)(A)(i) applies to written records of the activities of a public office or agency. The records that this subsection makes admissible pertain to a public agency's internal activities and operations. Examples of admissible Subsection A records include tickets for parking and moving violations, invoices and receipts, records concerning the posting of road signs, employment records, and documents relating to service of process.

Rule 803(8)(A)(ii) applies to records of matters observed by public servants pursuant to their official duty to observe and report. The phrase "matters observed" indicates that public employees must have personal knowledge of the information in their reports. Subsection B makes admissible reports pertaining to the infinite variety of tasks that public employees carry on as part of their duties. For example, it makes admissible the record of a health inspector's observations of conditions in a restaurant, a housing inspector's report about the condition of heaters in an apartment house, and a police officer's report indicating the lengths of the skid marks behind two vehicles that collided in an intersection.

An important exclusion in Rule 803(8)(A)(ii) is that the government cannot offer reports pertaining to "matters observed by police officers and other law enforcement personnel" against defendants in criminal cases. Subsection (ii) does not authorize admission of reports that police officers typically prepare in the course of criminal investigations, such as those that summarize witness interviews and describe other investigative information. The language of the statute has no provision allowing criminal defendants to offer police agency reports into evidence against the government, but most courts allow them to do so.[17] Like *Crawford* (see Chapter 10), Subsection (ii)'s exclusion protects criminal defendants' constitutional right to confront the witnesses against them.

Rule 803(8)(A)(iii) applies to records setting forth factual findings resulting from an authorized investigation. Such reports are admissible in civil cases and in criminal cases if offered by a defendant *against* the government. The absence of a "regularity" foundational requirement means that even "one-shot" investigations, such as the report of the Warren Commission's investigation into the death of President John F. Kennedy, might be admissible under this subsection.

Public records are admissible unless circumstances indicate a lack of trustworthiness. Again, this phrasing puts the burden on a party seeking to exclude otherwise admissible public records to convince a judge that they are unreliable.

Parties offering public records into evidence usually don't need to call "sponsoring" or "foundational" witnesses. In response to a subpoena, a public agency can mail a certified copy of a requested public record to the court. Under Rule 902, the certification stamp or seal establishes the public record's genuineness. Under Rule 1005, the copy is admissible to prove the contents of the original public record.

Example

Anne Athema sues Len Krocher, alleging that Len built a fence on her property. To prove that she owns the land on which Len built the fence, Anne subpoenas her Title Deed from the Office of the County Recorder. The County Recorder mails a copy of Anne's Title Deed to the court in which Anne has filed the case. The Deed bears a County Recorder's purple stamp, and a statement by an employee of the County Recorder's office certifying that the document is a copy of the original Deed on file in the County Recorder's office. The Deed is admissible without Anne having to call a sponsoring witness.

The broad language of subsection (iii) was liberally interpreted by *Beech Aircraft Corp. v. Rainey* (488 U.S. 153 (1988)). After the crash of a Navy training airplane, the flight instructor's husband sued the aircraft's manufacturer, claiming that equipment malfunction had caused the crash; the manufacturer claimed that pilot error was responsible. The Navy appointed a Naval officer to investigate and prepare a report on the cause of the crash. The manufacturer offered the report into evidence, and the Court held that it was admissible under Rule 803(8)(iii).

One issue concerned the meaning of the phrase "factual findings." The plaintiff asked the court to distinguish "factual findings" from "opinions," and contended that Rule 803(8)(A)(iii) made only the former admissible. Under the plaintiff's desired interpretation, the investigator's statement that "the aircraft's engine was

---

17. *See, e.g.*, U.S. v. DePeri, 778 F.2d 963 (3d Cir. 1985).

operating at the time of impact" might constitute an admissible "factual finding." By contrast, the investigator's statement that "the most probable cause of the accident was the pilot's failure to maintain proper interval" would constitute an inadmissible opinion.

The Court rejected the plaintiff's position based on the generally "liberal thrust" of the Federal Rules of Evidence, the legislative history of Rule 803(8)(A)(iii), and the linguistic difficulties inherent in trying to distinguish a "fact" from an "opinion."[18] The Court stated that "as long as the conclusion is based on a factual investigation and satisfies the Rule's trustworthiness requirement, it should be admissible along with other portions of the report." Thus, a judge may exclude an opinion in an investigatory report on the ground that it is unreliable, but not on the ground that it constitutes an opinion as opposed to a fact.

Most investigative reports have a "double hearsay" aspect. An investigator's observations and factual findings constitute one layer of hearsay, and information provided by "outsiders" on which the investigator bases those factual findings are another. For example, the Naval investigator in *Beech Aircraft* undoubtedly talked to non-public employees in the course of his investigation, and in his report undoubtedly referred to their statements as part of the justification for his findings. Investigative findings can be based on information provided by "outsiders," but "outsider" statements are not themselves admissible for the truth of their contents (unless of course they are independently admissible under some other hearsay exception). For example, if the investigator in *Beech Aircraft* had attached transcripts of his interviews with non-public employees to his report, those transcripts would not have been admissible for the truth of their contents. In effect, investigator's opinions under Rule 803(8)(A)(iii) are treated the same as experts' opinions under Rules 702 and 703. Both authorized investigators and experts may consider hearsay in the course of arriving at their opinions and conclusions, but the hearsay does not thereby become admissible.

Example

The parent of a child who was inoculated against measles sues the manufacturer of the drug, alleging that it caused the child's autism. The manufacturer offers into evidence a report of a government Institute of Health study concluding that the drug cannot cause autism. The report is likely to be admissible under Subsection (iii).

Problem 14-48: Reporting for Duty

1. Red Handed is charged with burglary. Betty Barty testifies for the prosecution that she is a police criminalist and that she compared the fingerprints found

---

18. Despite the Court's reliance on legislative history, the opinion recognized that some of that history was flatly contradictory. The House favored a narrow interpretation of the term "factual findings," whereas the Senate favored a broad interpretation. As is so often the case, Congress was able to pass the rule only by passing the buck to judges to figure out the meaning of legislation.

at the crime scene with those on file in police agencies for Red and concluded that they match. The prosecution offers into evidence under Rule 803(8)(A)(ii) Betty's written report describing the test and her conclusion. *How should the judge rule on Red's objections that Betty Barty's report as well as the record of his fingerprints in police agency files are inadmissible under* Rule 803(8)(A)(ii) *and the Confrontation Clause?*

2. Assume that Betty Barty is a criminalist employed by Whorls Inc., a private company that contracts with police agencies to do fingerprint analyses. The prosecutor offers Betty's report into evidence as a business record under Rule 803(6) rather than a public record under Rule 803(8)(A)(ii). *Should the judge determine the report's admissibility pursuant to Rule 803(6) rather than pursuant to Rule 803(8)(A)(ii)?*

Problem 14-49: Weather Report

Millie Barr sues Hugh Middity for personal injuries arising out of an auto accident. Millie offers the National Weather Bureau's rainfall records for the area in which the accident occurred to prove that there was no precipitation on the day of the accident. *Are the records admissible under Rule 803(8) over Hugh's hearsay objection? If so, under which subsection of Rule 803(8) would Millie offer the records into evidence?*

Problem 14-50: Bad Breath

Sal Lune is involved in an automobile accident. The results of a Breathalyzer test administered to Sal by the police following the accident show that his blood alcohol level at the time of the accident was .12, above the jurisdiction's legal limit of .08. *Determine the admissibility of the Breathalyzer test record under Rule 803(8)(A)(ii) in the following situations:*

1. The heirs of the other driver involved in the accident offer the record into evidence against Sal in a wrongful death case growing out of the accident.

2. The government offers the report against Sal in a vehicular manslaughter prosecution growing out of the accident.

3. Sal's attorney offers the report into evidence as part of Sal's defense to the vehicular manslaughter charges. Sal's defense is that the criminal charge is the result of police officer bias against him, and that inconsistencies and erasures in the report show that the police doctored it to support their claim that Sal was inebriated at the time of the accident.

Problem 14-51: Confrontation

Joe is charged in federal court with robbing the Last Federal Bank. *Determine the admissibility under Rule 803(8) and the Confrontation Clause of the following items of evidence:*

1. To prove that the bank was federally chartered (and therefore that the federal court has jurisdiction over the case), the prosecutor offers into evidence a certified copy of a record from the U.S. government bank chartering agency indicating that the Last Federal is a federally chartered bank.

2. To prove that the bills found in Joe's possession came from the Last Federal Bank, the prosecutor offers into evidence an FBI report that lists the serial numbers of the specially marked bills that have been allocated to each U.S. bank. The bills taken from Joe have the serial numbers identified in the report as having been allocated to the Last Federal.

3. As proof of Joe's identity as the robber, the prosecutor offers into evidence a certified copy of a record from the state's Department of Motor Vehicles indicating that the car that witnesses identified as the one that the robber sped away in after the bank robbery is registered to Joe.

4. As proof that a bullet that was fired during the robbery came from the gun taken from Joe pursuant to his arrest, the prosecutor offers into evidence a report from a police ballistics expert indicating that markings on the bullet show that it was fired by Joe's gun.

5. As evidence that Joe is guilty of a "gang activity" allegation that subjects him to enhanced punishment, the prosecutor calls Police Officer Joe Friday as an expert witness on local gangs and gang activities. The prosecutor seeks to elicit Officer Friday's opinion that Joe carried out the robbery as a member and for the benefit of the Hole in the Wall gang. Officer Friday is prepared to support this opinion by testifying to his lengthy experience as an investigator of local street gang activities and to conversations that he had with members of various local street gangs pertaining to the robbery with which Joe is charged.

Problem 14-52: Tread Lightly

Civil suit for personal injuries. Plaintiff Prince alleges that Defendant Dilg's negligent maintenance of Dilg's tires caused a tire to rupture and Dilg's car to swerve uncontrollably and crash into Prince's car. Dilg seeks to offer into evidence the citation that a police officer issued to Dilg following the collision for operating a motor vehicle with worn out tire treads. The police officer does not testify. *Under which subsection of Rule 803(8) should Prince offer the citation into evidence? Is the citation admissible in evidence?*

Problem 14-53: Guarded Remarks

Noah Bayle has sued Jay Lehr, a guard, and his employer, the County Sheriff, for damages in federal court, alleging that when Noah was a County Jail inmate, Lehr violated Noah's civil rights by knowingly permitting Bluto, another prisoner, to assault Noah. After Noah reported the assault, the Sheriff, whose office operates the County Jail, appointed a lawyer, Anna Turney, to investigate and prepare a report concerning the alleged incident. At trial, Noah seeks to offer Turney's report into evidence under Rule 803(8). *How should the judge rule on the following objections which the defendants might make?*

1. Objection; the report is inadmissible as a public record because the investigation was not authorized by a federal official.

2. Objection; the report is inadmissible as a public record because the investigator was a private individual and not a public employee.

3. Objection; the report is untrustworthy because the findings are based on information supplied by declarants who are not public employees.

4. Included in the report is a statement made to the investigator by Mark Time. The report indicates that Mark Time was a County Jail inmate at the time of the assault on Noah Bayle. Time told the investigator that he did not personally see the assault, but that on the day before it took place, Jay Lehr told him that he (Lehr) was going to see to it that Noah was beaten up for reporting that guards were selling drugs inside the jail. The defendants object to admission of the statement on the grounds of hearsay. Noah responds that it is admissible under a combination of the public records exception and hearsay exemptions for admissions (as to Lehr), and work-related statements by a party's employee (as to the Sheriff).

5. Assume that the judge sustains the objection in #4 and rules that Mark Time's statement is hearsay and therefore not admissible for the truth of its contents. One of the findings in the report is as follows: "Based in part on the information provided by Mark Time, the investigator concludes that Jay Lehr knowingly permitted the attack on Noah Bayle to occur as revenge for Mr. Bayle's having reported that guards were selling drugs inside the jail." The defendants object that this finding be excluded because it relies on inadmissible hearsay.

6. One of the findings in the report is as follows: "Jay Lehr and the Sheriff violated Noah Bayle's rights under 42 U.S.C. 1983, the federal civil rights law." The defendants object that this portion of the report is inadmissible.

7. Another one of the findings in the report is as follows: "Jay Lehr knew when he left Mr. Bayle alone with Bluto that Bluto would attack Mr. Bayle." The defendants object that this portion of the report is an inadmissible opinion regarding a matter as to which the investigator lacks personal knowledge.

8. When Noah offers a certified copy of Turney's report into evidence, the trial continues according to the transcript below. Please respond to the italicized questions. As you do so, consider that the Advisory Committee Note to Rule 803(8) states that in evaluating a report's trustworthiness, a judge may consider (1) the timeliness of the investigation, (2) the special skill or experience of the investigator, (3) whether a hearing was held, and (4) the motivations of the individuals who contributed to the report.

DEFENDANT'S ATTORNEY: (at the bench): We object to the report's admissibility, Your Honor. The report is untrustworthy and therefore should be excluded. We ask you to excuse the jury and hold a foundational hearing as to the report's trustworthiness.

JUDGE: Counsel, I have the authority not to excuse the jury, and I will not do so at this time. I will reconsider the matter if it looks like we'll be getting into the contents of the report during the hearing. (*Is this statement correct?*)

JUDGE: Also, I'll state for the record that the burden is on the defense to convince me that the report is untrustworthy. (*Is this statement correct?*)

DEFENDANT'S ATTORNEY: The defense calls Anna Turney, the investigator who prepared the report. Ms. Turney, how did you come to be named as the investigator in this matter?

A: The Sheriff phoned me about three weeks after the alleged assault took place.

DEFENDANT'S ATTORNEY: Had you ever been involved in an investigation on behalf of the Sheriff previously?

A: No.

DEFENDANT'S ATTORNEY: How about on behalf of any other law enforcement agency?

A: No.

PLAINTIFF'S ATTORNEY: Objection, irrelevant as to experience with other aspects of law enforcement.

JUDGE: Overruled. (*Is this ruling correct?*)

DEFENDANT'S ATTORNEY: In fact, didn't you give a speech about a year earlier in which you said that you thought that the County Jail was rife with corruption?

PLAINTIFF'S ATTORNEY: Objection, hearsay.

DEFENDANT'S ATTORNEY: Opposing party statement, Your Honor. (*Is this response correct?*)

DEFENDANT'S ATTORNEY: Also, admissible as non-hearsay as to state of mind. (*Is this response correct?*)

JUDGE: I'll overrule the objections. The witness may answer.

A: No, I said that I'd read some articles in the local paper about jail conditions, and suggested that a general review take place.

DEFENDANT'S ATTORNEY: Does your practice ever bring you into contact with defendants charged with crimes or incarcerated prisoners?

A: No. I'm sure that's one reason the Sheriff appointed me — the Sheriff would have wanted an unbiased investigator with no previous dealings with the criminal justice system.

DEFENDANT'S ATTORNEY: Objection, speculation as to the Sheriff's reasons. Move to strike.

JUDGE: Overruled. Evidence rules don't apply to foundational evidence. (*Is this ruling correct?*)

DEFENDANT'S ATTORNEY: What did you do after you became investigator?

A: I asked the Sheriff to send me any written material he had pertaining to the alleged assault.

DEFENDANT'S ATTORNEY: And were you sent any materials?

A: Yes. I received a file consisting of Mr. Bayle's original statement and Mr. Lehr's written response, the records of Mr. Bayle's medical treatment following the alleged assault, a roster of jail personnel and the names of the alleged assailant as well as other inmates who were potential witnesses.

DEFENDANT'S ATTORNEY: And then what happened?

A: Well, it took three or four weeks before this material was sent to me and I had a chance to review it. Then I had to be out of town on an unrelated trial for about a week. When I got back to my office, I went to County Jail a day or two later to interview Mr. Bayle.

DEFENDANT'S ATTORNEY: Who else did you talk to?

A: Mr. Lehr; an inmate named Mark Time; Bluto, the alleged assailant; and another inmate who was in the vicinity at the time of the alleged assault. I also talked to two guards.

DEFENDANT'S ATTORNEY: Is it true that Mr. Lehr asked you to talk to Pa Rolee, an inmate who'd been released after the date of the alleged assault, and that Mr. Lehr told you that Mr. Rolee had information about previous fights between Mr. Bayle and Bluto?

PLAINTIFF'S ATTORNEY: Objection, hearsay as to what Mr. Lehr said that Mr. Rolee might say.

JUDGE: Overruled. You may answer. (*Is this ruling correct?*)

A: Yes.

DEFENDANT'S ATTORNEY: Did you talk to Mr. Rolee?

A: No. He was not at the address listed in the County's release record.

DEFENDANT'S ATTORNEY: Did you try to locate him in other ways?

A: No.

DEFENDANT'S ATTORNEY: None of the people you talked to were placed under oath, correct?

A: Of course not. I didn't have the power to swear witnesses.

DEFENDANT'S ATTORNEY: And were Mr. Lehr or the Sheriff present when you spoke to Mr. Bayle?

A: No.

DEFENDANT'S ATTORNEY: You relied for your findings on information given to you by Mark Time, correct?

A: Well, along with a lot of other information.

DEFENDANT'S ATTORNEY: And Mr. Time admitted to you, did he not, that Mr. Lehr had previously cited him for misconduct, which caused Mr. Time to lose his good-time credits?

A: Yes, he said that.

DEFENDANT'S ATTORNEY: Nothing further. Your Honor, the defendants object to admission of the report on the grounds that the circumstances render it untrustworthy.

Student # 1: You are the defense counsel. Make a brief argument in support of your objection.

Student # 2: You are the plaintiff's attorney. Make a brief argument in support of admissibility of the report.

Student # 3: You are the judge. Preside over the arguments and rule on the report's admissibility.

§ 14.12 Other Rule 803 Hearsay Exceptions

The Rule 803 hearsay exceptions reviewed above, along with those examined in other chapters, are by far the ones most often used in actual trials. Among the remaining Rule 803 exceptions are the following:

A. Records of Vital Statistics (Rules 803(9), (11))

A variety of public agencies collect data from hospitals, clergy, and individuals regarding births, deaths, and marriages. This hearsay exception makes such records admissible for the truth of their contents. For example, to prove the date and place of a person's birth, an executor can offer into evidence a certified copy of a birth certificate Rule 803(11) creates a similar exception for regularly kept records of religious organizations containing information about personal or family history, such as births, deaths, and ancestry. For both subsections, trustworthiness emanates from the usual desire of family members to report this information accurately, and the official (subsection 9) or religious (subsection 11) duty to record the information accurately.

B. Family Records (Rule 803(13))

One of the mustier hearsay exceptions admits statements of fact concerning personal or family history written in family Bibles; inscribed on rings; engraved on urns, crypts, or tombstones; or found in other similar locations. As a rule, people do not inscribe family history in such meaningful and even sacred locations unless it is accurate. Dracula could rely on this exception to defend against a claim of unauthorized collection of blood by offering a tombstone into evidence to prove that he died centuries earlier. On the other hand, "P.B." could not prove that he loves "A.S." by offering evidence that this information was carved into the bark of a tree or sprayed on a building wall; those are not sufficiently respectful locales.

C. Statements in Dispositive Documents (Rule 803(15))

This hearsay exception admits statements in property-affecting documents such as deeds, mortgages, wills, security agreements, and the like. Such statements are likely to be reliable because the statements reflect important matters, and the documents are usually drawn with care. For example, a testator's statement in a will that "John is my only son" would be admissible for its truth. Similarly, a statement in a deed that property is owned by "Rhoda and Bernard, as community property" would be admissible for its truth.

D. Statements in Ancient Documents (Rule 803(16))

This exception admits statements in documents that are more than 20 years old, so long as foundational evidence demonstrates that the documents were prepared prior to January 1, 1998. Sorry, if you are reading this book, you (like the authors) are almost certainly older than an Ancient Document.

The exception's main justification is need. Age may be no guarantor of trustworthiness, but if a statement made many years earlier is relevant to a dispute, the fact that it was written down means that it may be superior to any other form of available proof. Thus, an entry in Noah's diary would (if properly authenticated, meaning established as genuine) be admissible to prove that "the animals, they came on, they came on by twosies twosies;" and a story in an old newspaper would be admissible to prove that "City Hall's clock tower was destroyed by a bolt of lightning" the day before the story was written.

The language limiting the scope of the exception to documents prepared before January 1, 1998, went into effect on December 1, 2017. Observe that the Ancient Documents exception does not include a reliability requirement beyond that implied by a document's age. The Advisory Committee on the Federal Rules of Evidence proposed the 1998 cutoff because as a result of "the exponential development and growth of electronic information since 1998," "vast amounts of unreliable electronically stored information" have been generated. The Committee feared that without the time restriction, the exception would be "a possible open door for large amounts of unreliable electronically stored information." The Committee acknowledged that the January 1, 1998, date is somewhat arbitrary, but stated that it was no more arbitrary than the 20-year period itself.

What about documents that are more than 20 years old when a party offers them into evidence but were produced after January 1, 1998? Any statements in those documents are not admissible under Rule 803(16). A proponent has to satisfy what the Committee referred to as a "reliability-based hearsay exception," such as other provisions in Rule 803 or Rule 807.

E. Market Reports and Commercial Publications (Rule 803(17))

This hearsay exception admits statements in commercially prepared publications in general use by the public and people in various occupations. For example, the price of a share of Disney stock on a certain day could be proved by a website's stock market quotations. And an entry in the *Martindale-Hubbell Lawyer's Directory* could be used to prove that Marx & Engels were partners in a law firm specializing in mergers and acquisitions.

§ 14.13 Multiple-Choice Review Questions

Review Problem 14-A

Edy Dreyer sells ice cream novelties door to door from her small truck. At the end of each day, Edy enters data into a computer file consisting of each day's gross receipts and how many units of each variety of ice cream she sold. She prints out the data for each day and stores it in a notebook. Edy's printout for November 17 contains this handwritten addition: "Today I observed a collision between a Saab and a BMW while I was selling ice cream on Elm Drive. A few minutes later, the drivers came over to buy ice cream. I heard one driver tell the other, 'Sorry, I blew the stop sign and hit your BMW with my Saab.'" None of the other printouts contain information beyond that relating to ice cream sales. The BMW driver sues the Saab driver for negligence and seeks to offer Edy's November 17 printout into evidence to prove that the Saab driver was negligent. *The judge should rule that:*

1. The printout is inadmissible hearsay because Edy's handwritten addition is not admissible under the business records exception.

2. The printout is inadmissible because the Saab driver's statement constitutes an offer to compromise that is barred under Rule 408.

3. The printout is admissible under Rules 801(d)(2) and 803(6) because the Saab driver's statement constitutes a party admission and the admission is incorporated into a business record.

4. The printout is inadmissible because Edy lacks personal knowledge of which driver caused the collision.

Review Problem 14-B

A defendant is charged with committing arson to a residence by pouring kerosene around the outside of the house and igniting it. The defendant seeks to offer evidence that moments before the fire broke out, one resident of the house said to the other, "Harry, is that gas that I smell?" *Which statement below is correct?*

1. The judge should sustain the prosecutor's "lack of personal knowledge" objection.

2. The judge should admit the statement as an excited utterance.

3. The judge should admit the statement because it does not constitute an assertion.

4. The judge should admit the statement as a present sense impression.

Review Problem 14-C

Samantha, a newspaper food critic, sues Lars's Taco Bar for intentionally serving her contaminated food that caused Samantha to become seriously ill with food poisoning. The alleged incident occurred when Samantha returned to the restaurant for lunch about two weeks after her scathing attack on the quality of Lars's food appeared in the paper. Lars's defense is that Samantha's illness was unrelated to the lunch meal. Samantha collapsed at work a couple of hours after she returned from lunch. She seeks to testify that she told the paramedic who attended to her in the ambulance on the way to the hospital that "I think I have food poisoning. I started feeling dizzy and nauseous as soon as I started eating Lars's Eel Special." *In response to Lars's objection, the judge should rule that:*

1. Samantha's statement to the ambulance attendant is inadmissible because as a lay witness she does not have the expertise to identify her illness as caused by food poisoning.

2. Samantha's statement to the ambulance attendant is admissible in its entirety under the state of mind and medical diagnosis hearsay exceptions.

3. Samantha's statement that "I think I have food poisoning" is admissible under the hearsay exception for then-existing state of mind or physical condition. However, the remainder is inadmissible because it is a statement of memory as to what Samantha did and how she felt prior to making the statement.

4. Samantha's statement to the ambulance attendant is inadmissible in its entirety because Samantha's motive to blame Lars's Taco Bar for her illness means that her statement lacks trustworthiness.

Review Problem 14-D

One Saturday night, six-year-old Joey's parents tell him that "Marty will be babysitting for you again tonight." Joey then told his parents that "I don't want Marty to babysit because the last time he babysat he took off his pants and made me play with his privates." Marty is charged with child sexual abuse; his defense is that no sexual abuse whatsoever took place when he babysat for Joey. The prosecution seeks to offer Joey's statement to his parents into evidence. *In response to Marty's objection, the judge should rule that:*

1. The statement is admissible as a present sense impression if no more than a few days had gone by since Marty had previously babysat for Joey.

2. The statement is admissible as "medical hearsay."

3. The statement is inadmissible hearsay.

4. The statement is admissible under the state of mind hearsay exception.

Review Problem 14-E

Patrol Officer Ritzik is parked when she hears the sound of a collision in the intersection about 50 yards away from her patrol vehicle. She immediately ran to the intersection to investigate. She later prepared a report stating in part that "I did not observe any skid marks behind the blue Acura, which was in the middle of the intersection facing south when I arrived at the intersection, which is controlled by traffic signals. Upon my arrival, bystander Finnegan told me that the driver of the Acura ran the red light. Finnegan also reported hearing the driver of the Acura say upon exiting the vehicle that "I shouldn't have had those last few martinis." Assume that the driver of the Acura is a defendant in a personal injury case brought by the driver of the other car, and that the plaintiff seeks to offer the quoted portion of the report into evidence. *Which of the statements below is accurate?*

1. The report is inadmissible hearsay in its entirety.

2. The portion of the report indicating the location of the Acura and the lack of skid marks is admissible, but the remainder of the report is inadmissible hearsay.

3. The portion of the report indicating the location of the Acura and the lack of skid marks, as well as Finnegan's statement that the Acura ran the red light, is admissible, but Finnegan's reference to the Acura driver's statement is inadmissible hearsay.

4. The report is admissible in its entirety.

Review Problem 14-F

Piper Wrench is working on neighbor Thomas' clogged drain when the pipe bursts without warning and causes extensive damage to Thomas' house. In Thomas' lawsuit against Piper and Piper's employer, Pat the Plumber, one issue is whether at the time of the incident Piper was doing the job as an employee or as a personal favor. As evidence that Piper was doing the job as an employee, Thomas seeks to testify that as soon as the pipe burst, Piper yelled, "Oh my God, I could get fired because of this." Pat the Plumber objects that Thomas' hearsay statement cannot be used as evidence that the incident occurred in the scope of Piper's employment. Pat the Plumber also objects under FRE 403, arguing that the statement is ambiguous on the issue of whether the job was within the scope of employment and therefore its probative value is substantially outweighed by the risk of unfair prejudice. How should the judge rule on these objections?

§ 14.14 Case Library

Mutual Life Ins. Co. v. Hillman
U.S. Supreme Court
145 U.S. 285 (1892)

Beech Aircraft Corp. v. Rainey
U.S. Supreme Court
488 U.S. 153 (1988)

Chapter 15

Admissibility of Hearsay Statements under Rules 804 and 807

§ 15.01 Chapter Checklist

1. What foundational element signals that Rule 804 hearsay exceptions are "second tier" exceptions?

2. In what circumstances can a person be physically present in court, yet be considered unavailable under Rule 804?

3. Is a person who breaks a promise to show up for trial unavailable under Rule 804?

4. Can deposition testimony qualify as former testimony if the deposition was taken in one case and the testimony is offered into evidence in another case?

5. Can testimony that a witness has previously given be admissible against a party who neither offered the testimony initially nor had an opportunity to cross-examine the witness who provided it?

6. In what types of cases are dying declarations admissible?

7. Can a dying declaration be admissible even if the declarant is alive?

8. What is the difference between an opposing party statement and a declaration against interest?

9. Does a self-serving statement qualify as against a declarant's interest so long as it is part of a larger set of statements that, taken as a whole, is against the declarant's interest?

10. In what way do the foundational requirements for statements against a declarant's penal interests differ from the requirements for statements against other interests?

11. What language in Rule 807 creates a "soft" unavailability requirement?

12. What is the "near miss" argument for residual hearsay?

13. What is the effect of a declarant's failure to testify at trial on the admissibility of hearsay under Rule 807?

14. How does the Confrontation Clause (*see* Chapter 10) affect the admissibility of hearsay offered into evidence under Rules 804 and 807?

§ 15.02 Relevant Federal Rules of Evidence

Rule 804. Exceptions to the Rule Against Hearsay — When the Declarant Is Unavailable as a Witness (partial text)

(a) Criteria for Being Unavailable. A declarant is considered to be unavailable as a witness if the declarant:

(1) is exempted from testifying about the subject matter of the declarant's statement because the court rules that a privilege applies;

(2) refuses to testify about the subject matter despite a court order to do so;

(3) testifies to not remembering the subject matter;

(4) cannot be present or testify at the trial or hearing because of death or a then-existing infirmity, physical illness, or mental illness; or

(5) is absent from the trial or hearing and the statement's proponent has not been able, by process or other reasonable means, to procure:

> (A) the declarant's attendance, in the case of a hearsay exception under Rule 804(b)(1) or (6); or

> (B) the declarant's attendance or testimony, in the case of a hearsay exception under Rule 804(b)(2), (3), or (4).

But this subdivision (a) does not apply if the statement's proponent procured or wrongfully caused the declarant's unavailability as a witness in order to prevent the declarant from attending or testifying.

(b) The Exceptions. The following are not excluded by the rule against hearsay if the declarant is unavailable as a witness:

(1) *Former Testimony.* Testimony that:

> (A) was given as a witness at a trial, hearing, or lawful deposition, whether given during the current proceeding or a different one; and

> (B) is now offered against a party who had — or, in a civil case, whose predecessor in interest had an opportunity and similar motive to develop it by direct, cross-, or redirect examination.

(2) *Statement Under the Belief of Imminent Death.* In a prosecution for homicide or in a civil case, a statement that the declarant, while believing the declarant's death to be imminent, made about its cause or circumstances.

(3) *Statement Against Interest.* A statement that:

> (A) a reasonable person in the declarant's position would have made only if the person believed it to be true because, when made, it was so

contrary to the declarant's proprietary or pecuniary interest or had so great a tendency to invalidate the declarant's claim against someone else or to expose the declarant to civil or criminal liability; and

(B) is supported by corroborating circumstances that clearly indicate its trustworthiness, if it is offered in a criminal case as one that tends to expose the declarant to criminal liability.

(4) *Statement of Personal or Family History.* A statement about:

(A) the declarant's own birth, adoption, legitimacy, ancestry, marriage, divorce, relationship by blood, adoption, or marriage, or similar facts of personal or family history, even though the declarant had no way of acquiring personal knowledge about that fact; or

(B) another person concerning any of these facts, as well as death, if the declarant was related to the person by blood, adoption, or marriage or was so intimately associated with the person's family that the declarant's information is likely to be accurate.

(5) *[Other Exceptions.]* [Transferred to Rule 807.]

(6) *Statement Offered Against a Party That Wrongfully Caused the Declarant's Unavailability.* A statement offered against a party that wrongfully caused — or acquiesced in wrongfully causing — the declarant's unavailability as a witness and did so intending that result.

Rule 807. Residual Exception

(a) In General. Under the following circumstances, a hearsay statement is not excluded by the rule against hearsay even if the statement is not admissible under a hearsay exception in Rule 803 or 804:

(1) the statement is supported by sufficient guarantees of trustworthiness- after considering the totality of circumstances under which it was made and evidence, if any, corroborating the statement; and

(2) it is more probative on the point for which it is offered than any other evidence that the proponent can obtain through reasonable efforts.

(b) Notice. The statement is admissible only if the proponent gives an adverse party reasonable notice of the intent to offer the statement — including its substance and the declarant's name — so that the party has a fair opportunity to meet it. The notice must be provided in writing before the trial or hearing — or in any form during the trial or hearing if the court, for good cause, excuses a lack of earlier notice.

§ 15.03 Introduction

Rule 804 consists of a small number of hearsay exceptions for which "unavailability of the declarant" is a common foundational element. In other words, whatever other foundational elements are necessary to prove, a party seeking to offer a hearsay assertion into evidence under Rule 804 must also prove pursuant to Rule 104(a) that the declarant is unavailable to testify at trial.

Compared to the hearsay exceptions established by Rule 803, those of Rule 804 constitute "second tier" exceptions. On the one hand, their existence demonstrates that the drafters of the Federal Rules are at least somewhat confident that statements made under the circumstances described in Rule 804 are likely to be trustworthy. On the other, the requirement that the proponent of hearsay prove a declarant's unavailability demonstrates a reluctance to admit the types of hearsay statements described in Rule 804 unless the only alternative is to do without the evidence altogether. Thus, a combination of trustworthiness and need underlies the Rule 804 exceptions.[1]

The chapter concludes by examining Rule 807, the "catch-all" or "residual" exception to the hearsay rule. Rule 807 fits nicely into this chapter because the language of Rule 807(B) ("the statement is more probative . . . than any other evidence that the proponent can obtain through reasonable efforts") creates a "soft" unavailability requirement.

§ 15.04 Unavailability

Establishing a witness' unavailability under Rule 804 requires more than showing that a hearsay declarant is not present in court when called to testify. For example, an attorney cannot prove unavailability by saying something like, "The bailiff and I have shouted the declarant's name three times now, Your Honor. We even wandered into the cafeteria. We had no response. How about we go with the hearsay?" Paradoxically, a declarant may actually have to appear as a witness for the declarant's unavailability to be established. The reason is that even if a declarant is *personally* present in court and testifying, the declarant's *testimony about the subject matter of a prior statement* may be unavailable.

Rule 804(a) allows a party to establish a declarant's unavailability in the following ways. Remember, however, that unavailability alone does not permit introduction of hearsay. Even if a declarant is unavailable within the meaning of Rule 804(a), a hearsay proponent also has to satisfy other foundational elements.

1. Under Rule 804(a)(1), a declarant is unavailable if a judge upholds the declarant's claim of privilege with respect to the subject matter of the declarant's prior statement.

---

1. Ironically, the more suspect a hearsay assertion's accuracy, the greater the need for cross-examination of a declarant. Yet Rule 804 premises admissibility on the declarant being unavailable, thus assuring that no cross-examination will occur.

(*See* Chapter 17 for a discussion of common privileges.) In this situation, it's possible that a declarant will testify in person on some matters yet be "unavailable" with regard to the subject matter of the prior statement.

Example 1

Abe is charged with burglarizing a computer parts warehouse. The police learn that Abe sold many of the computer parts to Cesar, and that Cesar had bragged to Tara about purchasing computer parts from Abe at a ridiculously low price. When the prosecutor calls Cesar as a witness, the testimony goes as follows:

PROSECUTOR: Cesar, I'd now like to ask you about a purchase you made from Abe on November 15. Did you meet with him on that date?

A: I refuse to answer that question on the ground that the answer might tend to incriminate me.

[After discussion out of the jury's hearing, the judge decides that by answering the questions Cesar might provide information that could be used against him in a criminal prosecution, and upholds his claim of privilege with respect to all questions concerning his purchasing allegedly stolen items from Abe.]

PROSECUTOR: In view of Your Honor's ruling, I submit that Cesar is unavailable with respect to the subject matter of purchasing computer parts from Abe.

JUDGE: I agree, and rule that Cesar is unavailable with respect to the subject matter of purchasing computer parts from Abe.

PROSECUTOR: In view of this ruling, we have no more questions for Cesar. Defense may cross-examine.

JUDGE: Defense counsel, any questions?

DEFENSE ATTORNEY: None.

PROSECUTOR: I now call Tara to testify to what Cesar told her about purchasing computer parts from Abe.

[If Cesar's statements to Tara qualify for admission under one of the Rule 804(b) exceptions, the unavailability of Cesar's testimony means that Tara could testify to them.]

[The prosecutor would also think about any other hearsay exceptions that might make Cesar's prior statement to Tara admissible. For example, if the statement qualified as a "co-conspirator statement," the prosecutor could offer it under Rule 801(d)(2)I, and if so would not have to establish Cesar's unavailability.]

2. Under Rule 804(a)(2), a declarant who improperly yet persistently refuses a judge's order to testify concerning the subject matter of the declarant's prior statement is unavailable. This basis of unavailability is similar to subsection (1), the difference here being that the declarant's refusal to testify is improper.

Example 2

Same case as the previous example. However, the prosecutor knew before trial that Cesar would claim his privilege against self-incrimination when asked about purchasing computer parts from Abe. To overcome the privilege claim, the prosecution granted Cesar "use immunity." As a result, nothing that Cesar testifies to in Abe's trial could be used against him in a future criminal case. When Cesar is asked to testify about his purchasing computer parts from Abe, the testimony goes as follows:

PROSECUTOR: Cesar, I'd now like to ask you about a purchase you made from Abe on November 15. Did you meet with him on that date?

A: I refuse to answer that question on the ground that the answer might tend to incriminate me.

[After discussion out of the jury's hearing, the judge decides that since Cesar was granted "use immunity," he no longer has a privilege to refuse to answer concerning his purchasing allegedly stolen items from Abe.]

JUDGE: The claim of privilege is invalid; the witness will answer the question.

PROSECUTOR: Cesar, do you remember the question?

A: Yes, and I will not answer it or any other questions about anything having to do with Abe.

JUDGE: Cesar, you have no choice. I have ordered you to answer the question and you have no legal excuse for failing to answer it.

A: I know, but I will not answer.

JUDGE: You understand that your refusal to answer is legally improper, and will result in my holding you in contempt of court and possibly ordering that you be taken to jail?

A: I understand, but I will not answer these questions.

PROSECUTOR: In view of the witness' persistent refusal, Your Honor, I submit that Cesar is unavailable with respect to the subject matter of purchasing computer parts from Abe.

JUDGE: I agree, and rule that Cesar is unavailable with respect to the subject matter of purchasing computer parts from Abe.

PROSECUTOR: In view of this ruling, we have no more questions for Cesar. Defense may cross-examine.

JUDGE: Defense counsel, any questions?

DEFENSE ATTORNEY: None.

PROSECUTOR: I now call Tara to testify to what Cesar told her about purchasing computer parts from Abe.

[If Cesar's statements to Tara qualify for admission under one of the Rule 804(b) exceptions, Tara could testify to them. And because his refusal to testify was improper, Cesar might well end up in jail.]

3. Rule 804(a)(3) provides that a declarant who is unable to remember the subject matter of the declarant's prior statement is unavailable.

Example 3

Same case as previous example. When Cesar is asked to testify about his purchasing computer parts from Abe, the testimony goes as follows:

PROSECUTOR: Cesar, I'd now like to ask you about a purchase you made from Abe on November 15. Did you meet with him on that date?

A: I'm sorry, I don't remember.

PROSECUTOR: Do you remember any dealings with Abe concerning computer parts in November?

A: No, I don't.

At this point the prosecutor tries to refresh Cesar's memory by showing him the police officer's notes regarding Cesar's conversation with Tara. (*See* Chapter 14 for additional information about refreshing recollection.)

PROSECUTOR: Cesar, is your memory now refreshed as to a meeting you had with Abe on November 15?

A: I'm sorry, I still don't remember it.

Cesar may well be feigning his inability to remember. It's often been said that "Failure of recollection is the last refuge of a scoundrel." As a foundational factor for unavailability, however, it matters little whether the failure of recollection is real or feigned. If the latter, inability to remember is essentially a refusal to testify, which constitutes unavailability under Rule 804(a)(2).

PROSECUTOR: In view of the witness' answers, Your Honor, I submit that Cesar is unavailable with respect to the subject matter of purchasing computer parts from Abe.

JUDGE: I agree, and rule that Cesar is unavailable with respect to the subject matter of purchasing computer parts from Abe.

PROSECUTOR: In view of this ruling, we have no more questions for Cesar. Defense may cross-examine.

JUDGE: Defense counsel, any questions?

DEFENSE ATTORNEY: Still can't think of any for Cesar. But somehow I'm beginning to feel that I know him.

PROSECUTOR: I now call Tara to testify to what Cesar told her about purchasing computer parts from Abe.

If Cesar's statements to Tara qualify for admission under one of the Rule 804(b) exceptions, Tara could testify to them.

4. Rule 804(a)(4) sensibly provides that a deceased declarant is unavailable. In addition, a declarant is unavailable if a physical or mental infirmity prevents the declarant from attending the trial or testifying. A party can offer a certified copy of a death certificate to establish with certainty that a declarant is deceased.

While the death certificate would be admissible as a public record under Rule 803(6), remember that Rule 104(a) provides that the rules of evidence (other than those relating to privilege) do not apply to foundational issues.) When a party claims that unavailability is due to physical or mental infirmity, however, judges often demand foundational testimony as to the extent of the infirmity from medical experts or others with knowledge of a declarant's condition.

The foundational testimony may allow a judge to tailor proceedings according to an infirmity's effects, rather than rule that a declarant is unavailable. If an infirmity is likely to be of short duration, the judge may continue a trial until the declarant is able to testify. For instance, if Cesar is unavailable to testify because of an adverse reaction to bee sting medication, and the prosecutor represents to the judge that Cesar will fully recover in a day or two, the judge may continue the case until Cesar is available. Similarly, if a declarant is physically unable to come to court, a judge may travel a short distance and hold court at the declarant's location. For example, assume that Cesar's bad reaction to the bee sting medication means that he'll have to remain in a hospital for a week, though he is fully able to communicate. The judge may decide to obtain Cesar's testimony at his bedside. In criminal cases, a defendant's constitutional right to confront and cross-examine adverse witnesses may force a judge to take such steps to secure an infirm declarant's testimony rather than to simply declare the declarant unavailable.

5. Finally, Rule 804(a)(5) provides that a declarant is unavailable if the declarant "is absent from the hearing and the proponent of a statement has been unable to procure the declarant's attendance or testimony . . . by process or other reasonable means."

One way to satisfy subsection (5) is to demonstrate that a witness is beyond a court's subpoena power and has refused to attend trial voluntarily. A second way is to demonstrate that efforts to locate a declarant have been futile. However, judges tend to require by way of foundation that a party claiming inability to secure a declarant's attendance offer evidence of genuine and timely efforts to locate and subpoena the declarant. In addition, by requiring that a proponent of hearsay procure either a "declarant's attendance or testimony," Rule 804(a)(5) expresses a preference for deposition testimony over unsworn hearsay. Thus, if a party has an opportunity to depose but chooses not to depose a declarant who is unavailable at trial, a judge might rule that the party has not shown an inability to procure the declarant's testimony.

The opinion in *Gordon v. D & G Escrow Corp.*[2] suggests the type of effort that parties may have to make to convince a judge that they have been unable to secure a declarant's attendance. In *Gordon*, an ex-husband sued an escrow company for wrongfully paying all the proceeds from the sale of the family home to his ex-wife. To prove that the house was community property, and that therefore he was entitled to half the sale proceeds, the ex-husband sought to enter his ex-wife's hearsay statement into evidence. (If the ex-wife were shown to be unavailable, the statement would have been admissible under California's equivalent of Rule 804(b)(3).) To prove that his ex-wife was unavailable, the ex-husband offered the following foundational evidence:

- He hadn't seen or spoken to his ex-wife in three years.
- Two years before trial, he sent his ex-wife a letter at the address where he was told she was living. The letter was returned as undeliverable, and it turned out that a creditor of the ex-wife had foreclosed on the house.
- A number of the ex-wife's creditors had contacted the ex-husband's attorney, asking for information on his ex-wife's whereabouts.
- He was unable to find a listing for his ex-wife in any local phone directory.
- He submitted an affidavit by his ex-wife's former attorney stating that the attorney did not know of her whereabouts. The court ruled that this foundational showing was insufficient to establish the ex-wife's unavailability. The ex-husband hadn't demonstrated sufficient "persevering and untiring efforts" to secure her attendance.

Even in criminal cases, judges should not insist that parties throw away time and money on obviously futile efforts to locate a declarant. *See Ohio v. Roberts*, described in Chapter 10 in the Confrontation Clause section. As *Gordon* suggests however, a claim that "I've done some checking and I have no idea where the declarant is" probably will not suffice. "Inability to secure a witness' attendance" requires a reasonable effort to locate a hearsay declarant. The investigatory steps that parties can take include checking hospital records and information from government motor vehicle agencies; contacting utility companies, Social Security, and welfare agencies; contacting a declarant's last known employer; and contacting any labor union or other employee organization of which the declarant was a member. Attorneys often hire professional investigators, and then call those investigators as foundational witnesses to testify to the efforts they made to locate a declarant whose attendance they have been unable to procure.

In some situations, it can be to a party's advantage for a hearsay declarant to be unavailable. For example, a party may prefer to offer a declarant's favorable hearsay

---

2. 48 Cal. App. 3d 616 (1975).

into evidence rather than have the declarant show up and offer unconvincing or even downright harmful testimony. To prevent parties from convincing declarants to take sudden holidays or suffer mysterious failures of recollection while testifying, Rule 804(a) concludes with the provision that a declarant is not unavailable if the hearsay statement's proponent "procured or wrongfully caused the declarant's unavailability as a witness in order to prevent the declarant from attending or testifying."

Example 4

Ma Barker is a plaintiff in a personal injury case. Ma deposed Elly Utness prior to trial. Elly's deposition testimony was quite favorable to Ma. Elly testified that the defendant Don Corleone was speeding and weaving in and out of lanes just prior to the accident. At trial, Ma claims that Elly is deceased (while hunting, she was accidentally shot by her hunting companion), and seeks to offer her deposition testimony into evidence. Corleone's attorney objects that the deposition testimony is inadmissible hearsay, and calls Ma in an effort to show that Ma procured Elly's unavailability. The foundational testimony goes as follows:

DEFENDANT'S ATTORNEY: Ma, am I correct that prior to her death you and Elly got together socially on a number of occasions?

A: That's true.

DEFENDANT'S ATTORNEY: And during one of these social occasions, Elly told you that she needed a vacation, correct?

A: That's right.

DEFENDANT'S ATTORNEY: And you suggested that she go hunting?

A: Well, she had told me previously that she'd gone once and enjoyed it. I reminded her of that and mentioned that Bonnie Clyde, a friend of mine, had talked about going hunting and that maybe they could go together.

DEFENDANT'S ATTORNEY: So it was you who convinced her to go hunting?

A: No. I just made the suggestion to Elly and gave her Bonnie's phone number. I had nothing more to do with it.

DEFENDANT'S ATTORNEY: And you knew that Bonnie's hunting license had been suspended twice previously for carelessness?

A: She'd told me something about that, but she said that she'd gotten it back.

DEFENDANT'S ATTORNEY: Did you talk to Bonnie before they left on the trip?

A: Just the night before they left, just to wish her good hunting. Nothing else.

DEFENDANT'S ATTORNEY: Nothing further. Your Honor, I submit that the timing leads to an inference that the plaintiff procured Elly's unavailability by sending her on a hunting trip from which the plaintiff was reasonably certain that Elly would never return.

JUDGE: Counsel, under Rule 104(a) the burden is on you to convince me that the plaintiff knowingly procured the witness' unavailability. The record does emit a faint aroma of planning, but I'm unable to say that you've convinced me. I conclude that Elly is unavailable, and that the plaintiff may read her deposition testimony into evidence.

Federal Rule of Civil Procedure 32(a)(3) is in effect an evidence rule providing alternative bases for establishing unavailability when a party to a civil lawsuit seeks to offer deposition testimony into evidence on the ground that the deponent is unavailable to testify at trial. Under Federal Rule of Civil Procedure 32(a)(4), a deponent is unavailable (and deposition testimony is therefore admissible) in any of the following situations if the court finds:

> (A) that the witness is dead;

> (B) that the witness is more than 100 miles from the place of hearing or trial or is outside the United States, unless it appears that the witness's absence was procured by the party offering the deposition;

> (C) that the witness cannot attend or testify because of age, illness, infirmity, or imprisonment;

> (D) that the party offering the deposition could not procure the witness's attendance by subpoena; or

> (E) on motion and notice, that exceptional circumstances make it desirable — in the interest of justice and with due regard to the importance of live testimony in open court — to permit the deposition to be used.

Perhaps because deposition testimony is given under oath and all parties have a right to attend depositions and question the deponents, the Federal Rule of Civil Procedure 32(a) grounds of unavailability are in general more relaxed than those listed in Rule 804(a). For example, under Rule 804(a), a declarant's distance from the place of trial is irrelevant. A party normally has to try to locate and subpoena a declarant anywhere within the court's jurisdiction, even if the declarant is in prison. (Interstate compacts sometimes allow a prisoner to be brought to another jurisdiction for the purpose of testifying.) Under Federal Rule of Civil Procedure 32(a), by contrast, unavailability is established by showing that a deponent is more than 100 miles from the place of trial.

Problem 15-1: Fair-Weather Friend

Dana is a plaintiff in a personal injury case. Jeff is Dana's close friend. He was with her when she was injured by an allegedly defective hedge cutter and can provide evidence that supports Dana's claims. Jeff orally assures Dana on many occasions that he will testify on her behalf. However, Jeff calls Dana on the morning of trial and tells her that he can't come to court because he had gone away for the weekend on a ski trip and is snowed in. *Is Jeff unavailable as a witness under Rule 804(a)?*

Is Jeff unavailable as a witness under Federal Rule of Civil Procedure 32(a)? What if the ski resort is located about 150 miles away from the courthouse?

Problem 15-2: Wherefore Art Thou, Waldo?

Consuela is charged with burglary of a home. Waldo identifies Consuela at her preliminary hearing as the person he saw running out the back door of the home when an alarm went off. Consuela is held for trial on the burglary charge, and the prosecution serves Waldo with a subpoena for the trial, set for five weeks later. A week before trial, the prosecutor calls Waldo at home to clarify a portion of his testimony and is told that "Waldo is no longer at this phone number. I don't know where he went." When Waldo doesn't appear for the trial, the prosecutor asks that the judge rule that Waldo is unavailable and that his preliminary hearing testimony can be read into the record as "former testimony" under Rule 804(b)(1). The defense objects and argues that the prosecution's failure to keep tabs on Waldo's whereabouts means that unavailability has not been shown.

You are the trial judge. *Has the prosecutor established Waldo's unavailability under Rule 804(a)(5)? How will you respond to the defense attorney's request that the trial be continued and the prosecution ordered to take steps to try to locate Waldo and bring him to court? Apart from Rule 804(b)(1), what is the effect of the Confrontation Clause on the prosecutor's request to read Waldo's deposition testimony into evidence?*

Problem 15-3: Doctor's Orders

Lester Sherr sues Devon Warwick for personal injuries and wants to offer into evidence a hearsay statement from Elizabeth. To prove that Elizabeth is unavailable as a witness, Lester's attorney hands the judge a letter written under the letterhead of "Anne Atomy, M.D.," and dated the day prior to trial. The letter reads as follows:

> To Whom It May Concern. I am a physician licensed to practice in this state and Board-Certified in obstetrics. Elizabeth is currently an obstetrical patient of mine in her fifth month of pregnancy. My medical opinion is that Elizabeth should not attend the trial because, due to complications of pregnancy, she needs complete bed rest and cannot participate in ordinary daily activities, including testifying as a witness. To do so would endanger both her health and that of her child. I expect this condition to continue indefinitely, possibly until she delivers the child. Anne Atomy, M.D.

The letter constitutes Dr. Atomy's out-of-court statement. *Is it admissible to prove that Elizabeth is unavailable? If so, does the letter establish that Elizabeth is unavailable within the meaning of Rule 804(a)?*

Problem 15-4: Try to Remember

Maisie Kreskin is a witness for the homeowner in a breach of warranty case against a builder based on construction defects in a new home. Maisie testifies to defects that she observed in the living room and one of the bathrooms when she visited the home just prior to the homeowner's moving in. When the homeowner's attorney asks her about problems that she observed in the kitchen, however, Maisie testifies only to seeing uneven countertops. At trial, Maisie is unable to recall problems with the kitchen floor that she testified to at her deposition, even after the homeowner's attorney tries to refresh her recollection with the deposition transcript. *Is Maisie unavailable as a witness under Rule 804(a) with respect to problems with the kitchen floor?*

Problem 15-5: Fear of Testifying

Basil is charged with sexually abusing his two stepchildren, A and B. A is eight years old at the time of trial; B is five. Both A and B have previously made statements that are non-testimonial and therefore would not be barred by the Confrontation Clause as interpreted by *Crawford v. Washington* (*see* Chapter 10), and would be admissible against Basil at trial if the judge rules under Rule 804(a) that they are unavailable. Consider A's and B's unavailability under each of the scenarios below.

1. The prosecutor tells the judge that "I've spoken to A and B. Neither of them is willing to testify. Frankly, they are both scared to death by the courtroom atmosphere, and also scared that the defendant will punish them if they testify. They are both crying. Your Honor; it would be psychologically devastating to require them to testify, so I ask that they be declared unavailable under Rule 804(a)(4)." *How should the judge rule on the prosecutor's request?*

2. The mother of A and B testifies that both children have told her that they are afraid of going to court. They both have had nightmares every night for the past two weeks, cry often, and have become withdrawn as the trial date approached. The judge then meets with A and B informally in chambers. The judge tells them that "I understand how you feel and will not let anything happen to you. I'm ordering you to testify, but anytime you want to stop for a timeout just let me know." However, A and B continue to say that they are scared of being in court and don't want to testify. *Should the judge rule that A and B are unavailable under Rule 804(a)(2), in that they have persistently refused to testify despite the judge's order that they do so? Should the judge rule that A and B are unavailable under Rule 804(a)(4), in that the emotional trauma of testifying constitutes a mental infirmity? Should the judge be allowed to talk to the children informally? Should both counsel be present? Should the judge ask A and B to testify via closed circuit TV?*[3]

3. The judge appoints a psychiatrist who specializes in child abuse to examine A. The psychiatrist testifies during a foundational mini-trial that testifying is stressful for young victims of abuse, that testifying would be harmful to A because it would trigger the memory of the abuse, that A expressed to the psychiatrist a strong desire not to testify, and that in the long run it would be

---

3. For a statute authorizing testimony via closed-circuit television, *see* 18 U.S.C. § 3509.

best for A's mental health not to testify. *Should the judge rule that A is unavailable under Rule 804(a)(4), in that the emotional trauma of testifying constitutes a mental infirmity?*

4. The same psychiatrist examines B, and testifies during a foundational hearing that B indicated a strong desire not to testify. The psychiatrist also testifies that especially because of B's age, B is extremely vulnerable to stress, that B is anxious and depressed, and spoke of suicide. In the psychiatrist's opinion, testifying could cause B to become psychotic. *Should the judge rule that B is unavailable under Rule 804(a)(4), in that the emotional trauma of testifying constitutes a mental infirmity?*

Problem 15-6: Building a Foundation

Polly Sigh sues a bus company for $60,000 for personal injuries she sustained when the bus in which she was a passenger collided with a car driven by Eben Flow. The bus company denies liability and seeks to offer Eben's hearsay statement into evidence under one of the subsections of Rule 804(b). The judge has granted the bus company attorney's request for a foundational mini-trial, during which the attorney will try to establish that Eben is unavailable as a witness under Rule 804(a)(5).

Student # 1: You are the attorney for the bus company. Meet outside of class with Student # 2, the investigator who you retained to locate and subpoena Eben. Plan the foundational testimony you will present through the investigator's testimony in an effort to convince the judge that Eben is unavailable. (Be careful not to overly gild the lily. The judge is aware of the amount that Polly seeks as damages, and may disbelieve testimony suggesting that the investigator went to extraordinary lengths to try to locate Eben.)

Student # 2: You are a professional investigator and were retained by Student #1 to locate and subpoena Eben Flow. You met with Eben at his apartment about a week after the accident and took his statement. However, you were informed by Student #1 that Eben was no longer at that address, and that he had quit his job, so could not be subpoenaed. Review the activities you engaged in to try to locate Eben with Student #1 prior to class, and be prepared to testify to those activities during a foundational hearing.

Student #3: You represent Polly Sigh. You may cross-examine the bus company's investigator in an effort to establish reasonable steps to locate Eben that the investigator neglected to take. (Insist on a pre-hearing meeting with the investigator so that you know what testimony to expect.) If reasonable to do so, make a brief argument to support a position that the investigator's testimony has not established Eben's unavailability.

Student # 4: You are the judge. Preside over the foundational hearing and rule on Eben Flow's unavailability.

§ 15.05 Former Testimony (Rule 804(b)(1))

Foundational Elements:

* The declarant is unavailable as a witness;

* The declarant has previously testified under oath in a hearing or deposition in the same or a different case;

* The party against whom the testimony is offered (or in civil cases, a predecessor in interest):

   * previously offered the testimony; or

   * previously had an opportunity to cross-examine the declarant.

* The party against whom the former testimony is offered has the same motive as when the party either offered it previously or had an opportunity to cross-examine the declarant.

Rule 804(b)(1) establishes a hearsay exception for unavailable declarants' "former testimony." The exception consists of two elements. The hearsay statement must have been made during a qualifying hearing or deposition. And the party against whom the testimony is offered (or in civil cases also a predecessor in interest) must have had an opportunity and similar motive to "develop" the testimony at the time the hearsay statement was made.

Former testimony seems almost the ideal hearsay exception: the prior statement is made under oath, in a formal setting, with the opportunity for cross-examination. On the other hand, prior testimony is typically given long after the occurrence of the events to which the testimony relates. Moreover, judges and juries lose the opportunity to observe a declarant's demeanor when testimony is read to them under the former testimony exception. The result is that former testimony is relegated to the second tier of hearsay exceptions.

The first element broadly defines former testimony as testimony given by a witness in a "hearing" or a "deposition," whether in the "same or a different proceeding." The term "hearing" incorporates almost any formalized legal proceeding in which a witness is placed under oath. For example, testimony given before a grand jury or in an administrative hearing may constitute "former testimony."

Example 1

Moe sues Larry for injuries that Moe sustained in a fall in Larry's store. Called as a witness by Moe, Shemp testifies to the slippery condition of the floor where Moe fell. Moe wins, but the judgment is reversed on appeal and a new trial is ordered. If Shemp is unavailable for the retrial, Shemp's testimony in the original trial qualifies as "former testimony" within the meaning of Rule 804(b)(1).

Example 2

Moe sues Larry for injuries sustained in a fall in Larry's store. Larry deposes Shemp, who testifies to the slippery condition of the floor where Moe fell. Shemp also signs an affidavit attesting to the floor's slipperiness, which Moe submits as part of a pretrial summary judgment motion. However, the case is settled prior to trial, and Shemp never testifies in court. In a separate case, Curly sues Larry for injuries that Curly sustained in a different fall on the same date in the same store. If Shemp is unavailable to testify in the trial of *Curly v. Larry*, Shemp's deposition testimony in the case of *Moe v. Larry* qualifies as "former testimony" within the meaning of Rule 804(b)(1). However, the statements in the affidavit do not constitute former testimony, as they were not made during a proceeding.

The second element requires a proponent of former testimony to show that the party against whom the testimony is offered (or in a civil case, that party's predecessor in interest) had a valid "opportunity and similar motive to develop the testimony" at the prior hearing "by direct, cross or redirect examination."

The "similar motive" foundational requirement promotes fairness by assuring that the party against whom former testimony is offered had an incentive to thoroughly probe the same topic on the earlier occasion when that party elicited (or had an opportunity to elicit) the testimony. When evaluating the similarity of a party's motivations in different proceedings, courts consider such factors as the amount of money in dispute and the purposes of the proceedings. For example, *United States v. DiNapoli*[4] involved a racketeering prosecution that was preceded by an extensive grand jury investigation. Hoping to elicit incriminating evidence of bid rigging in the construction industry against some of the "bigger fish" defendants, the government granted immunity to two of the alleged "smaller fish" and questioned them before the grand jury. The "smaller fish" testified that no bid rigging had occurred. Nevertheless, the defendants were indicted for racketeering based on other evidence. At trial, the defendants called the "smaller fish" as witnesses. When the "smaller fish" invoked the Fifth Amendment and refused to testify (thereby becoming unavailable), the defendants offered the "smaller fish's" grand jury testimony into evidence as former testimony. The defendants' argument was that the government's motivation in eliciting the testimony of the smaller fish before the grand jury was the same as it would have been at trial: to link the defendants to the bid rigging scheme.

The *DiNapoli* court disagreed, holding that the defense could not offer the "smaller fish's" grand jury testimony as former testimony. The court stated that "the proper approach ... in assessing similarity of motive under Rule 804(b)(1) must consider whether the party resisting the offered testimony at a pending proceeding had at a prior proceeding an interest of substantially similar intensity to prove (or disprove) the same side of a substantially similar issue. The nature of the two

---

4. 8 F.3d 909 (2d Cir. 1993).

proceedings — both what is at stake and the applicable burden of proof... will be relevant though not necessarily conclusive on the ultimate issue of similarity of motive." The court concluded that similarity of motive did not exist in this case because it was "beyond reasonable dispute that the prosecutor had no interest at the grand jury in proving the falsity of the witnesses' assertions." The court noted that the defendants had already been indicted at the time the smaller fish testified. Moreover, the grand jury record indicated that the grand jurors didn't believe the smaller fish's denials. According to the court, "a prosecutor has no interest in showing the falsity of testimony that a grand jury already disbelieves." However, the court refused to announce a bright line rule that the government's motive when eliciting grand jury testimony is always different than at trial. The court concluded that the similar motive inquiry must be "fact specific, and the grand jury context will sometimes, but not invariably, present circumstances that demonstrate the prosecutor's lack of a similar motive." (Can you alter the facts of *DiNapoli* so as to strengthen the defendant's argument that the government had similar motives before the grand jury and at trial with respect to the "smaller fish's" testimony?)

Notwithstanding outlier cases such as *DiNapoli*, the second element of Rule 804(b)(1) is generally satisfied when a declarant's former testimony is *offered against a party who previously offered the testimony*. Accordingly, a litigant who conducts a deposition or presents testimony at a trial or other formal hearing runs a risk that if the deponent or the witness becomes unavailable, some other party will be able to offer the deponent's or witness' testimony into evidence against the litigant in a future proceeding. But Rule 804(b)(1) offers some protection against unfair use of former testimony.

Example 3

Passenger #1 sued Bus Co. for injuries sustained when one of its buses struck a lamppost. During the trial of *Passenger #1 v. Bus Co.*, Bus Co. called Bystander as a witness. Bystander, however, testified that the bus was speeding at the time it struck the lamppost. Passenger #2 also sued Bus Co. for injuries sustained in the same incident. Bystander is unavailable by the time the case of *Passenger #2 v. Bus Co.* goes to trial. Passenger #2 can offer Bystander's former testimony against Bus Co., as follows:

PLAINTIFF'S ATTORNEY: At this time, Your Honor, I'd like to read into the record under Rule 804(b)(1) Bystander's testimony from the earlier trial of Passenger #1 v. Bus Co. As Your Honor can see from the transcript, Bus Co. offered Bystander's testimony in that case.

JUDGE: Counsel for Bus Co., is that correct?

DEFENDANT'S ATTORNEY: That's correct.

JUDGE: Counsel for Bus Co., is there an issue as to whether your client had a full opportunity to elicit testimony from Bystander during the earlier trial?

DEFENDANT'S ATTORNEY: No.

JUDGE: Counsel for Passenger # 2, did Bus Co. have a similar motive for questioning Bystander in both cases?

PLAINTIFF'S ATTORNEY: Clearly yes, Your Honor. Both cases involve personal injury claims made by passengers injured in the same accident, and in both cases Bus Co. would have wanted to elicit testimony from Bystander that the bus was being driven safely.

> [Rule 607 allows parties to impeach their own witnesses. Thus, when Bystander testified unfavorably to the bus company in *Passenger #1 v. Bus Co.*, the bus company had an opportunity and motive to attack Bystander's credibility and elicit evidence that the bus was being driven carefully.]

JUDGE: Counsel for Bus Co., any argument as to similarity of motive?

DEFENDANT'S ATTORNEY: No, Your Honor, though I would ask of course that Bystander's entire testimony from the earlier trial be read, including Bus Co.'s redirect examination.

JUDGE: So ordered. I find that Bystander's testimony offered by Bus Co. in *Passenger #1 v. Bus Co.* is admissible under Rule 804(b)(1) as former testimony in this case. Counsel for Passenger #2 can now commence reading of Bystander's testimony.

> [Bystander's testimony would normally be read into the record orally. If the written transcript of the testimony were admitted into evidence, jurors might give it undue weight. If the former testimony is at all lengthy, the offering attorney is likely to try to keep the judge's or jury's attention by asking a colleague or even the court clerk to serve as the witness and read the answers as the attorney reads the questions.]

Perhaps the most common use of former testimony under Rule 804(b)(1) arises when a declarant's former testimony is *offered against a party who previously had an opportunity to cross-examine the declarant.* Thus, a litigant who has an opportunity to or does cross-examine a witness at a deposition, trial or similar formal proceeding runs a risk that if the witness becomes unavailable, some other party can offer the witness' testimony into evidence against the litigant in a future proceeding. (Because this portion of the rule requires a previous opportunity to cross-examine, prosecutors who offer former testimony against criminal defendants under this provision also comply with the Confrontation Clause as interpreted by *Crawford v. Washington*.)

Example 4

Passenger #1 sued Bus Co. for injuries sustained when one of its buses struck a lamppost. During pretrial discovery, Passenger #1 deposed Bystander. At the deposition, Bystander testifies that the bus was speeding at the time it struck the lamppost. Passenger #1 and Bus Co. settled the case prior to trial. Passenger #2 also sues Bus Co. for injuries sustained in the same incident. Bystander is unavailable by the time the case of *Passenger #2 v. Bus Co.* goes to trial. Passenger #2 can offer Bystander's deposition testimony from *Passenger #1 v. Bus Co.* into evidence, as follows:

PLAINTIFF'S ATTORNEY: At this time, Your Honor, I'd like to read into the record pursuant to Rule 804(b)(1) Bystander's deposition testimony given in connection with the case of *Passenger #1 v. Bus Co.* Bystander was deposed by Passenger #1, and Bus. Co. had an opportunity to attend the deposition and question Bystander.

JUDGE: Counsel for Bus Co., is that correct?

DEFENDANT'S ATTORNEY: That's correct, Your Honor. However, as you can see from the transcript, counsel for Bus Co. did not in fact attend Bystander's deposition, so I would ask that the testimony not be used.

JUDGE: Counsel for Bus Co., is there any argument that Passenger #1's deposition notice was in any way deficient, or that your client would not have had a full opportunity to question Bystander at the deposition?

DEFENDANT'S ATTORNEY: No, Your Honor.

JUDGE: Counsel for Passenger #2, would Bus Co. have a similar motive for questioning Bystander in both cases?

PLAINTIFF'S ATTORNEY: Yes, Your Honor. Both cases involve personal injury claims made by passengers injured in the same accident, and in both cases Bus Co. would have wanted to elicit testimony from Bystander that the bus was being driven safely.

JUDGE: Counsel for Bus Co., any argument as to similarity of motive?

DEFENDANT'S ATTORNEY: None, Your Honor.

JUDGE: In that case, I find that Bystander's deposition testimony given in connection with the case of *Passenger #1 v. Bus Co.* is admissible under Rule 804(b)(1) as former testimony in this case. Bus Co. had an opportunity to attend the deposition and question Bystander, and under Rule 804(b)(1) it's irrelevant that Bus Co. failed to take advantage of that opportunity. Bus Co.'s motive was similar in both cases. Counsel for Passenger #2 can now commence reading of Bystander's testimony.

> [As the judge indicates, all that Rule 804(b)(1) requires is that the party against whom testimony is offered had the *opportunity* to question the declarant. In essence, the party against whom testimony is offered is locked into its earlier cross-examination if a deponent or witness becomes unavailable, even if the party conducted no cross-examination at all.]

A third and final situation that satisfies the second element of Rule 804(b)(1) arises in *civil cases only.* A witness' former testimony is admissible in a civil case if it is *offered against a party whose "predecessor in interest" had an opportunity and similar motive to cross-examine the declarant.* Under this somewhat extraordinary provision, former testimony can be offered against a party if a *different party* earlier had a chance to cross-examine a now-unavailable witness with a similar motive to that of the party against whom the former testimony is offered. As criminal defendants have a constitutional right to confront and cross-examine adverse witnesses, the statute sensibly provides that former testimony is admissible based on a different party's opportunity to cross-examine only in civil cases.

Rule 804(b)(1) offers the same protection against unfair use of former testimony in this situation as in the earlier ones. Before admitting former testimony, the judge must be satisfied that the cross-examiner had a valid "opportunity" and a "similar motive" to question the declarant. Because one party is in essence stuck with whatever cross-examination a different party conducted, the statute also offers an additional protection: the cross-examiner must be the "predecessor in interest" of the party against whom the former testimony is offered. The meaning of "predecessor in interest," however, is cloudy. According to most legal definitions, a predecessor in interest is a person who precedes another in an office or position. A strict, mechanistic interpretation of the term "predecessor in interest" would require the cross-examiner and the party against whom former testimony is offered to have a "mutuality of interest" in the same property. For example, the cross-examiner might have been a landowner who later deeded the property to the party against whom the former testimony is offered. While this situation probably won't arise often, perhaps it is the only fair reading if one party is to be stuck with testimony from an unavailable declarant based on some other party's opportunity to cross-examine. Many judges and commentators prefer a broader reading that regards "similar motive and opportunity" as sufficient to admit former testimony against a party who hasn't had an opportunity to cross-examine a declarant, thereby disregarding the "predecessor in interest" language entirely. Other judges pay lip service to the "predecessor in interest" requirement but regard any connection between two parties as sufficient to constitute "predecessor in interest" status. The legislative history of Rule 804(b)(1) is silent with respect to the meaning of "predecessor in interest," and the cases do not reach consistent outcomes.

How broadly or narrowly a judge chooses to interpret the meaning of "predecessor in interest" can be determinative as to whether hearsay is admitted as former testimony. For example, assume again that Passenger #1 sues Bus Co. for injuries sustained when one of its buses struck a lamppost. At trial, Bus Co. calls Bystander as a witness, and Bystander testifies favorably for Bus Co. that the bus hit the lamppost because the bus driver swerved to avoid a child who had suddenly darted into the bus' path. Passenger #1 cross-examines Bystander. Passenger #2 also sues Bus Co. for injuries sustained in the same incident. Bystander is unavailable by the time the case of *Passenger #2 v. Bus Co.* goes to trial. Can Bus Co. offer Bystander's testimony from *Passenger #1 v. Bus Co.* into evidence against Passenger #2? Under the strict interpretation of "predecessor in interest," the answer is probably "no." Passengers #1 and 2 do not have a mutuality of interest in common property. Under a broader interpretation emphasizing their common motive to attack Bystander's credibility, the testimony might be admissible as former testimony.

Once a judge has determined that former testimony is admissible, can the adversary ask the judge to exclude specific portions of a transcript? For example, can the adversary object to an answer on the ground that it is inadmissible hearsay, or that it is improperly speculative? Should the outcome depend on whether an objection was made at the time the testimony was first given? Neither Rule 804(b)(1) nor the Advisory Committee notes address these questions. The California version of the former testimony exception, Cal. Evid. Code §§ 1291–1292, does address it, and its provisions identify the majority approach. If former testimony is admitted against the party who earlier offered it in evidence or who had the opportunity to cross-examine the witness who provided the testimony, the former testimony is admitted subject to "substantive" objections (e.g., "improper hearsay") but is not subject to "form" objections (e.g., "leading") unless those objections were made when the former testimony was first given. If former testimony is admitted against a party based on a different party's opportunity to cross-examine, the former testimony is admitted subject to both types of objections. In all cases, objections based on competency or privilege cannot be made unless those infirmities existed at the time the former testimony was first given.

Practice Tip: Keep your audience in mind

Former testimony admitted into evidence is read to the jurors. The jurors do not read the transcripts themselves, out of fear that jurors may pore over the written testimony and give it greater weight than the oral testimony they've heard from the witness stand. But if the former testimony is at all lengthy, reading it to the jury may take hours or even days. If you are the proponent of lengthy former testimony, try to avoid lulling the jurors to sleep. A common and generally acceptable method is to use two readers; you may read the questions, for example, and ask an associate to read the answers. If your associate has previously received an Academy Award for Best Actor or Actress, so much the better.

Problem 15-7: You Go First

Alphonse and Gaston are indicted for jointly robbing a bank and are tried separately. In the trial of Alphonse, the government calls Hank Teller as a witness. Teller identifies Alphonse and Gaston as the robbers. By the time Gaston's case goes to trial, Teller is unavailable. *Can the government offer Teller's testimony from Alphonse's trial into evidence against Gaston?*

Problem 15-8: Play It Against Sam

After Sam allegedly holds up a fast food restaurant at gunpoint, the victimized cashier sues Sam for civil damages. As soon as the lawsuit is filed, the cashier's lawyer video records the deposition of an elderly patron who was in the restaurant at the time of the robbery, to perpetuate the patron's testimony for trial, pursuant to Federal Rule of Civil Procedure 27. In that deposition, which takes place in jail so that Sam can attend, the patron identifies Sam as the robber and describes how Sam committed the robbery. In separate criminal proceedings, the government charges Sam with armed robbery. The patron passes away before either the criminal or the civil case can go to trial.

Is the video recorded deposition admissible if offered into evidence by the cashier against Sam in the civil case?

What if it is offered into evidence by the government against Sam in the criminal case?

Problem 15-9: Blazing Objections

Kara Seene sues Insurance Co. in civil court to recover the proceeds of a fire insurance policy on her house. Kara had previously been charged with arson for setting the fire that burned the house down. In the criminal trial, Yvonne testified for the prosecution that she saw Kara set the fire. Bernie testified that he and Kara were eating together at a fondue restaurant when the fire broke out. Kara was found not guilty. With Yvonne and Bernie now unavailable for the civil trial, Insurance Co. seeks to read Yvonne's testimony from the criminal trial into evidence against Kara, and Kara seeks to read Bernie's testimony from the criminal trial into evidence against Insurance Co. *How should the court rule on the following objections?*

1. Kara objects to the reading of Yvonne's testimony from the criminal trial on the ground that her motives for cross-examining Yvonne in the criminal case are dissimilar from her motives in the civil case.

2. Insurance Co. objects to the reading of Bernie's testimony from the criminal trial on two grounds: (1) As it was not a party to the criminal case, it had no opportunity to cross-examine Bernie; and (2) its motives for cross-examining Bernie in the civil case are dissimilar from the prosecution's motives in the criminal case.

3. Kara makes a hearsay objection to the portion of Yvonne's testimony in the criminal trial in which she testified that Kara's next-door neighbor told Yvonne that the neighbor had also seen Kara set the fire." (Consider whether your answer depends on Kara having made this objection during the criminal trial.)

4. Insurance Co. objects to the portion of Bernie's testimony in the criminal trial in which Kara used a leading question to elicit Bernie's testimony that they were in the fondue restaurant between the hours of 7:00 and 9:00 PM. (Consider whether your answer depends on the prosecutor having objected during the criminal trial that the question was leading.)

5. Kara objects to the reading of Yvonne's testimony from the criminal trial under Rule 403, arguing that her acquittal in the criminal trial means that the jury found Yvonne's testimony unconvincing, and therefore the probative value of Yvonne's testimony is substantially outweighed by its prejudicial impact.

Problem 15-10: Bus Stop

Passenger #1 sued Bus Co. for injuries sustained when a bus hit a lamppost. At the ensuing trial, Bystander testified on behalf of Passenger #1 that the bus was speeding just before hitting the lamppost. When Bus Co.'s lawyer begins to cross-examine him, Bystander becomes ill and has to be hospitalized. To expedite the trial, counsel for Bus Co. waives the right to cross-examine Bystander after stipulating with counsel for Passenger #1 that "Bystander had drunk three beers in the hour preceding the accident and had previously been fired from Bystander's job as a Bus Co. maintenance worker due to excessive absence."

Later on, Passenger #2 sued Bus Co. for injuries sustained in the same accident. Bystander is now unavailable, and Passenger #2 seeks to offer Bystander's testimony from *Passenger #1 v. Bus Co.* (including the stipulations) into evidence. Bus Co. makes a hearsay objection. *Is Bystander's testimony from Action #1 admissible as former testimony?*

Problem 15-11: Fire Escape Clause

Bob has sued Tonedeaf Concert Promotions for personal injuries he sustained, allegedly due to Tonedeaf's failure to provide proper concert security. Bob was injured when a fire broke out mid-concert and members of the audience rushed to the exits. He contends that most of the exits were locked, and Tonedeaf disagrees. Bob was knocked down and trampled while trying to reach an open exit, sustaining two cracked ribs and a broken cheekbone. Bob's complaint asks for actual damages in the amount of $250,000 and punitive damages. Under Rule 804(b)(1), Bob seeks to offer into evidence against Tonedeaf testimony given by Ray in Ray's case against Tonedeaf for personal injuries that Ray sustained during the same concert. In the trial of that case, Ray testified that after the fire broke out, he tried to exit through four different doors, all of which were locked. Ray sustained only minor injuries, and asked for $25,000 in damages. Ray is now unavailable. Tonedeaf objects to the admissibility of Ray's testimony, and in a hearing out of the jury's presence the arguments of counsel proceed as follows:

DEFENDANT'S ATTORNEY: Your Honor, our objection is that Ray's testimony is hearsay that does not qualify for admission under Rule 804(b)(1). The statute requires similarity of motive, and clearly Tonedeaf did not have a similar motive in the two cases. Ray's suit asked for $25,000, so our motive to cross-examine to show that he was mistaken about the doors can't be compared to our motive to do so in a suit asking for $250,000 plus punitives.

PLAINTIFF'S ATTORNEY: Your Honor, the law doesn't require that the motives be exact, only that they be similar. Tonedeaf was the party in each case. This isn't a case where we're trying to hold Tonedeaf to the cross-examination conducted by an entirely different party. And in each case Tonedeaf had a similar motive-to try to show that the doors were open. Ray's testimony is clearly admissible under Rule 804(b)(1).

DEFENDANT'S ATTORNEY: Counsel's argument flies in the face of the economics of law practice. As Your Honor well knows, a lawyer can't invest a large amount of time and effort in a case worth at most $25,000, compared to one in which the plaintiff asks for $250,000 plus punitives. I'd also point out that my firm, with Tonedeaf's full cooperation, assigned a junior associate to handle the defense in Ray's case. We think that allowing new associates to handle small cases is important for their training and for the good of the profession as a whole. But if our clients are to be bound by their trial strategies, the policy is one that we and other firms would have to rethink.

PLAINTIFF'S ATTORNEY: Your Honor, $25,000 wasn't exactly chump change. Tonedeaf had a genuine motive in Ray's case to defend its security operations.

JUDGE: *Is an argument based on the economics of law practice one that you should consider? Would you be concerned about basing evidentiary rulings on lawyers' financial status and ability to finance cases? What ruling on the admissibility of Ray's testimony? Remember to indicate for the record which party has the burden of proof, and what that burden consists of.*

Problem 15-12: No Questions Asked 1

Lew Manion is charged with the attempted murder of Barney Quill. Manion's defense is that he stabbed Quill in self-defense. Eve Brooks testified for the prosecution at Manion's preliminary hearing that Manion attacked Quill. At the preliminary hearing, Manion was represented by a deputy public defender who had only a few minutes to meet with Manion and prepare for the hearing. The defense lawyer did not cross-examine Brooks even though Manion told the lawyer that Brooks was drunk at the time of the incident. Brooks is unavailable at the time of trial, and the prosecutor offers her preliminary examination testimony into evidence as former testimony under Rule 804(b)(1). The defense lawyer objects to the testimony's admissibility. The defense lawyer argues that Manion did not have a realistic opportunity to cross-examine Brooks at the preliminary hearing. Moreover, with Brooks unavailable to testify, the defense has no way of showing that she was drunk at the time of the incident other than through the testimony of Manion, who has a constitutional right not to testify. Thus, it would be unfair under the circumstances to admit Brooks' testimony into evidence. *Should the judge admit Brooks' preliminary examination testimony into evidence at trial?*

Problem 15-13: No Questions Asked 2

Mutt is on trial a second time on a charge of murdering Jeff. Mutt was convicted of murder after a first trial, but that conviction was reversed by the appellate court based on defense counsel's incompetent representation. One primary reason for the reversal was the defense counsel's failure to cross-examine Magoo, the prosecution's key eyewitness. Magoo is unavailable for the second trial, so the prosecution seeks to offer into evidence Magoo's testimony from the first trial under Rule 804(b)(1). Without Magoo's evidence, the case will have to be dismissed.

Student # 1: As the defense attorney, make a brief argument to support your position that Magoo's testimony is inadmissible.

Student # 2: As the prosecutor, respond to the defense objection with a brief argument supporting the admission of Magoo's testimony.

Student # 3: As the judge, preside over the arguments and rule on the admissibility of Magoo's testimony.

Practice Tip: Preliminary Hearings and Grand Jury Proceedings

Preliminary hearings and grand jury proceedings are key components of the criminal justice process when defendants are charged with felonies. In a preliminary hearing, a prosecutor has to present evidence sufficient to convince a judge that probable cause exists that a felony was committed and that the defendant committed it. The defendant has a right to appear with counsel at a preliminary hearing, to cross-examine witnesses, and to present exculpatory evidence. If the judge concludes that probable cause exists, the defendant is held or "bound over" for trial. In a grand jury proceeding, a prosecutor presents evidence supporting probable cause to a group of citizens sitting as a grand jury. A defendant has no right to appear at grand jury proceedings, either in person or through counsel. Indeed, grand jury proceedings are usually secret. Prosecutors typically seek indictments as defendants go about their daily lives, unaware that they are the subject of grand jury proceedings.

Whether prosecutors proceed via preliminary hearing or grand jury (and in some jurisdictions, prosecutors can choose one or the other) entails consequences under Rule 804(b)(1). Because defendants have the opportunity to question government witnesses at preliminary hearings, their testimony is likely to be admissible as former testimony (and not barred by the Confrontation Clause) should the witnesses be unavailable at the time of trial. As a result, defense attorneys may have to make difficult strategic decisions. They may not want to cross-examine government witnesses too aggressively, to avoid revealing information that they would rather save for trial. The risk of that strategy is that if the defense attorney has no means of offering evidence other than through cross-examination of an unavailable witness whose preliminary hearing testimony is read into the record by the prosecutor at trial, the defense has to do without the evidence entirely.

For prosecutors who conduct preliminary hearings, Rule 804(b)(1) may affect decisions as to what witnesses to call. Rules in many jurisdictions allow prosecutors to offer hearsay at preliminary hearings. Thus, rather than force a crime victim to testify at a preliminary hearing, a prosecutor can present the victim's story through the testimony of a police officer who talked to the victim as part of the investigation. The risk for the prosecutor is that if the victim is unavailable for trial, the prosecutor has no preliminary hearing testimony to offer as the victim's former testimony.

Grand jury testimony is not admissible against defendants under Rule 804(b)(1), as well as under the Confrontation Clause, as defendants have no opportunity to cross-examine the witnesses.

§ 15.06 Dying Declarations (Rule 804(b)(2))

Foundational Elements:

* The declarant is unavailable as a witness;

   The declarant needn't be deceased. This is a big break to declarants compared to the common-law rule that conditioned admissibility on their demise. However, some jurisdictions (including California) require a declarant to be deceased for hearsay to be admissible as a dying declaration.

* The statement is offered in either a homicide prosecution or a civil proceeding;

   Dying declarations are inadmissible in non-homicide criminal cases. *Is this sensible doctrine? If dying declarations are reliable enough for homicide cases, aren't they reliable enough for less serious crimes?*

* The declarant believed that death was imminent at the time the statement was made:

* The statement concerns the cause or circumstances of what the declarant believed to be imminent death.

Aided by scores of films and television shows, probably all of us can visualize one person comforting another who is facing certain death, with the latter uttering a final thought with his or her last breath.[5] The assumed trustworthiness of that final thought reflects the traditional belief of a "God-fearing" populace that "people would not want to meet their Maker with a lie on their lips." That belief was the foundation of the common law dying declaration exception to the hearsay rule. Whatever its current currency in more secular times, the belief continues to be reflected in Rule 804(b)(2), which refers to the exception as one for a "statement under belief of imminent death."

Despite its longevity, the rationale for the dying declaration exception is shaky. Granting that declarants' last words may be sincere, the ability of a person who is near death to perceive, recall, and communicate accurately may be uncertain. However, even sincerity cannot be assumed. Declarants may use their last words as an opportunity to get revenge on and vilify long-time enemies. Concerns such as these may explain why dying declarations are in the second tier of exceptions, and we must trust judges and jurors to discount their probative value appropriately according to circumstances.

---

5. For a classic example, *see* Alfred Hitchcock's suspense masterpiece, *The Man Who Knew Too Much* (Paramount Pictures 1956).

Example 1

A badly wounded Sangeeta tells a passerby, "Jones just shot me," at a time when Sangeeta believed that death was imminent. Sangeeta survived, but at her civil trial against Jones for damages, she cannot remember that Jones was the person who shot her. Sangeeta is unavailable within the meaning of Rule 804(a)(3), and the statement is likely to be admitted as a dying declaration because the other foundational elements are satisfied.

A declarant's subjective belief as to death's imminence can be shown directly, by the declarant's own statements ("I think I'm dying"). A declarant's subjective belief can also be inferred from statements made to the declarant ("Looks like you're dying"). Both types of statements are admissible despite the hearsay rule, which under Rule 104(a) does not apply to foundational issues. At any rate, such assertions would be admissible even in the absence of Rule 104(a). Declarants' assertions of their own belief ("I'm not going to make it") are admissible under the "state of mind" exception, Rule 803(3). And an outsider's statement affecting a declarant's subjective belief as to death's imminence ("Sorry, it doesn't look like you're going to make it") is admissible as non-hearsay for its "effect on the hearer."

A judge's foundational ruling will also be affected by a declarant's objective physical condition. A judge is unlikely to believe that a toothache caused a declarant to believe that death was imminent, no matter how distraught the declarant seemed to be at the time. This is not an exception that favors hypochondriacs.

Practice Tip: The Confrontation Clause and Dying Declarations

A police officer questions a fatally wounded crime victim. The victim provides information linking the defendant to the crime, then expires. Are the victim's assertions testimonial for hearsay rule purposes? Dictum in *Crawford* leaves the answer uncertain. Footnote 6 of the opinion states in part, "The existence of the (dying declaration) exception as a general rule of criminal hearsay law cannot be disputed. Although many dying declarations may not be testimonial, there is authority for admitting even those that clearly are. We need not decide in this case whether the Sixth Amendment incorporates an exception for testimonial dying declarations. If this exception must be accepted on historical grounds, it is *sui generis*." This far, the U.S. Supreme Court has not ruled on the admissibility of testimonial dying declarations.

Problem 15-14: Famous's Last Words

Ben Famous is walking along a street with Freddie Billity when he is grazed by a bullet fired from a passing car. Famous received only a slight flesh wound and immediately told Freddie, "That must have been Kwon who shot me; she made a threat against me last week. I'm lucky I got off so cheaply." Nevertheless, Famous decided to go to a hospital emergency room, where he was treated for the wound. Before he could leave the hospital, the wound became seriously infected and Famous lapsed into a coma. He died the next day, never having uttered another word. As a result, Kwon is charged with murder, and the prosecution calls Freddie to testify to Famous's statement. *Is the statement admissible under Rule 804(b)(2)?*

Problem 15-15: Bank Robbery

Virgil Starkwell is charged with murder and attempted murder as the result of his botched attempt to rob a bank. Starkwell is accused of shooting and killing bank teller Benitzi. Starkwell also shot bank customer Fernandez. Fernandez survived but was gravely injured and lapsed into a coma the day after the shooting. Moments before becoming comatose, Fernandez told a police officer, "Don't think I'm going to make it . . . that photo you're holding up, that's the guy who did this." (The photo depicts Starkwell.) The prosecutor seeks to offer Fernandez's identification of Starkwell into evidence as a dying declaration. Starkwell objects that Fernandez's statement does not constitute a dying declaration because the charge with respect to hearsay declarant Fernandez is attempted murder, not murder. *Could the prosecutor have offered Fernandez's statement into evidence as a prior identification under Rule 801? Is Fernandez's statement admissible as a dying declaration under Rule 804(b)(2)?*

Problem 15-16: Jesse and Billy

Jesse is close to death from a gunshot wound. Police Officer Wyatt arrives at the scene, calls an ambulance, and asks Jesse what happened. With his last breath Jesse tells Wyatt, "Billy shot me." At Billy's trial for murdering Jesse, the prosecutor calls Officer Wyatt to testify to Jesse's last words. Billy objects that because he did not have an opportunity to cross-examine Jesse, what Jesse told the police officer is inadmissible under the Confrontation Clause regardless of whether the statement constitutes a dying declaration. *How should the judge rule on the objection?*

Assume that despite what Jesse said, the government charges Frank with Jesse's murder. *Assuming all foundational requirements are met, can Frank offer Jesse's last words into evidence as a dying declaration?*

Problem 15-17: Capital Letter

Edwards is charged with the capital murder of Vic Timm. The prosecution contends that Edwards is subject to the death penalty because before killing Vic, Edwards robbed and kidnapped him. The prosecution calls a deputy sheriff to testify that "Following a lead, I found Timm in a remote mountain cabin. He was dead. Lying next to him I found a blood-stained letter, which reads as follows: 'I don't have long to live. Two days ago, Edwards kidnapped me at gunpoint and robbed me, then drove me to this cabin and left me tied up without food or water. Then Edwards returned and shot me.'" The parties stipulate that Timm died of the gunshot wound, and that the letter was written by Timm. The prosecution offers the entire letter as Timm's dying declaration under Rule 804(b)(2). The defense objects that the remarks about kidnapping and robbery must be stricken as they do not concern the cause and circumstances of Timm's death. The defense also objects on the ground that Timm was a lifelong atheist who spoke often against the existence of a Supreme Being. *How should the judge rule on these objections?*

Problem 15-18: On the Tube: Tight Squeeze

On the former television courtroom drama "The Practice," a wife is charged with the attempted murder of her husband. The prosecution contends that the wife intentionally drove her car into her husband after he got out of the passenger-side door to open the garage door. The husband is hospitalized both because of the injuries he suffered when hit by the car, and because he had a previously existing serious heart condition. The trial takes place in the husband's hospital room. The defense attorney's vigorous cross-examination attacks the husband's testimony that he could tell that his wife meant to hit him from her facial expression and the way the car sprang at him. The cross-examiner also angrily and repeatedly accuses the husband of committing perjury. The husband becomes so agitated that he goes into cardiac arrest. With emergency personnel rushing toward the husband, the prosecutor asks the husband to "squeeze the doctor's hand if your wife intended to kill you." The husband squeezes the doctor's hand, and then dies. The prosecutor offers the husband's squeezing of the doctor's hand as his dying declaration, meaning "my wife intended to kill me." *On what bases might the defense attorney object to the admissibility of the evidence? Should the judge admit the evidence as a dying declaration?*

Practice Tip: The Confrontation Clause and Adverse Witnesses Who Testify at Trial

The Confrontation Clause has a broader reach than situations involving the admission of hearsay as discussed in *Crawford v. Washington* and its progeny. The Confrontation Clause also ensures that criminal defendants have an adequate opportunity to cross-examine prosecution witnesses who testify at trial. If following a prosecution witness' direct examination the witness should die, disappear, or otherwise become unavailable before the defense has a legitimate opportunity to complete its cross-examination of the witness, upon defense motion the judge should strike the witness' direct examination testimony from the record and instruct the jurors to disregard it. In some circumstances, the judge may have to declare a mistrial.

Problem 15-19: Dying Declaration Mini-Trial

Smith is charged with murdering Wesson in a drive-by gang shooting. The prosecution offers Wesson's statement to a hospital nurse into evidence under Rule 804(b)(2); the defense objects that it is inadmissible hearsay. The judge has excused the jury and will conduct a mini-trial as to the statement's admissibility. The parties have

602   15 · ADMISSIBILITY OF HEARSAY STATEMENTS UNDER RULES 804 AND 807

stipulated that Wesson underwent emergency surgery at the hospital after he was shot and lived for a week, though he was comatose for most of that time.

Student # 1: You are the prosecutor. Elicit the foundational evidence below and make a brief argument supporting the statement's admissibility under Rule 804(b)(2).

Student # 2: You represent the defendant Smith. Cross-examine the prosecution's witnesses and make a brief argument that all or a portion of Wesson's statement is inadmissible.

Student # 3: You are the judge. Preside over the mini-trial and rule on the admissibility of all or part of the statement. As part of your ruling, indicate what the foundational burdens are with respect to the foundational elements such as personal knowledge and belief in imminent death.

Student # 4: You are witness Franklin, who can testify as follows: You and Wesson were walking down 3rd Street at about 11:00 p.m. on the night of the shooting after playing some pool. You heard a car pull up behind you, and heard a voice from the direction of the car say, "Get off our street." You instinctively ducked down, and saw Wesson do the same. You heard three gunshots come from the direction of the car, and heard the car drive off quickly. You are pretty sure there were three occupants inside the car, and you saw the shooter lean out the passenger window for a split second and point a gun, but not long enough for you to make an identification. You were walking to Wesson's right, so Wesson was a little nearer the car than you were. When you realized that Wesson had been shot, you called 911.

Student # 5: You are Metcalf, an ambulance attendant. You and your partner picked up Wesson at the scene of a shooting. Wesson was bleeding heavily from the chest and his left arm. After stabilizing him as best you could, you took him in the ambulance to the hospital. To give him the best chance of survival, you kept telling him, "You'll be all right, buddy. You'll be just fine." Most of the time, Wesson was fading in and out of consciousness and screaming in pain.

Student # 6: You are Nurse Hoolihan, employed at General Hospital. You first saw Wesson when he was wheeled into the emergency room. He was bleeding heavily from his chest and left arm, and was going in and out of consciousness. On the way to the surgical room, he asked you if he was going to make it, and you said, "It looks pretty serious, but we've got great doctors here and we'll do everything we can." About a minute later, Wesson said to you, "When is a doctor going to see me? I'm really in a lot of pain. I may not make it. Smith did this to me with a rifle. He's part of the 3rd Street Visigoths. He tried before, and this time he got me." Wesson then lapsed into unconsciousness again and one week later was pronounced dead, without having uttered another word.

§ 15.07 Statements against Interest
(Rule 804(b)(3))

Foundational Elements:

* The declarant is unavailable as a witness;

* The statement is sufficiently contrary to the declarant's interests (which may be pecuniary, proprietary, or penal in nature) that a reasonable person in the declarant's position would not have made the statement unless it was believed to be accurate.

* If a statement against penal interest is offered by either the prosecution or the defense in a criminal case, the offering party must also offer evidence of corroborating circumstances that clearly indicate that the statement is trustworthy.

Under Rule 804(b)(3), an unavailable declarant's out-of-court assertion constitutes a declaration against interest if "a reasonable person in the declarant's position would not have made the statement unless believing it to be true," because *at the time the statement was made* the statement: (1) was contrary to the declarant's "pecuniary or proprietary interest," (2) tended to subject the declarant to civil or criminal liability, or (3) tended to render invalid a claim by the declarant against another. The trustworthiness of statements against interest grows out of the belief that most people are self-interested. Therefore, people are unlikely to make statements harming their pecuniary or penal interests, so when they do so, the statements are likely to be accurate.

Determining whether statements were against declarants' interests at the time they were made often requires more than simply looking at statements' "four corners." Foundational evidence offered to oppose admissibility of a hearsay assertion may indicate either that a statement that on the surface appears to be against interest really is not. By the same token, foundational evidence offered to support admissibility of a hearsay assertion may indicate that a statement that on the surface appears not to be against interest really is. Thus, the admissibility of a declaration against interest often depends on surrounding circumstances as well as "what a declarant knew and when the declarant knew it."

Example 1

Mei-lan seeks to offer evidence of Quintos's out-of-court assertion, "I am the owner of Pesticide Playthings International." On its surface, a claim to own a business does not appear harmful to Quintos's pecuniary or proprietary interest. However, Mei-lan may be able to convince the judge that the statement was against Quintos's interest by offering foundational evidence showing that at the time Quintos spoke, Quintos was aware that government attorneys had begun criminal proceedings against the company and its officers for manufacturing dangerous children's toys.

A declarant whose assertion is offered as a declaration against interest will almost never be a party to the action in which the assertion is offered.[6] As a result, when a party seeks to offer an assertion into evidence as a declaration against interest, typically the party's reason for offering it grows out of what the declarant said about the party (or the adversary). Often, the result is uncertainty about whether the portions of out-of-court assertions that refer to other people are against the declarants' interests and therefore admissible under Rule 804(b)(3).

Example 2

Hamilton is charged with participating in the robbery of the Conglomerate Bank on October 9. Hamilton seeks to offer evidence that Burr, an unavailable declarant, said that "I robbed the Conglomerate Bank on October 9. Hamilton had nothing to do with it." Hamilton seeks to offer Burr's statement into evidence as a declaration against interest. The judge would have to decide whether the portion of the statement exculpating Hamilton was against Burr's interest.

Example 3

Hamilton is charged with participating in the robbery of the Conglomerate Bank on October 9. The prosecutor seeks to offer evidence that Burr, an unavailable declarant, said that "Hamilton and I robbed the Conglomerate Bank on October 9." The prosecutor seeks to offer Burr's statement into evidence as a declaration against interest. The judge would have to decide whether the portion of the statement inculpating Hamilton was against Burr's interest.

A badly divided United States Supreme Court provided an approach for analyzing statements in which declarants refer to themselves as well as others in *Williamson v. United States* (512 U.S. 594 (1994). In *Williamson*, a drug courier confessed to an arresting officer that he was transporting cocaine on behalf of Williamson, its owner. The prosecution offered the courier's statement into evidence against Williamson under Rule 804(b)(3). The majority opinion stated that Rule 804(b)(3) did not necessarily make the courier's confession admissible against Williamson. The Court took a line-by-line, "weeding the garden" approach and held that Rule 804(b)(3) makes admissible "only those declarations or remarks within the confession that are individually self-inculpatory . . . it does not allow admission of non-self-inculpatory statements, even if they are made within a broader narrative that is generally self-inculpatory."[7]

As interpreted by *Crawford v. Washington* (*see* Chapter 10), the Confrontation Clause prevents prosecutors from offering the evidence that was offered in

---

6. Were it otherwise, the declarant's assertion would normally be admissible as a party admission.

7. *Williamson* controls only the interpretation of Rule 804(b)(3) in federal courts. States that have an evidence rule identical to Rule 804(b)(3) are free to interpret their rule differently.

Williamson. The drug courier's confession to the police was clearly "testimonial" as that term is used in *Crawford.* Because Williamson had no opportunity to cross-examine the courier, the Confrontation Clause bars introduction of the courier's confession. However, *Williamson's* strict interpretation of Rule 804(b)(3) probably continues to operate in situations in which a declaration against interest might be admissible over a Confrontation Clause challenge.

When the Federal Rules of Evidence were first enacted, vestiges of the common law era hostility to admitting "declarations against penal interests" were evident in a foundational requirement that applied only to criminal defendants who offered statements exposing declarants to criminal liability into evidence for exculpatory purposes. In such situations, a statement was not admissible unless corroborating circumstances clearly indicated the trustworthiness of the statement. This foundational requirement reflected a fear that criminal defendants were likely to call nefarious cronies to swear falsely that conveniently unavailable declarants had confessed to committing the very crimes with which the defendants were charged. One way that a criminal defendant was able to corroborate a statement asserting that someone other than the defendant committed the charged crime was to offer additional foundational evidence linking the supposed perpetrator to the crime. A second form of corroboration consisted of foundational evidence pertaining to the circumstances under which the assertion was made.

Rule 804(b)(3) was subsequently amended so that it requires any party to a criminal case who offers a statement against penal interest into evidence to corroborate it. This was not as significant a change as it may appear to be, because, as the Committee note indicates, "A number of courts have applied the corroborating circumstances requirement to declarations against penal interest offered by the prosecution, even though the text of the Rule did not so provide."

The Committee also added a comment reminding judges that they are not to consider the credibility of the in-court witness who testifies to a declarant's statement against penal interest when determining whether corroborating circumstances exist. The Committee pointed out that "to base admission or exclusion of a hearsay statement on the witness' credibility would usurp the jury's role of determining the credibility of testifying witnesses."

Example 4

Hamilton is charged with participating in the robbery of the Conglomerate Bank on October 9. Pursuant to Rule 804(b)(3), the prosecutor seeks to offer evidence of a statement made by Adams, an unavailable declarant, in which Adams said, "I need to brush up on my getaway driver skills. I was a minute late picking up Hamilton after he robbed the bank; we're lucky we got away before the cops showed up." Pursuant to the same rule, Hamilton seeks to offer evidence that Burr, an unavailable declarant, said that "I single-handedly robbed the Conglomerate Bank on October 9." Both parties would have to convince the judge that the assertions were against the declarants' penal interests when they were spoken and that the foundational evidence clearly indicates that the statements are trustworthy. For example, the prosecutor might support trustworthiness with foundational evidence showing that Adams made the statement very shortly after the robbery took place while he was displaying the wad of bills that Adams said was his share of the robbery proceeds. Hamilton might support trustworthiness with foundational evidence consisting of testimony from an eyewitness, "Based on a picture of Burr that I have seen, I can tell you that Burr is the person I saw running out of the bank carrying a gun and a brown bag."

California's version of the declaration against interest exception, Cal. Evid. Code §1230, includes a hearsay statement that creates "a risk of making [a declarant] an object of hatred, ridicule, or social disgrace in the community." A similar provision was deleted from a draft of the Federal Rules of Evidence during the legislative process. Perhaps Congress was wise. In an era when people seemingly compete to see who can air the most sordid details of their lives on social media, perhaps the California expansion no longer makes sense. Can we have any confidence that a statement that creates a risk of making a declarant an object of social disgrace is trustworthy?

Problem 15-20: Spoke Too Soon

Sailing away from a cheering throng at the dock on the *Titanic*'s maiden voyage, John walks up to one of the passengers and says proudly, "I designed this ship." Later in the voyage, the ship strikes an iceberg and sinks, taking John with it. The passenger survives and sues John's estate, claiming that he negligently designed the *Titanic*. *Is John's statement admissible under Rule 804(b)(3) as a declaration against interest?*

Problem 15-21: Deep-Pocket Defendant

Lorinda is charged with possession of the cocaine that a police officer found in the pocket of the red jacket she was wearing. Lorinda's defense is that she had borrowed the jacket from Natasha and didn't know that the cocaine was in the pocket. Lorinda calls Carlos to testify that the night before Lorinda was arrested, Natasha told him that "I loaned my red jacket to Lorinda yesterday." *Natasha's statement is admissible:*

1. As a declaration against interest if Natasha is unavailable as a witness.

2. As a declaration against interest if Natasha is unavailable as a witness and if Carlos testifies that when he called Natasha to tell her that Lorinda had been arrested, Natasha said, "I hope it wasn't because of the cocaine I left in the pocket of the jacket that I loaned her."

3. As a prior inconsistent statement to prove that it was Natasha's jacket, if Natasha testifies and denies that the red jacket that Lorinda was wearing belonged to her.

4. As Natasha's present sense impression.

5. Under none of the above.

Problem 15-22: I Owe You?

Benny Fishiary (the executor of his late uncle's estate) sues Ellis Atey to enforce a promissory note for $50,000. Ellis had executed the note when he borrowed that amount of money from the uncle three years earlier.

1. Ellis calls Elle Satt, a friend of the uncle, to testify that about a year after Ellis signed the promissory note, the uncle told Satt that, "I told Ellis that he doesn't have to pay back the money I loaned to him; he should consider it a gift." *Is the uncle's statement to Satt admissible as his declaration against interest?*

2. Same situation as in # 1, except assume that the uncle and Satt are husband and wife. *Is the uncle's statement to Satt admissible as his declaration against interest?*

3. Ellis calls Elle Satt, a friend of the uncle, to testify that about a year after Ellis signed the promissory note, the uncle told Satt that, "Ellis still owes me $20,000 of the money that I loaned him." *Is the uncle's statement to Satt admissible as his declaration against interest?*

4. Assume that the uncle died from a self-inflicted gunshot wound. Ellis seeks to offer into evidence the portion of the uncle's suicide note that states, "Ellis paid off the note and owes nothing to me." *Is this portion of the suicide note admissible as the uncle's declaration against interest?*

Problem 15-23: Stool Pigeon 1

Jess Mist is on trial for the attempted murder of Hank O'Hare. The government claims that the attempt was carried out by Jess along with Robin Steele, who drove the car from which Jess shot at Hank. Yves Dropper, promised a recommendation of leniency by the government in Yves' upcoming sentencing hearing, is prepared to testify on behalf of the prosecution that "When I was in the cell next to Robin's in County Jail, I heard Robin tell his cellmate that Hank was lucky that Jess missed him, and that Jess wouldn't miss the next time." *Yves' testimony is:*

1. Admissible as a co-conspirator's admission under Rule 801(d)(2)(E), regardless of whether Robin is unavailable as a witness.

2. Inadmissible hearsay.

3. Admissible as Robin's declaration against interest if Robin exercises his Fifth Amendment privilege and refuses to testify.

4. Potentially admissible as Robin's declaration against interest if Robin exercises his Fifth Amendment privilege and refuses to testify, but barred by the Confrontation Clause.

5. Inadmissible if the judge concludes that Yves Dropper is an unreliable witness.

Problem 15-24: Stool Pigeon 2

Same case as the previous problem. Assume that Yves is prepared to testify for the government that "When I was in the cell next to Robin's in County Jail, I heard Robin tell his cellmate that Hank was lucky that Robin had to swerve to avoid hitting a gnatcatcher because it is an endangered species just as Jess shot at Hank, and that Hank won't be so lucky the next time." *Yves' testimony is:*

1. Admissible as a co-conspirator's admission under Rule 801(d)(2)(E), regardless of whether Robin is unavailable as a witness.

2. Admissible as Robin's declaration against interest if Robin exercises his Fifth Amendment privilege and refuses to testify, if the judge concludes that "Dropper's testimony is credible, and therefore the government has corroborated the trustworthiness of Robin's statement."

3. Potentially admissible as Robin's declaration against interest if Robin exercises his Fifth Amendment privilege and refuses to testify, but barred by the Confrontation Clause.

4. None of the above answers is accurate.

Problem 15-25: Defense Pigeon 1

Same case as the previous problem. Assume that Yves is prepared to testify for Jess, the defendant, that "When I was in the cell next to Robin's in County Jail, I heard Robin tell his cellmate that he and Joe tried to kill Hank as a way of getting into a gang, that Hank was lucky that Robin had to swerve to avoid an endangered gnatcatcher just as Joe shot at Hank, and that he and Joe wouldn't miss the next time." *Yves' testimony is:*

1. Admissible as a co-conspirator's admission under Rule 801(d)(2)(E), regardless of whether Robin is unavailable as a witness.

2. Inadmissible hearsay.

3. Admissible as Robin's declaration against interest if Robin exercises his Fifth Amendment privilege and refuses to testify.

4. Admissible as Robin's declaration against interest if Robin exercises his Fifth Amendment privilege and refuses to testify, and if Jess' attorney produces testimony from the person who was walking next to Hank at the time of the shooting that "I think that Robin and Joe were the occupants of the car from which the shots were fired."

Problem 15-26: Defense Pigeon 2

Same case as the previous problem, except that this time Hank O'Hare is the plaintiff in a civil suit that he filed against Jess Mist. Hank seeks damages from Jess resulting from Jess's alleged attempt to shoot Hank. Yves Dropper is prepared to testify for Jess that "When I was in the cell next to Robin's in County Jail, I heard Robin tell his cellmate that he and Joe tried to kill Hank as a way of getting into a gang, that Hank was lucky that Robin had to swerve to avoid an endangered gnat-catcher just as Joe shot at Hank, and that he and Joe wouldn't miss the next time." *Yves' testimony is:*

1. Admissible as a co-conspirator's admission under Rule 801(d)(2)(E), regardless of whether Robin is unavailable as a witness.

2. Inadmissible hearsay.

3. Admissible as Robin's declaration against interest if Robin exercises his Fifth Amendment privilege and refuses to testify.

4. Admissible as Robin's declaration against interest if Robin exercises his Fifth Amendment privilege and refuses to testify, and if Jess' attorney produces testimony from the person who was walking next to Hank at the time of the shooting that "I think that Robin and Joe were the occupants of the car from which the shots were fired."

Problem 15-27: At the Movies: Cell Talk

In the film *The Shawshank Redemption*,[8] Andy Dufresne is imprisoned after having been wrongly convicted of murder. Tommy Williams, another inmate, tells Dufresne that a former cellmate had confessed to Williams that he committed the murder for which Dufresne was convicted. The whereabouts of the confessor are unknown. Assume that Dufresne might be granted a new trial if the cellmate's confession is admissible in evidence. *What foundational elements do you have to satisfy for the confession to be admissible?*

After talking to Williams, Dufresne excitedly repeats Williams's statement to the warden. The warden, however, does not want Dufresne released because Dufresne might reveal that the warden has been ripping off the prison system. When the warden realizes that Williams is ready to testify in court to his former cellmate's confession, the warden arranges for Williams to be killed. *After Williams's death, does Dufresne have admissible evidence of the confession?*

Problem 15-28: No Smoking

Arsenio sues Fire Insurance Co. for denying coverage after Arsenio's house burned down, claiming that Arsenio set the fire intentionally to collect the insurance. As

---

8. Columbia Pictures, 1994. Thanks to Prof. David Schwartz for calling this example to our attention.

evidence that he did not set the fire, Arsenio calls Phil to testify to a statement made to Phil by Suzanne, who is stipulated to be unavailable as a witness. Phil will testify if permitted that when he and Suzanne walked past the still-smoldering remains of Arsenio's house, Suzanne said, "I wonder if this is the house I was walking past yesterday when I flipped a lit cigarette into the bushes." *Does Suzanne's statement constitute a declaration against interest?*

Problem 15-29: Driven

Hawkins is on trial for a gang-related drive-by murder of Edwards. The prosecution claims that Hawkins was a passenger in a car driven by Johnson. Hawkins shot and killed Edwards, a member of a rival gang who was standing on the sidewalk in front of his house as Johnson drove slowly past the house. To prove that Hawkins committed a premeditated murder, the prosecutor calls Wilson to testify to a statement made to him by his cellmate Johnson while Johnson was in jail awaiting trial. Johnson told Wilson (who secretly was a police informant), "I knew Hawkins was carrying a gun and was looking for Edwards. But I agreed to drive the car because I thought Hawkins had cooled off and just wanted to scare Edwards." The prosecution offers Johnson's statement as a declaration against interest after Johnson exercises his Fifth Amendment privilege and refuses to testify. *How should the judge rule on Hawkins' hearsay objection?*

Problem 15-30: Tainted Sauce

Rachel, a member of a religious community that adheres to traditional rules that forbid the consumption of pork, sues Leah for intentional infliction of emotional distress for knowingly concealing that spaghetti sauce that Leah served to Rachel was prepared with pork. Leah claims that she was unaware that the sauce was prepared with pork and that Isaac, a member of the same religious community, had given her the sauce as a gift. Leah calls Noah to testify, "My friend Isaac told me that he thinks the community's rules about consuming pork are outdated and that he frequently eats it and cooks with it." *If Isaac is unavailable as a witness, is his statement to Noah admissible as a declaration against interest? How might the fact that Noah is or is not a member of the same religious community affect your answer?*

Problem 15-31: Fishing Expedition

Jim Teacher and Ward Robey are charged with burgling a warehouse filled with sports equipment on August 1. Jim is tried first; he testifies that he had nothing to do with the burglary, and that he was shooting pool with Ed Fisical at the time it occurred. Ed testifies and corroborates Jim's alibi. Jim and the prosecutor stipulate that Ward is unavailable to testify, and Jim then calls Jose to testify to a statement that Ward made to Jose a few days after the burglary. Jim offers Ward's statement to Jose as Ward's declaration against interest under Rule 804(b)(3). The judge conducts a foundational mini-trial, which produces the evidence set forth in the transcript below.

DEFENSE ATTORNEY: Jose, where were you on the afternoon of August 4?

A: I was fishing out at the lake, with Dil Capote and Ward Robey.

DEFENSE ATTORNEY: Was this the first time the three of you had gone fishing together?

A: Oh, no. We've been going fishing together for a few years now. We go maybe 10–12 times a year in Dil's boat.

DEFENSE ATTORNEY: Do you know Jim Teacher?

A: I know him. Ward's brought him along on a few of the fishing trips, but I don't know him too well.

DEFENSE ATTORNEY: Was Jim with you on the August 4 fishing trip?

A: No.

DEFENSE ATTORNEY: While you were fishing on August 4, did Ward say anything about his fishing gear?

A: Yes. I said that I really liked the rod and reel he was using, that it looked brand new. Ward said he'd picked it up at a warehouse, and kind of smiled and winked at me. I asked him what was up with that, and he said, "Between the three of us, I got talked into doing something stupid. Me and this other guy took some stuff from a warehouse."

DEFENSE ATTORNEY: Did you respond in any way?

A: I said that was pretty dumb because he'd been clean for a long time, and that I hoped he wouldn't get in trouble. Dil asked him who the other guy was, was it that guy, Jim, he brings on the fishing trips sometimes. He said no, that the other guy suggested Jim, but that Jim had nothing to do with it.

DEFENSE ATTORNEY: Did Ward say anything else about Jim?

A: I don't know if I should say this, but Ward said that Jim had taken some masonry work away from him and that he realized that Jim was a jerk.

DEFENSE ATTORNEY: Was there any further discussion of taking stuff from the warehouse?

A: No, that was about it.

DEFENSE ATTORNEY: Nothing further.

JUDGE: Prosecutor, any questions as to foundation?

PROSECUTOR: Just a few, thank you. Jose, you would describe the three of you as good friends, correct?

A: Yes.

PROSECUTOR: If you mentioned to Dil or Ward that you had done something illegal, you wouldn't expect them to run to the police with the information, right?

A: I suppose that's true, depending on what it was.

PROSECUTOR: And when Ward talked to you about the warehouse, he undoubtedly had the same expectation about you and Dil, right?

A: I wouldn't know.

PROSECUTOR: When Ward made this statement about the warehouse, no other boats were in the area, correct?

A: That's right.

PROSECUTOR: Nothing further at this time.

JUDGE: If there's no additional evidence, I'll hear brief argument before ruling.

Student # 1: You represent Jim. Make a brief argument as to the admissibility of Ward's statement as a declaration against interest.

Student # 2: You are the prosecutor. Make a brief argument as to the inadmissibility of Ward's statement as a declaration against interest.

Student # 3: You are the judge. Preside over the arguments and rule on the admissibility of Ward's statement as a declaration against interest.

§ 15.08 Forfeiture by Wrongdoing (Rule 804(b)(6))

Foundational Elements:

* The declarant is unavailable as a witness;

* The party against whom the statement is offered engaged or acquiesced in wrongdoing that was intended to and did result in the declarant's unavailability.

Rule 804(b)(6) codified the rulings of many cases that hearsay from an unavailable declarant is admissible in evidence if the party procured the unavailability through wrongdoing that was intended to and did result in the declarant's unavailability. The rule typically applies to post-event conduct that is intended to and does prevent a witness from testifying or induce a witness not to testify. The wrongdoing need not constitute a crime. A party seeking to offer an unavailable declarant's hearsay statement into evidence under Rule 804(b)(6) has to convince a judge by a preponderance of the evidence under Rule 104(a) that the adversary's wrongdoing is responsible for the declarant's unavailability. A party claiming that forfeiture has occurred can also satisfy Rule 804(b)(6) with foundational evidence showing that the adversary acquiesced in another's wrongdoing that was intended to and did procure a declarant's unavailability.

Example

Following an automobile collision in which she was involved, celebrity Katie notices a bystander talking to a police officer and repeatedly and angrily pointing in Katie's direction. Sometime thereafter, Katie agrees to go along with an arrangement made by her personal manager for the bystander to have the free use of Katie's overseas villa in exchange for the bystander's promise to remain in the villa until after any litigation related to the collision concludes. Katie has acquiesced in conduct that interferes with the system of justice. If Katie is a defendant in either a civil or criminal case growing out of the collision and the bystander is unavailable to testify, the bystander's statement to the police officer is admissible under Rule 804(b)(6).

The U.S. Supreme Court decision in *Davis v. Washington* (*see* Chapter 10) suggests that Rule 804(b)(6) may be of particular importance in domestic violence cases. Domestic violence victims frequently call the police for help during or soon after an attack, but later refuse to testify against their attackers. In *Davis*, the Court ruled that the account of an attack that a domestic violence victim gave to a police officer was testimonial, and that since the victim did not appear for the trial, the Confrontation Clause prevented the prosecutor from offering her account into evidence against her abuser.

The Court in *Davis* acknowledged that domestic violence is a "type of crime notoriously susceptible to intimidation or coercion of the victim to ensure that she does not testify at trial. When this occurs, the Confrontation Clause gives the criminal a windfall." The opinion referred prosecutors of domestic violence cases to Rule 804(b)(6), noting, "one who obtains the absence of a witness by wrongdoing forfeits the constitutional right to confrontation." Leaving proof problems to lower courts, *Davis* took "no position on the standards necessary to demonstrate such forfeiture."

Two years after *Davis*, the Court did take a position on the forfeiture question in *Giles v. California* (554 U.S. 353 (2008)). In *Giles*, the defendant was charged with murdering Brenda Avie, his ex-girlfriend. To rebut the defendant's testimony that he was acting in self-defense when he shot Brenda, the prosecutor was allowed to call a police officer to testify to statements that Brenda had made to the officer about three weeks earlier when the officer responded to a domestic violence call. Brenda told the officer that the defendant had choked her, punched her in the face and head, and threatened to kill her. The California state courts ruled that the statements were admissible because the defendant had forfeited his right to confrontation by killing the declarant, Brenda.

In *Giles*, the U.S. Supreme Court ruled that the defendant's killing of Brenda resulted in a forfeiture *only* if he killed her *for the purpose of preventing her from testifying*. The Court acknowledged that it had often invoked the maxim that "a defendant should not be permitted to benefit from his own wrong," but concluded that to constitute forfeiture by wrongdoing, the "wrong" must consist of conduct designed to prevent a witness from testifying. The Court vacated Giles's conviction. Brenda Avie's hearsay might yet be admissible, if following remand the prosecution establishes by a preponderance of the evidence that Giles killed her for the purpose of preventing her from testifying against him. If so, Brenda's hearsay would be admissible to prove that Giles murdered her.

> [Giles was retried for and convicted of the murder of Brenda Avie. The Prosecutor who tried the case told one of the authors that she did not offer the contents of Brenda's domestic violence call into evidence during the retrial. One reason was the difficulty of establishing that the defendant's motive for killing Brenda was to prevent her from testifying against him in a domestic violence trial. The second reason was that the prosecutor correctly reasoned that she had ample proof of guilt without the contents of the domestic violence call.]

Though *Giles* reads an "intent to prevent from testifying" requirement into the jurisprudence of the Sixth Amendment and forfeiture doctrine, it also establishes that the prosecution can invoke the forfeiture doctrine when a defendant is prosecuted for the very act that causes the declarant's absence. That is, Brenda's hearsay account of Giles's prior attack could be admissible to prove that Giles murdered her, so long as the state can make a foundational showing that Giles killed her to prevent her from testifying against him. (Of course, the jury would not find out that in order for the hearsay statements to be admissible in evidence, the judge had to make a foundational finding that the defendant committed the very crime for which he or she is on trial.)

Problem 15-32: Owens' Flip Side

Johnny Angel, a prison inmate, is charged with attempting to kill Bob Owens, a correctional counselor. Angel admits striking Owens, but claims that he did so in self-defense after Owens dragged him into an empty cell and began to hit and kick him. Owens was so badly injured that he has remained hospitalized ever since the alleged attack, and is sometimes comatose. When police officers went to the hospital to interview Owens and gather information about what happened, he was unresponsive except for one occasion when he told Police Officer Shelley Faber that Angel "pulled me into an empty cell and beat me until other prisoners and correctional officers pulled him off me." After listening to the prosecution's foundational evidence, the judge rules that Owens is unavailable as a witness under Rule 804(a)(4). The prosecution then calls Officer Faber to testify to Owens's description of the incident in the hospital. In response to Angel's Confrontation Clause objection, the prosecutor argues that the statement is admissible under Rule 804(b)(6), because Angel forfeited his right to cross-examine Owens by attacking him so viciously that he remains hospitalized. *Is Faber's testimony admissible against Angel?*

Problem 15-33: Five-feiture

Pat Barron is charged with domestic violence. Two days after the alleged attack, Barron's wife Alita called the police and gave them a complete description of Barron's attack. Assume that the trial judge has correctly ruled that Alita is unavailable as a witness under one or more of the provisions of Rule 804(a)(5), and that the prosecutor offers Alita's statement to the police into evidence under the forfeiture provision, Rule 804(b)(6). *Which, if any, of the five circumstances below would support a judge's conclusion under Rule 104(a) that Barron forfeited his right to claim that Alita's statement is inadmissible under the Confrontation Clause? If you conclude that the foundational information provided in a sub-part is inadequate to support a finding of forfeiture, establish a sufficient foundation through the testimony of a new witness (who must be someone other than the defendant or Alita) who you will question in class. You and your witness should meet before class to develop the information that you will elicit.*

1. The prosecutor has no evidence of post-attack contact between Barron and Alita. However, the prosecutor calls a police officer to testify that when Alita contacted the police after a similar attack by Barron a few weeks earlier, Alita reported that Barron had said after striking her, "If you show up in court, you're a dead woman."

2. The prosecutor has no evidence of post-attack contact between Barron and Alita. Alita appears for Barron's trial, but refuses to testify to anything that Barron did to her despite the trial judge's repeatedly warning Alita of the consequences of wrongfully refusing to testify. All that Alita will say on the stand is: "I just can't testify. I'm scared. I came down here with good intentions, but I know my husband and his friends and you don't. I know that if I testify they'll do something terrible to me or my son."

3. The prosecutor has no evidence of post-attack contact between Barron and Alita. Despite having been subpoenaed, Alita fails to appear for trial and the prosecutor does not know her whereabouts. The prosecutor calls Alita's friend Marta to testify that two weeks before the trial, Alita phoned Marta and told her that "Oh my God, I just got off the phone with Joe, my husband's brother. Joe said he'd just come back from talking with Pat in jail, and Pat asked him to tell me that if I show up in court and testify about the argument, he's going to see to it that I'm killed. I know he means it. No way I'm showing up in court."

4. While out on bail awaiting trial on the domestic violence charges, Barron decides to raise money for his legal defense by burning down his house and fraudulently collecting the insurance proceeds. Alita was sleeping inside the house at the time and perished in the flames.

5. Assume now that Barron is charged with murdering Alita. After taking Alita's domestic violence report, the police searched for but were unable to arrest Barron. Two weeks later, Barron showed up at Alita's home and shot and killed

her. At trial, Barron testifies that he shot Alita in self-defense, thinking that she was advancing on him with a knife. To rebut the self-defense claim, the prosecution seeks to offer Alita's statement to the police following the domestic violence incident into evidence. In response to Barron's Confrontation Clause objection, the prosecutor argues that by killing Alita, Barron forfeited his right to confrontation. *How should the judge rule?*

When evaluating the admissibility of Alita's statements in the sub-parts above, consider this language from Justice Souter's concurring opinion in *Giles* (which Justice Breyer's dissent quotes):

> Examining the early cases and commentary, however, reveals two things that count in favor of the Court's understanding of forfeiture when the evidence shows domestic abuse ... The second is the absence from the early material of any reason to doubt that the element of intention would normally be satisfied by the intent inferred on the part of the domestic abuser in the classic abusive relationship, which is meant to isolate the victim from outside help, including the aid of law enforcement and the judicial process. If the evidence for admissibility shows a continuing relationship of this sort, it would make no sense to suggest that the oppressing defendant miraculously abandoned the dynamics of abuse the instant before he killed his victim, say in a fit of anger.

§ 15.09 Residual Hearsay (Rule 807)

Foundational Elements:

* A statement is supported by sufficient guarantees of trustworthiness — after considering the totality of circumstances under which it was made and evidence, if any, corroborating the statement;

This foundational element provides judges with discretion to admit hearsay that they consider trustworthy even if the hearsay would not be admissible under any of the gaggle of preceding hearsay exemptions and exceptions. Importantly, this element invites judges to consider both the circumstances surrounding the making of a hearsay statement and external circumstances when deciding whether a statement is trustworthy. The explicit power to consider external circumstances extends the scope of the residual exception beyond that of many of the preceding exceptions, which for the most part are based only on the circumstances under which a statement was made. For example, assume that a declarant's statement is, "A few hours ago I saw a man wearing a red sweater push someone off a rooftop as I was looking up at Halley's Comet." A judge could consider evidence that Halley's Comet was passing overhead at the time the declarant spoke as corroborative of trustworthiness.

* A statement is more probative on the point for which it is offered than any other evidence that the proponent can obtain through reasonable efforts.

This foundational element authorizes judges to exclude residual hearsay on the ground that a reasonable effort by the proponent might have produced either the declarant or more trustworthy hearsay (such as deposition testimony). Thus, as suggested earlier, the element imposes a soft unavailability requirement.

* The offering party gives the adversary adequate notice in advance of trial of the party's intent to offer the statement into evidence.

The notice must include information about a statement's content as well as contact information about the declarant, and must be given sufficiently in advance of trial to give the adversary "a fair opportunity to meet" the hearsay. An adversary who has a fair chance to investigate both the hearsay declarant and the circumstances under which the hearsay statement was made may be able to argue successfully that it lacks trustworthiness and so should either be not admitted or not believed.

The adoption of the Federal Rules of Evidence in the late 1970s generally moved evidence law in the direction of greater admissibility as compared to common law evidence principles. Increasing the discretion of trial judges when making evidentiary rulings was one of the tools that the Rules drafters used to promote admissibility, and this approach is perhaps nowhere more apparent than in Rule 807, the residual hearsay exception.[9]

A cartoon in a 1966 issue of the magazine *Saturday Review* depicts two judges on the bench in mid-hearing. Ignoring a lawyer's impassioned argument, one judge slyly whispers to the other: "Sure it's hearsay, but it's great hearsay." What seemed humorous about a decade before the enactment of the Federal Rules of Evidence is now good law under Rule 807. While many judges may use enacted hearsay exemptions and exceptions as guides when evaluating trustworthiness under Rule 807, it is possible to imagine a future time when the residual hearsay rule supplants all the rest.

The residual exception was quite controversial when it was first introduced. A number of commentators and legislators argued that a residual exception was unnecessary and would inject too much uncertainty into trials. Advocates of the residual exception argued that it was consistent with the general philosophy of the Federal Rules of Evidence as enunciated in Rule 102, to promote the "growth and development of the law of evidence." Advocates also tried to reassure the doubters that in practice, the residual exception's impact would be minimal. The Report of the Senate Committee on the Judiciary stated:

---

9. The residual or "catch-all" exception actually started life as two virtually identical exceptions, one a part of Rule 803 and the other part of Rule 804. They were combined as Rule 807 in 1997.

It is intended that the residual hearsay exception will be used very rarely, and only in exceptional circumstances. The committee does not intend to establish a broad license for trial judges to admit hearsay statements that do not fall within one of the other exceptions . . . the residual exceptions are not meant to authorize major judicial revisions of the hearsay rule.

Whether this statement reflected the Judiciary Committee's true expectations, a claim that judges have in practice used the catch-all sparingly is at least open to doubt.[10] Moreover, judges have excused parties' obligations to provide pretrial notice that they will offer hearsay under Rule 807, especially when the need for the hearsay is not apparent prior to trial and a short continuance provides an adversary with sufficient opportunity to prepare to counter it.[11]

Example

Ella Mentry, a third-grade teacher, sues Pete Teeyay, a parent of one of the children in Ella's class, for intentional infliction of emotional distress. Ella claims that Pete made verbal threats against her during an after-school conference. To prove that Pete made threats, Ella seeks to offer into evidence a note given to her by Bill Jones. The parties stipulate that Ella could not reasonably produce Bill Jones to testify, and that Ella's attorney notified Pete's attorney well before trial that Ella would seek to offer the contents of the note into evidence.

PLAINTIFF'S ATTORNEY: And what happened after Pete left the classroom?

A: I took a walk to try to calm my nerves. What he said really shook me up.

PLAINTIFF'S ATTORNEY: Did you talk to anyone?

A: No, I just walked around the campus by myself for about 15 or 20 minutes.

---

10. Perhaps the first case to do so was *United States v. Carlson*, 547 F.2d 1346 (8th Cir. 1976), *cert. denied*, 431 U.S. 914 (1977).

11. In *The Three Commandments of Amending the Federal Rules of Evidence*, 85 FORD-HAM L. REV. 1615 (2017), Victor Gold refers to a 2016 Advisory Committee note as follows at p. 1617:

> In the more than forty years since the enactment of the Rules, courts have been cautious when considering evidence under the residual exception. But it is not accurate to say that the exception has been used "very rarely." The Advisory Committee's Reporter collected all reported cases in the last ten years in which a court reviewed a claim that hearsay was admissible under Rule 807. He informed the Advisory Committee that he found 114 cases in which the court seriously addressed a Rule 807 objection and excluded the evidence. He also found seventy-one cases in which the hearsay was found admissible under Rule 807. While admitting that this data provides an imprecise picture of how the residual exception has been applied, the Reporter drew two conclusions: (1) the residual exception is being invoked with surprising frequency and (2) courts are excluding the proffered evidence more often they are admitting it. (footnotes excluded).

See also Myrna Raeder, *The Hearsay Rule at Work: Has It Been Abolished De Facto by Judicial Discretion?*, 76 MINN. L. REV. 507 (1992); D. Capra, *Memorandum Regarding Expanding the Residual Exception to the Hearsay Rule,* which is part of the October 2016 Agenda Book for the Advisory Comm. on Rules of Evidence.

PLAINTIFF'S ATTORNEY: Then what did you do?

A: I went back to my classroom. That's when Bill Jones, who at that time taught fourth grade across the hall, came in. He said he'd heard someone yelling at me and asked if I was OK.

> Bill's statement to Ella that he'd heard someone yelling may itself be hearsay, but if so is admissible under Rule 104(a) because it is foundational to show that he had personal knowledge.

PLAINTIFF'S ATTORNEY: What then happened?

A: I told him that I wasn't hurt, but that I had to get away. He said that he'd write down what he'd heard, in case I ever needed proof of what happened. I thanked him, gave him that piece of paper over there off my desk, and he wrote down what's on the paper.

> Ella's attorney marks the document to which Ella referred as Exhibit #1 and asks her to identify it as the one that she saw Bill prepare.

PLAINTIFF'S ATTORNEY: Nothing further at this time.

JUDGE: The defense may inquire.

DEFENDANT'S ATTORNEY: Ms. Mentry, I assume that you close the doors to your room during parent conferences?

A: Yes.

DEFENDANT'S ATTORNEY: Was Bill Jones also holding parent conferences that afternoon?

A: Probably. The whole school was that afternoon.

DEFENDANT'S ATTORNEY: And is it the principal's policy that teachers close their doors during parent conferences?

A: Yes.

DEFENDANT'S ATTORNEY: So if Bill Jones followed this policy, any sounds from your classroom would have had to travel through two sets of closed doors and a hallway?

A: I guess so.

DEFENDANT'S ATTORNEY: And you were walking for at least 15 or 20 minutes before you returned to your classroom and Bill Jones walked in?

A: No more than that.

DEFENDANT'S ATTORNEY: You weren't looking at your watch though, correct?

A: That's true.

DEFENDANT'S ATTORNEY: Nothing further.

PLAINTIFF'S ATTORNEY: Your Honor, I'd now like to read the contents of Exhibit #1 into evidence under Rule 807.

JUDGE: I'll hear argument from counsel.

PLAINTIFF'S ATTORNEY: I submit that Mr. Jones's note clearly has equivalent circumstantial guarantees of trustworthiness compared to the Rules 803 and 804 hearsay exceptions. Mr. Jones had personal knowledge of what took place, and he wrote the note shortly after the event. While the note may not have been prepared immediately after the shouting so as to qualify as a present sense impression under Rule 803(1) or pursuant to an excited state of mind so as to be admissible under Rule 803(2), it was made so soon after the events that Bill Jones's memory problems were nonexistent. Moreover, Bill was a neutral witness — he taught fourth grade and hadn't had any contact yet with the child or the parent. And given Ella's testimony as to the loudness of the defendant's voice, I don't believe that Mr. Jones's ability to hear is in serious question.

DEFENDANT'S ATTORNEY: To the contrary, Your Honor, the evidence suggests that Mr. Jones's ability to hear what happened in Ms. Mentry's classroom is in serious question. He didn't come in to check on the plaintiff until after she returned from her walk, so we can't be confident about what he heard or how accurately he heard it. Also, the plaintiff testified that she was very shaken by what had happened and was not looking at her watch, so we can't be sure that it wasn't more than 20 minutes between the incident and the time Mr. Jones wrote the note. The note is not trustworthy and should be excluded.

JUDGE: I'm satisfied that the note has equivalent reliability to statements admitted under other hearsay exceptions, so I'll admit its contents into evidence. Counsel may read it to the jury.

In this example, as is typically the case when parties offer hearsay pursuant to Rule 807, the attorneys' arguments center on the "hearsay dangers" that gave rise to the general rule proscribing hearsay in the first place: the declarant's sincerity, perception, and memory, and the risk of communication problems, such as ambiguity.

In the example above, Pete's attorney might also have tried to make what has been called a "near miss" argument. A "near miss" argument is that the residual exception should apply only to situations not contemplated by any of the specific exceptions listed in Rules 803 and 804. That is, if an out-of-court statement is of a type provided for by an existing hearsay exception and fails to meet that exception's foundational requirements, it should be inadmissible. For example, Pete's attorney's "near miss" argument might have gone as follows:

> Under Rule 803(1), a hearsay statement is admissible if it was made during or immediately after the event which it describes. Bill Jones's statement is of a type contemplated by Rule 803(1), but as Your Honor has correctly ruled, the statement does not qualify for admission under that exception.

Nor does his statement qualify as an excited utterance under Rule 803(2). Thus, you should not admit the statement under Rule 807. To admit it would be to flout the drafters' purpose in enacting Rules 803(1) and (2).

Some commentators would support such an argument.[12] However, judges have generally not accepted the "near miss" argument. A major problem with the "near miss" argument is that probably every hearsay statement can be analogized to at least one of the Rule 803 and 804 exceptions. For example, every out-of-court statement in which a declarant mentions a medical condition might be argued to be "admissible under the Rule 803(4) medical hearsay exception or not at all." Carried to its logical extent, therefore, the "near miss" argument could wipe out the residual exception altogether. Thus, the majority of court rulings implicitly recognize that if the residual exception is to admit any hearsay at all, admissibility cannot turn on whether a statement offered under Rule 807 is completely dissimilar to the types of statements admitted under Rules 803 or 804. The Committee Note to the 2019 amendment of Rule 807 said this about the "near miss" argument:

> [The] amendment makes the rule applicable to hearsay "not admissible under" those exceptions. This clarifies that a court assessing guarantees of trustworthiness may consider whether the statement is a "near-miss" of one of the Rule 803 or 804 exceptions. If the court employs a "near-miss" analysis it should—in addition to evaluating all relevant guarantees of trustworthiness—take into account the reasons that the hearsay misses the admissibility requirements of the standard exception.

The 2019 amendment to Rule 807 explicitly authorizes judges to consider both the circumstances under which a statement was made and corroborating circumstances when evaluating a statement's trustworthiness. Previously, many judges believed they could not consider corroborating circumstances when deciding to admit hearsay under Rule 807.

Problem 15-34: Hospital Hearsay

Florence Nighten, a nurse, has been civilly sued for battery by Maria Moore, a hospital patient; Florence denies striking Maria. To prove that Florence attacked her, Maria calls Dr. Killdear to testify to a statement made to the doctor by Dee Clarant, who at the time of the incident was a patient who shared Maria's hospital room. Dr. Killdear will testify that she spoke to Dee about 15 minutes after the attack on Maria. At the time Dr. Killdear spoke to Dee, Dee was semi-conscious, coming out of general anesthetic administered in connection with knee surgery for a torn meniscus. Dee told Dr. Killdear, "Heard yelling and hitting . . . next bed . . .

---

12. *See, e.g.*, G. Weissenberger & J. Duane, Federal Rules of Evidence: Rules, Legislative History, Commentary and Authority Sec. 807.3

thought imagining . . . saw nurse leaving room . . . scar right cheek." Other foundational evidence will show that:

- Florence has a scar on her right cheek, and is the only nurse who was on the floor at the time of the attack with such a mark.

- Because Maria's bed was closer to the door than Dee's, Dee at best could have seen Florence in profile and from behind.

- Dee had only a single previous contact with Florence, when Florence came into the room to check on Dee's blood pressure following the surgery and about 15 minutes before the time of the attack on Maria. Dee looked at Florence momentarily and raised her arm in response to Florence's request, then lapsed back to sleep.

- The day before the attack, Florence had told another nurse on the floor that "I've had all I can take of Maria Moore. She demands everything and then has the gall to file a complaint against me because I'm late with her dinner."

- A thin bracelet, of a type Florence usually wears, was found in Maria's bed following the attack.

Defense counsel objects to admission of Dee's statement to Dr. Killdear under Rule 807.

How should the judge rule if the judge evaluates the trustworthiness of Dee's statement by considering only the circumstances under which it was made? How might the admissibility of Dee's statement be affected by the amendment to Rule 807 that allows judges to consider corroborating evidence?

Problem 15-35: Home Work

Rip Toff has sued Bill Kem Construction Co. to set aside Kem's foreclosure on Rip's house, claiming that Kem fraudulently induced Rip to sign an agreement to pay for unnecessary home repairs and improvements that Rip could not afford. Rip contends, and Kem denies, that Kem told Rip, "the piece of paper you're signing is just my standard agreement under which you can never lose your house." To corroborate Rip's testimony that Kem did make this representation, Rip's attorney seeks to offer into evidence a signed out-of-court statement given under penalty of perjury to the attorney's investigator by Sue Porter. At the time she met with the investigator, Sue lived a block away from Rip. Sue's statement includes the assertion, "Two weeks ago, Kem knocked on my door and tried to talk me into doing some home repairs. Kem told me that under the standard home repair contract I would sign with Kem, I could never lose my house. I was planning to move, so I did not agree to have any work done." Sue moved out of state within weeks of talking to the investigator and is unavailable to testify.

1. Rip's attorney offers Sue's statement into evidence under Rule 807. Kem's lawyer has stipulated to receiving proper notice of the intent to offer the statement under Rule 807. What arguments might the parties make for and against admissibility?

2. You are Rip's attorney. Assume that Kem's lawyer has offered to settle the case for about one-third of what you have demanded. In your opinion, Kem's settlement offer is worth Rip's consideration if the judge excludes Sue's statement, but unacceptably low if Sue's statement is admitted into evidence. You have no information about the judge who will preside over the trial. *How might you explain to Rip the likelihood of the admissibility of Sue's statement and its impact on whether Rip should accept Kem's settlement offer?*

Problem 15-36: Cartune

Minnie Vann has sued Lex Sussman for injuries sustained in an auto accident. To prove that Lex's careless driving caused the accident, Minnie calls Ron to testify that a few hours after the accident, Ron's wife Pam told him, "I was lucky I wasn't hurt when I was in Lex Sussman's car today. Lex hit another car when he took his eyes off the road to change the radio station when a country and western song came on." *Under Rule 807, Ron's testimony is:*

1. Inadmissible because Pam's statement is of a type made admissible by Rules 803(1) and (2) and was not made soon enough after the accident to qualify as a present sense impression or an excited utterance.

2. Inadmissible if Minnie called Ron instead of Pam to testify because Ron has testified in court previously and would probably be more believable.

3. Admissible unless Lex can convince the judge that Pam's statement is untrustworthy.

4. Admissible if Minnie offers it for the non-hearsay purpose of showing why Ron believes that Lex was at fault.

Problem 15-37: Fireside Chat

You host an extremely popular Evidence Rules Podcast and managed to erase the sands of time in order to convene a group of experts to discuss the wisdom of Rule 807. Brief summaries of your guests' conflicting opinions are below. As is your practice, you will end the podcast with a statement of your views. What might you say?

Baron Parke: I wrote the key opinion in *Wright v. Tatham* nearly 200 years ago, and I'm still really upset that judges have interpreted the hearsay rule so that statements are not hearsay when they are offered for points that declarants did not intend to assert. (*See* Chapter 10.) Rule 807 is a disaster because it gives trial judges virtually unbridled discretion to admit hearsay. The rule thwarts effective trial planning and will lead to unjust verdicts. Get rid of Rule 807!

Jeremy Bentham: I've been around at least as long as Baron Parke. While I have great respect for his wisdom and experience, I champion the general movement of modern evidence law in the direction of greater discretion and admissibility. Rule 807 is absolutely necessary because decisions about the trustworthiness of hearsay are best made by judges in the context of concrete disputes, not in the abstract by remote rule-makers. I would allow judges to determine trustworthiness according to the lower threshold of Rule 104(b) — admit hearsay so long as jurors could rationally conclude that it is trustworthy.

Solomon: With all due respect to my learned friends, I suggest that we split the difference. Retain Rule 807, but direct judges to determine trustworthiness according to the factors most associated with trustworthiness as reflected in Rule 803. Judges should admit only if they are convinced of trustworthiness under Rule 104(a). That Bentham — always stirring the pot!

You: I'm really grateful to you all for traveling so far to address my vast numbers of podcast listeners who care so deeply about evidence rules. Here's what I suggest. . . . *How would you complete the thought?*

Problem 15-38: Voicemail

Rhoda Runner sues Wiley for personal injuries resulting from Wiley's allegedly unprovoked attack on Rhoda. Wiley has plead self-defense. Rhoda's attorney offers into evidence under Rule 807 a message left on Rhoda's home phone two days after the alleged attack. The message is as follows: "Rhoda, this is Ray Jacks. You don't know me, but I saw the notice in the local newspaper with your name and number asking for information from anyone who saw Wiley attack you. I was waiting to cross the street and I heard you honking your horn at Wiley, who was crossing the street really slowly. Then Wiley suddenly exploded, running over to your side of the car and hitting you a couple of times through the open window. Then Wiley ran off. At no time did you strike Wiley. I hope this is helpful, what I've said is the truth." *Is the voicemail message admissible under Rule 807?*

Problem 15-39: Mind the Gap 2

Problem 14-9 involved a lawsuit by Jean Yuss against The Gap, in which the plaintiff sought damages for allegedly hurting her knee when she tripped and fell in a Gap store when getting out of an elevator that stopped two inches below the level of the fourth floor. To prove that the elevator did not stop at floor level, Jean's attorney called a Gap customer service representative as an adverse witness to testify that about 30 minutes after Jean fell, a customer told the customer service representative that "You need to check your elevators. I just saw a woman trip getting out of an elevator on the fourth floor a little while earlier because the elevator didn't stop evenly with the floor." In response to the Gap's attorney's hearsay objection, the judge ruled that the hearsay statement is not admissible as a present sense impression or as an excited utterance. Jean's attorney now offers the hearsay statement into evidence under Rule 807. The defense attorney objects that since the statement does not qualify for admission under either of those exceptions, the judge should not admit it under the residual exception. *How should the judge rule on the objection?*

Problem 15-40: Building a Foundation

Shirin sues Kim's Auto Care for severe burns that Shirin sustained when having her car worked on at Kim's. Shirin claims that she was injured by an explosion that occurred on March 31 when Juan, a Kim's mechanic, poured gasoline directly into her car's carburetor when the engine was running. Kim's defense is that Shirin herself poured the gasoline into the carburetor despite Juan's warning her not to so do. To prove that Shirin's own carelessness was the cause of her injuries, Kim's seeks to offer into evidence under Rule 807 a note written by Guillermo, a customer who was waiting to pick up his car when the explosion occurred. After talking to Guillermo, Juan asked him to write down what happened. As Juan watched, Guillermo wrote the following: "March 31. I was at Kim's Auto Care waiting for my car when I saw a lady pour gasoline into her car's carburetor. I heard the mechanic, who was sitting in the car revving the engine, tell her not to, but she did anyway. Then there was an explosion and a fire, and the lady was burned. The mechanic and I put the fire out and called an ambulance. Guillermo. 823 Bolas Street, La Ronda Heights. E-mail: Guill@yabadabadoo.com. Tel: 438-555-1234." Kim's has been unable to locate Guillermo and so plans to offer the note into evidence pursuant to Rule 807.

Student # 1: You represent Kim's Auto Care and seek to offer Guillermo's handwritten note into evidence under Rule 807. Meet with Juan (Student # 2) before class and prepare foundational testimony that you will offer to make the contents of the note admissible in evidence. (Prior to class, notify Student # 3, who represents Shirin, of the testimony you plan to elicit.) You will call Juan as a witness at a foundational mini-trial during class, and after eliciting his testimony briefly argue for the admissibility of the note.

Student # 2: You are Juan, a mechanic employed by Kim's. Meet with Kim's lawyer before class and prepare the testimony you will provide during class.

Student # 3: You represent Shirin. Cross-examine Juan in an effort to undermine the note's trustworthiness, and at the conclusion of the testimony briefly argue against the note's admissibility if such an argument is warranted.

Student # 4: You are the judge. Preside at the foundational mini-trial, indicating which party has the burden of proving that the note is admissible under Rule 807 and what that burden consists of. After listening to brief arguments of counsel, rule on the note's admissibility.

All Students: As counsel for Kim's Auto Care, refer to the text of Rule 807 and draft a Notice that satisfies that section concerning your intention to offer Guillermo's note into evidence. Assume that you tried to contact Guillermo by phone and by regular and electronic mail. The phone number did not work, e-mails bounced back, and letters delivered by snail mail were returned marked "Addressee Unknown."

§ 15.10 Multiple-Choice Review Problems

Review Problem 15-A

O'Brien, the defendant in an automobile accident case, seeks to offer into evidence deposition testimony from Biscailuz stating that "I saw O'Brien's car make a full stop before entering the intersection where the collision took place." O'Brien can establish a foundation for reading this deposition testimony into the record at trial by offering evidence that:

1. Biscailuz is not present in the courtroom, and O'Brien sent Biscailuz at least three e-mail messages and left 4–5 telephone messages on Biscailuz's answering machine during the two weeks prior to trial informing Biscailuz of the trial date and the exact place and time of the trial.

2. Biscailuz is not present in the courtroom, and O'Brien produces a letter from Biscailuz's employer stating: "We have a deadline on a big project and since our place of business is 20 miles from the courthouse we simply can't allow Biscailuz to take the time to go to court."

3. Biscailuz appears at trial and testifies that "I have no recollection of anything leading up to or concerning the collision."

4. Biscailuz appears at trial and testifies as to the events leading up to the collision, but also testifies that "I have no recollection whatsoever of the testimony I gave at deposition."

Review Problem 15-B

Testifying on Rich's behalf in a lawsuit against a ski resort for personal injuries, Eileen testifies that "I know that it was 9:00 a.m. when the ski lift broke down because I looked at Rich's watch that was inside the pork pie-style hat that Rich always wears when he skis and that was lying on the lift chair between us." A year later, Rich is charged with armed robbery of a skier. The skier testifies that the robber wore a pork pie-style hat. The prosecution then offers evidence that Eileen is unavailable as a witness and seeks to offer her "former testimony" from the personal injury trial as evidence that Rich was the robber. *The judge should rule that:*

1. Eileen's testimony from the personal injury trial is inadmissible because Rich did not have a chance to cross-examine her in that trial.

2. Eileen's testimony from the personal injury trial is inadmissible because Rich's motives with respect to the pork pie hat testimony in the criminal trial are too dissimilar.

3. Eileen's testimony from the personal injury trial is inadmissible because former testimony from civil proceedings is inadmissible in criminal proceedings.

4. Eileen's testimony from the personal injury trial is admissible as former testimony because Rich had himself offered that testimony into evidence.

Review Problem 15-C

As Jelani is waiting for a traffic light to change to green, someone rips open the driver's side door, shoves Jelani to the side, and drives off. While the car is traveling at high speed, the driver opens the passenger side door and shoves Jelani out of the car. By the time Marie, another driver, sees Jelani and stops to help him, he is barely breathing and is bleeding profusely from multiple wounds. Jelani whispers to Marie, "I know I'm done for. Please just tell them that it was Eddie Malone who did this to me." Jelani then becomes unconscious. Eddie Malone is arrested, and when Jelani survives, Malone is charged with attempted murder and carjacking. However, by the time of trial Jelani has vanished and the judge rules that he is unavailable as a witness. The prosecution then offers Jelani's statement into evidence as a "dying declaration" by calling Marie as a witness. *In response to Malone's objection, the judge should rule that:*

1. The statement is inadmissible hearsay because it does not concern the cause and circumstances of Jelani's injuries.

2. The statement is inadmissible hearsay because dying declarations are not admissible in attempted murder and carjacking prosecutions.

3. The statement is inadmissible hearsay because Jelani survived the attack.

4. The statement is admissible under the dying declarations hearsay exception.

5. Jelani's statement is inadmissible under the Confrontation Clause.

Review Problem 15-D

Walt Whitman is arrested for cultivating a large quantity of marijuana in a national wilderness area. Whitman tells the arresting officer that "I didn't have any choice. The person you really want is John Barth, these are all his plants and he told me he'd have me killed if I didn't look after them." The government eventually charges Barth with illegally cultivating marijuana, and the judge rules that Whitman is unavailable as a witness after Whitman repeatedly refuses to testify though the government has granted him "use immunity." The government then seeks to offer Whitman's statement to the arresting officer implicating Barth into evidence. *In response to Barth's objection, the judge should rule that:*

1. The statement is inadmissible hearsay.

2. The statement is admissible as a declaration against interest.

3. The statement is admissible as a "co-conspirator party admission."

4. The statement is admissible under the state of mind hearsay exception.

5. The statement is inadmissible under the Confrontation Clause.

Review Problem 15-E

Lilly Calla is charged with receiving stolen property after police officers responding to a 911 call found a cache of stolen electronic equipment in her garage. Calla's defense is that she was unaware of the equipment's presence. Calla seeks to offer evidence that on the morning of the day that he was attacked by another prisoner and killed, Bob Newton told his cellmate, "Some associate of that weasel Lilly Calla may have me killed for doing this, but at least I got back at her a few days ago, just before they put me in the slammer. I stole some fancy electronic equipment and hid it in Calla's garage, then made sure the cops found it before she did." Calla seeks to offer evidence of Newton's statement into evidence by calling the cellmate as a witness. *Upon objection by the government, the judge should rule that:*

1. Newton's statement is admissible as a present sense impression.

2. Newton's statement is admissible as a declaration against interest.

3. Newton's statement is inadmissible hearsay.

4. Newton's statement is admissible as a dying declaration.

5. The statement is inadmissible under the Confrontation Clause.

Review Problem 15-F

Kobashian sues Dour Chemical Co. for personal injuries allegedly caused by a chemical leak. Kobashian calls Lewis, a next-door neighbor, to testify to an out-of-court statement made to Lewis by Kobashian about 24 hours after the leak occurred. In response to Dour's hearsay objection, Kobashian makes an offer of proof that Lewis will testify that when Lewis stopped by and asked how Kobashian was feeling, Kobashian said that "I'm really feeling nauseous and I've got ringing in my ears." Dour's counsel then makes a further offer of proof that "If Lewis is allowed to testify, I intend to call Clark to testify to an opinion that Kobashian is a dishonest scoundrel." *The judge should respond to these offers of proof by ruling that:*

1. Lewis' testimony is inadmissible in the absence of foundational evidence that Lewis has medical training and that Kobashian made the statement in order to obtain a medical diagnosis or receive treatment.

2. Lewis' testimony is admissible but Clark's testimony is inadmissible unless and until Kobashian testifies under oath at trial.

3. Lewis' testimony is admissible but Clark's testimony is not because character evidence is not admissible in civil cases.

4. Lewis's testimony is admissible, and after Lewis testifies, Clark's testimony is also admissible.

Review Problem 15-G

After returning to the office after eating lunch at Penny's Always Open Diner, Maysie tells a co-worker that "I slipped on some wet noodles near the salad bar." Maysie sues Penny's for personal injuries and calls the co-worker to testify to the statement she made when she came back from lunch. *In response to Penny's objection, the court should rule that:*

1. If the statement fails to meet the foundational requirements for a present sense impression, it is inadmissible under Rule 807.

2. Because Maysie is a party, her statement is admissible as an opposing party statement.

3. The statement is admissible under Rule 807 if the judge is convinced that it was made under circumstances demonstrating that it is trustworthy.

4. The statement is admissible as non-hearsay "words of independent legal significance."

5. The statement is admissible under Rule 807 if Maysie offers evidence sufficient to support a jury finding that it was made under circumstances demonstrating that it is trustworthy.

Review Problem 15-H

In a murder prosecution, the prosecutor seeks to offer a hearsay statement into evidence against the defendant under Rule 807. *Which statement below is correct?*

1. The statement is admissible only if the declarant is unavailable as a witness under Rule 804(a).

2. The prosecutor has to offer evidence showing that the statement has "indicia of reliability."

3. The statement is inadmissible if it was made during grand jury proceedings and the defendant has no opportunity to question the declarant.

4. If the statement is "testimonial," it is inadmissible regardless of whether the defendant has an opportunity to question the declarant.

§ 15.11 Case Library

Williamson v. United States

U.S. Supreme Court
512 U.S. 594 (1994)

Giles v. California

U.S. Supreme Court
554 U.S. 353 (2008)

Chapter 16

Shaping Outcomes: Burdens of Proof, Presumptions, and Judicial Notice

§ 16.01 Chapter Checklist

1. Do the Federal Rules of Evidence allocate burdens of proof or determine their content?

2. What is the difference between the "burden of producing evidence" and the "burden of persuasion"?

3. What is a "prima facie case"?

4. If a plaintiff makes out a prima facie case, does either the burden of producing evidence or the burden of persuasion then shift to the defendant?

5. How is a "presumption" different from a "permissive inference"?

6. How does a "social policy presumption" differ from a "common practice presumption"?

7. What does it mean to say that a presumption is "rebuttable"?

8. What is the effect of a "bursting bubble" presumption?

9. Does Rule 301 create any presumptions?

10. What is the distinction between "basic facts" and "presumed facts"?

11. How does the impact of presumptions differ in criminal versus civil cases?

12. What are the bases upon which judges can take judicial notice?

13. What is the distinction between "adjudicative" and "legislative facts"?

14. Can a party offer evidence that contravenes a judicially noticed fact?

§ 16.02 Relevant Federal Rules of Evidence

Rule 201. Judicial Notice of Adjudicative Facts

(a) Scope. This rule governs judicial notice of an adjudicative fact only, not a legislative fact.

(b) Kinds of Facts That May Be Judicially Noticed. The court may judicially notice a fact that is not subject to reasonable dispute because it:

(1) is generally known within the trial court's territorial jurisdiction;

or

(2) can be accurately and readily determined from sources whose accuracy cannot reasonably be questioned.

(c) Taking Notice. The court:

(1) may take judicial notice on its own; or

(2) must take judicial notice if a party requests it and the court is supplied with the necessary information.

(d) Timing. The court may take judicial notice at any stage of the proceeding.

(e) Opportunity to Be Heard. On timely request, a party is entitled to be heard on the propriety of taking judicial notice and the nature of the fact to be noticed. If the court takes judicial notice before notifying a party, the party, on request, is still entitled to be heard.

(f) Instructing the Jury. In a civil case, the court must instruct the jury to accept the noticed fact as conclusive. In a criminal case, the court must instruct the jury that it may or may not accept the noticed fact as conclusive.

Rule 301. Presumptions in Civil Actions Generally

In a civil case, unless a federal statute or these rules provide otherwise, the party against whom a presumption is directed has the burden of producing evidence to rebut the presumption. But this rule does not shift the burden of persuasion, which remains on the party who had it originally.

Rule 302. Applying State Law to Presumptions in Civil Cases

In a civil case, state law governs the effect of a presumption regarding a claim or defense for which state law supplies the rule of decision.

§ 16.03 Introduction

For the most part, evidence rules regulate only the information that judges and jurors are legally allowed to consider. If you think of a juror's mind as the proverbial "black box," evidence rules determine what case-specific information can enter the box. Through "admonishments" or "limiting instructions," judges can instruct jurors not to use evidence for forbidden purposes.[1]

---

1. For example, a judge may admonish jurors not to use an out-of-court statement admitted for a non-hearsay purpose for the truth of its contents. Similarly, a judge may admonish jurors not to use a past act admitted against a party for a non-character use under Rule 404(b) as evidence of the party's character.

However, once a case is turned over to jurors for decision, each juror decides for her, him or their self, what if any weight to attach to evidence. For example, assume that the defendant in a criminal case introduces evidence that the key prosecution witness is biased against the defendant. Jurors may choose to ignore the bias evidence, may decide that the witness is biased but truthful, may decide that the witness is truthful but mistaken, or may decide that the witness is lying. Even if a juror draws an improper inference from evidence (say, uses an out-of-court statement admitted as non-hearsay for its truth), a judge can do nothing about it once a verdict is reached.[2] The policy of allowing judges' and jurors' factual conclusions to be a product of their own experiences and reasoning processes rather than of legal strictures is confirmed by the general rule that those factual conclusions are for the most part binding on appellate court judges.

Within this broad terrain of factfinder freedom exist three important pockets of principles through which rule makers attempt to shape decision-making. These pockets represent legislative and judicial efforts to produce trial outcomes that are consistent with what they regard as rational principles and desirable social policies.

A. Burdens of Proof

One outcome-shaping principle is that the risk of uncertainty about which party is in the right should fall on the party asserting a legal claim. This social policy is reflected in the allocation of burdens of proof. Burdens of proof shape outcomes by instructing judges and jurors not to rule in a burdened party's favor unless that party discharges its predetermined quantum of proof. For example, in criminal cases judges instruct jurors not to reach guilty verdicts unless the government proves defendants guilty beyond a reasonable doubt. (Of course, one social policy can conquer another. No matter how strong the government's proof, criminal juries have the inherent power to "nullify" the law by acquitting a defendant.) In civil cases, judges instruct jurors not to hold defendants liable unless plaintiffs prove liability either by a preponderance of the evidence or by clear and convincing evidence, depending on applicable substantive law principles. A similar social policy explains why defendants often have the burden of proof when they rely on affirmative defenses, such as the defense of "accord and satisfaction" in breach of contract cases or "insanity" in criminal cases.

B. Presumptions (Rule 301)

Presumptions, a second outcome-shaping tool, reflect rule makers' desires that verdicts conform to their conceptions of accuracy and rationality. Presumptions are an attempt to ensure that particular foundational facts produce the same conclusions.

---

2. See FRE 606(b). If prior to the jury reaching a verdict a judge learns that a juror refuses to follow instructions, the judge may remove the juror from the jury.

As you know, most inferences are *permissive*, meaning that judges and jurors are normally free to draw or not draw inferences from circumstantial evidence as they see fit. For example, a judge or juror who hears evidence that Kelly was standing inside an office wearing a wet raincoat and carrying a wet umbrella may infer that Kelly was outside in the rain, that the office has a serious leaky roof problem, that Kelly was rehearsing for a revival of *Singing in the Rain*, or draw a different inference altogether.

Presumptions create *mandatory* inferences. If circumstantial evidence is subject to a presumption, a judge or juror *must* draw the inference created by the presumption unless the party burdened by the presumption adequately rebuts it. Thus, assume the unlikely existence of a presumption, "A person wearing a wet raincoat and carrying a wet umbrella is presumed to have been out in the rain." In that event, a judge or juror who believes that Kelly was wearing a wet raincoat and carrying a wet umbrella must conclude that Kelly was out in the rain, unless the adversary's evidence counters the presumption.

C. Judicial Notice (Rule 201)

Judicial notice also represents a tool for producing accurate and rational outcomes. When a judge concludes that a fact cannot be reasonably disputed, the judge may instruct jurors that they must accept that the fact is true. In addition to fostering rationality, judicial notice is a labor-saving device. Judges can instruct jurors to accept facts as true even in the absence of formal proof, thereby saving parties the trouble of having to "prove the obvious."

Practice Tip: Stipulations

Stipulations are shortcuts to proof that result from agreements between parties. Stipulations often focus on evidentiary matters. For example:

- In lieu of a party calling a witness, the attorneys may stipulate, "If the witness were called and sworn, the witness would testify as follows . . ." This form of stipulation allows a party to insert evidence into the record while allowing an opposing party to contest its credibility.

- In lieu of a party calling a witness, the attorneys may stipulate, "The witness was at home watching television at 9:00 p.m. on August 9." This form of stipulation both inserts evidence into the record and establishes its accuracy for the purpose of the case. The stipulation forecloses both parties from offering evidence to either bolster or attack the credibility of stipulated facts.

- The parties stipulate that a witness "is qualified as an expert in the field of . . ." This form of stipulation eliminates the need for a *voir dire* examination qualifying a witness as an expert.

Stipulations can also focus on legal matters. For example, the parties to a personal injury case may stipulate, "if the defendant is held to be liable, the damage award to the plaintiff shall be $125,000."

As stipulations are private agreements between parties, their use is not governed by the Federal Rules of Evidence. Nevertheless, stipulations are subject to some limits. For instance, parties cannot stipulate to jurisdiction that a court does not possess, or to a form of penalty that a judge cannot impose.

Lawyers may inform a judge orally in open court of a simple stipulation, but stipulations involving lengthy or complex matters may be negotiated by counsel and presented to a judge in writing for reading to a jury.

While stipulations are usually effective time-saving devices, judges do not usually force unwilling lawyers to accept opposing counsels' offers to stipulate. Subject to ultimate judicial control, lawyers are in charge of factual presentations and may not want to deprive stories of what the *Old Chief* case (*see* Chapter 4) referred to as "descriptive richness" by acceding even to helpful offers to stipulate. *Old Chief* was an exception in a case in which a prosecutor's refusal to accept a stipulation was reversible error because the result of the prosecutor's refusal to stipulate was that unduly prejudicial character evidence was put before the jury.

§ 16.04 Burdens of Proof

The Federal Rules of Evidence neither allocate burdens of proof nor set forth the degrees of proof required to prevail on a legal claim. (If you've been feverishly searching the Rules for provisions defining and allocating burdens of proof, you can stop now.) Rather, burdens of proof emanate from other sources.

For example, the so-called "Hinckley rule" was enacted after John Hinckley was found not guilty by reason of insanity of shooting then-President Reagan. At the time of Hinckley's trial in 1982, once Hinckley pled insanity the prosecution had the burden of proving beyond a reasonable doubt that Hinckley was sane. Following the trial, Congress changed the law to provide that criminal defendants relying on the insanity defense in federal court bear the burden of proving insanity by clear and convincing evidence. This burden of proof is set forth in 18 U.S.C. § 17(b), not in the Federal Rules of Evidence. Thus, a detailed examination of the social policies and processes underlying the allocation and degrees of burdens of proof is largely beyond the scope of an evidence course.[3]

The primary evidentiary issue concerning burdens of proof involves the sufficiency of a burdened party's evidence to discharge its burden. In this respect, a burdened party actually has to discharge two burdens, the burden of production and the burden of persuasion. Initially, a burdened party bears the *burden of production*,

---

3. For a useful overview of the subject, *see* the classic article by Edward Cleary, *Presuming and Pleading: An Essay on Juristic Immaturity*, 12 STAN. L. REV. 5 (1959).

sometimes also called the *burden of producing evidence* or the *burden of going forward with evidence.* This means that the burdened party will lose its claim or defense as a matter of law unless the party produces evidence that, if believed, is sufficient to sustain a verdict in the party's favor (i.e., evidence sufficient to constitute a "prima facie case"). Whether a burdened party has made out a prima facie case is a question of law for the trial judge. If the judge decides that the burdened party's evidence, even if it is believed, is not sufficient to constitute a prima facie case, the judge should enter judgment against that party before the case reaches the jury. *See* Federal Rule of Civil Procedure 50(a), authorizing "motions for judgment" when "there is no legally sufficient evidentiary basis for a reasonable jury to find for" the burdened party on an issue. *See also* Federal Rule of Criminal Procedure 29(a), providing for a defense "motion for judgment of acquittal" when "the evidence is insufficient to sustain a conviction" of an offense.

As you would imagine, in almost all the cases that survive to trial, a burdened party does offer sufficient evidence to sustain the burden of producing evidence.[4] The typical result is that the adversary then offers conflicting evidence, and the judge or jurors consider both parties' evidence when deciding whether the burdened party has carried its second burden, the more familiar *burden of persuasion* (aka *burden of proof*). Whereas a judge decides as a matter of law whether a party has sustained the burden of producing evidence, the issue of whether a burdened party has carried the burden of persuasion is a question of fact.

Example 1

Meg O'Bight sues Chip, a computer technician, for malpractice. Meg alleges that instead of increasing the memory capacity of her computer, Chip carelessly erased all the programs and files on her computer's hard drive. During her case-in-chief, Meg neglects to offer evidence that any programs or files were on her computer before Chip began working on it. The judge should grant Chip's motion for judgment at the close of Meg's case, because there is no legally sufficient basis for the judge or jurors to conclude that Chip erased anything from Meg's computer.

Example 2

Same case as previous example. As part of her case-in-chief, Meg elicits the following testimony from Mike Rohard: "I'm a computer dealer, and I personally installed [particular software programs and files] on Meg's computer before she left it with Chip for additional memory installation." Cross-examined by Chip, Mike admits that he's previously been convicted of perjury. Together with other evidence establishing Chip's negligence, Mike's testimony would probably be sufficient for Meg to establish a prima

---

4. A case in which a burdened party's evidence is too weak to sustain the burden of going forward is likely to be derailed before trial gets under way. For example, in civil cases, weak cases are often disposed of through the summary judgment process.

facie case. Whether Mike is telling the truth is a question of fact that the judge or jurors can consider when deciding whether the totality of the evidence establishes Chip's liability by a preponderance of the evidence.

Example 3

Cat Berger is charged with first-degree burglary for burglarizing a detached building near a lake on her next-door neighbor's property. Under the jurisdiction's law, to prove that a defendant committed first-degree burglary, the prosecution is required to prove that the building was being used as a residence. However, the prosecutor fails to offer evidence of such use. The judge should grant Cat's motion for judgment of acquittal of first-degree burglary at the close of the government's case, because the evidence is insufficient as a matter of law to sustain a conviction for that offense.

Example 4

Same case as previous example. Before concluding its case-in-chief, the prosecution elicits evidence from the building's owner that "members of my family often stay overnight in that building when we work down by the lake." Together with evidence satisfying the other elements of first-degree burglary, the prosecution has now made out a prima facie case and it's up to the judge or jurors to evaluate the prosecution's evidence along with any defense evidence and determine whether Cat's guilt has been proved beyond a reasonable doubt.

Once a burdened party makes out a prima facie case, does the burden of producing evidence then shift to the adversary so that the adversary's failure to produce evidence would result in judgment as a matter of law in the burdened party's favor? For example, if in a personal injury case the plaintiff makes out a prima facie case of the defendant's negligence, does the defendant have to counter the plaintiff's evidence to avoid judgment being automatically entered in the plaintiff's favor?

The general answer to this is "no." Of course, especially in civil cases, burdened parties' adversaries do typically offer evidence in support of their own versions of events. For example, a personal injury plaintiff's evidence that a defendant was driving carelessly is apt to be countered by evidence of the defendant's careful driving and the plaintiff's own carelessness. Nevertheless, the burden of producing evidence does not shift to the defendant; judgment will not be automatically entered against a defendant who fails to counter a plaintiff's prima facie case. Rather, the judge or jurors decide whether the burdened party's evidence, even in the unusual case in which it is unchallenged, is sufficiently persuasive to merit a favorable verdict.

The general rule that an uncontested prima facie case does not automatically satisfy the burden of persuasion is subject to two common "exceptions":

Exception 1. When the burdened party establishes the basic facts that give rise to a presumption (*see* §16.05), the judge or jury must find that the presumed fact is true. If the presumed fact is itself a fact of consequence, the burdened party's uncontested evidence automatically satisfies the burden of persuasion as to that fact. In such a situation, a presumption does more than shape a trial's outcome, it controls the outcome.

Example 5

A common presumption provides: "One who possesses an object is presumed to own it." (Perhaps you used to sneer at your little sibling who tried to grab a toy over which you claimed dominion that "possession is nine-tenths of the law." If so, you'll find comfort in this presumption, though the fact that the presumption is rebuttable means that your childhood estimate may have been a bit high.) Vincent sues Fire Insurance Co., seeking compensation for a valuable painting that hung in Vincent's house when it burned down. The insurance company denies that the picture belonged to Vincent. If the jury believes Vincent's evidence that the painting was in his house before the fire, and the insurance company fails to contest ownership, the existence of the presumption means that Vincent has carried the burden of persuasion on the issue of whether he owned the painting.

Exception 2. If the burdened party's evidence in a civil case is exceedingly compelling and the adversary fails to offer contrary evidence rationally worthy of belief, a judge may conclude that as a matter of law the burdened party has satisfied the burden of persuasion. Relatively few cases are decided under this exception, both because most civil parties contest the evidence offered against them and because most judges take parties' rights to jury trial very seriously. (This doctrine cannot of course be used at all in criminal cases, where defendants have a constitutional right to remain mute. No matter how strong a judge considers a prosecutor's case to be, a criminal defendant is entitled to have a case go to a jury.)

Problem 16-1: Allocating Burdens

You have been retained as Evidence Guru by the Civil Justice Council of the newly formed Republic of Xanadid. The Council has sent you an electronic message asking for your thoughts on the following issue: "In personal injury cases based on negligence, should we require plaintiffs to have to prove that they were not contributorily negligent in order to make out a prima facie case? Or should a plaintiff's contributory negligence be an affirmative defense as to which defendants have the burden of producing evidence? Thank you — have a nice day." When you reply by suggesting that the burden of responding be allocated to the republic's Civil Procedure Guru, the Council gently reminds you that it has not yet been able to totally eradicate the populace's ancient cannibalistic practices. *What recommendation as to allocation would you give to the Council and why?*

Problem 16-2: Into the Breach

Elgin Marbles sues Rose Ettastone for breach of contract; trial is to a jury. Elgin testifies that Rose agreed to publish his book on ancient hieroglyphics and then refused to go ahead with the project after Elgin turned down other offers of publication. *At this stage of the case, which of the statements below is correct?*

1. If the judge doesn't believe Elgin's testimony, the judge should enter a judgment in Rose's favor.

2. Even if Rose fails to offer additional evidence, Elgin has the burden of persuading the jury by a preponderance of the evidence that Rose breached the contract.

3. Rose now has the burden of producing evidence that she did not breach the contract.

4. If Elgin's evidence is sufficient to make out a prima facie case and Rose fails to offer additional evidence, the judge should enter judgment in Elgin's favor.

Problem 16-3: Don't Believe It

Ray sues Vivian for personal injuries that Ray sustained in an auto accident, allegedly due to Vivian's negligence. To prove that Vivian was negligent, Ray calls Derek as a witness and elicits the following testimony on direct examination:

PLAINTIFF'S ATTORNEY: Derek, did you see the collision involving Ray's and Vivian's cars last August 1?

A: Yes, I did.

PLAINTIFF'S ATTORNEY: Did you observe Vivian's car prior to the collision?

A: Yes. I was walking west on Piedmont, and I saw her make a right turn and go east on Piedmont, driving in my direction.

PLAINTIFF'S ATTORNEY: What, if anything, did you notice about Vivian's driving after she made the right turn?

A: Nothing in particular. She was driving slowly in the right-hand lane.

PLAINTIFF'S ATTORNEY: In your opinion, was she driving carefully?

A: Yes.

PLAINTIFF'S ATTORNEY: Derek, isn't it true that you told your friend Kent the next day that you thought Vivian ran into Ray's car because she was driving too fast?

A: I did say that. But I've thought more about it since then.

PLAINTIFF'S ATTORNEY: And what is your relationship with Vivian?

A: We're currently engaged to be married. I actually met her as a result of this accident.

PLAINTIFF'S ATTORNEY: What were you doing at the time you observed the collision?

A: I had just left a restaurant after eating lunch. Maybe drinking lunch is more accurate — I'd just been fired so I'd been drowning my sorrows in a few martinis.

PLAINTIFF'S ATTORNEY: No further questions. Plaintiff rests.

DEFENDANT'S ATTORNEY: (At sidebar): Your Honor, the defense makes a motion for judgment as a matter of law, based on the plaintiff's failure to establish a prima facie case of Vivian's negligence through Derek's testimony.

PLAINTIFF'S ATTORNEY: I submit that Derek's testimony does make out a prima facie case that Vivian was negligent. Sure, he testified that Vivian was driving carefully. But he was thoroughly impeached. He had been drinking heavily just before the collision, so his ability to have observed her driving carefully is highly doubtful. He's engaged to the defendant, so he's obviously biased in her favor. Moreover, consider his contradictory statement to his friend Kent the very next day. I realize that under Rule 801 the contradictory statement to Kent is not admissible for its truth, but it does cast extreme doubt on Derek's credibility. All in all, Derek's testimony supports an inference that exactly the opposite of what he testified to is true, and thus is sufficient to make out a prima facie case that Vivian was negligent.

JUDGE: *What ruling on the defense attorney's motion for judgment?*

Problem 16-4: Got the Blues

As Luke Outt crosses a dark Rocky Road late one night, a large vehicle strikes him and continues on its way. Luke sues the Blue Bus Co. to recover for his personal injuries. The Blue Bus Co. denies that one of its buses struck Luke. At trial, Luke testifies that the vehicle that struck him was a bus, but he does not remember any of its distinguishing features.

1. Luke also offers evidence that only two bus companies operate on Rocky Road, the Blue Bus Co. and the Brown Bus Co. The Blue Bus Co. operates 75 percent of the buses on Rocky Road while the Brown Bus Co. operates 25 percent of the buses. *If Luke presents no additional evidence, is his evidence (if believed) sufficient to demonstrate by a preponderance of the evidence that the Blue Bus Co. operated the bus that hit him?*

2. Assume that instead of the evidence described in question 1, Luke offers evidence that the Blue Bus Co. operates 90 percent of the buses that run along Rocky Road, and the Brown Bus Co. operates the other 10 percent. *If Luke presents no additional evidence, is his evidence (if believed) sufficient to demonstrate by a preponderance of the evidence that the Blue Bus Co. operated the bus that hit him?*

3. As in question 1, Luke offers evidence that the Blue Bus Co. operates 75 percent of the buses on Rocky Road while the Brown Bus Co. operates 25 percent of the buses. In addition, Luke offers into evidence a copy of the "Blue Bus Co. Schedule." According to the schedule for the Rocky Road Route, a Blue Bus Co. bus traveling in Luke's direction should have departed from a bus stop about five blocks away from where Luke was hit about five minutes before he was struck. *Is Luke's evidence (if believed) sufficient to demonstrate by*

a preponderance of the evidence that the Blue Bus Co. operated the bus that hit him?

Problem 16-5: High Witness Testimony

As Luke Outt crosses a dark Rocky Road late one night, a large vehicle strikes him and continues on its way. Luke sues the Blue Bus Co. to recover for his personal injuries. The Blue Bus Co. denies that one of its buses struck Luke. At trial, Luke testifies that the vehicle that struck him was a bus, but he does not remember any of its distinguishing features. Luke also offers evidence that only two bus companies operate on Rocky Road, the Blue Bus Co. and the Brown Bus Co.

Luke elicits testimony from Han Looker that Looker is a homeless individual who was asleep in a doorway about 20 yards away from where Luke was struck by what he testified was a bus. Looker awakened upon hearing the impact, and testifies on direct examination by Luke's attorney, "I saw what looked to me like a bus driving away. I think I saw the words, 'Blue Bus Co.' on the back of the bus." On cross-examination by the Blue Bus Co.'s lawyer, Looker testifies that he had drunk a bottle of Old Rotgut earlier in the evening and felt dizzy when he woke up, that the bus was at least 50 yards from him when he saw it, and that it was just barely light enough for him to make out that the vehicle was a bus. The cross-examiner also elicits testimony that Looker was angry upon learning shortly after the accident that the Blue Bus Co. had discontinued its policy of allowing homeless individuals to ride on its buses for free. Finally, the Blue Bus. Co. offers evidence that it operates only 25 percent of the buses on Rocky Road, whereas the Brown Bus Co. operates 75 percent of the buses. *Based on this evidence, should the judge grant the Blue Bus Co.'s motion for judgment based on Luke's failure to establish a prima facie case?*

Problem 16-6: Note Worthy?

Gotham Bank has sued Bruce Wayne for failure to pay any of the principal and interest of a Note. During its case-in-chief, the Bank introduced testimony and documentary evidence showing that the Bank was the holder of a Note in the principal amount of $50,000 signed by Wayne. The Bank's evidence further showed that the Note was in default, that Wayne had made no payments on the Note, and that Wayne owed the Bank $68,000 in unpaid principal and interest. Wayne had asked for a jury trial but rested without presenting evidence. The Bank moves for judgment, asking the judge to enter judgment in its favor in the amount of $68,000 plus costs and reasonable attorneys' fee (as the Note provides for). *Should the judge grant the motion?*

Problem 16-7: Cold Case

Jesse Eaton was brutally bludgeoned to death more than 25 years ago, but after trying unsuccessfully to find Eaton's killer, the police department closed the file. However, as the result of a "cold DNA hit," Evan Oaks was charged with killing Eaton. Oaks was charged with the murder on the basis of a DNA test indicating that Oaks' DNA matched the DNA left by Eaton's killer on crime scene evidence that was preserved in the police files. Other than showing that Oaks lived in the same general vicinity as Eaton at the time of the murder, the only evidence that the prosecutor can offer of Oaks' guilt consists of the testimony of a DNA expert analyst that "the chance that a random person in the population would match Oaks' DNA is one in a million, and given the match evidence the chance that Oaks is not the source of the DNA found at the crime scene is one in 1,000." *If the jurors believe the DNA expert's testimony, is it sufficient to prove Oaks guilty of the murder beyond a reasonable doubt?*

Problem 16-8: On the Defensive

Robert Berry is charged with robbery. Jones testifies for the prosecution that Berry ran up behind him on the street, grabbed a box of blueberries out of his grocery bag, and ran off. Berry's defenses are that he is not guilty of robbery because (1) the taking of the blueberries did not involve the use of force or intimidation, and (2) he was legally insane at the time that he took the blueberries.

The judge instructs the jurors that Berry has the burden of proving that the taking of the blueberries did not involve the use of force or intimidation. Following Berry's failure to offer evidence of insanity, the judge also refuses to give the jury any instruction pertaining to insanity. *What is the propriety of the judge's actions?*

§ 16.05 Presumptions in Civil Cases (Rule 301)

Rule 301 creates a general rule for civil cases that presumptions shift the burden of producing evidence to rebut the presumption but do not shift the burden of persuasion,

Presumptions, or mandatory inferences, represent legislators' and judges' desire for specified types of circumstantial evidence to produce pre-determined conclusions, at least in the absence of contrary evidence. Every presumption consists of two parts. One part is the "basic" or "foundational" facts, which are the facts that activate a presumption. The second part is the "presumed fact," the mandatory inference that follows from proof of the basic facts.

The party seeking the benefit of a presumption has the burden of offering evidence sufficient to establish (by a preponderance of evidence) that the basic facts are true.[5]

For example, a common presumption is, "A letter correctly addressed and properly mailed is presumed to have been received in the ordinary course of mail." (This presumption has been generally adapted for and extended to electronic versions of

---

5. By contrast, as you will shortly see, the burden of proof with respect to presumed facts can shift from one party to the other.

"snail mail" such as emails.) The basic or foundational facts of this presumption are that: (1) a letter was correctly addressed, and (2) the letter was properly mailed. The presumed fact—the mandatory inference—is that the letter was received in the ordinary course of mail. To be entitled to the benefit of the presumption, the party seeking to prove that a letter was received must establish by a preponderance of evidence that the letter was correctly addressed and properly mailed.

Presumptions exist to produce trial outcomes that either further desirable social policies or like the mailed letter presumption simply reflect objective reality.[6] These goals may be in conflict. For example, a "social policy presumption" may provide that when the contents of a package that has been shipped by more than one common carrier are damaged when the package arrives at its final destination, the last carrier is presumed to have caused the damage. The presumption may not reflect everyday experience that last carriers are the most likely cause of damaged goods. Rather, the presumption helps those who receive damaged goods to fasten liability on a specific carrier, and leave it to the carriers to decide where the damage occurred.

A second common "social policy presumption" is, "A person not heard from in five years is presumed dead." (Seven years was the traditional common-law period of time needed to activate this presumption. Modern living in some states has thus produced not only a quicker pace of life, but apparently of presumed death as well.) This presumption furthers social policies favoring the marketability of property and allowing the relatives of long-absent people to move on with their lives. Does it in your opinion comport with likely objective reality?

"Common practice presumptions" generally exist to conserve trial time while fostering outcomes that are consistent with "what really happened." For example, the ubiquitous "mailed letter" presumption is a common practice presumption. It does not owe its existence to a social policy favoring the receipt of mail. Rather, the presumption recognizes the objective reality that mail almost always reaches addressees according to predictable schedules. The presumption seeks to ensure that unless a genuine dispute exists as to whether a letter was received, a judge or jury must conclude that it was.

While none of this may seem astonishing, rest assured that major intellectual wars have been fought on the battleground of presumptions. Everyone in the pantheon of Great Evidence Scholars, including such giants as Wigmore, Thayer, and Morgan, has weighed in with a position. All have agreed that when the evidence giving rise to a presumption is uncontested, the presumed fact must be accepted. All have also agreed that evidentiary presumptions are "rebuttable." That is, the party on the wrong end of a presumption should normally have an opportunity to offer evidence contesting both the basic and presumed facts. The bickering has involved how much "staying power" presumptions should have when parties contest them.

---

6. At least, desirable or realistic in the eyes of presumptions' creators.

For example, return to the common practice presumption, "A letter correctly addressed and properly mailed is presumed to have been received in the ordinary course of mail." Assume that in a breach of contract case, Joe testifies, "I sent a written offer to Frank in a correctly addressed and properly mailed envelope." Frank then contests the presumption's mandatory inference by testifying, "I never received Joe's offer." At this point, what role should the "mailed letter" presumption play in the decisional process? The three primary competing positions have been these:

One strong view of presumptions. A presumption is itself evidence that judges and juries can consider when deciding whether to draw the inference that a presumption prescribes. A judge in our hypothetical case might instruct jurors along these lines: "In deciding whether Frank received Joe's offer, you may consider as evidence a presumption that a letter that is properly addressed and mailed was received by the addressee." However, the policy that a presumption is evidence never gained much traction and was abandoned long ago.

A second strong view of presumptions. Presumptions reflect important values of our system of justice, and should continue to influence outcomes even if parties contest a presumed fact. The best way to achieve this goal is to shift the burden of persuasion to the contesting party. Under this view, the judge in our hypothetical case might instruct jurors along these lines: "You are to conclude that Frank received Joe's offer, unless Frank convinces you by a preponderance of the evidence (or that it is "more likely than not") that he didn't receive it."

A weak view of presumptions. Presumptions are simply convenient procedural devices, mandating outcomes only in the absence of evidence to the contrary. Once contested, they should disappear. Advocates for this position have used colorful phrases (by evidence scholar standards, anyway), analogizing presumptions to "bursting bubbles" and "bats of the law, flitting in the twilight but disappearing in the sunshine of actual facts."[7] Under this view, Frank's testimony that he never received Joe's offer eliminates the presumption. Stated differently, the presumption has "done its work" by forcing the burdened party (Frank) to produce evidence countering the presumed fact on pain of the jury being told that they must find that the presumed fact has been proved. Having done its work, the presumption vanishes and all that remains is a permissive inference. Thus, the judge in our hypothetical case would say nothing to the jurors about whether Frank received Joe's letter. The jurors' everyday experiences may lead them to infer that Frank received Joe's offer. However, once Frank denies receiving the letter, the fact that Joe was at one time sailing with the wind of a presumption at his back is irrelevant under this view.[8]

---

7. The "bats" analogy is from *Mackowick v. Kansas City, St. Joseph & Council Bluffs R.R. Co.*, 196 Mo. 550, 94 S.W. 256, 262 (1906).

8. When a presumption is of the "bursting bubble" type, some jurisdictions authorize judges to pay homage to the remnants of a vanished presumption by informing jurors that they "can but don't have to" draw the inference that a presumption identifies. Thus, in the hypothetical in the text, a judge might instruct jurors that they "can but do not have to" conclude that Frank received

Aware of these and other possible approaches, the drafters of Rule 301 opted for the weak view of presumptions identified above (though they unfortunately left out the colorful language about bubbles and bats). Under Rule 301, a presumption "imposes on the party against whom it is directed the burden of going forward with evidence to rebut or meet the presumption, but does not shift to such party the burden of proof in the sense of the risk of non-persuasion, which remains throughout the trial upon the party on whom it was originally cast."

Applying Rule 301's language to the example involving Joe's testimony that he mailed an offer to Frank yields the following results:

- "A presumption imposes on the party against whom it is directed . . ." Frank is the party against whom the presumption is directed; because of the presumption, he will be found to have received the offer unless he contests Joe's testimony.

- "The burden of going forward with evidence to rebut or meet the presumption . . ." Frank went forward with evidence to rebut the presumed fact by testifying that he didn't get Joe's letter. Because he has satisfied the burden that Rule 301 imposed on him, it has burst and has no further force or effect.

- "But does not shift to such party the burden of proof in the sense of the risk of non-persuasion . . ." With the presumption gone, Joe retains the burden of persuading the judge or jury that Frank received the letter.

Even the weaker form of presumption provided for by Rule 301 can survive an evidentiary challenge if a burdened party's evidence contests only the basic fact. In such a situation, the response fails to "rebut or meet the presumption." As a result, the only issue for the judge or jury to decide is which party's version of the basic fact is accurate. If the judge or jury concludes that the basic fact exists, it must find the presumed fact. In other words, under Rule 301 the party opposing a presumption has to contest the *presumed* fact to cause the presumption to disappear. Consider the possibilities in the context of Joe's testimony that he mailed an offer to Frank.

- Frank contests only the basic facts. For example, assume that following Joe's testimony Frank calls Chet as a witness to testify, "I was with Joe when he mailed the offer to Frank. Just as Joe was putting the envelope in the mail slot, I noticed that he had put the wrong zip code on it." If this is the only evidence that Frank offers to refute Joe's testimony, a judge would instruct a jury, "If you find that Joe properly mailed a correctly addressed offer to Frank, you are to find that Frank received the offer."[9] (Reminder: the party seeking the benefit of a presumption—Joe, in this example—has the burden of persuasion with regard to the basic facts.)

Joe's letter. Of course, this is simply "permissive inference" language, and the same is true for any other item of circumstantial evidence.

  9. In a bench trial, the judge would of course adhere to the same principles.

- Frank contests only the presumed fact that he received the letter. Frank can do so by testifying, "I never received a letter from Joe." Frank has now satisfied the burden of going forward with evidence to "rebut or meet the presumed fact." The presumption disappears, and the judge or jury will decide whether Frank received Joe's letter without reference to a presumption.

- Frank contests both the basic and presumed facts. That is, Frank calls Chet to testify that the zip code was incorrect, and Frank testifies that he never received Joe's letter. Again, Frank has satisfied the burden of going forward so the presumption disappears.

Three-Step Civil Presumptions Matrix

Asking yourself the three questions below can help you analyze the effect of presumptions. (BPE = Burden of Producing Evidence; BP = Burden of Proof)

1. Does the language of a statute or court opinion create a presumption?

2. Does the presumption affect the BPE or the BP? Alternatively, is a person a BFP? (Sorry, this last question pertains to the Contracts course. You don't have to ask yourself this question in Evidence.)

3. Does the evidence offered by the party seeking the benefit of the presumption pertain to the basic fact or to the presumed fact? Example: Jones's spouse testifies, "Jones went to the market six years ago and I've neither seen nor heard from Jones since." This testimony pertains to the basic fact of the presumption, "A person who has not been seen or heard from for five years is presumed dead." (Sad fact: poor Jones.)

State laws on presumptions may differ from Rule 301. In California, for example, the consequences of presumptions differ depending on whether a presumption is of the "social policy" or the "common practice" variety. In California, social policy presumptions shift the burden of proof to the burdened party.[10] Common practice presumptions, like presumptions under Rule 301, reflect the weak view of presumptions and burst when contested.[11] Thus, if the California scheme is a bit more complicated than Rule 301, at least California honors the contributions of almost every evidence scholar who ever wrote about presumptions.

However, federal presumption practices are closer to California's than the language of Rule 301 suggests. Federal court judges often use presumptions to shift burdens of proof. A primary reason for this is that the Federal Rules of Evidence do not themselves create any presumptions. (As was true for rules allocating burdens of proof, if you've been flipping through the Rules looking for a list of presumptions, you can stop.) And Rule 301 provides that presumptions do not shift the burden of proof unless "otherwise provided for by Act of Congress." In fact, many

---

10. See Cal. Evid. Code § 605.
11. See Cal. Evid. Code § 603.

presumptions, perhaps numbering into the hundreds, are scattered through federal statutes. For example:

- 30 U.S.C. § 921: It is presumed that a person who's worked in a coal mine for at least 10 years and developed black lung disease developed the disease from working in the mine.

- 35 U.S.C. § 282: A patent is presumed to be valid.

- 18 U.S.C. § 343: A person with a blood alcohol content in excess of .10 is presumed to be under the influence of alcohol.

When construing such statutes, judges often decide that presumptions are entitled to greater weight than that established by Rule 301. As the U.S. Supreme Court stated in *Goldman Sachs Group v. Arkansas Teacher Retirement System* (594 U.S. ___ 2021), "Rule 301 in no way restricts the authority of a court to change the customary burdens of persuasion pursuant to a federal statute . . . and we have at times exercised that authority to reassign the burden of persuasion to the defendant upon a prima facie showing by the plaintiff." And in accord with the California scheme, federal judges generally treat a presumption as shifting the burden of persuasion when they believe that its purpose is to further social policies rather than simply to reflect common practices.

While statutes are the most common sources of presumptions, judges may also create presumptions through the common-law appellate court process. For example, the case of *Kaminsky v. Hertz Corp.*,[12] concerned a motorist who was hurt when a sheet of ice came loose from a truck bearing a Hertz logo that was traveling in front of the motorist and smashed into the windshield of the motorist's car. The motorist sued Hertz for negligence; Hertz denied that it owned the truck. The motorist's only proof that the truck was owned by Hertz was that it bore the Hertz logo. The court created a presumption that commercial logos on objects establish ownership. The presumption meant that Hertz had to produce evidence of non-ownership or lose on that issue.

Practice Tip: The Sometimes Confusing Terminology of Presumptions

Legislators and judges aren't always thoughtful enough to use the word "presumption" when they create these outcome-shaping devices. *Prima facie evidence* is an alternative term that may signal the presence of a presumption. For example, assume that a judicial opinion states that "performing open heart surgery without first anesthetizing the patient is prima facie evidence of negligence." You may take this to mean that the evidence creates a presumption of medical malpractice that shifts either the burden of producing evidence of non-negligence or the burden of proof of non-negligence to the doctor. On the other hand, judicial opinions may use the term "presumption" in a misleading way. For example, an opinion may

---

12. 94 Mich. App. 356, 288 N.W.2d 426 (1979).

refer to "a permissive presumption that the person wearing a white coat and a stethoscope was a doctor." The term "permissive presumption" is an oxymoron. You may take the opinion to mean merely that the judge or jury could reasonably *infer* that the person was a doctor, not that a formal burden-shifting presumption exists. Finally, a statute or judge may use the term "presumption" as meaning a *conclusive* or *mandatory* presumption rather than a *rebuttable* (or "evidentiary") presumption. While few conclusive presumptions exist, they are substantive principles clothed in the language of presumption. For example, a common substantive rule of criminal law states, "A child under the age of seven is conclusively presumed to be incapable of committing a crime." This is a conclusive and not an evidentiary presumption, because its presumed fact is irrebuttable. *Example:* In January 2023, a six-year-old student attending Richneck Elementary School in Virginia shot and wounded his teacher Abby Zwerner during class. The student could not be charged with a crime.

Under Rule 302, when federal judges apply a state's substantive laws (as is common when federal court jurisdiction is based on diversity of citizenship), they also apply the state's rules with regard to the effect of presumptions governing facts of consequence. Thus, if under a state's evidence rules the effect of a presumption governing a fact of consequence is to shift the burden of persuasion, a federal judge would give that presumption the same effect in a diversity case.

Example 1

Following an insured's death, a Maryland resident who is the beneficiary of a life insurance policy sues the Illinois insurance company that issued the policy. The insurance company claims that the insured committed suicide a few weeks after the policy was taken out, voiding the policy. Suit is in Illinois federal court based on diversity, but Illinois state law governs the case. The federal judge would be bound by an Illinois state law providing that a "presumption against suicide" is a burden-shifting presumption.

Example 2

Assume that the following presumption affects the burden of producing evidence: "People are presumed to be the owners of the things they possess." Party A, locked in a property battle with ex-spouse Party B, testifies in support of the basic fact, "The diamond ring that I claim is mine was in my safe deposit box."

1. Party B offers no evidence at all. Party A's testimony shifted the burden of producing evidence countering the presumed fact to Party B, who didn't meet the burden. Result: If Party A's testimony is believed, Party A has conclusively proved ownership of the ring. In a jury trial, the judge would instruct a jury, "If Party A convinces you by a preponderance of the

evidence that the ring was in Party A's safe deposit box, you are to find that Party A owns the ring."

2. Party B contests the basic fact only, calling a friend to testify, "Months ago, A and B gave the diamond ring to me for safe-keeping." Party A's testimony shifted the burden of producing evidence countering the presumed fact to Party B, who didn't meet the burden. Result: If Party A's testimony is believed, Party A has conclusively proved ownership of the ring. In a jury trial, the judge would instruct a jury, "If Party A convinces you by a preponderance of the evidence that the ring was in Party A's safe deposit box, you are to find that Party A owns the ring."[13]

3. Party B contests the presumed fact by testifying, "The diamond ring is mine; Party A gave it to me as a present." Whether or not Party B contests the basic fact, Party B has met the burden of producing evidence countering the presumed fact. Result: The presumption vanishes. Gone. Nada. Pffft. Nichts. Arrivederci. In a bench trial, the judge will decide which party owns the ring apart from any presumption. In a jury trial, the judge would not refer to the presumption.[14]

Example 3

Assume that the following presumption affects the burden of proof: "A person who has not been seen or heard from for five years is presumed dead." Party A, seeking to prove that his spouse Amelia Cooper is deceased, offers evidence from various family members and friends that they have neither heard from nor seen Amelia in more than five years.

1. Party B offers no evidence at all. Party A's evidence shifted the burden of producing evidence countering the presumed fact to Party B, who didn't meet the burden. Result: A judge who believes Party A's evidence must conclude that Amelia Cooper is dead. In a jury trial, the judge would instruct a jury, "If Party A convinces you by a preponderance of the evidence that Amelia Cooper has not been heard from in five years, you are to find that Amelia Cooper is dead."

2. Party B contests the basic fact only, calling a friend of Amelia to testify, "Amelia phoned me about three years ago. We had a nice chat." Party A's testimony shifted the burden of producing evidence countering the presumed fact to Party B, who didn't meet the burden. However, Party B did

---

13. If Party A fails to establish the presumption's basic facts by a preponderance of evidence, a judge or jury would simply decide which party owns the ring in the absence of any presumption.

14. When bubbles burst, some jurisdictions give judges the discretion to honor their former existence by telling jurors that they "may but are under no obligation to infer from Party A's testimony that the ring belongs to Party A." Of course, this is the language of a permissive inference, not a presumption.

contest the basic fact. Result: If Party A's testimony is believed, Party A has conclusively proved that Amelia is dead. In a jury trial, the judge would instruct a jury, "If Party A convinces you by a preponderance of the evidence that Amelia Cooper has not been heard from for over five years, you are to find that she is dead."

3. Party B contests the presumed fact only, calling a witness to testify, "My name is Amelia Cooper." Party A's testimony shifted the burden of producing evidence countering the presumed fact to Party B, who has met the burden. However, Party B did not contest the basic fact. Result: The burden of proof switches to Party B to convince the judge or jury that the presumed fact is not true. In a jury trial, the judge would instruct a jury, "You are to find that Amelia Cooper is dead, unless Party B convinces you by a preponderance of the evidence that she is alive."[15]

4. Party B contests both the basic fact and the presumed fact. Party B calls a friend of Amelia to testify, "Amelia phoned me about three years ago. We had a nice chat." Party B also calls a witness to testify, "My name is Amelia Cooper." Result: If Party A convinces the judge or jury that Amelia has been missing for more than five years, the burden of proving that Amelia is alive shifts to Party B. In a jury trial, the judge would instruct the jury, "If Party A convinces you by a preponderance of evidence that Amelia Cooper has not been heard from for more than five years, you are to find that she is dead unless Party B convinces you by a preponderance of the evidence that she is alive."

If you examine the language of the instructions in Examples 2 and 3, you will see that the word "presumption" appears nowhere in them. For example, the instruction in No. 4 immediately above does NOT say, "If Party A convinces you by a preponderance of evidence that Amelia Cooper has not been heard from for more than five years, you are to PRESUME that she is dead unless Party B convinces you by a preponderance of the evidence that she is alive." Judges generally believe that the term "presumption" carries too much weight and may confuse and mislead jurors, and so avoid using it when instructing jurors.

Problem 16-9: Party Smarty

Enjoying a veggie dip at a party, Law Professor Evy Denss is sought out by an anguished friend who tells her the following:

"I'm the plaintiff in a case that goes to trial next week. The other side is claiming that I received an important letter that I never got. A few minutes

---

15. As in this and the other examples in this chapter, an instruction can refer to the *effect* of a presumption without using the term "presumption" itself. Rules in many jurisdictions forbid use of the term "presumption" for the reason that the term may unfairly influence jurors.

ago one of your law students told me something about a presumption that I got the letter. I'm really upset — what can I do about the presumption?"

Evy replies, "Don't worry. Your lawyer will be able to eliminate that nasty old presumption with just one simple question."

What is that question?

Problem 16-10: Pick Your Own

Appellate court judges sometimes create new presumptions to reflect what they consider to be social policies or everyday truths not reflected in existing presumptions. For example, in a case involving Jones's alleged legal malpractice, a judge may decide to create a presumption that "A lawyer who has taken the course in Evidence is presumed to understand the declarations against interest exception to the hearsay rule." (Whether such a presumption would reflect social policy or common practice we leave to you!) *With that in mind, create a presumption that you might apply in an appropriate case concerning one of the following topics and state "for the record" whether you think that it reflects social policy or common practice:*

1. Law School

2. The Internet

3. Domestic Relations

4. Electronic Mail

5. Your Favorite Pet Peeve

Problem 16-11: Make-Up Case

Distinguish the basic facts from the presumed facts in the following presumptions, and develop a factual scenario that might give rise to the presumption:

1. "An obligation delivered up to the debtor is presumed to have been paid." (Cal. Evid. Code § 633)

2. "An employee who is involved in an accident while driving a vehicle owned by his or her employer is presumed to have been acting within the scope of employment."

3. "When an injury or accident occurs which ordinarily does not occur in the absence of negligence, which was caused by an agency or instrumentality in the defendant's exclusive control and was not due to any voluntary action or contribution on the part of the plaintiff, the injury or accident is presumed to have been caused by the defendant's negligence."

Problem 16-12: The Classifieds

Laws that create presumptions typically neglect to classify them as either a bursting-bubble presumption or one shifting the burden of persuasion. Judges may then have to decide into which category to place a presumption. *Make an argument as to how a judge should classify the following presumptions using the everyday experience/policy-based dichotomy described above.*

1. "A person who has worked in a coal mine for at least 10 years and develops black lung disease is presumed to have developed the disease from working in the mine."

2. "The driver of a car is presumed to be driving it with the owner's permission."

3. "A transaction between a trustee and a beneficiary by which the trustee gains an advantage is presumed to be the product of undue influence."

4. "If a will is shown to have been in the possession of a competent decedent prior to the decedent's death and cannot be found after death, it is presumed that the decedent revoked the will."

5. "A violent death caused by external means is presumed to have been the result of accident rather than suicide."

6. "A transfer of property without consideration made within three years of a person's death is presumed to have been made in contemplation of death." (A gift made in contemplation of death may be included in a taxpayer's estate, which could have estate tax consequences.)

7. "When goods are damaged during transit provided by more than one carrier, it is presumed that the last carrier caused the damage."

Problem 16-13: Donna For

Bella sues Donna to recover for personal injuries resulting from an automobile accident; trial is to a jury. Bella testifies that, "I had slowed down for a pedestrian when Donna's car rear-ended mine." A judicially created presumption in the jurisdiction where the trial takes place is that the driver of a car that rear-ends another car is presumed to have been negligent. Donna presents no evidence in her own behalf. In these circumstances, which of the following statements is correct?

1. If the jurors believe Bella's testimony that Donna's car rear-ended Bella's, they must conclude that Donna was negligent.

2. Bella has satisfied the burden of producing evidence of Donna's negligence, and it's up to the jury to decide whether Bella has carried the burden of persuasion on the issue of Donna's negligence.

3. The jury must conclude that Donna was negligent only if the presumption is one that shifts the burden of persuasion.

4. Bella has to offer evidence that the collision was the result of Donna's negligence in order to satisfy her burden of producing evidence.

5. The judge must take the case from the jury and rule that as a matter of law that Donna was negligent.

Problem 16-14: Basic Training

Same case as previous problem. As before, Donna presents no evidence as to her own driving. However, after Bella testified that Donna's car ran into hers, Donna's attorney cross-examined Bella as follows:

DEFENDANT'S ATTORNEY: Bella, up until the time of the collision you weren't aware that a car was behind yours, correct?

A: That's true.

DEFENDANT'S ATTORNEY: And after the collision, the driver of the car that hit yours drove off without stopping, correct?

A: Yes.

DEFENDANT'S ATTORNEY: So you can't be sure that my client, Donna, was driving the car the rear-ended you, right?

A: No. I know the driver was a woman. Also, I saw the car go by me, and the make and model match Donna's car. Also, I got a quick look at the license plate and the first two letters match Donna's license plate number.

DEFENDANT'S ATTORNEY: But as you've also admitted, the sun was directly in your eyes at the time of the collision, which made it more difficult for you to see, right?

A: Yes.

In the light of Bella's direct and cross-examination, which of the following statements is correct?

1. The judge must take the case from the jury and rule that as a matter of law Donna was negligent.

2. If the presumption is a bursting-bubble presumption, it has vanished as a result of Donna's cross-examination and the jury will decide the issue of Donna's negligence without regard to a presumption.

3. The judge should instruct the jury that if Bella proves by a preponderance of the evidence that Donna was driving the car that collided with Bella's, it must find that Donna was negligent.

4. If the presumption is one that shifts the burden of persuasion, the judge should instruct the jury that Donna has the burden of persuasion on the issues of whether she was driving the car that collided with Bella's car and whether she was negligent.

Problem 16-15: Donna Speaks

Same case as previous problem, except assume that the presumption is one affecting the burden of producing evidence. Donna's attorney does not cross-examine Bella. Instead, Donna testifies on her own behalf as follows:

DEFENDANT'S ATTORNEY: Donna, were you driving your car on the afternoon that Bella was rear-ended?

A: I was.

DEFENDANT'S ATTORNEY: And did your cars come into contact?

A: Yes. I was completely stopped for a red light a couple of feet behind Bella's car. Then a pick-up truck hit me from the rear so hard that it pushed my car into Bella's.

DEFENDANT'S ATTORNEY: Did you have any chance to avoid being hit by the pick-up truck?

A: None whatsoever. I never saw or heard it coming, and didn't know what happened until after I was hit.

DEFENDANT'S ATTORNEY: No further questions.

JUDGE: Plaintiff's counsel, any cross-examination?

PLAINTIFF'S ATTORNEY: Thank you, just one question. Donna, you were convicted of perjury last year, correct?

A: That's true.

PLAINTIFF'S ATTORNEY: That's all, Your Honor.

True or False: On this state of the record, the judge should instruct the jury that if they believe that Donna's car rear-ended Bella's, the jury must find that Donna was negligent.

Problem 16-16: Dueling Wills

Real estate tycoon Armand Giddy dies, leaving an estate of $3 billion. Two wills are found in his desk drawer. Will A is dated one year earlier than Will B. Will A leaves Giddy's entire estate to the Society for the Development of Marshmallows That Don't Melt in Hot Chocolate. Will B states that it revokes Will A and leaves Giddy's entire estate to family members. However, Will B also has a large red "X" drawn across the first page. The Society claims that Will A is valid; Giddy's family members file suit to establish the validity of Will B. A presumption exists, "A will that is made but mutilated is presumed revoked."

As the attorney for the Society, what evidence or arguments might you offer in order to get the benefit of this presumption?

As the attorney for Giddy's family members, you are about to begin factual investigation. *Identify evidence that you will look for to rebut the presumption. In addition, what difference does it make whether the presumption is a bursting-bubble presumption or one that shifts the burden of persuasion?*

Problem 16-17: A Permissive Inference

A medical malpractice action is underway in federal court based on diversity of citizenship. The plaintiff's prima facie case is sufficient to give rise to the presumption of *res ipsa loquitur*, which state law regards as a presumption affecting the burden of producing evidence. Assume that the defendant's evidence has contested the presumed fact that the plaintiff's injury was the result of the defendant's negligence. Can the judge instruct the jury they may draw an inference of negligence from the plaintiff's evidence, but the plaintiff has the burden of proving that it is more probable than not that the injury was caused by the defendant's negligence?

Problem 16-18: A Night at the Opera

Lem Ozine has sued Val's Parking Service for damage to his car; trial is to a jury. A presumption states, "Goods damaged or lost while in a bailee's possession are presumed to have been damaged or lost as a result of the bailee's negligence." The presumption has been construed as one shifting the burden of proof.

Lem testifies that he parked his brand new Megamobile with Val's Parking Service when he went to opening night at the opera. He offers into evidence a "Val's Claim Check" to substantiate his claim. He further testifies that when the car was brought to him after the opera concluded five long hours later, dents and scratches were all over it. Lem offers into evidence a photo of the car's appearance to substantiate this claim. He further testifies that none of this damage was present when he dropped the car off with Val's before the opera.

Val testifies and denies that Lem parked his car with her parking service. She knows that because she and her employees always stamp a distinctive "V" on a claim check before they give it to a customer, and the one offered into evidence by Lem doesn't have a "V" on it. Val further testifies that Lem could easily have picked up the claim check he offered into evidence without anyone noticing, as they are stacked on a table and it was a very busy night. Finally, Val calls John to testify that he is Lem's work colleague, and that in a conversation a week before opera opening night, Lem complained to John that "some vandals ruined my new Megamobile."

On rebuttal, Lem denies making the statement to John, and testifies that John is angry at him because Lem and not John got an important promotion.

Assume that trial is to the jury. *Based on the information set forth above, should the judge instruct the jury with respect to the presumption? If so, prepare the instruction that the judge should give.*

Problem 16-19: Dueling Presumptions

When Bobby is 10 years old, his mother Susan brings a paternity action against Phil seeking to prove that Phil is Bobby's father and asking for child support from Phil. The judge orders Phil to take a blood test. The results of the blood test show a very strong likelihood of at least 98 percent that Phil is Bobby's father, and give rise to a presumption of paternity that shifts to Phil the burden of proving that he is not Bobby's father. This presumption is based on the belief that blood test results are highly reliable and determine paternity with a high degree of certainty.

Phil offers evidence that at the time Bobby was conceived, Susan was lawfully married to and cohabiting with Jonah. This evidence gives rise to a presumption that Jonah is the father, a presumption that would shift the burden of proof to Jonah to prove that he is not Bobby's father. This presumption is based on a desire to legitimize children and provide them with a source of financial support.

Given these conflicting presumptions, should Susan have the burden of proving that Phil is the father, or should Phil have the burden of proving that he is not? What role should the presumptions play in the outcome of this case?

§ 16.06 Presumptions in Criminal Cases

Like civil statutes, criminal laws sometimes create presumptions. However, presumptions cannot operate against criminal defendants in the same way that they do against civil parties. To see why, assume that one element of a statute making it a crime to "receive stolen goods" is that the defendant acquired the goods with actual or constructive knowledge that they were stolen. The statute further provides that when a dealer in secondhand goods acquires stolen goods, "knowledge that the goods were stolen shall be presumed from evidence that the dealer acquired the goods in circumstances that should have caused the dealer to make a reasonable inquiry to determine whether the person from whom the goods were bought had legal title to them."

This statute would clearly be unconstitutional if it shifted the burden of proof to a defendant charged with violating this statute to prove lack of knowledge that secondhand goods were stolen. In criminal cases the government has to prove each and every element of a crime beyond a reasonable doubt. Criminal defendants may permissibly be assigned the burden of proof with respect to affirmative defenses, such as insanity. However, criminal defendants cannot be found guilty unless the government proves their guilt beyond a reasonable doubt. Thus, statutes cannot assign to criminal defendants the burden of disproving facts that constitute elements of crimes.

The statute would be similarly unconstitutional if it shifted the burden of producing evidence of lack of knowledge that secondhand goods were stolen to a defendant charged with violating this statute. Defendants in criminal cases have a Fifth Amendment right to remain silent in response to criminal charges. A presumption that required defendants to produce evidence on pain of having an element of a crime established as a matter of law would conflict with the right of silence.

The U.S. Supreme Court saved the many criminal statutes that purport to create presumptions from extinction by converting presumptions to permissive inferences in *County Court of Ulster v. Allen* (442 U.S. 140 (1979)). In that case, four occupants of a car (three adult males and one teenage female) were charged with possession of illegal weapons and drugs. The police found some of the contraband in the handbag of the 16-year-old female occupant; other items were in the trunk. All the occupants of the car were convicted with the aid of a statutory "presumption" that the presence of a firearm in a car is presumptive evidence of its illegal possession by all of the car's occupants. The U.S. Supreme Court upheld the convictions, ruling that the statute created only a "permissive statutory presumption" rather than a "mandatory presumption." The statute's presumption would have been "a far more troublesome evidentiary device" if it could "affect not only the strength of the 'no reasonable doubt' burden, but also the placement of that burden." This statute, however, created only a permissive presumption that "allows, but does not require, the trier of fact to infer the elemental fact from proof by the prosecutor of the basic one and which places no burden of any kind on the defendant." In other words, all that the "presumption" did was to inform the jurors that they could if they chose infer from the presence of the contraband in the car that all four of the car's occupants possessed it. Unlike the civil presumptions examined in § 16.05 above, which provide for mandatory inferences if uncontroverted, the Court's interpretation of the presumption in *Ulster County* as a permissive inference left the jurors free to reject the inference even if the defendants offered no evidence at all.

The *Ulster County* decision emphasized that to sustain a conviction, the inference identified by a "permissive statutory presumption" *must be rational when applied to the facts of a case.* A permissive statutory presumption would be improper "only if, under the facts of the case, there is no rational way the trier could make the connection permitted by the inference. For only in that situation is there any risk that an explanation of the permissible inference to a jury, or its use by a jury, has caused the presumptively rational fact finder to make an erroneous factual determination." Under the *Ulster County* facts, concluded the Court, the inference of possession by all occupants was entirely rational and sufficient to support the guilty verdict. None of the occupants were "hitchhikers or other casual passengers;" the guns partially in the girl's handbag were plainly visible to all occupants; and "a 16 year old girl in the company of three adult men . . . was the least likely of the four to be carrying one, let alone two, heavy handguns." Had the guns been locked in the trunk of the car, the inference of possession by all passengers would not have been rational. Thus, the permissive inference identified by a statutory presumption cannot support a guilty verdict when the prosecution's evidence is not strong enough to constitute guilt beyond a reasonable doubt without reference to the "presumption."

With these principles in mind, return to the presumption that a secondhand dealer's "knowledge that goods were stolen" is presumed from "evidence that the dealer acquired the goods in circumstances that should have caused the dealer to make a reasonable inquiry to determine whether the person from whom the goods were bought had legal title to them." Under the *Ulster County* reasoning, the statute's "presumption" would be valid only if (1) the judge instructed the jurors that they might, but did not have to, infer knowledge from a dealer's acquisition of goods in suspicious circumstances; and (2) the inference of knowledge was rational under the facts of the case.

Problem 16-20: Pet(ty) Offense

Al Falfa, a 12-year-old boy, is charged with criminal trespass. The owner of a pet store claims that a small group of boys who appeared to be between the ages of 11 and 13 ran into his shop, opened the cages of numerous dogs and cats, and ran out. The pet store owner's testimony with respect to Al was as follows:

PROSECUTOR: Did you see the defendant in the shop before the cages were opened?

A: I did. Moments before the other boys ran in, he was looking at various animals, including the birds and the fish.

PROSECUTOR: Was the defendant among the group of boys who you saw opening the cages?

A: I really couldn't say.

PROSECUTOR: Did the defendant run out along with the others?

A: No, he was laughing but he stayed in the store.

Assume that the criminal trespass statute provides, "Participation in a trespass by three or more people in a retail store shall be presumed from a person's presence in the store before and after the trespass takes place without making a purchase." Before the jurors began deliberating, the judge instructed them pursuant to the presumption that they "might, but were not required to, infer from the defendant's presence in the store before and after the attack that the defendant was acting as a lookout and was a participant in the trespass." *Is this instruction valid under the principles of the "Ulster County" case?*

Problem 16-21: Fire Escape

Penny Tenshery is charged with first degree murder. The prosecution contends that shortly before the killing, Penny had escaped from prison and was carrying a prison guard's gun. According to the prosecution, Penny came to the victim's house and demanded the victim's car keys. Penny shot and killed the victim when the victim started to slam the front door in Penny's face. Penny's defense is lack of intent to kill; Penny asserts that the gun fired accidentally when the door came into contact with it. *Which if any of the following jury instructions would be valid?*

1. "A person of sound mind is presumed to intend the acts that he or she performs."

2. "You may but are not required to infer from the fact that the defendant was in the process of escaping from prison at the time of the killing that the killing was intentional."

3. "All homicides are presumed intentional in the absence of evidence that would rebut the presumption. Thus, if the State has proved beyond a reasonable doubt

that a killing has occurred it is presumed that the killing was done intentionally, but the defendant may rebut this presumption either with direct or circumstantial evidence."

4. "The defendant is presumed innocent."

Assume that Penny was charged with first-degree murder under the following statute: "A killing that occurs in the course of escaping from prison is first-degree murder, unless the killing is the result of accident in which case the killing is murder in the second degree. The defendant shall have the burden of proving by clear and convincing evidence that a killing that occurred in the course of escaping from prison was the result of accident." The judge instructs the jurors in accordance with the statute that Penny has the burden of proof on the issue of whether the killing was accidental. *Is this a valid instruction?*

§ 16.07 Judicial Notice (Rule 201)

Rule 201 allows (and sometimes compels) judges to rule that adjudicative facts have been established. Subject to notice provisions and a party's right to contest the propriety of taking judicial notice, judges may judicially notice facts that are "generally known within the trial court's general jurisdiction" or facts that "can be accurately and readily determined from sources whose accuracy cannot reasonably be questioned."

Judicial notice is a shortcut by which parties can conclusively establish the accuracy of factual information while bypassing the usual proof process. For example, a judge supplied during a pretrial conference with reliable supporting information may take judicial notice that "The Florida Marlins won the baseball World Series for the second time in 2003." Once the judge judicially notices this fact, it need not be proved (and indeed cannot be proved) by witnesses or countered with conflicting evidence and is binding on the jury.

Like presumptions, judicial notice is both a shortcut to proof and an effort to further the rationality of trial outcomes. It is a shortcut to proof in that parties can establish the accuracy of factual information without having to call witnesses or otherwise go through the formal proof process. Judicial notice also furthers rationality by making information that is unquestionably accurate binding on judges and jurors.

Example 1

A judge sitting in Cook County (Chicago) could take judicial notice that "Michigan Avenue north of the Chicago River is a busy commercial thoroughfare." While this information might not be generally known throughout the country, it would certainly be generally known within the territorial jurisdiction of a judge sitting in Chicago.

Example 2

After referring to a smart phone's calendar, a judge could take judicial notice that "June 14 of last year was a Sunday." Few people would carry this information around in their heads, but it is readily established by reference to a reliable source. Similarly, a judge could rely on a physics textbook as a basis for taking judicial notice of the atomic number of krypton, if the judge ever cared to do so.

Rule 201 further provides as follows:

- If judicial notice is appropriate, a judge has the power to take judicial notice whether or not one of the parties asks the judge to do so.

- If judicial notice is appropriate, a judge *must* take judicial notice if requested by a party and supplied with the necessary supporting information.

- Whether a judge is about to take judicial notice on the judge's own motion or at the behest of a party, an adversary has a right to a hearing on the propriety of taking judicial notice.

- A judge may take judicial notice at any stage of a proceeding, even on appeal.

Example 3

A plaintiff suing for infringement of a trademark forgets to offer the legally necessary evidence that the trademark was registered with the federal government. The defendant fails to notice the omission until the case is on appeal, at which time the defendant asks the appellate court to dismiss the case. After the plaintiff provides the necessary documentation and the defendant has a chance to dispute it, the appellate court might take judicial notice that the trademark had been registered with the government.

- In civil jury trials, judges must instruct jurors to accept judicially noticed information as conclusive. In criminal jury trials, jurors are told that they "may but are not required to" accept judicially noticed information as conclusive.

Practice Tip: Stipulations and Requests for Admissions

Most of us love shortcuts so it is not surprising that lawyers have created shortcuts in addition to judicial notice. Parties may create non-contestable adjudicative facts by entering into stipulations before or during trial. For example, the parties to a defamation action may stipulate that an allegedly defamatory story about a plaintiff appeared in a journal's online edition on a specified date. Parties may also create non-contestable adjudicative facts by serving Requests for Admissions on adversaries during pretrial discovery.

Rule 201 governs only judicial notice of "adjudicative facts," but nowhere defines what constitutes an "adjudicative fact." This omission may unjustly unnerve you if you think that this is the sort of information you should have already known when you entered law school. You can perhaps best understand it to signify the case-specific factual information that constitutes parties' versions of "what happened." For instance, at trial you can elicit stories through a combination of oral testimony, documents, and judicially noticed facts. Thus, representing the plaintiff in an ordinary negligence case growing out of an automobile accident, two adjudicative facts in your story might consist of:

1. A witness' testimony that the defendant was driving at least 55 m.p.h. just prior to the accident; and

2. The judicially noticed adjudicative fact that it was raining at the time of the accident, as established by official Weather Bureau records.

The primary significance of Rule 201's adjudicative facts limitation is that it allows judges and jurors to make decisions based in part on factual information that is neither offered into evidence during the trial nor judicially noticed. Reference to such "outside the record" factual information occurs when judges and jurors use experience and common sense to make factual determinations. You might think of these bases of decision-making as "evaluative facts," because judges and jurors evaluate stories through the use of heuristics drawn from daily life. For example, a judge or juror might conclude that a defendant who was late for an appointment was speeding at the time of an accident, based in part on a heuristic that "people who are late for appointments often speed to get to the appointments as soon as possible." Information about the general behavior of people who are late to appointments will be neither offered into evidence during trial nor judicially noticed. Such information is the sort that we expect judges and jurors to "bring to the table." The information does not constitute an adjudicative fact, so judges and jurors can employ it because it is not subject to the strictures of Rule 201.

Judges, primarily appellate court judges, commonly also rely on "outside the record" information in the course of common law rule-making. Professor Kenneth Davis labeled such factual information "legislative facts," because like legislators considering new legislation, appellate court judges rely on generalizations drawn from everyday experience when making decisions. For example, when the U.S. Supreme Court in the famous case of *Miranda v. Arizona,* 384 U.S. 436 (1966), decided that statements resulting from police interrogations of prisoners were inadmissible at trial in the absence of "*Miranda* warnings," the Court relied in part on the fact, "the compulsion to speak in the isolated setting of the police station may well be greater than in courts." That fact was not drawn from evidence in the record. Rather, the fact reflected the majority justices' beliefs about the effect of arrest and confinement on arrestees. Judges commonly rely on such beliefs when making common-law decisions, and their ability to do so is not limited by Rule 201.

"Foreign law" is sometimes relevant to the outcome of a federal court case. For example, a federal court sitting in Florida might have to interpret a contract according to New York or German law. In such situations, the federal court judge has the power to determine and apply foreign law, whether contained in statutes or judicial opinions. Rule 201 does not govern the process, since laws are not adjudicative facts. For example, Federal Rule of Civil Procedure 44.1 provides in part that a "court, in determining foreign law, may consider any relevant material or source, including testimony, whether or not submitted by a party or admissible under the Federal Rules of Evidence. The court's determination shall be treated as a ruling on a question of law." This broad language allows a federal judge seeking foreign law to phone a knowledgeable friend in a foreign jurisdiction and obtain information as to the jurisdiction's law. Of course, all parties would be able to weigh in on the friend's information.

Problem 16-22: The Knowledgeable Judge

Personal injury case growing out of an automobile collision. When plaintiff's counsel asks the plaintiff to describe the intersection where the collision took place, the judge states, "I drive past that intersection every day. I take judicial notice that there was a four-way stop sign at that intersection at the time of the collision, and instruct the jury to accept that fact as conclusively established." *Has the judge properly taken judicial notice?*

After the plaintiff introduces evidence that the defendant was late for an important business meeting at the time of the collision, the judge states, "I take judicial notice that people who are late for important business meetings are likely to drive too fast, and instruct the jury to accept that fact as conclusively established." *Has the judge properly taken judicial notice?*

Problem 16-23: The Expert Judge

Cole Motose sues Dr. Frank Galvin, an anesthesiologist, for brain damage allegedly resulting from the doctor's use of an improper anesthetic during surgery. Cole claims that Dr. Galvin gave him the wrong anesthetic because Galvin misread the time of her last meal on the medical chart. The judge states, "I was an anesthesiologist before going to law school, and specialized in medical malpractice cases before going on the bench. It's hornbook medicine that the anesthetic administered by Dr. Galvin should not have been given to a patient who had eaten within an hour of surgery. I'll take judicial notice of that fact and instruct the jury to find that the anesthetic was improper if the jury concludes that Cole's medical chart accurately indicated that Cole had eaten within an hour of surgery." *Has the judge properly taken judicial notice?*

Problem 16-24: Consider the Source

Dustin Miojo is charged with a murder that took place on March 8 at 9:00 p.m., and testifies that he was at home watching "Cooking With Pearl Edna Gates" on Channel 5 at the time of the murder. To attack this alibi, the prosecutor wants the trial judge to take judicial notice that "Cooking With Pearl Edna Gates" was not showing on Channel 5 at the time of the murder. Indicate which if any of the following sources would provide adequate support for this request (more than one may be adequate):

1. A printout of the online version of the local area "TV Guide" for the week of the murder, indicating that *Barney Goes Undercover* was the program scheduled to be shown on Channel 5 at 9:00 p.m. on March 8.

2. The telephone number of Channel 5's program manager, who orally informs the judge that the cooking show did not begin airing on Channel 5 until March 15.

3. An affidavit of Pearl Edna Gates stating, "My cooking show did not begin airing in any market until March 15."

4. A story in the local newspaper for the date of March 15 downloaded off the paper's website, headlined "Pearl Edna Gates Cooking Show to Debut Tonight."

5. Testimony of a friend who accompanied Dustin's mother when she visited Dustin in jail that the mother fainted when Dustin told her that he'd been at home with her watching the *Pearl Edna Gates Cooking Show* at the time of the murder.

Problem 16-25: Source Spot

Same case as previous problem. In support of Dustin's alibi defense, Dustin's lawyer tries to discredit the identification by the prosecution's principal eyewitness. The defense lawyer's cross-examination emphasizes that Dustin and the eyewitness are of different ethnicities, and that the eyewitness feared being shot in the same incident. Defense counsel then furnishes the judge with the book *Eyewitness Identification* by Dr. Elizabeth Loftus, who the prosecutor stipulates is an authority in the field of eyewitness identification. Based on the results of experiments described in the book and the opinions of Dr. Loftus, defense counsel asks the judge to take judicial notice that the accuracy of identifications diminishes when people are of different ethnicities and the person making the identification is scared and nervous. *Should the judge accede to the defense counsel's request?*

Problem 16-26: Read My Clips

In a suit by City seeking to enjoin the holding of a rally by the Marching Tuba Players Asso. (MTPA), City furnishes the court with newspaper clippings reporting on recent MTPA rallies in other communities and asks the court to take judicial notice that the previous rallies have been extremely loud and disorganized and have led to violence. *Should the judge grant the request?*

Problem 16-27: Hear No Evil

In a child custody dispute, the son's father asks the judge to order that the son not be present while the parents testify. To support the request, which the mother opposes, the father asks the judge to take judicial notice that listening to each of the parents testify to the other's misdeeds would be harmful to the son.

1. Is the request for judicial notice proper?

2. Is the answer to the previous question different if the father furnishes the judge with a copy of *Child Development in a Nutshell* by Dr. Yung Sigmund, in which the author states that listening to parents accuse each other of misdeeds can cause irreparable damage to children's superegos?

3. Can the judge refuse to take judicial notice yet order that the child not be present during the parents' testimony on the ground that hearing their testimony might be harmful to the son?

4. To support his petition for custody of his son, the father cites an appellate court case decided in the same jurisdiction about 45 years earlier in which the court stated that in a child custody case, "the court takes judicial notice that all other things being equal it's better for a father to have custody of a son because as is generally known, they can then develop their mutual interests in such masculine activities as athletics, fishing, and working with mechanical devices." As the mother's attorney, what argument would you make in opposition to the father's request that the judge take judicial notice that it is generally in the best interests of a son to be in his father's custody?

Problem 16-28: *Power Play*

Wayne sues Katerina for intentionally injuring Wayne while they were playing in an adult league ice hockey game. Katerina asks the judge to take judicial notice and instruct the jurors that ice hockey is a rough physical contact sport.

1. Is Katerina's request proper?

2. If the request is proper, what supporting information, if any, would Katerina have to furnish to the judge?

Problem 16-29: *Attorney's Fees*

Anna Turney sues the *Local Gazette* for libel after the Gazette publishes an article stating that Turney was "the subject of numerous disciplinary complaints pending before the State Bar." Based on State Bar records furnished to the judge, the *Gazette* asks the judge to take judicial notice that six complaints against Turney for fee gouging are currently pending before the State Bar.

1. Is the *Gazette*'s request proper?

2. What is the propriety of these further requests for judicial notice by the *Gazette:*

   a. "Your Honor, we ask that you take judicial notice that six complaints constitute 'numerous complaints.'"

   b. "Your Honor, we ask that you take judicial notice that complaints for fee gouging constitute disciplinary complaints."

3. Assume that the *Gazette* article also stated, "a review of the complaints indicates that Turney routinely misleads clients as to the amount of fees they'll have to pay." The *Gazette* asks the judge to examine the complaints and take judicial notice that Turney misleads clients as to the amount of her fees. *Is the request proper? What if the article stated, "all of the complaints involve claims that Turney routinely misleads clients as to the amount of fees they'll have to pay," and the* Gazette *asks the judge to examine the complaints and take judicial notice that they involve claims about improper fees?*

4. Assume that the judge takes judicial notice that six complaints against Turney for fee gouging are currently pending before the State Bar. *May Turney then offer evidence that she was not the attorney named in those complaints?*

Problem 16-30: Fellin Down

Rex Fellin is charged with armed robbery and with being an ex-felon in possession of a firearm. Rex's defense to the armed robbery charge is mistaken identity; his defense to the possession of a firearm charge is that he knew nothing about the gun that the police found in his car at the time of his arrest and that the gun did not belong to him.

1. The prosecutor asks the judge to take judicial notice that Rex is an ex-felon and gives the judge a certified "Record of Judgment of Conviction" indicating that Rex had been convicted of armed robbery five years ago. *Can the judge take judicial notice as requested? If so, what instruction should the judge give the jury with respect to judicial notice?*

2. The prosecutor seeks to prove that Fellin committed both a previous armed robbery and the armed robbery for which he is now on trial by posing as a wedding guest, stealing the wedding presents at gunpoint and later writing thank you notes. Assume that such evidence would be admissible to prove identity as a "signature crime" under Rule 404 (b). The prosecutor asks the judge to take judicial notice that Fellin carried out the prior crime in this manner, and supports the request by offering a Certified Transcript of the sentencing hearing in Fellin's prior trial, during which the judge stated, "I find that Rex Fellin committed the crime by posing as a wedding guest, stealing the wedding presents at gunpoint and later writing thank you notes." *Is the prosecutor's request proper?*

3. Fellin is convicted of being an ex-felon in possession of a firearm, and appeals the conviction. The appellate court indicates its intention to reverse the conviction on the ground that the prosecutor's only evidence that Fellin was an ex-felon consisted of inadmissible hearsay. The prosecutor then submits to the appellate court a certified "Record of Judgment of Conviction" indicating that Rex had been convicted of armed robbery five years ago, and asks the appellate court to affirm the conviction by taking judicial notice that Fellin is an ex-felon. *Is the prosecutor's request proper?*

Problem 16-31: Pane and Simple

You are prosecuting Larry Burg for nighttime residential burglary. You claim that Larry broke into the burgled residence at midnight. Identification of Larry as the burglar rests in part on the results of fingerprint analysis, which according to the report of a police fingerprint analyst shows that fingerprints found on a windowsill of the burgled house are Larry's.

1. Proving that the burglary took place at night elevates the crime to a more serious felony. The next-door neighbor testifies, "It was midnight when I heard smashing glass and saw someone crawl through a broken window, and called the police." *Following this testimony, can the judge properly instruct the jurors, "If you conclude that a burglary took place at midnight, you are instructed to find that it took place at nighttime?"*

2. To establish the reliability of fingerprint analysis within the meaning of *Daubert* and FRE 702, can you properly ask the judge to take judicial notice of the general reliability of fingerprint analysis, or do you have to lay a foundation as to its reliability through expert testimony or by submitting relevant scientific studies to the judge?

3. You may properly offer into evidence a police fingerprint analyst's report indicating that the fingerprints found on a windowsill of the burgled house are Larry's by which of the following methods?

   a. Asking the judge to take judicial notice that the results of the fingerprint analysis are accurate.

   b. Calling the police fingerprint analyst as a witness to testify to how the analysis was performed and what results were obtained.

   c. Offering the report into evidence as a Public Record under Rule 803(8).

   d. All of the above.

Problem 16-32: Dicta

You are an Associate Justice of your state's Supreme Court (congratulations on your rapid ascent through the ranks). An 18-year-old male convicted of statutory rape, defined as "sexual intercourse with a female under the age of 16," has challenged the constitutionality of the statutory rape law on equal protection grounds because only males and not females can be convicted of statutory rape. Assume that the record from the courts below is silent as to the following statements. *Which could your opinion properly refer to either because you took judicial notice or because they constitute legislative facts not subject to judicial notice requirements? Which could you not properly refer to?*

1. "A recent study by the National Institute of Health found that more than half of the teenage girls who become pregnant fail to graduate from high school."

2. "Teenage females often seek the company of older males, and males often seek the company of younger females."

3. "The defendant accomplished the intercourse through subtle means of force and intimidation."

4. "Gender-neutral statutory rape laws are in force in 38 other states."

Problem 16-33: Transcript Analysis

Emma Lee is the beneficiary of a $1 million life insurance policy taken out by her late husband Phil three years before he died as the result of a self-inflicted gunshot wound. Emma claims that Phil shot himself accidentally in the course of cleaning his revolver, which under the terms of the policy obligates the life insurance company to pay double the face amount of the policy. The life insurance company claims that Phil committed suicide, which means that it only has to pay Emma the face value of the policy, which it has already done. Thus, Emma has filed this suit to recover the other $1 million that she believes the insurance company is obligated to pay. *Please answer the italicized questions embedded in the transcript below.*

PLAINTIFF'S ATTORNEY: Emma, do you recall what happened the day that your husband died?

A: I'll never forget it. We'd been watching TV at night, and were about to go upstairs to bed when he said that he'd be up in a minute, that he was going to the kitchen to clean his gun.

DEFENDANT'S ATTORNEY: Objection, move to strike what the husband said, hearsay.

JUDGE: *What ruling?*

PLAINTIFF'S ATTORNEY: And then what happened?

A: Well, I went upstairs and about five minutes later I heard a loud noise that sounded to me like a gunshot.

DEFENDANT'S ATTORNEY: Objection, move to strike, improper opinion, speculation.

JUDGE: Overruled. *Is this ruling correct?*

PLAINTIFF'S ATTORNEY: From the sound of the shot, could you tell what kind of gun it came from?

DEFENDANT'S ATTORNEY: *What objection, if any, might defense counsel make to this question?*

A: Yes, it came from a revolver.

PLAINTIFF'S ATTORNEY: What did you do then?

A: I screamed, "Oh my God, Phil has accidentally fired the gun!"

DEFENDANT'S ATTORNEY: Objection, hearsay.

PLAINTIFF'S ATTORNEY: The statement is admissible as an excited utterance.

JUDGE: *What ruling?*

PLAINTIFF'S ATTORNEY: Please continue.

A: I didn't hear Phil say anything in response, so I ran down the stairs and into the kitchen. I saw Phil sitting in a chair at the table with his head and the top part of his body slumped over onto the table, and I saw some blood on the table. It was awful.

PLAINTIFF'S ATTORNEY: Your Honor, it has been stipulated between the parties that Mr. Lee died of a gunshot wound to his left temple.

DEFENDANT'S ATTORNEY: That's correct, Your Honor. So stipulated.

JUDGE: Very well, I accept the stipulation. *Is this an appropriate matter for a stipulation?*

PLAINTIFF'S ATTORNEY: No further questions at this time.

DEFENDANT'S ATTORNEY: Just a couple of questions, Your Honor. Ms. Lee, from the date of your husband's death until the date you filed this lawsuit, you lost over half a million dollars in the stock market, correct?

A: That's true.

DEFENDANT'S ATTORNEY: And two days after your husband died, you told a neighbor that you didn't remember a thing about the events leading up to his death, correct?

A: That's true.

DEFENDANT'S ATTORNEY: No further questions.

PLAINTIFF'S ATTORNEY: No questions. Plaintiff rests.

DEFENDANT'S ATTORNEY: I move to dismiss. The plaintiff has the burden of producing evidence sufficient to establish a prima facie case that Mr. Lee's death was an accident. Here, the evidence is at least as consistent with suicide as it is with accident, and Ms. Lee's account of the events leading up to her husband's death was called seriously into question on cross-examination.

JUDGE: In ruling on that motion, I'll not consider the evidence elicited on cross-exam because I'm limited to deciding whether the plaintiff's evidence if believed is sufficient to establish a prima facie case. *Is this an accurate statement?*

JUDGE: Nevertheless, I conclude that the plaintiff's evidence, even were it not contradicted, is insufficient as a matter of law to support a finding that death was accidental, so I'll sustain the motion. *Is this ruling accurate?*

PLAINTIFF'S ATTORNEY: While I disagree with Your Honor's ruling, I am prepared to offer additional evidence, so do I have permission to reopen the plaintiff's case-in — chief? Thank you, Your Honor. Ms. Lee, what if anything did you and your husband talk about while you and he were watching TV on the night he died?

A: One thing he said was that his job as an accountant was getting boring and that middle-school teachers had much more satisfying lives.

DEFENDANT'S ATTORNEY: Objection and move to strike, hearsay.

JUDGE: Overruled. *Is this ruling correct?*

PLAINTIFF'S ATTORNEY: And did your husband seem depressed in the days prior to his death?

A: Not at all.

DEFENDANT'S ATTORNEY: Objection and move to strike, speculation, lack of foundation.

JUDGE: Overruled. *Is this ruling correct?*

PLAINTIFF'S ATTORNEY: Now, you've described seeing your husband slumped on the kitchen table after you heard the gunshot. What else did you notice about the table?

A: I saw a small pile of rags that Phil used to use for cleaning his gun and an open can of gun cleaning fluid.

PLAINTIFF'S ATTORNEY: I'd ask that the court take judicial notice that the presence of cleaning rags and cleaning fluid indicates that Mr. Lee was in the process of cleaning his gun rather than committing suicide when the gun fired. *Is this request proper?*

PLAINTIFF'S ATTORNEY: I'd also ask the court to take judicial notice of the rule in our jurisdiction that a violent death is presumed not to have been the result of suicide.

JUDGE: I will apply that rule to this case.

DEFENDANT'S ATTORNEY: Objection. Under Rule 201(e), I'm entitled to be heard as to the propriety of Your Honor's taking judicial notice.

JUDGE: The request is denied. Rule 201(e) is inapplicable in this situation. *Is this statement correct?*

PLAINTIFF'S ATTORNEY: Plaintiff rests.

DEFENDANT'S ATTORNEY: Renew the motion to dismiss for lack of a prima facie case.

JUDGE: That motion is denied; the plaintiff's evidence together with the presumption is sufficient to establish a prima facie case that Mr. Lee died as the result of an accidentally self-inflicted gunshot wound. *Is this ruling correct?*

PLAINTIFF'S ATTORNEY: Your Honor, it has never been determined in our jurisdiction whether the presumption is one affecting the burden of proof or the burden of producing evidence. Evidence rules in our jurisdiction give Your Honor the power to construe it as one or the other, and I ask that Your Honor take judicial notice that in our jurisdiction there exists a strong social policy disfavoring suicide and based on this social policy should construe the presumption as one affecting the burden of proof.

JUDGE: Based on the existence of a strong social policy against concluding that people have died as the result of suicide, I rule that the presumption is one that affects the burden of proof.

DEFENDANT'S ATTORNEY: Objection under Rule 201. The policy to which Your Honor refers is vague and neither generally known within this court's territorial jurisdiction nor capable of accurate and ready determination.

JUDGE: I'm not limited by Rule 201 in making this ruling, Counsel. *Is this statement correct?*

JUDGE: Based on my ruling that the presumption against suicide is one affecting the burden of proof, if the defendant fails to present evidence to rebut the presumed fact of non-suicide, I'll enter judgment as a matter of law in the plaintiff's favor. *Is this ruling correct?*

JUDGE: Also as a result of my ruling, I'll indicate for the record that if the defendant offers evidence from which the jury can rationally conclude that death occurred as the result of suicide, I'll instruct the jurors that the defendant has the burden of proving that Mr. Lee did not die of violent means and of proving that his death was the result of suicide. *Would this instruction be correct?*

§ 16.08 Multiple-Choice Review Problems

Review Problem 16-A

Suit for personal injuries growing out of an automobile accident. *Which if any of the following items of evidence could not be properly proved through the mechanism of judicial notice?*

1. That small children frequently play in the residential alleyway in which the collision occurred.

2. That the alleyway in which the collision occurred is located within the city limits of Phoenix, Arizona.

3. That at 5:00 p.m. on October 3, when the collision took place, the sun had not yet set.

4. That skid marks will be produced if the brakes are suddenly applied to a car going at least 40 m.p.h.

5. All of the above may be proper subjects for judicial notice.

Review Problem 16-B

Tom Paine sues Dr. Billie Burke for dental malpractice, alleging that Dr. Burke's negligence in extracting a dead tooth caused Paine to lose two additional teeth, one on either side of the extracted tooth. The jurisdiction in which the case is brought has a "*res ipsa loquitur*" presumption that negligence is presumed if, among other things, an injury is one that does not normally occur in the absence of negligence. (The other elements of the *res ipsa loquitur* presumption are not in dispute.) This presumption has been construed in accord with Rule 301, as one shifting the burden of producing evidence. During his case-in-chief, plaintiff Paine presents testimony from expert witness Dr. Don Dentin D.D.S. that Dr. Burke used improper extraction techniques, and that loss of additional teeth does not occur in the absence of negligence. The defense's case consists of testimony from expert witness Dr. Beth Moeller D.D.S. that "loss of surrounding teeth is a common side effect of dead tooth extractions, no matter how carefully they are performed." *As a result of the presumption and the testimony, the judge should:*

1. Ignore the presumption and instruct the jurors that the burden is on Paine to prove that Dr. Burke was negligent.

2. Instruct the jurors that if they conclude that loss of additional teeth does not occur in the absence of negligence, they must find that Dr. Burke was negligent unless they are convinced by a preponderance of the evidence that Dr. Burke was not negligent.

3. Instruct the jurors that if they conclude that loss of additional teeth does not occur in the absence of negligence, they must find that Dr. Burke was negligent.

4. Take judicial notice that loss of additional teeth is a common side effect of dead tooth extractions.

Review Problem 16-C

Alison Garvey is charged with uttering a bad check with intent to defraud. The prosecution offers evidence that Garvey paid by check for a variety of small electronic items at Sears. The check was in the amount of $83, and was returned unpaid, marked "not sufficient funds." The law under which Garvey is prosecuted provides that "intent to defraud shall be presumed from the utterance of a check in the amount of $50 or more when the maker of the check does not have sufficient funds in the account on which the check is drawn to cover the full amount of the check." *Based on the evidence and the presumption, the judge should:*

1. Instruct the jurors that Garvey is presumed to have uttered the check with the intent to defraud.

2. Instruct the jurors that the burden of proof is on Garvey to raise a reasonable doubt as to whether she uttered the check with intent to defraud.

3. Instruct the jurors that they may infer intent to defraud from the utterance of the bad check if they choose to do so.

4. Sustain Garvey's motion for judgment of acquittal if the prosecution is unable to offer additional evidence of Garvey's guilt.

Review Problem 16-D

A group of parents sues a school district in an effort to obtain a court order requiring the district to give children from lower-income areas a fair chance to gain entry into top colleges by offering additional Advanced Placement courses in inner-city high schools. *Which, if any, of the following trial court conclusions must have been either testified to at trial or have been properly judicially noticed?*

1. "Attending a top university is an important way of making connections that can open doors in later life."

2. "The competition to get into the country's top colleges and universities is fierce."

3. "Students admitted last year into a group of 25 universities typically ranked as among the top universities in the country took an average of nine Advanced Placement courses."

4. "A college education is as important for the maturation process that it stimulates as for the knowledge and skills that students obtain."

5. All of these conclusions must have been either testified to at trial or have been properly judicially noticed.

§ 16.09 Case Library

County Court of Ulster v. Allen

U.S. Supreme Court
442 U.S. 140 (1979)

Goldman Sachs Group v. Arkansas Teacher Retirement System

U.S. Supreme Court
594 U.S. ___ (2021)

Chapter 17

Privileges

§ 17.01 Chapter Checklist

1. Why do federal courts generally use federal common law to determine the privileges that apply?

2. What is the applicable privilege law in federal courts, the federal common law or the pertinent state law?

3. Is information privileged because it is a confidential communication associated with a special relationship, otherwise based on an important public policy or protected from disclosure by the Constitution?

4. If information is potentially privileged, has the privilege been expressly or impliedly waived?

5. If information is privileged, is there an exception that requires disclosure by the professional who received the information because of a competing public policy?

6. What do *Upjohn v. United States*, 449 U.S. 383, 101 S. Ct. 677, 66 L. Ed. 2d 584 (1981), *Nix v. Whiteside*, 475 U.S. 157, 106 S. Ct. 988, 89 L. Ed. 2d 123 (1986), and *Jaffee v. Redmond*, 518 U.S. 1, 116 S. Ct. 1923, 135 L. Ed. 2d 337 (1996), add to the body and scope of privilege law? These cases are referenced in the Case Library at the end of the chapter.

§ 17.02 Relevant Federal Rules of Evidence and Proposed (but Rejected) Rules

Rule 501. Privilege in General

The common law — as interpreted by United States courts in the light of reason and experience — governs a claim of privilege unless any of the following provides otherwise:

- the United States Constitution;

- a federal statute; or

- rules prescribed by the Supreme Court.

But in a civil case, state law governs privilege regarding a claim or defense for which state law supplies the rule of decision.

Rule 502. Attorney-Client Privilege and Work Product; Limitations on Waiver

The following provisions apply, in the circumstances set out, to disclosure of a communication or information covered by the attorney-client privilege or work-product protection.

(a) Disclosure Made in a Federal Proceeding or to a Federal Office or Agency; Scope of a Waiver. When the disclosure is made in a federal proceeding or to a federal office or agency and waives the attorney-client privilege or work-product protection, the waiver extends to an undisclosed communication or information in a federal or state proceeding only if:

(1) the waiver is intentional;

(2) the disclosed and undisclosed communications or information concern the same subject matter; and

(3) they ought in fairness to be considered together.

(b) Inadvertent Disclosure. When made in a federal proceeding or to a federal office or agency, the disclosure does not operate as a waiver in a federal or state proceeding if:

(1) the disclosure is inadvertent;

(2) the holder of the privilege or protection took reasonable steps to prevent disclosure; and

(3) the holder promptly took reasonable steps to rectify the error, including (if applicable) following Federal Rule of Civil Procedure 26 (b)(5)(B).

(c) Disclosure Made in a State Proceeding. When the disclosure is made in a state proceeding and is not the subject of a state-court order concerning waiver, the disclosure does not operate as a waiver in a federal proceeding if the disclosure:

(1) would not be a waiver under this rule if it had been made in a federal proceeding; or

(2) is not a waiver under the law of the state where the disclosure occurred.

(d) Controlling Effect of a Court Order. A federal court may order that the privilege or protection is not waived by disclosure connected with the litigation pending before the court — in which event the disclosure is also not a waiver in any other federal or state proceeding.

(e) Controlling Effect of a Party Agreement. An agreement on the effect of disclosure in a federal proceeding is binding only on the parties to the agreement, unless it is incorporated into a court order.

(f) Controlling Effect of this Rule. Notwithstanding Rules 101 and 1101, this rule applies to state proceedings and to federal court-annexed and federal court-mandated arbitration proceedings, in the circumstances set out in the rule. And notwithstanding Rule 501, this rule applies even if state law provides the rule of decision.

(g) Definitions. In this rule:

(1) "attorney-client privilege" means the protection that applicable law provides for confidential attorney-client communications; and

(2) "work-product protection" means the protection that applicable law provides for tangible material (or its intangible equivalent) prepared in anticipation of litigation or for trial.

* * *

(The following rules were proposed but not adopted.)

Proposed Rule 502. Required Reports Privileged by Statute [Not Enacted]

A person, corporation, association, or other organization or entity, either public or private, making a return or report required by law to be made has a privilege to refuse to disclose and to prevent any other person from disclosing the return or report, if the law requiring it to be made so provides. A public officer or agency to whom a return or report is required by law to be made has a privilege to refuse to disclose the return or report if the law requiring it to be made so provides. No privilege exists under this rule in actions involving perjury, false statements, fraud in the return or report, or other failure to comply with the law in question.

Proposed Rule 503. Lawyer-Client Privilege [Not Enacted]

(a) Definitions. As used in this rule:

(1) A "client" is a person, public officer, or corporation, association, or other organization or entity, either public or private, who is rendered professional legal services by a lawyer, or who consults a lawyer with a view to obtaining professional legal services from him.

(2) A "lawyer" is a person authorized, or reasonably believed by the client to be authorized, to practice law in any state or nation.

(3) A "representative of the lawyer" is one employed to assist the lawyer in the rendition of professional legal services.

(4) A communication is "confidential" if not intended to be disclosed to third persons other than those to whom disclosure is in furtherance of the rendition of professional legal services to the client or those reasonably necessary for the transmission of the communication.

(b) General rule of privilege. A client has a privilege to refuse to disclose and to prevent any other person from disclosing confidential communications made for the purpose of facilitating the rendition of professional legal services to the client, (1) between himself or his representative and his lawyer or his lawyer's representative, or (2) between his lawyer and the lawyer's representative, or (3) by him or his lawyer to a lawyer representing another in a matter of common interest, or (4) between representatives of the client or between the client and a representative of the client, or (5) between lawyers representing the client.

(c) Who may claim the privilege. The privilege may be claimed by the client, his guardian or conservator, the personal representative of a deceased client, or the successor, trustee, or similar representative of a corporation, association, or other organization, whether or not in existence. The person who was the lawyer at the time of the communication may claim the privilege but only on behalf of the client . . .

(d) Exceptions. There is no privilege under this rule:

(1) Furtherance of crime or fraud. If the services of the lawyer were sought or obtained to enable or aid anyone to commit or plan to commit what the client knew or reasonably should have known to be a crime or fraud; or

(2) Claimants through same deceased client. As to a communication relevant to an issue between parties who claim through the same deceased client, regardless of whether the claims are by testate or intestate succession or by inter vivos transaction; or

(3) Breach of duty by lawyer or client. As to a communication relevant to an issue of breach of duty by the lawyer to his client or by the client to his lawyer; or

(4) Document attested by lawyer. As to a communication relevant to an issue concerning an attested document to which the lawyer is an attesting witness; or

(5) Joint clients. As to a communication relevant to a matter of common interest between two or more clients if the communication was made by any of them to a lawyer retained or consulted in common, when offered in an action between any of the clients.

Proposed Rule 504. Psychotherapist-Patient Privilege [Not Enacted]

(a) Definitions

(1) A "patient" is a person who consults or is examined or interviewed by a psychotherapist.

(2) A "psychotherapist" is (A) a person authorized to practice medicine in any state or nation, or reasonably believed by the patient so to be, while engaged in the diagnosis or treatment of a mental or emotional condition, including drug addiction, or (B) a person licensed or certified as a psychologist under the laws of any state or nation, while similarly engaged.

(3) A communication is "confidential" if not intended to be disclosed to third persons other than those present to further the interest of the patient in the consultation, examination, or interview, or persons reasonably necessary for the transmission of the communication, or persons who are participating in the diagnosis and treatment under the direction of the psychotherapist, including members of the patient's family.

(b) General rule of privilege. A patient has a privilege to refuse to disclose and to prevent any other person from disclosing confidential communications, made for the purposes of diagnosis or treatment of his mental or emotional condition, including drug addiction, among himself, his psychotherapist, or persons who are participating in the diagnosis or treatment under the direction of the psychotherapist, including members of the patient's family.

(c) Who may claim the privilege. The privilege may be claimed by the patient, by his guardian or conservator, or by the personal representative of a deceased patient . . .

(d) Exceptions.

(1) Proceedings for hospitalization. There is no privilege under this rule for communications relevant to an issue in proceedings to hospitalize the patient for mental illness, if the psychotherapist in the course of diagnosis or treatment has determined that the patient is in need of hospitalization.

(2) Examination by order of judge. If the judge orders an examination of the mental or emotional condition of the patient, communications made in the course thereof are not privileged . . . .

(3) Condition an element of claim or defense. There is no privilege under this rule as to communications relevant to an issue of the mental or emotional condition of the patient in any proceeding in which he relies upon the condition as an element of his claim or defense, or, after the patient's death, in any proceeding in which any party relies upon the condition as an element of his claim or defense.

Proposed Rule 505. Husband-Wife [Not Enacted]

(a) General rule of privilege. An accused in a criminal proceeding has a privilege to prevent his spouse from testifying against him.

(b) Who may claim the privilege. The privilege may be claimed by the accused or by the spouse on his behalf. The authority of the spouse to do so is presumed in the absence of evidence to the contrary.

(c) Exceptions. There is no privilege under this rule (1) in proceedings in which one spouse is charged with a crime against the person or property of the other or of a child of either, or with a crime against the person or property of a third person committed in the course of committing a crime against the other, or (2) as to matters occurring prior to the marriage, or (3) in proceedings in which a spouse is charged with importing an alien for prostitution or other immoral purposes . . . .

Proposed Rule 506. Communications to Clergymen [Not Enacted]

(a) Definitions. As used in this rule:

(1) A "clergyman" is a minister, priest, rabbi, or other similar functionary of a religious organization, or an individual reasonably believed so to be by the person consulting him.

(2) A communication is "confidential" if made privately and not intended for further disclosure except to other persons present in furtherance of the purpose of the communication.

(b) General rule of privilege. A person has a privilege to refuse to disclose and to prevent another from disclosing a confidential communication by the person to a clergyman in his professional character as spiritual advisor.

(c) Who may claim the privilege. The privilege may be claimed by the person, by his guardian or conservator, or by his personal representative if he is deceased. The clergyman may claim the privilege on behalf of the person . . . .

Proposed Rule 507. Political Vote. [Not Enacted]

Every person has a privilege to refuse to disclose the tenor of his vote at a political election conducted by secret ballot unless the vote was cast illegally.

Proposed Rule 508. Trade Secrets. [Not Enacted]

A person has a privilege, which may be claimed by him or his agent or employee, to refuse to disclose and to prevent other persons from disclosing a trade secret owned by him, if the allowance of the privilege will not tend to conceal fraud or otherwise work injustice. When disclosure is directed, the judge shall take such protective measure as the interests of the holder of the privilege and of the parties and the furtherance of justice may require.

Proposed Rule 509. Secrets of State and Other Official Information. [Not Enacted]

(a) Definitions

(1) Secret of state. A "secret of state" is a governmental secret relating to the national defense or the international relations of the United States.

(2) Official information. "Official information" is information within the custody or control of a department or agency of the government the disclosure of which is shown to be contrary to the public interest . . .

(b) General rule of privilege. The government has a privilege to refuse to give evidence and to prevent any person from giving evidence upon a showing of reasonable likelihood of danger that the evidence will disclose a secret of state or official information, as defined in this rule.

Proposed Rule 510. Identity of Informer. [Not enacted]

(a) Rule of privilege. The government or a state or subdivision thereof has a privilege to refuse to disclose the identity of a person who has furnished information relating to or assisting in an investigation of a possible violation of law to a law enforcement officer or member of a legislative committee or its staff conducting an investigation.

(b) Who may claim. The privilege may be claimed by an appropriate representative of the government, regardless of whether the information was furnished to an officer of the government ... except that in a criminal case the privilege shall not be allowed if the government objects.

(c) Exceptions.

(1) Voluntary disclosure; informer a witness. No privilege exists under this rule if the identity of the informer or his interest in the subject matter of his communication has been disclosed to those who would have cause to resent the communication ... or if the informer appears as a witness for the government.

(2) Testimony on merits. If it appears from the evidence in the case or from other showing by a party that an informer may be able to give testimony necessary to a fair determination of the issue of guilt or innocence in a criminal case or of a material issue on the merits in a civil case ... the judge shall give the government an opportunity to show in camera facts relevant to determining whether the informer can, in fact, supply that testimony ....

(3) Legality of obtaining evidence. If information from an informer is relied upon to establish the legality of the means by which evidence was obtained and the judge is not satisfied that the information was received from an informer reasonably believed to be reliable or credible, he may require the identity of the informer to be disclosed ....

Proposed Rule 511. Waiver of Privilege by Voluntary Disclosure. [Not Enacted]

A person upon whom these rules confer a privilege against disclosure of the confidential matter or communication waives the privilege if he or his predecessor while holder of the privilege voluntarily discloses or consents to disclosure of any significant part of the matter or communication. This rule does not apply if the disclosure is itself a privileged communication.

§ 17.03 Introduction to Privileges

Privileges exclude otherwise relevant evidence in favor of public policies. As a former Supreme Court Justice stated, privileges are based on a "public good transcending the normally predominant principle of utilizing all rational means for ascertaining the truth." *Elkins v. United States*, 364 U.S. 206, 234, 80 S. Ct. 1437, 4 L. Ed. 2d 1669 (1960) (Frankfurter, J., dissenting). In effect, the existence of a privilege signifies a balancing of interests favoring the exclusion of information relevant to the case. The protected interests are variously described as promoting special relationships, privacy from disclosure, and the promotion of a greater external good. "Special relationship" is evidenced by the attorney-client, spousal, and psychotherapist privileges. Privacy is illustrated by the confidential communications privilege between spouses and the greater good by the adverse spousal testimony privilege, which keeps a spouse from testifying against the other spouse in a criminal case.

A. The Definition of Privileged Evidence

A privilege authorizes the non-disclosure of information. It can be framed as both a right and a power — a right to refuse the dissemination of information and the power to control that information, even after one's death. In effect, a privilege wraps potential evidence in a "cone of silence," much like the shield used to ensure private communications in a popular television show of the 1970s, and subsequent film of the same name, *Get Smart*.

Privileges can operate outside of the courtroom, as well as at trial. A privilege may be invoked in response to pretrial discovery requests, coerced interrogation, or an attempt to compel testimony. Thus, a deponent in a pretrial deposition may assert one privilege, a person being interrogated by the police may claim another privilege, and a person's estate may advance still another privilege on the decedent's behalf.

Significantly, a privilege continues to operate regardless of the relevance or importance of the information it shields from disclosure. Even if the information is crucial to the outcome of a case, such as the location of a murder victim's body, the privilege rules maintain the "cone of silence." This limitation on the search for truth is deemed warranted because of public policy considerations. In effect, privileges advance values thought to outweigh the need for a fair and accurate trial process. These values, such as the ability to speak in confidence to an attorney, therapist, spouse, or priest, are arguably essential to core relationships that should not be compromised.

As illustrated by the rejection of specific codified privileges by the drafters of the Federal Rules of Evidence, the decision as to what values to recognize through the law of privileges is a difficult one. Why, for example, should a patient's discussions with a psychotherapist be protected, but not an alleged sexual assault victim's conversation with a licensed sexual assault counselor? Why should the spousal relationship be protected by two privileges, the confidential communications and adverse testimony privileges, when there is absolutely no protection for conversations between parent and child? Much of the demarcation between what is privileged and what is not owes its existence to the historical development of the law. The fact that some privileges, such as attorney-client and husband-wife, are historically embedded in the common law has not stopped the debate. Some observers have argued that the relationship between parent and child needs as much fostering as spousal and attorney-client relationships.

The exclusion of useful information based on privilege is unusual but not unique. The law of privilege parallels the rules relating to several other evidentiary exclusions, including "relevant but inadmissible" evidence such as subsequent remedial measures, offers to compromise and completed compromises, offers to pay medical expenses, and plea negotiations. *See* Rules 407–410. Those exclusions are sometimes labeled "quasi-privileges," and also are based — at least in part — on public policy considerations designed to encourage certain conduct by the parties. (*See* Chapters 4 and 6, above.)

B. Federal and State Privileges

Privileges operate in both federal and state courts. The type of evidence that is considered privileged may vary from state to state, from federal to state courts, and within the same court over time. Yet, whether a privilege applies in federal or state court, it generally operates in the same way — to exclude information.

Significantly, state privilege rules sometimes operate in federal court proceedings, effectively replacing the federal common law at these times. Under Rule 501, state privileges apply when state law provides the rule of decision in a civil action or proceeding, which most often occurs in a case where federal jurisdiction is based on diversity of citizenship. *See Erie R. Co. v. Tompkins*, 304 U.S. 64.

C. Sources of Privilege

Privileges are created by courts through the common law, by legislatures through statutory enactments and by the Constitution. All three sources of privilege may be invoked at a single trial or hearing. An example of a privilege firmly entrenched within the common law is the attorney-client privilege. An example of a privilege essentially constructed by statute is the physician-patient privilege. An illustration of a constitutional privilege is the Fifth Amendment privilege against self-incrimination.

While privileges used to be created primarily through the common law, the law of privilege in most states is currently based on statute. The codified privileges often reflect the established common law, such as the attorney-client privilege. Sometimes, however, states have expanded the number of privileges through statutory enactments, adding such privileges as an accident report privilege, an accountant-client privilege, a sexual assault counselor-victim privilege and a domestic violence counselor-victim privilege. Some of these privileges are designed to encourage the free flow of information for public policy reasons. An apt illustration is the accident report privilege. Some states require a person who has been in an automobile accident to cooperate with a police officer who is writing a report about the accident. To promote cooperation, the privilege generally "immunizes" statements made by such persons involved in auto accidents from disclosure.

The third source of privilege, the United States Constitution, includes important express and implied privileges. The Fifth Amendment, as noted above, contains the privilege against self-incrimination. This privilege, often described as "taking the Fifth," is an important protection against coerced testimony. *See, e.g., United States v. Hubbell*, 167 F.3d 552 (D.C. Cir. 1999). Another important constitutional privilege is executive privilege, an implied privilege derived from the principle of the separation of powers. This privilege protects the interests of the United States government by exempting some presidential communications from disclosure in a trial or hearing. (*See United States v. Nixon*, 418 U.S. 683, in which the Supreme Court held that there was a constitutional basis for executive privilege, but that it was only a qualified privilege, depending on the subject matter.)

Example

In the early 1970s, the Committee to Reelect the President (C.R.E.E.P.), engaged in various surveillance and spying activities against political opponents. This group, whose mission was to re-elect President Richard M. Nixon, burglarized the office of the psychiatrist of Daniel Ellsberg, hoping to find incriminating information. (Ellsberg had leaked "The Pentagon Papers," government documents concerning the Vietnam War, to *The New York Times*.) The burglary, at an apartment complex called The Watergate, led to news reports about a cover-up of the relationship between the burglars and C.R.E.E.P.

The authors of most of the news reports were two reporters for *The Washington Post*, Robert Woodward and Carl Bernstein. The reporters refused to disclose their sources, particularly the main one, whom they called "Deep Throat." What is the basis for their refusal?

Answer: The basis for refusing to disclose sources, even in the face of a subpoena, is often called "the newsperson's privilege" or "journalist's privilege," and is traced to the First Amendment of the Constitution. The freedom of the press has been interpreted to include a qualified privilege for journalists that allows them to refuse to disclose their sources. The privilege is qualified, however, and not absolute. A judge might find the privilege outweighed by a particular interest in national security. Over the years, many reporters have voiced a preference for jail to disclosure, warning that forced disclosure would negatively impact the freedom of sources to provide information.

An additional illustration of the scope of the constitutionally based executive privilege resulted from the investigation of President William Jefferson Clinton and others in his administration by special prosecutor Kenneth Starr. In one case, the question arose as to whether Secret Service agents assigned to guard the President in the White House could invoke executive privilege. The Courts held that there was no such ancillary privilege, and that the agents would have to disclose what they saw and heard. Thus, Secret Service agents could be called to testify before a grand jury about the President. *See In re Sealed Case*, 148 F.3d 1073 (D.C. Cir. 1998), *cert. denied*, 119 S. Ct. 461 (1998).

D. The Operation of Privileges

Privileges do not operate automatically. A privilege will operate only upon a timely refusal to disclose information or to testify, usually occurring through an objection by counsel at trial or a motion *in limine* (in advance). When a privilege is asserted, the proponent of the privilege is generally assigned the burden of establishing the elements underlying a privilege. Without such action by counsel, an otherwise valid privilege may be waived. Waiver is a complicated concept. It can occur by implication as well as expressly. An implied waiver might occur under widely disparate circumstances, such as if a party reveals confidential communications to a third party or raises a claim at trial that creates a need for the privileged information (e.g., raising an insanity defense may result in waiver of the physician-patient privilege).

Even if counsel objects to disclosure, the objection must be timely. Once a timely objection is made, the court usually considers the merits of the claim *in camera*, outside the hearing of the jury. The need for secrecy is clear. Once jurors have heard information, it is extremely difficult for them to "unhear" it. Thus, judges have to determine whether information is privileged before the information can be disclosed to jurors.

Not all privileges exclude evidence in the same way. Some privileges extend only to confidential communications, such as the clergy-penitent privilege. For privileges based on communications, the witness must still testify and provide all relevant, non-privileged information. The witness may refuse to answer all questions whose answers come within the domain of the privilege.

Other privileges permit a witness to completely refuse to testify. An example of a privilege that offers the option of refusing to testify is the adverse spousal testimony privilege, which allows one spouse to refuse to testify against the other.

E. Confidential Communication Privileges Generally

Confidential communication privileges, such as attorney-client and clergy-penitent, are based on the following principles:

- A legally recognized *relationship* between the holder of the privilege and the person being consulted (i.e., husband-wife, attorney-client, priest-penitent) exists.

- A *communication* — written, oral, or nonverbal — took place between the holder and the person consulted.

- The communication is *confidential*.

- The *holder* of the privilege, generally the client, patient, or supplicant, can assert it, or the person consulted may assert it on the holder's behalf.

- The privilege does not operate if it has been expressly or impliedly *waived*.

- An *exception* to the privilege, such as using the privilege to commit a future crime, removes its protective cloak.

Waiver of a privilege generally does not result from an unknown eavesdropper overhearing a confidential communication. If a communication is intended to be confidential and the circumstances lead to a reasonable expectation of confidentiality, the law views the communication in the same way. For example, it is likely more reasonable to expect confidentiality in the privacy of one's own home than in a crowded rush-hour subway train.

As indicated above, not every important relationship is protected under the confidential communications privileges. While some relationships, such as marriage, are given extensive protection by allowing the spouses to refuse to testify at all, even to things other than confidential communications, other relationships, such as that of parent and child, receive no protection. *See In re Grand Jury*, 103 F.3d 1140, 1146 (3d Cir. 1997) ("Although legal academicians appear to favor adoption of a parent-child testimonial privilege, no federal Court of Appeals and no state supreme court has recognized such a privilege").

F. Public Policy-Based Privileges Generally

Many states create privileges based on public policy. These states want to encourage certain types of behavior and conclude that, without the privilege, the desired behavior will not be advanced. One example of a privilege generated by public policy is the domestic violence victim-domestic violence counselor privilege, which applies to confidential communications between the two parties for the purpose of counseling. Several states have made such communications privileged to promote disclosure and the free flow of information.

§ 17.04 The Federal Rules of Evidence Approach to Privilege

Privileges in federal court are generally derived from the federal common law, with one glaring exception. When state law supplies the rule of decision, particularly in cases based on the diversity of citizenship of the parties, the pertinent state privilege law applies. *See Erie R. v. Tompkins*, 304 U.S. 64. In this regard, privilege rules are considered "substantive" law and not simply "procedural rules relating to trial governance." The Senate Committee charged with reviewing the proposed rules concluded:

The [Senate Committee on the Judiciary] agrees . . . federal developed common law based on modern reason and experience shall apply except where the State nature of the issues renders deference to State privilege law the wiser course, as in the usual diversity case.[1]

At first glance, it is unclear why Congress decided to retain the traditional but evolving federal common law instead of enacting specific privilege rules, especially in light of the fairly specific codification in the other areas of the Federal Rules of Evidence. The reason may be due to the fact that privileges provided Congress with a particularly controversial and enigmatic subject, one firmly rooted in public policy. If any evidence area generated sparks of excitement in the general public as well as with trial lawyers and legal scholars, this was it. The controversial nature of the subject and thorniness of negotiating a consensus on what to include in the realm of exclusions provides some insight into why Congress might have decided to leave this area virtually untouched.

Under the common law process, demands by lawyers for new privileges regularly challenge the status quo. The demands offer judges the opportunity to adopt new directions, while at the same time forcing judges to face up to the limits of existing precedent. For the most part, judges dismiss the proposals, rejecting such additions as a parole officer-parolee privilege, a sexual assault counselor-victim privilege, a legislative privilege, and an academic peer-review privilege.

The drafters of the Federal Rules of Evidence had suggested adopting 13 distinct privilege rules (*see* §17.02). The proposed rules included a wide variety of privileges, many of which had been well established in the states and in the federal common law. Instead of adopting any or all of these specific privileges, Congress chose to adopt a single governing rule on privilege. Federal Rule of Evidence 501 perpetuates the use of the privileges previously recognized in the federal common law. Interestingly, the rejected proposed privileges have received different treatment by the courts. In some cases, the courts turn to the proposals for assistance in determining the parameters of federal common-law privilege. *See, e.g., United States v. McPartlin,* 595 F.2d 1321, 1335–1337 (7th Cir. 1979). In other cases, the courts do not give the proposals any weight at all. *See, e.g., United States v. Bizzard,* 674 F.2d 1382, 1387 (11th Cir. 1982).

The unease caused by leaving only the area of privilege tied to the common law, while subjecting the remaining rules of evidence to codification, led the Advisory Committee toward the end of 2003 to reconsider leaving privileges as the only significant area of evidence law governed by the common law. The lack of action by the Advisory Committee suggests its acceptance of the current framework.

Debate continues as to whether this approach to the law of privileges is appropriate. On the one hand, a single general rule casting a backward glance to established precedent incorporates the wisdom of the federal judiciary, which is already

---

1. Rule 501, Report of Senate Committee on the Judiciary.

responsible for applying the doctrine of privilege, while also permitting flexibility and responsiveness to changing times. On the other hand, the domain of privilege is the one area where Congress failed to codify bright-line rules and where historical precedent trumps modern ideas about what should be privileged, such as the statements made by victims of sexual abuse or domestic violence to respective counselors.

§ 17.05 Some Specific Privileges

A. The Husband-Wife Privileges — Adverse Spousal Testimony and Confidential Communications

Two well-recognized privileges in both federal and state law concern spouses. Each spousal privilege — adverse spousal testimony and confidential communications — has markedly different characteristics and must be distinguished from the other. The important distinctions include what triggers the privileges, their scope of application, the types of cases in which they apply, and who holds the privilege.

1. The Adverse Spousal Testimony Privilege

The adverse spousal testimony privilege is triggered at the time a spouse is called to testify against his or her spouse in a criminal case. As the word "spouse" suggests, a valid marriage is a prerequisite to asserting this privilege, specifically at the time of trial. The marriage requirement is met even if the spouses were separated at the time of trial, depending on the length and nature of the separation.

If the privilege is triggered, the husband and wife are afforded considerable protection. The adverse spousal testimony privilege allows the accused's spouse to avoid testifying by choosing not to take the witness stand. While the scope of the privilege is broad, the privilege is available only in criminal cases. In addition, the privilege is held only by the testifying spouse, and not the defendant spouse. This means that if the testifying spouse wishes to testify, the defendant spouse cannot stand in the witness spouse's way.

The privilege was not always held by the testifying spouse. Under earlier common law, it was the defendant spouse who held the key to opposing spousal testimony. This earlier rule was abandoned in *Trammel v. United States*, 445 U.S. 40, 53, 100 S. Ct. 906, 63 L. Ed. 2d 186 (1980), in which the Supreme Court held that the prevailing rule, enunciated in *Hawkins v. United States*, 358 U.S. 74, 78–79, 79 S. Ct. 136, 31 L. Ed. 2d 118 (1958), should be changed. *Hawkins* had perpetuated the common-law rule, barring testimony by one spouse against the other unless both consented. The court in *Trammel* found that the justification for the *Hawkins* rule no longer existed, and overruled it. The Court stated:

> Our consideration of the foundations for the privilege and its history satisfy us that "reason and experience" no longer justify so sweeping a rule as that

found acceptable by the Court in *Hawkins*. Accordingly, we conclude that the existing rule should be modified so that the witness spouse alone has a privilege to refuse to testify adversely; the witness may be neither compelled to testify nor foreclosed from testifying. This modification — vesting the privilege in the witness spouse — furthers the important public interest in marital harmony without unduly burdening legitimate law enforcement needs. 445 U.S. at 53.

What the justices appear to be saying here is that if a person wishes to testify against that person's spouse, the public policy of saving the marriage is not worth much, if anything at all. (One can only imagine the conversation at the breakfast table the day after one spouse voluntarily testifies against the other spouse.)

2. The Spousal Confidential Communications Privilege

Unlike the adverse spousal testimony privilege, the confidential communications privilege also is triggered by a valid marriage, but the marriage need only have existed *at the time of the communication*, not at the time of trial. Thus, a communication that occurred years prior to a trial still might be privileged, so long as it was made during the marriage, even if the husband and wife had been long-divorced by the time of trial.

The scope of the confidential communications privilege is narrower than that of the adverse spousal testimony privilege. The confidential communications privilege merely prohibits the disclosure by the spouse-witness of any confidential communications with the other spouse that occurs during the marriage. This means that a spouse can be called to the witness stand and asked to testify against the defendant spouse, including observations about the other spouse or non-confidential communications with the spouse.

The confidential communications privilege may apply in both criminal and civil cases and either spouse may assert the privilege. Thus, in a civil case, a spouse-defendant can prevent an adverse spouse-witness from testifying about confidential communications.

There are several important exceptions to the privilege. These exceptions include proceedings in which one spouse has been charged with crimes against the other spouse or against one or more of the spouse's children.

3. Problems

Problem 17-1: Bonnie and Clyde — Scenarios

1. *Bonnie and Clyde lived together for two years. During that time, Clyde told Bonnie that he robbed banks for a living. The two subsequently were married. Clyde was then charged with several bank robberies. Is Clyde's statement to Bonnie about robbing banks privileged?*

2. The prosecution calls Bonnie to testify that Clyde was wearing a red sweater and matching suede shoes on the day of one of the robberies.

   a. *Can Clyde prevent Bonnie from testifying to those facts if the husband-wife confidential communications privilege applies?*

   b. *Can Clyde prevent Bonnie from testifying to those facts if the adverse spousal testimony privilege applies?*

3. Clyde tells his secretary to take down the following letter, to be delivered to Bonnie: "Bonnie, meet me at the southeast corner of the bank right before closing time. Bring all of the 'stuff' for the bank; you know what I mean. Love and Kisses, Clyde." The government wishes to introduce this letter at the bank robbery trial in which Clyde is the defendant. *Is this letter admissible? Explain.*

4. Bonnie dies of a chronic illness during the trial. *Does Bonnie's death terminate the husband-wife confidential communications privilege?*

5. Based on bruises found on Bonnie, Clyde also is charged with aggravated spousal battery, a felony. At trial, Bonnie is called to testify by the prosecution. *Can Clyde assert one of the marital privileges? Can Bonnie claim privilege and refuse to testify?*

6. Suppose that after Clyde's death, Clyde's estate is sued by a third party claiming that Clyde had robbed her, buried the jewelry that he had taken, and informed Bonnie of the location of the jewelry before he had died. *If Bonnie had been told by Clyde that he had stolen the jewelry and had buried it in a certain place, must Bonnie disclose this information at trial?* Explain.

B. The Attorney-Client Privilege

1. Elements of Privilege

The attorney-client privilege extends to confidential communications between attorney and client. To promote the attorney-client relationship, even introductory confidential conversations are protected, as are communications that occur with necessary third parties, such as a paralegal, in attendance.

What is not protected, however, is material evidence. If a client gives the attorney potential evidence to hold or control, that evidence is not shielded by the privilege. In *State ex rel. Sowers v. Olwell*, 64 Wash. 2d 828, 394 P.2d 681, 684 (1964), an attorney was served with a subpoena asking him to produce "all knives in [his] possession and under [his] control relating to Henry LeRoy Gray, Gloria Pugh or John W. Warren." The attorney refused to comply, asserting the attorney-client privilege on behalf of his client. The Supreme Court of Washington held that the attorney's refusal was improper, stating:

> Here we must consider the balancing process between the attorney/ client privilege and the public interest in criminal investigation. We are in

agreement that the attorney/client privilege is applicable to the knife held by appellant, but do not agree that the privilege warrants the attorney, as an officer of the court, from withholding it after being properly requested to produce the same. The attorney should not be a depository for criminal evidence (such as a knife, other weapons, stolen property, etc.), which in itself has little, if any, material value for the purposes of aiding counsel in the preparation of the defense of his client's case. 64 Wash. 2d at 833.

Problem 17-2: Free Toaster Oven

Amy worries that she may have committed a crime, so she seeks legal advice. After going food shopping, she stops and speaks to a person named Mazzen, who is seated in a booth outside of the supermarket. The booth is decorated with a large sign stating, "Lawyer — reasonable fees. First consultation free." Amy discusses her situation with Mazzen, but decides not to hire him.

1. If Amy is later charged with a crime concerning the same situation she discussed with Mazzen, can the prosecutor call Mazzen to testify about what Amy had told him? What is the significance of Amy's decision not to hire Mazzen?

2. Suppose it turns out that Mazzen had passed the bar examination, but had never completed his bar application and thus was not a qualified lawyer at the time he offered his advice. Can the prosecutor now call Mazzen to testify?

3. If, during the same conversation, Amy sought business advice from Mazzen (who had earned an M.B.A. as well as a law degree) about a particular real estate investment that was quite successful, would the conversation be privileged?

4. If Amy's brother, Lenny, said to Amy, "Don't worry, I'll pay for your attorney," and as a result, Amy hires Mazzen, is there an attorney-client relationship between Amy and Mazzen? Is there an attorney-client relationship between Lenny and Mazzen? (*See, e.g., United States v. Edwards*, 39 F. Supp. 2d 716 (M.D. La. 1999).)

5. Suppose Amy hires Mazzen and there is immediate friction between them. After just one month of representation, Amy fired Mazzen, but not before providing him with incriminating information that could easily lead to her criminal conviction. Two months later, Amy is charged with a crime, and Mazzen is called to testify by the prosecution. Mazzen would love nothing better than to tell everyone what Amy had told him. Can Mazzen disclose all? Does it matter whether Amy had given Mazzen specific instructions regarding any subsequent disclosure of their conversations?

Problem 17-3: No Name

A defense lawyer, Paula, is subpoenaed by a grand jury investigating a stabbing leading to a person's death.

1. *Paula is asked about a knife allegedly given to Paula by her client. If, in fact, her client did give her a knife, can Paula refuse to acknowledge or disclose information about the knife? Does Paula have to turn the knife over to the prosecution?*

2. *Paula is asked by the grand jury about the name of the person who is paying her attorney's fees and the amount of those fees. Paula refuses to answer, claiming that the answer is privileged information. Is it? See Baird v. Koerner, 279 F.2d 623 (9th Cir. 1960).*

3. The prosecutor issues a subpoena for Paula's personal notes about the case. Must she disclose them?

4. Assuming that the name of Paula's client is disclosed, can her client be subpoenaed to provide a handwriting sample?

5. Can Paula's client be required to provide a hair sample, to see if hairs found at the crime scene match those of her client?

6. Paula's client asks Paula how best to lie before the grand jury. Does the attorney-client privilege apply?

Problem 17-4: Waiver?

Jimmy is charged with receiving stolen property after he purchased new televisions from a friend for a fraction of their cost. Jimmy decides to testify on his own behalf. During the course of his testimony, the following exchange occurs.

DEFENSE COUNSEL: Jimmy, what happened that led you to receive those television sets?

A: You know, my good friend Bernie said his friend George, who owned an electronics store, was going out of business.

PROSECUTOR: Objection. Hearsay.

JUDGE: Overruled. Please continue, counsel.

DEFENSE COUNSEL: Jimmy, what did you do in response to Bernie telling you about the television sets?

A: I wanted to buy them, naturally, and I did, for a fair price.

DEFENSE COUNSEL: I have no further questions, Your Honor.

JUDGE: Prosecutor, you may proceed with cross-examination.

PROSECUTOR: Thank you, Your Honor. Now Jimmy, you told your lawyer, did you not, that you knew those televisions were being sold for way under their fair price?

A: Yeah, I did, but only because I worked at a Great Buy Electronics store for a couple of years.

DEFENSE COUNSEL: Objection, your honor. May we approach the bench?

If defense counsel argues at the bench that any statements made by defendant to counsel are privileged and that the defendant was effectively tricked into revealing confidential communications, how should the judge rule?

2. The Attorney-Client Privilege and the Corporate Client

At common law, the paradigm for the attorney-client privilege involved a lawyer offering advice to an individual client. As businesses and corporate entities began to consult regularly with attorneys, issues relating to the scope of the attorney-client privilege arose — who in a corporation possessed the privilege? The early law granted a privilege only to the "control group" — those persons who had controlling power over the corporation.

The traditional rule proved to be less than satisfactory, however, given modern business practices. Often, many members of a corporation outside the control group consulted attorneys on legal matters for the company. These consultations were awkward at best, given the potential risk of disclosure. The apparent inconsistency was rectified in the case of *Upjohn v. United States*, 449 U.S. 383, 392–393, 101 S. Ct. 677, 66 L. Ed. 2d 584 (1981). *Upjohn* addressed the issue of the scope of the attorney-client privilege within the corporate setting. The Supreme Court adopted a more flexible test instead of the bright-line control group requirement. The Court stated:

> The narrow scope given the attorney client privilege [in the control group test] not only makes it difficult for corporate attorneys to formulate sound advice when their client is faced with a specific legal problem but also threatens to limit the valuable efforts of corporate counsel to ensure their client's compliance with the law . . . . The very terms of the [control group] test adopted by the court below suggest the unpredictability of its application. The test restricts the availability of the privilege to those officers who play a "substantial role" in deciding and directing a corporation's legal response. 449 U.S. at 384.

In light of this position, the Supreme Court held that middle-level and lower-level employees also could claim the attorney-client privilege, so long as they were acting in the course of their duties including legal advice about a subject relevant to the corporation. *See also Harper & Row Publishers, Inc. v. Decker*, 423 F.2d 487, 491–492 (7th Cir. 1970).

Problem 17-5: I.B.S.

The I.B.S. Corporation consults with its attorney, Bingem, Dingem, and Wingem, about pending litigation against the company. A technician employed by I.B.S. is subpoenaed to provide information about his communications with the attorneys for I.B.S. *Can the technician assert the attorney-client privilege?*

Problem 17-6: L.A. Cooke

A company named L.A. Cooke is charged with fraudulently violating security laws relating to a stock redemption. *Can the shareholders obtain the communications between the corporation's managers and its attorneys relating to the stock redemption? See Ward v. Succession of Freeman*, 854 F.2d 780 (5th Cir. 1988).

C. Other Privileges

There are several other well-established privileges worth reviewing, including the "work product" privilege, the psychotherapist-patient privilege and the Fifth Amendment privilege against self-incrimination.

1. "Work Product" Privilege

The so-called "work product" privilege is really an appendage of the litigation process. It prevents the discovery of mental impressions, conclusions, opinions, or legal theories of attorneys (or representatives of those attorneys) involved in, or preparing for, litigation. *See* F.R.C.P. 26(b)(3); *Hickman v. Taylor*, 329 U.S. 495, 67 S. Ct. 385, 91 L. Ed. 451 (1947). This protection of litigation strategy allows attorneys to try their own cases, and permits some secrecy in how evidence is offered, approached, and evaluated by the parties. Significantly, the work product privilege applies only to materials that are "otherwise discoverable." Thus, if materials are protected by another privilege, such as the attorney-client privilege, the issue of work product protection need never arise. *See, e.g., Miller v. Federal Express Corp.*, 186 F.R.D. 376 (W.D. Tenn. 1999).

Problem 17-7: The Union

James was the president of the largest union in New York City. During a difficult period, in which the Union threatened to strike, James met with several union representatives about their strategy regarding a potential strike. Before a strike could occur, the employer sued the union in federal court, claiming it violated several federal labor laws. James met with the Union's lawyer, Emily, who wrote down her thoughts about the situation, including the strategies and tactics that were legally available. During pretrial discovery, the employer sought disclosure of the meeting James had with his representatives and of Emily's notes of her meeting with James. *What must be disclosed, if anything?*

2. Psychotherapist-Patient Privilege

A psychotherapist-patient privilege is recognized under the common law of many states and under the federal common law. *See Jaffee v. Redmond*, 518 U.S. 1, 116 S. Ct. 1923, 135 L. Ed. 2d 337 (1996). In *Jaffee*, a police officer killed a man while on duty and was sued for violating that person's civil rights. The defendant officer received counseling following the incident from a licensed clinical social worker. The plaintiff sought the disclosure of the substance of that counseling, and the therapist was ordered to do so by the judge. The defendant and therapist refused, claiming they were protected by a psychotherapist-patient privilege. The Supreme Court agreed, finding that the federal law should reflect the states' enthusiastic endorsement of the privilege. The Court found that the privilege extended not only to psychiatrists and psychologists, but also to licensed clinical social workers administering psychotherapy.

Significantly, the privilege applies only to confidential communications made during the course of diagnosis or treatment of the patient. Statements made outside of diagnosis or treatment, such as those involving business matters or other unrelated subjects, are not privileged. Further, the privilege, like others, may be expressly or impliedly waived. An implied waiver may occur when litigants place their mental state at issue or sue the professional, necessitating the use of the psychotherapy records. In *Jaffee*, the officer refused to expressly waive the privilege and did not impliedly waive the privilege by raising an insanity defense.

Example

Mark David Chapman shot and killed John Lennon, a former member of the Beatles, outside of Lennon's apartment building in New York City in 1980. Instead of pleading guilty to the crime, Chapman could have sought a trial. If Chapman had asked for a trial and raised an insanity defense, his prior visits to a psychotherapist would have been subject to discovery by the prosecution because his assertion of insanity created an implied waiver of his psychotherapist-patient privilege — under either New York or federal law.

Problem 17-8: Crazy for You

Alex is charged with murder. Alex has been in therapy for nine years to treat his excessive and repetitive outbursts of anger against others.

If Alex raises an insanity defense at trial, can the prosecution call Alex's therapist, Marcy, to the witness stand to testify about what Alex told her in their therapy sessions? Why?

Problem 17-9: Bundy

The defendant, Bundy, is charged with a series of rapes. The prosecution attempts to discover what Bundy told his psychiatrist prior to the date charges were filed.

1. *Are the conversations between Bundy and his psychiatrist privileged?*

2. *Would the conversations be privileged if the psychiatrist's secretary was present during them?*

Problem 17-10: Still Crazy, After All These . . .

Paul, the defendant, objects to the admission of statements he made to his doctor, Dr. Simon, claiming that he believed Dr. Simon was also a psychotherapist. At a sidebar, the plaintiff's attorney makes the following proffer:

PLAINTIFF'S ATTORNEY: Your Honor, the evidence will show that Dr. Simon has been a practicing podiatrist for 21 years and planned on doing bunion surgery on the defendant. Paul knew Dr. Simon was a podiatrist and not a psychotherapist. Paul's statements to Dr. Simon are not part of the psychotherapist-patient relationship.

DEFENDANT'S ATTORNEY: Your honor, with all due respect, Dr. Simon discussed James Redfield's book, *The Tenth Insight*, with Paul, as well as the Dali Lama's book, *The Art of Happiness*. Everybody knows those books are within the realm of psychology.

How should the judge rule? See Henry v. Kernan, 177 F.3d 1152, 1159 (9th Cir. 1999).

3. The Physician-Patient Privilege

Under the federal common law, there was no privilege to avoid the compelled disclosure of confidential information shared in a physician-patient relationship. A majority of state jurisdictions have altered this rule, however, protecting confidential communications between a physician and her patient. *See, e.g.,* N.Y. Rev. Stat. 1828, 406 (pt. 3, ch. 7, Tit. 3, Art. 9, Section 73). Some of these states provide only limited protection to the doctor-patient relationship, requiring disclosure under a court subpoena or extending protection only during the course of litigation. *See, e.g.,* Florida Evidence Code, FL Stat., Chapter 90 et seq. Thus, the physician-patient rule of confidentiality is stronger outside of a court proceeding than in it.

Like most professional confidential communications privileges that belong to the layperson, the doctor-patient privilege, when it exists, is generally held by the patient. The privilege does not protect either the fact that the doctor has treated the patient or peripheral facts about the treatment (such as how many times treatment has occurred). In addition, the privilege may be abrogated for equally important public policy purposes, such as the disclosure of the existence of communicable or deadly diseases, like tuberculosis or AIDS. On the other hand, if the privilege attaches, it generally prevails even after the patient has died.

Problem 17-11: Booth

J.W. Booth woke up his family physician, claiming he was shot while hunting in Washington, D.C. The doctor examined the wound and saw that Booth was losing blood. Booth was taken to the doctor's adjoining office, where the doctor treated Booth. Booth then hurried away, despite remaining in a medically unstable condition.

If the treatment occurred in a state where the physician-patient privilege is recognized, and the state law supplies the rule of decision in a case where Booth's injury and its cause are relevant, can the doctor be required to testify about his treatment of Booth and the statements Booth made to him?

Problem: 17-12: Booth II

Assume the same facts as in the previous problem. Suppose that J.W. Booth's brother, Bob Booth, helped to carry Booth to the doctor's office and assisted during the treatment. *Can J.W.'s brother be required to testify about what he saw and heard in J.W.'s office?*

4. The Fifth Amendment Privilege Against Self-Incrimination

While it is amorphous in scope and heavily litigated, the privilege against self-incrimination is readily defined. It prohibits any compelled testimony that constitutes self-incrimination. *See, e.g., United States v. Hubbell*, 167 F.3d 552 (D.C. Cir. 1999). To invoke the privilege, the incrimination must result from the compelled testimony — and be "substantial and real." Thus, the modern interpretation is not tied so much to privacy, which focuses on the freedom from government snooping, as it is to autonomy and the freedom from governmental compulsion. *Id.* at 572. It is not a violation of the privilege to compel a defendant to provide a hair sample, voiceprint, or even blood, for example, because while the defendant is being compelled, it is not compelled testimony. On the other hand, it is a violation to force communications that implicate the defendant in a crime, such as confessions.

Problem 17-13: Lowering the Bar

Lynn filed a bar complaint against her attorney, Sam, alleging that he acted unethically in disclosing to her opponent certain confidential information that she gave him in the course of their attorney-client relationship. The Bar Disciplinary Commission wrote Sam, asking for his understanding of the facts. Sam claimed that his Fifth Amendment right against self-incrimination protected him from providing any information. Is Sam correct?

Problem 17-14: Illegal Gambling

To stop the proliferation of unlawful gambling in the United States, Congress enacts a law requiring "all proceeds from gambling, legal or otherwise, to be declared as income for tax purposes." Is this law constitutional? Why?

D. Additional Privilege Problems

Problem 17-15: Father and Son

John Sr. tells John Jr., "Look, I want you to keep a secret. Just between us, I cheated a bit on my taxes between 1995 and 2002 to help the family through hard times. Now the Internal Revenue Service is after me. Even if what I did was criminal, I never wanted to hurt you, got that? One more thing, if you would, try to minimize the expenses at college this semester; this fight is going to be a costly one."

If John Sr. is charged with tax evasion, can the prosecution call John Jr. as a witness to testify to the above conversation? Must John Jr. testify? What would you argue on John Sr.'s behalf?

Problem 17-16: Deep Throat

The identity of Deep Throat, the mysterious informant in the Watergate scandal who supposedly leaked information to journalists Woodward and Bernstein, becomes an issue in a subsequent trial. The media defendant in the trial subpoenas the Watergate reporters, Woodward and Bernstein. Can the reporters refuse to disclose the name of their informant? *See United States v. Caporale*, 806 F.2d 1487 (11th Cir. 1986). *Does it matter whether it is a criminal or civil case?* [Note: After 30 years of silence, Mr. W. Mark Felt, former Deputy Director of the FBI, disclosed publicly in 2005 that he was the "Deep Throat" who had provided Woodward and Bernstein with information.]

Problem 17-17: Confession

Joanne is charged with kidnapping. The prosecution attempts to introduce inculpatory statements Joanne made to her priest during a confession immediately prior to the kidnapping.

Are the statements Joanne made to her priest admissible? If Joanne had mentioned the substance of the confession to her mother, can the priest be subpoenaed to testify?

Problem 17-18: Accidental Discovery Disclosure

In a copyright and trademark infringement action by Burger King against McDonalds, discovery requests for documents and e-mails numbered in the tens of thousands. When Burger King realized it had turned over 20 documents it believed were privileged under the attorney-client privilege, it filed a motion to classify those documents as privileged and to have them returned. If the disclosure was indeed inadvertent, did Burger King waive its privilege?

§ 17.06 Examples of State Law Privileges

Georgia Chapter 24-9-21. Confidentiality of certain communications.

There are certain admissions and communications excluded on grounds of public policy. Among these are:

(1) Communications between husband and wife;

(2) Communications between attorney and client;

(3) Communications among grand jurors;

(4) Secrets of state; and

(5) Communications between psychiatrist and patient.

Florida Statute § 90.5035. Sexual assault counselor-victim privilege.

(1) For purposes of this section:

(a) a "rape crisis center" is any public or private agency that offers assistance to victims of sexual assault or sexual battery and their families.

(b) a "sexual counselor" is any employee of a rape crisis center whose primary purpose is the rendering of advice, counseling, or assistance to victims of sexual assault or sexual battery.

(2) A victim has a privilege to refuse to disclose and to prevent any other person from disclosing, a confidential communication made by the victim to a sexual assault counselor or any record made in the course of advising, counseling, or assisting the victim. Such confidential communication or record may be disclosed only with the prior written consent of the victim. This privilege includes any advice given by the sexual assault counselor in the course of that relationship.

Florida Statute § 90.5055. Accountant-client privilege.

(2) A client has a privilege to refuse to disclose, and to prevent any other person from disclosing, the contents of confidential communications with an accountant when such other person learned of the communications because they were made in the rendition of accounting services to the client. This privilege includes other confidential information obtained by the accountant from the client for the purpose of rendering accounting advice.

Nebraska § 27-504. Physician-patient privilege.

(2) A patient has a privilege to refuse to disclose and to prevent any other person from disclosing confidential communications made for the purposes of diagnosis or treatment of his or her physical, mental, or emotional condition among himself or herself, his or her physician, or persons who are participating in the diagnosis or treatment under the direction of the physician, including members of the patient's family.

Hawaii Rule 506. Communications to clergyman.

(a) Definitions. As used in this rule:

(1) A "clergyman" is a minister, priest, rabbi, Christian Science practitioner, or other similar functionary of a religious organization, or an individual reasonably believed so to be by the person consulting him.

(2) A communication is "confidential" if made privately and not intended for further disclosure except to other persons present in furtherance of the purpose of the communication.

(b) General rule of privilege. A person has a privilege to refuse to disclose and to prevent another from disclosing a confidential communication by the person to a clergyman in his professional character as spiritual advisor.

New Jersey § 2A:84A-21. Newspaperman's privilege.

Subject to Rule 37, a person engaged on, engaged in, connected with, or employed by a news media for the purpose of gathering, procuring, transmitting, compiling, editing or disseminating news for the general public or on whose behalf news is so gathered, procured, transmitted, compiled, edited or disseminated has a privilege to refuse to disclose, in any legal or quasi-legal proceeding or before any investigative body, including, but not limited to, any court, grand jury, petit jury, administrative agency, the Legislature or legislative committee, or elsewhere.

   a. The source, author, means, agency or person from or through whom any information was procured, obtained, supplied, furnished, gathered, transmitted, compiled, edited, disseminated, or delivered; and

   b. Any news or information obtained in the course of pursuing his professional activities whether or not it is disseminated.

§ 17.07 Summary and Review

1. How many privileges do the Federal Rules of Evidence expressly recognize?

2. How many marital privileges exist? Why?

3. Who should hold the adverse spousal privilege, the accused or the spouse who is called to testify? Why?

4. What are the various sources of federal privileges?

5. When does state privilege law apply in federal court?

6. Why have a privilege for the political vote?

7. Why have a privilege for the identity of an informer?

8. How can a privilege be waived?

9. Why don't the states and federal common law recognize a parent-child privilege?

§ 17.08 Chapter Review Problems

Problem 17-A

Barlie Thompson is called to testify against her husband, Artis Thompson, in a fraud action brought against Artis by a local bank, First National City Bank. Artis allegedly told Barlie he was cashing a check he knew to be fraudulent and was hiding the stolen money in his sock drawer. Artis asserts the spousal immunity privilege and attempts to keep Barlie off of the witness stand. *How should the judge rule?*

1. The judge should exclude Barlie from testifying, but only if Barlie asserts the privilege.

2. The judge should exclude Barlie from testifying because the privilege extends to the entire testimony about the events in question, before, during, and after the alleged fraud took place.

3. The judge should not exclude Barlie from testifying if she has competent and relevant information.

4. The judge should not exclude Barlie from testifying, but should prohibit any questions about her husband, Artis.

Problem 17-B

Biloxi Barnes was married to Harold Hines, an alleged member of a large crime syndicate in Chicago, Illinois. After Harold had passed away, Biloxi was called to testify in a criminal case involving her husband's business associates. The associates had been charged with mail fraud and conspiracy. Harold had allegedly told Biloxi, "Yeah, me and the boys had to take charge of our business and minimize the opportunities of our competitors, if you know what I mean." This statement:

1. Is not admissible as a co-conspirator admission if it was made in privacy by Harold to his wife.

2. Is not admissible as a statement against interest, because, now that Harold has passed away, it is not against his interest.

3. Is admissible as a co-conspirator admission, because Harold concedes he was working in concert with his business partners, those individuals on trial.

4. Is admissible as a statement against interest, because it was against Harold's interest when he made it.

Problem 17-C

Alice went to her massage therapist to work out the pain in her back after her car was rear-ended by another car. During the massage, Alice told her therapist, Adin, whom she had known for many years, "In the strictest of confidence, the pain in my lower back resulted from straining my back years ago at the supermarket, not from this accident." If, during a subsequent trial, the therapist is called to testify by the defendant against Alice, this testimony should be:

1. *Admitted, because Alice's statement is relevant and not hearsay.*

2. *Admitted, because it falls into an exception to the therapist's privilege.*

3. *Excluded, because the statement is privileged under the broad interpretation given the therapist privilege.*

4. *Excluded, because the promise to keep the information confidential binds the therapist in the face of the law.*

Problem 17-D

The Cinderella Cruise Line routinely reviews accidents on its ships after they occur. As part of the routine, an investigator is appointed, a file is created, and a confidential meeting is held to determine if safety standards have been met. After an accident in the dining room of one of the Cinderella ships and after a report has been prepared by Cinderella, a lawsuit is filed. The plaintiff seeks access to the report prepared by the cruise line, and the cruise line claims privilege. How should the court rule?

1. The document is privileged because it was intended to be confidential and was reviewed only by certain company employees.

2. The document is privileged under the attorney-client privilege.

3. The document is not privileged because there is only a qualified self-analysis privilege, at best, and this was a routine, habitual act by the company.

4. The document is not privileged because it is an admission by a party-opponent.

§ 17.09 Case Library

Upjohn v. United States

United States Supreme Court

449 U.S. 383, 101 S. Ct. 677, 66 L. Ed. 2d 584 (1981)

Nix v. Whiteside

United States Supreme Court

475 U.S. 157, 106 S. Ct. 988, 89 L. Ed. 2d 123 (1986)

Jaffee v. Redmond

United States Supreme Court

518 U.S. 1, 116 S. Ct. 1923, 135 L. Ed. 2d 337 (1996)

Chapter 18

Authentication, Identification, and the "Best Evidence" Rule

§ 18.01 Chapter Checklist

1. Is there sufficient proof that the thing offered into evidence is what it purports to be?

2. Have all of the "magic" foundation questions for authentication been asked of the witness in a recognizable form?

3. Does the so-called "best evidence" rule (really the original writings rule) apply to the case?

4. To determine the applicability of the best evidence rule, is a party proving the contents of a writing that is important to the case?

5. If the best evidence rule applies, is there an adequate alternative to the original writing that can serve as a substitute?

6. How is *Seiler v. Lucasfilm, Ltd.*, 808 F.2d 1316 (9th Cir. 1986), referenced in the Case Library at the end of the chapter, an apt illustration of the rationale underlying the "best evidence rule"?

§ 18.02 Relevant Federal Rules of Evidence
ARTICLE IX. AUTHENTICATION AND IDENTIFICATION

Rule 901. Authenticating or Identifying Evidence

(a) In General. To satisfy the requirement of authenticating or identifying an item of evidence, the proponent must produce evidence sufficient to support a finding that the item is what the proponent claims it is.

(b) Examples. The following are examples only — not a complete list — of evidence that satisfies the requirement:

(1) *Testimony of a Witness with Knowledge.* Testimony that an item is what it is claimed to be.

(2) *Nonexpert Opinion About Handwriting.* A nonexpert's opinion that handwriting is genuine, based on a familiarity with it that was not acquired for the current litigation.

(3) *Comparison by an Expert Witness or the Trier of Fact.* A comparison with an authenticated specimen by an expert witness or the trier of fact.

(4) *Distinctive Characteristics and the Like.* The appearance, contents, substance, internal patterns, or other distinctive characteristics of the item, taken together with all the circumstances.

(5) *Opinion About a Voice.* An opinion identifying a person's voice — whether heard firsthand or through mechanical or electronic transmission or recording — based on hearing the voice at any time under circumstances that connect it with the alleged speaker.

(6) *Evidence About a Telephone Conversation.* For a telephone conversation, evidence that a call was made to the number assigned at the time to:

(A) a particular person, if circumstances, including self-identification, show that the person answering was the one called; or

(B) a particular business, if the call was made to a business and the call related to business reasonably transacted over the telephone.

(7) *Evidence About Public Records.* Evidence that:

(A) a document was recorded or filed in a public office as authorized by law; or

(B) a purported public record or statement is from the office where items of this kind are kept.

(8) *Evidence About Ancient Documents or Data Compilations.* For a document or data compilation, evidence that it:

(A) is in a condition that creates no suspicion about its authenticity;

(B) was in a place where, if authentic, it would likely be; and

(C) is at least 20 years old when offered.

(9) *Evidence About a Process or System.* Evidence describing a process or system and showing that it produces an accurate result.

(10) *Methods Provided by a Statute or Rule.* Any method of authentication or identification allowed by a federal statute or a rule prescribed by the Supreme Court.

. . . .

Rule 902. Evidence That is Self-Authenticating

The following items of evidence are self-authenticating; they require no extrinsic evidence of authenticity in order to be admitted:

(1) Domestic Public Documents That Are Sealed and Signed. A document that bears:

(A) a seal purporting to be that of the United States; any state, district, commonwealth, territory, or insular possession of the United States; the former Panama Canal Zone; the Trust Territory of the Pacific Islands; a political subdivision of any of these entities; or a department, agency, or officer of any entity named above; and

(B) a signature purporting to be an execution or attestation.

(2) Domestic Public Documents That Are Not Sealed but Are Signed and Certified. A document that bears no seal if:

(A) it bears the signature of an officer or employee of an entity named in Rule 902(1)(A); and

(B) another public officer who has a seal and official duties within that same entity certifies under seal — or its equivalent — that the signer has the official capacity and that the signature is genuine.

(3) Foreign Public Documents. A document that purports to be signed or attested by a person who is authorized by a foreign country's law to do so. The document must be accompanied by a final certification that certifies the genuineness of the signature and official position of the signer or attester — or of any foreign official whose certificate of genuineness relates to the signature or attestation or is in a chain of certificates of genuineness relating to the signature or attestation. The certification may be made by a secretary of a United States embassy or legation; by a consul general, vice consul, or consular agent of the United States; or by a diplomatic or consular official of the foreign country assigned or accredited to the United States. If all parties have been given a reasonable opportunity to investigate the document's authenticity and accuracy, the court may, for good cause, either:

(A) order that it be treated as presumptively authentic without final certification; or

(B) allow it to be evidenced by an attested summary with or without final certification.

(4) Certified Copies of Public Records. A copy of an official record — or a copy of a document that was recorded or filed in a public office as authorized by law — if the copy is certified as correct by:

(A) the custodian or another person authorized to make the certification; or

(B) a certificate that complies with Rule 902(1), (2), or (3), a federal statute, or a rule prescribed by the Supreme Court.

(5) Official Publications. A book, pamphlet, or other publication purporting to be issued by a public authority.

(6) Newspapers and Periodicals. Printed material purporting to be a newspaper or periodical.

(7) Trade Inscriptions and the Like. An inscription, sign, tag, or label purporting to have been affixed in the course of business and indicating origin, ownership, or control.

(8) Acknowledged Documents. A document accompanied by a certificate of acknowledgment that is lawfully executed by a notary public or another officer who is authorized to take acknowledgments.

(9) Commercial Paper and Related Documents. Commercial paper, a signature on it, and related documents, to the extent allowed by general commercial law.

(10) Presumptions Under a Federal Statute. A signature, document, or anything else that a federal statute declares to be presumptively or prima facie genuine or authentic.

(11) Certified Domestic Records of a Regularly Conducted Activity. The original or a copy of a domestic record that meets the requirements of Rule 803(6)(A)-(C), as shown by a certification of the custodian or another qualified person that complies with a federal statute or a rule prescribed by the Supreme Court. Before the trial or hearing, the proponent must give an adverse party reasonable written notice of the intent to offer the record — and must make the record and certification available for inspection — so that the party has a fair opportunity to challenge them.

(12) Certified Foreign Records of a Regularly Conducted Activity. In a civil case, the original or a copy of a foreign record that meets the requirements of Rule 902(11), modified as follows: the certification, rather than complying with a federal statute or Supreme Court rule, must be signed in a manner that, if falsely made, would subject the maker to a criminal penalty in the country where the certification is signed. The proponent must also meet the notice requirements of Rule 902(11).

(13) Certified Records Generated by an Electronic Process or System. A record generated by an electronic process or system that produces an accurate result, as shown by a certification of a qualified person that complies with the certification requirements of Rule 902(11) or (12). The proponent must also meet the notice requirements of Rule 902(11).

(14) Certified Data Copied from an Electronic Device, Storage Medium, or File. Data copied from an electronic device, storage medium, or file, if authenticated by a process of digital identification, as shown by a certification of a qualified person that complies with the certification requirements of Rule 902(11) or (12). The proponent also must meet the notice requirements of Rule 902(11).

Rule 903. Subscribing Witness

A subscribing witness's testimony is necessary to authenticate a writing only if required by the law of the jurisdiction that governs its validity.

ARTICLE X. CONTENTS OF WRITINGS, RECORDINGS,
AND PHOTOGRAPHS

Rule 1001. Definitions That Apply to This Article

In this article:

(a) A "writing" consists of letters, words, numbers, or their equivalent set down in any form.

(b) A "recording" consists of letters, words, numbers, or their equivalent recorded in any manner.

(c) A "photograph" means a photographic image or its equivalent stored in any form.

(d) An "original" of a writing or recording means the writing or recording itself or any counterpart intended to have the same effect by the person who executed or issued it. For electronically stored information, "original" means any printout — or other output readable by sight — if it accurately reflects the information. An "original" of a photograph includes the negative or a print from it.

(e) A "duplicate" means a counterpart produced by a mechanical, photographic, chemical, electronic, or other equivalent process or technique that accurately reproduces the original.

Rule 1002. Requirement of the Original

An original writing, recording, or photograph is required in order to prove its content unless these rules or a federal statute provides otherwise.

Rule 1003 — Admissibility of Duplicates

A duplicate is admissible to the same extent as the original unless a genuine question is raised about the original's authenticity or the circumstances make it unfair to admit the duplicate.

Rule 1004. Admissibility of Other Evidence of Contents

An original is not required and other evidence of the content of a writing, recording, or photograph is admissible if:

(a) all the originals are lost or destroyed, and not by the proponent acting in bad faith;

(b) an original cannot be obtained by any available judicial process;

(c) the party against whom the original would be offered had control of the original; was at that time put on notice, by pleadings or otherwise, that the original would be a subject of proof at the trial or hearing; and fails to produce it at the trial or hearing; or

(d) the writing, recording, or photograph is not closely related to a controlling issue.

Rule 1005. Copies of Public Records to Prove Content

The proponent may use a copy to prove the content of an official record — or of a document that was recorded or filed in a public office as authorized by law — if these conditions are met: the record or document is otherwise admissible; and the copy is certified as correct in accordance with Rule 902(4) or is testified to be correct by a witness who has compared it with the original. If no such copy can be obtained by reasonable diligence, then the proponent may use other evidence to prove the content.

Rule 1006. Summaries

The proponent may use a summary, chart, or calculation to prove the content of voluminous writings, recordings, or photographs that cannot be conveniently examined in court. The proponent must make the originals or duplicates available for examination or copying, or both, by other parties at a reasonable time and place. And the court may order the proponent to produce them in court.

Rule 1007. Testimony or Statement of a Party to Prove Content

The proponent may prove the content of a writing, recording, or photograph by the testimony, deposition, or written statement of the party against whom the evidence is offered. The proponent need not account for the original.

Rule 1008. Functions of the Court and Jury

Ordinarily, the court determines whether the proponent has fulfilled the factual conditions for admitting other evidence of the content of a writing, recording, or photograph under Rule 1004 or 1005. But in a jury trial, the jury determines — in accordance with Rule 104(b) — any issue about whether:

(a) an asserted writing, recording, or photograph ever existed;

(b) another one produced at the trial or hearing is the original; or

(c) other evidence of content accurately reflects the content.

§ 18.03 Authentication and Identification

A. Requirement of Authentication

"Authentication and identification represent a special aspect of relevancy.... Wigmore describes the need for authentication as 'an inherent logical necessity.'" Advisory Committee Note, Rule 901.

In a sense, all evidence admitted at trial must first be authenticated. Authentication requires a basic showing that evidence is relevant to the case and to a minimum extent, reliable — that the evidence is what it purports to be. Authentication, as a threshold for admissibility, is a precursor to the trier of fact's subsequent job of weighing and evaluating the evidence to see if it helps to support the applicable burden of persuasion. For example, eyewitnesses to an event must show that they have personal knowledge of the event. The possessor of a radar gun must show the gun accurately assesses the speed of vehicles. Authentication, therefore, can be viewed as a special type of relevancy requirement that applies to a wide variety of evidence. Authentication is like requiring a list of ingredients on the side of a product sold in a supermarket. It is a form of truth in advertising, showing how the evidence connects to the issues in the case.

Authentication also addresses another type of relevancy problem: unfair prejudice. If the evidence is not authentic, it may well be misleading for the factfinder attempting to decide the case. To illustrate, a knife produced at trial in a murder case will be helpful only if it is relevant to resolving the issues in the case (e.g., it is the knife used in the killing at issue or it is sufficiently similar to the alleged knife to be used for demonstrative purposes). Similarly, a photograph must be a fair and accurate representation of whatever it depicts, or else it will be misleading. Even witnesses must be authenticated, by showing that they have relevant evidence to contribute. The admission of unauthenticated evidence would waste time and distract jurors from their fact-finding responsibilities.

The Federal Evidence Rules on the subject, 901 and 902, focus on specific authentication problems. Rule 901 assists with the recurring authentication issue of determining what methods are sufficient to authenticate different kinds of evidence. It lists some methods of authentication that are used in common situations, like ways to authenticate voices, handwriting, and telephone conversations.

Rule 902 provides help with a different issue — forms of evidence that everyone knows are authentic but would require considerable expenditures of time and effort to formally lay a foundation. The rule spares a party the trouble of formally offering foundational evidence and calling a stream of witnesses. Instead, like judicially noticed evidence, this category of evidence simply bypasses the formalities of laying the foundation. The party offers the evidence as self-authenticating under Rule 902. Rule 902, however, does not ensure automatic admissibility of the evidence. Other objections to the admissibility of the evidence can still be raised, just not one based on a lack of foundation.

The category of self-authenticating evidence provides a laundry list of examples. These include certified copies of public records, such as convictions of crimes, newspapers, periodicals, trade inscriptions, and commercial paper. *See* Rule 902.

In 2017, amendments to Rule 902 assisted with issues arising from the digitization of today's world, fast-forwarding the Rule into the 21st Century. The amendments allow electronic data to be authenticated in a predictable and efficient manner. The Rule states in pertinent part:

> *(13) Certified Records Generated by an Electronic Process or System.* A record generated by an electronic process or system that produces an accurate result, as shown by a certification of a quali-fied person that complies

with the certification requirements of Rule 902(11) or (12). The propo-nent must also meet the notice requirements of Rule 902(11).

(14) Certified Data Copied from an Electronic Device, Storage Medium, or File. Data copied from an electronic device, storage medium, or file, if authenticated by a process of digital identification, as shown by a certification of a qualified person that complies with the certification requirements of Rule (902(11) or (12). The proponent also must meet the notice requirements of Rule 902 (11).

B. Procedures for Authentication

The authentication of evidence — often called "laying the foundation" — generally proceeds in the following fashion. After evidence is marked, identified, and shown to opposing counsel, there are three traditional questions to ask a witness for authentication purposes:

Basic Question #1: Do you recognize prosecution/plaintiff/defendant's Exhibit #1 for identification purposes?

Basic Question #2: What is Exhibit #1 for identification purposes?

Basic Question #3: How do you recognize it?

Real or documentary evidence can be modified or altered. For example, a shotgun can be sawed off, a document can be erased or changed, and metal can rust or erode. Consequently, a fourth question is usually required to ensure that the real or documentary evidence has not changed in such a way as to make it unfairly prejudicial:

Basic Question #4: (Real Evidence): Witness, is Exhibit #1 for identification purposes in substantially the same condition as it was when you last saw it?

If the witness responds by saying that the condition of the evidence has been altered, the next question asked by counsel should probe how the alteration modified the evidence. For example, counsel could inquire, "What are the markings that have been added to the document?"

For representative evidence, the inquiry focuses on the accuracy of the evidence, not on the likelihood of tampering. Photographs, for example, can distort and not simply reproduce pertinent information. A photograph of an intersection on a bright, sunny day may be substantially different from a photograph of the same intersection during stormy conditions, which may have prevailed at the time in question. Further, the physical characteristics of an intersection can change dramatically over time. Thus, a fourth question is required to authenticate representative evidence.

Basic Question #5: (Representative Evidence): Is Exhibit #1 for identification purposes a fair and accurate representation of what it depicts as of a particular time and date [when the incident in question occurred]?

An additional foundational requirement may arise when evidence is susceptible to changes in its condition between the time the evidence is gathered and the time it is presented in court. When evidence is fungible, it is more susceptible to fraud. In such cases, authentication is not complete with the asking of the four "magic" questions. Instead, a *chain of custody* for the evidence must be shown as well.

A chain of custody means that the evidence is traced from its source, such as the crime scene in a criminal case or the accident scene in a personal injury action, all the way to the courtroom. The trace is intended to show that no custodian of the evidence has permitted alteration or tampering that would impugn the evidence's authenticity. For example, narcotics or an ordinary kitchen knife must be traced to the crime scene to ensure that the evidence has not been the subject of tampering.

Proof of a chain of custody is not always necessary. An item that is unique, non-fungible, or readily identifiable due to a special characteristic or context does not require such a foundation. To illustrate, a specially designed pearl-handled, neon green knife with the word "Mom" inlaid in jade on the handle likely will be considered unique, which would abrogating the need to establish a chain of custody. Further, non-unique real evidence sometimes can be made unique. A plain, ordinary kitchen knife may become unique if a witness' initials and the date are etched into it.

If evidence is authenticated, it may then be offered by a party "into evidence" at any time during the party's case. The offer need not occur when the authenticating witness is on the witness stand, although that is the most common and most appropriate time. Offering the evidence while the witness is on the stand affords the party the opportunity to repair any problems that might arise with the offer. The court usually will ask for objections prior to admitting the evidence. It also may permit a brief *voir dire* by the opposing party concerning authentication. A *voir dire* on an exhibit is essentially a miniature cross-examination restricted to the question of whether a proper foundation has been laid for admissibility.

If evidence is admitted, it is the offering party's responsibility to request that it be "published" (i.e., shown) to the jury. Generally, the court will allow admitted evidence to be published to the jury, subject to exceptions such as easily lost or fragile items. During publication, the questioning of a witness usually ceases, so the jury's attention can remain solely on the admitted evidence.

As noted above, the Rules categorize some evidence as self-authenticating. Self-authentication saves precious jury time and like judicial notice, permits the jury to focus on disputed issues of fact. *See* Rule 902. Self-authenticating evidence, such as domestic public documents, both under seal and not under seal, official publications, newspapers and periodicals, and trade inscriptions, also can be published to the jury.

> *Practice Tip — Make sure the jury has an unobstructed view*: When laying a foundation for an exhibit, be careful about where you stand. An attorney who is authenticating evidence should not block the jurors' ability to observe the witness or provide the jury with a view of the attorney's back.

(This principle applies to presenting witness testimony generally.) If standing near a witness while questioning the witness about a document, stand out of the way. The jury will appreciate it.

Problem 18-1: Yeah, That's the Ticket

In a complex commercial litigation case, the plaintiff offers various items in evidence. *What would the plaintiff have to do, if anything, to authenticate the following evidence? Briefly explain.*

1. A telephone conversation.

2. A business associate's handwriting.

3. A *Newsweek* magazine.

4. A Diet Coke label.

5. A photograph of the defendant.

6. A blueprint of a house.

Problem 18-2: Authenticate This . . .

After picking up his daughter from school in their green Town & Country van, Jean turned onto busy Commercial Boulevard. When he looked down to put a Raffi tape into the cassette player, he drifted into the left lane of the road. The driver in the left lane, Dirk, was speeding and not paying attention. In the ensuing crash, Dirk broke his leg, but everyone else was fine. Jean was sued by Dirk. *How would you authenticate the following evidence in the case? Briefly explain.*

1. A photograph of the scene of the auto accident.

2. The statement of a bystander, who happened to be a C.P.A.

3. The report of the emergency room physician who treated Jean.

4. The police officer's accident report.

5. A can of Budweiser recovered from the backseat of Dirk's car.

Problem 18-3: Not So Sweet

Rick and Associates, an advertising firm, sued Sarah's Pastries for breach of contract. Rick claimed that Sarah's owed him $4,000 for their performance under an agreement to create an advertising campaign. Rick's associate, Pam, had agreed on Rick's behalf to create a print advertising campaign for Sarah's products in several newspapers and trade publications. Pam signed the agreement after three telephone calls with Sarah's associate, Ben. Ben counter-signed and sent back the agreement with a separate piece of paper indicating that Sarah always reserved the right to review any advertising proposal "to her personal satisfaction." Three ads were created and ran in various papers after Pam had sent them to Ben via Bay State

Messenger Service. Rick requested payment from Sarah, but received no reply after four days.

You represent Sarah's Pastries at trial.

1. What evidence will you offer on her behalf? How will you authenticate that evidence?

2. What evidence will Rick offer? How will you oppose that evidence?

Problem 18-4: Making Money the Old-Fashioned Way

Sarah Gooding was an executive at Ortuna Web Systems, a business-to-business e-commerce company. During a highly contentious meeting, she observed a heated argument between Paul, the Chief Executive Officer, and Lisette, the Chief Financial Officer. Lisette subsequently sued Paul and the company, claiming she had been fired at the meeting. Paul rebutted her claims by alleging that Lisette had quit during the meeting. Sarah is questioned at trial:

PLAINTIFF'S ATTORNEY: Sarah, what did you see at the meeting that was held in the company boardroom at 3:00 p.m. on the 4th?

A: I saw a ferocious argument between Paul and Lisette over the company's direction. It was a real power struggle that I thought would come to blows.

PLAINTIFF'S ATTORNEY: Sarah, what, if anything, did you hear while you were at that meeting?

A: Bits and pieces of things. I heard Lisette say something like "we used to make money the old-fashioned way, by earning it," or something like that.

PLAINTIFF'S ATTORNEY: I show you what has been marked Plaintiff's Exhibit A for Identification Purposes. Do you recognize it?

A: It is a cassette tape.

PLAINTIFF'S ATTORNEY: How do you recognize that tape?

A: I've seen cassettes before; I own several, for that matter. I believe I have heard this one as well.

PLAINTIFF'S ATTORNEY: (playing it outside of the hearing of the jury) Do you recognize the contents of this cassette tape?

A: Parts. It sounded like the meeting on the 4th.

PLAINTIFF'S ATTORNEY: How do you recognize that it was the meeting on the 4th?

A: I was at the meeting and caught a lot of what they were saying.

PLAINTIFF'S ATTORNEY: Your Honor, I offer in evidence Plaintiff's Exhibit A for Identification Purposes.

JUDGE: Any objections?

DEFENDANT'S ATTORNEY: May I *voir dire* on the exhibit, Your Honor?

JUDGE: Certainly.

DEFENDANT'S ATTORNEY: You did not record this audiotape, did you, Sarah?

A: No, sir.

DEFENDANT'S ATTORNEY: You don't remember all of what was said on it, only parts, right?

A: True, but significant parts of it.

DEFENDANT'S ATTORNEY: You don't know who handled this tape prior to it being produced in court or whether it has been the subject of tampering?

A: True.

DEFENDANT'S ATTORNEY: I object, Your Honor, to the admission of the tape. There may be a break in the chain of custody, and Sarah cannot recollect all of the conversation.

If you are the judge, how would you rule on the admissibility of the audiotape? See United States v. Brown, 136 F.3d 1176 (7th Cir. 1998).

§ 18.04 The Best Evidence Rule

A. The Production of Original Documents

"In an earlier day, when discovery and other related procedures were strictly limited, the misleading[ly] named 'best evidence rule' afforded substantial guarantees against inaccuracies and fraud by its insistence upon production of original documents." Rule 1001, Advisory Committee's Note.

The best evidence rule imposes a special type of authentication requirement on some writings, which is why it is grouped with authentication in this chapter. As the Advisory Committee's Note to Rule 1001 indicates, writings can be susceptible to fraud and distortion. Consequently, the Federal Rules of Evidence continued the tradition of the common law, seeking to minimize potential problems by requiring the originals of writings that play a significant role at trial.

Objections based on the best evidence rule can cause quite a stir, if only because the rule's intricacies appear to be inscrutable. Because of its mystique, the rule often creates a formidable obstacle, much more formidable than the situation warrants.

As noted above, the so-called best evidence rule is actually a misnomer. While appearing to require the "best evidence," the rule really has a much more circumscribed application. It is more accurately described as "the original writings rule" or, as it is sometimes called, the "original documents rule." The rule applies only when a witness is testifying solely based on the contents of a writing or when a party attempts to prove the contents of a writing related to an issue in a case. For example, the rule would apply to a witness testifying about a written confession, the written contract in a breach of contract action, or a motion picture in an obscenity action.

The rule would not apply to an eyewitness to an automobile accident who took notes about the accident but left them at home, as the testimony is being offered to prove the circumstances of the accident, not the contents of the witness' notes.

Even in situations where the rule applies, it is perforated with exceptions. For example, a duplicate generally will suffice instead of the original. *See* Rules 1001(4), 1003.

While the rule may have limited applicability and is "fraught with exceptions," there is good reason to have it. One apt illustration of its value can be found in *Seiler v. Lucasfilm, Ltd.*, 808 F.2d 1316 (9th Cir. 1986), *cert. denied*, 484 U.S. 826 (1987), included at the end of the chapter in the Case Library. In *Seiler*, a graphic artist alleged that filmmaker George Lucas and others infringed the copyright on creatures the artist had created, called "Garthian Striders." Plaintiff contended that Lucas had used similar creatures, which Lucas called "Imperial Walkers," in the science fiction film, *The Empire Strikes Back*. At trial, the plaintiff intended to offer enlargements of the Garthian Striders. After a pretrial evidentiary hearing on the matter, the trial court held that the best evidence rule prevented the plaintiff from offering the enlargements and granted summary judgment for the defendants.

The trial court's ruling was based on the fact that the plaintiff could not produce the original drawings of the Garthian Striders, or in the alternative, any evidence of their existence prior to 1980, when *The Empire Strikes Back*, was released. Because of the danger of fraud, secondary evidence was excluded.

On appeal, the Ninth Circuit affirmed. The Court stated, "We hold that Seiler's drawings were 'writings' within the meaning of [the best evidence rule]; .... The contents of Seiler's work are at issue .... Since the contents are material and must be proved, Seiler must either produce the original or show that it is unavailable through no fault of his own .... This he could not do." 808 F.2d at 1318–1319. In fact, the Ninth Circuit noted that this case supported the very reason for the "best evidence" rule.

The best evidence rule applies to "writings," "recordings," and "photographs," which can include documents, x-rays, motion pictures, and videotapes. *See* Rules 1001(1), (2), 1002. Sometimes, it is unclear what constitutes a "writing" for the purposes of the rule. In *United States v. Duffy*, 454 F.2d 809 (5th Cir. 1972), for example, the defendant was convicted of transporting a stolen motor vehicle in interstate commerce. The car contained a suitcase that included a white shirt that had a laundry label reading, "D-U-F." The government offered testimony about the shirt at trial without producing it. In a decision handed down prior to the adoption of the Federal Rules of Evidence, the Fifth Circuit affirmed the trial court's decision to permit the testimony. The Court of Appeals stated:[1]

---

1. 454 F.2d at 812.

The [best evidence rule] is not, by its terms or because of the policies underlying it, applicable to the instant case. The shirt with a laundry mark would not, under ordinary understanding, be considered a writing, and would not, therefore, be covered by the "Best Evidence Rule." When the disputed evidence, such as the shirt in this case, is an object bearing a mark or inscription, and is therefore a chattel and a writing, the trial judge has discretion to treat the evidence as a chattel or as a writing. The shirt was collateral evidence of the crime. Furthermore, it was only one piece of evidence in a substantial case against Duffy.

Under the best evidence rule, disputes about whether a writing ever existed, whether a different writing is the original, or whether other evidence correctly reflects the writing's contents are considered questions of fact to be determined by the trier of fact. *See* Rule 1008. These are not admissibility questions to be decided by the judge pursuant to Rule 104(a).

Example

Princess Genevieve files an invasion of privacy action against *The Daily Star Mail* tabloid for publishing a photograph of her at a secluded Caribbean hideaway with her new boyfriend, Count Zigfried von Jonk. Does the best evidence rule apply to the production of the photograph at trial?

Answer: The best evidence rule likely applies to the photograph. The photograph is not collateral to the case, but rather is the basis of the cause of action. A photograph also is considered to be a writing pursuant to Federal Rule of Evidence 1001. Thus, *The Daily Star Mail* must produce the original photograph unless one of the numerous statutory exceptions governs.

B. Exceptions to the Requirement of an Original

The flexibility of the "original writing" rule is a prevailing characteristic. As the Advisory Committee stated, "[b]asically the rule requiring the production of the original as proof of contents has developed as a rule of preference: if failure to produce the original is satisfactorily explained, secondary evidence is admissible." Rule 1004, Advisory Committee's Note. The Advisory Committee's rationale is based on common sense. If a writing is at issue, the writing should be produced for a firsthand review. Production of the writing should not be required, however, if it would not be helpful to resolving the issues of the trial and would involve extra time and expense.

Even when the rule applies, the non-production of the original writing is allowed when:

- A duplicate is offered in lieu of the original. A "duplicate" is a counterpart produced from the original by a technique, such as photography or re-recording, that accurately reproduces the original. (Rule 1001(4).)

- The original has been lost or destroyed and no bad faith exists. (Rule 1004.)

- The original is not obtainable. For example, it is locked away in a safe in a foreign country and cannot be retrieved. (Rule 1004.)

- The original is in the possession of the opposing party. This exception prevents the rule from being used as both a sword and a shield, which would occur if a party possessing the original asks that the opposing party be penalized for not producing the original. (Rule 1004.)

- The writing whose contents are in question is collateral to the issues at trial. (Rule 1004.)

Other limitations on the requirement of providing the original are as follows:

- Copies of public records are permitted to promote judicial economy and avoid "serious inconvenience." (Rule 1005, Advisory Committee's Note.)

- Summaries of voluminous writings are allowed to promote judicial economy. (Rule 1006.)

- The testimony, deposition, or written admission of a party opponent about the contents of the writing may be used as proof of the contents without the production of the original. (Rule 1007.)

Despite the rule permitting the non-production of the original under a variety of circumstances, foundational limits to secondary evidence exist. Rule 1003 provides that a duplicate is allowed in all situations when proving the contents of a writing, except: (1) when there exists a genuine question as to the authenticity of the original writing, such as a dispute over which of the parties possesses the real contract in question; or (2) when the admission of a duplicate would be unfair under the circumstances. Thus, if a party challenges a document central to the case as a forgery, the document's authenticity is at issue and the original might be required. In addition, on fairness grounds, the original may be required if only a partial duplicate of a record is provided at trial. Under such circumstances, the opposing counsel would be at a disadvantage in countering the evidence and examining witnesses about it.

Destroying documents through bad faith also prohibits the proponent's admission of secondary evidence about the documents. Bad faith generally means more than the negligent loss or destruction of evidence and is usually the result of an intentional culpable act. Yet, not all intentional destruction of evidence qualifies as bad faith. For example, if a business routinely destroyed records after saving them for a certain period of time, such conduct might not satisfy the bad faith requirement.

Practice Tip: "If you haven't got a Ha'Penny . . ." The introduction to FRE 1004 states that if an original is not required, "other secondary evidence" of a writing's contents is admissible. This language means that if you're excused from having to offer the original of a writing, whether you prove its contents with a tangible copy (if one exists) or oral testimony is up to you. However, assuming that you have a choice, better practice is to follow the lyrics of an old English tune: "If you haven't got a penny, then a ha'penny will do; if you haven't got a ha'penny, then God bless you." As a general practice, prove the contents of an unavailable original writing through a tangible copy, if one is available. If a tangible copy is not available, then resort to oral testimony to the original's contents. (For more information about the tune, visit the web address *http://en.wikipedia.org/wiki/Christmas_Is_Coming*.)

Problem 18-5: Hagar

Harold Hagar was hired to build a porch on Paulette Pogo's house. Hagar claimed he was not paid for the job after completing it, so he brought suit. At trial, the only issue was whether Hagar completed the work. Hagar testified in his case-in-chief:

PLAINTIFF'S ATTORNEY: Hagar, are you employed?

A: Yes, I am a licensed building contractor.

DEFENDANT'S ATTORNEY: Objection. Since Hagar is testifying about a written contractor license, he is violating the best evidence rule. He must bring the license in for proper examination.

Is the defense counsel correct? Why?

PLAINTIFF'S ATTORNEY: Who did the work on the infrastructure of the deck?

A: Johnny Walker.

DEFENDANT'S ATTORNEY: Objection. Johnny Walker is the best witness to testify about who did the work on the deck. This testimony violates the best evidence rule.

Is the defense counsel correct? Why?

PLAINTIFF'S ATTORNEY: What was your role in the project?

A: I supervised construction, and kept copious records on a daily basis of who did what.

DEFENDANT'S ATTORNEY: Objection. Again, Your Honor, Hagar's testimony is in violation of the best evidence rule. Hagar must bring in the records and then properly authenticate them as business records.

Is the defense counsel correct? Why?

Problem 18-6: Sweet Suit

The plaintiff, Ethel, sued the defendant, Rose, for breach of contract involving the sale of chocolate bars on March 12. The sole issue at trial was whether the number of bars stated in the contract was 3,800 or 38,000. The defendant offers a duplicate of the contract at trial.

Will a duplicate suffice? Explain.

Problem 18-7: More Breach

In the same breach of contract action as in the previous problem, the defendant Rose contends that the original contract was washed away in a huge rainstorm that destroyed her office. She only was able to save a copy of it.

Will the defendant be able to offer a copy of the contract in lieu of the original? Explain.

Problem 18-8: Meet the Jetsons

Plaintiff, the Jetson Motor Credit Company, sued the defendant for allegedly failing to make a $5,500 payment on defendant's new Astro electric car. At trial, the defendant, Elroy, offers a duplicate of his payment receipt.

Will the duplicate receipt violate the best evidence rule? Explain.

Problem 18-9: Elroy Was Here

Elroy subsequently brings suit for an alleged overpayment to Jetson. Jetson defends by claiming that no overpayment occurred and that he had a receipt to prove it. At trial, Jetson forgets to bring in the receipt, but still testifies about the payment. Elroy objects to the testimony, claiming that any testimony about the payment without the receipt violates the best evidence rule.

How should the judge rule on this objection?

Problem 18-10: All Business

To prove that a famous person had been present on the San Diego boat, *All Business*, the plaintiff offers the duplicate of a photograph taken of the famous individual on the boat.

Is the duplicate admissible? Why?

Problem 18-11: I Confess!

Defendant Magoo is charged with a crime. After orally confessing to the police, the defendant signs a verbatim written version of his confession. At trial, the police forget to bring the written confession, but attempt to testify about the oral confession anyway.

Can a police officer who heard the confession testify to it? Why?

Can a police officer who read the confession testify to it? Explain.

Problem 18-12: Dat's Da Guy

Hillerich is charged with bank robbery of the National Bank. Bradley, the teller who was robbed, testifies for the prosecution. He is shown a copy of a photograph of the robbery taken by the bank surveillance camera. Bradley verifies that the people and their locations were as depicted in the photograph. Bradley also indicates that the photograph shows the robber carrying a gun in his belt. (Bradley does not independently remember seeing the gun on the assailant during the robbery because of Bradley's fear at the time.)

1. Does this testimony violate the best evidence rule? Why?

2. What is the significance, if any, of the defendant contesting the authenticity of the photograph?

Problem 18-13: Roll the Videotape, Please

Barnaby sues NBS Television for distributing a videotape in which NBS made allegedly libelous statements about him. At trial, Barnaby testifies about the tape but does not bring it with him.

1. Does Barnaby's testimony violate the best evidence rule? Explain.

2. If Barnaby brings a copy of the videotape, does this satisfy the best evidence rule? Explain.

3. The president of NBS was overheard two weeks prior to trial at a cocktail party saying, "Our employee said in that videotape that Barnaby was a slippery snake. So what?" Does Barnaby still have to offer the original videotape? Why?

4. If Barnaby has accidentally destroyed the videotape, what recourse does he have, if any, at trial? Explain.

Problem 18-14: Damages

In a workers' compensation action, the primary issue at trial was the plaintiff's earning capacity. Plaintiff testified on direct examination:

PLAINTIFF'S ATTORNEY: How much did you earn in the year 2005?

A: I earned the amount of—

DEFENDANT'S ATTORNEY: Objection. This testimony violates the best evidence rule, Your Honor.

1. Why does the defense counsel claim that this testimony violates the "best evidence" rule?

2. What ruling and why?

§ 18.05 Summary and Review

1. What kinds of evidence must be authenticated? Why?

2. What is the difference between the authentication of real evidence and the authentication of representative evidence?

3. Why is some evidence self-authenticating?

4. Why is the term "best evidence rule" a misnomer?

5. Describe two situations in which the best evidence rule applies.

6. Name three substitutes that may be offered in lieu of the original writing when the best evidence rule applies.

§ 18.06 Chapter Review Problems

Problem 18-A

Ann Larimore purchased a "Balancing" nutrition bar from the local supermarket, Everyday's Market. Shortly after eating the bar, Larimore became very ill. Upon recovering, she sued the maker of the bar. At trial, Larimore offered a bar in the identical wrapper to the one she purchased. While testifying, her own attorney asked her, "Ann, do you recognize plaintiff's Exhibit #11 for identification purposes?" Ann responded, "Yes, it is exactly the type of Balancing Bar I purchased that made me sick." The attorney then offered the bar in evidence. The defendant objected on several grounds, including lack of authentication. *As to the objection relating to authentication, how should the court rule?* Explain.

1. The exhibit should be excluded because the attorney failed to satisfy authentication requirements.

2. The exhibit should be excluded because it is unfairly prejudicial and will mislead the jury.

3. The exhibit should not be excluded based on a lack of authentication because under the circumstances, there is sufficient authentication.

4. The exhibit should not be excluded because the importance of the document outweighs the minor omissions by counsel in laying the foundation.

Problem 18-B

In a negligence action resulting from a collision between a sports utility vehicle and a truck, the plaintiff called an expert in accident reconstruction to describe what exactly occurred during the accident. The expert was admitted by the court and, after laying a foundation of how she constructed her demonstrative computer graphics, the expert attempted to use a computer reenactment of the accident to illustrate her testimony. The defense objects. *How should the court rule?*

1. Admit, if it is reasonably accurate and will aid in the witness' testimony.

2. Admit, if counsel shows the reenactment constitutes business records under the applicable hearsay exception.

3. Exclude, because such a reenactment is highly prejudicial.

4. Exclude, because the reenactment is not probative of a fact of consequence.

Problem 18-C

Johnny Epstein and Melissa Matsui were charged with wire fraud for allegedly selling millions of dollars of fraudulent bonds to retirees by telephone. At trial, the prosecutor offered transcripts of several wiretapped phone conversations on Melissa's phone between the defendants pursuant to a properly obtained warrant. The defense objects to the admission of the transcripts. *Which of the following statements is the most accurate?*

1. The best evidence rule applies, and the tape or a copy of the tape must be produced.

2. The tape is hearsay and inadmissible.

3. The phone conversations between the co-defendants are privileged.

4. The Rule of Completeness does not allow the conversations unless all of the conversations between the defendants were taped.

Problem 18-D

Serena Shelley was prosecuted for theft of Social Security checks from the United States mail. At trial, after laying the necessary foundation and authenticating its evidence, the prosecution offered four original checks and a partial photocopy of a fifth check. *If there is an objection to the admissibility of these five checks, how should the judge rule?*

1. The five checks should be admitted, so long as they were properly authenticated.

2. The partial photocopy should be admitted because the rule requiring the production of the remainder of a document does not apply to checks.

3. The partial photocopy should be admitted because the best evidence rule does not apply.

4. The partial photocopy should not be admitted, unless the remainder of the check is irrelevant or not useful to the opponent of the evidence.

§ 18.07 Case Library

Seiler v. Lucasfilm, Ltd.

United States Court of Appeals
Ninth Circuit 808 F.2d 1316 (1986)

Chapter 19

Review Problems

§ 19.01 Problems

This chapter helps you to prepare for law school exams by reviewing a variety of evidence issues. The first review problem, Problem 19-1, asks you to identify evidentiary issues in the context of a case file in the hypothetical criminal prosecution, *U.S. v. Rick O'Ruben*. The remainder of the chapter consists of sixty multiple-choice questions drawn from a variety of actual Evidence final examinations.

Problem 19-1: United States v. O'Ruben

This review problem is presented in the form of a mock trial that can be acted out by the participants. It involves the robbery of a convenience store, with one main witness for the prosecution and one for the defense. Additional witnesses can be added, such as a police officer for the prosecution or the spouse of Rick O'Ruben for the defense. The sworn statements of the store clerk, Sally Smith, and the defendant, Rick O'Ruben, provide the basis for each witness' testimony. Note that these statements are equivalent to a deposition and can be used to impeach the witnesses if they testify inconsistently with the sworn statements.

The problem is designed as a review of evidence law, touching on many subject areas of the course. Unlike previous problems where the subject matter is expressly labeled, this review is intended to promote issue-spotting skills as well as legal analysis.

The Prosecution's Case

1. The robbery note.

2. The gun.

3. A note written by Sally after the robbery containing the purported getaway car's license plate number.

4. The testimony of Sally Smith. (This testimony should be consistent with Sally Smith's statement below.)

5. The sworn statement of Sally Smith.

The following is the true signed and sworn statement of Sally Smith, made on January 25, within one month of the alleged robbery:

> My name is Sally Smith. I am 29 years old and I had been working on the night shift at Magruder's Convenience Store on Main Street for almost a

year. I was fired from Magruder's last Thursday for allegedly taking money from the cash register. They can't prove it, however, and that's because I did not do it.

I flunked out of high school and have had a few problems with the law. I was convicted of possessing marijuana, a misdemeanor, two years ago; of aggravated assault on my ex-husband, a felony, ten years ago; of embezzlement from my prior employer (although I was framed), a misdemeanor, last year; and of the unlawful possession of a firearm, a misdemeanor, twelve years ago. Also, I was arrested for the attempted murder of my ex-husband three years ago, but the charges were dropped.

I am now working as a receptionist in the Body Boutique, a nails and hair salon. I've been there for a week or so, and I like it a lot.

On the first Wednesday in January I was working the night shift at Magruder's. Magruder's is like any other convenience store—big on the beer, potato chips, muffins, and things like that. There is only one entrance into the store, and the clerk's counter is about ten yards or so from the front entrance. There are six aisles perpendicular to my counter, and mirrors near the ceiling so I can see the entire store. There is a surveillance camera as well, but it wasn't working that night. The lighting is pretty good, since the whole store has fluorescent lights.

I started that evening around 6:00 p.m. It was pretty quiet that night, only about fifteen customers each hour. I even had time to do inventory work, which took me into the back room for a short period of time, like ten minutes. At 9:00 p.m., I was the only person in the store. When this guy walked into the store, he seemed nervous; he looked around some.

He then came right up to me at the checkout counter, and put this note on the counter that said, "Your money or your life." I told my sister last week that when the fellow first walked in, he seemed like a nice guy, not the monster he turned out to be.

Anyway, he really was a creep. I guess I was going too slow for him, because he hit me on the shoulder real hard with his fist and said, "Faster, faster, sister, I mean it!" I thought I saw a gun in his hand, but I wasn't sure. After I gave him all of the money in the register, he started humming a song, I think it was Springsteen's "Tunnel of Love" or something like that. He then walked quickly out of the store. The whole thing lasted no more than five or ten minutes. I felt nauseous, and my knees buckled, but I took a deep breath and ran after him. I saw him get in his car and drive away. The lighting in the parking lot was pretty good; street lights near the car, you know. I wrote down his license plate number, but I can't remember what I wrote down—I was very nervous at the time. In looking at the paper I wrote it on, it says "license plate number: DDP 514."

I then ran back into the store and called the police. I told them I had just been robbed by a guy who was about 5 feet, 10 inches tall, and 140 pounds, white male, beard, shoulder length dark hair, with fingerless black gloves and an earring in his right ear. I told them the robbery probably took about a minute.

Several days after the robbery, the police showed me some photographs of people. I looked over all of them and pointed out the person who I thought was the robber. As sure as I am sitting here, it was that guy, Rick O'Ruben.

I had never seen him before, although I did see someone who looked just like him in the nearby supermarket about two months prior to the robbery.

This was one of the scariest things to ever happen to me. I will remember the robber's face as long as I live. I don't ever want to get robbed again; it still causes me nightmares.

As I ran out after the robber, I saw a gun lying on the floor just inside the store entrance. The robber must have dropped it. I had never seen the gun before. I picked up the gun, put my initials in the barrel along with the date, and turned it over to the police, Officer Smith, along with the robbery note and the paper on which I wrote down the license plate number. I put my initials and the date on the robbery note as well.

I swear that this statement is true and accurate to the best of my knowledge.

Signed

Sally Smith

The Defense Case

1. One of the defendant's blue fingerless gloves.

2. A letter from Rick O'Ruben's friend, Tim, a sailor in the Navy, which reads, "I look forward to playing tennis with you each Wednesday in January, at 8:00 p.m. at Holiday Park." The letter was dated December 1.

3. The testimony of Rick O'Ruben. (This testimony will be consistent with Rick O'Ruben's statement, below.)

4. The Statement of Rick O'Ruben.

The following is the signed and sworn statement of the defendant, Rick O'Ruben, taken on March 30th of the same year.

My name is Rick O'Ruben. I am 27 years old and I live on Talbot Street, right off of Main Street. I shop in the stores, restaurants, and bars in the area, including the Magruder's that they say had been robbed. I think Magruder's is overpriced so I don't go there often.

I am a white male, approximately 6 feet, 150 pounds, with dark shoulder-length hair, no beard or mustache, and I wear an earring in my left ear.

I have attended the local community college for one semester, and I am a licensed automobile mechanic. I work at the Shell Station over on 17th Street and own many blue fingerless gloves, which I often wear at work to protect my hands.

I have had a few problems with the law. Nine years ago, I was convicted as an adult of a felony robbery of a convenience store. I admit to committing that crime, but not to this one! I was just a kid hanging out with a bad crowd, and did not know better. I have grown up a lot since then. I was found guilty of misdemeanor shoplifting three years ago; was adjudicated a delinquent because of a heroin sale as a juvenile; and convicted of aggravated mayhem, a felony, ten years ago. The mayhem conviction resulted from a bar fight where I was just defending myself.

It took me a while to grow up. I've been arrested four times for fighting, three times for vandalism, and twice for suspicion of robbery, but I was pretty young and immature when those things happened and they couldn't make any of the charges stick.

On that night when the robbery supposedly took place I was playing tennis at Holiday Park from 8:00 to 9:00 p.m. with my buddy, Tim Lovell. He is in the Navy and presently at sea in the Indian Ocean. Every time Tim is in town, we play tennis every week on Wednesday night at Holi-day Park, unless the weather is really bad. I don't have a reserved court, but it is not too difficult to get a court at that time. Tim and I are pretty even, although he almost always wins. Actually, that Wednesday night I beat him and recall excitedly telling my wife that I won when I returned home that evening.

When the police arrested me at the Shell station where I work, I told them I did not do it. I have done some bad things in the past, but there is one thing I did not do — and that's rob the Magruder's like they say.

I have been married for six years to Becky and we have a wonderful four-year-old child named Sherri. I am trying to save some money so Sherri can go to a good school. I wouldn't do anything to hurt them. Becky used to be a bookkeeper, but had to quit because she has bad migraine headaches and has to lie down a lot. I wouldn't do anything to jeopardize my relationship with either of them. That is why I often work overtime at the Shell station. I want us to be able to afford a decent car. Right now I'm driving a junker with the license plate number, "PDD 514."

I was in the Magruder's once or twice in the month prior to that day to buy some beer and chips. It's on my way home from work.

I owned a gun at one time just like the handgun they told me they found at Magruder's. My gun was stolen from my car about two months ago along with some other stuff. I used it for protection; I often have to drive through some bad neighborhoods.

I swear the aforementioned is true and accurate to the best of my knowledge.

Signed,

Rick O'Ruben

Stipulations

1. The government tested the gun and the counter area for fingerprints. Four prints were found on the gun. One matched the defendant, two were of unknown persons, and one was too smudged to make an identification.

2. The alleged robbery note was smudged, which prevented any form of comparison with the defendant's handwriting.

3. The statements of Sally Smith and Rick O'Ruben were taken in depositions. After each deposition, the person making the statement was given an opportunity to review it for any inaccuracies.

4. The defendant was given *Miranda* warnings upon his arrest.

5. The defendant is being charged with one count of armed robbery. The judge will instruct the jury on the lesser included charge of robbery as well.

Brief Jury Instructions

Members of the jury, the defendant, Rick O'Ruben, stands charged by information of armed robbery, alleged to have been committed in the Magruder's convenience store on the first Wednesday of January of this year at approximately 9:00 p.m. The defendant has pleaded not guilty.

A defendant is presumed to be innocent until each and every element of the case is proven by the prosecution beyond a reasonable doubt. That means a doubt for which you can give a reason. If a reasonable doubt as to one or more of the elements of the crime charged exists in your mind, you must find the defendant not guilty.

In the present case, the defendant is charged with armed robbery. Robbery is the trespassory taking and carrying away of money or other personal property that may be the subject of a larceny from the person or custody of another person and, in the course of the taking, there is the use of force, violence, assault, or putting in fear.

If, in the course of committing the robbery, the offender possesses a firearm or other deadly weapon, then the robbery is considered to be an armed robbery.

An act shall be deemed "in the course of committing the robbery" if it occurs in an attempt to commit robbery or in flight after the attempt or commission.

If, based on the evidence presented at trial, you find beyond and to the exclusion of every reasonable doubt that on the 6th day of January, the defendant, Rick O'Ruben, did rob the Magruder's store, then you must find the defendant guilty as charged.

Please select a jury foreperson when you first begin to deliberate. You will be permitted to take with you all of the admitted evidence, a verdict form, and a copy of the charging document, the information, which is not evidence. You may now go to the jury room to deliberate.

Assignment

1. Prepare closing arguments for the prosecution and for the defense. What is the theory of each case? What is the most significant evidence for each side?

2. Which evidence offered by the prosecution likely will be admitted? Which evidence likely will not be admitted? Explain, describing the likely objections to each piece of evidence and the probable ruling on those objections.

3. Which evidence offered by the defense likely will be admitted? Which evidence likely will not be admitted? Explain, describing the likely objections to each piece of evidence and the probable rulings on those objections.

4. Prepare direct and cross-examinations of Sally Smith and Rick O'Ruben. Do your examinations comply with the applicable rules of evidence?

§ 19.02 Multiple-Choice Review Questions

1. Civil suit by P against Squibby (D), manufacturer of the drug Pharmacol, for failure to provide an adequate drug interaction warning. P allegedly developed a serious allergic reaction after taking Pharmacol in combination with another drug called "Lotrimin." D contends that Pharmacol did not cause P's reaction. P seeks to offer into evidence a report prepared by an independent consulting firm retained by D after P became ill that recommended that D change its warning label on Pharmacol to add that purchasers taking Lotrimin should contact their doctors before using Pharmacol. The consultant's report is:

A. Admissible to prove that the warning label was defective despite the quasi-privilege established by FRE 407 because no change to Pharmacol was actually made.

B. Inadmissible under the quasi-privilege established by FRE 407.

C. Inadmissible hearsay unless P offers additional foundational evidence showing that D authorized the consultant to make this recommendation.

D. Admissible only to impeach D's expert witness if the expert testifies that "the warning label that was on the pills at the time that P bought them was adequate."

E. Admissible if P's lawsuit is based on a product liability claim.

2. Same case. P also offers to prove that a year earlier, D paid $50,000 to another Lotrimin user who suffered an allergic reaction after taking Pharmacol. P's evidence is:

A. Admissible to prove D's liability if D made the payment voluntarily after reading in the newspaper that the other user developed an allergic reaction after taking Lotrimin and Pharmacol.

B. Admissible to prove D's liability only if the payment was made after the other user filed a lawsuit against D.

C. Admissible only for the limited purpose of impeaching D's medical expert who testifies that "Pharmacol was not the cause of P's allergic reaction."

D. Irrelevant.

3. Suit by P against Hospital (D) for medical malpractice by S, a staff doctor. Assume that to demonstrate D's liability, P has to prove (among other things) that S was incompetent when hired by D. P seeks to offer evidence from an expert, the County's Chief Medical Officer, that, "In my opinion S was incompetent when hired by D." The Chief Medical Officer's opinion is:

A. Inadmissible evidence of S's character.

B. Admissible only to impeach S's credibility as a witness if the doctor testifies.

C. Admissible under FRE 404(b) to show D's knowledge of S's incompetence.

D. Admissible to prove that S was incompetent when hired.

E. Inadmissible because it invades the province of the jury.

4. A common law rule that a type of evidence relating to an event was admissible only if there were no eyewitnesses to the event applied to:

A. Evidence of habit

B. Accusations

C. Lay witness opinions

D. Experts opinions

5. D is charged with bank robbery. The prosecution claims that S and D were co-conspirators, with S robbing the bank and D driving the getaway car. To prove that D was the driver of the getaway car, the prosecution seeks to offer evidence that S told his fiancée E that "With the cops right on our tail after I ran into the car with the loot from the bank job, D never should have made a full stop at that stop sign just to avoid getting a ticket." S's statement is admissible against D for this purpose if:

A. In S's earlier separate trial for robbing the bank, E testified on behalf of the prosecution that S said it. The judge in D's trial has ruled that E is unavailable, and the prosecution seeks to read E's testimony from S's trial into the record in D's trial under the hearsay exception for former testimony.

B. E testifies on behalf of the prosecution in D's trial that S said it, and the judge determines that the prosecution has offered evidence sufficient to support a finding that when S made the statement to E, S was hiding out in an effort to evade capture.

C. Instead of making the statement to E, S made the statement to the police officer who interrogated S after S was arrested for robbing the bank, at a time when D had not as yet been arrested.

D. E testifies in D's trial that E immediately wrote down exactly what S said on an envelope, and though E can no longer remember what S said, E authenticates the envelope shown to E by the prosecution as containing an accurate account of S's statement.

E. S's statement is not admissible against D under any of the circumstances described above.

6. Officer R was parked when she heard the sound of a collision in the intersection about 20 yards away from her patrol vehicle. R immediately ran to the intersection to investigate. R later prepared a report stating in part that "I did not observe any skidmarks behind the blue Acura, which was in the middle of the intersection facing south when I arrived at the intersection, which is controlled by traffic signals. Upon my arrival, bystander B told me that the driver of the Acura ran the red light. B also reported hearing the driver of the Acura say upon exiting the vehicle that 'I shouldn't have had those last few martinis.'" Assume that the driver of the Acura is a defendant in a personal injury case brought by the driver of the other car, and that the plaintiff seeks to offer the quoted portion of the report into evidence. Which of the statements below is accurate?

A. The report is inadmissible hearsay in its entirety.

B. The portion of the report indicating the location of the Acura and the lack of skidmarks is admissible, but the remainder of the report is inadmissible hearsay.

C. The portion of the report indicating the location of the Acura and the lack of skidmarks, as well as B's statement that the Acura ran the red light is admissible, but B's reference to the Acura driver's statement is inadmissible hearsay.

D. The report is admissible in its entirety.

7. P sues D, her former employer, for sexual harassment. P claims that M, who worked in the same department as P, regularly directed sexual remarks at P and displayed sexual materials in his office, and that D did nothing to stop M despite P's frequent complaints. J, who had worked in the same department as P, had previously sued D for sexual harassment. In J's case, D deposed J and the case later

settled without going to trial. In P's trial against D, P seeks to offer into evidence J's deposition testimony from the earlier case. Which of the statements below is accurate?

A. J's deposition testimony is admissible if P establishes by a preponderance of evidence that J is unavailable, and P can establish this by offering into evidence an email message from "J@msn.com" that says, "I've moved out of state, I can't come back for your trial."

B. J's deposition testimony is admissible if P establishes by a preponderance of evidence that J is unavailable, and P can establish this by offering evidence that a month before trial, P mailed a subpoena to the address for J that was listed in D's business records, and that it was returned "Moved — No Forwarding Address."

C. J's deposition testimony is admissible if P establishes by a preponderance of evidence that J is unavailable, and P can establish this by testifying that "The day after J settled her case, I got a phone call from a caller I know was J and J said that she'd already moved to another state and was never going to return."

D. P cannot offer J's deposition testimony into evidence regardless of whether J is unavailable.

E. If J is proved to be unavailable, D can offer J's deposition testimony into evidence against P.

8. Same case. During negotiations in J's earlier lawsuit against D that resulted in the parties resolving a dispute as to how much money J would receive, D's attorney told J's attorney, "We recognize that M has engaged in a lot of inappropriate behavior towards other employees." P seeks to offer D's attorney's statement into evidence against D. The judge should rule that:

A. The statement is admissible only if P also offers foundational evidence showing that D authorized its attorney to make the statement.

B. The statement is inadmissible because it was made in the course of compromise discussions.

C. The statement is admissible because it was made during compromise discussions in an unrelated case.

D. The statement is inadmissible because it was not made under oath.

9. P sues D for personal injuries resulting from D's alleged attack on P. D was also charged criminally with assault, and pleaded guilty. P seeks to testify to being present in the courtroom and hearing D plead guilty to assaulting P. P's testimony is:

A. Inadmissible under the Best Evidence Rule, because the Judgment of Conviction would be the best evidence of whether or not D pleaded guilty.

B. Admissible, but only to impeach D in the civil case should D deny committing the assault.

C. Inadmissible character evidence.

D. Admissible to prove that D assaulted P regardless of whether D testifies in the civil trial.

E. Inadmissible because criminal pleas are not admissible in civil cases.

10. Immediately after observing an armed bank robbery, a customer turns to a teller and says, "Oh my God, would you believe that same guy just finished doing time for another bank robbery?" If the prosecution seeks to offer the customer's statement into evidence against the defendant, the court should rule that the statement is:

A. Inadmissible character evidence.

B. Inadmissible under the Confrontation Clause as interpreted by *Crawford v. Washington* if the customer doesn't testify at trial and the defendant has not had an opportunity to cross-examine the customer.

C. Admissible as an excited utterance.

D. Admissible as a present sense impression.

E. Admissible to show that the defendant has a plan to rob banks.

11. The effect of the expansion of the common law version of the "medical hearsay exception" (FRE 803(4)) to apply to "statements made for purposes of diagnosis or treatment" was that:

A. Statements made by parties to forensic medical experts became admissible.

B. Hypothetical questions were no longer the exclusive method of eliciting opinions from medical experts.

C. Medical experts were able to testify to the information on which they based their opinions regardless of whether the information was admissible in evidence.

D. Statements made by medical experts to parties became admissible.

12. Prosecution of D for the murder of V; the defense is an alibi. To prove that D and V were together on the night that V died, the prosecution can offer evidence that:

A. Earlier on the day that V was killed, V's spouse told a friend, "I'm afraid that D is going to meet up with V tonight."

B. A few days after V was killed, V's spouse told a psychologist from whom the spouse was receiving counseling that "I've been depressed ever since D killed V."

C. A handwritten note that V's spouse testifies was written by V on the day that V was killed states that "I'm going to meet up with D later this evening."

D. The day after V was killed, V's spouse told a friend, "I was afraid that something bad was going to happen as soon as V told me yesterday morning that V planned to get together with D later in the day."

E. None of the above items is admissible to prove that D and V were together on the night that V died.

13. D is charged with assault and battery for striking L with a bottle of V-8 Juice during a fraternity party. L also files a civil suit against D for personal injuries that L suffered as a result of being struck. Some time after the alleged assault, D says that "I thought that L had insulted my frat house and I over-reacted." D's statement is:

A. Admissible in the *civil* case if D made this statement to the prosecutor during plea bargaining discussions.

B. Admissible in the *criminal* case if D made this statement to L when they met in a student cafeteria to try to resolve a disagreement about the seriousness of L's injuries.

C. Admissible in the *civil* case if D made this statement to the judge during a pre-plea colloquy that ended with D refusing to plead guilty after the judge refused to go along with the prosecutor's recommended sentence.

D. Admissible in the *criminal* case if D made this statement to the judge during a pre-plea colloquy that ended with D refusing to plead guilty after the judge refused to go along with the prosecutor's recommended sentence.

E. None of the above answers is correct.

14. P sues D for injuries sustained in a hit and run accident; D's defense is that a thief was driving D's car at the time of the accident. P seeks to testify, "D told me right after the accident that it was my fault because I was speeding." P's testimony is:

A. Admissible as D's opposing party statement.

B. Inadmissible under the Best Evidence Rule because D's statement is based on the contents of a writing, the speedometer in P's car.

C. Inadmissible as an opposing party statement because D's statement was exculpatory at the time it was made.

D. Inadmissible under the rule barring statements made during compromise negotiations.

15. D is charged with assaulting V with a deadly weapon. D claims self-defense and testifies that V initiated the attack. As a result:

A. D can call a witness to testify that "I have known D for many years, and in my opinion D is honest and truthful."

B. The prosecution can call a witness to testify that "About a year before V was attacked, I saw X challenge V to a fight; V just walked away from X."

C. The prosecution can call a witness to testify that "I have known V for years, and in my opinion V would never initiate an attack."

D. D can call a witness to testify that "I have known D and heard people talk about D for many years, and I know that D has a reputation for peacefulness."

E. All of the above evidence is admissible.

16. D is charged with rape of V; the defense is consent. At trial, the following takes place at the bench:

1. During its case-in-chief, the prosecution offers to prove through the testimony of G that D had raped G about a month before the alleged assault on V.

2. In response, D argues that G's testimony is inadmissible because G had consented to intercourse with D.

The judge should rule as follows:

A. G's testimony is admissible if the prosecution offers evidence sufficient to support a finding that D raped G.

B. Evidence that D had intercourse with G is admissible to prove that D raped V even if D and G engaged in consensual intercourse.

C. G's testimony is admissible only if the prosecution's evidence convinces the judge by a preponderance of the evidence that D raped G.

D. No matter what the circumstances, evidence of sexual relations between D and G is inadmissible evidence of D's character.

17. Which feature below distinguishes lay from expert opinions?

A. Experts can give opinions about ultimate issues but lay witnesses cannot.

B. Lay witnesses can testify to "collective facts" but expert witnesses cannot.

C. Experts can testify as to matters about which they lack personal knowledge.

D. Experts are allowed to draw inferences but lay witnesses are limited to factual observations.

E. Each of these features distinguishes lay from expert opinions.

18. D, the owner of a parking lot is criminally prosecuted for failing to maintain the lot in a safe condition. To prove D's guilt, the prosecution could offer evidence that:

A. During settlement negotiations aimed at resolving a civil suit filed against D by a patron who fell in the lot, D told P's lawyer that "I had a lot on my plate during that time period and couldn't worry about the condition of the parking lot."

B. Two years earlier, D pled guilty to being a slumlord.

C. In the opinion of D's secretary, D is an alcoholic.

D. A bystander who saw P fall told P that "I'm afraid that D is going to go to jail for ignoring the dreadful condition of the parking lot."

E. None of these answers is correct.

19. D is charged with felony possession of heroin for sale. The statute under which D is prosecuted states in part, "Possession of more than 5 grams of heroin is presumed to constitute possession for sale." The prosecutor offers evidence that D possessed 15 grams of heroin. Which statement below is accurate?

A. The jury can draw a permissive inference that D possessed the heroin for sale.

B. D has the burden of producing evidence that the heroin was for personal use and not for sale.

C. D has the burden of proving that the heroin was for personal use and not for sale.

D. The judge should dismiss the charge because presumptions are unconstitutional in criminal cases.

20. P sues D for civil damages for assault. Following the alleged assault, P received medical treatment from Dr. W, an emergency room physician. At trial, P offers Dr. W's testimony that "When I asked P what happened, P told me, 'I had argued with D on a couple of earlier occasions and feared that D would attack me if D got the opportunity.'" Dr. W's testimony is:

A. Inadmissible hearsay.

B. Inadmissible under the "medical hearsay" exception but admissible under the "state of mind" exception to prove that D assaulted P.

C. Admissible under the "medical hearsay" exception to prove that D assaulted P.

D. Admissible if D's defense is "self-defense" to prove that P would not have initiated an attack on D, but inadmissible if D's defense is "mistaken identity."

E. Admissible as non-hearsay to corroborate P after P testifies consistently with what P said to Dr. W.

21. D is on trial for armed robbery; the defense is mistaken identity. W, called as a prosecution witness, identifies D as the robber. After W testifies and the prosecution rests, D testifies to an alibi. On cross-examination, the prosecutor questions D as follows:

Q: You were nowhere near the bank at the time of the robbery?

A: That's right.

Q: But your attorney told the investigating police officer that you would plead guilty in exchange for a sentence of no longer than three years, isn't that right?

The prosecutor's last question is:

A. Improper because it exceeds the scope of direct.

B. Proper.

C. Proper if the prosecutor offers foundational evidence convincing the judge that D had explicitly authorized the attorney to conduct plea negotiations.

D. Improper because the statement was made during plea negotiations.

E. Improper because the question is argumentative.

22. P sues D for negligently driving D's car into P's ice cream truck. P seeks to offer evidence that after the accident, D told P, "I'm sorry, that was really negligent of me." In response to D's objection, the judge should rule that:

A. D's statement is inadmissible because the statement consists simply of a legal conclusion.

B. D's statement is admissible under the business records exception if P referred to D's statement in the daily ice cream sales report that P routinely prepares.

C. If D denies making the statement, P can testify to it only by convincing the judge by a preponderance of evidence that D made the statement.

D. After D denies making the statement, P can offer D's statement for its truth by calling W, D's next-door neighbor, to testify, "A week after the accident, D said to me 'I never should have told P that the accident was my fault.'"

E. D's statement is inadmissible because it constitutes an apology.

23. P sues D for injuries sustained in a hit and run accident. Called as a witness by P, W testifies, "I had just walked out of an Office Depot store when I saw D's car speeding moments before colliding with P's car." Cross-examining W, D's attorney asks, "Isn't it true that the store you had just walked out of when you saw the collision was a Staples store?" D's question is:

A. Proper impeachment, and if W answers "No" then D can call a witness to testify that W had been in Staples just prior to the collision.

B. Improper impeachment on a collateral issue.

C. Proper impeachment, but if W answers "No" then D must take the answer.

D. Proper impeachment, and regardless of W's answer D's attack on W's credibility, allows P to call a witness to testify to an opinion that W is honest.

24. A frequent impediment to the admissibility of "declarations against interests" is that:

A. The exception requires unavailability, and declarants who make such statements are typically available to testify.

B. Such statements are often offered to prove a fact about someone other than the declarant, and an assertion about another person's conduct is often not against the declarant's interests.

C. Whether an assertion was against a declarant's interest often depends on how events unfold long after the time the assertion was made.

D. The Confrontation Clause bars criminal defendants from using declarations against interest to prove that someone else may have committed the crime with which they are charged.

25. Which of the following now-existing evidentiary rules represents a *continuation* of common law evidentiary doctrine?

A. The residual exception to the hearsay rule.

B. The rule that "prior bad acts" are admissible to attack a witness' credibility only if they are probative of untruthfulness.

C. The rule that if foundational requirements are satisfied, prior inconsistent statements are admissible for their truth if they were made under oath.

D. The rule that witnesses may be impeached with prior felony convictions.

E. The rule that an expert's opinions may be admissible if they are helpful to the jury.

26. D is charged with murder of V in a state that allows previously hypnotized criminal defendants to testify without restriction. D testifies and claims to have stabbed V in self-defense. Cross-examining D, the prosecutor elicits evidence that prior to trial, D had undergone extensive case-related questioning while hypnotized. The prosecutor then furnishes the judge with a book called the Encyclopedia of Hypnosis and asks the judge to take judicial notice of a statement made in it that "the more closely a hypnotized subject is questioned, the greater the danger that the information recalled will be inaccurate." The judge should:

A. Refuse the request because judges cannot take judicial notice of adverse facts against defendants in criminal cases.

B. Refuse the request on the ground that the matter is not one that can be properly judicially noticed.

C. Refuse the request and strike D's testimony from the record and instruct the jury to disregard it because the hypnosis session rendered D incompetent to testify.

D. Take judicial notice, so long as the jury is told that it may, but need not, accept the judicially noticed fact as conclusive.

27. An attorney planning to impeach an adverse witness with the witness' prior inconsistent statement must:

A. Not excuse the witness from giving further testimony if the attorney plans to offer extrinsic evidence of the prior inconsistent statement instead of cross-examining the witness about it.

B. Ask questions regarding the context surrounding the making of the prior inconsistent statement before confronting the witness with the prior statement on cross-examination.

C. Make sure that the prior inconsistent statement was made under oath, because only then is extrinsic evidence of the statement admissible.

D. In all circumstances, take the witness' answer if the witness on cross-examination denies making the prior inconsistent statement.

28. W testifies on P's behalf in a civil breach of contract case. Cross-examining W, defendant D asks, "Isn't it true that you and P jointly operated an illegal internet file-sharing business?" Which statement below is accurate?

A. If W answers "No," D must take the answer.

B. The question improperly assumes facts not in evidence.

C. If W answers "No," D can offer extrinsic evidence that W and P jointly operate an illegal file-sharing business.

D. The question is improper as argumentative.

E. In order to ask the question, D has to provide the judge with a copy of a judgment of conviction showing that P and W were convicted of operating the illegal file-sharing business.

29. D is charged with masterminding a complex investor fraud scheme involving phony North Sea oil reserves. D may offer expert testimony from a clinical psychologist that due to severe learning difficulties and impaired mental functioning, D is unable to understand or process complex information. The prosecution may offer evidence that five years earlier, D had developed and marketed a complex consumer fraud scheme involving non-existent Argentinean gold mines. Which statement below is accurate?

A. The prosecution's evidence is admissible against D on a non-character theory, but only after D's expert testifies.

B. The prosecution's evidence constitutes inadmissible character evidence even if D's expert testifies.

C. D's expert testimony is inadmissible under FRE 704(b) because it concerns the mental state of a criminal defendant.

D. If D's expert testifies, any conversations that the expert had with acquaintances of D that the expert reasonably relied on are admissible for the truth of their contents.

E. Even if D does not offer the expert testimony, the prosecution can offer evidence of the earlier gold mine scheme as non-character evidence to prove that D intended to commit fraud.

30. D is charged with armed robbery; the defense is mistaken identity. Prosecution witness W identifies D as the robber. D then calls an eyewitness identification expert. Which statement below is accurate?

A. The expert can give an opinion concerning the accuracy of W's identification so long as eyewitness identification experts generally accept the principle that opinions about the accuracy of specific identifications are reliable.

B. The expert cannot give an opinion concerning the accuracy of W's identification, because the opinion would concern the ultimate issue in the case and invade the province of the jury.

C. The expert can give an opinion concerning the accuracy of W's identification so long as the expert has personally tested W's ability to observe and recollect.

D. The expert cannot give an opinion concerning the accuracy of W's identification, because the expert witness' expertise extends only to factors that in experimental studies have been shown to be associated with mistaken identifications.

E. None of the above answers is accurate.

31. P sues D for personal injuries resulting from an auto accident. P offers evidence that shortly before the collision, D had received a call on his car phone saying "D, someone has stolen your identity." True (A) or False (B): P's argument that "People who have just received disturbing personal news are often distracted" is an adjudicative fact that the judge can judicially notice.

32. D is charged with domestic violence for assaulting V. After D fled, V called 911 and described D's attack to a 911 operator. V does not testify at D's trial and D had no previous opportunity to cross-examine V. Which statement below is accurate?

A. A transcript of V's 911 call is admissible to prove D's guilt if V's statements constitute a present sense impression.

B. If D intentionally rendered V unavailable as a witness by threatening to harm V, a transcript of V's 911 call is admissible even if they were made too long after the attack to constitute a present sense impression.

C. A transcript of V's 911 call is admissible if the statements constitute a present sense impression and D's reputation for violence caused V's unavailability.

D. A transcript of V's 911 call is admissible if D killed V in a jealous rage a day after the charged acts of domestic violence took place.

E. A transcript of V's 911 call is admissible because a domestic violence victim's unavailability is presumed to have been caused by the abuser's threats.

33. D is charged with assaulting V with a deadly weapon. Prior to trial, D's lawyer meets with the prosecutor P in an attempt to resolve the case. During the plea negotiations, D's lawyer says that "D did throw a brick at V, but V had been taunting D all afternoon." If P seeks to offer the statement of D's lawyer's into evidence at trial, the statement is:

A. Admissible for the limited purpose of impeaching D's credibility should D testify to an alibi.

B. Admissible as D's opposing party statement during P's case-in-chief to prove that D threw the brick at V.

C. Inadmissible in the criminal case against D, but admissible in a civil suit brought by V against D for injuries that V sustained as a result of being struck by the brick.

D. Inadmissible in the criminal case as well as in the civil case referred to in Answer C.

34. When substantive law principles include "state of mind" elements, the usual evidentiary effect is to:

A. Narrow the scope of relevant evidence.

B. Expand the reach of the Confrontation Clause.

C. Expand the scope of relevant evidence.

D. Narrow the scope of the collateral evidence rule.

E. Allow criminal defendants to offer "mercy rule" evidence.

35. P sues D for personal injuries growing out of a traffic accident in an intersection. D was given a traffic ticket for entering the intersection against a red light. Which statement below is accurate?

A. If D went to trial in Traffic Court and was convicted of a red light violation, P can offer the conviction into evidence to prove that D entered the intersection against the red light.

B. If D went to trial in Traffic Court and was convicted of a red light violation, P can offer the conviction into evidence but only to attack D's credibility if D testifies to entering the intersection on a green light.

C. If D pleaded guilty in Traffic Court, P can call the Traffic Court Clerk as a witness to testify to the plea to prove that D entered the intersection against the red light.

D. Regardless of what happened in Traffic Court, P can offer the traffic ticket itself into evidence to prove that D entered the intersection against the red light.

36. Assume that Party A offers O's last words as a dying declaration; Party B opposes their introduction. Which of the following factual disputes should the judge resolve pursuant to FRE 104(b)?

A. Party A offers evidence that O had massive head injuries; Party B offers evidence that the head injuries were minor.

B. Party A offers evidence that O was the speaker of the words; Party B offers evidence that the words were actually spoken by a bystander.

C. Party A offers evidence that just before O spoke, a bystander said, "It doesn't look like you are going to make it"; Party B offers evidence that what the bystander said was, "You'll be up and around in no time."

D. All of the above.

E. None of the above.

37. Which of the following rules represents a break from common law evidence principles?

A. The rule that evidence is relevant if it has any tendency in reason to prove a material fact.

B. The rule that in a criminal case, a defendant can offer evidence attacking the character of a victim.

C. The rule that prior inconsistent statements are admissible for their truth if they were made under oath.

D. The rule that an expert witness can testify in the absence of personal knowledge.

38. D is charged with bank robbery. To show D's motive to rob the bank, the prosecution offers to prove that D is addicted to heroin. Upon D's objection that the evidence is irrelevant and unfairly prejudicial, the court should rule that:

A. The evidence is admissible under FRE 104(b) as long as there is sufficient evidence to sustain a finding that the evidence is relevant.

B. The evidence is inadmissible because "motive" is not an element of the crime of bank robbery.

C. The evidence is irrelevant.

D. The evidence is inadmissible to prove motive, but is admissible to impeach D if D testifies and denies robbing the bank.

39. D is charged with sexually molesting G, a nine-year-old girl. D testifies that he had some physical contact with G, but claims that it was incidental to his demonstrating self-defense techniques and was in no way sexual. On cross-examination, the prosecutor asks, "The doctor who examined the child found that G's genitalia were bruised. That's not consistent with your claim of accidental touching, is it?" This question is:

A. Proper cross-examination, because the doctor's findings are inconsistent with D's testimony.

B. Proper cross-examination, because the doctor's findings are admissible as a business record.

C. Improper cross-examination

D. Proper cross-examination if the doctor has already testified or if the prosecutor makes an offer of proof that the doctor will testify.

40. Same case. After testifying and denying G's allegations, D calls witness W to testify that in W's opinion, D is a peace-loving, passive individual. Upon objection by the prosecution, the court should rule that:

A. The evidence is inadmissible, because only the character trait of honesty and trustworthiness is admissible to support D's credibility.

B. The evidence is inadmissible because D can offer evidence to support his credibility only after the prosecution offers character evidence to attack D's credibility.

C. The evidence is admissible only if W can testify to specific instances of D's peaceable behavior.

D. The evidence is admissible to prove D's innocence of the charges.

41. Same case. D is convicted of sexually assaulting G. After the trial, D's counsel speaks with some of the jurors. The jurors inform D's counsel and sign affidavits indicating that the foreperson of the jury, a paralegal, said that under the law, any physical contact between D and G's private parts, even if unintentional, constitutes sexual assault. Assume that the paralegal's interpretation of the law is incorrect. If D's counsel asks the trial judge to consider the information in the affidavits when ruling on D's motion to set aside the guilty verdict, the court should rule that:

A. The request should be denied, because the paralegal's statement is hearsay.

B. The request should be granted under the FRE, because the paralegal's statement constitutes extraneous prejudicial information.

C. The request should be granted only if the jurors' affidavits also state that the paralegal's statement affected their votes.

D. None of these answers is correct.

42. P (beneficiary) sues D (trustee) for breach of fiduciary duty, alleging that D exercised undue influence in persuading P to transfer a valuable piece of real estate to D at a price well below its fair market value. D testified that D ceased acting as trustee of the trust one month before D bought the property from P, and D offers into evidence a letter that D testified was addressed properly to P and mailed one month before the transaction, informing P that D was no longer acting as a trustee. P denies receiving the letter. Based on the "mailed letter" presumption, at the conclusion of the case the court should:

A. Instruct the jury that if it concludes that D mailed the letter to P, P has the burden of proving that P did not receive it.

B. Instruct the jury without regard to that presumption.

C. Instruct the jury to find that P received the letter.

D. Instruct the jury that if it concludes that D mailed the letter to P, it is to find that P received it.

43. Civil suit in which P as guardian ad litem for P's child sues D for maintaining tree branches on D's residential property in an unsafe condition, as a result of which P's child was struck by a branch while bike riding, knocked off the bike and injured. P calls a witness, W, D's next door neighbor, to testify that about a week before the injury to P's child, W told D, "Those tree branches of yours are really dangerous, someone's going to get hurt." Upon objection by D, the court should rule that:

A. If D failed to deny the branches' dangerousness, W's statement should be admitted into evidence as D's opposing party statement.

B. W's testimony is improper as irrelevant and speculative, since W did not suffer any injuries.

C. W's testimony is inadmissible hearsay by a witness testifying to the witness' own out of court statement.

D. W's testimony is admissible to prove that D was aware of the dangerousness of the tree branches.

E. W's testimony is admissible to prove that the tree branches were dangerous.

44. P sues D-1, a police officer, and D-2 (D-1's employer) for using excessive force when arresting P on a shoplifting charge. After P testifies, D-1 and D-2 offer evidence from D-1 that three months earlier, D-1 had arrested P for an unrelated burglary, and that at that time P struck D-1 and said that he would get even with him and get him fired. Upon P's objection to this evidence, the court should rule that:

A. D-1's testimony about the unrelated burglary arrest is inadmissible character evidence.

B. D-1's testimony about the incident following the burglary arrest is admissible to impeach P's credibility.

C. D-1's testimony as to what P said following the burglary arrest is inadmissible hearsay.

D. D-1's testimony as to the earlier burglary incident is admissible because by making the excessive force claim, P has put his character in issue.

45. P sues to evict D as a tenant in a commercial property owned by P. P alleges that D breached the terms of the lease by selling drugs on the leased premises. P offers to testify that, "I sent my assistant, A, into the premises leased to D while I waited outside. A few minutes later, A came back out and told me that she answered the phone

and heard the caller say, 'I'm coming by in 10 minutes to pick up the cocaine.'" Upon D's objection to P's testimony, the court should rule that:

A. The testimony is inadmissible because the caller's statement to A is inadmissible hearsay.

B. The testimony is inadmissible because A's statement to P is inadmissible hearsay.

C. The testimony is inadmissible evidence of D's character.

D. The testimony is admissible because the caller's statement to A is non-hearsay, and A's statement to P is admissible as a present sense impression.

46. D is charged with rape of V; the defense is consent. Prosecutor P calls W as a pattern witness to testify to D's rape of W. D testifies that D's sexual encounter with W was consensual. Which statement below is accurate?

A. P can call D's work colleague M to testify that D has a reputation for sexual violence.

B. P can ask D on cross-examination, "Isn't it true that you were convicted of shoplifting two months ago?"

C. The judge has discretion to allow D to offer evidence that W has a reputation for sexual promiscuity.

D. D cannot attack W's sexual character.

47. If item of evidence E is conditionally relevant:

A. The proponent of E must offer foundational evidence sufficient to support a jury's finding that the condition has been fulfilled.

B. The proponent of E must offer foundational evidence that fulfills the condition before E can be admitted into evidence.

C. The proponent of E must offer foundational evidence convincing the judge by a preponderance of the evidence that the condition has been fulfilled.

D. The judge should admit E into evidence so long as the jury can reasonably conclude that E is relevant.

E. Once the proponent satisfies the condition, the adversary cannot attack the credibility of E.

48. D, a store clerk, is charged with illegally selling cigarettes to M, a minor under the age of 18. D seeks to testify that "Looking at M's driver's license led me to believe that M was over 18 years old." (A reasonable belief that M was an adult is a substantively valid defense.) Which statement below is accurate?

A. D's testimony is admissible.

B. D's testimony is inadmissible hearsay because the driver's license constitutes an out-of-court assertion that "M is over the age of 18."

C. D's testimony is inadmissible because D has failed to authenticate the driver's license as belonging to M.

D. The Best Evidence Rule requires D to offer M's driver's license into evidence or satisfactorily explain D's inability to do so.

49. D is charged with killing V in a drive-by shooting. The prosecution seeks to offer evidence from W that shortly before V was killed, V told W, "I'm afraid that D is going to kill me for talking to D's sister." V's statement to W is:

A. Inadmissible hearsay if offered to prove that D killed V.

B. Admissible as non-hearsay to prove that V feared D.

C. Admissible on a non-character theory to prove D's motive for killing V.

D. Admissible as non-hearsay to prove that W feared D.

E. Admissible under the state of mind exception to prove that D killed V.

50. D is charged with assaulting V. D and V each testify that the other person started the fight. At this point:

A. D can offer evidence that a week before the incident with D, V punched out a co-worker.

B. The prosecution can offer evidence that about a month before the incident, V had completed an anger management course.

C. The prosecution can call W to testify to an opinion that D is dishonest.

D. The prosecution can ask D on cross-examination, "Isn't it true that you punched out your next door neighbor a week before you attacked V?"

E. D can call W to testify that "About a week before the incident with V, I saw L challenge D to a fight and D walked away."

51. D is charged with rape of V on May 1; the defense is consent. V testifies that the rape took place in D's car, when V accepted D's offer of a ride home after they had met in a club. D calls W to testify that prior to leaving the club with D, V had been "hanging all over" and kissing a number of other men on the club's dance floor. W's testimony is:

A. Admissible if D testifies that V danced with and kissed D on the dance floor before D left the club with V.

B. Barred by the rape shield law.

C. Relevant to prove that V consented to sexual intercourse with D, and not barred by the rape shield law because W is not testifying to sexual behavior.

D. Admissible after V testifies, to impeach her credibility as a witness.

E. Admissible to prove that V's motive on the night of the alleged rape was to pick up D in the bar.

52. D is charged with murdering V; the defense is an alibi. The prosecution calls W, who was walking alongside V, to testify that "Moments before the shooting, V said

that 'I'm afraid that we might meet up with D, who has threatened to kill me.'" V's statement to W is:

A. Admissible under *Pheaster* to prove that D was at the murder scene, and that D was the shooter.

B. Admissible under *Pheaster* to prove only that D was at the murder scene.

C. Admissible to prove that D had threatened to shoot V.

D. Inadmissible hearsay.

E. Admissible for the limited purpose of proving that V feared D.

53. D, charged with murdering V, calls W to testify that V initiated the attack and that D struck V in self-defense. As a result:

A. Under both the CEC and the FRE, the prosecution can offer evidence of other specific instances of D's violent behavior.

B. Under the FRE but not the CEC, the prosecution can call a witness to testify to an opinion that V is peaceful and non-violent.

C. Under both the FRE and the CEC, the prosecution can offer evidence that D has a reputation for violence.

D. Under both the CEC and the FRE, the prosecution can call a witness to testify to D's reputation for dishonesty.

E. All of these statements are correct.

54. D is charged with embezzling $15,000 from D's former employer L. During P's case-in-chief, the judge has discretion to permit P to offer evidence that:

A. D has a previous felony conviction for embezzlement.

B. The embezzlement started after an angry investor who had lost money in D's phony Ponzi scheme threatened to report the scheme to the cops unless D paid back the investor.

C. D is a cocaine addict.

D. D falsified D's previous experience when applying for the job with L.

E. Each of the above answer choices is correct.

55. Same case. D testifies and denies embezzling any funds. At this point:

A. D can call D's co-worker W to testify that "A few weeks ago, the company's bookkeeper S told me, 'D didn't steal that $15,000, I did.'"

B. P can offer non-character "identity" evidence by calling D's former employer E to testify that D embezzled funds while in E's employ.

C. D can call W to testify to D's reputation for honesty.

D. D can offer evidence that co-worker M had access to the company's books and needed money to cover gambling losses.

E. P can call W to testify, "W's mother told me after D was arrested that she was afraid that D had been stealing from E."

56. Breach of contract case. P claims that D agreed to a contract during a meeting that took place on May 9; D denies attending a meeting with P on May 9. After a few background questions, P's lawyer asks P, "Did D attend a meeting with you on May 9?" This question is:

A. Leading and improper.

B. Leading, but proper because it pertains to a preliminary matter.

C. Proper as non-leading as it doesn't suggest a desired answer.

D. Improper as a compound question.

E. Improper as assuming facts not in evidence.

57. In a personal injury case, P seeks to testify that immediately after their cars collided, P ran over to D and yelled, "This was all your fault, and $1000 is a fair price for you to pay for the damage you did to my car," and that D made no reply. Which statement below is accurate?

A. P's statement is admissible as a verbal act.

B. D's silence constitutes an adoption of P's statement.

C. P's statement is admissible as an excited utterance.

D. P's statement is admissible as a present sense impression.

E. P's statement is inadmissible hearsay.

58. A and D are tried separately for jointly participating in a criminal scheme to defraud homeowners. With A unavailable to testify in D's trial, P offers into evidence A's recorded statement to a jailhouse cellmate in which A said, "I set up meetings with property owners for D, but D set up the whole operation and talked them out of their properties." A's statement is:

A. Admissible under the co-conspirator exemption.

B. Admissible as A's declaration against interest.

C. Inadmissible hearsay.

D. Admissible as A's declaration against interest so long as P offers additional evidence corroborating A's participation in the fraud.

E. Inadmissible under the Confrontation Clause.

59. D is charged with murdering V. P claims that V's murder was a "hit" ordered by M, a drug dealer to whom V owed a lot of money. During its case-in-chief, P seeks to offer evidence of two other instances in which M paid D to carry out "hits" of people who owed money to M. Evidence of the prior "hits" is:

A. Inadmissible "character to prove conduct" evidence.

B. Admissible to attack D's credibility as a witness after D testifies.

C. Admissible as non-character evidence during P's case-in-chief.

D. Admissible only to rebut D's testimony, "I shot V accidentally while demonstrating how to use a weapon."

E. Admissible to show D has a habit of committing contract killings.

60. D is charged with murdering V; the defense is an alibi. D's "mercy rule" witness W testifies, "D is peaceful and non-violent." Which statement below is accurate?

A. D can ask W to provide concrete examples of D's peaceful nature.

B. P can ask W, "Do you know that D committed perjury last year?"

C. P can ask W, "Do you know that D was arrested for attacking a supervisor at D's workplace?"

D. P can ask W, "Isn't it true that you made false statements in an application for unemployment benefits?"

E. D can ask W to testify to V's reputation for violence.

Chapter 20

Transcript Review Exercises

§ 20.01 Introduction

This chapter consists of two sets of transcript review exercises. The exercises provide you with opportunities to review evidence rules in the context of courtroom testimony, the primary activity in which judges and lawyers apply the rules. Each transcript includes bolded and numbered items of dialogue that raise evidentiary issues.

The transcripts in Section 20.02 consist of excerpts from actual trials that in their day drew intense attention and helped shape public attitudes about American justice. The trials are *People v. O.J. Simpson; United States v. Ethel and Julius Rosenberg; Anderson et al. v. W.R. Grace and Co.; People v. Erik and Lyle Menendez; the "Scottsboro Boys" trials, and the Leo Frank case.* The authors have gently edited the excerpts to enhance their value as vehicles for reviewing the rules of evidence.

The transcripts in Section 20.03 allow you to review evidentiary rules in the context of courtroom testimony in popular courtroom films. The films are *Anatomy of a Murder, A Few Good Men, Let Him Have It, A Civil Action, Philadelphia,* and *My Cousin Vinny.*

§ 20.02 Transcript Excerpts from Actual Trials

The transcripts in this section consist of excerpts from actual trials.

1. People v. O.J. Simpson

In 1995, O.J. Simpson was tried for murdering his ex-wife Nicole Brown Simpson and a companion, Ronald Goldman. Simpson was a former football star and at the time of the trial he was a celebrity who made films and was often featured in advertisements. The trial was an international media circus, televised live in virtually every country. Simpson was found not guilty in the criminal trial, but he was found liable for wrongful death in a subsequent (and much less noticed) civil trial.

The prosecution focused much of its case on forensic evidence linking Simpson to the knife-attack killings. The defense claimed that the police handling of the evidence was shoddy and that Simpson was framed by vengeful police officers. Other prosecution evidence concerned the defendant's previous acts of violence toward his ex-wife, and the two transcript excerpts below focus on that topic. The judge was Lance Ito; the prosecutors were Christopher Darden and Marsha Clark; the primary defense lawyer was Johnny Cochran; in this excerpt the defense lawyers were Robert Shapiro and Carl Douglas.

Transcript A

Prosecutor Darden's Direct Examination of Denise Brown

Q: Miss Brown, you are Nicole Brown's oldest — older sister?

1. *Is this an improper leading question?*

A: Yes, I am.

Q: Do you have other sisters?

A: Yes, I do.

Q: How many?

A: There's Dominique and Tanya and of course Nicole.

Q: And you are the oldest of the sisters; is that correct?

2. *Is this an improper leading question? How is the information relevant?*

A: Yes, I am.

Q: Do you know the defendant seated here at the end of counsel table?

A: Yes, I do.

Q: He's your former brother-in-law?

3. *Is this an improper leading question?*

A: Yes, he is.

Q: Miss Brown, your sister Nicole married the defendant in February 1985?

4. *Is this an improper leading question?*

A: Yes, she did.

Q: Do you recall an occasion when you and Ed McCabe and Nicole and the defendant went out to dinner?

A: Yes, I do.

Q: And where did the four of you go after you left the La Cantina restaurant?

A: We went to O.J.'S house, O.J. and Nicole's house.

Q: On Rockingham?

A: Yes.

Q: And what did you do when you returned to the defendant's home on Rockingham?

A: We were sitting at the bar talking, having some more drinks and talking.

Q: Okay. While you were talking, did you say something to the defendant?

A: Yes, I did.

Q: What did you say to him?

A: I told him he took Nicole for granted, and he blew up.

5. Def. Att: Your Honor, I'm going to object. Motion to strike the last response. *What would be a possible ground for the objection?*

6. Judge: *How should the Court rule on the objection?*

Q: You told the defendant that he took Nicole for granted?

A: Yes.

Q: Why did you tell him that?

A: Because she did have —

Def. Att: Objection. Irrelevant.

7. Judge: *How should the Court rule on the objection?*

Q: What reaction if any was there by the defendant when you told him that he took your sister Nicole for granted?

A: He got extremely upset. He started yelling at me, "I don't take her for granted. I do everything for her. I give her everything," and he continued, and then a whole fight broke out and pictures started flying off the walls, clothes started flying — he ran upstairs, got clothes, started flying down the stairs and grabbed Nicole, told her to get out of his house, wanted us all out of his house, picked her up, threw her against the wall, picked her up, threw her out of the house. She ended up falling. She ended up on her elbows and on her butt.

8. *Does this testimony constitute improper character evidence? What other objection might you have made?*

Q: Now, was his anger manifested in any way other than the fact that he became — other than the fact that he began screaming?

A: Yeah. His whole facial structure changed. I mean, everything changed about him.

Q: Okay. when you say his facial structure changed, what do you mean? Elaborate on that for us, please.

9. *Is this a proper question?*

A: It was calm, quiet, normal conversation, like we were sitting here right now, and then all of a sudden it turned into — the eyes got real angry. It was as — his whole jaw, everything started, you know — his whole face just changed completely when he got upset. Umm — it wasn't as if it was O.J. any more. He looked like a different person and that is what Nicole had always said when he gets angry.

10. *Are these appropriate opinions for the witness to give? Might the answer give rise to any other defense objection?*

Transcript B

Prosecutor Darden's Direct Examination of Ronald Shipp; Defense Lawyer Douglas' Cross-Examination

Direct Examination

Q: Mr. Shipp, are you acquainted with the defendant in this case?

A: Yes, I am.

Q: How long have you known him?

A: Approximately 26 years.

Q: You were an LAPD officer?

A: Yes.

Q: And you are no longer an LAPD officer?

A: No, I'm not.

1. *Are the last two questions improperly leading?*

Q: Did you ever meet Nicole Brown?

A: Yes.

Q: Okay. And did you consider Nicole Brown a friend?

A: Yes.

Q: As you did the defendant?

A: Yes.

Q: What kinds of things did you talk about [with the defendant] during those personal and intimate conversations?

Def. Att: Objection, Your Honor. Overbroad, vague.

2. Judge: *What ruling?*

Q: Were you still a member of the LAPD during the first week of January 1989?

A: Yes.

Q: And did you receive a telephone call from Nicole that week?

A: Yes.

Q: Did she ask you to do something?

A: Yes.

Q: What did she ask you to do?

Mr. Douglas: Objection, hearsay.

3. Judge: *What ruling?*

Q: Okay. Did she appear upset or sound upset at all?

Mr. Douglas: No foundation that he knows.

4. Judge: *What ruling?*

Q: You went to the defendant's home on Rockingham?

A: Yes.

Q: And did you see Nicole Brown at that time?

A: Yes.

Q: And did you notice anything unusual about her at that time?

A: Yes. Umm, if I remember, she had some injuries that had started to fade.

Def. Att: Objection, Your Honor. How does he know that? Calls for speculation. No foundation.

5. Judge: *What ruling?*

Q: What injuries did you see at that time, Mr. Shipp?

A: If I remember—I mean, I couldn't see that well because I remember she had make-up on, but if I remember there was some swelling about her head somewhere. I remember it was covered up pretty good.

6. *How does the witness' statement that he "couldn't see that well" affect the admissibility of the answer?*

Q: OK. And did you return to the house again?

A: The next day, yes, I did.

Q: OK. Did you bring anything with you at that time?

A: Yes.

Q: What did you bring with you?

A: I made copies of a portion of the domestic violence lesson plan.

Q: And when you arrived at the house was Nicole Brown there?

A: Yes.

Q: Was the defendant there?

A: No.

Q: Did you show her the profile of the battered woman?

A: Yes.

Q: So she focused mainly on the batterer's profile?

A: Right.

Q: And did she ask you to do something with that batterer's profile?

A: Yes.

Q: And did you do what she asked you to do?

A: Yes.

Q: When was the next time that you saw the defendant?

A: It might have been later on that week.

7. *Is this response objectionable as speculative or vague?*

Q: Do you recall where he was when you saw him?

A: At the house.

Q: And had you gone to the house for a specific reason that day?

A: Yes.

Q: And what was that reason?

A: To talk to O.J. about the profiles, at Nicole's request.

Q: And did you meet with the defendant?

A: Yes.

Q: Did you show him the batterer's profile?

A: Yes.

Q: And that profile does list certain characteristics of a batterer; is that right?

A: That's correct.

Q: Now, during that discussion did you discuss with him the events of January 1, 1989?

A: Yes.

Q: Relate to us the content of that conversation, please.

8. *Does this question improperly call for a narrative response?*

A: Umm, O.J. had said that they had gone out that night, he and Nicole, Marcus and Kathy, and they had had a pretty good time, that they had too much to drink, they were partying too much, and when they got back, they got in an argument.

Q: Did he say what the argument was about?

A: Yeah. I mean, he said that they had been kind of intimate and then that in the middle of it they started arguing for the most part.

Q: Did he tell you what happened next?

A: I believe at the time he told me that Nicole was the aggressor and came after him and that he was acting in self-defense.

Q: What did he say he did to Nicole in self-defense?

A: He had told me what he had — at the time that he had — was defending himself and then pushed her away and he didn't really hit her.

Q: He said that all he did was push her away?

A: At the time.

Q: Did he say what happened next?

A: Umm, I think he said, you know, she got hysterical and called the police on him.

9. *Does the witness' series of answers concerning the defendant's statements consti-tute inadmissible hearsay?*

Q: OK. Continue on then with your conversation you were having with the defen-dant regarding the batterer's profile.

A: At the time, after we went over all the profiles, he denied that any of those were him except for maybe one.

Q: And which one was that?

A: The jealous. He said "maybe I might be a little jealous" and that was it.

Q: Did he express to you at all that he was concerned about Nicole Brown's physical well-being?

A: Yes.

Q: What did he say?

A: Well, you know, he said he loved Nicole and he would never do anything to hurt her, and it was just — it was just an isolated incident.

Q: What did the defendant say about that?

A: Well, at the time he was very upset because he thought that he was going to lose Hertz [a rental car company for which Simpson was a celebrity spokesperson] and his image was going to be tarnished and, umm, he was just asking me to tell Nicole, you know, hey, this is never going to happen again, and you know, that he loved her.

Q: Well, the City Attorney was considering filing charges at that time, correct?

A: Correct.

Q: Did he ask you to say anything to Nicole about filing charges?

A: Yes. He had asked me to get a — to see if I could have her sign off — sign off the report, not press charges.

Q: Did you ever speak to any supervisor in the LAPD on the defendant's behalf?

A: Yes.

Q: Why did you do that?

A: Well, here once again I was caught between a rock and a hard place, and I was — I wanted to try and help O.J. out, but at the same time I felt that I didn't want to do it because of what I knew as far as, you know, that type of relationship, but I did bring — I brought the paper over to her.

Def. Att: Objection, Your Honor. that is nonresponsive.

10. Judge: *What ruling?*

Q: Did she sign it?

A: No, she didn't.

Q: Were you still friends with the defendant and Nicole on June 12, 1994?

A: Yes.

Q: At some point you learned that Nicole Brown was dead; is that right?

A: Yes.

Q: Well, when you went to the (O.J.) house the second time that evening, was he there?

A: Yes.

Q: Okay. And did you notice anything unusual about the defendant's hand at that time?

A: Yes. I noticed that he had one of his — on his left hand, I think one of his fingers was bandaged, white bandage on it.

Q: And did you pose any questions to him at that time?

A: Yes. I asked him how he cut his hand, how he cut his finger.

Q: And what did he say?

A: He said he did it in Chicago.

Q: Now, as you prepared to leave the defendant's home, did you walk towards the front door?

A: Yes.

Q: And did he say anything to you at that time?

A: Yeah. He said, "Ron, come upstairs for a minute."

Q: And did you go upstairs?

A: Yes.

Q: So what happened next?

A: He began to ask me a couple questions.

Q: What was the first —

A: No. excuse me. I take that back. The first thing he said, he told me what the police had done when they came out to his house.

Q: And what did he tell you the police had done when they came out to his house?

A: He said that they had gone through everything and that they told him that they had found a bloody glove, they told him something about a watch cap, something like that, and that they had — what was it? That's all I can remember at this time.

Q: Well, did he ask you any questions, any questions about the investigation?

A: After he told me about what they found at his house, he asked me how long does it take DNA to come back.

Q: And at that time, did you know the correct answer to that question?

A: No. But what I did say, I just off the cuff say two months.

Q: And what did he say in response to your indication that it takes DNA two months to come back?

A: He kind of jokingly just said, you know, "To be honest, Shipp — " that's what he called me, Shipp. He said, "I've had some dreams of killing her."

Q: Did he say how many dreams he had had of killing her?

A: No, he did not.

Q: You were interviewed by the LAPD back in June or July of 1994; is that correct?

A: That's correct.

Q: And did you reveal to the LAPD at that time that the defendant had told you that he had had dreams about killing Nicole Brown?

A: No, I did not.

11. *Can the prosecutor impeach his own witness with an inconsistency in the witness' story?*

Q: Well, you're an ex-police officer, right?

A: Yes.

Q: You understood that they were conducting a homicide investigation, correct?

A: Yes.

Q: Well, what was your reaction when you heard the defendant say that he had had dreams about killing Nicole Brown?

Def. Att: Irrelevant, Your Honor.

12. Judge: *What ruling?*

Q: Why didn't you tell the police detectives about the defendant's statement that he had had dreams of killing Nicole Brown?

A: At the time, when detective Vannatter approached me with the situation — you have to understand, I was in a state of shock for — up until that time, and I wanted nothing to do with any of this at the time. I just — I was just still thinking it was a dream like most of America.

Q: Well, did you think that you could somehow hurt the defendant or harm him by disclosing that information?

A: Yes, yes, yes, I did. I thought it was very — it was harmful.

Q: Mr. Shipp, do you still consider yourself a friend of this defendant?

Def. Att: Irrelevant, Your Honor.

13. Judge: *What ruling?*

A: I do. I don't know how he feels.

Q: Thank you, sir. No further questions, Your Honor.

Defense Cross-Examination

Q: Mr. Shipp, what did you review in preparation for your testimony today, sir?

A: The only thing I ever looked over was the domestic violence profiles.

Q: And you and I met in your attorney's office, didn't you?

A: That's correct.

Q: And during any time — withdrawn. You knew on that occasion that I was representing Mr. Simpson, didn't you?

A: Yes.

Q: During any part of the 45 minutes that you and I spoke, did you ever mention anything about this conversation with Mr. Simpson?

A: No sir.

Q: Didn't I ask you during that conversation to tell me the worst things that you knew about O.J. Simpson?

A: Yes.

Q: And wouldn't you agree that this statement about this supposed dream is a pretty bad thing about Mr. Simpson?

A: Yes.

Q: So did you lie when you didn't tell me about that dream?

A: I sure did.

14. *Is this an improper argumentative question?*

Q: You did. OK. You've lied a few times, haven't you, sir?

A: Never in court.

Q: But you've lied a few times concerning what you know about Mr. Simpson, true?

A: Well if holding back information — they never asked me about — if holding back information is lying. I don't think it is lying. I just didn't tell them everything.

Q: Well, you didn't tell the police and the district attorney about an important conversation that you claim occurred, true?

A: That's correct.

Q: So let me get this straight. You met for 90 minutes with Phil and Marcia and Bill and never mentioned this conversation, correct?

A: Never did.

Q: You met for 25 minutes with Joe Brown and never discussed this conversation, correct?

A: Did not.

Q: You met with me in your attorney's office for 45 minutes and never talked about this conversation, correct?

15. *Is this question objectionable as "asked and answered"?*

A: Correct.

Q: Now, you said that the reason why you didn't tell Phil about the conversation was because of what?

A: I said I didn't tell Phil because at the time, I really did not want to be really involved in all of this and I didn't want to be going down as a person to nail O.J.

Q: Well, you're not. So don't worry about that. But let me ask you this.

Pros: Ms. Clark: Objection to that editorial.

16. Judge: *What does the objection mean? How should the judge rule?*

Pros: Motion to strike.

17. Judge: *What does this request mean? What should the judge do in response to the request?*

Q: So I understand your version, there was a time when Mr. Simpson went to bed, correct?

A: Correct.

Q: And this was a man that had just lost the mother of his children, correct?

A: Correct.

Q: And he was grieving that evening, wasn't he?

A: Define grieve.

Pros: Objection.

Q: He was in grief, wasn't he?

Pros: This witness isn't competent to define who is grieving and who isn't, Your Honor.

18. Judge: *What ruling?*

Q: He was surrounded by his close friends, correct?

A: Correct.

Q: His family were concerned about his emotional state; were they not?

Pros: Objection.

19. Judge: *What ruling?*

Q: Isn't it true, sir, that you were hopeful that you would be able to garner some publicity by making up false allegations about Mr. Simpson?

A: No, that's not true at all.

Q: Didn't you think, sir, that by concocting this story about Mr. Simpson, it might enhance your own personal profile?

A: I put all my faith in God and my conscience. Since Nicole's been dead, I've felt nothing but guilt, my own personal guilt, that I didn't do as much as I probably should have.

20. *Is this answer responsive to the question?*

Q: Well, let me ask you this. Didn't you think that by being a witness in this case, it would enhance your own personal profile?

A: No, sir.

Q: Aren't you an actor?

A: Sir, I have done some acting, yes, I have.

Q: Have you gone to school for acting?

Def. Att: Objection. Is this relevant, Your Honor?

21. Judge: *Is the objection properly phrased? How should the judge rule?*

Q: Isn't it true, sir, that by being the witness who has a conversation with Mr. Simpson, that it is going to possibly enhance your profile around the world?

Pros: Objection, Your Honor.

22. Judge: *What ruling?*

A: There's no way, shape or form that I would sit here and go through all this, put my family through this for an acting career. I could care less if I do any acting.

Q: That's not the question. the question is —

Pros: Your Honor, He's answering the question.

23. Judge: *What ruling?*

2. <u>U.S. v. Julius and Ethel Rosenberg</u>

The transcript excerpts below are from the 1951 U.S. government prosecution of the Rosenbergs for espionage. At the time of the trial, the "Cold War" between the United States and the Soviet Union was in full swing and each country competed for supremacy in nuclear weapons technology. United States citizens Julius and Ethel Rosenberg, dubbed "the Atomic Spies," were charged with providing supposedly secret bomb-making information to an intermediary of the Soviet Union. They were convicted and executed in the electric chair after refusing government offers to spare their lives in exchange for information about their Soviet contacts. The judge was Irving Kaufman; the chief prosecutor was U.S. Attorney Irving Saypol; the defense attorney was Emanuel Bloch.

Transcript A: Government's Opening Statement

Pros: The evidence will show that the loyalty of the Rosenbergs was not to our country, but that it was to communism, communism in this country and throughout the world.

Def. Att: I object to these remarks as irrelevant to the charge before this Court because communism is not on trial here.

Judge: If the Government intends to establish that they had an interest in communism for the purpose of establishing a motive for what they were doing, I will when that question arises rule on that point.

Pros: That is the purpose of my remarks.

1. Def. Att: Defendants except to Your Honor's statement. *Does a lawyer have to "take exception" to a judge's ruling or statement in order to preserve the point for appeal?*

Transcript B: Prosecutor's Direct Examination of David Greenglass

David Greenglass (Ethel Rosenberg's brother) worked in the atomic bomb project, and he testified for the government that he gave information to the Rosenbergs that they allegedly passed along to Soviet Union agents.

Q: Did your wife Ruth visit you in Los Alamos to celebrate your anniversary?

A: Yes.

Q: Did she mention the Rosenbergs during that visit?

A: Yes. She said that they had asked her to tell me that if all nations have the same information about the most destructive weapon ever invented, then one nation couldn't use the bomb against another and we could prevent a third world war.

2. *Is this answer in any way objectionable?*

Q: Now Mr. Greenglass, at our request, have you prepared a copy of the sketch of the lens mold that you furnished to Julius Rosenberg when you were in New York?

A: Yes.

3. Q: Is this it? *Does this question reflect proper procedure for handling tangible exhibits?*

A: Yes.

Pros: We offer it in evidence.

Def. Att: May I inquire, Your Honor? Thank you. Mr. Greenglass, when did you prepare this sketch?

A: During the trial yesterday.

Q: This is a copy of the sketch that you turned over to Rosenberg?

A: Yes.

4. *Can defense counsel properly object to the copy's admissibility?*

Q: What happened then?

A. After I gave the sketch and some other handwritten papers to Rosenberg he took them into the next room to study them. Then he came back out with Ethel so that she could type up the information I had provided.

5. *Is this answer in any way objectionable?*

Q: Did Julius comment on your successfully providing this information to him?

A: He said that a few years earlier he had stolen a proximity fuse when he was working on national defense matters at Emerson Radio.

Def. Att: Objection, improper character evidence referring to an uncharged crime.

6. Judge: *What ruling?*

Transcript C: Defense Cross-Examination of David Greenglass

One defense tactic was to argue that Greenglass was an ordinary machinist and not a scientist, so that any information that he might have disclosed would be of little or no value.

Q: When you went to high school and Brooklyn Polytech, did you fail in your subjects?

A: I was quite young and I liked to play around, so I cut classes almost the whole time.

Q: How many of the eight courses that you took did you fail?

A: I failed them all. But I got good marks during my semester at Pratt Institute.

Q: You never got a science degree?

A: No.

Q: Did you ever study calculus, or thermodynamics, or atomic physics?

A: I did not.

7. *Are these questions relevant to the defense?*

Q: Do you know what an isotope is?

A: I do. It is an element having the same atomic structure but a different atomic weight.

8. *How would you analyze the wisdom of the defense lawyer's question?*

Transcript D: Defense Direct Examination of Julius Rosenberg

Q: Do you know what you are being charged with?

A: Yes. Conspiracy to commit espionage to aid a foreign government.

Q: As you have sat here throughout the trial, did you hear your brother-in-law David Greenglass and your sister-in-law Ruth Greenglass testify?

A: Yes.

Q: Now, Ruth Greenglass testified that in November 1944 you asked her to enlist her husband in getting information from the place he was working and giving it to you. Did you ever have any conversation with her at or about that time with respect to getting information from David Greenglass to you?

A: I did not.

9. *Is the previous question objectionable?*

Q: Based on your years-long familial relationship with Ruth Greenglass, why might she have testified to this if it weren't true?

10. *Is this question proper?*

A: She is trying to stay out of prison by blaming Ethel and me for her own crimes.

Transcript E: Prosecutor's Cross-Examination of Julius Rosenberg

The government claimed that Julius Rosenberg went to Washington, D.C., from New York to convince a former college classmate named Elitcher who worked at the Bureau of Standards to pass along government secrets. Rosenberg claimed that his visit to Elitcher was strictly social and casual.

Q: Four years later, when you were in Washington, you decided that you wanted to call him and pay him a visit?

A. That's right.

Q: What was it you wanted to see him about?

A: I was lonesome and I just wanted to see someone to talk to.

Q: Did you know Elitcher socially?

A: No, but he had been a former classmate.

Q: Now tell us, what did you talk about? Did you tell him why you came to see him? Didn't he ask you, "Just why out of the clear sky do you pick on me to pay a visit like this, I never really knew you?"

11. *Is this a proper question?*

A: He didn't say that.

3. <u>Anderson et al. v. W.R. Grace and Co., et al.</u>

This case, sometimes known as the "Woburn Toxic Trial," was a lawsuit filed by eight families from Woburn, Massachusetts against two manufacturers, W.R. Grace & Co. and Beatrice Foods (the parent company of Riley Tannery). The lawsuit claimed that the defendants had contaminated the town's water supply by knowingly disposing of toxic chemicals used in their manufacturing activities into the river that was the source of Woburn's water supply, causing serious illnesses and deaths. The jury found Beatrice Foods not liable, and W.R. Grace settled the case for $8 million. The U.S. Environmental Protection Agency independently filed lawsuits against both defendants, and they were forced to pay about $68 million to clean up the industrial contamination. Jerome Facher represented Beatrice Foods; Jan Schlichtmann represented the plaintiffs; federal court judge Walter Skinner presided over the trial. (This case was the basis of the Jonathan Harr book and the subsequent film, *A Civil Action*; an excerpt from that film appears below in Section 20.03.)

Transcript A: Cross-Examination by Beatrice Foods of Plaintiffs' Expert Witness Dr. Pinder

Q: Dr. Pinder, one thing that has been clear, since you have been hired as an expert, is that it was to give an opinion as to the travel time, is that right, of these contaminants?

A: I would say yes.

Q: And you were hired almost two years ago to give an opinion as to travel time, right?

A: No.

Q: You were hired several months — you were hired in 1984, is that what you stated?

A: Yes.

Q: And you have been prepared extensively for your testimony in this trial, have you not, not only by lawyers but on your own?

1. *Is this proper cross-examination?*

A: Yes.

Q: And you have reviewed all the documents or one-third of the documents in there?

2. *Is this a proper question?*

A: Yes.

Q: You have been doing computer computations for months?

A: Yes.

3. **Q: Are you telling this jury that you came in yesterday when you gave the opinion as a Ph.D. and as a chairman of a department that you made a little mistake in an opinion that you have been preparing for the last year and a half?** *Is this question objectionable?*

A: No.

Q: You made a mistake, though, didn't you, in these travel times?

A: Yes.

Q: That is the very opinion you knew you were going to give in this courtroom, right?

A: No.

Q: You knew you were going to be asked for travel times of these contaminants, weren't you?

A: No.

Q: Well, Dr. Pinder, you were engaged, were you not, to testify as to how long it would take for these contaminants to travel from one site to another?

A: No.

4. Q: That is the opinion you were preparing, wasn't it? *Are these questions objectionable as "asked and answered"?*

A: No.

Transcript B: Direct Examination by Beatrice Foods of Expert Witness Dr. Koch

5. Q: And after the pumping of — pumping test in December, 1985, what is your opinion whether Wells G and H, which were then pumping together, were drawing groundwater from underneath the Riley site which was passing under the river, supposed to be passing under the river, what is your opinion on that? *Is this question objectionable?*

A: My opinion is that water that was under the Riley site did not flow towards the Wells G and H at the end of the 30-day test.

Q: Can you tell us please what the bases or reasons for your opinion are?

A: Yes. There are several bases. One of the bases is the groundwater configuration that resulted after the 30 days of pumping had finished, and when I say after the 30-day test, what I really mean is just before the wells were shut down, a round of water levels was taken to show the maximum effect of these wells at the end of the 30-day period. The configuration of the — Now all the wells in the area that I had water levels for were used to prepare this water table map. And from that map, apparently it is easy to draw arrows showing the groundwater flow direction because groundwater will flow from the higher to lower elevation. In addition to that, there was other data collected to support the analysis that I had done as far as the groundwater flow map. One of the pieces of data was the discharge measurements collected by the United States Geological Survey of the Aberjona River. And when I say discharge measurements, what they have done is actually measured the amount of water in the river during the pumping test. And they have done it up by Olympia Ave. where the river first intersects the site and down by Salem Street where the river leaves the site. And from those measurements, you can tell whether or not the river is either gaining or losing water as it flows through the site. And at the end of the test, what the grouped water map showed me was that there was a high point created underneath the river which caused water to flow away from it. When I say away from it, I mean east of the river, groundwater flow towards Wells G and H. West of the river the groundwater flowed to the west. And the reason the mound was created was because the river at the end of the test was losing over 550 gallons a minute. And this water was seeping out of the river going into the groundwater system, and forming a long mound that caused groundwater to flow away in both directions.

6. *Is this a proper answer?*

Transcript C: Cross-Examination by Plaintiffs of Defendant's Expert Witness Dr. Guswa

Q: Now Dr. Guswa, do you agree with me if I told you that, in fact, the diagram below was done by Mr. Koch for Beatrice Foods?

A: Okay.

Q: And this overlay right here was done by yourself?

A: Yes.

Q: You and Mr. Koch seem to have a difference of opinion as to how the well flows from 13 to 14 from Well 92 to G, am I correct?

A: Yes. Well, there are different directions on the arrows.

Q: Yes, quite different, aren't they? Aren't they about as different as you can get? I mean, there is no mistake about it, your arrows are going straight over to G, and Mr. Koch's arrows are going straight away, am I right?

A: That's right.

Q: Well, who do you think is right, you or Mr. Koch?

Def. Att: I object to that, Your Honor.

7. Judge: *How should the judge rule on the objection?*

A: Well, I contoured these water level data. I don't know what water level data Mr. Koch contoured.

Q: Neither do I.

Def. Att: May that go out, your Honor?

8. Judge: *How should the judge rule on the objection?*

Q: Dr. Guswa, when we were over here, I asked you to make a determination of how the groundwater flowed based on this data from 13 over to 92, do you remember that?

A: I did that.

Q: That is what the data shows, is that right?

A: That's correct.

Q: Do you have any reason to doubt that these water levels are incorrect?

A: No.

Q: You used them in forming your opinions, didn't you?

A: No reason to doubt that they are incorrect other than dealing with the relative uncertainty I talked about earlier.

Q: Yes, but you used those values, didn't you, in forming your opinions?

A: That's correct.

Q: You didn't come into the courtroom when you did this and say, "Don't pay any attention to some of these values, these are the ones I used in forming my opinion?"

9. *Is the above question objectionable?*

Transcript D: Re-Direct Examination by Defendant Beatrice Foods of Defendant's Expert Witness Dr. Guswa

Q: Now, based on the model or your own general experience, are you able to determine where the movement of water in the bedrock actually occurs? I mean taking, for instance, the aquifer in East Woburn?

A: No, I am not.

Q: Is there movement, in your opinion, from the bedrock to the saturated zone when there is water within the bedrock?

A: Yes.

Q: And is that the reason why your model contemplates the fastest movement of water would be within the saturated zone?

10. Plain. Att: Objection as to form. *What impropriety is the basis of the "form" objection, and how should the judge rule?*

Sidebar: "Just one more question, please"

After Mr. Schlichtmann finished recross-examination of Dr. Guswa, a lighter moment in the trial occurred when defense counsel Facher sought permission to ask Dr. Guswa "one last question." The following dialogue ensued:

Mr. Schlichtmann: No more questions. Thank you very much.

Mr. Facher: Can I have one question based on the difference between the cone of influence and the cone of depression and the flow?

Judge: Well, I think your witness had explained it. I am going to, with this kind of testimony, I will stay with the two-round rule. There is no end to it, no end to the complexities that can be unraveled with each succeeding question.

Mr. Facher: I only wanted one question.

Judge: Nobody ever gets by with one question because one question produces one answer which leads to another question.

4. People v. Erik and Lyle Menendez

The Menendez brothers were charged with murder for killing their parents in their Beverly Hills, California, home in 1989. The brothers admitted that they killed their parents, but relied on a defense called "imperfect self-defense," claiming that they did so because they feared that their parents were just about to kill them. Their first trial was a nationally televised sensation, due to the family's wealth, the brutal circumstances of the killings, and the preppy brothers' claim that their well-known father was a violent sexual abuser. The first trial surprisingly ended in a mistrial, with the jurors equally divided between verdicts of manslaughter and murder.

The excerpts below are from the prosecutor's cross-examination of Erik Menendez in the 1995–96 non-televised retrial. This trial concluded with the jury convicting both brothers of first degree murder. They were sentenced to life in prison without possibility of parole. The excerpts focus on the prosecutor's contention that much of Erik's testimony and courtroom demeanor (especially his crying) was a phony ploy to gain sympathy with the jury. The judge was Stanley M. Weisburg; the prosecutor was Daniel Conn; the defense attorney was Barry Levin.

Pros: Mr. Menendez, you did a lot of crying on direct examination, didn't you?

A. I don't know what you mean by a lot of crying.

Q. Well, you cried, didn't you?

A. Yes.

Q. And you understand that tears can have an impact upon people, don't you?

Mr. Levin: Objection Your Honor. Calls for speculation.

1. Judge: Overruled. *Is this ruling correct?*

A. Many I'm not — I think that pain has an impact on people, I suppose. I really don't know. I never really thought about it.

Q. Well, no one can see your pain, they can only see your tears; is that correct, Mr. Menendez?

Def. Att: Objection Your Honor to the form of the question, and it also calls for speculation, what other people can see.

2. Judge: *What ruling?*

Q. What impact do you think that tears has on the average person, Mr. Menendez?

Def. Att: Objection. Argumentative.

3. Judge: *What ruling?*

A. I don't know.

Q. You have no idea that tears can influence people?

A. If you're asking if I cried on purpose, or if I tried to cry, I was actually doing just the opposite.

Q. Yes. The question I am asking you, Mr. Menendez, is do you think that crying in front of the jury has the potential of gaining sympathy from the right kind of juror?

A. I don't — I don't know how to answer the question. I don't know. I mean —

Q. It never occurred to you that if you cried in front of the jury, you might gain some sympathy from them?

A. Well, it's certainly not something that I was trying to do. I was actually asked by counsel to talk as little about the molestation as possible. It's not something I want to go into. It's not something I want to talk about, and whether my pain is expressed through tears, it doesn't make it any more real or any less real. There were times when I described it when I didn't cry; actually more painful incidents, what overwhelms me at the time. It's not something that I control.

4. *What is your analysis of this answer from the perspectives of the rules of evidence and rhetorical strategies?*

Q. The molestation is not something that you want to talk about?

A. No.

Q. But you have no hesitation telling the world about it if you think that it might get you your goal of manslaughter; is that correct?

Def. Att: Objection. Argumentative.

5. Judge: Overruled. *Is this ruling correct?*

A: There was a great deal of hesitation. It took my brother many years of therapy to even get to the point where he would discuss it with people, and this is not something that I want to speak about. My grandmother is in the courtroom, my relatives know what is happening, and this is not something that I enjoy talking about or enjoy discussing about my family.

Q. Do you use tears to manipulate people?

A. No.

Q. Have you ever done so?

A. No.

Q. You cried when you spoke to the police on the night of the killings, didn't you?

A. Yes.

Q. And Sergeant Edmonds let you leave the police station without even giving you a gunshot residue test; is that correct?

A. I don't think it had anything to do with my tears. I was crying when I asked him if my parents were dead, not when I was going through what I did that night.

Q. My question is just did Sergeant Edmonds let you leave the police station without giving you a gunshot residue test?

A. Yes.

6. *Is this question objectionable as "asked and answered"?*

Q. And would you say you were successful in gaining the sympathy of Sergeant Edmonds that night?

A. I never thought about it.

Q. You were trying to deceive him, weren't you?

A. I didn't want to tell him that I was responsible.

Q. And did you feel that the tears that you used may have helped you in deceiving him?

A. I cried for one sentence at the end of the interview. I don't think it had anything to do with him feeling sorry for me. He was a kind man, and my parents had just died, he's naturally going to feel sympathy for me.

Q. So you didn't feel that the tears were influential at all?

A. No.

Q. You want to gain the sympathy of this jury, don't you Mr. Menendez?

A. I am not here to gain sympathy, Mr. Conn. I am here to tell what happened, because I have no choice but to be here and to tell what happened.

Q. Well, weren't you trying to trick the police that evening and cause them to conclude that you had nothing to do with the killing?

A. Certainly by that time I did not want them to know.

Q. And to achieve that goal, you went through considerable efforts prior to calling the police to insure that you would not be suspects; is that correct?

Def. Att: Objection Your Honor, with respect to "considerable efforts" as vague.

7. Judge: Overruled. *Is this a correct ruling?*

A. You mean trying to get tickets and getting rid of the guns and so on?

Q. Correct.

A. Yes.

Q. And as you were driving around with your brother in the car, did you ever say to him "by the way, when you call the police, how are you going to sound? Are you going to be happy and cheerful, or are you going to be crying and make it sound more believable?"

8. *Is the cross-examiner improperly argumentative as trying to put words in the witness' mouth?*

A. We weren't in the frame of mind to think of these things. We were just doing the basic things of trying to get some tickets so that we could try to show we were at a theater and try to get rid of the guns.

Q. You said you were not in the frame of mind to do what things?

A. To think that far ahead on whether it's going to make a difference on a 911 call how you act in front of the police. I just didn't think that far ahead.

Q. You thought far enough ahead to get theater tickets that you could possibly use as an alibi, didn't you?

A. These were just — they were coming up and we were doing them. We were coming up with a better suggestion, and we would do that.

Q. And you thought far enough ahead to change your clothes and get rid of any bloody clothing, didn't you?

A. I didn't — I saw spots on my jeans and I said "I better take these off and get rid of them," and that's what we did.

Q. And you thought far enough ahead to pick up all of the gunshot shells, didn't you?

A. These things were happening — as someone would bring it up, we'd do it. They weren't thinking ahead of time and saying "maybe we should do this." We would just do it, and do it, and that's —

Q. And you thought far enough ahead to dump the weapons that you used to kill your parents; isn't that correct?

A. I don't know what you mean by far enough ahead, but certainly afterwards we wanted to do that, yes.

Q. And you're telling us you didn't think far enough ahead to talk to your brother about whether or not he was going to cry when he called the police?

Def. Att: Objection. Argumentative, your honor.

9. Judge: Overruled. *Is this a proper ruling*?

A. I never saw the point in what his demeanor — what it would matter what his demeanor was when he told the police that we had found my parents dead. I just — I still don't understand the importance of it, and I don't think it made a difference to me. It didn't even cross my mind to think about it.

Q. Now, you listened to the 911 recording when it was being played in court, didn't you?

A. Yes.

Q. And on that recording both you and your brother are very emotional at the time that the call is made; isn't that correct?

A. Yes.

Q. Now, you weren't emotional when you got out of the car at the movie theater and stood in line to purchase theater tickets, were you?

A. You mean was I crying at the time?

Q. Yeah.

A. No.

Q. You weren't emotional and crying when you got out of the car at the gas station and dumped clothing and ammunition in the dumpster, were you?

A. I'm not sure. If it happened after we arrived at the civic center, I was. If it happened before, I wasn't.

Q. And then when you got home, you became very emotional and you were crying just when your brother called the police and got them on the line; is that correct?

A. No. I got overly emotional when I realized and saw my parents and saw that there were no guns in the room, and saw the sight that horrified me, and that's when I completely lost control. My brother ran up the stairs, and I didn't know which 30 seconds or which 15 seconds he was calling the police. It just — at that point it wasn't on my mind.

Q. You weren't emotional right after the shooting when you turned on the lights and began to pick up the shotgun shells; is that correct?

A. You mean was I crying; is that what you mean by emotional?

Q. Yes.

A. No.

Q. Well, you do cry when you get in front of a jury, don't you, Mr. Menendez?

Def. Att: Objection, your honor. It's argumentative.

10. Judge: *What ruling?*

Q. Is there something about the sight of a jury sitting in judgment of you that brings tears to your eyes, Mr. Menendez?

A. No. A jury sitting in front of me scares me. It doesn't bring tears to my eyes.

Q. The tears that you were shedding, Mr. Menendez, are they tears for yourself or tears for your dead parents?

A. It's grief. It's sadness. It's regret and it's —

Q. Did you shed one tear for your mother before you shot her to death on August the 20th of 1989?

A. In that rushed state I wasn't — I don't know. No.

Q. Did you shed one tear for your father before you shot him to death on August the 20th of 1989?

A. I don't know what you mean by that question. You mean at the top of the stairs when I thought they were going to kill us?

Q. That's correct.

A. No. I was just — my brain was going crazy. I wasn't thinking about it.

Q. And you didn't feel any sorrow about the prospect of shooting your parents to death at that time, did you?

A. I thought they were going to kill us. I thought I was going to die.

Q. And you were going to shoot them to death; is that correct?

A. All I know is that I had to get to that room before they came out, or I was going to die. This is the only thing that I was thinking. I look back on it now, and I can say perhaps this or perhaps that, but at the time I was just reacting. I mean, I wasn't consciously making choices.

Q. But my question to you is did you shed one tear as you were going toward that room to shoot your parents to death?

A. No.

Q. At any time before you testified did you discuss with your brother that if he were to cry at the same time you cried, perhaps it would be even more effective than just one person crying at a time?

A. No. It's —

Def. Att: Objection. Hearsay, your honor.

11. Judge: Overruled. *Is this a proper ruling?*

A. It's the type of thing when he sees me hurt — it's painful for me in the last trial when he was up here and talking about the things that his father — dad did to Lyle. I was crying. I couldn't help but cry, because it's painful to see him in pain, and it's painful for me to think about these things. This is not — I am not a person who can just decide I want to cry right now. I'm not capable of that. I am not sure anyone is.

Q. Yes. Are you telling us that the tears of Lyle Menendez was not part of a plan to influence this jury?

Def. Att: Objection. He's never testified he's seen any tears in this trial.

12. Judge: Rephrase the question. *How was the question objectionable?*

Q. You did not discuss with your brother at any time whether you should cry on the witness stand or whether he should cry while he's listening to you?

A. No.

Q. Are you planning on crying during the cross-examination, Mr. Menendez?

Def. Att: Objection Your Honor. Calls for speculation. The question can't be answered.

13. Judge: Overruled. *Is this a correct ruling?*

A. Depends upon what we talk about, I suppose.

Q. Now, do you think your demeanor on the witness stand plays an important role in persuading the jury of your position, Mr. Menendez?

Def. Att: Objection, your honor. Calls for a conclusion.

14. Judge: Overruled. *Is this a proper ruling?*

A. It's a difficult question to answer. I had not thought about that before. I suppose the answer is how they view me in court and my — them learning about who I am as a person. I would think that would be important.

Q. Are you trying to convey a particular image to this jury, Mr. Menendez?

A. I don't think so.

Q. Are your facial expressions or signs of emotion matters that you consider before you testify, Mr. Menendez?

A. I think that being in the courtroom with the jury for three or four months, they get to know me and who I am, and I think that it would be impossible to try to portray myself as someone that I'm not.

Q. Did you ever take acting lessons, Mr. Menendez?

A. No.

Q. Did you study acting in school?

A. I took a year of theater in high school.

Q. And did you tell us that you wanted to study theater in college?

A. I enjoy the arts, and there's nothing more fun than that.

Q. My question was did you tell us that you wanted to study theater in college?

A. I did, yes.

Q. And did you consider having a career in acting?

A. I don't — I thought it would be fun. I meant stage acting. But I couldn't really think of that as a serious career. My father would laugh. And so I didn't seriously think about that.

Q. Did you tell Detective Zoeller that your mother thought you were a good actor?

A. She saw me in a play once and thought I was good.

15. *Does the reference to the mother's statement constitute hearsay?*

Q. You weren't a child when you shot your mother and father to death, were you, Mr. Menendez?

A. I don't think that I was a child.

Q. And is it part of the strategy of the defense to portray you as a helpless child, Mr. Menendez?

Def. Att: Objection Your Honor. It's argumentative.

16. Judge: *How should the judge rule on this objection?*

Q. Do you feel that the jury might have more sympathy for you if you emphasize your age?

Def. Att: Objection. Calls for a conclusion Your Honor. It's also speculation.

17. Judge: Overruled. *Is this a proper ruling?*

A. What the jury has sympathy for should not be my concern. I have — these are 17 people I have never met before, and I don't know what they find sympathy in and what they don't. I am here because I have to tell what happened in my life, and that's not my concern when I'm on the witness stand. What's in Mr. Levin's mind, I don't know. [Authors' note: the defendant includes the alternate jurors in the number of jurors.]

5. The Scottsboro Boys Trials

Nine Black men collectively known as the "Scottsboro Boys" were riding the rails in Alabama in 1931. They were charged with raping two white women, Victoria Price and Ruby Bates, who were in the same train car. Trials involving the charges took place between 1931 and 1937. In the first trial involving Powell and Patterson, the defendants were denied counsel and were quickly tried, convicted, and sentenced to death. The U.S. Supreme Court overturned the convictions, ruling that the denial of counsel deprived the defendants of due process of law. (*Powell v. Alabama*, 1932). Two of the defendants were then tried separately and represented by civil rights lawyer Samuel Liebowitz. Ruby Bates admitted at this trial that she had not been raped, but both defendants were again convicted and sentenced to death. This U.S. Supreme Court revered this conviction on the ground that Blacks were systematically excluded from the jury. (*Norris v. Alabama*, 1935) Other trials followed. Five of the defendants were eventually convicted of rape or other serious crimes; charges were dropped against the other four. The transcript excerpts below are from different Scottsboro Boys trials.

Transcript A. Direct and Cross-Examination of Prosecution Witness Ory Dobbins

(Dobbins testified to seeing the defendants in the same train car as Price and Bates.)

Prosecutor's Direct Examination

Q: About how far away were you from the track as the train passed?

A: Forty yards.

Q: Did you see anybody on that train?

A: I saw some negroes and there was two white girls.

Q: What sort of a car were they in?

A: On a gon.

Q: Gondola car?

1. Is this an improper leading question?

A: Yes sir.

Q: As the train passed did you see in that gondola car?

A: Yes sir.

Q: What did you see happen there between the negroes, among the negroes and anybody else in there?

2. On what basis might defense counsel have objected to this question?

A: I saw one of the girls setting up on the end of the gon fixing to jump off.

Def. Att: I move to strike out what she was fixing to do.

3. Judge: What basis might the defense counsel have had for objecting? *What ruling?*

Q: What did you see happen?

A: She was fixing to jump off.

Def. Att: I move to strike that out.

4. Judge: *What ruling?*

Defense Cross-Examination

Q: How many people were on this car?

A: I wouldn't be for sure.

Q: Just one?

A: No sir, looked like five or six.

Q: All together?

A: Yes sir.

Q: I am reading from page 44 of the Haywood Patterson record, you were asked this question: "Q. As it passed you all you saw was one colored man and one white boy on it?" "Yes sir." That is what you said at Scottsboro? [Authors' Note: The question refers to an earlier trial of Haywood and Patterson in Scottsboro.]

A: I didn't say it.

Def. Att: Will it be conceded that the official record of the trial that I have read is correct; that the official record of the trial before Judge Hawkins and the jury at Scottsboro shows that is exactly what he was asked and that is what he said. Have I read it correctly?

Pros: You read that part of it correctly.

5. *Is this proper use of extrinsic evidence (the excerpt from the record of a previous trial) for impeachment?*

Q: You testified here you were forty yards from the railroad didn't you, that is what you said several times in answer to my question.

6. *Is the cross-examiner improperly testifying to the witness' prior testimony?*

A: Forty yards is what it is.

Q: Let me ask you if you didn't say this at Scottsboro two years ago; I am reading from the official record taken down by the stenographer, page #43." "Q. How far from the track?" "A. About one hundred yards." That is what you said at Scottsboro. I am reading correctly am I not?

A: (no answer)

Q: You said one hundred yards from the track, that is what you swore two years ago instead of forty yards?

7. Is this question improper as argumentative or asked and answered?

A: I don't remember whether I said it or not, it has been so long.

Q: You only saw one girl?

A: Saw one girl.

Q: Not two girls, just saw one girl you spoke about, that is right, that is all you saw?

8. Is this question objectionable as argumentative?

A: The one I saw when he grabbed her.

Transcript B. Defense Cross-Examination of Victoria Price

Q: Ms. Price, you were raped by six different men?

A: Yes.

Q: Have you ever been convicted of a crime?

Pros. We object to that.

1. Judge: Sustained. *Was this a proper ruling?*

Def: I haven't finished my question.

Judge: It sounded like it to me.

Q: Were you ever convicted of a crime involving moral turpitude?

Pros: I object to that.

Judge: I doubt whether this witness knows what moral turpitude is; I doubt whether half the lawyers know it. Ask if she has been convicted and I can then determine whether that involves moral turpitude.

Q: What were you convicted of?

Pros: I object to that.

2. Judge: I sustain the objection. *Was this a proper ruling?*

Def Att: Your Honor just told me to ask it.

Court: No, not that way — you misunderstood me. You can ask her if she has ever been convicted of a certain offense, and I can then determine whether you can ask that kind of question.

Q: Were you ever convicted of the crime of adultery?

Pros: We object to that.

Judge: I sustain the objection. (To the Jury) Gentlemen of the jury, when a question is asked and I sustain an objection to that question, that question and all that involves and all inferences from it, it is out of the case, and not evidence in the case, and you must not consider it in arriving at your verdict.

Q: Were you ever convicted of the crime of fornication?

Pros: We object to that.

Judge: Sustained.

Q: Were you ever convicted for a violation of the prohibition law?

Pros: We object to that.

Judge: Sustained.

Q: Were you ever convicted of vagrancy and drunkenness?

Pros: We object to that.

Judge: Sustained.

3. Were the judge's rulings sustaining the prosecutor's objections correct under current law (assuming the questions refer to current offenses)?

Transcript C. Defense Direct Examination of Defense Witness Dallas Ramsey

(Ramsey testified that Victoria Price was in Chattanooga at a time when she testified that she was raped by the defendants.)

Q: The day or afternoon of the account referred to you say you saw those girls about six o'clock in the morning in the jungles (in Chattanooga)?

A: Yes sir.

1. COURT: How many girls did you see? *Is it appropriate for the judge to ask this question?*

A: Two

Def. Att: Will you bring Victoria Price in?

Pros: We object, let him first describe the girls.

COURT: Let her come in.

Pros: I don't mind her coming in, but I do think the jury should be able to test his accuracy, you see my cross examination on this is foreclosed.

2. *Should the judge have granted the prosecutor's request that the witness have to describe Victoria Price before she is brought into the courtroom for the witness to identify?*

Q: Is this the girl you saw?

Pros: We object.

3. *What ground for objection might have been appropriate? How should the judge have ruled?*

A: She seems like the same girl — it seems like she is a little heavier now that what she was then.

Q: It is the same girl?

A: Yes sir.

Q: Did this girl you have identified (for the record Victoria Price) say to you, when does the train for Huntsville leave?

4. *What if any objection might the prosecutor have made to this question?*

A: Yes sir.

Q: Or words to that effect?

A: Yes sir.

Q: Did you reply to that?

A: Yes sir.

Q: Tell these gentlemen what you said to her

A: I said it leaves somewhere around nine o'clock.

5. *Could defense counsel have offered the statement for a non-hearsay purpose?*

Q: What did she say then?

A: She said we came up here hunting a job, and I told her, I said about a month ago I says I left my job over there at the Hosiery Mill, at the Champion Hosiery Mill, I bought a dray and I had to quit, and they are hiring knitters over there, and I says they practically put on some every day and it might be you could get a job over there, and she said I have been all around the town and couldn't find no job.

6. *Could defense counsel have offered this statement for a non-hearsay purpose?*

Cross Examination by Prosecutor

Q: Do you know Mr. Chamlee? (a defense lawyer)

A: Yes sir.

Q: How long have you known him?

A: Oh, I have been knowing Mr. Chamlee for the last I reckon twelve or fifteen years.

Q: What did he say?

A: He asked me did I see these girls, and I told him, yes, I see them.

Q: Mr Chamlee is the first man that asked you did you see them, is that true?

A: He wasn't the first man, but he was the first man that was involved in the case that asked me anything, other people asked me about it.

Q: How did they happen to ask you about it?

Def. Att: I object.

7. COURT: *Overrule that objection. What might have been the basis of this objection? Was the judge's ruling correct?*

6. The Leo Frank Trial (1913)

Leo Frank was convicted and sentenced to death in Atlanta for killing 13-year-old Mary Phagan. Frank was the supervisor of a pencil factory in which Phagan worked.

Frank was a Jew. The evidence against him ranged from flimsy to nonexistent, and the conviction reflected the community's strong anti-Semitism. Georgia's governor commuted the death sentence, but a vigilante mob pulled Frank from a train and hanged him. *They Won't Forget is an excellent 1937 film about the case, though it makes Frank a northerner and ascribes the community's prejudice to anti-northerner sentiments rather than anti-Semitism.*

Transcript A. Prosecution Witness George Epps

(Epps was a 15-year-old friend of Mary Phagan who testified that he had ridden the streetcar with her in the morning of the day she was killed and planned to meet up with her in the afternoon to watch the Confederate Day Parade.)

Pros. Direct Examination

Q: What time was it when you and Mary got off the streetcar?

A: It was 12:07.

Q: Did Mary say anything about Mr. Frank as you both got off the streetcar?

1. Is this an improperly leading question?

A: Yes.

Q: What did she say?

A: She *said that she was afraid of Frank because he had been flirting with her.*

2. *Should a hearsay objection by the defense attorney have been sustained?*

Defense Cross-Examination

Q: How did you know what time it was when Mary Phagan joined you going downtown that morning?

A: I looked at a clock just before I took the car.

Q: You didn't say anything about a clock when you testified before the coroner's jury.

A: Nope, but I looked at one just the same.

3. *Is it proper for the cross-examiner to ask about the witness' failure to mention a clock when he testified before the coroner's jury? If so, on what basis? Had the witness claimed he had mentioned the clock when testifying before the coroner's jury, could the defense lawyer offer extrinsic evidence that he had not mentioned the clock?*

Q: How did you know what time it was when Miss Mary left you?

A: I estimated it from the time she got on the car, and I told it by the sun. I can tell time by the sun.

Q: You can tell the time to within seven minutes by the sun, then?

A: Yes, sir, I can.

4. *Is this proper cross-examination?*

Q: Do you know a reporter by the name of John Minar?

A: Yes.

Q: On the day that Mary Phagan was killed, didn't your sister tell Mr. Minar that you had told her that you had not seen Mary Phagan for a few days before she was killed?

5. How might the propriety of this question by affected by whether the witness Epps was present at the time his sister made this statement to the reporter?

Transcript B. Prosecution Witness Det. John Black

Detective John Black was a lead investigator on the murder case.

Pros. Direct Examination

Q: When you saw Frank the morning of Sunday April 27 did he seem nervous?

1. *Is this a permissible lay opinion?*

A: Yes.

Q: Why?

A: Because he had some considerable trouble putting on a collar. It seemed that he couldn't tie his necktie.

2. *Even if the opinion is one that a lay witness can give, is this an adequate foundation?*

Q: What did he say about going to the factory?

A: He kept on insisting on getting a cup of coffee, and I finally told him that I had been up until one o'clock the night before and had then been aroused at four o'clock in the morning and hadn't had any coffee or breakfast, either. I told him we'd better go to the factory and get that over with.

3. *What is the relevance of the testimony? Do Black's statements constitute hearsay?*

Q: Did you see him go the [factory punch] clock?

A: Yes. He looked at it, made an examination (of the slip inside the clock), and said it had been punched correctly up until 2:30 A.M.

Q: Did Frank produce a time slip at that time?

A: Yes, a slip which he gave to Chief Lanford on Monday.

Q: What became of the slip he had on Sunday?

A: He carried it into his office on Sunday morning.

Q: When did you first hear Frank state the slip was incorrect?

A: I cannot swear. It was Tuesday or Monday, one or the other.

4. *Is the question proper? Should Black's response be stricken as speculation?*

Defense Cross-Examination

Q: Who was present when you talked to Frank on the time previous to Sunday?

A: I don't remember.

Q: As a matter of fact, you can't swear truthfully that you spoke to him at all, can you?

A: Not positively.

5. *Is this question objectionable as argumentative?*

Q: You went through the factory with Frank?

A: I don't know — several people.

Q: And none of you saw the sketch said to be blood?

A: No, sir.

6. *Is this question beyond the scope of the direct examination?*

Q: How many of you went over the building?

A: I don't know exactly.

Q: Perhaps thirty people?

A: I don't know.

Q: This large horde made up of officers and curiosity seekers went over the factory and nobody saw these alleged blood spots?

7. *On what ground might the prosecutor have objected to this question?*

A: No, sir.

Q: You saw Frank at the clock?

A: Yes.

Q: He opened the clock band took out a slip?

A: Yes.

Q: When did Frank turn over this slip that he took out of the clock?

A: I don't know.

Q: Didn't you tell the prosecutor a few minutes ago that he turned over the slip on Monday morning?

A: I don't remember.

Q: Look here Black. Is your memory so bad you can't remember what you told the prosecutor twenty or thirty minutes ago? And yet you attempt here to state the words of conversations that occurred more than three months ago?

8. *Is this question objectionable?*

A: [No answer.]. . . .

Q: You also went to Lee's house? [Authors' Note: Newt Lee worked as a janitor in the pencil factory and many considered him to be Mary Phagan's killer.]

A: Yes.

Q: What did you find?

A: A bloody shirt.

Q: Is this the shirt, Mr. Black?

A: Yes, sir.

Q: What time did you find it?

A: Tuesday morning, about 9:00.

Q: Don't you know, Black, that as a matter of fact, that shirt was found before Frank ever said anything to you about the missed punch ins in that time slip?

9. *Is this question objectionable?*

A: [No answer.]

Q: Don't you know it?

A: [No answer.]

Q: [To Judge:] Give him time to answer, Your Honor.

A: I don't remember. I don't like to admit it, but I am so crossed up and worried that I don't know where I am at.

Q: No further questions.

§ 20.03 Transcript Excerpts from Courtroom Films

The transcripts in this section consist of excerpts from popular courtroom films.

1. *A Few Good Men*

The transcript below is an edited version of Lt. Kaffee's cross-examination of Col. Jessup in the classic courtroom drama, *A Few Good Men* (1992). Two Marines, Dawson and Downey, stationed at the U.S. military base in Guantanamo Bay, Cuba, face a court-martial for hazing Private Santiago so seriously that Santiago died. Dawson's and Downey's defense is that they should not be punished because their commanding officer, Col. Jessup, gave them a "Code Red" order to carry out the hazing. Col. Jessup insists that he gave no such order, and that in fact he had tried to protect Santiago from harm by ordering his transfer off the base the morning after the hazing. Following Capt. Jack Ross' examination of Col. Jessup, defense lawyer Lt. Kaffee seeks to show that Jessup did not order a transfer of Santiago.

1. Lt. Kaffee: Colonel, we have the transfer order that you signed ordering that Santiago be on a flight leaving Guantanamo at 6:00 the next day. Was that the first flight? *Is this a proper question?*

A: The 0600 was the first flight.

Q: You flew up to Washington this morning. Is that right?

A: Yes.

Q: You brought your dress uniform?

A: Yes.

Q: Toothbrush, shaving kit, underwear?

A: I brought a change of clothes and some personal items.

Q: After Dawson and Downey's arrest Santiago's barracks were sealed off and its contents inventoried. "Four pairs camouflage pants, three long-sleeve khaki shirts, three pairs of boots, four pairs green socks, three green T-shirts." I'm wondering why Santiago wasn't packed.

2. Capt. Ross: Objection. *Is the previous question objectionable? If so on what basis?*

A: (No answer)

3. Q: I'll tell you what. We'll get back to that one in a minute. This is a record of all phone calls made from your base in the past 24 hours. After being subpoenaed to Washington, you made three calls. *Is this a proper question?*

A: I called Colonel Fitzhughes to let him know that I would be in town. The second call was to arrange a meeting with Congressman Richmond of the House Armed Services Committee. And the third call was to my sister Elizabeth.

4. Q: These are phone records from Gitmo for September 6, and these are 14 letters that Santiago wrote in nine months requesting — in fact, begging — for a transfer. Upon hearing the news that he was finally getting his transfer Santiago was so excited that do you know how many people he called? Zero. Nobody. Not one call to his parents saying he was coming home. Not one call to a friend, saying, "Can you pick me up at the airport?" He was asleep in his bed at midnight, and according to you he was getting on a plane in six hours. Yet everything he owned was hanging neatly in his closet and folded neatly in his footlocker. You were leaving for one day. You packed a bag and made three calls. Santiago was leaving for the rest of his life and he hadn't called a soul and he hadn't packed a thing. Can you explain that? The fact is, there was no transfer order. Santiago wasn't going anywhere. Isn't that right, Colonel? *Does this constitute proper cross-examination?*

2. Let Him Have It

This film is based on a notorious 1953 English trial. Two teenagers, Derek Bentley and Chris Craig, were charged with conspiring to murder a police officer in the course of unsuccessfully attempting to burgle a warehouse. A surviving police officer, Sgt. Fairfax, testified for the prosecution that after Bentley was arrested, Craig pulled out a gun and pointed it at Fairfax. Sgt. Fairfax's testimony continued much as follows:

Q: How far from you was Craig when he pointed the gun at you?

A: Craig was standing about four feet in front of me.

Q: And what happened next?

A: Bentley shouted, Craig opened fire, I was hit in the shoulder.

Q: And what was it that Bentley shouted to cause Craig to open fire?

Defense Lawyer Cassels: My Lord, I really must object. My learned friend is clearly leading the witness.

1. Judge: It was a valid question Mr. Cassels. Please continue. *Is this a correct ruling?*

A: He shouted, "Let him have it, Chris."

Q: And what do you think he meant by that?

A: Shoot. Start firing.

2. *Is this a valid lay witness opinion?*

3. *Philadelphia*

Andrew Beckett sued the law firm that had employed him as an associate for illegally firing him because he had AIDS. (At the time of the film, AIDS was incurable, and widely considered to be easily transferable and virtually always fatal.) The law firm's defense was that Beckett was fired because he missed filing deadlines and made other serious mistakes. Beckett testified that the law firm partners knew that he had AIDS because one of them recognized the AIDS lesion on his face. To support the law firm partners' contention that they did not know that Beckett had AIDS, defense lawyer Belinda Conine conducted a live demonstration while cross-examining Beckett. This portion of the cross-examination proceeded as follows:

Ms. Conine: You've testified that the lesions on your face were visible to the people you worked with, correct?

A: That's right.

Q: And it's your contention that when the partners were made aware of the lesions, they jumped to the conclusion you had AIDS and fired you.

A: Absolutely.

Q: Do you have any lesions on your face at this time?

A: One. Here, in front of my ear (pointing to the side of his face).

Q: (An assistant hands Conine a small mirror, which she holds in front of Beckett) Remembering you are under oath, answering truthfully, can you see the lesion on your face, in this mirror, from three feet away? Answering truthfully.

1. *Is the form of this question objectionable?*

A: (Beckett examines his face in the mirror) When I was fired, there were four lesions on my face, much bigger . . .

Q: Answer the question, please.

A: No. I can't really see it.

2. *What objection, if any, might plaintiff's counsel have made to the defense lawyer's use of the mirror?*

Redirect Examination

Beckett's attorney Joe Miller responded with his own live demonstration on redirect examination. Miller borrowed the mirror from Conine and questioned Beckett as follows:

Mr. Miller: Andrew, do you have any lesions on any part of your body, at this time, that resemble the lesions that were on your face at the time you were fired?

A: Yes. On my torso.

Q: If it please the court, I'd like to ask Mr. Beckett to remove his shirt, so that the jury can have an accurate idea of what we're talking about.

Ms. Conine: We object Your Honor. It would unfairly influence the jury.

3. Judge: Overruled. *Is this ruling proper?*

Q: (Beckett removes his shirt to reveal a torso filled with purple lesions.) Can you see the lesions on your chest in this mirror?

A: Yes.

4. *What objection, if any, might defense counsel have made to the mirror demonstration?*

4. *Anatomy of a Murder*

Lt. Manion is charged with murdering Barney Quill. Manion admits shooting Quill, but claims that he did so when he developed a form of temporary insanity called irresistible impulse as a result of finding out that Quill had raped and beaten his wife. Prosecutor Claude Dancer contends that Manion invented the rape story to justify his killing of Quill. Surprise defense witness Mary Palant gives credence to the rape story however, when she testifies that the morning after Quill was killed, she found a torn pair of women's panties at the bottom of the laundry chute that is in the hallway right next to Quill's apartment door. (The panties belonged to Manion's wife.) Dancer furiously attacks Palant's credibility. The final portion of his cross-examination goes as follows:

Mr. Dancer: In the grip of what Mr. Biegler (defense counsel) might call irresistible impulse, you rushed in here because you wanted to crucify the character of the dead Barney Quill, isn't that true?

A: No, I thought it was my duty.

Q: Your pride was hurt, wasn't it?

A: I don't know what you mean.

Q: Ms. Palant, when you found the panties, was your first thought that Barney Quill might have raped Mrs. Manion or that he might have been stepping out with Mrs. Manion?

A: (To the judge) What does he mean? I don't know what he means.

Judge: Mr. Dancer, I must ask you to put straight questions to the witness.

1. *Can the judge make a ruling in the absence of an objection by the defense attorney?*

Q: Here is a straight question Your Honor. Ms. Palant, were you Barney Quill's mistress?

A: I was not.

Q: Do you know it was common knowledge in Thunder Bay that you were living with Quill?

2. *What objection, if any, to this question might have been proper?*

A: That's not true. Barney Quill was my . . .

Q: Was what, Ms. Palant? Barney Quill was what, Ms. Palant?

A: Barney Quill was my father.

Q: (in a stunned tone) No further questions.

5. *A Civil Action*

In the film version of Jonathan Harr's book *A Civil Action,* Jan Schlichtmann represents a class of plaintiffs in Woburn, Massachusetts who allege that two factories polluted their water supply by dumping toxic chemicals into a river. In this excerpt, Schlichtmann examines the owner of one of the factories.

Q: Experts have testified in this court that your land, your 15 acres, is the most grotesquely polluted land in all of New England. And you have no idea how it got that way?

1. *What is the propriety of this question?*

A: No sir.

Q: Does it upset you to learn this?

A: Very much so.

Q: Really. Why?

A: My factory is the oldest surviving business in Woburn. When the other tanners moved out, I stayed even though for me that was a very big financial burden. I stayed because Woburn is my home. My children's home.

Mr. Schlichtmann: This is not my question Your Honor. He's not answering my question.

2. **The Court:** He's trying to answer your question Mr. Schlichtmann. Just let him. *Is this a proper ruling?*

A: That land has been in my family for three generations. That land to me is hallowed ground. So when you ask me would I be upset if someone came onto that land and desecrated it, land that's part of the town that I love, my answer to your question Mr. Schlichtmann is yes.

3. *What is the tactical propriety of the question?*

6. *My Cousin Vinny*

In one of the funniest courtroom movies ever made (or one of the funniest movies ever made, period), a brash New York attorney defends his cousin Bill and Bill's friend Stan in a murder trial. Bill and Stan are driving cross-country to transfer to UCLA when they are arrested in Alabama for robbing a convenience store and killing the clerk. Vinny has never tried a case and knows virtually nothing about courtroom procedures. But Vinny proves to be an adept cross-examiner, and he brilliantly and comically undermines prosecutor Jim Trotter's eyewitnesses. But when an FBI agent links the defendants' car (a 1964 Buick Skylark) to the tire marks on the street in front of the store, Vinny finally has to ask for help from his fiancée Mona Lisa Vito. He calls her to testify as an expert in "general automotive mechanics." D.A. Trotter first unsuccessfully challenges Mona Lisa's expertise. Vinny then asks her to explain why Bill and Stan's car could not have been the source of the tire marks.

Transcript A. Prosecutor's *Voir Dire* **Questioning of Mona Lisa Vito**

Q: Your Honor, I object to this witness. Improper foundation. I'm not aware of this person's qualifications. I'd like to *voir dire* this witness as to the extent of her expertise.

Judge: Granted. Mr. Trotter, you may proceed.

Q: Miss Vito, what's your current profession?

A: I'm an out of work hairdresser.

Q: Out of work hairdresser? Now, in what way does that qualify you as an expert in automobiles?

A: It doesn't.

Q: In what way are you qualified?

1. *Is this a proper question?*

A: Well, my father was a mechanic, his father was a mechanic, my mother's father was a mechanic, my three brothers are mechanics, four uncles on my father's side are mechanics —

Q: Your family is obviously qualified, but have you ever worked as a mechanic?

A: Yeah, in my father's garage, yeah.

Q: As a mechanic? What did you do in your father's garage?

A: Tune-ups, oil changes, brake relining, engine rebuilds, rebuild some trannies, rear ends.

2. *What is the relationship of Mona Lisa's work experience to her qualifying as an expert witness under Rule 702?*

Q: Now, Miss Vito, being an expert on general automotive knowledge, can you tell me what would the correct ignition timing be on a 1955 Bel-Air Chevrolet with a 327 cubic inch engine and a four-barrel carburetor?

A: It's a bullshit question.

Q: Does that mean that you can't answer it?

A: It's a bullshit question. Nobody could answer that question

Q: Your Honor, I move to disqualify Miss Vito as an expert witness.

Judge: Can you answer the question?

A: No, it is a trick question.

Judge: Why is it a trick question?

A: Because Chevy didn't make a 327 in '55. The 327 didn't come out till '62, and it wasn't offered in a Bel-Air with a four-barrel carb 'til '64. However, in 1964 the correct ignition timing would be four degrees before top dead center.

3. *How does this answer support Mona Lisa's qualifications to testify as an expert under Rule 702?*

P: Well, uh, she's acceptable Your Honor.

Transcript B. Vinny's Direct Examination of Mona Lisa Vito

Q: Your Honor, this is a picture taken by my fiancée outside the Sack O' Suds. I'd like to submit this picture of the tire tracks as evidence.

Judge: Mr. Trotter?

P: No objection, Your Honor.

1. *Did Vinny lay a proper foundation for admission of the photograph as evidence? What if any objections might the prosecutor have made?*

Q: Miss Vito, did you take this picture?

A: You know I did.

Q: Miss Vito, it has been argued by me, the defense, that two sets of guys met up at the Sack O' Suds at the same time, driving identical metallic mint green 1964 Buick Skylark convertibles. Now, can you tell us, by looking at the picture, if the defense's case holds water?

A: No, the Defense is wrong! There is no way that these tire marks were made by a 1964 Buick Skylark. These marks were made by a 1963 Pontiac Tempest.

2. *Can the witness testify to this opinion without first testifying to its bases?*

Pros: Objection Your Honor, is the witness stating fact or opinion?

Judge: This is your opinion?

A: It's a fact.

3. *How does the fact/opinion dichotomy relate to expert opinions?*

Q: I find it hard to believe that this kind of information could be ascertained simply by looking at a picture.

A: Would you like me to explain?

Q: I would love to hear this.

A: The car that made these two equal length tire marks had Positraction, can't make those marks without Positraction, which was not available on the 1964 Buick Skylark

Q: And why not? What is Positraction?

A: It's a limited slip differential which distributes power equally to both the right and left tires. The '64 Skylark had a regular differential, which anyone who's been stuck in the mud in Alabama knows, you step on the gas, one tire spins, the other tire does nothing.

4. *How does this explanation relate to the witness' credibility?*

Q: Is that it?

A: No, there's more. When the left tire mark goes up on the curb, and the right tire mark stays flat and even, well, the '64 Skylark had a solid rear axle, so when the left tire would go up on the curb, the right tire would tilt out and ride along its edge, but that didn't happen here, the tire marks stayed flat and even. This car had an independent rear suspension. Now in the 60s there were only two other cars made in America that had Positraction and independent rear suspension and enough power to make these marks. One was the Corvette, which could never be confused with the Buick Skylark. The other had the same body length, height, width, weight, wheelbase, and wheel-track as the 64 Skylark, and that was the 1963 Pontiac Tempest.

5. *Is this an improper narrative answer?*

6. *In the language of Rule 702, did the photo provide sufficient facts or data for Mona Lisa's opinion? How does the judge know whether her opinion was the product of reliable principles and methods?*

Appendix 1

Federal Rules of Evidence

As amended to December 1, 2017

RULES OF EVIDENCE FOR UNITED STATES COURTS AND MAGISTRATES
ARTICLE I. GENERAL PROVISIONS

Rule 101. Scope; Definitions

(a) Scope. These rules apply to proceedings in United States courts. The specific courts and proceedings to which the rules apply, along with exceptions, are set out in Rule 1101.

(b) Definitions. In these rules:

(1) "civil case" means a civil action or proceeding;

(2) "criminal case" includes a criminal proceeding;

(3) "public office" includes a public agency;

(4) "record" includes a memorandum, report, or data compilation;

(5) a "rule prescribed by the Supreme Court" means a rule adopted by the Supreme Court under statutory authority; and

(6) a reference to any kind of written material or any other medium includes electronically stored information.

Rule 102. Purpose

These rules should be construed so as to administer every proceeding fairly, eliminate unjustifiable expense and delay, and promote the development of evidence law, to the end of ascertaining the truth and securing a just determination.

Rule 103. Rulings on Evidence

(a) Preserving a Claim of Error. A party may claim error in a ruling to admit or exclude evidence only if the error affects a substantial right of the party and:

(1) if the ruling admits evidence, a party, on the record:

(A) timely objects or moves to strike; and

(B) states the specific ground, unless it was apparent from the context; or

(2) if the ruling excludes evidence, a party informs the court of its substance by an offer of proof, unless the substance was apparent from the context.

(b) Not Needing to Renew an Objection or Offer of Proof. Once the court rules definitively on the record—either before or at trial—a party need not renew an objection or offer of proof to preserve a claim of error for appeal.

(c) Court's Statement About the Ruling; Directing an Offer of Proof. The court may make any statement about the character or form of the evidence, the objection made, and the ruling. The court may direct that an offer of proof be made in question-and-answer form.

(d) Preventing the Jury from Hearing Inadmissible Evidence. To the extent practicable, the court must conduct a jury trial so that inadmissible evidence is not suggested to the jury by any means.

(e) Taking Notice of Plain Error. A court may take notice of a plain error affecting a substantial right, even if the claim of error was not properly preserved.

Rule 104. Preliminary Questions

(a) In General. The court must decide any preliminary question about whether a witness is qualified, a privilege exists, or evidence is admissible. In so deciding, the court is not bound by evidence rules, except those on privilege.

(b) Relevance That Depends on a Fact. When the relevance of evidence depends on whether a fact exists, proof must be introduced sufficient to support a finding that the fact does exist. The court may admit the proposed evidence on the condition that the proof be introduced later.

(c) Conducting a Hearing So That the Jury Cannot Hear It. The court must conduct any hearing on a preliminary question so that the jury cannot hear it if:

> **(1)** the hearing involves the admissibility of a confession;

> **(2)** a defendant in a criminal case is a witness and so requests; or

> **(3)** justice so requires.

(d) Cross-Examining a Defendant in a Criminal Case. By testifying on a preliminary question, a defendant in a criminal case does not become subject to cross-examination on other issues in the case.

(e) Evidence Relevant to Weight and Credibility. This rule does not limit a party's right to introduce before the jury evidence that is relevant to the weight or credibility of other evidence.

Rule 105. Limiting Evidence That Is Not Admissible Against Other Parties or for Other Purposes

If the court admits evidence that is admissible against a party or for a purpose—but not against another party or for another purpose—the court, on timely request, must restrict the evidence to its proper scope and instruct the jury accordingly.

Rule 106. Remainder of or Related Writings or Recorded Statements

If a party introduces all or part of a writing or recorded statement, an adverse party may require the introduction, at that time, of any other part — or any other writing or recorded statement — that in fairness ought to be considered at the same time.

ARTICLE II. JUDICIAL NOTICE

Rule 201. Judicial Notice of Adjudicative Facts

(a) Scope. This rule governs judicial notice of an adjudicative fact only, not a legislative fact.

(b) Kinds of Facts That May Be Judicially Noticed. The court may judicially notice a fact that is not subject to reasonable dispute because it:

(1) is generally known within the trial court's territorial jurisdiction; or

(2) can be accurately and readily determined from sources whose accuracy cannot reasonably be questioned.

(c) Taking Notice. The court:

(1) may take judicial notice on its own; or

(2) must take judicial notice if a party requests it and the court is supplied with the necessary information.

(d) Timing. The court may take judicial notice at any stage of the proceeding.

(e) Opportunity to Be Heard. On timely request, a party is entitled to be heard on the propriety of taking judicial notice and the nature of the fact to be noticed. If the court takes judicial notice before notifying a party, the party, on request, is still entitled to be heard.

(f) Instructing the Jury. In a civil case, the court must instruct the jury to accept the noticed fact as conclusive. In a criminal case, the court must instruct the jury that it may or may not accept the noticed fact as conclusive.

ARTICLE III. PRESUMPTIONS IN CIVIL CASES

Rule 301. Presumptions in Civil Cases Generally

In a civil case, unless a federal statute or these rules provide otherwise, the party against whom a presumption is directed has the burden of producing evidence to rebut the presumption. But this rule does not shift the burden of persuasion, which remains on the party who had it originally.

Rule 302. Applying State Law to Presumptions in Civil Cases

In a civil case, state law governs the effect of a presumption regarding a claim or defense for which state law supplies the rule of decision.

ARTICLE IV. RELEVANCE AND ITS LIMITS

Rule 401. Test for Relevant Evidence

Evidence is relevant if:

(a) it has any tendency to make a fact more or less probable than it would be without the evidence; and

(b) the fact is of consequence in determining the action.

Rule 402. General Admissibility of Relevant Evidence

Relevant evidence is admissible unless any of the following provides otherwise:

- the United States Constitution;
- a federal statute;
- these rules; or
- other rules prescribed by the Supreme Court.

Irrelevant evidence is not admissible.

Rule 403. Excluding Relevant Evidence for Prejudice, Confusion, Waste of Time, or Other Reasons

The court may exclude relevant evidence if its probative value is substantially outweighed by a danger of one or more of the following: unfair prejudice, confusing the issues, misleading the jury, undue delay, wasting time, or needlessly presenting cumulative evidence.

Rule 404. Character Evidence; Crimes or Other Acts

(a) **Character Evidence.**

(1) *Prohibited Uses.* Evidence of a person's character or character trait is not admissible to prove that on a particular occasion the person acted in accordance with the character or trait.

(2) *Exceptions for a Defendant or Victim in a Criminal Case.* The following exceptions apply in a criminal case:

(A) a defendant may offer evidence of the defendant's pertinent trait, and if the evidence is admitted, the prosecutor may offer evidence to rebut it;

(B) subject to the limitations in Rule 412, a defendant may offer evidence of an alleged victim's pertinent trait, and if the evidence is admitted, the prosecutor may:

(i) offer evidence to rebut it; and

(ii) offer evidence of the defendant's same trait; and

(C) in a homicide case, the prosecutor may offer evidence of the alleged victim's trait of peacefulness to rebut evidence that the victim was the first aggressor.

(3) *Exceptions for a Witness.* Evidence of a witness's character may be admitted under Rules 607, 608, and 609.

(b) Crimes, Wrongs, or Other Acts.

(1) *Prohibited Uses.* Evidence of a crime, wrong, or other act is not admissible to prove a person's character in order to show that on a particular occasion the person acted in accordance with the character.

(2) *Permitted Uses; Notice in a Criminal Case.* This evidence may be admissible for another purpose, such as proving motive, opportunity, intent, preparation, plan, knowledge, identity, absence of mistake, or lack of accident. On request by a defendant in a criminal case, the prosecutor must:

> **(A)** provide reasonable notice of the general nature of any such evidence that the prosecutor intends to offer at trial; and

> **(B)** do so before trial — or during trial if the court, for good cause, excuses lack of pretrial notice.

Rule 405. Methods of Proving Character

(a) By Reputation or Opinion. When evidence of a person's character or character trait is admissible, it may be proved by testimony about the person's reputation or by testimony in the form of an opinion. On cross-examination of the character witness, the court may allow an inquiry into relevant specific instances of the person's conduct.

(b) By Specific Instances of Conduct. When a person's character or character trait is an essential element of a charge, claim, or defense, the character or trait may also be proved by relevant specific instances of the person's conduct.

Rule 406. Habit; Routine Practice

Evidence of a person's habit or an organization's routine practice may be admitted to prove that on a particular occasion the person or organization acted in accordance with the habit or routine practice. The court may admit this evidence regardless of whether it is corroborated or whether there was an eyewitness.

Rule 407. Subsequent Remedial Measures

When measures are taken that would have made an earlier injury or harm less likely to occur, evidence of the subsequent measures is not admissible to prove:

- negligence;
- culpable conduct;
- a defect in a product or its design; or
- a need for a warning or instruction.

But the court may admit this evidence for another purpose, such as impeachment or — if disputed — proving ownership, control, or the feasibility of precautionary measures.

Rule 408. Compromise Offers and Negotiations

(a) Prohibited Uses. Evidence of the following is not admissible — on behalf of any party — either to prove or disprove the validity or amount of a disputed claim or to impeach by a prior inconsistent statement or a contradiction:

(1) furnishing, promising, or offering — or accepting, promising to accept, or offering to accept — a valuable consideration in compromising or attempting to compromise the claim; and

(2) conduct or a statement made during compromise negotiations about the claim — except when offered in a criminal case and when the negotiations related to a claim by a public office in the exercise of its regulatory, investigative, or enforcement authority.

(b) Exceptions. The court may admit this evidence for another purpose, such as proving a witness's bias or prejudice, negating a contention of undue delay, or proving an effort to obstruct a criminal investigation or prosecution.

Rule 409. Offers to Pay Medical and Similar Expenses

Evidence of furnishing, promising to pay, or offering to pay medical, hospital, or similar expenses resulting from an injury is not admissible to prove liability for the injury.

Rule 410. Pleas, Plea Discussions, and Related Statements

(a) Prohibited Uses. In a civil or criminal case, evidence of the following is not admissible against the defendant who made the plea or participated in the plea discussions:

(1) a guilty plea that was later withdrawn;

(2) a nolo contendere plea;

(3) a statement made during a proceeding on either of those pleas under Federal Rule of Criminal Procedure 11 or a comparable state procedure; or

(4) a statement made during plea discussions with an attorney for the prosecuting authority if the discussions did not result in a guilty plea or they resulted in a later-withdrawn guilty plea.

(b) Exceptions. The court may admit a statement described in Rule 410(a)(3) or (4):

(1) in any proceeding in which another statement made during the same plea or plea discussions has been introduced, if in fairness the statements ought to be considered together; or

(2) in a criminal proceeding for perjury or false statement, if the defendant made the statement under oath, on the record, and with counsel present.

Rule 411. Liability Insurance

Evidence that a person was or was not insured against liability is not admissible to prove whether the person acted negligently or otherwise wrongfully. But the court may admit this evidence for another purpose, such as proving a witness's bias or prejudice or proving agency, ownership, or control.

Rule 412. Sex-Offense Cases: The Victim's Sexual Behavior or Predisposition

(a) Prohibited Uses. The following evidence is not admissible in a civil or criminal proceeding involving alleged sexual misconduct:

(1) evidence offered to prove that a victim engaged in other sexual behavior; or

(2) evidence offered to prove a victim's sexual predisposition.

(b) Exceptions.

(1) *Criminal Cases.* The court may admit the following evidence in a criminal case:

(A) evidence of specific instances of a victim's sexual behavior, if offered to prove that someone other than the defendant was the source of semen, injury, or other physical evidence;

(B) evidence of specific instances of a victim's sexual behavior with respect to the person accused of the sexual misconduct, if offered by the defendant to prove consent or if offered by the prosecutor; and

(C) evidence whose exclusion would violate the defendant's constitutional rights.

(2) *Civil Cases.* In a civil case, the court may admit evidence offered to prove a victim's sexual behavior or sexual predisposition if its probative value substantially outweighs the danger of harm to any victim and of unfair prejudice to any party. The court may admit evidence of a victim's reputation only if the victim has placed it in controversy.

(c) Procedure to Determine Admissibility.

(1) *Motion.* If a party intends to offer evidence under Rule 412(b), the party must:

(A) file a motion that specifically describes the evidence and states the purpose for which it is to be offered;

(B) do so at least 14 days before trial unless the court, for good cause, sets a different time;

(C) serve the motion on all parties; and

(D) notify the victim or, when appropriate, the victim's guardian or representative.

(2) *Hearing.* Before admitting evidence under this rule, the court must conduct an in camera hearing and give the victim and parties a right to attend and be heard. Unless the court orders otherwise, the motion, related materials, and the record of the hearing must be and remain sealed.

(d) Definition of "Victim." In this rule, "victim" includes an alleged victim.

Rule 413. Similar Crimes in Sexual-Assault Cases

(a) Permitted Uses. In a criminal case in which a defendant is accused of a sexual assault, the court may admit evidence that the defendant committed any other sexual assault. The evidence may be considered on any matter to which it is relevant.

(b) Disclosure to the Defendant. If the prosecutor intends to offer this evidence, the prosecutor must disclose it to the defendant, including witnesses' statements or a summary of the expected testimony. The prosecutor must do so at least 15 days before trial or at a later time that the court allows for good cause.

(c) Effect on Other Rules. This rule does not limit the admission or consideration of evidence under any other rule.

(d) Definition of "Sexual Assault." In this rule and Rule 415, "sexual assault" means a crime under federal law or under state law (as "state" is defined in 18 U.S.C. § 513) involving:

> (1) any conduct prohibited by 18 U.S.C. chapter 109A;

> (2) contact, without consent, between any part of the defendant's body — or an object — and another person's genitals or anus;

> (3) contact, without consent, between the defendant's genitals or anus and any part of another person's body;

> (4) deriving sexual pleasure or gratification from inflicting death, bodily injury, or physical pain on another person; or

> (5) an attempt or conspiracy to engage in conduct described in subparagraphs (1)–(4).

Rule 414. Similar Crimes in Child-Molestation Cases

(a) Permitted Uses. In a criminal case in which a defendant is accused of child molestation, the court may admit evidence that the defendant committed any other child molestation. The evidence may be considered on any matter to which it is relevant.

(b) Disclosure to the Defendant. If the prosecutor intends to offer this evidence, the prosecutor must disclose it to the defendant, including witnesses' statements or a summary of the expected testimony. The prosecutor must do so at least 15 days before trial or at a later time that the court allows for good cause.

(c) Effect on Other Rules. This rule does not limit the admission or consideration of evidence under any other rule.

(d) Definition of "Child" and "Child Molestation." In this rule and Rule 415:

(1) "child" means a person below the age of 14; and

(2) "child molestation" means a crime under federal law or under state law (as "state" is defined in 18 U.S.C. § 513) involving:

> (A) any conduct prohibited by 18 U.S.C. chapter 109A and committed with a child;

> (B) any conduct prohibited by 18 U.S.C. chapter 110;

> (C) contact between any part of the defendant's body — or an object — and a child's genitals or anus;

> (D) contact between the defendant's genitals or anus and any part of a child's body;

(E) deriving sexual pleasure or gratification from inflicting death, bodily injury, or physical pain on a child; or

(F) an attempt or conspiracy to engage in conduct described in subparagraphs (A)–(E).

Rule 415. Similar Acts in Civil Cases Involving Sexual Assault or Child Molestation

(a) **Permitted Uses.** In a civil case involving a claim for relief based on a party's alleged sexual assault or child molestation, the court may admit evidence that the party committed any other sexual assault or child molestation. The evidence may be considered as provided in Rules 413 and 414.

(b) **Disclosure to the Opponent.** If a party intends to offer this evidence, the party must disclose it to the party against whom it will be offered, including witnesses' statements or a summary of the expected testimony. The party must do so at least 15 days before trial or at a later time that the court allows for good cause.

(c) **Effect on Other Rules.** This rule does not limit the admission or consideration of evidence under any other rule.

ARTICLE V. PRIVILEGES

Rule 501. Privilege in General

The common law — as interpreted by United States courts in the light of reason and experience — governs a claim of privilege unless any of the following provides otherwise:

- the United States Constitution;
- a federal statute; or
- rules prescribed by the Supreme Court.

But in a civil case, state law governs privilege regarding a claim or defense for which state law supplies the rule of decision.

Rule 502. Attorney-Client Privilege and Work Product; Limitations on Waiver

The following provisions apply, in the circumstances set out, to disclosure of a communication or information covered by the attorney-client privilege or work-product protection.

(a) **Disclosure Made in a Federal Proceeding or to a Federal Office or Agency; Scope of a Waiver.** When the disclosure is made in a federal proceeding or to a federal office or agency and waives the attorney-client privilege or work-product protection, the waiver extends to an undisclosed communication or information in a federal or state proceeding only if:

(1) the waiver is intentional;

(2) the disclosed and undisclosed communications or information concern the same subject matter; and

(3) they ought in fairness to be considered together.

(b) Inadvertent Disclosure. When made in a federal proceeding or to a federal office or agency, the disclosure does not operate as a waiver in a federal or state proceeding if:

(1) the disclosure is inadvertent;

(2) the holder of the privilege or protection took reasonable steps to prevent disclosure; and

(3) the holder promptly took reasonable steps to rectify the error, including (if applicable) following Federal Rule of Civil Procedure 26(b)(5)(B).

(c) Disclosure Made in a State Proceeding. When the disclosure is made in a state proceeding and is not the subject of a state-court order concerning waiver, the disclosure does not operate as a waiver in a federal proceeding if the disclosure:

(1) would not be a waiver under this rule if it had been made in a federal proceeding; or

(2) is not a waiver under the law of the state where the disclosure occurred.

(d) Controlling Effect of a Court Order. A federal court may order that the privilege or protection is not waived by disclosure connected with the litigation pending before the court — in which event the disclosure is also not a waiver in any other federal or state proceeding.

(e) Controlling Effect of a Party Agreement. An agreement on the effect of disclosure in a federal proceeding is binding only on the parties to the agreement, unless it is incorporated into a court order.

(f) Controlling Effect of this Rule. Notwithstanding Rules 101 and 1101, this rule applies to state proceedings and to federal court-annexed and federal court-mandated arbitration proceedings, in the circumstances set out in the rule. And notwithstanding Rule 501, this rule applies even if state law provides the rule of decision.

(g) Definitions. In this rule:

(1) "attorney-client privilege" means the protection that applicable law provides for confidential attorney-client communications; and

(2) "work-product protection" means the protection that applicable law provides for tangible material (or its intangible equivalent) prepared in anticipation of litigation or for trial.

ARTICLE VI. WITNESSES

Rule 601. Competency to Testify in General

Every person is competent to be a witness unless these rules provide otherwise. But in a civil case, state law governs the witness's competency regarding a claim or defense for which state law supplies the rule of decision.

Rule 602. Need for Personal Knowledge

A witness may testify to a matter only if evidence is introduced sufficient to support a finding that the witness has personal knowledge of the matter. Evidence to prove personal knowledge may consist of the witness's own testimony. This rule does not apply to a witness's expert testimony under Rule 703.

Rule 603. Oath or Affirmation to Testify Truthfully

Before testifying, a witness must give an oath or affirmation to testify truthfully. It must be in a form designed to impress that duty on the witness's conscience.

Rule 604. Interpreter

An interpreter must be qualified and must give an oath or affirmation to make a true translation.

Rule 605. Judge's Competency as a Witness

The presiding judge may not testify as a witness at the trial. A party need not object to preserve the issue.

Rule 606. Juror's Competency as a Witness

(a) At the Trial. A juror may not testify as a witness before the other jurors at the trial. If a juror is called to testify, the court must give a party an opportunity to object outside the jury's presence.

(b) During an Inquiry into the Validity of a Verdict or Indictment.

(1) *Prohibited Testimony or Other Evidence.* During an inquiry into the validity of a verdict or indictment, a juror may not testify about any statement made or incident that occurred during the jury's deliberations; the effect of anything on that juror's or another juror's vote; or any juror's mental processes concerning the verdict or indictment. The court may not receive a juror's affidavit or evidence of a juror's statement on these matters.

(2) *Exceptions.* A juror may testify about whether:

(A) extraneous prejudicial information was improperly brought to the jury's attention;

(B) an outside influence was improperly brought to bear on any juror; or

(C) a mistake was made in entering the verdict on the verdict form.

Rule 607. Who May Impeach a Witness

Any party, including the party that called the witness, may attack the witness's credibility.

Rule 608. A Witness's Character for Truthfulness or Untruthfulness

(a) Reputation or Opinion Evidence. A witness's credibility may be attacked or supported by testimony about the witness's reputation for having a character for truthfulness or untruthfulness, or by testimony in the form of an opinion about that character. But evidence of truthful character is admissible only after the witness's character for truthfulness has been attacked.

(b) Specific Instances of Conduct. Except for a criminal conviction under Rule 609, extrinsic evidence is not admissible to prove specific instances of a witness's conduct in order to attack or support the witness's character for truthfulness. But the court may, on cross-examination, allow them to be inquired into if they are probative of the character for truthfulness or untruthfulness of:

(1) the witness; or

(2) another witness whose character the witness being cross-examined has testified about.

By testifying on another matter, a witness does not waive any privilege against self-incrimination for testimony that relates only to the witness's character for truthfulness.

Rule 609. Impeachment by Evidence of a Criminal Conviction

(a) In General. The following rules apply to attacking a witness's character for truthfulness by evidence of a criminal conviction:

(1) for a crime that, in the convicting jurisdiction, was punishable by death or by imprisonment for more than one year, the evidence:

(A) must be admitted, subject to Rule 403, in a civil case or in a criminal case in which the witness is not a defendant; and

(B) must be admitted in a criminal case in which the witness is a defendant, if the probative value of the evidence outweighs its prejudicial effect to that defendant; and

(2) for any crime regardless of the punishment, the evidence must be admitted if the court can readily determine that establishing the elements of the crime required proving — or the witness's admitting — a dishonest act or false statement.

(b) Limit on Using the Evidence After 10 Years. This subdivision (b) applies if more than 10 years have passed since the witness's conviction or release from confinement for it, whichever is later. Evidence of the conviction is admissible only if:

(1) its probative value, supported by specific facts and circumstances, substantially outweighs its prejudicial effect; and

(2) the proponent gives an adverse party reasonable written notice of the intent to use it so that the party has a fair opportunity to contest its use.

(c) Effect of a Pardon, Annulment, or Certificate of Rehabilitation. Evidence of a conviction is not admissible if:

(1) the conviction has been the subject of a pardon, annulment, certificate of rehabilitation, or other equivalent procedure based on a finding that the person

has been rehabilitated, and the person has not been convicted of a later crime punishable by death or by imprisonment for more than one year; or

(2) the conviction has been the subject of a pardon, annulment, or other equivalent procedure based on a finding of innocence.

(d) Juvenile Adjudications. Evidence of a juvenile adjudication is admissible under this rule only if:

(1) it is offered in a criminal case;

(2) the adjudication was of a witness other than the defendant;

(3) an adult's conviction for that offense would be admissible to attack the adult's credibility; and

(4) admitting the evidence is necessary to fairly determine guilt or innocence.

(e) Pendency of an Appeal. A conviction that satisfies this rule is admissible even if an appeal is pending. Evidence of the pendency is also admissible.

Rule 610. Religious Beliefs or Opinions

Evidence of a witness's religious beliefs or opinions is not admissible to attack or support the witness's credibility.

Rule 611. Mode and Order of Examining Witnesses and Presenting Evidence

(a) Control by the Court; Purposes. The court should exercise reasonable control over the mode and order of examining witnesses and presenting evidence so as to:

(1) make those procedures effective for determining the truth;

(2) avoid wasting time; and

(3) protect witnesses from harassment or undue embarrassment.

(b) Scope of Cross-Examination. Cross-examination should not go beyond the subject matter of the direct examination and matters affecting the witness's credibility. The court may allow inquiry into additional matters as if on direct examination.

(c) Leading Questions. Leading questions should not be used on direct examination except as necessary to develop the witness's testimony. Ordinarily, the court should allow leading questions:

(1) on cross-examination; and

(2) when a party calls a hostile witness, an adverse party, or a witness identified with an adverse party.

Rule 612. Writing Used to Refresh a Witness's Memory

(a) Scope. This rule gives an adverse party certain options when a witness uses a writing to refresh memory:

(1) while testifying; or

(2) before testifying, if the court decides that justice requires the party to have those options.

(b) Adverse Party's Options; Deleting Unrelated Matter. Unless 18 U.S.C. § 3500 provides otherwise in a criminal case, an adverse party is entitled to have the writing produced at the hearing, to inspect it, to cross-examine the witness about it, and to introduce in evidence any portion that relates to the witness's testimony. If the producing party claims that the writing includes unrelated matter, the court must examine the writing in camera, delete any unrelated portion, and order that the rest be delivered to the adverse party. Any portion deleted over objection must be preserved for the record.

(c) Failure to Produce or Deliver the Writing. If a writing is not produced or is not delivered as ordered, the court may issue any appropriate order. But if the prosecution does not comply in a criminal case, the court must strike the witness's testimony or — if justice so requires — declare a mistrial.

Rule 613. Witness's Prior Statement

(a) Showing or Disclosing the Statement During Examination. When examining a witness about the witness's prior statement, a party need not show it or disclose its contents to the witness. But the party must, on request, show it or disclose its contents to an adverse party's attorney.

(b) Extrinsic Evidence of a Prior Inconsistent Statement. Extrinsic evidence of a witness's prior inconsistent statement is admissible only if the witness is given an opportunity to explain or deny the statement and an adverse party is given an opportunity to examine the witness about it, or if justice so requires. This subdivision (b) does not apply to an opposing party's statement under Rule 801(d)(2).

Rule 614. Court's Calling or Examining a Witness

(a) Calling. The court may call a witness on its own or at a party's request. Each party is entitled to cross-examine the witness.

(b) Examining. The court may examine a witness regardless of who calls the witness.

(c) Objections. A party may object to the court's calling or examining a witness either at that time or at the next opportunity when the jury is not present.

Rule 615. Excluding Witnesses

At a party's request, the court must order witnesses excluded so that they cannot hear other witnesses' testimony. Or the court may do so on its own. But this rule does not authorize excluding:

    (a) a party who is a natural person;

    (b) an officer or employee of a party that is not a natural person, after being designated as the party's representative by its attorney;

    (c) a person whose presence a party shows to be essential to presenting the party's claim or defense; or

    (d) a person authorized by statute to be present.

ARTICLE VII. OPINIONS AND EXPERT TESTIMONY

Rule 701. Opinion Testimony by Lay Witnesses

If a witness is not testifying as an expert, testimony in the form of an opinion is limited to one that is:

(a) rationally based on the witness's perception;

(b) helpful to clearly understanding the witness's testimony or to determining a fact in issue; and

(c) not based on scientific, technical, or other specialized knowledge within the scope of Rule 702.

Rule 702. Testimony by Expert Witnesses

A witness who is qualified as an expert by knowledge, skill, experience, training, or education may testify in the form of an opinion or otherwise if:

(a) the expert's scientific, technical, or other specialized knowledge will help the trier of fact to understand the evidence or to determine a fact in issue;

(b) the testimony is based on sufficient facts or data;

(c) the testimony is the product of reliable principles and methods; and

(d) the expert has reliably applied the principles and methods to the facts of the case.

Rule 703. Bases of an Expert's Opinion Testimony

An expert may base an opinion on facts or data in the case that the expert has been made aware of or personally observed. If experts in the particular field would reasonably rely on those kinds of facts or data in forming an opinion on the subject, they need not be admissible for the opinion to be admitted. But if the facts or data would otherwise be inadmissible, the proponent of the opinion may disclose them to the jury only if their probative value in helping the jury evaluate the opinion substantially outweighs their prejudicial effect.

Rule 704. Opinion on an Ultimate Issue

(a) **In General — Not Automatically Objectionable.** An opinion is not objectionable just because it embraces an ultimate issue.

(b) **Exception.** In a criminal case, an expert witness must not state an opinion about whether the defendant did or did not have a mental state or condition that constitutes an element of the crime charged or of a defense. Those matters are for the trier of fact alone.

Rule 705. Disclosing the Facts or Data Underlying an Expert's Opinion

Unless the court orders otherwise, an expert may state an opinion—and give the reasons for it—without first testifying to the underlying facts or data. But the expert may be required to disclose those facts or data on cross-examination.

Rule 706. Court-Appointed Expert Witnesses

(a) Appointment Process. On a party's motion or on its own, the court may order the parties to show cause why expert witnesses should not be appointed and may ask the parties to submit nominations. The court may appoint any expert that the parties agree on and any of its own choosing. But the court may only appoint someone who consents to act.

(b) Expert's Role. The court must inform the expert of the expert's duties. The court may do so in writing and have a copy filed with the clerk or may do so orally at a conference in which the parties have an opportunity to participate. The expert:

> **(1)** must advise the parties of any findings the expert makes;

> **(2)** may be deposed by any party;

> **(3)** may be called to testify by the court or any party; and

> **(4)** may be cross-examined by any party, including the party that called the expert.

(c) Compensation. The expert is entitled to a reasonable compensation, as set by the court. The compensation is payable as follows:

> **(1)** in a criminal case or in a civil case involving just compensation under the Fifth Amendment, from any funds that are provided by law; and

> **(2)** in any other civil case, by the parties in the proportion and at the time that the court directs — and the compensation is then charged like other costs.

(d) Disclosing the Appointment to the Jury. The court may authorize disclosure to the jury that the court appointed the expert.

(e) Parties' Choice of Their Own Experts. This rule does not limit a party in calling its own experts.

ARTICLE VIII. HEARSAY

Rule 801. Definitions That Apply to This Article; Exclusions from Hearsay

(a) Statement. "Statement" means a person's oral assertion, written assertion, or nonverbal conduct, if the person intended it as an assertion.

(b) Declarant. "Declarant" means the person who made the statement.

(c) Hearsay. "Hearsay" means a statement that:

> **(1)** the declarant does not make while testifying at the current trial or hearing; and

> **(2)** a party offers in evidence to prove the truth of the matter asserted in the statement.

(d) Statements That Are Not Hearsay. A statement that meets the following conditions is not hearsay:

(1) *A Declarant-Witness's Prior Statement.* The declarant testifies and is subject to cross-examination about a prior statement, and the statement:

(A) is inconsistent with the declarant's testimony and was given under penalty of perjury at a trial, hearing, or other proceeding or in a deposition;

(B) is consistent with the declarant's testimony and is offered to rebut an express or implied charge that the declarant recently fabricated it or acted from a recent improper influence or motive in so testifying; or

(C) identifies a person as someone the declarant perceived earlier.

(2) *An Opposing Party's Statement.*

The statement is offered against an opposing party and:

(A) was made by the party in an individual or representative capacity;

(B) is one the party manifested that it adopted or believed to be true;

(C) was made by a person whom the party authorized to make a statement on the subject;

(D) was made by the party's agent or employee on a matter within the scope of that relationship and while it existed; or

(E) was made by the party's coconspirator during and in furtherance of the conspiracy.

The statement must be considered but does not by itself establish the declarant's authority under (C); the existence or scope of the relationship under (D); or the existence of the conspiracy or participation in it under (E).

Rule 802. The Rule Against Hearsay

Hearsay is not admissible unless any of the following provides otherwise:

- a federal statute;
- these rules; or
- other rules prescribed by the Supreme Court.

Rule 803. Exceptions to the Rule Against Hearsay — Regardless of Whether the Declarant Is Available as a Witness

The following are not excluded by the rule against hearsay, regardless of whether the declarant is available as a witness:

(1) *Present Sense Impression.* A statement describing or explaining an event or condition, made while or immediately after the declarant perceived it.

(2) *Excited Utterance.* A statement relating to a startling event or condition, made while the declarant was under the stress of excitement that it caused.

(3) *Then-Existing Mental, Emotional, or Physical Condition.* A statement of the declarant's then-existing state of mind (such as motive, intent, or plan) or emotional, sensory, or physical condition (such as mental feeling, pain, or bodily health),

but not including a statement of memory or belief to prove the fact remembered or believed unless it relates to the validity or terms of the declarant's will.

(4) *Statement Made for Medical Diagnosis or Treatment.* A statement that:

(A) is made for — and is reasonably pertinent to — medical diagnosis or treatment; and

(B) describes medical history; past or present symptoms or sensations; their inception; or their general cause.

(5) *Recorded Recollection.* A record that:

(A) is on a matter the witness once knew about but now cannot recall well enough to testify fully and accurately;

(B) was made or adopted by the witness when the matter was fresh in the witness's memory; and

(C) accurately reflects the witness's knowledge.

If admitted, the record may be read into evidence but may be received as an exhibit only if offered by an adverse party.

(6) *Records of a Regularly Conducted Activity.* A record of an act, event, condition, opinion, or diagnosis if:

(A) the record was made at or near the time by — or from information transmitted by — someone with knowledge;

(B) the record was kept in the course of a regularly conducted activity of a business, organization, occupation, or calling, whether or not for profit;

(C) making the record was a regular practice of that activity;

(D) all these conditions are shown by the testimony of the custodian or another qualified witness, or by a certification that complies with Rule 902 (11) or (12) or with a statute permitting certification; and

(E) the opponent does not show that the possible source of the information or other circumstances indicate a lack of trustworthiness.

(7) *Absence of a Record of a Regularly Conducted Activity.* Evidence that a matter is not included in a record described in paragraph (6) if:

(A) the evidence is admitted to prove that the matter did not occur or exist;

(B) a record was regularly kept for a matter of that kind; and

(C) the opponent does not show that the possible source of the information or other circumstances indicate a lack of trustworthiness.

(8) *Public Records.* A record or statement of a public office if:

(A) it sets out:

(i) the office's activities;

(ii) a matter observed while under a legal duty to report, but not including, in a criminal case, a matter observed by law-enforcement personnel; or

(iii) in a civil case or against the government in a criminal case, factual findings from a legally authorized investigation; and

(B) the opponent does not show that the source of information or other circumstances indicate a lack of trustworthiness.

(9) *Public Records of Vital Statistics.* A record of a birth, death, or marriage, if reported to a public office in accordance with a legal duty.

(10) *Absence of a Public Record.* Testimony — or a certification under Rule 902 — that a diligent search failed to disclose a public record or statement if:

(A) the testimony or certification is admitted to prove that

(i) the record or statement does not exist; or

(ii) a matter did not occur or exist, if a public office regularly kept a record or statement for a matter of that kind; and

(B) in a criminal case, a prosecutor who intends to offer a certification provides written notice of that intent at least 14 days before trial, and the defendant does not object in writing within 7 days of receiving the notice — unless the court sets a different time for the notice or the objection.

(11) *Records of Religious Organizations Concerning Personal or Family History.* A statement of birth, legitimacy, ancestry, marriage, divorce, death, relationship by blood or marriage, or similar facts of personal or family history, contained in a regularly kept record of a religious organization.

(12) *Certificates of Marriage, Baptism, and Similar Ceremonies.* A statement of fact contained in a certificate:

(A) made by a person who is authorized by a religious organization or by law to perform the act certified;

(B) attesting that the person performed a marriage or similar ceremony or administered a sacrament; and

(C) purporting to have been issued at the time of the act or within a reasonable time after it.

(13) *Family Records.* A statement of fact about personal or family history contained in a family record, such as a Bible, genealogy, chart, engraving on a ring, inscription on a portrait, or engraving on an urn or burial marker.

(14) *Records of Documents That Affect an Interest in Property.* The record of a document that purports to establish or affect an interest in property if:

(A) the record is admitted to prove the content of the original recorded document, along with its signing and its delivery by each person who purports to have signed it;

(B) the record is kept in a public office; and

(C) a statute authorizes recording documents of that kind in that office.

(15) *Statements in Documents That Affect an Interest in Property.* A statement contained in a document that purports to establish or affect an interest in property if the matter stated was relevant to the document's purpose — unless later dealings with the property are inconsistent with the truth of the statement or the purport of the document.

(16) *Statements in Ancient Documents.* A statement in a document that was prepared before January 1, 1998 and whose authenticity is established.

(17) *Market Reports and Similar Commercial Publications.* Market quotations, lists, directories, or other compilations that are generally relied on by the public or by persons in particular occupations.

(18) *Statements in Learned Treatises, Periodicals, or Pamphlets.* A statement contained in a treatise, periodical, or pamphlet if:

   (A) the statement is called to the attention of an expert witness on cross-examination or relied on by the expert on direct examination; and

   (B) the publication is established as a reliable authority by the expert's admission or testimony, by another expert's testimony, or by judicial notice.

If admitted, the statement may be read into evidence but not received as an exhibit.

(19) *Reputation Concerning Personal or Family History.* A reputation among a person's family by blood, adoption, or marriage — or among a person's associates or in the community — concerning the person's birth, adoption, legitimacy, ancestry, marriage, divorce, death, relationship by blood, adoption, or marriage, or similar facts of personal or family history.

(20) *Reputation Concerning Boundaries or General History.* A reputation in a community — arising before the controversy — concerning boundaries of land in the community or customs that affect the land, or concerning general historical events important to that community, state, or nation.

(21) *Reputation Concerning Character.* A reputation among a person's associates or in the community concerning the person's character.

(22) *Judgment of a Previous Conviction.* Evidence of a final judgment of conviction if:

   (A) the judgment was entered after a trial or guilty plea, but not a nolo contendere plea;

   (B) the conviction was for a crime punishable by death or by imprisonment for more than a year;

   (C) the evidence is admitted to prove any fact essential to the judgment; and

   (D) when offered by the prosecutor in a criminal case for a purpose other than impeachment, the judgment was against the defendant.

The pendency of an appeal may be shown but does not affect admissibility.

(23) *Judgments Involving Personal, Family, or General History, or a Boundary.* A judgment that is admitted to prove a matter of personal, family, or general history, or boundaries, if the matter:

> **(A)** was essential to the judgment; and

> **(B)** could be proved by evidence of reputation.

(24) [*Other Exceptions.*] [Transferred to Rule 807.]

Rule 804. Exceptions to the Rule Against Hearsay — When the Declarant Is Unavailable as a Witness

(a) Criteria for Being Unavailable. A declarant is considered to be unavailable as a witness if the declarant:

(1) is exempted from testifying about the subject matter of the declarant's statement because the court rules that a privilege applies;

(2) refuses to testify about the subject matter despite a court order to do so;

(3) testifies to not remembering the subject matter;

(4) cannot be present or testify at the trial or hearing because of death or a then-existing infirmity, physical illness, or mental illness; or

(5) is absent from the trial or hearing and the statement's proponent has not been able, by process or other reasonable means, to procure:

> **(A)** the declarant's attendance, in the case of a hearsay exception under Rule 804(b)(1) or (6); or

> **(B)** the declarant's attendance or testimony, in the case of a hearsay exception under Rule 804(b)(2), (3), or (4).

But this subdivision (a) does not apply if the statement's proponent procured or wrongfully caused the declarant's unavailability as a witness in order to prevent the declarant from attending or testifying.

(b) The Exceptions. The following are not excluded by the rule against hearsay if the declarant is unavailable as a witness:

(1) *Former Testimony.* Testimony that:

> **(A)** was given as a witness at a trial, hearing, or lawful deposition, whether given during the current proceeding or a different one; and

> **(B)** is now offered against a party who had — or, in a civil case, whose predecessor in interest had — an opportunity and similar motive to develop it by direct, cross-, or redirect examination.

(2) *Statement Under the Belief of Imminent Death.* In a prosecution for homicide or in a civil case, a statement that the declarant, while believing the declarant's death to be imminent, made about its cause or circumstances.

(3) *Statement Against Interest.* A statement that:

(A) a reasonable person in the declarant's position would have made only if the person believed it to be true because, when made, it was so contrary to the declarant's proprietary or pecuniary interest or had so great a tendency to invalidate the declarant's claim against someone else or to expose the declarant to civil or criminal liability; and

(B) is supported by corroborating circumstances that clearly indicate its trustworthiness, if it is offered in a criminal case as one that tends to expose the declarant to criminal liability.

(4) *Statement of Personal or Family History.* A statement about:

(A) the declarant's own birth, adoption, legitimacy, ancestry, marriage, divorce, relationship by blood, adoption, or marriage, or similar facts of personal or family history, even though the declarant had no way of acquiring personal knowledge about that fact; or

(B) another person concerning any of these facts, as well as death, if the declarant was related to the person by blood, adoption, or marriage or was so intimately associated with the person's family that the declarant's information is likely to be accurate.

(5) [*Other Exceptions.*] [Transferred to Rule 807.]

(6) *Statement Offered Against a Party That Wrongfully Caused the Declarant's Unavailability.* A statement offered against a party that wrongfully caused — or acquiesced in wrongfully causing — the declarant's unavailability as a witness, and did so intending that result.

Rule 805. Hearsay Within Hearsay

Hearsay within hearsay is not excluded by the rule against hearsay if each part of the combined statements conforms with an exception to the rule.

Rule 806. Attacking and Supporting the Declarant's Credibility

When a hearsay statement — or a statement described in Rule 801(d)(2)(C), (D), or (E) — has been admitted in evidence, the declarant's credibility may be attacked, and then supported, by any evidence that would be admissible for those purposes if the declarant had testified as a witness. The court may admit evidence of the declarant's inconsistent statement or conduct, regardless of when it occurred or whether the declarant had an opportunity to explain or deny it. If the party against whom the statement was admitted calls the declarant as a witness, the party may examine the declarant on the statement as if on cross-examination.

Rule 807. Residual Exception

(a) In General. Under the following circumstances, a hearsay statement is not excluded by the rule against hearsay even if the statement is not specifically covered by a hearsay exception in Rule 803 or 804:

(1) the statement has equivalent circumstantial guarantees of trustworthiness;

(2) it is offered as evidence of a material fact;

(3) it is more probative on the point for which it is offered than any other evidence that the proponent can obtain through reasonable efforts; and

(4) admitting it will best serve the purposes of these rules and the interests of justice.

(b) Notice. The statement is admissible only if, before the trial or hearing, the proponent gives an adverse party reasonable notice of the intent to offer the statement and its particulars, including the declarant's name and address, so that the party has a fair opportunity to meet it.

ARTICLE IX. AUTHENTICATION AND IDENTIFICATION

Rule 901. Authenticating or Identifying Evidence

(a) In General. To satisfy the requirement of authenticating or identifying an item of evidence, the proponent must produce evidence sufficient to support a finding that the item is what the proponent claims it is.

(b) Examples. The following are examples only — not a complete list — of evidence that satisfies the requirement:

(1) *Testimony of a Witness with Knowledge.* Testimony that an item is what it is claimed to be.

(2) *Nonexpert Opinion About Handwriting.* A nonexpert's opinion that handwriting is genuine, based on a familiarity with it that was not acquired for the current litigation.

(3) *Comparison by an Expert Witness or the Trier of Fact.* A comparison with an authenticated specimen by an expert witness or the trier of fact.

(4) *Distinctive Characteristics and the Like.* The appearance, contents, substance, internal patterns, or other distinctive characteristics of the item, taken together with all the circumstances.

(5) *Opinion About a Voice.* An opinion identifying a person's voice — whether heard firsthand or through mechanical or electronic transmission or recording — based on hearing the voice at any time under circumstances that connect it with the alleged speaker.

(6) *Evidence About a Telephone Conversation.* For a telephone conversation, evidence that a call was made to the number assigned at the time to:

(A) a particular person, if circumstances, including self-identification, show that the person answering was the one called; or

(B) a particular business, if the call was made to a business and the call related to business reasonably transacted over the telephone.

(7) *Evidence About Public Records.* Evidence that:

>   (A) a document was recorded or filed in a public office as authorized by law; or

>   (B) a purported public record or statement is from the office where items of this kind are kept.

(8) *Evidence About Ancient Documents or Data Compilations.* For a document or data compilation, evidence that it:

>   (A) is in a condition that creates no suspicion about its authenticity;

>   (B) was in a place where, if authentic, it would likely be; and

>   (C) is at least 20 years old when offered.

(9) *Evidence About a Process or System.* Evidence describing a process or system and showing that it produces an accurate result.

(10) *Methods Provided by a Statute or Rule.* Any method of authentication or identification allowed by a federal statute or a rule prescribed by the Supreme Court.

Rule 902. Evidence That Is Self-Authenticating

The following items of evidence are self-authenticating; they require no extrinsic evidence of authenticity in order to be admitted:

(1) *Domestic Public Documents That Are Sealed and Signed.* A document that bears:

>   (A) a seal purporting to be that of the United States; any state, district, commonwealth, territory, or insular possession of the United States; the former Panama Canal Zone; the Trust Territory of the Pacific Islands; a political subdivision of any of these entities; or a department, agency, or officer of any entity named above; and

>   (B) a signature purporting to be an execution or attestation.

(2) *Domestic Public Documents That Are Not Sealed but Are Signed and Certified.* A document that bears no seal if:

>   (A) it bears the signature of an officer or employee of an entity named in Rule 902(1)(A); and

>   (B) another public officer who has a seal and official duties within that same entity certifies under seal — or its equivalent — that the signer has the official capacity and that the signature is genuine.

(3) *Foreign Public Documents.* A document that purports to be signed or attested by a person who is authorized by a foreign country's law to do so. The document must be accompanied by a final certification that certifies the genuineness of the signature and official position of the signer or attester — or of any foreign official whose certificate of genuineness relates to the signature or attestation or is in a chain of certificates of genuineness relating to the signature or attestation. The certification may be made by a secretary of a United States embassy or legation; by a consul general, vice

consul, or consular agent of the United States; or by a diplomatic or consular official of the foreign country assigned or accredited to the United States. If all parties have been given a reasonable opportunity to investigate the document's authenticity and accuracy, the court may, for good cause, either:

(A) order that it be treated as presumptively authentic without final certification; or

(B) allow it to be evidenced by an attested summary with or without final certification.

(4) *Certified Copies of Public Records.*

A copy of an official record — or a copy of a document that was recorded or filed in a public office as authorized by law — if the copy is certified as correct by:

(A) the custodian or another person authorized to make the certification; or

(B) a certificate that complies with Rule 902(1), (2), or (3), a federal statute, or a rule prescribed by the Supreme Court.

(5) *Official Publications.* A book, pamphlet, or other publication purporting to be issued by a public authority.

(6) *Newspapers and Periodicals.* Printed material purporting to be a newspaper or periodical.

(7) *Trade Inscriptions and the Like.* An inscription, sign, tag, or label purporting to have been affixed in the course of business and indicating origin, ownership, or control.

(8) *Acknowledged Documents.* A document accompanied by a certificate of acknowledgment that is lawfully executed by a notary public or another officer who is authorized to take acknowledgments.

(9) *Commercial Paper and Related Documents.* Commercial paper, a signature on it, and related documents, to the extent allowed by general commercial law.

(10) *Presumptions Under a Federal Statute.* A signature, document, or anything else that a federal statute declares to be presumptively or prima facie genuine or authentic.

(11) *Certified Domestic Records of a Regularly Conducted Activity.* The original or a copy of a domestic record that meets the requirements of Rule 803(6)(A)-(C), as shown by a certification of the custodian or another qualified person that complies with a federal statute or a rule prescribed by the Supreme Court. Before the trial or hearing, the proponent must give an adverse party reasonable written notice of the intent to offer the record — and must make the record and certification available for inspection — so that the party has a fair opportunity to challenge them.

(12) *Certified Foreign Records of a Regularly Conducted Activity.* In a civil case, the original or a copy of a foreign record that meets the requirements of Rule 902(11), modified as follows: the certification, rather than complying with a federal statute or Supreme Court rule, must be signed in a manner that, if falsely made, would subject the maker to a criminal penalty in the country where the certification is signed. The proponent must also meet the notice requirements of Rule 902(11).

(13) Certified Records Generated by an Electronic Process or System. A record generated by an electronic process or system that produces an accurate result, as shown by a certification of a qualified person that complies with the certification requirements of Rule 902(11) or (12). The proponent must also meet the notice requirements of Rule 902(11).

(14) Certified Data Copied from an Electronic Device, Storage Medium, or File. Data copied from an electronic device, storage medium, or file, if authenticated by a process of digital identification, as shown by a certification of a qualified person that complies with the certification requirements of Rule 902(11) or (12). The proponent also must meet the notice requirements of Rule 902(11).

Rule 903. Subscribing Witness's Testimony

A subscribing witness's testimony is necessary to authenticate a writing only if required by the law of the jurisdiction that governs its validity.

ARTICLE X. CONTENTS OF WRITINGS, RECORDINGS, AND PHOTOGRAPHS

Rule 1001. Definitions That Apply to This Article

In this article:

(a) A "writing" consists of letters, words, numbers, or their equivalent set down in any form.

(b) A "recording" consists of letters, words, numbers, or their equivalent recorded in any manner.

(c) A "photograph" means a photographic image or its equivalent stored in any form.

(d) An "original" of a writing or recording means the writing or recording itself or any counterpart intended to have the same effect by the person who executed or issued it. For electronically stored information, "original" means any printout—or other output readable by sight—if it accurately reflects the information. An "original" of a photograph includes the negative or a print from it.

(e) A "duplicate" means a counterpart produced by a mechanical, photographic, chemical, electronic, or other equivalent process or technique that accurately reproduces the original.

Rule 1002. Requirement of the Original

An original writing, recording, or photograph is required in order to prove its content unless these rules or a federal statute provides otherwise.

Rule 1003. Admissibility of Duplicates

A duplicate is admissible to the same extent as the original unless a genuine question is raised about the original's authenticity or the circumstances make it unfair to admit the duplicate.

Rule 1004. Admissibility of Other Evidence of Content

An original is not required and other evidence of the content of a writing, recording, or photograph is admissible if:

(a) all the originals are lost or destroyed, and not by the proponent acting in bad faith;

(b) an original cannot be obtained by any available judicial process;

(c) the party against whom the original would be offered had control of the original; was at that time put on notice, by pleadings or otherwise, that the original would be a subject of proof at the trial or hearing; and fails to produce it at the trial or hearing; or

(d) the writing, recording, or photograph is not closely related to a controlling issue.

Rule 1005. Copies of Public Records to Prove Content

The proponent may use a copy to prove the content of an official record — or of a document that was recorded or filed in a public office as authorized by law — if these conditions are met: the record or document is otherwise admissible; and the copy is certified as correct in accordance with Rule 902(4) or is testified to be correct by a witness who has compared it with the original. If no such copy can be obtained by reasonable diligence, then the proponent may use other evidence to prove the content.

Rule 1006. Summaries to Prove Content

The proponent may use a summary, chart, or calculation to prove the content of voluminous writings, recordings, or photographs that cannot be conveniently examined in court. The proponent must make the originals or duplicates available for examination or copying, or both, by other parties at a reasonable time and place. And the court may order the proponent to produce them in court.

Rule 1007. Testimony or Statement of a Party to Prove Content

The proponent may prove the content of a writing, recording, or photograph by the testimony, deposition, or written statement of the party against whom the evidence is offered. The proponent need not account for the original.

Rule 1008. Functions of the Court and Jury

Ordinarily, the court determines whether the proponent has fulfilled the factual conditions for admitting other evidence of the content of a writing, recording, or photograph under Rule 1004 or 1005. But in a jury trial, the jury determines — in accordance with Rule 104(b) — any issue about whether:

> (a) an asserted writing, recording, or photograph ever existed;
>
> (b) another one produced at the trial or hearing is the original; or
>
> (c) other evidence of content accurately reflects the content.

ARTICLE XI. MISCELLANEOUS RULES

Rule 1101. Applicability of the Rules

(a) To Courts and Judges.

These rules apply to proceedings before:

- United States district courts;
- United States bankruptcy and magistrate judges;
- United States courts of appeals;
- the United States Court of Federal Court Claims; and
- the District courts of Guam, the Virgin Islands, and the Northern Mariana Islands.

(b) To Cases and Proceedings. These rules apply in:

- civil cases and proceedings, including bankruptcy, admiralty and maritime cases;
- criminal cases and proceedings; and
- contempt proceedings, except those in which the court may act summarily.

(c) Rules on Privilege. The rules on privilege apply to all stages of a case or proceeding.

(d) Exceptions. These rules — except for those on privilege — do not apply to the following:

(1) The court's determination, under Rule 104(a), on a preliminary question of a fact governing admissibility;

(2) grand-jury proceedings; and

(3) miscellaneous proceedings such as:

- extradition or rendition;
- issuing an arrest warrant, criminal summons, or search warrant;
- a preliminary examination in a criminal case;
- sentencing;
- granting or revoking probation or supervised release; and
- considering whether to release on bail or otherwise.

(e) Other Statutes and Rules. A federal statute or a rule prescribed by the Supreme Court may provide for admitting or excluding evidence independently from these rules.

Rule 1102. Amendments

These rules may be amended as provided in 28 U.S.C. § 2072.

Rule 1103. Title

These rules may be cited as the Federal Rules of Evidence.

Appendix 2

Federal Rules of Evidence — Proposed Amendments

Proposed Amendments — Effective Date December 1, 2023

Rule 106. Remainder of or Related Writings or Recorded Statements

If a party introduces all or part of a statement, an adverse party may require the introduction, at that time, of any other part — or any other statement — that in fairness ought to be considered at the same time. The adverse party may do so over a hearsay objection.

(Amended, eff 10-1-87; 12-1-11; 12-1-23)

Rule 615. Excluding Witnesses from the Courtroom; Preventing an Excluded Witness's Access to Trial Testimony

(a) Excluding Witnesses. At a party's request, the court must order witnesses excluded from the courtroom so that they cannot hear other witnesses' testimony. Or the court may do so on its own. But this rule does not authorize excluding:

(1) a party who is a natural person;

(2) one officer or employee of a party that is not a natural person if that officer or employee has been designated as the party's representative by its attorney;

(3) any person whose presence a party shows to be essential to presenting the party's claim or defense; or

(4) a person authorized by statute to be present.

(b) Additional Orders to Prevent Disclosing and Accessing Testimony. An order under (a) operates only to exclude witnesses from the courtroom. But the court may also, by order:

(1) prohibit disclosure of trial testimony to witnesses who are excluded from the courtroom; and

(2) prohibit excluded witnesses from accessing trial testimony.

(Amended, eff 10-1-87; 11-1-88; 11-18-88; 12-1-98; 12-1-11; 12-1-23)

Rule 702. Testimony by Expert Witnesses

A witness who is qualified as an expert by knowledge, skill, experience, training, or education may testify in the form of an opinion or otherwise if the proponent demonstrates to the court that it is more likely than not that:

(a) the expert's scientific, technical, or other specialized knowledge will help the trier of fact to understand the evidence or to determine a fact in issue;

(b) the testimony is based on sufficient facts or data;

(c) the testimony is the product of reliable principles and methods; and

(d) the expert's opinion reflects a reliable application of the principles and methods to the facts of the case.

(Amended, eff 12-1-00; 12-1-11; 12-1-23)

Proposed Amendments — Effective Date December 1, 2024

Rule 611. Mode and Order of Examining Witnesses and Presenting Evidence

Proposed amendment; new subsection (d):

(d) Illustrative Aids.

(1) **Permitted Uses.** The court may allow a party to present an illustrative aid to help the finder of fact understand admitted evidence if:

(A) its utility in assisting comprehension is not [substantially] outweighed by the danger of unfair prejudice, confusing the issues, misleading the jury, undue delay, or wasting time; and

(B) all parties are given notice and a reasonable opportunity to object to its use, unless the court, for good cause, orders otherwise.

(2) **Use in Jury Deliberations.** An illustrative aid must not be provided to the jury during deliberations unless:

(A) all parties consent; or

(B) the court, for good cause, orders otherwise.

(3) **Record.** When practicable, an illustrative aid that is used at trial must be entered into the record.

Rule 612. Writing Used to Refresh a Witness's Memory

Proposed amended version of subsection (b):

(b) Extrinsic Evidence of a Prior Inconsistent Statement. Unless the court orders otherwise, extrinsic evidence of a witness's prior inconsistent statement may not be admitted until after the witness is given an opportunity to explain or deny the statement and an adverse party is given an opportunity to examine the witness about it. This subdivision (b) does not apply to an opposing party's statement under Rule 801(d)(2).]

Rule 801. Definitions That Apply to This Article; Exclusions from Hearsay

Proposed amended version of subsection (d)(2):

(2) **An Opposing Party's Statement.** The statement is offered against an opposing party and:

(A) was made by the party in an individual or representative capacity;

(B) is one the party manifested that it adopted or believed to be true;

(C) was made by a person whom the party authorized to make a statement on the subject;

(D) was made by the party's agent or employee on a matter within the scope of that relationship and while it existed; or

(E) was made by the party's coconspirator during and in furtherance of the conspiracy.

The statement must be considered but does not by itself establish the declarant's authority under (C); the existence or scope of the relationship under (D); or the existence of the conspiracy or participation in it under (E).

If a party's claim or potential liability is directly derived from a declarant or the declarant's principal, a statement that would be admissible against the declarant or the principal under this rule 31 is also admissible against the party.]

Rule 804. Exceptions to the Rule Against Hearsay—When the Declarant Is Unavailable as a Witness

Proposed amendment to subsection (b)(3)(B):

(B) if offered in a criminal case as one that tends to expose the declarant to criminal liability, is supported by corroborating circumstances that clearly indicate its trustworthiness — after considering the totality of circumstances under which it was made and evidence, if any, corroborating it.]

Rule 1006. Summaries to Prove Content

Proposed amended Rule 1006:

(a) **Summaries of Voluminous Materials Admissible as Evidence.** The court may admit as evidence a summary, chart, or calculation to prove the content of voluminous writings, recordings, or photographs that cannot be conveniently examined in court, whether or not they have been introduced into evidence.

(b) **Procedures.** The proponent must make the underlying originals or duplicates available for examination or copying, or both, by other parties at a reasonable time and place. And the court may order the proponent to produce them in court.

(c) **Illustrative Aids Not Covered.** A summary, chart, or calculation that functions only as an illustrative aid is governed by Rule 611(d).]

Appendix 3

California Evidence Code: Selected Excerpts

The California Evidence Code (CEC) came into effect about a decade earlier than the Federal Rules of Evidence (FRE). Many of the federal evidence rules were modeled on those enacted in California, which in turn had been based on common law rules and various uniform evidence law proposals.

This Appendix includes CEC sections that represent interesting or significant variations between the CEC and the FRE with respect to issues that law school evidence courses commonly address. Among the omissions from this selection of CEC evidence rules are the many provisions that apply to specific scenarios that are beyond the scope of most law school Evidence courses.

Section 210 (Relevance)

"Relevant evidence" means evidence, including evidence relevant to the credibility of a witness or hearsay declarant, having any tendency in reason to prove or disprove any disputed fact that is of consequence to the determination of the action.

Section 351.1 (Lie Detectors)

(a) Notwithstanding any other provision of law, the results of a polygraph examination, the opinion of a polygraph examiner, or any reference to an offer to take, failure to take, or taking of a polygraph examination, shall not be admitted into evidence in any criminal proceeding, including pretrial and post conviction motions and hearings, or in any trial or hearing of a juvenile for a criminal offense, whether heard in juvenile or adult court, unless all parties stipulate to the admission of such results.

(b) Nothing in this section is intended to exclude from evidence statements made during a polygraph examination which are otherwise admissible.

Section 403 (Preliminary Facts)

(a) The proponent of the proffered evidence has the burden of producing evidence as to the existence of the preliminary fact, and the proffered evidence is inadmissible unless the court finds that there is evidence sufficient to sustain a finding of the existence of the preliminary fact, when:

(1) The relevance of the proffered evidence depends on the existence of the preliminary fact;

(2) The preliminary fact is the personal knowledge of a witness concerning the subject matter of his testimony;

(3) The preliminary fact is the authenticity of a writing; or

(4) The proffered evidence is of a statement or other conduct of a particular person and the preliminary fact is whether that person made the statement or so conducted himself.

(b) Subject to Section 702, the court may admit conditionally the proffered evidence under this section, subject to evidence of the preliminary fact being supplied later in the course of the trial.

(c) If the court admits the proffered evidence under this section, the court:

(1) May, and on request shall, instruct the jury to determine whether the preliminary fact exists and to disregard the proffered evidence unless the jury finds that the preliminary fact does exist.

(2) Shall instruct the jury to disregard the proffered evidence if the court subsequently determines that a jury could not reasonably find that the preliminary fact exists.

Section 457 (Judicial Notice)

If a matter judicially noticed is a matter which would otherwise have been for determination by the jury, the trial court may, and upon request shall, instruct the jury to accept as a fact the matter so noticed.

Section 602 (Presumptions)

A statute providing that a fact or group of facts is prima facie evidence of another fact establishes a rebuttable presumption.

Section 603 (Presumptions Affecting the Burden of Producing Evidence)

A presumption affecting the burden of producing evidence is a presumption established to implement no public policy other than to facilitate the determination of the particular action in which the presumption is applied.

Section 604 (Presumptions Affecting the Burden of Producing Evidence)

The effect of a presumption affecting the burden of producing evidence is to require the trier of fact to assume the existence of the presumed fact unless and until evidence is introduced which would support a finding of its nonexistence, in which case the trier of fact shall determine the existence or nonexistence of the presumed fact from the evidence and without regard to the presumption. Nothing in this section shall be construed to prevent the drawing of any inference that may be appropriate.

Section 605 (Presumptions Affecting the Burden of Proof)

A presumption affecting the burden of proof is a presumption established to implement some public policy other than to facilitate the determination of the particular action in which the presumption is applied, such as the policy in favor of establishment of a parent and child relationship, the validity of marriage, the stability of titles to property, or the security of those who entrust themselves or their property to the administration of others.

Section 606 (Presumptions Affecting the Burden of Proof)

The effect of a presumption affecting the burden of proof is to impose upon the party against whom it operates the burden of proof as to the nonexistence of the presumed fact.

Section 646 (Presumption — Res Ipsa Loquitor)

(a) As used in this section, "defendant" includes any party against whom the res ipsa loquitur presumption operates.

(b) The judicial doctrine of res ipsa loquitur is a presumption affecting the burden of producing evidence.

(c) If the evidence, or facts otherwise established, would support a res ipsa loquitur presumption and the defendant has introduced evidence which would support a finding that he was not negligent or that any negligence on his part was not a proximate cause of the occurrence, the court may, and upon request shall, instruct the jury to the effect that:

> (1) If the facts which would give rise to res ipsa loquitur presumption are found or otherwise established, the jury may draw the inference from such facts that a proximate cause of the occurrence was some negligent conduct on the part of the defendant; and

> (2) The jury shall not find that a proximate cause of the occurrence was some negligent conduct on the part of the defendant unless the jury believes, after weighing all the evidence in the case and drawing such inferences therefrom as the jury believes are warranted, that it is more probable than not that the occurrence was caused by some negligent conduct on the part of the defendant.

Section 667 (Presumption of Death)

A person not heard from in five years is presumed to be dead.

Section 788 (Character *re* Credibility)

For the purpose of attacking the credibility of a witness, it may be shown by the examination of the witness or by the record of the judgment that he has been convicted of a felony unless . . . .

Section 791 (Prior Consistent Statements)

Evidence of a statement previously made by a witness that is consistent with his testimony at the hearing is inadmissible to support his credibility unless it is offered after:

> (a) Evidence of a statement made by him that is inconsistent with any part of his testimony at the hearing has been admitted for the purpose of attacking his credibility, and the statement was made before the alleged inconsistent statement; or

(b) An express or implied charge has been made that his testimony at the hearing is recently fabricated or is influenced by bias or other improper motive, and the statement was made before the bias, motive for fabrication, or other improper motive is alleged to have arisen.

Section 795 (Hypnosis)

(a) The testimony of a witness is not inadmissible in a criminal proceeding by reason of the fact that the witness has previously undergone hypnosis for the purpose of recalling events that are the subject of the witness's testimony, if all of the following conditions are met:

(1) The testimony is limited to those matters that the witness recalled and related prior to the hypnosis.

(2) The substance of the pre-hypnotic memory was preserved in a writing, audio recording, or video recording prior to the hypnosis.

(3) The hypnosis was conducted in accordance with all of the following procedures:

(A) A written record was made prior to hypnosis documenting the subject's description of the event, and information that was provided to the hypnotist concerning the subject matter of the hypnosis.

(B) The subject gave informed consent to the hypnosis.

(C) The hypnosis session, including the pre- and post-hypnosis interviews, was video recorded for subsequent review.

(D) The hypnosis was performed by a licensed physician and surgeon, psychologist, licensed clinical social worker, licensed marriage and family therapist, or licensed professional clinical counselor experienced in the use of hypnosis and independent of and not in the presence of law enforcement, the prosecution, or the defense.

(4) Prior to admission of the testimony, the court holds a hearing . . . .

(b) Nothing in this section shall be construed to limit the ability of a party to attack the credibility of a witness who has undergone hypnosis, or to limit other legal grounds to admit or exclude the testimony of that witness.

Privileges. Division 8 Chapter 4 of the California Evidence Code provides for fifteen grounds of privilege. These range from the traditional (e.g., Lawyer-Client, Clergy-Penitent, Physician-Patient) to newer privileges such as the Sexual Assault Counselor-Victim Privilege and the Human Trafficking Caseworker-Victim Privilege. The excerpts below serve as examples of the treatment of privileges.

Section 912 (Waiver of Privileges)

[In addition to establishing a general rule of waiver, this section indicates the broad scope of CEC privilege provisions.]

(a) Except as otherwise provided in this section, the right of any person to claim a privilege provided by Section 954 (lawyer-client privilege), 966 (lawyer referral service-client privilege), 980 (privilege for confidential marital communications), 994 (physician-patient privilege), 1014 (psychotherapist-patient privilege), 1033 (privilege of penitent), 1034 (privilege of clergy member), 1035.8 (sexual assault counselor-victim privilege), or 1037.5 (domestic violence counselor-victim privilege) is waived with respect to a communication protected by the privilege if any holder of the privilege, without coercion, has disclosed a significant part of the communication or has consented to disclosure made by anyone. Consent to disclosure is manifested by any statement or other conduct of the holder of the privilege indicating consent to the disclosure, including failure to claim the privilege in any proceeding in which the holder has the legal standing and opportunity to claim the privilege.

Section 950 (Attorney-Client Privilege)

As used in this article, "lawyer" means a person authorized, or reasonably believed by the client to be authorized, to practice law in any state or nation.

Section 951 (Attorney-Client Privilege)

As used in this article, "client" means a person who, directly or through an authorized representative, consults a lawyer for the purpose of retaining the lawyer or securing legal service or advice from him in his professional capacity, and includes an incompetent (a) who himself so consults the lawyer or (b) whose guardian or conservator so consults the lawyer in behalf of the incompetent.

Section 952 (Attorney-Client Privilege)

As used in this article, "confidential communication between client and lawyer" means information transmitted between a client and his or her lawyer in the course of that relationship and in confidence by a means which, so far as the client is aware, discloses the information to no third persons other than those who are present to further the interest of the client in the consultation or those to whom disclosure is reasonably necessary for the transmission of the information or the accomplishment of the purpose for which the lawyer is consulted, and includes a legal opinion formed and the advice given by the lawyer in the course of that relationship.

Section 953 (Attorney-Client Privilege)

As used in this article, "holder of the privilege" means:

(a) The client, if the client has no guardian or conservator.

(b) A guardian or conservator of the client, if the client has a guardian or conservator.

(c) The personal representative of the client if the client is dead, including a personal representative appointed pursuant to Section 12252 of the Probate Code.

(d) A successor, assign, trustee in dissolution, or any similar representative of a firm, association, organization, partnership, business trust, corporation, or public entity that is no longer in existence.

Section 954 (Attorney-Client Privilege)

Subject to Section 912 and except as otherwise provided in this article, the client, whether or not a party, has a privilege to refuse to disclose, and to prevent another from disclosing, a confidential communication between client and lawyer if the privilege is claimed by:

(a) The holder of the privilege;

(b) A person who is authorized to claim the privilege by the holder of the privilege; or

(c) The person who was the lawyer at the time of the confidential communication, but such person may not claim the privilege if there is no holder of the privilege in existence or if he is otherwise instructed by a person authorized to permit disclosure. The relationship of attorney and client shall exist between a law corporation as defined in Article 10 (commencing with Section 6160) of Chapter 4 of Division 3 of the Business and Professions Code and the persons to whom it renders professional services, as well as between such persons and members of the State Bar employed by such corporation to render services to such persons. The word "persons" as used in this subdivision includes partnerships, corporations, limited liability companies, associations and other groups and entities.

Section 955 (Attorney-Client Privilege)

The lawyer who received or made a communication subject to the privilege under this article shall claim the privilege whenever he is present when the communication is sought to be disclosed and is authorized to claim the privilege under subdivision (c) of Section 954.

Section 956 (Attorney-Client Privilege)

There is no privilege under this article if the services of the lawyer were sought or obtained to enable or aid anyone to commit or plan to commit a crime or a fraud.

Section 956.5 (Attorney-Client Privilege)

There is no privilege under this article if the lawyer reasonably believes that disclosure of any confidential communication relating to representation of a client is necessary to prevent a criminal act that the lawyer reasonably believes is likely to result in the death of or substantial bodily harm to, an individual.

Section 957 (Attorney-Client Privilege)

There is no privilege under this article as to a communication relevant to an issue between parties all of whom claim through a deceased client, regardless of whether the claims are by testate or intestate succession, non-probate transfer, or inter vivos transaction.

Section 958 (Attorney-Client Privilege)

There is no privilege under this article as to a communication relevant to an issue of breach, by the lawyer or by the client, of a duty arising out of the lawyer-client relationship.

Section 959 (Attorney-Client Privilege)

There is no privilege under this article as to a communication relevant to an issue concerning the intention or competence of a client executing an attested document of which the lawyer is an attesting witness, or concerning the execution or attestation of such a document.

Section 960 (Attorney-Client Privilege)

There is no privilege under this article as to a communication relevant to an issue concerning the intention of a client, now deceased, with respect to a deed of conveyance, will, or other writing, executed by the client, purporting to affect an interest in property.

Section 961 (Attorney-Client Privilege)

There is no privilege under this article as to a communication relevant to an issue concerning the validity of a deed of conveyance, will, or other writing, executed by a client, now deceased, purporting to affect an interest in property.

Section 962 (Attorney-Client Privilege)

Where two or more clients have retained or consulted a lawyer upon a matter of common interest, none of them, nor the successor in interest of any of them, may claim a privilege under this article as to a communication made in the course of that relationship when such communication is offered in a civil proceeding between one of such clients (or his successor in interest) and another of such clients (or his successor in interest).

Section 1103 (Character Evidence in Criminal Cases; Rape Shield Law)

(a) In a criminal action, evidence of the character or a trait of character (in the form of an opinion, evidence of reputation, or evidence of specific instances of conduct) of the victim of the crime for which the defendant is being prosecuted is not made inadmissible by Section 1101 if the evidence is:

(1) Offered by the defendant to prove conduct of the victim in conformity with the character or trait of character.

(2) Offered by the prosecution to rebut evidence adduced by the defendant under paragraph (1).

(b) In a criminal action, evidence of the defendant's character for violence or trait of character for violence (in the form of an opinion, evidence of reputation, or evidence of specific instances of conduct) is not made inadmissible by Section 1101 if the evidence is offered by the prosecution to prove conduct of the defendant in conformity with the character or trait of character and is offered after evidence that the victim had a character for violence or a trait of character tending to show violence has been adduced by the defendant under paragraph (1) of subdivision (a).

(c)(1) Notwithstanding any other provision of this code to the contrary, and except as provided in this subdivision, in any prosecution under Section 261, 262, or 264.1 of the Penal Code, or under Section 286, 288a, or 289 of the Penal Code, or for assault with intent to commit, attempt to commit, or conspiracy to commit a crime defined in any of those sections, except where the crime is alleged to have occurred in a local detention facility, as defined in Section 6031.4, or in a state prison, as defined in Section 4504, opinion evidence, reputation evidence, and evidence of specific instances of the complaining witness' sexual conduct, or any of that evidence, is not admissible by the defendant in order to prove consent by the complaining witness.

(2) Notwithstanding paragraph (3), evidence of the manner in which the victim was dressed at the time of the commission of the offense shall not be admissible when offered by either party on the issue of consent in any prosecution for an offense specified in paragraph (1), unless the evidence is determined by the court to be relevant and admissible in the interests of justice. The proponent of the evidence shall make an offer of proof outside the hearing of the jury. The court shall then make its determination and at that time, state the reasons for its ruling on the record. For the purposes of this paragraph, "manner of dress" does not include the condition of the victim's clothing before, during, or after the commission of the offense.

(3) Paragraph (1) shall not be applicable to evidence of the complaining witness' sexual conduct with the defendant.

(4) If the prosecutor introduces evidence, including testimony of a witness, or the complaining witness as a witness gives testimony, and that evidence or testimony relates to the complaining witness' sexual conduct, the defendant may cross-examine the witness who gives the testimony and offer relevant evidence limited specifically to the rebuttal of the evidence introduced by the prosecutor or given by the complaining witness.

(5) Nothing in this subdivision shall be construed to make inadmissible any evidence offered to attack the credibility of the complaining witness as provided in Section 782.

(6) As used in this section, "complaining witness" means the alleged victim of the crime charged, the prosecution of which is subject to this subdivision.

Section 1107 (Expert Witness Testimony on Intimate Partner Battering and Its Effects)

(a) In a criminal action, expert testimony is admissible by either the prosecution or the defense regarding intimate partner battering and its effects, including the nature and effect of physical, emotional, or mental abuse on the beliefs, perceptions, or behavior of victims of domestic violence, except when offered against a criminal defendant to prove the occurrence of the act or acts of abuse which form the basis of the criminal charge.

(b) The foundation shall be sufficient for admission of this expert testimony if the proponent of the evidence establishes its relevancy and the proper qualifications of the expert witness. Expert opinion testimony on intimate partner battering and its effects shall not be considered a new scientific technique whose reliability is unproven.

. . .

Section 1109 (Character of Criminal Defendant — Domestic Violence, Elder Abuse, Dependent Person Abuse, Child Abuse prosecutions)

(a) (1) Except as provided in subdivision (e) or (f), in a criminal action in which the defendant is accused of an offense involving domestic violence, evidence of the defendant's commission of other domestic violence is not made inadmissible by Section 1101if the evidence is not inadmissible pursuant to Section 352.

(a) (2) Except as provided in subdivision (e) or (f), in a criminal action in which the defendant is accused of an offense involving abuse of an elder or dependent person, evidence of the defendant's commission of other abuse of an elder or dependent person is not made inadmissible by Section 1101 if the evidence is not inadmissible pursuant to Section 352.

(a) (3) Except as provided in subdivision (e) or (f) and subject to a hearing conducted pursuant to Section 352, which shall include consideration of any corroboration and remoteness in time, in a criminal action in which the defendant is accused of an offense involving child abuse, evidence of the defendant's commission of child abuse is not made inadmissible by Section 1101 if the evidence is not inadmissible pursuant to Section 352.

Section 1150 (Impeachment of a Jury Verdict)

(a) Upon an inquiry as to the validity of a verdict, any otherwise admissible evidence may be received as to statements made, or conduct, conditions, or events occurring, either within or without the jury room, of such a character as is likely to have influenced the verdict improperly. No evidence is admissible to show the effect of such statement, conduct, condition, or event upon a juror either in influencing him to assent to or dissent from the verdict or concerning the mental processes by which it was determined.

(b) Nothing in this code affects the law relating to the competence of a juror to give evidence to impeach or support a verdict.

Section 1151 (Remedial Measures)

When, after the occurrence of an event, remedial or precautionary measures are taken, which, if taken previously, would have tended to make the event less likely to occur, evidence of such subsequent measures is inadmissible to prove negligence or culpable conduct in connection with the event.

Section 1153 (Plea Negotiations)

Evidence of a plea of guilty, later withdrawn, or of an offer to plead guilty to the crime charged or to any other crime, made by the defendant in a criminal action is inadmissible in any action or in any proceeding of any nature, including proceedings before agencies, commissions, boards, and tribunals.

Section 1160 (Benevolent Gestures)

(a) The portion of statements, writings, or benevolent gestures expressing sympathy or a general sense of benevolence relating to the pain, suffering, or death of a person involved in an accident and made to that person or to the family of that person shall be inadmissible as evidence of an admission of liability in a civil action. <u>A statement of fault, however, which is part of, or in addition to, any of the above shall not be inadmissible pursuant to this section.</u>

(b) For purposes of this section:

(1) "Accident" means an occurrence resulting in injury or death to one or more persons which is not the result of willful action by a party.

(2) "Benevolent gestures" means actions which convey a sense of compassion or commiseration emanating from humane impulses.

(3) "Family" means the spouse, parent, grandparent, stepmother, stepfather, child, grandchild, brother, sister, half brother, half sister, adopted children of parent, or spouse's parents of an injured party.

Section 1222 (Authorized Admissions, Foundational Burden)

Evidence of a statement offered against a party is not made inadmissible by the hearsay rule if:

(a) The statement was made by a person authorized by the party to make a statement or statements for him concerning the subject matter of the statement; and

(b) The evidence is offered either after admission of evidence sufficient to sustain a finding of such authority or, in the court's discretion as to the order of proof, subject to the admission of such evidence.

Section 1223 (Co-Conspirator Statements, Foundational Burden)

Evidence of a statement offered against a party is not made inadmissible by the hearsay rule if:

(a) The statement was made by the declarant while participating in a conspiracy to commit a crime or civil wrong and in furtherance of the objective of that conspiracy;

(b) The statement was made prior to or during the time that the party was participating in that conspiracy; and

(c) The evidence is offered either after admission of evidence sufficient to sustain a finding of the facts specified in subdivisions (a) and (b) or, in the court's discretion as to the order of proof, subject to the admission of such evidence.

Section 1235 (Hearsay — Prior Inconsistent Statements)

Evidence of a statement made by a witness is not made inadmissible by the hearsay rule if the statement is inconsistent with his testimony at the hearing and is offered in compliance with Section 770.

Section 1237 (Hearsay — Recollection Recorded)

(a) Evidence of a statement previously made by a witness is not made inadmissible by the hearsay rule if the statement would have been admissible if made by him while testifying, the statement concerns a matter as to which the witness has insufficient present recollection to enable him to testify fully and accurately, and the statement is contained in a writing which:

(1) Was made at a time when the fact recorded in the writing actually occurred or was fresh in the witness' memory;

(2) Was made

(i) by the witness himself or under his direction or

(ii) by some other person for the purpose of recording the witness' statement at the time it was made;

(3) Is offered after the witness testifies that the statement he made was a true statement of such fact; and

(4) Is offered after the writing is authenticated as an accurate record of the statement.

(b) The writing may be read into evidence, but the writing itself may not be received in evidence unless offered by an adverse party.

Section 1238 (Hearsay — Prior Identification)

Evidence of a statement previously made by a witness is not made inadmissible by the hearsay rule if the statement would have been admissible if made by him while testifying and:

(a) The statement is an identification of a party or another as a person who participated in a crime or other occurrence;

(b) The statement was made at a time when the crime or other occurrence was fresh in the witness' memory; and

(c) The evidence of the statement is offered after the witness testifies that he made the identification and that it was a true reflection of his opinion at that time.

Section 1240 (Hearsay — Excited Utterances)

Evidence of a statement is not made inadmissible by the hearsay rule if the statement:

(a) Purports to narrate, describe, or explain an act, condition, or event perceived by the declarant; and

(b) Was made spontaneously while the declarant was under the stress of excitement caused by such perception.

Section 1242 (Hearsay — Dying Declarations)

Evidence of a statement made by a dying person respecting the cause and circumstances of his death is not made inadmissible by the hearsay rule if the statement was made upon his personal knowledge and under a sense of immediately impending death.

Section 1251 (Hearsay — Past State of Mind)

Subject to Section 1252, evidence of a statement of the declarant's state of mind, emotion, or physical sensation (including a statement of intent, plan, motive, design, mental feeling, pain, or bodily health) at a time prior to the statement is not made inadmissible by the hearsay rule if:

(a) The declarant is unavailable as a witness; and

(b) The evidence is offered to prove such prior state of mind, emotion, or physical sensation when it is itself an issue in the action and the evidence is not offered to prove any fact other than such state of mind, emotion, or physical sensation.

Section 1252 (Hearsay — State of Mind)

Evidence of a statement is inadmissible under this article [relating to present and state of mind] if the statement was made under circumstances such as to indicate its lack of trustworthiness.

Section 1271 (Hearsay — Business Records)

Evidence of a writing made as a record of an act, condition, or event is not made inadmissible by the hearsay rule when offered to prove the act, condition, or event if:

(a) The writing was made in the regular course of a business;

(b) The writing was made at or near the time of the act, condition, or event;

(c) The custodian or other qualified witness testifies to its identity and the mode of its preparation; and

(d) The sources of information and method and time of preparation were such as to indicate its trustworthiness.

Section 1280 (Hearsay — Official Records)

Evidence of a writing made as a record of an act, condition, or event is not made inadmissible by the hearsay rule when offered in any civil or criminal proceeding to prove the act, condition, or event if all of the following applies:

(a) The writing was made by and within the scope of duty of a public employee.

(b) The writing was made at or near the time of the act, condition, or event.

(c) The sources of information and method and time of preparation were such as to indicate its trustworthiness.

Section 1420 (Authentication)

A writing may be authenticated by evidence that the writing was received in response to a communication sent to the person who is claimed by the proponent of the evidence to be the author of the writing.

Section 1421 (Authentication)

A writing may be authenticated by evidence that the writing refers to or states matters that are unlikely to be known to anyone other than the person who is claimed by the proponent of the evidence to be the author of the writing.

Section 1521 (Secondary Evidence of a Writing)

(a) The content of a writing may be proved by otherwise admissible secondary evidence. The court shall exclude secondary evidence of the content of writing if the court determines either of the following:

(1) A genuine dispute exists concerning material terms of the writing and justice requires the exclusion.

(2) Admission of the secondary evidence would be unfair.

(b) Nothing in this section makes admissible oral testimony to prove the content of a writing if the testimony is inadmissible under Section 1523 (oral testimony of the content of a writing).

(c) Nothing in this section excuses compliance with Section 1401 (authentication).

(d) This section shall be known as the "Secondary Evidence Rule."

Index

[References are to pages]